FINANCE at FIELDS

FINANCE at FIELDS

Editors

Matheus R Grasselli

The Fields Institute & McMaster University, Canada

Lane P Hughston

University College London, United Kingdom

World Scientific

NEW JERSEY • LONDON • SINGAPORE • BEIJING • SHANGHAI • HONG KONG • TAIPEI • CHENNAI

Published by

World Scientific Publishing Co. Pte. Ltd.
5 Toh Tuck Link, Singapore 596224
USA office: 27 Warren Street, Suite 401-402, Hackensack, NJ 07601
UK office: 57 Shelton Street, Covent Garden, London WC2H 9HE

British Library Cataloguing-in-Publication Data
A catalogue record for this book is available from the British Library.

FINANCE AT FIELDS

ISBN 978-981-4407-88-5

In-house Editor: Sandhya Venkatesh

Typeset by Stallion Press
Email: enquiries@stallionpress.com

Printed in Singapore by B & Jo Enterprise Pte Ltd

PREFACE

Reflections on the Crisis and a Glimpse at the Future of Mathematical Finance

This distinguished collection of mathematical finance papers, largely based upon presentations made at the Fields Institute in 2010, at the height of the financial crisis, has an interesting history. Most of the readers of this book will know that the Fields Institute for Research in Mathematical Sciences, founded in 1992, based in a dedicated building located on the campus of the University of Toronto, and named after that visionary Canadian mathematician John Charles Fields (1863–1932), is famous for the series of thematic programs that it regularly hosts, ranging across the whole of mathematics and its applications. The Thematic Program on Quantitative Finance, held over the months of January to June 2010, leading up to the 2010 World Congress of the Bachelier Finance Society, also held in Toronto, was a major event for the mathematical finance community.

Plans for the 2010 program at Fields were already afoot some five years earlier. The skies of mathematical finance looked bright and clear around the year 2005. In the decade since the "fundamental theorem of asset pricing" had been established in great generality, the theoretical foundations of the subject had become broader and deeper, while at the same time its practical applications had expanded to varying degrees of assimilation to nearly all areas of banking and finance. The associated academic community had moved in great strides, with the proliferation of burgeoning research groups and blue-chip masters programs at top universities around the world, the establishment of several high-quality international journals devoted to the subject, and the creation of the Bachelier Finance Society and its galvanizing World Congresses. Apart from a few clouds on the distant horizon, the view of the future was one of financial markets with ever increasing mathematical sophistication, promoting research at a pace compatible with a mature subject entering that stage that Thomas Kuhn has called "normal science".

What were the distant clouds on this rhetorical panorama? Well, opinions differ on this, but one might certainly include: (1) the way in which superficially calibrated and largely untried mark-to-market methods were being applied by many financial institutions to the risk management of massively complex debt-related portfolios consisting of credit default swaps, collateralized debt obligations, and other such products, uncomfortably far removed from the hedging arguments that motivate risk management practice in the case of simpler derivatives; and (2) the gradual realization by many market participants of the possibility that the widespread entangled exchange of exotic derivatives and structured products between and amongst banks and other financial institutions might have the potential to make the entire system vulnerable to some kind of large-scale financial crisis. There were, of course, other dark patches in the sky as well, notably the anomalous rises in real estate prices, trade imbalances, and unregulated banking activities, coupled with what appeared at least to some to be a recklessly overabundant availability of credit to the not-so-credit-worthy. Issues such as these were thought to be mainly in the purview of economists, politicians, and regulators — and the mathematicians of finance were largely inclined to ignore such matters without quite being conscious of the fact that in doing so anything might be amiss; or, if not that, then at least to regard such issues as well outside their domain of professional competence. The mathematical finance community on the whole elected rather to focus primarily on its "core strengths", including: (i) foundational issues, (ii) computational challenges, and (iii) the design and implementation of new derivative products and risk management techniques.

Such was the landscape of the subject at the final days of that splendid six-month program on Developments in Quantitative Finance that took place (now so long ago it seems) over the period January to July 2005 at Cambridge's Isaac Newton Institute. Perhaps, in retrospect, it can be read as an omen that the closing conference of that program took place during the week of the tragic bombings of the London transport system on 7 July, leaving those of us who returned to London afterward to find a kind of ghost city, where nothing seemed to be as it should. At such somber times one questions everything one takes for granted; but the last thing on anyone's mind at that point was the thought that only a few years later the world of finance would seem to change forever.

Indeed, by 2005, the planning for a kind of sequel to the highly successful Isaac Newton event was well underway, and it was not long thereafter that arrangements were formalized to launch a six-month Thematic Program on "Quantitative Finance: Foundations and Applications" at the Fields Institute to take place during the first six months of the year 2010. The proposed agenda for the program was originally conceived on the basis that it would cover in a rather straightforward way the established three "domains of competence" of mathematical finance listed as (i), (ii), (iii) above. But by the time the meeting was due to begin, the subject was no longer what it had been. As we all know now, those dark clouds on the horizon eventually coalesced to form a perfect storm: a hurricane of plummeting asset prices, massive disruption of the credit markets, collapse of confidence, slowdown of economic activity — and, more recently, imminent threats of sovereign debt degradation, default, or worse, in greater Europe — stormy conditions that have yet to abate at the time we write. A funny thing happened on the way to the Fields Institute, one might say, and the realized agenda for the program reacted accordingly.

The history of so-called mathematical finance will seem to younger mathematicians as if it stretches back to antiquity — that is to say, all the way to the 1950s. It is a matter of definitions to determine exactly when finance became "mathematical". It may have been when geometric Brownian motion was introduced to model stock prices, or when stochastic calculus was introduced into the subject. It may have been when the Black-Scholes formula was discovered, or when Vasicek proposed his famous model for interest rates. It may have been when martingale theory became prominent and the change-of measure technique was used to give a rigorous basis to so-called risk-neutral pricing. Who is to say? The French would probably even claim (and perhaps not unjustifiably) that finance became mathematical decades earlier when Bachelier wrote his famous thesis! In any case, by the late 1980s the subject of mathematical finance had clearly begun to establish a life of its own, and was no longer necessarily "still living at home with its parents" in economics departments or the finance departments of business schools. What caught both academics and industry practitioners alike by surprise was the full extent of the applicability of the subject in a banking context — and this was just at the time that the depth and generality of the mathematical framework was first beginning to be fully appreciated as well. Indeed, to paraphrase the physicist Eugene Wigner, one can now speak of "the unusual effectiveness of mathematics in the theory of finance".

Science as a whole can be likened unto a vast Tower of Babel, and as each new community of research develops it is perhaps only natural that each establishes its own language, its own culture, its own criteria of quality and legitimacy, thus keeping other communities apart; and even now one bristles at shallow interdisciplinarianism. Further, after all, there is only so much one can master, and no one expects a cobbler also then to be a plumber. But is this always so? In the uncommon time of national emergency, it is not uncommon to see scientists of one calling quickly adapting their skills to another. And one might rightly say the financial crisis was — and for some time yet will continue to be — a kind of international emergency. It is not unreasonable to invite those whose work has in the main been devoted to the essentially microeconomic pricing theories of "traditional" mathematical finance to raise their ambitions with a view to having a go at issues on a larger scale. This is not, of course, to say that micro-issues are in any way pedestrian — rather, that greater challenges remain that are still well within our scope and skill-set as mathematical finance theorists.

It is often said that anything, once it becomes sufficiently important, becomes political; and it is also sometimes said that science ends where politics begins. These adages harbor truth, no doubt; but that does not mean that mathematicians should stand by and let others supposedly more competent and worldly-wise deal with the seemingly messy non-mathematical realities of global risk management and financial regulation. On the contrary, if we may speak normatively, what the world-wide finance community much needs is an application at the macroeconomic scale, and indeed also at what might appropriately be called the mesoeconomic scale, of that same intellectual force of mathematical rationality and clarity that has proven so effective at the microeconomic scale in those problems hitherto tackled by financial mathematicians. By an application at the mesoeconomic level, we do not mean anything like that black-box treatment of the economy as a whole pursued in modern macroeconomics — which considers, so to speak, the equilibrium interface of the ocean and the atmosphere to be a smooth surface, a model of no use to the captain of a ship down amongst the threatening waves, when there is a storm on the horizon. Many of the issues faced by the regulators of financial institutions engaged with large portfolios of complex products are squarely on the mesoeconomic scale. Examples of such issues include the determination of rational policies for capital adequacy requirements, how best to avoid or at least mitigate financial contagion, and the formulation of optimally fair rules for the regulation of price-sensitive information dissemination in what we must acknowledge is an information obsessed society that as time goes by will more so be.

Our view, if we may say so, is that at both the macro and the meso levels of the economy there are roles to be played by modern mathematical modellers. Macroeconomics is too important to be left in the hands of the macroeconomists. The bitter public debate in the so-called "macro wars" involving diverse academic economists arguing for radically different policy approaches has exposed a profession torn at its core and in dire need of new tools and fresh thinking. One might let this be a Call to Arms for mathematicians to join the fight. And this is a battle that will be waged on more than one front. That such problems of large and intermediate scale are tough there is no doubt, and half the work is that of saying first just what it is that needs to be done. The popular image of the "professional" mathematician as a kind of bearded and bespectacled boffin who knows all the answers and, when presented with problems, waves his slide-rule and applies the appropriate techniques to produce suitably salubrious solutions, is rather remote from the reality of the present situation in mathematical finance. It may be that one has to think back to the spirit of the eighteenth and nineteenth centuries, when the distinction between the "natural scientist" and the "mathematician" was not so sharp. Certainly, one cannot simply sit back and assume that someone else will say what it is that needs to be sorted out. One must think these things through for oneself.

By the time the details of the 2010 Fields Institute program were being drawn up, such weighty issues were very much in the air. Talks, panels, and informal discussions abounded on systemic risk, the limits of arbitrage, models for liquidity, price bubbles, financial fragility, Knightian uncertainty, the role of information, heterogeneous agents, behaviourism, algorithmic trading, high-frequency trading, high-throughput computing, regulatory finance, structured incentives, and much more. Many of these topics permeate the papers presented in this volume, solidly grounded in the intellectual rigor and scientific independence that have been the hallmarks of mathematical finance since its origins, but charting undeniably new territory. One might even venture to suggest that these are times of paradigm shift. Whether this is so is for a future generation to decide. In the meantime, we (collectively and mathematically speaking) have work to do, much work.

The articles collected in this book have all appeared in International Journal of Theoretical and Applied Finance (IJTAF), the majority in a set of special issues of the journal dedicated to papers arising from a series of workshops that took place during the course of the 2010 Fields Institute program. One of us (MRG) had overall responsibility for the organization of the 2010 Thematic Program on Quantitative Finance, while the other (LPH) has been for some years Editor-in-Chief of IJTAF. In collaborating in the preparation of the special issues and more recently in the compilation of this volume, we were greatly assisted by the staff of the World Scientific Publishing Company, to whom we express our thanks. In presenting readers with this worthy sample of Finance at Fields we remain impressed with the exciting range of topics under display, and yet conscious of goals yet to be gained implicit in so much that is said therein.

Matheus R. Grasselli
Lane P. Hughston

CONTENTS

HEAT KERNEL INTEREST RATE MODELS WITH TIME-INHOMOGENEOUS MARKOV PROCESSES*

JIRÔ AKAHORI

Department of Mathematical Sciences
Ritsumeikan University
1-1-1 Nojihigashi, Kusatsu 52-8577, Shiga, Japan

ANDREA MACRINA

Department of Mathematics, King's College London
London WC2R 2LS, United Kingdom
and
Institute of Economic Research, Kyoto University
Yoshida-Honmachi, Sakyo-Ku, Kyoto 606-8501, Japan

We consider a heat kernel approach for the development of stochastic pricing kernels. The kernels are constructed by positive propagators, which are driven by time-inhomogeneous Markov processes. We multiply such a propagator with a positive, time-dependent and decreasing weight function, and integrate the product over time. The result is a so-called weighted heat kernel that by construction is a supermartingale with respect to the filtration generated by the time-inhomogeneous Markov processes. As an application, we show how this framework naturally fits the information-based asset pricing framework where time-inhomogeneous Markov processes are utilized to model partial information about random economic factors. We present examples of pricing kernel models which lead to analytical formulae for bond prices along with explicit expressions for the associated interest rate and market price of risk. Furthermore, we also address the pricing of fixed-income derivatives within this framework.

Keywords: Time-inhomogeneous Markov processes; Lévy processes; heat kernels; pricing kernels; information-based pricing; interest rate models; fixed-income assets.

1. Introduction

In work by Hughston and Macrina [8], and Macrina and Parbhoo [10], the information-based asset pricing framework developed by Brody *et al.* [2, 3] is applied

*This chapter was originally published under the same title in *International Journal of Theoretical and Applied Finance*, Vol.15, No.1, 1250007-1–15 (2012). Singapore: World Scientific Publishing.

to the modelling of the pricing kernel with the goal to price fixed-income securities. The view taken is that interest rates and market prices of risk fluctuate due to noisy information about economic factors that becomes available to investors as time passes. Another reason for proposing information-based pricing kernels is the necessity to develop stochastic discount models which naturally combine with, e.g., the equity, credit and insurance pricing models presented in Brody *et al.* [2–4] and in Hoyle *et al.* [7]. A first, albeit different, extension of information-based pricing to include stochastic discount factors can be found in Rutkowski and Yu [13]. The theory of pricing kernels is treated in, e.g., Cochrane [5] and in Duffie [6].

We briefly summarise the information-based method for the construction of pricing kernels. The financial market is modelled by a filtered probability space $(\Omega, \mathcal{F}, \{\mathcal{F}_t\}, \mathbb{P})$ where $\mathbb{P}$ is the real probability measure. The filtration $\{\mathcal{F}_t\}_{0\leq t}$ is assumed to be generated by so-called information processes which model the noisy information about economic factors that market investors may observe. An information process $\{L_{tU}\}_{0\leq t\leq U}$ is constructed such that the associated economic factor X_U is revealed at some fixed future time U. In order to ensure that the derived asset price processes are adapted to the market filtration, it is postulated that the pricing kernel $\{\pi_t\}$ be a functional of the information processes which generate $\{\mathcal{F}_t\}$.

We shall consider the simpler situation where the filtration is generated by a single information process that has the Markov property, and where the pricing kernel can be expressed by a positive function of time and the value of the information process at that time:

$$\pi_t = \pi(t, L_{tU}). \tag{1.1}$$

The function $\pi(t, L_{tU})$ needs to be specified in such a way that the resulting pricing kernel process is a positive supermartingale. To find explicit pricing kernel models, it is also necessary to specify the information process. For example one can choose $\{L_{tU}\}$ to be a Brownian bridge information process defined by

$$L_{tU} = \sigma t X_U + \beta_{tU} \tag{1.2}$$

where σ is a constant parameter and $\{\beta_{tU}\}_{0\leq t\leq U}$ is an independent standard Brownian bridge. In this case it is convenient to assume that the pricing kernel is expressed by

$$\pi_t = \pi(t, L_{tU}) = M_t f(t, L_{tU}), \tag{1.3}$$

where $\{M_t\}_{0\leq t<U}$ is a positive $\mathbb{P}$-martingale that induces a change of measure to the so-called bridge measure $\mathbb{B}$ under which $\{L_{tU}\}$ has the law of a Brownian bridge. It is then shown in Hughston and Macrina [8] that $\{\pi_t\}$ is a positive $\mathbb{P}$-supermartingale if and only if the function $f(t, x)$ is positive and it satisfies the following partial differential inequality:

$$\frac{x}{U-t}\partial_x f(t,x) - \frac{1}{2}\partial_{xx} f(t,x) - \partial_t f(t,x) > 0. \tag{1.4}$$

The short rate of interest $\{r_t\}$ and the market price of risk $\{\lambda_t\}$ associated with a pricing kernel of the form (1.3) are given by

$$r_t = \frac{1}{f(t,x)} \left(\frac{x}{U-t} \partial_x f(t,x) - \frac{1}{2} \partial_{xx} f(t,x) - \partial_t f(t,x) \right) \Bigg|_{x=L_{tU}}, \tag{1.5}$$

$$\lambda_t = \frac{\sigma U}{U-t} \mathbb{E}[X_U | L_{tU}] - \frac{\partial_x f(t,x)}{f(t,x)} \Bigg|_{x=L_{tU}}. \tag{1.6}$$

The condition (1.4) is equivalent to requiring that the short rate of interest be a positive process. This is evident if (1.5) is compared with (1.4). The expectation in (1.6) can be worked out analytically by utilizing the Bayes formula.

In this paper we present a method that enables us to produce pricing kernel models which by construction are supermartingales adapted to the market filtration generated by information processes. We then show, as an example, that in the case of pricing kernels driven by Brownian bridge information processes (1.2), the function $f(t,x)$ associated with the constructed pricing kernel automatically satisfies the partial differential inequality (1.4). Thus we also obtain a class of positive interest rate models which are driven by time-inhomogenous Markov processes. The heat kernel approach for the construction of supermartingales that we consider, is introduced in Akahori *et al.* [1] for the case that the pricing kernel is driven by time-homogeneous Markov processes. We point to references therein for further background on the modelling of pricing kernels, and highlight work by Rogers [12] and material in Hunt *et al.* [9]. Since we generate the market filtration by information processes which by construction are time-inhomogeneous Markov processes, we need to modify the heat kernel approach used by Akahori *et al.* [1]. We focus on the weighted heat kernel approach that for our purpose turns out to be perhaps the more natural of the heat kernel methods. The Brownian bridge information process, the gamma bridge information process introduced in Brody *et al.* [3], and more generally the Lévy random bridge information processes proposed in Hoyle *et al.* [7] are all examples of time-inhomogeneous processes that possess the Markov property with respect to their natural filtration.

We shall denote a general time-inhomogeneous Markov process by $\{X_t\}$. A Lévy random bridge is denoted by $\{L_{tU}\}_{0\leq t\leq U}$ where the subscript reminds us that $\{L_{tU}\}$ has a stochastic dynamics for $t \in [0, U]$, and that after time U it "freezes" at the value L_{UU} for all $t > U$. For example, the Brownian bridge information process (1.2) takes the value $L_{UU} = \sigma\, U\, X_U$ for all $t \geq U$. In Sec. 2 we present the heat kernel approach adapted for time-inhomogeneous Markov processes and introduce weighted heat kernels which will form the basis for the construction of information-based pricing kernels. In Sec. 3 we summarise the theory of Lévy random bridges and apply it to the modelling of pricing kernels by use of weighted heat kernels. Furthermore we provide the dynamics of bond prices, and show how to price fixed income vanilla options. In Sec. 4 we focus on the situation where the time-inhomogeneous Markov process is a Brownian bridge information process. This example is developed in detail, offering analytical pricing kernel models. We also provide the associated explicit stochastic interest rate and market price of risk models.

2. Heat Kernels for Supermartingales

The heat kernel approach introduced in Akahori *et al.* [1] is a systematic method for the construction of Markov functionals for interest rate models. Pricing kernel processes are modelled by assuming that they are functionals of Markov processes which generate the market filtration. The pricing kernel models give rise to the Markov functionals of the related interest rate models. Bond pricing and in general the pricing of fixed-income instruments is performed by applying the pricing kernel models. We propose the same scheme for the construction of pricing kernels driven by information processes. However, we adapt the heat kernel scheme to the case in which the driving Markov processes are time-inhomogeneous.

Let $\{X_t\}_{0\leq t}$ be a Markov process, and let $q(s,t,x,y)$ be its transition function, where $0 \leq s \leq t$. Then we have:

$$\mathbb{P}[X_{t+s} \in \mathrm{d}y | X_s = x] = q(s,t,x,\mathrm{d}y). \tag{2.1}$$

A Markov process is said to be time-homogeneous (or simply homogeneous) if its transition function is independent of s; see for instance [11]. If the transition function admits the form

$$q(s,t,x,\mathrm{d}y) = p(s,t,x,y)\mathrm{d}y, \tag{2.2}$$

then the function $p(s,t,x,y)$ is often called a "heat kernel". Usually $p(s,t,x,y)$ is not defined on the set $s = t$. For the construction of pricing kernels, we consider so-called "propagators" defined as follows:

Definition 2.1. Let $\mathcal{S}$ be a Polish space, and $\mathcal{U} := \{(u,t) \in [0,U)^2 : u+t < U, u \neq 0\}$. Let $\{X_t\}_{0\leq t<U}$ be a Markov process with state space $\mathcal{S}$. A measurable function $p : \mathcal{U} \times \mathcal{S} \to \mathbb{R}$ is a propagator if it satisfies

$$\mathbb{E}[p(u,t,X_t)|X_s = x] = p(u+t-s,s,x) \tag{2.3}$$

for arbitrary $(u,t) \in \mathcal{U}$ and $0 \leq s \leq t$.

Remark 2.1. By excluding $u = 0$ from $\mathcal{U}$, we allow for the class of propagators to include heat kernels.

Proposition 2.1. *Let $F : [0,U) \to \mathbb{R}^+$ be a measurable function. Set*

$$p(u,t,x) := \mathbb{E}[F(u+t,X_{u+t})|X_t = x], \tag{2.4}$$

where $x \in \mathcal{S}$ and $0 \leq t$, $0 \leq u$. Then $p(u,t,x)$ is a propagator.

Proof. We have:

$$\begin{aligned}\mathbb{E}[p(u,t,X_t)|X_s] &= \mathbb{E}[\mathbb{E}[F(u+t,X_{u+t})|X_t]|X_s],\\ &= \mathbb{E}[F(u+t,X_{u+t})|X_s],\\ &= \mathbb{E}[F((u+t-s)+s,X_{(u+t-s)+s})|X_s],\\ &= p(u+t-s,s,X_s). \end{aligned} \tag{2.5}$$

□

Remark 2.2. If we allow $u = 0$ in (2.3), then the converse of Proposition 2.1 holds. Namely, the propagator is represented by some measurable function $F : [0, U) \to \mathbb{R}^+$ as given in (2.4). More precisely, we have

$$p(u,t,X_t) = \mathbb{E}[p(0,u+t,X_{u+t})|X_t], \tag{2.6}$$

by letting $u \to 0$, $t \to u + t$ and $s \to t$. That is, $F(t, x) = p(0, t, x)$.

Definition 2.2. Let a measurable function $w : [0, U]^2 \to \mathbb{R}^+$ that satisfies

$$w(t,u-s) \leq w(t-s,u) \tag{2.7}$$

for $0 < U \leq \infty$ and $s \leq t \wedge u$, be called a "weight function". A "weighted heat kernel" $f(t, x)$ is defined by

$$f(t,x) = \int_0^{U-t} p(u,t,x)w(t,u)\mathrm{d}u, \tag{2.8}$$

for $0 \leq t < U$, $u \neq 0$, and where $p(u, t, x)$ is a propagator.

Proposition 2.2. *Consider the propagator* (2.4). *Assume that* $\mathbb{P}[f(t, X_t) < \infty] = 1$ *for all* $t \in [0, U)$, *and let* $0 \leq u + t < U$. *Then*

$$f(t,X_t) = \int_0^{U-t} \mathbb{E}[F(u+t,X_{u+t})|X_t]w(t,u)\mathrm{d}u \tag{2.9}$$

is a positive supermartingale.

Proof. For $0 \leq s \leq t$, we have

$$\mathbb{E}[f(t,X_t)|X_s] = \int_0^{U-t} \mathbb{E}[\mathbb{E}[F(u+t,X_{u+t})|X_t]|X_s]w(t,u)\mathrm{d}u \tag{2.10}$$

where we make use of Fubini's theorem. By the propagation property and the change of variables $u = v - t + s$, we obtain

$$\mathbb{E}[f(t,X_t)|X_s] = \int_{t-s}^{U-s} \mathbb{E}[F(v+s,X_{v+s})|X_s]w(t,v-t+s)\mathrm{d}v. \tag{2.11}$$

We complete the proof by applying the property (2.7):

$$\begin{aligned}\mathbb{E}[f(t,X_t)|X_s] &\le \int_{t-s}^{U-s} \mathbb{E}[F(v+s,X_{v+s})|X_s]w(t-(t-s),v)\mathrm{d}v \\ &\le \int_0^{U-s} \mathbb{E}[F(v+s,X_{v+s})|X_s]w(s,v)\mathrm{d}v \\ &\le f(s,X_s). \end{aligned} \tag{2.12}$$

□

Remark 2.3.

1. Let $w_1(t,u)$ and $w_2(t,u)$ be weight functions, and c be a positive constant. Then $c\,w_1(t,u)$, $w_1(t,u)+w_2(t,u)$, and $w_1(t,u)\,w_2(t,u)$ are weight functions.
2. If $w(t,u)$ is non-increasing in t and non-decreasing in u, then $w(t,u)$ is a weight function.
3. If $w(t,u)=\bar{w}(t+u)$ for some measurable function $\bar{w}:\mathbb{R}\to\mathbb{R}^+$, then $w(t,u)$ is a weight function.

The assertions 1 and 2 are obvious. The assertion 3 is shown by observing that $w(t,u-s)=\bar{w}(t+u-s)=w(t-s,u)$.

Remark 2.4. Since the state space of the time-inhomogeneous Markov processes is a Polish space, the heat kernel approach may also be applied to construct pricing kernel models which are driven by multiple information processes. The development of explicit multi-factor models is deferred to future research. We refer to Hughston and Macrina [8], and Macrina and Parbhoo [10] for further material on multi-factor interest rate models, and emphasize that multi-factor pricing kernels may have dynamics simultaneously driven by time-inhomogeneous Markov processes based, for instance, on various different Lévy processes.

3. Pricing with Time-Inhomogeneous Markov Information

Fixed-income assets can be priced by use of pricing kernel models. Let us consider a single-dividend-paying asset which, at a fixed future date T, has a random cash flow H_T. The price H_t at time $t\le T$ of such an asset is

$$H_t=\frac{1}{\pi_t}\mathbb{E}[\pi_T H_T|\mathcal{F}_t], \tag{3.1}$$

where $\{\pi_t\}$ is the pricing kernel. For $H_T=1$ we recover the pricing formula for a discount bond with maturity T. In order to obtain specific processes for the discount bond system, we need to develop explicit pricing kernel models. Let us denote the price process of the discount bond by $\{P_{tT}\}_{0\le t\le T}$, and let us consider pricing kernel models of the form $\pi_t=\pi(t,X_t)$ where $\{X_t\}$ is a Markov process that generates the market filtration $\{\mathcal{F}_t\}$. Hence we have

$$P_{tT} = \frac{\mathbb{E}[\pi(T, X_T)|X_t]}{\pi(t, X_t)}. \tag{3.2}$$

No-arbitrage requires the pricing kernel to be a positive supermartingale. We can thus apply Proposition 2.2 to construct these pricing kernels:

$$\pi(t, X_t) = \int_0^{U-t} \mathbb{E}[F(u+t, X_{u+t})|X_t]w(t, u)\mathrm{d}u. \tag{3.3}$$

Assuming $0 \le t \le T < U$, the price of the discount bond is

$$P_{tT} = \frac{\int_{T-t}^{U-t} \mathbb{E}[F(u+t, X_{u+t})|X_t]w(T, u-T+t)\mathrm{d}u}{\int_0^{U-t} \mathbb{E}[F(u+t, X_{u+t})|X_t]w(t, u)\mathrm{d}u}, \tag{3.4}$$

where (2.11) is used in order to work out the conditional expectation in (3.2).

There are three ingredients which need to be specified so that explicit pricing models can be derived: (i) the Markov process $\{X_t\}$, (ii) the positive function $F(t, x)$, and (iii) the weight function $w(t, u)$. The specification of $\{X_t\}$ is rather crucial since it also determines the model for the market filtration. As an example of a class of Markov processes which can be applied to model the market information flow, we take the Lévy random bridges proposed in Hoyle *et al.* [7]. These Markov processes are manifestly time-inhomogeneous since their transition function depends explicitly on the time variable. We shall adopt the notation in Hoyle *et al.* [7], that is also useful in making a distinction between a general Markov process $\{X_t\}$ and a Lévy random bridge denoted $\{L_{tU}\}$.

Definition 3.1. A Lévy random bridge $\{L_{tU}\}_{0\le t\le U}$ that takes values in a continuous state space, is a process with the following properties:

1. L_{UU} has marginal law ν.
2. There exists a Lévy process $\{L_t\}$ such that L_t has density $\rho_t(x)$ for all $t \in (0, U]$.
3. ν concentrates mass where $\rho_U(z)$ is positive and finite, i.e. $0 < \rho_U(z) < \infty$ for ν-almost every z.
4. For every $n \in \mathbb{N}_+$, every $0 < t_1 < \cdots < t_n < U$, every $(x_1, \ldots, x_n) \in \mathbb{R}^n$, and ν-almost every z, we have

$$\begin{aligned}&\mathbb{P}[L_{t_1U} \le x_1, \ldots, L_{t_nU} \le x_n | L_{UU} = z]\\ &\qquad = \mathbb{P}[L_{t_1} \le x_1, \ldots, L_{t_n} \le x_n | L_U = z].\end{aligned}$$

For the computation of the conditional expectation involved in (3.3) and (3.4), the following result in Hoyle *et al.* (2011) is useful: For $0 \le s < t < U$,

$$\mathbb{P}[L_{tU} \in \mathrm{d}y | L_{sU} = x] = \frac{\psi_{tU}(\mathbb{R}; y)}{\psi_{sU}(\mathbb{R}, x)} \rho_{t-s}(y-x)\mathrm{d}y, \tag{3.5}$$

where

$$\psi_{tU}(\mathbb{R};y) := \int_{-\infty}^{\infty} \frac{\rho_{U-t}(z-y)}{\rho_U(z)}\nu(\mathrm{d}z), \quad \psi_{0U}(\mathrm{d}z;y) := \nu(\mathrm{d}z). \tag{3.6}$$

If we assume that the Markov process $\{X_t\}$ driving the bond price process (3.4) is a Lévy random bridge, then the conditional expectation in (3.4) is given by

$$\mathbb{E}[F(u+t, L_{u+t,U})|L_{tU}] = \int_{-\infty}^{\infty} F(u+t,y)\frac{\psi_{u+t,U}(\mathbb{R};y)}{\psi_{tU}(\mathbb{R},L_{tU})}\rho_u(y-L_{tU})\mathrm{d}y. \tag{3.7}$$

In this case, the evolution of the bond price is determined by the conditional law of ρ_t of the Lévy process $\{L_t\}$. The density ρ_t is given by a function of time t and the value of L_{tU} prevailing at t.

Before we go on to work out explicitly the price of a fixed-income security, e.g., a discount bond, by choosing a specific Lévy random bridge, we show how in this framework one can also price derivatives. In particular, we show how to calculate a bond option via (3.1). Let $\{C_{st}\}$, $0 \leq s \leq t \leq T < U$, be the price process of a European-style call bond option with maturity t and strike K. The option price at time s is

$$C_{st} = \frac{1}{\pi(s, L_{sU})}\mathbb{E}^{\mathbb{P}}\left[\pi(t, L_{tU})(P_{tT} - K)^+|L_{sU}\right], \tag{3.8}$$

where here P_{tT} is defined by (3.2) for $X_t = L_{tU}$. Since the pricing kernel is a positive process, we may take $\pi(t, L_{tU})$ inside the max-function. We obtain

$$C_{st} = \frac{1}{\pi(s, L_{sU})}\mathbb{E}^{\mathbb{P}}\left[(\mathbb{E}^{\mathbb{P}}[\pi(T, L_{TU})|L_{tU}] - K\pi(t, L_{tU}))^+|L_{sU}\right]. \tag{3.9}$$

For $\pi(t, L_{tU})$, we use formula (3.3) where $X_t = L_{tU}$. Furthermore,

$$\mathbb{E}^{\mathbb{P}}[\pi(T, L_{TU} \,|\, L_{tU})] = \int_{T-t}^{U-t} \mathbb{E}^{\mathbb{P}}\left[F(u+t, L_{u+t,U})|L_{tU}\right] w(T, u-T+t)\mathrm{d}u, \tag{3.10}$$

which can be simplified by (3.7). The implicit result is a function of time t and L_{tU} that we denote $I(t, L_{tU})$. We rewrite the option price in the form

$$C_{st} = \frac{1}{\pi(t, L_{sU})}\mathbb{E}^{\mathbb{P}}[(I(t, L_{tU}) - K\pi(t, L_{tU}))^+|L_{sU}]. \tag{3.11}$$

For fixed t, let z^* be the set defined by

$$z^* := \{z|I(t,z) - K\pi(t,z) > 0\}. \tag{3.12}$$

Then we have

$$C_{st} = \frac{1}{\pi(s, L_{sU})}\int_{z^*}^{\infty}(I(t,z) - K\pi(t,z))\mathbb{P}[L_{tU} \in \mathrm{d}z|L_{sU}], \tag{3.13}$$

where $\mathbb{P}[L_{tU} \in \mathrm{d}z|L_{sU}]$ is given by (3.5). We observe that the option price is determined by a function of time and the value at time s of the time-inhomogeneous Markov process $\{L_{tU}\}_{0\leq s\leq t\leq U}$.

4. Explicit Pricing Kernel Models

We reconsider the case in which the Lévy random bridge is a Brownian random bridge (Brownian bridge information process) as defined in (1.2). As shown in Hoyle *et al.* [7], the conditional density (3.5) can be computed in closed form. We can thus utilize this result in order to directly write down the expression for the bond price process (3.4) driven, e.g., by Brownian random bridge information. In this case we need working out a Gaussian integral over the range of the variable u. However, we shall apply a change-of-measure technique introduced in Brody *et al.* [2, 3].

Recall that the Brownian bridge information process is a Lévy random bridge of the form

$$L_{tU} = \sigma t X_U + \beta_{tU}, \tag{4.1}$$

where $\{\beta_{tU}\}_{0\leq t\leq U}$ is a Brownian bridge that is independent of X_U. Let $\{M_t\}_{0\leq t<U}$ be defined by

$$\frac{\mathrm{d}M_t}{M_t} = -\frac{\sigma U}{U-t}\mathbb{E}[X_U|L_{tU}]\mathrm{d}W_t, \tag{4.2}$$

where

$$W_t = L_{tU} + \int_0^t \frac{L_{sU}}{U-s}\mathrm{d}s - \sigma U\int_0^t \frac{1}{U-s}\mathbb{E}[X_U|L_{sU}]\mathrm{d}s. \tag{4.3}$$

The $(\{\mathcal{F}_t\},\mathbb{P})$-martingale $\{M_t\}$ induces a change of measure from $\mathbb{P}$ to the so-called bridge measure $\mathbb{B}$ under which $\{L_{tU}\}$ has the distribution of a Brownian bridge. We emphasize that the process $\{W_t\}$ is an $(\{\mathcal{F}_t\},\mathbb{P})$-Brownian motion on $[0,U)$. The bond price is modelled by

$$P_{tT} = \frac{\mathbb{E}[\pi(T,L_{TU})|L_{tU}]}{\pi(t,L_{tU})}. \tag{4.4}$$

Next we assume, with no loss of generality, that

$$\pi(t,L_{tU}) = M_t f(t,L_{tU}), \tag{4.5}$$

and perform the change of measure $\mathbb{P}$ to $\mathbb{B}$ so that

$$P_{tT} = \frac{\mathbb{E}^{\mathbb{B}}[f(T,L_{TU})|L_{tU}]}{f(t,L_{tU})}. \tag{4.6}$$

The pricing kernel $\{\pi(t,L_{tU})\}$ is a positive $\mathbb{P}$-supermartingale if and only if $\{f(t,L_{tU})\}$ is a positive supermartingale under $\mathbb{B}$. That is, for $0\leq s\leq t$,

$$\mathbb{E}^{\mathbb{P}}[\pi_t|\mathcal{F}_s] = M_s\mathbb{E}^{\mathbb{B}}[f(t,L_{tU})|L_{sU}] \leq M_s f(s,L_{sU}) = \pi_s. \tag{4.7}$$

The positive $\mathbb{B}$-supermartingale $\{f(t,L_{tU})\}_{0\leq t<U}$ can now be constructed by positive weighted heat kernels according to Proposition 2.2, where the conditional expectation is taken with respect to the $\mathbb{B}$-measure. The price P_{tT} is thus calculated by

the formula

$$P_{tT} = \frac{\int_{T-t}^{U-t} \mathbb{E}^{\mathbb{B}}[F(u+t, L_{u+t,U})|L_{tU}]w(T, u-T+t)\mathrm{d}u}{\int_0^{U-t} \mathbb{E}^{\mathbb{B}}[F(u+t, L_{u+t,U})|L_{tU}]w(t,u)\mathrm{d}u}. \tag{4.8}$$

Since, under the $\mathbb{B}$-measure, L_{tU} has the law of a Brownian bridge, the conditional expectation involves the Gaussian density function. Explicit expressions for the bond price are obtained by specifying $F(t,x)$ and the weight function $w(t,u)$. Depending on the combination of $F(t,x)$ and $w(t,u)$, the integration with respect to u in (4.8) can be performed in closed form. Some examples follow:

Quadratic models. We consider the positive function $F(x) = x^2$, and a weight function $w(t,u) = U - t - u$. As we shall see shortly, such a combination leads to a stochastic interest model and a closed-form expression for the bond price. The propagator (3.7) that gives rise to the stochastic dynamics of the bond price is given by

$$\mathbb{E}^{\mathbb{B}}\left[(L_{u+t,U})^2|L_{tU}\right] = \frac{u(U-t-u)}{U-t} + \left(\frac{U-t-u}{U-t}\right)L_{tU}^2. \tag{4.9}$$

Here we use the property that L_{tU} has the law of a Brownian bridge over $[0,U)$ under the $\mathbb{B}$-measure. The weighted heat kernel takes the form

$$\begin{aligned} f(t, L_{tU}) &= \int_0^{U-t} \mathbb{E}^{\mathbb{B}}[F(L_{u+t,U})|L_{tU}]w(t,u)\mathrm{d}u, \\ &= \frac{1}{12}(U-t)^3 + \frac{1}{4}(U-t)^2 L_{tU}^2, \end{aligned} \tag{4.10}$$

which ensures that the pricing kernel (4.5) is, via (4.7), a positive $\mathbb{P}$-supermartingale. Inserting (4.9) and (4.10) in (4.8), we obtain the bond price

$$P_{tT} = \frac{\frac{1}{12}(U-T)^3 + \frac{1}{4}\frac{(T-t)(U-T)^3}{(U-t)} + \frac{1}{4}\frac{(U-T)^4}{(U-t)^2}L_{tU}^2}{\frac{1}{12}(U-t)^3 + \frac{1}{4}(U-t)^2 L_{tU}^2}. \tag{4.11}$$

The associated short rate of interest $\{r_t\}$ can be obtained by calculating the instantaneous forward rate associated with the bond price $\{P_{tT}\}_{0 \le t \le T < U}$. Alternatively, (4.10) can be inserted in formula (1.5) for the short rate process. We get

$$r(t, L_{tU}) = \frac{L_{tU}^2}{\frac{1}{4}(U-t)\left[\frac{1}{3}(U-t) + L_{tU}^2\right]}, \tag{4.12}$$

for $0 \le t < U$. We emphasize that this is, by construction, a positive interest rate model. The market price of risk $\{\lambda_t\}$ can be obtained via (1.6). We have

$$\lambda(t, L_{tU}) = \frac{\sigma U}{U-t}\mathbb{E}^{\mathbb{P}}[X_U|L_{tU}] - \frac{\frac{1}{2}(U-t)^2 L_{tU}}{\frac{1}{12}(U-t)^3 + \frac{1}{4}(U-t)^2 L_{tU}^2}. \tag{4.13}$$

The expectation $\mathbb{E}^{\mathbb{P}}[X_U|L_{tU}]$ can be calculated in closed form by applying the Bayes formula.

Exponential quadratic models. We consider a positive function $F(t,x)$ that depends explicitly on time, unlike in the previous example. Let

$$F(u+t,x) = \exp\left(\frac{1}{2}\gamma_{t+u}x^2\right), \tag{4.14}$$

where γ_{t+u} is positive and deterministic. In this case the propagator takes the form

$$\mathbb{E}^{\mathbb{B}}\left[\exp\left(\frac{1}{2}\gamma_{t+u}L^2_{t+u,U}\right)\middle|L_{tU}\right]$$
$$= \frac{1}{\sqrt{1-u\gamma_{t+u}a_{t+u}}}\exp\left(\frac{\gamma_{t+u}a^2_{t+u}}{2\,(1-u\gamma_{t+u}a_{t+u})}L^2_{tU}\right), \tag{4.15}$$

where $a_{t+u} = (U-t-u)/(U-t)$. By setting $\gamma_{t+u} = (U-t-u)^{-1}$, and by choosing the weight function

$$w(t,u) = (U-t-u)^{\eta-\frac{1}{2}} \quad \left(\eta > \tfrac{1}{2}\right), \tag{4.16}$$

we obtain an analytical expression for the $\mathbb{B}$-supermartingale $\{f(t,L_{tU})\}$:

$$f(t,L_{tU}) = \frac{1}{\eta-\frac{1}{2}}(U-t)^{\eta}\exp\left(\frac{L^2_{tU}}{2(U-t)}\right). \tag{4.17}$$

This supermartingale leads to a deterministic bond price, even though the related pricing kernel is stochastic. However, we can modify $\{f(t,L_{tU})\}$ slightly. Let $g_0(t)$ and $g_1(t)$ be positive, decreasing, and differentiable functions. Consider the supermartingale

$$\tilde{f}(t,L_{tU}) = g_0(t) + g_1(t)(U-t)^{\eta}\exp\left(\frac{L^2_{tU}}{2(U-t)}\right). \tag{4.18}$$

Then the associated bond price system has the following stochastic dynamics:

$$P_{tT} = \frac{g_0(T) + g_1(T)(U-T)^{\eta-1/2}(U-t)^{1/2}\exp\left(\frac{L^2_{tU}}{2(U-t)}\right)}{g_0(t) + g_1(t)(U-t)^{\eta}\exp\left(\frac{L^2_{tU}}{2(U-t)}\right)}, \tag{4.19}$$

for $t \in [0,U)$ and $u \in [0,U-t]$. By use of (1.5) we work out the short rate process, and obtain

$$r_t = \frac{g_1(t)(U-t)^{\eta}\exp\left[\frac{L^2_{tU}}{2(U-t)}\right]}{g_0(t) + g_1(t)(U-t)^{\eta}\exp\left[\frac{L^2_{tU}}{2(U-t)}\right]}$$
$$\times\left[\left(\eta-\frac{1}{2}\right)(U-t)^{-1} - \frac{\partial_t g_1(t)}{g_1(t)} - \frac{\partial_t g_0(t)}{g_1(t)(U-t)^{\eta}\exp\left[\frac{L^2_{tU}}{2(U-t)}\right]}\right]. \tag{4.20}$$

Next we consider a particular choice for $g_1(t)$. If

$$g_1(t) = (U-t)^{-(\eta-\frac{1}{2})}, \tag{4.21}$$

then (4.20) reduces to

$$r_t = -\frac{\partial_t g_0(t)}{g_0(t) + (U-t)^{1/2}\exp\left[\frac{L_{tU}^2}{2(U-t)}\right]}. \tag{4.22}$$

Since $g_0(t)$ is a positive decreasing function, its derivative is negative. Thus the interest rate process (4.22) is positive. The market price of risk model can of course also be derived in closed form — e.g., via (1.6) — and it is given in terms of a function of time and L_{tU}. We conclude this section by noting that further examples can be constructed. A semi-analytic formula is obtained for the exponential linear family where, for instance, $F(x) = \exp(-\mu x)$ may be chosen.

5. Fixed-Income Derivatives with Brownian Bridge Information

In Sec. 3 we introduced formula (3.8) for the pricing of a European-style bond option with strike K and maturity t. The market information is modelled by a Lévy random bridge process, and the pricing kernel is assumed to be of the form $\pi_t = \pi(t, L_{tU})$. The price process of the bond option is then given implicitly in terms of a function of time and the Lévy random bridge.

In this section we go one step further, and price the bond option under the assumption that the market filtration is generated by a Brownian bridge information process (4.1). In order to derive an explicit price process for the option, we need to specify the price process of the underlying bond. We shall use the quadratic models as an example, and thus apply (4.11). The related pricing kernel model is

$$\pi_t = M_t f(t, L_{tU}), \tag{5.1}$$

where $\{M_t\}_{0\le t<U}$ is defined by (4.2), and $\{f(t, L_{tU})\}$ is given by (4.10). We write down equation (3.8) for the option price under the bridge measure $\mathbb{B}$, that is

$$C_{st} = \frac{1}{f(s, L_{sU})}\mathbb{E}^{\mathbb{B}}[f(t, L_{tU})(P_{tT} - K)^+ | L_{sU}]. \tag{5.2}$$

We take the positive $\mathbb{B}$-supermartingale $\{f(t, L_{tU})\}$ inside the max-function where, on one hand it cancels with the denominator of P_{tT}, and on the other hand, it is multiplied with the strike price K. We re-arrange the resulting terms, and obtain

$$C_{st} = \frac{1}{f(s, L_{sU})}\mathbb{E}^{\mathbb{B}}\left[\left(\frac{1}{4}\frac{(T-t)(U-T)^3}{U-t} + \frac{1}{12}[(U-T)^3 - K(U-t)^3]\right.\right.$$
$$\left.\left. + \frac{1}{4}\left[\frac{(U-T)^4}{(U-t)^2} - K(U-t)^2\right]L_{tU}^2\right)^+ \middle| L_{sU}\right] \tag{5.3}$$

In order to work out the conditional expectation, we make the substitution

$$L_{tU} = \nu_{st} Y + \frac{U-t}{U-s} L_{sU}, \tag{5.4}$$

where Y is a standard normally-distributed random variable that is $\mathbb{B}$-independent of L_{sU}. Furthermore,

$$\nu_{st} = \sqrt{\frac{(t-s)(U-t)}{U-s}}. \tag{5.5}$$

Due to the properties of Y, the expression for the option price reduces to the following Gaussian integral:

$$C_{st} = \frac{1}{f(s, L_{sU})} \int_{-\infty}^{\infty} \left(A + B \left(\nu_{st} y + \frac{U-t}{U-s} L_{sU} \right)^2 \right)^+ \frac{1}{\sqrt{2\pi}} \exp\left(-\frac{1}{2} y^2 \right) \mathrm{d}y, \tag{5.6}$$

where

$$A = \frac{1}{4} \frac{(T-t)(U-T)^3}{U-t} + \frac{1}{12} [(U-T)^3 - K(U-t)^3] \tag{5.7}$$

$$B = \frac{1}{4} \left[\frac{(U-T)^4}{(U-t)^2} - K(U-t)^2 \right]. \tag{5.8}$$

Next we integrate over the range of y for which the max-function does not vanish. This can be written as follows:

$$C_{st} = \frac{1}{f(s, L_{sU})} \int_{cy^2+by+a>0}^{\infty} (cy^2 + by + a) \frac{1}{\sqrt{2\pi}} \exp\left(-\frac{1}{2} y^2 \right) \mathrm{d}y, \tag{5.9}$$

where

$$a = A + B \left(\frac{U-t}{U-s} \right)^2 L_{sU}^2, \quad b = 2B\nu_{st} \frac{U-t}{U-s} L_{sU}, \quad c = B\nu_{st}^2. \tag{5.10}$$

Next we solve for the values y that satisfy the inequality $cy^2 + by + a > 0$. Let $N(x)$ denote the cumulative normal distribution function. Then:

1. Case $c = 0$. For $b > 0$ we obtain

$$C_{st} = \frac{1}{f(s, L_{sU})} \left[aN\left(\frac{a}{b}\right) + \frac{b}{\sqrt{2\pi}} \exp\left(-\frac{1}{2} \left(\frac{a}{b}\right)^2 \right) \right], \tag{5.11}$$

   and for $b < 0$ we have

$$C_{st} = \frac{1}{f(s, L_{sU})} \left[aN\left(-\frac{a}{b}\right) - \frac{b}{\sqrt{2\pi}} \exp\left(-\frac{1}{2} \left(\frac{a}{b}\right)^2 \right) \right]. \tag{5.12}$$

2. Case $c \neq 0$ and $b^2 - 4ac = -4AB\nu_{st}^2 > 0$. For $c < 0$ we have

$$y_{\pm} = \frac{1}{2c}\left(-b \pm \sqrt{b^2 - 4ac}\right), \tag{5.13}$$

and thus

$$C_{st} = \frac{1}{f(s, L_{sU})}\left[(a+b)[N(y_+) - N(y_-)] + (b + cy_-)\exp\left(-\frac{1}{2}(y_-)^2\right)\right.$$
$$\left. - (b + cy_+)\exp\left(-\frac{1}{2}(y_+)^2\right)\right]. \tag{5.14}$$

For $c > 0$ we have either $y \leq y_-$ or $y \geq y_+$ and thus

$$C_{st} = \frac{1}{f(s, L_{sU})}\left[(a+c)[N(y_-) + N(y_+)] - (b + cy_-)\frac{1}{\sqrt{2\pi}}\exp\left(-\frac{1}{2}(y_-)^2\right)\right.$$
$$\left. + (b + cy_+)\frac{1}{\sqrt{2\pi}}\exp\left(-\frac{1}{2}(y_+)^2\right)\right]. \tag{5.15}$$

3. Case $c \neq 0$ and $b^2 - 4ac = -4AB\nu_{st}^2 \leq 0$. For $c < 0$ the probability that $cy^2 + by + a > 0$ is zero. This means that in such a case the option at time s is almost always out of the money, and we have $C_{st} = 0$. For $c > 0$ we have $cy^2 + by + a > 0$ with probability one, and thus the option is almost always in the money. Hence we have

$$C_{st} = \frac{a + c}{f(s, L_{sU})}. \tag{5.16}$$

Acknowledgments

The authors are grateful to seminar participants at the KIER-TMU International Workshop on Financial Engineering 2009, the Vienna Institute of Finance (September 2009), Hitotsubashi University (November 2009), and at the Workshop on Financial Derivatives and Risk Management at the Fields Institute in Toronto (May 2010) for helpful comments and suggestions. In particular, we thank P. A. Parbhoo and J. Sekine for stimulating and fruitful discussions. AM thanks Ritsumeikan University in Kusatsu, Japan, for their hospitality and friendly work environment.

References

[1] J. Akahori, Y. Hishida, J. Teichmann and T. Tsuchiya, A heat kernel approach to interest rate models, arXiv.org: 0910.5033 (2009).

[2] D. C. Brody, L. P. Hughston and A. Macrina, Beyond hazard rates: a new framework for credit-risk modelling, in *Advances in Mathematical Finance*, Festschrift volume in honour of D. Madan, R. Elliot, M. Fu, R. Jarrow and J. Y. Yen, eds. (Birkhäuser, Springer Verlag, 2007).

[3] D. C. Brody, L. P. Hughston and A. Macrina, Information-based asset pricing, *International Journal of Theoretical and Applied Finance* **1** (2008) 107–142.

[4] D. C. Brody, L. P. Hughston and A. Macrina, Dam rain and cumulative gain, *Proceedings of the Royal Society A* **464** (2008) 1801–1822.

[5] J. H. Cochrane, *Asset Pricing*, Revised edition (Princeton University Press, 2005).

[6] D. Duffie, *Dynamic Asset Pricing*, Third edition (Princeton University Press, 2001).

[7] E. Hoyle, L. P. Hughston and A. Macrina, Lévy random bridges and the modelling of financial information, *Stochastic Processes and their Applications* **121** (2011) 856–884.

[8] L. P. Hughston and A. Macrina, Pricing fixed-income securities in an information-based framework, *Applied Mathematical Finance*, DOI: 10.1080/1350486X.2011.631757 (2012).

[9] P. J. Hunt, J. E. Kennedy and A. Pelsser, Markov-functional interest rate models, *Finance and Stochastics* **4**(4) (2000) 391–408.

[10] A. Macrina and P. A. Parbhoo, Security pricing with information-sensitive discounting, in *Recent Advances in Financial Engineering 2009, Proceedings of the KIER-TMU International Workshop on Financial Engineering 2009*, M. Kijima, C. Hara, K. Tanaka, eds. (World Scientific Publishing Company, 2010).

[11] D. Revuz and M. Yor, *Continuous Martingales and Brownian Motion*, 3rd edition (Springer Verlag, 1999).

[12] L. C. G. Rogers, The potential approach to the term structure of interest rates and foreign exchange rates, *Mathematical Finance* **7**(2) (1997) 157–176.

[13] M. Rutkowski and N. Yu, On the Brody-Hughston-Macrina approach to modelling of defaultable term structure, *International Journal of Theoretical and Applied Finance* **10** (2007) 557–589.

STRESS TESTING THE RESILIENCE OF FINANCIAL NETWORKS¶

HAMED AMINI*,†, RAMA CONT‡,§
and ANDREEA MINCA*,‡

*INRIA, Domaine de Voluceau, Rocquencourt
78153 Le Chesnay Cedex, France

†École Normale Supérieure
Rue d'Ulm, F-75230 Paris Cedex 05, France

‡Laboratoire de Probabilités et Modèles Aléatoires
CNRS – Université Pierre et Marie Curie, Paris, France

§Deparment of Industrial Engineering and Operations Research
Columbia University, New York, NY 10027, USA

We propose a simulation-free framework for stress testing the resilience of a financial network to external shocks affecting balance sheets. Whereas previous studies of contagion effects in financial networks have relied on large scale simulations, our approach uses a simple analytical criterion for resilience to contagion, based on an asymptotic analysis of default cascades in heterogeneous networks. In particular, our methodology does not require to observe the whole network but focuses on the characteristics of the network which contribute to its resilience. Applying this framework to a sample network, we observe that the size of the default cascade generated by a macroeconomic shock across balance sheets may exhibit a sharp transition when the magnitude of the shock reaches a certain threshold: Beyond this threshold, contagion spreads to a large fraction of the financial system. An upper bound is given for the threshold in terms of the characteristics of the network.

Keywords: Systemic risk; random graphs; stress test; default risk; macro-prudential regulation.

1. Introduction

In the Supervisory Capital Assessment Program, implemented by the Board of Governors of the Federal Reserve System in 2009 [21], the 19 largest US banks were asked to project their losses and resources under various macroeconomic shock scenarios. The program determined which of the large banks needed to augment its capital base in order to withstand the projected losses. Although underlying this

¶This chapter was originally published under the same title in *International Journal of Theoretical and Applied Finance*, Vol.15, No.1, 1250006-1–20 (2012). Singapore: World Scientific Publishing.

stress test was the concern that the failure of these large banks might generate contagion in the US financial system, contagion effects were not directly taken into account when designing the stress tests nor in evaluating the magnitude of losses in the stress scenarios.

Various models for default contagion in banking systems have been proposed in the recent literature, in the framework of *network* models. In this approach, a banking system is modeled as a weighted directed graph in which nodes represent the financial institutions and edges represent exposures between institutions [12, 13]. The fundamental default of certain banks propagates to their counterparties as these write down from their capital the exposures to the defaulted banks [1, 11].

The literature contains many simulation-based studies of contagion in banking networks conducted using central bank data — examples include Elsinger *et al.* [13] for Austria, Cont *et al.* [11] for Brazil, Upper [23] for Germany — as well as similar studies on simulated networks [10, 20]. The conclusions regarding the magnitude of contagion differ across studies, as network topology and regulatory limits, differ from one country to another, but the complexity of the models involved prevent simple insights into the influence of different network characteristics on the results. For the Austrian network, the authors find that among the sources of systemic risk, the direct effect of correlation in the external shocks is far more important than direct contagion effects, which are only secondary. In their case contagious defaults occur only in scenarios where a large number of fundamental defaults occur. In the German network, on the contrary, the default of a single bank can wipe out a significant fraction of the system, so contagion risk is by no means secondary [23].

These studies suggest that some networks are intrinsically fragile and the default of a single bank may trigger a large cascade, whereas other networks might be more resilient to contagion. This intuition is supported by theoretical results on the resilience of networks to contagion [1], and the aim of this work is to integrate such theoretical insights into the stress testing framework, thus shedding some light on the results of such stress tests.

We propose in this work a simple framework for stress-testing the resilience to contagion in a financial network under macroeconomic shocks. Instead of relying on computationally intensive simulations, our approach relies on analytical insights obtained from the asymptotic analysis of the magnitude of default contagion in large networks [1]. Based on the asymptotic analysis of [1], we propose a measure of resilience to contagion, which involves the connectivity of nodes and the proportion of "contagious" links in the network and use it to assess the resilience of the network under macroeconomic shocks. In particular, our methodology does not require to observe the whole network but focuses on the characteristics of the network which contribute to its resilience. Applying this framework to a sample network, we observe that the size of the default cascade generated by a macroeconomic shock across balance sheets may exhibit a sharp transition when the magnitude of the shock reaches a certain threshold: beyond this threshold, contagion spreads to a large fraction of the financial system. An upper bound is given for the threshold in terms of the characteristics of the network. As the resilience measure is a decreasing function of each bank's connectivity and fraction of contagious links, it can be used for monitoring/regulating the financial institutions that pose the highest systemic risk.

The paper is organized as follows. Section 2 presents a model for default contagion in a financial network, following [1, 9]. Section 2.1 presents a probabilistic framework for studying asymptotic behavior of cascades in large networks and recalls the main results of Amini *et al.* [1]. Section 2.2 presents some new results on the size of the default cascade generated by a single node. Section 3 presents a stress testing framework for analyzing the resilience of a network to macroeconomic shocks and discusses two examples: a random infinite network (Sec. 3.2) and a scale-free network whose size is comparable to existing banking networks (Sec. 3.3).

2. Network Models of Banking Systems

Interlinkages across balance sheets of financial institutions may be modeled by a weighted directed graph $\mathbf{g} = (\mathbf{v}, \mathbf{e})$ on the vertex set $\mathbf{v} = [1, \ldots, n]$, whose elements represent financial institutions. Table 1 displays a stylized balance sheet of a financial institution: denoting by $e_{i,j}$ the exposure (in monetary units) of institution i to institution j, the interbank assets of i are given by $A_i = \sum_j e_{i,j}$, whereas $L_i = \sum_j e_{j,i}$ represents the interbank liabilities of i. In addition to these interbank assets and liabilities, a bank may hold other assets and liabilities (such as deposits). The net worth of the bank, given by its **capital** c_i, represents its capacity for absorbing losses before it becomes insolvent. We define the ratio γ_i as

$$c_i = \gamma_i A_i.$$

We will refer to γ_i as "capital ratio" although technically it is the ratio of capital to interbank assets and not total assets. An institution is *insolvent* if its net worth is negative or zero, in which case we set $\gamma_i = 0$.

Definition 2.1. A **financial network** $(\mathbf{e}, \gamma)$ is defined by

- a matrix of exposures $\{e_{i,j}\}_{1 \leq i,j \leq n}$,

Table 1. Stylized balance sheet of a bank.

Assets	Liabilities
Interbank assets $A_i = \sum_j e_{i,j}$	Interbank liabilities $L_i = \sum_j e_{j,i}$ Deposits D_i
Other assets x_i	Net worth $c_i = \gamma_i A_i$

- a set of capital ratios $\{\gamma_i\}_{1\le i\le n}$ with $\gamma_i > 0$.

The number of an institution's creditors is called its *in-degree*

$$d^-(i) = \#\{j \in \mathbf{v}\, s.t.\, e_{j,i} > 0\},$$

while the *out-degree* of a node i is the number of it's debtors

$$d^+(i) = \#\{j \in \mathbf{v}\, s.t.\, e_{i,j} > 0\}.$$

In a network $(\mathbf{e}, \gamma)$, the set of initially insolvent institutions is represented by

$$\mathbb{D}_0(e, \gamma) = \{i \in \mathbf{v} \,|\, \gamma_i = 0\}.$$

If we denote by R_j the recovery rate for the debt of a market participant j, then j's default induces a loss equal to $(1 - R_j)e_{i,j}$ to its counterparty i. If this loss is greater then i's capital, then i defaults. The set of nodes which become insolvent due to their exposures to initial defaults is

$$\mathbb{D}_1(e, \gamma) = \left\{ i \in \mathbf{v} \,|\, \gamma_i A_i < \sum_{j\in\mathbb{D}_0} (1 - R_j)e_{i,j} \right\},$$

and generally $\mathbb{D}_r$ represents the set of nodes defaulting in round r due to exposures to nodes defaulted in rounds $0, \ldots, r-1$.
It is easy to see that the process finishes at most after $n-1$ time steps, if the network is of size n, and gives the increasing sequence of default sets

$$\mathbb{D}_0(e, \gamma) \subseteq \mathbb{D}_1(e, \gamma) \subseteq \cdots \subseteq \mathbb{D}_{n-1}(e, \gamma).$$

We assume in what follows that the recovery rate is constant over all nodes and equal to R. Over a short time horizon the recovery rate can be approximated by zero, which is the value we will use in the numerical examples in the next section. The final fraction of defaults at the end of the cascade process is a deterministic function of the exposure matrix and sequence of capital ratios, that we denote

$$\alpha_n(\mathbf{e}, \gamma) = \frac{|\mathbb{D}_{n-1}(e, \gamma)|}{n}.$$

2.1. *Asymptotic analysis of default cascades in large networks*

We summarize here the main results of Amini *et al.* [1]. The financial network $(\mathbf{e}, \gamma)$ is embedded in a sequence of financial networks, indexed by their size $(\mathbf{e_n}, \gamma_\mathbf{n})$. The sequences of in and out-degrees in these networks, also indexed by n, are denoted $\mathbf{d_n^+} = \{d_n^+(i)\}_{i=1}^n$ and respectively $\mathbf{d_n^-} = \{d_n^-(i)\}_{i=1}^n$. Their empirical distribution is given by

$$\mu_n(j, k) := \frac{1}{n}\#\{i : d_n^+(i) = j, d_n^-(i) = k\},$$

and the total number of links in the network of size n by

$$m_n := \sum_i d_n^+(i) = \sum_i d_n^-(i).$$

We assume that the degree sequence $\mathbf{d}_\mathbf{n}^+ = \{d_n^+(i)\}_{i=1}^n$ and $\mathbf{d}_\mathbf{n}^- = \{d_n^-(i)\}_{i=1}^n$ are sequences of nonnegative integers satisfying the following assumptions:

Assumption 2.1. There exists a probability distribution μ on $\mathbb{N}^2$ such that:

1. The empirical proportion of nodes of degree (j,k) tends to $\mu(j,k)$:
$$\mu_n(j,k) \to \mu(j,k) \quad \text{as } n \to \infty;$$
2. Finite average degree property:
$$\exists \lambda \in (0,\infty), \quad \sum_{j,k} j\mu(j,k) = \sum_{j,k} k\mu(j,k) =: \lambda;$$
3. $\sum_{i=1}^n d_n^+(i) = \sum_{i=1}^n d_n^-(i)$;
4. $\sum_{i=1}^n (d_n^+(i))^2 + (d_n^-(i))^2 = O(n)$.

The sequences of continuous exposures and capital ratios are mapped into discrete sequences representing the default threshold for each node. We denote by $\Sigma_i^\mathbf{e}$ the set of permutations of node i's counterparties in a network $\mathbf{e}$. For each node i and permutation $\tau \in \Sigma_i^\mathbf{e}$, we define

$$\Theta(i,\tau,\mathbf{e}) := \min\left\{ k \geq 0, \gamma_i \sum_{j=1}^{d^+(i)} e_{i,j} < \sum_{j=1}^{k} (1-R) e_{i,\tau(j)} \right\}, \tag{2.1}$$

which represents the threshold function: conditional on the order τ in which the counterparties of i may default, this function determines how many defaults i's capital buffer can withstand before i defaults.

Let us define

$$p_n(j,k,\theta) := \frac{\#\{(i,\tau) \,|\, 1 \leq i \leq n, \tau \in \Sigma_i^{\mathbf{e_n}}, d_n^+(i) = j, d_n^-(i) = k, \Theta(i,\tau,\mathbf{e_n}) = \theta\}}{n\mu_n(j,k) j!}. \tag{2.2}$$

Assumption 2.2. There exists a function $p : \mathbb{N}^3 \to [0,1]$ such that for all $j,k,\theta \in \mathbb{N}$ $(\theta \leq j)$

$$p_n(j,k,\theta) \overset{n\to\infty}{\to} p(j,k,\theta).$$

Remark 2.1 (Contagious links). We say that a link is "contagious" if it represents an exposure of a node larger than its capital. It is easy to see that $p_n(j,k,1)$ represents the proportion of "contagious" links leaving nodes with degree (j,k). The limit $p(j,k,1)$ also represents the fraction of nodes with degree (j,k) that default when one counterparty defaults.

Definition 2.2 (Random network ensemble). Let $\mathbb{G}_n(\mathbf{e_n}, \mathbf{d}_\mathbf{n}^+, \mathbf{d}_\mathbf{n}^-)$ be the set of all weighted directed graphs with degree sequence $\mathbf{d}_\mathbf{n}^+, \mathbf{d}_\mathbf{n}^-$ such that, for any node i, the set of exposures is given by the non-zero elements of line i in the exposure matrix $\mathbf{e_n}$. On a probability space $(\Omega, \mathcal{A}, \mathbb{P})$, we define $\mathbf{E_n}$ as a random network uniformly distributed on $\mathbb{G}_n(\mathbf{e_n}, \mathbf{d}_\mathbf{n}^+, \mathbf{d}_\mathbf{n}^-)$.

We endow the nodes in $\mathbf{E_n}$ with the capital ratios $\gamma_\mathbf{n}$. Then:

$$\forall i = 1, \dots, n; \quad \{\mathbf{E_n}(i,j), \quad \mathbf{E_n}(i,j) \neq 0\} = \{\mathbf{e_n}(i,j), \quad \mathbf{e_n}(i,j) \neq 0\} \quad \mathbb{P} - a.s.$$

$$\#\{j \in \mathbf{v}, \mathbf{E_n}(j,i) \neq 0\} = d_n^+(j), \quad \text{and} \quad \#\{j \in \mathbf{v}, \mathbf{E_n}(i,j) \neq 0\} = d_n^-(i).$$

The quantity $\alpha_n(\mathbf{E_n}, \gamma_\mathbf{n})$ represents the size of the cascade generated by the default of nodes in the set $\mathbb{D}_0(\mathbf{E_n}, \gamma_\mathbf{n}) = \{i, \gamma_n(i) = 0\}$. The following theorems give the asymptotic behavior of this quantity.

Theorem 2.1. *Define the function*

$$I(\pi) := \sum_{j,k} \frac{k\mu(j,k)}{\lambda} \sum_{\theta=0}^{j} p(j,k,\theta)\mathbb{P}(\text{Bin}(j,\pi) \geq \theta), \tag{2.3}$$

where $\text{Bin}(j,\pi)$ *denotes a binomial variable with parameters* j *and* π.

Consider a sequence of exposure matrices and capital ratios $\{(\mathbf{e_n})_{\mathbf{n}\geq 1}, (\gamma_\mathbf{n})_{\mathbf{n}\geq 1}\}$ *satisfying Assumptions* 2.1 *and* 2.2 *and the corresponding sequence of random matrices* $(\mathbf{E_n})_{n\geq 1}$ *defined on* $(\Omega, \mathcal{A}, \mathbb{P})$ *as in Definition* 2.2. *Let* π^* *be the smallest fixed point of* I *in* $[0,1]$, *i.e.*

$$\pi^* = \inf\{\pi \in [0,1] \,|\, I(\pi) = \pi\}.$$

1. *If* $\pi^* = 1$, *i.e. if* $I(\pi) > \pi$ *for all* $\pi \in [0,1)$, *then asymptotically all nodes default during the cascades:*

$$\alpha_n(\mathbf{E_n}, \gamma_\mathbf{n}) \xrightarrow{p} 1.$$

2. *If* $\pi^* < 1$ *and furthermore* π^* *is a stable fixed point of* I $(I'(\pi^*) < 1)$, *then the asymptotic fraction of defaults satisfies:*

$$\alpha_n(\mathbf{E_n}, \gamma_\mathbf{n}) \xrightarrow{p} \sum_{j,k} \mu(j,k) \sum_{\theta=0}^{j} p(j,k,\theta)\mathbb{P}(\text{Bin}(j,\pi^*) \geq \theta).$$

Definition 2.3 (Resilience measure). We define as the resilience measure the following function of the network's features, which takes values in $(-\infty, 1]$:

$$1 - \sum_{j,k} \frac{jk}{\lambda} \mu(j,k) p(j,k,1).$$

Theorem 2.2. *Under the assumptions of Theorem* 2.1:

- *If the resilience measure is positive, i.e.*

$$1 - \sum_{j,k} \frac{jk}{\lambda} \mu(j,k) p(j,k,1) > 0, \tag{2.4}$$

then for every $\epsilon > 0$, *there exists* N_ϵ *and* ρ_ϵ *such that if the initial fraction of defaults is smaller than* ρ_ϵ, *then* $\mathbb{P}(\alpha_n(\mathbf{E_n}, \gamma_\mathbf{n}) \leq \epsilon) > 1 - \epsilon$ *for all* $n \geq N_\epsilon$.

- *If the resilience measure is negative, i.e.*

$$1 - \sum_{j,k} \frac{jk}{\lambda} \mu(j,k) p(j,k,1) < 0, \tag{2.5}$$

then there exists a connected set C_n of nodes representing a positive fraction of the financial system, i.e. $|C_n|/n \xrightarrow{p} c > 0$ such that, with high probability, any node belonging to this set can trigger the default of all nodes in the set: for any sequence $(\gamma_n)_{n\geq 1}$ such that $\{i, \gamma_n(i) = 0\} \cap C_n \neq \emptyset$,

$$\liminf_n \alpha_n(E_n, \gamma_n) \geq c > 0.$$

Similar results have been obtained using heuristic methods or mean-field approximations in epidemic models on unweighted graphs with arbitrary degree distributions. Gai and Kapadia [14], extending previous work by Watts [24] to the directed graph case, give the following cascade condition:

$$1 - \sum_{j,k} \frac{jk}{\lambda} \mu(j,k) v_j < 0, \tag{2.6}$$

with v_j being the probability that a bank with out-degree j is vulnerable, i.e. exposed to the default of a single neighbor. This condition can be seen as a special case of Condition (2.5) in which the assets and capital buffers are i.i.d. sequences. In such case the convergence Assumption 2.2 is satisfied by the law of large numbers. The results in [14] are derived using generating function methods (see Newman [19]); under the assumption that component sizes are finite, one finds the generating function of the size of a connected component; the point at which the expected size of a connected component diverges marks the phase transition when the giant component appears. The arguments used in [14] are valid for graphs without cycles, i.e. trees. Rigorous proofs of these results and their extension to inhomogeneous weighted directed graphs with prescribed degree sequences are given in [1].

Note that these results are stated in term of the divergence of the **expected** size of a cascade starting from a randomly chosen node, the expectation being computed with respect to the law of a random graph with the given degree distribution. Theorems 2.1 and 2.2 are stronger statements: they show convergence in probability, not just in expectation, of the number of defaults for large networks.

More importantly, we do not assume a specific probabilistic model for the degree sequence or the balance sheet data: actual balance sheet data may be used as an input, under the mild Assumptions 2.1 and 2.2. As such, what appears in other models as the probability of a node to be vulnerable represents here the limit when $n \to \infty$ of the fraction of contagious links, a directly measurable quantity. Moreover as the capital ratios can be prescribed, it suffices to set to zero the capital ratio of certain banks in order to have prescribed defaults. All this is crucial if one wants to use the resilience measure in a stress testing framework.

We note that results closely related to those appearing in Theorems 2.1 and 2.2 have been used in the physics literature to study the size of cascades in networks.

Studies like [6–8] focus on the resilience of scale free networks and specifically the Internet and its robustness to targeted attacks. Meyers *et al.* [18] model the spread of infectious diseases in a semi-directed network, in which the asymmetry of disease transmission is captured by the presence of both undirected and directed edges. Their model generalizes previous work on undirected networks [19] and fully directed networks [22]. The resilience condition in these studies reduces to the existence of a giant component in the percolated graph.

Recently, Gleeson [15] finds the mean size of avalanches on directed unweighted networks in a model in which damage propagates from a fraction ρ of initially damaged nodes and a non-damaged node becomes damaged according to a random threshold depending on its in-degree (we note that damage propagates in [15] in the direction of edges, while in our case in the inverse direction due to our convention to model exposures). The damage propagation functions [15, Eqs. (4) and (5)] are equivalent to the function I in Eq. (2.3) and respectively the limit value for α in Theorem 2.1. The underlying assumption that is made in [15] is that, for large networks with well-behaved degree distributions the state of an input is independent for distinct inputs of a node. In [1] we prove that under the mild Assumptions 2.1 and 2.2 on the degree and exposure sequences, the size of a cascade behaves, in the large limit, as if, at each step, the counterparties of a node default independently of each other. Furthermore, while we prove that the weighted case reduces to the unweighted case, this is not trivial: the function p in Eq. (2.2) is directly computable from balance sheet data and accounts for the heterogeneity of exposures. The model is thus much more general than models with independent degrees and thresholds.

2.2. *Size of default cascade*

We now consider the structure of the skeleton of contagious links. Define the *susceptibility* of a random financial network

$$\chi(\mathbf{E_n}, \gamma_\mathbf{n}) := \frac{1}{n} \sum_{v \in [1,\ldots,n]} |C(v)|, \tag{2.7}$$

with $C(v)$ the default cluster of v containing all nodes from which v is reachable by a directed path of contagious links.

The skeleton of contagious links is the subgraph obtained by retaining only the contagious links in the initial network. Thus, if we consider the new degree sequence for this subgraph, it is still a random graph chosen uniformly from all graphs with this degree sequence [1], so we can still apply asymptotic results for the random configuration model [4, 16]. In particular, Janson [16] shows that the susceptibility of the random graph with given vertex degrees converges under mild conditions to the expected cluster size in the corresponding branching process, which may be defined as a Galton-Watson branching process with initial offspring ξ_0 and general offspring ξ. We define

$$\tilde{\lambda} := \sum_{j,k} j\mu(j,k)p(j,k,1),$$

the average number of contagious links and note that the fraction of contagious links is $T := \frac{\tilde{\lambda}}{\lambda}$. The generating function of the initial offspring ξ_0 is

$$G_0(y) = \sum_{k_0,j,k\geq k_0} \mu(j,k)\binom{k}{k_0}(1-T)^{k-k_0}T^{k_0}y^{k_0} = \sum_{j,k}\mu(j,k)(1-T+Ty)^k,$$

while the generating function of the general offspring is

$$G(y) = \sum_{j,k} \frac{j\mu(j,k)p(j,k,1)}{\tilde{\lambda}}(1-T+Ty)^k.$$

It is easy to see that G_0 represents the generating function of the number of links pointing into a randomly chosen node after bond percolation with probability T (each incoming edge is removed with probability $1-T$ independently of all other incoming edges). In terms of our network model, G represents the generating function of the number of contagious links ending in a node which is start of a randomly chosen contagious link. The probability that such a node has degree (j,k) is given by a weighted version of μ: $\frac{j\mu(j,k)p(j,k,1)}{\tilde{\lambda}}$. We have that

$$\mathbb{E}(\xi) = G'(1) = \sum_{j,k} \frac{j\mu(j,k)p(j,k,1)}{\tilde{\lambda}}kT = \sum_{j,k}\frac{jk\mu(j,k)}{\lambda}p(j,k,1),$$

and

$$\mathbb{E}(\xi_0) = G_0'(1) = \sum_{j,k} k\mu(j,k)T = \tilde{\lambda}$$

For a branching process with initial offspring ξ_0 and general offspring ξ, its susceptibility is given by $1+\frac{\mathbb{E}\xi_0}{(1-\mathbb{E}\xi)_+}$ (see [16, Theorem 3.1], [19]). By virtue of [16, Theorem 3.3] applied to the skeleton of contagious links, under Conditions 2.1 and 2.2, the average cascade size converges in probability (and in fact in L^1, in the subcritical case when $\mathbb{E}(\xi) < 1$) to the susceptibility of the corresponding branching process. We have:

- If the resilience measure is strictly positive,

$$\chi(\mathbf{E_n},\gamma_\mathbf{n}) \xrightarrow{L^1} \chi_\infty := 1 + \frac{\sum_{j,k} j\mu(j,k)p(j,k,1)}{1-\sum_{j,k}\frac{jk}{\lambda}\mu(j,k)p(j,k,1)}.$$

- If the resilience measure is zero or negative,

$$\chi(\mathbf{E_n},\gamma_\mathbf{n}) \xrightarrow{p} \infty.$$

We show thus by a different method that the positivity of the resilience measure is a necessary condition for the non-occurrence of global cascades: this condition is equivalent to the non-explosion of the branching process associated to the skeleton of contagious links

$$\mathbb{E}(\xi) < 1.$$

The full distribution of the size of the default cluster can be computed once the generating functions G_0 and G are known (see Bertoin and Sidoravicius [2, Theorem 1] which connects the structure of clusters in random graphs with prescribed degree distributions to branching processes and Newman *et al.* [19] for the derivation in case of branching processes). We define the generating function H of the size of the default cluster generated by a randomly chosen contagious edge, which verifies the condition $H(y) = yG(H(y))$. The generating function H_0 of the size of a default cluster is then given by $H_0(y) = yG_0(H(y))$. If the resilience measure is negative, then the probability of a large scale epidemic triggered by a single node is equal to the explosion probability of the branching process. If we let y^* be the smallest solution of

$$y = \sum_{j,k} \frac{j\mu(j,k)p(j,k,1)}{\tilde{\lambda}}(1 - T + Ty)^k,$$

then the probability of a global cascade is given by

$$1 - \sum_{j,k} \mu(j,k)(1 - T + Ty^*)^k.$$

This last formula confirms the observations in Gleeson [15] that the probability of occurrence of a global cascade strongly depends on the out-degree distribution even when the average cascade size does not, such as in cases where the degree distribution factorizes and the fraction of contagious links does not depend on the out-degrees.

3. Stress Testing

The analytical results presented above may be used to investigate the resilience of a financial network in a stress scenario, without the need for large scale simulation of default cascades. The idea is simply to apply shocks to balance sheets and to compute the impact of these shocks on the resilience measure (Definition (2.3)). Interestingly, it is observed that the final fraction of defaults generated by a fraction ϵ of fundamental defaults undergoes a sharp transition when the size of the shocks exceeds a certain threshold.

We explain how such a stress test may be done and apply the stress test to two example of networks: an infinite random network, and a finite scale-free network whose properties mimic the empirical properties of banking networks [5, 11].

3.1. *Stress testing resilience to macroeconomic shocks*

Consider a banking system in which the ratio $\gamma(i)$ of each bank's capital to its total assets is restricted to be greater than a minimal capital ratio: $\gamma(i) \geq \gamma_{\min}$. If the ratio of institution i's interbank assets to its total assets is denoted by LR_i, then

$$c_i = \gamma_i A_i \frac{1}{LR_i} > 0. \tag{3.1}$$

In a stress testing framework, we consider scenarios in which a given shock is applied to balance sheets of banks, resulting in the loss of a fraction $0 \leq S \leq 1$ of their external assets. To assess how such a stress scenario affects the resilience of the network to contagion, we evaluate the impact on the network of the default of a (small) fraction ϵ of nodes under stress scenarios of variable severity.

Using the notations in Table 1, the remaining capital of bank i is then given by

$$\begin{aligned} c_i(S) &= (A_i + x_i \cdot (1 - S) - L_i) \cdot \epsilon(i) \\ &= \left(A_i + A_i \left(\frac{1}{LR_i} - 1 \right) \cdot (1 - S) - \frac{A_i}{LR_i}(1 - \gamma_i) \right) \epsilon(i), \end{aligned}$$

where $\epsilon(i)$ are independent variables with

$$\mathbb{P}(\epsilon(i) = 1) = \epsilon = 1 - \mathbb{P}(\epsilon(i) = 0),$$

where $\epsilon(i) = 1$ indicating thats i is in default in the stress scenario under consideration.

This can be re-written so as to underline the effect of the shock S on the capital

$$c_i(S) = \gamma_i A_i \frac{1}{LR_i} \left(1 - \frac{S}{\gamma_i}(1 - LR_i) \right) \epsilon(i),$$

which means that a loss equal to a fraction S of the external assets translates into a loss equal to a fraction $Z_i := \frac{S}{\gamma_i}(1 - LR_i)$ of the capital buffer. Thus, in the stress scenario characterized by a macroeconomic shock (S, ϵ), the ratio of capital to interbank assets is given by

$$\gamma_i(S, \epsilon) = \gamma_i \left(1 - \frac{S}{\gamma_i}(1 - LR_i) \right) \epsilon(i). \tag{3.2}$$

Starting from this expression, one can use the results of Sec. 2 to evaluate the resilience of the network and the fraction of final defaults as a function of the size of the macroeconomic shock S, without resorting to large scale simulations. In particular, given that the conditions (2.4) and (2.5) will depend on the shock size S, we will see that there is a *threshold* for the magnitude of S above which it destabilizes the network and makes it vulnerable to contagion. This 'phase transition' indicates that a given network has a maximal tolerance for stress; we will see in fact that this threshold may be easily computed from the characteristics of the network.

This approach is applicable to any large network, with an arbitrary distribution of exposures and degrees. To provide some analytical insight into the impact of macroeconomic shocks on the resilience to contagion, we will consider in the next two examples the case where both LR_i and γ_i are constant and equal to LR and γ_{min} respectively. Figures for the lending ratio LR have been given by [14, 17, 23]. We will take $LR = 20\%$ and $\gamma_{min} = 10\%$.

Then the fraction of capital lost in the stress scenario is given by

$$Z = \frac{S}{\gamma_{min}}(1 - LR),$$

so we have

$$\gamma_i(Z) = \gamma_{min}(1 - Z)\epsilon(i).$$

One can observe that in this model, if $Z = 1$, a trivial global cascade ensues, in which all nodes are fundamental defaults: $\forall i, \gamma_i(Z) = 0$. However, as we shall see in the examples in the next sections, a sharp transition in the magnitude of the cascade occur for a threshold value of Z well below 1, which depends on the network characteristics.

3.2. *An example of infinite network*

We first apply the results to an infinite random scale-free network. Such a network may be obtained as the limit when $n \to \infty$ in Blanchard's random graph model [3]. In this model, the limit distribution of the out-degree d^+ is a power law with tail coefficient γ^+

$$\mu^+(j) := P(d^+ = j),$$

while the conditional law of the in-degree is a Poisson distribution

$$P(d^- = k|d^+ = j) = e^{-\lambda(j)}\frac{\lambda(j)^k}{k!},$$

with $\lambda(j) = \frac{j^\alpha \mathbb{E}^{\mu^+}(d^+)}{\mathbb{E}^{\mu^+}((d^+)^\alpha)}$, and α a real parameter. The main theorem in [3] states that the marginal distribution of the in-degree has a Pareto tail with exponent $\gamma^- = \frac{\gamma^+}{\alpha}$, provided $1 \leq \alpha < \gamma^+$. For $\alpha > 0$, one obtains positive correlation between in and out-degrees.

The exposures of each bank with out-degree j are assumed to be independent, and follow a Pareto law. The average exposure is an increasing deterministic function of j. We denote this law F_j.

Note that in this case the limit function $p(j, k, \theta)$ does not depend on the in-degree k (we denote this simply by $p(j, \theta)$), and the function I, whose smallest zero determines the final fraction of defaults (see Theorem 2.1), simplifies to

$$I(\pi) = \sum_j \mu^+(j)\frac{\lambda(j)}{\lambda}\sum_{\theta=0}^{j} p(j, \theta)\beta(j, \pi, \theta)$$

$$= \sum_j \mu^+(j) \frac{j^\alpha}{\mathbb{E}^{\mu^+}((d^+)^\alpha)} \sum_{\theta=0}^{j} p(j,\theta)\beta(j,\pi,\theta)$$

$$= \sum_j \hat{\mu}^+(j) \sum_{\theta=0}^{j} p(j,\theta)\beta(j,\pi,\theta), \tag{3.3}$$

with $\alpha = \gamma^+/\gamma^-$, and $\hat{\mu}^+$ the size-weighted out-degree distribution given by

$$\hat{\mu}^+(j) = \mu^+(j) \frac{j^\alpha}{\mathbb{E}^{\mu^+}((d^+)^\alpha)},$$

which is the probability that the end node of a randomly chosen edge has an out-degree equal to j. Since the out-degree distribution is a Pareto distribution, the size biased out-degree distribution is also Pareto, but with a heavier tail with exponent $\gamma^+ - \alpha$. The resilience condition 2.4 then simplifies to

$$\sum_j \hat{\mu}^+(j) j p(j,1) < 1. \tag{3.4}$$

Under the macroeconomic shock Z, the function $p(j,\theta)$ is given by

$$p(j,\theta) = \mathbb{P}(X(\theta) > \gamma(Z) \sum_{l=1}^{j} X(l) - \sum_{l=1}^{\theta-1} (1-R)X(l) \geq 0),$$

where $(X(l))_{l=1}^{j}$ are i.i.d. random variables with law F_j under $\mathbb{P}$ and $\gamma(Z)$ is given by (3.2). The function $p(j,\theta)$ is plotted in Fig. 1 for a given value of the macroeconomic shock Z. The steep increase with the number of counterparty defaults θ shows how much the system is prone to contagion, especially for the institutions whose assets are concentrated across a small number of counterparties (i.e nodes with small out-degrees).

We consider that a node defaults in the first round with probability ϵ, such that $p(j,0) = \epsilon$, for all j. We plot the function I given by (3.3) for several values of the macroeconomic shock Z in Fig. 2. We notice that the function I has three zeros for smaller values of Z, the smallest being close to zero, and as Z reaches a threshold value Z_c (in this case 42%) its only zero is close to one.

As stated in Theorem 2.1, if the resilience measure is positive, then with high probability, as the initial fraction of defaults tends to 0, no global cascades appear. On the other hand, if the resilience measure is negative, the skeleton of "contagious" links percolates, i.e. represents a positive fraction of the whole system, and we observe global cascades for any arbitrarily small fraction $\epsilon > 0$ of initial defaults chosen uniformly among all nodes. The verification of Theorem 2.1 is shown in Fig. 3. In the non-resilient regime global cascades may occur no matter how small the initial fraction of defaults is. On the contrary, in the resilient regime of the infinite network, if the initial fraction of defaults is small enough, global cascades are not possible. Therefore, the condition of positivity of the resilience measure is a necessary, but not sufficient condition for non occurrence of global cascades.

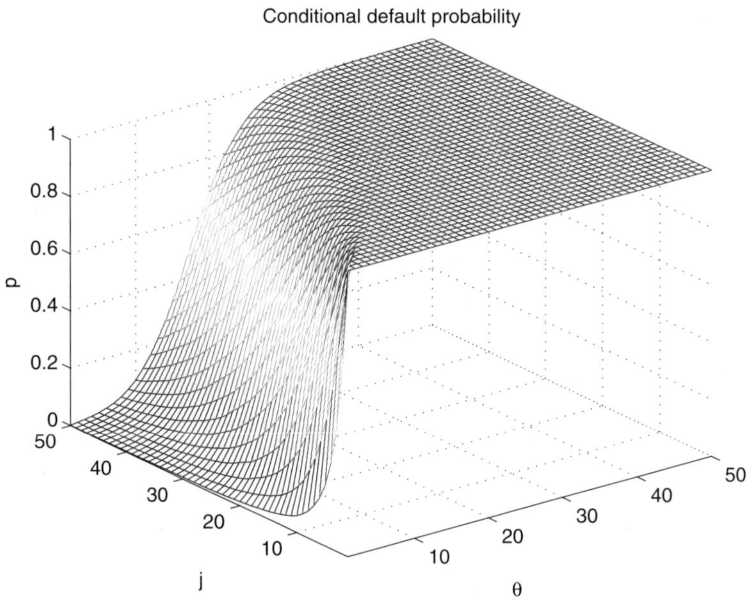

Fig. 1. The conditional probability of default, Minimal capital ratio = 8%, Macroeconomic shock = 20%, Recovery rate = 0.

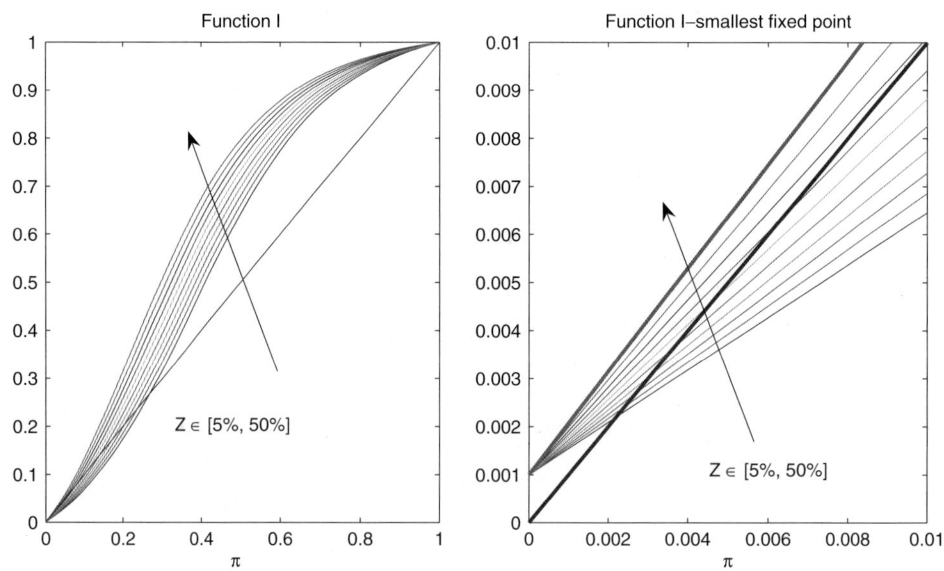

Fig. 2. Function I for varying size of macroeconomic shock. Fraction of initial defaults = 0.1%.

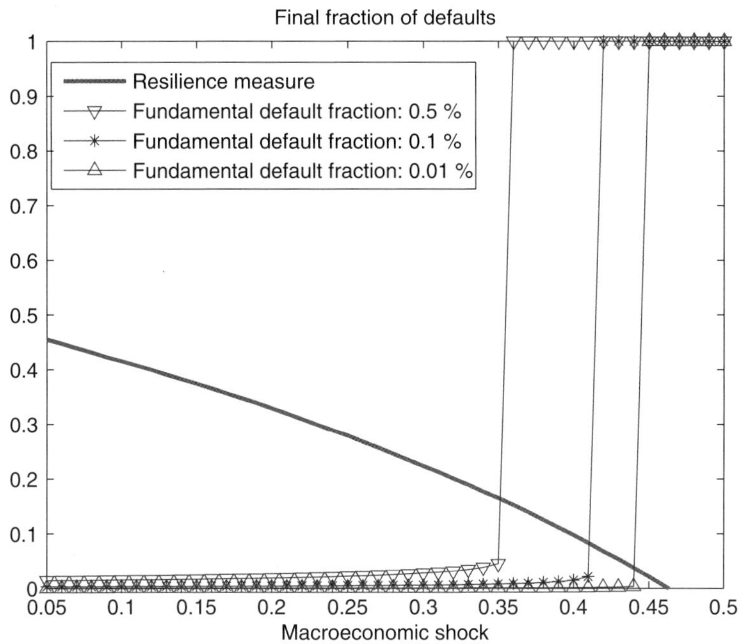

Fig. 3. Final fraction of defaults: infinite network.

3.3. *A finite scale-free network*

We apply the results to a sample scale free network of 2000 nodes with heterogeneous degrees and exposures, generated from Blanchard's random graph model [3]. The empirical distribution of the sample network's degrees and exposures is shown in Fig. 4, and its parameters were based on the analysis of the Brazilian [11] and Austrian [5] networks.

As Fig. 5 shows, we obtain highly correlated asset and liabilities sizes and the average exposure is increasing with the number of debtors for the more connected nodes. These properties are both observed in the empirical data.

In the finite sample, condition 3.4 translates to a condition on the average over all nodes of their number of 'contagious' links with a weight proportional to the out-degree to the power α:

$$\frac{1}{n}\sum_i w_i q_i < 1 \tag{3.5}$$

with $q_i := \#\{j \in v \mid e_{i,j} > c_i\}$ and $w_i := \frac{(d^+(i))^\alpha}{\sum_l (d^+(l))^\alpha}$.

If α is positive, so the more correlated the in-degree and the out-degree are, the more weight is given to the most interconnected nodes. This confirms the intuition that the nodes posing the highest systemic risk are those both overexposed and interconnected, but not necessarily the largest in terms of balance sheet size.

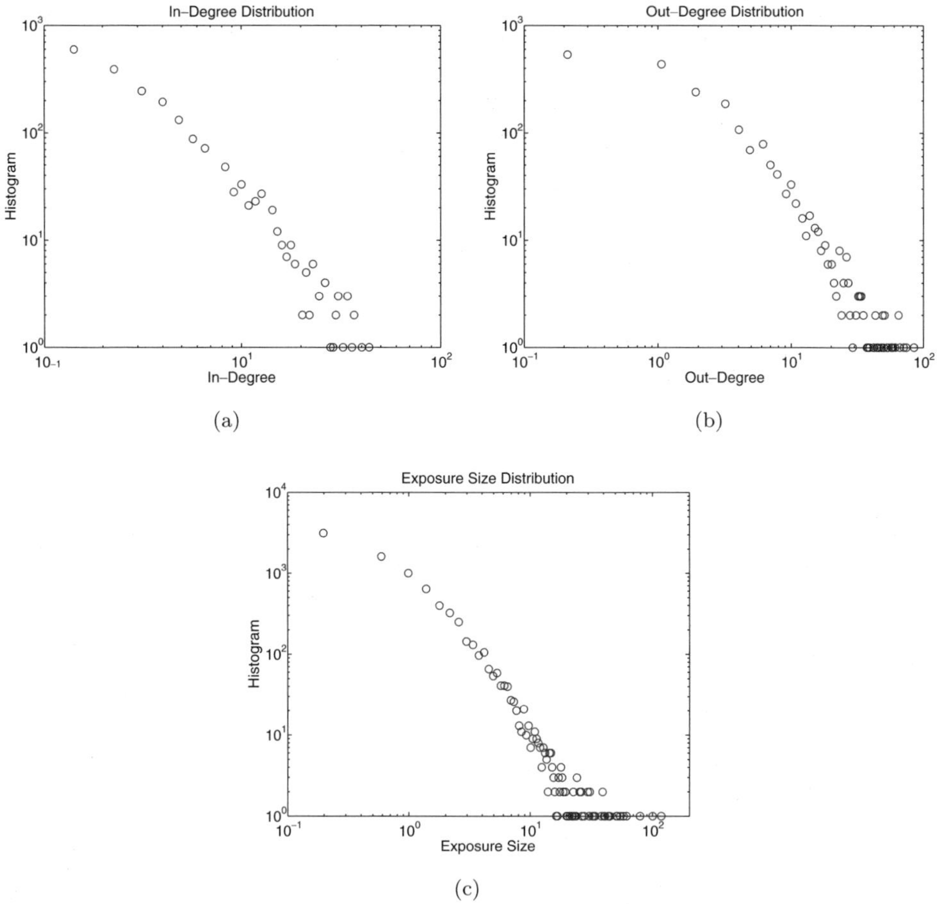

Fig. 4. (a) The distribution of out-degree has a Pareto tail with exponent 3.5, (b) The distribution of the in-degree has a Pareto tail with exponent 2.5, (c) The distribution of the exposures has a Pareto tail with exponent 2.1.

The value $p(j, 1)$ represents the limit fraction of contagious links entering nodes with out-degree j in the limit network. Fig. 6 shows the good accordance between the theoretical values and the values computed in the sample network. This suggests that in practice, there is no need to estimate the parameters of the limit distribution, but instead work directly with the empirical data.

Definition 3.1 (Empirical resilience measure). In a network $(\mathbf{e}, \gamma)$ of size n, we define the empirical resilience measure

$$1 - \frac{1}{m_n} \sum_i d^-(i) q_i, \tag{3.6}$$

where m_n is the total number of links in the network.

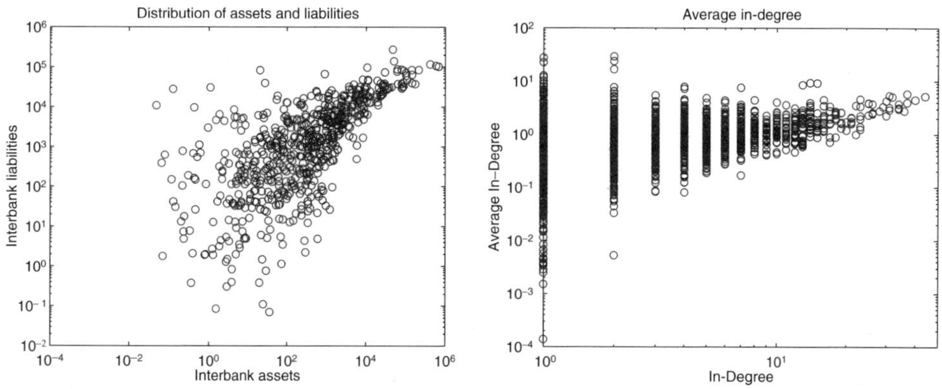

(a) (b)

Fig. 5. (a) Assets and liabilities, (b) Average exposures and connectivity.

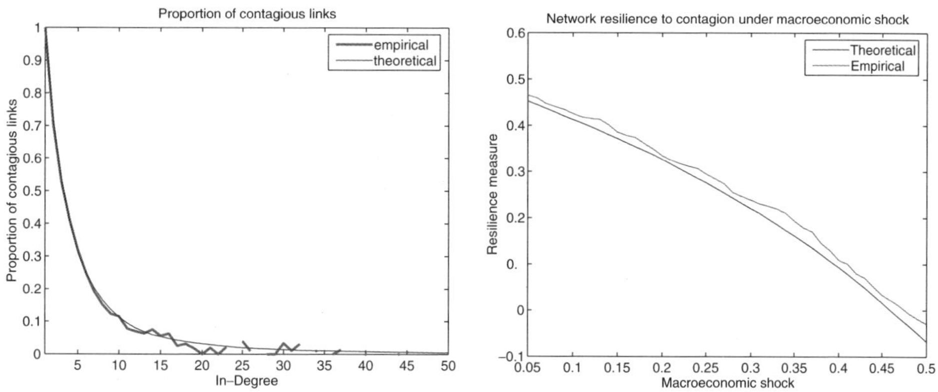

(a) (b)

Fig. 6. (a)Proportion of contagious links, (b)Resilience measure for varying size of macroeconomic shock in the sample and limit random network.

We conduct the following simulation on the sample network: two nodes, uniformly selected among all nodes of the network initially default. Then for each value of the macroeconomic shock Z and the corresponding sizes of the capital buffers, we compute the final fraction of defaults. In light of Fig. 3, in the infinite network, for an initial fraction of defaults representing 0.1% of the network, the positivity of the resilience measure is also sufficient for global cascades not to occur.

The results are plotted in Fig. 7 along with the "empirical" resilience measure.

We observe that for the given network and set of initial defaults, there exists a threshold value of the macroeconomic shock, beyond which the contagion spreads to essentially the whole network. By virtue of Theorem 2.1, the threshold value is

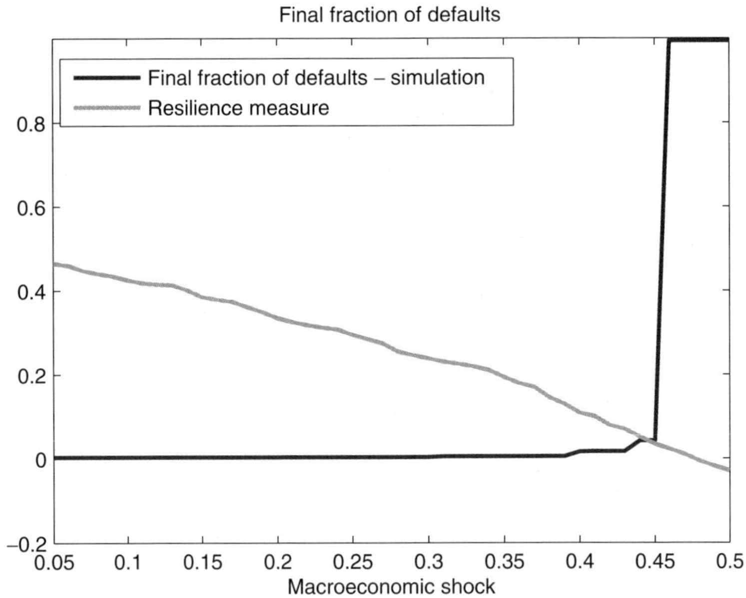

Fig. 7. Final fraction of defaults triggered by an initial fraction of defaults representing 0.1% of the total network.

smaller than the value of Z, for which the empirical resilience measure becomes zero. Also, the proximity of those two values depends strongly on the initial set of defaults. In the considered example, there is a good agreement between the two values, as the initial fraction of defaults is very small.

4. Discussion

We have proposed a framework for evaluating the impact of a macroeconomic shock on the resilience of a banking network to contagion effects. Our approach complements existing stress tests used by regulators [21] and suggests to monitor the capital adequacy of each institution with regard to its *largest exposures*.

In practice, such a stress tests may be implemented in a decentralized fashion by requesting banks to project the effect of a macroeconomic stress scenario on their balance sheets, and report the quantities of interest — mainly the number of exposures exceeding capital in the stress scenario — to the regulator, who can then assess the resilience of the network using our proposed resilience measure. Our criterion for resilience suggests that one need not monitor/know the *entire* network of counterparty exposures, but simply the subgraph of "contagious" links, which is much smaller. This intuition is indeed confirmed by simulation studies on a wide variety of networks [10, 11].

Acknowledgments

We thank M. Crouhy, J. Gleeson, the participants of the MITACS Workshop on Financial Networks and Risk Assessment and the Workshop on Financial Derivatives and Risk Management (Toronto, May 2010), the 6th World Congress of the Bachelier Finance Society (Toronto, June 2010) and the Workshop on Counterparty Risk, Systemic Risk and CCPs (Paris, September 2010) for helpful comments and discussions. We also thank an anonymous referee whose comments improved the first version of this paper. Andreea Minca's work is supported by the Natixis Foundation for Quantitative Research. This work was partially supported by a grant from the Europlace Institute of Finance.

References

[1] H. Amini, R. Cont and A. Minca, Resilience to contagion in financial networks, working paper. Available at http://ssrn.com/abstract=1865997 (2010).

[2] J. Bertoin and V. Sidoravicius, The structure of typical clusters in large sparse random configurations, *Journal of Statistical Physics* **135**(1) (2009) 87–105.

[3] P. Blanchard, C.-H. Chang and T. Krüger, Epidemic thresholds on scale-free graphs: the interplay between exponent and preferential choice, *Ann. Henri Poincaré* **4**(2) (2003) 957–970.

[4] B. Bollobás, *Random Graphs* (Cambridge University Press, 2001).

[5] M. Boss, H. Elsinger, M. Summer and S. Thurner, The network topology of the interbank market, *Quantitative Finance* **4** (2004) 677–684.

[6] D. S. Callaway, M. E. J. Newman, S. H. Strogatz and D. J. Watts, Network robustness and fragility: Percolation on random graphs, *Phys. Rev. Lett.* **85**(25) (2000) 5468–5471.

[7] R. Cohen, K. Erez, D. ben Avraham and S. Havlin, Resilience of the internet to random breakdowns, *Phys. Rev. Lett.* **85**(21) (2000) 4626–4628.

[8] R. Cohen, K. Erez, D. ben Avraham and S. Havlin, Breakdown of the internet under intentional attack, *Phys. Rev. Lett.* **86**(16) (2001) 3682–3685.

[9] R. Cont, Measuring systemic risk, to appear in J. P. Fouque and J. Langsam (eds.), *Handbook of Systemic Risk* (2009).

[10] R. Cont and A. Moussa, Too interconnected to fail: contagion and systemic risk in financial networks, Working Paper (2010).

[11] R. Cont, A. Moussa and E. B. e Santos, Network structure and systemic risk in banking system, working paper. Available at http://ssrn.com/abstract=1733528 (2010).

[12] L. Eisenberg and T. H. Noe, Systemic risk in financial systems, *Management Science* **47**(2) (2001) 236–249.

[13] H. Elsinger, A. Lehar and M. Summer, Risk assessment for banking systems, *Management Science* **52**(9) (2006) 1301–1314.

[14] P. Gai and S. Kapadia, Contagion in financial networks, SSRN eLibrary (2010).

[15] J. P. Gleeson, Mean size of avalanches on directed random networks with arbitrary degree distributions, *Phys. Rev. E* **77**(5) (2008) 057101.

[16] S. Janson, Susceptibility of random graphs with given vertex degrees, to appear in *Journal of Combinatorics*.

[17] R. M. May and N. Arinaminpathy, Systemic risk: the dynamics of model banking systems, *Journal of The Royal Society Interface* **7**(46) (2010) 823–838.

[18] L. A. Meyers, M. Newman and B. Pourbohloul, Predicting epidemics on directed contact networks, *Journal of Theoretical Biology* **240**(3) (2006) 400–418.

[19] M. E. J. Newman, S. H. Strogatz and D. J. Watts, Random graphs with arbitrary degree distributions and their applications, *Physical Review E* **64** (2001) 026118.

[20] E. Nier, J. Yang, T. Yorulmazer and A. Alentorn, Network models and finacial stability, *Journal of Economic Dynamics and Control* **31**(6) (2007) 2033–2060.

[21] Board of Governors of the Federal Reserve System. The supervisory capital assessment program: Design and implementation, April 24 (2009).

[22] N. Schwartz, R. Cohen, D. ben Avraham, A.-L. Barabási and S. Havlin, Percolation in directed scale-free networks, *Phys. Rev. E* **66**(1) (2002) 015104.

[23] C. Upper and A. Worms, Estimating bilateral exposures in the german interbank market: Is there a danger of contagion? Deutsche Bundesbank Discussion Paper No 09/02, February (2002).

[24] D. J. Watts, A simple model of global cascades on random networks, *Proc. Natl. Acad. Sci. USA* **99**(9) (2002) 5766–5771.

MANAGING CORPORATE LIQUIDITY: STRATEGIES AND PRICING IMPLICATIONS*

ATTAKRIT ASVANUNT

AQR Capital Management
2 Greenwich Plaza, 3rd Floor, Greenwich, CT 06830, USA

MARK BROADIE and SURESH SUNDARESAN

Graduate School of Business, Columbia University
New York, NY 10027, USA

Defaults arising from illiquidity can lead to private workouts, formal bankruptcy proceedings or even liquidation. All these outcomes can result in deadweight losses. Corporate illiquidity in the presence of realistic capital market frictions can be managed by (a) equity dilution, (b) carrying positive cash balances, or (c) entering into loan commitments with a syndicate of lenders. An efficient way to manage illiquidity is to rely on mechanisms that transfer cash from "good states" into "bad states" (i.e., financial distress) without wasting liquidity in the process. In this paper, we first investigate the impact of costly equity dilution as a method to deal with illiquidity, and characterize its effects on corporate debt prices and optimal capital structure. We show that equity dilution produces lower firm value in general. Next, we consider two alternative mechanisms: cash balances and loan commitments. Abstracting from future investment opportunities and share re-purchases, which are strong reasons for corporate cash holdings, we show that carrying positive cash balances for managing illiquidity is in general inefficient relative to entering into loan commitments, since cash balances (a) may have agency costs, (b) reduce the riskiness of the firm thereby lowering the option value to default, (c) postpone or reduce dividends in good states, and (d) tend to inject liquidity in both good and bad states. Loan commitments, on the other hand, (a) reduce agency costs, and (b) permit injection of liquidity in bad states as and when needed. Then, we study the trade-offs between these alternative approaches to managing corporate illiquidity. We show that loan commitments can lead to an improvement in overall welfare and reduction in spreads on existing debt for a broad range of parameter values. We derive explicit pricing formulas for debt and equity prices. In addition, we characterize the optimal draw down strategy for loan commitments, and study its impact on optimal capital structure.

Keywords: Loan commitment; cash reserve; liquidity management; security pricing.

*This chapter was originally published under the same title in *International Journal of Theoretical and Applied Finance*, Vol.14, No.3, 369–406 (2011). Singapore: World Scientific Publishing.

1. Introduction

Theory of optimal capital structure and debt valuation has made rapid strides in recent years. Beginning with the pioneering work of [29], which provided the first structural formulation of debt pricing, a number of recent papers have extended the analysis to consider the valuation of multiple issues of debt, optimal capital structure, debt renegotiation, and the effects of Chapters 7 and 11 provisions on debt valuation and optimal capital structure.[1] These models have tended to abstract from cash holdings by companies or loan commitments held by the companies. Yet these are important ways in which companies deal with illiquidity and avoid potentially costly liquidations or financial distress. In the banking literature, researchers have examined the role of loan commitments and their effects on the welfare of corporate borrowers both in theoretical and empirical work. Papers by [26, 34, 35, 37, 38] have explored the important role played by loan commitments under capital market frictions. The insights of these papers have not yet been brought to bear on the pricing and optimal capital structure implications. This is one of the goals of our paper. A typical company often issues multiple types of debt, with different seniority and covenants. As a result, cash flows to creditors are complicated to model when the firm enters bad states (as in financial distress). In the case of default, the U.S. Bankruptcy Codes (Chapters 11, 13, etc.) allow companies to postpone liquidation by providing the borrowing firm with protection while it undergoes reorganization and debt renegotiation with the creditors. Alternatively, companies can also enter into financial contracts such as loan commitments in good states (when they are solvent), to alleviate their financial distress and thus postponing or avoiding bankruptcy. In this paper, we propose a structural model that incorporates loan commitments as an alternative source of liquidity. We contrast this strategy with two other mechanisms that have been studied in the literature for managing illiquidity: cash balances and costly equity dilution. Our paper does not consider dynamic investment opportunities (future growth options), and this assumption precludes an important incentive for holding cash: the model presented is more relevant for mature firms.

1.1. *Overview of major results*

In our paper we integrate the insights of the banking literature on loan commitments with the insights of debt pricing literature and provide a framework for analyzing loan commitments as a part of optimal capital structure. Our paper also formally explores three distinct ways in which companies deal with illiquidity – equity dilution, cash balances and loan commitments. To our knowledge, this is the first paper to undertake this comprehensive examination of corporate strategies for managing liquidity. In so doing, we extend the theory of optimal capital structure to permit

[1] An important subset of this literature includes the papers by [4, 9, 12, 25].

junior and senior debt, where the corporate borrower can optimally select the "draw down" and "repayment" strategy of loan commitments.

We provide an analytical characterization of credit spreads, optimal capital structure and debt capacity when equity dilution is costly, subject to the endogenous default boundary as a solution to a nonlinear equation. Using the base case of zero cost of equity dilution, we characterize the welfare losses due to dilution costs when equity holders decide on the choice of the optimal default boundary.

We show, through an induction argument, that it is never optimal to carry cash balances to guard against default when equity issuance is costless. More importantly, we characterize the threshold levels of managerial frictions associated with holding cash *and* equity dilution costs over which it is never optimal to hold cash balances. Our results show that the dilution costs of equity have to be very significant and the costs of holding cash have to be very low in order for the firm to curtail dividends and hold cash balances.

In the context of previous results, we explore contingent transfer of liquidity through the use of loan commitments where the borrower is able to pay a commitment fee in good states and draw down cash in bad states as needed. We develop a model and computational methodology needed for loan commitments. Using this approach, we characterize the optimal draw down and repayment strategy and the effects of loan commitments on existing debt spreads and the welfare of the borrowing firm. We find that entering into a loan commitment agreement can benefit both equity and debt holders. We also study the impact of a loan commitment on the firm's optimal capital structure.

Our results should be viewed in the context of our model assumptions. We treat the firm's investment policy as fixed and exogenous. Availability of future investment and growth options may provide a strong motive for accumulating cash balances when equity dilution costs are significant. We abstract from this important consideration. Our paper does not model strategic debt service considerations. Since strategic debt service (especially when renegotiations are not costly) allows for underperformance in bad states, it acts as a substitute to holding cash balances. This has been noted by [1]. Our analysis, however, can be modified to incorporate strategic debt service. Finally, we do not model the Chapter 11 provision of the bankruptcy code, which also allows illiquid firms to seek bankruptcy protection and coordinate their liquidity problems with lenders and avoid potential liquidation.

1.2. *Review of the literature*

The structural approach to modeling corporate debt begins with the seminal work of [29]. He indicates that risky zero-coupon bonds may be valued using the Black-Scholes-Merton option pricing approach. In this model, default occurs if the asset value of the firm falls below the debt principal at maturity. [9] extend this model for coupon bonds with finite maturity, where they impose that the firm must issue equity to make the coupon payments, and that default is endogenously chosen by the firm at any time prior to maturity. [25] derives a closed-form solution for prices of perpetual coupon bonds. His model incorporates bankruptcy cost, tax benefit of coupon payments, and dividend payouts. He also derives the expressions for optimal capital structure, debt capacity, and optimal default boundary. [12] consider the presence of Chapters 7 and 11, which leads to reorganization upon bankruptcy prior to liquidation. All of these models restrict the firm from selling its asset.

The work mentioned above implicitly assume that liquidity has no value. This follows from the assumption that the firm can dilute equity freely to finance shortfall of cash from operations to fund the coupon payments. Equity issuance, however, is quite costly in practice, and hence many firms maintain cash reserves or enter into agreements such as a loan commitment to manage liquidity crises.

The literature of cash reserves is related to that of dividend policies. Since the work of [30], who show that dividend policy is irrelevant to the firm value in perfect (frictionless) markets, extensive research has emerged in the study of optimal dividend policies by means of optimization and stochastic optimal control under more realistic market conditions. Examples of stochastic control models include [5, 22, and 33]. These models choose a policy that maximizes the present value of a future dividend stream subject to various cost structures associated with the distribution. [39] provides a more detailed discussion of the literature in this area. In a recent paper, [14] model the cash process as a mean-reverting process, and characterize optimal dividend policy in terms of the amount and timing of dividend distributions. Our model is more similar in spirit to those of [23] and [1], where the focus is on liquidity. [23] develop a three-period model that investigates the trade-offs between holding liquid assets (cash) with lower returns versus facing future uncertainty and costly external funding (equity issuance). They find that the optimal level of cash is increasing with the cost of equity issuance and the volatility of future cash flows. [1] develop a multi-period model that allows the firm to simultaneously keep cash reserves and service debt strategically. They find that the option to carry cash is valuable if the firm also has the option for strategic debt-service. We provide a fully dynamic model of endogenous default and derive implications for cash balances and line of credit.

Existing literature on loan commitments dates back to [19] and [20]. [19] develops a pricing framework for loan commitment contracts under two different models. The first model assumes that the firm's assets are bought or sold when the loan commitment is drawn down or repaid, respectively. The second assumes that the shareholders receive dividends when loan commitment is drawn down, and new shares are issued when it is repaid. [20] focus on the hedging of a loan commitment with bond futures contracts. In their model, they assume that the firm has an option to draw down at a fixed time, and cannot repay it before maturity. [32] discusses these two papers in more detail. [27] formulate an optimization problem for a firm which enters into a loan commitment for future financing of investment opportunities that arrive stochastically. They discuss the optimal size of the loan commitment, the determinants of the size, and the average usage by the firm. [32] investigates the impact of loan commitment on existing debt. He imposes a covenant that restricts dividend payouts to shareholders when the loan commitment is drawn. In this model, excess cash from revenue after making coupon payments must go back to repay the loan commitment immediately. Our model differs from the above, with the exception of [32], in terms of the purpose of the loan commitment. We use loan commitment solely for managing liquidity, and not for financing investment opportunities. In addition, our model accounts for both the optimal draw down *and* repayment strategies of the loan commitment.

There is also a body of literature that discusses the roles and benefits of loan commitments. [26] argues that loan commitments can increase individual firm's profit in an imperfectly competitive market, when they are used to finance the firm's strategic position as a response to its rival's decisions. [8] develop a two-period model to show that a loan commitment may be an optimal way to finance risky investments. [34] demonstrates that a loan commitment leads to higher optimal debt level and lower cost of debt under similar settings. [36] argues that a loan commitment is a strictly better source of financing than a standard debt, in the presence of the debt overhang problem originally proposed by [31], because of its fixed-fee and low interest rate features. Under our model assumptions, we also find that the loan commitment increases the optimal level of existing debt and may reduce its spread.

On the empirical side, [28] provide empirical analysis on "packages" of loan commitment terms from surveyed data of 132 U.S. non-financial firms. They find that the loan commitment size is positively correlated with the interest mark-up, commitment fee, length of contracts, current ratios, and firm size. [35] provide similar analysis based on data of 2,513 bank loan commitment contracts sold to publicly traded U.S. firms. The data were collected from Securities and Exchange Commission filings by the Loan Pricing Corporation. [2] test the model of [27] empirically against the data for loan commitments made to 712 privately-owned firms, and find the results consistent with the model's predictions. In a recent paper [37] has presented evidence that suggests that banks are unwilling to provide loan commitments to firms that do not have sufficient operating cash flows. In other words, there is a supply side constraint on the ability of borrowing firms to get loan commitment.

Loan commitments often carry Material Adverse Change (MAC) provisions, which may allow the bank to withdraw the lines under specified economic circumstances. This said, MAC is rarely invoked: firms such as Enron were able to draw their lines before they eventually declared bankruptcy[2]. [21] notes that the draw-down of credit lines may help explain the fact that bank commercial and industrial (C&I) lending increased during the fall of 2008 when borrowers and bankers were reporting extremely tight credit market conditions. C&I loans held by U.S. domestic

[2]See [21], for example.

banks increased from \$1.514 trillion in August 2008 to \$1.582 trillion by year-end, while the Federal Reserves Senior Loan Officer Opinion Survey on Bank Lending Practices found that a record net 83.2% of respondents reported that their institutions had tightened loan standards for large and medium borrowers in the fourth quarter. This pattern of usage of loan commitments is consistent with the theory developed in our paper.

The remainder of the paper is organized as follows. Section 2 describes the basic setup of the model. In Sec. 3, we study the welfare and pricing of the firm's securities under costly equity dilution. We introduce the loan commitment into the model in in Sec. 4. Section 5 concludes and the Appendices contain technical proofs and our computational methodology.

2. The Model

In a perfect capital market where there are no frictions and where distress can be resolved costlessly, the question of corporate liquidity is not relevant. Empirical evidence suggests, however, that there are at least two important sources of frictions which render corporate liquidity a very important question. First, there are costs associated with security issuance. Such costs reflect not only the costs associated with underwriting and distribution, but also with asymmetric information that characterize the relationship between the suppliers of capital and corporations. A survey by [24] finds that direct equity issuance cost (underwriter spreads and administrative fees) on average is over 13% for \$2–10 million and over 8% for \$10–20 million of seasoned equity offerings. The average cost for initial public offerings is even higher, 17% for \$2–10 million and over 11% for \$10–20 million. In addition, financial distress can lead to private workouts, bankruptcy proceedings and even liquidation, all of which are known to be costly. [10] reports total bankruptcy-related costs to firm and claimholders to be between 13% and 21% of pre-distressed value. [11] provide a detailed analysis of bankruptcy costs under Chapters 7 and 11. They find that the average change in asset value maybe as high as 84% before and after the filing of Chapter 7. In this paper, we construct a simple trade-off model of capital structure, where corporate liquidity plays a pivotal role. Our structural model is an extension of [25] with net cash payouts by the firm (Sec. VI. B). We introduce two costs explicitly. First, we model the cost of maintaining liquidity by introducing an exogenous cost on cash balances. In addition, we also recognize that equity dilution is costly. A corporate borrower chooses a level of debt by trading off tax benefits and the possibility of costly liquidation in the future. We ask how this decision is informed by managing the liquidity of the firm through three possible tools: (a) equity dilution, (b) carrying cash balances, and (c) using loan commitment, which are fairly priced. In order to focus squarely on liquidity strategies of the corporation in a trade-off model, we abstract from a detailed modeling of the bankruptcy code, which in itself is an institution that is designed, in part, to address the question of resolving illiquidity. It will be of interest to extend our analysis to examine how the liquidity strategies of a firm will be influenced by the availability of a well designed bankruptcy code.[3]

Since the investment policy is fixed, we restrict the sale and purchase of the firm's assets, and hence the firm can only use its revenue or proceeds from equity dilution to make the coupon payments in absence of cash balances or loan commitments. We consider costs associated with holding cash explicitly. As an alternative to cash or equity dilution, the firm may also enter into a loan commitment to transfer cash from the solvent state to the state when the firm is not generating enough revenue to cover the coupon payment. We assume that the firm has to pay a one-time fee at the time the loan commitment contract is signed. Since the firm's asset cannot be purchased or sold, the sole purpose of cash and a loan commitment is to provide liquidity when the firm is in distress, and not for investment purposes.

2.1. *Basic setup*

We assume that the firm's asset value, denoted by V_t, is independent of its capital structure, and follows a diffusion process whose evolution under the risk neutral measure $\mathbb{Q}$ is given by:

$$dV_t = (r - q)V_t dt + \sigma V_t dW_t$$

where r is the risk-free rate, q is the instantaneous rate of the return on asset, σ is the volatility of asset value, and W_t is a standard Brownian motion under $\mathbb{Q}$. The instantaneous revenue generated by the firm is given by:

$$\delta_t = qV_t.$$

The parameter q determines the internal liquidity of the firm from its cash flow. Holding the current asset value fixed, a higher value of q implies that the firm produces more cash flow per unit time than a lower value of q. In this regard, lower q is consistent with a higher growth rate, holding other factors constant.

The firm issues debt with principal P, a continuous coupon rate c, and a maturity T. The firm uses its revenue δ_t to make the coupon payment, and uses any surplus to pay dividends to the shareholders. In absence of cash balances and loan commitment, when revenue is not enough to cover the payment, the firm can either dilute equity to raise money to make the payment or declare bankruptcy. In the latter case, the firm liquidates its assets and the proceeds go to the debt holders. There is an equity dilution cost of γ and a liquidation cost of α, which will be explained in the next section. We next describe the three strategies to manage corporate illiquidity.

[3]Examples of papers that examine alternative bankruptcy procedures include [3, 6, 7, 17]. [18] summarizes the general consensus on the goals and the characteristics of efficient bankruptcy procedures.

2.2. *Equity dilution*

When faced with a liquidity crisis, the firm may raise capital by issuing additional equity. We assume that the cost of equity dilution is proportional to the proceeds from the issuance. Let γ be the proportion of the proceeds lost due to deadweight costs of issuance. In other words, if x is the percentage of outstanding shares to be issued, then the proceeds from equity dilution are $\frac{x}{1+x}E$. However, the firm only receives $(1-\gamma)\frac{x}{1+x}E$. The claim value of the original shareholders reduces to $\frac{1}{1+x}E$.

Suppose the firm needs to raise $\bar{C}$ dollars from equity dilution, then the percentage of shares it needs to issue is given by:

$$x = \frac{\bar{C}}{(1-\gamma)E - \bar{C}}$$

and the claim value of the original shareholders reduces to:

$$\frac{1}{1+x}E = \left(\frac{1}{1 + (\bar{C}/((1-\gamma)E - \bar{C}))}\right)E = E - \frac{\bar{C}}{1-\gamma}$$

which is equivalent to the shareholders receiving a *negative dividend* of $\frac{\bar{C}}{1-\gamma}$. In our model, equity issuance would not be undertaken if it does not lead to an increase in the value of equity.

2.3. *Cash balance*

An alternative to issuing equity is to build up a cash balance. The firm may choose a dividend payout rate d strictly less than the revenue rate δ in the good states when the revenues exceed coupon payments, and thus accumulate a cash balance, x, over time. On this cash balance, we assume that the firm earns an interest at rate $r_x \leq r$, reflecting the possible costs associated with leaving cash inside the firm. In our model, the firm chooses the payout rate d that maximizes its equity value.

2.4. *Loan commitment*

Finally, the firm may enter into a loan commitment with another lender. A loan commitment is a contractual agreement between lender (the "bank") and the firm, that gives the right, but not an obligation, to the firm to borrow in the future at the pre-specified terms. The terms may include, but are not limited to, the size of a loan commitment P^l, a rate of interest (coupon rate) c^l, and an expiration date. Generally, there are *drawn* and *undrawn* fees associated with the loan commitment.

In our model, the bank imposes a covenant that forbids the firm from using the proceeds of the loan to pay shareholder dividends. The firm does not keep a cash balance, so as a result, it only considers drawing down the loan when revenue is not sufficient to cover the coupon payment. Furthermore, the firm can at most draw down the amount of the shortfall. The bank also allows the firm to repay any amount of the loan at any time prior to maturity. We assume that the firm makes all its decisions to maximize the equity value.

We describe in detail how the firm makes the decisions, and how the fees are determined in Sec. 5.

3. Welfare and Pricing Under Costly Equity Dilution

In this section, we show how equity, debt and total firm value can be determined when equity dilution is costly. We derive closed-form solutions for these values for the infinite maturity case. We show how equity dilution cost affects credit spread, debt capacity and optimal capital structure.

3.1. *Exogenous bankruptcy boundary*

First, we derive closed-form solutions for equity, debt and total firm values when the bankruptcy boundary is determined exogenously. We assume that there is an asset value boundary V_B, below which the firm will declare bankruptcy. Upon bankruptcy, the firm liquidates its assets and incurs a liquidation cost of α, i.e., the proceeds from liquidation are $(1-\alpha)(V+\delta)$.

It is well known (e.g. [15]) that the value, $f(V_t, t)$, of any security whose payoff depends on the asset value, V_t, must satisfy the following PDE:

$$\frac{1}{2}\sigma^2 V_t^2 f_{VV} + (r-q)V_t f_V - rf + f_t + g(V_t, t) = 0 \tag{3.1}$$

where $g(V_t, t)$ is the payout received by holders of security f.

In the perpetuity case, the security becomes time-independent, and hence the above PDE reduces to the following ODE:

$$\frac{1}{2}\sigma^2 V^2 f_{VV} + (r-q)V f_V - rf + g(V) = 0 \tag{3.2}$$

Equation (3.2) has the general solution:

$$f(V) = A_0 + A_1 V + A_2 V^{-Y} + A_3 V^{-X} \tag{3.3}$$

where

$$X = \frac{\left(r-q-\frac{\sigma^2}{2}\right) + \sqrt{\left(r-q-\frac{\sigma^2}{2}\right)^2 + 2\sigma^2 r}}{\sigma^2} \tag{3.4}$$

$$Y = \frac{\left(r-q-\frac{\sigma^2}{2}\right) - \sqrt{\left(r-q-\frac{\sigma^2}{2}\right)^2 + 2\sigma^2 r}}{\sigma^2} \tag{3.5}$$

3.1.1. *Equity value*

Consider a firm that issues perpetual debt which pays a continuous coupon at the rate C. When the firm's revenue rate exceeds the coupon rate, $qV \geq C$, equity holders receive dividends at rate $(qV - C)$, otherwise the firm dilutes equity to make the coupon payment. As explained above, the latter is equivalent to a negative dividend of $\beta(qV - C)$, where $\beta = 1/(1-\gamma)$.

Therefore, the equity value, E, must satisfy:

$$\frac{1}{2}\sigma^2 V^2 E_{VV} + (r-q)VE_V - rE + \beta(qV - C) = 0 \quad \text{for } V_B \le V < C/q \tag{3.6}$$

$$\frac{1}{2}\sigma^2 V^2 E_{VV} + (r-q)VE_V - rE + qV - C = 0 \quad \text{for } V \ge C/q \tag{3.7}$$

The general solution (3.3) becomes:

$$E(V) = \begin{cases} A_0 + A_1 V + A_2 V^{-Y} + A_3 V^{-X} & \text{for } V_B \le V < C/q \\ \tilde{A}_0 + \tilde{A}_1 V + \tilde{A}_2 V^{-Y} + \tilde{A}_3 V^{-X} & \text{for } V \ge C/q \end{cases} \tag{3.8}$$

To solve for the coefficients in (3.8), we use the fact that $E(V)$ must also satisfy the following boundary, continuity and smooth pasting conditions:

$$\begin{aligned} &\text{(BC I):} && E(V_B) = 0 \\ &\text{(BC II):} && \lim_{V\to\infty} E(V) = V - \tfrac{C}{r} \\ &\text{(CC):} && E((C/q)^-) = E(C/q) \\ &\text{(SP):} && E_V((C/q)^-) = E_V(C/q) \end{aligned} \tag{3.9}$$

(BC I) follows from our assumption that the shareholders get nothing when the firm declares bankruptcy. (BC II) is the value of equity when the firm becomes riskless as the asset value approaches infinity. (CC) and (SP) ensures a smooth and continuous transition in and out of equity dilution region. This follows from the fact that the equity value fully anticipates the future events.

By solving the system of equations above, the equity value is given by:

$$E(V) = \begin{cases} \beta\left(V - \dfrac{C}{r}\right) + A_2 V^{-Y} + A_3 V^{-X} & \text{for } V_B \le V < C/q \\ \left(V - \dfrac{C}{r}\right) + \tilde{A}_3 V^{-X} & \text{for } V \ge C/q \end{cases} \tag{3.10}$$

where

$$A_2 = \frac{(\beta-1)\left(\frac{C}{q}\right)^Y \left(X\frac{C}{r} - X\frac{C}{q} - \frac{C}{q}\right)}{X - Y}$$

$$A_3 = \left[\beta\left(\frac{C}{r} - V_B\right) - A_2 V_B^{-Y}\right] V_B^X$$

$$\tilde{A}_3 = \left[(\beta-1)\left(\frac{C}{q} - \frac{C}{r}\right) V_B^{-X} + \beta\left(\frac{C}{q}\right)^{-X}\left(\frac{C}{r} - V_B\right)\right] V_B^{X+Y}$$

$$+ \frac{(\beta-1)\left(X\frac{C}{r} - X\frac{C}{q} - \frac{C}{q}\right)\left(V_B^{-X} - V_B^{-Y}\left(\frac{C}{q}\right)^{Y-X}\right)}{X - Y} V_B^{X+Y}$$

The details of this derivation can be found in Appendix A.

3.1.2. *Debt value*

Debt holders receive a constant payout rate of C as long as the firm remains solvent, i.e., when $V \geq V_B$. Therefore the debt value, D, must satisfy:

$$\frac{1}{2}\sigma^2 V^2 D_{VV} + (r-q)VD_V - rE + C = 0 \quad \text{for } V \geq V_B \tag{3.11}$$

Equation (3.11) has a general solution:

$$D(V) = B_0 + B_1 V + B_2 V^{-X} \tag{3.12}$$

where X is given by (3.4).

Similar to solving for the equity value, we use the fact that $D(V)$ must satisfy the following boundary conditions:

$$\begin{aligned} &\text{(BC I):} && D(V_B) = (1-\alpha)V_B \\ &\text{(BC II):} && \lim_{V\to\infty} D(V) = \frac{C}{r} \end{aligned} \tag{3.13}$$

(BC I) follows from our assumption on bankruptcy cost, and (BC II) is the value of a perpetual debt as it becomes riskless.

Then we can show that the debt value is given by:

$$D(V) = \frac{C}{r} + \left((1-\alpha)V_B - \frac{C}{r}\right)\left(\frac{V}{V_B}\right)^{-X} \quad \text{for } V \geq V_B \tag{3.14}$$

The details of this derivation can be found in Appendix A.

3.2. *Endogenous bankruptcy boundary*

In the previous section, we assume that the bankruptcy boundary is determined exogenously. In practice, the management of the firm acts in the best interest of its shareholders. Thus in the absence of a covenant imposed by the debt holders, the firm will choose a bankruptcy boundary that maximizes its equity value. From the expression of equity value given in (3.10), we can see that the equity value only depends on V_B through A_3 (assuming that optimal V_B is in the equity dilution region, $V < \frac{C}{q}$). Thus, the optimal V_B can be found by solving $\frac{\partial E}{\partial V_B} = 0$, which is equivalent to solving $\frac{\partial A_3}{\partial V_B} = 0$. Consequently, the optimal bankruptcy boundary, V_B^*, is given by the following implicit expression:

$$X\beta\frac{C}{r}(V_B^*)^{-1} - (1+X)\beta - (X-Y)A_2(V_B^*)^{-Y-1} = 0 \tag{3.15}$$

The equity and debt values with endogenous bankruptcy boundary is therefore given by (3.8) and (3.14), evaluated at V_B^*.

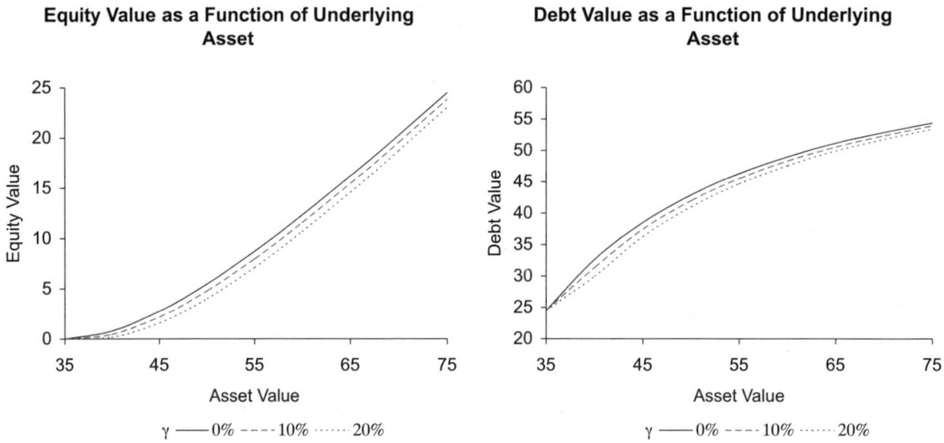

Fig. 1. Plots of equity, $E(V)$, and debt values, $D(V)$, as a function asset value at different levels equity dilution cost, γ. Both $E(V)$ and $D(V)$ are increasing in V, decreasing in γ, and converge to the Leland results as $V \to \infty$ for all values of γ. ($V = 100, C = 3.36, \sigma = 0.2, r = 0.05, q = 0.03, \alpha = 0.3, \tau = 0.15$).

3.3. *Impacts of costly equity dilution*

3.3.1. *Security values*

Figure 1 plots equity and debt values as a function of the underlying asset value as given by (3.8) and (3.14). We observe that the optimal bankruptcy boundary, V_B, increases as γ increases. This makes sense because as asset value declines, the equity value declines at a faster rate with costly equity diltuion, and hence bankruptcy is declared at a higher asset value. Equity value is also decreasing in γ. The impact of dilution cost converges to zero as $V \to \infty$.

We observe that debt value is decreasing in γ. Since $D(V)$ is only a function of γ through V_B and V_B is increasing in γ, from (3.14), we can deduce that $D(V)$ is decreasing in γ if and only if $(1-\alpha)V_B \leq \frac{C}{r}\frac{X}{1+X}$. Similar to the equity value, the effect of dilution cost converges to zero as $V \to \infty$.

3.3.2. *Debt capacity and optimal capital structure*

The debt capacity of a firm is defined as the maximum value of debt that can be sustained by the firm. This is determined by the value of coupon, $C^{\max}$, which maximizes the debt value, denoted by $D^{\max}$. In this section, we illustrate numerically how the cost of equity dilution, γ, affects $D^{\max}$. The left panel of Fig. 2 shows that $C^{\max}$, as well as $D^{\max}$, decreases as equity dilution becomes more costly. In this example, a dilution cost of 10% reduces the debt capacity from \$86 to \$84.

The optimal capital structure of the firm is defined as the coupon value, C^*, that maximizes the total firm value, denoted by v^*. The right panel of Fig. 2 illustrates how the optimal coupon, C^*, as well as the firm value, v^*, decreases as equity

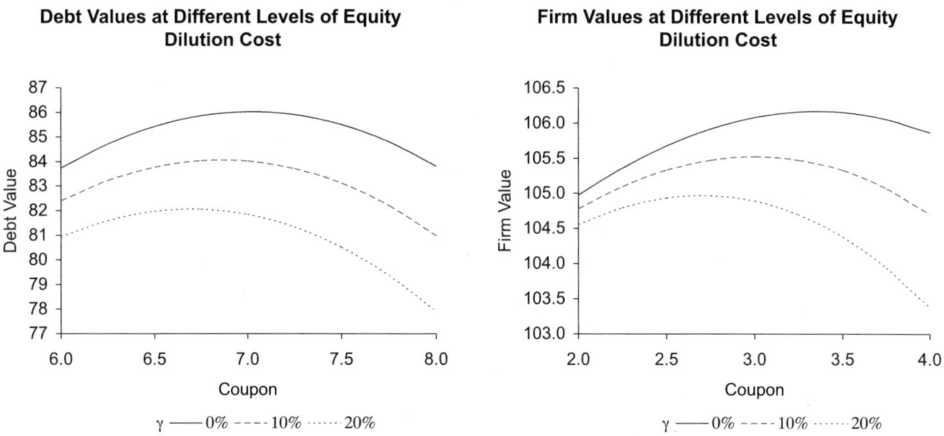

Fig. 2. The left panel plots debt value vs. coupon rate. This illustrates how the debt capacity is affected by the equity dilution cost. The debt capacity decreases as equity dilution becomes more costly. The right panel plots total firm value vs. coupon rate. This illustrates how the optimal capital structure is affected by the dilution cost. The firm issues lower coupon when dilution cost is higher under the optimal structure. ($V = 100, \sigma = 0.2, r = 0.05, q = 0.03, \alpha = 0.3, \tau = 0.15$).

dilution becomes more costly. Therefore, neglecting the costliness of equity dilution can result in over-leveraging the firm. In this example, a dilution cost of 10% reduces the optimal coupon from \$3.3 to \$3 (9%). This translates to a 0.6% change in the firm value.

4. Cash Balances to Manage Illiquidity

In this section, we explore the optimality of building cash balances in good states in order to confront illiquidity in bad states of the world. This strategy may make sense when equity dilution costs are high and the costs of holding cash balances are low. We model the costs of holding cash by assigning a rate of return r_x on cash balances, where $r_x \leq r$, and r is the risk-free rate. We refer to the difference, $r_x - r$, as the cost associated with holding cash inside the firm. We continue to model equity dilution costs as in the previous section. Note that the strategy of building cash balances has several disadvantages. First, building cash balances requires that the equity holders forego some dividends in good states. Second, the firm wastes liquidity by carrying cash in good states when it is not needed. Third, the accumulation of cash balances makes the existing debt less risky and thereby may induce a transfer of wealth from the equity holders to the existing creditors. We prove the following general result:

Proposition 4.1. *If there is no equity dilution cost and the interest on cash reserve is not greater than the risk-free rate, then paying out the entire cash reserve as dividend is an optimal strategy when the firm wishes to maximize its equity value.*

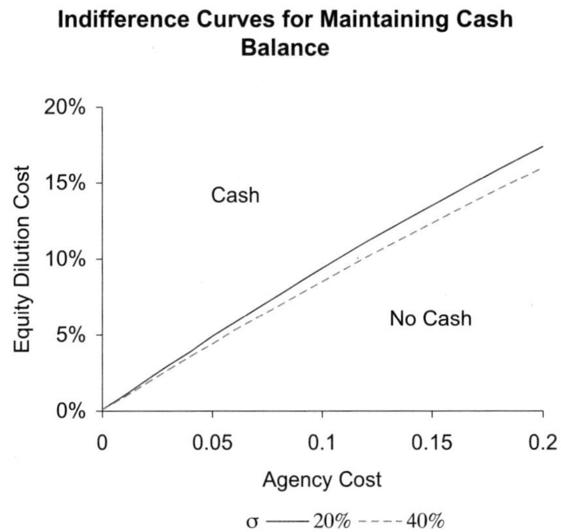

Fig. 3. This figure plots an indifference region for maintaining a positive cash balance for different levels of equity dilution and costs.of holding cash balances. The upper-left region is where it is optimal to carry a positive cash balance, while the lower-right region is where it is optimal to always pay everything out as dividend. The plot shows that the region for keeping cash is larger for firms with higher volatility. ($V = 100, \sigma = 0.2, r = 0.05, q = 0.03, \alpha = 0.3, \tau = 0.15$).

The proof of this proposition is in Appendix B.[4]

This base case result establishes a benchmark for evaluating the following question: how high must the equity dilution costs be in order for the firm to hold cash? Note here that there are no other motives such as growth options or investments for carrying cash in our setting. The results presented in the remainder of this section are obtained using the binomial approach described in Appendix C. We use the infinite horizon implementation with $T = 200$, $N = 2,400$ and $M = 40$.

Figure 3 shows the magnitude of equity dilution costs for various costs of carrying cash under which it is optimal for the firm to carry cash balances. The indifference curve shows that for high costs of equity dilution and low costs of holding cash inside the firm, cash balances will be carried by the firm to avoid illiquidity induced liquidation. It also shows that the region for holding cash is larger for the more volatile firm.

4.1. *Optimal level of cash*

In this section, we discuss the optimal level of cash for a firm that maximizes equity value. Note that cash has the following pros and cons: carrying cash exposes the firm

[4]This result is similar to the Proposition 4 of [16] where it is shown that it is optimal to pay all extra cash flows in good states as dividends. But their result assumes that the cash flows are reinvested in the technology of the firm and no cash balances were modeled. Similar result has been shown by [23] in a static setting.

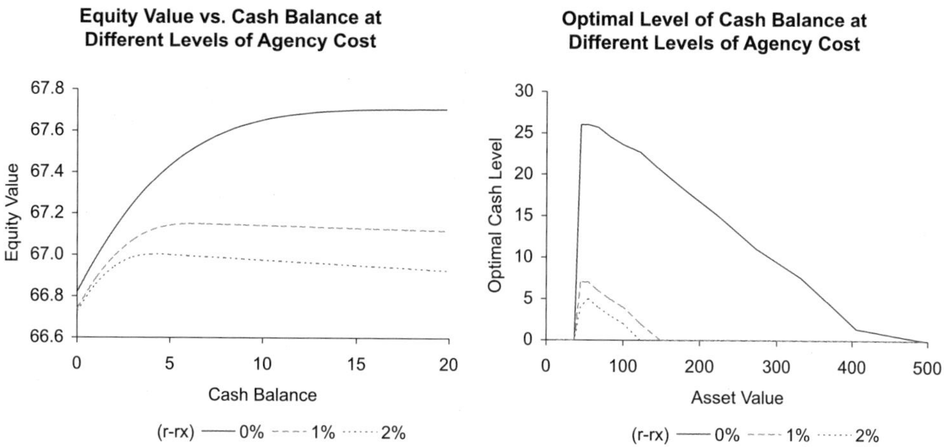

Fig. 4. The left panel plots equity value, E, vs. cash balance, x, for different levels of costs. With no cost, E is increasing in x and levels off beyond a certain value of x. With positive cost, E is increasing in x up to a critical value of x when it starts to decrease. This results in a unique optimal level of x that maximizes E. The right panel plots the optimal level of cash balance, x^*, vs. asset value, V. $x^* = 0$ for values of V below a certain critical level, and it is decreasing in V beyond that level. This critical level is close to the bankruptcy boundary. ($V = 67, \sigma = 0.2, r = 0.05, q = 0.03, C = 3.36, \alpha = 0.3, \tau = 0.15, \gamma = 0.15$).

to costs and forces equity holders to forgo dividends in good states. This makes the firm relatively safe, benefiting the debt, ex-post. But, this latter effect also results in lower spreads, ex-ante, which is good for the equity holders. The left panel of Fig. 4 plots the equity values as a function of the cash balance for different levels of costs of holding cash balances. It shows that when there is no cost to holding cash balances, equity value is maximized as long as the cash balance is above a certain level.[5] However, with strictly positive agency cost, there is a unique optimal level of cash. The right panel of Fig. 4 plots the optimal level of cash as a function of asset values for different levels of costs of holding cash balances. As expected, the optimal level is decreasing with the asset value. We also observe that below a certain level of asset value, the optimal cash level is zero. This is because the firm is anticipating bankruptcy and is passing the cash to shareholders so that debt holders will not receive it upon liquidation.

Furthermore, we observe that optimal level of cash decreases drastically when the cost of holding cash balances increases from 0% to 1%. Later, we will see that the impact of cash quickly diminishes as the cost increases for this reason.

4.2. *Impacts of cash balance*

In this section we discuss the effect of cash balances on debt and total firm value. The left panel of Fig. 5 shows that optimally carrying a cash balance increases debt

[5]The equity value converges to a constant as cash balance increases.

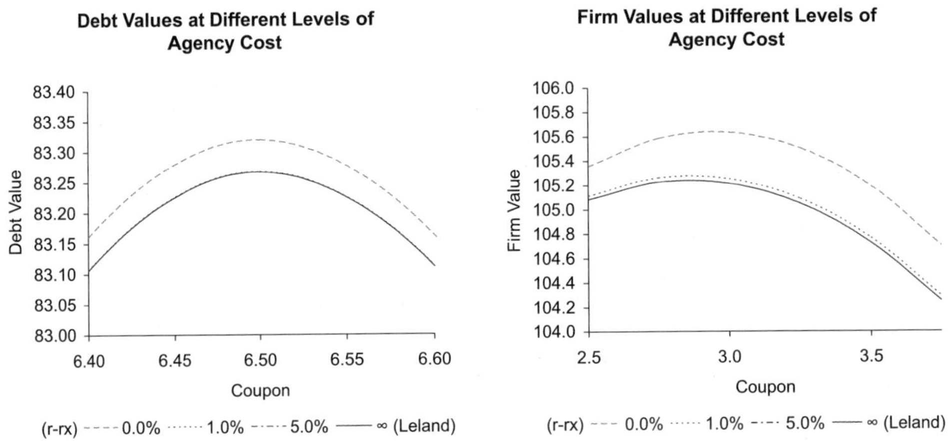

Fig. 5. The left panel plots debt value vs. coupon rate. This illustrates how debt capacity is affected by cash balance. Cash balance virtually has no effect on debt value when there is a positive cost of holding cash. At zero cost, it increases the debt value. The right panel plots total firm value vs. coupon rate. This illustrates how the optimal capital structure is affected by the cash balance. Cash balance increases the value of the firm and also increases the optimal coupon rate. ($V = 100, \sigma = 0.2, r = 0.05, q = 0.03, \alpha = 0.3, \tau = 0.15, \gamma = 0.15$).

value as well as equity values. However, the impact becomes negligible when the cost is strictly positive.

When the cash balance is carried optimally, it can alter the optimal capital structure of the firm as well. The right panel of Fig. 5 illustrates this effect. The optimal capital structure increases relative to the Leland benchmark (i.e., no cash balance or infinite cost of holding cash). The availability of cash enables the firm to increase the proportion of debt it holds in the optimal capital structure. Note that when the cost increases from zero to 1% there is a dramatic shift in the firm value as well as in the optimal level of coupon. For subsequent increases in costs, there is only a marginal variation in the firm values and optimal coupon. This is because the optimal level of cash decreases rapidly when cost increases, as illustrated in the right panel of Fig. 4.

We characterize the impact of optimal cash balances on spreads in Fig. 6. We have seen earlier that as costs of holding cash increase, the debt value decreases and the optimal capital structure carries a lower proportion of debt. Note that the spreads decline as the costs decline. This is due to the fact that higher cash balances can be optimally carried at low costs. This makes the firm less risky and provides it with cushions from premature liquidation, and the firm's debt consequently becomes more attractive to investors.

Although the cash balance helps the firm avoid equity dilution, it does not significantly postpone the expected time to default, or its distribution, when carried optimally. This result is somewhat surprising. But as we mentioned before, as the firm approaches bankruptcy, it depletes the cash balance by paying shareholders

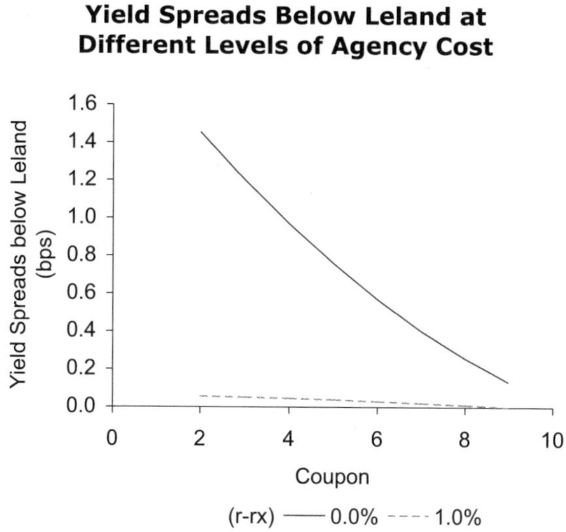

Fig. 6. This figure shows how much cash balance reduces the spread of the existing debt. ($V = 100, \sigma = 0.2, r = 0.05, q = 0.03, \alpha = 0.3, \tau = 0.15, \gamma = 0.15$).

dividend. The result is different when the firm is maximizing total firm value instead of equity value. Appendix F discusses this difference in more detail. Also in Sec. 5.2, we will see that a loan commitment significantly impacts the distribution of default times even in the equity maximizing case.

We have characterized in this section how cash balances may be optimally used to manage illiquidity in the presence of costs of holding cash balance and equity dilution costs. We now turn to the use of a loan commitment as an alternative to managing illiquidity.

5. Loan Commitment

In this section, we show how the firm can use a loan commitment to manage its liquidity problem and relieve it from expensive equity dilution costs and costs associated with carrying cash.

We first define a stylized loan commitment contract. The firm pays a one-time fee (*undrawn fee*), F, at the time it enters into the loan commitment. Let p be the amount of loan commitment outstanding, and $C^l(p)$ be the associated coupon obligation (*drawn fee*). Then when the firm faces a cash flow shortage, i.e., when its revenue is not sufficient to cover the coupon payments, the firm has the option to draw down the loan commitment as long as $p < P^l$. We assume that the firm chooses between drawing down the loan and diluting equity to maximize its equity value. The decision that the firm faces is how much to draw down or repay the loan commitment at each time. We denote this decision variable by λ, where $\lambda > 0$ corresponds to drawing down the loan and $\lambda < 0$ corresponds to repaying the loan.

At any given time, if the firm is still solvent, then one of the following events can happen:

First, in the case where there is no cash flow shortage, i.e., $\delta \geq C + C^l(p)$, the firm can decide how much of the outstanding loan commitment to repay, and the remaining cash surplus goes to the shareholders as dividends. Note that since the firm can neither use the proceeds from the loan for dividends, nor keep a cash balance, it cannot draw down the loan commitment in this case. Hence λ must be in the interval $[-p, 0]$. If $|\lambda| > \delta - C + C^l(p)$, then the firm is also diluting equity to repay the loan commitment.

Second, in the case where there is a cash flow shortage, i.e., $\delta < C + C^l(p)$, the firm has to decide how to manage this shortfall. It needs to raise an additional $C + C^l(p) - \delta$ to meet its coupon obligations. The firm can decide between diluting equity or drawing down the loan commitment, or both. Again, since we restrict the firm from using the proceeds from the loan for dividends, it can draw down at most the shortfall amount, as long as it does not exceed the credit line. We also restrict the firm from repaying the loan commitment in this case. Thus λ must be in the interval $[0, \min\{C + C^l(p) - \delta, P^l - p\}]$.

If the firm declares bankruptcy, then we apply an absolute priority rule to the distribution of proceeds from liquidation. The bankruptcy cost is shared between the bank and the debt holders. Let $L(V, p)$ be the value of the loan commitment. Then the value of the debt and the loan commitment before liquidation costs are:

$$\hat{L}(V, p) = \min\{V + \delta, p\}$$
$$\hat{D}(V, p) = V + \delta - L(V, p)$$

And then we apply the bankruptcy cost pro rata. Thus the debt and loan commitment values ex-liquidation costs are:

$$L(V, p) = \hat{L}(V, p) - \frac{\hat{L}(V, p)}{\hat{L}(V, p) + \hat{D}(V, p)}\alpha(V + \delta)$$
$$D(V, p) = \hat{D}(V, p) - \frac{\hat{D}(V, p)}{\hat{L}(V, p) + \hat{D}(V, p)}\alpha(V + \delta)$$

The one-time fee, F, is chosen such that the loan commitment has zero value to the bank at the time of signing. Therefore, it is the difference between the present value of the loan commitment and the present value of all expected future draws on the loan commitment:

$$F = \int_0^T e^{-rt}\lambda_t^+ dt - L(V_0, 0) \tag{5.1}$$

The coupon rate of the loan commitment, c^l, is determined as follows. Given the current capital structure of the firm, the bank first determines the level of firm's asset value at which it will start drawing down the loan ($qV \leq C$). Then for a loan commitment of size P^l, the bank decides what the cost of borrowing for the firm should be in that state. In particular, it chooses c^l to solve

$$P^l = D(C/q, c^l P^l),$$

where $D(V, C)$ is the value of a perpetual debt that pays continuous coupon of rate C dollars issued by the firm with asset value V.

This choice of c^l is reasonable because when the firm faces a liquidity crisis at $V = C/q$, its alternative to a loan commitment is to issue additional perpetual debt. If the bank charges any amount greater than c^l, the firm might as well issue additional perpetual debt instead of using a loan commitment.

The size of the loan commitment P^l is usually chosen by the firm. Larger P^l provides more liquidity to the firm, but it also requires larger coupon C^l and larger fee F. Thus the firm chooses P^l that maximizes the benefit to the shareholders. The left panel of Fig. 7 illustrate this result for different levels of α, at the respective level of optimal coupon in absence of the loan commitment. There is also a maximum value of P^l that the firm can support. This is similar to the concept of debt capacity. The right panel of Fig. 7 shows how the loan commitment capacity changes with liquidation cost, α.

The results in this section are obtained by using the binomial approach described in Appendix D. We use the infinite horizon implementation with $T = 200$, $N = 2{,}400$ and $M = 40$.

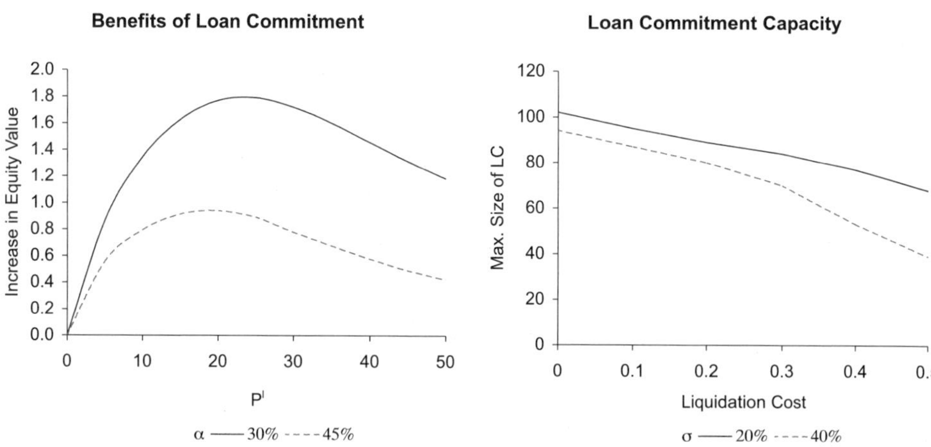

Fig. 7. The left panel plots impact of loan commitment on equity value vs. size of the loan commitment, P^l. The figure shows that there is an optimal value, P^{l*}, where shareholders benefit the most. Furthermore, P^{l*} as well as the impact itself decreases as liquidation cost, α, increases. The right panel plots firm's capacity for loan commitment vs. liquidation cost. The firm is able to take on smaller size of loan commitment as α gets larger. ($V = 100, C = 3.17, \sigma = 0.2, r = 0.05, q = 0.03, \tau = 0.15, \gamma = 0.05$).

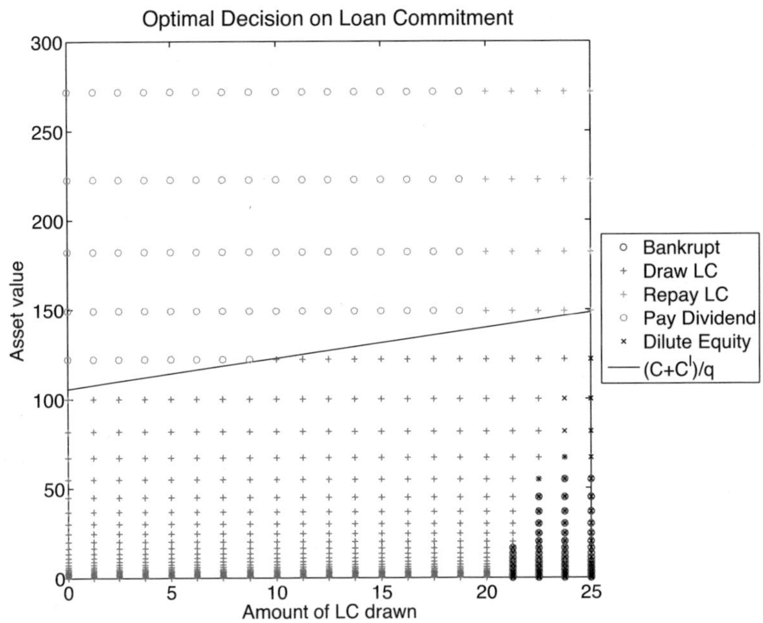

Fig. 8. This figure shows the optimal decisions on the loan commitment. The black solid line is the boundary below which the firm does not generate enough revenue to cover coupon payments. The firm draws down the loan commitment below this line, and only dilutes equity or declare bankruptcy when the credit limit is reached. Above this line, there is a critical level of amount the loan commitment drawn, below which the firm uses excess revenue to pay dividend and above which the firm uses it to repay loan commitment. ($V = 100, \sigma = 0.2, r = 0.05, q = 0.03, \alpha = 0.3, \tau = 0, \gamma = 0.05, C = 3.17, P^l = 25, C^l = 1.285$ (5.14%)).

5.1. *Optimal draw down and repayment decisions*

When a loan commitment is available to the firm, we find that it will gradually draw it down until the credit limit is reached before diluting equity. The firm will not declare bankruptcy as long as the loan commitment is still available. While the firm is above the cash flow shortage line $(C + C^l(p_t))/q$, there is a level of drawn amount, p_R, above which the it will use excess revenue to repay the principle of the loan commitment, and below which it will use it to pay dividend. Figure 8 illustrates these observations.

5.2. *Impacts of loan commitment*

In this section, we first discuss the impact of the loan commitment on existing debt and firm values. The left panel of Fig. 9 shows how equity value changes for various sizes of the loan commitment. We find that the presence of the loan commitment increases the equity value. This result is intuitive since the loan commitment helps the firm avoid costly equity dilution. However, we observe that the size of the

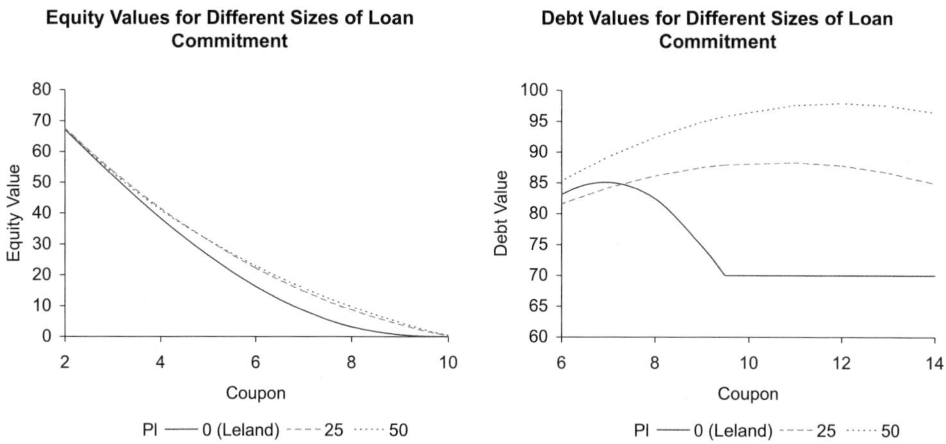

Fig. 9. The left panel plots equity value vs. coupon rate for different sizes of loan commitment. Loan commitment always increases the equity value but its size has little impact on the difference. The right panel plots debt value vs. coupon rate. Debt holders do not always benefit from the loan commitment. High leveraged firms benefit more than low leveraged firms. The debt capacity of the firm increases significantly in presence of loan commitment, and is increasing in its size, P^l. ($V = 100, \sigma = 0.2, r = 0.05, q = 0.03, \alpha = 0.3, \tau = 0.15, \gamma = 0.05$).

loan commitment has very small impact on the change in equity value, just as we previously observed in Fig. 7.

We find more interesting results for debt values. While the shareholders benefit from the loan commitment regardless of the size of the existing debt, we find that the existing debt holders only benefit if its size, as characterized by the coupon C, is larger than a certain level. When C is small, the debt holders are better off without the loan commitment. The right panel of Fig. 9 shows that with a loan commitment of size \$25, the debt holders are better of if the coupon is greater than \$7, whereas for a loan commitment of size \$50, the debt holders are always better off. The loan commitment has both positive and negative impacts on the debt holders. First, since it is more senior than the existing debt, in the case of bankruptcy, the debt holders receive less money when the firm is liquidated. This, and the cost of the loan commitment itself, reduces the existing debt value. Second, it can help the firm avoid or postpone bankruptcy and hence increase the existing debt value. Therefore, it is not surprising that the debt holders are worse off when C is small. This is because the firm is not likely to declare bankruptcy in the future and the costs of having the loan commitment outweigh the benefits. However, at higher leverage, the probability of declaring bankruptcy is more significant and the benefits of the loan commitment dominates the costs.

Notice also in the absence of loan commitments, the debt value is constant when the coupon is above a certain level (\$9 in our example). At this level of coupon, the optimal bankruptcy boundary is above the current asset value, and thus the firm declares bankruptcy immediately, leaving the debt holder with only

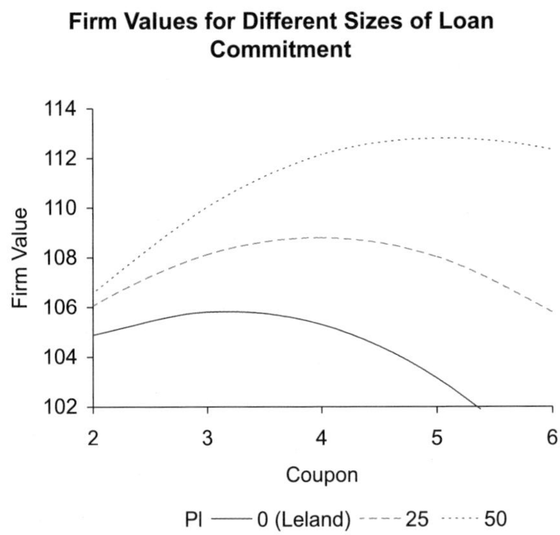

Fig. 10. This figure plots total firm value vs. coupon rate for different sizes of loan commitment. The firm value increases with the size of the loan commitment. This figure also illustrates how loan commitment impacts the optimal capital structure of the firm. The firm with loan commitment will issue debt with much higher coupon rate at optimal capital structure. ($V = 100, \sigma = 0.2, r = 0.05, q = 0.03, \alpha = 0.3, \tau = 0.15, \gamma = 0.05$).

the liquidated asset value less bankruptcy cost, $(1-\alpha)V$. As we discussed previously, it is never optimal to declare bankruptcy when the firm can still draw down the loan commitment. For this reason, we observe that the debt value does not behave the same way when a loan commitment is present. Furthermore, the benefit of a loan commitment increases with its size, because it can prolong the life of the firm further, and the debt holder gets to collect more coupon payments. In addition, the debt capacity of the firm significantly increases in the presence of a loan commitment for the same reason.

Figure 10 shows how the loan commitment increases the total firm value. What is more interesting here is how it impacts the optimal capital structure. We observe that the optimal leverage of the firm increases with the size of the loan commitment. This can be explained by the fact that the loan commitment allows the firm take on more debt to utilize the tax benefits, while providing it with protection from bankruptcy.

The results from this section leads to the following important observation.

Even in the absence of equity dilution and liquidation costs, it is generally beneficial for the firm to enter into a loan commitment contract.

Note that the firm is able derive benefits by exercising the loan commitment in bad states to meet any liquidity needs. The critical point is that the firm can optimally stagger the draw on a loan commitment and only pay (higher) interest on the drawn portion of it. It is this property that makes the loan commitment

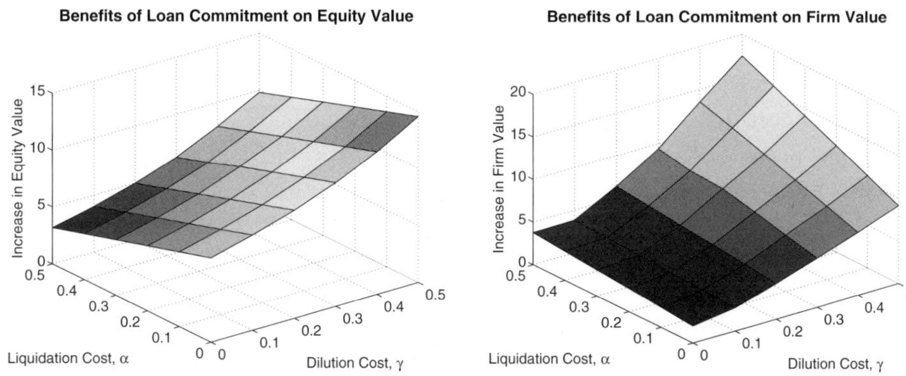

Fig. 11. The left panel plots the increase in equity values from loan commitment for different level of dilution and liquidation costs. The increase in equity value is increasing in γ, but decreasing in α. The right panel plots the increase in total firm value. The increase in the firm value is increasing in γ and α. In both plots, we fix the coupon rate of original debt to \$5.27, which is the optimal level for $\alpha = 0$ and $\gamma = 0$. ($V = 100, \sigma = 0.2, r = 0.05, q = 0.03, C = 5.27, \alpha = 0.3, \tau = 0.15, \gamma = 0.05$).

attractive. Figure 11 plots the increase in equity and total firm value from the loan commitment. The left panel shows that the increase in equity value is increasing in γ, but decreasing in α. This is because equity holders benefit mostly from avoiding costly dilution. Hence as liquidation cost increases, the increase in cost of loan commitment outweighs the increase in benefits. On the other hand, the right panel shows that the increase total firm value is increasing in both γ and α. This is

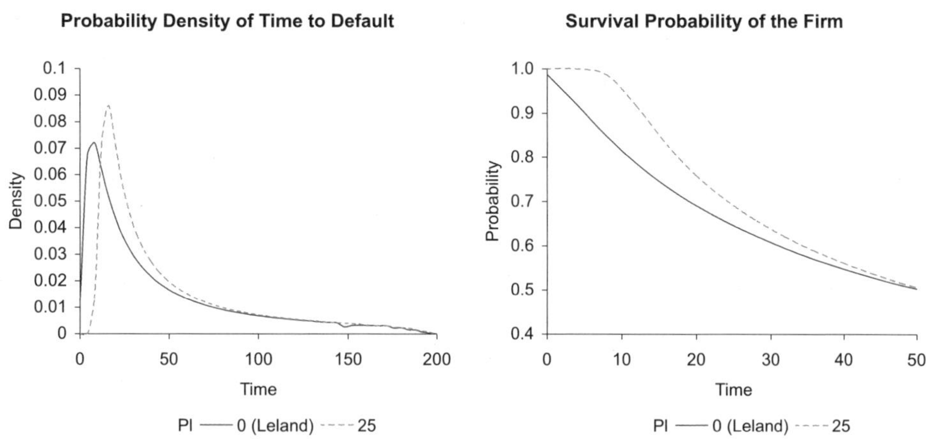

Fig. 12. The left panel plots the probability density function of the default time with and without the loan commitment. The right panel plots the firm's survival probability, or the probability that the firm will not default before a certain time. The expect default time conditioned on ever defaulting increases from 47 to 50 years. Moreover, the survival probability over the *near* future increases significantly in the presence of loan commitment. ($V = 100, \sigma = 0.2, r = 0.05, q = 0.03, \alpha = 0.3, \tau = 0.15, \gamma = 0.05$).

intuitive because the loan commitment helps to avoid both equity dilution and liquidation costs.

As stated above, entering into a loan commitment is generally beneficial for the firm since it postpones costly equity dilutions and liquidations. Figure 12 shows the probability density of the time of default with and without the loan commitment. In this example, the expected time to default increases from 47 to 50 years with a \$25 loan commitment. More importantly, it significantly increases the survival probability in the near future. In this example, the survival probability is one up to almost ten years, compared with 80% at ten years without the loan commitment. The probability remains higher for about 50 years. The methodology for determining the default time distribution is described in Appendix E. The results were obtained by using $T = 200$, $N = 2{,}400$ and $K = 50$.

In contrast to cash balance, a loan commitment postpones the default time because the firm does not need to worry about debt holders taking cash upon liquidation. Moreover, the firm must first accumulate the cash balance before it can be of any use, while the loan commitment is available immediately.

6. Conclusion

Our paper characterizes liquidity management strategies and their impact on pricing. We provide an analytical solution to pricing of the firm's securities when equity dilution is costly, and show that costly dilution reduces the firm's debt capacity and optimal level of debt. We provide a methodology to investigate the effectiveness of cash balances and loan commitments as means of managing illiquidity. We find that carrying cash is generally not efficient even in absence of costs associated with holding cash. This is because (a) it is not immediately available since the firm must accumulate cash first, and (b) in doing so, equity holders forego dividends in good states. On the contrary, we show that loan commitments provide an efficient way to manage illiquidity and can be a better strategy when equity dilution and liquidation costs are significant. The staggered draw feature of the loan commitment allows the firm to inject liquidity when needed without foregoing dividends in the good states. Furthermore, we find that the loan commitment increases both the debt capacity and the optimal level of debt, reduces default probability, and increases the expected time to default of the firm.

An interesting extension might be to incorporate strategic debt service in our framework. This is likely to provide a lower incentive to hold cash balances as strategic debt service is another way to deal with illiquidity which imposes greater costs ex-ante to the borrower. Another extension would be to model the Chapter 11 provisions explicitly in our framework as Chapter 11 is yet another institution to deal with liquidity problems of companies. We have not modeled the possibility of carrying cash balances to take advantage of future investment opportunities. In addition, we have not addressed the fact that companies issue debt to raise cash for "general corporate purposes." These are fruitful avenues for further research.

Appendix A

Derivation of equity value from Section 3.1.1

Substituting the general solution (3.8) into (3.6), we get:

$$\begin{aligned}
&\frac{1}{2}\sigma^2 A_2 Y(Y+1)V^{-Y} + \frac{1}{2}\sigma^2 A_3 X(X+1)V^{-X} - (r-q)A_1 V \\
&\quad - (r-q)A_2 Y V^{-Y} - (r-q)A_3 X V^{-X} \\
&\quad - r(A_0 + A_1 V + A_2 V^{-Y} + A_3 V^{-X}) + \beta(qV - C) = 0 \qquad \text{(A.1)}
\end{aligned}$$

We solve for X and Y by collecting the coefficients of V^{-X} and V^{-Y} in (A.1) and setting it to zero:

$$\begin{aligned}
&\frac{1}{2}\sigma^2 A_2 X(X+1) - (r-q)A_2 X - rA_2 = 0 \\
&\quad \Rightarrow \frac{1}{2}\sigma^2 X^2 + \left(\frac{1}{2}\sigma^2 - (r-q)\right) X - r = 0 \\
&\quad \Rightarrow X = \frac{\left(r - q - \frac{\sigma^2}{2}\right) + \sqrt{\left(r - q - \frac{\sigma^2}{2}\right)^2 + 2\sigma^2 r}}{\sigma^2} \\
&\quad \text{and } Y = \frac{\left(r - q - \frac{\sigma^2}{2}\right) - \sqrt{\left(r - q - \frac{\sigma^2}{2}\right)^2 + 2\sigma^2 r}}{\sigma^2}
\end{aligned}$$

A_0 and A_1 can be solved by collecting the constant and the coefficient of the linear term in (A.1) as follows:

$$-rA_0 - \beta C = 0 \Rightarrow A_0 = -\frac{\beta C}{r}$$

$$(r-q)A_1 - rA_1 + \beta q = 0 \Rightarrow A_1 = \beta$$

Similarly, substituting (3.8) into (3.7), and solve for $\tilde{A}_0$ and $\tilde{A}_1$ we get:

$$-r\tilde{A}_0 - C = 0 \Rightarrow \tilde{A}_0 = -\frac{C}{r}$$

$$(r-q)\tilde{A}_1 - r\tilde{A}_1 + q = 0 \Rightarrow \tilde{A}_1 = 1$$

Since $Y \leq -1$, the condition (BC II) in (3.9) implies that $\tilde{A}_2 = 0$. The remaining coefficients are determined by solving the system of linear equations imposed by the other three conditions in (3.9).

$$\text{(BC I):} \qquad \beta\left(-\frac{C}{r} + V_B\right) + A_2 V_B^{-Y} + A_3 V_B^{-X} = 0$$

$$\text{(CC):} \quad \beta\left(-\frac{C}{r} + \frac{C}{q}\right) + A_2\left(\frac{C}{q}\right)^{-Y} + A_3\left(\frac{C}{q}\right)^{-X} = -\frac{C}{r} + \frac{C}{q} + \tilde{A}_3\left(\frac{C}{q}\right)$$

$$\text{(SP):} \qquad \beta - A_2 Y\left(\frac{C}{q}\right)^{-Y-1} - A_3 X\left(\frac{C}{q}\right)^{-X-1} = 1 - \tilde{A}_3 X\left(\frac{C}{q}\right)^{-X-1}$$

And we get the expression for A_2, A_3 and $\tilde{A}_3$ as given in (3.10).

Derivation of debt value from Section 3.1.2

Substituting the general solution (3.12) into (3.11), we get:

$$\frac{1}{2}\sigma^2 B_2 X(X+1)V^{-X} + (r-q)B_1 V - (r-q)B_2 X V^{-X} - r(B_0 + B_1 V + B_2 V^{-X}) + C = 0 \tag{A.2}$$

B_0 and B_1 can be solved by collecting the constant and the coefficient of the linear term in (A.2) as follows:

$$-rB_0 + C = 0 \Rightarrow B_0 = \frac{C}{r}$$
$$(r-q)B_1 - rB_1 = 0 \Rightarrow B_1 = 0$$

The condition (BC I) in (3.13) implies that:

$$\frac{C}{r} + B_2 V_B^{-X} = (1-\alpha)V_B \Rightarrow B_2 = \left((1-\alpha)V_B - \frac{C}{r}\right)\frac{1}{V_B^{-X}}$$

Hence the debt value is as given in (3.14).

Appendix B

Proof of Proposition 4.1

Define the notation:

$$\begin{aligned} x_t &= \text{cash balance} \\ \delta_t &= \text{revenue generated during time interval } (t-h, t] \\ \zeta_t &= \text{coupon payment during time interval } (t-h, t] \\ d &= \text{dividend payout} \\ E_t(x_t, d) &= \text{Equity value at time } t\text{, with cash balance } x\text{, and dividend payout } d \\ r_x &= \text{interest earned on cash balance} \\ p &= \text{probability of an up move} \end{aligned}$$

Proof. We will establish by induction that $E_t(x,d)$ in increasing in d for all t and x, and hence it is optimal to pay as much dividend as possible, leaving no cash inside the firm. For convenience, we set $\tau = 0$ without loss of generality.

Let x^+ be the value of cash balance at the next time period, i.e.

$$x^+ = e^{r_x h}(\delta_t + x - \zeta - d) \tag{B.1}$$

At maturity,

$$E_T(x) = (x + \delta_T + V_T - \zeta - P)^+ \tag{B.2}$$

Let $\mathbb{E}_t[E_{t+h}(x)] = pE^u_{t+h}(x) + (1-p)E^d_{t+h}(x)$, where $E^u_{t+h}(x)$ and $E^d_{t+h}(x)$ are the equity values at the up and down node at time $t+h$ respectively.

Then, for non-bankruptcy nodes at time $T-h$,

$$\begin{aligned} E_{T-h}(x,d) &= e^{-rh}\mathbb{E}_{T-h}[E_T(x^+)] + d \\ &= e^{-rh}\mathbb{E}_{T-h}[(x^+ + V_T + \delta_T - \zeta - P)^+] + d \end{aligned}$$

Case I: For a range of d such that both $E_T^u(x^+)$ and $E_T^d(x^+)$ are not bankrupt,

$$\begin{aligned} E_{T-h}(x,d) &= e^{-rh}\mathbb{E}_{T-h}[x^+ + V_T + \delta_T - \zeta - P] + d \\ &= e^{-rh}(x^+ + \mathbb{E}_{T-h}[V_T + \delta_T] - \zeta - P) + d \\ \Rightarrow \frac{\partial E_{T-h}}{\partial d} &= e^{-rh}\frac{\partial x^+}{\partial d} + 1 \\ &= 1 - e^{-(r-r_x)h} \geq 0 \quad \text{for } r_x \leq r \end{aligned} \tag{B.3}$$

Case II: $E_T^d(x^+)$ is bankrupt, but $E_T^u(x^+)$ is not,

$$\begin{aligned} E_{T-h}(x,d) &= e^{-rh}p(x^+ + V_T^u + \delta_T^u - \zeta - P) + d \\ \Rightarrow \frac{\partial E_{T-h}}{\partial d} &= 1 - pe^{-(r-r_x)h} \geq 0 \quad \text{for } r_x \leq r \end{aligned}$$

Case III: Both $E_T^u(x^+)$ and $E_T^d(x^+)$ are bankrupt

$$E_{T-h}(x,d) = d \Rightarrow \frac{\partial E_{T-h}}{\partial d} = 1$$

Since, E_{T-h} is increasing in d for all cases, the optimal dividend at time $T-h$, d_{T-h}^* is given by

$$d_{T-h}^* = (x + \delta_{T-h} - \zeta)^+ \tag{B.4}$$

When the firm does not have enough revenue and cash to cover the coupon payments, it has to dilution equity, which is equivalent to paying a negative dividend. So to cover the case where dilution occurs, we simply write the optimal dividend as

$$d_{T-h}^* = x + \delta_{T-h} - \zeta \tag{B.5}$$

Let $E_{T-h}^*(x) = E_{T-h}(x, d_{T-h}^*)$. Then for the three cases above, we have

$$E_{T-h}^*(x) = \begin{cases} e^{-rh}(\mathbb{E}_{T-h}[V_T + \delta_T] - \zeta - P) + x + \delta_{T-h} - \zeta \\ e^{-rh}p(V_T^u + \delta_T^u - \zeta - P) + x + \delta_{T-h} - \zeta \\ x + \delta_{T-h} - \zeta \end{cases}$$

$$\Rightarrow \frac{\partial E_{T-h}^*}{\partial x} = 1$$

Assume that for non-bankruptcy nodes at time $t+h$, $\frac{\partial E_{t+h}^*}{\partial x} = 1$. Then at time t,

Case I: For a range of d such that both $E^u_{t+h}(x^+)$ and $E^d_{t+h}(x^+)$ are not bankrupt,

$$\begin{aligned} E_t(x,d) &= e^{-rh}\mathbb{E}_t[E^*_{t+h}(x^+)] + d \\ \Rightarrow \frac{\partial E^*_t}{\partial d} &= e^{-rh}\left(\frac{\partial E^*_{t+h}}{\partial x^+}\frac{\partial x^+}{\partial d}\right) + 1 \\ &= 1 - e^{-(r-r_x)h} \geq 0 \quad \text{for } r_x \leq r \end{aligned}$$

Case II: $E^d_{t+h}(x^+)$ is bankrupt, but $E^u_{t+h}(x^+)$ is not,

$$\begin{aligned} E_t(x,d) &= e^{-rh} p E^{u*}_{t+h}(x^+) + d \\ \Rightarrow \frac{\partial E_t}{\partial d} &= pe^{-rh}\left(\frac{\partial E^*_{t+h}}{\partial x^+}\frac{\partial x^+}{\partial d}\right) + 1 \\ &= 1 - pe^{-(r-r_x)h} \geq 0 \quad \text{for } r_x \leq r \end{aligned}$$

Case III: Both nodes $E^u_{t+h}(x^+)$ and $E^d_{t+h}(x^+)$ are bankrupt

$$\begin{aligned} E_t(x,d) &= d \\ \Rightarrow \frac{\partial E_t}{\partial d} &= 1 \end{aligned}$$

Hence $E_t(x,d)$ is increasing in d, and $d^*_t = x + \delta_t - \zeta$ is the optimal dividend payout. We can write the optimal equity value for the three cases as,

$$\begin{aligned} E^*_t(x) &= \begin{cases} e^{-rh}\mathbb{E}_t[E^*_{t+h}(0)] + x + \delta_t - \zeta \\ e^{-r} p E^{u*}_{t+h}(0) + x + \delta_t - \zeta \\ x + \delta_t - \zeta \end{cases} \\ \Rightarrow \frac{\partial E^*_t}{\partial x} &= 1 \end{aligned}$$

which completes the proof. □

Appendix C

Binomial lattice for cash balance

We extend the binomial lattice method of [13] to price corporate debt in the presence of cash balances. Following Cox, Ross and Rubinstein (1979), we divide time into N increments of length $h = T/N$, then we write the evolution of the firm asset value V_t as follows:

$$V_{t+h} = \begin{cases} uV_t & \text{with risk-neutral probability } p \\ dV_t & \text{with risk-neutral probability } 1-p \end{cases} \tag{C.1}$$

Let $V_t^u = uV_t$ and $V_t^d = dV_t$. By imposing that $u = 1/d$, we have:

$$u = e^{\sigma\sqrt{h}} \tag{C.2}$$

$$d = e^{-\sigma\sqrt{h}} \tag{C.3}$$

$$a = e^{(r-q)h} \tag{C.4}$$

$$p = \frac{a-d}{u-d} \tag{C.5}$$

In this setting, we approximate revenue during time interval h by:

$$\int_t^{t+h} qV_t dt \approx V_t(e^{qh} - 1) =: \delta_t$$

Similarly, we approximate the coupon payment by:

$$\int_t^{t+h} cPdt \approx P(e^{ch} - 1) =: \zeta \tag{C.6}$$

Incorporating the tax benefit of rate τ, the effective coupon payment is $(1-\tau)\zeta$.

Each node in the lattice is a vector of dimension M, where each element in the vector corresponds to a different level of cash balance, x. The values of x are linearly spaced from 0 to $x^{\max}$.[6]

We distinguish the cash before and cash after revenue and dividend by x and x^+, respectively.

Let $E_t(V_t, x_t)$ be the equity value at time t when the firm's asset value is V_t, and its cash balance level is x_t. Similarly, $D_t(V_t, x_t)$ is the corresponding debt value. We also let $\mathbb{E}_t[f_{t+h}(V_{t+h}, x_{t+h})]$ be the expected value of the security $f(\cdot)$ at the next time period $t+h$, given the information at time t, where $f(\cdot)$ can represent the equity value, $E(\cdot)$, or the debt value, $D(\cdot)$, namely,

$$\mathbb{E}_t[f_{t+h}(V_{t+h}, x_{t+h})] = pf_{t+h}(V_{t+h}^u, x_{t+h}) + (1-p)f_{t+h}(V_{t+h}^d, x_{t+h}).$$

Note that x_{t+h} is deterministic because it only depends on the decision at time t. Since we only know the values of $f_{t+h}(V, x)$ for a discrete set of values of x, we use linear interpolation to estimate $f_{t+h}(V_{t+h}^u, x_{t+h})$ and $f_{t+h}(V_{t+h}^d, x_{t+h})$.

Figure C.1 illustrates what each node in the lattice represents.

At maturity, the firm returns everything to shareholders after meeting its debt obligations.

If $V_T + x_T + \delta_T \geq (1-\tau)\zeta + P$:

$$E_T(V_T, x_T) = V_T + x_T + \delta_T - (1-\tau)\zeta - P$$
$$D_T(V_T, x_T) = \zeta + P$$

If (V_T, x_T) is such that the firm does not have enough value to meet its debt obligation, it declares bankruptcy and liquidates its assets.

[6]In our routine, we pick $x^{\max}$ arbitrarily and check if the optimal cash balance, x^*, is attained at $x^{\max}$. If it does, then we increase $x^{\max}$ and repeat the routine.

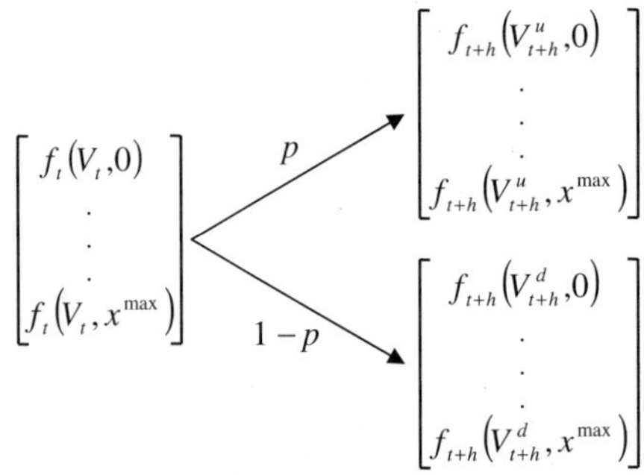

Fig. C.1. This figure illustrates the vector in each node of the lattice. $f_t(\cdot)$ represents the security value at each element of the vector, where f_t can represent the equity value, E_t, or the debt value, D_t.

If $V_T + x_T + \delta_T < (1-\tau)\zeta + P$:

$$\begin{aligned} E_T(V_T, x_T) &= 0 \\ D_T(V_T, x_T) &= (1-\alpha)(V_T + x_T + \delta_T) \end{aligned}$$

At other times t, if (V_t, x_t) is such that the firm has enough cash from revenue and cash balance to meet its debt obligations, then it has an option to retain some excess revenue in the cash balance, or pay it out to shareholders as dividend.

(1) If $x_t + \delta_t \geq (1-\tau)\zeta$:

$$\begin{aligned} &\text{Choose } x_t^+ \in [0, x_t + \delta_t - (1-\tau)\zeta] \\ &x_{t+h} = e^{r_x h} x_t^+ \\ &E_t(V_t, x_t) = e^{-rh}\mathbb{E}_t[E_{t+h}(V_{t+h}, x_{t+h})] + x_t + \delta_t - (1-\tau)\zeta - x_t^+ \\ &D_t(V_t, x_t) = e^{-rh}\mathbb{E}_t[D_{t+h}(V_{t+h}, x_{t+h})] + \zeta \end{aligned}$$

x_t^+ is chosen such that the objective value (equity or firm value) is maximized at time t. The optimization is done by performing a search over K discrete points of feasible values of x_t^+ as given above.
If (V_t, x_t) is such that the firm does not have enough from revenue and cash balance, then it has to raise money by diluting equity.

(2) If $x_t + \delta_t < (1-\tau)\zeta$:
If (V_t, x_t) is such that the firm has enough equity to cover the shortfall:
2A. If $(1-\gamma)e^{-rh}\mathbb{E}_t[E_{t+h}(V_{t+h}, 0)] \geq (1-\tau)\zeta - x_t - \delta_t$:

$$\begin{aligned} E_t(V_t, x_t) &= e^{-rh}\mathbb{E}_t[E_{t+h}(V_{t+h}, 0)] + (x_t + \delta_t - (1-\tau)\zeta)/(1-\gamma) \\ D_t(V_t, x_t) &= e^{-rh}\mathbb{E}_t[D_{t+h}(V_{t+h}, 0)] + \zeta \end{aligned}$$

If (V_t, x_t) is such that the firm does not have enough equity value to cover the shortfall, then it declares bankruptcy:

2B. If $(1-\tau)\zeta - x_t - \delta_t > (1-\gamma)e^{-rh}\mathbb{E}_t[E_{t+h}(V_{t+h}, 0)]$

$$E_t(V_t, x_t) = 0$$

$$D_t(V_t, x_t) = (1-\alpha)(V_t + x_t + \delta_t)$$

In the infinite maturity case, we use an arbitrarily large maturity T and modify the terminal values of states (V_T, x_T) such that the firm is not bankrupt as follows:

If $V_T + x_T + \delta_T \geq (1-\tau)\zeta + P$:

$$E_T(V_T, x_T) = V_T + x_T - (1-\tau)\zeta/(1-r)$$
$$D_T(V_T, x_T) = \zeta/(1-r)$$

We use the infinite horizon implementation with $T = 200$, $N = 2{,}400$ and $M = 40$ for the results in Figs. 3–6.

Appendix D

Binomial lattice for loan commitment

The basic setup of the lattice is as described in Appendix C. Each node in the lattice is a vector of dimension M, where each element in the vector corresponds to the different level of outstanding loan commitment, p. The values of p are linearly spaced from 0 to P^l.

Let λ_t be the amount the loan commitment drawn at time t. In addition to $E_t(p_t)$ and $D_t(p_t)$, we let $L_t(p_t)$ be the loan commitment value to the bank at time t, with the drawn amount of p_t, and $\Lambda_t(p_t)$ be its value to the firm (i.e., future cash flow from the loan commitment to the firm). Again, we let $\mathbb{E}_t[f_{t+h}(V_{t+h}, x_{t+h})]$ be the expected value of the security $f(\cdot)$ at the next time period $t+h$, given the information at time t, where $f(\cdot)$ can represent $L(\cdot)$ or $\Lambda(\cdot)$, in addition to $E(\cdot)$ and $D(\cdot)$.

At maturity, the firm returns everything to shareholders after meeting all of its debt obligations.

If $V_T + \delta_T \geq (1-\tau)(\zeta + \zeta^l(p_T)) + P + p_T$:

$$E_T(V_T, p_T) = V_T + \delta_T - (1-\tau)(\zeta + \zeta^l(p_T)) - (P + p_T)$$
$$L_T(V_T, p_T) = \zeta^l(p_T) + p_T$$
$$D_T(V_T, p_T) = \zeta + P$$
$$\Lambda_T(V_T, p_T) = 0$$

If (V_T, p_T) is such that the firm does not have enough value to meet its debt obligation, then it declares bankruptcy and the liquidation cost is shared among the debt holders as described in Sec. 5.

If $V_T + \delta_T < (1-\tau)(\zeta + \zeta^l(p_T)) + P + p_T$:

$$E_T(V_T, p_T) = 0$$
$$\hat{L}_T(V_T, p_T) = \min\left\{V_T + \delta_T, \zeta^l(p_T) + p_T\right\}$$

$$
\begin{aligned}
\hat{D}_T(V_T, p_T) &= V_T + \delta_T - \hat{L}_T(V_T, p_T) \\
L_T(V_T, p_T) &= \hat{L}_T(V_T, p_T) - \frac{\hat{L}_T(V_T, p_T)}{\hat{L}_T(V_T, p_T) + \hat{D}_T(V_T, p_T)}\alpha(V_T + \delta_T) \\
D_T(V_T, p_T) &= \hat{D}_T(V_T, p_T) - \frac{\hat{D}_T(V_T, p_T)}{\hat{L}_T(V_T, p_T) + \hat{D}_T(V_T, p_T)}\alpha(V_T + \delta_T) \\
\Lambda_T(V_T, p_T) &= 0
\end{aligned}
$$

At other times t, if (V_T, p_T) is such that the firm generates enough revenue to meet its debt obligations, then it has an option to repay some of the loan commitment by using excess cash from revenue or equity dilution, or both. Any remaining cash goes to shareholders as dividend.

(1) If $\delta_t \geq (1 - \tau)(\zeta + \zeta^l(p_t))$:

$$
\begin{aligned}
\text{Choose } \lambda_t &\in [-p_t, 0] \\
p_{t+h} &= p_t + \lambda_t \\
\Lambda_t(V_t, p_t) &= e^{-rh}\mathbb{E}_t[\Lambda_{t+h}(V_{t+h}, p_{t+h})]
\end{aligned}
$$

If (V_t, p_t) is such that the firm has enough equity value to repay the chosen amount of loan commitment, λ_t:

(1A) If $(1 - \gamma)\mathbb{E}_t[E_{t+h}(V_{t+h}, p_{t+h})] \geq (1 - \tau)(\zeta + \zeta^l(p_t)) - \delta_t - \lambda_t$:

$$
\begin{aligned}
E_t(V_t, p_t) &= e^{-rh}\mathbb{E}_t[E_{t+h}(V_{t+h}, p_{t+h})] + \min\{\delta_t - (1 - \tau)(\zeta + \zeta^l(p_t)) + \lambda_t, \\
&\qquad (\delta_t - (1 - \tau)(\zeta + \zeta^l(p_t)) + \lambda_t) / (1 - \gamma)\} \\
L_t(V_t, p_t) &= e^{-rh}\mathbb{E}_t[L_{t+h}(V_{t+h}, p_{t+h})] + \zeta^l(p_t) - \lambda_t \\
D_t(V_t, p_t) &= e^{-rh}\mathbb{E}_t[D_{t+h}(V_{t+h}, p_{t+h})] + \zeta
\end{aligned}
$$

If (V_t, p_t) is such that the firm does not have enough equity value, it declares bankruptcy:

(1B) If $(1 - \tau)(\zeta h + \zeta^l(p_t)) - \delta_t - \lambda_t > (1 - \gamma)e^{-rh}\mathbb{E}_t[E_{t+h}(V_{t+h}, p_{t+h})]$:

$$
\begin{aligned}
E_t(V_t, p_t) &= 0 \\
\hat{L}_t(V_t, p_t) &= \min\left\{V_t + \delta_t, \zeta^l(p_t) + p_t\right\} \\
\hat{D}_t(V_t, p_t) &= V_t + \delta_t - \hat{L}_t(V_t, p_t) \\
L_t(V_t, p_t) &= \hat{L}_t(V_t, p_t) - \frac{\hat{L}_t(V_t, p_t)}{\hat{L}_t(V_t, p_t) + \hat{D}_t(V_t, p_t)}\alpha(V_t + \delta_t) \\
D_t(V_t, p_t) &= \hat{D}_t(V_t, p_t) - \frac{\hat{D}_t(V_t, p_t)}{\hat{L}_t(V_t, p_t) + \hat{D}_t(V_t, p_t)}\alpha(V_t + \delta_t)
\end{aligned}
$$

If (V_t, p_t) is such that the firm does not generate enough revenue, then it has to raise money by either drawing down the loan commitment or diluting equity. The maximum it can draw from the loan commitment is limited by the credit limit P^l, and the maximum it can raise from equity dilution is limited by its equity value.

(2) If $\delta_t < (1-\tau)(\zeta + \zeta^l(p_t))$:

$$\begin{aligned} &\text{Choose } \lambda_t \in [0, \min\{(1-\tau)(\zeta+\zeta^l(p_t)) - \delta_t, P^l_{\max} - p_t] \\ &p_{t+h} = p_t + \lambda_t \\ &\Lambda_t(V_t, p_t) = e^{-rh}\mathbb{E}_t[\Lambda_{t+h}(V_{t+h}, p_{t+h})] + \lambda_t \end{aligned}$$

(2A) If (V_t, p_t) is such that λ_t alone is enough to cover the shortfall, i.e., $\lambda_t = (1-\tau)(\zeta+\zeta^l(p_t)) - \delta_t$, then:

$$\begin{aligned} E_t(p_t) &= e^{-rh}\mathbb{E}_t[E_{t+h}(p_{t+h})] \\ L_t(p_t) &= e^{-rh}\mathbb{E}_t[L_{t+h}(p_{t+h})] + \zeta^l(p_t) \\ D_t(p_t) &= e^{-rh}\mathbb{E}_t[D_{t+h}(p_{t+h})] + \zeta \end{aligned}$$

If (V_t, p_t) is such that λ_t is not enough to cover the shortfall, i.e., $\lambda_t < (1-\tau)(\zeta+\zeta^l(p_t)) - \delta_t$, and the firm has enough equity to cover the difference:

(2B) If $(1-\gamma)e^{-rh}\mathbb{E}_t[E_{t+h}(V_{t+h}, p_{t+h})] \geq (1-\tau)(\zeta+\zeta^l(p_t)) - \delta_t - \lambda_t$:

$$\begin{aligned} E_t(V_t, p_t) &= e^{-rh}\mathbb{E}_t[E_{t+h}(V_{t+h}, p_{t+h})] \\ &\quad + (\delta_t - (1-\tau)(\zeta+\zeta^l(p_t)) + \lambda_t)/(1-\gamma) \\ L_t(V_t, p_t) &= e^{-rh}\mathbb{E}_t[L_{t+h}(V_{t+h}, p_{t+h})] + \zeta^l(p_t) \\ D_t(V_t, p_t) &= e^{-rh}\mathbb{E}_t[D_{t+h}(V_{t+h}, p_{t+h})] + \zeta \end{aligned}$$

If at the chosen level of λ_t, (V_t, p_t) is such that the firm does not have enough equity value to cover the shortfall, then it declares bankruptcy:

(2C) If $(1-\tau)(\zeta+\zeta^l(p_t)) - \delta_t - \lambda_t > (1-\gamma)e^{-rh}\mathbb{E}_t[E_{t+h}(V_{t+h}, p_{t+h})]$

$$\begin{aligned} E_t(V_t, p_t) &= 0 \\ \hat{L}_t(V_t, p_t) &= \min\left\{V_t + \delta_t, \zeta^l(p_t) + p_t\right\} \\ \hat{D}_t(V_t, p_t) &= V_t + \delta_t - \hat{L}_t(p_t) \\ L_t(V_t, p_t) &= \hat{L}_t(V_t, p_t) - \frac{\hat{L}_t(V_t, p_t)}{\hat{L}_t(V_t, p_t) + \hat{D}_t(V_t, p_t)}\alpha(V_t + \delta_t) \\ D_t(V_t, p_t) &= \hat{D}_t(V_t, p_t) - \frac{\hat{D}_t(V_t, p_t)}{\hat{L}_t(V_t, p_t) + \hat{D}_t(V_t, p_t)}\alpha(V_t + \delta_t) \end{aligned}$$

In the infinite maturity case, we use an arbitrarily large maturity T and modify the terminal values of states (V_T, x_T) such that the firm is not bankrupt as follows:

If $V_T + \delta_T \geq (1-\tau)(\zeta+\zeta^l(p_T)) + P + p_T$:

$$\begin{aligned} E_T(V_T, p_T) &= V_T + \delta_T - (1-\tau)(\zeta+\zeta^l(p_T))/(1-r) \\ L_T(V_T, p_T) &= \zeta^l(p_T)/(1-r) \\ D_T(V_T, p_T) &= \zeta/(1-r) \end{aligned}$$

We use the infinite horizon implementation with $T = 200$, $N = 2{,}400$ and $M = 40$ for the results in Figs. 7–12.

Appendix E

Estimating default distribution in binomial lattice

In this section, we describe a method for estimating the distribution of default time in the binomial lattice. For simplicity, we assume that there is no cash balance or loan commitment, but the method can be easily applied to both cases.

We discretize the probability density of default time into K buckets of time intervals of length $\Delta = T/K$. The kth bucket corresponds to the time interval $(t_k, t_{k+1}]$, for $k = 0, 1, \ldots, K-1$, where $t_k = k\Delta$. K can be any positive integer no greater than the number of discrete time steps, N, in the lattice. Let $\Pi_t(V_t, k)$ be the time t probability of defaulting during the kth interval when the firm's asset value is V_t.

At maturity, if V_T is such that the firm is not bankrupt, then the default probability is zero for all intervals k.

$$\Pi_T(V_T, k) = 0 \quad \text{for all } k$$

Otherwise, if V_T is such that the firm is bankrupt, then the probability of defaulting at $t = T$ is one, and is zero everywhere else:

$$\Pi_T(V_T, k) = \begin{cases} 0 & \text{for } k \neq K-1 \\ 1 & \text{for } k = K-1 \end{cases}$$

because T is in the $(K-1)$st interval (the last interval).

At other times t, if V_t is such that the firm is not bankrupt, then the time t distribution of default time is the expected value of time $t+h$ distribution.

$$\Pi_t(V_t, k) = \mathbb{E}_t[\Pi_{t+h}(V_{t+h}, k)] \quad \text{for all } k$$

Otherwise, if V_t is such that the firm is bankrupt, then probability of defaulting during the interval where t belongs in is one, and is zero everywhere else.

$$\Pi_t(V_t, k) = \begin{cases} 0 & \text{for } k \text{ such that } t \notin (t_k, t_{k+1}] \\ 1 & \text{for } k \text{ such that } t \in (t_k, t_{k+1}] \end{cases}$$

Figure E.1 provides an example of the default time distribution in a binomial lattice with $K = N = 4$ and $p = 0.5$.

We use $T = 200$, $N = 2{,}400$ and $K = 50$ for the results in Figs. 12 and F.2.

Appendix F

Effects of cash balance on default time

As discussed in Sec. 4.2, cash balance does not have a significant impact on default time when the firm is maximizing the equity value. This is because the firm

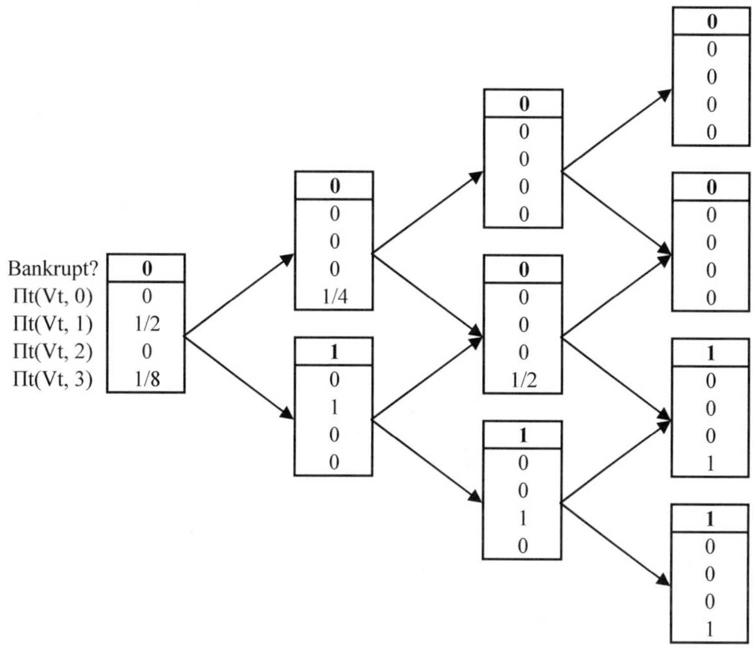

Fig. E.1. This figure shows the default time distribution at each node of the binomial lattice for $K = N = 4$ and $p = 0.5$. Each box represents a node in the lattice. The first (bold) number is 1 if the firm is bankrupt at that node, or is 0 otherwise. The remaining four elements are the probabilities of defaulting at time $0, 1, \ldots, 4$, respectively.

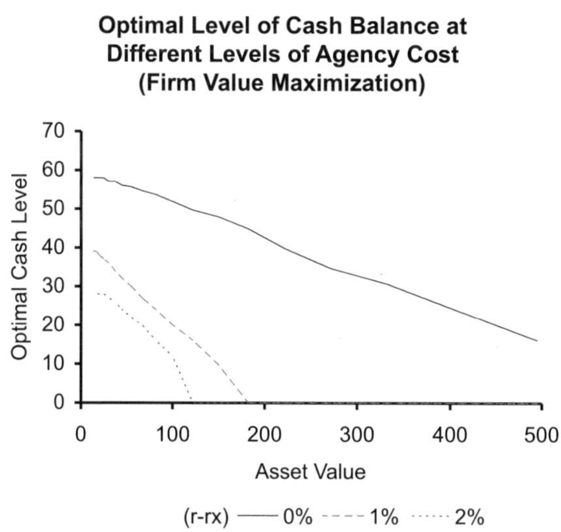

Fig. F.1. This figure plots the optimal level of cash balance, x^*, vs. asset value, V, under firm value maximization. Unlike equity value maximization, x^* is decreasing in V for all values of V. ($V = 100, C = 3.36, \sigma = 0.2, r = 0.05, q = 0.03, \alpha = 0.3, \tau = 0.15$).

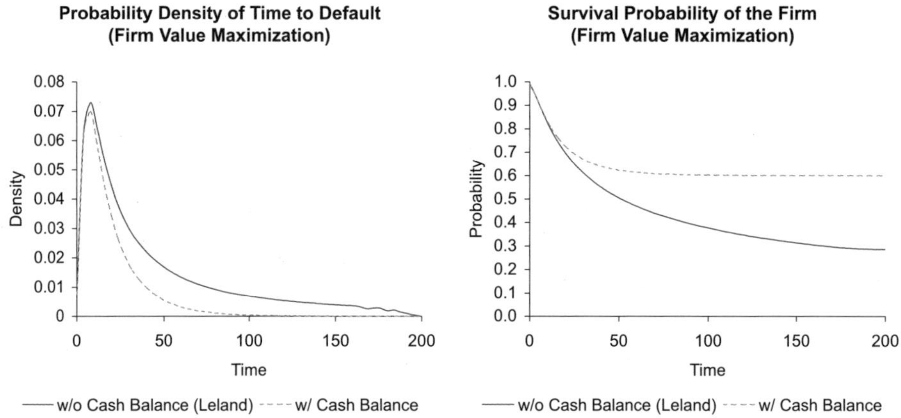

Fig. F.2. The left panel plots the probability density function of the default time with and without cash balance under firm value maximization. The distribution is significantly different because the firm keeps cash inside even as it approaches bankruptcy. The right panel plots the survival probability. The survival probability is almost the same for $t \leq 10$, but starts to deviate (upward) significantly for larger values of t. ($V = 100, C = 3.36, \sigma = 0.2, r = 0.05, q = 0.03, \alpha = 0.3, \tau = 0.15$).

depletes the cash balance so that shareholders can receive more dividends prior to bankruptcy. The impact of cash balance on default time is significantly different under total firm value maximization. Figure F.1 plots the optimal level of cash balance as a function of asset value. Unlike the equity maximization case, the optimal cash level increases as the asset value decreases, regardless of how close it is to bankruptcy. Consequently, as the firm heads towards bankruptcy, it will not empty out the cash balance and will be able to remain solvent longer. This has a big impact on the probability of default. In our example, the probability of default reduces from 71.3% to 40.0%. However, since there is a huge reduction in probability of default, the expected default time, conditioned on ever defaulting, reduces from 44.6 to 19.6. Figure F.2 shows the distribution of default time and the survival probability. We find that the probability of defaulting within ten years is practically the same in both cases. The probabilities start to deviate at later times. The reason for this is because in the next few years, the firm is not likely to be able to accumulate significant amount of cash to make a difference. If the firm survives the initial period, then the survival probability is significantly different.

Acknowledgment

This work was supported by NSF grant DMS-0914539.

References

[1] V. Acharya, J.-Z. Huang, M. Subrahmanyam and R. K. Sundaram, When does strategic debt-service matter?, *Economic Theory* **29**(2) (2006) 363–378.

[2] S. Agarwal, S. Chomsisengphet and J. C. Driscoll, Loan commitments and private firms, Finance and Economics Discussion Series 2004–27, Board of Governors of the Federal Reserve System (U.S.) 2004.

[3] P. Aghion, O. Hart and J. Moore, The economics of bankruptcy reform, *Journal of Law, Economics and Organization* **8** (1992) 523–546.

[4] R. W. Anderson and S. M. Sundaresan, Design and valuation of debt contracts, *Review of Financial Studies* **9**(1) (1996) 37–68.

[5] S. Asmussen and M. I. Taksar, Controlled diffusion models for optimal dividend payout, *Insurance: Mathematics and Economics* **20**(1) (1997) 1–15.

[6] L. A. Bebchuk, A new approach to corporate reorganization, *Havard Law Review* **101** (1988) 775–804.

[7] L. A. Bebchuk and J. M. Fried, The uneasy case for the priority of secured claims in bankruptcy, *Yale Law Journal* **105** (1996) 857–934.

[8] E. Berkovitch and S. I. Greenbaum, The loan commitment as an optimal financing contract, *Journal of Financial and Quantitative Analysis* **26**(1) (1991) 83–95.

[9] F. Black and J. C. Cox, Valuing corporate securities: Some effects of bond indenture provisions, *Journal of Finance* **31**(2) (1976) 351–367.

[10] B. Branch, The costs of bankruptcy: A review, *International Review of Financial Analysis* **11**(1) (2002) 39–57.

[11] A. Bris, I. Welch and N. Zhu, The costs of bankruptcy: Chapter 7 liquidation versus Chapter 11 reorganization, *Journal of Finance* **61**(3) (2006) 1253–1303.

[12] M. Broadie, M. Chernov and S. M. Sundaresan, Optimal debt and equity values in the presence of Chapter 7 and Chapter 11, *Journal of Finance* **62** (2007).

[13] M. Broadie and O. Kaya, A binomial lattice method for pricing. Corporate debt and modeling Chapter 11 proceedings, *Journal of Financial and Quantitative Analysis* **42**(2) (2007).

[14] A. Cadenillas, S. Sarkar and F. Zapatero, Optimal dividend policy with mean-reverting cash reservoir, *Mathematical Finance* **17**(1) (2007) 81–109.

[15] D. Duffie, An extension of the black-scholes model of security valuation, *Journal of Economic Theory* **46**(1) (1988) 194–204.

[16] H. Fan and S. M. Sundaresan, Debt valuation, renegotiations, and optimal dividend policy, *The Review of Financial Studies* **13**(4) (2000) 1057–1099.

[17] O. Hart, R. La Porta Drago, F. Lopez-de Silane and J. Moore, A new bankruptcy procedure that uses multiple auctions, *European Economic Review* **41**(3) (1997) 461–473.

[18] O. Hart, Different approaches to bankruptcy, Harvard Institute of Economic Research Paper 1903, Harvard Institute of Economic Research (2000).

[19] G. D. Hawkins, An analysis of revolving credit agreements, *Journal of Financial Economics* **10**(1) (1982) 59–81.

[20] T. S. Y. Ho and A. Saunders, Fixed rate loan commitments, take-down risk, and the dynamics of hedging with futures, *Journal of Financial and Quantitative Analysis* **18**(4) (1983) 499–516.

[21] C. M. James, Credit market conditions and the use of bank lines of credit, *Federal Reserve Bank of San Francisco Economic Letter* **27** (2009).

[22] M. Jeanblanc-Picque and A. N. Shiryaev, Optimization of the flow of dividends, *Russian Mathematical Surveys* **50** (1995) 257–277.

[23] C.-S. Kim, D. C. Mauer and A. E. Sherman, The determinants of corporate liquidity: Theory and Evidence, *Journal of Financial and Quantitative Analysis* **33**(3) (1998) 335–359.

[24] I. Lee, S. Lochhead, J. Ritter and Q. Zhao, The costs of raising capital, *Journal of Financial Research* **19**(1) (1996) 59–74.
[25] H. E. Leland, Corporate debt value, bond covenants, and optimal capital structure, *Journal of Finance* **49**(4) (1994) 1213–1252.
[26] V. Maksimovic, Product market imperfections and loan commitments, *Journal of Finance* **45**(5) (1990) 1641–1653.
[27] J. S. Martin and A. M. Santomero, Investment opportunities and corporate demand for lines of credit, *Journal of Banking & Finance* **21**(10) (1997) 1331–1350.
[28] A. Melnik and S. Plaut, Loan commitment contracts, terms of lending, and credit allocation, *Journal of Finance* **41**(2) (1986) 425–435.
[29] R. C. Merton, On the pricing of corporate debt: The risk structure of interest rates, *Journal of Finance* **29**(2) (1974) 449–470.
[30] M. H. Miller and F. Modigliani, Dividend policy, growth, and the valuation of shares, *Journal of Business* **34**(4) (1961) 411–433.
[31] S. C. Myers, Determinants of corporate borrowing, *Journal of Financial Economics* **5**(2) (1977) 147–175.
[32] C. M. Pedersen, On corporate debt and credit risk, PhD thesis, Columbia University (2004).
[33] R. Radner and L. Shepp, Risk vs. profit potential: A model for corporate strategy, *Journal of Economic Dynamics and Control* **20**(8) (1996) 1373–1393.
[34] R. L. Shockley, Bank loan commitments and corporate leverage, *Journal of Financial Intermediation* **4**(3) (1995) 272–301.
[35] R. L. Shockley and A. V. Thakor, Bank loan commitment contracts: Data, theory, and tests, *Journal of Money, Credit and Banking*, **29**(4) (1997) 517–534.
[36] C. M. Snyder, Loan commitments and the debt overhang problem, *Journal of Financial and Quantitative Analysis* **33**(1) (1998) 87–116.
[37] A. Sufi, Information asymmetry and financing arrangements: Evidence from syndicated loans, *Journal of Finance* **62**(2) (2007).
[38] A. Sufi, Bank lines of credit in corporate finance: An empirical analysis, *Forthcoming in Review of Financial Studies* (2007).
[39] M. I. Taksar, Optimal risk and dividend distribution controls models for an insurance company, *Mathematical Methods of Operations Research* **51** (2000) 1–42.

VALUATION AND HEDGING OF CDS COUNTERPARTY EXPOSURE IN A MARKOV COPULA MODEL[§]

T. R. BIELECKI*, S. CRÉPEY[†],
M. JEANBLANC[†] and B. ZARGARI[†,‡]

*Department of Applied Mathematics
Illinois Institute of Technology
10 W 32nd Street, Chicago, IL 60616, USA

[†]Université d'Evry, Laboratoire d'Analyse & Probabilitiés
23 Boulevard de France, 91037 Evry, France

[‡]Sharif University of Technology, Tehran, Iran

A Markov model is constructed for studying the counterparty risk in a CDS contract. The "wrong-way risk" in this model is accounted for by the possibility of the common default of the reference name and of the counterparty. A dynamic copula property as well as affine model specifications make pricing and calibration very efficient. We also consider the issue of dynamically hedging the CVA with a rolling CDS written on the counterparty. Numerical results are presented to show the adequacy of the behavior of CVA in the model with stylized features.

Keywords: Counterparty credit risk; CDS; CVA; wrong-way risk; dynamic hedging.

1. Introduction

The sub-prime crisis has highlighted the importance of counterparty risk in OTC derivative markets, particularly in the case of credit derivatives. We consider in this paper the case of a Credit Default Swap with counterparty risk. This topic, which corresponds to the emblematic case of CDSs between Lehman and AIG, already received a lot of attention in the literature. It can thus be considered as a benchmark problem of counterparty credit risk.

There has been a lot of research activity in the recent years devoted to valuation of counterparty risk. To quote but a few references:

- Huge and Lando [21] propose a rating-based approach,
- Hull and White [20] study this problem in the set-up of a static copula model,

[§]This chapter was originally published under the same title in *International Journal of Theoretical and Applied Finance*, Vol.15, No.1, 1250004-1–39 (2012). Singapore: World Scientific Publishing.

- Jarrow and Yu [22] use an intensity contagion model, further considered in Leung and Kwok [26],
- Brigo and Chourdakis [11] work in the set-up of their Gaussian copula and CIR++ intensity model, extended to the issue of bilateral counterparty credit risk in Brigo and Capponi [10],
- Blanchet-Scalliet and Patras [8] or Lipton and Sepp [25] develop structural approaches,
- Stein and Lee [29] give a discussion of theoretical and practical issues regarding computations of credit valuation adjustment in the fixed income markets,
- Recent monographs of Cesari *et al.* [13] and Gregory [19] provide discussion of modeling and computational aspects regarding managing of exposure to counterparty risk.

In this paper (see [15] for a preparatory study in the set-up of a deterministic intensities model), we shall work in a Markovian copula set-up [5] with marginals auto-calibrated to the related CDS curves, the model dependence structure being determined by the possibility of simultaneous defaults of the counterparty and of the firm underlying the CDS. Here we apply the Markov copula approach to model joint default between counterparty and the reference name in a CDS contract. Exactly the same approach can be applied to modeling the "double-default" effect (cf. [2]).

Note that we limit ourselves to the so called *unilateral* counterparty risk, not considering the counterparty risk due to the possibility of 'one's own default'. Whether counterparty risk should be assessed on a unilateral or bilateral basis is a controversial issue. For discussion of bilateral counterparty risk we refer the reader to, for instance, Brigo and Capponi [10], Assefa *et al.* [1], or to Bielecki *et al.* [7].

There has been a lot of research activity in the recent years devoted to valuation of counter-party risk. In contrast, almost no attention has been devoted to quantitative studies of the problem of (dynamic) hedging of this form of risk. There is some discussion devoted to dynamic hedging of counterparty exposure in Cesari *et al.* [13] and in Gregory [19].

In this paper, we present formal mathematical results that provide analytical basis for the quantitative methodology of dynamic hedging of counterparty risk. Due to space limitation, we only provide a rather preliminary and incomplete study. But, we address the main theoretical issues of dynamic hedging of CVA, nevertheless. In particular, we provide formulae for mean-variance delta for a combined hedging of spread risk and jump-to-default risk, as well as a formula for mean-variance delta for hedging of the jump-to-default risk.

It needs to be stressed though that in this pilot study we only focus on hedging against exposure to the specific credit risk of the counterparty. So, in essence, we are only concerned with the credit deltas relative to the counterparty (sensitivities to counterparty spread, and counterparty jump-to-default). Credit deltas relative to the reference name, as well as the market deltas (specifically, sensitivities to rates), and also the so called cross-gammas, i.e. the change in market sensitivities due to change in spread (cf. [14]), will be considered in a separate study.

1.1. *Outline of the paper*

Section 2 recalls the basics of a CDS with counterparty credit risk. In Sec. 3, we present our Markov model. In Sec. 4, the main valuation results are derived. Hedging is discussed in Sec. 5. In Sec. 6, we propose an affine intensities specification of the model, and discuss its calibration. A variant of the model using extended CIR intensity processes is devised in Sec. 7. Section 8 presents numerical results.

2. Cash Flows and Pricing in a General Set-Up

In this section, we briefly recall the basics of CDS (unilateral) counterparty risk, referring the reader to [15] for every detail. Let us thus be given a CDS with maturity T and contractual spread κ, as considered from the perspective of the investor, assumed by default to be buyer of default protection on the reference firm of the CDS (case of payer CDS). In the case of a receiver CDS all the related quantities will be denoted with a "bar", like $\overline{\text{CDS}}$.

Indices 1 and 2 will refer to quantities related to the firm and to the counterparty, respectively. For instance, τ_1 and τ_2 will denote their respective default times, whereas R_1 and R_2 will stand for the corresponding recoveries upon default.

The default times τ_1 and τ_2 cannot occur at fixed times, but may occur simultaneously. The recovery rates R_1 and R_2 are assumed to be constant for simplicity. Finally one assumes a deterministic discount factor $\beta(t) = \exp(-rt)$, for a constant short-term interest-rate function r. Given a risk neutral pricing model $(\Omega, \mathbb{F}, \mathbb{P})$, where $\mathbb{F} = (\mathcal{F}_t)_{t\in[0,T]}$ is a given filtration for which the τ_is are stopping times, let $\mathbb{E}_\theta$ stand for the conditional expectation under $\mathbb{P}$ given $\mathcal{F}_\theta$, for any stopping time θ. Let "risky CDS" and "risk-free CDS" respectively refer to a CDS with and without consideration of the counterparty risk.

Definition 2.1. (i) The *price* process of a risk-free CDS is given by $P_t = \mathbb{E}_t p^t$, where the *discounted cumulative risk-free cash flows* on $(t, T]$ are given by

$$\beta(t)p^t = -\kappa \int_t^{\tau_1 \wedge T} \beta(s)ds + (1 - R_1)\beta(\tau_1)\mathbb{1}_{t<\tau_1<T}. \tag{2.1}$$

For $\overline{\text{CDS}}$, the risk-free cash flows are $\bar{p}^t = -p^t$ and the corresponding price process is $\bar{P}_t = \mathbb{E}_t[\bar{p}^t] = -P_t$.

(ii) The *price* process of a risky CDS is given by $\Pi_t = \mathbb{E}_t \pi^t$, where the *discounted cumulative risky cash flows* on $(t, T]$ are given by

$$\beta(t)\pi^t = -\kappa \int_t^{\tau_1\wedge\tau_2\wedge T} \beta(s)ds + \beta(\tau_1)(1 - R_1)\mathbb{1}_{t<\tau_1<T}[\mathbb{1}_{\tau_1<\tau_2} + R_2\mathbb{1}_{\tau_1=\tau_2}]$$
$$+ \beta(\tau_2)\mathbb{1}_{t<\tau_2<\tau_1\wedge T}[R_2 P_{\tau_2}^+ - P_{\tau_2}^-], \tag{2.2}$$

in which P^+ (resp. P^-) stands for the positive (resp. negative) part of P. The corresponding risky cumulative cash flows and price process for $\overline{\text{CDS}}$ are given by

$$\beta(t)\bar{\pi}^t = \kappa \int_t^{\tau_1\wedge\tau_2\wedge T} \beta(s)ds - (1-R_1)\beta(\tau_1)\mathbb{1}_{t<\tau_1\leq\tau_2\wedge T}$$
$$+ \beta(\tau_2)\mathbb{1}_{t<\tau_2<\tau_1\wedge T}[R_2 P^-_{\tau_2} - P^+_{\tau_2}],$$

and $\bar{\Pi}_t = \mathbb{E}_t[\bar{\pi}^t]$.

(iii) The Credit Valuation Adjustments are the processes defined by, for $t \in [0,T]$,

$$\Theta_t = \mathbb{1}_{\{t<\tau_2\}}(P_t - \Pi_t), \quad \bar{\Theta}_t = \mathbb{1}_{\{t<\tau_2\}}(\bar{P}_t - \bar{\Pi}_t).$$

Note that $p^t = \bar{p}^t = P_t = \bar{P}_t = 0$ for $t \geq \tau_1 \wedge T$, and $\pi^t = \bar{\pi}^t = \Pi_t = \bar{\Pi}_t = \Theta_t = \bar{\Theta}_t = 0$ for $t \geq \tau_1 \wedge \tau_2 \wedge T$.

Proposition 2.1 (See [1, 12, 15]). *One has, on* $\{t < \tau_2\}$,

$$\beta(t)\Theta_t = \mathbb{1}_{\{t<\tau_2\}}\mathbb{E}_t[\beta(\tau_2)\xi_{(\tau_2)}], \quad \beta(t)\bar{\Theta}_t = \mathbb{1}_{\{t<\tau_2\}}\mathbb{E}_t[\beta(\tau_2)\bar{\xi}_{(\tau_2)}],$$

for the $\mathcal{F}_{\tau_2}$*-measurable Potential Future Exposures (PFEs) defined by*

$$\xi_{(\tau_2)} := (1-R_2)(\mathbb{1}_{\tau_2<\tau_1\wedge T}P^+_{\tau_2} + \mathbb{1}_{\tau_2=\tau_1<T}(1-R_1)),$$
$$\bar{\xi}_{(\tau_2)} := (1-R_2)P^-_{\tau_2}\mathbb{1}_{\tau_2<\tau_1\wedge T}.$$

Remark 2.1. A major issue in regard to counterparty credit risk is the so-called *wrong-way risk*. In general the wrong-way risk is understood as follows: Wrong-way risk occurs when exposure to a counterparty is adversely correlated with the credit quality of that counterparty. This can be rephrased as the risk that the value of the contract may be particularly high from the perspective of the other party at the moment of default of the counterparty. In our model the wrong-way risk is accounted for by the two terms in $\xi_{(\tau_2)}$ for the payer CDS: by the "large" term $1 - R_1$, as well as by possibly large term $P^+_{\tau_2}$.

Roughly speaking, the wrong-way risk manifests itself in two regimes:

Regime 1:
$\mathbb{P}(\tau_2$ is small) is large, and $\mathbb{P}(\tau_2 < \tau_1)$ is large. So, indeed, it would be the (large) term $P^+_{\tau_2}$ that accounts for the wrong-way risk. [As an extreme case one could consider the case where $\tau_2 = \varepsilon > 0$ with probability nearly one, and $\tau_1 = \tau_2 + \varepsilon'$. Then, correlation is 1 between τ_1 and τ_2, and, clearly, $P^+_{\tau_2}$ is the only term in the exposure, and it is large. This is a clear cut case of wrong-way risk: the fact that $\tau_2 = \varepsilon$ with probability nearly one means that the counterparty is of low credit quality, and the exposure is large.]

Regime 2:
$\mathbb{P}(\tau_2$ is small) is large, and $\mathbb{P}(\tau_2 = \tau_1)$ is large. So, indeed, it would be the (large) term $(1 - R_1)$ that accounts for the wrong-way risk. [As an extreme case one could consider the case where $\tau_2 = \varepsilon > 0$ with probability nearly one,

and $\tau_1 = \tau_2$. Here the only exposure term is $(1 - R_1)$. Again this is the clear cut case of the wrong-way risk.]

For the receiver CDS there is no wrong-way risk, at least not of this type.

3. Model

Let $\mathrm{H} = (H^1, H^2)$ denote the pair of the default indicator processes, so $H_t^i = \mathbb{1}_{\tau_i \le t}$. Given a *factor process* $\mathrm{X} = (X_1, X_2)$, to be made precise below, we consider a Markovian model of the pair (X, H) relative to its own filtration $\mathbb{F} = \mathbb{X} \vee \mathbb{H}$, with generator given by, for $u = u(t, x, e)$ with $t \in \mathbb{R}_+, x = (x_1, x_2) \in \mathbb{R}^2, e = (e_1, e_2) \in \{0, 1\}^2$:

$$\begin{aligned}\mathcal{A}u(t,x,e) &= \partial_t u(t,x,e) + \sum_{1\le i\le 2} l_i(t,x_i)(u(t,x,e^i) - u(t,x,e)) \\ &\quad + l_3(t)(u(t,x,1,1) - u(t,x,e)) \\ &\quad + \sum_{1\le i\le 2}\left(b_i(t,x_i)\partial_{x_i}u(t,x,e) + \frac{1}{2}\sigma_i^2(t,x_i)\partial^2_{x_i^2}u(t,x,e)\right) \\ &\quad + \varrho\sigma_1(t,x_1)\sigma_2(t,x_2)\partial^2_{x_1,x_2}u(t,x,e), \end{aligned} \tag{3.1}$$

where, for $i = 1, 2$:

- e^i denotes the vector obtained from e, by replacing the component i by number one,
- b_i and σ_i^2 denote factor *drift* and *variance* functions, and l_i is an *individual default intensity* function,
- ϱ and $l_3(t)$ respectively stand for a *factor correlation* and a *joint defaults intensity* function. The choice $\varrho = 0$ will thus correspond to independent factor processes X^1 and X^2, whereas it is also possible to consider a *common factor process* $X^1 = X^2 = X$ by letting $b_1 = b_2$, $\sigma_1 = \sigma_2$, $X_0^1 = X_0^2$ and $\varrho = 1$.

The $\mathbb{F}$-*intensity-matrix function* of H (see, e.g., Bielecki and Rutkowski [4]) is thus given by the following 4×4 matrix $A(t, x)$, where the first to fourth rows (or columns) correspond to the four possible states $(0, 0)$, $(1, 0)$, $(0, 1)$ and $(1, 1)$ of H_t:

$$A(t,x) = \begin{bmatrix} -l(t,x) & l_1(t,x_1) & l_2(t,x_2) & l_3(t) \\ 0 & -q_2(t,x_2) & 0 & q_2(t,x_2) \\ 0 & 0 & -q_1(t,x_1) & q_1(t,x_1) \\ 0 & 0 & 0 & 0 \end{bmatrix},$$

with, for every $i = 1, 2$,

$$q_i(t, x_i) = l_i(t, x_i) + l_3(t) \tag{3.2}$$

and $l(t, x) = l_1(t, x_1) + l_2(t, x_2) + l_3(t)$. We assume standard regularity and growth assumptions on the coefficients of $\mathcal{A}$ so as to ensure well-posedness of the related martingale problem (see, e.g., Ethier and Kurtz [18]). One then has,

Proposition 3.1. (i) *For every $i = 1, 2$, the process (X^i, H^i) is an $\mathbb{F}$-Markov process with generator given by, for $u_i = u_i(t, x_i, e_i)$, with $t \in \mathbb{R}_+, x_i \in \mathbb{R}, e_i \in \{0, 1\}$:*

$$\begin{aligned}\mathcal{A}_i u_i(t, x_i, e_i) &= \partial_t u_i(t, x_i, e_i) + b_i(t, x_i)\partial_{x_i} u_i(t, x_i, e_i) + \frac{1}{2}\sigma_i^2(t, x_i)\partial^2_{x_i^2} u_i(t, x_i, e_i) \\ &\quad + q_i(t, x_i)\left(u_i(t, x_i, 1) - u_i(t, x_i, e_i)\right).\end{aligned} \tag{3.3}$$

The $\mathbb{F}$-intensity matrix function of H^i is thus given by

$$A_i(t, x_i) = \begin{bmatrix} -q_i(t, x_i) & q_i(t, x_i) \\ 0 & 0 \end{bmatrix}$$

In other words, the process M^i defined by, for $i = 1, 2$,

$$M_t^i = H_t^i - \int_0^t (1 - H_s^i) q_i(s, X_s^i) ds, \tag{3.4}$$

is an $\mathbb{F}$-martingale.

(ii) *One has, for every $t \geq 0$,*

$$\begin{aligned}\mathbb{P}(\tau_i > t) &= \mathbb{E}\exp\left(-\int_0^t q_i(u, X_u^i) du\right), \\ \mathbb{P}(\tau_1 \wedge \tau_2 > t) &= \mathbb{E}\exp\left(-\int_0^t l(u, \mathrm{X}_u) du\right).\end{aligned} \tag{3.5}$$

Proof. (i) Applying the operator $\mathcal{A}$ in (3.1) to $u(t, x, e) := u_i(t, x_i, e_i)$, one gets,

$$\mathcal{A}u(t, x, e) = \mathcal{A}_i u_i(t, x_i, e_i),$$

where $\mathcal{A}_i$ is the operator defined in (3.3). In view of the Markov property of (X, H), the process $\mathcal{M}^i$ defined by

$$\begin{aligned}\mathcal{M}_t^i &:= u_i(t, X_t^i, H_t^i) - \int_0^t \mathcal{A}_i u_i(s, X_s^i, H_s^i) ds \\ &= u(t, \mathrm{X}_t, \mathrm{H}_t) - \int_0^t \mathcal{A}u(s, \mathrm{X}_s, \mathrm{H}_s) ds,\end{aligned}$$

is an $\mathbb{F}$-martingale. By the martingale characterization of Markov processes, the process (t, X^i, H^i) is thus $\mathbb{F}$-Markovian with generator $\mathcal{A}_i$. In particular for $u_i(t, x_i, e_i) := e_i$, one has $\mathcal{A}_i u_i(t, x_i, e_i) = q_i(t, x_i)(1 - e_i)$ and the martingale $\mathcal{M}^i$ coincides with M^i as of (3.4).

(ii) Since $\mathbb{P}(\tau_i > t) = \mathbb{E}\mathbb{1}_{H^i_t=0}$ and $\mathbb{P}(\tau_1 \wedge \tau_2 > t) = \mathbb{E}\mathbb{1}_{H^1_t=H^2_t=0}$, and in view of the Markov properties of (X^i, H^i) and (X, H), identities (3.5) can be checked by verification in the related Kolmogorov equations. □

In the terminology of [5], the model (X, H) is a Markovian copula model with marginals (X^i, H^i)s, or, in the common factor case $X^1 = X^2 = X$, marginals (X, H^i)s.

4. Pricing

Lemma 4.1. (i) *For every $i = 1, 2$ and function $p = p(t, x_i)$, one has, for $t \in [0, T]$,*

$$\mathbb{E}_t \int_t^T \beta(s)(1 - H^i_s)p(s, X^i_s)ds = (1 - H^i_t)\beta(t)v(t, X^i_t), \tag{4.1}$$

for a function $v = v(t, x_i)$ solving the following pricing PDE:

$$\begin{cases} v(T, x_i) = 0, \quad x_i \in \mathbb{R} \\ \left(\partial_t + b_i(t, x_i)\partial_{x_i} + \frac{1}{2}\sigma_i^2(t, x_i)\partial^2_{x_i^2}\right) v(t, x_i) \\ \qquad - (r + q_i(t, x_i))v(t, x_i) + p(t, x_i) = 0, \\ \qquad\qquad t \in [0, T), \quad x_i \in \mathbb{R}, \end{cases} \tag{4.2}$$

or, equivalently to (4.2),

$$v(t, x_i) = \mathbb{E}\left(\int_t^T e^{-\int_t^s (r+q_i(\zeta, X^i_\zeta))d\zeta} p(s, X^i_s)ds \,\middle|\, X^i_t = x_i\right). \tag{4.3}$$

(ii) *For every function $\pi = \pi(t, x)$, one has, for $t \in [0, T]$,*

$$\mathbb{E}_t \int_t^T \beta(s)(1 - H^1_s)(1 - H^2_s)\pi(s, \mathrm{X}_s)ds = (1 - H^1_t)(1 - H^2_t)\beta(t)u(t, \mathrm{X}_t),$$

for a function $u = u(t, x)$ solving the following pricing PDE:

$$\begin{cases} u(T, x) = 0, \quad x \in \mathbb{R}^2 \\ \left(\partial_t + \sum_{1\le i\le 2} \left(b_i(t, x_i)\partial_{x_i} + \frac{1}{2}\sigma_i^2(t, x_i)\partial^2_{x_i^2}\right) + \varrho\sigma_1(t, x_1)\sigma_2(t, x_2)\partial^2_{x_1,x_2}\right) u(t, x) \\ \qquad - (r + l(t, x))u(t, x) + \pi(t, x) = 0, \quad t \in [0, T), \quad x \in \mathbb{R}^2, \end{cases} \tag{4.4}$$

or, equivalently to (4.4),

$$u(t, x) = \mathbb{E}\left(\int_t^T e^{-\int_t^s (r+l(\zeta, \mathrm{X}_\zeta))d\zeta} \pi(s, \mathrm{X}_s)ds \,\middle|\, \mathrm{X}_t = x\right).$$

Proof. (i) The Markov property of (X^1, H^1) stated at Proposition 3.1(i) implies (4.1). Moreover, in view of the form (3.3) of the generator of (X^1, H^1), the function v has to satisfy (4.2). From Feynman-Kač formula, one then obtains (4.3).

(ii) The result follows as in point (i), using the form (3.1) of the generator of (X, H). □

Remark 4.1. Validity of this result and the related proof are in fact subject to suitable regularity and growth assumptions on the data, including the coefficient functions p and π. The strength of these assumptions depends on the meaning in which a solution to the pricing equations is sought for. Since these kinds of technicalities are not the main issue of the present paper, we refer the reader to the literature in this regard (see, for instance, Karatzas and Shreve [23] for classical solutions).

Let further $H^{\{1\}}$, $H^{\{2\}}$ and $H^{\{1,2\}}$ stand for the indicator processes of a default of the firm alone, of the counterparty alone, and of a simultaneous default of the firm and the counterparty, respectively. So

$$H^{\{1,2\}} = [H^1, H^2], \quad H^{\{1\}} = H^1 - H^{\{1,2\}}, \quad H^{\{2\}} = H^2 - H^{\{1,2\}},$$

where $[H^1, H^2]_t = \mathbb{1}_{\tau_1 = \tau_2 \leq t}$ stands for the quadratic covariation of the default indicator processes H^1 and H^2.

Lemma 4.2. *The $\mathbb{F}$-intensity of H^ι is of the form $q_\iota(t, \mathrm{X}_t, \mathrm{H}_t)$ for a suitable function $q_\iota(t, x, e)$ for every $\iota \in I = \{\{1\}, \{2\}, \{1,2\}\}$, namely,*

$$\begin{aligned} q_{\{1\}}(t, x, e) &= \mathbb{1}_{e_1=0}(\mathbb{1}_{e_2=0} l_1(t, x_1) + \mathbb{1}_{e_2=1} q_1(t, x_1)) \\ q_{\{2\}}(t, x, e) &= \mathbb{1}_{e_2=0}(\mathbb{1}_{e_1=0} l_2(t, x_2) + \mathbb{1}_{e_1=1} q_2(t, x_2)) \\ q_{\{1,2\}}(t, x, e) &= \mathbb{1}_{e=(0,0)} l_3(t). \end{aligned}$$

Put another way, for every $\iota \in I$, the process M^ι defined by,

$$M_t^\iota = H_t^\iota - \int_0^t q_\iota(s, \mathrm{X}_s, \mathrm{H}_s) ds,$$

is an $\mathbb{F}$-martingale, where the intensity processes $q_\iota(t, X_t, H_t)s$ are given by

$$\begin{aligned} q_{\{1\}}(t, \mathrm{X}_t, \mathrm{H}_t) &= (1 - H_t^1)((1 - H_t^2) l_1(t, X_t^1) + H_t^2 q_1(t, X_t^1)) \\ q_{\{2\}}(t, \mathrm{X}_t, \mathrm{H}_t) &= (1 - H_t^2)((1 - H_t^1) l_2(t, X_t^2) + H_t^1 q_2(t, X_t^2)) \\ q_{\{1,2\}}(t, \mathrm{X}_t, \mathrm{H}_t) &= (1 - H_t^1)(1 - H_t^2) l_3(t). \end{aligned}$$

Proof. An application of the $\mathbb{F}$-local martingale characterization of the $\mathbb{F}$-Markov process (X, H) with generator $\mathcal{A}$ in (3.1) yields the $\mathbb{F}$-intensity γ of process $H^1 H^2$:

$$\gamma_t = (1 - H_t^1) H_t^2 l_1(t, X_t^1) + (1 - H_t^2) H_t^1 l_2(t, X_t^2) + (1 - H_t^1 H_t^2) l_3(t).$$

Using Proposition 3.1(i), one deduces the desired expression for the $\mathbb{F}$-intensity process of

$$H^{\{1,2\}} = [H^1, H^2] = -\int_0^{\cdot} H^1_{t-} dH^2_t - \int_0^{\cdot} H^2_{t-} dH^1_t + H^1 H^2,$$

and then the $\mathbb{F}$-intensity processes of $H^{\{i\}}$ is obtained using $H^{\{i\}} = H^i - H^{\{1,2\}}$, for $i = 1, 2$. □

We are now in a position to derive the risk-free and risky CDS pricing equations.

Proposition 4.1. (i) *The price of the risk-free CDS admits the representation:*

$$P_t = (1 - H^1_t) v(t, X^1_t),$$

for a pre-default pricing function $v = v(t, x_1)$ *as of Lemma* 4.1(i), *with* $i = 1$ *and*

$$p(t, x_1) = (1 - R_1) q_1(t, x_1) - \kappa. \tag{4.5}$$

(ii) *The price of the risky CDS admits the representation:*

$$\Pi_t = (1 - H^1_t)(1 - H^2_t) u(t, \mathrm{X}_t),$$

for a pre-default pricing function $u = u(t, x)$ *as of Lemma* 4.1(ii) *with*

$$\begin{aligned} \pi(t, x) = (1 - R_1)&[l_1(t, x_1) + R_2 l_3(t)] \\ &+ l_2(t, x_2)[R_2 v^+(t, x_1) - v^-(t, x_1)] - \kappa. \end{aligned} \tag{4.6}$$

(iii) *The price of the risky* $\overline{\text{CDS}}$ *admits the representation:*

$$\bar{\Pi}_t = (1 - H^1_t)(1 - H^2_t) \bar{u}(t, \mathrm{X}_t),$$

for a pre-default pricing function $\bar{u} = \bar{u}(t, x)$ *as of Lemma* 4.1(ii) *with*

$$\bar{\pi}(t, x) = \kappa - (1 - R_1) q_1(t, x_1) + l_2(t, x_2)[R_2 v^-(t, x_1) - v^+(t, x_1)]. \tag{4.7}$$

Proof. (i) One has $P_t = \mathbb{E}_t(p^t)$, with

$$\begin{aligned} \beta(t) p^t &= -\kappa \int_t^T \beta(s)(1 - H^1_s) ds + (1 - R_1) \int_t^T \beta(s) dH^1_s \\ &= \int_t^T \beta(s)(1 - H^1_s) p(s, X^1_s) ds + (1 - R_1) \int_t^T \beta(s) dM^1_s, \end{aligned}$$

with p defined by (4.5). Since $\mathbb{E}_t(\int_t^T \beta(s) dM^1_s) = 0$, the result follows by an application of Lemma 4.1(i).

(ii) One has $\Pi_t = \mathbb{E}_t(\pi^t)$, with π^t defined in (2.2). As in part (i), we write π^t in terms of integrals with respect to H^ιs:

$$\beta(t)\pi^t = -\kappa \int_t^T \beta(s)(1-H_s^1)(1-H_s^2)ds + (1-R_1)\int_t^T \beta(s)(1-H_{s-}^2)dH_s^{\{1\}}$$

$$+ R_2(1-R_1)\int_t^T \beta(s)dH_s^{\{1,2\}}$$

$$+ \int_t^T \beta(s)[R_2 v^+(s,X_s^1) - v^-(s,X_s^1)](1-H_{s-}^1)dH_s^{\{2\}},$$

where (i) was used in the last term. But in view of Lemma 4.2, this expression coincides, up to a martingale term, with

$$\int_t^T \beta(s)(1-H_s^1)(1-H_s^2)\pi(s,\mathrm{X}_s)ds,$$

where π is given by (4.6). The result then follows by an application of Lemma 4.1(ii).

(iii) can be proved similarly to (ii). □

Note finally that in the case of time-deterministic intensities, the valuation PDEs reduce to ODEs, and semi-explicit formulas in the form of integrals with respect to time can be obtained for most quantities of interest, including the CVAs (see [15]).

5. Hedging of Counterparty Exposure

In order to discuss hedging of counterparty exposure we introduce now the cumulative CVA process. We first focus on the payer CDS, the main results for $\overline{\text{CDS}}$ being then given in Proposition 5.3.

Definition 5.1. The cumulative CVA process $\widehat{\Theta}$ is given as, for $t \in [0,T]$,

$$\beta(t)\widehat{\Theta}_t = \beta(t\wedge\tau_2)(\widehat{P}_{t\wedge\tau_2} - \widehat{\Pi}_{t\wedge\tau_2}),$$

where $\widehat{P}$ (resp. $\widehat{\Pi}$) denotes the *cumulative* risk-free (resp. risky) CDS price process such that $\beta(t)\widehat{P}_t = \mathbb{E}_t p^0$ (resp. $\beta(t)\widehat{\Pi}_t = \mathbb{E}_t\pi^0$).

Here, we shall focus on the cumulative CVA as it is this process that enjoys the martingale properties (after discounting) which are important for the hedging endeavor. One has by application of Proposition 2.1:

$$\beta(t)\widehat{\Theta}_t = \mathbb{E}_t[\beta(\tau_2)\xi_{(\tau_2)}].$$

Note that on the set $\{\tau_2 \le T\}$, the random variable $\xi_{(\tau_2)}$ can be represented as the value at time $t = \tau_2$ of the process ξ defined by, for $t \in [0,T]$,

$$\xi_t = (1-R_2)(P_t^+ + (H_t^1 - H_{t-}^1)(1-R_1))$$

$$= (1-R_2)((1-H_t^1)v^+(t,X_t^1) + (H_t^1 - H_{t-}^1)(1-R_1)), \tag{5.1}$$

where the second equality follows from Proposition 4.1.

In this section, we set henceforth $\beta = 1$ (null interest rate) for notational simplicity.

5.1. *Dynamics of cumulative CVA*

The first step consists in deriving dynamics of the cumulative CVA. We start with the following elementary result,

Lemma 5.1. *For any $t \in (0, T]$, we have*

$$\begin{aligned} d\widehat{\Theta}_t &= (1 - H^2_{t-})(d\widehat{P}_t - d\widehat{\Pi}_t) \\ &= (1 - H^2_t)(dP_t - d\Pi_t) + (\Delta\widehat{P}_{\tau_2} - \Delta\widehat{\Pi}_{\tau_2})dH^2_t \\ &= (1 - H^2_t)(dP_t - d\Pi_t) + (\xi_{\tau_2} - \widehat{\Theta}_{\tau_2 -})dH^2_t \\ &= (1 - H^2_t)(dP_t - d\Pi_t) + (\xi_t - \widehat{\Theta}_{t-})dH^2_t \\ &= (1 - H^2_t)(dP_t - d\Pi_t) + (\xi_t - \Theta_{t-})dH^2_t. \end{aligned} \tag{5.2}$$

Proof. The first line holds by definition of $\widehat{\Theta}$ and by application of Itô's formula. The second one follows from the fact that $p^0 - p^t = \pi^0 - \pi^t$ for any $t < \tau_2$. The remaining three equalities follow easily. □

Equation (5.2) is the key to hedging of counterparty risk. The dynamics of $\widehat{\Theta}$ splits into the "pre-counter-party-default" part $(1 - H^2_t)(dP_t - d\Pi_t)$, and the "at-counter-party-default" part $(\xi_t - \widehat{\Theta}_{t-})dH^2_t$.

Specification of the above dynamics, that is specification of all martingale terms, is not easy in general. We now provide exact formulae for these coefficients, in our stylized Markovian copula model.

5.1.1. *Markovian case*

We are in position now to particularize dynamics of the cumulative CVA for the model of Sec. 3.

Proposition 5.1. *For any $t \in [0, T]$, we have:*

$$\begin{aligned} d\widehat{\Theta}_t = &-(1 - H^2_{t-})(v - u)dM^1_t \\ &+ \{(1 - R_2)(1 - H^1_{t-})v^+ - (1 - H^1_{t-})(v - (1 - H^2_{t-})u\}dM^2_t \\ &+ (v - u + (1 - R_2)(1 - R_1) - (1 - R_2)v^+)dM^{\{1,2\}}_t \\ &+ (1 - H^1_t)(1 - H^2_t)((\partial_{x_1} v - \partial_{x_1} u)\sigma_1 dW^1_t - (\partial_{x_2} u)\sigma_2 dW^2_t). \end{aligned}$$

where u and v stand for $u(t, \mathrm{X}_t)$ and $v(t, X^1_t)$.

Proof. Recall (5.2). Using Proposition 4.1 we obtain, for $0 \le t \le T$,

$$\begin{aligned}(1-H_t^2)dP_t &= (1-H_t^2)d((1-H_t^1)v(t,X_t^1)) \\ &= (1-H_t^1)(1-H_t^2)(\partial_{x_1}v)\sigma_1 dW_t^1 - (1-H_{t-}^2)v dM_t^1 \\ &\quad + (H_t^2 - H_{t-}^2)v dH_t^1 - (1-H_t^1)(1-H_t^2)((1-R_1)q_1 - \kappa)dt,\end{aligned}$$

where the term $(1-H_{t-}^2)v dM_t^1$ defines a martingale. In the same way,

$$\begin{aligned}(1-H_t^2)d\Pi_t &= (1-H_t^2)d\big((1-H_t^1)(1-H_t^2)u(t,X_t^1,X_t^2)\big) \\ &= -(1-H_{t-}^2)u dM_t^1 + (H_t^2 - H_{t-}^2)u dH_t^1 \\ &\quad + (1-H_t^1)(1-H_t^2)(l_2 u - (1-R_1)(l_1 + R_2 l_3) \\ &\quad - l_2(R_2 v^+ - v^-) + \kappa)dt \\ &\quad + (1-H_t^1)(1-H_t^2)((\partial_{x_1}u)\sigma_1 dW_t^1 + (\partial_{x_2}u)\sigma_2 dW_t^2),\end{aligned}$$

and

$$\begin{aligned}(\xi_t - \widehat{\Theta}_{t-})dH_t^2 &= \{(1-R_2)((1-H_t^1)v^+ + (H_t^1 - H_{t-}^1)(1-R_1)) \\ &\quad - (1-H_{t-}^1)v + (1-H_{t-}^1)(1-H_{t-}^2)u\}dH_t^2.\end{aligned}$$

This, combined with Lemma 5.1, leads to

$$\begin{aligned}d\widehat{\Theta}_t &= -(1-H_{t-}^2)(v-u)dM_t^1 + (H_t^2 - H_{t-}^2)(v-u)dH_t^1 \\ &\quad + (1-H_t^1)(1-H_t^2)((\partial_{x_1}v - \partial_{x_1}u)\sigma_1 dW_t^1 - (\partial_{x_2}u)\sigma_2 dW_t^2) \\ &\quad - (1-H_t^1)(1-H_t^2)(((1-R_1)q_1 - \kappa) + (l_2 u - (1-R_1)(l_1 + R_2 l_3) \\ &\quad - l_2(R_2 v^+ - v^-) + \kappa))dt + \{(1-R_2)\big((1-H_t^1)v^+ + (H_t^1 - H_{t-}^1)(1-R_1)\big) \\ &\quad - (1-H_{t-}^1)v + (1-H_{t-}^1)(1-H_{t-}^2)u\}dH_t^2.\end{aligned}$$

We now observe that

$$\begin{aligned}(H_t^2 - H_{t-}^2)(v-u)dH_t^1 &= (v-u)dH_t^{\{1,2\}}, \\ (1-H_t^1)v^+ dH_t^1 &= (1-H_{t-}^1)v^+ dH_t^1 - v^+ dH_t^{\{1,2\}}.\end{aligned}$$

Consequently,

$$\begin{aligned}d\widehat{\Theta}_t &= -(1-H_{t-}^2)(v-u)dM_t^1 + (1-H_t^1)(1-H_t^2)((\partial_{x_1}v - \partial_{x_1}u)\sigma_1 dW_t^1 \\ &\quad - (\partial_{x_2}u)\sigma_2 dW_t^2) + (v - u + (1-R_1)(1-R_2) - (1-R_2)v^+)dH_t^{\{1,2\}} \\ &\quad - (1-H_t^1)(1-H_t^2)((1-R_1)(q_1 - l_1 - R_2 l_3) - l_2(v - u + (R_2 - 1)v^+))dt \\ &\quad + \{(1-R_2)(1-H_{t-}^1)v^+ - (1-H_{t-}^1)(v - (1-H_{t-}^2)u)\}dH_t^2.\end{aligned}$$

Now, using

$$dH_t^{\{1,2\}} = dM_t^{\{1,2\}} + l_3(1-H_t^1)(1-H_t^2)dt, \quad dH^2 = dM_t^2 + q_2(1-H_t^2)dt,$$

the last expression can be rewritten as

$$
\begin{aligned}
d\widehat{\Theta}_t &= -(1-H^2_{t-})(v-u)dM^1_t + (1-H^1_t)(1-H^2_t)((\partial_{x_1}v - \partial_{x_1}u)\sigma_1 dW^1_t \\
&\quad - (\partial_{x_2}u)\sigma_2 dW^2_t) + (v-u+(1-R_1)(1-R_2)-(1-R_2)v^+)dM^{\{1,2\}}_t \\
&\quad + \{(1-R_2)(1-H^1_{t-})v^+ - (1-H^1_{t-})(v-(1-H^2_{t-})u\}dM^2_t \\
&\quad + (1-H^1_t)(1-H^2_t)\{(v-u+(1-R_1)(1-R_2)-(1-R_2)v^+)l_3 \\
&\quad - (1-R_1)\big(q_1 - l_1 - R_2 l_3\big) + l_2(v-u+(R_2-1)v^+) \\
&\quad + ((1-R_2)v^+ - v + u)q_2\}dt,
\end{aligned}
$$

where the dt-coefficient simplifies to zero, which proves the result. □

As a corollary, we obtain the following representation for the dynamics of CVA, which will be used in Sec. 5.2,

Corollary 5.1. *For any $t \in [0,T]$ we have*

$$
\begin{aligned}
d\,\widehat{\Theta}_t &= -(1-H^1_{t-})(1-H^2_{t-})(v-u)dM^{\{1\}}_t \\
&\quad + (1-H^1_{t-})(1-H^2_{t-})((1-R_2)v^+ - (v-u))dM^{\{2\}}_t \\
&\quad + (1-H^1_{t-})(1-H^2_{t-})((1-R_1)(1-R_2) - (v-u))dM^{\{1,2\}}_t \\
&\quad + (1-H^1_t)(1-H^2_t)((\partial_{x_1}v - \partial_{x_1}u)\sigma_1 dW^1_t - (\partial_{x_2}u)\sigma_2 dW^2_t) \\
&=: \widetilde{\eta}^{\{1\}}_t dM^{\{1\}}_t + \widetilde{\eta}^{\{2\}}_t dM^{\{2\}}_t + \widetilde{\eta}^{\{1,2\}}_t dM^{\{1,2\}}_t + \widetilde{\gamma}^1_t dW^1_t + \widetilde{\gamma}^2_t dW^2_t. \qquad (5.3)
\end{aligned}
$$

Recall that if $R_2 = 1$ then $v = u$ so that in this case $\widetilde{\eta}^{\{1\}} = \widetilde{\eta}^{\{2\}} = \widetilde{\eta}^{\{1,2\}} = \widetilde{\gamma}^1 = \widetilde{\gamma}^2 = 0$. In particular, $\Theta_t = \widehat{\Theta}_t = 0$ for all t. Now, using the convention that $\frac{0}{0} = 1$ we can write

$$
d\,\widehat{\Theta}_t =: (1-R_2)(\eta^{\{1\}}_t dM^{\{1\}}_t + \eta^{\{2\}}_t dM^{\{2\}}_t + \eta^{\{1,2\}}_t dM^{\{1,2\}}_t + \gamma^1_t dW^1_t + \gamma^2_t dW^2_t), \qquad (5.4)
$$

where $\eta^{\{1\}} = \frac{\widetilde{\eta}^{\{1\}}}{1-R_2}$, and accordingly for the remaining coefficients.

5.2. *Hedging of CVA*

We shall apply the above results to the problem of dynamically hedging the CDS counterparty risk in our Markovian copula model.

As it is seen from Corollary 5.1 there are five martingale terms to hedge in the dynamics for $\widehat{\Theta}$. Three of them, namely those in $dM^{\{1,2\}}_t$, $dM^{\{2\}}_t$ and dW^2_t, induce the risk directly related to the counterparty. In this paper, we are only concerned with hedging of these three terms in the mean variance sense, using a single hedging instrument taken as a rolling CDS contract written on the counterparty. Of course we also implicitly trade in the savings account (which is worth a constant, in the present nil interest rates set-up) for the purpose of making the strategy self-financing.

5.2.1. *Rolling CDS*

For the purpose of dynamically hedging the CVA on the CDS on name one, we shall now consider a *rolling CDS*[1] referencing the counterparty, that is corresponding to the default time τ_2. The concept of the rolling CDS contract was formally introduced and studied in [6]. A rolling CDS is an "abstract" contract which at any time t has similar features as the T-maturity CDS issued at this date t, in particular, its ex-dividend price is equal to zero at every t. Intuitively, one can think of the rolling CDS of a constant maturity T as a stream of CDSs of constant maturities equal to T that are continuously entered into and immediately unwound. Thus, a rolling CDS contract is equivalent to a self-financing trading strategy that at any given time t enters into a CDS contract of maturity T and then unwinds the contract at time $t + dt$.

Remark 5.1. We shall use here a simplifying assumption that the recovery R_2 is generic, that is, it is the same for all CDS contracts referencing the same default τ_2 and with the same maturity T. Otherwise, for every fixed maturity date T, we would need to consider the whole class of protection payment processes, indexed by the initiation date.

The main result regarding the dynamics of the mark-to-market value of a rolling CDS contract is the following.

Lemma 5.2 ([6]). *The cumulative value process, say $\widehat{Q}$, of a rolling CDS referencing the counterparty, is an $\mathbb{F}$-martingale, and its dynamics are given as*

$$\begin{aligned} d\widehat{Q}_t &= (1 - H_t^2)((1 - R_2)\partial_x g(t, X_t^2) - \kappa(t, X_t^2)\partial_x f(t, X_t^2)) \\ &\quad \times \sigma_2(t, X_t^2)dW_t^2 + (1 - R_2)dM_t^2 \\ &=: (1 - R_2)((1 - H_t^2)\psi_t dW_t^2 + dM_t^{\{2\}} + dM_t^{\{1,2\}}) \end{aligned} \tag{5.5}$$

where g and f denote the pre-default pricing functions of the unit protection and fee legs of the ordinary CDS contract initiated at time t, so that

$$f(t, X_t^2) = \mathbb{E}\left(\int_t^T e^{-\int_t^u q_2(v, X_v^2)dv} du \,|\, X_t^2\right),$$

$$g(t, X_t^2) = \mathbb{E}\left(\int_t^T e^{-\int_t^u q_2(v, X_v^2)dv} q_2(u, X_u^2) du \,|\, X_t^2\right),$$

and $\kappa = (1 - R_2)g/f$ is the corresponding CDS fair spread function.

[1]It is clear that for the hedging purposes one needs to use rolling CDS contracts, which are entered into with counterparties that are remote from default.

5.2.2. *Mean-variance hedging*

In principle, given that one has at one's disposal sufficiently many liquid traded instruments, one can dynamically replicate all risk sources that show up in the CVA in (5.3), namely $M^{\{1\}}$, $M^{\{2\}}$, $M^{\{1,2\}}$, W^1 and W^2.

In this paper we shall not discuss this dynamic replication though, but rather we shall focus on mean-variance hedging of CVA, using the rolling CDS on the counterparty (along with the savings account) as hedging instrument. Let thus ζ be a real-valued process, representing the number of units of rolling CDS which are held in a self-financing hedging strategy of CVA. Invoking (5.3) and (5.5) we conclude that the tracking error process e_t of the hedged portfolio satisfies, for $t \in [0, T]$,

$$de_t = d\widehat{\Theta}_t - (1 - H^1_{t-})\zeta_t d\widehat{Q}_t$$

$$\frac{de_t}{1 - R_2} = \eta^{\{1\}}_t dM^{\{1\}}_t + (\eta^{\{1,2\}}_t - \zeta_t)dM^{\{1,2\}}_t + (\eta^{\{2\}}_t - (1 - H^1_{t-})\zeta_t)dM^{\{2\}}_t$$
$$+ \gamma^1_t dW^1_t + (\gamma^2_t - \zeta_t \psi^2_t)dW^2_t.$$

where the η and γ's were defined in (5.3) and ψ in (5.5). We thus obtain the following result,

Proposition 5.2. *For a payer CDS*: (i) *the self-financing strategy that minimizes the risk neutral variance of the tracking error is given, on the set* $\{t \le \tau_1 \wedge \tau_2\}$, *as*

$$\zeta^{va}_t = \frac{\eta^{\{2\}}_t d\langle M^{\{2\}}\rangle_t + \eta^{\{1,2\}}_t d\langle M^{\{1,2\}}\rangle_t + (\varrho\gamma^1_t + \gamma^2_t)\psi_t dt}{d\langle M^{\{2\}}\rangle_t + d\langle M^{\{1,2\}}\rangle_t + \psi^2_t dt}$$
$$= \frac{l_2(t, X^2_t)\eta^{\{2\}}_t + l_3(t)\eta^{\{1,2\}}_t + (\varrho\gamma^1_t + \gamma^2_t)\psi_t}{l_2(t, X^2_t) + l_3(t) + \psi^2_t};$$

(ii) *The self-financing strategy that minimizes the risk neutral variance of the jump-to-counterparty-default risk is given, on the set* $\{t \le \tau_1 \wedge \tau_2\}$, *as*

$$\zeta^{jd}_t = \frac{l_2(t, X^2_t)\eta^{\{2\}}_t + l_3(t)\eta^{\{1,2\}}_t}{l_2(t, X^2_t) + l_3(t)}$$
$$= \left(P^+_t - \frac{\Theta_{t-}}{1 - R_2}\right)\frac{l_2(t, X^2_t)}{l_2(t, X^2_t) + l_3(t)} + \left((1 - R_1) - \frac{\Theta_{t-}}{1 - R_2}\right)\frac{l_3(t)}{l_2(t, X^2_t) + l_3(t)}$$
$$= \frac{1}{1 - R_2}\left(\mathbb{E}(\xi \,|\, \mathcal{F}_{\tau_2-}) \,|_{\tau_2 = t} - \Theta_{t-}\right).$$

The ζ^{jd} *hedging strategy changes the counterparty jump-to-default exposure from* $\xi - \Theta_{\tau_2-}$ *to* $\xi - \mathbb{E}(\xi \,|\, \mathcal{F}_{\tau_2-})$, *where* $\mathbb{E}(\xi \,|\, \mathcal{F}_{\tau_2-})$ *is the "best guess" of* ξ *available right before* τ_2.

Remark 5.2. Since τ_2 is an $\mathbb{F}$-stopping time, the $\mathcal{F}_{\tau_2-}$-measurable random variable $\mathbb{E}(\xi|\mathcal{F}_{\tau_2-})$ can be represented as Y_{τ_2}, for some $\mathbb{F}$-predictable process Y (see Dellacherie and Meyer [16], Thm 67.b). In the above proposition, we denote

$\mathbb{E}(\xi|\mathcal{F}_{\tau_2-})|_{\tau_2=t} = Y_t$. A similar remark applies to the notation $\mathbb{E}(\bar{\xi}|\mathcal{F}_{\tau_2-})|_{\tau_2=t} = \bar{Y}_t$ in Proposition 5.3.

In the case of the receiver CDS, let

$$\begin{aligned}
\bar{\eta}_t^{\{1\}} &= (1 - H_{t-}^1)(1 - H_{t-}^2)(v + \bar{u}) \\
\bar{\eta}_t^{\{2\}} &= (1 - H_{t-}^1)(1 - H_{t-}^2)((1 - R_2)v^- + (v + \bar{u})) \\
\bar{\eta}_t^{\{1,2\}} &= (1 - H_{t-}^1)(1 - H_{t-}^2)(v + \bar{u}) \\
\bar{\gamma}_t^1 &= -(1 - H_t^1)(1 - H_t^2)\sigma_1(\partial_{x_1} v + \partial_{x_1} \bar{u}) \\
\bar{\gamma}_t^2 &= -(1 - H_t^1)(1 - H_t^2)\sigma_2\partial_{x_2}\bar{u},
\end{aligned}$$

Proposition 5.3. *For a receiver CDS:* (i) *The self-financing strategy that minimizes the risk neutral variance of the tracking error is given, on the set* $\{t \leq \tau_1 \wedge \tau_2\}$, *as*

$$\begin{aligned}
\bar{\zeta}_t^{va} &= \frac{\bar{\eta}_t^{\{2\}} d\langle M^{\{2\}}\rangle_t + \bar{\eta}_t^{\{1,2\}} d\langle M^{\{1,2\}}\rangle_t + (\varrho\gamma_t^1 + \gamma_t^2)\bar{\psi}_t dt}{d\langle M^{\{2\}}\rangle_t + d\langle M^{\{1,2\}}\rangle_t + \bar{\psi}_t^2 dt} \\
&= \frac{l_2(t, X_t^2)\bar{\eta}_t^{\{2\}} + l_3(t)\bar{\eta}_t^{\{1,2\}} + (\varrho\gamma_t^1 + \gamma_t^2)\bar{\psi}_t}{l_2(t, X_t^2) + l_3(t) + \bar{\psi}_t^2};
\end{aligned}$$

(ii) *The self-financing strategy that minimizes the risk neutral variance of the jump–to–counterparty–default risk is given, on the set* $\{t \leq \tau_1 \wedge \tau_2\}$, *as*

$$\begin{aligned}
\bar{\zeta}_t^{jd} &= \frac{l_2(t, X_t^2)\bar{\eta}_t^{\{2\}} + l_3(t)\bar{\eta}_t^{\{1,2\}}}{l_2(t, X_t^2) + l_3(t)} = \left(P_t^- - \frac{\bar{\Theta}_{t-}}{1 - R_2}\right)\frac{l_2(t, X_t^2)}{l_2(t, X_t^2) + l_3(t)} \\
&= \frac{1}{1 - R_2}(\mathbb{E}(\bar{\xi} \mid \mathcal{F}_{\tau_2-})|_{\tau_2=t} - \bar{\Theta}_{t-}).
\end{aligned}$$

The $\bar{\zeta}^{jd}$ *hedging strategy changes the counterparty jump-to-default exposure from* $\bar{\xi} - \bar{\Theta}_{\tau_2-}$ *to* $\bar{\xi} - \mathbb{E}(\bar{\xi} \mid \mathcal{F}_{\tau_2-})$, *where* $\mathbb{E}(\bar{\xi} \mid \mathcal{F}_{\tau_2-})$ *is the "best guess" of* ξ *available right before* τ_2.

6. Model Implementation

In view of the model generator (3.1), the model primitives are the factor coefficients b and σ and the intensity functions l_is for $i = 1$ to 3, or, equivalently to the latter via (3.2), the marginal intensity functions $q_1 = q_1(t, x_1)$ and $q_2 = q_2(t, x_2)$ and the joint defaults intensity function $l_3 = l_3(t)$. In this section, following the lines of Brigo *et al.* [10, 11], we shall specify the factors in the form of CIR++ processes. Let thus the X^is be affine processes of the form

$$dX_t^i = \eta(\mu_i - X_t^i)dt + \nu\sqrt{X_t^i}dW_t^i,$$

for non-negative coefficients η, μ_i and ν. One then sets

$$q_i(t, x_i) = f_i(t) + \delta x_i, \tag{6.1}$$

for functions $f_i(t)$ such that $f_i(t) \geq l_3(t)$ and $\delta \in \{0, 1\}$.

Remark 6.1. (i) As in Brigo *et al.* [10, 11], we shall not restrict ourselves to the inaccessible origin case $2\eta\mu_i > \nu^2$, in order not to limit the range of the model CDS implied volatility.[2]

(ii) The restriction $f_i(t) \geq l_3(t)$ is imposed to guarantee that, consistently with (3.2), $q_i(t, X_t^i)$ defined by (6.1) is never smaller than $l_3(t)$.

In the sequel, by (2F), we mean the parametrization (6.1) with $\delta = 1$ and independent affine factors X^1 and X^2, that is two independent CIR++ factors. Also, we denote by (0F), the parametrization (6.1) with $\delta = 0$, that is without stochastic factors (case of time-deterministic, piecewise constant intensities).

6.1. *Marginals*

Under the model specification (6.1), one can derive a more explicit formula for the pricing function $v = v(t, x_1)$. Let $F_1(t) = \int_0^t f_1(s)ds$.

Proposition 6.1. *Assuming* (6.1), *one has*

$$\beta(t)v(t, x_1) = \int_t^T \beta(s)\big((1 - R_1)\mathcal{D}_\delta(s, t, x_1) - \kappa\big)\mathcal{E}_\delta(s, t, x_1)ds,$$

where we set, for $s \geq t$,

$$\begin{aligned}
\mathcal{E}_\delta(s, t, x_1) &= \exp(-\big(F_1(s) - F_1(t) + \delta\phi(s - t, 0)x_1 + \delta\xi(s - t, 0)\mu_1\big)), \\
\mathcal{D}_\delta(s, t, x_1) &= f_1(s) + \delta\eta\mu_1\phi(s - t, 0) \\
&\quad + \delta\left(-\eta\phi(s - t, 0) - \frac{1}{2}\nu^2(\phi(s - t, 0))^2 + 1\right)x_1,
\end{aligned}$$

in which the functions ϕ *and* ξ *are those of Lemma* A.1.

Proof. Recall from Proposition 4.1 that

$$\beta(t)v(t, x_1) = \int_t^T \beta(s)\mathbb{E}\big(e^{-\int_t^s q_1(\zeta, X_\zeta^1)d\zeta}p(s, X_s^1)|X_t^1 = x_1\big)ds$$

with

$$p(s, X_s^1) = (1 - R_1)q_1(s, X_s^1) - \kappa, \quad q_1(t, X_t^1) = f_1(t) + \delta X_t^1.$$

[2]Indeed in our numerical tests the calibrated parameters do not always satisfy $2\eta\mu_i > \nu^2$.

For $\delta = 0$, the result follows immediately and for $\delta = 1$, it is obtained by an application of Lemma A.1. □

In particular the model break-even spread at time 0 of a risk-free CDS of maturity T on the firm, is given by

$$\kappa_0(T) = (1 - R_1)\frac{\int_0^T \beta(s)\mathcal{D}_\delta(s,0,X_0^1)\mathcal{E}_\delta(s,0,X_0^1)ds}{\int_0^T \beta(s)\mathcal{E}_\delta(s,0,X_0^1)ds}.$$

We denote by p_1 the cumulative distribution function (c.d.f. hereafter) of τ_1, namely,

$$p_1(t) := \mathbb{P}(\tau_1 \leq t) = 1 - \mathcal{E}_\delta(t,0,X_0^1). \tag{6.2}$$

In the same way, one can obtain semi-explicit formulae for the forward spread and CDS option price. As we will see in Sec. 8, such formulae are useful while computing the associated implied volatility.

For $0 \leq T_a < T_b$, the forward spread (at time 0) of a CDS issued at time T_a with maturity T_b is given by

$$\kappa_0(T_a, T_b) = (1 - R_1)\frac{\int_{T_a}^{T_b} e^{-rs}\mathcal{D}_\delta(s,0,X_0^1)\mathcal{E}_\delta(s,0,X_0^1)ds}{\int_{T_a}^{T_b} e^{-rs}\mathcal{E}_\delta(s,0,X_0^1)ds}. \tag{6.3}$$

Now we consider a payer (resp. receiver) CDS option which gives the right to enter at time T_a a payer (resp. receiver) CDS with maturity T_b and the contractual spread κ.[3] Then the price at time 0 of these CDS options are given by

$$e^{-rT_a}\mathbb{E}\big[(1 - H_{T_a}^1)v(T_a, X_{T_a}^1)^+\big] \quad \text{for a payer CDS option,} \tag{6.4}$$

$$e^{-rT_a}\mathbb{E}\big[(1 - H_{T_a}^1)v(T_a, X_{T_a}^1)^-\big] \quad \text{for a receiver CDS option,} \tag{6.5}$$

where $v(t, x_1)$ is the CDS price function as in Proposition 6.1.

Of course analogous formulae hold for a risk-free CDS and CDS options on the counterparty.

6.2. *Joint defaults*

In case market prices of instrument sensitive to the dependence structure of default times are available (basket credit instrument on the firm and the counterparty), these can be used to calibrate l_3. Admittedly however, this situation is an exception rather than the rule. It is thus important to devise a practical way of calibrating l_3 in case such market data are not available.

Note that under parameterizations (0F) and (2F), one has

$$\mathbb{P}(\tau_1 > t, \tau_2 > t) = \mathbb{P}(\tau_1 > t)\mathbb{P}(\tau_2 > t)e^{L_3(t)}, \tag{6.6}$$

for $L_3(t) = \int_0^t l_3(s)ds$. A possible procedure thus consists in "calibrating" l_3 to target values for the model probabilities $p_{1,2}(t) = \mathbb{P}(\tau_1 < t, \tau_2 < t)$ of default of

[3] To avoid ambiguity, we call this contractual spread ,"the strike".

both names up to various time horizons t. More precisely, given a target for the function $p_{1,2}(t)$, one plugs it, together with the functions $p_1(t)$ and $p_2(t)$, into (6.6), to deduce $L_3(t)$.

Remark 6.2. Regarding the derivation of a target for $p_{1,2}(t)$, note the following relation between $p_{1,2}(t)$ and a standard static Gaussian copula *asset correlation* ρ at the horizon t:

$$p_{1,2}(t) = \mathcal{N}_2^{\rho}(\mathcal{N}_1^{-1}(p_1(t)), \mathcal{N}_1^{-1}(p_2(t))), \tag{6.7}$$

where $\mathcal{N}_1$ denotes the standard Gaussian c.d.f., and $\mathcal{N}_2^{\rho}$ denotes a bivariate centered Gaussian c.d.f. with one-factor Gaussian copula correlation matrix of parameter ρ. A target value for $p_{1,2}(t)$ can thus be obtained by plugging values extracted from the market for ρ, $p_1(t)$ and $p_2(t)$ into the RHS of (6.7). In particular a "market" static Gaussian asset correlation ρ can be retrieved from the Basel II correlations per asset class (cf. [3, pages 63 to 66]).

6.3. *Calibration*

We aim at calibrating the model to marginal CDS curves and to an asset correlation ρ (see Remark 6.2). We assume that the functions f_1, f_2 and l_3 are piecewise constant functions of time.

We denote by $(T_1, \ldots, T_m)$ the term structure of the maturities of the market CDS written on the counterparty and on the reference entity, and we set $\Delta_j = T_j - T_{j-1}$, with the convention $T_0 = 0$. One then proceeds in four steps as follows:

- One bootstraps the CDS curve for both names i into a piecewise constant c.d.f. $p_i(\cdot)$, for $i = 1, 2$, yielding

$$p_i(t) = p_i(T_j) \quad \text{on } T_{j-1} \le t < T_j,$$

- Next, given $p_1(t)$, $p_2(t)$ and ρ, one computes $p_{1,2}(t) = \mathbb{P}(\tau_1 < t, \tau_2 < t)$ via (6.7).
- The relation (6.6) yields a system of m linear equations in the m unknowns $l_{3,1}, \ldots, l_{3,m}$.

$$\begin{cases} \Delta_1 l_{3,1} + \cdots + \Delta_j l_{3,j} = -\ln \dfrac{\mathbb{P}(\tau_1 > T_j, \tau_2 > T_j)}{\mathbb{P}(\tau_1 > T_j)\mathbb{P}(\tau_2 > T_j)} \\ \text{subject to } l_{3,j} \ge 0, \quad j = 1, \ldots, m \end{cases}$$

- At last, formula (6.2) results in two systems of m linear equations in the $m + 2$ unknowns $X_0^i, \mu_i, f_{i,1}, \ldots, f_{i,m}$. That is, for $i = 1, 2$,

$$\begin{cases} \delta\phi(T_j)X_0^i + \delta\xi(T_j)\mu_i + \Delta_1 f_{i,1} + \cdots + \Delta_j f_{i,j} = -\ln\ \mathbb{P}(\tau_i > T_j) \\ \text{subject to } X_0^i \ge 0, \quad \mu_i \ge 0, \quad f_{i,j} \ge l_{3,j}, \quad j = 1, \ldots, m. \end{cases}$$

In practice these equations are solved in the sense of mean-square minimization under constraints.

7. A Variant of the Model with Extended CIR Intensities

In this section, we propose a variant of the general model of Sec. 3, defined in terms of extended CIR factor processes. By comparison with (3.1), one thus chooses a specific, affine form of the factors, but one also lets the joint defaults intensity l_3 be stochastic, via a "new" factor X^3. In particular, one models the factors X^is as affine processes of the form

$$dX_t^i = \eta(\mu_i(t) - X_t^i)dt + \nu\sqrt{X_t^i}dW_t^i,$$

with W_1 and W_2 correlated at the level ϱ and W_3 independent from W_1 and W_2. Note in this regard that the factors X^is have the same coefficients but for $\mu_i(t)$, to the effect that $\widetilde{X}^i := X^i + X^3$, for $i = 1, 2$, is again an extended CIR process, with parameters η, $\widetilde{\mu}_i(t) = \mu_i(t) + \mu_3(t)$ and ν.

Let as before $\mathrm{H} = (H^1, H^2)$ and let now $\mathrm{X} = (X^1, X^2, X^3)$.

One thus considers a Markovian model of the pair (X, H) relative to its natural filtration $\mathbb{F}$, with generator of (X, H) given by, for $u = u(t, x, e)$ with $t \in \mathbb{R}_+, x = (x_1, x_2, x_3) \in \mathbb{R}^3, e = (e_1, e_2) \in \{0, 1\}^2$:

$$\begin{aligned}\mathcal{A}u(t,x,e) &= \partial u(t,x,e) + \sum_{1\leq i\leq 2} l_i(t,x_i)(u(t,x,e^i) - u(t,x,e)) \\ &\quad + l_3(t,x_3)(u(t,x,1,1) - u(t,x,e)) \\ &\quad + \sum_{1\leq i\leq 3}\left(\eta(\mu_i(t) - x_i)\partial_{x_i}u(t,x,e) + \frac{1}{2}\nu^2 x_i \partial^2_{x_i^2}u(t,x,e)\right) \\ &\quad + \varrho\nu^2\sqrt{x_1x_2}\partial^2_{x_1,x_2}u(t,x,e),\end{aligned}$$

where, for $i = 1$ to 3:

- the default intensity function l_i is of the form

$$l_i(t, x_i) = x_i + g_i(t), \tag{7.1}$$

- the coefficients η, ν are non-negative constants and $\mu_i(\cdot)$s are non-negative functions of time.

The $\mathbb{F}$ — intensity matrix-function of H is now given by

$$A(t,x) = \begin{bmatrix} -l(t,x) & l_1(t,x_1) & l_2(t,x_2) & l_3(t,x_3) \\ 0 & -q_2(t,\widetilde{x}_2) & 0 & q_2(t,\widetilde{x}_2) \\ 0 & 0 & -q_1(t,\widetilde{x}_1) & q_1(t,\widetilde{x}_1) \\ 0 & 0 & 0 & 0 \end{bmatrix},$$

with, for every $i = 1, 2$,

$$\widetilde{x}_i = x_i + x_3, \quad q_i(t,\widetilde{x}_i) = l_i(t,x_i) + l_3(t,x_3) = \widetilde{x}_i + g_i(t) + g_3(t)$$

and $l = l_1 + l_2 + l_3$. Under standard regularity and growth assumptions on the coefficients of $\mathcal{A}$, one then has the following variant of Proposition 3.1,

Proposition 7.1. (i) *For every $i = 1, 2$, the process $(\widetilde{X}^i, H^i)$ is an $\mathbb{F}$-Markov process, with generator of $(\widetilde{X}^i, H^i)$ given by, for $u_i = u_i(t, \widetilde{x}_i, e_i)$, with $t \in \mathbb{R}_+, \widetilde{x}_i \in \mathbb{R}, e_i \in \{0, 1\}$:*

$$\mathcal{A}^i u_i(t, \widetilde{x}_i, e_i) = \partial_t u_i(t, \widetilde{x}_i, e_i) + \eta(\widetilde{\mu}_i(t) - \widetilde{x}_i)\partial_{\widetilde{x}_i} u_i(t, \widetilde{x}_i, e_i) + \frac{1}{2}\nu^2 x_i \partial^2_{\widetilde{x}_i^2} u_i(t, \widetilde{x}_i, e_i)$$
$$+ q_i(t, \widetilde{x}_i)(u_i(t, \widetilde{x}_i, 1) - u_i(t, \widetilde{x}_i, e_i)). \tag{7.2}$$

The $\mathbb{F}$ — intensity matrix function of H^i is thus given by

$$A_i(t, \widetilde{x}_i) = \begin{bmatrix} -q_i(t, \widetilde{x}_i) & q_i(t, \widetilde{x}_i) \\ 0 & 0 \end{bmatrix}$$

In other words, the process M^i defined by, for $i = 1, 2$,

$$M^i_t = H^i_t - \int_0^t (1 - H^i_s) q_i(s, \widetilde{X}^i_s) ds,$$

is an $\mathbb{F}$-martingale.
(ii) *One has, for every $t \geq 0$,*

$$\begin{aligned} \mathbb{P}(\tau_i > t) &= \mathbb{E} \exp\left(-\int_0^t q_i(u, \widetilde{X}^i_u) du\right), \\ \mathbb{P}(\tau_1 \wedge \tau_2 > t) &= \mathbb{E} \exp\left(-\int_0^t l(u, \mathrm{X}_u) du\right) \end{aligned} \tag{7.3}$$

One thus gets in the terminology of [5] *a Markovian copula model* (X, H) *with marginals* $(\widetilde{X}^i, H^i)$, for $i = 1, 2$ — or, in the 'common factor case' $X^1 = X^2 = X$, with marginals $(\widetilde{X}, H^i)$, where we set $\widetilde{X} = X + X^3$.

Let, for $\widetilde{x}_1 \in \mathbb{R}_+$,

$$p(t, \widetilde{x}_1) = (1 - R_1) q_1(t, \widetilde{x}_1) - \kappa.$$

One then has much like in Proposition 4.1(i) (analogs of Propositions 4.1(ii) and (iii) could be derived as well if wished),

Proposition 7.2. *The price of the risk-free CDS admits the representation:*

$$P_t = (1 - H^1_t) v(t, \widetilde{X}^1_t),$$

for a pre-default pricing function $v = v(t, \widetilde{x}_1)$ solving the following pricing PDE:

$$\begin{cases} v(T, \widetilde{x}_1) = 0, \quad \widetilde{x}_1 \in \mathbb{R} \\ \left(\partial_t + \eta(\widetilde{\mu}_1(t) - \widetilde{x}_1)\partial_{\widetilde{x}_1} + \frac{1}{2}\nu^2 \widetilde{x}_1 \partial^2_{\widetilde{x}_1^2}\right) v(t, \widetilde{x}_1) \\ \qquad - \big(r + q_1(t, \widetilde{x}_1)\big) v(t, \widetilde{x}_1) + p(t, \widetilde{x}_1) = 0, \\ t \in [0, T), \; \widetilde{x}_1 \in \mathbb{R}; \end{cases}$$

Hedging could also be discussed analogously as in Sec. 5 for (2F).

7.1. *Implementation*

Let us consider the parametrization stated in (7.1), with $g_i = 0$, therein. We assume that the $\mu_i(\cdot)$s are piecewise constant functions,

$$\mu_i(t) = \mu_{i,j}, \quad \text{for } t \in [T_{j-1}, T_j).$$

The marginal intensity processes $q_i(t, \widetilde{X}_t^i)$s are then extended CIR processes (cf. (7.2)) with the following piecewise constant 'long-term mean' function $\widetilde{\mu}_i(\cdot)$,

$$\widetilde{\mu}_i(t) = \mu_{i,j} + \mu_{3,j}, \quad \text{for } t \in [T_{j-1}, T_j).$$

We will refer to this model parametrization as (3F). Under this specification, one has the following proposition for the pricing function of a risk-free CDS on the firm. Let the functions $\widetilde{\mathcal{D}}_1$ and $\widetilde{\mathcal{E}}_1$ be defined as in Proposition A.1, with $\mu(\cdot) = \widetilde{\mu}_1(\cdot)$ therein.

Proposition 7.3. *Assuming* (3F), *one has,*

$$\beta(t)v(t, \widetilde{x}_1) = \int_t^T \beta(s)\big((1 - R_1)\widetilde{\mathcal{D}}(s, t, \widetilde{x}_1) - \kappa\big)\widetilde{\mathcal{E}}(s, t, \widetilde{x}_1, 0)ds.$$

Proof. Recall from Proposition 7.2(i) that

$$v(t, \widetilde{x}_1) = \mathbb{E}\left(\int_t^T e^{-\int_t^s (r + q_1(\zeta, \widetilde{X}_\zeta^1))d\zeta} p(s, \widetilde{X}_s^1)ds \,\middle|\, \widetilde{X}_t^1 = \widetilde{x}_1\right),$$

with

$$p(s, \widetilde{X}_s^1) = (1 - R_1)\widetilde{X}_s^1 - \kappa.$$

The result thus follows by an application of Proposition A.1. □

Also, the spread at time 0 of a risk-free CDS of maturity T on the firm, is given by

$$\kappa_0(T) = (1 - R_1)\frac{\int_0^T \beta(s)\widetilde{\mathcal{D}}_1(s, 0, X_0^1)\widetilde{\mathcal{E}}_1(s, 0, X_0^1, 0)ds}{\int_0^T \beta(s)\widetilde{\mathcal{E}}_1(s, 0, X_0^1, 0)ds}.$$

As for the forward spread, the counterparty of formulae (6.3) for this variant of the model, is

$$\kappa_0(T_a, T_b) = (1 - R_1)\frac{\int_{T_a}^{T_b} e^{-rs}\widetilde{\mathcal{D}}_\delta(s, 0, X_0^1)\widetilde{\mathcal{E}}_\delta(s, 0, X_0^1)ds}{\int_{T_a}^{T_b} e^{-rs}\widetilde{\mathcal{E}}_\delta(s, 0, X_0^1)ds}. \tag{7.4}$$

Also, the price at time 0 of CDS options with strike κ are given by

$$e^{-rT_a}\mathbb{E}\big[(1 - H_{T_a}^1)v(T_a, \widetilde{X}_{T_a}^1)^+\big] \quad \text{for a payer CDS option,} \tag{7.5}$$

$$e^{-rT_a}\mathbb{E}\big[(1 - H_{T_a}^1)v(T_a, \widetilde{X}_{T_a}^1)^-\big] \quad \text{for a receiver CDS option,} \tag{7.6}$$

where $v(t, \widetilde{x}_1)$ is the price function given by Proposition 7.3.

As in the previous case, the input to the calibration is an asset correlation ρ and the piecewise constant marginal cumulative default probabilities obtained by bootstrapping from the related CDS curves. For simplicity of calibration, the volatility parameter ν and the mean-reversion η are assumed to be given (as opposed to calibrated), whereas for each factor X^i the initial value X_0^i and $\mu_{i,1}, \ldots, \mu_{i,m}$ are calibrated.

Using identities (7.3) and Corollary A.1, the following expressions follows for the marginal and joint survival probabilities:

$$\mathbb{P}(\tau_i > T_j) = \mathbb{E}\left(\exp\left(-\int_0^{T_j} \widetilde{X}_s^i ds\right)\right) = \exp\left(-a_{j,0}\widetilde{X}_0^i - \sum_{k=1}^{j} \widetilde{\mu}_{i,k}\xi(\Delta_k, a_{j,k})\right)$$

and

$$\begin{aligned}\mathbb{P}(\tau_1 > T_j, \tau_2 > T_j) &= \mathbb{E}\left(\exp\left(-\int_0^{T_j} (X_s^1 + X_s^2 + X_s^3)ds\right)\right) \\ &= \mathbb{P}(\tau_1 > T_j)\mathbb{P}(\tau_2 > T_j)\exp\left(a_{j,0}X_0^3 + \sum_{k=1}^{j} \mu_{3,k}\xi(\Delta_k, a_{j,k})\right).\end{aligned}$$

where the coefficients $a_{j,k}$ are given in (A.6).

One can then follow the same lines as in Sec. 6.3, to obtain the following three systems of linear equations with constraints. Each system consists of m equations in $m + 1$ unknowns:

For $j = 1, \ldots, m$,

$$\begin{cases} a_{j,0}X_0^3 + \displaystyle\sum_{k=1}^{j} \xi(\Delta_k, a_{j,k})\mu_{3,k} = \ln \frac{\mathbb{P}(\tau_1 > T_j, \tau_2 > T_j)}{\mathbb{P}(\tau_1 > T_j)\mathbb{P}(\tau_2 > T_j)} \\ \text{subject to } X_0^3 \geq 0, \;\; \mu_{3,k} \geq 0, \;\; k = 1, \ldots, m. \end{cases}$$

For $i = 1, 2$,

$$\begin{cases} a_{j,0}\widetilde{X}_0^i + \displaystyle\sum_{k=1}^{j} \xi(\Delta_k, a_{j,k})\widetilde{\mu}_{i,k} = -\ln\, \mathbb{P}(\tau_i > T_j) \\ \text{subject to } \widetilde{X}_0^i \geq X_0^3, \;\; \widetilde{\mu}_{i,k} \geq \mu_{3,k}, \;\; k = 1, \ldots, m. \end{cases}$$

In practice these equations are solved in the sense of mean-square minimization under constraints.

8. Numerical Results

Our aim is to assess by means of numerical experiments the impact on the counterparty risk exposure of:

- ρ, a constant asset correlation between the firm and the counterparty,
- p_2, the cumulative distribution function of the default time τ_2 of the counterparty,
- ν, the volatility of the factors.

The numerical tests below have been done using the following model parameterizations:

(0F) No stochastic factor, as in (6.1) with $\delta = 0$,
(2F) Two independent CIR++ factors, as in (6.1) with $\delta = 1$,
(3F) Three independent extended CIR factors as of Sec. 7.1 with $\varrho = 0$.

The mean-reversion parameter η is fixed to 10%. The recovery rates are set to 40% and the risk-free rate r is taken equal to 5%.

8.1. *Calibration to market data*

In the following example, we consider four CDSs written on the reference name UBS AG, with different counterparties: Gaz de France, Carrefour, AXA and Telecom Italia SpA, referred to in the sequel as CP1, CP2, CP3 and CP4. For each counterparty we consider six CDSs with maturities of one, two, three, five, seven and ten years, corresponding to data of March 30, 2008. Table 1 includes market CDS spreads on the five names in consideration and for the six different maturities. The bootstrapped piecewise constant c.d.f. of the five names are represented in Table 2. The counterparties are ordered form the less risky one, CP1, to the most risky one, CP4.

Tables 3 and 4 represent the calibration error in basis points of (2F) and (3F), respectively. Precisely, in each table, we consider

$$\mathrm{er}_i(t) = 10^4 \times \frac{|p_i(t) - \widehat{p}_i(t)|}{p_i(t)}, \quad \mathrm{er}_{1,2}(t) = 10^4 \times \frac{|p_{1,2}(t) - \widehat{p}_{1,2}(t)|}{p_{1,2}(t)}$$

where $\widehat{p}_1, \widehat{p}_2, \widehat{p}_{1,2}$ are obtained from equations (3.5) and (7.3) using the calibrated parameters. The corresponding errors in the case of (0F) are 0.0000 bp. The

Table 1. Market spreads in bps for different time horizons on March 30, 2008.

Ref	UBS AG	1 Year	2 Years	3 Years	5 Years	7 Years	10 Years
		90	109	129	147	148	146
CP1	Gaz de France	27	35	42	53	57	61
CP2	Carrefour	34	42	53	67	71	76
CP3	AXA	72	83	105	128	129	128
CP4	Telecom Italia SpA	99	157	210	243	255	262

Table 2. Default probabilities for different maturities.

	1 Year	2 Years	3 Years	5 Years	7 Years	10 Years
Ref	0.0146	0.0355	0.0631	0.1185	0.1612	0.2193
CP1	0.0044	0.0116	0.0212	0.0445	0.0664	0.1005
CP2	0.0056	0.0138	0.0264	0.0558	0.0822	0.1246
CP3	0.0118	0.0269	0.0517	0.1042	0.1434	0.1964
CP4	0.0155	0.0504	0.1026	0.1903	0.2662	0.3670

Table 3. Relative error in bps of the cumulative probabilities p_1, p_2 and $p_{1,2}$ in the case (2F) with $\rho = 40\%$.

		Maturities						Mean	Max
		1 Year	2 Years	3 Years	5 Years	7 Years	10 Years		
CP1	er_1	0.2500	0.9630	0.8560	1.1390	2.1600	1.7600	1.1880	2.1600
	er_2	0.0191	0.0112	0.3790	0.0612	0.4027	0.0198	0.1488	0.4027
	$\mathrm{er}_{1,2}$	0.1790	0.7700	0.5350	1.2040	1.1120	0.7610	0.7600	1.2040
CP2	er_1	1.9240	1.8000	1.0500	1.3020	0.2590	2.1340	1.4110	2.1340
	er_2	0.3817	0.0726	0.0714	0.7904	0.3275	0.3992	0.3404	0.7904
	$\mathrm{er}_{1,2}$	0.2471	0.1127	0.0644	0.0442	0.0990	0.0213	0.0981	0.2471
CP3	er_1	0.4150	1.2380	0.4110	0.3430	1.3280	0.3410	0.6790	1.3280
	er_2	0.4730	0.8080	0.5390	0.6290	3.9800	0.8040	1.2050	3.9800
	$\mathrm{er}_{1,2}$	0.0494	0.0437	0.0065	0.0011	0.0116	0.0029	0.0192	0.0494
CP4	er_1	0.0364	0.1808	0.2382	0.1823	0.0988	0.3502	0.1811	0.3502
	er_2	0.0586	0.0167	0.0095	0.0376	0.0206	0.0285	0.0286	0.0586
	$\mathrm{er}_{1,2}$	0.2097	0.3922	0.2680	0.0917	0.0815	0.1537	0.1994	0.3922

Table 4. Relative error in bps of the cumulative probabilities p_1, p_2 and $p_{1,2}$ in the case (3F) with $\rho = 40\%$.

		Maturities						Mean	Max
		1 Year	2 Years	3 Years	5 Years	7 Years	10 Years		
CP1	er_1	5.0422	14.190	2.1420	15.050	15.920	0.4151	8.7940	15.920
	er_2	0.7888	1.6940	2.4450	0.0024	2.7510	1.0728	1.4591	2.7515
	$\mathrm{er}_{1,2}$	0.0000	0.0000	0.0000	0.0000	0.0000	0.0000	0.0000	0.0000
CP2	er_1	0.5700	2.1950	2.6910	1.4200	0.4247	0.0426	1.2240	2.6910
	er_2	0.3025	0.1581	0.4489	0.4358	0.0444	0.4780	0.3113	0.4780
	$\mathrm{er}_{1,2}$	0.0000	0.0000	0.0000	0.0006	0.0006	0.0002	0.0002	0.0006
CP3	er_1	0.0434	0.3486	0.4462	0.1976	0.1464	0.0282	0.2018	0.4462
	er_2	25.809	82.406	87.861	34.909	68.141	0.0325	49.860	87.861
	$\mathrm{er}_{1,2}$	0.0001	0.0012	0.0020	0.0036	0.0063	0.0054	0.0032	0.0063
CP4	er_1	1.5396	5.3363	24.188	59.728	40.733	0.9771	22.084	59.728
	er_2	0.0652	3.8962	4.6377	4.6433	3.8499	0.9716	3.0106	4.6432
	$\mathrm{er}_{1,2}$	0.0002	0.0030	0.0102	0.0176	0.0263	0.0081	0.0109	0.0263

difference between market spreads and calibrated model spreads are represented in Tables 5, 6 and 7, respectively.

8.2. *CVA stylized features*

Figure 1 shows the Credit Valuation Adjustment at time 0 of a risky CDS on the reference name UBS AG, as a function of the volatility parameter ν of the CIR factors X^is.

The graphs on the left of this figure show the results obtained from the parametrization (2F) while the graphs on the right correspond to the case of (3F). On each graph the asset correlation ρ is fixed, with from top to down $\rho = 5\%$, 10%,

Table 5. bp-Differences between market spreads and calibrated spreads in the case of (0F) with $\rho = 40\%$.

	1 Year	2 Years	3 Years	5 Years	7 Years	10 Years	Mean	Max
Ref	0.2920	0.1622	0.3957	0.3296	0.2537	0.1964	0.2716	0.3957
CP1	0.1285	0.0693	0.1556	0.1080	0.0829	0.0639	0.1014	0.1556
CP2	0.1067	0.0576	0.1897	0.1370	0.1054	0.0819	0.1130	0.1897
CP3	0.0096	0.0052	0.3108	0.2665	0.2052	0.1586	0.1593	0.3108
CP4	0.0098	0.0060	0.4711	0.5125	0.4097	0.3310	0.2900	0.5125

Table 6. bp-Differences between market spreads and calibrated spreads in the case of (2F) with $\rho = 40\%$.

	1 Year	2 Years	3 Years	5 Years	7 Years	10 Years	Mean	Max
Ref	0.3343	0.2167	0.4315	0.3980	0.3120	0.3489	0.3402	0.4315
CP1	0.0719	0.0781	0.0131	0.0150	0.0305	0.1040	0.0521	0.1040
CP2	0.0345	0.0028	0.1352	0.0852	0.0598	0.0833	0.0668	0.1352
CP3	0.0203	0.0088	0.2876	0.2426	0.1461	0.1855	0.1485	0.2876
CP4	0.0698	0.0537	0.5219	0.5614	0.4584	0.3976	0.3438	0.5614

Table 7. bp-Differences between market spreads and calibrated spreads in the case of (3F) with $\rho = 40\%$.

	1 Year	2 Years	3 Years	5 Years	7 Years	10 Years	Mean	Max
Ref	1.8110	1.6440	0.6820	0.8820	0.4950	0.4790	0.9988	1.8110
CP1	0.7730	0.6560	0.4300	0.2370	0.2130	0.0750	0.3973	0.7730
CP2	0.7400	0.8190	0.4300	0.2030	0.2140	0.1250	0.4218	0.8190
CP3	1.1690	0.9320	1.4230	0.5160	0.6940	0.4710	0.8675	1.4230
CP4	5.6840	3.5300	1.7190	0.6740	0.5720	0.4910	2.1117	5.6840

40% and 70%. The four curves on each graph of Fig. 1 correspond to Θ_0 calculated for a risky CDS of maturity $T = 10$ years between Ref and CP1, CP2, CP3, CP4, respectively.

On this data set we observe that Θ_0 is:

- increasing in the default risk of the counterparty,
- increasing in the asset correlation ρ,
- slowly increasing in the volatility ν of the common factor.

In Table 8, one can see the values of Θ_0 calculated within the parametrization (0F), that is with no stochastic factor. Note that for a CDS written on Ref, the risk-free value of the default leg is equal to $\mathrm{DL}_0 = 0.1031$.

For the receiver case, $\bar{\Theta}_0$ on the reference name UBS AG is shown in Fig. 2 as a function of the volatility parameter ν, for both parameterizations (2F) and (3F). Note that $\bar{\Theta}_0$ is much smaller (for a common unit nominal), and more dependent on ν, than Θ_0. This is mostly due to the absence of the common jump term in the $\overline{\mathrm{CVA}}$ (see Remark 2.1). Also, $\bar{\Theta}_0$ is *decreasing* in the asset correlation ρ.

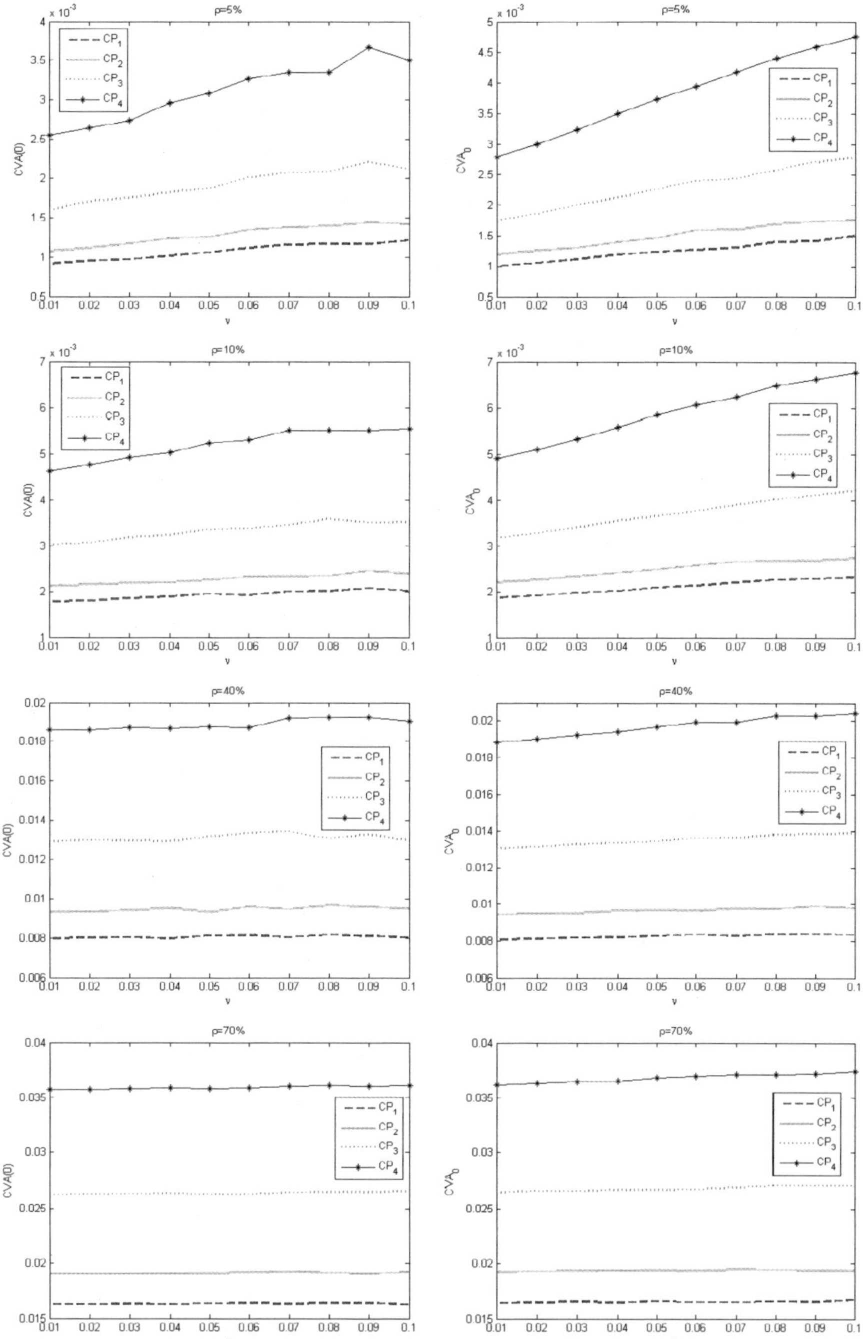

Fig. 1. Θ_0 versus ν for the payer CDS on Ref. The graphs on the left column correspond to the case (2F) and those of the right column correspond to (3F). In each graph ρ is fixed. From top to down $\rho = 5\%$, $\rho = 10\%$, $\rho = 40\%$ and $\rho = 70\%$.

Table 8. Θ_0 for CDSs written on Ref in the case (0F).

	$\rho = 5\%$	$\rho = 10\%$	$\rho = 40\%$	$\rho = 70\%$
CP1	0.0009	0.0018	0.0080	0.0163
CP2	0.0011	0.0021	0.0093	0.0190
CP3	0.0016	0.0030	0.0129	0.0262
CP4	0.0025	0.0047	0.0186	0.0358

To give an idea about the **execution times** of the three model parameterizations, it is worth mentioning that, in these experiments:

- a calibration takes about 0.01, 0.30 and 0.35 seconds for the case of (0F), (2F) and (3F), respectively;
- a computation of CVA takes about 0.015, 5.0 and 12 seconds for the cases of (0F), (2F) and (3F), respectively.

8.3. *Case of a low-risk reference entity*

In the previous example, except in the low ρ cases, the dependency of Θ_0 on ν was rather limited (see Fig. 1). For a low-risk reference entity, however, ν is expected to have more impact on Θ_0, including for larger ρ's. To assess this numerically we thus now consider a low-risk obligor, referred to as Ref', whose piecewise constant c.d.f. is given in Table 9. For a CDS written on Ref', the risk-free value of the default leg is equal to $\mathrm{DL}_0' = 0.0240$. On each graph of Fig. 3, the asset correlation is fixed to $\rho = 5\%, 10\%, 40\%$ or 70%. One can see that Θ_0 is significantly sensitive to ν, and even extremely so in the case of low correlations ρ. For comparison Table 10 shows the values of Θ_0 calculated within the parametrization (0F).

8.4. *Spread options implied volatilities*

The goal of this subsection is to assess the level of spreads' volatility implied by the alternative model parameterizations. To this end we will compute the implied volatility of payer and receiver CDS options written on individual names.

The explicit Black formula for the price of a CDS option can be found in Brigo [9] (see for example Eq. (7.2) therein). The Markov copula model prices are given by formulae (6.4) and (6.5) for the case of (0F) and (2F) and by formulae (7.5) and (7.6) for the case of (3F).

For numerical tests we consider CDSs of 7 year maturity on credit names CP1, Ref and CP4 (cf. Table 1). Also, we consider payer and receiver CDS options with maturity of 3 years on these three names and with strike $K = 65$, 150 and 250 bp, respectively. So, with notation introduced for forward spread, $T_a = 3$ and $T_b = 10$.

Figure 4 shows the implied volatility versus ν of receiver CDS options written on the three names and for the parameterizations (2F) and (3F), the case of (0F) corresponding essentially to ν tending to 0 in (2F) or (3F) (in particular the implied volatility of all the three receiver CDS options is then equal to zero).

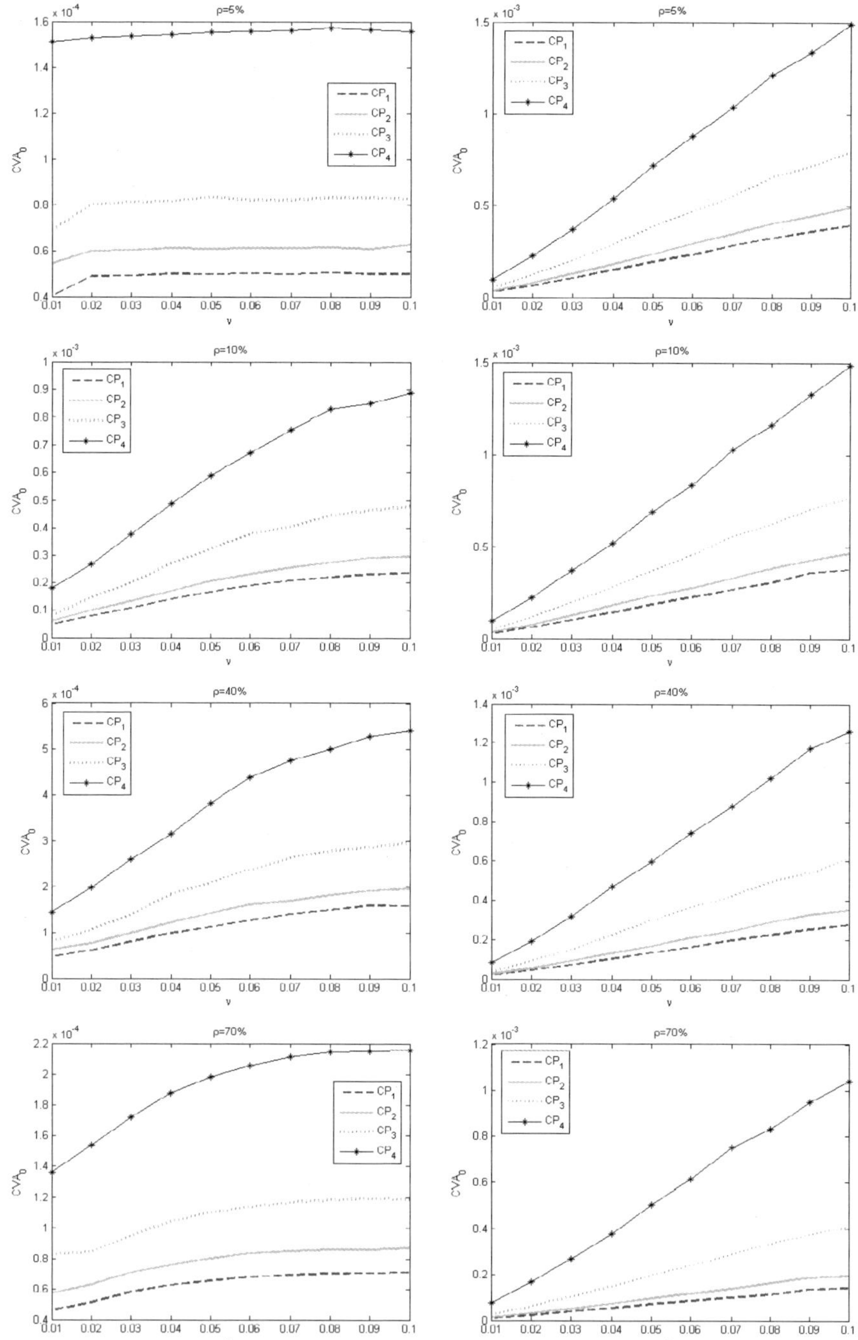

Fig. 2. $\bar{\Theta}_0$ versus ν for the receiver CDS on Ref. The graphs on the left column correspond to the case (2F) and those of the right column correspond to (3F). In each graph ρ is fixed. From top to down $\rho = 5\%$, $\rho = 10\%$, $\rho = 40\%$ and $\rho = 70\%$.

Table 9. Default probabilities of Ref'.

1 Year	2 Years	3 Years	5 Years	7 Years	10 Years
0.0100	0.01500	0.0200	0.0300	0.0400	0.0500

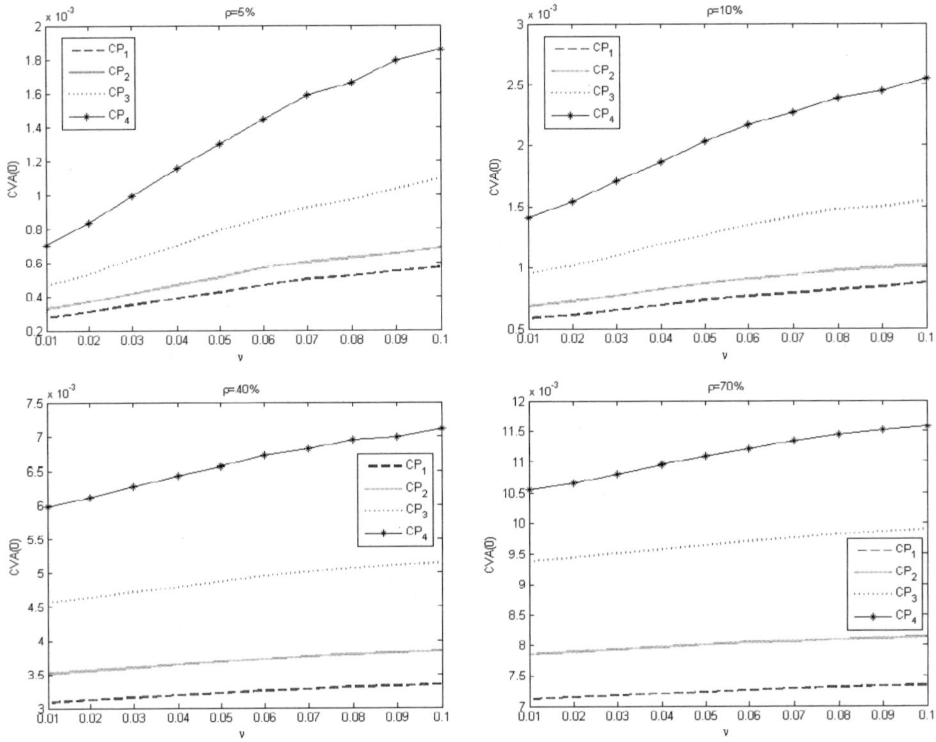

Fig. 3. Θ_0 versus ν for a CDS written on Ref' in the case (2F). In each graph ρ is fixed.

Table 10. Θ_0 for CDSs written on Ref' in the case (0F).

	$\rho = 5\%$	$\rho = 10\%$	$\rho = 40\%$	$\rho = 70\%$
CP1	0.0002	0.0006	0.0031	0.0073
CP2	0.0003	0.0007	0.0035	0.0080
CP3	0.0004	0.0009	0.0046	0.0096
CP4	0.0007	0.0014	0.0061	0.0108

The curves in the case (2F) are represented on the left column and those of (3F) are on the right column. The graphs on the top, middle and bottom of this figure correspond, respectively, to receiver CDS option written on names CP1, Ref and CP4. Recall from Table 1 that CP1, Ref and CP4 are, respectively, low-risk, middle-risk and high-risk names, in the sense of their 10-years CDS spread. On Fig. 5 the same graphs for payer CDS options are represented.

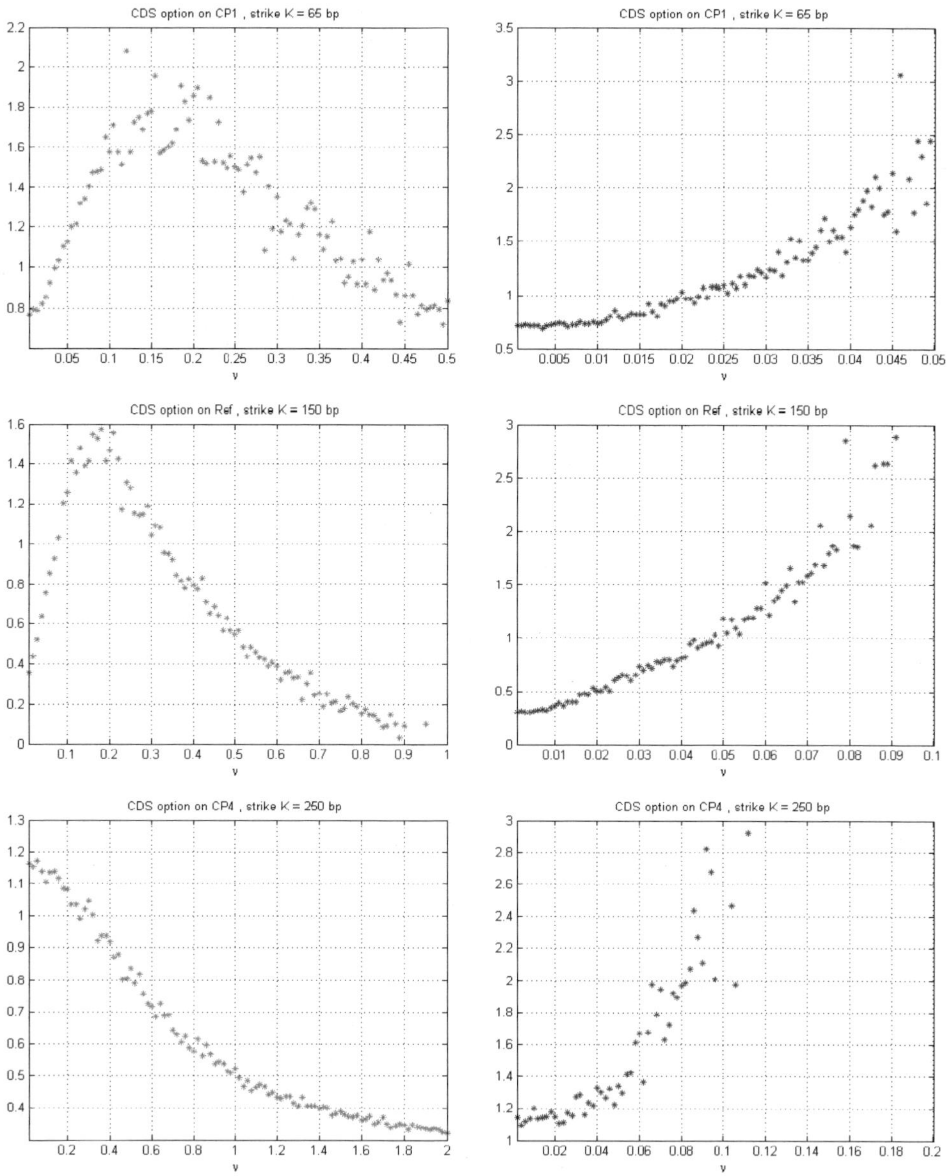

Fig. 4. Implied volatility versus ν of payer CDS option written on individual names. The graphs on the left column correspond to the case (2F) and those of the right column correspond to (3F). The graphs on the top, middle and bottom correspond to payer CDS options written on names CP1, Ref and CP4 (with strike $K = 65$bp, 150bp and 250bp), respectively.

One observes that for the same level of ν, implied volatility in the case of (3F) is typically much higher than that of (2F), which was expected since the joint defaults intensity l_3 is deterministic in (2F), whereas intensities are "fully stochastic" in (3F). Also, for a fixed level of ν, the implied volatility is decreasing in riskiness of the

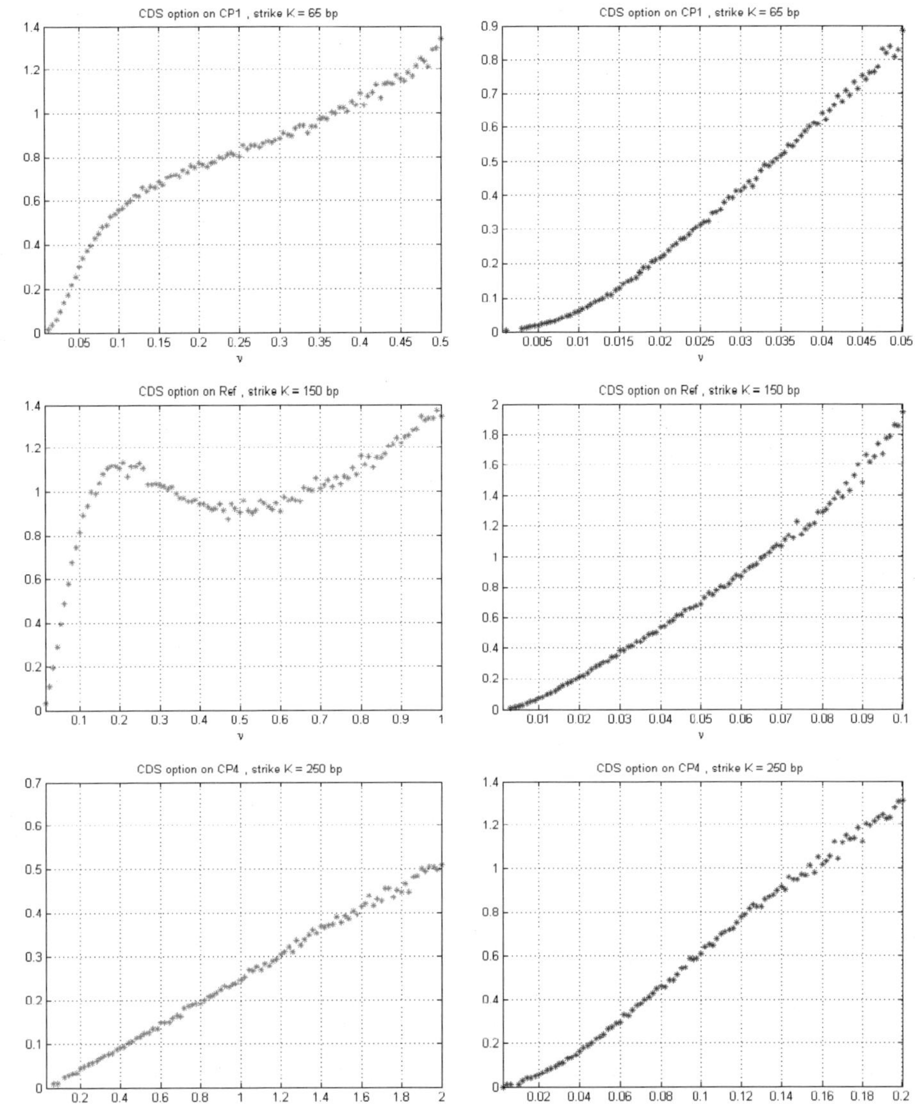

Fig. 5. Implied volatility versus ν of receiver CDS option written on individual names. The graphs on the left column correspond to the case (2F) and those of the right column correspond to (3F). The graphs on the top, middle and bottom correspond to receiver CDS options written on names CP1, Ref and CP4 (with strike $K = 65$bp, 150bp and 250bp), respectively.

credit name. In other words, to achieve a given implied volatility, the riskier the credit name, the lower the implied ν.

For the parametrization (3F), the implied volatility curves are non-decreasing in ν, in both payer and receiver cases. As is observed, this is not the case for the parametrization (2F).

8.5. *The analysis of the contribution of the joint default*

In this subsection, drawing on the same data set as before, we make a numerical test to assess the contribution of the joint default to the payer credit valuation adjustment (parameter α below), and its contribution to the default scenarios of the counterparty (parameter $\widetilde{\alpha}$ below).

Recall that in our model, Θ_0 has two components, one of which is due to the simultaneous default of the reference entity and the counterparty. Introducing the notation

$$\widehat{\xi}_{(\tau_2)} := (1-R_1)(1-R_2)\,\mathbb{1}_{\tau_2=\tau_1<T}, \quad \beta(t)\widehat{\Theta}_t = \mathbb{1}_{\{t<\tau_2\}}\mathbb{E}_t\big[\beta(\tau_2)\widehat{\xi}_{(\tau_2)}\big],$$

we define the parameter α which measures the contribution of the joint default to Θ_0,

$$\alpha = \frac{\widehat{\Theta}_0}{\Theta_0}.$$

Inspired by Remark 2.1 (Regime 1), it is interesting to investigate the behavior of the parameter α with respect to the asset correlation ρ, in the case where both $\mathbb{P}(\tau_2$ is small) and $\mathbb{P}(\tau_2 < \tau_1)$ are large. Figure 6, represents α as a function of ρ, for the most risky counterparty CP4, and for the reference entity Ref (on the left) and Ref' (on the right). The three curves on each figure, correspond to the cases (0F), (2F) and (3F). We observe that, even in the case of "Regime 1", and in all the three model parameterizations, α is increasing in ρ and that for $\rho = 1$, one has $\alpha \approx 1$. This means that, in our model, it is the joint default that plays the essential role in the credit valuation adjustment, Θ_0.

As we have already observed, for a payer CDS, the volatility parameter has a more important impact on Θ_0, in the case of a less risky reference name, and of a lower correlation between the counterparty and the reference name (cf. Figs. 1

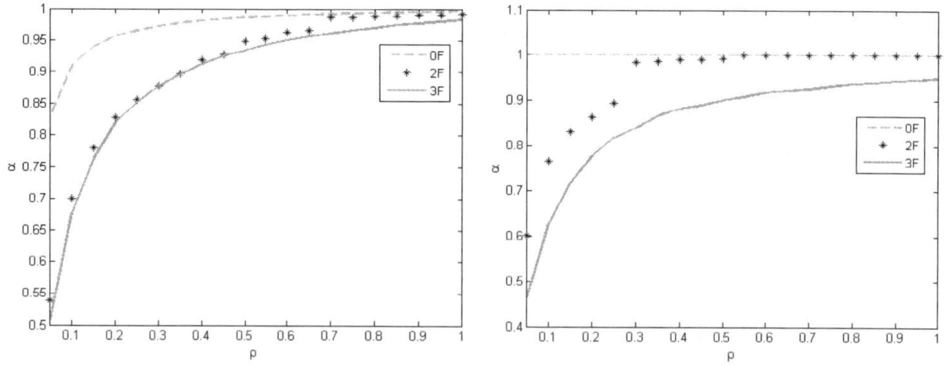

Fig. 6. α as a function of ρ for the counterparty CP4, in the case of deterministic intensities (0F), and stochastic intensities (2F) and (3F), both with $\nu = 0.1$. The left graphs correspond to the reference name Ref, and the right graphs correspond to Ref'.

and 3). This motivates us to define another parameter, $\widetilde{\alpha}$, which represents the proportion of default scenarios of the counterparty due to its simultaneous default with the reference entity

$$\widetilde{\alpha} := \frac{\sharp\{\tau_2 = \tau_1 < T\}}{\sharp\{\tau_2 = \tau_1 < T\} + \sharp\{\tau_2 < \tau_1 \wedge T\}} \approx \frac{\mathbb{P}(\tau_2 = \tau_1 < T)}{\mathbb{P}(\tau_2 = \tau_1 < T) + \mathbb{P}(\tau_2 < \tau_1 \wedge T)}.$$

Thus, in the following numerical experiences, we are interested in the behavior of $\widetilde{\alpha}$ as a function of the asset correlation ρ, for the less risky reference name, Ref'. Table 11 shows $\widetilde{\alpha}$ in the case of deterministic intensities (0F), for the reference name Ref', different counterparties and different levels of the correlation ρ. It is seen that for all counterparties, $\widetilde{\alpha}$ is increasing in the correlation.

The curves in Fig. 7 represent $\widetilde{\alpha}$ as a function of the asset correlation ρ, for the less risky reference entity, Ref', and four different counterparties. The graph on the left corresponds to (2F) and the graph on the right corresponds to (3F), with the volatility parameter ν fixed and equal to 0.1 for both parameterizations. It is observed that $\widetilde{\alpha}$ is increasing in ρ. This is inline with the our previous observation: For the less risky reference entity and lower level of the correlation ρ, there are more scenarios where the counterparty defaults prior to the reference entity, and hence, the impact on CVA of the volatility parameter, ν, is more important.

Table 11. $\widetilde{\alpha}$ as a function of ρ for Ref', and the parametrization (0F).

	$\rho = 5\%$	$\rho = 10\%$	$\rho = 40\%$	$\rho = 70\%$
CP1	0.0105	0.0220	0.1160	0.2636
CP2	0.0099	0.0208	0.1062	0.2333
CP3	0.0087	0.0180	0.0857	0.1725
CP4	0.0070	0.0141	0.0596	0.1023

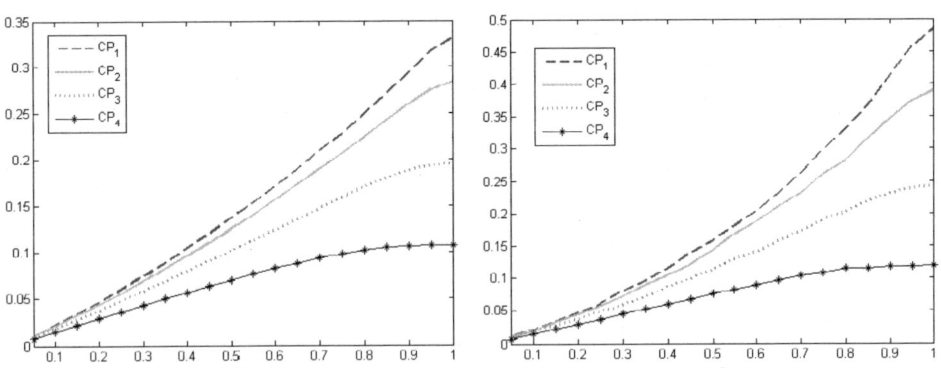

Fig. 7. $\widetilde{\alpha}$ as a function of ρ for Ref'. The graph on the left corresponds to (2F), and that on the right corresponds to (3F). In each graph $\nu = 0.1$.

9. Conclusions

One develops in this paper a Markovian model of counterparty credit risk on a CDS. The issue of "wrong-way risk", which is particularly important in the case of a payer CDS, is represented in the model by the possibility of simultaneous defaults of the counterparty and of the reference firm of the CDS. Since this is a dynamic model of counterparty credit risk, prices and CVAs can be connected to dynamic hedging arguments, as illustrated by our study of mean-variance hedging the CVA of the CDS on the firm by a rolling CDS on the counterparty.

Moreover, we devise, implement and discuss three model specifications.

Our numeric results show that in the case of a payer CDS on a "risky enough" reference entity and for a sufficient level of correlation between the counterparty and the reference entity, a time-deterministic specification of intensities does a good and quick job in estimating the CVA.

In case of a receiver CDS, or of a payer CDS with low risk reference entity or low level of correlation between the counterparty and the reference entity, the time-deterministic specification of intensities "misses" a non-negligible component of CVA, due to spreads' volatility. In this case, a stochastic specification of the intensities is preferred (cf. Figs. 2, 3 and 1), like a CIR++ specification of the intensities with marginal default intensities given as sums of affine processes and deterministic functions of time.

In this specification the joint defaults intensity of the counterparty and the reference firm is time-deterministic, so that one might wonder whether a fully stochastic specification of the intensities would lead to even higher (possibly more realistic) CVAs. This led us to investigate a third specification of the intensities in the form of extended CIR processes with time-dependent parameters, and no deterministic component anymore. In case of a payer CDS the levels of CVA happen to be quite similar to those got through the CIR++ specification, however for the receiver CDS they may be much larger (as is seen in Fig. 2).

Appendix A

Let X be an extended CIR process with dynamics

$$dX_t = \eta(\mu(t) - X_t)dt + \nu\sqrt{X_t}dW_t \tag{A.1}$$

where η and ν are positive constants and $\mu(\cdot)$ is a non-negative deterministic function.

The following lemma is a standard result in the affine processes literature (see e.g. [17]). Notice that (A.3) is obtained from (A.2) with $y = 0$, by differentiating with respect to t.

Lemma A.1. *Consider the process X in* (A.1). *If $\mu(\cdot)$ is constant on $[t_0, t]$, then for every $y \geq 0$,*

$$\mathbb{E}(e^{-\int_{t_0}^{t} X_s ds - yX_t} | X_{t_0}) = e^{-\phi(t-t_0,y)X_{t_0} - \xi(t-t_0,y)\mu}, \tag{A.2}$$

$$\mathbb{E}(X_t e^{-\int_{t_0}^t X_s ds}|X_{t_0})$$
$$= \big(\dot{\phi}(t-t_0,0)X_{t_0} + \dot{\xi}(t-t_0,0)\mu\big)e^{-\phi(t-t_0,0)X_{t_0}-\xi(t-t_0,0)\mu}, \qquad (A.3)$$

where ϕ and ξ satisfy the following system of ODE:

$$\begin{cases} \dot{\phi}(s,y) = -\eta\phi(s,y) - \dfrac{\nu^2}{2}(\phi(s,y))^2 + 1; & \phi(0,y) = y \\ \dot{\xi}(s,y) = \eta\phi(s,y); & \xi(0,y) = 0. \end{cases}$$

Explicitly,

$$\phi(s,y) = \frac{1 + D(y)e^{-A(y)s}}{B + C(y)e^{-A(y)s}},$$

$$\xi(s,y) = \frac{\eta}{B}\left\{\frac{C(y) - BD(y)}{A(y)C(y)} \log \frac{B + C(y)e^{-A(y)s}}{B + C(y)} + s\right\}.$$

where A, B, C and D are given by

$$B = \frac{1}{2}\big(\eta + \sqrt{\eta^2 + 2\nu^2}\big), \quad C(y) = (1 - By)\frac{\eta + \nu^2 y - \sqrt{\eta^2 + 2\nu^2}}{2\eta y + \nu^2 y - 2},$$

$$D(y) = (B + C(y))y - 1, \quad A(y) = \frac{-C(y)(2B - \eta) + D(y)(\nu^2 + \eta B)}{BD(y) - C(y)}.$$

In the following proposition (see also Shirakawa [28]), we generalize Lemma A.1 to the case of a piecewise constant function $\mu(\cdot)$. We denote $T_0 = 0$ and $\Delta_j = T_j - T_{j-1}$. The functions ϕ and ξ are those of Lemma A.1.

Proposition A.1. *Assume that $\mu(\cdot)$ is a piecewise constant function: $\mu(t) = \mu_k$ on $t \in [T_{k-1}, T_k]$ for $k = 1, \ldots, m$. For $t < s$, let $i \leq j$ such that $t \in [T_{i-1}, T_i)$ and $s \in (T_j, T_{j+1}]$. Then*

(i) *For any $x \geq 0$ and $y \geq 0$,*

$$\widetilde{\mathcal{E}}(s,t,x,y) := \mathbb{E}\Big(\exp\Big(-\int_t^s X_u du - yX_s\Big)\,|X_t = x\Big)$$
$$= \exp\Big\{-\mu_i\xi(T_i - t, y_i) - x\phi(T_i - t, y_i)$$
$$- \sum_{k=i+1}^{j} \mu_k\xi(\Delta_k, y_k) - \mu_{j+1}\xi(s - T_j, y)\Big\} \qquad (A.4)$$

with

$$y_j = y_j(s) := \phi(s - T_j, y),$$
$$y_k = y_k(s) := \phi(\Delta_{k+1}, y_{k+1}(s)), \quad k < j. \qquad (A.5)$$

(ii) *One has,*

$$\mathbb{E}\Big(X_s \exp\Big(-\int_t^s X_u du\Big)\,|X_t\Big) = \widetilde{\mathcal{D}}(s,t,X_t)\mathbb{E}\Big(\exp\Big(-\int_t^s X_u du\Big)\,|X_t\Big)$$

where

$$\widetilde{\mathcal{D}}(s,t,x) = \mu_i \frac{\partial \xi}{\partial y}(T_i - t, y_i)\frac{dy_i}{ds} + x\frac{\partial \phi}{\partial y}(T_i - t, y_i)\frac{dy_i}{ds}$$
$$+ \sum_{k=i+1}^{j} \mu_k \frac{\partial \xi}{\partial y}(\Delta_k, y_k)\frac{dy_k}{ds} + \mu_{j+1}\frac{\partial \xi}{\partial s}(s - T_j, 0),$$

and the y_ks are as in (A.5) *with* $y = 0$.

Setting $t = 0$ and $s = T_j$ in the first part of the above proposition, one obtains:

Corollary A.1. *One has*

$$\mathbb{E}\Big(\exp\Big(-\int_0^{T_j} X_u du\Big)\Big) = \exp\Big(-a_{j,0}X_0 - \sum_{k=1}^{j} \mu_k \xi(\Delta_k, a_{j,k})\Big)$$

with

$$a_{j,j} = 0, \quad a_{j,k} = \phi(\Delta_{k+1}, a_{j,k+1}) \quad \text{for } k < j. \tag{A.6}$$

Acknowledgments

The authors thank S. Assefa and J.-P. Lardy for interesting discussions during the preparation of this article. The research of T.R. Bielecki was supported by NSF Grant DMS–0604789 and NSF Grant DMS–0908099. The research of S. Crépey and M. Jeanblanc benefited from the support of the DGE.

References

[1] S. Assefa, T. R. Bielecki, S. Crépey and M. Jeanblanc, CVA computation for counterparty risk assessment in credit portfolios, in *Credit Risk Frontiers: Subprime Crisis, Pricing and Hedging, CVA, MBS, Ratings and Liquidity*, T. R. Bielecki, D. Brigo and F. Patras eds. (Wiley, 2011), pp. 397–436.

[2] Basel Committee on Banking Supervision, The application of basel II to trading activities and the treatment of double default effects, Bank for International Settlements (2005).

[3] Basel Committee on Banking Supervision, International convergence of capital measurement and capital standards, *Bank for International Settlements* (2006).

[4] T. R. Bielecki and M. Rutkowski, *Credit Risk: Modeling, Valuation and Hedging* (Springer-Verlag, Berlin, 2002).

[5] T. R. Bielecki, A. Vidozzi and L. Vidozzi, A Markov copulae approach to pricing and hedging of credit index derivatives and ratings triggered step–up bonds, *Journal of Credit Risk* **4**(1) (2008) 47–76.

[6] T. R. Bielecki, M. Jeanblanc and M. Rutkowski, Pricing and trading credit default swaps in a hazard process model, *Annals of Applied Probability* **18**(6) (2008) 2495–2529.

[7] T. R. Bielecki, I. Cialenco and I. Iyigunler, Counterparty risk and the impact of collateralization in CDS contracts, Forthcoming in *Festschrift in Honour of Robert Elliott*, S. Cohen, D. Madan, T. K. Siu and H. Yan, eds. (World Scientific, 2011).

[8] Ch. Blanchet-Scalliet and F. Patras, Structural counterparty risk valuation for CDS, in *Credit Risk Frontiers: Subprime Crisis, Pricing and Hedging, CVA, MBS, Ratings and Liquidity*, T. R. Bielecki, D. Brigo and F. Patras, eds. (Wiley, 2011), pp. 437–455.

[9] D. Brigo, Candidate market models and the calibrated CIR++ stochastic intensity model for credit default swap options and callable floaters, *Risk Magazine* (2005).

[10] D. Brigo and A. Capponi, Bilateral counterparty risk valuation with stochastic dynamical models and application to credit default swaps, Working Paper. Available at http://arXiv.org/pdf/0812.3705.pdf (2008).

[11] D. Brigo and K. Chourdakis, Counterparty risk for credit default swaps: Impact of spread volatility and default correlation, *International Journal of Theoretical and Applied Finance* **12**(7) (2009) 1007–1026.

[12] D. Brigo and M. Masetti, Risk neutral pricing of counterparty risk, *Counterparty Credit Risk Modeling: Risk Management, Pricing and Regulation*, M. Pykhtin, ed. (Risk Books, London, 2006).

[13] G. Cesari, J. Aquilina and N. Charpillon, *Modelling, Pricing, and Hedging Counterparty Credit Exposure* (Springer Finance, 2010).

[14] G. Cesari, Personal Communication.

[15] S. Crépey, M. Jeanblanc and B. Zargari, Counterparty risk on a CDS in a markov chain copula model with joint defaults, *Recent Advances in Financial Engineering 2009*, M. Kijima, C. Hara, Y. Muromachi and K. Tanaka, eds. (World Scientific Publishing Co. Pte., 2010), pp. 91–126. Available on http://grozny.maths.univ-evry.fr/pages_perso/crepey/.

[16] C. Dellacherie and P.-A. Meyer, *Probabilité et Potentiel*, Vol. I (Hermann, 1975).

[17] D. Duffie and N. Gârleanu, Risk and the valuation of collateralized debt obligations, *Financial Analysts Journal* **57**(1) (2001) 41–62.

[18] H. J. Ethier and T. G. Kurtz, *Markov Processes, Characterization and Convergence* (Wiley, 1986).

[19] J. Gregory *Counterparty Credit Risk: The New Challenge for Global Financial Markets* (Wiley, 2009).

[20] J. Hull and A. White, Valuing credit default swaps II: Modeling default correlation, *The Journal of Derivatives* **8**(3) (2001) 12–22.

[21] B. Huge and D. Lando, Swap pricing with two-sided default risk in a rating-based model, *European Finance Review* **3** (1999) 239–268.

[22] R. Jarrow and F. Yu, Counterparty risk and the pricing of defaultable securities, *Journal of Finance* **56** (2001) 1765–1799.

[23] I. Karatzas and S. Shreve, *Brownian Motion and Stochastic Calculus* (Springer-Verlag, 1988).

[24] J. P. Lardy, Counterparty risk on CDS: A composite spread method example, CRIS Seminar (2008).

[25] A. Lipton and A. Sepp, Credit value adjustment for credit default swaps via the structural default model, *The Journal of Credit Risk* **5**(2) (2009) 123–146.

[26] S. Y. Leung and Y. K. Kwok, Credit default swap valuation with counterparty risk, *Kyoto Economic Review* **74**(1) (2005) 25–45.

[27] C. Redon, Wrong-way risk modelling, *Risk Magazine* (April, 2006).

[28] H. Shirakawa, A squared bessel processes and their applications to the square root interest rate model, *Financial Engineering and the Japanese Markets* **9**(3–4) (2002) 169–190.

[29] H. Stein and K. P. Lee, Counterparty valuation adjustments, in *Credit Risk Frontiers: Subprime crisis, Pricing and Hedging, CVA, MBS, Ratings and Liquidity*, T. R. Bielecki, D. Brigo and F. Patras, eds. (Wiley, 2011).

INFORMATION-BASED ASSET PRICING*

DORJE C. BRODY
Department of Mathematics, Imperial College London
London SW7 2AZ, United Kingdom

LANE P. HUGHSTON and ANDREA MACRINA
Department of Mathematics, King's College London
London WC2R 2LS, United Kingdom

A new framework for asset price dynamics is introduced in which the concept of noisy information about future cash flows is used to derive the corresponding price processes. In this framework an asset is defined by its cash-flow structure. Each cash flow is modelled by a random variable that can be expressed as a function of a collection of independent random variables called market factors. With each such "X-factor" we associate a market information process, the values of which we assume are accessible to market participants. Each information process consists of a sum of two terms; one contains true information about the value of the associated market factor, and the other represents "noise". The noise term is modelled by an independent Brownian bridge that spans the interval from the present to the time at which the value of the factor is revealed. The market filtration is assumed to be that generated by the aggregate of the independent information processes. The price of an asset is given by the expectation of the discounted cash flows in the risk-neutral measure, conditional on the information provided by the market filtration. In the case where the cash flows are the dividend payments associated with equities, an explicit model is obtained for the share-price process. Dividend growth is taken into account by introducing appropriate structure on the market factors. The prices of options on dividend-paying assets are derived. Remarkably, the resulting formula for the price of a European-style call option is of the Black–Scholes–Merton type. We consider the case where the rate at which information is revealed to the market is constant, and the case where the information rate varies in time. Option pricing formulae are obtained for both cases. The information-based framework generates a natural explanation for the origin of stochastic volatility in financial markets, without the need for specifying on an *ad hoc* basis the dynamics of the volatility.

Keywords: Asset pricing; partial information; stochastic volatility; correlation; dividend growth; Brownian bridge; nonlinear filtering; market microstructure.

*This chapter was originally published under the same title in *International Journal of Theoretical and Applied Finance*, Vol.11, No.1, 107–142 (2008). Singapore: World Scientific Publishing.

1. Introduction

In derivative pricing, the starting point is usually the specification of a model for the price process of the underlying asset. Such models tend to be of an *ad hoc* nature. For example, in the Black–Scholes–Merton theory, the underlying asset has a geometric Brownian motion as its price process. More generally, the economy is often modelled by a probability space equipped with the filtration generated by a multi-dimensional Brownian motion, and it is assumed that asset prices are adapted to this filtration. This example is of course the "standard" model within which a great deal of financial engineering has been carried out. The basic problem with the standard model (and the same applies to various generalisations thereof) is that the market filtration is fixed, and no comment is offered on the issue of "where it comes from". In other words, the filtration, which represents the revelation of information to market participants, is modelled first, in an *ad hoc* manner, and then it is assumed that price processes are adapted to it. But no indication is given about the nature of this "information", and it is not obvious, *a priori*, why the Brownian filtration, for example, should be regarded as providing information rather than noise.

In a complete market there is a sense in which the Brownian filtration provides no irrelevant information. That is to say, in a complete market based on a Brownian filtration the asset price movements reflect the information content of the filtration. Nevertheless, the notion that the market filtration should be "prespecified" is an unsatisfactory one in financial modelling. The intuition behind the "prespecified-filtration" approach is that the filtration represents the unfolding in time of a succession of random events that "influence" the markets, causing prices to change. For example, bad weather in South America results in a decrease in the supply of coffee beans and hence an increase in the price of coffee. Or, say, a spate of bad derivative deals causes a drop in confidence in banks, and hence a downgrade in earnings projections, and thus a drop in their prices. The idea is that one "abstractifies" these influences in the form of a prespecified filtration to which price processes are adapted. What is unsatisfactory about this is that little structure is given to the filtration: price movements behave as though they were spontaneous. In reality, we expect the price-formation process to exhibit more structure.

It would be out of place in the present context to attempt an account of the process of price formation. Nevertheless, we can improve on the "prespecified" approach. In that spirit we proceed as follows. We note that price changes arise from two sources. The first is that resulting from changes in agent preferences—that is to say, changes in the pricing kernel. Movements in the pricing kernel are associated with (a) changes in investor attitudes towards risk, and (b) changes in investor "impatience", the subjective discounting of future cash flows. Equally important are changes in price resulting from the revelation of information about the future cash flows derivable from a given asset. When a market agent decides to buy or sell an asset, the decision is made in accordance with the information available to the agent concerning the likely future cash flows associated with the asset. A change in the information available to the agent about a future cash flow will typically have an effect on the price at which they are willing to buy or sell, even if the agent's preferences remain unchanged. Consider the situation where one is thinking of purchasing an item at a price that seems attractive. But then, one reads an article pointing out an undesirable feature of the product. After reflection, one decides that the price is too high, given the deficiencies that one is now aware of. As a result, one decides not to buy, not at that price, and eventually—because other individuals will have read the same report—the price drops.

The movement of the price of an asset should, therefore, be regarded as *an emergent phenomenon.* To put the matter another way, the price process of an asset should be viewed as the output of (rather than an input into) the decisions made relating to possible transactions in the asset, and these decisions should be understood as being induced primarily by the flow of information to market participants. Taking into account this observation we propose in this paper a new framework for asset pricing based on *modelling of the flow of market information.* The information is that concerning the values of the future cash flows associated with the given assets. For example, if the asset represents a share in a firm that will make a single distribution at some agreed date, then there is a single cash flow. If the asset is a credit-risky discount bond, then the future cash flow is the payout of the bond at maturity. In each case, based on the information available relating to the likely payouts of the given financial instrument, market participants determine estimates for the value of the right to the impending cash flows. These estimates lead to the decisions concerning transactions that trigger movements in the price.

In this paper we present a class of models capturing the essence of the scenario described above. In building the framework we have several criteria in mind that we would like to see satisfied. The first of these is that our model for the flow of market information should be intuitively appealing, and should allow for a reasonably sophisticated account of aggregate investor behaviour. At the same time, the model should be simple enough to allow one to derive explicit expressions for the asset price processes thus induced, in a suitably rich range of examples, as well as for various associated derivative price processes. The framework should also be flexible enough to allow for the modelling of assets having complex cash-flow structures. Furthermore, it should be suitable for practical implementation. The framework should be mathematically sound, and manifestly arbitrage-free. In what follows we show how our modelling framework goes a long way towards satisfying these criteria.

The role of information in financial modelling has long been appreciated, particularly in the theory of market microstructure (see, e.g., Back [1], Back and Baruch [2], O'Hara [21], and references cited therein). The present framework is perhaps most closely related to the line of investigation represented, e.g., in Cetin *et al.* [5], Duffie and Lando [8], Geman *et al.* [10], Giesecke [11], Giesecke and Goldberg [12], and Jarrow and Protter [14]. The work in this paper, in particular, develops that described in Brody *et al.* [3] and Macrina [20], where preliminary accounts of some of this material appear (see also Rutkowski and Yu [23]).

The paper is organised as follows. In Secs. 2, 3, and 4 we illustrate the framework for information-based pricing by considering the scenario in which there is a single random cash flow. An elementary model for market information is presented, based on the specification of a process composed of two parts: a "signal" component containing true information about the upcoming cash flow, and an independent "noise" component which we model in a specific way. A closed-form expression for the asset price is obtained in terms of the market information available at the time the price is being specified. This result is summarised in Proposition 4.1. In Sec. 5 we show that the resulting asset price process is driven by a Brownian motion, an expression for which can be obtained in terms of the market information process: this construction indicates in explicit terms the sense in which the price process can be viewed as an "emergent" phenomenon. In Sec. 6 we show that the value of a European-style call option, in the case of an asset with a single cash flow, admits a simple formula analogous to that of the Black–Scholes–Merton model. In Sec. 7 we derive pricing formulae for the situation when the random variable associated with the single cash flow has an exponential distribution or, more generally, a gamma distribution.

The extension of the framework to assets associated with multiple cash flows is established in Sec. 8. We show that once the relevant cash flows are decomposed in terms of a collection of independent market factors, then a closed-form expression for the asset price associated with a complex cash-flow structure can be obtained. In Sec. 9 we show how the standard geometric Brownian motion model can be derived in an information-based setting. This remarkable result motivates the specific choice of information process given in Eq. (4.1). In Sec. 10 we present a simple model for dividend growth. In Sec. 11 we show that by allowing distinct assets to share one or more common market factors in the determination of one or more of their respective cash flows we obtain a natural correlation structure for the associated asset price processes. This method for introducing correlation in asset price movements contrasts with the *ad hoc* approach adopted in most financial modelling. In Sec. 12 we demonstrate that if two or more market factors affect the future cash flows of an asset, then the corresponding price process will exhibit unhedgeable stochastic volatility. This result is noteworthy since even for the class of relatively simple models considered here it is possible to identify a candidate for *the origin of stochasticity in price volatility*, as well as the form it should take, which is given in Proposition 12.1.

In the remaining sections of the paper we consider the case where the rate at which the information concerning the true value of an impending cash flow is revealed is time dependent. The introduction of a time-dependent information rate adds additional flexibility to the modelling framework, and opens the door to the possibility of calibrating the model to the market prices of options. We consider the single-factor case first, and obtain a closed-form expression for the conditional expectation of the cash flow. The result is stated first in Sec. 13 as Proposition 13.1, and the derivation is then given in the two sections that follow. In Sec. 14 we introduce a new measure appropriate for the consideration of a Brownian bridge with a random drift, which is used in Sec. 15 to obtain an expression for the conditional density of the random cash flow. The consistency of the resulting price process is established in Sec. 16. We show, in particular, that, for the given information process, if we re-initialise the model at some specified future time, the dynamics of the model moving forward from that time can be represented by a suitably re-initialised information process. This result is given in Proposition 16.1. The dynamical equation satisfied by the price is analysed in Sec. 17, where we demonstrate in Proposition 17.1 that the driving process is a Brownian motion, just as in the constant parameter case. In Sec. 18 we derive the price of a European-style call option in the case for which the information rate is time dependent.

Our approach is based on the idea that first one models the cash flows, then the information processes, then the filtration, and finally the prices. In Sec. 19, we solve the corresponding "inverse" problem. The result is stated in Proposition 19.1. Starting from the dynamics of the conditional distribution of the impending payoff, which is driven by a Brownian motion adapted to the market filtration, we construct (a) the random variable that represents the relevant market factor, and (b) an independent Brownian bridge representing irrelevant information. These two combine to generate the market filtration. We conclude in Sec. 20 with a general multi-factor extension of the time-dependent setup, for which the dynamics of the resulting price processes are given in Propositions 20.1 and 20.2.

2. The Modelling Framework

In asset pricing we require three ingredients: (a) the cash flows, (b) the investor preferences, and (c) the flow of information to market participants. Translated into a mathematical language, these ingredients amount to the following: (a′) cash flows are modelled as random variables; (b′) investor preferences are modelled with the determination of a pricing kernel; and (c′) the market information flow is modelled with the specification of a filtration. As we have indicated above, asset pricing theory conventionally attaches more weight to (a) and (b) than to (c). In this paper we emphasise the importance of ingredient (c).

Our theory will be based on modelling the flow of information accessible to market participants concerning the future cash flows associated with a position in a financial asset. We start by introducing the notation and assumptions employed in this paper. We model the financial markets with the specification of a probability space $(\Omega, \mathcal{F}, \mathbb{Q})$ on which a filtration $\{\mathcal{F}_t\}_{0\leq t<\infty}$ will be constructed. The probability measure $\mathbb{Q}$ is understood to be the risk-neutral measure, and $\{\mathcal{F}_t\}$ is understood to be the market filtration. All asset-price processes and other information-providing processes accessible to market participants will be adapted to $\{\mathcal{F}_t\}$.

Several simplifying assumptions will be made that will enable us to concentrate our efforts on the problems associated with the flow of market information. The first of these assumptions is the use of the risk-neutral measure. The "real" probability measure does not enter into the present investigation. Expectation in the measure $\mathbb{Q}$ will be denoted by $\mathbb{E}[-]$. Our second assumption is that we take the default-free system of interest rates to be deterministic. The absence of arbitrage then implies that the corresponding system of discount functions $\{P_{tT}\}_{0\leq t\leq T<\infty}$ can be written in the form $P_{tT} = P_{0T}/P_{0t}$ for $t \leq T$, where $\{P_{0t}\}_{0\leq t<\infty}$ is the initial discount function, which we take to be part of the initial data of the model. The function $\{P_{0t}\}_{0\leq t<\infty}$ is assumed to be differentiable and strictly decreasing, and to satisfy $0 < P_{0t} \leq 1$ and $\lim_{t\to\infty} P_{0t} = 0$.

We also assume, for simplicity, that cash flows occur at pre-determined dates. Now clearly for some purposes we would like to allow for cash flows occurring effectively at random times—in particular, at stopping times associated with the market filtration. But in the present exposition we want to avoid the idea of a "prespecified" filtration with respect to which stopping times are defined. We take the view that the market filtration is a "derived" notion, generated by information about upcoming cash flows, and by the values of cash flows when they occur. We shall therefore regard a "randomly-timed" cash flow as being a *set* of random cash flows occurring at various times, and with a joint distribution function that ensures only one of these flows is non-zero. Hence in our view the ontological status of a cash flow is that its timing is definite, only the amount is random—and that cash flows occurring at different times are, by their nature, different cash flows.

3. Modelling the Cash Flows

First we consider the case of an asset that provides a single isolated cash flow occurring at time T, represented by a random variable D_T. We assume that $D_T \geq 0$. The value S_t of the cash flow at any earlier time t in the interval $0 \leq t < T$ is then given by the discounted conditional expectation of D_T:

$$S_t = P_{tT}\mathbb{E}\left[D_T|\mathcal{F}_t\right]. \tag{3.1}$$

In this way we model the price process $\{S_t\}_{0\leq t<T}$ of a limited-liability asset that pays a single dividend D_T at time T. The construction of the price process here is carried out in such a way as to guarantee an arbitrage-free market if other assets are priced by the same method (see Davis [6] for a closely related point of view). We shall use the terms "cash flow" and "dividend" more or less interchangeably. If a more specific use of one of these terms is needed, then this will be evident from the context. We adopt the convention that when the dividend is paid the asset price goes "ex-dividend" immediately. Hence in the example above we have $\lim_{t\to T} S_t = D_T$ and $S_T = 0$.

In the case where the asset pays a sequence of dividends D_{T_k} $(k = 1, 2, \ldots, n)$ on the dates T_k the price (for $t < T_1$) is given by

$$S_t = \sum_{k=1}^{n} P_{tT_k}\mathbb{E}\left[D_{T_k}|\mathcal{F}_t\right]. \tag{3.2}$$

More generally, for all $t \geq 0$, and taking into account the ex-dividend behaviour, we have

$$S_t = \sum_{k=1}^{n} \mathbb{1}_{\{t<T_k\}} P_{tT_k} \mathbb{E}\left[D_{T_k} | \mathcal{F}_t\right]. \tag{3.3}$$

It will be useful if we adopt the convention that a discount bond also goes ex-dividend on its maturity date. Thus in the case of a discount bond we assume that the price of the bond is given, for dates earlier than the maturity date, by the product of the principal and the relevant discount factor. But at maturity (when the principal is paid) the value of the bond drops to zero. In the case of a coupon bond, there is a downward jump in the price of the bond at the time a coupon is paid (the value lost may be captured back in the form of an "accrued interest" payment). In this way we obtain a consistent treatment of the "ex-dividend" behaviour of all of the asset price processes under consideration. With this convention it follows that price processes are right continuous with left limits.

4. Modelling the Information Flow

Now we present a simple model for the flow of market information, following Brody *et al.* [3]. We consider first the case of a single distribution, occurring at time T, and assume that market participants have only partial information about the upcoming cash flow D_T. The information available in the market about the cash flow is assumed to be contained in a process $\{\xi_t\}_{0\leq t\leq T}$ defined by

$$\xi_t = \sigma t D_T + \beta_{tT}. \tag{4.1}$$

We call $\{\xi_t\}$ the *market information process*. This process is composed of two parts. The term $\sigma t D_T$ contains the "true information" about the dividend, and grows in magnitude as t increases. The process $\{\beta_{tT}\}_{0\leq t\leq T}$ is a standard Brownian bridge over the time interval $[0, T]$. Thus $\{\beta_{tT}\}$ is Gaussian, $\beta_{0T} = 0$, $\beta_{TT} = 0$, the random variable β_{tT} has mean zero, and the covariance of β_{sT} and β_{tT} for $s \leq t$ is $s(T-t)/T$. We assume that D_T and $\{\beta_{tT}\}$ are independent. Thus the information contained in the bridge process is "pure noise".

We assume that the market filtration $\{\mathcal{F}_t\}$ is generated by the market information process: $\mathcal{F}_t = \sigma(\{\xi_s\}_{0\leq s\leq t})$. The dividend D_T is therefore $\mathcal{F}_T$-measurable, but is not $\mathcal{F}_t$-measurable for $t < T$. Thus the value of D_T becomes "known" at time T, but not earlier. The bridge process $\{\beta_{tT}\}$ is not adapted to $\{\mathcal{F}_t\}$ and thus is not directly accessible to market participants. This reflects the fact that until the dividend is paid the market participants cannot distinguish the "true information" from the "noise" in the market. The introduction of the Brownian bridge models the fact that market perceptions, whether valid or not, play a role in determining asset prices. Initially, all available information is used to determine the *a priori* probability distribution for D_T. The parameter σ represents the rate at which information about the true value of D_T is revealed as time progresses. If σ is low, the value of

D_T is effectively hidden until very near the time of the dividend payment; whereas if σ is high, then the value of the cash flow is for all practical purposes revealed quickly.

In the example under consideration we have made some simplifying assumptions concerning the information structure. For instance, we assume that σ is constant. In Sec. 13, however, we consider a time-dependent information flow rate. We have also assumed that the random dividend D_T enters directly into the structure of the information process, and enters linearly. As we shall indicate later, a more general and natural setup is to let the information process depend on a random variable X_T which we call a "market factor"; then the dividend is regarded as a function of the market factor. This arrangement has the advantage that it easily generalises to the situation where a cash flow might depend on several independent market factors, or indeed where cash flows associated with different financial instruments have one or more factors in common.

Given the market information structure described above for a single cash flow, we proceed to construct the associated price dynamics. The price process $\{S_t\}$ for a share in the firm paying the specified dividend is given by formula (3.1). It is assumed that the *a priori* probability distribution of the dividend D_T is known. This distribution is regarded as part of the initial data of the problem, which in some cases can be calibrated from knowledge of the initial price of the asset along with other price data. The general problem of how the *a priori* distribution is obtained is an important one—any asset pricing model has to confront this issue—which we defer for later consideration. The initial distribution is not to be understood as being "absolutely" determined, but rather represents the "best estimate" for the distribution given the data available at that time, in accordance with what one might call a Bayesian point of view. We note the fact that the information process $\{\xi_t\}$ is Markovian (see Brody *et al.* [3], and Rutkowski and Yu [23]). Making use of this property together with the fact that D_T is $\mathcal{F}_T$-measurable we deduce that

$$S_t = \mathbb{1}_{\{t<T\}} P_{tT} \mathbb{E}\left[D_T | \xi_t\right]. \tag{4.2}$$

If the random variable D_T that represents the payoff has a continuous distribution, then the conditional expectation in (4.2) can be expressed in the form

$$\mathbb{E}\left[D_T | \xi_t\right] = \int_0^\infty x \pi_t(x) \, \mathrm{d}x. \tag{4.3}$$

Here $\pi_t(x)$ is the conditional probability density for the random variable D_T:

$$\pi_t(x) = \frac{\mathrm{d}}{\mathrm{d}x} \mathbb{Q}(D_T \leq x | \xi_t). \tag{4.4}$$

We implicitly assume appropriate technical conditions on the distribution of the dividend that will suffice to ensure the existence of the expressions under consideration. Also, for convenience we use a notation appropriate for continuous distributions, though corresponding results can be inferred for discrete distributions, or more general distributions, by slightly modifying the stated assumptions and conclusions.

Bearing in mind these points, we note that the conditional probability density process for the dividend can be worked out by use of a form of the Bayes formula:

$$\pi_t(x) = \frac{p(x)\rho(\xi_t|D_T = x)}{\int_0^\infty p(x)\rho(\xi_t|D_T = x)\mathrm{d}x}. \tag{4.5}$$

Here $p(x)$ denotes the *a priori* density for D_T, which we assume is known as an initial condition, and $\rho(\xi_t|D_T = x)$ denotes the conditional density for the random variable ξ_t given that $D_T = x$. Since β_{tT} is a Gaussian random variable with mean zero and variance $t(T-t)/T$, we deduce that the conditional density for ξ_t is

$$\rho(\xi_t|D_T = x) = \sqrt{\frac{T}{2\pi t(T-t)}}\exp\left(-\frac{(\xi_t - \sigma t x)^2 T}{2t(T-t)}\right). \tag{4.6}$$

Inserting this expression into the Bayes formula we get

$$\pi_t(x) = \frac{p(x)\exp\left[\frac{T}{T-t}(\sigma x \xi_t - \frac{1}{2}\sigma^2 x^2 t)\right]}{\int_0^\infty p(x)\exp\left[\frac{T}{T-t}(\sigma x \xi_t - \frac{1}{2}\sigma^2 x^2 t)\right]\mathrm{d}x}. \tag{4.7}$$

We thus obtain the following result for the asset price:

Proposition 4.1. *The information-based price process $\{S_t\}_{0\leq t\leq T}$ of a limited-liability asset that pays a single dividend D_T at time T with a priori distribution*

$$\mathbb{Q}(D_T \leq y) = \int_0^y p(x)\,\mathrm{d}x \tag{4.8}$$

is given by

$$S_t = \mathbb{1}_{\{t<T\}} P_{tT} \frac{\int_0^\infty x p(x)\exp\left[\frac{T}{T-t}(\sigma x \xi_t - \frac{1}{2}\sigma^2 x^2 t)\right]\mathrm{d}x}{\int_0^\infty p(x)\exp\left[\frac{T}{T-t}(\sigma x \xi_t - \frac{1}{2}\sigma^2 x^2 t)\right]\mathrm{d}x}, \tag{4.9}$$

where $\xi_t = \sigma t D_T + \beta_{tT}$ is the market information.

5. Asset Price Dynamics in the Case of a Single Cash Flow

In order to analyse the properties of the price process deduced above, and to be able to compare it with other models, we need to work out the dynamics of $\{S_t\}$. One of the advantages of the model under consideration is that we have an explicit expression for the price at our disposal. Thus in obtaining the dynamics we need to find the stochastic differential equation of which $\{S_t\}$ is the solution. This turns out to be an interesting exercise because it offers some insights into what we mean by the assertion that market price dynamics should be regarded as an "emergent phenomenon". To obtain the dynamics associated with the price process $\{S_t\}$ of a single-dividend paying asset let us write

$$D_{tT} = \mathbb{E}[D_T|\xi_t]. \tag{5.1}$$

Evidently, D_{tT} can be expressed in the form $D_{tT} = D(\xi_t, t)$, where

$$D(\xi, t) = \frac{\int_0^\infty x p(x) \exp\left[\frac{T}{T-t}(\sigma x \xi - \frac{1}{2}\sigma^2 x^2 t)\right] \mathrm{d}x}{\int_0^\infty p(x) \exp\left[\frac{T}{T-t}(\sigma x \xi - \frac{1}{2}\sigma^2 x^2 t)\right] \mathrm{d}x}. \tag{5.2}$$

A straightforward calculation making use of the Ito rules shows that the dynamical equation for $\{D_{tT}\}$ is given by

$$\mathrm{d}D_{tT} = \frac{\sigma T}{T-t} V_t \left[\frac{1}{T-t}\left(\xi_t - \sigma T D_{tT}\right)\mathrm{d}t + \mathrm{d}\xi_t\right]. \tag{5.3}$$

Here V_t is the conditional variance of the dividend:

$$V_t = \mathbb{E}_t[(D_T - \mathbb{E}_t[D_T])^2] = \int_0^\infty x^2 \pi_t(x)\,\mathrm{d}x - \left(\int_0^\infty x \pi_t(x)\,\mathrm{d}x\right)^2. \tag{5.4}$$

Therefore, if we define a new process $\{W_t\}_{0 \le t < T}$ by setting

$$W_t = \xi_t - \int_0^t \frac{1}{T-s}(\sigma T D_{tT} - \xi_s)\mathrm{d}s, \tag{5.5}$$

we find, after some rearrangement, that

$$\mathrm{d}D_{tT} = \frac{\sigma T}{T-t} V_t \mathrm{d}W_t. \tag{5.6}$$

For the dynamics of the asset price we thus have

$$\mathrm{d}S_t = r_t S_t \mathrm{d}t + \Gamma_{tT}\mathrm{d}W_t, \tag{5.7}$$

where $r_t = -\mathrm{d}\ln P_{0t}/\mathrm{d}t$ is the short rate, and the absolute price volatility Γ_{tT} is

$$\Gamma_{tT} = P_{tT}\frac{\sigma T}{T-t} V_t. \tag{5.8}$$

A slightly different way of arriving at this result is as follows. We start with the conditional probability $\pi_t(x)$. Then, using the notation above, for its dynamics we obtain

$$\mathrm{d}\pi_t(x) = \frac{\sigma T}{T-t}(x - D_{tT})\pi_t(x)\,\mathrm{d}W_t. \tag{5.9}$$

Since according to (4.2) the asset price is given by

$$S_t = \mathbb{1}_{\{t<T\}} P_{tT} \int_0^\infty x \pi_t(x)\,\mathrm{d}x, \tag{5.10}$$

we can infer the dynamics of $\{S_t\}$ from the dynamics of the conditional probability $\{\pi_t(x)\}$, once we take into account formula (5.4) for the conditional variance.

As we shall demonstrate later, the process $\{W_t\}$ defined in (5.5) is an $\{\mathcal{F}_t\}$-Brownian motion. Hence *from the point of view of the market it is the process* $\{W_t\}$ *that drives the asset price dynamics.* In this way our framework resolves the paradoxical point of view usually adopted in financial modelling in which $\{W_t\}$ is regarded on the one hand as "noise", and yet on the other hand also generates the market information flow. And thus, instead of hypothesising the existence of a driving process for the dynamics of the markets, we are able from the information-based perspective to *deduce* the existence of such a process.

The information-flow parameter σ determines the overall magnitude of the volatility. In fact, σ plays a role analogous to the similarly-labelled parameter in the Black–Scholes–Merton theory. Thus, we can say that the rate at which information is revealed in the market determines the magnitude of the volatility. Everything else being the same, if we increase the information-flow rate, then the market volatility will increase as well. According to this point of view, those mechanisms that one might have thought were destined to make markets more efficient—e.g., globalisation of the financial markets, reduction of trade barriers, improved communications, a robust regulatory environment, and so on—can have the effect of increasing market volatility, and hence market risk, rather than reducing it.

6. European-Style Call Options

Before we turn to the consideration of more general cash flows and market information structures, let us consider the pricing of a derivative on an asset for which the price process is governed by (5.7). Specifically, we consider the valuation of a European call option on such an asset, with strike price K, and exercisable at a fixed date t. The option is written on an asset that pays a single dividend D_T at time $T > t$. The initial value of the option is

$$C_0 = P_{0t}\mathbb{E}\left[(S_t - K)^+\right]. \tag{6.1}$$

Inserting the expression for S_t derived in the previous section, we obtain

$$C_0 = P_{0t}\,\mathbb{E}\left[\left(P_{tT}\int_0^\infty x\,\pi_t(x)\mathrm{d}x - K\right)^+\right]. \tag{6.2}$$

For convenience we write the conditional probability $\pi_t(x)$ in the form

$$\pi_t(x) = \frac{p_t(x)}{\int_0^\infty p_t(x)\mathrm{d}x}, \tag{6.3}$$

where the "unnormalised" density $p_t(x)$ is defined by

$$p_t(x) = p(x)\exp\left[\frac{T}{T-t}\left(\sigma x\xi_t - \tfrac{1}{2}\sigma^2 x^2 t\right)\right]. \tag{6.4}$$

Substituting (6.4) into (6.2) we find that the value of the option is

$$C_0 = P_{0t}\mathbb{E}\left[\frac{1}{\Phi_t}\left(\int_0^\infty (P_{tT}x - K)\,p_t(x)\mathrm{d}x\right)^+\right], \tag{6.5}$$

where

$$\Phi_t = \int_0^\infty p_t(x)\mathrm{d}x. \tag{6.6}$$

The random variable $1/\Phi_t$ can be used to introduce a measure $\mathbb{B}$ on $(\Omega, \mathcal{F}_t)$, which we call the "bridge measure". The option price can then be written:

$$C_0 = P_{0t}\mathbb{E}^{\mathbb{B}}\left[\left(\int_0^\infty (P_{tT}x - K)\, p_t(x)\mathrm{d}x\right)^+\right]. \tag{6.7}$$

The special feature of the bridge measure, as we establish in Sec. 14 in a more general context, is that the random variable ξ_t is Gaussian under $\mathbb{B}$. In particular, under $\mathbb{B}$ we find that ξ_t has mean 0 and variance $t(T-t)/T$. Since $p_t(x)$ can be expressed as a function of ξ_t, when we calculate the expectation in (6.7) we obtain a tractable formula for C_0.

To determine the value of the option we define a constant ξ^* (the critical value) by the following condition:

$$\int_0^\infty (P_{tT}x - K)\, p(x) \exp\left[\frac{T}{T-t}\left(\sigma x \xi^* - \frac{1}{2}\sigma^2 x^2 t\right)\right] \mathrm{d}x = 0. \tag{6.8}$$

Then the expectation in (6.7) can be performed and we find that the option price is given by

$$C_0 = P_{0T}\int_0^\infty x\, p(x)\, N(-z^* + \sigma x\sqrt{\tau})\mathrm{d}x - P_{0t}K\int_0^\infty p(x)\, N(-z^* + \sigma x\sqrt{\tau})\mathrm{d}x, \tag{6.9}$$

where $N(x)$ is the standard normal distribution function, and

$$\tau = \frac{tT}{T-t}, \qquad z^* = \xi^*\sqrt{\frac{T}{t(T-t)}}. \tag{6.10}$$

We see that a tractable expression of the Black–Scholes–Merton type is obtained. The option pricing problem, even for general $p(x)$, reduces to an elementary numerical problem. It is interesting to note that although the probability distribution for the price S_t is not of a "standard" type, nevertheless the option valuation problem remains a solvable one.

7. Examples of Specific Dividend Structures

In this section we consider the dynamics of assets with various dividend structures. First we look at a simple asset for which the cash flow is exponentially distributed. The *a priori* probability density for D_T is thus of the form

$$p(x) = \frac{1}{\delta}\exp(-x/\delta), \tag{7.1}$$

where δ is a constant. We can regard an exponentially distributed payout as a model for the situation where little is known about the distribution of the dividend, apart from its mean. Then from formula (4.9) we find that the price is:

$$S_t = \mathbb{1}_{\{t<T\}} P_{tT} \frac{\int_0^\infty x \exp(-x/\delta) \exp\left[\frac{T}{T-t}(\sigma x \xi_t - \frac{1}{2}\sigma^2 x^2 t)\right] \mathrm{d}x}{\int_0^\infty \exp(-x/\delta) \exp\left[\frac{T}{T-t}(\sigma x \xi_t - \frac{1}{2}\sigma^2 x^2 t)\right] \mathrm{d}x}. \tag{7.2}$$

We note that $S_0 = P_{0T}\delta$, so we can calibrate δ by use of the initial price. The integrals in the numerator and denominator in the expression above can be worked out explicitly. Hence, we obtain a closed-form expression for the price in the case of a simple asset with an exponentially-distributed cash flow:

$$S_t = \mathbb{1}_{\{t<T\}} P_{tT} \left[\frac{\exp(-\frac{1}{2}B_t^2/A_t)}{\sqrt{2\pi A_t}\; N(B_t/\sqrt{A_t})} + \frac{B_t}{A_t} \right], \tag{7.3}$$

where $A_t = \sigma^2 tT/(T-t)$ and $B_t = \sigma T\xi_t/(T-t) - \delta^{-1}$.

Next we consider the case of an asset for which the single dividend paid at T is gamma-distributed. More specifically, we assume the density is of the form

$$p(x) = \frac{\delta^n}{(n-1)!} x^{n-1} \exp(-\delta x), \tag{7.4}$$

where δ is a positive real number and n is a positive integer. This choice for the density also leads to a closed-form expression for the share price. We find that

$$S_t = \mathbb{1}_{\{t<T\}} P_{tT} \frac{\sum_{k=0}^{n} \binom{n}{k} A_t^{\frac{1}{2}k-n} B_t^{n-k} F_k(-B_t/\sqrt{A_t})}{\sum_{k=0}^{n-1} \binom{n-1}{k} A_t^{\frac{1}{2}k-n+1} B_t^{n-k-1} F_k(-B_t/\sqrt{A_t})}, \tag{7.5}$$

where A_t and B_t are as above, and

$$F_k(x) = \int_x^\infty z^k \exp\left(-\frac{1}{2}z^2\right) dz. \tag{7.6}$$

A recursion formula can be worked out for the function $F_k(x)$. This is given by

$$(k+1)F_k(x) = F_{k+2}(x) - x^{k+1} \exp\left(-\frac{1}{2}x^2\right), \tag{7.7}$$

from which it follows that $F_0(x) = \sqrt{2\pi}N(-x)$, $F_1(x) = \mathrm{e}^{-\frac{1}{2}x^2}$, $F_2(x) = x\mathrm{e}^{-\frac{1}{2}x^2} + \sqrt{2\pi}N(-x)$, $F_3(x) = (x^2+2)\mathrm{e}^{-\frac{1}{2}x^2}$, and so on. In general, the polynomial parts of $\{F_k(x)\}_{k=0,1,2,\ldots}$ are related to the Legendre polynomials.

8. Market Factors and Multiple Cash Flows

We proceed to consider the more general situation where the asset pays multiple dividends. This will allow us to consider a wider range of financial instruments. Let us write D_{T_k} $(k = 1, \ldots, n)$ for a set of random dividends paid at the pre-designated dates T_k $(k = 1, \ldots, n)$. Possession of the asset at time t entitles the bearer to the cash flows occurring at times $T_k > t$. For simplicity we assume n is finite. For each value of k we introduce a set of independent random variables $X_{T_k}^{\alpha}$ $(\alpha = 1, \ldots, m_k)$, which we call market factors or X-factors. For each value of α we assume that the market factor $X^{\alpha}_{T_k}$ is $\mathcal{F}_{T_k}$-measurable, where $\{\mathcal{F}_t\}$ is the market filtration.

For each value of k, the market factors $\{X^{\alpha}_{T_j}\}_{j\leq k}$ represent the independent elements that determine the cash flow occurring at time T_k. Thus the cash flow D_{T_k} is assumed to have the following structure:

$$D_{T_k} = \Delta_{T_k}(X^{\alpha}_{T_1}, X^{\alpha}_{T_2}, \ldots, X^{\alpha}_{T_k}), \tag{8.1}$$

where $\Delta_{T_k}(X^{\alpha}_{T_1}, X^{\alpha}_{T_2}, \ldots, X^{\alpha}_{T_k})$ is a function of $\sum_{j=1}^{k} m_j$ variables. For each cash flow it is, so to speak, the job of the financial analyst (or actuary) to determine the relevant independent market factors, and the form of the cash-flow function Δ_{T_k}. With each market factor $X^{\alpha}_{T_k}$ we associate an information process $\{\xi^{\alpha}_{tT_k}\}_{0\leq t\leq T_k}$ of the form

$$\xi^{\alpha}_{tT_k} = \sigma^{\alpha}_{T_k} X^{\alpha}_{T_k} t + \beta^{\alpha}_{tT_k}. \tag{8.2}$$

Here $\sigma^{\alpha}_{T_k}$ is a parameter, and $\{\beta^{\alpha}_{tT_k}\}$ is a standard Brownian bridge over the interval $[0, T_k]$. We assume that the X-factors and the Brownian bridge processes are independent. The parameter $\sigma^{\alpha}_{T_k}$ determines the rate at which the market factor $X^{\alpha}_{T_k}$ is revealed. The Brownian bridge represents the associated noise. We assume that the market filtration $\{\mathcal{F}_t\}$ is generated by the totality of the independent information processes $\{\xi^{\alpha}_{tT_k}\}_{0\leq t\leq T_k}$ for $k = 1, 2, \ldots, n$ and $\alpha = 1, 2, \ldots, m_k$. Hence, the price of the asset is given by

$$S_t = \sum_{k=1}^{n} \mathbb{1}_{\{t<T_k\}} P_{tT_k} \mathbb{E}_t\left[D_{T_k}\right]. \tag{8.3}$$

9. Geometric Brownian Motion Model

The simplest application of the X-factor technique arises in the case of geometric Brownian motion models. We consider a limited-liability asset that makes a single cash distribution S_T at time T. We assume that S_T has a log-normal distribution under $\mathbb{Q}$, and can be written in the form

$$S_T = S_0 \exp\left(rT + \nu\sqrt{T}X_T - \frac{1}{2}\nu^2 T\right), \tag{9.1}$$

where the market factor X_T is normally distributed with mean zero and variance one, and $r > 0$ and $\nu > 0$ are constants. The information process $\{\xi_t\}$ is taken to be of the form

$$\xi_t = \sigma t X_T + \beta_{tT}, \tag{9.2}$$

where the Brownian bridge $\{\beta_{tT}\}$ is independent of X_T, and where the information flow rate is of the special form

$$\sigma = \frac{1}{\sqrt{T}}. \tag{9.3}$$

By use of the Bayes formula we find that the conditional probability density is of the Gaussian form

$$\pi_t(x) = \sqrt{\frac{T}{2\pi(T-t)}} \exp\left(-\frac{1}{2(T-t)}(\sqrt{T}x - \xi_t)^2\right), \tag{9.4}$$

and has the following dynamics:

$$\mathrm{d}\pi_t(x) = \frac{1}{T-t}(\sqrt{T}x - \xi_t)\pi_t(x)\mathrm{d}\xi_t. \tag{9.5}$$

A short calculation then shows that the value of the asset at time $t < T$ is given by

$$\begin{aligned} S_t &= \mathrm{e}^{-r(T-t)}\mathbb{E}_t[S_T] \\ &= \mathrm{e}^{-r(T-t)} \int_{-\infty}^{\infty} S_0 \mathrm{e}^{rT+\nu\sqrt{T}x-\frac{1}{2}\nu^2 T} \pi_t(x)\mathrm{d}x \\ &= S_0 \exp\left(rt + \nu\xi_t - \frac{1}{2}\nu^2 t\right). \end{aligned} \tag{9.6}$$

The surprising fact in this example is that $\{\xi_t\}$ itself turns out to be the innovation process. Indeed, it is not too difficult to verify that $\{\xi_t\}$ is an $\{\mathcal{F}_t\}$-Brownian motion. Hence, setting $W_t = \xi_t$ for $0 \leq t < T$ we obtain the standard geometric Brownian motion model:

$$S_t = S_0 \exp\left(rt + \nu W_t - \frac{1}{2}\nu^2 t\right). \tag{9.7}$$

We see therefore that starting with an information process of the form (9.2) we are able to recover the familiar asset price dynamics given by (9.7).

An important point to note here is that the Brownian bridge process $\{\beta_{tT}\}$ appears quite naturally in this context. In fact, if we start with (9.7) then we can make use of the following orthogonal decomposition of the Brownian motion (see, e.g., Yor [24]):

$$W_t = \frac{t}{T} W_T + \left(W_t - \frac{t}{T} W_T\right). \tag{9.8}$$

The second term in the right, independent of the first term on the right, is a standard representation for a Brownian bridge process:

$$\beta_{tT} = W_t - \frac{t}{T} W_T. \tag{9.9}$$

Thus by writing $X_T = W_T/\sqrt{T}$ and $\sigma = 1/\sqrt{T}$ we find that the right side of (9.8) is indeed the market information. In other words, formulated in the information-based framework, the standard Black–Scholes–Merton theory can be expressed in terms of a normally distributed X-factor and an independent Brownian bridge noise process.

10. Dividend Growth

As an elementary example of a multi-dividend structure, we shall look at a simple growth model for dividends in the equity markets. We consider an asset that pays a sequence of dividends D_{T_k}, where each dividend date has an associated X-factor. Let $\{X_{T_k}\}_{k=1,\ldots,n}$ be a set of independent, identically-distributed X-factors, each with mean $1+g$. The dividend structure is assumed to be of the form

$$D_{T_k} = D_0 \prod_{j=1}^{k} X_{T_j}, \tag{10.1}$$

where D_0 is a constant. The parameter g can be interpreted as the dividend growth factor, and D_0 can be understood as representing the most recent dividend before time zero. For the price of the asset we have:

$$S_t = D_0 \sum_{k=1}^{n} \mathbb{1}_{\{t<T_k\}} P_{tT_k} \mathbb{E}_t \left[\prod_{j=1}^{k} X_{T_j} \right]. \tag{10.2}$$

Since the X-factors are independent, the conditional expectation of the product appearing in this expression factorises into a product of conditional expectations, and each such conditional expectation can be written in the form of an expression of the type we have already considered. As a consequence we are led to a tractable family of dividend growth models.

11. Assets with Common Factors

The multiple-dividend asset pricing model introduced in Sec. 8 can be extended in a very natural way to the situation where two or more assets are being priced. In this case we consider a collection of N assets with price processes $\{S_t^{(i)}\}_{i=1,2,\ldots,N}$. With asset number (i) we associate the cash flows $\{D_{T_k}^{(i)}\}$ paid at the dates $\{T_k\}_{k=1,2,\ldots,n}$. We note that the dates $\{T_k\}_{k=1,2,\ldots,n}$ are not tied to any specific asset, but rather represent the totality of possible cash-flow dates of any of the given assets. If a particular asset has no cash flow on one of the dates, then it is assigned a zero cash-flow for that date. From this point, the theory proceeds exactly as in the single asset case. That is to say, with each value of k we associate a set of X-factors $X_{T_k}^{\alpha}$ $(\alpha = 1, 2, \ldots, m_k)$, and a system of market information processes $\{\xi_{tT_k}^{\alpha}\}$. The X-factors and the information processes are not tied to any particular asset. The cash flow $D_{T_k}^{(i)}$ occurring at time T_k for asset number (i) is given by a cash flow function of the form

$$D_{T_k}^{(i)} = \Delta_{T_k}^{(i)}(X_{T_1}^{\alpha}, X_{T_2}^{\alpha}, \ldots, X_{T_k}^{\alpha}). \tag{11.1}$$

In other words, for each asset each cash flow can depend on all of the X-factors that have been "activated" at that point. Thus for the general multi-asset model we have the following price process system:

$$S_t^{(i)} = \sum_{k=1}^{n} \mathbb{1}_{\{t<T_k\}} P_{tT_k} \mathbb{E}_t[D_{T_k}^{(i)}]. \tag{11.2}$$

It is possible in general for two or more assets to "share" an X-factor in association with one or more of the cash flows of each of the assets. This in turn implies that the various assets will have at least one Brownian motion in common in the dynamics of their price processes. We thus obtain a natural model for the correlation structures in the prices of these assets. The intuition is that as new information comes in (whether "true" or "bogus") there will be several different assets all affected by the news, and as a consequence there will be a correlated movement in their prices.

12. Origin of Unhedgeable Stochastic Volatility

Based on the general model introduced in the previous sections, we are now in a position to make an observation concerning the nature of stochastic volatility in the equity markets. In particular, we shall show how a natural framework for *stochastic volatility* arises in the information-based framework. This is achieved without the need for any *ad hoc* assumptions concerning the dynamics of the stochastic volatility. In fact, a very specific dynamical model for stochastic volatility is obtained—thus leading to a possible means by which the theory proposed here might be tested.

We shall work out the volatility associated with the dynamics of the asset price process $\{S_t\}$ given by (8.3). The result is given in Proposition 12.1 below. First, as an example, we consider the dynamics of an asset that pays a single dividend D_T at T. We assume that the dividend depends on the market factors $\{X_T^\alpha\}_{\alpha=1,\ldots,m}$. For $t < T$ we then have:

$$S_t = P_{tT}\mathbb{E}^{\mathbb{Q}}[\Delta_T(X_T^1,\ldots,X_T^m)|\xi_{tT}^1,\ldots,\xi_{tT}^m]$$

$$= P_{tT}\int\cdots\int\Delta_T(x^1,\ldots,x^m)\,\pi_{tT}^1(x_1)\cdots\pi_{tT}^m(x_m)\,\mathrm{d}x_1\cdots\mathrm{d}x_m. \quad (12.1)$$

Here the conditional density functions $\pi_{tT}^\alpha(x)$ for $\alpha = 1,\ldots,m$ are given by

$$\pi_{tT}^\alpha(x) = \frac{p^\alpha(x)\exp\left[\frac{T}{T-t}\left(\sigma^\alpha\, x\,\xi_{tT}^\alpha - \frac{1}{2}(\sigma^\alpha)^2\, x^2 t\right)\right]}{\int_0^\infty p^\alpha(x)\exp\left[\frac{T}{T-t}\left(\sigma^\alpha\, x\,\xi_{tT}^\alpha - \frac{1}{2}(\sigma^\alpha)^2\, x^2 t\right)\right]\mathrm{d}x}, \quad (12.2)$$

where $p^\alpha(x)$ denotes the *a priori* probability density function for the factor X_T^α. The drift of $\{S_t\}_{0\leq t<T}$ is given by the short rate. This is because $\mathbb{Q}$ is the risk-neutral measure, and no dividend is paid before T. Thus, we are left with the problem of determining the volatility of $\{S_t\}$. We find that for $t < T$ the dynamical equation of $\{S_t\}$ assumes the form:

$$\mathrm{d}S_t = r_t S_t \mathrm{d}t + \sum_{\alpha=1}^m \Gamma_{tT}^\alpha \mathrm{d}W_t^\alpha. \quad (12.3)$$

Here the volatility term associated with factor number α is given by

$$\Gamma_{tT}^\alpha = \sigma^\alpha \frac{T}{T-t} P_{tT}\,\mathrm{Cov}[\Delta_T(X_T^1,\ldots,X_T^m), X_T^\alpha|\mathcal{F}_t], \quad (12.4)$$

and $\{W_t^\alpha\}$ denotes the Brownian motion associated with the information process $\{\xi_t^\alpha\}$, defined as in (5.5). The absolute volatility of $\{S_t\}$ is of the form

$$\Gamma_t = \left(\sum_{\alpha=1}^{m} (\Gamma_{tT}^\alpha)^2 \right)^{1/2}. \tag{12.5}$$

For the dynamics of a multi-factor single-dividend paying asset we can thus write $\mathrm{d}S_t = r_t S_t \mathrm{d}t + \Gamma_t \mathrm{d}Z_t$, where the $\{\mathcal{F}_t\}$-Brownian motion $\{Z_t\}$ that drives the asset-price process is

$$Z_t = \int_0^t \frac{1}{\Gamma_s} \sum_{\alpha=1}^{m} \Gamma_{sT}^\alpha \, \mathrm{d}W_s^\alpha. \tag{12.6}$$

The point to note here is that in the case of a multi-factor model we obtain an unhedgeable stochastic volatility. That is to say, although the asset price is in effect driven by a single Brownian motion, its volatility in general depends on a multiplicity of Brownian motions. This means that in general an option position cannot be hedged with a position in the underlying asset. The components of the volatility vector are given by the covariances of the cash flow and the independent market factors. Unhedgeable stochastic volatility thus emerges from the multiplicity of uncertain elements in the market that affect the value of the future cash flow. As a consequence we see that *in this framework we obtain a natural explanation for the origin of stochastic volatility.*

This result can be contrasted with, say, the Heston model [13], which despite its popularity suffers from the fact that it is *ad hoc* in nature. Much the same can be said for the various generalisations of the Heston model used in commercial applications. The approach to stochastic volatility proposed in the present paper is thus of a new character. Expression (12.3) generalises to the case for which the asset pays a set of dividends D_{T_k} $(k = 1, \ldots, n)$, and for each k the dividend depends on the X-factors $\{\{X_{T_j}^\alpha\}_{j=1,\ldots,k}^{\alpha=1,\ldots,m_j}\}$. The result can be summarised as follows.

Proposition 12.1. *The price process of a multi-dividend asset has the following dynamics*:

$$\mathrm{d}S_t = r_t\, S_t\, \mathrm{d}t + \sum_{k=1}^{n} \sum_{j=1}^{k} \sum_{\alpha=1}^{m_j} \mathbb{1}_{\{t<T_k\}} P_{tT_k} \frac{\sigma_j^\alpha T_j}{T_j - t} \,\mathrm{Cov}[D_{T_k}, X_{T_j}^\alpha | \mathcal{F}_t] \mathrm{d}W_t^{\alpha j}$$
$$+ \sum_{k=1}^{n} D_{T_k} \mathrm{d}\mathbb{1}_{\{t<T_k\}}, \tag{12.7}$$

where $D_{T_k} = \Delta_{T_k}(X_{T_1}^\alpha, X_{T_2}^\alpha, \cdots, X_{T_k}^\alpha)$ *is the dividend at time* T_k $(k = 1, 2, \ldots, n)$.

13. Time-Dependent Information Flow

We consider now a generalisation of the foregoing material to the situation in which the information-flow rate varies in time. The time-dependent problem is of relevance to many circumstances. For example, there will typically be more activity in a market during the day than at night—such a consideration is important for short-term investments. Alternatively, it may be that the annual report of a firm is going to be published on a specified day—in this case much more information concerning the future of the firm may be made available on that day than normal.

We begin our analysis of the time-dependent case by considering the situation where there is a single cash flow D_T occurring at T, and the associated market factor is the cash flow itself. In this way we can focus our attention on mathematical issues arising from the time dependence of the information flow rate. Once these issues have been dealt with, we shall consider more complicated cash-flow structures. For the market information process we propose an expression of the form

$$\xi_t = D_T \int_0^t \sigma_s \mathrm{d}s + \beta_{tT}, \tag{13.1}$$

where the function $\{\sigma_s\}_{o\leq s\leq T}$ is taken to be deterministic and nonnegative. We assume that $0 < \int_0^T \sigma_s^2 ds < \infty$. The price process $\{S_t\}$ of the asset is then given by

$$S_t = \mathbb{1}_{\{t<T\}} P_{tT} \mathbb{E}[D_T|\mathcal{F}_t], \tag{13.2}$$

where the market filtration is, as in the previous sections, assumed to be generated by the information process.

Our first task is to work out the conditional expectation in (13.2). This can be achieved by use of a change-of-measure technique, which will be outlined in Sec. 14. It will be useful, however, to state the result first. We define the conditional probability density process $\{\pi_t(x)\}$ by setting

$$\pi_t(x) = \frac{\mathrm{d}}{\mathrm{d}x} \mathbb{Q}(D_T \leq x|\mathcal{F}_t). \tag{13.3}$$

The following result is obtained:

Proposition 13.1. *Let the information process $\{\xi_t\}$ be given by (13.1). Then the conditional probability density process $\{\pi_t(x)\}$ for the random variable D_T is*

$$\pi_t(x) = \frac{p(x)\,\mathrm{e}^{x\left(\frac{1}{T-t}\xi_t \int_0^t \sigma_s \mathrm{d}s + \int_0^t \sigma_s \mathrm{d}\xi_s\right) - \frac{1}{2}x^2\left(\frac{1}{T-t}\left(\int_0^t \sigma_s \mathrm{d}s\right)^2 + \int_0^t \sigma_s^2 \mathrm{d}s\right)}}{\int_0^\infty p(x)\,\mathrm{e}^{x\left(\frac{1}{T-t}\xi_t \int_0^t \sigma_s \mathrm{d}s + \int_0^t \sigma_s \mathrm{d}\xi_s\right) - \frac{1}{2}x^2\left(\frac{1}{T-t}\left(\int_0^t \sigma_s \mathrm{d}s\right)^2 + \int_0^t \sigma_s^2 \mathrm{d}s\right)}\mathrm{d}x}. \tag{13.4}$$

We deduce at once from Proposition 3 that the conditional expectation of the random variable D_T is

$$D_{tT} = \frac{\int_0^\infty x p(x)\,\mathrm{e}^{x\left(\frac{1}{T-t}\xi_t \int_0^t \sigma_s \mathrm{d}s + \int_0^t \sigma_s \mathrm{d}\xi_s\right) - \frac{1}{2}x^2\left(\frac{1}{T-t}\left(\int_0^t \sigma_s \mathrm{d}s\right)^2 + \int_0^t \sigma_s^2 \mathrm{d}s\right)}\mathrm{d}x}{\int_0^\infty p(x)\,\mathrm{e}^{x\left(\frac{1}{T-t}\xi_t \int_0^t \sigma_s \mathrm{d}s + \int_0^t \sigma_s \mathrm{d}\xi_s\right) - \frac{1}{2}x^2\left(\frac{1}{T-t}\left(\int_0^t \sigma_s \mathrm{d}s\right)^2 + \int_0^t \sigma_s^2 \mathrm{d}s\right)}\mathrm{d}x}. \tag{13.5}$$

The associated price process $\{S_t\}$ is then given by $S_t = \mathbb{1}_{\{t<T\}} P_{tT} D_{tT}$.

14. Changes of Measure for Brownian Bridges

Since the information process is a Brownian bridge with a random drift, we shall require formulae relating a Brownian bridge with drift in one measure to a standard Brownian bridge in another measure to establish Proposition 13.1. We proceed as follows. First we recall a well-known integral representation for the Brownian bridge. Let the probability space $(\Omega, \mathcal{F}, \mathbb{Q})$ be given, with a filtration $\{\mathcal{G}_t\}_{0\le t<\infty}$, and let $\{B_t\}$ be a standard $\{\mathcal{G}_t\}$-Brownian motion. Then the process $\{\beta_{tT}\}$, defined by

$$\beta_{tT} = (T-t)\int_0^t \frac{1}{T-s}\,\mathrm{d}B_s, \tag{14.1}$$

for $0 \le t < T$, and by $\beta_{tT} = 0$ for $t = T$, is a standard Brownian bridge over the interval $[0, T]$. Expression (14.1) converges to zero as $t \to T$; see, e.g., Karatzas and Shreve [17], Protter [22]. The filtration $\{\mathcal{G}_t\}$ is larger than the market filtration $\{\mathcal{F}_t\}$. In particular, since $\{\beta_{tT}\}$ is adapted to $\{\mathcal{G}_t\}$ we can think of $\{\mathcal{G}_t\}$ as the filtration describing the information available to an "insider" who can distinguish between what is noise and what is not.

Let D_T be a random variable on $(\Omega, \mathcal{F}, \mathbb{Q})$. We assume that D_T is $\mathcal{G}_0$-measurable and that D_T is independent of $\{\beta_{tT}\}$. Thus the value of D_T is known "all along" to the insider, but not to the typical market participant. For simplicity in what follows we assume that D_T is bounded; this condition can be relaxed with the introduction of an appropriate Novikov-type condition; but we will not pursue the more general situation here. Define the deterministic nonnegative process $\{\nu_t\}_{0\le t\le T}$ by

$$\nu_t = \sigma_t + \frac{1}{T-t}\int_0^t \sigma_s \mathrm{d}s, \tag{14.2}$$

and let $\{\xi_t\}$ be defined as in (13.1). We define the process $\{\Lambda_t\}_{0\le t<T}$ by the relation

$$\frac{1}{\Lambda_t} = \exp\left(-D_T\int_0^t \nu_s \mathrm{d}B_s - \frac{1}{2}D_T^2\int_0^t \nu_s^2 \mathrm{d}s\right). \tag{14.3}$$

With these elements in hand, we fix a time horizon $U \in (0, T)$ and introduce a probability measure $\mathbb{B}$ on $\mathcal{G}_U$ by the relation

$$\mathrm{d}\mathbb{B} = \Lambda_U^{-1}\mathrm{d}\mathbb{Q}. \tag{14.4}$$

Then we have the following facts: (i) The process $\{W_t^*\}_{0\le t<U}$ defined by

$$W_t^* = D_T\int_0^t \nu_s \mathrm{d}s + B_t \tag{14.5}$$

is a $\mathbb{B}$-Brownian motion. (ii) The process $\{\xi_t\}$ defined by (13.1) is a $\mathbb{B}$-Brownian bridge and is independent of D_T. (iii) The random variable D_T has the same probability law with respect to $\mathbb{B}$ and $\mathbb{Q}$. (iv) The conditional expectation for any integrable function $f(D_T)$ of the random variable D_T can be expressed in the form

$$\mathbb{E}^{\mathbb{Q}}[f(D_T)|\mathcal{F}_t^{\xi}] = \frac{\mathbb{E}^{\mathbb{B}}[f(D_T)\Lambda_t|\mathcal{F}_t^{\xi}]}{\mathbb{E}^{\mathbb{B}}[\Lambda_t|\mathcal{F}_t^{\xi}]}. \tag{14.6}$$

We note that the measure $\mathbb{B}$ is independent of the specific choice of the time horizon U in the sense that if $\mathbb{B}$ is defined on $\mathcal{G}_{U'}$ for some $U' > U$, then the restriction of that measure to $\mathcal{G}_U$ agrees with the measure $\mathbb{B}$ as already defined.

When we say that $\{\xi_t\}$ is a $\mathbb{B}$-Brownian bridge what we mean, more precisely, is that $\xi_0 = 0$, that $\{\xi_t\}$ is $\mathbb{B}$-Gaussian, that $\mathbb{E}^{\mathbb{B}}[\xi_t] = 0$, and that

$$\mathbb{E}^{\mathbb{B}}[\xi_s\xi_t] = \frac{s(T-t)}{T} \tag{14.7}$$

for $0 \le s \le t \le U$. Thus with respect to the measure $\mathbb{B}$ the process $\{\xi_t\}_{0\le t\le U}$ has the properties of a standard $[0,T]$-Brownian bridge that has been truncated at time U. The fact that $\{\xi_t\}$ is a $\mathbb{B}$-Brownian bridge can be verified as follows. By (13.1), (14.1), and (14.5) we have

$$\begin{aligned}
\xi_t &= D_T\int_0^t \sigma_s \mathrm{d}s + (T-t)\int_0^t \frac{1}{T-s}\,\mathrm{d}B_s \\
&= D_T\int_0^t \sigma_s \mathrm{d}s + (T-t)\int_0^t \frac{1}{T-s}\,(\mathrm{d}W_s^* - D_T\nu_s\mathrm{d}s) \\
&= D_T\left(\int_0^t \sigma_s \mathrm{d}s - (T-t)\int_0^t \frac{1}{T-s}\,\nu_s\mathrm{d}s\right) + (T-t)\int_0^t \frac{1}{T-s}\,\mathrm{d}W_s^* \\
&= (T-t)\int_0^t \frac{1}{T-s}\,\mathrm{d}W_s^*,
\end{aligned} \tag{14.8}$$

where in the final step we used the relation

$$\int_0^t \frac{1}{T-s}\,\nu_s\mathrm{d}s = \frac{1}{T-t}\int_0^t \sigma_s\mathrm{d}s. \tag{14.9}$$

This formula can be verified by differentiation, which gives (14.2). In (14.8) we see that $\{\xi_t\}$ has been given the standard integral representation of a Brownian bridge.

We remark, incidentally, that (14.6) can be thought of a variation of the Kallianpur-Striebel formula appearing in the literature of nonlinear filtering (see, for example, Bucy and Joseph [4], Davis and Marcus [7], Fujisaki *et al.* [9], Kailath [15], Kallianpur and Striebel [16], Krishnan [18], and Liptser and Shiryaev [19]).

15. Derivation of the Conditional Density

We have introduced the idea of measure changes associated with Brownian bridges in order to introduce formula (14.6), which involves the density process $\{\Lambda_t\}$, which in (14.3) is defined in terms of the $\mathbb{Q}$-Brownian motion $\{B_t\}$. On the other hand, the expectations in (14.6) are conditional with respect to the information generated by $\{\xi_t\}$. Therefore, it will be convenient to express $\{\Lambda_t\}$ in terms of $\{\xi_t\}$. To do this we substitute (14.5) in (14.3) to obtain

$$\Lambda_t = \exp\left(D_T \int_0^t \nu_s \mathrm{d}W_s^* - \frac{1}{2} D_T^2 \int_0^t \nu_s^2 \mathrm{d}s \right). \tag{15.1}$$

We then observe, by differentiating (14.8), that

$$\mathrm{d}\xi_t = -\frac{\xi_t}{T-t}\,\mathrm{d}t + \mathrm{d}W_t^*. \tag{15.2}$$

Substituting this relation in (15.1) we obtain

$$\Lambda_t = \exp\left[D_T \left(\int_0^t \nu_s \mathrm{d}\xi_s + \int_0^t \frac{1}{T-s} \nu_s \xi_s \mathrm{d}s \right) - \frac{1}{2} D_T^2 \int_0^t \nu_s^2 \mathrm{d}s \right]. \tag{15.3}$$

In principle at this point all we need to do is to substitute (14.2) into (15.3) to obtain the result for $\{\Lambda_t\}$. In practice, further simplification can be achieved. To this end, we note that by taking the differential of the coefficient of D_T in the exponent of (15.3) we get

$$\begin{aligned} \mathrm{d}\left(\int_0^t \nu_s \mathrm{d}\xi_s + \int_0^t \frac{1}{T-s} \nu_s \xi_s \mathrm{d}s \right) &= \nu_t \left(\mathrm{d}\xi_t + \frac{1}{T-t} \xi_t \mathrm{d}t \right) \\ &= \left(\sigma_t + \frac{1}{T-t} \int_0^t \sigma_s \mathrm{d}s \right) \left(\mathrm{d}\xi_t + \frac{1}{T-t} \xi_t \mathrm{d}t \right) \\ &= \mathrm{d}\left(\frac{1}{T-t} \xi_t \int_0^t \sigma_s \mathrm{d}s + \int_0^t \sigma_s \mathrm{d}\xi_s \right). \end{aligned} \tag{15.4}$$

Then integrating both sides of (15.4) we obtain:

$$\int_0^t \nu_s \mathrm{d}\xi_s + \int_0^t \frac{1}{T-s} \nu_s \xi_s \mathrm{d}s = \frac{1}{T-t} \xi_t \int_0^t \sigma_s \mathrm{d}s + \int_0^t \sigma_s \mathrm{d}\xi_s. \tag{15.5}$$

Similarly, by taking the differential of the coefficient of $-\frac{1}{2}D_T^2$ in the exponent of (15.3) and making use of (14.2), we find

$$\begin{aligned} \nu_t^2 \mathrm{d}t &= \left[\sigma_t^2 + 2\frac{1}{T-t} \sigma_t \int_0^t \sigma_s \mathrm{d}s + \frac{1}{(T-t)^2} \left(\int_0^t \sigma_s \mathrm{d}s \right)^2 \right] dt \\ &= \mathrm{d}\left[\frac{1}{T-t} \left(\int_0^t \sigma_s \mathrm{d}s \right)^2 + \int_0^t \sigma_s^2 \mathrm{d}s \right]. \end{aligned} \tag{15.6}$$

Therefore, by integrating both sides of (15.6) we obtain an identity for the coefficient of the term $-\frac{1}{2}D_T^2$.

It follows by virtue of the two identities just obtained that $\{\Lambda_t\}$ can be expressed in terms of $\{\xi_t\}$. More explicitly, we have

$$\Lambda_t = \exp\Bigg[D_T\left(\frac{1}{T-t}\,\xi_t\int_0^t \sigma_s \mathrm{d}s + \int_0^t \sigma_s \mathrm{d}\xi_s\right) \\ -\frac{1}{2}D_T^2\left(\frac{1}{T-t}\left(\int_0^t \sigma_s \mathrm{d}s\right)^2 + \int_0^t \sigma_s^2 \mathrm{d}s\right)\Bigg]. \tag{15.7}$$

Note that by transforming (15.3) into (15.7) we have eliminated a term having $\{\xi_t\}$ in the integrand, thus achieving a considerable simplification. Proposition 13.1 can then be deduced if we use equation (14.9) and the basic relation

$$\mathbb{Q}(D_T \le x|\mathcal{F}_t) = \mathbb{E}^{\mathbb{Q}}[\mathbb{1}_{\{D_T\le x\}}|\mathcal{F}_t]. \tag{15.8}$$

In particular, since D_T and $\{\xi_t\}$ are independent under the bridge measure, by virtue of (14.6), (15.7), and (15.8) we obtain

$$\mathbb{Q}(D_T \le x|\mathcal{F}_t) = \frac{\int_0^x p(y)\,\mathrm{e}^{y\left(\frac{1}{T-t}\xi_t\int_0^t\sigma_s\mathrm{d}s+\int_0^t\sigma_s\mathrm{d}\xi_s\right)-\frac{1}{2}y^2\left(\frac{1}{T-t}\left(\int_0^t\sigma_s\mathrm{d}s\right)^2+\int_0^t\sigma_s^2\mathrm{d}s\right)}\mathrm{d}y}{\int_0^\infty p(y)\,\mathrm{e}^{y\left(\frac{1}{T-t}\xi_t\int_0^t\sigma_s\mathrm{d}s+\int_0^t\sigma_s\mathrm{d}\xi_s\right)-\frac{1}{2}y^2\left(\frac{1}{T-t}\left(\int_0^t\sigma_s\mathrm{d}s\right)^2+\int_0^t\sigma_s^2\mathrm{d}s\right)}\mathrm{d}y}, \tag{15.9}$$

from which we infer Proposition 13.1 by differentiation with respect to x.

We conclude this section by noting that an alternative expression for $\{\pi_t(x)\}$, written in terms of $\{W_t^*\}$, is given by

$$\pi_t(x) = \frac{p(x)\,\exp\left(x\int_0^t \nu_u \mathrm{d}W_u^* - \frac{1}{2}x^2\int_0^t \nu_u^2\mathrm{d}u\right)}{\int_0^\infty p(x)\,\exp\left(x\int_0^t \nu_u \mathrm{d}W_u^* - \frac{1}{2}x^2\int_0^t \nu_u^2\mathrm{d}u\right)\mathrm{d}x}. \tag{15.10}$$

16. Consistency Relations

Before we proceed to analyse in detail the dynamics of the price process $\{S_t\}$, first we shall establish a useful *dynamical consistency* relation satisfied by prices obtained in the information-based framework. By "consistency" we have in mind the following. Suppose that we re-initialise the information process at an intermediate time $s \in (0, T)$ by specifying the value ξ_s of the information at that time. For the framework to be dynamically consistent, we require that the remainder of the period $[s, T]$ admits a representation in terms of a suitably "renormalised" information process. Specifically, we have:

Proposition 16.1. *Let $0 \leq s \leq t \leq T$. The conditional probability $\pi_t(x)$ can be written in terms of the intermediate conditional probability $\pi_s(x)$ in the form*

$$\pi_t(x) = \frac{\pi_s(x)\, \mathrm{e}^{x\left(\frac{1}{T-t}\eta_t \int_s^t \tilde{\sigma}_u \mathrm{d}u + \int_s^t \tilde{\sigma}_u \mathrm{d}\eta_u\right) - \frac{1}{2}x^2\left(\frac{1}{T-t}\left(\int_s^t \tilde{\sigma}_u \mathrm{d}u\right)^2 + \int_s^t \tilde{\sigma}_u^2 \mathrm{d}u\right)}}{\int_0^\infty \pi_s(x)\, \mathrm{e}^{x\left(\frac{1}{T-t}\eta_t \int_s^t \tilde{\sigma}_u \mathrm{d}u + \int_s^t \tilde{\sigma}_u \mathrm{d}\eta_u\right) - \frac{1}{2}x^2\left(\frac{1}{T-t}\left(\int_s^t \tilde{\sigma}_u \mathrm{d}u\right)^2 + \int_s^t \tilde{\sigma}_u^2 \mathrm{d}u\right)} \mathrm{d}x}, \tag{16.1}$$

where

$$\tilde{\sigma}_u = \sigma_u + \frac{1}{T-s}\int_0^s \sigma_v \mathrm{d}v \tag{16.2}$$

is the re-initialised market information-flow rate, and

$$\eta_t = \xi_t - \frac{T-t}{T-s}\xi_s \tag{16.3}$$

is the re-initialised information process.

The fact that $\{\eta_t\}_{s\leq t\leq T}$ represents the updated information process bridging the interval $[s,T]$ can be seen as follows. First, we note that $\eta_s = 0$ and that $\eta_T = \xi_T$. Substituting (13.1) in (16.3) we find that

$$\eta_t = D_T \int_s^t \tilde{\sigma}_u \mathrm{d}u + \gamma_{tT}, \tag{16.4}$$

where $\tilde{\sigma}_u$ is as defined in (16.2), and

$$\gamma_{tT} = \beta_{tT} - \frac{T-t}{T-s}\beta_{sT}. \tag{16.5}$$

A calculation making use of the covariance of $\{\beta_{tT}\}$ shows that the Gaussian process $\{\gamma_{tT}\}_{s\leq t\leq T}$ is a standard Brownian bridge over the interval $[s,T]$. It follows that $\{\eta_t\}$ is the information bridge interpolating the interval $[s,T]$.

To verify (16.1) we note that (15.10) can be written in the form

$$\pi_t(x) = \frac{\pi_s(x)\,\exp\left(x\int_s^t \nu_u \mathrm{d}W_u^* - \frac{1}{2}x^2\int_s^t \nu_u^2 \mathrm{d}u\right)}{\int_0^\infty \pi_s(x)\,\exp\left(x\int_s^t \nu_u \mathrm{d}W_u^* - \frac{1}{2}x^2\int_s^t \nu_u^2 \mathrm{d}u\right)\mathrm{d}x}. \tag{16.6}$$

The identity (15.4) then implies that

$$\begin{aligned}\int_s^t \nu_u \mathrm{d}W_u^* &= \frac{1}{T-t}\xi_t \int_s^t \sigma_u \mathrm{d}u + \int_s^t \sigma_u \mathrm{d}\xi_u + \left(\frac{\xi_t}{T-t} - \frac{\xi_s}{T-s}\right)\int_0^s \sigma_u \mathrm{d}u \\ &= \frac{1}{T-t}\eta_t \int_s^t \tilde{\sigma}_u \mathrm{d}u + \int_s^t \tilde{\sigma}_u \mathrm{d}\eta_u,\end{aligned} \tag{16.7}$$

where we have made use of (16.2) and (16.3). Similarly, (15.5) implies that

$$\begin{aligned}\int_s^t \nu_u^2 \mathrm{d}u &= \frac{1}{T-t}\left(\int_0^t \sigma_u \mathrm{d}u\right)^2 - \frac{1}{T-s}\left(\int_0^s \sigma_u \mathrm{d}u\right)^2 + \int_s^t \sigma_u^2 \mathrm{d}u \\ &= \frac{1}{T-t}\left(\int_s^t \tilde{\sigma}_u \mathrm{d}u\right)^2 + \int_s^t \tilde{\sigma}_u^2 \mathrm{d}u. \end{aligned} \tag{16.8}$$

Substitution of (16.7) and (16.8) into (16.6) establishes (16.1). In particular, the form of (16.1) is identical to the original formula (13.4), modulo the indicated renormalisation of the information process and the associated information flow rate.

17. Expected Dividend

The goal of Secs. 13, 14, and 15 was to obtain an expression for the conditional expectation (5.1) in the case of a single-dividend asset when one has a time-dependent information-flow rate. In the analysis of the price process it will be useful to work out the dynamics of the conditional expectation of the dividend. In particular, an application of Ito's rule to (13.5), after some rearrangement, shows that

$$\mathrm{d}D_{tT} = \nu_t V_t \left(\frac{1}{T-t}\xi_t - \nu_t D_{tT}\right)\mathrm{d}t + \nu_t V_t \mathrm{d}\xi_t, \tag{17.1}$$

where $\{V_t\}$ is the conditional variance of the random variable D_T, given by (5.4). Let us define a new process $\{W_t\}$ by

$$W_t = \xi_t + \int_0^t \frac{1}{T-s}\xi_s \mathrm{d}s - \int_0^t \nu_s D_{sT} \mathrm{d}s. \tag{17.2}$$

We refer to $\{W_t\}$ as the "innovation process". It follows from the definition of $\{W_t\}$ that

$$\mathrm{d}D_{tT} = \nu_t V_t \,\mathrm{d}W_t. \tag{17.3}$$

Since $\{D_{tT}\}$ is an $\{\mathcal{F}_t\}$-martingale we are thus led to conjecture that $\{W_t\}$ must also be an $\{\mathcal{F}_t\}$-martingale. In fact, we have the following result:

Proposition 17.1. *The process $\{W_t\}$ defined by (17.2) is an $\{\mathcal{F}_t\}$-Brownian motion under $\mathbb{Q}$.*

Proof. We need to establish that (i) $\{W_t\}$ is an $\{\mathcal{F}_t\}$-martingale, and that (ii) $(\mathrm{d}W_t)^2 = \mathrm{d}t$. Writing $\mathbb{E}_t[-] = \mathbb{E}^{\mathbb{Q}}[-|\mathcal{F}_t]$ and letting $t \le u$ we have

$$\mathbb{E}_t[W_u] = \mathbb{E}_t[\xi_u] + \mathbb{E}_t\left[\int_0^u \frac{1}{T-s}\xi_s \mathrm{d}s\right] - \mathbb{E}_t\left[\int_0^u \nu_s D_{sT} \mathrm{d}s\right]. \tag{17.4}$$

Splitting the second two terms on the right into integrals between 0 and t, and between t and u, we obtain

$$\mathbb{E}_t[W_u] = \mathbb{E}_t[\xi_u] + \int_0^t \frac{1}{T-s}\,\xi_s \mathrm{d}s - \int_0^t \nu_s D_{sT} \mathrm{d}s$$

$$+ \int_t^u \frac{1}{T-s}\,\mathbb{E}_t[\xi_s] \mathrm{d}s - \int_t^u \nu_s \mathbb{E}_t[D_{sT}] \mathrm{d}s. \tag{17.5}$$

The martingale property of the conditional expectation implies that $\mathbb{E}_t[D_{sT}] = D_{tT}$ for $t \leq s$, which allows us to simplify the last term. To simplify the expression for the expectation $\mathbb{E}_t[\xi_s]$ for $t \leq s$ we use the tower property:

$$\mathbb{E}_t[\beta_{sT}] = \mathbb{E}_t[\mathbb{E}[\beta_{sT}|H_T, \beta_{tT}]] = \mathbb{E}_t[\mathbb{E}[\beta_{sT}|\beta_{tT}]]. \tag{17.6}$$

To calculate the inner expectation $\mathbb{E}[\beta_{sT}|\beta_{tT}]$ we use the fact that the random variable $\beta_{sT}/(T-s) - \beta_{tT}/(T-t)$ is independent of β_{tT} and deduce that

$$\mathbb{E}[\beta_{sT}|\beta_{tT}] = \frac{T-s}{T-t}\,\beta_{tT}, \tag{17.7}$$

from which it follows that

$$\mathbb{E}_t[\beta_{sT}] = \frac{T-s}{T-t}\,\mathbb{E}_t[\beta_{tT}]. \tag{17.8}$$

As a result we obtain

$$\mathbb{E}_t[\xi_s] = D_{tT} \int_0^s \sigma_v \mathrm{d}v + \frac{T-s}{T-t}\,\mathbb{E}_t[\beta_{tT}]. \tag{17.9}$$

We also recall the definition of $\{W_t\}$ given by (17.2), which implies that

$$\int_0^t \frac{1}{T-s}\,\xi_s \mathrm{d}s - \int_0^t \nu_s D_{sT} \mathrm{d}s = W_t - \xi_t. \tag{17.10}$$

Therefore, substituting (17.9) and (17.10) into (17.5) we obtain

$$\mathbb{E}_t[W_u] = D_{tT} \int_0^u \sigma_s \mathrm{d}s + W_t - \xi_t + D_{tT} \int_t^u \frac{1}{T-s} \left(\int_0^s \sigma_v \mathrm{d}v \right) \mathrm{d}s$$

$$- D_{tT} \int_t^u \nu_s \mathrm{d}s + \mathbb{E}_t[\beta_{tT}]. \tag{17.11}$$

Next we split the first term into an integral from 0 to t and an integral from t to u, and we insert the definition (14.2) of $\{\nu_t\}$ into the fifth term. The result is:

$$\mathbb{E}_t[W_u] = W_t + D_{tT} \int_0^t \sigma_s \mathrm{d}s + \mathbb{E}_t[\beta_{tT}] - \xi_t. \tag{17.12}$$

Finally, if we make use of the fact that $\xi_t = \mathbb{E}_t[\xi_t]$, and hence that

$$\xi_t = D_{tT} \int_0^t \sigma_s \mathrm{d}s + \mathbb{E}_t[\beta_{tT}], \tag{17.13}$$

we see that $\{W_t\}$ satisfies the martingale condition. On the other hand, by virtue of (17.2) we have $(\mathrm{d}W_t)^2 = \mathrm{d}t$. We conclude that $\{W_t\}$ is an $\{\mathcal{F}_t\}$-Brownian motion under the measure $\mathbb{Q}$. □

18. Asset Prices and Derivative Prices

We are now in a position to consider in more detail the dynamics of the price process of an asset paying a single dividend D_T in the case of a time-dependent information flow. For $\{S_t\}$ we have $S_t = \mathbb{1}_{\{t<T\}} P_{tT} D_{tT}$, or equivalently

$$S_t = \mathbb{1}_{\{t<T\}} P_{tT} \frac{\int_0^\infty x p(x)\, \mathrm{e}^{x\left(\frac{1}{T-t}\xi_t \int_0^t \sigma_s \mathrm{d}s + \int_0^t \sigma_s \mathrm{d}\xi_s\right) - \frac{1}{2}x^2\left(\frac{1}{T-t}\left(\int_0^t \sigma_s \mathrm{d}s\right)^2 + \int_0^t \sigma_s^2 \mathrm{d}s\right)} \mathrm{d}x}{\int_0^\infty p(x)\, \mathrm{e}^{x\left(\frac{1}{T-t}\xi_t \int_0^t \sigma_s \mathrm{d}s + \int_0^t \sigma_s \mathrm{d}\xi_s\right) - \frac{1}{2}x^2\left(\frac{1}{T-t}\left(\int_0^t \sigma_s \mathrm{d}s\right)^2 + \int_0^t \sigma_s^2 \mathrm{d}s\right)} \mathrm{d}x}. \tag{18.1}$$

A calculation making use of (17.3) shows that for the dynamics of the price we have

$$\mathrm{d}S_t = r_t S_t \mathrm{d}t + \Gamma_{tT} \mathrm{d}W_t, \tag{18.2}$$

where the asset price volatility is given by $\Gamma_{tT} = \nu_t P_{tT} V_t$, and V_t is the conditional variance of the dividend, given by (5.4). It should be evident by virtue of its definition that $\{V_t\}$ is a supermartingale. More specifically, for the dynamics of $\{V_t\}$ we obtain

$$\mathrm{d}V_t = -\nu_t^2 V_t^2 \mathrm{d}t + \nu_t \kappa_t \mathrm{d}W_t, \tag{18.3}$$

where κ_t denotes the third conditional moment of the random variable D_T, given by the expression $\kappa_t = \mathbb{E}_t\left[(D_T - D_{tT})^3\right]$.

Although we have derived (18.1) by assuming that the price process is induced by the market information $\{\xi_t\}$, the result to be shown in Sec. 19 demonstrates that we can regard the dynamical equation (18.2) for the price process as given, and then deduce the structure of the underlying information. The information-based interpretation of the modelling framework, however, is more appealing. According to this interpretation there is a flow of market information, which is available to all market participants and is represented by the filtration generated by $\{\xi_t\}$. Given this information, each participant will "act", in our interpretation, so as to minimise the risk adjusted future P&L variance associated with the cash flow under consideration. The future P&L is determined by the value of D_T, and the estimate of D_T that minimises its variance is indeed given by the conditional expectation (5.1). By discounting this expectation with P_{tT} we recover the price process $\{S_t\}$.

We note that $\{\Gamma_{tT}\}$ is "infinitely stochastic" in the sense that all of the higher-order volatilities (the volatility of the volatility, and so on) are stochastic. These higher-order volatilities have a natural interpretation: the volatility of the asset price is determined by the variance of the random cash flow; the volatility of the volatility is determined by the skewness of D_T; its volatility is determined by the kurtosis of D_T; and so on.

The fact that the asset price in the bridge measure is given by a function of a Gaussian random variable means that the pricing of derivatives is numerically straightforward. We have seen this in the case of a constant information-flow rate, but the result holds in the time-dependent case as well. For example, consider a

European-style call option with strike K and maturity t, where $t \le T$, for which the value is (6.1). If we express the asset price S_t on the option maturity date in terms of the $\mathbb{B}$-Brownian motion $\{W_t^*\}$ we find

$$C_0 = P_{0t}\mathbb{E}^{\mathbb{Q}}\left[\frac{1}{\Phi_t}\left\{\int_0^\infty (P_{tT}x - K)p(x)\exp\left(x\int_0^t \nu_s \mathrm{d}W_s^* - \frac{1}{2}x^2\int_0^t \nu_s^2 \mathrm{d}s\right)\mathrm{d}x\right\}^+\right], \tag{18.4}$$

where

$$\Phi_t = \int_0^\infty p(x)\exp\left(x\int_0^t \nu_s \mathrm{d}W_s^* - \frac{1}{2}x^2\int_0^t \nu_s^2 \mathrm{d}s\right)\mathrm{d}x. \tag{18.5}$$

To proceed we shall use the factor $1/\Phi_t$ in (18.4) to make a change of measure on $(\Omega, \mathcal{F}_t)$. The idea is as follows. We fix a time horizon u at or beyond the option expiration but before the bond maturity, so $t \le u < T$, and define a process $\{\Phi_t\}_{0\le t\le u}$ by use of the expression (18.5), where now we let t vary in the range $[0, u]$. By an application of Ito calculus on (18.5) we see that $\mathrm{d}\Phi_t = \nu_t D_{tT}\Phi_t\,\mathrm{d}W_t^*$. On the other hand, it follows from (15.2) and (17.2) that the $\mathbb{B}$-Brownian motion $\{W_t^*\}$ and the $\mathbb{Q}$-Brownian motion $\{W_t\}$ are related by

$$\mathrm{d}W_t^* = \mathrm{d}W_t + \nu_t D_{tT}\mathrm{d}t. \tag{18.6}$$

Therefore, in terms of $\{W_t\}$ we have

$$\mathrm{d}\Phi_t = \nu_t^2 D_{tT}^2\Phi_t \mathrm{d}t + \nu_t D_{tT}\Phi_t\,\mathrm{d}W_t, \tag{18.7}$$

from which it follows that

$$\mathrm{d}\Phi_t^{-1} = -\nu_t D_{tT}\Phi_t^{-1}\mathrm{d}W_t. \tag{18.8}$$

Upon integration we deduce

$$\Phi_t^{-1} = \exp\left(-\int_0^t \nu_s D_{sT}\,\mathrm{d}W_s - \frac{1}{2}\int_0^t \nu_s^2 D_{sT}^2\,\mathrm{d}s\right). \tag{18.9}$$

Since $\{\nu_s D_{sT}\}$ is bounded, and $s \le u < T$, we see that $\{\Phi_s^{-1}\}_{0\le s\le u}$ is a $\mathbb{Q}$-martingale with $\mathbb{E}^{\mathbb{Q}}[\Phi_t^{-1}] = 1$, where t is the option maturity date. Therefore, the factor $1/\Phi_t$ in (18.4) can be used to effect a change of measure $\mathbb{Q} \to \mathbb{B}$ on $(\Omega, \mathcal{F}_t)$. We note that while on the space $(\Omega, \mathcal{G}_t)$ it is the process $\{\Lambda_t\}$ introduced in (14.3) that defines the measure change from $\mathbb{B}$ and $\mathbb{Q}$, on $(\Omega, \mathcal{F}_t)$ it is $\Phi_t = \mathbb{E}^{\mathbb{Q}}[\Lambda_t|\mathcal{F}_t]$ that defines the relevant measure change. As a consequence, by changing the measure in (18.4) we obtain

$$C_0 = P_{0t}\mathbb{E}^{\mathbb{B}}\left[\left\{\int_0^\infty (P_{tT}x - K)p(x)\exp\left(x\int_0^t \nu_s \mathrm{d}W_s^* - \frac{1}{2}x^2\int_0^t \nu_s^2 \mathrm{d}s\right)\mathrm{d}x\right\}^+\right]. \tag{18.10}$$

This result should be compared with (6.5). We note that in the bridge measure the expression $\int_0^t \nu_s \mathrm{d}W_s^*$ is a Gaussian random variable with mean zero and variance

$$\omega_t^2 = \int_0^t \nu_s^2 \mathrm{d}s = \frac{1}{T-t}\left(\int_0^t \sigma_s \mathrm{d}s\right)^2 + \int_0^t \sigma_s^2 \mathrm{d}s. \tag{18.11}$$

Here we have used the relation (15.6). Therefore, if we set

$$Y = \omega_t^{-1} \int_0^t \nu_s \mathrm{d}W_s^*, \tag{18.12}$$

it follows that Y is $\mathbb{B}$-Gaussian. For the call price we thus have

$$C_0 = P_{0t}\mathbb{E}^{\mathbb{B}}\left[\left\{\int_0^\infty (P_{tT}x - K)p(x)\mathrm{e}^{\omega_t xY - \frac{1}{2}\omega_t^2 x^2}\mathrm{d}x\right\}^+\right], \tag{18.13}$$

and hence

$$C_0 = P_{0t}\frac{1}{\sqrt{2\pi}}\int_{y=-\infty}^\infty \mathrm{e}^{-\frac{1}{2}y^2}\left(\int_{x=0}^\infty (P_{tT}x - K)p(x)\mathrm{e}^{\omega_t xy - \frac{1}{2}\omega_t^2 x^2}\mathrm{d}x\right)^+ \mathrm{d}y. \tag{18.14}$$

We observe that there exists a critical value $y = y^*$ such that the argument of the "plus" function vanishes in the expression above. Thus y^* is given by

$$\int_0^\infty (P_{tT}x - K)p(x)\,\mathrm{e}^{\omega_t xy^* - \frac{1}{2}\omega_t^2 x^2}\mathrm{d}x = 0. \tag{18.15}$$

As a consequence the call price can be written

$$C_0 = P_{0t}\frac{1}{\sqrt{2\pi}}\int_{y=y^*}^\infty \mathrm{e}^{-\frac{1}{2}y^2}\left(\int_{x=0}^\infty (P_{tT}x - K)p(x)\mathrm{e}^{\omega_t xy - \frac{1}{2}\omega_t^2 x^2}\mathrm{d}x\right)\mathrm{d}y. \tag{18.16}$$

The integration in the y variable can be performed, and we deduce the following representation for the call price:

$$C_0 = P_{0t}\int_0^\infty (P_{tT}x - K)p(x)N(\omega_t x - y^*)\mathrm{d}x. \tag{18.17}$$

When the cash flow is represented by a discrete random variable and the information-flow rate is constant, this result reduces to an expression equivalent to the option pricing formula derived in Brody *et al.* [3]. If the cash flow is a continuous random variable and the information flow rate is constant then we recover the expression (6.9) given in Sec. IV (see also Rutkowski and Yu [23]).

We conclude this section with the remark that the simulation of $\{S_t\}$ is straightforward. First, we generate a Brownian trajectory, and form the associated Brownian bridge $\{\beta_{tT}(\omega)\}$. We then select a value for D_T by a method consistent with the *a priori* probability density $p(x)$, and substitute these in the formula $\xi_t(\omega) = D_T(\omega)\int_0^t \sigma_s \mathrm{d}s + \beta_{tT}(\omega)$ for some choice of $\{\sigma_t\}$. Finally, substitution of $\{\xi_t(\omega)\}$ in (18.1) gives us a simulated path $\{S_t(\omega)\}$. The statistics of the process $\{S_t\}$ are obtained by repeating this procedure, the results of which can be used to price derivatives, or to calibrate the information-flow rate $\{\sigma_t\}$.

19. Existence of the Information Process

We consider now what might be called the "inverse problem" for information-based asset pricing. The idea is to begin with the conditional density process $\{\pi_t(x)\}$ and to construct from it the independent degrees of freedom represented by the X-factor D_T and the noise $\{\beta_{tT}\}$. The setup is as follows. On the probability space $(\Omega, \mathcal{F}, \mathbb{Q})$ let $\{W_t\}$ be a Brownian motion and let $\{\mathcal{F}_t\}$ be the filtration generated by $\{W_t\}$. Let D_T be $\mathcal{F}_T$-measurable, and let $\{\pi_t(x)\}$ denote the associated conditional probability density process. We assume that $\{\pi_t(x)\}$ satisfies the stochastic differential equation

$$\mathrm{d}\pi_t(x) = \nu_t(x - D_{tT})\pi_t(x)\,\mathrm{d}W_t, \tag{19.1}$$

with the initial condition $\pi_0(x) = p(x)$, where $\{\nu_t\}$ is given by (14.2), and where

$$D_{tT} = \int_0^\infty x\pi_t(x)\,\mathrm{d}x. \tag{19.2}$$

We define the process $\{\xi_t\}$ as follows:

$$\xi_t = (T-t)\int_0^t \frac{1}{T-s}(\mathrm{d}W_s + \nu_s D_{sT}\mathrm{d}s). \tag{19.3}$$

Then we have the following result:

Proposition 19.1. *The random variables D_T and $\beta_{tT} = \xi_t - D_T\int_0^t \sigma_s \mathrm{d}s$ are $\mathbb{Q}$-independent for $t \in [0,T]$. Furthermore, the process $\{\beta_{tT}\}$ is a $\mathbb{Q}$-Brownian bridge.*

Proof. To establish the independence of D_T and β_{tT} it suffices to verify that

$$\mathbb{E}^{\mathbb{Q}}[\mathrm{e}^{x\beta_{tT}+yD_T}] = \mathbb{E}^{\mathbb{Q}}[\mathrm{e}^{x\beta_{tT}}]\,\mathbb{E}^{\mathbb{Q}}[\mathrm{e}^{yD_T}] \tag{19.4}$$

for arbitrary x, y. Using the tower property we have

$$\mathbb{E}^{\mathbb{Q}}[\mathrm{e}^{x\beta_{tT}+yD_T}] = \mathbb{E}^{\mathbb{Q}}[\mathrm{e}^{x\xi_t}\,\mathbb{E}_t^{\mathbb{Q}}[\mathrm{e}^{(y-x\int_0^t \sigma_s \mathrm{d}s)D_T}]], \tag{19.5}$$

where we have inserted the definition of β_{tT} given in the statement of the Proposition. We consider the inner expectation first. From equation (14.6) for the conditional expectation of a function of D_T we deduce that

$$\mathbb{E}_t^{\mathbb{Q}}[\mathrm{e}^{(y-x\int_0^t \sigma_s \mathrm{d}s)D_T}] = \Phi_t^{-1}\int_0^\infty p(z)\,\mathrm{e}^{(y-x\int_0^t \sigma_s \mathrm{d}s)z}\,\mathrm{e}^{z\int_0^t \nu_u \mathrm{d}W_u^* - \frac{1}{2}z^2\int_0^t \nu_u^2 \mathrm{d}u}\mathrm{d}z, \tag{19.6}$$

where the process $\{\Phi_t\}$ is defined by (18.5). We now change the probability measure from $\mathbb{Q}$ to $\mathbb{B}$, so that the term Φ_t^{-1} appearing in (19.6) drops out to give us

$$
\begin{aligned}
&\mathbb{E}^{\mathbb{Q}}[\mathrm{e}^{x\xi_t}\,\mathbb{E}_t^{\mathbb{Q}}[\mathrm{e}^{(y-x\int_0^t\sigma_s\mathrm{d}s)D_T}]]\\
&\quad=\mathbb{E}^{\mathbb{B}}\left[\mathrm{e}^{x\xi_t}\int_0^\infty p(z)\,\mathrm{e}^{(y-x\int_0^t\sigma_s\mathrm{d}s)z}\,\mathrm{e}^{z\int_0^t\nu_u\mathrm{d}W_u^*-\frac{1}{2}z^2\int_0^t\nu_u^2\mathrm{d}u}\mathrm{d}z\right]\\
&\quad=\int_0^\infty p(z)\,\mathbb{E}^{\mathbb{B}}\left[\mathrm{e}^{x(T-t)\int_0^t\frac{1}{T-s}\mathrm{d}W_s^*+(y-x\int_0^t\sigma_s\mathrm{d}s)z+z\int_0^t\nu_s\mathrm{d}W_s^*-\frac{1}{2}z^2\int_0^t\nu_s^2\mathrm{d}s}\right]\mathrm{d}z\\
&\quad=\int_0^\infty p(z)\,\mathrm{e}^{(y-x\int_0^t\sigma_s\mathrm{d}s)z-\frac{1}{2}z^2\int_0^t\nu_s^2\mathrm{d}s+\frac{1}{2}\int_0^t\alpha_s^2\mathrm{d}s}\,\mathbb{E}^{\mathbb{B}}\left[\mathrm{e}^{\int_0^t\alpha_s\mathrm{d}W_s^*-\frac{1}{2}\int_0^t\alpha_s^2\mathrm{d}s}\right]\mathrm{d}z,
\end{aligned}
\tag{19.7}
$$

where $\alpha_s = x(T-t)/(T-s) + z\nu_s$, and therefore

$$
\mathbb{E}^{\mathbb{Q}}[\mathrm{e}^{x\beta_{tT}+yD_T}]=\int_0^\infty p(z)\,\mathrm{e}^{(y-x\int_0^t\sigma_s\mathrm{d}s)z-\frac{1}{2}z^2\int_0^t\nu_s^2\mathrm{d}s+\frac{1}{2}\int_0^t\alpha_s^2\mathrm{d}s}\mathrm{d}z. \tag{19.8}
$$

Furthermore, making use of relation (14.9) we have

$$
\exp\left(-xz\int_0^t\sigma_s\mathrm{d}s-\frac{1}{2}z^2\int_0^t\nu_s^2\mathrm{d}s+\frac{1}{2}\int_0^t\alpha_s^2\mathrm{d}s\right)=\exp\left(\frac{t(T-t)}{2T}\,x^2\right). \tag{19.9}
$$

As a consequence, it follows from (19.8) that

$$
\mathbb{E}^{\mathbb{Q}}[\mathrm{e}^{x\beta_{tT}+yD_T}]=\left(\int_0^\infty p(z)\,\mathrm{e}^{yz}\mathrm{d}z\right)\exp\left(\frac{t(T-t)}{2T}x^2\right). \tag{19.10}
$$

This establishes the independence of $\{\beta_{tT}\}$ and D_T.

The factorisation (19.10) also shows that the process $\{\beta_{tT}\}$ is $\mathbb{Q}$-Gaussian, with mean zero and variance $t(T-t)/T$. To establish that $\{\beta_{tT}\}$ is a Brownian bridge, we must show that for $s \le t$ the covariance of β_{sT} and β_{tT} is given by $s(T-t)/T$. Alternatively, it suffices to analyse the moment generating function $\mathbb{E}[\mathrm{e}^{x\beta_{sT}+y\beta_{tT}}]$. We proceed as follows. First, using the tower property we have

$$
\begin{aligned}
\mathbb{E}^{\mathbb{Q}}[\mathrm{e}^{x\beta_{sT}+y\beta_{tT}}]&=\mathbb{E}[\mathrm{e}^{x\xi_s+y\xi_t-(x\int_0^s\sigma_u\mathrm{d}u+y\int_0^t\sigma_u\mathrm{d}u)D_T}]\\
&=\mathbb{E}[\mathrm{e}^{x\xi_s+y\xi_t}\mathbb{E}_t^{\mathbb{Q}}[\mathrm{e}^{-(x\int_0^s\sigma_u\mathrm{d}u+y\int_0^t\sigma_u\mathrm{d}u)D_T}]].
\end{aligned}
\tag{19.11}
$$

Next, by use of formula (14.6), the inner expectation can be carried out to give

$$
\begin{aligned}
&\mathbb{E}^{\mathbb{Q}}[\mathrm{e}^{x\beta_{sT}+y\beta_{tT}}]\\
&\quad=\mathbb{E}\left[\mathrm{e}^{x\xi_s+y\xi_t}\Phi_t^{-1}\int_0^\infty p(z)\,\mathrm{e}^{-(x\int_0^s\sigma_u\mathrm{d}u+y\int_0^t\sigma_u\mathrm{d}u)z}\,\mathrm{e}^{z\int_0^t\nu_u\mathrm{d}W_u^*-\frac{1}{2}z^2\int_0^t\nu_u^2\mathrm{d}u}\mathrm{d}z\right].
\end{aligned}
\tag{19.12}
$$

If we change the probability measure to $\mathbb{B}$ the random variable Φ_t in the denominator drops out, and we have

$$\mathbb{E}^{\mathbb{Q}}[\mathrm{e}^{x\beta_{sT}+y\beta_{tT}}] \\ = \int_0^\infty p(z)\,\mathrm{e}^{-(x\int_0^s \sigma_u \mathrm{d}u + y\int_0^t \sigma_u \mathrm{d}u)z - \frac{1}{2}z^2\int_0^t \nu_u^2 \mathrm{d}u}\,\mathbb{E}^{\mathbb{B}}[\mathrm{e}^{x\xi_s + y\xi_t + z\int_0^t \nu_s \mathrm{d}W_s^*}]\mathrm{d}z. \tag{19.13}$$

Let us consider the inner expectation first. By defining $a_u = x(T-s)/(T-u)$ and $b_u = y(T-t)/(T-u) + z\nu_u$ we can write

$$\mathbb{E}^{\mathbb{B}}[\mathrm{e}^{x\xi_s + y\xi_t + z\int_0^t \nu_s \mathrm{d}W_s^*}] = \mathbb{E}^{\mathbb{B}}[\mathrm{e}^{\int_0^s a_u \mathrm{d}W_u^* + \int_0^t b_u \mathrm{d}W_u^*}]. \tag{19.14}$$

However, since $\{W_t^*\}$ is a $\mathbb{B}$-Brownian motion, using the properties of Gaussian random variable we find that

$$\mathbb{E}^{\mathbb{B}}[\mathrm{e}^{\int_0^s a_u \mathrm{d}W_u^* + \int_0^t b_u \mathrm{d}W_u^*}] = \exp\left\{\frac{1}{2}\left(\int_0^s a_u^2 \mathrm{d}u + \int_0^t b_u^2 \mathrm{d}u + 2\int_0^s a_u b_u \mathrm{d}u\right)\right\}. \tag{19.15}$$

Substituting the definitions of $\{a_u\}$ and $\{b_u\}$ into the right side of (19.15) and combining the result with the remaining terms in the exponent of the right side of (19.13) we find that the terms involving the integration variable z drop out, and we are left with the integral of the density function $p(z)$, which is unity. Gathering the remaining terms we obtain

$$\mathbb{E}^{\mathbb{Q}}[\mathrm{e}^{x\beta_{sT}+y\beta_{tT}}] = \exp\left\{\frac{1}{2}\left(x^2\,\frac{s(T-s)}{T} + y^2\,\frac{t(T-t)}{T} + 2xy\,\frac{s(T-t)}{T}\right)\right\}. \tag{19.16}$$

It follows that the covariance of β_{sT} and β_{tT} for $s \leq t$ is given by

$$\frac{\partial^2}{\partial x \partial y}\mathbb{E}^{\mathbb{Q}}\left[\mathrm{e}^{x}\,\beta_{sT} + y\beta_{tT}\right]\bigg|_{x=y=0} = \frac{s(T-t)}{T}. \tag{19.17}$$

This establishes the assertion that $\{\beta_{tT}\}$ is a $\mathbb{Q}$-Brownian bridge. □

The result above shows that, for the class of price processes we are considering, even if at the outset we take the "usual" point of view in financial modelling, and regard the price process of the asset as being adapted to some "prespecified" filtration, nevertheless it is possible to *deduce* the structure of the underlying information-based model.

20. Multi-Factor Models with a Time-Dependent Information Flow Rate

Let us now turn to consider the case of a single cash flow D_T that depends on a *multiplicity* of market factors $\{X_{T_k}^{\alpha}\}_{k=1,\dots,n}^{\alpha=1,\dots,m_k}$, where we have the n pre-designated information dates $\{T_k\}_{k=1,2,\dots,n}$, and where for each value of k we have a set of m_k

market factors. For simplicity we set $T = T_n$. Each market factor $X^{\alpha}_{T_k}$ is associated with an information process

$$\xi^{\alpha}_{tT_k} = X^{\alpha}_{T_k} \int_0^t \sigma^{\alpha}_{sT_k} \mathrm{d}s + \beta^{\alpha}_{tT_k}, \tag{20.1}$$

where $X^{\alpha}_{T_k}$ and $\{\beta^{\alpha}_{tT_k}\}$ are independent. It should be evident that although the random variable D_T representing the cash flow is $\mathcal{F}_T$-measurable, the values of some of the X-factors upon which it depends may be revealed at earlier times. That is to say, the uncertainties arising from some of the economic elements affecting the value of the cash flow at time T may be resolved before that time.

Since the X-factors are independent, it follows that for each market factor the associated conditional density process $\pi^{\alpha}_{tT_k}(x)$ takes the form given in (13.4), and the corresponding dynamical equation is given by

$$\mathrm{d}\pi^{\alpha}_{tT_k} = \nu^{\alpha}_{tT_k}(x^{\alpha}_k - \mathbb{E}^{\mathbb{Q}}[X^{\alpha}_{T_k}|\mathcal{F}_t])\pi^{\alpha}_{tT_k}\, \mathrm{d}W^{\alpha k}_t. \tag{20.2}$$

The function $\nu^{\alpha}_{tT_k}$ appearing here is given by an expression of the form (14.2):

$$\nu^{\alpha}_{tT_k} = \sigma^{\alpha}_{tT_k} + \frac{1}{T_k - t}\int_0^t \sigma^{\alpha}_{sT_k} \mathrm{d}s. \tag{20.3}$$

The innovation process $\{W^{\alpha k}_t\}$ is defined in terms of $\{\xi^{\alpha}_{tT_k}\}$ via the relation

$$W^{\alpha k}_t = \xi^{\alpha}_{tT_k} + \int_0^t \frac{1}{T_k - s}\xi^{\alpha}_{sT_k} \mathrm{d}s - \int_0^t \nu^{\alpha}_{sT_k} X^{\alpha}_{T_k} \mathrm{d}s. \tag{20.4}$$

The expectation $\mathbb{E}^{\mathbb{Q}}[D_T|\mathcal{F}_t]$ is thus given by the multi-dimensional integral

$$\begin{aligned} D_{tT} = \int_0^{\infty} \cdots \int_0^{\infty} & \Delta_T(x^1_1, \ldots, x^{m_1}_1, \ldots, x^1_n, \ldots, x^{m_n}_n) \\ & \times \pi_{t1}(x^1_1)\cdots\pi_{t1}(x^{m_1}_1)\cdots\pi_{tn}(x^1_n)\cdots\pi_{tn}(x^{m_n}_n)\,\mathrm{d}x^1_1\cdots\mathrm{d}x^{m_1}_1\cdots\mathrm{d}x^1_n\cdots\mathrm{d}x^{m_n}_n, \end{aligned} \tag{20.5}$$

and the price of the asset for $t < T$ is $S_t = P_{tT}D_{tT}$. A straightforward application of Ito's rule then establishes the following result:

Proposition 20.1. *The price process $\{S_t\}_{0\leq t<T}$ of an asset that pays a single dividend D_T at time $T(= T_n)$ depending on the market factors $\{X^{\alpha}_{T_k}\}^{\alpha=1,2,\ldots,m_k}_{k=1,2,\ldots n}$, satisfies the dynamical equation*

$$\mathrm{d}S_t = r_t S_t \mathrm{d}t + \sum_{k=1}^{n}\sum_{\alpha=1}^{m_k} \nu^{\alpha}_{tT_k}\,\mathrm{Cov}_t[D_T, X^{\alpha}_{T_k}]\,\mathrm{d}W^{\alpha k}_t, \tag{20.6}$$

where

$$D_T = \Delta_T(X^{\alpha}_{T_1}, \ldots, X^{\alpha}_{T_n}). \tag{20.7}$$

Here $\mathrm{Cov}_t[D_T, X^{\alpha}_{T_k}]$ denotes the covariance between the cash-flow D_T and the market factor $X^{\alpha}_{T_k}$, conditional on the information $\mathcal{F}_t$ generated by the information processes $\{\xi^{\alpha}_{sT_k}\}_{0\leq s\leq t}$, for $k = 1, 2, \ldots, n$ and $\alpha = 1, 2, \ldots, m_k$.

In the more general case of an asset that pays multiple dividends (see Sec. 8) the price is given by

$$S_t = \sum_{k=1}^{n} \mathbb{1}_{\{t<T_k\}} P_{tT_k} \mathbb{E}^{\mathbb{Q}}[\Delta_{T_k}(\{X^{\alpha}_{T_j}\}^{\alpha=1,2,\ldots,m_j}_{j=1,\ldots,k})|\mathcal{F}_t]. \tag{20.8}$$

Proposition 20.2. *The price process* $\{S_t\}$ *of an asset that pays the random dividends* D_{T_k} *on the dates* T_k $(k = 1, \ldots, n)$ *satisfies the dynamical equation*

$$\mathrm{d}S_t = r_t S_t \mathrm{d}t + \sum_{k=1}^{n}\sum_{j=1}^{k}\sum_{\alpha=1}^{m_j} \mathbb{1}_{\{t<T_k\}} P_t T_k \nu^{\alpha}_{tT_j} \mathrm{Cov}_t[D_{T_k}, X^{\alpha}_{T_j}]\mathrm{d}W^{\alpha j}_t + \sum_{k=1}^{n} D_{T_k} \mathrm{d}\mathbb{1}_{\{t<T_k\}}, \tag{20.9}$$

where

$$D_{T_k} = \Delta_{T_k}(\{X^{\alpha}_{T_j}\}^{\alpha=1,\ldots,m_j}_{j=1,\ldots,k}). \tag{20.10}$$

Here $\mathrm{Cov}_t[D_{T_k}, X^{\alpha}_{T_j}]$ *denotes the covariance between the dividend* D_{T_k} *and the market factor* $X^{\alpha}_{T_j}$*, conditional on the market information* $\mathcal{F}_t$*.*

We conclude that the multi-factor, multi-dividend situation is fully tractable when the information-flow rates associated with the various market factors are time dependent. A straightforward extension of Proposition 20.2 allows us to formulate the joint price dynamics of a system of assets, the associated dividend flows of which may depend on common market factors. As a consequence, a specific model for stochastic volatility and correlation emerges for such a system of assets, and it is one of the main conclusions of this paper that such a model can be formulated. The information-based "X-factor" approach presented here thus offers a new insights into the nature of volatility and correlation, and as such may find applications in a number of different areas of financial risk analysis. We have in mind, in particular, applications to equity portfolios, credit portfolios, and insurance, all of which exhibit intertemporal market correlation effects. We also have in mind the problem of firm-wide risk management and optimal capital allocation for banking institutions.

Acknowledgments

The authors thank T. Bielecki, T. Björk, I. Buckley, H. Bühlmann, S. Carter, I. Constantinou, M. Davis, J. Dear, A. Elizalde, B. Flesaker, H. Geman, V. Henderson, D. Hobson, T. Hurd, M. Jeanblanc, A. Lokka, J. Mao, B. Meister, M. Monoyios, M. Pistorius, M. Rutkowski, D. Taylor, and M. Zervos for stimulating discussions. The authors are grateful for comments made by seminar participants at meetings where parts of this work have been presented, including: the Developments in Quantitative Finance conference, July 2005, Isaac Newton Institute, Cambridge; the Mathematics in Finance conference, August 2005, Kruger National Park; University of the Witwatersrand, August 2005; Centro de Estudios Monetarios y Financieros (CEMFI), Madrid, October 2005; Heriot-Watt University, December 2005; King's

College London, December 2005; Bank of Japan, Tokyo, December 2005; Nomura, Tokyo, December 2005; the 16th Annual Derivatives Securities and Risk Management Conference, Federal Deposit Insurance Corporation, Virginia, April 2006; and ETH Zurich, June 2006. DCB acknowledges support from The Royal Society; LPH and AM acknowledge support from EPSRC (grant number GR/S22998/01); AM thanks the Public Education Authority of the Canton of Bern, Switzerland, and the UK Universities ORS scheme, for support.

References

[1] K. Back, Insider trading in continuous time, *Review of Financial Studies* **5** (1992) 387–407.

[2] K. Back and S. Baruch, Information in securities markets: Kyle meets Glosten and Milgrom, *Econometrica* **72** (2004) 433–465.

[3] D. C. Brody, L. P. Hughston and A. Macrina, Beyond hazard rates: A new framework for credit-risk modelling, in *Advances in Mathematical Finance: Festschrift Volume in Honour of Dilip Madan*, M. Fu, J.-Y. Yen, R. Jarrow and R. Elliott, eds. (Birkhäuser, Basel, 2007).

[4] R. S. Bucy and P. D. Joseph, *Filtering for Stochastic Processes with Applications to Guidance* (Interscience Publishers, New York, 1968).

[5] U. Cetin, R. Jarrow, P. Protter and Y. Yildrim, Modelling credit risk with partial information, *Annals of Applied Probability* **14** (2004) 1167–1172.

[6] M. H. A. Davis, Complete-market models of stochastic volatility, *Proceedings of the Royal Society London A* **460** (2004) 11–26.

[7] M. H. A. Davis and S. I. Marcus, An introduction to nonlinear filtering, in *Stochastic Systems: The Mathematics of Filtering and Identification and Application*, M. Hazewinkel and J. C. Willems, eds. (D. Reidel, Dordrecht, 1981).

[8] D. Duffie and D. Lando, Term structure of credit spreads with incomplete accounting information, *Econometrica* **69** (2001) 633–664.

[9] M. Fujisaki, G. Kallianpur and H. Kunita Stochastic differential equations for the non linear filtering problem, *Osaka Journal of Mathematics* **9** (1972) 19–40.

[10] H. Geman, D. B. Madan and M. Yor, Probing option prices for information, *Methodology and Computing in Applied Probability* **9** (2007) 115–131.

[11] K. Giesecke, Correlated default with incomplete information, *Journal of Banking and Finance* **28** (2004) 1521–1545.

[12] K. Giesecke and L. R. Goldberg, Sequential default and incomplete information, *Journal of Risk* **7** (2004) 1–26.

[13] S. L. Heston, A closed-form solution for options with stochastic volatility with applications to bond and currency options, *Review of Financial Studies* **6** (1993) 327–343.

[14] R. A. Jarrow and P. Protter, Structural versus reduced form models: A new information based perspective, *Journal of Investment Management* **2** (2004) 34–43.

[15] T. Kailath, A view of three decades of linear filtering theory, *IEEE Transactions on Information Theory* **IT-20** (1974) 146–181.

[16] G. Kallianpur and C. Striebel, Estimation of stochastic systems: Arbitrary system process with additive white noise observation errors, *Annals of Mathematical Statisics* **39** (1968) 785–801.

[17] I. Karatzas and S. E. Shreve, *Brownian Motion and Stochastic Calculus* (Springer, Berlin, 1997).

[18] V. Krishnan, *Nonlinear Filtering and Smoothing* (Dover, New York, 2005).

[19] R. S. Liptser and A. N. Shiryaev, *Statistics of Random Processes*, Vols. I and II, 2nd ed. (Springer, Berlin, 2000).
[20] A. Macrina, An information-based framework for asset pricing: X-factor theory and its applications, PhD thesis, King's College London (2006).
[21] M. O'Hara, *Market Microstructure Theory* (Blackwell, Cambridge, Massachusetts, 1995).
[22] P. Protter *Stochastic Integration and Differential Equations: A New Approach*, 2nd ed. (Springer, Berlin, 2003).
[23] M. Rutkowski and N. Yu, An extension of the Brody–Hughston–Macrina approach to modelling of defaultable bonds, *International Journal of Theoretical and Applied Finance* **10** (2007) 557–589.
[24] M. Yor, *Some Aspects of Brownian Motion, Part I: Some Special Functionals* (Birkhäuser, Basel, 1992).

TANGENT MODELS AS A MATHEMATICAL FRAMEWORK FOR DYNAMIC CALIBRATION*

RENÉ CARMONA and SERGEY NADTOCHIY
Bendheim Center for Finance, ORFE
Princeton University
Princeton, NJ 08544, USA

Motivated by the desire to integrate repeated calibration procedures into a single dynamic *market model*, we introduce the notion of a "tangent model" in an abstract set up, and we show that this new mathematical paradigm accommodates all the recent attempts to study consistency and absence of arbitrage in market models. For the sake of illustration, we concentrate on the case when market quotes provide the prices of European call options for a specific set of strikes and maturities. While reviewing our recent results on dynamic local volatility and tangent Lévy models, we present a theory of *tangent models* unifying these two approaches and construct a new class of tangent Lévy models, which allows the underlying to have both continuous and pure jump components.

Keywords: Market models; Heath–Jarrow–Morton approach; implied volatility; local volatility; tangent Lévy models.

1. Introduction

Calibration of a financial model is most often understood as a procedure to choose the model parameters so that the theoretical prices produced by the model match the market quotes. In most cases, the market quotes span a term structure of maturities, and by nature, the calibration procedure introduces an extra time-dependence in the parameters that are *calibrated*. Introducing such a time dependence in the parameters changes dramatically the interpretation of the original equations. Indeed, even if these equations were originally introduced to capture the dynamics (whether they are historical or risk neutral) of the prices or index values underlying derivatives, the equations with the *calibrated* parameters lost their interpretations as providing the time evolutions of the underlying prices and indexes. The purpose of market models is to restore this interpretation, and the notion of tangent models which we introduce formally in this paper appears as a general framework to do just that.

*This chapter was originally published under the same title in *International Journal of Theoretical and Applied Finance*, Vol.14, No.1, 107–135 (2011). Singapore: World Scientific Publishing.

In order to illustrate clearly the point of the matter, we review a standard example from interest rate theory used routinely as a justification for the introduction of the HJM approach to fixed income models. If we consider Vasicek's model for example

$$dr_t = \kappa(\overline{r} - r_t)dt + \sigma dW_t,$$

because of the linear and Gaussian nature of the process, it is possible to derive explicit formulas for many derivatives and in particular for the forward and yield curves. However, the term structure given by these formulas is too rigid, and on most days, one cannot find reasonable values of the 3 parameters κ, $\overline{r}$ and σ giving a *theoretical* forward curve matching, in a satisfactory manner, the forward curve $\tau \hookrightarrow f(\tau)$ observed on that day. This is a serious shortcoming as, whether it is for hedging and risk management purposes, or for valuing non-vanilla instruments, using a model consistent with the market quotes is imperative. Clever people found a fix to this hindrance: *replace the constant parameter* $\overline{r}$ *by a deterministic function of time* $t \hookrightarrow \overline{r}(t)$. Indeed, this function being deterministic, the interest rate process remains Gaussian (at least as long as we do not change the initial condition) and we can still obtain explicit formulas for the forward curves given by the model. Moreover, if we choose the time dependent parameter to be given by

$$\overline{r}(\tau) = f'(\tau) + \kappa f(\tau) - \frac{\sigma^2}{2\kappa}(1 - e^{-\kappa\tau})(3e^{-\kappa\tau} - 1)$$

then the model provides a *perfect* match to the curve observed on the market, in the sense that the forward rate with time to maturity τ produced by the model (1.1) with a time dependent $\overline{r}$, is exactly equal to $f(\tau)$. Our contention is that even though it provides a stochastic differential equation (SDE for short)

$$dr_t = \kappa(\overline{r}(t) - r_t)dt + \sigma dW_t, \tag{1.1}$$

this procedure can be misleading, looking as if this SDE actually relates to the dynamics of the short interest rate. Indeed, this is not a model in the sense that when the next day comes along, one has to restart the whole calibration procedure from scratch, and use equation (1.1) with a different function $t \hookrightarrow \overline{r}(t)$. Despite the fact that its left hand side contains the infinitesimal "dr_t", which could leave us to believe that the time evolution of r_t is prescribed by its right hand side, formula (1.1) does not provides a dynamic model, it is a mere artifact designed to capture the prices observed on the market: it is what we call a *tangent model.*

The main goal of this paper is to identify a framework in which dynamic models for the underlying indexes and the quoted prices can coexist and in which their consistency can be assessed. Despite its generality, this framework can be used to offer concrete solutions to practical problems. Case in point, one of the nagging challenges of *quant* groups supporting equity trading is to be able to generate Monte Carlo scenarios of implied volatility surfaces which are consistent with historical observations while being arbitrage free at the same time. We show in Sec. 4.5 how tangent Lévy models can be used to construct such simulation models.

The paper is organized as follows. Section 2 introduces the notation and the definitions used throughout. In particular, the general notion of tangent model is described and illustrated. Sections 3 and 4 recast the results of [4–6] in the present framework of tangent models, and for this reason, they are mostly of a review nature. Section 5 introduces and characterizes the consistency of new tangent models that combine the features of the diffusion tangent models of Sec. 3 and the pure jump tangent models of Sec. 4. These models bear some similarities to those appearing in a recent technical report [21] where Kallsen and Krühner study a form of Heath-Jarrow-Morton approach to dynamic stock option price modeling. However, their approach does not seem to lead to constructive models like the one proposed in Sec. 4.5.

2. Tangent Models and Calibration

2.1. *Market models for equity derivatives: Problem formulation*

We now describe the framework of the paper more precisely. First of all, as it is done in a typical set-up for a mathematical model, we assume that we are given a stochastic basis $(\Omega, \mathcal{F}, (\mathcal{F}_t)_{t\geq 0}, \mathbb{Q})$ and that pricing is linear in the sense that the time t prices of all contingent claims are given as (conditional) expectations of discounted payoffs under the pricing measure $\mathbb{Q}$, with respect to the market filtration $\mathcal{F}_t$. We assume, for simplicity, that the discounting factor is one, and unless otherwise specified, all stochastic processes are defined on the above stochastic basis and $\mathbb{E} \equiv \mathbb{E}^{\mathbb{Q}}$. Interest rates do not have to be zero for the results of this paper to still hold. Any positive deterministic function of time would do. However, we refrain from working in this generality for the sake of notation. We denote by $(S_t)_{t\geq 0}$ the true risk-neutral (stochastic) dynamics of the value of the index or security underlying the derivatives whose prices are quoted in the market. We denote by $\mathcal{D}_t$ the set of derivatives available at time t. Naturally, we identify each element of $\mathcal{D}_t$ with its maturity T and the payoff h (which may be a function of the entire path of $(S_t)_{t\in[0,T]}$). We assume that the market for these derivatives is liquid in the sense that each of them can be bought or sold, in any desired quantity, at the price quoted in the market. Thus, we denote by $P_t(T, h)$ the market price of a corresponding derivative at time t, and introduce the set of all market prices

$$\mathcal{P}_t = \{P_t(T, h)\}_{(T,h)\in\mathcal{D}_t}$$

In the most commonly used example, S_t is the price at time t of a share and $\mathcal{D}_t$ is the set of European call options for all strikes $K > 0$ and maturities $T > t$ at time t, having price $C_t(T, K)$, so that in this case,

$$\mathcal{P}_t = \{C_t(T, K)\}_{T>t,K>0} \tag{2.1}$$

Our goal is to describe explicitly a large class of time-consistent *market models*, i.e. stochastic models (say, SDE's) giving the joint arbitrage-free time evolution of S and $\mathcal{P}$. One would like to start the model from "almost" any initial condition, typically the set of currently observed market prices, and prescribe "almost" any dynamics for the model provided it doesn't contradict the no-arbitrage property. Of course, the above formulation of the problem is rather idealistic. This explains our use of the word "almost" whose specific meaning is different for each class of *market models.*

The need for financial models consistent with the observed option prices has been exacerbated by the fact that call options have become liquid and provide reliable price signals to market participants. Stochastic volatility models (e.g. Hull-White, Heston, etc.) are very popular tools in this respect, namely as a means to capture this signal. Involving a small number of parameters, they are relatively easy to implement, and they can *capture the smile* reasonably well for a given maturity. However, the fit to the entire term structure of *implied volatility* is not always satisfactory as they cannot reproduce market prices for *all* strikes and maturities. See for example [15].

The preferred solution for over 15 years has been based on the so-called *local volatility* models introduced by Dupire in [14]. It says that if the true model for the risk neutral dynamics of the underlying is given by an equation of the form $dS_t = \sigma_t dW_t$. (recall that we assume zero interest rate for the sake of simplicity), and if we assume that the function $C(T, K)$ giving the price of an European call options with maturity T and strike K is smooth, then the stochastic process $\tilde{S}$ solving the equation

$$\tilde{S}_t = S_0 + \int_0^t \tilde{S}_u \tilde{a}(u, \tilde{S}_u) dW_u,$$

with

$$\tilde{a}^2(T, K) := \frac{2\frac{\partial}{\partial T}C(T, K)}{K^2 \frac{\partial^2}{\partial K^2}C(T, K)}, \tag{2.2}$$

produces at time $t = 0$, the *same exact call prices* $C(T, K)$! In other words, for all $T > 0$ and $K > 0$, we have $\mathbb{E}(\tilde{S}_T - K)^+ = C(T, K)$. The function $(T, K) \hookrightarrow \tilde{a}^2(T, K)$ so defined is called the local volatility. For the sake of illustration, we computed and plotted the graph of this function in the case of the two most popular stochastic volatility models mentioned earlier, the Heston and the Hull-White models. These plots are given in Fig. 1. In the terminology which we develop below, the *artificial* financial model given by the process $(\tilde{S}_t)_{t \geq 0}$, introduced for the sole purpose of reproducing the prices of options at time zero (in other words, the result of *calibration* at time zero), is said to be *tangent* to the true model $(S_t)_{t \geq 0}$ at $t = 0$. Together with the simple interest rate model reviewed in the introduction, this discussion of Dupire's approach provides the second example of a SDE introduced for

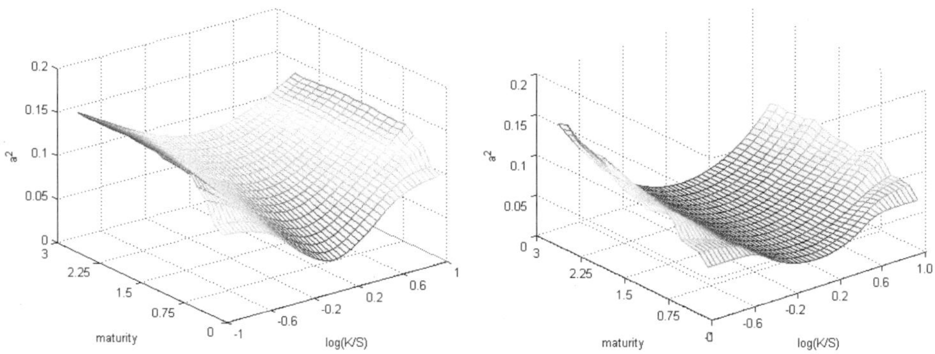

(a) (b)

Fig. 1. Local volatility surfaces for the Heston (a) and Hull-White (b) models as functions of the time to maturity $\tau = T - t$ and log-moneyness $\log(K/S)$.

the sole purpose of capturing the prices quoted on the market. We now formalize this concept in a set of mathematical definitions.

One of the major problems with calibration is its frequency: stochastic volatility models have different "optimal" parameters most every day, and the *local volatility* surface calibrated on a daily basis changes as well. In order to incorporate these changes in a model, we focus on the "daily" capture of the price signals given by the market through the quotes of the liquidly traded derivatives.

2.2. *Examples of the sets of derivatives*

The theoretical framework of this paper was inspired by earlier works on the original market models which pioneered the analysis of joint dynamics for a large class of derivatives written on a common underlying index. Most appropriate references (given the spirit of the present paper) include [9] for the HJM approach to bond markets, [28] and [16] for the BGM approach to the LIBOR markets, [1] for the markets of variance swaps, and [32] and [35] for the markets of synthetic CDOs and credit portfolios. See also [2] for a review.

However, for the sake of definiteness and notation, we restrict the discussion of this paper to the models used for the markets of equity derivatives. The following list is a sample of examples which can be found in the existing literature, and for which the above formalism applies:

- $\mathcal{P}_t = \{S_t, C_t(T, K);\ T > t\}$ for some fixed $K > 0$ — considered by Schoenbucher in [31];
- $\mathcal{P}_t = \{S_t, C_t(T);\ T > t\}$ where $C_t(T)$ represents the price at time t of a European call option when the *hockey-stick* function $x \hookrightarrow (x - K)^+$ is replaced by a fixed convex payoff function — considered by Jacod and Protter in [20] and Schweizer and Wissel in [34];

- $\mathcal{P}_t = \{S_t, C_t(T, K);\ K > 0\}$ for some fixed $T > t$ — considered by Schweizer and Wissel in [33];
- $\mathcal{P}_t = \{S_t, C_t(T_i, K_j);\ i = 1, \ldots, m,\ j = 1, \ldots, n\}$ — considered by Schweizer and Wissel in [33];
- $\mathcal{P}_t = \{S_t, C_t(T, K);\ T > t,\ K > 0\}$ — considered by Cont *et al.* in [11] and Carmona and Nadtochiy in [5].

For the most part of this paper we concentrate on the last example where the prices of the liquidly traded instruments are:

$$\mathcal{P}_t = \{S_t, C_t(T, K);\ T \in (t, \bar{T}],\ K > 0\}, \tag{2.3}$$

where we assume, in addition, that both maturity T and calendar time t are bounded above by some finite $\bar{T} > 0$. Notice that such a set $\mathcal{P}_t$ is infinite (even of continuum power), even though the set $\mathcal{P}_t$ is finite in practice. This abstraction is standard in the financial mathematic and engineering literature.

2.3. *Tangent models*

Recall that we use the notation T and h for the typical maturity and payoff function of a derivative in $\mathcal{D}_t$ (h may be path dependent) and $P_t(T, h)$ for its price at time $t \geq 0$. Each process $(P_t(T, h))$ is adapted and, due to our standing assumption of risk-neutrality, we have, almost surely

$$P_t(T, h) = \mathbb{E}(h((S_u)_{u \in [0,T]}) \,|\, \mathcal{F}_t)$$

Motivated by Dupire's result of *exact static calibration*, we say that the stochastic model given by an auxiliary stochastic process $(\tilde{S}_u)_{u \geq 0}$ defined on a (possibly different) stochastic basis $(\tilde{\Omega}, \tilde{\mathcal{F}}, \tilde{\mathbb{P}})$ is $\mathcal{D}_t$*-tangent to the true model* (or just *tangent* when no ambiguity is possible) at time t for a given $\omega \in \Omega$, if

$$\forall\,(T, h) \in \mathcal{D}_t \quad P_{t,\omega}(T, h) = \mathbb{E}^{\tilde{\mathbb{P}}}(h(\bar{S}^{t,\omega})), \tag{2.4}$$

where

$$\bar{S}^{t,\omega} = (\bar{S}^{t,\omega}_{u,\tilde{\omega}})_{u \in [0,T],\, \tilde{\omega} \in \tilde{\Omega}} \quad \text{and} \quad \bar{S}^{t,\omega}_{u,\tilde{\omega}} = \mathbf{1}_{u \leq t} S_{u,\omega} + \mathbf{1}_{u > t} \tilde{S}_{u-t,\tilde{\omega}},$$

and the expectation in (2.4) is computed over $\tilde{\Omega}$ for t and ω fixed. The payoff appearing in the above expectation is computed over a path which coincides with the path of the underlying index S up to time t and with the path of the *tangent* process $\tilde{S}$ after that time. The expression of $\bar{S}^{t,\omega}$ used in (2.4) is involved only because we allow the payoff h to depend upon the entire path of the underlying index. However, in all particular applications we discuss below, we deal with payoffs that depend only upon S_T, for some maturity T, and in that case we can simply change the maturities of the payoffs from T to $T - t$, and use $\tilde{S}$ instead of $\bar{S}^{t,\omega}$ in (2.4).

We want to think of the above notion of tangent model as an analog of the notion of tangent vector in classical differential geometry: the two models are tangent in the sense that, locally, at a fixed point in time, they produce the same prices of derivatives in a chosen family. Recall that tangent vectors in differential geometry are often used as a convenient way to describe the time dynamics. In the same way, we hope that the tangent models introduced above will help in a better understanding of *market models*.

2.4. *Code books*

Let us assume that the martingale models considered for the underlying index can be parameterized explicitly, say in the form:

$$\mathbb{M} = \{\mathcal{M}(\theta)\}_{\theta \in \Theta},$$

and that $P^\theta(h)$, the price at time $t = 0$ of a claim with payoff function h in the model $\mathcal{M}(\theta)$, is fairly easy to compute. If, in addition, the relation

$$\theta \hookrightarrow \{P^\theta(h)\}_{h \in \mathcal{D}_0}, \tag{2.5}$$

is invertible, we obtain a one-to-one correspondence between a set of prices for the derivatives in $\mathcal{D}_0$ and the parameter space Θ. When this is the case, we also assume that this one-to-one correspondence can be extended to hold at each time t. More precisely, at each time $t > 0$ the derivatives we consider can be viewed as contingent claims depending on the future evolution of the underlying (since the past is known), hence we define the "effective" maturity and payoff at time t by

$$\tau = T - t \quad \text{and} \quad \tilde{h}((\tilde{S}_u)_{u \in (0, T-t]}) := h((S_u)_{u \in [0,t]} \sqcup (\tilde{S}_{u-t})_{u \in (t,T]})$$

respectively. In the above we used "$\sqcup$" to denote the concatenation of paths. Thus, given time t and the evolution of the underlying $(S_u)_{u \in [0,t]}$ up to time t, for each pair $(T, h) \in \mathcal{D}_t$ there is a unique corresponding pair $(\tau, \tilde{h})$. Therefore we define $\tilde{\mathcal{D}}_t$, the set of target derivative contracts expressed in the "centered" (around current time) variables, via

$$\tilde{\mathcal{D}}_t := \{(\tau, \tilde{h}) \mid (T, h) \in \mathcal{D}_t\}$$

The models $\mathcal{M}(\theta)$ are now viewed as the models for $\tilde{S}$, which are used to compute $P^\theta(\tau, \tilde{h})$, the time zero prices of derivatives in $\tilde{\mathcal{D}}_t$. Hence, we assume that at each time t there exists a one-to-one mapping

$$\Theta \ni \theta \leftrightarrow \mathcal{P}_t^\theta := \{P^\theta(\tau, \tilde{h})\}_{(\tau, \tilde{h}) \in \tilde{\mathcal{D}}_t} \tag{2.6}$$

Then we call the set Θ a *code-book* and the above bijective correspondence a *code*. Recall that set $\tilde{\mathcal{D}}_t$ contains the same derivatives as $\mathcal{D}_t$, but in the new time coordinates: with the current moment of time t being the origin. Hence, the existence of bijection (2.6) means that at each moment of time there exists a model $\mathcal{M}(\theta)$ such that the market price $P_t(T,h)$ of any contract in $\mathcal{D}_t$ coincides with the time zero *model-implied* price of a corresponding contract in $\tilde{\mathcal{D}}_t$. Then the above mapping allows us to think of the set of market prices $\mathcal{P}_t$ in terms of its code value $\theta \in \Theta$. We can reformulate the notion of a tangent model in terms of code-books in the following way: *if at time t for a given $\omega \in \Omega$ there exists a code value $\theta_{t,\omega} \in \Theta$ which reproduces the market prices (i.e. $\mathcal{P}_t = \mathcal{P}_t^{\theta_{t,\omega}}$), then the model $\mathcal{M}(\theta_{t,\omega})$ is tangent to the true model in the sense of* (2.4).

When the set Θ is simple enough (for example an open subset of a linear space), the construction of market models reduces to putting in motion the initial code θ_0, which captures the initial prices of the liquidly traded derivatives, and obtaining (θ_t) (whenever possible, we drop the dependence upon "ω" in our notation, as most probabilists do). One can then go from the code-book space to the original domain by computing the resulting derivatives prices for any future time t in the model $\mathcal{M}(\theta_t)$. Code-books, as more convenient representations of derivatives prices, have been used by practitioners for a very long time: the examples include *yield curve* in the Treasury bond market, *implied term structure of default probabilities* for CDO tranches and *implied volatility* for the European options, etc.

Remark 2.1. Due to the specific form of our abstract definition of a tangent model, we can identify any such model with the law of the underlying process it produces, as opposed to the general case when a financial model is defined by the pair: "underlying process" and "market filtration". In the same way, by model $\mathcal{M}(\theta)$ we will understand a specific distribution of the process $\tilde{S}$ used instantaneously as a proxy for the underlying index. In this respect, the construction of consistent stochastic dynamics for tangent models is not without similarities with the foundations of Knight's prediction process [22].

We now define two important classes of tangent models and we review their main properties in the following two sections.

2.5. *Tangent diffusion models*

We say that a tangent model is a *tangent diffusion model* if at any given time, the tangent process $\tilde{S}$ is a possibly inhomogeneous *diffusion* process. More precisely, we shall assume that the process $\tilde{S}$ is of the form

$$\tilde{S}_t = s + \int_0^t \tilde{S}_u \tilde{a}(u, \tilde{S}_u) dB_u,$$

for some initial condition s, *local volatility* function $\tilde{a}(.,.)$ and a Brownian motion B. The law of $\tilde{S}$ is then uniquely determined by $(s, \tilde{a}(.,.))$, where the surface $\tilde{a}$ has to satisfy mild regularity assumptions (see [5] and [4] for details). Clearly, the values at time $t = 0$ of the underlying index and the call prices in any such model are given by s and

$$C^{s,\tilde{a}}(\tau, x) = \mathbb{E}(\tilde{S}_\tau - e^x)^+, \tag{2.7}$$

respectively, if we use the notation $K = e^x$ for the strike. From Dupire's formula (2.2), we can conclude that the above mapping from $(s, \tilde{a})$ to the couple ("value of the underlying", "prices of call options") is one-to-one, thus producing a code-book.

For a given $\omega \in \Omega$, if at time t there exists a value of the code $\theta_{t,\omega} = (s_{t,\omega}, \tilde{a}_{t,\omega})$, which reproduces the true market prices of all the call options and the underlying, then the model given by $(s_{t,\omega}, \tilde{a}_{t,\omega})$ is a tangent diffusion model at time t. In that case $s_{t,\omega}$ has to coincide with the current value of the underlying index $S_t(\omega)$ and $\tilde{a}_{t,\omega}(.,.)$ can be viewed as the local volatility surface calibrated (fitted) to match the observed call prices at time t.

2.6. *Tangent Lévy models*

We say that a tangent model is a *tangent Lévy model* if the tangent process $\tilde{S}$ is given by an additive (i.e. a (possibly) *time-inhomogeneous Lévy process*). To be more specific, a given model is a tangent Lévy model if it is tangent (in the sense of (2.4)) and the corresponding tangent process $\tilde{S}$ is a pure jump additive process satisfying

$$\tilde{S}_t = s + \int_0^t \int_{\mathbb{R}} \tilde{S}_{u-}(e^x - 1)[N(dx, du) - \eta(dx, du)], \tag{2.8}$$

where $N(dx, du)$ is a *Poisson random measure* — associated with the jumps of $\log(\tilde{S})$ — having an absolutely continuous (deterministic) *intensity*

$$\eta(dx, du) = \tilde{\kappa}(u, x)dxdu.$$

The law of $\tilde{S}$ is then uniquely determined by $(s, \tilde{\kappa})$. As before, the values at time $t = 0$ of the underlying index and the call prices in any such model are given by s and

$$C^{s,\tilde{\kappa}}(\tau, x) = \mathbb{E}(\tilde{S}_\tau - e^x)^+ \tag{2.9}$$

respectively. From the analytic representation of (2.9) provided in Sec. 4 (and discussed in more detail in [6]), it is not hard to see that the above mapping from $(s, \tilde{\kappa})$ to ("value of the underlying", "prices of the call options") is one-to-one, thus producing a code-book.

As before, for a given $\omega \in \Omega$, if at time t there exists a value of the code $\theta_{t,\omega} = (s_{t,\omega}, \tilde{\kappa}_{t,\omega})$, which reproduces the market prices of all the European call options and the value of the underlying index, then the model given by $(s_{t,\omega}, \tilde{\kappa}_{t,\omega})$ is a tangent Lévy model at time t.

2.7. *Time-consistency of calibration*

It is important to remember that our standing assumption is that the prices of all contingent claims are given by conditional expectations in the true (unknown) model. Therefore, when prescribing the (stochastic) dynamics of the code θ_t, we have to make sure that the derivative prices produced by θ_t at each future time t are indeed "the market prices". In other words, they have to coincide with the corresponding conditional expectations, or, equivalently, $\mathcal{M}(\theta_{t,\omega})$ has to be tangent to the true model at each time t, for almost all $\omega \in \Omega$. This condition reflects the internal time-consistency of the dynamic calibration, and therefore, we further refer to it as the *consistency* of the code dynamics (or simply "consistency"). If the dynamics of θ_t are consistent with a true model, then we say that the true model and (θ_t) form a *dynamic tangent model.*

3. Dynamic Tangent Diffusion Models

In this section we assume that the filtration $(\mathcal{F}_t)_{t\geq 0}$ is Brownian in the sense that it is generated by a (possibly infinite dimensional) Wiener process, and that the set $\mathcal{P}_t$ of prices of liquidly traded derivatives is given by (2.3).

3.1. *The local volatility code book*

We capture the prices of all the European call options with the local volatility $\tilde{a}_t(.,.)$ defined with what is known as Dupire's formula, which we recalled earlier in the static case $t = 0$:

$$\tilde{a}_t^2(\tau, K) := \frac{2\frac{\partial}{\partial T} C_t(t+\tau, K)}{K^2 \frac{\partial^2}{\partial K^2} C_t(t+\tau, K)}, \tag{3.1}$$

where $C_t(T, K)$ is the (true) market price of a call option with strike K and maturity T at time t. As discussed above, this formula defines a mapping from the surfaces of call prices to the local volatility functions producing a code-book. We switch to the log-moneyness x, writing

$$h(\tau, x) := \log \tilde{a}^2(\tau, se^x) \tag{3.2}$$

for the logarithm of the square of local volatility. Recall the definition of $C^{s,\tilde{a}}$, call prices produced by local volatility, given by (2.7). Using the normalized call prices

$$c^{s,\tilde{a}}(\tau, x) = \frac{1}{s} C^{s,\tilde{a}}(\tau, \log s + x), \tag{3.3}$$

the analytic representation of the call prices produced by the code value $(s, \tilde{a})$ takes the form of the Partial Differential Equation (PDE)

$$\begin{cases} \partial_\tau c^{s,\tilde{a}}(\tau, x) = e^{h(\tau,x)} D_x c^{s,\tilde{a}}(\tau, x), \quad \tau > 0, \;\; x \in \mathbb{R} \\ c^{s,\tilde{a}}(\tau, x)|_{\tau=0} = (1 - e^x)^+. \end{cases} \tag{3.4}$$

where we used notation D_x for the differential operator $D_x = \frac{1}{2}(\partial^2_{x^2} - \partial_x)$. Starting from a squared local volatility function $\tilde{a}^2$ (or equivalently its logarithm h) and ending with the solution of the above PDE defines an operator $\mathbf{F}: h \mapsto c$ which plays a crucial role in the analysis of tangent diffusion models.

Once specific function spaces are chosen (see Sec. 2.2 of [4] for the definitions of the domain and range of $\mathbf{F}$), formula (3.1) and the operator $\mathbf{F}$ provide a one-to-one correspondence between call option price surfaces and local volatility surfaces. This defines the local volatility code-book for call prices. See also [4] and [5] for more details.

3.2. *Formal definition of dynamic tangent diffusion models*

As explained earlier, we assume that a pricing measure has been chosen (it does not have to be uniquely determined as the "martingale measure", i.e. we allow for an incomplete market), and that under the probability structure it defines, the underlying index is a martingale as we ignore interest rate and dividend payments for the sake of simplicity. Consequently, the underlying index value is a martingale of the form:

$$dS_t = S_t \sigma_t dW_t,$$

for some scalar adapted *spot volatility* process (σ_t) and a one-dimensional Wiener process $(W_t)_t$ which we will identify, without any loss of generality with the first component $(B^1_t)_t$ of the multidimensional Wiener process $(B_t)_t$ generating the market filtration. In order to specify the dynamics of the code $(s_t, \tilde{a}_t)$, we notice that if we want these dynamics to be consistent (see the discussion in Sec. 2.7), we need to have $s_t = S_t$. Thus we define the dynamics (time evolution) of the codes by

$$\begin{cases} s_t = S_t, \quad dS_t = S_t \sigma_t dB^1_t, \\ \tilde{a}_t(\tau, K) = \exp\left(\dfrac{1}{2} h_t\left(\tau, \log K/s_t\right)\right), \quad dh_t = \alpha_t dt + \displaystyle\sum_{n=1}^{m} \beta^n_t dB^n_t, \end{cases} \tag{3.5}$$

where $B = (B^1, \ldots, B^m)$ is an m-dimensional Brownian motion (m could be ∞), the stochastic processes α and $\{\beta^n\}_{n=1}^m$ take values in spaces of functions of τ and x (see Sec. 3 of [4] for the exact definitions of function spaces for α and β), and σ is a (scalar) locally square integrable adapted stochastic process, such that S is a true martingale.

A *tangent diffusion model* is defined by the dynamics (3.5) in such a way that for any $(T, x) \in (0, \bar{T}] \times \mathbb{R}$ the following equality is satisfied almost surely for all $t \in [0, T)$

$$C^{s_t, \tilde{a}_t}(T - t, x) = \mathbb{E}((S_T - K)^+ \,|\, \mathcal{F}_t), \tag{3.6}$$

where $C^{s,\tilde{a}}$ is defined in (2.7). Such a constraint is called *consistency condition.*

This type of model was first proposed by Derman and Kani in [12] and studied mathematically by Carmona and Nadtochiy in [5] and [4]. Notice that the consistency condition defined by (3.6) is rather implicit and makes it very hard to construct dynamic tangent diffusion models explicitly. Therefore, the main goal of the following subsection is to express the consistency condition (3.6) in terms of the input parameters of the model: σ, α and β.

3.3. *Consistency of dynamic tangent diffusion models*

The above question turns out to be equivalent to obtaining a necessary and sufficient conditions for the call prices $C^{S_t,\tilde{a}_t}$ produced by the code-book to be martingales.

Starting from Itô's dynamics for h (or equivalently $\tilde{a}$), an infinite dimensional version of Itô's formula shows that call prices are semi-martingales, and being able to compute their drifts should lead to consistency conditions merely stating that the call prices are martingales (i.e. setting the drifts to zero, since the local martingale property is enough in this case). Clearly, this reasoning depends upon proving that the mapping provided by the operator $\mathbf{F}$ is twice Fréchet differentiable. This strategy for the analysis of no-arbitrage was used in [5], and a more transparent proof fo the Fréchet-differentiability is presented in [4], whose main result we state below after we agree to denote by $p(h)$ the fundamental solution of the forward PDE

$$\partial_\tau w(\tau, x) = e^{h(\tau,x)} D_x w(\tau, x)$$

and by $q(h)$ the fundamental solution of the dual (backward) PDE

$$\partial_\tau w(\tau, x) = -e^{h(\tau,x)} D_x w(\tau, x)$$

It is proven in [4] that once the proper function spaces are chosen, the operator $\mathbf{F}$ (acting on appropriate domain $\tilde{\mathcal{B}}$, defined in Sec. 2.2 of [4]) is twice continuously Frechét-differentiable, and that for any $h, h', h'' \in \tilde{\mathcal{B}}$, we have

$$\mathbf{F}'(h)[h'] = \frac{1}{2} K[p(h), h'e^h, q(h)],$$

and

$$\mathbf{F}''(h)[h', h''] = \frac{1}{2}(K[I[p(h), h''e^h, p(h)], h'e^h, q(h)] + K[p(h), h'e^h, J[q(h), h''e^h, q(h)]])$$

where the operators I, J, and K are defined by

- $I[\Gamma_2, f, \Gamma_1](\tau_2, x_2; \tau_1, x_1)$
$$:= \int_{\tau_1}^{\tau_2} \int_{\mathbb{R}} \Gamma_2(\tau_2, x_2; u, y) f(u, y) D_y \Gamma_1(u, y; \tau_1, x_1) dy du,$$
- $J[\Gamma_2, f, \Gamma_1](\tau_2, x_2; \tau_1, x_1)$
$$:= \int_{\tau_1}^{\tau_2} \int_{\mathbb{R}} D_y \Gamma_2(\tau_2, x_2; u, y) f(u, y) \Gamma_1(u, y; \tau_1, x_1) dy du,$$

- $K[\Gamma_2, f, \Gamma_1](\tau_2, x_2; \tau_1, x_1)$

$$:= \int_{\tau_1}^{\tau_2} \int_{\mathbb{R}} \Gamma_2(\tau_2, x_2; u, y) e^y f(u, y) \Gamma_1(u, y; \tau_1, x_1) dy du.$$

Finally, as it is shown in [4] and [5], if we use the notations $D_x^* := \frac{1}{2}(\partial_x^2 + \partial_x)$, $L(h_t) := \log q(h_t)$, and L' for the Fréchet derivative of L, and provided that S is a martingale and processes α and β are chosen to take values in appropriate spaces (again, see Sec. 3 of [4] for the definitions of appropriate spaces), then we have a *dynamic tangent diffusion model* if and only if the following two conditions are satisfied:

(1) *Drift restriction*:

$$\alpha_t = \partial_T h_t - \sigma_t^2 D_x^* h_t + \sigma_t \partial_x \beta^1 - \frac{1}{2}(\beta_t^1 + \sigma_t \partial_x h_t)^2 - \frac{1}{2}\sum_{n=2}^{\infty} \beta_t^{n2}$$
$$- (\beta_t^1 - \sigma_t \partial_x h_t)(L'(h_t)[\beta_t^1] - \sigma_t \partial_x L(h_t)) - \sum_{n=2}^{\infty} \beta_t^n L'(h_t)[\beta_t^n] \quad (3.7)$$

(2) *Spot volatility specification*:

$$2 \log \sigma_t = h_t(0, 0). \quad (3.8)$$

From the form of the above drift condition (3.7) and the spot volatility specification condition (3.8), it looks like β is a free parameter whose choice completely determines both α and σ. And the following strategy appears as a natural method of constructing dynamic tangent diffusion models: choose a vector of random processes β and define process h as the solution of the following SDE

$$dh_t = \alpha(h_t, \beta_t)dt + \beta_t \cdot dB_t, \quad (3.9)$$

where $\alpha(h_t, \beta_t)$ is given by the right hand side of (3.7). Having the dynamics of h, we obtain the time evolution of σ (via (3.8)) and, therefore, S. However, studying equation (3.9) is extremely difficult due to the complicated structure of the drift condition (3.7), and in particular the operator L involved in it. Therefore, the problem of existence of the solution to the above SDE is still open. In addition, to the best of our knowledge, the only explicit example of β_t and h_t which produce a tractable expression for the drift in the right hand side of (3.7) is the "flat" case: $\beta_t^n(.,.) \equiv$ const and $h_t(.,.) \equiv$ const. However, as discussed at the end of Sec. 6 in [5], any regular enough stochastic volatility model falls within the framework of dynamic local volatility and, therefore, gives an implicit example of α and β that satisfy condition (3.7). This set of examples, of course, is not satisfactory since the way such (classical) models are constructed does not agree with the market model philosophy (discussed in the introduction) and, hence, produces very rigid dynamics of local volatility.

Even though we don't have a formal proof of the existence of the solution to (3.9) for any admissible β, we have everything needed in order to approximate the solution (assuming it exists) with an explicit Euler scheme: given the input, h_0 and β, make the step from h_t to $h_{t+\Delta t}$ by "freezing" the coefficients of the equation, $\alpha(h_t, \beta_t)$ and β_t. This method allows one to simulate (approximately, due to the numerical error of the Euler method) future arbitrage-free evolution of h (and hence the call prices) by choosing its diffusion coefficient β. The Euler scheme itself is guaranteed to work, in the sense that it will always produce future values of $h_t(.,.)$, however, in order for these values to make sense, they need to satisfy the conditions imposed on the code-book values: in other words, $h_t(.,.)$ has to be a regular enough surface so that one could compute the corresponding call prices via (2.7). The regularity of $h_t(.,.)$, simulated via the above Euler scheme, can be violated if the drift $\alpha(h_t, \beta_t)$ does not always produce a regular enough surface. It turns out that, in order to make sure that the right hand side of drift restriction (3.7) is regular enough at time t, one has to choose $\beta_t(\tau, x)$ satisfying certain additional restrictions as $\tau \to 0$, i.e. β is not a completely free parameter (see Sec. 5.2 of [5] for precise conditions $\beta_t(0, x)$ has to satisfy).

3.4. *When shouldn't local volatility models be used?*

Leaving aside the problem of existence of a solution to (3.9), another, more fundamental, question is the applicability of the diffusion-based code-book: "*Given a set of call option prices, when can we use the local volatility as a (static) code-book?*" A classical result of Gyöngy [18] shows that this is possible if the true underlying S is an Itô process satisfying some mild regularity conditions. However, if the true underlying dynamics have a non-trivial jump component, the local volatility function $\tilde{a}(T, K)$ given by Dupire's equation (2.2) will be singular as $T \searrow 0$. To see this, recall that for all $K \neq S_0$, the denominator of the right hand side of (2.2) converges to zero as $T \searrow 0$. Indeed, the second derivative of the call price with respect to strike is given by the density of the marginal distribution of the underlying index at time T whenever this density exists. To conclude, it is enough to notice (and this can be done by an application of the Itô's formula, or using (5.3) in the case of exponential Lévy processes) that, in the presence of jumps, the T-derivative of call prices does not necessarily vanish as $T \searrow 0$, which yields the explosion mentioned above. In fact, one can detect (at least in theory) the presence of jumps in the underlying (or the lack of thereof) by observing the short-maturity behavior of the implied volatility: it also explodes when the underlying has a non-trivial jumps component. In addition, at-the-money short-maturity behavior of the implied volatility may allow us to test for the presence of continuous component as in the pure jump models, at-the-money implied volatility vanishes as $T \searrow 0$. The detailed discussion of the above can be found in [10, 17, 27, 30] and references therein.

Our work [6] on tangent Lévy models was a natural attempt to depart from the assumption that S is an Itô process, and introduce jumps in its dynamics. The natural question: "*What is the right substitute for the local volatility code-book in this case?*" is addressed in the next section.

4. Dynamic Tangent Lévy Models

Using processes with jumps in financial modeling goes back to the pioneering work of Merton [26]. Fitting option prices with Lévy-based models has also a long history. At the risk of missing important contributions, we mention for example the series of works by Carr, Geman, Madan, Yor and Seneta between 1990 and 2005 [7, 9, 25] on models with jumps of infinite activity, such as the Variance Gamma (VG) and $CGMY$ models, and the easy to use double exponential model of Kou [23]. Still in the static case at time $t = 0$, Carr *et al.* noticed in their 2004 paper [8] that Dupire's local volatility can be interpreted as an S_t-dependent time change. On this ground, they introduced *Local Lévy* models which they defined as Markovian time changes of a Lévy process. However, following their approach to define a code-book would lead to the same level of complexity in the formulation of the consistency of the models. For this reason, we chose to define the code-book in a different way — via the *tangent Leévy models* (see the definition in Sec. 2.6).

4.1. *The Lévy measure code book*

Formula (2.9) defining the notation $C^{s,\tilde{\kappa}}(\tau, x)$ for the European call prices in pure jump exponential additive models can be used, together with the specification of "s" as the current value of the underlying, to establish a code-book, and as it was demonstrated above, in order to construct a *dynamic tangent model* we only need to prescribe the dynamics of the code value $(s, \tilde{\kappa})$ and make sure they are *consistent*. However, in order to study consistency of the code-book dynamics, we need to have a convenient analytic representation of the *code*: the associated transform between call prices and $(s, \tilde{\kappa})$. With this goal in mind, we introduce the Partial Integral Differential Equation (PIDE) representation of the call prices in pure jump exponential additive models:

$$\begin{cases} \partial_\tau C^{s,\tilde{\kappa}}(\tau, x) = \displaystyle\int_{\mathbb{R}} \psi(\tilde{\kappa}(\tau, \cdot); x - y) D_y C^{s,\tilde{\kappa}}(\tau, y) dy \\ C^{s,\tilde{\kappa}}(\tau, x)|_{\tau=0} = (s - e^x)^+, \end{cases} \tag{4.1}$$

where the double exponential tail function ψ is defined by

$$\psi(f; x) = \begin{cases} \displaystyle\int_{-\infty}^{x} (e^x - e^z) f(z) dz & x < 0 \\ \displaystyle\int_{x}^{\infty} (e^z - e^x) f(z) dz & x > 0. \end{cases} \tag{4.2}$$

Clearly, the presence of convolutions and constant coefficient differential operators in (5.3) are screaming for the use of Fourier transform.

4.2. *Fourier transform*

Unfortunately, the setup is not *Fourier transform friendly* as the initial condition in (5.3) is not an integrable function! In order to overcome this difficulty, we work with derivatives. Before taking Fourier transform (we use a "hat" for functions in Fourier space), we differentiate both sides of the PIDE (5.3) using the notation $\Delta^{s,\tilde{\kappa}}(\tau,x) = -\partial_x C^{s,\tilde{\kappa}}(\tau,x)$.

$$\begin{cases} \partial_\tau \hat{\Delta}^{s,\tilde{\kappa}}(\tau,\xi) = -(4\pi^2\xi^2 + 2\pi i\xi)\hat{\psi}(\tilde{\kappa}(\tau,\cdot),\xi)\hat{\Delta}^{s,\tilde{\kappa}}(\tau,\xi) \\ \hat{\Delta}^{s,\tilde{\kappa}}(\tau,\xi)|_{\tau=0} = \dfrac{\exp\{\log s(1-2\pi i\xi)\}}{1-2\pi i\xi} \end{cases} \tag{4.3}$$

The above equation gives us a mapping:

$$C^{s,\tilde{\kappa}} \hookrightarrow \hat{\Delta}^{s,\tilde{\kappa}} \hookrightarrow \hat{\psi} \hookrightarrow \tilde{\kappa}.$$

Conversely, in order to go from $\tilde{\kappa}$ and s to call prices we only need to solve the evolution equation in Fourier domain (4.3), and obtain $\hat{\Delta}^{s,\tilde{\kappa}}$ in closed form. We recover $\Delta^{s,\tilde{\kappa}}(T,x) = -\partial_x C^{s,\tilde{\kappa}}(T,x)$ by inverting the Fourier transform. A plain integration gives

$$\begin{aligned} C^{s,\tilde{\kappa}}(\tau,x) = s \lim_{\lambda\to+\infty} \int_{\mathbb{R}} & \frac{e^{2\pi i\xi\lambda} - e^{2\pi i\xi(x-\log s)}}{2\pi i\xi(1-2\pi i\xi)} \\ & \cdot \exp\left(-2\pi(2\pi\xi^2 + i\xi)\int_0^T \hat{\psi}(\tilde{\kappa}(u,\cdot),\xi)du\right) d\xi \end{aligned}$$

providing the required inverse mapping: $\tilde{\kappa} \hookrightarrow \hat{\psi} \hookrightarrow C^{s,\tilde{\kappa}}$.

4.3. *Formal definition of dynamic tangent Lévy models and consistency results*

In this case we assume that the set of liquid derivatives consists of call options with all possible strikes and with maturities not exceeding some fixed $\bar{T} > 0$. As in the case of tangent diffusion models we need to put the code value $(s,\tilde{\kappa})$ in motion by constructing a pair of stochastic processes $(s_t,\tilde{\kappa}_t)_{t\in[0,\bar{T}]}$ under the pricing measure. As before, we would like to keep the true model for the dynamics of the underlying index as general as possible while keeping the computations at a reasonable level of complexity. In this section, we assume that under the pricing measure, the underlying index S is a positive pure jump martingale given by

$$S_t = S_0 + \int_0^t \int_{\mathbb{R}} S_{u-}(e^x - 1)(M(dx,du) - K_u(x)dxdu) \tag{4.4}$$

for some (unknown) *integer valued random measure* M whose predictable compensator is absolutely continuous, i.e. of the form $K_{u,\omega}(x)dxdu$ for some stochastic process (K_u) with values in the Banach space $\mathcal{B}^0$ constructed in Sec. 3.1 of [6].

It may seem too restrictive to assume that the underlying process has no continuous martingale component and that the compensator of M is absolutely continuous. These assumptions are dictated by our choice of the code-book, which is based on pure jump processes without fixed points of discontinuity. Indeed, as we explained earlier, the short-maturity properties of call prices produced by pure jump models are incompatible with the presence of a continuous component in the underlying dynamics. Nevertheless, we propose an extension of the present code-book in the next section, and as a result, allow for slightly more general dynamics of the underlying.

If we want the model corresponding to $(s_t, \tilde{\kappa}_t)$ to be almost surely tangent to the true model at time t (in other words, if we want $(s_{t,\omega}, \tilde{\kappa}_{t,\omega})$ to be a code value that reproduces the market prices at time t, for almost all $\omega \in \Omega$), then s_t has to coincide with S_t, and its dynamics must be given by (4.4). Therefore, the only additional process whose time-evolution we need to specify is $(\tilde{\kappa}_t)_{t\in[0,\bar{T}]}$. In this case, it is more convenient to use the time-of-maturity T instead of the time-to-maturity τ, so we introduce the Lévy density $\kappa_t(T, x)$ defined by

$$\kappa_t(T, x) = \tilde{\kappa}_t(T - t, x),$$

and we specify its dynamics by an equation of the form

$$\kappa_t = \kappa_0 + \int_0^t \alpha_u du + \sum_{n=1}^{m} \int_0^t \beta_u^n dB_u^n \tag{4.5}$$

where $B = (B^1, \dots, B^m)$ is an m-dimensional Brownian motion (m can be ∞), α is a progressively measurable integrable stochastic process with values in a Banach space $\mathcal{B}$ defined in Sec. 3.1 of [6], and $\beta = (\beta^1, \dots, \beta^m)$ is a vector of progressively measurable square integrable stochastic processes taking values in a Hilbert space $\mathcal{H}$ defined also in Sec. 3.1 of [6].

Notice again, that the dynamics of κ_t could, in principle, include jumps. However, we chose to restrict our framework to the continuous evolution of κ in order to keep the results and their derivations more transparent.

Thus, a *dynamic tangent Lévy model* is defined by the pair of equations (4.4) and (4.5), given that such dynamics are consistent, or in other words, given that for any $(T, x) \in (0, \bar{T}] \times \mathbb{R}$ the following equality is satisfied almost surely for all $t \in [0, T)$

$$C^{S_t, \tilde{\kappa}_t}(T - t, x) = \mathbb{E}((S_T - K)^+ \,|\, \mathcal{F}_t)$$

As in Sec. 3, the above formulation of the consistency condition is not very convenient. It is important to characterize the consistency of code-book dynamics, (4.4) and (4.5), explicitly in terms of the input parameters: α, β and K. Such an explicit formulation of the consistency condition is one of the main results of [6], and it is given in Theorem 12 of the above mentioned paper. In order to state this result we introduce the notation:

$$\bar{\beta}_t^n(T,x) := \int_{t\wedge T}^{T} \beta_t^n(u,x)du, \quad \Psi(f;x) = -e^x \int_x^{\mathrm{sign}(x)\infty} f(y)dy. \tag{4.6}$$

Assuming that S is a true martingale, $\kappa \geq 0$ and β satisfies the *regularity assumptions RA1–RA4* given in Sec. 3.2 of [6], the code-book dynamics given by (4.4) and (4.5) are consistent if and only if the following conditions are satisfied:

(1) *Drift restriction*:

$$\begin{aligned}\alpha_t(T,x) = -e^{-x}\sum_{n=1}^{m}\int_{\mathbb{R}} &\partial_{y^2}^2 \Psi(\bar{\beta}_t^n(T);y)\\ &\times[\Psi(\beta_t^n(T);x-y) - (1-y\partial_x)\Psi(\beta_t^n(T);x)]\\ &-2\partial_y\Psi(\bar{\beta}_t^n(T);y)[\Psi(\beta_t^n(T);x-y) - \Psi(\beta_t^n(T);x)]\\ &+\Psi(\bar{\beta}_t^n(T);y)\Psi(\beta_t^n(T);x-y)dy,\end{aligned} \tag{4.7}$$

(2) *Compensator specification*: $K_t(x) = \kappa_t(t,x)$.

4.4. *Model specification and existence result*

Denoting by ρ the weight function

$$\rho(x) := e^{-\lambda|x|}(|x|^{-1-\delta} \vee 1),$$

with some $\lambda > 1$ and $\delta \in (0,1)$, and switching from κ_t to $\breve{\kappa}_t$ given by $\breve{\kappa}_t(T,x) = \kappa_t(T,x)/\rho(x)$, we can easily force $\breve{\kappa}_t$ to take values in a more convenient space of continuous functions, in which its maximal and minimal values can be controlled. Introducing the weighted drift $\breve{\alpha}_t = \alpha_t/\rho$, weighted diffusion terms $\{\breve{\beta}_t^n = \beta_t^n/\rho\}_{n=1}^m$ (which take values in corresponding function spaces, $\tilde{\mathcal{B}}$ and $\tilde{\mathcal{H}}$, defined in Sec. 5.1 of [6]) and the stopping time

$$\tau_0 = \inf\left\{t \geq 0 : \inf_{T\in[t,\bar{T}],x\in\mathbb{R}} \breve{\kappa}_t(T,x) \leq 0\right\},$$

(τ_0 is predictable and $\breve{\kappa}_{t\wedge\tau_0}$ is nonnegative), we can specify the model as follows:

- Assume that the market filtration supports a Brownian motion $\{B^n\}_{n=1}^m$ and an independent Poisson random measure N with compensator $\rho(x)dxdt$.
- Denote by $\{(t_n,x_n)\}_{n=1}^\infty$ the atoms of N. Then measure M (recall (4.4)) can be defined by its atoms

  $$\{(t_n, W[\breve{\kappa}_{t_n}(t_n,\cdot)](x_n))\}_{n=1}^\infty,$$

  for some deterministic mapping $f(\cdot) \mapsto W[f](\cdot)$, so that it has the desired compensator $\rho(x)\breve{\kappa}_t(t,x)dxdt$, and therefore, the *compensator specification* is satisfied. An explicit expression for W is given in Sec. 5 of [6].

- Rewrite the right hand side of *drift restriction* (4.7) using $\check{\beta}$ instead of β, and denote the resulting quadratic operator by $Q^{\check{\beta}_t}(T,x)$. Construct $\check{\kappa}_t$ by integrating "$Q^{\check{\beta}_t}dt + \check{\beta}_t \cdot dB_t$", and stop it at τ_0. Such $\check{\kappa}$ will satisfy the drift restriction and the nonnegativity property.

  In addition, $\beta_t = \rho\check{\beta}_t$ satisfies the *regularity assumptions RA1–RA4* in Sec. 3.2 of [6] due to the choice of state space for $\check{\beta}_t$ (the Hilbert space $\tilde{\mathcal{H}}$ defined in Sec. 5.1 of [6]).
- If we also choose $\check{\beta}$ to be independent of N, we can guarantee that S, produced by (4.4) and the above choice of M, is a true martingale. Thus, the above specification allows to determine the model uniquely through N, B and $\check{\beta}$.

As a result we obtain the following class of code-book dynamics:

$$\begin{cases} S_t = S_0 + \displaystyle\int_0^t \int_{\mathbb{R}} S_{u-}(\exp(W[\check{\kappa}_u(u,\cdot)](x)) - 1)(N(dx,du) - \rho(x)dxdu), \\ \tilde{\kappa}_t(\tau,x) = \rho(x)\check{\kappa}_t(t+\tau,x), \quad \check{\kappa}_t = \check{\kappa}_0 + \displaystyle\int_0^t Q^{\check{\beta}_u}\mathbf{1}_{u\le\tau_0}du + \sum_{n=1}^m \int_0^t \check{\beta}_u^n \mathbf{1}_{u\le\tau_0}dB_u^n \end{cases} \tag{4.8}$$

Theorem 2 in [6] states that for any square integrable stochastic process $\check{\beta}$ the above system has a unique solution, and if, in addition, $\check{\beta}$ is independent of N, then the resulting processes $(S_t)_{t\in[0,\bar{T}]}$ and $(\tilde{\kappa}_t)_{t\in[0,\bar{T}]}$ are consistent, and, therefore, form a *dynamic tangent Lévy model.*

This "local existence" result, albeit limited (the presence of stopping time τ_0 and the independence assumption should eventually be relaxed, as it is demonstrated by the example that follows), provides a method for construction of the future evolution of the code value, starting from any given one. In practice, it means that, if we are able to calibrate a model from the chosen space of pure jump exponential additive models to the currently observed option prices, we can use the above result to generate a large family of dynamic stochastic models for the future joint evolution of the option prices (or, equivalently, the *implied volatility* surface) and the underlying.

4.5. *Example of a dynamic tangent Lévy model*

The following tangent Lévy model was proposed in [6]. Its analysis and implementation on real market data is being carried out in [3]. Here we outline the main steps of the analysis to illustrate the versatility of the model, and the fact that it does provide an answer to the nagging question of the Monte Carlo simulation of arbitrage free time evolutions of implied volatility surfaces.

- Choose $m = 1$, and $\check{\beta}_t(T,x) = \gamma_t C(x)$,
- Let $\gamma_t = \gamma(\check{\kappa}_t, t) := \frac{\sigma}{\epsilon}(\inf_{T\in[t,\bar{T}],x\in\mathbb{R}} \check{\kappa}_t(T,x) \wedge \epsilon)$, for some $\sigma, \epsilon > 0$,

- and $C(x) = e^{-\lambda'|x|}(|x| \wedge 1)^{1+\delta}\tilde{C}(x)$, for some $\lambda' > 0, \delta \in (0,1)$ and some bounded absolutely continuous function $\tilde{C}$, with bounded derivative, such that

$$\int_{\mathbb{R}} (e^x - 1)e^{-(\lambda+\lambda')|x|}(|x| \wedge 1)^{-\delta}\tilde{C}(x)dx = 0,$$

and

$$\int_{\mathbb{R}} e^{-(\lambda+\lambda')|x|}(|x| \wedge 1)^{-\delta}\tilde{C}(x)dx = 0$$

- Then

$$d\breve{\kappa}_t(T,x) = \gamma^2(\breve{\kappa}_t,t)(T - t \wedge T)A(x)dt + \gamma(\breve{\kappa}_t,t)C(x)dB_t, \tag{4.9}$$

where A is obtained from C via the "drift restriction", which in this case (due to the properties of $\tilde{C}$ presented above) takes its simplest form, namely:

$$A(x) = -\frac{1}{\rho(x)} \int_{\mathbb{R}} \rho(y)C(y)\rho(x-y)C(x-y)dy$$

Please, see Sec. 6 of [6] for the derivation of the above formulae.

It is worth mentioning that, as shown in Proposition 17 of [6], the process $\breve{\kappa}$ defined by (4.9) always stays positive. In addition, as discussed in [6], the above example can be extended to diffusion coefficients of the form $\gamma_t C(T,x)$, and, of course, one can consider $\breve{\beta}^n(\cdot,\cdot)$'s given by functions "$C$" of different shapes. These functions, $\{C^n\}$, would correspond to different Brownian motions and can be estimated, for example, via the analysis in principal components (or an alternative statistical method) of the time series of $\tilde{\kappa}_t(\cdot,\cdot)$, fitted to the historical call prices on dates t of a recent past.

5. Extension of Dynamic Tangent Lévy Models

Notice that the dynamic tangent Lévy models introduced above do not allow for a continuous martingale component in the evolution of the underlying. This is a direct consequence of our choice of the space of tangent models: by being *pure jump* martingales, they force the evolution of the underlying index to have pure jump dynamics since short time asymptotic properties of the marginal distributions of pure jump processes are incompatible with the presence of continuous martingale component (recall the discussion in Sec. 3.4). In this section we consider an extension of the space of tangent Lévy models introduced above, which includes underlying processes with nontrivial continuous martingale components.

In the definition of tangent Lévy models given in Sec. 2.6, we now allow the tangent processes $\tilde{S}$ to be given by an equation of the form

$$\tilde{S}_t = s + \int_0^t \tilde{\Sigma}(u)d\tilde{B}_u + \int_0^t \int_{\mathbb{R}} \tilde{S}_{u-}(e^x - 1)[N(dx,du) - \tilde{\kappa}(u,x)dxdu], \tag{5.1}$$

for a one-dimensional Brownian motion $\tilde{B}$ and an independent Poisson random measure N whose compensator we denote $\tilde{\kappa}(u,x)dxdu$. The class of such models is then parameterized by $(s, \tilde{\Sigma}(\cdot), \tilde{\kappa}(.,.))$. As before, we introduce the call prices produced by $(s, \tilde{\Sigma}, \tilde{\kappa})$

$$C^{s,\tilde{\Sigma},\tilde{\kappa}}(\tau, x) = \mathbb{E}(\tilde{S}_\tau - e^x)^+, \tag{5.2}$$

and derive their analytic representation via the following PIDE:

$$\begin{cases} \partial_\tau C^{s,\tilde{\Sigma},\tilde{\kappa}}(\tau,x) = \dfrac{1}{2}\tilde{\Sigma}(\tau) D_x C^{s,\tilde{\Sigma},\tilde{\kappa}}(T,x) + \displaystyle\int_{\mathbb{R}} \psi(\tilde{\kappa}(\tau,\cdot); x-y) D_y C^{s,\tilde{\Sigma},\tilde{\kappa}}(\tau,y)dy \\ C^{s,\tilde{\kappa}}(\tau,x)|_{\tau=0} = (s-e^x)^+, \end{cases} \tag{5.3}$$

where $D_x = \partial^2_{x^2} - \partial_x$ and ψ is defined in (4.2). Analogous to the case of pure jump Lévy code-book, we introduce $\Delta^{s,\tilde{\Sigma},\tilde{\kappa}}(\tau,x) = -\partial_x C^{s,\tilde{\Sigma},\tilde{\kappa}}(\tau,x)$, and $\hat{\Delta}^{s,\tilde{\Sigma},\tilde{\kappa}}(\tau,\xi)$ as the Fourier transform of $\Delta^{s,\tilde{\Sigma},\tilde{\kappa}}(\tau,\cdot)$. Then we can rewrite (4.3) in the present setup (with one additional term on the right hand side of the equation) and obtain

$$\hat{\Delta}^{s,\tilde{\Sigma},\tilde{\kappa}}(\tau,\xi) = \frac{e^{(1-2\pi i\xi)\log s}}{1-2\pi i\xi} \exp\left(-2\pi(2\pi\xi^2 + i\xi)\int_0^\tau \frac{1}{2}\tilde{\Sigma}_t^2(u) + \hat{\psi}(\tilde{\kappa}_t(u,\cdot);\xi)du\right), \tag{5.4}$$

where $\hat{\psi}$ is the Fourier transform of ψ.

Given s, we obtain the desired one-to-one correspondence:

$$C^{s,\tilde{\Sigma},\tilde{\kappa}} \leftrightarrow \hat{\Delta}^{s,\tilde{\Sigma},\tilde{\kappa}} \leftrightarrow (\tilde{\Sigma},\hat{\psi}) \hookrightarrow (\tilde{\Sigma},\tilde{\kappa}).$$

Finally, we choose a stochastic motion in the code-book, producing the following dynamics of the code value:

$$\begin{cases} s_t = S_t, \quad S_t = S_0 + \displaystyle\int_0^t S_u\sigma_u dB_u^1 + \int_0^t\int_{\mathbb{R}} S_{u-}(e^x-1)(M(dx,du) - K_u(x)dxdu), \\ \tilde{\kappa}_t(\tau,x) = \kappa_t(t+\tau,x), \quad \kappa_t = \kappa_0 + \displaystyle\int_0^t \alpha_u du + \sum_{n=1}^m \int_0^t \beta_u^n dB_u^n, \\ \tilde{\Sigma}_t(\tau) = \Sigma_t(t+\tau), \quad \Sigma_t = \Sigma_0 + \displaystyle\int_0^t \mu_u du + \sum_{n=1}^m \int_0^t \nu_u^n dB_u^n, \end{cases} \tag{5.5}$$

where $B = (B^1, \ldots, B^m)$ is a multidimensional Brownian motion, M is an integer valued random measure with predictable compensator $K_{u,\omega}(x)dxdu$; $(K_t)_{t\in[0,\bar{T}]}$ is a predictable integrable stochastic process with values in the Banach space $\mathcal{B}^0$; $(\alpha_t)_{t\in[0,\bar{T}]}$ and $(\mu_t)_{t\in[0,\bar{T}]}$ are progressively measurable integrable stochastic processes with values in Banach spaces $\mathcal{B}$ and $C([0,\bar{T}])$ respectively; $(\beta^n)_{t\in[0,\bar{T}]}$ and $(\nu^n)_{t\in[0,\bar{T}]}$ are progressively measurable square integrable stochastic processes taking values in the Hilbert spaces $\mathcal{H}$ and $W^{1,2}([0,\bar{T}])$ respectively. Recall that $C([0,\bar{T}])$ is the space of continuous functions on $[0,\bar{T}]$, equipped with "sup" norm, and $W^{1,2}([0,\bar{T}])$ is the space of absolutely continuous functions on $[0,\bar{T}]$ with square integrable derivatives. Spaces $\mathcal{B}^0$, $\mathcal{B}$ and $\mathcal{H}$ are constructed in Sec. 3.1 of [6], and their definitions are presented in Appendix A. The following result characterizes the consistency of the above dynamics.

Theorem 5.1. *Assume that $(S_t)_{t\in[0,\bar{T}]}$ is a martingale, β satisfies the regularity assumptions RA1–RA4 in Sec.* 3.2 *of* [6] *(see Appendix A for their exact formulations) and $\kappa_t(T,x)\geq 0$, almost surely for all $t\in[0,\bar{T})$ and almost all $(T,x)\in[t,\bar{T}]\times\mathbb{R}$. Then processes $(S_t,\tilde{\Sigma}_t,\tilde{\kappa}_t)_{t\in[0,\bar{T}]}$ satisfying* (5.5) *are* consistent, *in the sense that*

$$C^{S_t,\tilde{\Sigma}_t,\tilde{\kappa}_t}(T-t,x)=\mathbb{E}((S_T-e^x)^+\,|\,\mathcal{F}_t)\,\text{almost surely,}$$
$$\text{for all } x\in\mathbb{R} \quad \text{and} \quad 0\leq t<T\leq\bar{T},$$

if and only if the following conditions hold almost surely for almost every $x\in\mathbb{R}$ and $t\in[0,\bar{T})$, and all $T\in(t,\bar{T}]$:

(1) *Drift restriction*:

$$\begin{aligned}\alpha_t(T,x)=-e^{-x}\sum_{n=1}^{m}\int_{\mathbb{R}}&\partial^2_{y^2}\Psi(\bar{\beta}^n_t(T,\cdot);y)\\&\times[\Psi(\beta^n_t(T,\cdot);x-y)-(1-y\partial_x)\Psi(\beta^n_t(T,\cdot);x)]\\&-2\partial_y\Psi(\bar{\beta}^n_t(T,\cdot);y)\Psi(\beta^n_t(T,\cdot);x-y)-\Psi(\beta^n_t(T,\cdot);x)]\\&+\Psi(\bar{\beta}^n_t(T,\cdot);y)\Psi(\beta^n_t(T,\cdot);x-y)dy+\sigma_t\partial_x\beta^1_t(T,x),\end{aligned}$$

(2) *Compensator specification*: $K_t(x)=\kappa_t(t,x)$,
(3) *Volatility specification*: $\sigma_t^2=\Sigma_t^2(t)$,
(4) *Stability of volatility*: $\mu\equiv 0,\nu\equiv 0$,

where Ψ and $\bar{\beta}$ are defined in (4.6).

Proof. First we prove that consistency of the code-book dynamics (5.5) is equivalent to the local martingale property of $(\hat{\Delta}^{S_t,\tilde{\Sigma}_t,\tilde{\kappa}_t}(T-t,\xi))_{t\in[0,T)}$, for all $\xi\in\mathbb{R}$ (see (5.4) for the definition of $\hat{\Delta}^{s,\tilde{\Sigma},\tilde{\kappa}}$). The proof of this equivalence is, essentially, a repetition of the propositions and corollaries from Sec. 4 of [6] and the first part of the proof of Theorem 12 in the above mentioned paper.

Recall Proposition 6 from Sec. 4 of [6], which states that the code-book dynamics are consistent if and only if the call prices $(C^{S_t,\tilde{\Sigma}_t,\tilde{\kappa}_t}(T-t,x))_{t\in[0,\bar{T})}$ produced by the code values are martingales. It is not hard to see, by essentially repeating the proof of the proposition, that its statement holds in the present setup. The necessity of the martingale property is obvious, let's prove the sufficiency. Notice that, as it is shown in [6], ψ is a bounded linear operator from $\mathcal{B}^0$ to $\mathbb{L}^1(\mathbb{R})$, and since $\|\kappa_t(T,\cdot)\|_{\mathcal{B}^0}$ and $\|\Sigma_t\|_{C([0,\bar{T}])}$ are almost surely bounded over $t \in [0,T]$, we conclude that

$$\hat{\Delta}^{S_t,\tilde{\Sigma}_t,\tilde{\kappa}_t}(T-t,\xi) \to \frac{e^{\log S_{T-}(1-2\pi i\xi)}}{(1-2\pi i\xi)},$$

in $\mathbb{L}^2(\mathbb{R})$ as a function of ξ, as $t \nearrow T$. Then we invert the fourier transform on both sides of the above to obtain that $\Delta^{S_t,\tilde{\Sigma}_t,\tilde{\kappa}_t}(T-t,x)$ converges to $e^x \mathbf{1}_{(-\infty,\log S_{T-}]}(x)$. Passing to the call prices $C^{S_t,\tilde{\Sigma}_t,\tilde{\kappa}_t}(T-t,x)$ via integration we conclude that they converge to the payoff $(S_T - e^x)^+$ as $t \nearrow T$ (recall that $S_{T-} = S_T$ almost surely). Thus, we conclude that, by construction of the code and due to the regularity of the code-book dynamics, the call prices produced by the code values converge to the right payoffs. Therefore, since call price processes $(C^{S_t,\tilde{\Sigma}_t,\tilde{\kappa}_t}(T-t,x))_{t\in[0,\bar{T})}$ are uniformly integrable (bounded by S_t), whenever they are martingales they have to coincide with the corresponding conditional expectations, which implies consistency of the model.

Now we need to prove that the martingale property of call prices $(C^{S_t,\tilde{\Sigma}_t,\tilde{\kappa}_t}(T-t,x))_{t\in[0,\bar{T})}$ is equivalent to the local martingale property of $(\hat{\Delta}^{S_t,\tilde{\Sigma}_t,\tilde{\kappa}_t}(T-t,\xi))_{t\in[0,\bar{T})}$. This, again, can be done along the lines presented in Sec. 4 of [6]. First, since $C^{S_t,\tilde{\Sigma}_t,\tilde{\kappa}_t}$ is bounded by S_t as shown above, the martingale property can indeed be substituted to the local martingale property. Next, we notice that $\hat{\Delta}^{S_t,\tilde{\Sigma}_t,\tilde{\kappa}_t}(\tau,\cdot)$ can be obtained from $C^{S_t,\tilde{\Sigma}_t,\tilde{\kappa}_t}(\tau,\cdot)$ by a composition of differentiation and Fourier transform, which is a linear operator and hence, in principle, should preserve the local martingale property. However, in order to apply this logic one needs to choose the right function spaces on which the above linear operator is bounded. A typical choice would be to embed the above processes into some Banach space such that the corresponding operator maps this space into itself. This approach turns out to be quite problematic since in the present case the Fourier transform is understood in the *generalized* sense, and there is no standard Banach space it would preserve. Hence, we consider $(\hat{\Delta}^{S_t,\tilde{\Sigma}_t,\tilde{\kappa}_t}(T-t,\cdot))_{t\in[0,\bar{T})}$ as a process in $\mathcal{S}^*$, and show that its local martingale property in the "weak sense" is equivalent to the local martingale property of the call prices. Recall that $\mathcal{S}^*$ is the topological dual of $\mathcal{S}$, the *Schwartz space* of (complex-valued) C^∞ functions on $\mathbb{R}$ whose derivatives of all orders decay at infinity faster than any negative power of $|x|$. Then any polynomially bounded Borel function f is an element of $\mathcal{S}^*$ since it can be viewed as a continuous functional on $\mathcal{S}$ via the duality

$$\langle f, \phi \rangle = \int_{\mathbb{R}} f(x)\overline{\phi(x)}dx. \tag{5.6}$$

This particular choice of the function space is dictated by the fact that both differentiation and Fourier transform map $\mathcal{S}^*$ into itself and are invertible on this space. We then define the "weak" local martingale property of a stochastic process (X_t) with values in $\mathcal{S}^*$ as the local martingale property of $(\langle X_t, \phi \rangle)$ for all $\phi \in \mathcal{S}$. It is shown in the first part of the proof of Theorem 12 in [6] that the local martingale property of $(C^{S_t,\tilde{\Sigma}_t,\tilde{\kappa}_t}(T-t,x))_{t\in[0,\bar{T})}$, for all $x \in \mathbb{R}$, is equivalent to the weak local martingale property of $(\hat{\Delta}^{S_t,\tilde{\Sigma}_t,\tilde{\kappa}_t}(T-t,\cdot))_{t\in[0,\bar{T})}$.

Thus, we need to characterize the weak local martingale property of $(\hat{\Delta}^{S_t,\tilde{\Sigma}_t,\tilde{\kappa}_t}(T-t,\cdot))_{t\in[0,\bar{T})}$ in terms of the input parameters of the model. Recall that (5.3) provides an explicit formula for $\hat{\Delta}^{S_t,\tilde{\Sigma}_t,\tilde{\kappa}_t}(T-t,\xi)$ in terms of (S_t,Σ_t,κ_t). Then, for fixed (T,ξ), we can apply an infinite dimensional Itô's formula to the process $(\hat{\Delta}^{S_t,\tilde{\Sigma}_t,\tilde{\kappa}_t}(T-t,\xi))_{t\in[0,\bar{T})}$ (the process itself is one dimensional but the input, (S_t,Σ_t,κ_t) is infinite dimensional) to compute its drift. Notice that

$$\hat{\Delta}^{S_t,\tilde{\Sigma}_t,\tilde{\kappa}_t}(T-t,\xi) = \hat{\Delta}^{S_t,\tilde{\kappa}_t}(T-t,\xi)\exp\left(-\pi(2\pi\xi^2+i\xi)\int_t^T \Sigma_t^2(u)du\right),$$

where $\hat{\Delta}^{s,\tilde{\kappa}}$ is defined by (4.3), or more explicitly in equation (13) of [6]. The semimartingale decomposition of $\hat{\Delta}^{S_t,\tilde{\kappa}_t}(T-t,\xi)$ is provided in Corollary 9 of [6], therefore we only need to compute the semimartingale decomposition of the additional factor. Applying Itô's lemma for conditional Banach spaces (see, for example, Theorem III.5.4 in [24]), we obtain

$$\begin{aligned} d&\left[\exp\left(-\pi(2\pi\xi^2+i\xi)\int_t^T \Sigma_t^2(u)du\right)\right] \\ &= \exp\left(-\pi(2\pi\xi^2+i\xi)\int_t^T \Sigma_t^2(u)du\right)\pi(2\pi\xi^2+i\xi) \\ &\quad\cdot\Bigg[\Bigg(\Sigma_t^2(t) - \int_t^T 2\Sigma_t(u)\mu_t(u) + \sum_{n=1}^m \nu_t^n(u)^2 du \\ &\quad + 2\pi(2\pi\xi^2+i\xi)\sum_{n=1}^m\left(\int_t^T \Sigma_t(u)\nu_t^n(u)du\right)^2\Bigg)dt \\ &\quad - \sum_{n=1}^m \int_t^T 2\Sigma_t(u)\nu_t^n(u)du\, dB_t^n\Bigg] \end{aligned}$$

Combining the above decomposition with Corollary 9 and Proposition 7 of [6] we apply classical Itô's rule to a product of two processes to obtain

$$\begin{aligned} d(\hat{\Delta}^{S_t,\tilde{\Sigma}_t,\tilde{\kappa}_t}(T-t,\xi)) &= \hat{\Delta}^{S_t,\tilde{\Sigma}_t,\tilde{\kappa}_t}(T-t,\xi)2\pi i\xi(1-2\pi i\xi) \\ &\quad\cdot\Bigg[\Bigg(\hat{\psi}(\kappa_t(t,\cdot)-K_t(\cdot);\xi) + \frac{1}{2}(\Sigma_t^2(t)-\sigma_t^2) - \int_t^T \Sigma_t(u)\mu_t(u) \\ &\quad + \frac{1}{2}\sum_{n=1}^m \nu_t^n(u)^2 du - \int_t^T \hat{\psi}(\alpha_t(u,\cdot);\xi)du + \pi i\xi(1-2\pi i\xi) \\ &\quad \times \sum_{n=1}^m \left(\int_t^T \Sigma_t(u)\nu_t^n(u) + \hat{\psi}(\beta_t^n(u,\cdot);\xi)du\right)^2 \end{aligned}$$

$$
\begin{aligned}
&- (1 - 2\pi i\xi)\sigma_t \int_t^T \Sigma_t(u)\nu_t^1(u) + \hat{\psi}(\beta_t^1(u,\cdot);\xi)du \Bigg) dt \\
&- \sum_{n=1}^m \int_t^T \Sigma_t(u)\nu_t^n(u) + \hat{\psi}(\beta_t^n(u,\cdot);\xi)du\, dB_t^n \Bigg] \\
&+ \int_{\mathbb{R}} \hat{\Delta}^{S_{t-},\tilde{\Sigma}_t,\tilde{\kappa}_t}(T-t,\xi)(e^{x(1-2\pi i\xi)} - 1) \\
&\times [M(dx,dt) - K_t(x)dxdt]
\end{aligned}
$$

Denote the drift in the right hand side of the above equation by $\Gamma_t(T,\xi)$. Notice that the above decomposition holds almost surely for ξ fixed. However, since $\hat{\Delta}^{S_t,\tilde{\Sigma}_t,\tilde{\kappa}_t}(T-t,\cdot)$ is continuous, we conclude that this decomposition holds almost surely for all $\xi \in \mathbb{R}$. Then we can apply stochastic Fubini's theorem (see, for example, Theorem 65 in [29]) to obtain, for any $\phi \in \mathcal{S}$

$$
d\langle \hat{\Delta}^{S_t,\tilde{\Sigma}_t,\tilde{\kappa}_t}(T-t,\cdot),\phi\rangle = \langle \Gamma_t(T,\cdot),\phi\rangle dt + dZ_t,
$$

where Z is a local martingale. The conditions needed for the application of stochastic Fubini's theorem can be verified by repeating the proof of Proposition 10 in [6].

We have shown that the model is consistent if and only if, for any $\phi \in \mathcal{S}$ and $T \in (0,\bar{T}]$, $\langle \Gamma_t(T,\cdot),\phi\rangle = 0$ almost surely for almost all $t \in [0,T)$. We can choose a dense countable subset of $\mathcal{S}$ and recall that $\Gamma_t(\cdot,\cdot)$ is continuous to conclude that consistency is equivalent to: *almost surely,* $\Gamma_t(T,\xi) = 0$ *for all* $\xi \in \mathbb{R}$ *and* $T \in (0,\bar{T}]$ *and almost all* $t \in [0,T)$. Since $\hat{\Delta}^{S_t,\tilde{\Sigma}_t,\tilde{\kappa}_t}(T-t,\xi) \neq 0$, we will search for necessary and sufficient conditions for $\Gamma_t(T,\xi)/\hat{\Delta}^{S_t,\tilde{\Sigma}_t,\tilde{\kappa}_t}(T-t,\xi)$ to be zero, for all $T \in (t,\bar{T})$ and $\xi \in \mathbb{R}$. Since this expression is absolutely continuous as a function of $T \in [t,\bar{T}]$, it vanishes if and only if its value at $T = t$ is zero and the value of its T-derivative is zero for all $(T,\xi) \in (t,\bar{T}) \times \mathbb{R}$. Thus, we obtain a system of two equations:

$$
\begin{aligned}
&\hat{\psi}(\kappa_t(t,\cdot) - K_t(\cdot);\xi) + \frac{1}{2}\left(\Sigma_t^2(t) - \sigma_t^2\right) = 0, \\
&2\pi i\xi(1-2\pi i\xi)\sum_{n=1}^m (\Sigma_t(T)\nu_t^n(T) + \hat{\psi}(\beta_t^n(T,\cdot);\xi)) \\
&\quad \times \int_t^T \Sigma_t(u)\nu_t^n(u) + \hat{\psi}(\beta_t^n(u,\cdot);\xi)du \\
&\quad - \Sigma_t(T)\mu_t(T) - \hat{\psi}(\alpha_t(T,\cdot,);\xi) + \frac{1}{2}\sum_{n=1}^m \nu_t^n(T)^2 \\
&\quad - (1-2\pi i\xi)\sigma_t(\Sigma_t(T)\nu_t^1(T) + \hat{\psi}(\beta_t^1(T,\cdot);\xi)) = 0
\end{aligned}
$$

Now, recall that Fourier transform of an absolutely integrable function converges to zero as the argument goes to infinity. Also notice that multiplication by "$2\pi i\xi$" in the Fourier domain corresponds to taking derivative in the original domain. Due to the regularity assumptions RA1–RA4 (see Appendix A),

$\partial_x \psi(\beta_t^n(T,\cdot);x) = \Psi(\beta_t^n(T,\cdot);x)$ is absolutely integrable in $x \in \mathbb{R}$, therefore, $\xi\hat{\psi}(\beta_t^n(T,\cdot);\xi) \to 0$, as $|\xi| \to \infty$. Using this observation, we can split the above system into the following parts

$$\kappa_t(t,x) - K_t(x) = 0, \quad \Sigma_t^2(t) - \sigma_t^2 = 0,$$

$$\sum_{n=1}^{m} \Sigma_t(T)\nu_t^n(T) \int_{t\wedge T}^{T} \Sigma_t(u)\nu_t^n(u)du = 0, \quad \Sigma_t(T)\mu_t(T) - \frac{1}{2}\sum_{n=1}^{m} \nu_t^n(T)^2 = 0,$$

$$2\pi i\xi(1-2\pi i\xi)\sum_{n=1}^{m} \hat{\psi}(\beta_t^n(u,\cdot);\xi) \int_{t\wedge T}^{T} \hat{\psi}(\beta_t^n(u,\cdot);\xi)du$$
$$-(1-2\pi i\xi)\sigma_t\hat{\psi}(\beta_t^1(T,\cdot);\xi) - \hat{\psi}(\alpha_t(T,\cdot);\xi) = 0,$$

which, after inverting the Fourier transform and operator ψ (see the end of the proof of Theorem 12 in Sec. 4 of [6]), yields the statement of the theorem. □

As one can see, the parameter Σ_t in the above tangent models cannot change as a continuous stochastic process in t, and therefore, the spot volatility σ_t has to be deterministic. This surprising result can be interpreted as follows: calibrating exponential additive model to the call option market at each time, assuming that the parameters of the calibration change continuously, one has to keep the same continuous quadratic variation component $\Sigma^2(\cdot)$ in order to avoid arbitrage.

6. Conclusions

In this paper we introduce the general formalism of *tangent models* for construction of *market models* for the time evolution of the prices of a specified set of liquidly traded derivatives. According to this methodology, a market model is defined by the choice of a *code-book* for the prices of the target set of derivatives (the "market prices") and by prescribing statistics of the market prices through a stochastic process for the code value. The above construction is motivated by the *dynamic calibration* frequently used by the practitioners and provides a rigorous mathematical framework for this phenomenon.

We illustrate the above formalism by a review of recent work based on the following representations of the call price surface:

- via *Local Volatility* surface,
- via *Tangent Lévy Density.*

Each of the above classes of models corresponds to a different type of dynamics of the underlying: *continuous* in the first case and *pure jump* in the second, while keeping the semimartingale property. Our description of tangent Lévy models is complete in the sense that for any admissible value of the free parameter (taking values in a given linear space), we can construct a unique arbitrage-free model for the future stochastic evolution of the call price surface.

Finally, the last contribution of this paper is to generalize the class of tangent Lévy models to include underlying processes with a continuous martingale component, and to extend the characterization of the consistency of the model (including the classical *drift condition*) to this enlarged class of models going beyond the pure jump underlying models studied in [6].

Appendix A

Here we recall the definitions of spaces $\mathcal{B}^0$, $\mathcal{B}$ and $\mathcal{H}$, as well as the regularity assumptions RA1–RA4, presented in Sec. 3.1 of [6].

Banach space $\mathcal{B}^0$ is the space of equivalence classes of Borel measurable functions $f : \mathbb{R} \hookrightarrow \mathbb{R}$ satisfying

$$\|f\|_{\mathcal{B}^0} := \int_{\mathbb{R}} (|x| \wedge 1)|x|(1 + e^x)|f(x)|dx < \infty.$$

Banach space $\mathcal{B}$ consists of *absolutely continuous* functions $f : [0, \bar{T}] \hookrightarrow \mathcal{B}^0$ satisfying

$$\|f\|_{\mathcal{B}} := \|f(0)\|_{\mathcal{B}^0} + \int_0^{\bar{T}} \left\| \frac{d}{du} f(u) \right\|_{\mathcal{B}^0} du < \infty.$$

Recall that a Borel function $f : [0, \bar{T}] \hookrightarrow \mathcal{B}^0$ is said to be absolutely continuous if there exists a measurable function $g : [0, \bar{T}] \hookrightarrow \mathcal{B}^0$, such that for any $t \in [0, \bar{T}]$ we have

$$f(t) := f(0) + \int_0^t g(u)du,$$

where the above integral is understood as the *Bochner integral* (see p. 44 in [13] for a definition) of a $\mathcal{B}^0$-valued function. In such a case, the equivalence class of such functions g is denoted $\frac{d}{dt} f$.

Hilbert space $\mathcal{H}^0$ is defined as the space of equivalence classes of functions satisfying

$$\|f\|^2_{\mathcal{H}^0} := \int_{\mathbb{R}} |x|^4 (1 + e^x)^2 |f(x)|^2 dx < \infty$$

(the inner product of $\mathcal{H}^0$ being obtained by polarization), and the Hilbert space $\mathcal{H}$ consists of absolutely continuous functions $f : [0, \bar{T}] \hookrightarrow \mathcal{H}^0$ satisfying

$$\|f\|^2_{\mathcal{H}} := \|f(0)\|^2_{\mathcal{H}^0} + \int_0^{\bar{T}} \left\| \frac{d}{du} f(u) \right\|^2_{\mathcal{H}^0} du < \infty.$$

Finally, we introduce

$$\begin{aligned} I^{n,k}_{t,\varepsilon} := \sup_{T \in [t, \bar{T}]} &\left[\operatorname{esssup}_{x \in \mathbb{R} \setminus [-\varepsilon, \varepsilon]} (e^x + 1)|\partial^k_{x^k} \beta^n_t(T, x)| \right. \\ &\left. + \int_{\mathbb{R}} (e^x + 1)|x|^3 (|x| \wedge 1)^{k-1} |\partial^k_{x^k} \beta^n_t(T, x)| dx \right], \end{aligned}$$

whenever the derivatives appearing in right hand side are well defined, and recall the

Regularity Assumptions. For each $n \le m$, almost surely, for almost every $t \in [0, \bar{T}]$, we have:

RA1: $\sup_{T\in[t,\bar{T}]} \int_{-1}^{1} |x||\beta_t^n(T,x)|dx < \infty$
RA2: For every $T \in [t, \bar{T}]$, the function $\beta_t^n(T, \cdot)$ is absolutely continuous on $\mathbb{R} \setminus \{0\}$.
RA3: For any $\varepsilon > 0$, $I_{t,\varepsilon}^{n,0} + I_{t,\varepsilon}^{n,1} < \infty$.
RA4: For any $T \in [t, \bar{T}]$, $\int_{\mathbb{R}} (e^x - 1)\beta_t^n(T, x) = 0$.

References

[1] H. Buehler, Consistent variance carve models, Technical report (2006).
[2] R. Carmona, HJM: A unified approach to dynamic models for fixed income, credit and equity markets, in *Paris-Princeton Lectures in Mathematical Finance*, 2005, Vol. 1919 of Lecture Notes in Mathematics (Springer-Verlag, 2007), pp. 3–45.
[3] R. Carmona, Y. Ma and S. Nadtochiy, Calibration and simulation of arbitrage free implied volatility dynamic models, Technical report, Princeton University (2010).
[4] R. Carmona and S. Nadtochiy, An infinite dimensional stochastic analysis approach to local volatility dynamic models, *Communications on Stochastic Analysis* **2**(1) (2008) 109–123.
[5] R. Carmona and S. Nadtochiy, Local volatility dynamic models, *Finance and Stochastics* **13** (2009) 1–48.
[6] R. Carmona and S. Nadtochiy, Tangent Lévy models, to appear *Finance and Stochastics* (2010).
[7] P. Carr, H. Geman, D. Madan and M. Yor, The fine structure of asset returns: An empirical investigation, *Journal of Business* **75**(2) (2002) 305–332.
[8] P. Carr, H. Geman, D. Madan, and M. Yor, From local volatility to local Lévy models, *Quantitative Finance* **4** (2005) 581–588.
[9] P. Carr and D. Madan, Option valuation using the fast Fourier transform, *Journal of Computational Finance* **2**(5) (1998) 61–73.
[10] P. Carr and L. Wu, What type of process underlies options? a simple robust test, *J. Finance* **58**(6) (2003) 2581–2610.
[11] R. Cont, I. da Fonseca and V. Durrleman, Stochastic models of implied volatility surfaces, *Economic Notes* **31**(2) (2002).
[12] E. Derman and I. Kani, Stochastic implied trees: Arbitrage pricing with stochastic term and strike structure of volatility, *International Journal of Theoretical and Applied Finance* **1** (1998) 61–110.
[13] J. Diestel and J. Uhl, *Vector Measures* (American Mathematical Society, 1979).
[14] B. Dupire, Pricing with a smile, *Risk* **7** (1994) 32–39.
[15] J. P. Fouque, G. Papanicolaou and R. Sircar, *Derivatives in Financial Markets with Stochastic Volatility* (Cambridge University Press, 2000).
[16] D. Gatarek, *The LIBOR Market Models in Practice* (Wiley, 2007).
[17] J. Gatheral, E. P. Hsu, P. M. Laurence, C. Ouyang and T.-H. Wang, Asymptotics of implied volatility in local volatility models, Technical report, http://www.math.northwestern.edu/~ehsu/ImpliedVolatilityExpansionRevisedDecemer23.pdf (2009).
[18] I. Gyöngyi, Mimicking the one-dimensional marginal distributions of processes having an ito differential, *Probability Theory and Related Fields* **71**(4) (1986) 501–516.

[19] D. Heath, R. Jarrow and A. Morton, Bond pricing and the term structure of interest rates: A new methodology for contingent claims valuation, *Econometrica* **60** (1992) 77–105.

[20] J. Jacod and P. Protter, Risk neutral compatibility with option prices, *Finance and Stochastics* **14** (2010) 285–315.

[21] J. Kallsen and P. Krüner, A Heath-Jarrow-Morton approach for stock options, Technical report, Kiel University (2010).

[22] F. Knight, *Foundations of the Prediction Process* (Oxford University Press, 1992).

[23] S. Kou, A jump-diffusion model for option pricing, *Management Science* **48**(8) (2002) 1086–1101.

[24] H. Kuo, *Gaussian Measures in Banach Spaces*, Lecture Notes in Mathematics (Springer-Verlag, Berlin, 1975).

[25] D. Madan and E. Seneta, The Variance Gamma (V.G.) model for share market returns, *Journal of Business* **63**(4) (1990) 511–524.

[26] R. Merton, Option pricing when underlying stock returns are discontinuous, *Journal of Financial Economics* **3** (1976) 125–144.

[27] J. Muhle-Karbe and M. Nutz, Small-time asymptotics of option prices and first absolute moments, Technical report, http://www.mat.univie.ac.at/~muhlekarbe/optasym.pdf (2010).

[28] M. Musiela and M. Rutkowski, *Martingale Methods in Financial Modelling*, 2nd Ed. (Springer Verlag, 2004).

[29] P. Protter, *Stochastic Integration and Differential Equations* (Springer-Verlag, Berlin, Heidelberg, 2005).

[30] M. Roper, Implied volatility explosions: European calls and implied volatilites close to expiry in exponential lévy models, Technical report, http://arxiv.org/PS_cache/arxiv/pdf/0809/0809.3305v2.pdf (2008).

[31] P. Schönbucher, A market model for stochastic implied volatility, *Phil. Trans. of the Royal Society, Series A* **357** (1999) 2071–2092.

[32] P. Schönbucher, Portfolio losses and the term structure of loss transition rates: A new methodology for the pricing of portfolio credit derivatives, Technical report, ETH Zürich (2005).

[33] M. Schweizer and J. Wissel, Arbitrage-free market models for option prices: The multi-strike case, Technical report (2008).

[34] M. Schweizer and J. Wissel, Term structures of implied volatilities: Absence of arbitrage and existence results, *Mathematical Finance* **18** (2008) 77–114.

[35] J. Sidenius, V. Piterbarg and L. Andersen, A new framework for dynamic credit portfolio loss modelling, *International Journal of Theoretical and Applied Finance* **11** (2008) 163–197.

COMPOSITION OF TIME-CONSISTENT DYNAMIC MONETARY RISK MEASURES IN DISCRETE TIME*

PATRICK CHERIDITO

ORFE, Princeton University
Princeton, NJ 08544, USA

MICHAEL KUPPER

Department of Mathematics
Humboldt University Berlin
10099 Berlin, Germany

In discrete time, every time-consistent dynamic monetary risk measure can be written as a composition of one-step risk measures. We exploit this structure to give new dual representation results for time-consistent convex monetary risk measures in terms of one-step penalty functions. We first study risk measures for random variables modelling financial positions at a fixed future time. Then we consider the more general case of risk measures that depend on stochastic processes describing the evolution of financial positions or cumulated cash flows. In both cases the new representations allow for a simple composition of one-step risk measures in the dual. We discuss several explicit examples and provide connections to the recently introduced class of dynamic variational preferences.

Keywords: Dynamic risk measures; time-consistency; dual representations.

1. Introduction

Following the introduction of coherent, convex and monetary risk measures in [2, 3, 19–21], different dynamic extensions have been proposed. This has led to the study of conditional representations and time-consistency properties of dynamic risk measures in various setups. We refer to [1, 4, 7, 10, 14, 18, 23, 25, 32–34, 36] for the discrete time case and [5, 6, 12, 13, 22, 28, 31] for risk measures in continuous time; see also [16] and [29] for related results for dynamic preferences in discrete time.

In this paper we provide representations of time-consistent dynamic monetary risk measures in discrete time that are similar in spirit to the continuous-time representations of [5, 6, 13, 22, 31]. Rather than looking at general dynamic monetary

*This chapter was originally published under the same title in *International Journal of Theoretical and Applied Finance*, Vol.14, No.1, 137–162 (2011). Singapore: World Scientific Publishing.

risk measures and trying to establish conditions for time-consistency, we here only consider time-consistent ones and view them as compositions of one-step risk measures. For time-consistent dynamic convex monetary risk measures, we exploit this structure to derive new dual representations in terms of the penalty functions of the one-step risk measures. These representations permit a simple construction of time-consistent dynamic convex monetary risk measures by composing one-step risk measures in the dual.

The structure of the paper is as follows. In Sec. 2, we study time-consistent dynamic monetary risk measures for random variables. They can be written as simple concatenations of one-step risk measures. In Theorem 2.1, Lemma 2.1 and Corollary 2.1 we give dual representations for time-consistent dynamic convex monetary risk measures for random variables. The time-consistency is reflected by an additive structure in the dual. We illustrate this with examples and provide connections to the dynamic variational preferences of [29]. In Sec. 3, we consider dynamic monetary risk measures that depend on stochastic processes describing the evolution of financial positions over time. In this case, the composition of one-step risk measures involves the aggregation of current and future risk. For time-consistent dynamic convex monetary risk measures, we translate this structure into a dual representation in terms of supermartingales; see Theorem 3.1, Lemma 3.2 and Corollary 3.1. We conclude by introducing a special class of one-step aggregators of composed form and discussing several related examples of risk measures that depend on the whole path of a stochastic process.

2. Dynamic Risk Measures for Bounded Random Variables

We fix a finite time horizon $T \in \mathbb{N}$ and let $(\Omega, \mathcal{F}, (\mathcal{F}_t)_{t=0}^T, \mathbb{P})$ be a filtered probability space such that $\mathbb{P}[A] \in \{0, 1\}$ for all $A \in \mathcal{F}_0$. $\mathbb{P}$ is not necessarily understood as a physical probability measure. We use it as reference measure that specifies the negligible events. Equalities and inequalities between random variables as well as equalities and inclusions betweens events are understood in the $\mathbb{P}$-almost sure sense. For instance, $A \subset B$ for $A, B \in \mathcal{F}$ means $\mathbb{P}[A \backslash B] = 0$. $L^\infty(\mathcal{F}_t)$ is the space of essentially bounded $\mathcal{F}_t$-measurable random variables. By $\mathcal{P}^a$ we denote the set of all probability measures on $(\Omega, \mathcal{F})$ that are absolutely continuous with respect to $\mathbb{P}$.

In this section the risky objects are financial positions at time T modelled by the set $L^\infty(\mathcal{F}_T)$ of essentially bounded $\mathcal{F}_T$-measurable random variables. We assume that there exists a money market account and use it as numeraire, that is, money at later times is expressed in multiples of the value of one dollar put into the money market account at time 0. A risk measure at time t is a mapping $\rho_t : L^\infty(\mathcal{F}_T) \to L^\infty(\mathcal{F}_t)$. $\rho_t(X)$ is interpreted as a capital requirement at time t for the financial position X conditional on the information given by $\mathcal{F}_t$. For the study of dynamic risk measures, it is more convenient to work with the negative $\phi_t = -\rho_t$ of a monetary risk measure. We call ϕ_t a monetary utility function. Alternative names are risk adjusted valuation ([4]) or acceptance measure ([33]).

Definition 2.1. Let $t \in \{0, \ldots, T\}$. We call a mapping $\phi_t : L^\infty(\mathcal{F}_T) \to L^\infty(\mathcal{F}_t)$ a monetary utility function at time t, if it has the following properties:

(N) **Normalization:** $\phi_t(0) = 0$
(M) **Monotonicity:** $\phi_t(X) \geq \phi_t(Y)$ for all $X, Y \in L^\infty(\mathcal{F}_T)$ such that $X \geq Y$
(T) **Translation property:** $\phi_t(X + m) = \phi_t(X) + m$ for all $X \in L^\infty(\mathcal{F}_T)$ and $m \in L^\infty(\mathcal{F}_t)$

We call ϕ_t a concave monetary utility function at time t, if it also satisfies

(C) **$\mathcal{F}_t$-concavity:** $\phi_t(\lambda X + (1-\lambda)Y) \geq \lambda \phi_t(X) + (1-\lambda)\phi_t(Y)$ for all $X, Y \in L^\infty(\mathcal{F}_t)$ and $\lambda \in L^\infty(\mathcal{F}_t)$ such that $0 \leq \lambda \leq 1$.

A dynamic monetary utility function is a family of monetary utility functions $(\phi_t)_{t=0}^T$. If all ϕ_t are concave, then we call $(\phi_t)_{t=0}^T$ a dynamic concave monetary utility function.

The normalization property (N) is convenient for the study of time-consistency questions. Every function $\phi_t : L^\infty(\mathcal{F}_T) \to L^\infty(\mathcal{F}_t)$ satisfying (M) and (T) can readily be normalized by passing to $\phi_t(.) - \phi_t(0)$. Note that the properties (M) and (T) imply the

(LP) **Local property:**

$$\phi_t(1_A X + 1_{A^c} Y) = 1_A \phi_t(X) + 1_{A^c} \phi_t(Y)$$

for all $X, Y \in L^\infty(\mathcal{F}_T)$ and $A \in \mathcal{F}_t$.

Indeed, it follows from (M) and (T) that

$$\begin{aligned}\phi_t(1_A X) - 1_{A^c} \|X\|_\infty &= \phi_t(1_A X - 1_{A^c} \|X\|_\infty) \leq \phi_t(X) \leq \phi_t(1_A X + 1_{A^c} \|X\|_\infty) \\ &= \phi_t(1_A X) + 1_{A^c} \|X\|_\infty .\end{aligned}$$

By multiplying through with 1_A, one obtains $1_A \phi_t(X) = 1_A \phi_t(1_A X)$, which is equivalent to (LP).

Definition 2.2. We call a dynamic monetary utility function $(\phi_t)_{t=0}^T$ time-consistent if

$$\phi_{t+1}(X) \geq \phi_{t+1}(Y) \quad \text{implies } \phi_t(X) \geq \phi_t(Y) \tag{2.1}$$

for all $X, Y \in L^\infty(\mathcal{F}_T)$ and $t = 0, \ldots, T-1$.

Due to the properties (N), (M) and (T), time-consistency of dynamic monetary utility functions on $L^\infty(\mathcal{F}_T)$ is equivalent to the dynamic programming principle

$$\phi_t(X) = \phi_t(\phi_{t+1}(X)) \quad \text{for all } X \in L^\infty(\mathcal{F}_T) \quad \text{and} \quad t = 0, \ldots, T-1. \tag{2.2}$$

Concepts equivalent or similar to (2.1) or (2.2) have been studied in different contexts, see for instance [4–6, 10, 12, 14–18, 25–29, 31–36].

2.1. *Generators*

For a dynamic monetary utility function $(\phi_t)_{t=0}^T$, we denote by φ_t the restriction of ϕ_t to $L^\infty(\mathcal{F}_{t+1})$ and call $(\varphi_t)_{t=0}^{T-1}$ the generator of $(\phi_t)_{t=0}^T$. It follows from (2.2) that a time-consistent dynamic monetary utility function is uniquely given by its generator. One can also start with an arbitrary family

$$\varphi_t : L^\infty(\mathcal{F}_{t+1}) \to L^\infty(\mathcal{F}_t), \quad t = 0, \dots, T-1,$$

of monetary utility functions and define the time-consistent monetary utility function $(\phi_t)_{t=0}^T$ by backwards induction:

$$\phi_T(X) = X \quad \text{and} \quad \phi_t(X) = \varphi_t(\phi_{t+1}(X)), \quad t \le T-1.$$

It is clear that every ϕ_t is $\mathcal{F}_t$-concave if and only if all φ_t are so.

2.2. *Duality*

In this section, we provide duality results for time-consistent dynamic concave monetary utility functions on $L^\infty(\mathcal{F}_T)$ in terms of one-step penalty functions. We need the sets of one-step transition densities

$$\mathcal{D}_t := \{\xi \in L^1_+(\mathcal{F}_t) : \mathrm{E}_{\mathbb{P}}[\xi \,|\, \mathcal{F}_{t-1}] = 1\}, \quad t = 1, \dots, T.$$

Every sequence $(\xi_1, \dots, \xi_T) \in \mathcal{D}_1 \times \cdots \times \mathcal{D}_T$ defines a probability measure $\mathbb{Q}^\xi$ in $\mathcal{P}^a$ with density

$$\frac{d\mathbb{Q}^\xi}{d\mathbb{P}} = \xi_1 \cdots \xi_T.$$

On the other hand, every probability measure $\mathbb{Q}$ in $\mathcal{P}^a$ induces a non-negative martingale

$$M_t^{\mathbb{Q}} := \mathrm{E}_{\mathbb{P}}\left[\frac{d\mathbb{Q}}{d\mathbb{P}} \,\middle|\, \mathcal{F}_t\right], \quad t = 0, \dots, T.$$

One has

$$\{M_{t-1}^{\mathbb{Q}} = 0\} \subset \{M_t^{\mathbb{Q}} = 0\} \quad \text{for all } 1 \le t \le T,$$

and the sequence

$$\xi_t^{\mathbb{Q}} := \begin{cases} \dfrac{M_t^{\mathbb{Q}}}{M_{t-1}^{\mathbb{Q}}} & \text{on } \{M_{t-1}^{\mathbb{Q}} > 0\} \\ 1 & \text{on } \{M_{t-1}^{\mathbb{Q}} = 0\} \end{cases} \qquad \text{for } t = 1, \dots, T,$$

is an element in $\mathcal{D}_1 \times \cdots \times \mathcal{D}_T$ with the property

$$\frac{d\mathbb{Q}}{d\mathbb{P}} = \xi_1^{\mathbb{Q}} \cdots \xi_T^{\mathbb{Q}}.$$

We will work with the convention

$$\mathrm{E}_{\mathbb{Q}}[X \,|\, \mathcal{F}_t] := \mathrm{E}_{\mathbb{P}}[\xi_{t+1}^{\mathbb{Q}} \cdots \xi_T^{\mathbb{Q}} X \,|\, \mathcal{F}_t], \quad X \in L^\infty(\mathcal{F}_T), \quad t = 0, \dots, T-1.$$

This is consistent with the standard definition of the conditional expectation. But according to the standard definition, $\mathrm{E}_{\mathbb{Q}}[X \mid \mathcal{F}_t]$ is only defined up to $\mathbb{Q}$-almost sure equality, whereas $\mathrm{E}_{\mathbb{P}}[\xi^{\mathbb{Q}}_{t+1} \cdots \xi^{\mathbb{Q}}_T X \mid \mathcal{F}_t]$ is a version of $\mathrm{E}_{\mathbb{Q}}[X \mid \mathcal{F}_t]$ which is defined up to $\mathbb{P}$-almost sure equality. This will be important for formulas like (2.3) and (2.12) below, which involve the essential infimum or supremum of random variables. We denote the essential infimum by ess inf and the essential supremum by ess sup. Both are understood with respect to the reference measure $\mathbb{P}$; for the definition and properties of the essential infumum and supremum, see for instance, Proposition VI.1.1 of Neveu [30] or the Appendix in Föllmer and Schied [20].

By $\bar{L}_+(\mathcal{F}_t)$ we denote all $\mathcal{F}_t$-measurable functions $X : \Omega \to [0, \infty]$. The conditional expectation of $X \in \bar{L}_+(\mathcal{F}_t)$ is, as usual, understood as

$$\mathrm{E}_{\mathbb{P}}[X \mid \mathcal{F}_t] := \lim_{n \to \infty} \mathrm{E}_{\mathbb{P}}[X \wedge n \mid \mathcal{F}_t].$$

Definition 2.3. For $t \in \{0, \ldots, T-1\}$, we call a mapping

$$\psi_t : \mathcal{D}_{t+1} \to \bar{L}_+(\mathcal{F}_t)$$

a one-step penalty function if it satisfies the following two conditions:

(i) $\operatorname{ess\,inf}_{\xi \in \mathcal{D}_{t+1}} \psi_t(\xi) = 0$
(ii) $\psi_t(1_A \xi + 1_{A^c} \xi') = 1_A \psi_t(\xi) + 1_{A^c} \psi_t(\xi')$ for all $\xi, \xi' \in \mathcal{D}_{t+1}$ and $A \in \mathcal{F}_t$.

For $\mathbb{Q} \in \mathcal{P}^a$, we set

$$\psi_t(\mathbb{Q}) := \psi_t(\xi^{\mathbb{Q}}_{t+1}).$$

A dynamic penalty function consists of a sequence $(\psi_t)_{t=0}^{T-1}$ of one-step penalty functions. It induces the mapping $\Psi : \mathcal{P}^a \to \bar{L}_+(\mathcal{F}_{T-1})$ given by $\Psi(\mathbb{Q}) = \sum_{t=0}^{T-1} \psi_t(\mathbb{Q})$.

In the following theorem we provide different dual representations through which a dynamic penalty function induces a time-consistent dynamic concave monetary utility function. A new feature of Theorem 2.1 compared to other representations of time-consistent dynamic convex monetary risk measures is that (2.5) provides a dual representation of a whole family of risk measures $(\phi_t)_{t=0}^T$ in terms of the single penalty function $\Psi = \sum_{j=0}^{T-1} \psi_j$. This extends the dual representation of a time-consistent dynamic coherent risk measure with one m-stable (or rectangular) set of probability measures (see [4, 10, 12, 16, 32]). Formula (2.4) can be seen as a discrete version of the continuous-time representation (37) in [6].

Theorem 2.1. *Let $(\psi_t)_{t=0}^{T-1}$ be a dynamic penalty function. Then*

$$\varphi_t(X) = \operatorname*{ess\,inf}_{\mathbb{Q} \in \mathcal{P}^a} \{\mathrm{E}_{\mathbb{Q}}[X \mid \mathcal{F}_t] + \psi_t(\mathbb{Q})\}, \quad t = 0, \ldots, T-1, \;\; X \in L^\infty(\mathcal{F}_{t+1}), \tag{2.3}$$

defines a generator of a time-consistent concave monetary utility function $(\phi_t)_{t=0}^T$ *with the following representations*:

$$\phi_t(X) = \operatorname*{ess\,inf}_{\mathbb{Q}\in\mathcal{P}^a} \mathrm{E}_{\mathbb{Q}}\left[X + \sum_{j=t+1}^{T} \psi_{j-1}(\mathbb{Q}) \,|\, \mathcal{F}_t\right] \tag{2.4}$$

$$= \operatorname*{ess\,inf}_{\mathbb{Q}\in\mathcal{P}^a} \mathrm{E}_{\mathbb{Q}}[X + \Psi(\mathbb{Q}) \,|\, \mathcal{F}_t] \tag{2.5}$$

for all $t \le T-1$ *and* $X \in L^\infty(\mathcal{F}_T)$.

Proof. It can easily be checked that for all $t \le T-1$,

$$\varphi_t(X) = \operatorname*{ess\,inf}_{\mathbb{Q}\in\mathcal{P}^a} \{\mathrm{E}_{\mathbb{Q}}[X \,|\, \mathcal{F}_t] + \psi_t(\mathbb{Q})\}$$

defines a concave monetary utility function from $L^\infty(\mathcal{F}_{t+1})$ to $L^\infty(\mathcal{F}_t)$. Therefore, $(\varphi_t)_{t=0}^{T-1}$ is the generator of a time-consistent dynamic concave monetary utility function $(\phi_t)_{t=0}^T$. It remains to show (2.4) and (2.5). To do this we denote (2.5) by $\tilde{\phi}_t(X)$. If $X \in L^\infty(\mathcal{F}_s)$ for $0 \le t < s \le T$, then

$$\tilde{\phi}_t(X) = \operatorname*{ess\,inf}_{(\xi_1,\ldots,\xi_T)\in\mathcal{D}_1\times\cdots\times\mathcal{D}_T} \mathrm{E}_{\mathbb{P}}\left[\xi_{t+1}\cdots\xi_T\left(X + \sum_{j=1}^{T}\psi_{j-1}(\xi_j)\right)\middle|\,\mathcal{F}_t\right]$$

$$= \sum_{j=1}^{t} \operatorname*{ess\,inf}_{\xi_j\in\mathcal{D}_j} \psi_{j-1}(\xi_j) \tag{2.6}$$

$$+ \operatorname*{ess\,inf}_{(\xi_{t+1},\ldots,\xi_s)\in\mathcal{D}_{t+1}\times\cdots\times\mathcal{D}_s} \left\{ \mathrm{E}_{\mathbb{P}}\left[\xi_{t+1}\cdots\xi_s\left(X + \sum_{j=t+1}^{s}\psi_{j-1}(\xi_j)\right)\middle|\,\mathcal{F}_t\right]\right.$$

$$\left. + \operatorname*{ess\,inf}_{(\xi_{s+1},\ldots,\xi_T)\in\mathcal{D}_{s+1}\times\cdots\times\mathcal{D}_T} \sum_{j=s+1}^{T} \mathrm{E}_{\mathbb{P}}[\xi_{t+1}\cdots\xi_{j-1}\,\psi_{j-1}(\xi_j) \,|\, \mathcal{F}_t]\right\}. \tag{2.7}$$

The terms (2.6) and (2.7) are both equal to 0. For (2.6) this follows directly from condition (i) of Definition 2.3. For (2.7) we prove it by induction over T: Fix $(\xi_{t+1},\ldots,\xi_s) \in \mathcal{D}_{t+1}\times\cdots\times\mathcal{D}_s$. If $T = s$, then the sum in (2.7) contains no terms and is equal to zero. If $T = s+1$, then (2.7) equals

$$\operatorname*{ess\,inf}_{\xi_{s+1}\in\mathcal{D}_{s+1}} \mathrm{E}_{\mathbb{P}}[\xi_{t+1}\cdots\xi_s\,\psi_s(\xi_{s+1}) \,|\, \mathcal{F}_t]. \tag{2.8}$$

By condition (ii) of Definition 2.3, the family $\{\psi_s(\xi_{s+1}) : \xi_{s+1} \in \mathcal{D}_{s+1}\}$ is directed downwards. Therefore, the ess inf in (2.8) can be taken over a decreasing sequence and, by Beppo Levi's dominated convergence theorem, commutes with the conditional expectation. By condition (i) of Definition 2.3, this shows that (2.8) is equal to zero. Now, assume $T \geq s+2$ and

$$\operatorname*{ess\,inf}_{(\xi_{s+1},\dots,\xi_{T-1})\in\mathcal{D}_{s+1}\times\cdots\times\mathcal{D}_{T-1}} \sum_{j=s+1}^{T-1} \mathrm{E}_{\mathbb{P}}[\xi_{t+1}\cdots\xi_{j-1}\,\psi_{j-1}(\xi_j)\,|\,\mathcal{F}_t] = 0.$$

Then, to prove that (2.7) is equal to zero, it is enough to show that for fixed $(\xi_{t+1},\dots,\xi_{T-1}) \in \mathcal{D}_{t+1}\times\cdots\times\mathcal{D}_{T-1}$, the term

$$\operatorname*{ess\,inf}_{\xi_T\in\mathcal{D}_T} \mathrm{E}_{\mathbb{P}}[\xi_{t+1}\cdots\xi_{T-1}\,\psi_{T-1}(\xi_T)\,|\,\mathcal{F}_t]$$

is zero. As above, this follows because ψ_{T-1} satisfies condition (ii) of Definition 2.3 and therefore, the ess inf can be taken inside the conditional expectation.

Since (2.6) and (2.7) are both equal to zero, one has

$$\begin{aligned}\tilde{\phi}_t(X) &= \operatorname*{ess\,inf}_{\mathbb{Q}\in\mathcal{P}^a} \mathrm{E}_{\mathbb{Q}}\left[X + \sum_{j=t+1}^{T} \psi_{j-1}(\mathbb{Q})\,\Big|\,\mathcal{F}_t\right]\\ &= \operatorname*{ess\,inf}_{\mathbb{Q}\in\mathcal{P}^a} \mathrm{E}_{\mathbb{Q}}\left[X + \sum_{j=t+1}^{s} \psi_{j-1}(\mathbb{Q})\,\Big|\,\mathcal{F}_t\right].\end{aligned} \tag{2.9}$$

Next, we show $\phi_t = \tilde{\phi}_t$ by induction over s. If $s = t+1$, then we obtain from (2.9) that

$$\phi_t(X) = \varphi_t(X) = \operatorname*{ess\,inf}_{\mathbb{Q}\in\mathcal{P}^a} \mathrm{E}_{\mathbb{Q}}[X + \psi_t(\mathbb{Q})\,|\,\mathcal{F}_t] = \tilde{\phi}_t(X) \quad \text{for all } X \in L^\infty(\mathcal{F}_s).$$

Now, assume $s \geq t+2$ and $\phi_t(Y) = \tilde{\phi}_t(Y)$ for all $Y \in L^\infty(\mathcal{F}_{s-1})$. If $X \in L^\infty(\mathcal{F}_s)$, then $\varphi_{s-1}(X) \in L^\infty(\mathcal{F}_{s-1})$, and we get

$$\begin{aligned}\phi_t(X) &= \phi_t(\varphi_{s-1}(X)) = \tilde{\phi}_t(\varphi_{s-1}(X))\\ &= \operatorname*{ess\,inf}_{\xi_{t+1},\dots,\xi_{s-1}\in\mathcal{D}_{t+1}\times\cdots\times\mathcal{D}_{s-1}} \mathrm{E}_{\mathbb{P}}\left[\xi_{t+1}\cdots\xi_{s-1}\left(\varphi_{s-1}(X) + \sum_{j=t+1}^{s-1}\psi_{j-1}(\xi_j)\right)\Bigg|\,\mathcal{F}_t\right]\end{aligned} \tag{2.10}$$

$$\begin{aligned}&= \operatorname*{ess\,inf}_{\xi_{t+1},\dots,\xi_{s-1}\in\mathcal{D}_{t+1}\times\cdots\times\mathcal{D}_{s-1}} \mathrm{E}_{\mathbb{P}}\Bigg[\xi_{t+1}\cdots\xi_{s-1}\\ &\quad\times \operatorname*{ess\,inf}_{\xi_s\in\mathcal{D}_s}\left\{\mathrm{E}_{\mathbb{P}}[\xi_s X\,|\,\mathcal{F}_{s-1}] + \sum_{j=t+1}^{s}\psi_{j-1}(\xi_j)\right\}\Bigg|\,\mathcal{F}_t\Bigg].\end{aligned} \tag{2.11}$$

By condition (ii) of Definition 2.3, the family

$$\mathrm{E}_{\mathbb{P}}[\xi_s X\,|\,\mathcal{F}_{s-1}] + \psi_{s-1}(\xi_s), \quad \xi_s \in \mathcal{D}_s$$

is directed downwards. Therefore, we can take the ess inf in (2.11) outside of the conditional expectation and arrive at

$$\phi_t(X) = \operatorname*{ess\,inf}_{\xi_{t+1},\dots,\xi_s \in \mathcal{D}_{t+1}\times\cdots\times\mathcal{D}_s} \mathrm{E}_{\mathbb{P}}\left[\xi_{t+1}\cdots\xi_s\left(X + \sum_{j=t+1}^{s}\psi_{j-1}(\xi_j)\right)\middle|\mathcal{F}_t\right]$$

$$= \tilde{\phi}_t(X),$$

which concludes the proof. □

Remark 2.1. The generator $(\varphi_t)_{t=0}^{T-1}$ and dynamic utility function $(\phi_t)_{t=0}^{T-1}$ in Theorem 2.1 can also be represented by the variants of (2.3)–(2.5), where $\mathcal{P}^a$ is replaced with the smaller set

$$\mathcal{P}^{\Psi} := \{\mathbb{Q} \in \mathcal{P}^a : \Psi(\mathbb{Q}) < \infty\}.$$

Indeed, it follows from conditions (i) and (ii) of Definition 2.3 that for all $t \le T-1$, there exists a sequence $(\xi^n_{t+1})_{n\ge1}$ in $\mathcal{D}_{t+1}$ such that $\psi_t(\xi^n_{t+1}) \downarrow 0$ $\mathbb{P}$-almost surely. Set $A^n_t := \{\psi_t(\xi^n_{t+1}) < \infty\}$ and define

$$\xi^*_{t+1} := \xi^1_{t+1}1_{A^1_t} + \sum_{n\ge2}\xi^n_{t+1}1_{\{A^n_t\setminus A^{n-1}_t\}}.$$

Then

$$\xi^*_{t+1} \in \mathcal{D}^{\psi_t}_{t+1} := \{\xi_{t+1} \in \mathcal{D}_{t+1} : \psi_t(\xi_{t+1}) < \infty\}.$$

For arbitrary $\xi_{t+1} \in \mathcal{D}_{t+1}$, the element $\tilde{\xi}_{t+1} := \xi_{t+1}1_{\{\psi_t(\xi_{t+1})<\infty\}} + \xi^*_{t+1}$ $1_{\{\psi_t(\xi_{t+1})=\infty\}}$ is in $\mathcal{D}^{\psi_t}_{t+1}$, and

$$\mathrm{E}_{\mathbb{P}}[\xi_{t+1}X \mid \mathcal{F}_t] + \psi_t(\xi_{t+1}) \ge \mathrm{E}_{\mathbb{P}}[\tilde{\xi}_{t+1}X \mid \mathcal{F}_t] + \psi_t(\tilde{\xi}_{t+1}) \quad \text{for } X \in L^\infty(\mathcal{F}_{t+1}).$$

Since

$$\mathcal{P}^{\Psi} = \mathcal{D}^{\psi_0}_1 \cdots \mathcal{D}^{\psi_{T-1}}_T,$$

this shows that

$$\varphi_t(X) = \operatorname*{ess\,inf}_{\mathbb{Q}\in\mathcal{P}^{\Psi}}\{\mathrm{E}_{\mathbb{Q}}[X \mid \mathcal{F}_t] + \psi_t(\mathbb{Q})\}, \quad X \in L^\infty(\mathcal{F}_{t+1}).$$

From here, exactly the same arguments as in the proof of Theorem 2.1 lead to

$$\phi_t(X) = \operatorname*{ess\,inf}_{\mathbb{Q}\in\mathcal{P}^{\Psi}} \mathrm{E}_{\mathbb{Q}}\left[X + \sum_{j=t+1}^{T}\psi_{j-1}(\mathbb{Q}) \mid \mathcal{F}_t\right] = \operatorname*{ess\,inf}_{\mathbb{Q}\in\mathcal{P}^{\Psi}} \mathrm{E}_{\mathbb{Q}}[X + \Psi(\mathbb{Q}) \mid \mathcal{F}_t]$$

for $t \le T-1$ and $X \in L^\infty(\mathcal{F}_T)$. Note that the second identity can be written in the alternative form

$$\phi_t(X) = \operatorname*{ess\,inf}_{(\mathbb{Q},q)\in\mathcal{Q}^{\Psi}} \mathrm{E}_{\mathbb{Q}}[X + q \mid \mathcal{F}_t],$$

for the set

$$\mathcal{Q}^{\Psi} := \{(\mathbb{Q}, q) \in \mathcal{P}^a \times L^0_+(\mathcal{F}_T) : q \ge \Psi(\mathbb{Q})\}.$$

It can easily be checked that generators with a dual representation of the form (2.3) and the corresponding dynamic monetary utility functions (2.4)–(2.5) have the following continuity property:

Definition 2.4. For $0 \le t \le s \le T$, we call a mapping $I : L^\infty(\mathcal{F}_s) \to L^\infty(\mathcal{F}_t)$ continuous from above if

$$I(X^n) \to I(X) \quad \mathbb{P}\text{-almost surely}$$

for every sequence $(X^n)_{n\in\mathbb{N}}$ in $L^\infty(\mathcal{F}_s)$ that decreases $\mathbb{P}$-almost surely to $X \in L^\infty(\mathcal{F}_s)$. We call a generator $(\varphi_t)_{t=0}^{T-1}$ or a dynamic monetary utility function $(\phi_t)_{t=0}^{T}$ on $L^\infty(\mathcal{F}_T)$ continuous from above if all φ_t or ϕ_t are continuous from above, respectively.

Next we are going to show that every time-consistent dynamic concave monetary utility function with generator that is continuous from above has representations of the form (2.4)–(2.5). This will be shown in Corollary 2.1 below. First we need the following definition and lemma.

Definition 2.5. For a time-consistent dynamic concave monetary utility function $(\phi_t)_{t=0}^{T-1}$ with generator $(\varphi_t)_{t=0}^{T-1}$ that is continuous from above we define for all $t = 0, \dots, T-1$,

$$\varphi_t^{\#}(\xi_{t+1}) := \operatorname*{ess\,sup}_{X\in L^\infty(\mathcal{F}_{t+1})} \{\varphi_t(X) - \mathrm{E}_{\mathbb{P}}[\xi_{t+1}X \,|\, \mathcal{F}_t]\}, \quad \xi_{t+1} \in \mathcal{D}_{t+1}. \tag{2.12}$$

Up to a sign, $\varphi_t^{\#}$ is the conditional concave conjugate of φ_t. In the next lemma we provide a conditional dual representation result for concave generators φ_t in terms of $\varphi_t^{\#}$. Similar results are proved in [4, 7, 10, 14, 28, 32, 34]. Since our setup is slightly different, we provide a proof.

Lemma 2.1. *Let $(\phi_t)_{t=0}^{T}$ be a time-consistent dynamic concave monetary utility function on $L^\infty(\mathcal{F}_T)$ with generator $(\varphi_t)_{t=0}^{T-1}$ that is continuous from above. Then $(\varphi_t^{\#})_{t=0}^{T-1}$ is the smallest dynamic penalty function such that*

$$\varphi_t(X) = \operatorname*{ess\,inf}_{\mathbb{Q}\in\mathcal{P}^a}\{\mathrm{E}_{\mathbb{Q}}[X \,|\, \mathcal{F}_t] + \varphi_t^{\#}(\mathbb{Q})\} \tag{2.13}$$

for all $t = 0, \dots, T-1$ and $X \in L^\infty(\mathcal{F}_{t+1})$.

Proof. We fix $t \in \{0, \dots, T-1\}$ and introduce the sets

$$\mathcal{B}_t := \{X \in L^\infty(\mathcal{F}_{t+1}) : \varphi_t(X) \ge 0\}$$

and

$$\mathcal{C}_t := \{X \in L^\infty(\mathcal{F}_{t+1}) : \mathrm{E}_{\mathbb{Q}}[X \,|\, \mathcal{F}_t] + \varphi_t^{\#}(\mathbb{Q}) \ge 0 \text{ for all } \mathbb{Q} \in \mathcal{P}^a\}.$$

It follows directly from the definition of $\varphi_t^{\#}$ that

$$\mathrm{E}_{\mathbb{Q}}[X \,|\, \mathcal{F}_t] + \varphi_t^{\#}(\mathbb{Q}) \ge \varphi_t(X)$$

for all $X \in L^\infty(\mathcal{F}_{t+1})$ and $\mathbb{Q} \in \mathcal{P}^a$. This shows that $\mathcal{B}_t \subset \mathcal{C}_t$. In the following we are going to prove $\mathcal{C}_t \subset \mathcal{B}_t$. Assume this is not the case. Then there exists $X^* \in \mathcal{C}_t \backslash \mathcal{B}_t$. Hence, the set $A := \{\varphi_t(X^*) < 0\}$ has positive $\mathbb{P}$-measure and $1_A X^*$ is still in $\mathcal{C}_t \backslash \mathcal{B}_t$. The mapping

$$X \mapsto I(X) := \mathrm{E}\left[\varphi_t(X)\right]$$

is a concave monetary utility function from $L^\infty(\mathcal{F}_{t+1})$ to $\mathbb{R}$ that is continuous from above. Hence, it can be deduced from the Krein–Šmulian theorem that

$$\mathcal{B} := \{X \in L^\infty(\mathcal{F}_{t+1}) : I(X) \geq 0\}$$

is $\sigma(L^\infty(\mathcal{F}_{t+1}), L^1(\mathcal{F}_{t+1}))$-closed, see for instance, the proof of Theorem 3.2 in Delbaen [11] or Remark 4.3 in Cheridito *et al.* [10]. Since it does not contain $1_A X^*$, it follows from the separating hyperplane theorem that there exists a $\mathbb{Q} \in \mathcal{P}^a$ such that

$$\mathrm{E}_{\mathbb{Q}}[1_A X^*] < \inf_{X \in \mathcal{B}} \mathrm{E}_{\mathbb{Q}}[X] \leq \inf_{X \in \mathcal{B}_t} \mathrm{E}_{\mathbb{Q}}[X] . \tag{2.14}$$

Since the family $\{\mathrm{E}_{\mathbb{Q}}[X \mid \mathcal{F}_t] : X \in \mathcal{B}_t\}$ is directed downwards, we obtain from Beppo Levi's monotone convergence theorem that

$$\inf_{X \in \mathcal{B}_t} \mathrm{E}_{\mathbb{Q}}[X] = \mathrm{E}_{\mathbb{Q}}\left[\operatorname*{ess\,inf}_{X \in \mathcal{B}_t} \mathrm{E}_{\mathbb{Q}}[X \mid \mathcal{F}_t]\right] .$$

Moreover, by the translation property of φ_t, $\varphi_t^{\#}$ can be written as

$$\varphi_t^{\#}(\mathbb{Q}) = \operatorname*{ess\,sup}_{X \in \mathcal{B}_t} \mathrm{E}_{\mathbb{Q}}[-X \mid \mathcal{F}_t] .$$

Therefore, it follows from (2.14) that

$$\mathrm{E}_{\mathbb{Q}}[1_A X^*] < \mathrm{E}_{\mathbb{Q}}[-\varphi_t^{\#}(\mathbb{Q})],$$

and hence,

$$\mathrm{E}_{\mathbb{Q}}[\mathrm{E}_{\mathbb{Q}}[1_A X^* \mid \mathcal{F}_t] + \varphi_t^{\#}(\mathbb{Q})] < 0.$$

But this contradicts $1_A X^* \in \mathcal{C}_t$. Thus, we must have $\mathcal{B}_t = \mathcal{C}_t$. Now note that for all $X \in L^\infty(\mathcal{F}_{t+1})$,

$$\varphi_t(X) = \operatorname{ess\,sup}\{m \in L^\infty(\mathcal{F}_t) : X - m \in \mathcal{B}_t\},$$

and therefore,

$$\begin{aligned}
\varphi_t(X) &= \operatorname{ess\,sup}\{m \in L^\infty(\mathcal{F}_t) : \mathrm{E}_{\mathbb{Q}}[X - m \mid \mathcal{F}_t] + \varphi_t^{\#}(\mathbb{Q}) \geq 0 \text{ for all } \mathbb{Q} \in \mathcal{P}^a\} \\
&= \operatorname{ess\,sup}\{m \in L^\infty(\mathcal{F}_t) : \mathrm{E}_{\mathbb{Q}}[X \mid \mathcal{F}_t] + \varphi_t^{\#}(\mathbb{Q}) \geq m \text{ for all } \mathbb{Q} \in \mathcal{P}^a\} \\
&= \operatorname*{ess\,inf}_{\mathbb{Q} \in \mathcal{P}^a} \{\mathrm{E}_{\mathbb{Q}}[X \mid \mathcal{F}_t] + \varphi_t^{\#}(\mathbb{Q})\}.
\end{aligned}$$

Finally, observe that for every function ψ_t from $\mathcal{D}_{t+1}$ to $\bar{L}_+(\mathcal{F}_t)$ satisfying

$$\varphi_t(X) = \operatorname*{ess\,inf}_{\xi_{t+1} \in \mathcal{D}_{t+1}} \{\mathrm{E}_{\mathbb{P}}[\xi_{t+1} X \mid \mathcal{F}_t] + \psi_t(\xi_{t+1})\}$$

for all $X \in L^\infty(\mathcal{F}_{t+1})$, one has

$$\varphi_t(X) - \mathrm{E}_{\mathbb{P}}[\xi_{t+1}X \mid \mathcal{F}_t] \le \psi_t(\xi_{t+1})$$

for all $X \in L^\infty(\mathcal{F}_{t+1})$ and $\xi_{t+1} \in \mathcal{D}_{t+1}$, and hence, $\varphi_t^\# \le \varphi_t$. □

The following corollary is an immediate consequence of Theorem 2.1 and Lemma 2.1.

Corollary 2.1. *Let $(\phi_t)_{t=0}^T$ be a time-consistent dynamic concave monetary utility function that is continuous from above. Then*

$$\phi_t(X) = \operatorname*{ess\,inf}_{\mathbb{Q}\in\mathcal{P}^a} \mathrm{E}_{\mathbb{Q}}\left[X + \sum_{j=t+1}^{T} \varphi_{j-1}^\#(\mathbb{Q}) \,\Big|\, \mathcal{F}_t\right] = \operatorname*{ess\,inf}_{\mathbb{Q}\in\mathcal{P}^a} \mathrm{E}_{\mathbb{Q}}\left[X + \phi^\#(\mathbb{Q}) \mid \mathcal{F}_t\right]$$

for all $t \le T-1$ and $X \in L^\infty(\mathcal{F}_T)$, where $\phi^\#(\mathbb{Q}) = \sum_{j=1}^T \varphi_{j-1}^\#(\mathbb{Q})$.

2.3. *Examples*

2.3.1. *Dynamic average-value-at-risk*

For every $t = 0,\ldots,T-1$, let α_t be an element of $L^\infty(\mathcal{F}_t)$ such that $0 < \alpha_t \le 1$ and consider the generators

$$\varphi_t(X) = \operatorname*{ess\,inf}_{\xi_{t+1}\in\mathcal{D}_{t+1},\, \xi_{t+1}\le\alpha_t^{-1}} \mathrm{E}_{\mathbb{P}}[\xi_{t+1}\, X \mid \mathcal{F}_t], \quad X \in L^\infty(\mathcal{F}_{t+1}).$$

Then, $-\varphi_t$ is a conditional Average-Value-at-Risk on $L^\infty(\mathcal{F}_{t+1})$ at the level α_t; see [20] for the definition of the unconditional Average-Value-at-Risk. The minimal dynamic penalty function $(\varphi_t^\#)_{t=0}^{T-1}$ of the induced time-consistent dynamic concave monetary utility function $(\phi_t)_{t=0}^T$ is given by

$$\begin{aligned}\varphi_t^\#(\xi_{t+1}) &= \operatorname*{ess\,sup}_{X\in L^\infty(\mathcal{F}_{t+1})} \{\varphi_t(X) - \mathrm{E}_{\mathbb{P}}[\xi_{t+1}X \mid \mathcal{F}_t]\} \\ &= \begin{cases} 0 & \text{on } \{\mathbb{P}[\xi_{t+1} > \alpha_t^{-1} \mid \mathcal{F}_t] = 0\} \\ \infty & \text{on } \{\mathbb{P}[\xi_{t+1} > \alpha_t^{-1} \mid \mathcal{F}_t] > 0\} \end{cases}.\end{aligned}$$

Hence,

$$\phi^\#(\mathbb{Q}) = \sum_{j=1}^T \varphi_{j-1}^\#(\mathbb{Q}) = \begin{cases} 0 & \text{if } \mathbb{P}[\xi_j^{\mathbb{Q}} > \alpha_{j-1}^{-1} \mid \mathcal{F}_{j-1}] = 0 \quad \text{for all } j = 1,\ldots,T \\ \infty & \text{else} \end{cases},$$

and

$$\phi_t(X) = \operatorname*{ess\,inf}_{\mathbb{Q}\in\mathcal{P}^a} \mathrm{E}_{\mathbb{Q}}\left[X + \phi^\#(\mathbb{Q}) \mid \mathcal{F}_t\right] = \operatorname*{ess\,inf}_{\mathbb{Q}\in\mathcal{Q}} \mathrm{E}_{\mathbb{Q}}[X \mid \mathcal{F}_t],$$

where

$$\mathcal{Q} := \{\mathbb{Q} \in \mathcal{P}^a : \xi_j^{\mathbb{Q}} \le \alpha_{j-1}^{-1} \text{ for all } j = 1,\ldots,T\}.$$

$(\rho_t)_{t=0}^T = (-\phi_t)_{t=0}^T$ is a time-consistent dynamic Average-Value-at-Risk at the dynamic level $(\alpha_0,\ldots,\alpha_{T-1})$.

2.3.2. *Dynamic entropic risk measure*

For all $t = 0, \dots, T-1$, let $\alpha_t \in L^\infty(\mathcal{F}_t)$ with $\alpha_t > 0$ and define φ_t by

$$\varphi_t(X) = -\alpha_t^{-1} \log \mathrm{E}_{\mathbb{P}}[\exp(-\alpha_t X) \,|\, \mathcal{F}_t], \quad X \in L^\infty(\mathcal{F}_{t+1}).$$

Then, $-\varphi_t$ is a conditional entropic risk measure on $L^\infty(\mathcal{F}_{t+1})$ with risk aversion parameter α_t; see [5, 6, 10, 14, 19, 20]. It is well known that the minimal dynamic penalty function $(\varphi_t^\#)_{t=0}^{T-1}$ of the induced time-consistent concave monetary utility function $(\phi_t)_{t=0}^T$ is given by

$$\varphi_t^\#(\xi_{t+1}) = \alpha_t^{-1} \mathrm{E}_{\mathbb{P}}[\xi_{t+1} \log(\xi_{t+1}) \,|\, \mathcal{F}_t].$$

Hence,

$$\phi^\#(\mathbb{Q}) = \sum_{j=1}^T \varphi_{j-1}^\#(\mathbb{Q}) = \sum_{j=1}^T \frac{1}{\alpha_j} \mathrm{E}_{\mathbb{Q}}\left[\log\left(\xi_{j+1}^{\mathbb{Q}}\right) \,|\, \mathcal{F}_j\right],$$

and

$$\phi_t(X) = \operatorname*{ess\,inf}_{\mathbb{Q} \in \mathcal{P}^a} \mathrm{E}_{\mathbb{Q}}\left[X + \phi^\#(\mathbb{Q}) \,|\, \mathcal{F}_t\right], \quad X \in L^\infty(\mathcal{F}_T), \quad t = 0, \dots, T.$$

2.3.3. *Dynamic variational preferences*

Denote by $\mathcal{R}^\infty$ the space of all essentially bounded adapted processes $(X_t)_{t=0}^T$ on $(\Omega, \mathcal{F}, (\mathcal{F}_t)_{t=0}^T, \mathbb{P})$. We here understand X_t as a (not necessarily discounted) cash-flow at time t. Let $(\phi_t)_{t=0}^T$ be a time-consistent dynamic concave monetary utility function on $L^\infty(\mathcal{F}_T)$ and $\beta > 0$ a depreciation factor. The transform

$$W_t(.) := \beta^{-t} \phi_t(\beta^t .), \quad t = 0, \dots, T,$$

is still a dynamic concave monetary utility function on $L^\infty(\mathcal{F}_T)$. It satisfies the β-time-consistency condition

$$W_{t+1}(Y) \geq W_{t+1}(Z) \quad \text{implies } W_t(\beta Y) \geq W_t(\beta Z) \quad \text{for } Y, Z \in L^\infty(\mathcal{F}_T).$$

or equivalently, the β-dynamic programming principle

$$W_t(Y) = W_t(\beta W_{t+1}(\beta^{-1} Y)) \quad \text{for } Y \in L^\infty(\mathcal{F}_T).$$

Now, let u be an increasing continuous function from $\mathbb{R}$ to $\mathbb{R}$. Then, the functionals

$$V_t(X) := W_t\left(\sum_{j=t}^T \beta^{j-t} u(X_j)\right), \quad X \in \mathcal{R}^\infty, \ t = 0, \dots, T,$$

satisfy the recursive relation

$$V_t(X) = u(X_t) + W_t(\beta V_{t+1}(X)), \quad t = 0, \dots, T-1.$$

In the simpler framework of finite sample spaces, this class of dynamic preferences is axiomatized in [29], where they are called dynamic variational preferences.

3. Dynamic Monetary Risk Measures for Stochastic Processes

In this section the risky objects are stochastic processes $X \in \mathcal{R}^\infty$ modelling discounted value processes or discounted cumulated cash flows; for instance, the discounted market value of a portfolio, the discounted equity value of a firm or the discounted surplus of an insurance company. This interpretation of $X \in \mathcal{R}^\infty$ is the same as in [4, 8–10, 25] but different from the one in Sec. 2.3.3 above, where X is understood as a sequence of cash flows. However, in discrete time it is easy to pass from cash flows to cumulated cash flows and back (see Sec. 3.1 below). As before, we are interested in monetary risk measures ρ_t but find it more convenient to work with the corresponding monetary utility functions $\phi_t = -\rho_t$. In the following, we generalize the definitions of Sec. 2 to this more general setup. For $0 \le t \le s \le T$, we define the projection $\pi_{t,s} : \mathcal{R}^\infty \to \mathcal{R}^\infty$ by

$$\pi_{t,s}(X)_r := 1_{\{t \le r\}} X_{r \wedge s}, \quad r = 0, \ldots, T.$$

and denote

$$\mathcal{R}^\infty_{t,s} := \pi_{t,s}(\mathcal{R}^\infty).$$

Definition 3.1. Let $t \in \{0, \ldots, T\}$. A monetary utility function on $\mathcal{R}^\infty_{t,T}$ is a mapping $\phi_t : \mathcal{R}^\infty_{t,T} \to L^\infty(\mathcal{F}_t)$ with the following properties:

(N) **Normalization:** $\phi_t(0) = 0$
(M) **Monotonicity:** $\phi_t(X) \ge \phi_t(Y)$ for all $X, Y \in \mathcal{R}^\infty_{t,T}$ such that $X \ge Y$
(T) **Translation property:** $\phi_t(X + m1_{[t,T]}) = \phi_t(X) + m$ for all $X \in \mathcal{R}^\infty_{t,T}$ and $m \in L^\infty(\mathcal{F}_t)$.
We call ϕ_t $\mathcal{F}_t$-concave if it satisfies
(C) **$\mathcal{F}_t$-concavity:** $\phi_t(\lambda X + (1-\lambda)Y) \ge \lambda\phi_t(X) + (1-\lambda)\phi_t(Y)$ for all $X, Y \in \mathcal{R}^\infty_{t,T}$ and $\lambda \in L^\infty(\mathcal{F}_t)$ such that $0 \le \lambda \le 1$

For $X \in \mathcal{R}^\infty$ we set

$$\phi_t(X) := \phi_t \circ \pi_{t,T}(X).$$

A dynamic monetary utility function on $\mathcal{R}^\infty$ is a family $(\phi_t)_{t=0}^T$ such that each ϕ_t is a monetary utility function on $\mathcal{R}^\infty_{t,T}$. If all ϕ_t satisfy (C), then we call $(\phi_t)_{t=0}^T$ a dynamic concave monetary utility function on $\mathcal{R}^\infty$.

As in the case of risk measures for random variables, it can be deduced from (M) and (T) that ϕ_t satisfies the

(LP) **Local property:** $\phi_t(1_A X + 1_{A^c} Y) = 1_A \phi_t(X) + 1_{A^c}\phi_t(Y)$ for all $X, Y \in \mathcal{R}^\infty$ and $A \in \mathcal{F}_t$.

Definition 3.2. We call a dynamic monetary utility function $(\phi_t)_{t=0}^T$ on $\mathcal{R}^\infty$ time-consistent if for all $X, Y \in \mathcal{R}^\infty$ and $t = 0, \ldots, T-1$,

$$X_t = Y_t \quad \text{and} \quad \phi_{t+1}(X) \ge \phi_{t+1}(Y)$$

imply

$$\phi_t(X) \geq \phi_t(Y).$$

It can easily be deduced from (N), (M) and (T) that time-consistency of a dynamic monetary risk measure on $\mathcal{R}^\infty$ is equivalent to the following dynamic programming principle:

$$\phi_t(X) = \phi_t(X_t 1_{\{t\}} + \phi_{t+1}(X) 1_{[t+1,T]}) \quad \text{for all } X \in \mathcal{R}^\infty \text{ and } t = 0, \dots, T-1. \tag{3.1}$$

3.1. *Cash flow streams*

In discrete time, one can easily pass from discounted value processes or cumulated discounted cash flows $X \in \mathcal{R}^\infty$ to discounted increments or discounted cash flows $C_0 = X_0$, $C_t = \Delta X_t = X_t - X_{t-1}$, $t \geq 1$. A monetary utility function $\phi_t : \mathcal{R}^\infty_{t,T} \to L^\infty(\mathcal{F}_t)$ induces the following functional for future discounted cash flows

$$\tilde{\phi}_t(C_{t+1}, \dots, C_T) = \phi_t\left(0, \dots, 0, C_{t+1}, C_{t+1} + C_{t+2}, \dots, \sum_{j=t+1}^{T} C_j\right).$$

The dynamic programming principle (3.1) translates into

$$\tilde{\phi}_t(C_{t+1}, \dots, C_T) = \tilde{\phi}_t(C_{t+1} + \tilde{\phi}_{t+1}(C_{t+2}, \dots, C_T), 0, \dots, 0),$$

and ϕ_t can be recovered from $\tilde{\phi}_t$ through

$$\phi_t(X) = X_t + \tilde{\phi}_t(\Delta X_{t+1}, \dots, \Delta X_T).$$

So in discrete time, the two formulations are equivalent.

3.2. *Aggregators and generators*

For a time-consistent dynamic monetary utility function $(\phi_t)_{t=0}^T$ on $\mathcal{R}^\infty$, we define the aggregators

$$G_t : L^\infty(\mathcal{F}_t) \times L^\infty(\mathcal{F}_{t+1}) \to L^\infty(\mathcal{F}_t), \quad t = 0, \dots, T-1$$

by

$$G_t(X_t, X_{t+1}) := \phi_t(X),$$

where X is the process in $\mathcal{R}^\infty_{t,t+1}$ given by

$$X_r := \begin{cases} 0 & \text{for } r < t \\ X_t & \text{for } r = t \\ X_{t+1} & \text{for } r \geq t+1 \end{cases}.$$

Clearly, G_t has the following three properties:

(G1) $G_t(0, 0) = 0$
(G2) $G_t(X_t, X_{t+1}) \geq G_t(Y_t, Y_{t+1})$ if $X_t \geq Y_t$ and $X_{t+1} \geq Y_{t+1}$
(G3) $G_t(X_t + m, X_{t+1} + m) = G_t(X_t, X_{t+1}) + m$ for all $m \in L(\mathcal{F}_t)$,

and it can be seen from (3.1) that the whole dynamic functional $(\phi_t)_{t=0}^T$ is uniquely determined by the aggregators $(G_t)_{t=0}^{T-1}$. In fact, every sequence of functionals $(G_t)_{t=0}^{T-1}$ satisfying (G1)–(G3) defines a time-consistent dynamic monetary utility function $(\phi_t)_{t=0}^T$ by

$$\phi_T(X) = X$$

$$\phi_t(X) = G_t(X_t, \phi_{t+1}(X)), \quad t \le T-1.$$

It is clear that $(\phi_t)_{t=0}^T$ is concave if and only if all G_t satisfy

(G4) $G_t(\lambda X_t + (1-\lambda)Y_t, \lambda X_{t+1} + (1-\lambda)Y_{t+1}) \ge \lambda G_t(X_t, X_{t+1}) + (1-\lambda)G_t(Y_t, Y_{t+1})$ for all $X_t, Y_t \in L^\infty(\mathcal{F}_t)$, $X_{t+1}, Y_{t+1} \in L^\infty(\mathcal{F}_{t+1})$ and $\lambda \in L^\infty(\mathcal{F}_t)$ such that $0 \le \lambda \le 1$.

By (G3), we can write G_t as

$$G_t(X_t, X_{t+1}) = X_t + G_t(0, X_{t+1} - X_t) = X_t + H_t(X_{t+1} - X_t), \tag{3.2}$$

for the mapping $H_t : L^\infty(\mathcal{F}_{t+1}) \to L^\infty(\mathcal{F}_t)$ given by

$$H_t(X) := G_t(0, X).$$

It follows from (G1)–(G3) that H_t has the following three properties:

(H1) $H_t(0) = 0$
(H2) $H_t(X) \ge H_t(Y)$ for $X, Y \in L^\infty(\mathcal{F}_{t+1})$ with $X \ge Y$
(H3) $H_t(X + m) \le H_t(X) + m$ for all $X \in L^\infty(\mathcal{F}_{t+1})$ and $m \in L^\infty_+(\mathcal{F}_t)$

(H1) and (H2) are clear, and (H3) holds because for $X \in L^\infty(\mathcal{F}_{t+1})$ and $m \in L^\infty_+(\mathcal{F}_t)$ one has

$$H_t(X + m) = G_t(0, X + m) = m + G_t(-m, X) \le m + G_t(0, X) = m + H_t(X).$$

On the other hand, every sequence $(H_t)_{t=0}^{T-1}$ of mappings satisfying (H1)–(H3) induces aggregators $(G_t)_{t=0}^{T-1}$ of a time-consistent dynamic monetary utility function $(\phi_t)_{t=0}^T$ on $\mathcal{R}^\infty$. Indeed, if H_t satisfies (H1)–(H3), then

$$G_t(X_t, X_{t+1}) = X_t + H_t(X_{t+1} - X_t)$$

satisfies (G1)–(G3). (G1) and (G3) are clear, and (G2) holds because for $X_t, Y_t \in L^\infty(\mathcal{F}_t)$ and $X_{t+1}, Y_{t+1} \in L^\infty(\mathcal{F}_{t+1})$ such that $X_t \ge Y_t$ and $X_{t+1} \ge Y_{t+1}$, one obtains from (H2) and (H3) that

$$\begin{aligned} G_t(X_t, X_{t+1}) &= X_t + H_t(X_{t+1} - X_t) \\ &\ge X_t + H_t(Y_{t+1} - X_t) \\ &\ge Y_t + H_t(Y_{t+1} - Y_t). \end{aligned}$$

We call $(H_t)_{t=0}^{T-1}$ the generators of $(\phi_t)_{t=0}^T$. It is clear that G_t satisfies (G4) if and only if H_t fulfils

(H4) $H_t(\lambda X + (1-\lambda)Y) \ge \lambda H_t(X) + (1-\lambda)H_t(Y)$ for all $\lambda \in L^\infty(\mathcal{F}_t)$ such that $0 \le \lambda \le 1$.

3.3. *Duality*

For $t = 1, \dots, T$, we define the set

$$\mathcal{E}_t := \{\xi \in L^1_+(\mathcal{F}_t) : \mathrm{E}_{\mathbb{P}}[\xi \,|\, \mathcal{F}_{t-1}] \leq 1\}.$$

Every sequence $(\xi_{t+1}, \dots, \xi_T) \in \mathcal{E}_{t+1} \times \cdots \times \mathcal{E}_T$ induces a $\mathbb{P}$-supermartingale $(M^\xi_r)_{r=0}^T$ by

$$M^\xi_r := \begin{cases} 1 & \text{for } r \leq t \\ \xi_{t+1} \cdots \xi_r & \text{for } r = t+1, \dots, T. \end{cases}$$

Definition 3.3. A one-step penalty function on $\mathcal{E}_{t+1}$ is a mapping

$$\psi_t : \mathcal{E}_{t+1} \to \bar{L}_+(\mathcal{F}_t)$$

that satisfies the two properties:

(i) $\operatorname{ess\,inf}_{\xi \in \mathcal{E}_{t+1}} \psi_t(\xi) = 0$
(ii) $\psi_t(1_A \xi + 1_{A^c} \xi') = 1_A \psi_t(\xi) + 1_{A^c} \psi_t(\xi')$ for all $\xi, \xi' \in \mathcal{E}_{t+1}$ and $A \in \mathcal{F}_t$

A dynamic penalty function on $\mathcal{E}$ is a sequence $(\psi_t)_{t=0}^{T-1}$ of one-step penalty functions.

Theorem 3.1. *Let $(\psi_t)_{t=0}^{T-1}$ be a dynamic penalty function on $\mathcal{E}$. Then*

$$H_t(X) = \operatorname*{ess\,inf}_{\xi_{t+1} \in \mathcal{E}_{t+1}} \{\mathrm{E}_{\mathbb{P}}[\xi_{t+1} X \,|\, \mathcal{F}_t] + \psi_t(\xi_{t+1})\}, \quad t = 0, \dots, T-1, \tag{3.3}$$

defines generators of a time-consistent dynamic concave monetary utility function $(\phi_t)_{t=0}^T$ on $\mathcal{R}^\infty$ with the following representation:

$$\phi_t(X) = X_t + \operatorname*{ess\,inf}_{(\xi_{t+1}, \dots, \xi_T) \in \mathcal{E}_{t+1} \times \cdots \times \mathcal{E}_T} \mathrm{E}_{\mathbb{P}}\left[\sum_{j=t+1}^T M^\xi_j \Delta X_j + M^\xi_{j-1} \psi_{j-1}(\xi_j) \,|\, \mathcal{F}_t\right] \tag{3.4}$$

for all $t \leq T-1$ and $X \in \mathcal{R}^\infty$.

Proof. It can easily be checked that for every $t = 0, \dots, T-1$,

$$H_t(X) = \operatorname*{ess\,inf}_{\xi_{t+1} \in \mathcal{E}_{t+1}} \{\mathrm{E}_{\mathbb{P}}[\xi_{t+1} X \,|\, \mathcal{F}_t] + \psi_t(\xi_{t+1})\}$$

defines a mapping from $L^\infty(\mathcal{F}_{t+1})$ to $L^\infty(\mathcal{F}_t)$ satisfying (H1)–(H4). Therefore, the family $(H_t)_{t=0}^{T-1}$ induces a time-consistent dynamic concave monetary utility function $(\phi_t)_{t=0}^T$ on $\mathcal{R}^\infty$. Let $X \in \mathcal{R}^\infty_{t,s}$ for some $t < s \leq T$ and denote

$$\phi_{t,s}(X) = X_t + \operatorname*{ess\,inf}_{(\xi_{t+1},\dots,\xi_s)\in\mathcal{E}_{t+1}\times\cdots\times\mathcal{E}_s} \mathrm{E}_{\mathbb{P}}\left[\sum_{j=t+1}^{s} M_j^\xi \Delta X_j + M_{j-1}^\xi \psi_{j-1}(\xi_j) \,|\, \mathcal{F}_t\right].$$

Since

$$\operatorname*{ess\,inf}_{(\xi_{s+1},\dots,\xi_T)\in\mathcal{E}_{s+1}\times\cdots\times\mathcal{E}_T} \mathrm{E}_{\mathbb{P}}\left[\sum_{j=s+1}^{T} M_{j-1}^\xi \psi_{j-1}(\xi_j) \,|\, \mathcal{F}_t\right] = 0,$$

for all $s \leq T-1$, one has

$$\phi_{t,s}(X) = X_t + \operatorname*{ess\,inf}_{(\xi_{t+1},\dots,\xi_T)\in\mathcal{E}_{t+1}\times\cdots\times\mathcal{E}_T} \mathrm{E}_{\mathbb{P}}\left[\sum_{j=t+1}^{T} M_j^\xi \Delta X_j + M_{j-1}^\xi \psi_{j-1}(\xi_j) \,|\, \mathcal{F}_t\right].$$

So it is enough to show that $\phi_t(X) = \phi_{t,s}(X)$. We prove this by induction over s. First, assume that $X \in \mathcal{R}^\infty_{t,t+1}$. Then,

$$\begin{aligned}\phi_t(X) &= G_t(X_t, \phi_{t+1}(X)) = G_t(X_t, X_{t+1}) = X_t + H_t(\Delta X_{t+1})\\ &= X_t + \operatorname*{ess\,inf}_{\xi_{t+1}\in\mathcal{E}_{t+1}} \{\mathrm{E}_{\mathbb{P}}[\xi_{t+1}\Delta X_{t+1} \,|\, \mathcal{F}_t] + \psi_t(\xi_{t+1})\} = \phi_{t,t+1}(X).\end{aligned}$$

Now, assume $X \in \mathcal{R}^\infty_{t,s}$ for $s \geq t+2$ and $\phi_t(Y) = \phi_{t,s-1}(Y)$ for all $Y \in \mathcal{R}^\infty_{t,s-1}$. By (3.1), we have $\phi_t(X) = \phi_t(Y)$ for

$$Y = 1_{[t,s-1)}X + 1_{[s-1,T]}\phi_{s-1}(X) \in \mathcal{R}^\infty_{t,s-1},$$

and therefore,

$$\begin{aligned}\phi_t(X) &= \phi_t(Y) = \phi_{t,s-1}(Y)\\ &= X_t + \operatorname*{ess\,inf}_{(\xi_{t+1},\dots,\xi_{s-1})\in\mathcal{E}_{t+1}\times\cdots\times\mathcal{E}_{s-1}} \mathrm{E}_{\mathbb{P}}\left[\sum_{j=t+1}^{s-1} M_j^\xi \Delta Y_j + M_{j-1}^\xi \psi_{j-1}(\xi_j) \,|\, \mathcal{F}_t\right]\\ &= X_t + \operatorname*{ess\,inf}_{(\xi_{t+1},\dots,\xi_{s-1})\in\mathcal{E}_{t+1}\times\cdots\times\mathcal{E}_{s-1}} \mathrm{E}_{\mathbb{P}}\Bigg[\sum_{j=t+1}^{s-2} M_j^\xi \Delta X_j + M_{s-1}^\xi [\phi_{s-1}(X) - X_{s-2}]\\ &\quad + \sum_{j=t+1}^{s-1} M_{j-1}^\xi \psi_{j-1}(\xi_j) \,|\, \mathcal{F}_t\Bigg]\end{aligned}$$

$$= X_t + \operatorname*{ess\,inf}_{(\xi_{t+1},\dots,\xi_{s-1})\in\mathcal{E}_{t+1}\times\cdots\times\mathcal{E}_{s-1}} \mathrm{E}_{\mathbb{P}}\left[\sum_{j=t+1}^{s-2} M_j^{\xi}\Delta X_j + M_{s-1}^{\xi}\left[\Delta X_{s-1}\right.\right.$$

$$\left.\left. + \operatorname*{ess\,inf}_{\xi_s\in\mathcal{E}_s}\{\mathrm{E}_{\mathbb{P}}[\xi_s\Delta X_s \,|\, \mathcal{F}_{s-1}] + \psi_{s-1}(\xi_s)\}\right] + \sum_{j=t+1}^{s-1} M_{j-1}^{\xi}\psi_{j-1}(\xi_j) \,\Big|\, \mathcal{F}_t\right], \quad (3.5)$$

where for $s = t+2$, the term $\sum_{j=t+1}^{s-2} M_j^{\xi}\Delta X_j$ is understood as 0. By condition (ii) of Definition 3.3, the family

$$\mathrm{E}_{\mathbb{P}}[\xi_s\Delta X_s \,|\, \mathcal{F}_{s-1}] + \psi_{s-1}(\xi_s), \quad \xi_s \in \mathcal{E}_s,$$

is directed downwards. Therefore, we can take the ess inf in (3.5) outside of the conditional expectation $\mathrm{E}_{\mathbb{P}}[. \,|\, \mathcal{F}_t]$ and arrive at

$$\begin{aligned}\phi_t(X) &= X_t + \operatorname*{ess\,inf}_{(\xi_{t+1},\dots,\xi_s)\in\mathcal{E}_{t+1}\times\cdots\times\mathcal{E}_s} \mathrm{E}_{\mathbb{P}}\left[\sum_{j=t+1}^{s} M_j^{\xi}\Delta X_j + M_{j-1}^{\xi}\psi_{j-1}(\xi_j)\right] \\ &= \phi_{t,s}(X).\end{aligned}$$

□

It is easy to see that aggregators of the form (3.3) are continuous from above in the sense of Definition 2.4 and utility functions of the form (3.4) are continuous from above in the following more general sense:

Definition 3.4. Let $0 \le t \le s \le T$. We call a mapping $I : \mathcal{R}_{t,s}^{\infty} \to L^{\infty}(\mathcal{F}_t)$ continuous from above if $I(X^n) \to I(X)$ $\mathbb{P}$-almost surely for all $(X^n)_{n\in\mathbb{N}}$ and X in $\mathcal{R}_{t,s}^{\infty}$ such that X_r^n decreases to X_r $\mathbb{P}$-almost surely for all $r = t,\dots,s$. We call a dynamic monetary utility function $(\phi_t)_{t=0}^T$ on $\mathcal{R}^{\infty}$ continuous from above if every ϕ_t is continuous from above.

Lemma 3.1. *A time-consistent dynamic monetary utility function $(\phi_t)_{t=0}^T$ is continuous from above if and only if all of the corresponding aggregators $(G_t)_{t=0}^{T-1}$ are continuous from above, which is the case if and only if all of the associated generators $(H_t)_{t=0}^{T-1}$ are continuous from above.*

Proof. It is obvious that $(\phi_t)_{t=0}^T$ is continuous from above if and only if all aggregators $(G_t)_{t=0}^{T-1}$ are continuous from above. Now, fix t and assume that G_t is continuous from above. If $(X^n)_{n\in\mathbb{N}}$ and X are in $L^{\infty}(\mathcal{F}_{t+1})$ such that $(X^n)_{n\in\mathbb{N}}$ decreases to X $\mathbb{P}$-almost surely, then we have

$$H_t(X^n) = G_t(0, X^n) \downarrow G_t(0, X) = H_t(X) \quad \mathbb{P}\text{-almost surely.}$$

Hence, H_t is continuous from above. On the other hand, if we assume that H_t is continuous from above and $(X_t^n, X_{t+1}^n)_{n\in\mathbb{N}}$ is a sequence in $L^{\infty}(\mathcal{F}_t) \times L^{\infty}(\mathcal{F}_{t+1})$

that decreases to $(X_t, X_{t+1}) \in L^\infty(\mathcal{F}_t) \times L^\infty(\mathcal{F}_{t+1})$ $\mathbb{P}$-almost surely, then

$$\begin{aligned} G_t(X_t^n, X_{t+1}^n) &= X_t^n + H_t(X_{t+1}^n - X_t^n) \\ &\le X_t^n + H_t(X_{t+1}^n - X_t) \downarrow X_t + H_t(X_{t+1} - X_t) \\ &= G_t(X_t, X_{t+1}) \end{aligned}$$

$\mathbb{P}$-almost surely. This shows that G_t is continuous from above. □

Definition 3.5. For a time-consistent dynamic concave monetary utility function $(\phi_t)_{t=0}^T$ on $\mathcal{R}^\infty$ with generators $(H_t)_{t=0}^{T-1}$ that are continuous from above, we define for $\xi_{t+1} \in \mathcal{E}_{t+1}$ and $t = 0, \dots, T-1$,

$$H_t^\#(\xi_{t+1}) := \operatorname*{ess\,sup}_{X \in L^\infty(\mathcal{F}_{t+1})} \{H_t(X) - \mathrm{E}_\mathbb{P}[\xi_{t+1} X \mid \mathcal{F}_t]\}.$$

Lemma 3.2. *Let $(\phi_t)_{t=0}^T$ be a time-consistent dynamic concave monetary utility function on $\mathcal{R}^\infty$ with generators $(H_t)_{t=0}^{T-1}$ that are continuous from above. Then $(H_t^\#)_{t=0}^{T-1}$ is the smallest dynamic penalty function on $\mathcal{E}$ such that*

$$H_t(X) = \operatorname*{ess\,inf}_{\xi_{t+1} \in \mathcal{E}_{t+1}} \{\mathrm{E}_\mathbb{P}[\xi_{t+1} X \mid \mathcal{F}_t] + H_t^\#(\xi_{t+1})\} \tag{3.6}$$

for all $t = 0, \dots, T-1$ and $X \in L^\infty(\mathcal{F}_{t+1})$.

Proof. Fix $t \in \{0, \dots, T-1\}$ and consider $\hat{\Omega} := \{t, t+1\} \times \Omega$ with the σ-algebra $\hat{\mathcal{F}}_{t+1}$ generated by all sets of the form $\{j\} \times A_j$ for $j = t, t+1$ and $A_j \in \mathcal{F}_j$. Let $\hat{\mathbb{P}}$ be the probability measure on $(\hat{\Omega}, \hat{\mathcal{F}}_{t+1})$ given by $\hat{\mathbb{P}}[\{j\} \times A_j] := \frac{1}{2}\mathbb{P}[A_j]$ for $j = t, t+1$ and $A_j \in \mathcal{F}_j$. By $\hat{\mathcal{F}}_t$ we denote the σ-algebra on $\hat{\Omega}$ generated by all sets of the form $\{t, t+1\} \times A_t$ for $A_t \in \mathcal{F}_t$. Then one has

$$L^\infty(\mathcal{F}_t) \times L^\infty(\mathcal{F}_{t+1}) = L^\infty(\hat{\Omega}, \hat{\mathcal{F}}_{t+1}, \hat{\mathbb{P}}),$$

and the aggregator G_t can be viewed as a concave monetary utility function from $L^\infty(\hat{\Omega}, \hat{\mathcal{F}}_{t+1}, \hat{\mathbb{P}})$ to $L^\infty(\hat{\Omega}, \hat{\mathcal{F}}_t, \hat{\mathbb{P}})$. Clearly, it is continuous from above. Therefore, it follows from Lemma 2.1 that

$$\begin{aligned} &G_t(X_t, X_{t+1}) \\ &\quad = \operatorname*{ess\,inf}_{(a, \xi_{t+1}) \in L^\infty_{[0,1]}(\mathcal{F}_t) \times \mathcal{D}_{t+1}} \{\mathrm{E}_\mathbb{P}[(1-a)X_t + a\xi_{t+1} X_{t+1} \mid \mathcal{F}_t] + \zeta_t(a, \xi_{t+1})\}, \end{aligned} \tag{3.7}$$

where

$$L^\infty_{[0,1]}(\mathcal{F}_t) := \{a \in L^\infty(\mathcal{F}_t) : 0 \le a \le 1\}$$

and

$$\begin{aligned} &\zeta_t(a, \xi_{t+1}) \\ &\quad := \operatorname*{ess\,sup}_{(X_t, X_{t+1}) \in L^\infty(\mathcal{F}_t) \times L^\infty(\mathcal{F}_{t+1})} \{G_t(X_t, X_{t+1}) - \mathrm{E}_\mathbb{P}[(1-a)X_t + a\,\xi_{t+1} X_{t+1} \mid \mathcal{F}_t]\} \\ &\quad = \operatorname*{ess\,sup}_{(X_t, X_{t+1}) \in L^\infty(\mathcal{F}_t) \times L^\infty(\mathcal{F}_{t+1})} \{G_t(0, \Delta X_{t+1}) - \mathrm{E}_\mathbb{P}[a\,\xi_{t+1} \Delta X_{t+1} \mid \mathcal{F}_t]\} \\ &\quad = \operatorname*{ess\,sup}_{X \in L^\infty(\mathcal{F}_{t+1})} \{H_t(X) - \mathrm{E}_\mathbb{P}[a\,\xi_{t+1} X \mid \mathcal{F}_t]\}. \end{aligned}$$

Hence,

$$H_t(X) = G_t(0, X) = \operatorname*{ess\,inf}_{\xi_{t+1} \in \mathcal{E}_{t+1}} \{\mathrm{E}_{\mathbb{P}}[\xi_{t+1} X \mid \mathcal{F}_t] + H_t^{\#}(\xi_{t+1})\}$$

for all $X \in L^\infty(\mathcal{F}_{t+1})$. The minimality of $H_t^{\#}$ follows because every function $\psi_t : \mathcal{E}_{t+1} \to \bar{L}_+(\mathcal{F}_t)$ fulfilling

$$H_t(X) = \operatorname*{ess\,inf}_{\xi_{t+1} \in \mathcal{E}_{t+1}} \{\mathrm{E}_{\mathbb{P}}[\xi_{t+1} X \mid \mathcal{F}_t] + \psi_t(\xi_{t+1})\} \quad \text{for all } X \in L^\infty(\mathcal{F}_{t+1})$$

must also satisfy

$$H_t(X) - \mathrm{E}_{\mathbb{P}}[\xi_{t+1} X \mid \mathcal{F}_t] \le \psi_t(\xi_{t+1}) \quad \text{for all } X \in L^\infty(\mathcal{F}_{t+1}) \text{ and } \xi_{t+1} \in \mathcal{E}_{t+1},$$

and therefore, $H_t^{\#} \le \psi_t$. □

The following corollary is an immediate consequence of Theorem 3.1 and Lemma 3.2.

Corollary 3.1. *Let $(\phi_t)_{t=0}^T$ be a time-consistent dynamic concave monetary utility function that is continuous from above. Then*

$$\phi_t(X) = X_t + \operatorname*{ess\,inf}_{(\xi_{t+1},\dots,\xi_T) \in \mathcal{E}_{t+1} \times \cdots \times \mathcal{E}_T} \mathrm{E}_{\mathbb{P}}\left[\sum_{j=t+1}^{T} M_j^{\xi} \Delta X_j + M_{j-1}^{\xi} H_{j-1}^{\#}(\xi_j) \mid \mathcal{F}_t\right]$$

for all $t \le T-1$ and $X \in R^\infty$.

3.4. *Composed generators*

We now consider generators of the special form

$$H_t(X) = h_t(\varphi_t(X)), \tag{3.8}$$

where $\varphi_t : L^\infty(\mathcal{F}_{t+1}) \to L^\infty(\mathcal{F}_t)$ is a monetary utility function from $L^\infty(\mathcal{F}_{t+1})$ to $L^\infty(\mathcal{F}_t)$ and $h_t : \mathbb{R} \to \mathbb{R}$ is a function satisfying

(h1) $h_t(0) = 0$
(h2) $h_t(x) \ge h_t(y)$ for $x \ge y$
(h3) $|h_t(x) - h_t(y)| \le |x - y|$ for all $x, y \in \mathbb{R}$.

Then $H_t = h_t \circ \varphi_t : L^\infty(\mathcal{F}_{t+1}) \to L^\infty(\mathcal{F}_t)$ satisfies the properties (H1), (H2) and (H3). Hence, $(h_t, \varphi_t)_{t=0}^{T-1}$ induces a time-consistent dynamic monetary utility function $(\phi_t)_{t=0}^T$ on $\mathcal{R}^\infty$. If in addition to (h1)–(h3), h_t is concave and φ_t $\mathcal{F}_t$-concave, then H_t satisfies (H4), and $(\phi_t)_{t=0}^T$ is a time-consistent dynamic concave monetary utility function on $\mathcal{R}^\infty$.

By standard convex duality, every concave function $h : \mathbb{R} \to \mathbb{R}$ can be represented as

$$h(x) = \min_{y \in \mathbb{R}} xy - h^*(y),$$

where h^* is the concave conjugate given by

$$h^*(y) := \inf_{x \in \mathbb{R}} xy - h(x).$$

As a consequence, the following representation result holds:

Proposition 3.1. *If* $\varphi_t : L^\infty(\mathcal{F}_{t+1}) \to L^\infty(\mathcal{F}_t)$ *is given by*

$$\varphi_t(X) = \operatorname*{ess\,inf}_{\xi_{t+1} \in \mathcal{D}_{t+1}} \{\mathrm{E}_\mathbb{P}[\xi_{t+1} X \,|\, \mathcal{F}_t] + \eta_t(\xi_{t+1})\}$$

for a one-step penalty function η_t *on* $\mathcal{D}_{t+1}$ *and* $h_t : \mathbb{R} \to \mathbb{R}$ *is a concave function satisfying* (h1)–(h3). *Then* $H_t = h_t(\varphi_t(X))$ *can be represented as*

$$H_t(X) = \operatorname*{ess\,inf}_{\xi_{t+1} \in \mathcal{E}_{t+1}} \{\mathrm{E}_\mathbb{P}[\xi_{t+1} X \,|\, \mathcal{F}_t] + \psi_t(\xi_{t+1})\}, \quad X \in L^\infty(\mathcal{F}_{t+1}),$$

for the one-step penalty function ψ_t *on* $\mathcal{E}_{t+1}$ *given by*

$$\psi_t(\xi_{t+1}) = \mathrm{E}_\mathbb{P}[\xi_{t+1} \,|\, \mathcal{F}_t]\, \eta_t\left(\frac{\xi_{t+1}}{\mathrm{E}_\mathbb{P}[\xi_{t+1} \,|\, \mathcal{F}_t]}\right) - h_t^*(\mathrm{E}_\mathbb{P}[\xi_{t+1} \,|\, \mathcal{F}_t]).$$

Proof. Since h_t satisfies (h2) and (h3), we have $h_t^*(y) = -\infty$ for $y \notin [0,1]$, and therefore

$$\begin{aligned} H_t(X) &= h_t(\eta_t(X)) \\ &= h_t\left(\operatorname*{ess\,inf}_{\xi_{t+1} \in \mathcal{D}_{t+1}} \{\mathrm{E}_\mathbb{P}[\xi_{t+1} X \,|\, \mathcal{F}_t] + \eta_t(\xi_{t+1})\}\right) \\ &= \operatorname*{ess\,inf}_{0 \le y \le 1,\, \xi_{t+1} \in \mathcal{D}_{t+1}} \{y\, [\mathrm{E}_\mathbb{P}[\xi_{t+1} X \,|\, \mathcal{F}_t] + \eta_t(\xi_{t+1})] - h_t^*(y)\} \\ &= \operatorname*{ess\,inf}_{\xi_{t+1} \in \mathcal{E}_{t+1}} \left\{\mathrm{E}_\mathbb{P}[\xi_{t+1} X \,|\, \mathcal{F}_t] + \mathrm{E}_\mathbb{P}[\xi_{t+1} \,|\, \mathcal{F}_t] \eta_t\left(\frac{\xi_{t+1}}{\mathrm{E}_\mathbb{P}[\xi_{t+1} \,|\, \mathcal{F}_t]}\right)\right. \\ &\quad \left. - h_t^*(\mathrm{E}_\mathbb{P}[\xi_{t+1} \,|\, \mathcal{F}_t])\right\}. \end{aligned}$$

□

In the following we are going to discuss different specifications of the function h_t. This leads to extensions of some of the examples of Sec. 5 of Cheridito *et al.* [10].

3.4.1. *Risk measures which only depend on the final value*

If $h_t(x) = x$, then the aggregators reduce to

$$G_t(X_t, X_{t+1}) = X_t + h_t(\varphi_t(X_{t+1} - X_t)) = \varphi_t(X_{t+1}).$$

So one has

$$\phi_t(X) = G_t(X_t, \phi_{t+1}(X)) = \varphi_t(\phi_{t+1}(X)) = \varphi_t \circ \cdots \circ \varphi_{T-1}(X_T),$$

that is, $(\phi_t)_{t=0}^T$ is a time-consistent dynamic utility function which only depends on the final value X_T of X.

3.4.2. *Risk measures that depend on a weighted average over time*

If $h_t(x) = \gamma_t x$ for $\gamma_t \in L^\infty(\mathcal{F}_t)$ such that $0 < \gamma_t \le 1$, then

$$G_t(X_t, X_{t+1}) = X_t + h_t(\varphi_t(X_{t+1} - X_t)) = (1-\gamma_t)X_t + \gamma_t\varphi_t(X_{t+1}).$$

Consider the mappings $\phi_t^\gamma : L^\infty(\mathcal{F}_T) \to L^\infty(\mathcal{F}_t)$ given by

$$\phi_t^\gamma(X) = \gamma_t\varphi_t \circ \gamma_{t+1}\varphi_{t+1} \circ \cdots \circ \gamma_{T-1}\varphi_{T-1}\left(\frac{X}{\gamma_t \cdots \gamma_{T-1}}\right).$$

Then the time-consistent dynamic monetary utility function $(\phi_t)_{t=0}^T$ on $\mathcal{R}^\infty$ induced by the aggregators $(G_t)_{t=0}^T$ is given by

$$\phi_t(X) = \phi_t^\gamma\left(\sum_{j=t}^T \delta_j^t X_j\right), \quad t = 0, \ldots, T-1,$$

where

$$\delta_j^t = \begin{cases} 1-\gamma_t & \text{for } j = t \\ \gamma_t \cdots \gamma_{j-1}(1-\gamma_j) & \text{for } t < j < T. \\ \gamma_t \cdots \gamma_{T-1} & \text{for } j = T \end{cases}$$

In particular, for $\gamma_t = \frac{T-t}{T-t+1}$, one obtains

$$\phi_t(X) = \phi_t^\gamma\left(\frac{1}{T-t+1}\sum_{j=t}^T X_j\right).$$

Observe that for the special case, where all φ_t have the scaling property $\varphi_t(\gamma_t X) = \gamma_t\varphi_t(X)$, the ϕ_t^γ are of the form $\phi_t^\gamma = \varphi_t \circ \cdots \circ \varphi_{T-1}$.

3.4.3. *Risk measures defined by worst stopping*

For $h_t(x) = x \wedge 0$, the aggregators become

$$G_t(X_t, X_{t+1}) = X_t + h_t(\varphi_t(X_{t+1} - X_t)) = X_t \wedge \varphi_t(X_{t+1}), \tag{3.9}$$

and the ϕ_t are of the form

$$\phi_t(X) = \operatorname*{ess\,inf}_{\tau \in \Theta_t} \tilde{\phi}_t(X_\tau), \quad X \in \mathcal{R}^\infty,$$

where Θ_t is the set of all $\{t, \dots, T\}$-valued stopping times and $(\tilde{\phi}_t)_{t=0}^T$ is the time-consistent dynamic concave monetary utility function on $L^\infty(\mathcal{F}_T)$ given by

$$\tilde{\phi}_t(X) = \varphi_t \circ \cdots \circ \varphi_{T-1}(X), \quad X \in L^\infty(\mathcal{F}_T).$$

This can be seen by checking that

$$\operatorname*{ess\,inf}_{\tau \in \Theta_t} \tilde{\phi}_t(X_\tau), \quad t = 0, \dots, T$$

is a time-consistent dynamic monetary utility function on $\mathcal{R}^\infty$ whose aggregators are given by (3.9).

3.4.4. *Trade-off functions*

Instead of specifying the function h_t directly, one can start with a continuous decreasing function $g_t : \mathbb{R} \to \mathbb{R}$ such that $g_t(0) = 0$ and define the corresponding aggregator G_t by

$$G_t(X_t, X_{t+1}) = \operatorname{ess\,sup}\{m \in L^\infty(\mathcal{F}_t) : (X_t - m, X_{t+1} - m) \in \mathcal{B}_t\},$$

where the one-step acceptance set $\mathcal{B}_t$ is given by

$$\mathcal{B}_t = \{(X_t, X_{t+1}) \in L^\infty(\mathcal{F}_t) \times L^\infty(\mathcal{F}_{t+1}) : g_t(X_t) \le \varphi_t(X_{t+1})\}.$$

The function g_t specifies the trade-off between risk at time t and $t+1$ of an acceptable process $X \in \mathcal{R}^\infty_{t,t+1}$. It can easily be checked that the inverse h_t of the strictly increasing function $g_t(-x) + x$ satisfies (h1)–(h3), and $\mathcal{B}_t$ can be written as

$$\mathcal{B}_t = \{(X_t, X_{t+1}) \in L^\infty(\mathcal{F}_t) \times L^\infty(\mathcal{F}_{t+1}) : X_t + h_t \circ \varphi_t(X_{t+1} - X_t) \ge 0\}.$$

Hence, the generator H_t is given by $h_t \circ \varphi_t$. Note h_t is concave if and only if g_t is convex. For $g_t(x) = 0$ we get $h_t(x) = x$, and we are back in the case of Sec. 3.4.1. The case $g_t(x) = (1 - 1/\gamma_t)x$ for $0 < \gamma_t < 1$ corresponds to $h_t(x) = \gamma_t x$ of Sec. 3.4.2. The function $h_t(x) = x \wedge 0$ of Sec. 3.4.3 is not bijective. Therefore, it cannot be obtained from a trade-off function g_t.

Example 3.1. Our last example is built on trade-off functions of the form $g_t(x) := \exp(-\gamma_t x) - 1$ for $\gamma_t > 0$. In this case there exists no closed form expression for h_t. But one has the following relation between h_t^* and the convex conjugate $g_t^*(y) = \sup_{x \in \mathbb{R}} xy - g_t(x)$ of g_t:

$$h_t^*(y) = \begin{cases} -y g_t^*(1 - 1/y) & \text{for } y \in (0,1] \\ -\infty & \text{for } y \notin (0,1] \end{cases}.$$

Indeed, $h_t^*(y) = -\infty$ for $y \notin (0,1]$ is an immediate consequence of the fact that h_t satisfies $\lim_{x \to \infty} h_t(x) = \infty$ as well as (h2) and (h3). For $y \in (0,1]$, one can write

$$
\begin{aligned}
h_t^*(y) &= \inf_{x\in\mathbb{R}} xy - h_t(x) = \inf_{x\in\mathbb{R}} h_t^{-1}(-x)y - h_t(h_t^{-1}(-x)) \\
&= y \inf_{x\in\mathbb{R}} h_t^{-1}(-x) + x/y = y \inf_{x\in\mathbb{R}} h_t^{-1}(-x) + x + (1/y - 1)\,x \\
&= -y \sup_{x\in\mathbb{R}} (1 - 1/y)\,x - g_t(x) = -y g_t^*\,(1 - 1/y).
\end{aligned}
$$

For $z < 0$, one has

$$
g_t^*(z) = \frac{z}{\gamma_t}\left(1 - \log\left(-\frac{z}{\gamma_t}\right)\right) + 1,
$$

and therefore,

$$
h_t^*(y) = \frac{1-y}{\gamma_t}\left[1 - \log\left(\frac{1-y}{\gamma_t y}\right)\right] - y.
$$

We now combine h_t with the entropic generator

$$
\varphi_t(X) = -\alpha_t^{-1} \log \mathrm{E}_{\mathbb{P}}[\exp(-\alpha_t X) \,|\, \mathcal{F}_t], \quad X \in L^\infty(\mathcal{F}_{t+1})
$$

with minimal penalty function

$$
\varphi_t^{\#}(\xi_{t+1}) = \alpha_t^{-1} \mathrm{E}_{\mathbb{P}}[\xi_{t+1} \log(\xi_{t+1}) \,|\, \mathcal{F}_t].
$$

It follows from Proposition 3.1 that the minimal dynamic penalty function of the dynamic concave monetary utility function $(\phi_t)_{t=0}^T$ on $\mathcal{R}^\infty$ induced by $(h_t, \varphi_t)_{t=0}^{T-1}$ is given by

$$
\begin{aligned}
\psi_t(\xi_{t+1}) &= \alpha_t^{-1} \mathrm{E}_{\mathbb{P}}[\xi_{t+1} \log(\xi_{t+1}) \,|\, \mathcal{F}_t] - \alpha_t^{-1} \lambda \log(\lambda) \\
&\quad + \lambda + \frac{1-\lambda}{\gamma_t} \log\left(\frac{1-\lambda}{\gamma_t \lambda}\right) - \frac{1-\lambda}{\gamma_t},
\end{aligned}
$$

for $\xi_{t+1} \in \mathcal{E}_{t+1}$ and $\lambda = \mathrm{E}_{\mathbb{P}}[\xi_{t+1} \,|\, \mathcal{F}_t]$.

Acknowledgments

We thank Irina Penner and an anonymous referee for valuable comments. P. Cheridito was supported by NSF Grant DMS-0642361. M. Kupper was supported by the Swiss National Science Foundation.

References

[1] B. Acciaio, H. Föllmer and I. Penner, Risk assessment for uncertain cash flows: Model ambiguity, discounting ambiguity, and the role of bubbles, Preprints (2010).

[2] P. Artzner, F. Delbaen, J. M. Eber and D. Heath, Thinking coherently, *RISK* **10** (1997) 68–71.

[3] P. Artzner, F. Delbaen, J. M. Eber and D. Heath, Coherent measures of risk, *Math. Finance* **9**(3) (1999) 203–228.

[4] P. Artzner, F. Delbaen, J. M. Eber, D. Heath and H. Ku, Coherent multiperiod risk adjusted values and Bellman's principle, *Ann. Oper. Res.* **152** (2007) 5–22.

[5] P. Barrieu and N. El Karoui, Optimal derivatives design under dynamic risk measures, in *Mathematics of Finance*, 13–25, Contemp. Math., 351 (Amer. Math. Soc., Providence, RI, 2004).
[6] P. Barrieu and N. El Karoui, Pricing, hedging and optimally designing derivatives via minimization of risk measures, in *Volume on Indifference Pricing*, R. Carmona, ed. (Princeton University Press, 2009).
[7] J. Bion-Nadal, Conditional risk measures and robust representation of convex risk measures, Ecole Polytechnique, CMAP, preprint no. 557 (2004).
[8] P. Cheridito, F. Delbaen and M. Kupper, Coherent and convex risk measures for bounded càdlàg processes, *Stoch. Proc. Appl.* **112**(1) (2004) 1–22.
[9] P. Cheridito, F. Delbaen and M. Kupper, Coherent and convex risk measures for unbounded càdlàg processes, *Fin. Stoch.* **10**(3) (2006) 427–448.
[10] P. Cheridito, F. Delbaen and M. Kupper, Dynamic monetary risk measures for bounded discrete-time processes, *Electr. J. Probability* **11** (2006) 57–106.
[11] F. Delbaen, Coherent risk measures on general probability spaces, in *Advances in Finance and Stochastics*, 1–37 (Springer-Verlag, Berlin, 2002).
[12] F. Delbaen, The structure of m-stable sets and in particular of the set of risk neutral measures, in *Memoriam Paul-André Meyer: Séminaire de Probabilités XXXIX*, 215–258, Lecture Notes in Math., 1874 (Springer, Berlin, 2006).
[13] F. Delbaen, S. Peng and E. Rosazza Gianin, Representation of the penalty term of dynamic concave utilities, *Fin. Stoch* **14**(3) (2010) 449–472.
[14] K. Detlefsen and G. Scandolo, Conditional and dynamic convex risk measures, *Fin. Stoch.* **9**(4) (2005) 539–561.
[15] D. Duffie and L. G. Epstein, Stochastic differential utility, *Econometrica* **60**(2) (1992) 353–394.
[16] L. G. Epstein and M. Schneider, Recursive multiple-priors, *J. Econom. Theory* **113**(1) (2003) 1–31.
[17] L. G. Epstein and S. E. Zin, Substitution, risk aversion, and the temporal behavior of consumption and asset returns: A theoretical framework, *Econometrica* **57**(4) (1989) 937–969.
[18] H. Föllmer and I. Penner, Convex risk measures and the dynamics of their penalty functions, *Statistics and Decisions* **24**(1) (2006) 61–96.
[19] H. Föllmer and A. Schied, Convex measures of risk and trading constraints, *Fin. Stoch.* **6**(4) (2002) 429–447.
[20] H. Föllmer and A. Schied, *Stochastic Finance, An Introduction in Discrete Time.* 36 Second ed., de Gruyter Studies in Mathematics 27 (2004).
[21] M. Frittelli and E. Rosazza Gianin, Putting order in risk measures, *J. Bank. Fin.* **26**(7) (2002) 1473–1486.
[22] M. Frittelli and E. Rosazza Gianin, Dynamic convex risk measures, in *Risk Measures for the 21st Century*, Chapter 12 (Wiley Finance, 2004).
[23] M. Frittelli and G. Scandolo, Risk measures and capital requirements for processes, *Math. Finance* **16**(4) (2006) 589–612.
[24] I. Gilboa and D. Schmeidler, Maxmin expected utility with non-unique priop, *J. Math. Econom.* **18** (1989) 141–153.
[25] A. Jobert and L. C. G. Rogers, Valuations and dynamic convex risk measures, *Math. Finance* **18**(1) (2008) 1–22.
[26] T. C. Koopmans, Stationary ordinal utility and impatience, *Econometrica* **28**(2) (1960) 287–309.
[27] M. K. Kreps and E. L. Porteus, Temporal resolution of uncertainty and dynamic choice theory, *Econometrica* **46**(1) (1978) 185–200.

[28] S. Klöppel and M. Schweizer, Dynamic indifference valuation via convex risk measures, *Math. Finance* **17** (2005) 599–627.
[29] F. Maccheroni, M. Marinacci and A. Rustichini, Dynamic variational preferences, *J. Econom. Theory* **128**(1) (2006) 4–44.
[30] J. Neveu, *Discrete-Parameter Martingales* (North-Holland Publishing Company-Amsterdam, Oxford, 1975).
[31] S. Peng, Non-linear expectations, non-linear evaluations and risk measures, in *Lecture Notes in Mathematics 1856* (Springer, 2004).
[32] F. Riedel, Dynamic coherent risk measures, *Stoch. Proc. Appl.* **112**(2) (2004) 185–200.
[33] B. Roorda, J. M. Schumacher and J. Engwerda, Coherent acceptability measures in multiperiod models, *Math. Finance* **15**(4) (2005) 589–612.
[34] A. Ruszczyński and A. Shapiro, Conditional risk mappings, *Math. Op. Res.* **31** (2006) 544–561.
[35] T. Wang, Conditional preferences and updating, *J. Econ. Theory* **108**(2) (2003) 286–321.
[36] S. Weber, Distribution-invariant risk measures, information, and dynamic consistency, *Math. Finance* **16**(2) (2006) 419–441.

TARGET VOLATILITY OPTION PRICING*

GIUSEPPE DI GRAZIANO

Deutsche Bank AG
1 Great Winchester Street
London EC2N 2DB, United Kingdom
and
Department of Mathematics
King's College London
London WC2R 2LS, United Kingdom

LORENZO TORRICELLI

Department of Mathematics
University College London
London WC1E 6BT, United Kingdom

In this paper we present two methods for the pricing of Target Volatility Options (TVOs), a recent market innovation in the field of volatility derivative. TVOs allow investors to take a joint view on the future price of a given underlying (e.g. stocks, commodities, etc) and its realized volatility. For example, a target volatility call pays at maturity the terminal value of the asset minus the strike, floored at zero, scaled by the ratio of the target volatility (an arbitrary constant) and the realized volatility of the underlying over the life of the option. TVOs are popular with investors and hedgers because they are typically cheaper than their vanilla equivalent. We present two approaches for the pricing of TVOs: a power series expansion and a Laplace transform method. We also provide both model dependent and model independent solutions. The pricing methodologies have been tested numerically and results are provided.

Keywords: Volatility derivatives; target volatility; robust hedging; quadratic variation; Taylor expansion; Black and Scholes.

1. Introduction

Variance and volatility swaps were the first instances of volatility derivatives. They were introduced in the late nineties to allow investors to trade pure volatility risk (see Derman *et al.* [7] for a detailed account).

*This chapter was originally published under the same title in *International Journal of Theoretical and Applied Finance*, Vol.15, No.1, 1250005-1–17 (2012). Singapore: World Scientific Publishing.

Over the past few years, volatility products have become very liquid and widely traded instruments. Investors use volatility derivatives to hedge the volatility risk of their portfolios or to speculate on future realized volatility levels.

Variance and volatility swaps have been extensively studied in the literature. Derman *et al.* [7] show how to price and statically hedge variance swaps in a model independent fashion by investing in a portfolio of calls and puts when the underlying exhibits continuous sample paths. In a seminal paper, Carr and Lee [4] provide several methods for pricing and hedging a large class of functions on quadratic variation. Prices and hedges of quadratic variation claims are expressed in terms of weighted portfolios of European contracts on the terminal value of the underlying. Friz and Gatheral [11] study some ill-posed problems connected with the replication strategy of certain pay-offs suggested by Carr and Lee [4] and propose some regularization scheme.

A new type of volatility derivative was introduced around 2008 under the name of Target Volatility Options (TVOs). TVOs allow investors to take a joint view on the realized volatility of a given asset and its price. For example, a target volatility call pays at maturity the terminal value of the underlying S_T minus the strike K, floored at zero, rescaled by the ratio of the target volatility (an arbitrary constant, say $\bar{\sigma}$) and the asset's realized volatility RV_T over the life of the option

$$\phi(S_T, RV_T) = \frac{\bar{\sigma}}{RV_T}(S_T - K)^+ . \tag{1.1}$$

TVOs are popular with investors and hedgers because they are typically cheaper than vanilla options. As long as the realized volatility is lower than the target volatility, the pay-off of the former is higher than the pay-off of the corresponding vanilla option.

During the 2008 financial crisis for example, implied volatilities across asset classes experienced a steep increase, with a significant impact on (long vega) option costs. The generalized increase in implied volatilities was in part a consequence of higher expected future realized volatilities, but was also connected with banks' reluctance to increase their short vega positions. TVOs were introduced to allow investors to take a bullish/bearish view on the underlying asset in an option format at a relatively low cost.

In this paper we provide two methodologies for the pricing of TVOs. We shall assume that volatility is independent from the Brownian motion driving the returns of the asset. This assumption is in general quite restrictive and its relaxation will be topic of further research. The assumption of independence however allows us to reduce the TVO pricing problem to calculating the expectation of a portfolio of quadratic variation claims.

The paper is structured as follows: in the next section we state the main assumptions and introduce some notation. In Sec. 3 we derive the first approximation method which is based on Taylor expansions. The price of a TVO at inception is approximated by a sum of integrals of certain functions of the underlying asset variance. The subsequent section extends the result of section 3 to a generic time t to take into account the effect of the cumulated variance. A second pricing methodology based on the log-strike Laplace transform of the option pay-off is introduced in sec. 5. The results of the section can be applied to a large class of stochastic volatility models. In Sec. 6 we provide a representation of the price of the TVO in terms of a weighted portfolio of vanilla calls and puts. In particular we show that the TVO price is equal to the expectation of some linear combination of functions of the terminal value S_T. We then apply the Breeden and Litzenberg [3] formula to decompose the expectation above in a weighted portfolio of calls and puts and provide a formula for the weights. Numerical results are provided in Sec. 7. Both the Taylor and the Laplace transform methods exhibit high levels of accuracy. Proofs of the main results are provided in Appendix A.

2. Assumptions

Our market is represented by a filtered probability space $(\Omega, \mathcal{F}, \mathcal{F}_t, \mathbb{P})$ satisfying the usual conditions. Throughout the paper we will assume that there exist a money market account process B_t paying zero interest rates. We shall also assume that there exists a probability measure $\mathbb{Q}$ under which any non-dividend-paying asset S_t satisfies the stochastic differential equation

$$dS_t = \sigma_t S_t dW_t, \tag{2.1}$$

where W_t is a $\mathbb{Q}$-Brownian motion and $\sigma_t > 0$ is a stochastic volatility process. All expectations are taken with respect to the risk neutral measure $\mathbb{Q}$.

We will restrict our attention to volatility processes satisfying diffusion equations of the type

$$d\sigma_t = \mu_t(\sigma_t, t)dt + \nu_t(\sigma_t, t)dZ_t, \quad \sigma_0 > 0, \tag{2.2}$$

where the $\mathbb{Q}$-Brownian motion Z_t is independent of W_t.

Let $X_t = \log(S_t/S_0)$; the *quadratic variation* of the process X_t is given by

$$\langle X \rangle_t = \int_0^t \sigma_u^2 du. \tag{2.3}$$

We shall assume that the quadratic variation $\langle X \rangle_t$ is bounded from below for any $t > 0$.

Define an arbitrary constant $\bar{\sigma} > 0$, which we shall refer to as the *target volatility*. A *target volatility call option* with strike K is a contingent claim on S_T and $\langle X \rangle_T$ with time-t price given by

$$\bar{C}_t^{TV}(S_t, K, \langle X \rangle_t) = E_t\left[\frac{\bar{\sigma}\sqrt{T}}{\sqrt{\langle X \rangle_T}}(S_T - K)^+\right]. \tag{2.4}$$

Similarly the time-t price of a put TVO can be obtained by calculating the following expectation:

$$\bar{P}_t^{TV}(S_t, K, \langle X\rangle_t) = E_t\left[\frac{\bar{\sigma}\sqrt{T}}{\sqrt{\langle X\rangle_T}}(K - S_T)^+\right]. \tag{2.5}$$

TVOs allow option buyers to take a joint bet on the price of the underlying and its volatility. The target volatility typically represents the option buyer's expectation of the future average realized volatility of S_t during the life of the option. In particular, if volatility realizes at or below the target level, the pay-off of the option will be greater or equal than the pay-off of the corresponding vanilla option. If implied volatilities are relatively high compared to the buyer's expectations, TVOs provide a way to gain exposure to the underlying at a reduced premium.

3. Taylor Expansion Approximation

We begin this section with a simple motivating example. Consider the pricing of an at the money (ATM) call (or put) TVO. Using the well known Bachelier approximation formula, it is straightforward to see that the price of the ATM TVO is approximately equal to the price of the equivalent vanilla option with implied volatility $\bar{\sigma}$:

$$\begin{aligned}
\bar{C}_0^{TV}(S_0, S_0, 0) &= E_0\left[\frac{\bar{\sigma}\sqrt{T}}{\sqrt{\langle X\rangle_T}}E[(S_T - S_0)^+ \mid \mathcal{F}_T^\sigma]\right] \\
&= E_0\left[\frac{\bar{\sigma}\sqrt{T}}{\sqrt{\langle X\rangle_T}}C^{BS}(S_0, S_0, \langle X\rangle_T)\right] \\
&\approx S_0 E_0\left[\frac{\bar{\sigma}\sqrt{T}}{\sqrt{\langle X\rangle_T}}\sqrt{\frac{\langle X\rangle_T}{2\pi}}\right] \\
&= S_0\bar{\sigma}\sqrt{\frac{T}{2\pi}} \\
&\approx C^{BS}(S_0, S_0, \bar{\sigma}^2 T).
\end{aligned} \tag{3.1}$$

Here $(\mathcal{F}^\sigma)_{t\geq 0}$ is the filtration generated by the volatility process and $C^{BS}(S_0, K, x)$ is the Black-Scholes price of a vanilla European call option with cumulative variance x, spot price S_0 and strike K, that is

$$C^{BS}(S_0, K, x) \equiv S_0 N(d^+(x)) - KN(d^-(x)), \tag{3.2}$$

and

$$d^\pm(x) = \frac{\log(S_0/K) \pm x/2}{\sqrt{x}}, \tag{3.3}$$

where $N(\cdot)$ is the cumulative normal distribution function.

A slightly more general version of the problem above involves calculating the initial price of TVOs for a generic strike K,

$$\bar{C}_0^{TV}(S_0, K, 0) = E_0\left[\frac{\bar{\sigma}\sqrt{T}}{\sqrt{\langle X\rangle_T}} C^{BS}(S_0, K, \langle X\rangle_T)\right]. \tag{3.4}$$

The TVO price can be calculated by approximating the Black and Scholes formula appearing on the right-hand side of equation (3.4) by its Taylor expansion around the ATM level S_0. We shall show that each term of the expansion can be written as an integral of some exponential function of the quadratic variation $\langle X\rangle_T$. Expectations of such quantities can be calculated explicitly for a large class of parametric models or can be derived using a non-parametric approach *à la* Bredeen and Litzenberger [3]. The following Lemma allows us to express the Black and Scholes price as a weighted sum of functions of the cumulative variance:

Lemma 3.1. *The Black and Scholes (call) formula, considered as a function of the strike K, admits the following Taylor expansion around the ATM point S,*

$$C^{BS}(S,K,x) = S - (S+K)N\left(-\frac{\sqrt{x}}{2}\right) + e^{-x/8}\sum_{j=0}^{f(n)} x^{-(1/2+j)}W^{n,j}(K) + \mathcal{O}((K-S)^{n+3}), \tag{3.5}$$

where

$$W^{n,j}(K) \equiv \frac{1}{\sqrt{2\pi}}\sum_{k=2j}^{n}(-1)^k c^{f(k)-j,k}\frac{(K-S)^{k+2}}{S^{k+1}(k+2)!}, \tag{3.6}$$

and

$$f(k) = \begin{cases} \dfrac{k}{2}, & k \text{ even;} \\ \dfrac{k-1}{2}, & k \text{ odd.} \end{cases} \tag{3.7}$$

The coefficients $c^{j,n}$ can be derived explicitly by solving a simple recursive equation (see Appendix A for details). In order to calculate the TVO price we need to substitute (3.5) back into (3.4). The following lemma will allow us to simplify the calculations.

Lemma 3.2. *For any $x, r > 0$ the following equalities hold:*

$$\frac{1}{\sqrt{x}}N\left(-\frac{\sqrt{x}}{2}\right) = \frac{1}{2\sqrt{\pi}}\int_0^\infty \frac{e^{-(z+1/8)x}}{\sqrt{z+1/8}}dz, \tag{3.8}$$

and

$$x^{-r} = \frac{1}{r\Gamma(r)} \int_0^\infty e^{-z^{1/r}x} dz. \tag{3.9}$$

Substituting equation (3.5) into (3.4) and using (3.8) and (3.9), we have the following Proposition:

Proposition 3.1. *The price of a call TVO can be approximated by a linear combination of integrals of some exponential function of the quadratic variation,*

$$C_0^{TV}(K) \approx \bar{\sigma}\sqrt{T}\left[\frac{2S_0}{\sqrt{\pi}} I_0^{1/2,0} - \frac{S_0 + K}{2\sqrt{\pi}} \Phi_0^{1,1/8} + \sum_{j=0}^{f(n)} \tilde{W}^{n,j}(K) I_0^{j+1,1/8}\right], \tag{3.10}$$

where we have defined

$$I_0^{r,a} \equiv \int_0^\infty E_0[e^{\lambda^{r,a}(z)\langle X\rangle_T}]dz, \tag{3.11}$$

$$\Phi_0^{1,1/8} \equiv \int_0^\infty \frac{E_0[e^{\lambda^{1,1/8}(z)\langle X\rangle_T}]}{\sqrt{z+1/8}} dz, \tag{3.12}$$

$$\lambda^{r,a}(z) \equiv -(z^{1/r} + a), \tag{3.13}$$

and

$$\tilde{W}^{n,j} \equiv \frac{W^{n,j}(K)}{(j+1)!}. \tag{3.14}$$

The use of Fubini's Theorem to interchange the order of integration in the formula above is justified by the fact that the process $(\langle X\rangle)_{t>0}$ is bounded from below. Integrals $I_0^{r,a}$ and $\Phi_0^{1,1/8}$ can be calculated explicitly for a variety of parametric models for which the Laplace transform of the quadratic variation is known in closed form. For example we could model the instantaneous variance σ_t^2 as a CIR process. More generally we can make use of the abundant literature on affine processes (see Duffie *et al.* [8] for a detailed treatment) to derive closed form solutions for the price of the TVO.

In Sec. 6 we shall use a model independent approach in the spirit of Carr and Lee [4] to express integrals (3.11) and (3.12) and thus the TVO price as a weighted portfolio of traded options.

4. Taylor Expansion for $t > 0$

So far we have dealt with the pricing problem at time zero. As variance cumulates during the life of the option, the pricing problem changes slightly and formulae become more involved but the solution remains similar in nature.

Let us consider the price of a TVO at time $t > 0$. We need to calculate an expectation of the form

$$\bar{C}^{TV}(S_t, K, \langle X \rangle_t) = E_t\left[\frac{\bar{\sigma}\sqrt{T}}{\sqrt{\langle X \rangle_T}}(S_T - K)^+\right]$$

$$= E_t\left[\frac{\bar{\sigma}\sqrt{T}}{\sqrt{\epsilon_t + \langle X \rangle_T - \langle X \rangle_t}} C^{BS}(S_t, K, \langle X \rangle_T - \langle X \rangle_t)\right], \qquad (4.1)$$

where we have set $\epsilon_t \equiv \langle X \rangle_t$. Thanks to the Markovian structure of the stock price and volatility, the $t > 0$ pricing problem is very similar to the one encountered in the previous section. However the presence of the term ϵ_t causes a lack of symmetry between the powers of $\langle X \rangle_T - \langle X \rangle_t$ in the numerator and the square root in the denominator when substituting the Black and Scholes formula with its Taylor series. In particular, after expanding the time-t Black and Scholes formula around the strike K, we are left with expressions of the form

$$q_1(x) \equiv \frac{N(-\sqrt{x}/2)}{\sqrt{\epsilon + x}}, \qquad (4.2)$$

$$q_2(x) \equiv \frac{x^{-(j+1/2)}}{\sqrt{\epsilon + x}}. \qquad (4.3)$$

In principle, we could represents $q_1(x)$ and $q_2(x)$ as double integrals of exponential functions of x by considering the numerator and denominator separately. However, because of singularities in some of the integrals involved, this approach does not allow us to derive model independent prices. An alternative approach is to consider the Taylor expansion of $N(-\sqrt{x}/2)$ and $x^{-(j+1/2)}$ around the point $x + \epsilon$:

$$q_1(x) = \frac{N(-\frac{\sqrt{\epsilon+x}}{2})}{\sqrt{\epsilon + x}} + \frac{e^{-(\epsilon+x)/8}}{\sqrt{2\pi}} \sum_{i=0}^{m} \omega^{i,m}(\epsilon)(\epsilon + x)^{-(i+1)} + \mathcal{O}(\epsilon^{m+2}), \qquad (4.4)$$

where

$$\omega^{i,m}(\epsilon) \equiv \sum_{k=i}^{m} (-1)^{k+1} \gamma^{i,k} \frac{\epsilon^{k+1}}{k + 1!}, \qquad (4.5)$$

and $\gamma^{i,k}$ satisfies the following recursion[1]:

$$\begin{aligned}
\gamma^{0,0} &= -1/4 \\
\gamma^{0,k} &= \left(-\tfrac{1}{8}\right)\gamma^{0,k-1}, \quad k = 1, \ldots, m \\
\gamma^{k,k} &= (1/2 - k)\gamma^{k-1,k-1}, \quad k = 1, \ldots, m \\
\gamma^{i,k} &= \left(-\tfrac{1}{8}\right)\gamma^{i,k-1} + (1/2 - i)\gamma^{i-1,k-1}, \quad i = 1, \ldots, m, \; k = i + 1, \ldots, m.
\end{aligned} \qquad (4.6)$$

[1] The closed form solution of the recursion is $\gamma^{i,k} = -\frac{1}{4}\prod_{i=1}^{j} \frac{1-2i}{2}(-\frac{1}{8})^{k-j}\binom{k}{j}$ for $j \geq 1$ and $k \geq j$.

Similarly,

$$q_2(x) = \sum_{k=0}^{m} \zeta^{k,j}(\epsilon)(\epsilon + x)^{-(j+k+1)} + \mathcal{O}(\epsilon^{m+1}), \tag{4.7}$$

where we have defined $\zeta^{0,j}(\epsilon) = 1$ and

$$\zeta^{k,j}(\epsilon) = \frac{\epsilon^k}{k!} \prod_{i=0}^{k-1} (j + i + 1/2), \tag{4.8}$$

for $k \geq 1$.

These approximations can be substituted into the Taylor expansion of the time-t Black and Scholes price. By putting all terms $\langle X \rangle_T - \langle X \rangle_t$ as common factor, after some rearrangement we obtain

Proposition 4.1.

$$C_t^{TV}(K) \approx \bar{\sigma}\sqrt{T} \left[\frac{2S_t}{\sqrt{\pi}} I_t^{1/2,0,0} - \frac{S_t + K}{2\sqrt{\pi}} \Phi_t^{1,1/8} \right.$$
$$\left. + \sum_{j=0}^{m+f(n)} \hat{W}_t^{n,m,j}(K, \langle X \rangle_t) I_t^{j+1,1/8,0} \right], \tag{4.9}$$

where

$$I_t^{r,a,b} = \int_0^\infty e^{-(z^{1/r}+b)\langle X \rangle_t} E_t \left[e^{\lambda^{r,a}(\langle X \rangle_T - \langle X \rangle_t)} \right] dz, \tag{4.10}$$

$$\Phi_t^{1,a} = \int_0^\infty \frac{e^{-(z+a)\langle X \rangle_t}}{\sqrt{z+a}} E_t \left[e^{\lambda^{1,a}(\langle X \rangle_T - \langle X \rangle_t)} \right] dz, \tag{4.11}$$

$$\lambda^{r,a}(z) \equiv -(z^{1/r} + a), \tag{4.12}$$

and the weights of the linear combination are given by

$$\hat{W}_t^{n,m,j}(K,\epsilon) \equiv \frac{1}{(j+1)!} \left\{ -\frac{S_t + K}{\sqrt{2\pi}} e^{-\epsilon/8} \omega^{j,m}(\epsilon) \right.$$
$$+ \sum_{k=0}^{\min(j,f(n))} W^{n,k}(K) \zeta^{j-k,k}(\epsilon) I_{j \leq m}$$
$$\left. + \sum_{k=0}^{\min(m,f(n)-j+m)} W^{n,j-m+k}(K) \zeta^{m-k,j-m+k}(\epsilon) I_{j>m} \right\}. \tag{4.13}$$

Note that to simplify the notation, we have imposed that the summation in the Taylor expansion of $q_1(x)$ and $q_2(x)$ is up to m for both functions.

5. TVO Pricing using Laplace Transforms

An alternative approach to derive the price of TVOs is to consider the log-strike Laplace transform of the pay-off. As we will show later in this section, this approach leads to very simple semi-analytical solutions which are also computationally efficient. The main drawback of the methodology is that our model independent approach cannot be applied.

Let us consider the pricing problem of a put TVO. It is convenient to express the pay-off of the option is in terms of the log-strike $k \equiv \log K$

$$\bar{P}_t(S_t, e^k, \langle X\rangle_t) = E_t\left[\frac{\bar{\sigma}\sqrt{T}}{\sqrt{\langle X\rangle_T}}(e^k - S_T)^+\right] \equiv P_t(k). \tag{5.1}$$

By Laplace transforming the option price in the k, we can eliminate the max function appearing in the pay-off of the TVO. This will allow us to reduce the problem to the pricing of a quadratic variation claim rather than a joint claim on the terminal value of the stock and the quadratic variation.

For any complex α such that $\mathrm{Re}(\alpha) > 1$, the Laplace transform of $P_t(k)$ is equal to

$$\begin{aligned}\hat{P}_t(\alpha) &\equiv \int_0^\infty e^{-\alpha k} P_t(k)dk \\ &= \bar{\sigma}\sqrt{T}S_t^{1-\alpha}E_t\left[\frac{1}{\sqrt{\epsilon_t + \langle X\rangle_T - \langle X\rangle_t}}\frac{e^{(1-\alpha)(X_T - X_t)}}{\alpha(\alpha-1)}\right].\end{aligned} \tag{5.2}$$

Using formula (3.9) we can represent the denominator of (5.2) in integral form:

$$\frac{1}{\sqrt{\epsilon + x}} = \frac{2}{\sqrt{\pi}}\int_0^\infty e^{-z^2(\epsilon+x)}dz. \tag{5.3}$$

Under the assumption of independence of σ_t and W_t, after applying Fubini's Theorem, we can write $\hat{P}(\alpha)$ in terms of S_t and the quadratic variation

$$\begin{aligned}\hat{P}_t(\alpha) &= 2\bar{\sigma}\sqrt{\frac{T}{\pi}}S_t^{1-\alpha}\int_0^\infty e^{-z^2\langle X\rangle_t}E_t\left[\frac{e^{-z^2(\langle X\rangle_T - \langle X\rangle_t) + (1-\alpha)(X_T - X_t)}}{\alpha(\alpha-1)}\right]dz \\ &= 2\bar{\sigma}\sqrt{\frac{T}{\pi}}S_t^{1-\alpha}\int_0^\infty \frac{e^{-z^2\langle X\rangle_t}E_t[e^{\lambda_{z,\alpha}(\langle X\rangle_T - \langle X\rangle_t)}]}{\alpha(\alpha-1)}dz,\end{aligned} \tag{5.4}$$

where we have defined the function

$$\lambda_{z,\alpha} = -(z^2 + \alpha(1-\alpha)/2). \tag{5.5}$$

The Laplace transform (5.4) can be calculated explicitly for a variety stochastic volatility models (e.g., affine models). The price of the TVO can be obtained by inverting (5.4) numerically. In particular, pricing the option amounts to calculating the following double integral

$$P_t(k) = \frac{4e^{ak}\bar{\sigma}\sqrt{T}}{\pi^{3/2}} \int_0^\infty \int_0^\infty e^{-z^2\langle X\rangle_t} \mathrm{Re}$$

$$\times \left(\frac{S_t^{1-a-iu} E_t \left[e^{\lambda_{z,a+iu}(\langle X\rangle_T - \langle X\rangle_t)} \right]}{(a+iu)(a+iu-1)} \right) \cos(uk) dz du. \tag{5.6}$$

Numerical integration can be achieved by using, for example, the Abate-Whitt method [1] which is based on a smart application of the trapezium rule combined with the Euler summation. The Laplace method is fast, easy to implement and produces accurate and stable results.

6. Robust Pricing

Many authors in recent years (see for example Schoutens *et al.* [15]) have highlighted various problems related to model dependence in the context of exotic option pricing and hedging. For example, local volatility and stochastic volatility models are known to give different results when pricing forward starting and cliquet options. Even within the stochastic volatility class, different models lead to different prices for path dependent options when calibrated to the same volatility surface.

In a pioneering paper, Breeden and Litzenberger [3] showed how to obtain the risk-neutral density of prices of the underlying asset from traded European option prices. Model-independent prices for European-style claims on the underlying with sufficiently smooth second derivatives may then be obtained by forming a portfolio of traded call and put options (see e.g. Carr and Madan [5]). These results are not immediately applicable to volatility derivatives which cannot in general be expressed as portfolios of European-style claims on the underlying.

Carr and Lee [4] however proved that under the assumption of independence, expectations of exponential functions of the quadratic variation are equal to expectations of some function of the terminal value of the underlying. The results of [4] allow us to calculate the price of a special class of path dependent options by taking expectations of an equivalent European claim. For any complex λ we have

$$E_t[e^{\lambda(\langle X\rangle_T - \langle X\rangle_t)}] = E_t\left[e^{(X_T - X_t)p(\lambda)}\right] = E_t\left(\frac{S_T}{S_t}\right)^{p(\lambda)}, \tag{6.1}$$

where

$$p(\lambda) = \frac{1}{2} \pm \sqrt{\frac{1}{4} + 2\lambda}. \tag{6.2}$$

In Secs. 3 and 4 we showed how to approximate TVO prices by a linear combination of integrals involving expressions of the form (6.1). We shall now show how to apply Breeden-Litzenberger formula (6.3) to represent the TVO price in terms of traded option prices. Let $f(S)$ be a twice-differentiable pay-off. For some arbitrary constant η we have,

$$f(S) = f(\eta) + f'(k)[S - \eta] + \int_\eta^\infty f''(x)(S - x)^+ dx + \int_0^\eta f''(x)(x - S)^+ dx. \quad (6.3)$$

By taking conditional expectations on both sides of (6.3), we obtain a representation of the price of the claim $f(S)$ in terms of vanilla call and put prices

$$E_t[f(S_T)] = f(\eta) + f'(\eta)[S_t - \eta] + \int_\eta^\infty f''(x) C_t^M(S_t, x)dx + \int_0^\eta f''(x) P_t^M(S_t, x)dx, \quad (6.4)$$

where $C_t^M(S_t, x)$ and $P_t^M(S_t, x)$ are call and put prices with strike x.

6.1. *Robust pricing via Taylor*

In order to apply formula (6.4) to price TVOs, we need to find a function $f(S)$ such that $E_t[f(S_T)]$ equals the TVO price. As shown in formula (4.9), the price of a call TVO can be approximated by a linear combination of terms of the form $I_t^{r,a,b}$ and $\Phi_t^{1,a}$. In order to derive model independent prices for TVOs it is sufficient to apply Breeden-Litzenberger formula to $I_t^{r,a,b}$ and $\Phi_t^{1,a}$. In particular, Carr-Lee formula (6.1) can be used to express $I_t^{r,a,b}$ and $\Phi_t^{1,a}$ as expectations of some functional of S_T. It is straightforward to show that

$$\begin{aligned} I_t^{r,a,b} &= \int_0^\infty e^{-(z^{1/r}+b)\langle X\rangle_t} E_t[e^{\lambda^{r,a}(\langle X\rangle_T - \langle X\rangle_t)}] \\ &= E_t \int_0^\infty e^{-(z^{1/r}+b)\langle X\rangle_t} \mathrm{Re}\left(\frac{S_T}{S_t}\right)^{p^{r,a}(z)} dz, \end{aligned} \quad (6.5)$$

where we have applied Fubini's Theorem to interchange the order of integration and defined

$$p^{r,a} \equiv 1/2 \pm \sqrt{1/4 - 2z^{1/r} - 2a}. \quad (6.6)$$

Similarly,

$$\begin{aligned} \Phi_t^{1,a} &= \int_0^\infty \frac{e^{-(z+a)\langle X\rangle_t}}{\sqrt{z+a}} E_t[e^{\lambda^{1,a}(\langle X\rangle_T - \langle X\rangle_t)}]dz \\ &= E_t \int_0^\infty \frac{e^{-(z+a)\langle X\rangle_t}}{\sqrt{z+a}} \mathrm{Re}\left(\frac{S_T}{S_t}\right)^{p^{1,a}(z)} dz. \end{aligned} \quad (6.7)$$

The last step is to define the following functions of the terminal value of the underlying S,

$$\tilde{I}_t^{r,a,b}(S) \equiv \int_0^\infty e^{-(z^{1/r}+b)\langle X\rangle_t}\mathrm{Re}\left(\frac{S}{S_t}\right)^{p^{r,a}(z)} dz \tag{6.8}$$

$$\tilde{\Phi}_t^{1,a}(S) \equiv \int_0^\infty \frac{e^{-(z+a)\langle X\rangle_t}}{\sqrt{z+a}}\mathrm{Re}\left(\frac{S}{S_t}\right)^{p^{1,a}(z)} dz. \tag{6.9}$$

For $t > 0$, the second derivative in S of $\tilde{I}_t^{r,a,b}(S)$ and $\tilde{\Phi}_t^{1,a}(S)$ is well defined since $\langle X\rangle_t$ is strictly positive. Moreover, the left-hand sides of (6.5) and (6.7) are equal to the conditional expectation of $\tilde{I}_t^{r,a,b}(S)$ and $\tilde{\Phi}_t^{1,a}(S)$ respectively. We can now apply formula (6.4) to the functions above with $\eta = S_t$ and substitute the result in (4.9) to obtain a representation of the TVO price in terms of traded call and put options.

Note that for $t = 0$ the integrals in expressions (6.8) and (6.9) do not converge and we cannot use Fubini's Theorem to interchange the order of integration in equations (6.5) and (6.7). It is therefore not always possible to calculate the TVO price using formula (6.4).

However, if the TVO contract is redefined as

$$\bar{C}_0^{TV}(S_0, K, 0) = E_0\left[\frac{\bar{\sigma}\sqrt{T}}{\sqrt{c+\langle X\rangle_T}}(S_T - K)^+\right] \tag{6.10}$$

for some small arbitrary constant c, a "robust price", in the sense defined in this paper, does exist.

6.2. *Robust pricing via Laplace transforms*

Can the robust pricing approach be applied to the Laplace transform method introduced in Sec. 5? Using the Carr-Lee formula (6.1) we can express the Laplace transform of the TVO as the conditional expectation of some function of the terminal value S_T

$$P_t(k) = \frac{4e^{ak}\bar{\sigma}\sqrt{T}}{\pi^{3/2}}E_t\left[\int_0^\infty e^{-z^2\langle X\rangle_t}\int_0^\infty \mathrm{Re}\left(\frac{S_t^{1-a-iu}(S_T/S_t)^{p^{\pm}_{z,\alpha}}}{(a+iu)(a+iu-1)}\right)\cos(uk)du dz\right], \tag{6.11}$$

where we have set $\alpha = a + iu$ and defined

$$p^{\pm}_{z,\alpha} \equiv 1/2 \pm \sqrt{1/4 - 2z^2 - \alpha(1-\alpha)}. \tag{6.12}$$

In principle, we could define the function $f(S)$ as

$$f(S) \equiv \frac{4e^{ak}\bar{\sigma}\sqrt{T}}{\pi^{3/2}}\int_0^\infty e^{-z^2\langle X\rangle_t}\int_0^\infty \mathrm{Re}\left(\frac{S_t^{1-a-iu}(S/S_t)^{p^{\pm}_{z,\alpha}}}{(a+iu)(a+iu-1)}\right)\cos(uk)du dz. \tag{6.13}$$

However the second derivative of $f(S)$ does not exist, because the dz-integral we obtain after differentiating (6.13) twice does not converge. It is therefore not possible to apply the Breeden-Litzenberger decomposition to derive a model independent price for the TVO using the Laplace transform method introduced in Sec. 5.

7. Numerical Results

We have implemented and tested the pricing formulae presented in the previous sections using MATLAB. In particular, we have assumed Heston dynamics for the underlying asset process

$$dS_t = v_t^{1/2} S_t dW_t, \tag{7.1}$$

$$dv_t = \kappa(\theta - v_t)dt + \eta v_t^{1/2} dZ_t, \tag{7.2}$$

where W_t and Z_t are independent Brownian motions.

Unless otherwise specified, we have used the following parameters:

$$S_0 = 100, \quad v_0 = 0.2, \quad \overline{\sigma} = 0.1, \quad \kappa = 0.5, \quad \theta = 0.2, \quad \eta = 0.3. \tag{7.3}$$

In order to test the accuracy of our results we checked formulae (3.10), (4.9) and (5.6) against a Monte Carlo simulation of the pay-off across various strikes, maturities and cumulative realized volatilies. Both the Taylor approximation and the Laplace transform method proved to be very accurate.

Table 1. Maturity $T = 3$, $t = 0$. TVOs prices for different strikes, using different pricing methods

Strike	Taylor Polynomial of Order n					Laplace Transform	Monte Carlo Simulation
	$n = 1$	$n = 2$	$n = 3$	$n = 4$	$n = 5$		
60	10.1534	11.1768	11.3814	11.4006	11.3958	11.3919	11.3897
80	8.4475	8.7033	8.7289	8.7301	8.7300	8.7301	8.7281
100	6.7416	6.7416	6.7416	6.7416	6.7416	6.7416	6.7415
120	5.0357	5.2915	5.2659	5.2671	5.2673	5.2672	5.2618
140	3.3298	4.3532	4.1485	4.1677	4.1725	4.1699	4.1643

Table 2. Maturity $T = 0.25$, $t = 0$. TVOs prices for different strikes, using different pricing methods

Strike	Taylor Polynomial of Order n					Laplace Transform	Monte Carlo Simulation
	$n = 1$	$n = 2$	$n = 3$	$n = 4$	$n = 5$		
60	6.1232	9.4084	10.0654	9.9672	9.8556	9.0774	9.1058
80	4.0569	4.8782	4.9603	4.9542	4.9507	4.8989	4.9051
100	1.9906	1.9906	1.9906	1.9906	1.9906	1.9906	1.9906
120	−0.0757	0.7456	0.6634	0.6573	0.6608	0.6310	0.6291
140	−2.1420	1.1431	0.4861	0.3879	0.4994	0.1706	0.1703

Table 3. Maturity $T = 4$, $t = 3$, $\langle X\rangle_t = 0.3$. TVOs prices for different strikes, using different pricing methods.

Strike	Taylor Polynomial of Order n					Laplace Transform	Monte Carlo Simulation
	$n=1$	$n=2$	$n=3$	$n=4$	$n=5$		
60	9.7467	11.4962	11.8461	11.8810	11.8740	11.9816	11.9827
80	7.4080	7.8454	7.8892	7.8913	7.8911	7.8390	7.8400
100	5.0694	5.0694	5.0694	5.0694	5.0694	4.9175	4.9067
120	2.7307	3.1681	3.1243	3.1265	3.1267	3.0313	3.0338
140	0.3920	2.1415	1.7916	1.8266	1.8336	1.8690	1.8680

Table 4. Maturity $T = 5$, $t = 2$, $K = 100$, $S_t = 120$. TVOs prices for various realized volatility levels.

$\langle X\rangle_t$	Taylor polynomial of order n					Laplace Transform	Monte Carlo Simulation
	$n=1$	$n=2$	$n=3$	$n=4$	$n=5$		
0.2	10.7404	10.9632	10.9817	10.9828	10.9828	10.9780	10.9772
0.4	9.5530	9.7438	9.7597	9.7607	9.7607	9.7416	9.7391
0.6	8.7105	8.8795	8.8935	8.8945	8.8945	8.8601	8.8577
0.8	8.0694	8.2222	8.2349	8.2358	8.2358	8.1872	8.1894
1	7.5591	7.6993	7.7110	7.7118	7.7118	7.6503	7.6416

Appendix A

Proposition A.1.

Proof. Consider first the Taylor expansion of the Black and Scholes formula $C^{BS}(S,K,x) \equiv C(K)$ with respect to the strike K around the ATM point S

$$C(K) = C(S) + C^{(1)}(K-S) + \sum_{k=0}^{\infty} C^{(k+2)}(S)\frac{(K-S)^{k+2}}{(k+2)!}, \tag{A.1}$$

where $C^i(S)$ represents the ith derivative with respect to the strike K evaluated at the ATM point S. Following Estrella [10], the Taylor series converges for $0 < K < 2S$, and it is possible to derive explicitly derivatives $C^{k+2}(S)$ for all $k \geq 0$:

$$C^{k+2}(S) = \frac{1}{\sqrt{2\pi}}\exp\left(-\frac{\hat{\sigma}^2}{8}\right)\frac{P_k(d^+)}{S^{k+1}\hat{\sigma}^{k+1}}(-1)^k, \tag{A.2}$$

where we have defined the time scaled volatility $\hat{\sigma} \equiv \sigma\sqrt{t} = \sqrt{x}$. It can be shown that $P_n(d^+)$ satisfies the following recursive equation: $P_0(d^+) = 1$ and

$$P_k(d^+) = (d^+ + k\hat{\sigma})P_{k-1}(d^+) - P'_{k-1}(d^+), \tag{A.3}$$

where d^+ is defined in (3.3). Noting that for $K = S$ then $d^+ = \hat{\sigma}/2$, we can write the generic term P_n as a sum of powers of the volatility term, namely

$$P_k = \sum_{j=0}^{f(k)} c^{j,k}\hat{\sigma}^{\gamma(j,k)}, \tag{A.4}$$

where $c^{j,k}$ is the jth term of the polynomial P_k, $f(k)$ is defined in (3.7) and

$$\gamma(j,k) = \begin{cases} 2j, & k \text{ even;} \\ 2j+1, & k \text{ odd.} \end{cases} \tag{A.5}$$

Polynomials P_k consist of a sum of even (odd) powers of $\hat{\sigma}$ for k even (odd) and are of degree k. The scaled polynomials

$$\bar{P}_k \equiv \frac{P_k}{\hat{\sigma}^{k+1}}, \tag{A.6}$$

consist only of odd powers of the volatility term $\hat{\sigma}$ and are equal to

$$\bar{P}_k = \sum_{j=0}^{f(k)} c^{f(k)-j,k} \hat{\sigma}^{-(1+2j)}. \tag{A.7}$$

Substituting (A.7) into (A.2) and using the result in the Taylor expansion of the Black and Scholes formula, we obtain

$$C(K) = C(S) + C^{(1)}(K-S) + e^{-\hat{\sigma}^2/8} \sum_{k=0}^{n} (-1)^k \frac{(K-S)^{k+2}}{(k+2)!}$$
$$\times \sum_{j=0}^{f(k)} c^{f(k)-j,n} \hat{\sigma}^{-(1+2j)} + \mathcal{O}((K-S)^{n+3}). \tag{A.8}$$

Inverting the order of summation, taking $\hat{\sigma}$ as a common factor and using the definition of $C^0(S)$ and $C^1(S)$, we obtain

$$C(K) = S\left\{N\left(\frac{\hat{\sigma}}{2}\right) - N\left(-\frac{\hat{\sigma}}{2}\right)\right\} - N\left(-\frac{\hat{\sigma}}{2}\right)(K-S)$$
$$+ \frac{e^{-\hat{\sigma}^2/8}}{\sqrt{2\pi}} \sum_{j=0}^{f(n)} \hat{\sigma}^{-(1+2j)} \sum_{k=2j}^{n} (-1)^k c^{f(k)-j,k} \frac{(K-S)^{k+2}}{S^{k+1}(k+2)!} + \mathcal{O}((K-S)^{n+3}). \tag{A.9}$$

Formula (3.5) follows. □

Lemma A.2.

Proof. For any $a > 0$, the Laplace transform of the function $g(z) \equiv 1/\sqrt{\pi(z+a)}$ is equal to

$$\begin{aligned} \hat{g}(x,a) &\equiv \int_0^\infty \frac{e^{-xz}}{\sqrt{\pi(z+a)}} dz \\ &= \frac{e^{xa}}{\sqrt{x}} \text{erfc}(\sqrt{ax}) \\ &= \frac{2e^{ax}}{\sqrt{x}} N\left(-\frac{\sqrt{x}}{2}\right). \end{aligned} \tag{A.10}$$

Setting $a = 1/8$ and rearranging we obtain formula (3.8).

The proof of the second equality can be found in Schuerger [16]. □

Proposition A.4.

Proof. Let us first calculate the quantity

$$\tilde{C}^{BS}(S,K,x,\epsilon) \equiv \frac{C^{BS}(S,K,x)}{\sqrt{\epsilon+x}}. \tag{A.11}$$

Substituting (3.5) in the right-hand side of (A.11) and using (4.4) and (4.7), we can approximate the rescaled Black and Scholes price (A.11) as follows:

$$\begin{aligned}\tilde{C}^{BS}(S,K,x,\epsilon) \approx{}& \frac{S}{\sqrt{\epsilon+x}} - \frac{(S+K)}{\sqrt{\epsilon+x}}N\left(-\frac{\sqrt{\epsilon+x}}{2}\right)\\ &-(S+K)e^{-(x+\epsilon)/8}\sum_{j=0}^{m}\omega^{j,m}(\epsilon+x)^{-(1+j)}\\ &+e^{-x/8}\sum_{j=0}^{f(n)}W^{n,j}(K)\sum_{k=0}^{m}\zeta^{k,j}(\epsilon+x)^{-(1+k+j)}.\end{aligned} \tag{A.12}$$

Expanding the sum in the equation above and putting all terms in $(\epsilon+x)^{-(1+j)}$ as common factor, after a bit of algebra we obtain

$$\begin{aligned}\tilde{C}^{BS}(S,K,x) \approx{}& \frac{S}{\sqrt{\epsilon+x}} - \frac{(S+K)}{\sqrt{\epsilon+x}}N\left(-\frac{\sqrt{\epsilon+x}}{2}\right)\\ &-(S+K)e^{-x/8}\sum_{j=0}^{m}(j+1)!\hat{W}(n,m,j)(K,\epsilon)(\epsilon+x)^{-(1+j)}.\end{aligned} \tag{A.13}$$

The time-t TVO price is equal to the t-conditional expectation

$$C_t^{TV}(K) = E_t\left[\tilde{C}^{BS}(S_t,K,\langle X\rangle_T-\langle X\rangle_t,\langle X\rangle_t)\right]; \tag{A.14}$$

substituting (A.13) into the right-hand side of (A.14), making use of integral representations (3.9) and (3.2) and applying Fubini's Theorem to exchange the expectation with the integral in dz, we obtain the desired result. □

Applicability of Fubini's Theorem to Formulae (6.5) and (6.7).

Proof. In order to justify the interchange of the order of integration in equation (6.5), it is sufficient to prove that that

$$\int_0^\infty E_t\left[\left|e^{-(z^{1/r}+b)\langle X\rangle_t}\mathrm{Re}\left(\frac{S_T}{S_t}\right)^{1/2\pm\sqrt{1/4-2z^{1/r}-4a}}\right|\right]dz < \infty. \tag{A.15}$$

Without loss of generality, set $b = 0$. For $z \to \infty$ the function

$$I(z) \equiv E_t\left[\left| e^{-z^{1/r}\langle X\rangle_t}\mathrm{Re}\left(\frac{S_T}{S_t}\right)^{1/2\pm\sqrt{1/4-2z^{1/r}-4a}}\right|\right]$$

$$\sim e^{-z^{1/r}\langle X\rangle_t}E_t\left(\frac{S_T}{S_t}\right)^{1/2} \to 0 \tag{A.16}$$

decays exponentially since $E_t(S_T/S_t)^{1/2} < \infty$. □

The justification of equality (6.7) is similar.

Acknowledgment

The authors would like to thank Lane Hughston, Jim Gatheral, Roger Lee and an anonymous referee for their useful comments.

References

[1] J. Abate and W. Whitt, Numerical inversion of laplace transforms of probability distributions, *ORSA Journal on Computing* **7** (1995) 36–43.

[2] M. Abramowitz and I. A. Stegun, *Handbook of Mathematical Functions* (Dover, 1970).

[3] D. Breeden and R. Litzenberger, Prices of state contingent claims implicit in options prices, *Journal of Business* **51** (1978) 621–651.

[4] P. Carr and R. Lee, Robust replication of volatility derivatives, Mathematics in finance working paper series, New York University, Courant Institute of Mathematical Sciences (2008).

[5] P. Carr and D. Madan, Towards a theory of volatility trading, Reprinted in *Option Pricing, Interest Rates, and Risk Management* (University Press, 1998), pp. 417–427.

[6] P. Carr, D. Madan and R. H. Smith, Option valuation using the fast fourier transform, *Journal of Computational Finance* **2** (1999) 61–73.

[7] E. Derman, M. Kamal, K. Demeterfi and J. Zou, More than you ever wanted to know about volatility swaps, *The Journal of Derivatives* **6–4** (1999) 9–22.

[8] D. Filipovic, D Duffie and W. Schachermayer, Affine processes and applications in finance, *The Annals of Applied Probability* **13** (2003) 984–1053.

[9] D. Dufresne, The integrated square-root process, Research Paper 90, University of Montreal (2001).

[10] A. Estrella, Taylor, Black and Scholes, series approximations and risk management pitfalls, Research Paper 9501, Federal Reserve Bank of New York (1995).

[11] P. Friz and J. Gatheral, Valuation of volatility derivatives as an inverse problem, *Quantitative Finance* **5** (2005) 531–542.

[12] J. Gatheral, *The Volatility Surface: A Practitioner's Guide* (Wiley Finance, 2006).

[13] J. Hull and A. White, The pricing of options on assets with stochastic volatility, *Journal of Finance* **42**(2) June (1987) 281–300.

[14] W. Schachermayer and T. Teichmann, How close are the option pricing formulas of Bachelier and Black-Merton-Scholes? *Mathematical Finance* **18**(1) (2008) 155–170.

[15] W. Schoutens, E. Simons and J. Tistaert, A perfect calibration! Now what? *Wilmott Magazine*, March (2004).

[16] K. Schuerger, Laplace transforms and suprema of stochastic processes, University of Bonn (2002).

CONDITIONAL DENSITY MODELS FOR ASSET PRICING*

DAMIR FILIPOVIĆ

Swiss Finance Institute
and
École Polytechnique Fédérale de Lausanne,
1015 Lausanne, Switzerland

LANE P. HUGHSTON

Department of Mathematics, University College London
London WC1E 6BT, United Kingdom
and
Department of Mathematics, Imperial College London
London SW7 2AZ, United Kingdom

ANDREA MACRINA

Department of Mathematics, King's College London
London WC2R 2LS, United Kingdom
and
Institute of Economic Research
Kyoto University, Kyoto 606-8501, Japan

We model the dynamics of asset prices and associated derivatives by consideration of the dynamics of the conditional probability density process for the value of an asset at some specified time in the future. In the case where the price process is driven by Brownian motion, an associated "master equation" for the dynamics of the conditional probability density is derived and expressed in integral form. By a "model" for the conditional density process we mean a solution to the master equation along with the specification of (a) the initial density, and (b) the volatility structure of the density. The volatility structure is assumed at any time and for each value of the argument of the density to be a functional of the history of the density up to that time. In practice one specifies the functional modulo sufficient parametric freedom to allow for the input of additional option data apart from that implicit in the initial density. The scheme is sufficiently flexible to allow for the input of various types of data depending on the nature of the options market and the class of valuation problem being undertaken. Various examples are studied in detail, with exact solutions provided in some cases.

Keywords: Volatility surface; option pricing; implied volatility; Bachelier model; information-based asset pricing; nonlinear filtering; Breeden-Litzenberger equation.

*This chapter was originally published under the same title in *International Journal of Theoretical and Applied Finance*, Vol.15, No.1, 1250002-1–24 (2012). Singapore: World Scientific Publishing.

1. Introduction

This paper is concerned with modelling the dynamics of the volatility surface. The problem is of great practical interest to traders, and as a consequence has an extensive mathematical literature associated with it. In this brief report, we shall not attempt to review earlier work in the area, but refer the reader, for example, to Schönbucher [18], Gatheral [14], Schweizer and Wissel [19, 20], Carmona and Nadtochiy [8, 9], and references therein. Put informally, the general idea of the paper is as follows. We fix a numeraire, and write $\{A_t\}$ for the value process of some tradable financial asset expressed in units of that numeraire. We fix a time T and assume that no dividends are paid from time 0 up to T. Letting $\mathbb{Q}$ denote the martingale measure associated with the chosen numeraire, we have

$$A_t = \mathbb{E}^{\mathbb{Q}}[A_T|\mathcal{F}_t], \tag{1.1}$$

for $t \leq T$, and

$$C_{tT}(K) = \mathbb{E}^{\mathbb{Q}}[(A_T - K)^+|\mathcal{F}_t], \tag{1.2}$$

where $C_{tT}(K)$ denotes the price at time t of a T-maturity call option with strike K. The associated conditional density process $\{f_t(x)\}$ for the random variable A_T is defined by

$$\int_{-\infty}^{y} f_t(x)\mathrm{d}x = \mathbb{E}^{\mathbb{Q}}[\mathbb{1}\{y > A_T\}|\mathcal{F}_t]. \tag{1.3}$$

Then for the asset price we have

$$A_t = \int_{\mathbb{R}} x f_t(x)\mathrm{d}x, \tag{1.4}$$

and the corresponding option prices are given by

$$C_{tT}(K) = \int_{\mathbb{R}} (x - K)^+ f_t(x)\mathrm{d}x. \tag{1.5}$$

Instead of modelling $\{A_t\}$ and then determining $\{C_{tT}(K)\}$, our strategy is to model the conditional density process. Then the underlying asset price process and the associated option prices are determined by (1.4) and (1.5). Roughly speaking, the idea is to model $\{f_t(x)\}$ in such a way that it contains some parametric freedom that can be calibrated to a specified range of initial option prices. Models for conditional densities have been considered in various contexts in finance. These include for example applications to interest rates [3–5], and to credit risk [12]. Although mostly different from what has previously appeared in the literature, our approach to modelling the volatility surface is similar in spirit in some respects to that of Davis (2004).

Let us consider in more detail the class of assets that will form the basis of our investigation. We introduce a probability space $(\Omega, \mathcal{F}, \mathbb{P})$ with filtration $\{\mathcal{F}_t\}_{t\geq 0}$, where $\mathbb{P}$ is the "physical" measure and $\{\mathcal{F}_t\}$ is the market filtration. We assume that price processes are adapted to $\{\mathcal{F}_t\}$. We assume the absence of arbitrage, and the existence of an established pricing kernel $\{\pi_t\}$ associated with some choice of base currency as numeraire. We work in the setting of a multi-asset market, and do not assume that the market is complete.

We write $\{A_t^i\}_{i=0,1,\ldots,N}$ for the price processes of a collection of non-dividend-paying tradable financial assets. Prices are expressed in units of the base currency. We refer to asset i as A^i. We model the $\{A_t^i\}$ as Ito processes, and for each A^i we require that

$$\pi_s A_s^i = \mathbb{E}^{\mathbb{P}}[\pi_t A_t^i | \mathcal{F}_s] \tag{1.6}$$

for $s \leq t$. Such an asset is characterized by its value A_T^i at some terminal date T. In some situations it is useful to regard the asset as offering a single payment at T. In that case $\{A_t^i\}_{0\leq t<T}$ represents the price process of the asset that offers such a payment. In other situations we can consider A_T as being a "snapshot" of the value of the asset at time T. Usually the context will make it clear which meaning is intended.

Let $\{A_t^0\}$ be a money-market account in the base currency, initialised to unity. If we set $\rho_t = \pi_t A_t^0$ for $t \geq 0$, it follows that $\{\rho_t\}$ is a $\mathbb{P}$-martingale. A standard argument shows that $\{\rho_t\}$ can be used to make a change of measure. The resulting measure $\mathbb{Q}^0$ is the "risk-neutral" measure associated with the base currency, and has the property that if the price of any non-dividend-paying asset is expressed in units of the money-market account, then the resulting process is a $\mathbb{Q}^0$-martingale. Thus, for each i we have

$$A_s^i = A_s^0 \mathbb{E}^{\mathbb{Q}^0}\left[\left.\frac{A_t^i}{A_t^0}\right| \mathcal{F}_s\right]. \tag{1.7}$$

A similar situation arises with other choices of numeraire. Specifically, for any non-dividend-paying asset A^i of limited liability ($A_t^i > 0$), with price $\{A_t^i\}$, there is an associated measure $\mathbb{Q}^i$ with the property that if the price of any non-dividend-paying asset is expressed in units of A^i then the result is a $\mathbb{Q}^i$-martingale. Thus for $0 \leq s \leq t$ and for all i, j for which the price of A^i is strictly positive we have:

$$A_s^j = A_s^i \mathbb{E}^{\mathbb{Q}^i}\left[\left.\frac{A_t^j}{A_t^i}\right| \mathcal{F}_s\right]. \tag{1.8}$$

Bearing these points in mind, we observe that the option pricing problem can be formulated in the following context. We consider European-style options of a "Margrabe" type, for a pair of non-dividend-paying assets A^i and A^j, where the option-holder has the right at time t to exchange K units of A^i for one unit of A^j. The payoff H_t^{ij} of such an option, in units of the base currency, is of the form

$$H_t^{ij}(K) = (A_t^j - KA_t^i)^+. \tag{1.9}$$

The value of the option at $s \leq t$, expressed in units of the base currency, is given by

$$C_{st}^{ij}(K) = \frac{1}{\pi_s}\mathbb{E}^{\mathbb{P}}[\pi_t(A_t^j - KA_t^i)^+ | \mathcal{F}_s]. \tag{1.10}$$

If A^i is of limited liability, then the option value, expressed in units of A^i, is a $\mathbb{Q}^i$-martingale:

$$\frac{C^{ij}_{st}(K)}{A^i_s} = \mathbb{E}^{\mathbb{Q}^i}\left[\left(\frac{A^j_t}{A^i_t} - K\right)^+ \middle| \mathcal{F}_s\right]. \tag{1.11}$$

This relation can be expressed more compactly as follows. Write A_s for the price at time $s \leq t$ of a "generic asset" expressed in units of a "generic numeraire", and $C_{st}(K)$ for the price, in units of the chosen numeraire, at time $s \leq t$, of a t-maturity K-strike option. Then the option payoff is given (in numeraire units) by

$$H_t(K) = (A_t - K)^+. \tag{1.12}$$

The value of the option at time $s \leq t$ is

$$C_{st}(K) = \mathbb{E}^{\mathbb{Q}}[(A_t - K)^+ | \mathcal{F}_s], \tag{1.13}$$

where $\mathbb{Q}$ is the martingale measure associated with the numeraire. By "generic" we mean any choice of a non-dividend-paying assets A^i and A^j such that A^i is of limited liability.

Standard options are not included in the category discussed above. A standard call has the payoff $H_t = (A_t - K)^+$ where A_t is the price of the underlying at time t in currency units, and K is a fixed strike in currency units. This is not an option to exchange K units of a non-dividend-paying asset for one unit of another non-dividend-paying asset. One should think of the fixed strike as being K units of a unit floating rate note. The only asset that maintains a constant value (in base-currency units) is a floating rate note — and such an asset pays a dividend. The dividend is the interest rate. In a given currency, by a floating rate note we mean an idealised note that pays interest continuously (rather than in lumps). The associated dividend is the short rate. One might argue that the strike on a standard option is cash, and that cash is a non-dividend-paying asset: this point of view leads to paradoxes. In the standard theory we regard cash as paying an implicit dividend, a convenience yield, in the form of a liquidity benefit equivalent to the interest rate. In summary, a standard option is an option to exchange the asset with a floating-rate note, which pays a "dividend".

Thus a standard option is a complicated entity — it is an option to exchange a certain number of units of a dividend-paying asset for one unit of a non-dividend-paying asset. It is more logical first to examine an option based on a pair of *non-dividend-paying* assets. In the literature this approach is implicitly adopted through the device of "setting the interest rate equal to zero". In that situation the floating rate note is non-dividend-paying; thus, the setting we operate within includes the zero-interest case. One would like to tackle the general problem of an option to exchange K units of one dividend-paying asset for one unit of another dividend-paying asset (a "standard" foreign exchange option falls into that category); but, unless the dividend (or the interest rate) systems are deterministic, this is a more difficult problem than the one we propose to consider here.

The structure of the paper is as follows. In Sec. 2 we derive a dynamical equation for the conditional density, which we call the "master equation", given by (2.13). An integral form of the equation is presented in (2.14), which forms the basis of the solutions presented in later sections. In Sec. 3 we specify the general form we require the volatility structure of the conditional density to take, and give a characterization of what we mean by a "conditional density model" for asset pricing. In Sec. 4 we consider in detail the class of models for which the volatility structure of the conditional density is a deterministic function of two variables. This family of models admits a complete solution by use of a filtering technique. The resulting asset prices exhibit a stochastic volatility that is adapted to the market filtration but that is not in general of the local-volatility type. In Sec. 5 we consider the case when the volatility structure is linear in the terminal value of the asset. In that case the resulting models are Markovian, and can be calibrated to an arbitrary initial density. In Sec. 6 an alternative representation of the semi-linear case is presented using a Brownian-bridge technique. In Sec. 7 we show that the Bachelier model and the geometric Brownian motion model arise as special cases of the semilinear models, for particular choices of the initial density. We conclude in Sec. 8 with the calculation of option prices.

2. Conditional Density Processes

The market is understood as having the setup described in the previous section. We have a probability space $(\Omega, \mathcal{F}, \mathbb{Q})$ with filtration $\{\mathcal{F}_t\}$. A non-dividend-paying limited-liability asset is chosen as numeraire, and all prices are expressed in units of that numeraire. The measure $\mathbb{Q}$ has the property that the price process of a non-dividend-paying asset, when expressed in units of the numeraire, is a martingale. We refer to $\mathbb{Q}$ as the martingale measure associated with this numeraire.

We fix $T > 0$, and assume for $0 \leq t < T$ the existence of an $\mathcal{F}_t$-conditional $\mathbb{Q}$-density $f_t(x)$ for A_T. In our applications we have in mind the cases $x \in \mathbb{R}$ and $x \in \mathbb{R}^+$, but it is useful to be flexible as regards the choice of the domain of the density function. In what follows we treat the case $x \in \mathbb{R}$, and leave it to the reader to supply the necessary adjustments for other domains. Thus we assume the existence of a density process $\{f_t(x)\}$, $x \in \mathbb{R}$, $0 \leq t < T$, such that (1.3) holds. It follows that for any bounded, measurable function $g(x)$, $x \in \mathbb{R}$, we have

$$\int_{\mathbb{R}} g(x) f_t(x) \mathrm{d}x = \mathbb{E}[g(A_T)|\mathcal{F}_t]. \tag{2.1}$$

We ask that $\{f_t(x)\}$ should have those properties that follow heuristically as consequence of the formula obtained by formally differentiating (1.3), namely:

$$f_t(x) = \mathbb{E}[\delta(x - A_T)|\mathcal{F}_t]. \tag{2.2}$$

In particular, we require the following: (a) that for each $x \in \mathbb{R}$ the process $\{f_t(x)\}_{0 \leq t < T}$ is an $\{\mathcal{F}_t\}$-martingale, and hence $f_s(x) = \mathbb{E}[f_t(x)|\mathcal{F}_s]$ for $0 \leq s \leq$

$t < T$; (b) that the price of the asset can be expressed in terms of the density by (1.4) for $t < T$; and (c) that

$$\lim_{t \to T} \int_{\mathbb{R}} x f_t(x) \mathrm{d}x = A_T. \tag{2.3}$$

We also assume, where required, that expressions analogous to (1.4) can be written for claims based on A_T. For example, if $C_{tT}(K)$ denotes the price at t of a T-maturity, K-strike European call option, then we assume that (1.5) holds.

In the applications that follow, we introduce a $\mathbb{Q}$-Brownian motion $\{W_t\}$, which we take to be adapted to $\{\mathcal{F}_t\}$, and specialize to the case for which the dynamical equation of $\{f_t(x)\}$ is of the form

$$f_t(x) = f_0(x) + \int_0^t \sigma_s^f(x) f_s(x) \mathrm{d}W_s, \tag{2.4}$$

for some process $\{\sigma_t^f(x)\}$, $x \in \mathbb{R}$, $0 \leq t < T$, representing the volatility of the density. It follows that

$$A_t = A_0 + \int_0^t \sigma_s^A \mathrm{d}W_s, \tag{2.5}$$

where $A_0 = \int_{\mathbb{R}} x f_0(x) \mathrm{d}x$, and where the volatility of A_t is given by

$$\sigma_t^A = \int_{\mathbb{R}} x \sigma_t^f(x) f_t(x) \mathrm{d}x. \tag{2.6}$$

For simplicity, we consider in this paper the case where $\{W_t\}$ is a one-dimensional Brownian motion. The extension to the multi-dimensional situation is unproblematic.

Lemma 2.1. *The normalisation condition*

$$\int_{\mathbb{R}} f_t(x) \mathrm{d}x = 1 \tag{2.7}$$

holds for all $t \in [0, T)$ if and only if there exists a process $\{\sigma_t(x)\}$ such that

$$\sigma_t^f(x) = \sigma_t(x) \int_{\mathbb{R}} f_t(y) \mathrm{d}y - \int_{\mathbb{R}} \sigma_t(y) f_t(y) \mathrm{d}y \tag{2.8}$$

for almost all $t \in [0, T)$, and we have the initial condition

$$\int_{\mathbb{R}} f_0(x) \mathrm{d}x = 1. \tag{2.9}$$

Proof. First we show that (2.8) and (2.9) imply (2.7). Starting with (2.4), we integrate with respect to x to obtain

$$\int_{\mathbb{R}} f_t(x) \mathrm{d}x = \int_{\mathbb{R}} f_0(x) \mathrm{d}x + \int_0^t \int_{\mathbb{R}} \sigma_s^f(x) f_s(x) \mathrm{d}x \, \mathrm{d}W_s. \tag{2.10}$$

Inserting (2.8) and using (2.9) we obtain (2.7). Conversely, if we assume (2.7) then (2.9) holds as well, and hence

$$\int_0^t \int_{\mathbb{R}} \sigma_s^f(x) f_s(x) \mathrm{d}x \, \mathrm{d}W_s = 0, \tag{2.11}$$

from which it follows that

$$\int_{\mathbb{R}} \sigma_t^f(x) f_t(x) \mathrm{d}x = 0 \tag{2.12}$$

for almost all $t \in [0, T)$, and thus that (2.8) holds for almost all $t \in [0, T)$ for some $\sigma_t(x)$. □

Thus, once we specify $\{\sigma_t(x)\}$ and $\{f_0(x)\}$, the dynamical equation for the density — the so-called master equation — takes the form

$$f_t(x) = f_0(x) + \int_0^t \left[\sigma_s(x) - \int_{\mathbb{R}} \sigma_s(y) f_s(y) \mathrm{d}y \right] f_s(x) \mathrm{d}W_s. \tag{2.13}$$

Lemma 2.2. *The conditional density process* $\{f_t(x)\}$ *satisfies the master equation* (2.13) *with initial density* $\{f_0(x)\}$ *and volatility structure* $\{\sigma_t(x)\}$ *if and only if*

$$f_t(x) = \frac{f_0(x) \exp(\int_0^t \sigma_s(x) \mathrm{d}Z_s - \frac{1}{2} \int_0^t \sigma_s{}^2(x) \mathrm{d}s)}{\int_{\mathbb{R}} f_0(y) \exp(\int_0^t \sigma_s(y) \mathrm{d}Z_s - \frac{1}{2} \int_0^t \sigma_s{}^2(y) \mathrm{d}s) \mathrm{d}y}, \tag{2.14}$$

where

$$Z_t = W_t + \int_0^t \int_{\mathbb{R}} \sigma_s(y) f_s(y) \mathrm{d}y \mathrm{d}s. \tag{2.15}$$

Proof. Writing (2.13) in differential form, we have

$$\mathrm{d}f_t(x) = f_t(x)(\sigma_t(x) - \langle \sigma_t \rangle) \mathrm{d}W_t, \tag{2.16}$$

where for convenience we write

$$\langle \sigma_t \rangle = \int_{\mathbb{R}} \sigma_t(x) f_t(x) \mathrm{d}x \tag{2.17}$$

for the conditional "mean" of the volatility. We integrate (2.16) to obtain

$$f_t(x) = f_0(x) \exp\left[\int_0^t (\sigma_s(x) - \langle \sigma_s \rangle) \mathrm{d}W_s - \frac{1}{2} \int_0^t (\sigma_s(x) - \langle \sigma_s \rangle)^2 \mathrm{d}s \right]. \tag{2.18}$$

Expanding the exponent, we have

$$f_t(x) = f_0(x) \frac{\exp[\int_0^t \sigma_s(x)(\mathrm{d}W_s + \langle \sigma_s \rangle \mathrm{d}s) - \frac{1}{2} \int_0^t \sigma_s{}^2(x) \mathrm{d}s]}{\exp[\int_0^t \langle \sigma_s \rangle \, (\mathrm{d}W_s + \langle \sigma_s \rangle \mathrm{d}s) - \frac{1}{2} \int_0^t \langle \sigma_s \rangle^2 \mathrm{d}s]}. \tag{2.19}$$

Then we introduce a process $\{Z_t\}$ by writing

$$Z_t = W_t + \int_0^t \langle \sigma_s \rangle \mathrm{d}s, \tag{2.20}$$

and it follows that

$$f_t(x) = f_0(x)\frac{\exp[\int_0^t \sigma_s(x)\mathrm{d}Z_s - \frac{1}{2}\int_0^t {\sigma_s}^2(x)\mathrm{d}s]}{\exp[\int_0^t \langle\sigma_s\rangle\mathrm{d}Z_s - \frac{1}{2}\int_0^t \langle\sigma_s\rangle^2\mathrm{d}s]}. \tag{2.21}$$

Applying the normalization condition (2.7) to equation (2.21) above, we see that

$$\exp\left(\int_0^t \langle\sigma_s\rangle\mathrm{d}Z_s - \frac{1}{2}\int_0^t \langle\sigma_s\rangle^2\mathrm{d}s\right) = \int_{\mathbb{R}} f_0(x)\exp\left(\int_0^t \sigma_s(x)\mathrm{d}Z_s - \frac{1}{2}\int_0^t {\sigma_s}^2(x)\mathrm{d}s\right)\mathrm{d}x. \tag{2.22}$$

It follows that (2.21) reduces to (2.14). Conversely, if $f_t(x)$ is given by (2.14), then it is a straightforward exercise in Ito calculus to check that the master equation is satisfied. □

3. Conditional Density Models

We are in a position now to say more precisely what we mean by a "conditional density model". In doing so, we are motivated in part by advances in the study of infinite-dimensional stochastic differential equations (see, e.g., [13]). By a "model" for the density process we understand the following. We consider solutions of the master equation (2.13) satisfying the normalization condition (2.7), in conjunction with the specification of: (a) the *initial density* $f_0(x)$; and (b) the *volatility structure* $\{\sigma_t(x)\}$ in the form of a functional

$$\sigma_t(x) = \Phi[f_t(\cdot), t, x]. \tag{3.1}$$

For each x and t the volatility $\sigma_t(x)$ depends on $f_t(y)$ for all $y \in \mathbb{R}$. Hence (2.13), thus specified, determines the dynamics of an infinite-dimensional Markov process.

The initial density $f_0(x)$ can be determined if one supplies initial option price data for the maturity date T and for all strikes $K \in \mathbb{R}$. In particular, we have

$$C_{0T}(K) = \mathbb{E}[(A_T - K)^+] = \int_{\mathbb{R}} (x - K)^+ f_0(x)\mathrm{d}x. \tag{3.2}$$

By use of the idea of Breeden and Litzenberger [2] we see, in the present context, that for each value of x one has

$$f_0(x) = \frac{\partial^2 C_{0T}(x)}{\partial x^2}. \tag{3.3}$$

Here $f_0(x)$ is not generally the risk-neutral density, but rather the $\mathbb{Q}$-density of the value at time T of the asset in units of the chosen numeraire. For simple practical applications, we take — in common with much of the literature — the numeraire to be the money-market account, and set the interest rate to zero. Then $f_0(x)$ is the risk-neutral density. Once $f_0(x)$ has been supplied, the choice of the functional Φ determines the model for the conditional density: we give some examples later in the paper.

In practice, one would like to specify Φ modulo sufficient parametric freedom to allow the input of additional option price data. What form this additional data might take depends on the nature of the market and the class of valuation problems being pursued. For example, a standard problem would be to look at a limited-liability asset and consider additional data in the form of initial option prices for all strikes in $\mathbb{R}^+$ and all maturities in the strip $0 < t \leq T$. We require that Φ should be specified in such a way that once the data are provided, then Φ is determined and the "master equation" provides an evolution of the conditional density. Once we have the conditional density process, we can work out the evolution of the option price system for the specified strip, and hence the evolution of the associated implied volatility surface.

The data do not have to be presented exactly in the way specified in the previous paragraph — there may be situations where more data are available (e.g., in the form of barrier option prices or other derivative prices) or where less data are available (less well-developed markets). One should think of the parametric form of Φ as being adapted in a flexible way to the nature of a specific problem. The philosophy is that there are many different markets for options, and one needs a methodology that can accommodate these with reasonable generality.

It should be evident that an arbitrary solution to the master equation need not be a density process for an $\mathcal{F}_t$-measurable random variable — additional assumptions are required concerning the nature of the volatility structure in order to ensure that $f_t(x)$ converges in an appropriate sense to a suitable Dirac distribution. In the examples given, we indicate how this can be achieved, in various situations, by the choice of the volatility structure.

4. Models with Deterministic Volatility Structures

We proceed to present a rather general class of conditional density models characterized by a deterministic volatility structure. These are models for which $\{\sigma_t(x)\}$ is of the form

$$\sigma_t(x) = v(t, x) \tag{4.1}$$

for some deterministic function $v(t, x)$ defined for appropriate values of t and x. We are able to give a more or less complete construction of such models in the form of a "weak" solution of the master equation. By a weak solution we mean that on a probability space $(\Omega, \mathcal{F}, \mathbb{Q})$ we construct a filtration $\{\mathcal{F}_t\}$, a Brownian motion $\{W_t\}$, and a conditional density process $\{f_t(x)\}$ satisfying the master equation and having the desired properties. More specifically, let $T \in (0, \infty)$ be fixed, and let $f_0(x) : \mathbb{R} \to \mathbb{R}^+$ be a prescribed initial density. Let $v(t, x)$ be a function on $[0, T) \times \mathbb{R}$ satisfying

$$\int_0^t v(s, x)^2 \mathrm{d}s < \infty \tag{4.2}$$

for $t < T$ and $x \in \mathbb{R}$, and let $\gamma(t)$ be a function on $[0,T)$ such that

$$\lim_{t\to T} \gamma(t) = 0, \quad \lim_{t\to T} \gamma(t) \int_0^t v(s,x)\mathrm{d}s = g(x), \tag{4.3}$$

for some invertible function $g(x)$ on $\mathbb{R}$. We have the following:

Proposition 4.1. *Let X have density $f_0(x)$, and let $\{B_t\}$ be an independent Brownian motion. Let $\{\mathcal{F}_t\}$ be the filtration generated by the "information" process $\{I_t\}$ defined by*

$$I_t = B_t + \int_0^t v(s,X)\mathrm{d}s. \tag{4.4}$$

Let $\{f_t(x)\}$ be defined by

$$f_t(x) = \frac{f_0(x)\exp[\int_0^t v(s,x)\mathrm{d}I_s - \frac{1}{2}\int_0^t v^2(s,x)\mathrm{d}s]}{\int_{-\infty}^{\infty} f_0(y)\exp[\int_0^t v(s,y)\mathrm{d}I_s - \frac{1}{2}\int_0^t v^2(s,y)\mathrm{d}s]\mathrm{d}y}, \tag{4.5}$$

and define $\{W_t\}$ by setting

$$W_t = I_t - \int_0^t \mathbb{E}^{\mathbb{Q}}[v(s,X)|\mathcal{F}_s]\mathrm{d}s. \tag{4.6}$$

Then: (a) *the random variable X is $\mathcal{F}_T$-measurable, and $f_t(x)$ is the associated conditional density;* (b) *the process $\{W_t\}$ is an $\{\mathcal{F}_t\}$-adapted Brownian motion; and* (c) *for $t \in [0,T)$, the density process $\{f_t(x)\}$ satisfies the master equation*

$$f_t(x) = f_0(x) + \int_0^t f_s(x)\left[v(s,x) - \int_{-\infty}^{\infty} v(s,y)f_s(y)\mathrm{d}y\right]\mathrm{d}W_s. \tag{4.7}$$

Proof. It follows from (4.3) that $g(X) = \lim_{t\to T}\gamma(t)I_t$ is $\mathcal{F}_T$-measurable. Since $g(x)$ is invertible, we conclude that X is $\mathcal{F}_T$-measurable. Now let the filtration $\{\mathcal{G}_t\}$ be defined by

$$\mathcal{G}_t = \sigma(\{B_s\}_{0\le s\le t}, X). \tag{4.8}$$

Clearly $\mathcal{F}_t \subset \mathcal{G}_t$. The random variable X is $\mathcal{G}_t$-measurable, and $\{B_t\}$ is a $(\{\mathcal{G}_t\},\mathbb{Q})$-Brownian motion. We introduce a $(\{\mathcal{G}_t\},\mathbb{Q})$-martingale $\{M_t\}$ by setting

$$M_t = \exp\left[-\int_0^t v(s,X)\mathrm{d}B_s - \frac{1}{2}\int_0^t v^2(s,X)\mathrm{d}s\right], \tag{4.9}$$

for $t \in [0,T)$, and we let the probability measure $\mathbb{B}$ be defined by

$$\left.\frac{\mathrm{d}\mathbb{B}}{\mathrm{d}\mathbb{Q}}\right|_{\mathcal{G}_t} = M_t. \tag{4.10}$$

We observe that $\mathrm{d}I_t = \mathrm{d}B_t + v(t,X)\mathrm{d}t$. By Girsanov's theorem, $\{I_t\}$ is a $(\{\mathcal{G}_t\},\mathbb{B})$-Brownian motion. We note that $\{M_t^{-1}\}$ is a $(\{\mathcal{G}_t\},\mathbb{B})$-martingale. Let H be a bounded measurable function on $\mathbb{R}$. Since $H(X)$ is $\mathcal{G}_t$-measurable, we have the generalised Bayes formula

$$\mathbb{E}^{\mathbb{Q}}[H(X)|\mathcal{F}_t] = \frac{\mathbb{E}^{\mathbb{B}}[M_t^{-1}H(X)|\mathcal{F}_t]}{\mathbb{E}^{\mathbb{B}}[M_t^{-1}|\mathcal{F}_t]}. \tag{4.11}$$

Let us work out the right-hand side of this equation. To this end we show that X and I_t are $\mathbb{B}$-independent for all t. In particular, we show that the generating function

$$\mathbb{E}^{\mathbb{B}}[\exp(yI_t + zX)] \tag{4.12}$$

factorises. We have:

$$\begin{aligned}
\mathbb{E}^{\mathbb{B}}[\exp(yI_t + zX)] &= \mathbb{E}^{\mathbb{Q}}[M_t \exp(yI_t + zX)] &(4.13)\\
&= \mathbb{E}^{\mathbb{Q}}\left[\exp\left(-\int_0^t v(s,X)\mathrm{d}B_s - \frac{1}{2}\int_0^t v^2(s,X)\mathrm{d}s\right.\right.\\
&\quad \left.\left. + y\left[B_t + \int_0^t v(s,X)\mathrm{d}s\right]\right)\exp(zX)\right], &(4.14)\\
&= \mathbb{E}^{\mathbb{Q}}\left[m_t \exp\left(\frac{1}{2}y^2 t\right)\exp(zX)\right], &(4.15)
\end{aligned}$$

where

$$m_t = \exp\left(\int_0^t [-v(s,X)+y]\mathrm{d}B_s - \frac{1}{2}\int_0^t [-v(s,X)+y]^2\mathrm{d}s\right). \tag{4.16}$$

By use of the tower property and the independence of $\{B_t\}$ and X under $\mathbb{Q}$, we have

$$\begin{aligned}
\mathbb{E}^{\mathbb{B}}[\exp(yI_t + zX)] &= \mathbb{E}^{\mathbb{Q}}\left[m_t \exp\left(\frac{1}{2}y^2 t\right)\exp(zX)\right], &(4.17)\\
&= \exp\left(\frac{1}{2}y^2 t\right)\mathbb{E}^{\mathbb{Q}}[\mathbb{E}^{\mathbb{Q}}[m_t \exp(zX)|X]], &(4.18)\\
&= \exp\left(\frac{1}{2}y^2 t\right)\mathbb{E}^{\mathbb{Q}}[\mathbb{E}^{\mathbb{Q}}[m_t|X]\mathbb{E}^{\mathbb{Q}}[\exp(zX)]]. &(4.19)
\end{aligned}$$

One observes that $\mathbb{E}^{\mathbb{Q}}[m_t|X] = 1$. Thus we obtain the desired factorization:

$$\mathbb{E}^{\mathbb{B}}[\exp(yI_t + zX)] = \exp\left(\frac{1}{2}y^2 t\right)\mathbb{E}^{\mathbb{Q}}[\exp(zX)]. \tag{4.20}$$

Now that we have shown that X is $\mathbb{B}$-independent of I_t (and thus of $\mathcal{F}_t$), we can work out the right-hand side of (4.11). We have:

$$\mathbb{E}^{\mathbb{Q}}[H(X)|\mathcal{F}_t] = \frac{\mathbb{E}^{\mathbb{B}}[M_t^{-1}H(X)|\mathcal{F}_t]}{\mathbb{E}^{\mathbb{B}}[M_t^{-1}|\mathcal{F}_t]}, \tag{4.21}$$

$$= \frac{\mathbb{E}^{\mathbb{B}}[H(X)\exp(\int_0^t v(s,X)\mathrm{d}I_s - \frac{1}{2}\int_0^t v^2(s,X)\mathrm{d}s)|\mathcal{F}_t]}{\mathbb{E}^{\mathbb{B}}[\exp(\int_0^t v(s,X)\mathrm{d}I_s - \frac{1}{2}\int_0^t v^2(s,X)\mathrm{d}s)|\mathcal{F}_t]}, \tag{4.22}$$

$$= \frac{\int_{-\infty}^{\infty} f_0(x)H(x)\exp(\int_0^t v(s,x)\mathrm{d}I_s - \frac{1}{2}\int_0^t v^2(s,x)\mathrm{d}s)\,\mathrm{d}x}{\int_{-\infty}^{\infty} f_0(y)\exp(\int_0^t v(s,y)\mathrm{d}I_s - \frac{1}{2}\int_0^t v^2(s,y)\mathrm{d}s)\,\mathrm{d}y}. \tag{4.23}$$

In particular, setting $H(X) = \mathbf{1}(X \leq x)$, we deduce that $f_t(x)$ is the $\mathcal{F}_t$-conditional density of X, as required. That proves the first part of the proposition.

Next we show that $\{W_t\}$ is an $(\{\mathcal{F}_t\}, \mathbb{Q})$-Brownian motion. We need to show (1) that $(\mathrm{d}W_t)^2 = \mathrm{d}t$, and (2) that $\mathbb{E}^{\mathbb{Q}}[W_u|\mathcal{F}_t] = W_t$ for $0 \leq t \leq u$. The first condition is evidently satisfied. The second condition can be shown to be satisfied as follows. For simplicity, we suppress the superscript $\mathbb{Q}$. We have

$$\mathbb{E}[W_u|\mathcal{F}_t] = \mathbb{E}[I_u|\mathcal{F}_t] - \mathbb{E}\left[\int_0^u \mathbb{E}[v(s,X)|\mathcal{F}_s]\mathrm{d}s|\mathcal{F}_t\right]. \tag{4.24}$$

First we work out $\mathbb{E}[I_u|\mathcal{F}_t]$. Since $\{B_t\}$ is a $(\{\mathcal{G}_t\}, \mathbb{Q})$-Brownian motion, we have

$$\mathbb{E}[I_u|\mathcal{F}_t] = \mathbb{E}\left[B_u + \int_0^u v(s,X)\mathrm{d}s|\mathcal{F}_t\right] \tag{4.25}$$

$$= \mathbb{E}[B_u|\mathcal{F}_t] + \mathbb{E}\left[\int_0^u v(s,X)\mathrm{d}s|\mathcal{F}_t\right] \tag{4.26}$$

$$= \mathbb{E}[\mathbb{E}[B_u|\mathcal{G}_t]|\mathcal{F}_t] + \mathbb{E}\left[\int_0^u v(s,X)\mathrm{d}s|\mathcal{F}_t\right] \tag{4.27}$$

$$= \mathbb{E}[B_t|\mathcal{F}_t] + \mathbb{E}\left[\int_0^u v(s,X)\mathrm{d}s|\mathcal{F}_t\right]. \tag{4.28}$$

We insert this intermediate result in (4.24) to obtain

$$\mathbb{E}[W_u|\mathcal{F}_t] = \mathbb{E}[I_u|\mathcal{F}_t] - \mathbb{E}\left[\int_0^u \mathbb{E}[v(s,X)|\mathcal{F}_s]\mathrm{d}s|\mathcal{F}_t\right] \tag{4.29}$$

$$= \mathbb{E}[B_t|\mathcal{F}_t] + \mathbb{E}\left[\int_0^u v(s,X)\mathrm{d}s|\mathcal{F}_t\right] - \mathbb{E}\left[\int_0^u \mathbb{E}[v(s,X)|\mathcal{F}_s]\mathrm{d}s|\mathcal{F}_t\right]. \tag{4.30}$$

Next we split the integrals in the last two expectations by writing,

$$\mathbb{E}[W_u|\mathcal{F}_t] = \mathbb{E}[B_t|\mathcal{F}_t] + \mathbb{E}\left[\int_0^t v(s,X)\mathrm{d}s|\mathcal{F}_t\right] + \mathbb{E}\left[\int_t^u v(s,X)\mathrm{d}s|\mathcal{F}_t\right]$$
$$-\mathbb{E}\left[\int_0^t \mathbb{E}[v(s,X)|\mathcal{F}_s]\,\mathrm{d}s|\mathcal{F}_t\right] - \mathbb{E}\left[\int_t^u \mathbb{E}[v(s,X)|\mathcal{F}_s]\,\mathrm{d}s|\mathcal{F}_t\right]. \tag{4.31}$$

Observing that

$$\mathbb{E}[B_t|\mathcal{F}_t] + \mathbb{E}\left[\int_0^t v(s,X)\mathrm{d}s|\mathcal{F}_t\right] = I_t, \tag{4.32}$$

and that

$$\mathbb{E}\left[\int_t^u v(s,X)\mathrm{d}s|\mathcal{F}_t\right] = \mathbb{E}\left[\int_t^u \mathbb{E}[v(s,X)|\mathcal{F}_s]\mathrm{d}s|\mathcal{F}_t\right], \tag{4.33}$$

we see that the expectation $\mathbb{E}[W_u|\mathcal{F}_t]$ reduces to

$$\mathbb{E}[W_u|\mathcal{F}_t] = I_t - \mathbb{E}\left[\int_0^t \mathbb{E}[v(s,X)|\mathcal{F}_s]\mathrm{d}s|\mathcal{F}_t\right] = I_t - \int_0^t \mathbb{E}[v(s,X)|\mathcal{F}_s]\mathrm{d}s = W_t. \tag{4.34}$$

That shows that $\{W_t\}$ is an $\{\mathcal{F}_t\}$-Brownian motion. An application of Ito calculus shows that the density process (4.5) satisfies the SDE (4.7). □

Remark 4.1. For simplicity we have presented Proposition 4.1 for the case of a one-dimensional state space. It should be clear from the proof how the results carry over to conditional densities on higher-dimensional state spaces.

Remark 4.2. For simulations of the dynamics of the conditional density process, the following alternative representation for (4.5) may prove useful:

$$f_t(x) = \frac{f_0(x)\exp(\int_0^t [v(s,x) - v(s,X)]\mathrm{d}B_s - \frac{1}{2}\int_0^t [v(s,x) - v(s,X)]^2 \mathrm{d}s)}{\int_{\mathbb{R}} f_0(y)\exp(\int_0^t [v(s,y) - v(s,X)]\mathrm{d}B_s - \frac{1}{2}\int_0^t [v(s,y) - v(s,X)]^2 \mathrm{d}s)\,\mathrm{d}y}. \tag{4.35}$$

The unnormalised density — the numerator in (4.35) — is for all $x \in \mathbb{R}$ conditionally log-normal given X. The simulation of the density requires only the numerical implementation of the standard Brownian motion and of the random variable X.

Remark 4.3. The density models with deterministic volatility structure presented in Proposition 4.1 can be extended to a class of models that satisfy the following system:

Let $f_0(x) : \mathbb{R} \to \mathbb{R}^+$ be a density function. A filtered probability space $(\Omega, \mathcal{F}, \{\mathcal{F}_t\}, \mathbb{Q})$ can be constructed along with (i) an $\mathcal{F}_\infty$-measurable random variable X with density $f_0(x)$, (ii) an $\{\mathcal{F}_t\}$-adapted density process $\{f_t(x)\}$, and (iii) an $\{\mathcal{F}_t\}$-adapted Brownian motion $\{W_t\}$, such that (a) for some function $\gamma(t)$ on

$[0, \infty)$, (b) for some function $g(x)$ that is invertible onto $\mathbb{R}$, and (c) for some suitably integrable function $v(t, x)$ on $[0, \infty) \times \mathbb{R}$ with the properties

$$\lim_{t \to \infty} \sqrt{t}\gamma(t) = 0, \quad \lim_{t \to \infty} \gamma(t) \int_0^t v(s, x)\mathrm{d}s = g(x), \tag{4.36}$$

the following relations hold for all $t \in [0, \infty)$. We have $\mathbb{Q}[X \in \mathrm{d}x|\mathcal{F}_t] = f_t(x)\mathrm{d}x$ and

$$f_t(x) = f_0(x) + \int_0^t f_s(x) \left[v(s, x) - \int_{-\infty}^{\infty} v(s, y) f_s(y)\mathrm{d}y \right] \mathrm{d}W_s. \tag{4.37}$$

Remark 4.4. The construction of conditional density models admits an interpretation as a kind of a filtering problem. The process (4.4) plays the role of an "observation process", and (4.6) has the interpretation of being an "innovation process". See [1, 15, 16].

Remark 4.5. It is reasonable on a heuristic basis to expect that the general deterministic volatility structure model can be calibrated to the specification of an essentially arbitrary volatility surface. In particular, the parametric freedom implicit in a deterministic volatility structure coincides with that of a volatility surface. The situation is rather similar to that of the relation arising in the Dupire [11] model between the local volatility (which is determined by a deterministic function of two variables, one with the dimensionality of price and the other with that of time) and the initial volatility surface (which represents a two-parameter family of option prices, labelled by strike and maturity). The precise characterisation of such relations constitutes a non-trivial and important inverse problem.

Remark 4.6. In the general deterministic volatility structure model, the dynamics of the underlying asset price $\{A_t\}$ are of the form $\mathrm{d}A_t = V_t\mathrm{d}W_t$, with

$$V_t = \int_{\mathbb{R}} xv(t, x)f_t(x)\mathrm{d}x - \int_{\mathbb{R}} xf_t(x)\mathrm{d}x \int_{\mathbb{R}} v(t, x)f_t(x)\mathrm{d}x, \tag{4.38}$$

where $f_t(x)$ is given by (4.5). Thus the absolute volatility V_t at time t takes the form of a conditional covariance between X and $v(t, X)$. In general, $\{V_t\}$ is an $\{\mathcal{F}_t\}$-adapted stochastic volatility process that cannot be expressed in the form $\Sigma(t, A_t)$ for some function $\Sigma(t, x)$, and the dynamics do not constitute a simple diffusion of the Dupire (local volatility) type. In the "semilinear" case $v(t, x) = \sigma Tx/(T - t)$, however, the associated information process is Markovian, and V_t can indeed be expressed in the form $\Sigma(t, A_t)$.

5. Semilinear Volatility Structure

We consider in this section the case where A_T has a prescribed unconditional density $f_{0T}(x)$, and construct a family of conditional density processes $\{f_{tT}\}$ that solve the master Eq. (2.13) over the time interval $[0, T)$. The filtration with respect to which $\{f_{tT}\}$ is defined will be constructed as follows. We introduce a process $\{\xi_{tT}\}_{0 \leq t \leq T}$

given by $\xi_{tT} = \sigma A_T t + \beta_{tT}$, where σ is a constant and $\{\beta_{tT}\}_{0\le t\le T}$ is a standard Brownian bridge, taken to be independent from A_T. We assume that $\{\mathcal{F}_t\}$ is given by

$$\mathcal{F}_t = \sigma(\{\xi_{sT}\}_{0\le s\le t}). \tag{5.1}$$

Clearly $\{\xi_{tT}\}$ is $\{\mathcal{F}_t\}$-adapted, and A_T is $\mathcal{F}_T$-measurable. It is shown in Brody *et al.* [6, 7] that $\{\xi_{tT}\}$ is an $\{\mathcal{F}_t\}$-Markov process (see also [17]).

Proposition 5.1. *Let the initial density $f_{0T}(x)$ be prescribed, and let the volatility structure be of the semilinear form*

$$\sigma_{tT}(x) = \sigma\frac{T}{T-t}x, \tag{5.2}$$

for $0 \le t < T$, and let $\{\mathcal{F}_t\}$ be defined by (5.1). Then the process $\{W_t\}_{0\le t<T}$ defined by

$$W_t = \xi_{tT} - \int_0^t \frac{1}{T-s}(\sigma T\mathbb{E}[A_T|\xi_{sT}] - \xi_{sT})\mathrm{d}s \tag{5.3}$$

is an $\{\mathcal{F}_t\}$-Brownian motion, and the process $\{f_{tT}(x)\}$, given by

$$f_{tT}(x) = \frac{f_{0T}(x)\exp[\frac{T}{T-t}(\sigma\xi_{tT}x - \frac{1}{2}\sigma^2x^2t)]}{\int_{-\infty}^{\infty} f_{0T}(y)\exp[\frac{T}{T-t}\,(\sigma\xi_{tT}y - \frac{1}{2}\sigma^2y^2t)]\mathrm{d}y}, \tag{5.4}$$

satisfies the master equation (2.13) with the given initial condition.

Proof. The fact that $\{W_t\}_{0\le t<T}$ is an $\{\mathcal{F}_t\}$-Brownian motion is shown in Brody *et al.* [6, 7]. We work out $\mathbb{E}[A_T|\xi_{tT}]$ by use of the Bayes formula,

$$\mathbb{E}[A_T|\xi_{tT}] = \int_{\mathbb{R}} x f_{tT}(x)\mathrm{d}x, \tag{5.5}$$

where

$$f_{tT}(x) = \frac{f_{0T}(x)\rho(\xi_{tT}|A_T = x)}{\int_{\mathbb{R}} f_{0T}(y)\rho(\xi_{tT}|A_T = y)\mathrm{d}y}. \tag{5.6}$$

Here $\rho(\xi_{tT}|A_T = x)$ is the conditional density of ξ_{tT} given the value of A_T. We observe that ξ_{tT} is conditionally Gaussian:

$$\rho(\xi_{tT}|A_T = x) = \sqrt{\frac{T}{2\pi t(T-t)}}\exp\left[-\frac{1}{2}\frac{T}{t(T-t)}(\xi_{tT} - \sigma t x)^2\right]. \tag{5.7}$$

Thus the density process is given by

$$f_{tT}(x) = \frac{f_{0T}(x)\exp[-\frac{1}{2}\frac{T}{t(T-t)}(\xi_{tT} - \sigma t x)^2]}{\int_{-\infty}^{\infty} f_{0T}(y)\exp[-\frac{1}{2}\frac{T}{t(T-t)}(\xi_{tT} - \sigma t y)^2]\mathrm{d}y}. \tag{5.8}$$

The last expression can be simplified after some rearrangement so as to take the form

$$f_{tT}(x) = \frac{f_{0T}(x)\exp[\frac{T}{T-t}\left(\sigma\xi_{tT}x - \frac{1}{2}\sigma^2x^2t\right)]}{\int_{-\infty}^{\infty} f_{0T}(y)\exp[\frac{T}{T-t}\left(\sigma\xi_{tT}y - \frac{1}{2}\sigma^2y^2t\right)]\mathrm{d}y}. \tag{5.9}$$

With this result at hand, we can write the process $\{W_t\}_{0\le t<T}$ in the form

$$W_t = \xi_{tT} - \int_0^t \frac{1}{T-s}\left(\sigma T\int_{\mathbb{R}} x f_{sT}(x)\mathrm{d}x - \xi_{sT}\right)\mathrm{d}s. \tag{5.10}$$

We recall that the master equation (2.13) can be written as (2.14). We shall prove that (5.4) satisfies (2.13) by showing that (2.14) reduces to (5.4) if we insert (5.3) in (2.20) and choose the volatility structure to be (5.2). For the process $\{Z_t\}$ in (2.20) we obtain

$$Z_t = \xi_{tT} + \int_0^t \frac{\xi_{sT}}{T-s}\mathrm{d}s. \tag{5.11}$$

The next step is to insert $\{Z_t\}$ in the exponent

$$\int_0^t \sigma_{sT}(x)\mathrm{d}Z_s - \frac{1}{2}\int_0^t \sigma_{sT}(x)^2\mathrm{d}s \tag{5.12}$$

appearing in equation (2.14). Expression (5.12) can be simplified by use of (5.2) to give

$$\begin{aligned}\sigma Tx\int_0^t \frac{1}{T-s}\left(\mathrm{d}\xi_{sT} + \frac{\xi_{sT}}{T-s}\mathrm{d}s\right) - \frac{1}{2}(\sigma Tx)^2\int_0^t \frac{1}{(T-s)^2}\mathrm{d}s \\ = \frac{T}{T-t}\left(\sigma x\xi_{tT} - \frac{1}{2}\sigma^2x^2t\right).\end{aligned} \tag{5.13}$$

To derive this result, we make use of the relation

$$\int_0^t \frac{\mathrm{d}\xi_{sT}}{T-s} = \frac{\xi_{tT}}{T-t} - \int_0^t \frac{\xi_{sT}}{(T-s)^2}\mathrm{d}s. \tag{5.14}$$

With equation (5.13) at hand, we see that (2.14) reduces to (5.4) if (5.2) holds. □

6. Semilinear Volatility: Brownian Motion Approach

We proceed to show how the models constructed in Sec. 5 are related to the density models with deterministic volatility structure treated in Sec. 4. In particular, we consider a deterministic semilinear volatility function of the form

$$v(t,x) = \sigma\frac{T}{T-t}x, \tag{6.1}$$

where $0 \le t < T$. For this volatility function the process $\{I_t\}$ has the dynamics

$$\mathrm{d}I_t = \sigma\frac{T}{T-t}X\mathrm{d}t + \mathrm{d}B_t. \tag{6.2}$$

We are thus able to work out the exponent

$$\int_0^t v(s,x)\mathrm{d}I_s - \frac{1}{2}\int_0^t v^2(s,x)\mathrm{d}s \tag{6.3}$$

in Eq. (4.5) making use of (6.1) and (6.2). We have:

$$\begin{aligned}&\int_0^t v(s,x)\mathrm{d}I_s - \frac{1}{2}\int_0^t v^2(s,x)\mathrm{d}s\\&\quad= \frac{T}{T-t}\sigma x\left[(T-t)\int_0^t \frac{\mathrm{d}B_s}{T-s} + T(T-t)\sigma X\int_0^t \frac{\mathrm{d}s}{(T-s)^2}\right]\\&\quad-\frac{1}{2}T^2\sigma^2x^2\int_0^t \frac{\mathrm{d}s}{(T-s)^2}.\end{aligned} \tag{6.4}$$

The first integral gives rise to a $(\{\mathcal{G}_t\},\mathbb{Q})$-Brownian bridge $\{\beta_{tT}\}$ over the interval $[0,T]$. More specifically, we have

$$\beta_{tT} = (T-t)\int_0^t \frac{\mathrm{d}B_s}{T-s}. \tag{6.5}$$

The deterministic integral in (6.4) gives

$$\int_0^t \frac{\mathrm{d}s}{(T-s)^2} = \frac{t}{T(T-t)}. \tag{6.6}$$

Armed with these results, one can write (6.3) as follows:

$$\int_0^t v(s,x)\mathrm{d}I_s - \frac{1}{2}\int_0^t v^2(s,x)\mathrm{d}s = \frac{T}{T-t}\sigma x(\sigma Xt+\beta_{tT}) - \frac{1}{2}\frac{T}{T-t}\sigma^2x^2t. \tag{6.7}$$

Let $\{\xi_{tT}\}$ be defined for $t\in[0,T]$ by $\xi_{tT}=\sigma Xt+\beta_{tT}$. Then for (6.7) we obtain

$$\int_0^t v(s,x)\mathrm{d}I_s - \frac{1}{2}\int_0^t v^2(s,x)\mathrm{d}s = \frac{T}{T-t}\left(\sigma x\xi_{tT} - \frac{1}{2}\sigma^2x^2t\right). \tag{6.8}$$

We conclude that the conditional density process $\{f_t(x)\}$ in (4.5) reduces to the following expression in the case for which the volatility structure is given by (6.1):

$$f_t(x) = \frac{f_0(x)\exp[\frac{T}{T-t}\left(\sigma x\xi_{tT} - \frac{1}{2}\sigma^2x^2t\right)]}{\int_{-\infty}^{\infty} f_0(y)\exp[\frac{T}{T-t}\left(\sigma y\xi_{tT} - \frac{1}{2}\sigma^2y^2t\right)]\mathrm{d}y}. \tag{6.9}$$

From Eq. (6.8) we see that $\{\xi_{tT}\}$ takes the role of the information process that generates $\{\mathcal{F}_t\}$. Since $\{\beta_{tT}\}$ vanishes for $t=T$, the random variable X is "revealed" at T. Thus X is $\mathcal{F}_T$-measurable, and $\{\xi_{tT}\}$ is the process generating the information-based models of Brody *et al.* [6, 7]. This conclusion is supported by the following construction.

We consider the measure $\mathbb{B}$ defined in (4.10). Under $\mathbb{B}$ the process $\{I_t\}$ is a Brownian motion over the interval $[0,T)$. We construct a $\mathbb{B}$-Brownian bridge by use of the $\mathbb{B}$-Brownian motion $\{I_t\}$ as follows. On $[0,T)$ we set

$$\xi_{tT} = (T-t)\int_0^t \frac{1}{T-s}\mathrm{d}I_s. \tag{6.10}$$

Next we recall Definition (4.4) and insert this in the expression above. The result is

$$\xi_{tT} = (T-t)\int_0^t \frac{\mathrm{d}B_s}{T-s} + (T-t)\int_0^t \frac{1}{T-s}v(s,X)\mathrm{d}s. \tag{6.11}$$

The first integral defines a $(\{\mathcal{G}_t\},\mathbb{Q})$-Brownian bridge over the interval $[0,T)$ which we denote $\{\beta_{tT}\}$. For the volatility function we set

$$v(t,x) = \sigma\frac{T}{T-t}x. \tag{6.12}$$

This leads to

$$\xi_{tT} = \sigma X(T-t)T\int_0^t \frac{1}{(T-s)^2}\mathrm{d}s + \beta_{tT}, \tag{6.13}$$

and thence to (6.8).

7. Bachelier Model

The Bachelier model is obtained by setting $A_t = \gamma W_t$ where γ is a constant. We shall show that the class of models defined by Proposition 5.1 contains the Bachelier model. We consider a random variable A_T associated with a fixed date T. We assume that $A_T \sim N[0, 1/(T\sigma^2)]$, where $N[m,v]$ is the class of Gaussian random variables with mean m and variance v. In the notation of Sec. 5, we have

$$f_{0T}(x) = \frac{\sigma\sqrt{T}}{\sqrt{2\pi}}\exp\left(-\frac{1}{2}\sigma^2 T x^2\right). \tag{7.1}$$

We recall the process $\{\xi_{tT}\}_{0\le t\le T}$ defined by $\xi_{tT} = \sigma A_T t + \beta_{tT}$. If $A_T \sim N(0, 1/(T\sigma^2))$, then $\{\xi_{tT}\}$ is an $\{\mathcal{F}_t\}$-Brownian motion over $[0,T]$. This is because $\{\xi_{tT}\}$ is a continuous Gaussian process with $\xi_{0T} = 0$ and $\mathrm{Cov}[\xi_{sT},\xi_{tT}] = s$ for $0 \le s \le t \le T$. We recall the definition of the Brownian motion $\{W_t\}$ associated with $\{\xi_{tT}\}$, given by (5.3). Since for $A_T \sim N(0, 1/T\sigma^2)$ the process $\{\xi_{tT}\}$ is a Brownian motion, it follows that

$$\mathbb{E}[A_T|\xi_{sT}] = \frac{1}{\sigma T}\mathbb{E}[\xi_{TT}|\xi_{sT}] = \frac{1}{\sigma T}\xi_{sT}. \tag{7.2}$$

Thus we see that $W_t = \xi_{tT}$. As a consequence we have

$$A_t = \mathbb{E}[A_T|\xi_{tT}] = \frac{1}{\sigma T}\mathbb{E}[W_T|W_t] = \frac{1}{\sigma T}W_t. \tag{7.3}$$

Hence to match the Bachelier model with an element in the class of models constructed in Sec. 5, it suffices to set $\sigma = 1/(\gamma T)$.

Proposition 7.1. *The conditional density process* $\{f^B_{tT}(x)\}$ *of the Bachelier price process, defined over the interval* $[0, T)$, *given by*

$$f^B_{tT}(x) = \frac{\exp[-\frac{1}{2}\frac{1}{\gamma^2(T-t)}(x-\gamma W_t)^2]}{\int_{-\infty}^{\infty}\exp[-\frac{1}{2}\frac{1}{\gamma^2(T-t)}(y-\gamma W_t)^2]\mathrm{d}y}, \tag{7.4}$$

is a special case of the family of the models of Proposition 5.1, *and is obtained by setting*

$$f_{0T}(x) = \frac{\sigma\sqrt{T}}{\sqrt{2\pi}}\exp\left(-\frac{1}{2}\sigma^2 T x^2\right), \quad \sigma_{tT}(x) = \sigma\frac{T}{T-t}x, \quad \textit{and} \quad \sigma = 1/(\gamma T). \tag{7.5}$$

Proof. We insert (7.5) in (5.4). Completion of squares gives

$$\begin{aligned} f_{tT}(x) &= \frac{f_{0T}(x)\exp[\frac{T}{T-t}(\sigma\xi_{tT}x - \frac{1}{2}\sigma^2x^2t)]}{\int_{-\infty}^{\infty}f_{0T}(y)\exp[\frac{T}{T-t}(\sigma\xi_{tT}y-\frac{1}{2}\sigma^2y^2t)]\mathrm{d}y} \\ &= \frac{\exp[-\frac{1}{2}\frac{\sigma^2T^2}{T-t}(x-\frac{1}{\sigma T}\xi_{tT})^2]}{\int_{-\infty}^{\infty}\exp[-\frac{1}{2}\frac{\sigma^2T^2}{T-t}(y-\frac{1}{\sigma T}\xi_{tT})^2]\mathrm{d}y}. \end{aligned} \tag{7.6}$$

Recalling that $\xi_{tT} = W_t$, and setting $\sigma = 1/(\gamma T)$, we obtain the desired result. □

Remark 7.1. Let the initial density $f_{0T}(x)$, the volatility structure $\sigma_{tT}(x)$, and the parameter σ be given as in (7.5). Then the Bachelier conditional density $\{f^B_{tT}(x)\}$ satisfies the master equation (2.13), and $\{W_t\}$ coincides with $\{\xi_{tT}\}$.

Remark 7.2. Suppose we chose an asset price model with a certain law. Then we know that we can derive the corresponding conditional density process where the related volatility structure and initial density are specified. We may then wonder how the conditional density transforms, and what the new volatility structure looks like, if we consider a new law for the asset price model. For instance, we may begin with the Bachelier model and ask what is the conditional density and volatility structure associated with a log-normal model. We present a "transformation formula" for the conditional density. This result allows for the construction of a variety of conditional density processes from a given one. Let $\{f_t(x)\}$ solve (2.13), and let $\psi : \mathbb{R} \to \mathbb{R}$ be a C^1-bijection. Then it is known that if X has conditional density $f_t(x)$ then $Z = \psi(X)$ has conditional density $g_t(z)$ given by

$$g_t(z) = \frac{f_t(\psi^{-1}(z))}{\psi'(\psi^{-1}(z))}, \tag{7.7}$$

where $\psi^{-1}(z)$ is the inverse function and $\psi'(x)$ is the derivative of $\psi(x)$. The conditional density $\{g_t(z)\}$ satisfies

$$\mathrm{d}g_t(z) = g_t(z)[\nu(t,z) - \langle\nu_t\rangle]\mathrm{d}W_t, \tag{7.8}$$

where $\nu(t,z) = v(t,\psi^{-1}(z))$ and

$$\langle\nu_t\rangle = \int_{\mathbb{R}} v(t,y)g_t(y)\mathrm{d}y. \tag{7.9}$$

We see that the volatility structure $v(t,x)$ associated with $f_t(x)$ becomes the volatility structure $\nu(t,z)$ associated with $g_t(z)$. For example, consider the Bachelier model where $A_T \sim N(0, 1/(T\sigma^2))$. The associated initial density and volatility structure are given in (7.5). Now suppose that $Z = \exp(A_T)$, so $\psi(x) = \exp(x)$. The price process $\{A_t\}$ is then given by the log-normal model

$$A_t = \exp(\gamma W_t), \tag{7.10}$$

where $W_t = \xi_{tT}$. It follows by (7.7) that the conditional density process $\{g_{tT}(x)\}$ associated with the log-normal price process (7.10) is

$$g_{tT}(z) = \frac{\exp[-\frac{1}{2}\frac{1}{\gamma^2(T-t)}(\ln(z) - \gamma W_t)^2]}{z\int_0^\infty \exp[-\frac{1}{2}\frac{1}{\gamma^2(T-t)}(\ln(y) - \gamma W_t)^2]\mathrm{d}y}, \tag{7.11}$$

for $z > 0$. Indeed we see that $g_{tT}(z)$ is the log-normal conditional density. The associated volatility structure is

$$\nu(t,z) = v(t,\ln(z)) = \sigma_{tT}(z) = \sigma\frac{T}{T-t}\ln(z). \tag{7.12}$$

8. Option Prices

We consider a European-style call option with maturity t, strike K, and price as determined by equation (1.13). The price process $\{A_t\}_{0\le t<\infty}$ of the underlying asset is given by

$$A_t = \mathbb{E}^{\mathbb{Q}}[X|\mathcal{F}_t] = \frac{\int_{-\infty}^{\infty} x f_0(x)\exp(\int_0^t v(s,x)\mathrm{d}I_s - \frac{1}{2}\int_0^t v^2(s,x)\mathrm{d}s)\mathrm{d}x}{\int_{-\infty}^{\infty} f_0(y)\exp(\int_0^t v(s,y)\mathrm{d}I_s - \frac{1}{2}\int_0^t v^2(s,y)\mathrm{d}s)\mathrm{d}y}, \tag{8.1}$$

where $\{\mathcal{F}_t\}_{0\le s\le t<\infty}$ is generated by (4.4). We recall that $\{B_t\}$ is a $(\{\mathcal{G}_t\},\mathbb{Q})$-Brownian motion, and that there exists an $(\{\mathcal{F}_t\},\mathbb{Q})$-Brownian motion $\{W_t\}$ such that

$$\mathrm{d}I_t = \mathrm{d}W_t + \langle v_t\rangle\mathrm{d}t, \tag{8.2}$$

where the bracket notation is defined by (2.17). We introduce a positive $(\{\mathcal{F}_t\}, \mathbb{Q})$-martingale

$$\Lambda_t = \exp\left(\int_0^t \langle v_s\rangle \mathrm{d}W_s + \frac{1}{2}\int_0^t \langle v_s\rangle^2 \mathrm{d}s\right), \tag{8.3}$$

which induces a change of measure from $\mathbb{Q}$ to measure $\mathbb{Q}^*$ given by

$$\left.\frac{\mathrm{d}\mathbb{Q}^*}{\mathrm{d}\mathbb{Q}}\right|_{\mathcal{F}_t} = \Lambda_t. \tag{8.4}$$

The $\mathbb{Q}^*$-measure is characterised by the fact that $\{I_t\}$ is an $(\{\mathcal{F}_t\}, \mathbb{Q}^*)$-Brownian motion. We observe that by the relationship

$$\begin{aligned}\int_{\mathbb{R}} f_0(x)\exp&\left(\int_0^t v(s,x)\mathrm{d}I_s - \frac{1}{2}\int_0^t v^2(s,x)\mathrm{d}s\right)\mathrm{d}x\\ &= \exp\left(\int_0^t \langle v_s\rangle \mathrm{d}I_s - \frac{1}{2}\int_0^t \langle v_s\rangle^2 \mathrm{d}s\right) &(8.5)\\ &= \Lambda_t, &(8.6)\end{aligned}$$

we can use the denominator in (8.1) to write the option price C_{st} in terms of a conditional expectation taken with respect to $\mathbb{Q}^*$ under which $\{I_t\}$ is a Brownian motion. Equation (8.6) is obtained by applying the relationship (8.2). We then have

$$\begin{aligned}C_{st} &= \mathbb{E}^{\mathbb{Q}}[(A_t - K)^+|\mathcal{F}_s] &(8.7)\\ &= \mathbb{E}^{\mathbb{Q}}[(N_t\Lambda_t^{-1} - K)^+|\mathcal{F}_s] &(8.8)\\ &= \mathbb{E}^{\mathbb{Q}}[\Lambda_t^{-1}(N_t - K\Lambda_t)^+|\mathcal{F}_s] &(8.9)\\ &= \Lambda_s^{-1}\mathbb{E}^{\mathbb{Q}^*}[(N_t - K\Lambda_t)^+|\mathcal{F}_s], &(8.10)\end{aligned}$$

where

$$N_t = \int_{-\infty}^{\infty} x f_0(x)\exp\left(\int_0^t v(s,x)\mathrm{d}I_s - \frac{1}{2}\int_0^t v^2(s,x)\mathrm{d}s\right)\mathrm{d}x, \tag{8.11}$$

$$\Lambda_t = \int_{-\infty}^{\infty} f_0(x)\exp\left(\int_0^t v(s,x)\mathrm{d}I_s - \frac{1}{2}\int_0^t v^2(s,x)\mathrm{d}s\right)\mathrm{d}x. \tag{8.12}$$

Since $\{I_t\}$ is an $(\{\mathcal{F}_t\}, \mathbb{Q}^*)$-Brownian motion, the conditional expectation simplifies to the calculation of a Gaussian integral provided the zero of the max function can be computed.

With these formulae in hand, we observe that a closed-form expression for the conditional expectation can be worked out in the case of a binary initial density function of the form

$$f_0(x) = q_1\delta(x - x_1) + q_2\delta(x - x_2). \tag{8.13}$$

Here $\delta(x)$ is the Dirac distribution and $q_i = \mathbb{Q}[X = x_i]$ for $i = 1, 2$. It follows that

$$N_t = \sum_{i=1}^{2} x_i q_i \mathcal{E}_t(x_i), \quad \Lambda_t = \sum_{i=1}^{2} q_i \mathcal{E}_t(x_i), \tag{8.14}$$

where we introduce the process

$$\mathcal{E}_t(x_i) = \exp\left[\int_0^t v(s,x_i)\mathrm{d}I_s - \frac{1}{2}\int_0^t v^2(s,x_i)\mathrm{d}s\right]. \tag{8.15}$$

In the case where the random variable X takes the values x_1 and x_2, the option price is

$$C_{st} = \Lambda_s^{-1}\mathbb{E}_s^{\mathbb{Q}^*}\left[\left.\left(\sum_{i=1}^{2}(x_i - K)q_i\mathcal{E}_t(x_i)\right)^+\right|\mathcal{F}_s\right]. \tag{8.16}$$

We observe that $\{\mathcal{E}(x_i)\}$ is positive and has the property $\mathbb{E}^{\mathbb{Q}^*}[\mathcal{E}_t(x_i)] = 1$. In particular, we can use $\{\mathcal{E}_t(x_1)\}$ to define a change of measure from $\mathbb{Q}^*$ to a new measure $\tilde{\mathbb{Q}}$ by setting

$$\left.\frac{\mathrm{d}\tilde{\mathbb{Q}}}{\mathrm{d}\mathbb{Q}^*}\right|_{\mathcal{F}_t} = \mathcal{E}_t(x_1), \tag{8.17}$$

together with $\mathrm{d}I_t = \mathrm{d}\tilde{I}_t + v(t,x_1)\mathrm{d}t$. Next we pull $\mathcal{E}_t(x_1)$ out to the front of the max function in equation (8.16) to obtain

$$C_{st} = \Lambda_s^{-1}\mathbb{E}^{\mathbb{Q}^*}\left[\left.\mathcal{E}_t(x_1)\left(q_1(x_1 - K) + q_2(x_2 - K)\frac{\mathcal{E}_t(x_2)}{\mathcal{E}_t(x_1)}\right)^+\right|\mathcal{F}_s\right]. \tag{8.18}$$

By use of the Bayes formula we express the option price in terms of $\tilde{\mathbb{Q}}$:

$$C_{st} = \Lambda_s^{-1}\mathcal{E}_s(x_1)\mathbb{E}^{\tilde{\mathbb{Q}}}\left[\left.\left(q_1(x_1 - K) + q_2(x_2 - K)\frac{\mathcal{E}_t(x_2)}{\mathcal{E}_t(x_1)}\right)^+\right|\mathcal{F}_s\right]. \tag{8.19}$$

For the sake of a simplified notation we define $R_{0t} = \mathcal{E}_t(x_2)/\mathcal{E}_t(x_1)$, and we observe that the process $\{R_{0t}\}$ is an exponential $(\{\mathcal{F}_t\},\tilde{\mathbb{Q}})$-martingale:

$$R_{0t} = \exp\left(\int_0^t [v(s,x_2) - v(s,x_1)]\mathrm{d}\tilde{I}_s - \frac{1}{2}\int_0^t [v(s,x_2) - v(s,x_1)]^2\mathrm{d}s\right). \tag{8.20}$$

We write $R_{0t} = R_{0s}R_{st}$ so that

$$C_{st} = \Lambda_s^{-1}\mathcal{E}_s(x_1)\mathbb{E}^{\tilde{\mathbb{Q}}}[(q_1(x_1 - K) + q_2(x_2 - K)R_{0s}R_{st})^+|\mathcal{F}_s], \tag{8.21}$$

and we note that R_{0s} is $\mathcal{F}_s$-measurable. One is thus left with the task of finding the range of values of R_{st} for which the max function vanishes. Then we calculate the Gaussian integral arising from the conditional expectation. Recalling that $\{\tilde{I}_t\}$ is an $(\{\mathcal{F}_t\},\tilde{\mathbb{Q}})$-Brownian motion, we note that the logarithm of R_{st} is Gaussian. Let Y be a standard Gaussian variable. Then we can write

$$\ln(R_{st}) = \sqrt{\int_s^t [v(u,x_2) - v(u,x_1)]^2\mathrm{d}u}\,Y - \frac{1}{2}\int_s^t [v(u,x_2) - v(u,x_1)]^2\mathrm{d}u. \tag{8.22}$$

By solving for the logarithm of R_{st} in the argument of the max function in (8.21), we deduce that the max function is zero for all values y^* that Y may take for which

$$y^* \leq \frac{\ln[\frac{q_1(K-x_1)}{q_2(K-x_2)R_{0s}}] + \frac{1}{2}\int_s^t [v(u,x_2)-v(u,x_1)]^2 \mathrm{d}u}{\sqrt{\int_s^t [v(u,x_2)-v(u,x_1)]^2 \mathrm{d}u}}. \tag{8.23}$$

It follows therefore that the option price can be written in the form

$$C_{st} = \Lambda_s^{-1}\mathcal{E}_s(x_1)\left[q_1(x_1-K)\frac{1}{\sqrt{2\pi}}\int_{y^*}^{\infty}\exp\left(-\frac{1}{2}y^2\right)\mathrm{d}y \right.$$
$$\left. + q_2(x_2-K)R_{0s}\frac{1}{\sqrt{2\pi}}\int_{y^*}^{\infty}\exp\left(-\frac{1}{2}\eta^2(y)\right)\mathrm{d}y\right], \tag{8.24}$$

where

$$\eta(y) = y - \sqrt{\int_s^t [v(u,x_2)-v(u,x_1)]^2 \mathrm{d}u}. \tag{8.25}$$

The two Gaussian integrals can be written in terms of the normal distribution function $N(x)$. To highlight the similarity with the Black-Scholes option price formula, we define

$$d_{st}^- = -y^*, \quad d_{st}^+ = d_{st}^- + \sqrt{\int_s^t [v(u,x_2)-v(u,x_1)]^2 \mathrm{d}u}, \tag{8.26}$$

so that one can write

$$C_{st} = \Lambda_s^{-1}\mathcal{E}_s(x_1)[q_1(x_1-K)N(d_{st}^-) + q_2(x_2-K)R_{0s}N(d_{st}^+)]. \tag{8.27}$$

We can simplify this expression further by use of (8.14). Finally, we conclude that the price of the call option is given by the following compact formula:

$$C_{st} = (x_1-K)\frac{q_1}{q_1+q_2R_{0s}}N(d_{st}^-) + (x_2-K)\frac{q_2}{q_1R_{0s}^{-1}+q_2}N(d_{st}^+). \tag{8.28}$$

Acknowledgments

The authors thank T. Björk, Y. Kabanov, M. Monoiyos, M. Schweizer, J. Sekine, J. Zubelli, and participants at the Sixth World Congress of the Bachelier Finance Society for useful discussions. Part of this research has been carried out as part of the project “Dynamic Asset Pricing”, National Centre of Competence in Research “Financial Valuation and Risk Management” (NCCR FINRISK), a research instrument of the Swiss National Science Foundation. LPH and AM are grateful to the Ludwig-Maximilians-Universität, München, and the Fields Institute, Toronto, for hospitality. LPH acknowledges support from Lloyds TSB Bank Plc, Kyoto University, Shell UK Ltd, and the Aspen Center for Physics. AM acknowledges support by ESF through AMaMeF grant 2863, and thanks the Vienna Institute of Finance and EPFL for the stimulating work environment. Part of this research was carried out while AM was a member of the Department of Mathematics, ETH Zürich.

References

[1] A. Bensoussan, *Stochastic Control of Partially Observable Systems* (Cambridge University Press, 1992).
[2] D. T. Breeden and R. H. Litzenberger, Prices of state-contingent claims implicit in option prices, *Journal of Business* **51** (1978) 621–651.
[3] D. C. Brody and L. P. Hughston, Interest rates and information geometry, *Proceedings of the Royal Society A* **457** (2001a) 1343–1364.
[4] D. C. Brody and L. P. Hughston, Applications of information geometry to interest rate theory, in *Disordered and Complex Systems*, P. Sollich, A. C. C. Coolen, L. P. Hughston and R. F. Streater, eds. (AIP, New York, 2001).
[5] D. C. Brody and L. P. Hughston, Entropy and information in the interest rate term structure, *Quantitative Finance* **2** (2002) 70–80.
[6] D. C. Brody, L. P. Hughston and A. Macrina, Beyond hazard rates: a new approach to credit risk modelling, in *Advances in Mathematical Finance, Festschrift Volume in Honour of Dilip Madan*, R. Elliott, M. Fu, R. Jarrow and Ju-Yi Yen, eds. (Birkhäuser, 2007).
[7] D. C. Brody, L. P. Hughston and A. Macrina, Information-based asset pricing, *International Journal of Theoretical and Applied Finance* **11**(1) (2008) 107–142.
[8] R. Carmona and S. Nadtochiy, Local volatility dynamic models, *Finance and Stochastics* **13** (2009) 1–48.
[9] R. Carmona and S. Nadtochiy, Tangent models as a mathematical framework for dynamic calibration, *International Journal of Theoretical and Applied Finance* **14**(1) (2011) 107–135.
[10] M. Davis, Complete-market models of stochastic volatility, in *Proceedings of the Royal Society London A* **460** (2004) 11–26.
[11] B. Dupire, Pricing with a smile, *Risk* **7** (1994) 18–20.
[12] N. El Karoui, M. Jeanblanc and Y. Jiao, What happens after a default: the conditional density approach, *Stochastic Processes and Their Applications* **120**(7) (2010) 1011–1032.
[13] D. Filipović, S. Tappe, and J. Teichmann, Term structure models driven by Wiener process and Poisson measures: existence and positivity, *SIAM Journal on Financial Mathematics* **1** (2010) 523–554.
[14] J. Gatheral, *The Implied Volatility Surface: A Practitioner's Guide* (Wiley, 2006).
[15] N. V. Krylov, *Controlled Diffusion Processes* (Springer, 1980).
[16] R. S. Liptser and A. N. Shiryaev, *Statistics of Random Processes, I. General Theory, and II. Applications*, 2nd edn. (Springer, 2001).
[17] M. Rutkowski and N. Yu, An extension of the Brody-Hughston-Macrina approach to modeling of defaultable bonds, *International Journal of Theoretical and Applied Finance* **10**(3) (2007) 557–589.
[18] P. J. Schönbucher, A market model for stochastic implied volatility, *Philosophical Transactions of the Royal Society A* **357** (1999) 2071–2092.
[19] M. Schweizer and J. Wissel, Term structure of implied volatilities: absence of arbitrage and existence results, *Mathematical Finance* **18**(1) (2008a) 77–114.
[20] M. Schweizer and J. Wissel, Arbitrage-free market models for option prices: the multi-strike case, *Finance and Stochastics* **12** (2008b) 469–505.

MONETARY VALUATION OF CASH FLOWS UNDER KNIGHTIAN UNCERTAINTY*

HANS FÖLLMER and IRINA PENNER

Humboldt-Universität zu Berlin, Institut für Mathematik
Unter den Linden 6, 10099 Berlin, Germany

The classical valuation of an uncertain cash flow in discrete time consists in taking the expectation of the sum of the discounted future payoffs under a fixed probability measure, which is assumed to be known. Here we discuss the valuation problem in the context of Knightian uncertainty. Using results from the theory of convex risk measures, but without assuming the existence of a global reference measure, we derive a robust representation of concave valuations with an infinite time horizon, which specifies the interplay between model uncertainty and uncertainty about the time value of money.

Keywords: Cash flows; dynamic convex risk measures; concave monetary valuations; Knightian uncertainty; robust representation; model ambiguity; discounting ambiguity; bubbles.

1. Introduction

For an uncertain nonnegative cash flow $(\tilde{C}_t)_{t=0,1,\dots}$, for a risk free interest rate $r > 0$, and at any time t, the classical risk neutral valuation of the future cash flow takes the form

$$\tilde{V}_t := E_P\left[\sum_{s=t}^{\infty} \frac{\tilde{C}_s}{(1+r)^{s-t}} \,\middle|\, \mathcal{F}_t\right]. \tag{1.1}$$

Here $\mathcal{F}_t$ denotes the information available at time t, and P is a given probability measure assumed to be known. Passing to the discounted quantities

$$V_t := \frac{\tilde{V}_t}{(1+r)^t} \quad \text{and} \quad C_t := \frac{\tilde{C}_t}{(1+r)^t},$$

*This chapter was originally published under the same title in *International Journal of Theoretical and Applied Finance*, Vol.14, No.1, 1–15 (2011). Singapore: World Scientific Publishing.

the valuation formula (1.1) takes the simpler form

$$V_t = E_P\left[\sum_{s=t}^{\infty} C_s \,|\, \mathcal{F}_t\right]. \tag{1.2}$$

In this paper we discuss the valuation problem in a situation of "Knightian uncertainty", or model ambiguity, where there is no canonical choice of an underlying probability measure P. A systematic approach to such situations has been developed in the theory of coherent and, more generally, convex risk measures; cf. [3, 4, 9–11, 13–15]. This suggests to focus on concave monetary valuations defined in terms of convex risk measure on the space of bounded adapted processes; cf. [1, 5, 7, 8, 16, 18]. From this general point of view, the valuation formula (1.2) turns out to be a special case of the robust valuation formula

$$V_t(C) = \min_{Q,D}\left(E_Q\left[\sum_{s=t}^{\infty} C_s D_s \,|\, \mathcal{F}_t\right] + \alpha_t(Q,D)\right) \tag{1.3}$$

in terms of a whole class of probability measures Q, a class of predictable discounting processes $D = (D_t)_{t=0,1,\ldots}$, and a penalty function α_t. Such a representation involves both model ambiguity, as reflected in the multiplicity of Q, and discounting ambiguity, as described by different discounting processes D, which come on top of the classical discounting by the money market account.

In Sec. 3, we focus on the unconditional case at the initial time 0. Here the valuation $V := V_0$ takes the form

$$V(C) = U(X) := -\rho(X),$$

where $X = (X_t)_{t=0,1,\ldots}$ is the cumulated cash flow associated to $C = (C_t)_{t=0,1,\ldots}$ by $X_t = \sum_{s=0}^{t} C_s$, and where ρ is a convex risk measure on the space of bounded processes which are adapted to the given filtration. Our aim is to derive the valuation formula (1.3) under full model uncertainty. This means that, in contrast to the closely related representation results in [1], we do *not* assume the existence of a global reference measure P which fixes the class of null sets, and thus allows one to use the standard techniques of risk measures on L^∞ as in [1, 2, 6–12, 14, 15]. Under a regularity assumption which is weaker than global continuity from below, we prove the representation (1.3) for the concave monetary valuation V, viewed as a functional on a suitable class of discounted cash flows. This involves a careful look at a class of finitely additive probability measures on the optional σ-field, and in particular a decomposition theorem for the corresponding σ-additive probability measures on an enlarged product space.

In Sec. 4, we sketch the extension to dynamic valuations. Using results from [1, 2, 12], we discuss the characterization of time consistency by supermartingale properties of the penalty processes arising in the robust representation (1.3). In this context we identify two potential sources of "bubbles". The first source is the penalization process $(\alpha_t(Q,D))_{t=0,1,\ldots}$. Time consistency implies that it can be decomposed into a potential and into an additional martingale which may be viewed as an excessive neglect of the model (Q, D), and which may introduce a component of "exuberance" in the valuation. The second source already appears in the classical case, where we have fixed a probability model P. It consists in taking into account the option to sell the cash flow at some future time, and this may create a bubble on top of the fundamental "buy and hold" valuation in (1.2) and (1.3).

2. Preliminaries

Consider a filtration $(\mathcal{F}_t)_{t=0,1,...}$ on some measurable space $(\Omega, \mathcal{F})$, such that $\mathcal{F}_0 = \{\emptyset, \Omega\}$ and

$$\mathcal{F} = \mathcal{F}_\infty := \sigma\left(\bigcup_{t=0}^{\infty} \mathcal{F}_t\right).$$

Note that we do not fix a reference measure P on $(\Omega, \mathcal{F})$.

Let $\mathcal{X}$ denote the space of all adapted processes $X = (X_t)_{t=0,1,...}$ such that

$$\|X\| := \sup_{\omega,t} |X_t(\omega)| < \infty.$$

We also consider the subspaces

$$\mathcal{X}_t := \{X \in \mathcal{X} \mid X_s = X_t \, \forall \, s \geq t\}, \quad t = 0, 1, \ldots$$

and

$$\mathcal{X}_\infty := \left\{X \in \mathcal{X} \mid \exists \, X_\infty(\omega) := \lim_{t\to\infty} X_t(\omega) \, \forall \, \omega \in \Omega\right\}.$$

The processes in $\mathcal{X}$ are regarded as cumulated discounted cash flows. Via

$$C_t := X_t - X_{t-1}, \quad X_t := \sum_{s=0}^{t} C_s,$$

the space $\mathcal{X}_\infty$ can be identified with the space

$$\mathcal{C} := \left\{C = (C_t)_{t=0,1,...} \in \mathcal{X} \mid \exists \sum_{t=0}^{\infty} C_t(\omega) \forall \, \omega \in \Omega\right\}$$

of discounted cash flows whose sum converges pointwise. As explained in the following remark, any bounded adapted cash flow discounted by a suitable numéraire is in fact an element of $\mathcal{C}$.

Remark 2.1. Assume that there is a money market account

$$N_t := \prod_{s=1}^{t} (1 + r_s) \quad t = 0, 1, \ldots$$

generated by a predictable process $(r_t)_{t=0,1,...}$ of nonnegative short rates bounded away from zero by some constant $\delta > 0$. Consider an uncertain adapted cash flow $\tilde{C} = (\tilde{C}_t)_{t=0,1,...}$ such that $\|\tilde{C}\| < \infty$. Using $N = (N_t)_{t=0,1,...}$ as a numéraire, the *discounted cash flow* $C = (C_t)_{t=0,1,...}$ defined by

$$C_t = N_t^{-1} \tilde{C}_t$$

satisfies

$$\sum_{t=0}^{\infty} \|C_t\| \leq \frac{1}{\delta}\|\tilde{C}\| < \infty,$$

and hence belongs to the space $\mathcal{C}$.

We focus on the valuation of a cumulated cash flow at the initial time $t = 0$, using the notation $U(X) := V(C)$, where $X \in \mathcal{X}$ is the cumulated cash flow associated to C.

Definition 2.1. A map $U : \mathcal{X} \to \mathbb{R}$ is called a *concave monetary valuation* if U is

- cash invariant, i.e.,

$$U(X + m1_{\{0,1,\ldots\}}) = U(X) + m$$

  for all $m \in \mathbb{R}$;
- monotone, i.e.,

$$X \leq Y \Rightarrow U(X) \leq U(Y);$$

- concave, i.e.,

$$U(\lambda X + (1-\lambda)Y) \geq \lambda U(X) + (1-\lambda)U(Y)$$

  for $X, Y \in \mathcal{X}$ and $\lambda \in [0, 1]$;
- normalized, i.e., $U(0I_{\{0,1,\ldots\}}) = 0$.

The concave set

$$\mathcal{A} := \{X \in \mathcal{X} \mid U(X) \geq 0\}$$

is called the *acceptance set* of U.

Let us fix a concave monetary valuation U on $\mathcal{X}$. Note that $\mathcal{X}$ can be identified with the Banach space of all bounded measurable functions on the product space

$$\bar{\Omega} = \Omega \times \{0, 1, \ldots\}$$

endowed with the optional σ-field

$$\bar{\mathcal{F}} = \sigma(\mathcal{X}) = \sigma(\{A_t \times \{t\} \mid A_t \in \mathcal{F}_t, t = 0, 1, \ldots),$$

and that the functional $\rho := -U$ can be viewed as a convex risk measure on this Banach space; cf. [14, Secs. 4.1 and 4.2]. Applying the representation theorem [14, Theorem 4.15], and denoting by $\bar{\mathcal{M}}_{1,f}$ the class of finitely additive probability measures on $(\bar{\Omega}, \bar{\mathcal{F}})$, we obtain the following representation of U:

Proposition 2.1. *For any $X \in \mathcal{X}$ we have*

$$U(X) = \min_{\bar{Q} \in \bar{\mathcal{M}}_{1,f}} (E_{\bar{Q}}[X] + \alpha(\bar{Q})), \tag{2.1}$$

where the penalty function $\alpha : \bar{\mathcal{M}}_{1,f} \to (-\infty, \infty]$ *is given by*

$$\alpha(\bar{Q}) = \sup_{X \in \mathcal{A}} E_{\bar{Q}}[-X] = \sup_{X \in \mathcal{X}} (E_{\bar{Q}}[-X] + U(X)). \tag{2.2}$$

Our aim is to clarify the probabilistic structure of this representation if U is regarded as a functional on the subspace $\mathcal{X}_\infty$, or, equivalently, as a functional V on the space $\mathcal{C}$. To this end we introduce the following

Assumption 2.1. The filtration $(\mathcal{F}_t)_{t=0,1,\dots}$ is a *standard system* in the sense of Parthasarathy [20], i.e.,

(i) Each σ-field $\mathcal{F}_t$ is σ-isomorphic to the Borel σ-field on some complete separable metric space,
(ii) Any decreasing sequence of atoms $A_t \in \mathcal{F}_t$, $t = 0, 1, \dots$ has a non-void intersection.

This assumption guarantees that any consistent sequence of probability measures Q_t on $(\Omega, \mathcal{F}_t)$, $t = 0, 1, \dots$, has a (unique) extension to a probability measure Q on $(\Omega, \mathcal{F})$; cf. Parthasarathy [20, Theorem 4.1].

Example 2.1. Consider the path space $\Omega = S^{\{1,2,\dots\}}$, where S is a Polish state space, and where $\mathcal{F}_t$ is generated by the coordinate maps $\omega \to \omega(s)$, $s = 1, \dots, t$. Then $(\mathcal{F}_t)_{t=0,1,\dots}$ is indeed a standard system, and Parthasarathy's extension theorem reduces to the classical extension theorem of Kolmogorov.

3. Robust Representation of Concave Monetary Valuations on $\mathcal{X}_\infty$

Let $\mathcal{M}_1$ denote the class of probability measures on $(\Omega, \mathcal{F})$. For any $Q \in \mathcal{M}_1$, we denote by $\Gamma(Q)$ the class of all *optional random measures* γ on the extended time axis $\{0, \dots, \infty\}$ which are normalized under Q, i.e., $\gamma = (\gamma_t)_{t=0,\dots,\infty}$ is an adapted process such that $\gamma_t \geq 0$ and

$$\sum_{t=0}^{\infty} \gamma_t + \gamma_\infty = 1 \quad Q\text{-a.s.}.$$

Via

$$D_t := 1 - \sum_{s=0}^{t-1} \gamma_s, \quad \gamma_t := D_t - D_{t+1}, \quad t = 0, 1, \dots, \quad D_\infty := \gamma_\infty, \tag{3.1}$$

the class $\Gamma(Q)$ can be identified with the class $\mathcal{D}(Q)$ of *predictable discounting processes* $D = (D_t)_{t=0,\dots,\infty}$ under Q, i.e., D is a predictable process such that $D_0 = 1$ and $D_t \geq D_{t+1} \geq 0$ Q-a.s.. Note that

$$D_\infty = \lim_{t \to \infty} D_t = \gamma_\infty \quad Q\text{-a.s.},$$

and that the "integration by parts" formula

$$\sum_{s=0}^{\infty} \gamma_s X_s + \gamma_\infty X_\infty = \sum_{s=0}^{\infty} D_s(X_s - X_{s-1}) \quad Q\text{-a.s.} \tag{3.2}$$

holds, for any $X \in \mathcal{X}_\infty$ where we put $X_{-1} := 0$.

Let U be a concave monetary utility valuation on $\mathcal{X}$.

Definition 3.1. Let us say that U is *regular on* $\mathcal{X}_\infty$ if

$$U(X) = \lim_{n\to\infty} U(X^n),$$

whenever $(X^n)_{n=0,1,\ldots}$ is a sequence in $\mathcal{X}_\infty$ which increases to $X \in \mathcal{X}_\infty$ uniformly in t in the sense that

$$\lim_{n\to\infty} \sup_t (X - X^n)_t(\omega) = 0 \quad \forall\, \omega \in \Omega.$$

Remark 3.1. Regularity on $\mathcal{X}_\infty$ is a relaxed version of continuity from below. Note that it implies *local* continuity from below, i.e., continuity from below on the subspace $\mathcal{X}_t$ for any finite t. On the other hand, it is weaker than *global* continuity from below on $\mathcal{X}$. By [14, Proposition 4.21], the latter condition would immediately allow us to replace the finitely additive measures in (2.1) by σ-additive probability measures on $(\bar{\Omega}, \bar{\mathcal{F}})$. It turns out, however, that this would be too restrictive. For example, as explained in [1, Example 48], global continuity from below (or even from above) would not allow to calibrate the valuation to a given term structure. The point is that finitely additive measures such as Banach limits play an important role by creating mass at infinity. As a result, our representation theorem will involve probability measures on the extended product space $(\tilde{\Omega}, \tilde{\mathcal{F}})$ introduced below.

The following representation of U, viewed as a functional on the subspace $\mathcal{X}_\infty$, is the main result of this paper. It describes the interplay of model ambiguity, as specified by the measures $Q \in \mathcal{M}_1$, and of discounting ambiguity, as specified by the discounting processes $D \in \mathcal{D}(Q)$. In contrast to [1, Theorem 3.8], we neither assume the existence of a global reference measure P on $(\Omega, \mathcal{F})$, nor a global continuity condition on $\mathcal{X}$.

Theorem 3.1. *Suppose that U is regular on $\mathcal{X}_\infty$. Then, for each $X \in \mathcal{X}_\infty$, the valuation U takes the form*

$$U(X) = \min_{Q\in\mathcal{M}_1} \min_{\gamma\in\Gamma(Q)} \left(E_Q\left[\sum_{t=0}^{\infty} X_t\gamma_t + X_\infty\gamma_\infty \right] + \alpha(Q,\gamma) \right), \tag{3.3}$$

where

$$\alpha(Q,\gamma) := \sup_{X\in\mathcal{X}_\infty} \left(E_Q\left[-\sum_{t=0}^{\infty} X_t\gamma_t - X_\infty\gamma_\infty \right] + U(X) \right). \tag{3.4}$$

Alternatively, replacing $X \in \mathcal{X}_\infty$ by the corresponding discounted cash flow $C \in \mathcal{C}$, the valuation $V(C) := U(X)$ takes the form

$$V(C) = \min_{Q \in \mathcal{M}_1} \min_{D \in \mathcal{D}(Q)} \left(E_Q \left[\sum_{t=0}^{\infty} C_t D_t \right] + \alpha(Q, D) \right), \tag{3.5}$$

where

$$\alpha(Q, D) := \sup_{X \in \mathcal{C}} \left(E_Q \left[- \sum_{t=0}^{\infty} C_t D_t \right] + V(C) \right).$$

The proof will be given in several steps. In the first step, we are going to show that each finitely additive measure $\bar{Q} \in \bar{\mathcal{M}}_{1,f}$, which is relevant for the representation (2.1), can be replaced by a σ-additive probability measure on the extended product space

$$\tilde{\Omega} := \Omega \times \{0, \ldots, \infty\},$$

endowed with the σ-field

$$\tilde{\mathcal{F}} := \sigma(\{A_t \times \{t, \ldots, \infty\} \mid A_t \in \mathcal{F}_t, t = 0, 1, \ldots\}).$$

Let $\tilde{\mathcal{M}}_1$ denote the class of σ-additive probability measures on $(\tilde{\Omega}, \tilde{\mathcal{F}})$.

Proposition 3.1. *For each $\bar{Q} \in \bar{\mathcal{M}}_{1,f}$ such that $\alpha(\bar{Q}) < \infty$, there exists a probability measure $\tilde{Q} \in \tilde{\mathcal{M}}_1$, such that*

$$E_{\bar{Q}}[X] = E_{\tilde{Q}}[\tilde{X}],$$

for any $X \in \mathcal{X}_\infty$, where $\tilde{X}$ denotes the measurable bounded function on $(\tilde{\Omega}, \tilde{\mathcal{F}})$ corresponding to X via $\tilde{X}(\omega, s) := X_s(\omega)$ for $s = 0, 1, \ldots,$ and $\tilde{X}(\omega, \infty) := X_\infty(\omega) :=$ $\lim_{s \to \infty} X_s(\omega)$.

Proof. (1) Our assumption $\alpha(\bar{Q}) < \infty$ clearly implies

$$\alpha^t(\bar{Q}) := \sup_{X \in \mathcal{X}_t} (E_{\bar{Q}}[-X] + U(X)) \leq \alpha(\bar{Q}) < \infty.$$

Note that $\alpha^t(\bar{Q})$ is the minimal penalty function in the robust representation of the convex risk measure ρ^t, defined as the restriction of $-U$ to $\mathcal{X}_t$. Note also that $\mathcal{X}_t$ can be identified with the Banach space of bounded measurable functions on $(\bar{\Omega}, \bar{\mathcal{F}}_t)$, where

$$\bar{\mathcal{F}}_t := \sigma(\{A_s \times \{s, s+1, \ldots\} \mid A_s \in \mathcal{F}_s, s \leq t\}),$$

and that our assumption on U implies that ρ^t is continuous from below. By [14, Proposition 4.21], we can conclude that the restriction of $\bar{Q}$ to $\bar{\mathcal{F}}_t$ is σ-additive.

(2) We introduce the optional filtration $(\tilde{\mathcal{F}}_t)_{t=0,1,\ldots}$ on $(\tilde{\Omega}, \tilde{\mathcal{F}})$, where

$$\tilde{\mathcal{F}}_t := \sigma(\{A_s \times \{s, \ldots, \infty\} \mid A_s \in \mathcal{F}_s, s \leq t\}).$$

Define $\tilde{Q}$ consistently on each σ-field $\tilde{\mathcal{F}}_t$ by

$$\tilde{Q}[A_s \times \{s\}] = \bar{Q}[A_s \times \{s\}] \quad \text{for } s < t, \quad \text{and}$$
$$\tilde{Q}[A_t \times \{t, \ldots, \infty\}] = \bar{Q}[A_t \times \{t, t+1, \ldots\}].$$

Due to (1), $\tilde{Q}$ is σ-additive on each $\tilde{\mathcal{F}}_t$. Since $(\mathcal{F}_t)_{t=0,1,\ldots}$ is assumed to be a standard system, it follows that $(\tilde{\mathcal{F}}_t)_{t=0,1,\ldots}$ is also a standard system. In particular, any decreasing sequence of atoms $\tilde{A}_t = A_t \times \{t, \ldots, \infty\} \in \tilde{\mathcal{F}}_t$, $t = 0, 1, \ldots$, has a non-void intersection of the form $\cap_t A_t \times \{\infty\}$. Due to Parthasarathy's extension theorem [20, Theorem 4.1], there exists exactly one extension of $\tilde{Q}$ to the σ-field

$$\tilde{\mathcal{F}} := \tilde{\mathcal{F}}_\infty = \sigma\left(\bigcup_{t=0}^{\infty} \tilde{\mathcal{F}}_t\right)$$

such that

$$E_{\tilde{Q}}[\tilde{X}] = E_{\bar{Q}}[X]$$

for any $X \in \mathcal{X}_t$. Now take $X \in \mathcal{X}_\infty$, and note that the functions $X^n \in \mathcal{X}_n$ defined by $X^n_t := X_t$ for $t < n$ and $X^n_t = X_n$ for $t \geq n$, converge to X uniformly in t. Applying Lebesgue's convergence theorem for $\tilde{Q}$ in the last step, we obtain

$$E_{\bar{Q}}[X] = \lim_{n\to\infty} E_{\bar{Q}}[X^n] = \lim_{n\to\infty} E_{\tilde{Q}}[\tilde{X}^n] = E_{\tilde{Q}}[\tilde{X}].$$

In order to justify the first step, define $Z^n := \sup_{k\geq n} |X^k - X| \in \mathcal{X}_\infty$. Since Z^n decreases to 0 uniformly in t, regularity of U implies that $U(-\lambda Z^n)$ converges to 0 for any $\lambda > 0$. But

$$|E_{\bar{Q}}[X^n] - E_{\bar{Q}}[X]| \leq E_{\bar{Q}}[Z^n] \leq \lambda^{-1}(\alpha(\bar{Q}) - U(-\lambda Z^n))$$

due to Proposition 2.1. Passing to ∞ first with n and then with λ, we obtain the desired convergence of $E_{\bar{Q}}[X^n]$ to $E_{\bar{Q}}[X]$. □

Our next step consists in representing any probability measure on $(\tilde{\Omega}, \tilde{\mathcal{F}})$ in terms of a probability measure on $(\Omega, \mathcal{F})$ and a predictable discounting process; for a related decomposition in continuous time cf. Kardaras [19].

Proposition 3.2. *Any probability measure $\tilde{Q} \in \tilde{\mathcal{M}}_1$ admits a decomposition*

$$\tilde{Q} = Q \otimes \gamma = Q \otimes D,$$

where Q is a probability measure on $(\Omega, \mathcal{F}), \gamma \in \Gamma(Q)$, and $D \in \mathcal{D}(Q)$ corresponds to γ via (3.1). *More precisely,*

$$E_{\tilde{Q}}[\tilde{X}] = E_{Q\otimes\gamma}[\tilde{X}] := E_Q\left[\sum_{t=0}^{\infty} \tilde{X}_t\gamma_t + \tilde{X}_\infty\gamma_\infty\right] \tag{3.6}$$

for any bounded measurable function $\tilde{X}$ on $(\tilde{\Omega}, \tilde{\mathcal{F}})$, and we can also write

$$E_{\tilde{Q}}[\tilde{X}] = E_{Q\otimes D}[\tilde{X}] := E_Q\left[\sum_{t=0}^{\infty} D_t(\tilde{X}_t - \tilde{X}_{t-1})\right], \tag{3.7}$$

if $\tilde{X}_\infty = \lim_{t\to\infty} \tilde{X}_t$.

The proof is similar to the proof of [1, Theorem 3.4], but here we do not have a reference measure P as in [1]. For the convenience of the reader we sketch the argument.

Proof. For each $t \in \{0, \dots, \infty\}$, the restriction of $\tilde{Q}$ to $\Omega\times\{t\}$ is of the form $Q_t \otimes \delta_t$ for some subprobability measure Q_t on $\mathcal{F}_t$ such that $\sum_{t=1}^{\infty} Q_t(\Omega) + Q_\infty(\Omega) = 1$. Choose some extension of Q_t to $\mathcal{F}$, take

$$R := \sum_{t=1}^{\infty} Q_t + Q_\infty$$

as a reference measure on $(\Omega, \mathcal{F})$, and denote by Z_t the density of Q_t with respect to R. Then

$$\sum_{t=0}^{\infty} Z_t + Z_\infty = 1 \quad R\text{-a.s.},$$

and

$$S_t := E_R\left[\sum_{s=t}^{\infty} Z_s + Z_\infty \,|\, \mathcal{F}_t\right], \quad t = 0, \dots, \infty,$$

defines an R-supermartingale $S = (S_t)_{t=0,\dots,\infty}$ such that $S_0 = 1$ and

$$S_\infty = \lim_{t\to\infty} S_t = Z_\infty \quad R\text{-a.s.}.$$

Now consider the Itô-Watanabe factorization

$$S_t = M_t D_t, \quad t = 0, 1, \dots,$$

where $M = (M_t)$ is a nonnegative R-martingale with $M_0 = 1$, and $D = (D_t)$ is a nonnegative predictable decreasing process with $D_0 = 1$.; cf. [1, Proposition A.1]. The martingale M induces a unique probability measure Q on $(\Omega, \mathcal{F}_\infty)$, due to Parthasarathy's extension theorem [20, Theorem 4.1]. The limits $M_\infty := \lim_{t\to\infty} M_t$ and $D_\infty := \lim_{t\to\infty} D_t$ exist and satisfy $S_\infty = M_\infty D_\infty$, both R- and Q-a.s..

We define the process $\gamma = (\gamma_t)_{t \in \mathbb{T}}$ via (3.1). Now take $X \in \mathcal{X}_\infty$ with $X \geq 0$. By monotone convergence,

$$E_{\bar{Q}}[X] = E_R\left[\sum_{t=0}^{\infty} X_t Z_t + Z_\infty X_\infty\right] = \sum_{t=0}^{\infty} E_R[X_t E_R[S_t - S_{t+1} \,|\, \mathcal{F}_t]] + E_R[S_\infty X_\infty]$$

$$= \sum_{t=0}^{\infty} E_R[X_t(M_t D_t - M_{t+1} D_{t+1})] + E_R[M_\infty D_\infty X_\infty]$$

$$= E_Q\left[\sum_{t=0}^{\infty} X_t \gamma_t\right] + E_R[M_\infty D_\infty X_\infty]. \tag{3.8}$$

Using the Lebesgue decomposition

$$Q[A] = E_R[I_A M_\infty] + Q[A \cap \{M_\infty = \infty\}], \quad A \in \mathcal{F}_\infty$$

of Q with respect to R on $(\Omega, \mathcal{F}_\infty)$ (cf., e.g., [21, Theorem VII.6.1]), (3.8) takes the form

$$E_{\bar{Q}}[X] = E_Q\left[\sum_{t=0}^{\infty} X_t \gamma_t\right] + E_Q[X_\infty \gamma_\infty] - E_Q[\gamma_\infty X_\infty I_{\{M_\infty = \infty\}}]. \tag{3.9}$$

For $X = 1$ this yields

$$1 = E_{\bar{Q}}[1] = E_Q\left[\sum_{t=0}^{\infty} \gamma_t + \gamma_\infty\right] - E_Q[\gamma_\infty I_{\{M_\infty = \infty\}}]$$

$$= 1 - E_Q[\gamma_\infty I_{\{M_\infty = \infty\}}].$$

Thus $\gamma_\infty = 0$ Q-a.s. on $\{M_\infty = \infty\}$, and (3.9) reduces to (3.6). □

We are now ready to conclude the proof of Theorem 3.1.

Proof. [Proof of Theorem 3.1] Recall the representation (2.1), and take any $\bar{Q} \in \bar{\mathcal{M}}_{1,f}$ such that $\alpha(\bar{Q}) < \infty$. Let $\tilde{Q} \in \tilde{\mathcal{M}}_1$ be the probability measure on $(\tilde{\Omega}, \tilde{\mathcal{F}})$ associated to $\bar{Q}$ via Proposition 3.1, and consider the decomposition $\tilde{Q} = Q \otimes \gamma$ with $Q \in \mathcal{M}_1$ and $\gamma \in \Gamma(Q)$ as in Proposition 3.2. For any $X \in \mathcal{X}_\infty$, we can thus write

$$E_{\bar{Q}}[X] = E_{\tilde{Q}}[\tilde{X}] = E_Q\left[\sum_{t=0}^{\infty} X_t \gamma_t + X_\infty \gamma_\infty\right], \tag{3.10}$$

Note that, in view of (2.2) and (3.4),

$$\alpha(Q, \gamma) = \sup_{X \in \mathcal{X}_\infty} (E_{\tilde{Q}}[-X] + U(X)) \leq \alpha(\bar{Q}). \tag{3.11}$$

Now fix $X \in \mathcal{X}_\infty$. Since

$$\alpha(Q, \gamma) \geq E_{\tilde{Q}}[-X] + U(X)$$

for any $\tilde{Q} = Q \otimes \gamma \in \tilde{\mathcal{M}}_1$, we obtain

$$U(X) \leq \inf_{\tilde{Q}=Q\otimes\gamma\in\tilde{\mathcal{M}}_1} (E_{\tilde{Q}}[\tilde{X}] + \alpha(Q,\gamma)). \tag{3.12}$$

On the other hand, take $\bar{Q}^X$ such that the minimum in (2.1) is attained. The corresponding probability measure $\tilde{Q}^X = Q^X \otimes \gamma^X$ satisfies

$$U(X) = E_{\tilde{Q}^X}[\tilde{X}] + \alpha(\bar{Q}) \geq E_{\tilde{Q}^X}[\tilde{X}] + \alpha(Q^X, \gamma^X),$$

due to (3.11). In view of (3.10) and (3.12), this implies the representation (3.3). Alternatively, using the predictable discounting process $D = (D_t) \in \mathcal{D}(Q)$ induced by γ and the integration by parts formula (3.2), we can write

$$E_{\tilde{Q}}[\tilde{X}] = E_Q\left[\sum_{t=0}^{\infty} D_t(X_t - X_{t-1})\right]$$

for any $X \in \mathcal{X}_\infty$, and this yields the valuation formula (3.5) for the cash flow $C = (C_t)$ associated to X via $C_t := X_t - X_{t-1}$. □

4. Time Consistency and the Appearance of Bubbles

In this section we sketch the extension to dynamic valuations, adapting results from [1, 2, 12] to our present context of Knightian uncertainty. In order to simplify the discussion we assume that we are in the situation of Example 2.1 with a countable state space S; a more thorough analysis will appear elsewhere.

At a given time t, the valuation of a future cash flow should be based on the information available at that time. Using the obvious conditional formulation of the properties in Sec. 2, we obtain the notion of a *conditional concave monetary valuation* U_t at time t, defined as a map from $\mathcal{X}$ to the space of bounded measurable functions on $(\Omega, \mathcal{F}_t)$. Adding the condition of *regularity on* $\mathcal{X}_\infty$, and repeating the construction of Sec. 3 on each atom of $\mathcal{F}_t$, we obtain the following conditional valuation formula for a cumulated cash flow $X \in \mathcal{X}_\infty$:

$$U_t(X) = \min_{Q\in\mathcal{M}_1} \min_{\gamma\in\Gamma(Q)} \left(E_Q\left[\sum_{s=t}^{\infty} X_s \frac{\gamma_s}{D_t} + X_\infty \frac{\gamma_\infty}{D_t}\middle| \mathcal{F}_t\right] + \alpha_t(Q,\gamma)\right), \tag{4.1}$$

where

$$\alpha_t(Q,\gamma) = \sup_{X\in\mathcal{X}_\infty} \left(E_Q\left[-\sum_{s=t}^{\infty} X_s \frac{\gamma_s}{D_t} - X_\infty \frac{\gamma_\infty}{D_t}\middle| \mathcal{F}_t\right] + U_t(X)\right),$$

and $D_t = 1 - \sum_{s=0}^{t-1} \gamma_s$; cf. [1, Theorem 3.8], where the formula is derived for the conditional risk measure $\rho_t := -U_t$, but under different assumptions.

Translating the conditional valuation formula for $U_t(X)$ to the level of cash flows $C \in \mathcal{C}$ and using the integration by parts formula (3.2), we obtain the following result:

Theorem 4.1. *For any $C \in \mathcal{C}$, the conditional valuation at time t of the future cash flow defined by*

$$V_t(C) := U_t(X) - X_{t-1},$$

where $X \in \mathcal{X}_\infty$ is the cumulated cash flow induced by C, takes the form

$$V_t(C) = \min_{Q\in\mathcal{M}_1} \min_{D\in\mathcal{D}(Q)} \left(E_Q\left[\sum_{s=t}^{\infty} C_s \frac{D_s}{D_t} \middle| \mathcal{F}_t \right] + \alpha_t(Q,D) \right), \tag{4.2}$$

where

$$\alpha_t(Q,D) = \sup_{C\in\mathcal{C}} \left(E_Q\left[-\sum_{s=t}^{\infty} C_s \frac{D_s}{D_t} \middle| \mathcal{F}_t \right] + V_t(C) \right),$$

The sequence $(U_t)_{t=0,1,\dots}$, and also the corresponding sequence $(V_t)_{t=0,1,\dots}$ on the level of cash flows, will be called a *dynamic concave valuation.*

Definition 4.1. A dynamic concave valuation $(V_t)_{t=0,1,\dots}$ is called (strongly) *time consistent* if it satisfies the recursion

$$V_t(C) = C_t + V_t(V_{t+1}(C) I_{\{t+1\}}), \quad t = 0, 1, \dots \tag{4.3}$$

for any $C \in \mathcal{C}$.

From now on we assume that (V_t) is time consistent. In order to focus on the supermartingale aspects of time consistency, let us introduce the subspace

$$\mathcal{C}_{t,t+1} := \{C \in \mathcal{C} \,|\, C_s = 0 \quad \text{for } s \notin \{t, t+1\}\}$$

and the corresponding one-step penalty function

$$\alpha_{t,t+1}(Q,D) = \sup_{C\in\mathcal{C}_{t,t+1}} \left(E_Q\left[-C_t - \frac{D_{t+1}}{D_t} C_{t+1} \middle| \mathcal{F}_t \right] + V_t(C) \right). \tag{4.4}$$

A straightforward translation of [1, Theorem 4.2] yields the following result.

Proposition 4.1. *Time consistency of $(V_t)_{t=0,1,\dots}$ implies, for any $Q \in \mathcal{M}_1$ and any $D \in \mathcal{D}(Q)$,*

$$D_t \alpha_t(Q,D) = D_t \alpha_{t,t+1}(Q,D) + E_Q[D_{t+1}\alpha_{t+1}(Q,D) \,|\, \mathcal{F}_t] \quad Q\text{-a.s.} \tag{4.5}$$

and

$$E_Q[D_{t+1}(V_t(C) - \alpha_{t+1}(Q,D)) \,|\, \mathcal{F}_t] \geq D_t(V_t(C) - C_t - \alpha_t(Q,D)) \quad Q\text{-a.s.}.$$

for $t = 0, 1, \dots$.

For any $Q \otimes D$ such that $\alpha_0(Q, D) < \infty$, Proposition 4.1 shows that the process

$$D_t V_t(C) + \sum_{s=0}^{t-1} D_s C_s - D_t \alpha_t(Q, D), \quad t = 0, 1, \ldots$$

is a Q-submartingale, and that the process $(D_t \alpha_t(Q, D))_{t=0,1,\ldots}$ is a nonnegative Q-supermartingale. Moreover, (4.5) yields the *Doob decomposition*

$$D_t \alpha_t(Q, D) = M_t^{Q,D} - A_t^{Q,D}, \quad t = 0, 1, \ldots$$

into a nonnegative Q-martingale $(M_t^{Q,D})$ and the predictable increasing process

$$A_t^{Q,D} := \sum_{k=0}^{t-1} D_k \alpha_{k,k+1}(Q, D), \quad t = 0, 1, \ldots.$$

Splitting the martingale

$$M_t^{Q,D} = E_Q[A_\infty^{Q,D} \,|\, \mathcal{F}_t] + B_t^{Q,D}$$

into the "fundamental" component generated by the one-step penalties and into an additional nonnegative martingale $B^{Q,D}$, we obtain the *Riesz decomposition*

$$D_t \alpha_t(Q, D) = E_Q[A_\infty^{Q,D} - A_t^{Q,D} \,|\, \mathcal{F}_t] + B_t^{Q,D}, \quad t = 0, 1, \ldots.$$

into the potential generated by the process $A^{Q,D}$ and into a non-negative martingale. The martingale $(B_t^{Q,D})$ may be viewed as a "bubble" in the penalization of the model (Q, D): It comes on top of the fundamental component in the Riesz decomposition of the penalty process, and may thus lead to an excessive neglect of that model; cf. the discussion in [1, Section 4.3], and in particular [1, Theorem 4.8], where it is shown that the appearance of a bubble $(B_t^{Q,D})$ amounts to a breakdown of asymptotic safety of the valuation procedure under the model (Q, D).

There is, of course, an additional source of "bubbles" which appears already in the classical case under a fixed probability model P. So far, we have discussed the valuation of the future cash flow under the assumption that the cash flow will be held indefinitely ("buy and hold"). If we take into account the option to sell the cash flow at some future time, it is plausible to replace the classical valuation

$$V_t(C) = E_P\left[\sum_{k=t}^{\infty} C_k \,|\, \mathcal{F}_t\right]$$

by

$$\bar{V}_t(C) = \sup_{\tau \geq t} E_P\left[\sum_{k=t}^{\tau-1} C_k + \pi_\tau(C) I_{\{\tau < \infty\}} \,|\, \mathcal{F}_t\right], \tag{4.6}$$

where the supremum is taken over all stopping times $\tau \geq t$, and where $\pi_\tau(C)$ is the uncertain price of the future cash flow at time τ (usually assumed to satisfy the equilibrium condition $\pi_\tau(C) = \bar{V}_\tau(C)$; cf., e.g., [17]). The difference

$$B_t(C) := \bar{V}_t(C) - V_t(C), \quad t = 0, 1, \ldots,$$

is often called a bubble. Clearly, the same kind of bubble may appear in our setting of Knightian uncertainty if we replace (4.6) by

$$\bar{V}_t(C) = \sup_{\tau \geq t} \min_{Q \in \mathcal{M}_1} \min_{D \in \mathcal{D}(Q)} \left(E_Q\left[\sum_{k=t}^{\tau-1} C_k \frac{D_k}{D_t} + \pi_\tau(C) I_{\{\tau<\infty\}} \,|\, \mathcal{F}_t \right] - \alpha_t(Q, D) \right).$$

A detailed analysis of these two sources of bubbles and of their interplay will appear elsewhere.

Acknowledgments

We thank two anonymous referees for their comments which helped us to improve the presentation of this paper.

References

[1] B. Acciaio, H. Föllmer and I. Penner, Risk assessment for uncertain cash flows: Model ambiguity, discounting ambiguity, and the role of bubbles, *submitted.*

[2] B. Acciaio and I. Penner, Dynamic risk measures, *forthcoming.*

[3] P. Artzner, F. Delbaen, J. M. Eber and D. Heath, Thinking coherently, *RISK* **10** (1997) 68–71.

[4] P. Artzner, F. Delbaen, J. M. Eber and D. Heath, Coherent measures of risk, *Math. Finance* **9**(3) (1999) 203–228.

[5] P. Artzner, F. Delbaen, J. M. Eber, D. Heath and H. Ku, Coherent multiperiod risk adjusted values and Bellman's principle, *Ann. Oper. Res.* **152** (2007) 5–22.

[6] J. Bion-Nadal, Dynamic risk measures: Time consistency and risk measures from BMO martingales, *Finance Stoch.* **12**(2) (2008) 219–244.

[7] P. Cheridito, F. Delbaen and M. Kupper, Dynamic monetary risk measures for bounded discrete-time processes, *Electron. J. Probab.* **11**(3) (2006) 57–106.

[8] P. Cheridito and M. Kupper, Composition of time-consistent dynamic monetary risk measures in discrete time, forthcoming in *International Journal of Theoretical and Applied Finance.*

[9] F. Delbaen, Coherent risk measures, *Cattedra Galileiana, Scuola Normale Superiore, Classe di Scienze* Pisa (2000).

[10] F. Delbaen, Coherent risk measures on general probability spaces, in *Advances in Finance and Stochastics* (Springer, Berlin, 2002), pp. 1–37.

[11] K. Detlefsen and G. Scandolo, Conditional and dynamic convex risk measures, *Finance Stoch.* **9**(4) (2005) 539–561.

[12] H. Föllmer and I. Penner, Convex risk measures and the dynamics of their penalty functions, *Statist. Decisions* **24**(1) (2006) 61–96.

[13] H. Föllmer and A. Schied, Convex measures of risk and trading constraints, *Finance Stoch.* **6**(4) (2002) 429–447.

[14] H. Föllmer and A. Schied, Stochastic finance: An introduction in discrete time, *De Gruyter Studies in Mathematics* **27** (2004) Berlin.

[15] M. Frittelli and E. Rosazza Gianin, Putting order in risk measures, *Journal of Banking Finance* **26**(7) (2002) 1473–1486.

[16] M. Frittelli and G. Scandolo, Risk measures and capital requirements for processes, *Math. Finance* **16**(4) (2006) 589–612.

[17] J. M. Harrison and D. M. Kreps, Speculative investor behavior in a stock market with heterogeneous expectations, *Q. J. Econ.* **92** (1978) 323–336.

[18] A. Jobert and L. C. G. Rogers, Valuations and dynamic convex risk measures, *Math. Finance* **18**(1) (2008) 1–22.

[19] C. Kardaras, Numéraire-invariant preferences in financial modeling, to appear in *Annals of Applied Probability.*

[20] K. R. Parthasarathy, *Probability Measures on Metric Spaces* (Academic Press, New York, London, 1967).

[21] A. N. Shiryaev, Probability, *Graduate Texts in Mathematics* (Springer, New York, 1996).

PORTFOLIO OPTIMIZATION UNDER PARTIAL INFORMATION WITH EXPERT OPINIONS*

RÜDIGER FREY

Institute for Statistics and Mathematics
Vienna University of Economics and Business
Augasse 2-6, A-1090 Vienna, Austria

ABDELALI GABIH

Laboratoire de Technologie de l'Information et Modélisation (TIM)
ENSA-Université de Marrakech, Boulvard Abdelkrim
El Khattabi BP 575, Marrakech, Morocco

RALF WUNDERLICH

Mathematical Institute, Brandenburg University of Technology
Postfach 101344, D-03013 Cottbus, Germany

This paper investigates optimal portfolio strategies in a market with partial information on the drift. The drift is modelled as a function of a continuous-time Markov chain with finitely many states which is not directly observable. Information on the drift is obtained from the observation of stock prices. Moreover, expert opinions in the form of signals at random discrete time points are included in the analysis. We derive the filtering equation for the return process and incorporate the filter into the state variables of the optimization problem. This problem is studied with dynamic programming methods. In particular, we propose a policy improvement method to obtain computable approximations of the optimal strategy. Numerical results are presented at the end.

Keywords: Portfolio optimization; hidden Markov model; dynamic programming.

1. Introduction

It is well-known that the drift of asset prices has a crucial impact on the optimal trading strategy in dynamic portfolio optimization problems. At the same time this parameter is notoriously difficult to estimate from historical asset price data: first,

*This chapter was originally published under the same title in *International Journal of Theoretical and Applied Finance*, Vol.15, No.1, 1250009-1–18 (2012). Singapore: World Scientific Publishing.

drifts tend to fluctuate randomly over time; second, even if drifts were constant, a long time series is needed to estimate this parameter with a reasonable degree of precision as drift effects are usually dominated by volatility. For these reasons practitioners rely mostly on external sources of information such as news, company reports or ratings and on their own intuitive views when determining an estimate for the future growth rate of an asset; these outside sources of information are labelled expert opinions in this paper. The popular Black-Litterman model (see [2, 19] where subjective views are used to update equilibrium-implied returns in a Bayesian way is a typical example for the use of expert opinions in *static* (one-period) models. However, to the best of our knowledge expected utility maximization in *dynamic* portfolio optimization models with expert opinions has so far not been studied.

In the present paper we set out to do exactly that. We consider a hidden Markov model (HMM) where asset prices follow a diffusion process whose drift is driven by an unobservable finite-state Markov chain Y. Information on the hidden chain is of mixed type. First, investors observe stock prices. Moreover, and this is the novel feature of this paper, expert opinions are included in the analysis as a second source of information. Mathematically, expert opinions are represented by a marked point process with jump-size distribution depending on the current state of Y. Standard filtering results for HMMs and Bayesian updating are used to derive a finite-dimensional filter for the state of the hidden Markov chain. This allows us to reduce the portfolio optimization problem to a problem under complete information where the new state variables are the filter distribution and the wealth of the investor. In this model the market is incomplete, as the investor filtration is partly generated by the non-tradable marked point process that models the expert opinions. This makes the application of duality methods and of the martingale approach to portfolio optimization relatively involved. Hence we resort to dynamic programming and work with the associated Hamilton-Jacobi-Bellman (HJB) equation instead. We consider the case of logarithmic and power utilities. In the latter case the HJB equation can be simplified by a change of measure and we end up with a quasi-linear integro-differential equation. Finally we propose a policy improvement method to obtain an approximation of the optimal strategy.

Portfolio optimization under partial information on the drift has been studied extensively over the last years. There are two popular model classes for the drift, linear Gaussian dynamics and HMMs. For Gaussian dynamics explicit solutions for the problem of optimizing the expected utility of terminal wealth are provided for example in Lakner [11], Brendle [4], Danilova *et al.* [5], where the last paper focuses on additional insider information. Utility maximization for a HMM model is investigated for example in Rieder and Bäuerle [16], Sass and Haussmann [17], Sass and Wunderlich [18] and Gabih *et al.* [10]. These approaches are generalized in Björk *et al.* [1]. In the present paper we follow Rieder and Bäuerle [16] for the setup of the HJB equation in a model with an unobservable drift modelled by a finite-state Markov chain. Moreover, we were inspired by the change of measure technique used among others by Nagai and Runggaldier [14] and Davis and Lleo [6].

The paper is organized as follows. In Sec. 2 we introduce our model of the financial market and formulate the portfolio optimization problem. Section 3 is devoted to the filtering problem for the unobservable drift. Section 4 treats the optimization problem for the special case of logarithmic utility, Sec. 5 is devoted to the case of power utility. In Sec. 6 we discuss approximation methods for the optimal strategy; numerical results are presented in Sec. 7.

2. Financial Market Model

Fix some date $T > 0$ representing the investment horizon. We work on a filtered probability space $(\Omega, \mathcal{G}, \mathbb{G}, P)$, with filtration $\mathbb{G} = (\mathcal{G}_t)_{t\in[0,T]}$ satisfying the usual conditions. All processes are assumed to be $\mathbb{G}$-adapted. For a generic $\mathbb{G}$-adapted process H we denote by $\mathbb{G}^H$ the filtration generated by H.

Price dynamics. We consider a market model for one risk-free bond with price $S_t^0 = 1$ and n risky securities with prices $S_t = (S_t^1, \ldots, S_t^n)^\top$ given by

$$dS_t^i = S_t^i \left(\mu^i(Y_t)dt + \sum_{j=1}^n \sigma^{ij} dW_t^j \right), \quad S_0^i = s^i, \quad i = 1, \ldots, n. \tag{2.1}$$

Here $\mu = \mu(Y_t) \in \mathbb{R}^n$ denotes the mean stock return or drift which is driven by some factor process Y described below. The volatility $\sigma = (\sigma^{ij})_{1\le i,j\le n}$ is assumed to be a constant invertible matrix and $W_t = (W_t^1, \ldots, W_t^n)$ is an n-dimensional $\mathbb{G}$-adapted Brownian motion. The invertibility of σ always can be ensured by a suitable parametrization if the covariance matrix $\sigma\sigma^\top$ is positive definite. The factor process Y is a finite-state Markov chain independent of the Brownian motion W with state space $\{e_1, \ldots, e_d\}$ where e_i is the ith unit vector in $\mathbb{R}^d$. The generator matrix is denoted by Q and the initial distribution by $\pi = (\pi^1, \ldots, \pi^d)^\top$. The states of the factor process Y are mapped onto the states $\mu_1, \ldots, \mu_d$ of the drift by the function $\mu(Y_t) = MY_t$, where $M_{lk} = \mu^l(e_k)$, $1 \le l \le n$, $1 \le k \le d$.

Define the return process R associated with the price process S by $dR_t^i = dS_t^i/S_t^i, i = 1, \ldots, n$. Note that R satisfies

$$dR_t = \mu(Y_t)dt + \sigma dW_t,$$

so that the quadratic variation of R^i and of $\log S^i$ coincide, $[R^i]_t = [\log S^i]_t$. Since moreover $R_t^i = \log(S_t^i) + \frac{1}{2}[R^i]_t$ we have the equality $\mathbb{G}^R = \mathbb{G}^{\log S} = \mathbb{G}^S$. This is useful, since it allows us to work with R instead of S in the filtering part.

Investor Information. We assume that the investor does not observe the factor process Y directly; he does however know the model parameters, in particular the initial distribution π, the generator matrix Q and the functions $\mu^i(\cdot)$. Moreover, he has noisy observations of the hidden process Y at his disposal. More precisely we assume that the investor observes the return process R and that he receives at discrete points in time T_n noisy signals about the current state of Y. These signals are to be interpreted as expert opinions; a number of examples is given below.

We model expert opinions by a marked point process $I = (T_n, Z_n)$, so that at T_n the investor observes the realisation of a random variable Z_n whose distribution depends on the current state Y_{T_n} of the factor process. The T_n are modelled as jump times of a standard Poisson process with intensity λ, independent of Y, so that the timing of the information arrival does not carry any useful information. The signal Z_n takes values in some measurable space $\mathcal{Z}$ with reference measure dz. Examples are a discrete space with the counting measure or $\mathcal{Z} = \mathbb{R}^N$ with the Lebesgue measure. We assume that the Z_n are conditionally independent given $\mathcal{F}_T^Y$ and that the distribution of Z_n is absolutely continuous w.r.t. the reference measure dz with density $f(Y_{T_n}, z)$. We identify the marked point process $I = (T_n, Z_n)$ with the associated counting measure denoted by $I(dt \times dz)$. Note that the $\mathbb{G}$-compensator of I is $\lambda dt f(Y_t, z)dz$.

Summarizing, the information available to the investor is given by the *investor filtration* $\mathbb{F}$ with

$$\mathcal{F}_t = \mathcal{G}_t^R \vee \mathcal{G}_t^I, \quad 0 \leq t \leq T. \tag{2.2}$$

Next we give some simple examples for the random variables Z_n that are inspired by the Black-Litterman approach, see for example Schöttle *et al.* [19].

Example 2.1. In the Black-Litterman framework one distinguishes so-called absolute and relative views of an investor. An *absolute view* is a prediction on the return of a single asset; it might take the form "asset i has a return of 5%". Moreover, the investor might specify the confidence in his views. This can be modelled by taking

$$Z_n = (Z_n^{(1)}, Z_n^{(2)}) \quad \text{with } Z_n^{(1)} = \mu_i(Y_{T_n}) + Z_n^{(2)}\varepsilon_n.$$

Here (ε_n, Z_n) is an iid sequence that is independent of Y; $\varepsilon_n \sim \mathcal{N}(0,1)$; $Z_n^{(2)}$ follows a given distribution on $(0, \infty)$ and $Z_n^{(1)}$ and $Z_n^{(2)}$ are independent. A realization $Z_n = (0.05, 0.02)$ means that the investor forecasts a growth rate of 5% and that he believes that the standard deviation of the prediction error of his forecast is 2% (which would correspond to a high level of confidence); a realization $Z_n = (0.05, 0.05)$ on the other hand corresponds to an investor who believes that the standard deviation of his prediction error is 5% reflecting a low level of confidence. A high (low) level of confidence implies that the current view of the investor has a strong (weak) impact on his filter estimate for the drift as can be seen formally from the Bayesian updating formula (3.2) below. The special case where the investors' confidence does not vary is included by setting $Z_n^{(2)} = \sigma_\varepsilon$ for some constant $\sigma_\varepsilon > 0$.

A *relative* view might take the form "on average asset i outperforms asset j by 2%". This can be modelled by taking

$$Z_n^{(1)} = \mu_i(Y_{T_n}) - \mu_j(Y_{T_n}) + Z_n^{(2)}\varepsilon_n,$$

where, as before, $Z_n^{(2)}$ is used to model the investors' confidence.

Finally we remark that in the Black-Litterman approach the measure P should be seen as the subjective probability measure of the investor. We do not claim that his views are in fact correct or that his predictions are actually unbiased. Rather we only assume that the investor *believes* that his predictions are unbiased.

Portfolios and optimization problem. We describe the self-financing trading strategy of an investor by the initial capital $x_0 > 0$ and the n-dimensional $\mathbb{F}$-adapted process h where $h_t^i, i = 1, \ldots, n$, is the proportion of wealth invested in stock i at time t. It is well-known that in this setting the wealth process $X^{(h)}$ has the dynamics

$$\frac{dX_t^{(h)}}{X_t^{(h)}} = \sum_{i=0}^{n} h_t^i \frac{dS_t^i}{S_t^i} = h_t^\top \mu(Y_t)dt + h_t^\top \sigma dW_t, \quad X_0^{(h)} = x_0. \tag{2.3}$$

Since $\mu(Y_t)$ is bounded and σ is constant, equation (2.3) is well defined if $\int_0^T \|h_s\|^2 ds < \infty$. It will be useful to impose the stronger requirement

$$E\left(\exp\left\{\int_0^T \|h_s\|^2 ds\right\}\right) < \infty. \tag{2.4}$$

A trading strategy satisfying this condition is called admissible; the class of *admissible trading strategies* will be denoted by $\mathcal{H}$.

We assume that the investor wants to maximize the expected utility of terminal wealth for logarithmic utility $U(x) = \log(x)$ and power utility $U(x) = \frac{1}{\theta}x^\theta$, $\theta < 1$, $\theta \neq 0$. The optimization problem thus reads as

$$\max\{E(U(X_T^{(h)})) \colon h \in \mathcal{H}\}. \tag{2.5}$$

This is a maximization problem under partial information since we have required that the strategy h is adapted to the investor filtration $\mathbb{F}$. Note that for $x_0 > 0$ the solution of the SDE (2.3) is strictly positive. This guarantees that $X_T^{(h)}$ is in the domain of logarithmic and power utility.

3. Partial Information and Filtering

In this section we explain how the control problem (2.5) can be reduced to a control problem with complete information via filtering arguments. We use the following notation: for a generic process H we denote by $\widehat{H}_t = E(H|\mathcal{F}_t)$ its optional projection on the filtration $\mathbb{F}$, and the filter for the Markov chain Y_t is denoted by $p_t = (p_t^1, \ldots, p_t^d)$ with $p_t^k = P(Y_t = e_k \,|\, \mathcal{F}_t), k = 1, \ldots, d$. Note that for a process of the form $H_t = h(Y_t)$ the optional projection is given by $\widehat{h(Y_t)} = \sum_{k=1}^d h(e_k)p_t^k$. In particular, the projection of the drift is given by

$$\widehat{\mu(Y_t)} = \sum_{k=1}^{d} \mu_k p_t^k = M p_t.$$

The following two processes will drive the dynamics of p_t. First, let

$$\widetilde{W}_t := \sigma^{-1}\left(R_t - \int_0^t M p_s ds\right).$$

By standard results from filtering theory $\widetilde{W}$ is an $\mathbb{F}$-Brownian motion (the so-called innovations process). Second, define the predictable random measure

$$\nu(dt \times dz) = \lambda dt \sum_{k=1}^{d} p_{t-}^{k} f(e_k, z)dz.$$

By standard results on point processes ν is the $\mathbb{F}$-compensator of I, see for instance Bremaud [3]. The compensated random measure will be denoted by $\gamma(dt \times dz) := I(dt \times dz) - \nu(dt \times dz)$.

Filtering. Next we use filtering results in order to derive a stochastic differential equation (SDE) for the filter p_t. We start with the situation where the investor can only observe the return process R. In that case we are in the classical situation of a hidden Markov model and we can use the standard filter for that case (see for example [7, 12, 20]: It is well-known that p_t solves the SDE system

$$dp_t^k = \sum_{j=1}^{d} Q^{jk} p_t^j dt + p_t^k \left(\sigma^{-1} \left(\mu_k - \sum_{j=1}^{d} p_t^j \mu_j \right) \right)^{\top} d\widetilde{W}_t, \quad p_0^k = \pi^k. \tag{3.1}$$

In the presence of the additional information contained in I we have to add an correction term to the above equation. Assume that at time T_n the investor observes Z_n. Denote by $p_{T_n-} = (p_{T_n-}^1, \dots, p_{T_n-}^d)$ the a-priori probabilities before the arrival of this new observation. Then the a-posteriori probabilities $p_{T_n}^k, k = 1, \dots, d$, are determined from Bayes formula as follows:

$$p_{T_n}^k = \frac{p_{T_n-}^k f(e_k, Z_n)}{\overline{f}(p_{T_n-}, Z_n)} \quad \text{with } \overline{f}(p, z) := \sum_{j=1}^{d} p^j f(e_j, z). \tag{3.2}$$

The increment $\Delta p_{T_n}^k := p_{T_n}^k - p_{T_n-}^k$ is thus given by

$$\Delta p_{T_n}^k = p_{T_n-}^k \left(\frac{f(e_k, Z_n)}{\overline{f}(p_{T_n-}, Z_n)} - 1 \right) = p_{T_n-}^k \int_{\mathcal{Z}} \left(\frac{f(e_k, z)}{\overline{f}(p_{T_n-}, z)} - 1 \right) I(\{T_n\} \times dz). \tag{3.3}$$

By combining (3.1) and (3.3) we arrive at the following result.

Proposition 3.1. *The filter p solves the following d-dimensional SDE system*

$$\begin{aligned} dp_t^k &= \sum_{j=1}^{d} Q^{jk} p_t^j dt + p_t^k \left(\sigma^{-1} \left(\mu_k - \sum_{j=1}^{d} p_t^j \mu_j \right) \right)^{\top} d\widetilde{W}_t \\ &\quad + p_{t-}^k \int_{\mathcal{Z}} \left(\frac{f(e_k, z)}{\overline{f}(p_{t-}, z)} - 1 \right) \gamma(dt \times dz), \end{aligned} \tag{3.4}$$

with initial condition $p_0^k = \pi^k$. and compensated jump measure $\gamma = I - \nu$.

Proof. In view of (3.1) and (3.3), all that remains to show is the relation

$$\int_{[0,t]\times\mathcal{Z}} \left(\frac{f(e_k,z)}{\overline{f}(p_{s-},z)} - 1\right)\nu(ds\times dz) = 0 \quad \text{for all } t; \tag{3.5}$$

this allows us to replace the integral with respect to I in (3.3) by an integral with respect to the compensated jump measure γ. Using the representation $\nu(ds \times dz) = \lambda ds\overline{f}(p_{s-},z)dz$ and $\overline{f}(p_{s-},z) = \sum_{j=1}^{d} p_{s-}^{j} f(e_j,z)$ we get

$$\begin{aligned}
&\int_{[0,t]\times\mathcal{Z}} \left(\frac{f(e_k,z)}{\overline{f}(p_{s-},z)} - 1\right)\nu(ds\times dz) \\
&\quad = \int_{[0,t]\times\mathcal{Z}} (f(e_k,z) - \overline{f}(p_{s-},z))\lambda ds dz \\
&\quad = \int_{[0,t]} \left(\int_{\mathcal{Z}} f(e_k,z)\,dz - \sum_{j=1}^{d} p_{s-}^{j} \int_{\mathcal{Z}} f(e_j,z)dz\right)\lambda ds \\
&\quad = \int_{[0,t]} \left(1 - \sum_{j=1}^{d} p_{s-}^{j}\cdot 1\right)\lambda ds = 0,
\end{aligned}$$

where we used the normalization properties $\int_{\mathcal{Z}} f(e_k,z)dz = 1$ and $\sum_{j=1}^{d} p_{s-}^{j} = 1$. □

It is well-known (see for example [11, 17] that the $\mathbb{F}$-semimartingale decomposition of $X^{(h)}$ is given by

$$\frac{dX_t^{(h)}}{X_t^{(h)}} = h_t^{\top} M p_t\, dt + h_t^{\top}\sigma d\widetilde{W}_t. \tag{3.6}$$

Now note that for given $h \in \mathbb{R}^n$ the $(d+1)$-dimensional process $(X^{(h)},p)$ is an $\mathbb{F}$-Markov process as is immediate from the dynamics in (3.4) and (3.6). Hence the optimization problem (2.5) can be considered as a control problem under complete information with the $(d+1)$-dimensional state variable process $(X^{(h)},p)$. In Sec. 5 we will study this problem using dynamic programming techniques.

4. Logarithmic Utility

In the case of logarithmic utility the optimization problem can be solved directly.

Lemma 4.1. *Suppose that* $U(x) = \log x$, *then the optimal strategy for problem* (2.5) *equals* $h_t^* = (\sigma\sigma^{\top})^{-1}\widehat{\mu(Y_s)}$.

Proof. From (3.6) it follows that

$$U(X_T^{(h)}) = \log X_T^{(h)} = \log x_0 + \int_0^T \left(h_s^\top \widehat{\mu(Y_s)} - \frac{1}{2}\|\sigma^\top h_s\|^2 \right) ds + \int_0^T h_s^\top \sigma d\widetilde{W}_s.$$

For $h \in \mathcal{H}$ we have $E(\int_0^T h_s^\top \sigma d\widetilde{W}_s) = 0$ and hence

$$E[U(X_T^{(h)})] = \log x_0 + E\left(\int_0^T \left(h_s^\top \widehat{\mu(Y_s)} - \frac{1}{2}\|\sigma^\top h_s\|^2 \right) ds \right). \tag{4.1}$$

Since $\widehat{\mu(Y_t)} = Mp_t$ is bounded, the strategy h^* given in the lemma is bounded; in particular $h^* \in \mathcal{H}$. Moreover, for all $s \in [0, T]$ the quantity h_s^* maximizes the integrand in (4.1), which implies that h^* is the maximizer of $E(\log(X_T^{(h)}))$. □

Remark 4.1. If the factor process Y_t and hence the drift $\mu(Y_t)$ is observable then the optimal strategy is well-known — at time t one has to invest the fractions $(\sigma\sigma^\top)^{-1}\mu(Y_t)$ of wealth in the risky stocks. So for logarithmic utility the so-called *certainty equivalence principle* holds, i.e. the optimal strategy under partial information is obtained by replacing the unknown drift $\mu(Y_t)$ by the filter estimate $\widehat{\mu(Y_t)}$ in the formula for the optimal strategy under full information.

5. Dynamic Programming Equation for the Case of Power Utility

A simplified optimization problem. In Sec. 3 we have shown that using filtering theory the original problem (2.5) can be transformed into a problem under complete information where the state variables are $X^{(h)}$ and p. In principle this problem could be attacked with dynamic programming methods. However, it turns out that the resulting HJB equation is fully nonlinear. Following Nagai and Runggaldier [14] we simplify the problem by a change of measure. This will lead to a new problem where the set of state variables is reduced to p and where the HJB equation takes on a simpler quasi-linear form.

First we compute the utility of terminal wealth $U(X_T^{(h)}) = \frac{1}{\theta}(X_T^{(h)})^\theta$. From (3.6) it follows that

$$\frac{1}{\theta}(X_T^{(h)})^\theta = \frac{x_0^\theta}{\theta} \exp\left\{ \theta \int_0^T \left(h_s^\top \widehat{\mu(Y_s)} - \frac{1}{2}\|\sigma^\top h_s\|^2 \right) ds + \theta \int_0^T h_s^\top \sigma d\widetilde{W}_s \right\}. \tag{5.1}$$

Define now the random variable $Z_T^{(h)} = \exp\{\int_0^T \theta h_s^\top \sigma d\widetilde{W}_s - \frac{1}{2}\int_0^T \|\theta\sigma^\top h_s\|^2 ds\}$ and the function

$$b(p, h) = b(p, h; \theta) = -\theta\left(h^\top Mp - \frac{1-\theta}{2}\|\sigma^\top h\|^2 \right). \tag{5.2}$$

Recall that $\widehat{\mu(Y_s)} = \sum_{k=1}^d \mu_k p_s^k = Mp_s$. Hence (5.1) can be written in the form

$$\frac{1}{\theta}(X_T^{(h)})^\theta = \frac{x_0^\theta}{\theta} Z_T^{(h)} \exp\left\{ \int_0^T -b(p_s, h_s; \theta) ds \right\}. \tag{5.3}$$

Since σ is deterministic, the Novikov condition together with (2.4) implies that $E(Z_T^{(h)}) = 1$. Hence we can define an equivalent measure $P^{(h)}$ on $\mathcal{F}_T$ by $dP^{(h)}/dP = Z_T^{(h)}$, and Girsanov's theorem guarantees that $B_t := \widetilde{W}_t - \theta \int_0^t \sigma^\top h_s ds$ is a standard $(P^{(h)}, \mathbb{F})$-Brownian motion. We set

$$a_k(p) = p^k \sigma^{-1} \left(\mu_k - \sum_{j=1}^{d} \mu_j p^j \right) = p^k \sigma^{-1} M(e_k - p) \in \mathbb{R}^n, \tag{5.4}$$

and let as before $\overline{f}(p,z) = \sum_{k=1}^d p^k f(e_k, z)$. Hence we have the following dynamics for the filter under $P^{(h)}$

$$dp_t^k = ((Q^\top p_t)_k + \theta a_k^\top (p_t) \sigma^\top h_t) dt + a_k^\top (p_t) dB_t + p_t^k \int_{\mathcal{Z}} \left(\frac{f(x_k, z)}{\overline{f}(p_{t-}, z)} - 1 \right) \gamma(dt \times dz). \tag{5.5}$$

In view of these transformations, for $0 < \theta < 1$ the optimization problem (2.5) is equivalent to the new optimization problem

$$\max \left\{ E\left(\exp\left\{ \int_0^T -b(p_s^{(h)}, h_s; \theta) ds \right\} \right) : h \in \mathcal{H} \right\} \tag{5.6}$$

where for $h \in \mathcal{H}$ the process $p^{(h)}$ has the dynamics (5.5) with initial condition $p_0^{(h)} = \pi$.

For $\theta < 0$ on the other hand (2.5) is equivalent to minimizing the expectation in (5.6). In the sequel we will concentrate on the case $0 < \theta < 1$; the necessary changes for $\theta < 0$ will be indicated where appropriate. Moreover, θ will be largely removed from the notation. The reward function for this control problem equals

$$v(t,p,h) = E_{t,p} \left(\exp\left\{ \int_t^T -b(p_s^{(h)}, h_s) ds \right\} \right) \quad \text{for } h \in \mathcal{H},$$

and the value function is given by $V(t,p) = \sup\{v(t,p,h) \colon h \in \mathcal{H}\}$. Note that $v(T,p,h) = V(T,p) = 1$.

The HJB equation. As a first step in the derivation of the HJB equation we compute the generator of the process $p_t^{(h)}$ with dynamics (5.5) for a constant strategy $h_t \equiv h \in \mathbb{R}^n$. In that case $p^{(h)}$ is obviously Markovian and a standard application of the Ito-formula shows that the generator $\mathcal{L}^h$ operates on $g \in \mathcal{C}^2(\mathcal{S})$ as follows

$$\mathcal{L}^h g(p) = \frac{1}{2} \sum_{i,j=1}^{d} a_i^\top (p) a_j(p) g_{p^i p^j} + \sum_{i=1}^{d} \left\{ \sum_{j=1}^{d} Q^{ji} p^j + \theta a_i^\top (p) \sigma^\top h \right\} g_{p^i}$$
$$+ \lambda \int_{\mathcal{Z}} \{ g(p + \Delta(p,z)) - g(p) \} \overline{f}(p,z) dz. \tag{5.7}$$

Here $\mathcal{S} = \{p \in [0,1]^d : \sum_{i=1}^d p^i = 1\}$ denotes the unit simplex in $\mathbb{R}^d$ and $\Delta(p,z)$ is defined via

$$\Delta^k(p,z) = p^k \left(\frac{f(x_k,z)}{\overline{f}(p,z)} - 1 \right), \quad k = 1, \ldots, d. \tag{5.8}$$

Next we turn to a heuristic derivation of the HJB equation for the optimization problem (5.6). Consider an arbitrary admissible strategy h and time points $t \le u \le T$. We obtain, by conditioning on $\mathcal{F}_u$

$$V(t,p) \ge v(t,p,h) = E_{t,p}\left(\exp\left\{ - \int_t^u b(p_s^{(h)}, h_s) ds \right\} v(u, p_u^{(h)}, h) \right). \tag{5.9}$$

Consider now a sequence of strategies h^n on the time interval $[u,T]$ such that $v(u, p_u^{(h)}, h^n)$ converges monotonically to $V(u, p_u^{(h)})$. Then we get by passing to the limit in (5.9) that

$$V(t,p) \ge E_{t,p}\left(\exp\left\{ - \int_t^u b(p_s^{(h)}, h_s) ds \right\} V(u, p_u^{(h)}) \right). \tag{5.10}$$

Define $\beta_t^h = \exp\{-\int_0^t b(p_s^{(h)}, h_s) ds\}$. It is immediate from (5.10) that $\beta_t^h V(t, p_t^{(h)})$ is a supermartingale. Suppose now that h^* is an optimal strategy. In that case we have equality in (5.9) and $\beta_t^{h^*} V(t, p_t^{(h^*)})$ is a martingale. If we moreover assume that $V(t,\cdot) \in \operatorname{dom} \mathcal{L}^h$ for all $t \in [0,T)$, we get from the Dynkin formula the following HJB equation

$$V_t(t,p) + \sup_{h \in \mathbb{R}^n} \{ \mathcal{L}^h V(t,p) - b(p,h;\theta) V(t,p) \} = 0, \quad (t,p) \in [0,T) \times \mathcal{S}, \tag{5.11}$$

with terminal condition $V(T,p) = 1$. In case that $\theta < 0$ the equation is similar, but the sup is replaced by an inf. Plugging in $\mathcal{L}^h$ as given in (5.7) and $b(p,h)$ as given in (5.2) into (5.11) the HJB equation can be written more explicitly as

$$\left.\begin{aligned} 0 = V_t(t,p) &+ \frac{1}{2} \sum_{k,l=1}^d a_k^\top(p_t) a_l(p_t) V_{p^k p^l}(t,p) + \sum_{k=1}^d \left\{ \sum_{l=1}^d Q^{lk} p^l \right\} V_{p^k}(t,p) \\ &+ \sup_h \left\{ \sum_{k=1}^d a_k^\top(p_t) \sigma^\top \theta h V_{p^k}(t,p) + \theta V(t,p) \left(h^\top M p - \frac{1}{2} \|\sigma^\top h\|^2 (1-\theta) \right) \right\} \\ &+ \lambda \int_{\mathcal{Z}} \{ V(t, p + \Delta(p,z)) - V(t,p) \} \overline{f}(p,z) dz. \end{aligned}\right\} \tag{5.12}$$

Now the second line of (5.12) is quadratic in h so that the optimum is attained at the solution h^* of the following linear equation (the first-order condition)

$$\sigma \sum_{k=1}^d a_k(p) V_{p^k}(t,p) + V(t,p)(Mp - \sigma\sigma^\top h(1-\theta)) = 0.$$

Since σ is an invertible matrix, h^* is given by

$$h^* = h^*(t,p) = \frac{1}{(1-\theta)}(\sigma\sigma^\top)^{-1}\left\{Mp + \frac{1}{V(t,p)}\sigma\sum_{k=1}^{d} a_k(p)V_{p^k}(t,p)\right\}. \quad (5.13)$$

If we plug this form of h^* back in the HJB equation (5.12) we obtain a *quasi-linear* integro-differential equation since the resulting equation is linear in the second derivatives $V_{p^k p^l}$ and in the integral part.

Remark 5.1 (On the formal justification of the Bellman equation). So far, our derivation of the HJB equation and of the candidate optimal strategy h^* in (5.13) is purely heuristic. A possible approach to give a precise mathematical meaning to the equation is to use *verification arguments*: if we can find a classical solution $V \in \mathcal{C}^{1,2}([0,T) \times \mathcal{S})$ of equation (5.12) with bounded derivatives, the function h^* introduced in (5.13) is bounded. Hence there exists a solution p^* of the SDE (5.5) with $h_t = h^*(t, p_t^*)$. Then a standard verification result such as Theorem 3.1 of Fleming and Soner [8] immediately gives that V is the value function of the control problem (5.6) and that $h_t^* := h^*(t, p_t^*)$ is the optimal strategy.

However, the existence of a classical solution of equation (5.12) is an open issue. The main problem is the fact that one cannot guarantee that the equation is *uniformly elliptic.* To see this note that the coefficient matrix of the second derivatives in (5.12) is given by $C = A^\top A$ where the matrix A is given by

$$A = A(p) = (a_1(p), \ldots, a_d(p)) \in \mathbb{R}^{n\times d}.$$

By definition equation (5.12) is uniformly elliptic if we can find some $c > 0$ such that for all $\xi \in \mathbb{R}^d$ we have $\xi^\top C\xi \geq c\|\xi\|^2$; in particular the matrix C needs to be strictly positive definite. This is possible only if there are no non-trivial solutions of the linear equation $Ax = 0$ so that we need to have the inequality $n \geq d$ (at least as many assets as states of the Markov chain Y). Such an assumption is hard to justify economically; imposing it nonetheless out of mathematical necessity would severely limit the applicability of our approach.

At present we therefore study an alternative route to justifying equations (5.12) and (5.13), see Frey *et al.* [9]. First, using results from Pham [15], it is possible to show that V is a *viscosity solution* of (5.12). Moreover, we are currently working on a homogenization argument that will show that (5.13) can be used to compute an approximately optimal strategy. For this we add a term $\sqrt{\varepsilon}d\widetilde{B}_t$, with $\varepsilon > 0$ and $\widetilde{B}$ a d-dimensional Brownian motion independent of B, to the dynamics of the state equation (5.5). The HJB equation associated with these modified dynamics has an additional term $\varepsilon\sum_{k=1}^{d} V_{p^k p^k}$ and is therefore uniformly elliptic. Hence the results of Davis and Lleo [6] apply directly to the modified equation, yielding the existence of a classical solution V^ε. Moreover, the optimal strategy $h^{\varepsilon,*}$ of the modified problem is given by (5.13) with V^ε instead of V. Clearly, one expects that for ε sufficiently small $h^{\varepsilon,*}$ is approximately optimal in the original problem. We are currently working on a formal proof of this statement.

Remark 5.2. Inspection of equation (5.13) shows that in the case of power utility the candidate optimal strategy consists of two parts. The first part

$$h_t^{(0)} = \frac{1}{1-\theta}(\sigma\sigma^\top)^{-1} M p_t \tag{5.14}$$

is the so-called *myopic strategy*; it is obtained by replacing the unknown drift $\mu(Y_t)$ with the filter estimate Mp_t in the classical formula for the optimal strategy under full information. Moreover, there is a correction term

$$\frac{1}{(1-\theta)V(t,p)}(\sigma^\top)^{-1}\sum_{k=1}^{d} a_k(p)V_{p^k}(t,p)$$

which is called *drift risk* in Rieder and Bäuerle [16]. In particular, in the case of power utility the certainty equivalence principle does not hold.

6. Policy Improvement

Solving the Bellman equation (5.12) numerically with finite difference methods is feasible only if d (the number of states of the hidden Markov chain Y) is small. In this section we therefore propose a policy improvement procedure that permits to find an approximation of the optimal strategy which is computable using Monte-Carlo methods. The starting point is the myopic strategy $h_t^{(0)}$ from (5.14) with corresponding reward function

$$v^{(0)}(t,p) := v(t,p,h^{(0)}) = E_{t,p}\left(\exp\left\{-\int_t^T b(p_s^{(h^{(0)})}, h_s^{(0)})ds\right\}\right). \tag{6.1}$$

Assume that $v^{(0)}$ is a $\mathcal{C}^{1,2}$ function. Motivated by the derivation of the HJB equation in the previous section we compute a new strategy $h^{(1)}$ by maximizing (for $0<\theta<1$) resp. minimizing (for $\theta<0$) the drift of $\beta_t^h v^{(0)}(t,p_t^{(h)})$. This leads to the following optimization problem

$$\max\{\mathrm{sign}(\theta)(\mathcal{L}^h v^{(0)}(t,p) - b(p,h)v^{(0)}(t,p))\colon h\in\mathbb{R}^n\}. \tag{6.2}$$

By analogous arguments as in the derivation of the candidate optimal strategy h^* in the previous section we obtain

$$h^{(1)}(t,p) = h^{(0)}(t,p) + \frac{1}{(1-\theta)v^{(0)}(t,p)}(\sigma^\top)^{-1}\sum_{k=1}^{d} a_k(p)v_{p^k}^{(0)}(t,p). \tag{6.3}$$

Note that $h^{(1)}$ has a similar structural form as the optimal strategy h^*, but with $v^{(0)}$ instead of the value function V in the correction term for the drift risk. The reward function corresponding to the strategy $h^{(1)}$ is given by $v^{(1)}(t,p) := v(t,p,h^{(1)})$. The next lemma shows that $h^{(1)}$ is in fact an improvement of $h^{(0)}$.

Lemma 6.1. *Suppose that the reward functions $v^{(0)}$ and $v^{(1)}$ are $\mathcal{C}^{1,2}$ functions. Then it holds that $v^{(1)}(t,p) \geq v^{(0)}(t,p)$, $(t,p)\in[0,T)\times\mathcal{S}$.*

Proof. We concentrate on the case $\theta > 0$. Here we have the following inequalities

$$0 = v_t^{(0)} + (\mathcal{L}^{h^{(0)}} v^{(0)} - b(p, h^{(0)})v^{(0)}) \leq v_t^{(0)} + (\mathcal{L}^{h^{(1)}} v^{(0)} - b(p, h^{(1)})v^{(0)})$$

where the first equality follows from the fact that $\beta_t^{h^{(0)}} v^{(0)}(t, p_t^{(h^{(0)})})$ is a martingale while the inequality follows from the fact, that $h^{(1)}$ is the maximum of (6.2). This implies that the process $\beta_t^{h^{(1)}} v^{(0)}(t, p_t^{(h^{(1)})})$ has a non-negative drift, consequently it is a submartingale. Since $v^{(0)}(T, \cdot) = v^{(1)}(T, \cdot) \equiv 1$ we obtain

$$\begin{aligned}\beta_t^{h^{(1)}} v^{(0)}(t, p) &\leq E_{t,p}(\beta_T^{h^{(1)}} v^{(0)}(T, p_T^{h^{(1)}})) \\ &= E_{t,p}(\beta_T^{h^{(1)}} v^{(1)}(T, p_T^{h^{(1)}})) = \beta_t^{h^{(1)}} v^{(1)}(t, p),\end{aligned}$$

where the last equality follows since $\beta_t^{h^{(1)}} v^{(1)}(t, p_t^{h^{(1)}})$ is a martingale. Division by $\beta_t^{h^{(1)}}$ yields the assertion. □

In order to compute $h^{(1)}$ one needs to compute the reward function $v^{(0)}$ and its partial derivatives. Since $h^{(0)}$ is known this can be done with standard Monte-Carlo methods.

Remark 6.1. The assumption that $v^{(0)}$ and $v^{(1)}$ are $\mathcal{C}^{1,2}$ functions can be verified for the modified version of the state equation introduced in Remark 5.1, since the Kolmogorov backward equation associated with the modified version of the state process is strictly elliptical. The argument outlined at the end of Remark 5.1 shows that for ε sufficiently small $h^{(\varepsilon,1)}$ (the policy improvement in the modified model) is also a "good" strategy for the original problem.

7. Numerical Example

In this section we illustrate the findings of the previous sections. We consider a market with $n = 1$ stock with volatility $\sigma = 0.2$. The drift process $\mu(Y_t)$ is modelled by a Markov chain with $d = 2$ states, $\mu_1 = 0.4$ and $\mu_2 = -0.2$. The transition intensities of Y are set as $\lambda_{12} = 1.5$ and $\lambda_{21} = 1$, yielding the stationary distribution $(0.4, 0.6)$ and the ergodic mean $\lim_{t\to\infty} E[\mu(Y_t)] = 0.06$. The trading horizon is $T = 2$ years, time discretization works with $M = 250$ time steps.

We consider absolute views for the drift as described in Example 2.1. At the jump times T_n of a Poisson process with intensity λ the views Z_n are generated according to $Z_n = \mu(Y_{T_n}) + \sigma_\varepsilon \varepsilon_n$ where the constant $\sigma_\varepsilon > 0$ describes the confidence of the prediction.

We have simulated a path of the drift process $\mu(Y_t)$, predictions Z_n with confidence parameter $\sigma_\varepsilon = 0.1$ arriving with intensity $\lambda = 2$ and stock returns using $\Delta S_t/S_t = \mu(Y_t)\Delta t + \sigma \Delta W_t$. The upper panel of Fig. 1 shows the non-observable drift path $\mu(Y_t)$. The quantities which are observable to the investor are divided into two parts. First, the path of the stock price S_t shown in the lower panel together with the (non-observable) path of $\exp(\int_0^t \mu(Y_s)ds)$ representing the drift component.

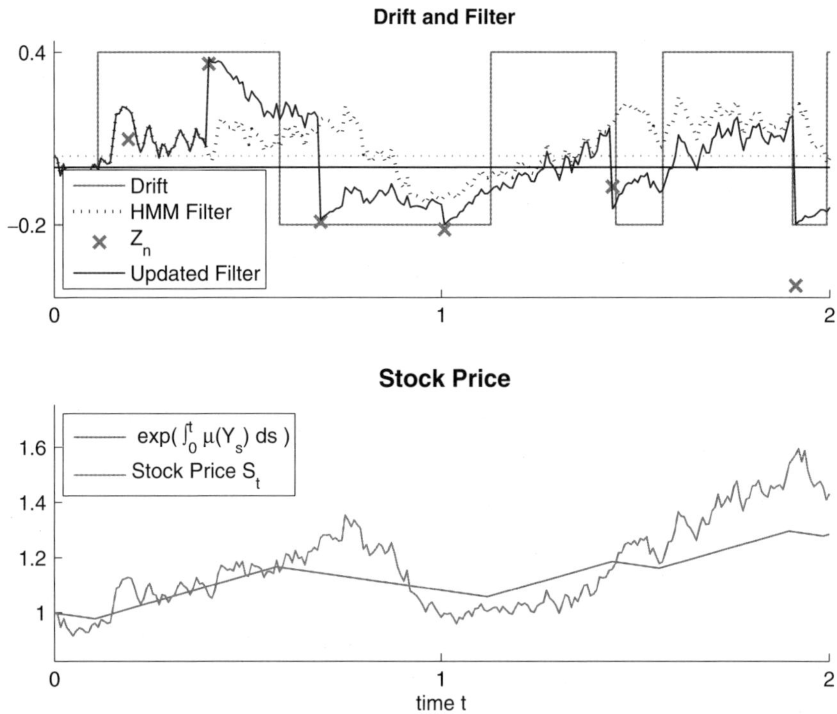

Fig. 1. Top: drift $\mu(Y_t)$, classical HMM filter, predictions Z_n and updated filter $\widehat{\mu(Y_t)}$ Bottom: stock price S_t and drift component $\exp(\int_0^t \mu(Y_s)ds)$.

Second, the predictions Z_n constituting the extra information, which are represented by crosses in the upper panel.

Filter. Given the observations of the stock prices respective returns and the marked point process (T_n, Z_n) the investor can compute the filter p_t by integrating the filter equation (3.4). As initial distribution π we use the stationary distribution of the Markov chain. The resulting filter for the drift $\widehat{\mu(Y_t)} = \sum_{k=1}^{d} \mu_k p_t^k$ is drawn in the upper panel of Fig. 1. For the sake of comparison we also show the classical HMM filter which is based on the observed stock returns only, but not on the extra information.

It can be seen that for the chosen parameters the observed drift predictions Z_n arriving at the information dates T_n are very informative for the investor since for $t = T_n$ the filter is quite close to the actual value of the drift. That means, for $t = T_n$ and for the chosen distribution of Z_n, the investor has nearly full information on the drift. Between the information dates the filter is pushed back towards the ergodic mean.

For the computation of the filter p_t we apply the procedure described in Sec. 3. We integrate filter equation (3.4) between two jumps, i.e. in the interval (T_{n-1}, T_n), using a Euler scheme with time step size $\Delta t = T/M$ and add at T_n the correction term resulting from Bayesian updating. In order to reduce time-discretization errors in the integration of the filter equation between the jumps we work instead of the nonlinear Wonham filter equation (3.1) for the normalized filter p_t with a linear filter equation for the unnormalized filter and apply robust filter techniques, see Sass and Wunderlich [18].

Information gain for log-utility. In order to quantify the value of the additional information from the expert opinions we compare two utility maximizing investors. First, the "non-informed" investor can only observe stock returns. Second, the "informed" investor additionally has access to expert opinions. Now we consider the initial capital which the non-informed investor needs to obtain the same maximized expected utility at time T as the informed investor who started at time 0 with unit wealth. The difference between this capital and one can be interpreted as information gain for the informed investor. This comparison is restricted to logarithmic utility. Here the optimal strategy h^* given in Lemma 4.1 coincides with the strategy $h^{(0)}$ and expected utility $E(U(X_T^{(h^*)}))$ can be computed easily via Monte-Carlo simulation using representation (4.1).

Denote by X_T^I and X_T^N the optimal terminal wealth of the informed and of the non-informed investor starting both with an initial wealth of one. Then the additional initial capital required by the non-informed investor is given by $x_0^N = \exp\{E(\log(X_T^I)) - E(\log(X_T^N))\}$. Figure 2 shows this initial capital as a function of the intensity λ for different values of the confidence parameter $\sigma_\varepsilon = 0.1, 0.3, 0.5$ representing high, moderate and low confidence. As expected the information gain increases with λ and decreases with σ_ε. The figure also shows the result for the fully informed investor which is obtained for $\lambda \to \infty$.

Optimal strategy for power utility: Next, we consider an investor who maximizes expected power utility $U(x) = x^\theta/\theta$ of terminal wealth with $\theta = 2/3$.

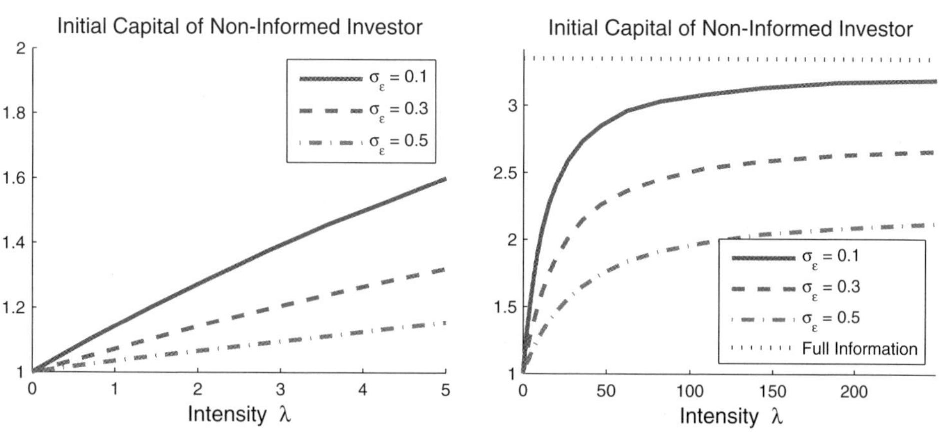

Fig. 2. Initial capital of the non-informed investor which is required to obtain the same maximized expected log-utility at time T as the informed investor who started at time 0 with unit wealth.

For computing an approximation of the optimal strategy h^* we apply the policy improvement described in the preceding section. We start with the myopic strategy $h^{(0)}$ given in (5.14) which can be computed directly from the filter for the drift $\widehat{\mu(Y_t)} = \overline{\mu}(p_t)$. For the computation of the first improvement $h^{(1)}$ given in (6.3) we need the reward function $v^{(0)}$ and its partial derivatives. Here we use representation (6.1) of $v^{(0)}$ as conditional expectation. Assume that at time t^* based on observations of the stock prices S_t and the marked point process I in $[0, t^*]$ we have obtained the filter $p_{t^*} = p^*$. Then a Monte-Carlo approximation of $v^{(0)}(t^*, p^*)$ is computed from $N = 1000$ paths of $p_s^{h^{(0)}}$ on $[t^*, T]$ which are solutions of the filter equation (5.5) starting at time t^* with p^*. The partial derivatives of $v^{(0)}(t, p)$ with respect to $p^k, k = 1, \ldots, d$ are approximated using central differences.

Figure 3 shows in the second panel the myopic strategy $h^{(0)}$ and the first approximation $h^{(1)}$ of the policy improvement. For the chosen parameters the myopic strategy $h^{(0)}$ is very close to the first approximation $h^{(1)}$ of the policy improvement. The lower panel shows the correction term $h^{(1)} - h^{(0)}$ of the policy improvement. It turns out, that this difference vanishes for $t = T_n$ (marked by dotted vertical lines)

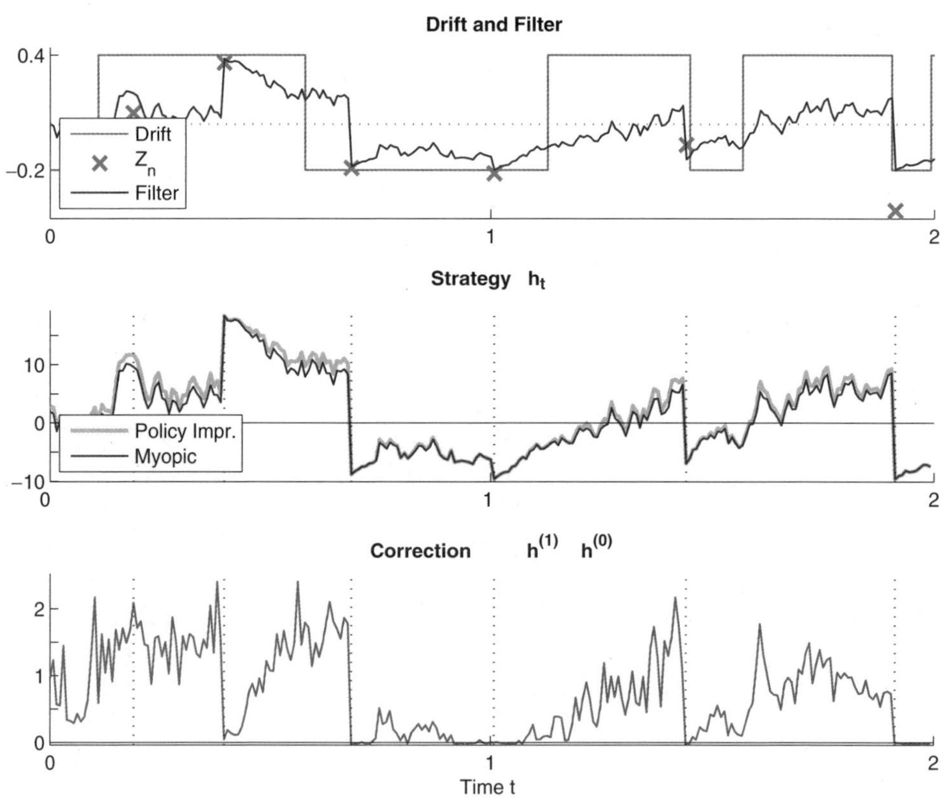

Fig. 3. Top: drift $\mu(Y_t)$, filter $\widehat{\mu(Y_t)}$ and predictions Z_n, Center: myopic strategy $h^{(0)}$ and first approximation $h^{(1)}$, Bottom: correction term $h^{(1)} - h^{(0)}$.

where additional information allows for quite accurate estimates for the drift which are close to the actual values. So the investor has nearly full information on the drift, and both, the optimal strategy under incomplete information and the myopic strategy are close to the optimal strategy under full information. Moreover, the correction term tends to zero for $t \to T$ as one would expect.

Acknowledgments

The work on this paper was done while Rüdiger Frey was at the Department of Mathematics, University of Leipzig, and the support of the department is gratefully acknowledged.

References

[1] T. Björk, M. H. A. Davis and C. Landén, Optimal investment with partial information, *Mathematical Methods of Operations Research* **71** (2010) 371–399.

[2] F. Black and R. Litterman, Global portfolio optimization, *Financial Analysts Journal* **48**(5) (1992) 28–43.

[3] P. Bremaud, *Point Processes and Queues: Martingale Dynamics* (Springer, New York, 1981).

[4] S. Brendle, Portfolio selection under incomplete information, *Stochastic Processes and Their Applications* **116** (2006) 701–723.

[5] A. Danilova, M. Monoyios and A. Ng, Optimal investment with inside information and parameter uncertainty, *Mathematics and Financial Economics*, **3** (2010) 13–38.

[6] M. Davis and S. Lleo, Risk-sensitive asset management in a jump-diffusion factor model, Working Paper, arXiv:1001.1379v2 (2010).

[7] R. J. Elliott, L. Aggoun and J. B. Moore, *Hidden Markov Models* (Springer, New York, 1994).

[8] W. H. Fleming and H. M. Soner, *Controlled Markov Processes and Viscosity Solutions*, 2nd edn (Springer, New York, 2006).

[9] R. Frey, A. Gabih and R. Wunderlich, Portfolio Optimization under Partial Information with Expert Opinions: Mathematical Aspects. In preparation (2011).

[10] A. Gabih, J. Sass and R. Wunderlich, Utility maximization under bounded expected loss, *Stochastic Models*, **3**(25) (2009) 375–407.

[11] P. Lakner, Optimal trading strategy for an investor: the case of partial information, *Stochastic Processes and their Applications* **76** (1998) 77–97.

[12] R. S. Liptser and A. N. Shiryaev, *Statistics of Random Processes: General Theory*, 2nd edn (Springer, New York, 2001).

[13] H. Nagai and S. Peng, Risk-sensitive dynamic portfolio optimization with partial information on infinite time horizon, *The Annals of Applied Probability* **12** (2002) 173–195.

[14] H. Nagai and W. J. Runggaldier, PDE approach to utility maximization for market models with hidden Markov factors, in *Seminar on Stochastic Analysis, Random Fields and Applications V*, Progress in Probability, Vol. 59, R. C. Dalang, M. Dozzi, F. Russo, eds. (Birkhäuser Verlag, 2008), pp. 493–506.

[15] H. Pham, Optimal stopping of controlled jump diffusion proicesses: a viscosity solution approach, *Journal of Mathematical Systems, Estimation and Control* **8** (1998) 1–27.

[16] U. Rieder and N. Bäuerle, Portfolio optimization with unobservable Markov-modulated drift process, *Journal of Applied Probability* **43** (2005) 362–378.
[17] J. Sass and U. G. Haussmann, Optimizing the terminal wealth under partial information: The drift process as a continuous time Markov chain, *Finance and Stochastics* **8** (2004) 553–577.
[18] J. Sass and R. Wunderlich, Optimal portfolio policies under bounded expected loss and partial information, *Mathematical Methods of Operations Research* **72** (2010) 25–61.
[19] K. Schöttle, R. Werner and R. Zagst, Comparison and robustification of Bayes and Black-Litterman models, *Mathematical Methods of Operations Research* **71** (2010) 453–475.
[20] W. M. Wonham, Some applications of stochastic differential equations to optimal non-linear filtering, *SIAM J. Control Opt.* 347–369 (1965).

ON THE PENALTY FUNCTION AND ON CONTINUITY PROPERTIES OF RISK MEASURES*

MARCO FRITTELLI

Dipartimento di Matematica
Università degli Studi di Milano
Via C. Saldini 50, 20122 Milano, Italy

EMANUELA ROSAZZA GIANIN

Dipartimento di Metodi Quantitativi
Università di Milano-Bicocca
Via Bicocca degli Arcimboldi 8, 20126 Milano, Italy

We discuss two issues about risk measures: we first point out an alternative interpretation of the penalty function in the dual representation of a risk measure; then we analyze the continuity properties of comonotone convex risk measures. In particular, due to the loss of convexity, local and global continuity are no more equivalent and many implications true for convex risk measures do not hold any more.

Keywords: Risk measures; penalty function; continuity.

1. Introduction

This analysis arises from the financial need of weakening the axiom of convexity (or the stronger one of sublinearity) imposed on risk measures (see Delbaen [8, 9], Föllmer and Schied [11, 12] and Frittelli and Rosazza Gianin [18], among many others) and motivated by diversification reasons.

On one hand, indeed, convexity of a real-valued map π defined on a space of random variables implies that for $\alpha \in [0,1]$

$$\pi(\alpha X + (1-\alpha)Y) \leq \alpha\pi(X) + (1-\alpha)\pi(Y) \leq \max(\pi(X), \pi(Y)).$$

However, to control the risk of the diversified position it is sufficient to assume only quasiconvexity, i.e. $\pi(\alpha X + (1-\alpha)Y) \leq \max(\pi(X), \pi(Y))$. This indeed is one of the motivations behind the recent approach proposed in [5], where the notion of a quasiconvex cash subadditive risk measure was introduced. The dual representation

*This chapter was originally published under the same title in *International Journal of Theoretical and Applied Finance*, Vol.14, No.1, 163–185 (2011). Singapore: World Scientific Publishing.

of such risk measures (see Proposition 2.1) may be written in terms of a function $R = R(q, Q)$, which assigns the risk that is hedgeable with a level of wealth $q \in \mathbb{R}$, once a pricing functional Q is fixed. In the quasiconvex case, this function R replaces the role of the penalty component in the dual representation of a convex risk measure. In the first part of this paper (Proposition 2.3) we show that the penalty term π^* of *any* map π can be recovered from the function R by computing $R^*(1, Q)$, where $R^*(p, Q) := \sup_{q \in \mathbb{R}}\{pq - R(q, Q)\}$, thus proving an alternative interpretation for the penalty function.

On the other hand, insurance premium principles are sometimes assumed to satisfy additivity only for comonotone risks (see Wang *et al.* [29]). Song and Yan [25] and Heyde *et al.* [19] proposed therefore to replace convexity with *comonotone convexity*, that is convexity for comonotone risks. It has been proved by Song and Yan [25] that a risk measure ρ satisfying comonotone convexity (plus some additional assumptions, but without any assumptions on continuity) may be represented as the maximum of the penalized Choquet integrals over a suitable set $\mathcal{M}$ of set functions. In the second part of the paper we show that when continuity from above in 0 is imposed to $\pi(X) \triangleq \rho(-X)$, then in the representation of π the set $\mathcal{M}$ may be relaxed with its subset $\mathcal{M}_{ca0}$ of set functions that are continuous from above in 0 (see Proposition 3.2). This result will be applied to some functionals that are law invariant and consistent with different orders. We will consider then different notions of continuity and show that many implications true for convex risk measures fail to hold once convexity is relaxed with comonotone convexity.

In Sec. 2 we will work in the general setting described below. However, the results of Secs. 3.1 and 3.2 hold for the specific case of bounded random variables and therefore there we will confine our study to risk measures defined on $L^\infty(\Omega, \mathcal{F}, P)$.

1.1. *Notations and setting*

We consider a lattice $L_\mathcal{F} \triangleq L(\Omega, \mathcal{F}, P) \subseteq L^0(\Omega, \mathcal{F}, P)$ of $\mathcal{F}$-measurable random variables, on the probability space $(\Omega, \mathcal{F}, P)$, that is endowed with the usual — P-a.s. — order relation $\geq$ and we suppose that $L_\mathcal{F}$ contains the space $L^\infty_\mathcal{F}$ of essentially bounded r.v.'s.

The order continuous dual of $(L_\mathcal{F}, \geq)$, denoted by $L^*_\mathcal{F} = (L_\mathcal{F}, \geq)^*$, is a lattice and we assume that it satisfies: $L^*_\mathcal{F} \hookrightarrow L^1_\mathcal{F}$. The vector space $L^*_\mathcal{F}$ is required to be not trivial, so that $(L_\mathcal{F}, \sigma(L_\mathcal{F}, L^*_\mathcal{F}))$ is a locally convex TVS.

Many important classes of spaces satisfy these conditions, as for example:

- The L^p-spaces, $p \in [1, \infty]$: $L_\mathcal{F} = L^p_\mathcal{F}$, $L^*_\mathcal{F} = L^q_\mathcal{F} \hookrightarrow L^1_\mathcal{F}$.
- The Orlicz spaces L^Ψ for any Young function Ψ: $L_\mathcal{F} = L^\Psi_\mathcal{F}$, $L^*_\mathcal{F} = L^{\Psi^*}_\mathcal{F} \hookrightarrow L^1_\mathcal{F}$, where Ψ^* denotes the conjugate function of Ψ.

From now on, the dual system $(L_\mathcal{F}, L^*_\mathcal{F})$ is fixed.

We also consider the set of densities of probability measures given by $\mathcal{P} \triangleq \{\frac{dQ}{dP} \in (L^1_\mathcal{F})_+ \mid E[\frac{dQ}{dP}] = 1, Q \ll P\}$ and, with an abuse of notation, we will write $Q \in \mathcal{P}$ instead of $\frac{dQ}{dP} \in \mathcal{P}$.

Consider the following list of properties on a functional π associated to a risk measure ρ, that is $\pi(X) \triangleq \rho(-X)$.

Properties of $\pi : L_{\mathcal{F}} \to \overline{\mathbb{R}} \triangleq \mathbb{R} \cup \{-\infty\} \cup \{\infty\}$.

— monotonicity: $\pi(X) \leq \pi(Y)$ for all $X, Y \in L_{\mathcal{F}}$ such that $X \leq Y$
— convexity: $\pi(\alpha X + (1-\alpha)Y) \leq \alpha\pi(X) + (1-\alpha)\pi(Y)$ for all $X, Y \in L_{\mathcal{F}}$, $\alpha \in [0, 1]$
— quasiconvexity: the lower level sets $\mathcal{A}_a \triangleq \{X \in L_{\mathcal{F}} \mid \pi(X) \leq a\}$ are convex for all $a \in \mathbb{R}$
— additivity: $\pi(X+Y) = \pi(X) + \pi(Y)$ for all $X, Y \in L_{\mathcal{F}}$
— subadditivity: $\pi(X+Y) \leq \pi(X) + \pi(Y)$ for all $X, Y \in L_{\mathcal{F}}$
— positive homogeneity: $\pi(\lambda X) = \lambda\pi(X)$ for all $X \in L_{\mathcal{F}}$, $\lambda \geq 0$
— cash additivity: $\pi(X + a) = \pi(X) + a$ for all $X \in L_{\mathcal{F}}$, $a \in \mathbb{R}$
— constant-preserving: $\pi(a) = a$ for all $a \in \mathbb{R}$
— law invariance: $\pi(X) = \pi(Y)$ if $X, Y \in L_{\mathcal{F}}$ have the same distribution (notation: $X \sim Y$)
— lower semicontinuity (lsc): the lower level sets $\mathcal{A}_a$ are closed for all $a \in \mathbb{R}$.

We remind that two random variables X and Y are called comonotone if $(X(\omega) - X(\omega'))(Y(\omega) - Y(\omega')) \geq 0$, $(P \times P)$-almost surely. When we add to a property the label "comonotone" it means that the property holds (only) for comonotone r.v.'s.

As mentioned, Sec. 2 is devoted to the analysis of the penalty term for general maps $\pi : L_{\mathcal{F}} \to \overline{\mathbb{R}}$. In Sec. 3.1 a representation of comonotone convex functionals with a continuity property is established. Other notions of continuity and several examples that underline what happens for non-convex functionals are presented in Sec. 3.2. A sufficient condition for continuity of monotone real-valued functionals is provided in Sec. 3.3.

2. On the Penalty Function of Risk Measures

In this section we consider maps $\pi : L_{\mathcal{F}} \to \overline{\mathbb{R}} \triangleq \mathbb{R} \cup \{-\infty\} \cup \{\infty\}$. The dual representation of "quasiconvex risk measures" (see [5] in the static case and [16] in a dynamic setting) is written in terms of the following functions of two variables.

Definition 2.1. Let $\pi : L_{\mathcal{F}} \to \overline{\mathbb{R}}$ and set for $Z \in L^*_{\mathcal{F}}$ and $q \in \mathbb{R}$

$$R(q, Z) \triangleq \inf_{\xi \in L_{\mathcal{F}}} \{\pi(\xi) \mid E[Z\xi] = q\},$$

$$\mathcal{R}(q, Z) \triangleq \inf_{\xi \in L_{\mathcal{F}}} \{\pi(\xi) \mid E[Z\xi] \geq q\},$$

and $R(q, Q) \triangleq R(q, \frac{dQ}{dP})$, if $Q \in \mathcal{P}$.

Interpretation of $R(q, Q)$

For a given level of wealth q and for a given "pricing functional" Q, $R(q, Q)$ assigns the "value" or "risk" — depending on the meaning of the map π, either as value or as risk — that is "attainable" or "hedgeable" from q.

Notice that if $Z \in (L^*_{\mathcal{F}})_+$ with $E[Z] > 0$ and $\frac{dQ}{dP} \triangleq \frac{Z}{E[Z]}$ then

$$R(E[ZX], Z) = R\left(\frac{E[ZX]}{E[Z]}, \frac{Z}{E[Z]}\right) = R(E_Q[X], Q).$$

The following Proposition is known: it collects some of the results in [5] and [16], which are essentially based on those proved in [28], on the dual representation of *quasiconvex* functions. We recall that $\pi : L_{\mathcal{F}} \to \overline{\mathbb{R}}$ is quasiconvex if and only if $\pi(\alpha X + (1-\alpha)Y) \leq \max(\pi(X), \pi(Y))$, for all $X, Y \in L_{\mathcal{F}}$, $\alpha \in [0,1]$.

Proposition 2.1. (i) *If $\pi : L_{\mathcal{F}} \to \overline{\mathbb{R}}$ is quasiconvex and $(L_{\mathcal{F}}, L^*_{\mathcal{F}})$–lsc then*

$$\pi(X) = \sup_{Z \in L^*_{\mathcal{F}}} \mathcal{R}(E[ZX], Z). \tag{2.1}$$

(ii) *If in addition π is monotone increasing then*

$$\pi(X) = \sup_{Z \in L^*_{\mathcal{F}} \cap \mathcal{P}} R(E[ZX], Z). \tag{2.2}$$

(iii) *If in addition π is cash additive then*

$$R(q, Q) = q - \pi^*(Q) \tag{2.3}$$

and, from (2.2) *and* (2.3):

$$\pi(X) = \sup_{Q \in L^*_{\mathcal{F}} \cap \mathcal{P}} \{E_Q[X] - \pi^*(Q)\}, \tag{2.4}$$

where

$$\pi^*(Z) = \sup_{\xi \in L_{\mathcal{F}}} \{E[Z\xi] - \pi(\xi)\}$$

is the convex conjugate of π.

Remark 2.1. The formula (2.4) can be deduced from the equality $\pi = \pi^{**}$, which holds for any *convex* lsc proper function — as stated by the Fenchel-Moreau theorem — and using monotonicity and cash additivity (see [18]). The fact that it is possible to obtain (2.4) from quasiconvexity is not a surprise since quasiconvexity and cash additivity imply convexity. This last sentence is well known (see for example [5]) and can be proved in a direct way as follows. By quasiconvexity, the lower level set $\mathcal{A}_0$ is convex and, by cash additivity, $(X - \pi(X)) \in \mathcal{A}_0$ for any $X \in L_{\mathcal{F}}$. Therefore, $\{\lambda(X - \pi(X)) + (1-\lambda)(Y - \pi(Y))\} \in \mathcal{A}_0$ for any $X, Y \in L_{\mathcal{F}}$ and $\lambda \in [0,1]$ and:

$$\begin{aligned} 0 &\geq \pi\{\lambda(X - \pi(X)) + (1-\lambda)(Y - \pi(Y))\} \\ &= \pi(\lambda X + (1-\lambda)Y) - \lambda\pi(X) - (1-\lambda)\pi(Y) \end{aligned}$$

by cash additivity.

Remark 2.2. Setting $\rho(X) = \pi(-X)$ we obtain from (2.4) the well known (see [11] and [18]) representation of a lsc convex risk measure

$$\rho(X) = \sup_{Q \in L^*_{\mathcal{F}} \cap \mathcal{P}} \{E_Q[-X] - \rho^*(-Q)\}.$$

Example 2.1. For a given utility function u, that is a strictly increasing concave function $u : \mathbb{R} \to \mathbb{R}$, consider the certainty equivalent operator $\pi^u(\cdot) = u^{-1}(E_P[u(\cdot)])$. Notice that π^u is a quasiconcave map, that in general is not concave, and we assume that $\pi^u : L_{\mathcal{F}} \to \overline{\mathbb{R}}$ is well defined (this is the case, for example, if $L_{\mathcal{F}}$ is the Orlicz space associated to the utility function u, see [17] for details, or if $L_{\mathcal{F}} = L^{\infty}_{\mathcal{F}}$). In the presence of a financial market, the no arbitrage principle guarantees that the set of equivalent martingale (or pricing) measures is not empty. For an assigned "pricing" measure $Q \in L^*_{\mathcal{F}} \cap \mathcal{P}$ consider the price $E_Q[X]$ of the claim X. As in [2] and [3], we compare two components: the artificial linear pricing operator $E_Q[\cdot]$ and the subjective valuation $\pi^u(\cdot)$ based on the preference relation $\succeq$ associated to u (and P):

$$E_Q[X] - \pi^u(X) = E_Q[X] - u^{-1}(E_P[u(X)]).$$

The maximum of this difference, for a fixed level q, is

$$\begin{aligned}\sup_{\xi \in L_{\mathcal{F}} : E_Q[\xi]=q} \{E_Q[\xi] - u^{-1}(E_P[u(\xi)])\} &= \sup_{\xi \in L_{\mathcal{F}} : E_Q[\xi]=q} \{q - \pi^u(\xi)\} \\ &= q - R(q, Q).\end{aligned}$$

In general, this difference will depend on the level of wealth q, as well as on Q, and its maximum, with respect to all $q \in \mathbb{R}$,

$$R^*(Q) \triangleq \sup_{q \in \mathbb{R}} \{q - R(q, Q)\} = \sup_{q \in \mathbb{R}} \sup_{\{\xi \in L_{\mathcal{F}} : E_Q[\xi]=q\}} \{E_Q[\xi] - u^{-1}(E_P[u(\xi)])\},$$

gives the "distance" between the certainty equivalent operator π^u and the expectation operator w.r.to the fixed Q.

This example suggests to define the following penalty function R^* of R.

Definition 2.2. Let $\pi : L_{\mathcal{F}} \to \overline{\mathbb{R}}$, $Z \in L^*_{\mathcal{F}}$ and $p \in \mathbb{R}$ and set:

$$R^*(p, Z) \triangleq \sup_{q \in \mathbb{R}} \{pq - R(q, Z)\},$$

$$R^*(Z) \triangleq R^*(1, Z) = \sup_{q \in \mathbb{R}} \{q - R(q, Z)\}.$$

For each $Z \in L^*_{\mathcal{F}}$, $R^*(\cdot, Z)$ is the convex conjugate of the function $R(\cdot, Z) : \mathbb{R} \to \overline{\mathbb{R}}$. Notice that when $Z = 0$, $R(q, 0)$ and $\mathcal{R}(q, 0)$ are equal to $+\infty$ for $q \neq 0$ and $R(0, 0) = \mathcal{R}(0, 0) = \inf_{\xi \in L_{\mathcal{F}}} \{\pi(\xi)\} = -\pi^*(0)$, $R^*(0) = -R(0, 0) = \pi^*(0)$.

Let us also consider the symmetric notations and state the corresponding dual representation in the *concave* upper semicontinuous (usc) case.

Definition 2.3. Let $\pi : L_{\mathcal{F}} \to \overline{\mathbb{R}}$ and set for $Z \in L^*_{\mathcal{F}}$ and $q \in \mathbb{R}$

$$\begin{aligned} r(q, Z) &\triangleq \sup_{\xi \in L_{\mathcal{F}}} \{\pi(\xi) \,|\, E[Z\xi] = q\}, \\ r_*(Z) &\triangleq \inf_{q \in \mathbb{R}} \{q - r(q, Z)\} \end{aligned} \tag{2.5}$$

and let $\pi_* : L^*_{\mathcal{F}} \to \overline{\mathbb{R}}$ be the concave conjugate of π:

$$\pi_*(Z) = \inf_{\xi \in L_{\mathcal{F}}} \{E[Z\xi] - \pi(\xi)\}.$$

By applying Proposition 2.1 to the map $-\pi(-X)$ one can easily deduce the following result.

Proposition 2.2. (i) *If $\pi : L_{\mathcal{F}} \to \overline{\mathbb{R}}$ is quasiconcave, monotone increasing and $(L_{\mathcal{F}}, L^*_{\mathcal{F}})-$usc then*

$$\pi(X) = \inf_{Q \in L^*_{\mathcal{F}} \cap \mathcal{P}} r(E_Q[X], Q).$$

(ii) *If in addition π is cash additive then*

$$\begin{aligned} r(q, Q) &= q - \pi_*(Q), \\ \pi(X) &= \inf_{Q \in L^*_{\mathcal{F}} \cap \mathcal{P}} \{E_Q[X] - \pi_*(Q)\}. \end{aligned} \tag{2.6}$$

The main contribution of this section is the next proposition, where we show that for *any* map π (in particular we do not assume that π is quasiconvex, monotone or cash additive) R^* coincides with the convex conjugate π^*; moreover, when π is cash additive, then

$$R^\pi(q, Q) \triangleq q - R(q, Z)$$

does not depend on q, so that $R^*(Q) = -R(0, Q) = R^\pi(q, Q)$, for any q.

Proposition 2.3. *Let $\pi : L_{\mathcal{F}} \to \overline{\mathbb{R}}$, $Q \in L^*_{\mathcal{F}} \cap \mathcal{P}$ and $q \in \mathbb{R}$.*

(1) $\pi_* = r_* \le R^* = \pi^*$.
(2) *If π is cash additive then $R(\cdot, Q)$ and $r(\cdot, Q)$ are affine and*

$$\begin{gathered} R(q, Q) = q - \pi^*(Q), \quad r(q, Q) = q - \pi_*(Q) \\ \pi_*(Q) = r_*(Q) = -r(0, Q) \le -R(0, Q) = R^*(Q) = \pi^*(Q). \end{gathered}$$

Proof. The statements regarding $R(\cdot, Q)$, R^* and π^* are proved in Lemma 2.1, where few additional items are also showed. The statements concerning $r(\cdot, Q)$, r_* and π_* can be proved in a similar way. The two inequalities are simple consequences of the definitions. □

Example 2.2. In the case of the exponential utility function it is known (see [14], Proposition 3.2) that

$$\frac{1}{a}H(Q,P) = \sup_{\xi \in L_{\mathcal{F}}:E_Q[\xi]=0} u_a^{-1}(E_P[u_a(\xi)]),$$

where: $u_a(x) = -\frac{1}{a}e^{-ax}$, $a > 0$, $H(Q,P) = E\left[\frac{dQ}{dP}\log\left(\frac{dQ}{dP}\right)\right]$ is the relative entropy and $L_{\mathcal{F}} = L_{\mathcal{F}}^{\infty}$.

Here, $\pi^a(X) \triangleq u_a^{-1}(E_P[u_a(X)]) = -\frac{1}{a}\ln(E[e^{-aX}])$ is cash additive and therefore from item (2) of Proposition 2.3 and from the definition of r in equation (2.5) we get

$$-\pi_*^a(Q) = -r_*^a(Q) = r^a(0,Q) \triangleq \sup_{\xi \in L_{\mathcal{F}}:E_Q[\xi]=0} u_a^{-1}(E_P[u_a(\xi)]) = \frac{1}{a}H(Q,P),$$

and we recover the well known penalty function of the entropic risk measure ρ^a defined by

$$\rho^a(X) \triangleq -\pi^a(X) = \frac{1}{a}\ln(E[e^{-aX}]).$$

Notice indeed that, since π^a is quasiconcave, $(L_{\mathcal{F}}^{\infty}, L_{\mathcal{F}}^{1})-$usc, monotone increasing and cash additive, the equation (2.6) and $\pi_*^a(Q) = -\frac{1}{a}H(Q,P)$ imply

$$\rho^a(X) = -\pi^a(X) = -\inf_{Q \in L_{\mathcal{F}}^1 \cap \mathcal{P}} \{E_Q[X] - \pi_*^a(Q)\} = \sup_{Q \ll P}\left\{E_Q[-X] - \frac{1}{a}H(Q,P)\right\}.$$

But the circumstance that $q - r(q,Z)$ does not depend on q is specific of the selection of the exponential utility, as in this example; in general to recover the penalty function $\pi_* = r_*$ a further optimization with respect to q is needed.

Proposition 2.4. *Let $\pi : L_{\mathcal{F}} \to \overline{\mathbb{R}}$, $Z \in L_{\mathcal{F}}^*$. Then*

$$R^*(Z) = \sup_{X \in L_{\mathcal{F}}} R^{\pi}(E[ZX], Z) = \pi^*(Z). \tag{2.7}$$

For $X \in L_{\mathcal{F}}$, the duality relation

$$\pi(X) = \sup_{Z \in (L_{\mathcal{F}}^*)_+} \{E[ZX] - R^{\pi}(E[ZX], Z)\} \tag{2.8}$$

holds true under the conditions that π is quasiconvex, $(L_{\mathcal{F}}, L_{\mathcal{F}}^*)-$lower semicontinuous and monotone increasing.

Proof. Equation (2.7) holds true if $Z = 0$, and so we now suppose $Z \neq 0$. Since $L_{\mathcal{F}}^{\infty} \subseteq L_{\mathcal{F}}$, the range of $X \to E[ZX]$ is $\mathbb{R}$ and so:

$$R^*(Z) \triangleq \sup_{q \in \mathbb{R}}\{R^{\pi}(q,Z)\} = \sup_{X \in L_{\mathcal{F}}} R^{\pi}(E[ZX], Z).$$

Equation (2.8) is a reformulation of equation (2.2). □

Remark 2.3. Suppose that π is a convex lsc proper monotone increasing function. From the Fenchel-Moreau theorem $\pi^{**} = \pi$ and from (2.8) we get:

$$\sup_{Z\in(L^*_{\mathcal{F}})_+} \{E[ZX] - \pi^*(Z)\} = \pi(X) = \sup_{Z\in(L^*_{\mathcal{F}})_+} \{E[ZX] - R^{\pi}(E[ZX], Z)\}.$$

In general $\pi^*(Z) \neq R^{\pi}(E[ZX], Z)$, while if π is cash additive then $\pi^*(Z) = R^{\pi}(q, Z)$, for any q.

Lemma 2.1. *Let* $\pi : L_{\mathcal{F}} \to \overline{\mathbb{R}}$, $Z \in L^*_{\mathcal{F}}$ *and* $q \in \mathbb{R}$.

(1)

$$R(q, Z) \geq \mathcal{R}(q, Z) \geq q - \pi^*(Z),$$
$$\sup_{q\in\mathbb{R}}\{q - R(q, Z)\} = \sup_{q\in\mathbb{R}}\{q - \mathcal{R}(q, Z)\},$$
$$R^*(Z) = \pi^*(Z).$$

(2) *Suppose that* π *is cash additive. For all* $E[Z] \neq 0$ *and* $q, c \in \mathbb{R}$

$$R(c + q, Z) = R(c, Z) + \frac{q}{E[Z]}$$

and:

$$R\left(q, \frac{Z}{E[Z]}\right) = q - \pi^*\left(\frac{Z}{E[Z]}\right) = q + R(0, Z).$$

(3) *Suppose that* π *is cash sub-additive, i.e.* $\pi(X + q) \leq \pi(X) + q$, *for all* $q \geq 0$ *and* $X \in L_{\mathcal{F}}$. *For all* $E[Z] > 0$, $c \in \mathbb{R}$ *and* $q \in \mathbb{R}_+$

$$\mathcal{R}(c + q, Z) \leq \mathcal{R}(c, Z) + \frac{q}{E[Z]}, \qquad R(c + q, Z) \leq R(c, Z) + \frac{q}{E[Z]}.$$

Proof. (1) We may assume that $Z \neq 0$, since for $Z = 0$ the statements in item 1 are obvious. For all $\xi \in L_{\mathcal{F}}$ we have: $\pi^*(Z) \triangleq \sup_{\xi\in L_{\mathcal{F}}}\{E[Z\xi] - \pi(\xi)\} \geq E[Z\xi] - \pi(\xi)$. Hence: $q - \pi^*(Z) \leq q - E[Z\xi] + \pi(\xi) \leq \pi(\xi)$ for all $\xi \in L_{\mathcal{F}}$ s.t. $E[Z\xi] \geq q$. Therefore: $q - \pi^*(Z) \leq \inf_{\xi\in L_{\mathcal{F}}}\{\pi(\xi) \,|\, E[Z\xi] \geq q\} = \mathcal{R}(q, Z) \leq R(q, Z)$. Then $q - \mathcal{R}(q, Z) \leq \pi^*(Z)$ and

$$R^*(Z) = \sup_{q\in\mathbb{R}}\{q - R(q, Z)\} \leq \sup_{q\in\mathbb{R}}\{q - \mathcal{R}(q, Z)\} \leq \pi^*(Z). \tag{2.9}$$

Now let $X \in L_{\mathcal{F}}$. Notice that (since $Z \neq 0$) the range of $X \to E[ZX]$ is $\mathbb{R}$ and so:

$$R^*(Z) \triangleq \sup_{q\in\mathbb{R}}\{R^{\pi}(q, Z)\} = \sup_{X\in L_{\mathcal{F}}} R^{\pi}(E[ZX], Z). \tag{2.10}$$

Since $\inf_{\xi\in L_{\mathcal{F}}}\{\pi(\xi)\,|\,E[Z\xi]=E[ZX]\}\leq\pi(X)$ we have:

$$R^{\pi}(E[ZX],Z)=E[ZX]-\inf_{\xi\in L_{\mathcal{F}}}\{\pi(\xi)\,|\,E[Z\xi]=E[ZX]\}\geq E[ZX]-\pi(X),$$

which implies

$$\sup_{X\in L_{\mathcal{F}}}R^{\pi}(E[ZX],Z)\geq\sup_{X\in L_{\mathcal{F}}}\{E[ZX]-\pi(X)\}=\pi^{*}(Z)$$

and taking into consideration (2.10) and (2.9) we deduce

$$R^{*}(Z)=\sup_{X\in L_{\mathcal{F}}}R^{\pi}(E[ZX],Z)\geq\pi^{*}(Z)\geq\sup_{q\in\mathbb{R}}\{q-\mathcal{R}(q,Z)\}\geq R^{*}(Z)$$

which concludes the proof of item 1.

(2) Since π is cash additive, it is easy to check that for $q,c\in\mathbb{R}$ and $E[Z]\neq0$

$$R(c+q,Z)=R(c,Z)+\frac{q}{E[Z]},$$

and therefore, letting $c=0$,

$$R\left(q,\frac{Z}{E[Z]}\right)=R\left(0,\frac{Z}{E[Z]}\right)+q=R(0,Z)+q.$$

From $\pi^{*}=R^{*}$ we then deduce:

$$\pi^{*}\left(\frac{Z}{E[Z]}\right)=R^{*}\left(\frac{Z}{E[Z]}\right)\triangleq\sup_{q\in\mathbb{R}}\left\{q-R\left(q,\frac{Z}{E[Z]}\right)\right\}=-R(0,Z).$$

and therefore

$$R\left(q,\frac{Z}{E[Z]}\right)=q+R(0,Z)=q-\pi^{*}\left(\frac{Z}{E[Z]}\right).$$

(3) We prove only the first inequality, since the same argument can be used to prove the second one. Let $\eta\triangleq\xi-\frac{q}{E[Z]}$, then we have

$$\mathcal{R}(c+q,Z)\triangleq\inf_{\xi\in L_{\mathcal{F}}}\{\pi(\xi)|E[Z\xi]\geq c+q\}=\inf_{\xi\in L_{\mathcal{F}}}\left\{\pi(\xi)|E\left[Z\left(\xi-\frac{q}{E[Z]}\right)\right]\geq c\right\}$$

$$=\inf_{\eta\in L_{\mathcal{F}}}\left\{\pi\left(\eta+\frac{q}{E[Z]}\right)|E[Z\eta]\geq c\right\}.$$

Notice that $\frac{q}{E[Z]}\geq0$ then, from cash sub-additivity of π, we obtain

$$\mathcal{R}(c+q,Z)\leq\inf_{\eta\in L_{\mathcal{F}}}\{\pi(\eta)|E[Z\eta]\geq c\}+\frac{q}{E[Z]}\triangleq\mathcal{R}(c,Z)+\frac{q}{E[Z]}$$ □

3. On Continuity Properties of Risk Measures

It is well known that a convex function bounded above on a neighbourhood of a point is continuous at that point. This in particular implies that for convex functions local and global continuity are equivalent (see, for instance, Aliprantis and Border [1]).

In this section we analyze the continuity properties of comonotone convex risk measures, where the above equivalence (as well as many other implications true for convex risk measures) does not hold true any more, due to the loss of convexity. In the last subsection we also provide a simple criterium for continuity of monotone real-valued maps.

In the sequel of the paper we assume $L_{\mathcal{F}} = L^{\infty}_{\mathcal{F}}$.

There are some trivial implications among some of the properties of π listed in the introduction. Obviously convexity implies comonotone convexity; furthermore, comonotone additivity and constant-preserving imply cash additivity. Indeed, it is straightforward to check that a constant random variable a is comonotone with any random variable $X \in L_{\mathcal{F}}$.

Subadditivity, positive homogeneity and $\pi(\pm 1) = \pm 1$ imply cash additivity (see [15]). More generally, it is easy to check that comonotone subadditivity, positive homogeneity and $\pi(\pm 1) = \pm 1$ imply cash additivity.

In order to show the dual representation of comonotone risk measures we still need to introduce some properties (see for reference Denneberg [10], Aliprantis and Border [1], among many others) of set functions $\mu : \mathcal{F} \to [0, +\infty]$. We assume that each set function μ satisfies $\mu(\varnothing) = 0$.

Properties on μ

- monotone: if $A, B \in \mathcal{F}$, $A \subseteq B$, then $\mu(A) \leq \mu(B)$
- finite: if $\mu(A) < +\infty$ for any $A \in \mathcal{F}$. In particular, μ is said to be normalized if $\mu(\Omega) = 1$
- submodular (or 2−alternating): if $A, B \in \mathcal{F}$ ($A \cup B, A \cap B \in \mathcal{F}$), then $\mu(A \cup B) + \mu(A \cap B) \leq \mu(A) + \mu(B)$
- continuous from below: if $(A_n)_{n \geq 0} \subseteq \mathcal{F}$, $A_n \subseteq A_{n+1}$ for any $n \geq 0$ (and $A = \cup_{n=0}^{\infty} A_n \in \mathcal{F}$), then $\lim_{n \to +\infty} \mu(A_n) = \mu(A)$
- continuous from above: if $(B_n)_{n \geq 0} \subseteq \mathcal{F}$, $B_n \supseteq B_{n+1}$ for any $n \geq 0$ (and $B = \cap_{n=0}^{\infty} B_n \in \mathcal{F}$), then $\lim_{n \to +\infty} \mu(B_n) = \mu(B)$
- absolutely continuous with respect to P ($\mu \ll P$): if μ is a normalized monotone set function such that: for any $A, B \in \mathcal{F}$ with $P(A \triangle B) = 0$ it holds that $\mu(A) = \mu(B)$.

Consider, for instance, an increasing function $f : [0, 1] \to [0, 1]$ satisfying $f(0) = 0$ and $f(1) = 1$. Such a function f is called *distortion* and the (monotone and normalized) set function $\mu \triangleq f \circ P$ associated to f is called *distorted probability*. Moreover, if f is concave and continuous (that is, continuous in 0) then the distorted probability $\mu \triangleq f \circ P$ is monotone, submodular and continuous from below (see Delbaen [8, 9], Denneberg [10], Kunze [23] for the proof, for further details and for applications to risk measures).

We recall (see Choquet [6] and Denneberg [10] for an exhaustive treatment) that for a normalized, monotone set function $\mu : \mathcal{F} \to [0, 1]$ such that $\mu \ll P$ the

Choquet integral of X, defined as

$$E_\mu[X] \triangleq \int_{-\infty}^{0} [\mu(X \geq x) - 1]dx + \int_{0}^{+\infty} \mu(X \geq x)dx, \tag{3.1}$$

satisfies the properties of monotonicity, positive homogeneity, comonotone additivity, cash additivity and $E_\mu[1_A] = \mu(A)$. Subadditivity holds iff μ is submodular. In particular, when μ is a probability measure then E_μ reduces to the classical expectation.

Set

$$\mathcal{M}(P) \triangleq \left\{ \mu : \mathcal{F} \to [0; +\infty] \;\middle|\; \begin{array}{c} \mu \text{ monotone set function such that} \\ \mu(\Omega) = 1 \text{ and } \mu \ll P \end{array} \right\}$$

It is clear that $\mathcal{M}(P)$ contains the set of all probability measures $Q \ll P$. In the following we will simply write $\mathcal{M}$ instead of $\mathcal{M}(P)$.

Song and Yan [25, 26] represented suitable functionals (without any axiom of continuity) in terms of set functions belonging to $\mathcal{M}$. More precisely, they proved that:

- if $\pi : L^\infty_\mathcal{F} \to \mathbb{R}$ satisfies monotonicity, *comonotone subadditivity*, positive homogeneity and cash additivity, then

$$\pi(X) = \max_{\mu \in \mathcal{M}^*} E_\mu[X] \tag{3.2}$$

  where $\mathcal{M}^* \triangleq \{\mu \in \mathcal{M} : E_\mu[Y] \leq \pi(Y) \; \forall Y \in L^\infty_\mathcal{F}\}$;
- if $\pi : L^\infty_\mathcal{F} \to \mathbb{R}$ satisfies monotonicity, *comonotone convexity* and cash additivity, then

$$\pi(X) = \max_{\mu \in \mathcal{M}} \{E_\mu[X] - F(\mu)\}, \tag{3.3}$$

  where the penalty functional F is defined as

$$F(\mu) \triangleq \sup_{X \in L^\infty_\mathcal{F} : \pi(X) \leq 0} E_\mu[X]. \tag{3.4}$$

By imposing $\pi(0) = 0$, it follows that $F(\mu) \geq 0$ and $\min_{\mu \in \mathcal{M}} F(\mu) = 0$.

Remark 3.1. We show now that the following relation (proved by Föllmer and Schied [11, 12] in the convex case)

$$F(\mu) = \sup_{X \in L^\infty_\mathcal{F}} \{E_\mu[X] - \pi(X)\} \tag{3.5}$$

also holds for functionals satisfying comonotone convexity, monotonicity and cash additivity.

By comonotone additivity of E_μ and by cash additivity of π it follows indeed that

$$\begin{aligned}\sup_{X\in L^\infty_{\mathcal{F}}}\{E_\mu[X]-\pi(X)\} &= \sup_{Y\in L^\infty_{\mathcal{F}}:Y=X-\pi(X)} E_\mu[Y]\\ &\le \sup_{Y\in L^\infty_{\mathcal{F}}:\pi(Y)\le 0} E_\mu[Y]\\ &\le \sup_{X\in L^\infty_{\mathcal{F}}}\{E_\mu[X]-\pi(X)\}.\end{aligned}$$

As a consequence of equation (3.5), the representation (3.2) can be rewritten as in (3.3) with

$$F(\mu)\triangleq\begin{cases}0; & \text{if } \mu\in\mathcal{M}^*\\ +\infty; & \text{otherwise}\end{cases}.$$

3.1. *On the dual representation of certain classes of risk measures*

Our aim is to represent functionals π satisfying the properties above (comonotone convexity, monotonicity, cash additivity and $\pi(0)=0$) plus some kind of continuity. The assumption that $\pi(0)=0$ just implies that the penalty functional F in the representation (3.3) is such that $\min_{\mu\in\mathcal{M}} F(\mu)=0$.

Further axioms

- *continuity from above in* 0 (shortly, ca0) of π: for any sequence $(Y_n)_{n\in\mathbb{N}}$ such that $Y_n\searrow 0$, then $\lim_{n\to+\infty}\pi(Y_n)=\pi(0)=0$
- *continuity from above in* 0 of μ : for any sequence $(B_n)_{n\in\mathbb{N}}$ of sets such that $B_n\searrow\emptyset$, then $\lim_{n\to+\infty}\mu(B_n)=0$

By cash additivity of π and $\pi(0)=0$, it is clear that continuity from above in 0 of π is equivalent to the following axiom: for any sequence $(Y_n)_{n\in\mathbb{N}}$ such that $Y_n\searrow k$ with $k\in\mathbb{R}$, then $\lim_{n\to+\infty}\pi(Y_n)=k$.

In the following, $\mathcal{M}_{ca0}$ will denote the subset of $\mathcal{M}$ formed by all normalized, monotone set functions $\mu\ll P$ that are continuous from above in 0, i.e. $\mathcal{M}_{ca_0}=\{\mu\in\mathcal{M}:\mu \text{ is ca0}\}$.

The following result (and its proof) is an extension of Lemma 19 of Föllmer and Schied [12] to the comonotone case.

Proposition 3.1. *Let $\pi: L^\infty_{\mathcal{F}}\to\mathbb{R}$ satisfy monotonicity, comonotone convexity, cash additivity and $\pi(0)=0$.*

For any sequence $(Y_n)_{n\in\mathbb{N}}$ such that $0\le Y_n\le 1$ for any $n\in\mathbb{N}$, the following are equivalent:

(a) $\pi(\lambda Y_n)\to_{n\to+\infty} 0$ *for any* $\lambda>0$;

(b) $\sup_{\mu\in\Lambda_c} E_\mu[Y_n] \to_{n\to+\infty} 0$ *for any* $c>0$,

where $\Lambda_c \triangleq \{\mu \in \mathcal{M} : F(\mu) \le c\}$.

Proof. Consider an arbitrary sequence $(Y_n)_{n\in\mathbb{N}}$ such that $0 \le Y_n \le 1$ for any $n \in \mathbb{N}$.

(a) $\Rightarrow$ (b): by the formulation of F in (3.5), for any $\mu \in \Lambda_c$ (with fixed $c > 0$) and for any $\lambda > 0$ it holds

$$c \ge F(\mu) \ge E_\mu[\lambda Y_n] - \pi(\lambda Y_n).$$

Hence:

$$E_\mu[Y_n] \le \frac{c}{\lambda} + \frac{\pi(\lambda Y_n)}{\lambda}$$

By positivity of Y_n, we get

$$0 \le \sup_{\mu\in\Lambda_c} E_\mu[Y_n] \le \frac{c}{\lambda} + \frac{\pi(\lambda Y_n)}{\lambda}.$$

By (a), it follows therefore that

$$0 \le \overline{\lim_{n\to+\infty}} \sup_{\mu\in\Lambda_c} E_\mu[Y_n] \le \lim_{n\to+\infty} \left(\frac{c}{\lambda} + \frac{\pi(\lambda Y_n)}{\lambda}\right) = \frac{c}{\lambda}.$$

It is therefore sufficient to pass to the limit (as $\lambda \to +\infty$) to obtain (b).

(b) $\Rightarrow$ (a): Again by positivity of Y_n and by the representation of π in (3.3):

$$\begin{aligned} 0 \le \pi(\lambda Y_n) &= \sup_{\mu\in\mathcal{M}} \{E_\mu[\lambda Y_n] - F(\mu)\} \\ &= \sup_{\mu\in\Lambda_\lambda} \{E_\mu[\lambda Y_n] - F(\mu)\} && (3.6) \\ &\le \lambda \sup_{\mu\in\Lambda_\lambda} E_\mu[Y_n] \to_{n\to+\infty} 0 && (3.7) \end{aligned}$$

where the limit in (3.7) is due to (b) and (3.6) is due to the fact that if $\mu \notin \Lambda_\lambda$ then $F(\mu) > \lambda$, hence $E_\mu[\lambda Y_n] - F(\mu) < E_\mu[\lambda Y_n] - \lambda \le 0$.

From the inequalities above it follows $\pi(\lambda Y_n) \to_{n\to+\infty} 0$ for any $\lambda > 0$. □

The following result is an extension of Proposition 18 of Föllmer and Schied [12] to the comonotone case.

Proposition 3.2. *Let* $\pi : L^\infty_\mathcal{F} \to \mathbb{R}$ *satisfy monotonicity, comonotone convexity, cash additivity and* $\pi(0) = 0$.

If π *is continuous from above in* 0, *then:*

$$F(\mu) < +\infty \Rightarrow \mu \in \mathcal{M}_{ca0}.$$

Hence, π *can be represented as*

$$\pi(X) = \max_{\mu\in\mathcal{M}_{ca0}} \{E_\mu[X] - F(\mu)\}. \tag{3.8}$$

Proof. In order to prove that the set $\mathcal{M}$ can be relaxed with $\mathcal{M}_{ca0}$, it is sufficient to consider an arbitrary sequence $(B_n)_{n\in\mathbb{N}}$ such that $B_n \searrow \emptyset$ and to take $Y_n = 1_{B_n}$. In such a case, indeed, the sequence $(Y_n)_{n\in\mathbb{N}}$ satisfies the hypothesis of Proposition 3.1 and, because of the continuity from above in 0 of π, (a) is verified. Hence, $\sup_{\mu\in\Lambda_c} E_\mu[1_{B_n}] \to_{n\to+\infty} 0$ for any $c > 0$. Therefore: if $F(\mu) < +\infty$ then there exists $c_0 > 0$ such that $F(\mu) \leq c_0$, hence $\mu \in \Lambda_{c_0}$ and $\mu(B_n) \to 0$ as $n \to +\infty$, that is continuity from above of μ in 0.

The last statement is immediate. □

Corollary 3.1. *Let $\pi : L^\infty_{\mathcal{F}} \to \mathbb{R}$ satisfy monotonicity, comonotone subadditivity, positive homogeneity and cash additivity.*

If π is continuous from above in 0, then it can be represented as

$$\pi(X) = \max_{\mu\in\mathcal{M}^*} E_\mu[X] \tag{3.9}$$

for a suitable $\mathcal{M}^* \subseteq \mathcal{M}_{ca0}$.

Proof. Since comonotone subadditivity plus positive homogeneity imply comonotone convexity, by Proposition 3.2 $\pi(X) = \max_{\mu\in\mathcal{M}_{ca0}}\{E_\mu[X] - F(\mu)\}$.

Consider now an arbitrary $\mu \in \mathcal{M}_{ca0}$ and suppose that $F(\mu) > 0$. Since $F(\mu) = \sup_{X\in L^\infty_{\mathcal{F}}}\{E_\mu[X] - \pi(X)\}$, we may suppose that there exists a $\overline{X} \in L^\infty_{\mathcal{F}}$ such that $E_\mu[\overline{X}] - \pi(\overline{X}) > 0$. Hence, by positive homogeneity of π,

$$F(\mu) \geq \sup_{\lambda>0}\{E_\mu[\lambda\overline{X}] - \pi(\lambda\overline{X})\} = \sup_{\lambda>0}\{\lambda[E_\mu[\overline{X}] - \pi(\overline{X})]\} = +\infty \tag{3.10}$$

The representation (3.9) then follows from the arguments above by taking $\mathcal{M}^* = \{\mu \in \mathcal{M}_{ca0} : F(\mu) < +\infty\}$. □

3.1.1. *Law invariance and consistency with respect to different orders*

In this section we will assume that the probability space $(\Omega, \mathcal{F}, P)$ is atomless.

We recall the following definitions on different orders. For further details, see Dana [7], Kusuoka [24] and Song and Yan [26], among many others.

Definition 3.1 (see [7, 24, 26]). A random variable X is said to be dominated by Y

— in the First Stochastic Dominance Order ($X \preceq_1 Y$) if $F_X(x) \geq F_Y(x)$ for any $x \in \mathbb{R}$
— in the Stop-Loss Order ($X \preceq_{sl} Y$) if $E[(X-x)^+] \leq E[(Y-x)^+]$ for any $x \in \mathbb{R}$

Definition 3.2 (see [7, 24, 26]). A functional π is said to be consistent with the First Stochastic Dominance (resp. Stop-Loss) Order if:

$$X \preceq_1 Y \text{ (resp. } X \preceq_{sl} Y) \Rightarrow \pi(X) \leq \pi(Y)$$

It is clear that consistency with the First Order Stochastic Dominance implies law invariance and monotonicity. The converse is also true in atomless spaces (see Kaas *et al.* [21] and Wang *et al.* [29], among many others).

Denote by $\mathcal{G}$ the set of all distortions, i.e. of all increasing functions $g : [0,1] \to [0,1]$ satisfying $g(0) = 0$ and $g(1) = 1$, and by $\mathcal{G}^{cc}$ the set of all concave distortions.

We remind the result of Song and Yan [26] on comonotone convex risk measure. The only difference between the formulation below and that in [26] is that here $\pi(0) = 0$ is imposed, hence $\min_{g\in\mathcal{G}} F(g \circ P) = 0$.

Proposition 3.3 (Song and Yan, Theorem 3.5, [26]). *$\pi : L^\infty \to \mathbb{R}$ satisfies consistency with respect to $\preceq_1$ (or, equivalently in atomless space, law invariance and monotonicity), comonotone convexity, cash additivity and $\pi(0) = 0$ if and only if*

$$\pi(X) = \max_{g\in\mathcal{G}}\{E_{(g\circ P)}[X] - F(g \circ P)\}, \tag{3.11}$$

where $F(g \circ P) = \sup_{X\in L^\infty_{\mathcal{F}}} \{E_{(g\circ P)}[X] - \pi(X)\}$ and $\min_{g\in\mathcal{G}} F(g \circ P) = 0$.

A similar result holds also for the comonotone subadditive case (see [26]).

When continuity from above in 0 is imposed to π, from Proposition 3.2 we obtain the following particular cases.

Proposition 3.4. *Let $\pi : L^\infty_{\mathcal{F}} \to \mathbb{R}$ satisfy consistency with respect to $\preceq_1$ (or, equivalently in atomless space, law invariance and monotonicity).*

(i) *(comonotone convexity) If π satisfies comonotone convexity, cash additivity, $\pi(0) = 0$ and continuity from above in 0, then π can be represented as in (3.11) by replacing $\mathcal{G}$ with*

$$\mathcal{G}_{ca0} \triangleq \{g \in \mathcal{G} : g \text{ is continuous in } 0\}. \tag{3.12}$$

(ii) *(comonotone subadditivity and positive homogeneity) If π satisfies comonotone subadditivity, positive homogeneity, cash additivity and continuity from above in 0, then*

$$\pi(X) = \max_{g\in\mathcal{G}^*_{ca0}} E_{(g\circ P)}[X]$$

for a suitable $\mathcal{G}^*_{ca0} \subseteq \mathcal{G}_{ca0}$.

An inspection between (3.11) and (3.13) in the next Proposition shows that the only difference between these representations is given by the set of distortions ($\mathcal{G}$ in the former case, $\mathcal{G}^{cc}$ in the latter case) over which the maximum is attained.

Proposition 3.5 (Song and Yan, Theorems 3.6 and 3.7, [26]). *$\pi : L^\infty \to \mathbb{R}$ satisfies cash additivity, comonotone convexity and consistency wrt $\preceq_{sl}$ iff π satisfies cash additivity, convexity and consistency wrt $\preceq_1$.*

Moreover, if π *satisfies all the assumptions of Proposition* 3.3 *except for comonotonic convexity that is replaced by convexity, then:*

$$\pi(X) = \max_{g \in \mathcal{G}^{cc}} \{E_{(g \circ P)}[X] - F(g \circ P)\}, \tag{3.13}$$

where $F(g \circ P) = \sup_{X \in L^\infty_{\mathcal{F}}} \{E_{(g \circ P)}[X] - \pi(X)\}$ *and* $\min_{g \in \mathcal{G}^{cc}} F(g \circ P) = 0$.

An example of a comonotonic convex risk functional that is not convex is given by the Wang Transform risk measure with parameter $\alpha < 0$ (see Wang [30] for a detailed treatment). In the following example we clarify the difference between comonotonic convex and convex risk functionals.

Example 3.1. Consider the following distortions

$$g_1(x) = x; \quad g_2(x) = \begin{cases} 0; & 0 \le x < \dfrac{1}{2} \\ x; & \dfrac{1}{2} \le x \le 1 \end{cases}; \quad g_3(x) = x^2$$

restricted on the interval $[0, 1]$ and $F(g_1 \circ P) = 0$, $F(g_2 \circ P) = \frac{1}{12}$ and $F(g_3 \circ P) = 0$ as penalties. Set

$$\hat{\pi}(X) = \max_{g \in \{g_1, g_2\}} \{E_{g \circ P}[X] - F(g \circ P)\}$$

$$\bar{\pi}(X) = \max_{g \in \{g_2, g_3\}} \{E_{g \circ P}[X] - F(g \circ P)\}.$$

It is clear that both $\hat{\pi}$ and $\bar{\pi}$ satisfy monotonicity, cash additivity, law invariance, constant-preserving and $\hat{\pi}(0) = \bar{\pi}(0) = 0$.

On one hand, since $g_1 \ge g_2$ and $F(g_1 \circ P) \le F(g_2 \circ P)$, then $\hat{\pi}(X) = E_{g_1 \circ P}[X] - F(g_1 \circ P)$ for any X. Because of concavity of g_1, it follows that $\hat{\pi}$ is also convex.

On the other hand, by taking X distributed as a Uniform on $[0, 1]$ and $Y = -2X + 1$, one can easily check that $\bar{\pi}(X) = \frac{1}{3}$, $\bar{\pi}(Y) = -\frac{1}{3}$ and $\bar{\pi}(\frac{1}{2}X + \frac{1}{2}Y) = \frac{1}{6}$, hence convexity fails to be satisfied by such a $\bar{\pi}$.

A result similar to Proposition 3.5 holds also for the comonotone subadditive case (see [26]). The representation (3.13) can be found also in Theorem 4.12 of Kunze [23] under the additional assumption of continuity from below of π (already guaranteed by the other hypothesis — see Jouini *et al.* [20]).

By imposing continuity from above in 0 to π and by applying Proposition 3.2, we obtain the following particular cases.

Corollary 3.2. (i) (*convexity*) *Let* $\pi : L^\infty_{\mathcal{F}} \to \mathbb{R}$ *satisfy law invariance, monotonicity, convexity, cash additivity* (*or, equivalently, consistency wrt* $\preceq_1$*, convexity and cash additivity; or, equivalently by Proposition* 3.5*, comonotone convexity, consistency wrt* $\preceq_{sl}$ *and cash additivity*) *and* $\pi(0) = 0$.

If π is continuous from above in 0*, then π can be represented as in* (3.13) *by replacing $\mathcal{G}^{cc}$ with*

$$\mathcal{G}_c^{cc} \triangleq \{g \in \mathcal{G}^{cc} : g \text{ is continuous in } [0,1]\}.$$

(ii) (*subadditivity and positive homogeneity*) *Let $\pi : L_{\mathcal{F}}^{\infty} \to \mathbb{R}$ satisfy law invariance, monotonicity, subadditivity, positive homogeneity and cash additivity* (*or, equivalently, consistency wrt $\preceq_1$, subadditivity, positive homogeneity and cash additivity; or, equivalently by* [26], *comonotone subadditivity, positive homogeneity, consistency wrt $\preceq_{sl}$ and cash additivity*).

If π is continuous from above in 0 (*hence, see later, also continuous from above*), *then*

$$\pi(X) = \max_{g \in \mathcal{G}_c^{*,cc}} E_{(g \circ P)}[X]$$

for a suitable $\mathcal{G}_c^{*,cc} \subseteq \mathcal{G}_c^{cc}$.

Take note that in the last two particular cases law invariance, monotonicity, convexity, cash additivity and $\pi(0) = 0$ already guarantee that π is continuous from below (see Theorem 1.2 of Jouini *et al.* [20]). Here we impose the additional property of continuity from above in 0. See the next subsection for further details on the definition and on the comparison between different notions of continuity.

3.2. *Comparison between different kinds of continuity in the comonotone case*

Continuity from above of π in 0 has been investigated previously. We consider now the following further notions of continuity for π:

- *continuity from above* (shortly, ca): if $(X_n)_{n \geq 0} \subseteq L_{\mathcal{F}}^{\infty}$, $X_n \searrow X \in L_{\mathcal{F}}^{\infty}$, then $\lim_{n \to +\infty} \pi(X_n) = \pi(X)$
- *continuity from below* (shortly, cb): if $(Y_n)_{n \geq 0} \subseteq L_{\mathcal{F}}^{\infty}$, $Y_n \nearrow Y \in L_{\mathcal{F}}^{\infty}$, then $\lim_{n \to +\infty} \pi(Y_n) = \pi(Y)$
- *continuity from below in* 1 (shortly, cb1): for any sequence $(Y_n)_{n \in \mathbb{N}}$ such that $Y_n \nearrow 1$, then $\lim_{n \to +\infty} \pi(Y_n) = \pi(1)$.

With *continuity from below in* 1 *of* μ we mean that for any sequence $(A_n)_{n \in \mathbb{N}}$ of sets such that $A_n \nearrow \Omega$, then $\lim_{n \to +\infty} \mu(A_n) = 1$.

By cash additivity of π and $\pi(0) = 0$, it is clear that continuity from below in 1 of π is equivalent to the following axiom: for any sequence $(Y_n)_{n \in \mathbb{N}}$ such that $Y_n \nearrow k$ with $k \in \mathbb{R}$, then $\lim_{n \to +\infty} \pi(Y_n) = k$.

We recall that $\pi : L_{\mathcal{F}}^{\infty} \to \mathbb{R}$ is said to be *order lower semi-continuous* with respect to the weak topology $\sigma(L_{\mathcal{F}}^{\infty}, L_{\mathcal{F}}^{1})$ (or to satisfy the Fatou property) if for any uniformly bounded sequence $(X_n)_{n \geq 0}$ such that $X_n \to X$, P-a.s. it holds $\pi(X) \leq \liminf_{n \to +\infty} \pi(X_n)$.

See Delbaen [8], Föllmer and Schied [11] and Biagini and Frittelli [4], among many others, for further details.

By translating well known results true for convex risk measures ρ (see Delbaen [8, 9], Föllmer and Schied [11, 12], Klöppel and Schweizer [22] and Jouini *et al.* [20]) to $\pi(X) \triangleq \rho(-X)$, it follows that for $\pi : L^\infty_{\mathcal{F}} \to \mathbb{R}$ satisfying convexity, monotonicity, cash additivity and $\pi(0) = 0$ the following implications are true:

<table>
<tr><td>continuity from above in 0</td><td></td><td>continuity from below in 1</td></tr>
<tr><td>$\Uparrow$</td><td></td><td>$\Uparrow$</td></tr>
<tr><td>continuity from above</td><td>$\Rightarrow$</td><td>continuity from below</td></tr>
<tr><td></td><td></td><td>$\Updownarrow$</td></tr>
<tr><td></td><td></td><td>order lower semi-continuity (or Fatou)</td></tr>
<tr><td></td><td></td><td>$\Uparrow$</td></tr>
<tr><td></td><td></td><td>law invariance (in an atomless space)</td></tr>
</table>

Furthermore, for π satisfying also positive homogeneity: continuity from above is equivalent to continuity from above in 0 (see [8] and Sec. 3.2.1).

We investigate now if implications similar to the ones above hold also for comonotone convex π and/or for continuity from above in 0 and from below in 1.

3.2.1. *Continuity from above (in* 0*) and continuity from below in* 1

We recall from Denneberg [10] that the conjugate set function $\overline{\mu} : \mathcal{F} \to [0, +\infty)$ of a normalized μ is defined as $\overline{\mu}(A) \triangleq 1 - \mu(A^c)$, for any $A \in \mathcal{F}$, and that for a normalized monotone set function, continuity from above of μ is equivalent to continuity from below of $\overline{\mu}$ (see Proposition 2.3 of Denneberg [10]).

We omit the simple proof of the following Lemma.

Lemma 3.1. *Let μ be a normalized monotone set function such that $\mu \ll P$.*

(i) *μ is continuous from above in* 0 *iff $\overline{\mu}$ is continuous from below in* 1.
(ii) *if μ is continuous from above in* 0 *(respectively, continuous from below in* 1*), then E_μ is continuous from above in* 0 *(respectively, continuous from below in* 1*).*

Lemma 3.2. *Let π satisfy convexity and $\pi(0) = 0$, monotonicity and cash additivity. If π is continuous from above in* 0*, then it is also continuous from below in* 1.

Proof. Suppose that π is continuous from above in 0 and take an arbitrary sequence $(Y_n)_{n \in \mathbb{N}}$ such that $Y_n \nearrow 1$. Then $0 \geq \pi(Y_n) - 1 = \pi(Y_n - 1) = \pi(-(1 - Y_n)) \geq -\pi(1 - Y_n)$, where the last inequality is due to convexity and $\pi(0) = 0$. From $1 - Y_n \searrow 0$ and continuity from above of π in 0 it follows that $\pi(1 - Y_n) \to 0$ as $n \to +\infty$, hence the thesis. $\square$

Under the additional hypothesis of positive homogeneity on π a result similar to the previous one (formulated for risk measures) can be found in Delbaen [8].

It is easy to check that if π is monotone, subadditive and continuous from above in 0, then it is also continuous from above (see Delbaen [8]). Take indeed a sequence $(X_n)_{n\geq 0}$ such that $X_n \searrow X$. Then

$$\pi(X) \leq \pi(X_n) = \pi(X_n - X + X) \leq \pi(X_n - X) + \pi(X) \to \pi(X),$$

hence $\pi(X_n) \to \pi(X)$ as $n \to +\infty$.

In the following example, we show that when convexity (or sublinearity) is weakened by comonotone convexity (in particular: comonotone additivity): (i) continuity from above in 0 does not imply continuity from below in 1; (ii) continuity from above in 0 does not imply continuity from above even if π is monotone, comonotone subadditive and positively homogeneous; (iii) in an atomless space: law invariance is no more sufficient to guarantee continuity from below in 1.

Example 3.2 (ca0 and law invariant but neither cb1 nor ca). Consider

$$f(x) = \begin{cases} \dfrac{x^2}{2}; & \text{if } 0 \leq x \leq \frac{1}{2} \\ \dfrac{x}{2}; & \text{if } \dfrac{1}{2} < x < 1 \\ 1; & \text{if } x = 1 \end{cases}.$$

Take $([0,1), \mathcal{B}[0,1), Lebesgue[0,1))$ as an atomless probability space and set $\pi(X) = E_{(f\circ P)}[X]$ for any $X \in L^\infty_{\mathcal{F}}$.

Hence $\mu = f \circ P$ is a monotone, normalized set function and $\mu \ll P$, so π satisfies law invariance, monotonicity, positive homogeneity, comonotone additivity and cash additivity. Moreover, it is easy to check that continuity of f in 0 implies continuity from above in 0 of μ. Hence, by Lemma 3.1, π is continuous from above in 0.

- *π is not continuous from below in* 1

For any $n \in \mathbb{N}$, $n \geq 2$, take now $A_n = [0; 1 - \frac{1}{n}]$ and $Y_n = 1_{A_n}$. Hence, $A_n \nearrow \Omega$ and $Y_n \nearrow 1$. It is immediate to check that $\pi(1) = 1$. Nevertheless, for any $n > 2$ one gets $\pi(Y_n) = \frac{1}{2} - \frac{1}{2n} \to \frac{1}{2} \neq \pi(1)$.

The motivation why π is continuous from above in 0 but not continuous from below in 1 is essentially that it is not subadditive. By taking $A = [0, \frac{1}{4})$ and $B = [\frac{1}{2}, 1)$, it is easy to check that μ is not submodular and, therefore, π is not subadditive.

- *π is not continuous from above*

For any $n \in \mathbb{N}$, $n \geq 1$, take now $B_n = [0; \frac{1}{2} + \frac{1}{4n}]$ and $X_n = 1_{B_n}$. Hence, $B_n \searrow B = [0, \frac{1}{2}]$ and $X_n \searrow 1_B$. Nevertheless, for any $n \geq 1$ one gets $\pi(X_n) = \frac{1}{4} + \frac{1}{8n} \to \frac{1}{4}$, while $\pi(1_B) = \frac{1}{8}$. It is also clear that the distorted probability $\mu = f \circ P$ is continuous from above in 0 but not continuous from above.

The following counterexample is not surprising since cb1 $\nRightarrow$ ca0 even for π induced by a coherent risk measure.

Example 3.3 (cb1 but not ca0). Take an increasing continuous function $f_0 : (0,1] \to (0,1]$ such that $f_0(0^+) = \lim_{x \searrow 0} f_0(x) > 0$ and $f_0(1) = 1$ and consider

$$f(x) = \begin{cases} 0; & \text{if } x = 0 \\ f_0(x); & \text{if } 0 < x \leq 1 \end{cases}.$$

Take $((0,1], \mathcal{B}(0,1], Lebesgue(0,1])$ as a probability space and set $\pi(X) = E_{(f \circ P)}[X]$ for any $X \in L^\infty_{\mathcal{F}}$.

As in Example 3.2, π satisfies law invariance, monotonicity, positive homogeneity, comonotone additivity, cash additivity and $\pi(0) = 0$. Moreover, it is easy to check that continuity of f in 1 implies continuity from below in 1 of $\mu = f \circ P$. Hence, by Lemma 3.1, π is continuous from below in 1.

For any $n \in \mathbb{N}$, $n \geq 1$, take now $B_n = (0; \frac{1}{n}]$ and $X_n = 1_{B_n}$. Hence, $B_n \searrow \emptyset$ and $X_n \searrow 0$. Nevertheless, for any $n \geq 1$ one gets $\pi(X_n) = f_0(\frac{1}{n}) \to f_0(0^+) > \pi(0)$.

3.2.2. *Order lower semi-continuity and continuity from below/above*

We focus now on the relationship between order lower semi-continuity (order lsc, for short) and continuity from below. It is well known that on $L^\infty_{\mathcal{F}}$ order lower semi-continuity and continuity from below are equivalent for functionals π induced by convex risk measures (see Föllmer and Schied [13], among many others) and, more in general, for functionals π satisfying monotonicity (see Lemma 15 of Biagini and Frittelli [4]).

In particular, by the arguments above for any $\pi : L^\infty_{\mathcal{F}} \to \mathbb{R}$ satisfying monotonicity:

$$\text{order lsc} \Leftrightarrow \text{continuous from below} \Rightarrow \text{continuity from below in 1.}$$

The counterexample below shows that for π satisfying monotonicity, comonotone convexity, cash additivity and $\pi(0) = 0$:

$$\text{continuity from below in 1} \nRightarrow \text{order lsc}$$

$$\text{continuity from above} \nRightarrow \text{order lsc}$$

even if we remember that the last implication is true at least when π is convex.

It is also well known that (even for π induced by coherent risk measures): cb $\nRightarrow$ ca. Hence: order lsc $\nRightarrow$ ca.

Example 3.4 (cb1 and ca but not order lsc). Take $x_0 \in (0,1)$, an increasing continuous function $f_1 : [x_0, 1] \to (0,1]$ such that $f_1(x_0) > x_0$ and $f_1(1) = 1$ and consider

$$f(x) = \begin{cases} x; & \text{if } 0 \leq x < x_0 \\ f_1(x); & \text{if } x_0 \leq x \leq 1 \end{cases}.$$

Take $([0,1], \mathcal{B}[0,1], \textit{Lebesgue}\,[0,1])$ as a probability space and set $\pi(X) = E_{(f\circ P)}[X]$ for any $X \in L^\infty_{\mathcal{F}}$.

As usual, π satisfies law invariance, monotonicity, positive homogeneity, comonotone additivity, cash additivity and $\pi(0) = 0$. Moreover, it is easy to check that π is continuous from below in 1 and continuous from above.

For any $n \in \mathbb{N}$, $n \geq [1/x_0] + 1$, set $A_n = [0; x_0 - \frac{1}{n}]$ and $Y_n = 1_{A_n}$. Hence, $A_n \nearrow [0; x_0) = A$ and $Y_n \nearrow 1_A$. π is not order lower semi-continuous, indeed for any $n \geq [1/x_0] + 1$ it is easy to check that $\pi(Y_n) = \int_0^1 f(x_0 - \frac{1}{n})dx = x_0 - \frac{1}{n} \to x_0$, while $\pi(1_A) = \int_0^1 f(x_0)dx = f_1(x_0) > x_0 = \liminf_{n\to+\infty} \pi(Y_n)$.

Example 3.2 (together with the results recalled above on order lsc) shows also that, for a monotone, cash additive, comonotone convex functional π with $\pi(0) = 0$ and in an atomless space, law invariance does not imply order lower semi-continuity.

3.3. *A sufficient condition for continuity*

Let $\mathcal{X}$ be a Frechet lattice. Biagini and Frittelli [4] proved that any proper convex and monotone $\pi : \mathcal{X} \to (-\infty, +\infty]$ is continuous on the interior of the domain of π (Extended Namioka-Klee Theorem — Theorem 1 in [4]). It is easy to check (see Lemma 1, [4]) that if $\pi : \mathcal{X} \to (-\infty, +\infty]$ is convex and satisfies $\pi(0) = 0$ then

$$n|\pi(X)| \leq \pi(n|X|), \quad \forall n \geq 1, \quad \forall X \in \mathcal{X}. \tag{3.14}$$

Notice that (3.14) alone implies $\pi(0) = 0$. Moreover, we observe that, in the proof of the mentioned Extended Namioka-Klee Theorem, only the properties

$$|\pi(X)| \leq \frac{1}{n}\pi(n|X|), \quad \forall X \in \mathcal{X} \text{ and for all large } n \tag{3.15}$$

and monotonicity are used to prove the continuity in 0 of π. As stated before, (3.15) is satisfied by convex maps null in 0, but may be satisfied by functionals that are not convex. We therefore obtain a sufficient criterium for continuity:

Lemma 3.3. *Let $\mathcal{X}$ be a Frechet lattice and $\pi : \mathcal{X} \to \mathbb{R}$ be a monotone real-valued functional. If π satisfies* (3.15) *then it is continuous in* 0.

As the following example illustrates, monotone and quasiconvex functional $\pi : L^\infty_{\mathcal{F}} \to \mathbb{R}$ may not be continuous in 0.

Example 3.5. Let $\mathcal{X} = (L^\infty_{\mathcal{F}}, \|\cdot\|_\infty)$ and consider a strictly increasing function $\nu : \mathbb{R} \to \mathbb{R}$ satisfying $\nu(0) = 0$. Then the functional $\pi : L^\infty_{\mathcal{F}} \to \mathbb{R}$

$$\pi(X) \triangleq \nu(E[X])$$

is increasing, satisfies $\pi(0) = 0$ and is quasiconvex. In this case, (3.15) reduces to:

$$|\nu(E[X])| \leq \frac{1}{n}\nu(nE[|X|]), \quad \forall X \in \mathcal{X} \text{ and for all large } n. \tag{3.16}$$

If ν does not grow too fast (i.e. if $\frac{\nu(|x|)}{|x|} \leq k \in \mathbb{R}_+$ for large x) then $0 \leq \frac{1}{n}\nu(nE[|X|]) \leq kE[|X|]$ and $\frac{1}{n}\nu(nE[|X|])$ is small if $E[|X|]$ is small. On the other hand, if ν is left discontinuous at 0 (i.e. $\nu(0^-) \triangleq \lim_{x\uparrow 0}\nu(x) < \nu(0) = 0$), then $|\nu(E[X])| \geq |\nu(0^-)|$ for all $E[X] < 0$ and therefore property (3.16) is not satisfied. Clearly the discontinuity of ν implies that π is not norm continuous in 0.

References

[1] C. D. Aliprantis and K. C. Border, *Infinite Dimensional Analysis*, 2nd edition (Springer, 1999).

[2] F. Bellini and M. Frittelli, Certainty equivalent and no arbitrage: a reconciliation via duality theory, Technical Report # 139, Dept. "Metodi Quantitativi", University of Brescia (1998).

[3] F. Bellini and M. Frittelli, On the existence of minimax martingale measures, *Mathematical Finance* **12** (2002) 1–21.

[4] S. Biagini and M. Frittelli, On the extension of the Namioka-Klee theorem and on the Fatou property for risk measures, in *Optimality and Risk: Modern Trends in Mathematical Finance, The Kabanov Festschrift*, F. Delbaen, M. Rasonyi, Ch. Stricker eds. (2009), pp. 1–28.

[5] S. Cerreia-Vioglio, F. Maccheroni, M. Marinacci and L. Montrucchio, Risk measures: rationality and diversification, Forthcoming in *Math. Fin.* (2009).

[6] G. Choquet, Theory of capacities, *Annales de l'Institut Fourier* (Grenoble) **5** (1953) 131–295.

[7] R. A. Dana, A representation result for concave Schur concave functions, *Mathematical Finance* **15** (2005) 613–634.

[8] F. Delbaen, Coherent risk measures, Lecture notes, Scuola Normale Superiore, Pisa, Italy (2000).

[9] F. Delbaen, Coherent Risk Measures on General Probability Spaces, in *Advances in Finance and Stochastics*, K. Sandmann and P. J. Schönbucher eds. (Springer-Verlag, 2002), pp. 1–37.

[10] D. Denneberg, *Non-Additive Measure and Integral* (Kluwer Academic Publishers, 1994).

[11] H. Föllmer and A. Schied, Convex measures of risk and trading constraints, *Finance & Stochastics* **6** (2002a) 429–447.

[12] H. Föllmer and A. Schied, Robust preferences and convex measures of risk, in *Advances in Finance and Stochastics*, K. Sandmann and P. J. Schönbucher eds. (Springer-Verlag, 2002), pp. 39–56.

[13] H. Föllmer and A. Schied, *Stochastic Finance. An Introduction in Discrete Time*, 2nd Ed. (De Gruyter, Berlin, New York, 2004).

[14] M. Frittelli, The minimal entropy martingale measure and the valuation problem in incomplete markets, *Mathematical Finance* **10** (2000) 39–52.

[15] M. Frittelli, Representing sublinear risk measures and pricing rules, Working paper no. 10 (2000), Università di Milano Bicocca, Italy.

[16] M. Frittelli and M. Maggis, Dual representation of quasiconvex conditional maps, Preprint (2009): arXiv:1001.3644.

[17] M. Frittelli and M. Maggis, Conditional certainty equivalent, *International Journal of Theoretical and Applied Finance* **14**(1) (2011).

[18] M. Frittelli and E. Rosazza Gianin, Putting order in risk measures, *Journal of Banking & Finance* **26** (2002) 1473–1486.

[19] C. C. Heyde, S. G. Kou and X. H. Peng, What is a good risk measure: bridging the gaps between data, coherent risk measure and insurance risk measure, preprint (2006).

[20] E. Jouini, W. Schachermayer and N. Touzi, Law invariant risk measures have the Fatou property, in *Advances in Mathematical Economics*, S. Kusuoka and A. Yamazaki, eds. (2006) 49–71.

[21] R. Kaas, A. E. van Heerwaaden and M. J. Goovaerts, *Ordering of Actuarial Risks*, Education Series 1 (CAIRE, Brussels, 1994).

[22] S. Klöppel and M. Schweizer, Dynamic utility indifference valuation via convex risk measures, Working Paper FINRISK no. 209, ETH Zürich (2005).

[23] M. Kunze, Verteilungsinvariante konvexe Risikomaße, Diplomarbeit, Humboldt-Universität, Berlin (2003).

[24] S. Kusuoka, On law invariant coherent risk measures. In: Kusuoka, S., Maruyama, T. (eds.), *Advances in Mathematical Economics* **3** (2001) 83–95.

[25] Y. Song and J.-A. Yan, The representations of two types of functionals on $L^\infty(\Omega, \mathcal{F})$ and $L^\infty(\Omega, \mathcal{F}, P)$, *Science in China: Series A Mathematics* **49** (2006) 1376–1382.

[26] Y. Song and J.-A. Yan, Risk measures with comonotonic subaddivity or convexity and respecting stochastic orders, *Insurance: Mathematics and Economics* **45** (2009) 459–465.

[27] Y. Song and J.-A. Yan, An overview of representation theorems for static risk measures, *Science in China: Series A Mathematics* **52** (2009) 1412–1422.

[28] M. Volle, Duality for the level sum of quasiconvex functions and applications, *Control, Optimisation and Calculus of Variations* **3** (1998) 329–343.

[29] S. S. Wang, V. R. Young and H. H. Panjer, Axiomatic characterization of insurance prices, *Insurance: Mathematics and Economics* **21** (1997) 173–183.

[30] S. S. Wang, A class of distortion operators for pricing financial and insurance risks, *The Journal of Risk and Insurance* **67** (2000) 15–36.

CONDITIONAL CERTAINTY EQUIVALENT*

MARCO FRITTELLI and MARCO MAGGIS
Department of Mathematics, University of Milan
via C. Saldini 50 Milan, 20134, Italy

In a dynamic framework, we study the conditional version of the classical notion of certainty equivalent when the preferences are described by a stochastic dynamic utility $u(x, t, \omega)$. We introduce an appropriate mathematical setting, namely Orlicz spaces determined by the underlying preferences and thus provide a systematic method to go beyond the case of bounded random variables. Finally we prove a conditional version of the dual representation which is a crucial prerequisite for discussing the dynamics of certainty equivalents.

Keywords: Stochastic dynamic utility; conditional certainty equivalent; Musielak-Orlicz spaces; quasiconcavity; dual representation.

1. Introduction

In the last decade many methodologies for pricing in incomplete markets were built on expected utility maximization with respect to terminal wealth: classic examples of this approach are the notions of fair price [8], certainty equivalent [14] and indifference price [4, 9, 16].

These techniques were developed both in a static framework and in a dynamic context [10]. In the dynamic case however, the utility function represents preferences at a fixed time T, while the pricing occurs at any time between today and the expiration T (backward pricing). The martingale property of the indirect utility (the value function of the optimization problem [11]) is an automatic consequence of the dynamic programming principle.

This classic backward approach has recently been argued in [3, 15, 22, 23] and a novel forward theory has been proposed: the utility function is stochastic, time dependent and moves forward.

In this theory, the forward utility (which replaces the indirect utility of the classic case) is built through the underlying financial market and must satisfy some appropriate martingale conditions.

*This chapter was originally published under the same title in *International Journal of Theoretical and Applied Finance*, Vol.14, No.1, 41–59 (2011). Singapore: World Scientific Publishing.

Our research is inspired by the theory just mentioned, but a different approach is here developed: our preliminary object will be a stochastic dynamic utility $u(x,t,\omega)$ — i.e. a stochastic field [19] — representing the evolution of the preferences of the agent (see Definition 1.1).

The definition of the Conditional Certainty Equivalent (CCE) that we propose and analyze in this paper (Definition 1.6), is the natural generalization to the dynamic and stochastic environment of the classical notion of the certainty equivalent, as given in [25]. The CCE, denoted by $C_{s,t}(\cdot)$, provides the time s value of an F_t measurable claim ($s \leq t$) in terms only of the Stochastic Dynamic Utility (SDU) and the filtration.

The SDU that we consider does not require *a priori* the presence of a financial market; neither it will have any specific recursive structure, nor will necessarily be an indirect utility function based on optimal trading in the market. However, as studied in Sec. 1.1, appropriate conditions are required on the SDU in order to deduce interesting properties for the CCE.

The next step, which is left for future research, would be the investigation of the compatibility conditions between the value assigned by the CCE and existing prices when an underlying market indeed exists. Clearly, not all SDU are compatible with the market. One extreme case is when the SDU can be determined by the market and the initial preferences structure, as in the case of the forward utility theory.

The second part of the paper is devoted to the dual representation of the CCE, considered as a monotone and quasiconcave operator between vector lattices (see Sec. 3). Recently, the dual representation of such operators has been obtained in [13]. Due to the particular form of the CCE, we are able to provide here a direct proof which is also less demanding than the general one.

However, in order to show the dual representation of the CCE we must first define it on appropriate vector lattices. A common approach is to restrict the view to bounded random variables, so that no further integrability conditions are requested. But as soon as we try to extend the scenario to unbounded random variables it immediately appears that the distortion provoked by utility function can be mastered only in *ad hoc* frameworks.

To this end we introduce in Sec. 2, in the spirit of [5], a generalized class of Orlicz spaces which are naturally associated to the SDU taken into account. We show (Sec. 2.3) with some examples that these spaces also play a fundamental role for time compatibility of the CCE, since $C_{s,t} : M^{\widehat{u}_t} \to M^{\widehat{u}_s}$, where $M^{\widehat{u}_t}$ is the generalized Orlicz space of $\mathcal{F}_t$ measurable random variables associated to the SDU $u(x,t,\omega)$.

1.1. *Definitions and first properties*

A non-atomic probability space $(\Omega, \mathcal{F}, \mathbb{P})$ and a right continuous filtration $\{\mathcal{F}_t\}_{t\geq 0}$ are fixed throughout this paper. As usual we denote with $L^0(\Omega, \mathcal{F}, \mathbb{P})$ the space of $\mathcal{F}$ measurable random variables that are $\mathbb{P}$ almost surely finite and with $\bar{L}^0(\Omega, \mathcal{F}, \mathbb{P})$

the space of extended r.v. which take values in $\mathbb{R} \cup \{\infty\}$. The $L^p(\Omega, \mathcal{F}, \mathbb{P})$ spaces, $p \in [0, \infty]$, will simply be denoted by L^p, unless it is necessary to specify the sigma algebra, in which case we write $L^p_{\mathcal{F}}$. All equalities and inequalities are intended to be $\mathbb{P}$ almost surely: by $X > Y$ we mean that $\mathbb{P}(X > Y) = 1$. Otherwise, for any $\mathbb{Q} \ll \mathbb{P}$ we explicitly write $X >_{\mathbb{Q}} Y$. Moreover the essential ($\mathbb{P}$ a.s.) *supremum* $ess\sup(X_\lambda)$ of a family of random variables X_λ will be simply denoted by $\sup(X_\lambda)$, and similarly for the essential *infimum* (see [12] Sec. A.5 for reference). Hereafter the symbol $\hookrightarrow$ denotes inclusion and lattice embedding between two lattices, and $\vee$ (resp. $\wedge$) the essential ($\mathbb{P}$ a.s.) *maximum* (resp. the essential *minimum*) between two random variables, which are the usual lattice operations.

Definition 1.1. A stochastic dynamic utility (SDU)

$$u : \mathbb{R} \times [0, \infty) \times \Omega \to \mathbb{R} \cup \{-\infty\}$$

satisfies the following conditions: for any $t \in [0, +\infty)$ there exists $A_t \in \mathcal{F}_t$ such that $\mathbb{P}(A_t) = 1$ and

(a) the effective domain, $\mathcal{D}(t) := \{x \in \mathbb{R} : u(x, t, \omega) > -\infty\}$ and the range $\mathcal{R}(t) := \{u(x, t, \omega) \mid x \in \mathcal{D}(t)\}$ do not depend on $\omega \in A_t$; moreover $0 \in int\mathcal{D}(t)$, $E[u(0, t)] < +\infty$ and $\mathcal{R}(t) \subseteq \mathcal{R}(s)$;
(b) for all $\omega \in A_t$ and $t \in [0, +\infty)$ the function $x \to u(x, t, \omega)$ is strictly increasing on $\mathcal{D}(t)$ and increasing, concave and upper semicontinuous on $\mathbb{R}$.
(c) $\omega \to u(x, t, \cdot)$ is $\mathcal{F}_t$-measurable for all $(x, t) \in \mathcal{D}(t) \times [0, +\infty)$

The following assumption may turn out to be relevant in the sequel of the paper, even if not necessary for the definition of SDU.

(d) For any fixed $x \in \mathcal{D}(t)$, $u(x, t, \cdot) \leq u(x, s, \cdot)$ for every $s \leq t$.

Remark 1.1. We identify two SDU, $u \sim \widetilde{u}$, if for every $t \in [0, +\infty)$, the two domains are equal ($\mathcal{D}(t) = \widetilde{\mathcal{D}}(t)$) and there exists an $\mathcal{F}_t$-measurable set B_t such that $\mathbb{P}(B_t) = 1$ and $u(x, t, \omega) = \widetilde{u}(x, t, \omega)$ for every $(x, \omega) \in \mathcal{D}(t) \times B_t$.

In the sequel, we denote $u(x, t, \cdot)$ simply by $u(x, t)$, unless confusion may arise.

In order to define the conditional certainty equivalent we introduce the set

$$\mathcal{U}(t) = \{X \in L^0(\Omega, \mathcal{F}_t, \mathbb{P}) \mid u(X, t) \in L^1(\Omega, \mathcal{F}, \mathbb{P})\}.$$

Lemma 1.1. *Let u be a SDU.*

(i) (*Inverse*) *Let $t \in [0, \infty)$ and $A_t \in \mathcal{F}_t$ as in Definition* 1.1: *the inverse function $u^{-1} : \mathcal{R}(t) \times [0, \infty) \times A_t \to \mathcal{D}(t)$*

$$u^{-1}(u(x, t, \omega), t, \omega) = x \tag{1.1}$$

is well defined. For each $\omega \in A_t$, the function $u^{-1}(\cdot, t, \omega)$ is continuous and strictly increasing on $\mathcal{R}(t)$ and $u^{-1}(y, t, \cdot)$ is $\mathcal{F}_t$-measurable for all $y \in \mathcal{R}(t)$.

(ii) (*Comparison*) *Fix any* $t \in [0, \infty)$; *if* $X, Y \in \mathcal{U}(t)$ *then* $u(X,t) \leq u(Y,t)$ *if and only if* $X \leq Y$. *The same holds if the inequalities are replaced by equalities.*

(iii) (*Jensen*) *If* $X \in L^1_{\mathcal{F}_t}$ *and* $u(X,s)$ *is integrable, then, for all* $s \leq t$,

$$E\left[u(X,s) \,|\, \mathcal{F}_s\right] \leq u(E[X \,|\, \mathcal{F}_s], s).$$

(iv) (*Extended Jensen*) *Suppose* $u(x,s)$ *is integrable for every* $x \in \mathcal{D}(s)$. *Let* $X \in L^0_{\mathcal{F}_t}$, *such that* $u(X,s)^-$ *is integrable. Then*

$$E\left[u(X,s) \,|\, \mathcal{F}_s\right] \leq u(E[X \,|\, \mathcal{F}_s], s). \tag{1.2}$$

where the conditional expectation is meant in an extended way.

Proof. (i) Since both assumptions (a) and (b) hold on A_t, the existence of a continuous, increasing inverse function follows straightforwardly. From assumption (c) we can deduce that $u^{-1}(y,t,\cdot)$ is $\mathcal{F}_t$-measurable for all $y \in \mathcal{R}(t)$.
(ii) Is also immediate since u is strictly increasing as a function of x.
(iii) This property follows from the Theorem p.79 in [21].
(iv) First we suppose that $u(0,s) = 0$. This implies that $u(X,s)\mathbf{1}_A = u(X\mathbf{1}_A, s)$ for every $A \in \mathcal{F}_t$. Recall that if $Y \in L^0_{\mathcal{F}_t}$ and $Y \geq 0$ then $E[Y \,|\, \mathcal{F}_s] := \lim_n E[Y\mathbf{1}_{Y \leq n} \,|\, \mathcal{F}_s]$ is well defined.

First we show that $u(X,s)^-$ integrable implies $E[X\mathbf{1}_{\{X<0\}} \,|\, \mathcal{F}_s] > -\infty$ and therefore both terms in (1.2) are well defined. From the equality $-u(X,s)\mathbf{1}_{\{X<0\}} = u(X,s)^-$ we get that $u(X,s)\mathbf{1}_{\{X<0\}}$ is integrable. From (iii) we have that $u(0,s) \geq u(X\mathbf{1}_{\{0>X\geq -n\}}, s) \geq u(-n,s)$ implies:

$$E[u(X\mathbf{1}_{\{0>X\geq -n\}}, s) \,|\, \mathcal{F}_s] \leq u(E[X\mathbf{1}_{\{0>X\geq -n\}} \,|\, \mathcal{F}_s], s). \tag{1.3}$$

By monotone convergence, from (1.3) we then get our claim:

$$-\infty < E[u(X\mathbf{1}_{\{X<0\}}, s) \,|\, \mathcal{F}_s] \leq u(E[X\mathbf{1}_{\{X<0\}} \,|\, \mathcal{F}_s], s).$$

Applying (iii) in the second inequality below we get:

$$\begin{aligned} E[u(X,s) \,|\, \mathcal{F}_s] &= \lim_n E[u(X,s)\mathbf{1}_{\{0\leq u(X,s)\leq n\}} \,|\, \mathcal{F}_s] + E[u(X,s)\mathbf{1}_{\{u(X,s)<0\}} \,|\, \mathcal{F}_s] \quad (1.4)\\ &\leq \lim_n E[u(X,s)\mathbf{1}_{\{0\leq X\leq n\}} \,|\, \mathcal{F}_s] = \lim_n E[u(X\mathbf{1}_{\{0\leq X\leq n\}}, s) \,|\, \mathcal{F}_s]\\ &\leq \lim_n u(E[X\mathbf{1}_{\{0\leq X\leq n\}} \,|\, \mathcal{F}_s], s) = u(E[X^+ \,|\, \mathcal{F}_s], s). \quad (1.5) \end{aligned}$$

Notice that on the $\mathcal{F}_s$-measurable set $G^\infty := \{E[X \,|\, \mathcal{F}_s] = +\infty\}$ the equation (1.2) is trivial. Since $E[-X^- \,|\, \mathcal{F}_s] > -\infty$, it is clear that $E[|X| \,|\, \mathcal{F}_s] = +\infty$ on a set $A \in \mathcal{F}$ iff $E[X \,|\, \mathcal{F}_s] = +\infty$ on the same set A. Therefore, by defining $G_n := \{\omega \in \Omega \backslash G^\infty \,|\, E[|X| \,|\, \mathcal{F}_s](\omega) \leq n\}$, we have: $G_n \uparrow \Omega \backslash G^\infty$. Since each G_n is $\mathcal{F}_s$-measurable, the inequality (1.4)–(1.5) guarantees that

$$-E[u(X\mathbf{1}_{G_n},s)^- \,|\, \mathcal{F}_s] \le E[u(X\mathbf{1}_{G_n},s) \,|\, \mathcal{F}_s] \le u(E[X^+\mathbf{1}_{G_n} \,|\, \mathcal{F}_s],s)$$
$$\le u(E[\,|\,X\,|\,|\mathcal{F}_s],s)\mathbf{1}_{G_n} \le u(n,s)$$

and therefore $u(X\mathbf{1}_{G_n},s)$ is integrable. Obviously, $X\mathbf{1}_{G_n}$ is also integrable and we may apply (iii) (replacing X with $X\mathbf{1}_{G_n}$) and deduce

$$E[u(X,s) \,|\, \mathcal{F}_s]\mathbf{1}_{G_n} = E[u(X\mathbf{1}_{G_n},s) \,|\, \mathcal{F}_s] \le u(E[X\mathbf{1}_{G_n} \,|\, \mathcal{F}_s],s) = u(E[X \,|\, \mathcal{F}_s],s)\mathbf{1}_{G_n}.$$

The thesis follows immediately by taking the limit as $n \to \infty$, since $G_n \uparrow \Omega \backslash G^\infty$.

For a general $u(x,s)$, apply the above argument to $v(x,s) =: u(x,s) - u(0,s)$. □

A SDU allows us to define the backward conditional certainty equivalent, that represents the time-s-value of the time-t-claim X, for $0 \le s \le t < \infty$.

Definition 1.2 (Conditional Certainty Equivalent). Let u be a SDU. The backward Conditional Certainty Equivalent $C_{s,t}(X)$ of the random variable $X \in \mathcal{U}(t)$, is the random variable in $\mathcal{U}(s)$ solution of the equation:

$$u(C_{s,t}(X),s) = E\left[u(X,t) \,|\, \mathcal{F}_s\right]. \tag{1.6}$$

Thus the CCE defines the *valuation* operator

$$C_{s,t} : \mathcal{U}(t) \to \mathcal{U}(s), \quad C_{s,t}(X) = u^{-1}\left(E\left[u(X,t) \,|\, \mathcal{F}_s\right]\right), s). \tag{1.7}$$

Observe that $E\left[u(C_{s,t}(X),s)\right] = E[u(X,t)]$ and so indeed $C_{s,t}(X) \in \mathcal{U}(s)$.

The definition is well posed:

(1) For any given $X \in \mathcal{U}(t)$, $E\left[u(X,t) \,|\, \mathcal{F}_s\right] \in L^1(\Omega,\mathcal{F}_s,P)$.
(2) Choose two arbitrary versions of the conditional expectation and of the SDU at time s, namely $\widetilde{E}\left[u(X,t) \,|\, \mathcal{F}_s\right]$, $\widehat{E}\left[u(X,t) \,|\, \mathcal{F}_s\right]$ and $\widetilde{u}(x,s)$, $\widehat{u}(x,s)$.
(3) For all $\omega \in A_t$, $\widetilde{E}\left[u(X,t) \,|\, \mathcal{F}_s\right](\omega) \in \mathcal{R}(t) \subseteq \mathcal{R}(s)$. We find a unique solution of $\widetilde{u}(\widetilde{C}_{s,t}(X),s) = \widetilde{E}\left[u(X,t) \,|\, \mathcal{F}_s\right]$ defined as
$$\widetilde{C}_{s,t}(X)(\omega) = \widetilde{u}^{-1}(\widetilde{E}\left[u(X,t)| \,|\, \mathcal{F}_s\right](\omega),s,\omega) \quad \forall \omega \in A_t.$$
(4) Repeat the previous argument for the second version and find $\widehat{C}_{s,t}(X)$ which differs from $\widetilde{C}_{s,t}(X)$ only on a $\mathbb{P}$-null set.

We could equivalently reformulate the definition of the CCE as follows:

Definition 1.3. The conditional certainty equivalent process is the only process $\{Y_s\}_{0\le s\le t}$ such that $Y_t \equiv X$ and the process $\{u(Y_s,s)\}_{0\le s\le t}$ is a martingale.

In the following proposition we show some elementary properties of the CCE, which have however very convenient interpretations. In (i) we show the semigroup property of the valuation operator; (iii) show the time consistency of the CCE: if the time-v-values of two time t claims are equal, then the two values should be equal at any previous time; (iv) and (v) are the key properties to obtain a dual representation of the map $C_{s,t}$ as shown in [13]; property (vi) shows that the expectation of the valuation operator is increasing, as a function of the *valuation time* s and the second issue expresses the risk aversion of the economic agent.

Proposition 1.1. *Let u be a SDU, $0 \le s \le v \le t < \infty$ and $X, Y \in \mathcal{U}(t)$.*

(i) $C_{s,t}(X) = C_{s,v}(C_{v,t}(X))$.
(ii) $C_{t,t}(X) = X$.
(iii) *If $C_{v,t}(X) \le C_{v,t}(Y)$ then for all $0 \le s \le v$ we have: $C_{s,t}(X) \le C_{s,t}(Y)$. Therefore, $X \le Y$ implies that for all $0 \le s \le t$ we have: $C_{s,t}(X) \le C_{s,t}(Y)$. The same holds if the inequalities are replaced by equalities.*
(iv) *Regularity: for every $A \in F_s$ we have*

$$C_{s,t}(X\mathbf{1}_A + Y\mathbf{1}_{A^C}) = C_{s,t}(X)\mathbf{1}_A + C_{s,t}(Y)\mathbf{1}_{A^C}$$

and then $C_{s,t}(X)\mathbf{1}_A = C_{s,t}(X\mathbf{1}_A)\mathbf{1}_A$.
(v) *Quasiconcavity: the upper level set $\{X \in \mathcal{U}_t \mid C_{s,t}(X) \ge Y\}$ is conditionally convex for every $Y \in L^0_{\mathcal{F}_s}$.*
(vi) *Suppose u satisfies (d) and for every $t \in [0, +\infty)$, $u(x,t)$ is integrable for every $x \in \mathcal{D}(t)$. Then $C_{s,t}(X) \le E[C_{v,t}(X) \mid \mathcal{F}_s]$ and $E[C_{s,t}(X)] \le E[C_{v,t}(X)]$. Moreover $C_{s,t}(X) \le E[X \mid \mathcal{F}_s]$ and therefore $E[C_{s,t}(X)] \le E[X]$.*

Proof. By definition:

$$u(C_{v,t}(X), v) \overset{(\cdot)}{=} E[u(X,t) \mid \mathcal{F}_v], \quad X \in \mathcal{U}(t)$$

$$u(C_{s,t}(X), s) \overset{(+)}{=} E[u(X,t) \mid \mathcal{F}_s], \quad X \in \mathcal{U}(t)$$

$$u(C_{s,v}(Z), s) \overset{(\times)}{=} E[u(Z,v) \mid \mathcal{F}_s], \quad Z \in \mathcal{U}(v)$$

(i) Let $Z = C_{v,t}(X)$ and compute:

$$u(C_{s,v}(C_{v,t}(X)), s) = u(C_{s,v}(Z), s) \overset{(\times)}{=} E[u(Z,v) \mid \mathcal{F}_s]$$

$$\overset{(\cdot)}{=} E[E[u(X,t) \mid \mathcal{F}_v] \mid \mathcal{F}_s] = E[u(X,t) \mid \mathcal{F}_s] \overset{(+)}{=} u(C_{s,t}(X), s)$$

(ii) Obvious, since $u(C_{t,t}(X), t) \overset{(\cdot)}{=} E[u(X,t) \mid \mathcal{F}_t] \overset{(c)}{=} u(X,t)$.
(iii)

$$u(C_{s,t}(X), s) \overset{(+)}{=} E[u(X,t) \mid \mathcal{F}_s] = E[E[u(X,t) \mid \mathcal{F}_v] \mid \mathcal{F}_s]$$

$$\overset{(\cdot)}{=} E[u(C_{v,t}(X), v) \mid \mathcal{F}_s] \le E[u(C_{v,t}(Y), v) \mid \mathcal{F}_s]$$

$$\overset{(\cdot)}{=} E[E[u(Y,t) \mid \mathcal{F}_v] \mid \mathcal{F}_s] \overset{(+)}{=} u(C_{s,t}(Y), s).$$

If $X \le Y$ then $C_{t,t}(X) \le C_{t,t}(Y)$ and the statement follows from what we just proved. The same for equalities.

(iv) Consider every $A \in \mathcal{F}_s$ and notice that

$$\begin{aligned} C_{s,t}(X\mathbf{1}_A + Y\mathbf{1}_{A^C}) &= u^{-1}\left(E[u(X,t)\mathbf{1}_A + u(Y,t)\mathbf{1}_{A^C} \,|\, \mathcal{F}_s], s\right) \\ &= u^{-1}(E[u(X,t) \,|\, \mathcal{F}_s]\mathbf{1}_A, s) + u^{-1}(E[u(Y,t) \,|\, \mathcal{F}_s]\mathbf{1}_{A^C}, s) \\ &= C_{s,t}(X)\mathbf{1}_A + C_{s,t}(Y)\mathbf{1}_{A^C} \end{aligned}$$

(v) Fix an arbitrary $Y \in L^0_{\mathcal{F}_s}$ and consider the set $\mathcal{Y} = \{X \in \mathcal{U}_t \,|\, C_{s,t}(X) \geq Y\}$. Take $X_1, X_2 \in \mathcal{Y}$ and $\Lambda \in L^0_{\mathcal{F}_s}$, $0 \leq \Lambda \leq 1$:

$$\begin{aligned} &E[u(\Lambda X_1 + (1-\Lambda)X_2, t) \,|\, \mathcal{F}_s] \\ &\quad \geq \Lambda E[u(X_1,t) \,|\, \mathcal{F}_s] + (1-\Lambda)E[u(X_2,t) \,|\, \mathcal{F}_s] \geq u(Y,s) \end{aligned}$$

hence we get the thesis composing both sides with $u^{-1}(\cdot, s)$.

(vi)

$$\begin{aligned} u(C_{s,t}(X), s) &\overset{(+)}{=} E\left[u(X,t) \,|\, \mathcal{F}_s\right] = E\left[E\left[u(X,t) \,|\, \mathcal{F}_v\right] \,|\, \mathcal{F}_s\right] \\ &\overset{(\cdot)}{=} E\left[u(C_{v,t}(X), v) \,|\, \mathcal{F}_s\right] \overset{(d)}{\leq} E\left[u(C_{v,t}(X), s) \,|\, \mathcal{F}_s\right] \\ &\leq u(E\left[C_{v,t}(X) \,|\, \mathcal{F}_s\right], s). \end{aligned}$$

We applied in the last inequality the extended Jensen inequality, since $(u(C_{v,t}(X), s))^-$ is integrable. The second property follows by taking $v = t$ and observing that $C_{t,t}(X) = X$. □

Remark 1.2. Comparing the definition of SDU with the existing literature about forward performances ([3, 22, 23]), we may notice that the CCE does not rely on the existence of a market: this allows a higher level of generality and freedom in the choice of the preferences of the agent. If one takes into account the class of forward utilities and compute the CCE of a self-financing discounted portfolios X^π (see [22] for the notations), then only for an optimal strategy π^*_t we have that $C_{s,t}(X^{\pi^*}_t) = X^{\pi^*}_s$ whereas in general $C_{s,t}\left(X^\pi_t\right) \leq X^\pi_s$. This points out an economic interpretation of the CCE: given the final outcome of some risky position we backwardly build up a process which takes into account the agent's random risk-aversion. For replicable contingent claims it means that $X^\pi_s - C_{s,t}(X^\pi_t)$ measures the gap between the real value of the claim at time s, and the smallest amount for which the decision maker would willingly sell the claim if he had it. The gap will be deleted whenever we move through an optimal strategy.

2. The Right Framework for the CCE

Until now we have considered $C_{s,t}$ as a map defined on the set of random variables $\mathcal{U}(t)$ which is not in general a vector space. In order to show the dual representation of the CCE it is convenient to define it on a Banach lattice. Therefore we now introduce the general class of Musielak-Orlicz spaces induced by the SDU taken into account.

2.1. *Generalities on Musielak-Orlicz spaces*

Given a non-atomic probability space $(\Omega, \mathcal{F}, \mathbb{P})$ and a function $\Psi : \mathbb{R} \times \Omega \to \mathbb{R} \cup \{+\infty\}$, with $\mathcal{D} = \{x \in \mathbb{R} \mid \Psi(x, \omega) < +\infty\} \neq \emptyset$, we say that Ψ is a (generalized) Young function if $\Psi(x, \cdot)$ is $\mathcal{F}$-measurable and for $\mathbb{P}$ a.e. $\omega \in \Omega$

(1) $\Psi(\cdot, \omega)$ is even and convex;
(2) the effective domain $\mathcal{D}$ does not depend on ω and $0 \in \mathrm{int}(\mathcal{D})$;
(3) $\Psi(\infty, \omega) = +\infty$, $\Psi(0, \omega) = 0$.

Note that Ψ may jump to $+\infty$ outside of a bounded neighborhood of 0. In case Ψ is finite valued however, it is also continuous w.r.t. x by convexity. Whenever possible, we will suppress the explicit dependence of Ψ from ω.

The Musielak-Orlicz space L^Ψ, on $(\Omega, \mathcal{F}, \mathbb{P})$ is then defined as

$$L^\Psi = \left\{X \in L^0 \mid \exists\, \alpha > 0\, E[\Psi(\alpha X)] < +\infty\right\}.$$

endowed with the Luxemburg norm

$$N_\Psi(X) = \inf\left\{c > 0 \mid E\left[\Psi\left(X \cdot c^{-1}\right)\right] \leq 1\right\}.$$

Although there are no particular differences with Musielak work (see [24]), here we are dropping the hypothesis on Ψ to be finite (and so continuous). But since the domain $\mathcal{D}$ does not depend on ω we have that non continuous Ψs always induce the space $L^\infty(\Omega, \mathcal{F}, \mathbb{P})$ and the Luxemburg norm is equivalent to the supremum norm.

It is known that (L^Ψ, N_Ψ) is a Banach space (Theorem 7.7 in [24]), and with the usual pointwise lattice operations, L^Ψ is a Banach lattice.

There is an important linear subspace of L^Ψ, which is also a Banach lattice

$$M^\Psi = \left\{X \in L^0 \mid E\left[\Psi(\alpha X)\right] < +\infty \;\forall\, \alpha > 0\right\}.$$

In general, $M^\Psi \subsetneq L^\Psi$ and this can be easily seen when Ψ is non continuous since in this case $M^\Psi = \{0\}$, but there are also non trivial examples of the strict containment with finite-valued, continuous Young functions, that we will consider soon.

Other convenient assumptions on Ψ that we will use in the forthcoming discussion are

(int) $E[\Psi(x)]$ is finite for every $x \in \mathcal{D}$;
(sub) there exists a Young function $g : \mathbb{R} \to \mathbb{R} \cup \{+\infty\}$ such that $g(x) \leq \Psi(x, \omega)$ for $\mathbb{P}$-a.e. $\omega \in \Omega$
(Δ_2) There exists $K \in \mathbb{R}$, $h \in L^1$ and $x_0 \in \mathbb{R}$ such that

$$\Psi(2x, \cdot) \leq K\Psi(x, \cdot) + h(\cdot) \quad \text{for all } x > x_0,\ \mathbb{P}\text{-}a.s.$$

When Ψ satisfies (int) and the (Δ_2) condition (and it is henceforth finite-valued and continuous) the two spaces M^Ψ, L^Ψ coincide and L^Ψ can simply be written as $\{X \in L^0 \mid E[\Psi(X)] < +\infty\}$ (see [24], Theorem 8.14). This is the case of the L^p spaces when Ψ does not depend on ω.

In [24] (Theorem 7.6) it is also shown that when Ψ is (int) and continuous on $\mathbb{R}$, then $M^\Psi = \overline{L^\infty}^\Psi$ with closure taken in the Luxemburg norm. When Ψ is continuous but grows too quickly, it may happen that $M^\Psi = \overline{L^\infty}^\Psi \subsetneq L^\Psi$. As a consequence, simple functions are not necessarily dense in L^Ψ.

If both (int) and (sub) hold, it is not difficult to prove that

$$L^\infty \hookrightarrow M^\Psi \hookrightarrow L^\Psi \hookrightarrow L^g \hookrightarrow L^1$$

with linear lattice embeddings (the inclusions).

As usual, the convex conjugate function Ψ^* of Ψ is defined as

$$\Psi^*(y,\omega) =: \sup_{x\in\mathbb{R}} \{xy - \Psi(x,\omega)\}$$

and it is also a Young function. The function Ψ^* in general does not satisfy (int), but a sufficient condition for it is that Ψ is (sub). The Musielak-Orlicz space L^{Ψ^*} will be endowed with the Orlicz (or dual) norm

$$\|X\|_{\Psi^*} = \sup\{\, E[\,|Xf|\,] \,|\, f \in L^\Psi : E[\Psi(f)] \le 1\},$$

which is equivalent to the Luxemburg norm.

2.2. *The Musielak-Orlicz space $L^{\widehat{u}}$ induced by an SDU*

In the spirit of [5], we now build the time-dependent stochastic Orlicz space induced by the SDU $u(x,t,\omega)$. The even function $\widehat{u}:\mathbb{R}\times[0,+\infty)\times\Omega \to \mathbb{R}\cup\{+\infty\}$ defined by

$$\widehat{u}(x,t,\omega) = u(0,t) - u(-|x|,t,\omega)$$

is a Young function and the induced Orlicz spaces are

$$L^{\widehat{u}_t} = \{X \in L^0_{\mathcal{F}_t} \,|\, \exists \alpha > 0\, E[\widehat{u}(\alpha X,t)] < +\infty\}$$

$$M^{\widehat{u}_t} = \{X \in L^0_{\mathcal{F}_t} \,|\, E[\widehat{u}(\alpha X,t)] < +\infty \;\forall\, \alpha > 0\}$$

endowed with the Luxemburg norm $N_{\widehat{u}_t}(\cdot)$.

Notice the following important fact:

$$M^{\widehat{u}_t} \subseteq \mathcal{U}(t).$$

Indeed, for any given $\lambda > 0$ and $X \in L^0_{\mathcal{F}_t}$ such that $E[\widehat{u}(\lambda X,t)] < +\infty$ we have: $E[u(\lambda X,t)] \ge E[u(-\lambda|X|,t)] > -\infty$. On the other hand $u(x,t) - u(0,t) \le \widehat{u}(x,t)$ so that $E[u(\lambda X,t)] \le E[\widehat{u}(\lambda X,t) + u(0,t)] < +\infty$ and the claim follows. In particular this means that (int) implies $u(x,t)$ is integrable for every $x \in \mathcal{D}(t)$.

This argument highlights one relevant feature: every $X \in M^{\widehat{u}_t}$ belongs to the set $\mathcal{U}(t)$ so that the CCE is well defined on $M^{\widehat{u}_t}$. In the following examples also $C_{s,t}(X) \in M^{\widehat{u}_s}$ holds true, so that $C_{s,t} : M^{\widehat{u}_t} \to M^{\widehat{u}_s}$ and it make sense to study the time consistency of $C_{s,t}$.

2.3. *Examples*

Exponential random utilities. Let us consider $u : \mathbb{R}\times[0,\infty)\times\Omega \to \mathbb{R}$ defined by

$$u(x,t,\omega) = -e^{-\alpha_t(\omega)x+\beta_t(\omega)}$$

where $\alpha_t > 0$ and β_t are adapted stochastic processes.

In this example the CCE may be simply computed inverting the function $u(\cdot,t,\omega)$:

$$C_{s,t}(X) = -\frac{1}{\alpha_s}\ln\left\{E[e^{-\alpha_t X+\beta_t}\,|\,\mathcal{F}_s]\right\} + \frac{\beta_s}{\alpha_s} \tag{2.1}$$

Notice the measurability requirement on the risk aversion process α_t, which is different from what can be found in some examples in the literature related to dynamic risk measures, as e.g. in [1], where the α_t in (2.1) is replaced by α_s.

Assumptions. We suppose that β_t belongs to $L^\infty(\mathcal{F}_t)$ for any $t > 0$ and that $e^{\alpha_t x} \in L^1_{\mathcal{F}_t}$ for every $x \in \mathbb{R}$.

These assumptions guarantee that (int) holds. In particular if $\alpha_t(\omega) \equiv \alpha \in \mathbb{R}$ and $\beta_t \equiv 0$ then $C_{s,t}(X) = -\rho_{s,t}(X)$, where $\rho_{s,t}$ is the dynamic entropic risk measure induced by the exponential utility. Unfortunately when the risk aversion coefficient is stochastic we have no chance that $C_{s,t}$ has any monetary property. On the other hand monotonicity and concavity keep standing. The first is due to Proposition 1.1, whereas the second is a straightforward application of Holder-conditional inequality. This means that in general $\rho_{s,t}(X) =: -C_{s,t}(X)$ satisfies all the usual assumptions of dynamic risk measures, only failing the cash additive property. We now show a sufficient condition by which $\rho_{s,t}(X)$ is at least cash subadditive, i.e. $\rho_{s,t}(X+Y) \geq \rho_{s,t}(X) - Y$ where $Y \in L^\infty_{\mathcal{F}_s}$ and $Y \geq 0$.

Proposition 2.1. *Under the previous assumptions, the functional*

$$\rho_{s,t}(X) = \frac{1}{\alpha_s}\ln\left\{E[e^{-\alpha_t X+\beta_t}\,|\,\mathcal{F}_s]\right\} + \frac{\beta_s}{\alpha_s}$$

is cash subadditive if the process $\{\alpha_t\}_{t\geq 0}$ *is almost surely decreasing.*

Proof. For every $Y \in L^\infty_{\mathcal{F}_s}$ and $Y \geq 0$:

$$\begin{aligned}\rho_{s,t}(X+Y) &= \frac{1}{\alpha_s}\ln\left\{E[e^{-\frac{\alpha_t}{\alpha_s}\alpha_s Y}e^{-\alpha_t X+\beta_t}\,|\,\mathcal{F}_s]\right\} - \frac{\beta_s}{\alpha_s} \\ &\geq \frac{1}{\alpha_s}\ln\left\{E[e^{-\alpha_s Y}e^{-\alpha_t X+\beta_t}\,|\,\mathcal{F}_s]\right\} - \frac{\beta_s}{\alpha_s} = \rho_{s,t}(X) - Y.\end{aligned}$$

□

Proposition 2.2. *Under the the previous assumptions*

$$C_{s,t} : M^{\widehat{u}_t} \to M^{\widehat{u}_s}$$

Proof. Let $\lambda \geq 1$, and since no confusion arises we denote by $u_t(x) \doteq u(x,t)$. Define $A = \{\ln E[e^{-\alpha_t X+\beta_t} \,|\, \mathcal{F}_s] \leq \beta_s\}$ and notice that

$$\begin{aligned}
\widehat{u}_s(\lambda C_{s,t}(X)) - u_s(0) &= -u_s\left(-\frac{\lambda}{\alpha_s}\left|-\ln E[e^{-\alpha_t X+\beta_t} \,|\, \mathcal{F}_s] + \beta_s\right|\right) \\
&= e^{\beta_s}\exp(\lambda|-\ln E[e^{-\alpha_t X+\beta_t} \,|\, \mathcal{F}_s] + \beta_s|) \\
&= e^{\beta_s}\exp(\lambda(\beta_s - \ln E[e^{-\alpha_t X+\beta_t} \,|\, \mathcal{F}_s]))\mathbf{1}_A \\
&\quad + e^{\beta_s}\exp(\lambda(\ln E[e^{-\alpha_t X+\beta_t} \,|\, \mathcal{F}_s] - \beta_s))\mathbf{1}_{A^C} \\
&= e^{\beta_s(1+\lambda)}E[e^{-\alpha_t X+\beta_t} \,|\, \mathcal{F}_s]^{-\lambda}\mathbf{1}_A + e^{\beta_s(1-\lambda)}E[e^{-\alpha_t X+\beta_t} \,|\, \mathcal{F}_s]^{\lambda}\mathbf{1}_{A^C}
\end{aligned}$$

Since on A we have $E[e^{-\alpha_t X+\beta_t} \,|\, \mathcal{F}_s] \leq e^{\beta_s}$ and in general $e^{\beta_s(1-\lambda)} \leq a \in \mathbb{R}_+$ then

$$\begin{aligned}
E[\widehat{u}_s(\lambda C_{s,t}(X))] &\leq E[e^{\beta_s(1+\lambda-\lambda)}\mathbf{1}_A] + aE\{E[e^{-\alpha_t X+\beta_t} \,|\, \mathcal{F}_s]^{\lambda}\mathbf{1}_{A^C}\} + E[u_s(0)] \\
&\leq -E[u_s(0)] + aE[e^{\lambda(-\alpha_t X+\beta_t)}] + E[u_s(0)] \\
&\leq +a\|(e^{(\lambda-1)\beta_t})\|_\infty E[\widehat{u}_t(\lambda X) + e^{\beta_t}] \leq KE[\widehat{u}_t(\lambda X)]
\end{aligned}$$

Notice that the second step is a simple application of Jensen's inequality, in fact: $E[Y \,|\, \mathcal{G}]^\lambda \leq E[Y^\lambda \,|\, \mathcal{G}]$ $\forall \lambda \geq 1$. Moreover we have that for $0 < \lambda < 1$ $E[\widehat{u}_s(\lambda C_{s,t}(X))] \leq E[\widehat{u}_s(C_{s,t}(X))] < \infty$ and then $C_{s,t}(X) \in M^{\widehat{u}_s}$. □

Random-power utility. Consider the utility function given by

$$u(x,t,\omega) = -\gamma_t(\omega)|x|^{p_t(\omega)}\mathbf{1}_{(-\infty,0)}$$

where γ_t, p_t are adapted stochastic processes satisfying $\gamma_t > 0$ and $p_t > 1$. We have $\widehat{u}(x,t) = \gamma_t|x|^{p_t}$. Here assumption (int) is troublesome but not needed for what follows. On the other hand the utility fails to be strictly increasing so that we won't have uniqueness of the solution for the equation defining the CCE, namely

$$-\gamma_s|C_{s,t}(X)|^{p_s}\mathbf{1}_{\{C_{s,t}(X)<0\}} = E\left[-\gamma_t|X|^{p_t}\mathbf{1}_{\{X<0\}} \,|\, \mathcal{F}_s\right] \tag{2.2}$$

Notice that $C_{s,t}(X) = C_{s,t}(X^- + K\mathbf{1}_{X\geq 0})$ where K is any positive $\mathcal{F}_t$ r.v.; moreover if $G := \{E[\gamma_t\,|X|^{p_t}\mathbf{1}_{\{X<0\}} \,|\, \mathcal{F}_s] > 0\}$ then $\mathbb{P}(G \backslash \{C_{s,t}(X) < 0\}) = 0$. If we decompose X as $X^+ - X^-$ we can conclude that

$$C_{s,t}(X) = -\frac{1}{\gamma_s}\left(E[\gamma_t(X^-)^{p_t} \,|\, \mathcal{F}_s]\right)^{\frac{1}{p_s}} + K\mathbf{1}_{G^C}$$

it's the class of solutions of (2.2) where $K \in L^0_{\mathcal{F}_s}$ and $K > 0$. This is a natural consequence of the choice of a preference system in which the agent is indifferent among all the positive variables. If in particular $K \in M^{\hat{u}_s}$ then it is easy to check that $C_{s,t} : M^{\widehat{u}_t} \to M^{\widehat{u}_s}$.

A general result. One may wonder what happens for an arbitrary SDU. Clearly the fact that $C_{s,t}$ is a map between the the two corresponding Orlicz spaces at time t and s is a key feature for the time-consistency. We take into account a particular class of SDU, which are a stochastic transformation of a standard utility function.

Let $V : \mathbb{R} \to \mathbb{R}$ a concave, strictly increasing function: take an adapted stochastic process, $\{\alpha_t\}_{t\geq 0}$, such that for every $t \geq 0$, $\alpha_t > 0$. Then $u(x,t,\omega) = V(\alpha_t(\omega)x)$ is a SDU and

$$C_{s,t}(X) = \frac{1}{\alpha_s} V^{-1}\left(E[V(\alpha_t X) \,|\, \mathcal{F}_s]\right)$$

Proposition 2.3. *Let* $\Theta_t = \{X \in L^{\widehat{u}_t} \,|\, E[u(-X^-, t)] > -\infty\} \supseteq M^{\widehat{u}_t}$. *Then*

$$C_{s,t} : \Theta_t \to \Theta_s$$

Moreover if $\widehat{u}(x,s)$ *satisfies the* (Δ_2) *condition, then*

$$C_{s,t} : M^{\widehat{u}_t} \to M^{\widehat{u}_s}.$$

Proof. Denote $\widehat{u}_t(x) = \widehat{u}(x,t)$; from Jensen inequality we have

$$\frac{1}{\alpha_s} V^{-1}\left(E[V(\alpha_t X) \,|\, \mathcal{F}_s]\right) \leq \frac{1}{\alpha_s} E[\alpha_t X \,|\, \mathcal{F}_s] \tag{2.3}$$

Define the $\mathcal{F}_s$ measurable sets

$$F = \{E[V(\alpha_t X) \,|\, \mathcal{F}_s] \geq V(0)\}, \quad G = \{E[\alpha_t X \,|\, \mathcal{F}_s] \geq 0\}$$

and deduce from equation (2.3) that

$$0 \leq C_{s,t}(X)^+ = \frac{1}{\alpha_s} V^{-1}\left(E[V(\alpha_t X) \,|\, \mathcal{F}_s]\right) \mathbf{1}_F \leq \frac{1}{\alpha_s} E[(\alpha_t X)\mathbf{1}_G \,|\, \mathcal{F}_s]$$

For every $X \in L^{\widehat{u}_t}$ we may find a $\lambda > 0$ such that $E[\hat{u}_t(\lambda X \mathbf{1}_G)] < +\infty$:

$$\begin{aligned}
E&\left[\hat{u}_s\left(\frac{\lambda}{\alpha_s} V^{-1}\left(E[V(\alpha_t X) \,|\, \mathcal{F}_s]\right) \mathbf{1}_F\right)\right] \\
&\leq E\left[\hat{u}_s\left(\frac{\lambda}{\alpha_s} E[(\alpha_t X)\mathbf{1}_G \,|\, \mathcal{F}_s]\right)\right] \\
&= E[V(0) - V(-E[(\lambda\alpha_t X)\mathbf{1}_G \,|\, \mathcal{F}_s])] \\
&\leq E[V(0) - V(-\lambda\alpha_t X \mathbf{1}_G)] \leq E[\widehat{u}_t(\lambda X \mathbf{1}_G)].
\end{aligned}$$

Hence $X \in L^{\widehat{u}_t}$ implies $C_{s,t}(X)^+ \in L^{\widehat{u}_s}$.

Now let's consider a r.v. $X \in \Theta_t$: $-C_{s,t}(X)^- = \frac{1}{\alpha_s} V^{-1}\left(E[V(\alpha_t X) \,|\, \mathcal{F}_s]\right) \mathbf{1}_{F^C}$. We can conclude that

$$\begin{aligned}
0 \leq E[\widehat{u}_s(-C_{s,t}(X)^-)] &= E\left[-V \circ V^{-1}\left(E[V(\alpha_t X)\mathbf{1}_{F^C} \,|\, \mathcal{F}_s]\right) + V(0)\right] \\
&= E[-V(\alpha_t X)\mathbf{1}_{F^C} + V(0)] < +\infty
\end{aligned}$$

where the last inequality follows from $X \in \Theta_t$, $\{X \geq 0\} \subseteq F$ and

$$V(\alpha_t X)\mathbf{1}_{F^C} = \left(V(\alpha_t X^+)\mathbf{1}_{\{X\geq 0\}} + V(-\alpha_t X^-)\mathbf{1}_{\{X<0\}}\right)\mathbf{1}_{F^C}$$
$$= V(-\alpha_t X^-)\mathbf{1}_{\{X<0\}\cap F^C}$$

This shows that surely $C_{s,t}(X) \in \Theta_s$, if $X \in \Theta_t$. □

3. Dual Representation of CCE

In this section we prove a dual formula for the CCE, which is similar to the general result that can be found in [13]: due to the particular structure of the CCE the proof is simpler and more readable.

Consider the condition:

$$\text{there exists } X^* \in (L^{\widehat{u}_t})^* \quad \text{s.t. } E[f^*(X^*, t)] < +\infty \tag{3.1}$$

where $f^*(x, t, \omega) = \sup_{y\in\mathbb{R}} \{xy + u(y, t, \omega)\}$.

As a consequence of Theorem 1 [26], we may deduce that if (3.1) holds, if $\widehat{u}(x, t)$ is (int) and $X \in L^{\widehat{u}_t}$ then $E[u(\lambda X, t)] < +\infty$ for every $\lambda > 0$.

Remark 3.1. The condition (3.1) is quite weak: it is satisfied, for example, if $u(x, t, \omega) \leq ax + b$ with $a, b \in \mathbb{R}$ since

$$f^*(-a, t, \omega) \leq \sup_{y\in\mathbb{R}}\{(-a + a)y + b\} = b.$$

We now take into account $(L^\Psi)^*$, the norm dual of L^Ψ and consider the following three cases which cover a pretty large class of possible Young functions.

(1) $\Psi(\cdot, \omega)$ is (int) and discontinuous, i.e. $\mathcal{D} \subsetneq \mathbb{R}$.

In this case, $L^\Psi = L^\infty$ and from the Yosida-Hewitt decomposition for elements of $ba(\Omega, \mathcal{F}, P)$ we have

$$ba = (L^\infty)^* = L^1 \oplus \mathcal{A}^d,$$

where $\mathcal{A}^d$ consists of pure charges, i.e. purely finitely additive measures (which are not order continuous).

(2) $\Psi(\cdot, \omega)$ is continuous, Ψ and Ψ^* are (int) and satisfy:

$$\frac{\Psi(x, \omega)}{x} \to +\infty \ \mathbb{P} - a.s, \quad \text{as } x \to \infty.$$

These conditions are not restrictive and hold as soon as Ψ is (int) and (sub) with $\lim_{x\to\infty} \frac{g(x)}{x} \to +\infty$. For such Young functions it can be easily deduced from Theorem 13.17 in [24] that $(M^\Psi)^* = L^{\Psi^*}$: $\mu_r \in (M^\Psi)^*$ can be identified with its density $\frac{d\mu_r}{dP} \in L^{\Psi^*}$ so that we will write its action on $X \in L^\Psi$ as $\mu_r(X) = E[\mu_r X]$. Moreover $(M^\Psi)^*$ is a band in the dual space $(L^\Psi)^*$ (see [2] Sec. 8) so that we may decompose

$$(L^\Psi)^* = (M^\Psi)^* \oplus (M^\Psi)^\perp$$

i.e. every $X^* \in (L^\Psi)^*$ can be uniquely represented as $X^* = \mu_r + \mu_s$ where μ_s belongs to the annihilator of M^Ψ ($\mu_s(X) = 0$ for every $X \in M^\Psi$) and $\mu_r \in (M^\Psi)^* = L^{\Psi^*}$. Notice that every element $\mu_r \in (M^\Psi)^*$ is clearly order continuous. Moreover it can be shown, applying an argument similar to the one used in Lemma 10 [5], that every $\mu_s \in (M^\Psi)^\perp$ is not order continuous.

(3) $\Psi(\cdot,\omega)$ is continuous and

$$0 < a = ess\inf_{\omega\in\Omega}\lim_{x\to\infty}\frac{\Psi(x,\omega)}{x} \le ess\sup_{\omega\in\Omega}\lim_{x\to\infty}\frac{\Psi(x,\omega)}{x} = b < +\infty$$

Here (int) automatically holds for both Ψ and Ψ^*. It follows that $L^\Psi = L^1$ and the L^1-norm is equivalent to the Luxemburg norm, so that $(L^\Psi)^* = L^{\Psi^*} = L^\infty$.

Assumptions for the dual result. In this section $u(x,t,\omega)$ is a SDU, such that:

(1) For all $t \ge 0$, the induced Young function $\widehat{u}(x,t,\omega)$ belongs to one of the three classes mentioned above
(2) The condition (3.1) holds true.

As shown above, under the assumption (1) the order dual space of $L^{\widehat{u}_t}$ is known and is contained in L^1. This will also allow us to apply Proposition A.1. The second assumption implies that $E[u(\cdot,t)] : L^{\widehat{u}_t} \to [-\infty,+\infty)$ is a well defined convex functional ([26]).

Thus we have $u(X^+,t) \in L^1_{\mathcal{F}_t}$, but in general we do not have integrability for $u(-X^-,t)$. This means that if $X \notin \Theta_t = \{X \in L^{\widehat{u}_t} \mid E[u(-X^-,t)] > -\infty\}$ we are forced to consider the generalized conditional expectation

$$E[u(X,t)\,|\,\mathcal{F}_s] := E[u(X,t)^+\,|\,\mathcal{F}_s] - \lim_n E[u(X,t)^- \mathbf{1}_{\{-n\le -u(X,s)^-<0\}}\,|\,\mathcal{F}_s],$$

which can be equivalently written as:

$$E[u(X,t)\,|\,\mathcal{F}_s] = E[u(X^+,t)\mathbf{1}_{\{X\ge 0\}}\,|\,\mathcal{F}_s] + \lim_n E[u(-X^-,t)\mathbf{1}_{\{-n\le X<0\}}\,|\,\mathcal{F}_s].$$

Therefore, $E[u(X,t)\,|\,\mathcal{F}_s] \in \bar{L}^0_{\mathcal{F}_s}$ and $C_{s,t}(\cdot)$ is defined on the entire space $L^{\widehat{u}_t}$. We fix throughout this section $0 < s \le t$ and define

$$\mathcal{P}_{\mathcal{F}_t} = \{X^* \in (L^{\widehat{u}_t^*})_+ \mid E[X^*] = 1\} \subseteq \{Q \ll \mathbb{P} \mid Q \text{ probability}\}$$

$$U : L^{\widehat{u}_t} \to \bar{L}^0_{\mathcal{F}_s} \text{ given by } U(X) := E[u(X,t)\,|\,\mathcal{F}_s]$$

The map U is concave and increasing and admits the dual representation stated in Lemma 3.1. From equation (3.3) we deduce the dual representation of $C_{s,t}(\cdot) = u^{-1}(U(\cdot),s)$ as follows.

Theorem 3.1. *Fix $s \le t$. For every $X \in L^{\widehat{u}_t}$*

$$C_{s,t}(X) = \inf_{Q\in\mathcal{P}_{\mathcal{F}_t}} G(E_Q[X\,|\,\mathcal{F}_s], Q) \tag{3.2}$$

where for every $Y \in L^0_{\mathcal{F}_s}$,

$$G(Y,Q) = \sup_{\xi \in L^{\hat{u}_t}} \{C_{s,t}(\xi) \,|\, E_Q[\xi \,|\, \mathcal{F}_s] =_Q Y\}.$$

Moreover if $X \in M^{\widehat{u}_t}$ *then the essential* infimum *in* (3.2) *is actually a* minimum.

The proof is based on the following lemma.

Lemma 3.1. *Let* $s \leq t$. *For every* $X \in L^{\widehat{u}_t}$

$$U(X) = \inf_{Q \in \mathcal{P}_{\mathcal{F}_t}} S(E_Q[X \,|\, \mathcal{F}_s], Q) \tag{3.3}$$

where $S(Y,Q) = \sup_{\xi \in L^{\hat{u}_t}} \{U(\xi) \,|\, E_Q[\xi \,|\, \mathcal{F}_s] =_Q Y\}$ *for any* $Y \in L^0_{\mathcal{F}_s}$.

Moreover if $X \in M^{\widehat{u}_t}$ *then the essential* infimum *in* (3.3) *is actually a* minimum.

Proof. Obviously $\forall\, Q \in \mathcal{P}_{\mathcal{F}_t}$

$$E[u(X,t) \,|\, \mathcal{F}_s] \leq \sup_{\xi \in L^{\hat{u}_t}} \{U(\xi) \,|\, E_Q[\xi \,|\, \mathcal{F}_s] =_Q E_Q[X \,|\, \mathcal{F}_s]\}$$

and then

$$E[u(X,t) \,|\, \mathcal{F}_s] \leq \inf_{Q \in \mathcal{P}_{\mathcal{F}_t}} \sup_{\xi \in L^{\hat{u}_t}} \{U(\xi) \,|\, E_Q[\xi \,|\, \mathcal{F}_s] =_Q E_Q[X \,|\, \mathcal{F}_s]\}. \tag{3.4}$$

Important remark: we have that $E(U(X)) = E(u(X,t))$; this means that

$$E(U(\cdot)) : L^{\widehat{u}_t} \to [-\infty, +\infty)$$

is a concave functional. From the monotone convergence theorem and Jensen inequality the functional $E(u(X,t))$ is continuous from above (i.e. $X_n \downarrow X \Rightarrow E(u(X_n,t)) \downarrow E(u(X,t))$). Applying Lemma 15 in [6], $E(U(X))$ is order u.s.c. and thus $\sigma(L^{\widehat{u}_t}, L^{\widehat{u}_t^*})$-u.s.c. (Proposition 24 [6]).

From Proposition A.1 in the Appendix:

$$\begin{aligned} E(U(X)) &= \inf_{Q \in \mathcal{P}_{\mathcal{F}_t}} \sup_{\xi \in L^{\hat{u}_t}} \{E[U(\xi)] \,|\, E_Q[\xi] = E_Q[X]\} \\ &\geq \inf_{Q \in \mathcal{P}_{\mathcal{F}_t}} \sup_{\xi \in L^{\hat{u}_t}} \{E(U(\xi)) \,|\, E_Q[\xi \,|\, \mathcal{F}_s] =_Q E_Q[X \,|\, \mathcal{F}_s]\} \geq E(U(X)) \end{aligned}$$

i.e.

$$E(U(X)) = \inf_{Q \in \mathcal{P}_{\mathcal{F}_t}} \sup_{\xi \in L^{\hat{u}_t}} \{E(U(\xi)) \,|\, E_Q[\xi \,|\, \mathcal{F}_s] =_Q E_Q[X \,|\, \mathcal{F}_s]\} \tag{3.5}$$

Surely the map U is regular (i.e. for every $A \in \mathcal{F}_s$, $U(X\mathbf{1}_A + Y\mathbf{1}_{A^C}) = U(X)\mathbf{1}_A + U(Y)\mathbf{1}_{A^C}$) and then the set $\mathcal{A} = \{U(\xi) \,|\, E_Q[\xi \,|\, \mathcal{F}_s] =_Q E_Q[X \,|\, \mathcal{F}_s]\}$ is upward directed. In fact given $\xi_1, \xi_2 \in \mathcal{A}$ we have

$$U(\xi_1) \vee U(\xi_2) = U(\xi_1)\mathbf{1}_F + U(\xi_2)\mathbf{1}_{F^C} = U(\xi_1\mathbf{1}_F + \xi_2\mathbf{1}_{F^C})$$

where $F = \{U(\xi_1) \geq U(\xi_2)\}$ and $E_Q[\xi_1 \mathbf{1}_F + \xi_2 \mathbf{1}_{F^C} \,|\, \mathcal{F}_s] =_Q E_Q[X \,|\, \mathcal{F}_s]$. By this last property and the monotone convergence theorem we deduce

$$E[S(E_Q[X \,|\, \mathcal{F}_s], Q)] = \sup_{\xi \in L^{\widehat{u}_t}} \{E[U(\xi)] \,|\, E_Q[\xi \,|\, \mathcal{F}_s] =_Q E_Q[X \,|\, \mathcal{F}_s]\}$$

Hence

$$\begin{aligned} E(U(X)) &= \inf_{Q \in \mathcal{P}_{\mathcal{F}_t}} \sup_{\xi \in L^{\widehat{u}_t}} \{E(U(\xi)) \,|\, E_Q[\xi \,|\, \mathcal{F}_s] =_Q E_Q[X \,|\, \mathcal{F}_s]\} \\ &= \inf_{Q \in \mathcal{P}_{\mathcal{F}_t}} E\left(\sup_{\xi \in L^{\widehat{u}_t}} \{U(\xi) \,|\, E_Q[\xi \,|\, \mathcal{F}_s] =_Q E_Q[X \,|\, \mathcal{F}_s]\} \right) \\ &\geq E\left(\inf_{Q \in \mathcal{P}_{\mathcal{F}_t}} \sup_{\xi \in L^{\widehat{u}_t}} \{U(\xi) \,|\, E_Q[\xi \,|\, \mathcal{F}_s] =_Q E_Q[X \,|\, \mathcal{F}_s]\} \right) \end{aligned}$$

This last chain of inequalities together with inequality (3.4) gives

$$U(X) = \inf_{Q \in \mathcal{P}_{\mathcal{F}_t}} \sup_{\xi \in L^{\widehat{u}_t}} \{U(\xi) \,|\, E_Q[\xi \,|\, \mathcal{F}_s] =_Q E_Q[X \,|\, \mathcal{F}_s]\} \quad \forall X \in L^{\widehat{u}_t} \tag{3.6}$$

Moreover from generalized Namioka-Klee theorem, the functional $E(u(\cdot)) : L^{\widehat{u}_t}$ is norm continuous on $int(\Theta_u) \supseteq M^{\widehat{u}_t}$ (see [6] Lemma 32) and then $E(U(X))$ as well since $E(U(X)) = E(u(X))$.

From Proposition A.1 we have that:

$$\begin{aligned} E(U(X)) &= \min_{Q \in \mathcal{P}_{\mathcal{F}_t}} \sup_{\xi \in M^{\widehat{u}_t}} \{E(U(\xi)) \,|\, E_Q[\xi] = E_Q[X]\} \\ &= \sup_{\xi \in M^{\widehat{u}_t}} \{E[U(\xi)] \,|\, E_{Q_{\min}}[\xi] = E_{Q_{\min}}[X]\} \\ &\geq \sup_{\xi \in M^{\widehat{u}_t}} \{E[U(\xi)] \,|\, E_{Q_{\min}}[\xi \,|\, \mathcal{F}_s] =_{Q_{\min}} E_{Q_{\min}}[X \,|\, \mathcal{F}_s]\} \geq E[(U(X)) \end{aligned}$$

The remaining proof matches the previous case and then we get

$$U(X) = \min_{Q \in \mathcal{P}_{\mathcal{F}_t}} \sup_{\xi \in M^{\widehat{u}_t}} \{U(\xi) \,|\, E_Q[\xi \,|\, \mathcal{F}_s] =_Q E_Q[X \,|\, \mathcal{F}_s]\} \quad \forall X \in M^{\widehat{u}_t} \tag{3.7}$$

where the minimizer is exactly $Q_{\min}$. □

Proof. [of Theorem 3.1] Since s, t are fixed throughout this proof we redefine $C_{s,t}(\cdot) = C(\cdot)$, $u(x,t) = u(x)$ and $u(x,s) = v(x)$. We show that for every fixed $Q \in \mathcal{P}_{\mathcal{F}_t}$, $v^{-1} S(E_Q[X \,|\, \mathcal{F}_s], Q) = G(E_Q[X \,|\, \mathcal{F}_s], Q)$.

Since C, U are regular, for every fixed $Q \in \mathcal{P}_{\mathcal{F}}$ the sets

$$\begin{aligned} &\{C(\xi) \,|\, \xi \in L^{\widehat{u}_t},\, E_Q[\xi \,|\, \mathcal{F}_s] =_Q E_Q[X \,|\, \mathcal{F}_s]\}, \\ &\{U(\xi) \,|\, \xi \in L^{\widehat{u}_t},\, E_Q[\xi \,|\, \mathcal{F}_s] =_Q E_Q[X \,|\, \mathcal{F}_s]\} \end{aligned}$$

are upward directed and then there exist ξ_h^Q, η_h^Q such that $E_Q[\xi_h^Q \mid \mathcal{F}_s] =_Q E_Q[X \mid \mathcal{F}_s]$, $E_Q[\eta_h^Q \mid \mathcal{F}_s] =_Q E_Q[X \mid \mathcal{F}_s]$, for every $h > 0$, and

$$C(\xi_h^Q) \uparrow G(E_Q[X \mid \mathcal{F}_s], Q)\,, \quad U(\eta_h^Q) \uparrow S(E_Q[X \mid \mathcal{F}_s], Q) \quad \mathbb{P}\text{-a.s.}$$

Thus since v^{-1} is continuous in the interior of its domain:

$$\begin{aligned} G(E_Q[X \mid \mathcal{F}_s], Q) &\geq \lim_h C(\eta_h^Q) = v^{-1} \lim_h U(\eta_h^Q) = v^{-1} S(E_Q[X \mid \mathcal{F}_s], Q) \\ &\geq v^{-1} \lim_h U(\xi_h^Q) = \lim_h C(\xi_h^Q) = G(E_Q[X \mid \mathcal{F}_s], Q) \end{aligned}$$

and this ends the first claim.

It's not hard to prove that the infimum is actually a limit (using the property of downward directness of the set as has been shown in Lemma 19 (iv) in [13]): therefore we deduce from the continuity of v^{-1} that

$$\begin{aligned} C(X) &= v^{-1} \inf_{Q \in \mathcal{P}_{\mathcal{F}_t}} S(E_Q[X \mid \mathcal{F}_s], Q) \\ &= \inf_{Q \in \mathcal{P}_{\mathcal{F}_t}} v^{-1} S(E_Q[X \mid \mathcal{F}_s], Q) = \inf_{Q \in \mathcal{P}_{\mathcal{F}_t}} G(E_Q[X \mid \mathcal{F}_s], Q). \end{aligned}$$

□

Appendix

A.1. *On quasiconvex real valued maps*

Let L be a locally convex topological vector space, L^* be its dual space and $f : L \to \overline{\mathbb{R}} := \mathbb{R} \cup \{-\infty\} \cup \{\infty\}$. Define: $R : L^* \times \mathbb{R} \to \overline{\mathbb{R}}$ by

$$R(X^*, t) := \sup\{f(X) \mid X \in L \text{ such that } X^*(X) \geq t\}.$$

Theorem A.1. *Let f as before*

(i) *If f is lsc then*: $f(X) = \sup_{X^* \in L^*} R(X^*, X^*(X))$.
(ii) *If f is usc then*: $f(X) = \max_{X^* \in L^*} R(X^*, X^*(X))$.

Proof. By definition, for any $X^* \in L^*$, $R(X^*, X^*(X)) \leq f(X)$ and therefore

$$\sup_{X^* \in L^*} R(X^*, X^*(X)) \leq f(X), \quad X \in L.$$

(i) See [13] Theorem 1.1.
(ii) For any fixed $X \in L$, the set $\{\xi \in L : f(\xi) < f(X)\} := \mathcal{E}$ is convex open and $X \notin \mathcal{E}$. By the Hahn Banach theorem there exists a continuous linear functional that properly separates X and $\mathcal{E}$, i.e. there exists $\alpha \in \mathbb{R}$ and $X^* \in L^*$ such that: $X^*(X) > \alpha \geq X^*(\xi)$ for all $\xi \in \mathcal{E}$.

Hence: $\{\xi \in L : X^*(\xi) \geq X^*(X)\} \subseteq (\mathcal{E})^C = \{\xi \in L : f(\xi) \geq f(X)\}$ and

$$\begin{aligned} f(X) &\geq \sup_{Y^* \in L^*} R(Y^*, Y^*(X)) \geq R(X^*, X^*(X)) \\ &= \inf\{f(\xi) \mid \xi \in L \text{ such that } X^*(\xi) \geq X^*(X)\} \\ &\geq \inf\{f(\xi) \mid \xi \in (\mathcal{E})^C\} \geq f(X). \end{aligned}$$

□

Proposition A.1. *Suppose L is a lattice, $L^* = (L, \geq)^*$ is the order continuous dual space satisfying $L^* \hookrightarrow L^1$ and $(L, \sigma(L, L^*))$ is a locally convex TVS. If $f : L \to \overline{\mathbb{R}}$ is quasiconvex, $\sigma(L, L^*)$-lsc (resp usc) and monotone increasing then*

$$f(X) = \sup_{Q \in L^*_+ \,|\, Q(\mathbf{1})=1} R(Q(X), Q), \quad \textit{resp. } f(X) = \max_{Q \in L^*_+ \,|\, Q(\mathbf{1})=1} R(Q(X), Q).$$

Proof. See [13] Proposition 5.4. □

References

[1] B. Acciaio and I. Penner, Dynamic risk measures, Preprint (2009).

[2] C. D. Aliprantis and K. C. Border, *Infinite Dimensional Analysis*, 3rd edn. (Springer, Berlin, 2005).

[3] F. P. Y. S. Berrier, L. C. G. Rogers and M. R. Theranchi, A characterization of forward utility functions, Preprint (2007).

[4] F. Bellini and M. Frittelli, On the existence of minimax martingale measures, *Mathematical Finance* **12**(1) (2008) 1–21.

[5] S. Biagini and M. Frittelli, A unified frameork for utility maximization problems: An Orlicz space approach, *Ann. Appl. Prob.* **18**(3) (2008) 929–966.

[6] S. Biagini and M. Frittelli, On the extension of the Namioka-Klee theorem and on the Fatou property for risk measures, in *Optimality and Risk: Modern Trends in Mathematical Finance, The Kabanov Festschrift*, F. Delbaen, M. Rasonyi and CH. Stricker (eds.) (2009).

[7] S. Cerreia-Vioglio, F. Maccheroni, M. Marinacci and L. Montrucchio, Risk measures: Rationality and diversification, The Carlo Alberto Working Papers No. 100 (2009).

[8] M. H. A. Davis, Option pricing in incomplete markets, in *Mathematics of Derivative Securities* (Newton Institute, Cambridge University Press, 1997), pp. 216–226.

[9] F. Delbaen, P. Grandits, T. Rheinlander, D. Samperi, M. Schweizer and C. Stricker, Exponential hedging and entropic penalties, *Mathematical Finance* **12**(2) (1997) 99–123.

[10] N. El Karoui and R. Rouge, Pricing via utility maximization and entropy, *Mathematical Finance* **10**(2) (2000) 259–276.

[11] N. El Karoui, S. Peng and M. C. Quenez, A dynamic maximum principle for the optimization of recursive utilities under constraints, *Ann. Appl. Prob.* **11**(3) (2001) 664–693.

[12] H. Föllmer and A. Schied, Stochastic Finance, An introduction in discrete time, 2nd edn., *de Gruyter Studies in Mathematics*, Vol. 27 (2004).

[13] M. Frittelli and M. Maggis, Dual representation of quasiconvex conditional maps, Preprint (2009).

[14] M. Frittelli, Introduction to a theory of value coherent with the no arbitrage principle, *Finance and Stochastics* **4**(3) (2000) 275–297.

[15] V. Henderson and D. Hobson, Horizon-unbiased utility functions, *Stoch. Proc & Appl.* **117**(11) (2007) 1621–1641.

[16] S. D. Hodges and A. Neuberger, Optimal replication of contingent claims under transaction costs, *Re. Futures Markets* **8** (1989) 222–239.

[17] H. Hudzik and Z. Zbaszyniak, Smoothness in Musielak-Orlicz spaces equipped with the Orlicz norm, *Collect. Math.* **48** (1997) 543–561.

[18] D. M. Kreps and E. L. Porteus, Dynamic choice theory and dynamic programming, *Econometrica* **47**(1) (1979) 91–100.

[19] H. Kunita, Stochastic Flows and Stochastic Differential Equations, Cambridge University Press (1964).

[20] A. Lazrak and M. C. Quenez, A generalized stochastic differential utility, *Mathematics of Operations Research* **28**(1) (2003) 154–180.

[21] P. A. Meyer, *Probability and Potentials* (Blaisdell Publishing Col, London, 1966).

[22] M. Musiela and T. Zariphopoulou, Investment and valuation under backward and forward dynamic exponential utilities in a stochastic factor model, in *Advances in Mathematical Finance*, Applied and Numerical Harmonic Series (2006), pp. 303–334.

[23] M. Musiela and T. Zariphopoulou, Optimal asset allocation under forward exponential criteria, *Markov Processes and Related Topics: A Festschrift for T.G. Kurtz*, IMS Collections, Institute of Mathematical statistics **4** (2008) 285–300.

[24] J. Musielak, *Orlicz Spaces and Modular Spaces*, Lectures Notes in Mathematics, Vol. 1034 (Springer, 1983).

[25] A. Pratt, Risk aversion in the small and in the large, *Econometrica* **32**(1/2) (1964) 122–136.

[26] R. T. Rockafellar, Integrals which are convex functionals, *Pacific Journal of Mathematics* **24**(3) (1968) 525–539.

PRICING OF PERPETUAL AMERICAN OPTIONS IN A MODEL WITH PARTIAL INFORMATION[†]

PAVEL V. GAPEEV*

Department of Mathematics, London School of Economics
Houghton Street, London WC2A 2AE, United Kingdom

We study the perpetual American call option pricing problem in a model of a financial market in which the firm issuing a traded asset can regulate the dividend rate by switching it between two constant values. The firm dividend policy is unknown for small investors, who can only observe the prices available from the market. The asset price dynamics are described by a geometric Brownian motion with a random drift rate modeled by a continuous time Markov chain with two states. The optimal exercise time of the option for small investors is found as the first time at which the asset price hits a boundary depending on the current state of the filtering dividend rate estimate. The proof is based on an embedding of the initial problem into a two-dimensional optimal stopping problem and the analysis of the associated parabolic-type free-boundary problem. We also provide closed form estimates for the rational option price and the optimal exercise boundary.

Keywords: Perpetual American option; stochastic dividend rate; discounted two-dimensional optimal stopping problem; stochastic boundary; diffusion process; hidden Markov chain; filtering estimate; innovation process; parabolic-type free-boundary problem; change-of-variable formula with local time on surfaces.

1. Introduction

The problem of pricing of American options is an important problem of the mathematical theory of modern finance. This problem consists of finding a rational (no-arbitrage) price of the option as well as an optimal stopping time at which the option should be exercised. For the case of perpetual American put options in the Black-Merton-Scholes model, this problem was first studied by McKean [22], who proved the optimality of the first time at which the price of the underlying risky asset hits a constant boundary (see also Shiryaev [28, Chapter VIII; Sec. 2a] and Peskir and Shiryaev [25, Chapter VII; Sec. 25] for an extensive overview of other related results in the area). More recently, Guo [15] and Guo and Zhang [16]

*Supported by ESF AMaMeF Short Visit Grant No. 1505.

[†]This chapter was originally published under the same title in *International Journal of Theoretical and Applied Finance*, Vol.15, No.1, 1250010-1–21 (2012). Singapore: World Scientific Publishing.

obtained closed form solutions of the perpetual American lookback and put option pricing problems in an extension of that model to the case in which the drift and volatility coefficients switch their values between two constant ones, according to the change of the state of a continuous time Markov chain. Jobert and Rogers [18] considered the perpetual American put option problem within an extension of that model to the case of several states for the Markov chain and solved the corresponding problem with finite expiry numerically. In the model with a two-state Markov chain and no diffusion part, Dalang and Hongler [6] presented a complete and essentially explicit solution to a similar problem, which exhibited a surprisingly rich structure. These results were further extended by Jiang and Pistorius [17], who studied the perpetual American put option problem within the framework of an exponential jump-diffusion model with *observable* dynamics of regime-switching behaving parameters. In the present paper, we study the problem of pricing of perpetual American call options on assets *continuously* paying dividends in a model with a *hidden* continuous time Markov chain describing the dynamics of the dividend rate. This stays within the general framework of the information-based approach for derivative pricing introduced by Brody, Hughston and Macrina [5]. The efficient pricing of derivatives on assets with *discretely* paid dividends was recently studied by Vellekoop and Nieuwenhuis [30].

We consider a model of a financial market in which the firm issuing the asset can regulate the dividend rate paid to share holders. To simplify the exposition, we assume that the firm policy allows only two possible states for the dividend rate. Roughly speaking, the firm can be either in a *good* or *bad* economic state, so that the dividend rate may take only two values, accordingly. We further assume that, being inaccessible to small investors trading in the market, the future dividend policy of the issuing firm is hidden into the dynamics of the underlying asset prices, under the risk-neutral probability measure. From the point of view of such investors, the firm future dividend policy and thus the dynamics of the dividend rate can be described by a continuous Markov chain with two states.

Suppose that the dynamics of the underlying asset prices are described by a geometric Brownian motion with a random drift rate having the following structure with respect to the risk-neutral probability measure. We assume that the drift switches its rate from one constant value to another, according to the change of the state of the continuous time Markov chain. Such a switching model for the description of the interest rate dynamics was proposed by Shiryaev [28, Chapter III, Sec. 4a]. More general hidden continuous time Markov chains were recently used by Elliott and Wilson [8] for modeling of the interest rate dynamics. A model for several asset prices with one-time switching random dividends, that reflects an influence of certain unobservable external events, was recently considered in Gapeev and Jeanblanc [10], where the rational prices of European contingent claims were computed. Some other models with random dividends were earlier considered in the literature (see, e.g. Geske [13]), where the possibility of significance of stochastic dividend effects on the rational values of contingent claims was emphasized.

The paper is organized as follows. In Sec. 2, we make an embedding of the initial perpetual American option pricing problem into an extended optimal stopping problem for a two-dimensional Markov diffusion process, having the asset price and the filtering dividend rate estimate as its state space components. We show that the optimal time of exercise is expressed as the first time at which the asset price process hits a stochastic boundary depending on the current state of the dividend rate estimate. We also formulate the associated free-boundary problem for a parabolic-type second order partial differential operator. Moreover, we construct some closed form estimates for the value function and the stopping boundary. In Sec. 3, we reduce the resulting parabolic-type partial differential operator to the normal form. We verify that the solution of the free-boundary problem, which satisfies certain additional conditions, provides the solution of the initial optimal stopping problem. For this, we apply the change-of-variable formula with local time on surfaces, obtained by Peskir [24]. In Sec. 4, we construct other related estimates, which coincide with the true value function and the exercise boundary, under certain relations between the parameters of the model. We also clarify the validity of the smooth-fit principle for the underlying two-dimensional optimal stopping problem. The main results of the paper are stated in Theorem 3.1, Remark 3.1, and Corollary 4.1.

Note that other optimal stopping problems for diffusions under partial information were earlier considered by Beibel and Lerche [3, Sec. 2.6], Rishel [26], and Shiryaev and Novikov [29] for underlying one-dimensional processes, and, more recently, in Gapeev and Shiryaev [11, 12] for essentially two-dimensional models.

2. Preliminaries

In this section, we introduce the setting and notation of the two-dimensional optimal stopping problem, which is related to the pricing of perpetual American call options under partial information, and formulate the associated free-boundary problem.

2.1. *Formulation of the problem*

Let us suppose that on a probability space $(\Omega, \mathcal{G}, P)$ there exist a standard Brownian motion $B = (B_t)_{t \geq 0}$ and a continuous-time Markov chain $\Theta = (\Theta_t)_{t \geq 0}$ with two states 0 and 1. Assume that Θ has initial distribution $\{1 - \pi, \pi\}$ for $\pi \in [0, 1]$, transition probability matrix $\{e^{-\lambda t}, 1 - e^{-\lambda t}; 1 - e^{-\lambda t}, e^{-\lambda t}\}$ for $t \geq 0$, and intensity matrix $\{-\lambda, \lambda; \lambda, -\lambda\}$ for some $\lambda \geq 0$ fixed. Suppose that the processes B and Θ are independent. Let us define the process $S = (S_t)_{t \geq 0}$ started at some $s > 0$ by:

$$S_t = s \exp\left(\int_0^t \left(r - \frac{\sigma^2}{2} - \delta_0 - (\delta_1 - \delta_0)\Theta_u \right) du + \sigma B_t \right) \tag{2.1}$$

which solves the stochastic differential equation:

$$dS_t = (r - \delta_0 - (\delta_1 - \delta_0)\Theta_t) S_t dt + \sigma S_t dB_t \quad (S_0 = s) \tag{2.2}$$

where $\sigma > 0$ and $0 < \delta_i < r$ are some given constants, for every $i = 0, 1$.

Assume that the process S describes the risk-neutral dynamics of the price of a dividend paying asset changing its dividend rate at the switching times of the process Θ. Suppose that Θ reflects the switching behavior of the economic state of the firm issuing the asset from 0 (the firm is in the so-called *bad* state) to 1 (the firm is in the so-called *good* state) and vice versa. In those cases, the asset pays dividends at the rate δ_0 if $\Theta_t = 0$, and the dividend rate is δ_1 if $\Theta_t = 1$, for all $t \geq 0$. We let the time of each stay be exponentially distributed with parameter λ. Here, r is the interest rate of a riskless bank account and σ is the volatility coefficient.

Suppose that the dividend rate regulation process $\delta_0 + (\delta_1 - \delta_0)\Theta$ is unknown to small investors trading at the market, who can only observe the dynamics of the asset prices S. The main purpose of the present paper is to derive a solution to the optimal stopping problem:

$$V_* = \sup_{\tau} E[e^{-r\tau}(S_\tau - K)^+] \tag{2.3}$$

where the supremum is taken over all stopping times τ with respect to the natural filtration $\mathcal{F}_t = \sigma(S_u \,|\, 0 \leq u \leq t) \subseteq \mathcal{G}$, $t \geq 0$, of the asset price process S. Since we work under the martingale probability measure P on the filtration $(\mathcal{F}_t)_{t\geq 0}$, the value of (2.3) represents a *rational* (*no-arbitrage*) *price* of a perpetual American call option with the strike price $K > 0$ in a model with *partial information.*

It is shown by means of standard arguments (see, e.g. [21, Chapter IX] or [7, Chapter VIII]) that the asset price process S from (2.2) admits the representation:

$$dS_t = (r - \delta_0 - (\delta_1 - \delta_0)\Pi_t)S_t dt + \sigma S_t d\overline{B}_t \quad (S_0 = s) \tag{2.4}$$

and the filtering estimate $\Pi = (\Pi_t)_{t\geq 0}$ defined by $\Pi_t = E[\Theta_t \,|\, \mathcal{F}_t] \equiv P(\Theta_t = 1 \,|\, \mathcal{F}_t)$ solves the stochastic differential equation:

$$d\Pi_t = \lambda(1 - 2\Pi_t)dt - \frac{\delta_1 - \delta_0}{\sigma}\Pi_t(1 - \Pi_t)d\overline{B}_t \quad (\Pi_0 = \pi) \tag{2.5}$$

for some $(s, \pi) \in (0, \infty) \times [0, 1]$ fixed. Here, the innovation process $\overline{B} = (\overline{B}_t)_{t\geq 0}$ defined by:

$$\overline{B}_t = \int_0^t \frac{dS_u}{\sigma S_u} - \frac{1}{\sigma}\int_0^t (r - \delta_0 - (\delta_1 - \delta_0)\Pi_u)du \tag{2.6}$$

is a standard Brownian motion, according to P. Lévy's characterization theorem (see, e.g. [21, Theorem 4.1]). It can be verified that (S, Π) is a (time-homogeneous strong) Markov process under P with respect to its natural filtration $(\mathcal{F}_t)_{t\geq 0}$ as a unique strong solution of the system of stochastic differential equations in (2.4) and (2.5) (see, e.g. [23, Theorem 7.2.4]).

2.2. *The optimal stopping problem*

For the problem of (2.3), let us consider the following *extended* optimal stopping problem:

$$V_*(s,\pi) = \sup_{\tau} E_{s,\pi}[e^{-r\tau}(S_\tau - K)^+] \tag{2.7}$$

where $P_{s,\pi}$ is a measure of the diffusion process (S, Π) started at some $(s,\pi) \in (0,\infty) \times [0,1]$ and solving the two-dimensional system of equations in (2.4) and (2.5). The supremum in (2.7) is therefore taken over all stopping times τ of (S, Π) being a Markovian sufficient statistic in the problem (see [27, Chapter II, Sec. 15] for a discussion of this notion). By means of the results of general theory of optimal stopping (see, e.g. [27, Chapter III] or [25, Chapter I, Sec. 2.1]), it follows from the structure of the reward function in (2.7) that the optimal stopping time is given by:

$$\tau_* = \inf\{t \geq 0 \,|\, V_*(S_t, \Pi_t) = (S_t - K)^+\} \tag{2.8}$$

so that the continuation region has the form:

$$C_* = \{(s,\pi) \in (0,\infty) \times [0,1] \,|\, V_*(s,\pi) > (s-K)^+\}. \tag{2.9}$$

In order to specify the structure of the optimal stopping time in (2.8), we apply the change-of-variable formula from [24] to the function $e^{-rt}(s-K)^+$ to get:

$$\begin{aligned} e^{-rt}(S_t - K)^+ &= (s-K)^+ + M_t^K \\ &\quad + \int_0^t e^{-ru} H(S_u, \Pi_u) I(S_u > K)\, du + \frac{1}{2}\int_0^t e^{-ru} I(S_u = K)\, d\ell_u^K(S) \end{aligned} \tag{2.10}$$

where we set $H(s,\pi) = rK - (\delta_0 + (\delta_1 - \delta_0)\pi)s$, and the process $\ell^K(S) = (\ell_t^K(S))_{t\geq 0}$ is the local time of S at the point K given by:

$$\ell_t^K(S) = \lim_{\varepsilon \downarrow 0} \frac{1}{2\varepsilon} \int_0^t I(K - \varepsilon < S_u < K + \varepsilon)\sigma^2 S_u^2\, du \tag{2.11}$$

as a limit in probability. Here, the process $M^K = (M_t^K)_{t\geq 0}$ defined by:

$$M_t^K = \int_0^t e^{-ru} I(S_u > K)\sigma S_u\, d\overline{B}_u \tag{2.12}$$

is a continuous square integrable martingale under $P_{s,\pi}$, and $I(\cdot)$ denotes the indicator function. Therefore, applying Doob's optional sampling theorem (see, e.g. [21, Theorem 3.6]) and using the expression in (2.10), we get that:

$$\begin{aligned} E_{s,\pi}[e^{-r\tau}(S_\tau - K)^+] &= (s-K)^+ \\ &\quad + E_{s,\pi}\left[\int_0^\tau e^{-ru} H(S_u, \Pi_u) I(S_u > K)\, du + \frac{1}{2}\int_0^\tau e^{-ru} I(S_u = K)\, d\ell_u^K(S)\right] \end{aligned} \tag{2.13}$$

holds for any stopping time τ and all $(s,\pi) \in (0,\infty) \times [0,1]$. Choosing τ to be the exit time of S from a small ball, it is seen from (2.13) that it is never optimal to stop when $H(S_t, \Pi_t) \geq 0$ and $S_t > K$, for $t \geq 0$. In other words, this shows that all points (s, π) such that $K < s \leq \underline{b}(\pi)$ with $\underline{b}(\pi) = rK/(\delta_0 + (\delta_1 - \delta_0)\pi)$ for $\pi \in [0, 1]$ belong to the continuation region in (2.9), which clearly contains the rectangle $\{(s, \pi) \in (0, K] \times [0, 1]\}$.

Let us fix some (s, π) from the continuation region C_* in (2.9) and let $\tau_* = \tau_*(s, \pi)$ denote the optimal stopping time in the problem of (2.7). Then, by means of the general optimal stopping theory for Markov processes (see, e.g. [27, Chapter III] or [25, Chapter I, Sec. 2.2]), we conclude from the expression in (2.13) that:

$$V_*(s, \pi) - (s - K)^+ \\ = E_{s,\pi}\left[\int_0^{\tau_*} e^{-ru} H(S_u, \Pi_u) I(S_u > K) du + \frac{1}{2}\int_0^{\tau_*} e^{-ru} I(S_u = K) d\ell_u^K(S)\right] > 0 \tag{2.14}$$

holds. Hence, taking any s' such that $K < \underline{b}(\pi) < s' < s$ and using the explicit expression for the process S through its starting point in (2.1), we obtain from (2.13) that the inequalities:

$$\begin{aligned} &V_*(s', \pi) - (s' - K)^+ \\ &\quad \geq E_{s',\pi}\left[\int_0^{\tau_*} e^{-ru} H(S_u, \Pi_u) I(S_u > K) du + \frac{1}{2}\int_0^{\tau_*} e^{-ru} I(S_u = K) d\ell_u^K(S)\right] \\ &\quad \geq E_{s,\pi}\left[\int_0^{\tau_*} e^{-ru} H(S_u, \Pi_u) I(S_u > K) du + \frac{1}{2}\int_0^{\tau_*} e^{-ru} I(S_u = K) d\ell_u^K(S)\right] \end{aligned} \tag{2.15}$$

are satisfied. Thus, taking into account the fact that $0 < \delta_i < r$, by virtue of the inequality in (2.14) we see that $(s', \pi) \in C_*$. These arguments, together with the easily proved convexity of the function $s \mapsto V_*(s, \pi)$ on $(0, \infty)$, show that there exists a function $b_*(\pi)$ such that $K < \underline{b}(\pi) \leq b_*(\pi)$ holds for all $\pi \in [0, 1]$. Therefore, the continuation region in (2.9) for the optimal stopping problem of (2.7) takes the form:

$$C_* = \{(s, \pi) \in (0, \infty) \times [0, 1] | s < b_*(\pi)\} \tag{2.16}$$

and the corresponding stopping region is the closure of the set:

$$D_* = \{(s, \pi) \in (0, \infty) \times [0, 1] | s > b_*(\pi)\}. \tag{2.17}$$

For any $(s, \pi) \in C_*$ fixed, let us now take π' such that $\pi' < \pi$ if $\delta_0 < \delta_1$ (or $\pi < \pi'$ if $\delta_0 > \delta_1$), whenever $s > K$. Then, using the facts that (S, Π) is a time-homogeneous Markov process and $\tau_* = \tau_*(s, \pi)$ does not depend on π', taking into account the comparison results for solutions of stochastic differential equations, we obtain from the expression in (2.10) and the structure of the process $\ell^K(S)$ in (2.11) that:

$$
\begin{aligned}
&V_*(s,\pi') - (s-K)^+ \\
&\quad \geq E_{s,\pi'}\left[\int_0^{\tau_*} e^{-ru} H(S_u,\Pi_u) I(S_u > K)\, du + \frac{1}{2}\int_0^{\tau_*} e^{-ru} I(S_u = K)\, d\ell_u^K(S)\right] \\
&\quad \geq E_{s,\pi}\left[\int_0^{\tau_*} e^{-ru} H(S_u,\Pi_u) I(S_u > K)\, du + \frac{1}{2}\int_0^{\tau_*} e^{-ru} I(S_u = K)\, d\ell_u^K(S)\right]
\end{aligned}
\tag{2.18}
$$

holds. By virtue of the inequality in (2.14), we may conclude that $(s,\pi') \in C_*$, so that the boundary $b_*(\pi)$ is decreasing (increasing) on $[0,1]$ in (2.16)–(2.17) whenever $\delta_0 < \delta_1$ ($\delta_0 > \delta_1$), respectively.

Summarizing the facts proved above, we are now ready to formulate the following assertion.

Lemma 2.1. *Suppose that $\sigma > 0$ and $0 < \delta_i < r$ for every $i = 0, 1$ in (2.1)–(2.2). Then, in the perpetual American call option pricing problem of (2.3) and (2.7) under partial information, the optimal exercise time has the structure:*

$$\tau_* = \inf\{t \geq 0 \,|\, S_t \geq b_*(\Pi_t)\} \tag{2.19}$$

where the function $b_*(\pi)$ satisfies the properties:

$$b_*(\pi) : [0,1] \to (K,\infty) \text{ is decreasing/increasing if } \delta_0 < \delta_1/\delta_0 > \delta_1 \tag{2.20}$$

$$K < \underline{b}(\pi) \leq b_*(\pi) \text{ with } \underline{b}(\pi) = rK/(\delta_0 + (\delta_1 - \delta_0)\pi) \tag{2.21}$$

for all $\pi \in [0,1]$.

2.3. *The free-boundary problem*

By means of standard arguments based on the application of Itô's formula, it is shown that the infinitesimal operator $\mathbb{L}_{(S,\Pi)}$ of the process (S,Π) from (2.4)–(2.5) acts on an arbitrary locally bounded function $F(s,\pi)$ from the class $C^{2,2}$ on the set $(0,\infty)\times[0,1]$ according to the rule:

$$
\begin{aligned}
(\mathbb{L}_{(S,\Pi)}F)(s,\pi) = \Bigg(&(r - \delta_0 - (\delta_1-\delta_0)\pi) s F_s + \frac{1}{2}\sigma^2 s^2 F_{ss} \\
&- (\delta_1 - \delta_0) s\pi(1-\pi) F_{s\pi} + \lambda(1-2\pi)F_\pi + \frac{1}{2}\left(\frac{\delta_1-\delta_0}{\sigma}\right)^2 \pi^2(1-\pi)^2 F_{\pi\pi}\Bigg)(s,\pi)
\end{aligned}
\tag{2.22}
$$

for all $(s,\pi) \in (0,\infty)\times[0,1]$. In order to find analytic expressions for the unknown value function $V_*(s,\pi)$ from (2.7) and the boundary $b_*(\pi)$ from (2.16)–(2.17), we use the results of the general theory of optimal stopping problems for continuous time Markov processes (see, e.g. [14], [27, Chapter III, Sec. 8] and [25, Chapter IV, Sec. 8]) to formulate the associated *free-boundary problem*:

$$(\mathbb{L}_{(S,\Pi)}V)(s,\pi) = rV(s,\pi) \quad \text{for} \quad (s,\pi) \in C \tag{2.23}$$

$$V(s,\pi)|_{s=b(\pi)-} = b(\pi) - K \quad (\textit{instantaneous stopping}) \tag{2.24}$$

$$V(s,\pi) = (s-K)^+ \quad \text{for} \quad (s,\pi) \in D \tag{2.25}$$

$$V(s,\pi) > (s-K)^+ \quad \text{for} \quad (s,\pi) \in C \tag{2.26}$$

where C and D are defined as C_* and D_* in (2.16) and (2.17) with $b(\pi)$ instead of $b_*(\pi)$, and the condition in (2.24) is satisfied for all $\pi \in (0,1)$. Note that the superharmonic characterization of the value function (see [27, Chapter III, Sec. 8] or [25, Chapter IV, Sec. 9]) implies that $V_*(s,\pi)$ from (2.7) is the smallest function satisfying (2.23)–(2.26) with the boundary $b_*(\pi)$.

Remark 2.1. Observe that, since the system in (2.23)–(2.26) admits multiple solutions, we need to find some additional conditions which would specify the appropriate solution providing the value function and the optimal stopping boundary for the initial problem of (2.7). In order to derive such conditions, in the following section, we shall reduce the operator in (2.23) to the normal form. We also note that the fact that the stochastic differential equations for the asset price and the filtering estimate in (2.4) and (2.5) are driven by the same (one-dimensional) innovation Brownian motion yields the property that the infinitesimal operator in (2.22) turns out to be of parabolic type.

2.4. *The case of full information*

Let us now recall the corresponding problem with *full information*, which consists of computing the value function:

$$W_*(s,\theta) = \sup_{\zeta} E_{s,\theta}[e^{-r\zeta}(S_\zeta - K)^+] \tag{2.27}$$

where $P_{s,\theta}$ is a measure of the process (S,Θ) started at some $(s,\theta) \in (0,\infty) \times \{0,1\}$. The supremum in (2.27) is taken over all stopping times ζ with respect to the filtration $\mathcal{G}_t = \sigma(S_u, \Theta_u \,|\, 0 \le u \le t)$, $t \ge 0$. Since the continuous time Markov chain Θ is observable in this formulation, the optimal stopping time for the problem of (2.27) should be of the form:

$$\zeta_* = \inf\{t \ge 0 \,|\, S_t \ge a_*(\Theta_t)\} \tag{2.28}$$

for some points $a_*(\theta)$, $\theta = 0, 1$, to be determined.

By means of standard arguments based on the application of Itô's formula, it is shown that the infinitesimal operator $\mathbb{L}_{(S,\Theta)}$ of the process (S,Θ) from (2.1)–(2.2) acts on an arbitrary locally bounded function $F(s,\theta)$, which is twice continuously differentiable on $(0, \infty)$ for $\theta = 0, 1$ fixed, according to the rule:

$$(\mathbb{L}_{(S,\Theta)}F)(s,\theta) = (r - \delta_0 - (\delta_1 - \delta_0)\theta)sF_s(s,\theta) + \frac{1}{2}\sigma^2 s^2 F_{ss}(s,\theta) + \lambda(F(s, 1-\theta) - F(s,\theta)) \tag{2.29}$$

for all $(s, \theta) \in (0, \infty) \times \{0, 1\}$. Following the way of arguments from [16] (see also [17] for a more general model), we conclude that the function $W_*(s,\theta)$ and the boundary $a_*(\theta)$ solve the coupled system of *ordinary* differential free-boundary problems:

$$(\mathbb{L}_{(S,\Theta)}W)(s,\theta) = rW(s,\theta) \quad \text{for} \quad 0 < s < a(\theta) \quad \text{such that} \quad s \neq a(1-\theta) \tag{2.30}$$

$$W(s,\theta)|_{s=a(\theta)-} = a(\theta) - K \quad (\textit{instantaneous stopping}) \tag{2.31}$$

$$W(s,\theta) = (s-K)^+ \quad \text{for} \quad s > a(\theta) \tag{2.32}$$

$$W(s,\theta) > (s-K)^+ \quad \text{for} \quad s < a(\theta) \tag{2.33}$$

where the condition in (2.31) is satisfied for $\theta = 0, 1$. Moreover, we assume that the following conditions:

$$W(s,\theta)|_{s=0+} = 0 \quad (\textit{natural boundary}) \tag{2.34}$$

$$W_s(s,\theta)|_{s=a(\theta)-} = 1 \quad (\textit{smooth fit}) \tag{2.35}$$

hold for every $\theta = 0, 1$.

To simplify the notation, we further assume that $\delta_0 > \delta_1$, without loss of generality. By means of straightforward computations, we obtain that the general solutions of the two-dimensional system of second order ordinary differential equations in (2.30) satisfying the conditions in (2.34) are given by:

$$W(s,\theta) = C_1(\theta)s^{\beta_1} + C_2(\theta)s^{\beta_2} + C_3(\theta)s^{\beta_3} + C_4(\theta)s^{\beta_4} \tag{2.36}$$

for $0 < s < a(0)$ and $\theta = 0, 1$, as well as

$$W(s,1) = D_1(1)s^{\gamma_1} + D_2(1)s^{\gamma_2} + G(s) \tag{2.37}$$

for $a(0) < s < a(1)$ with

$$G(s) = \frac{\lambda s}{\delta_1 + \lambda} - \frac{\lambda K}{r + \lambda} \tag{2.38}$$

for $s > 0$. Here, $\beta_4 < \beta_3 < 0 < \beta_2 < \beta_1$ are the roots of the corresponding characteristic equation:

$$Q_0(\beta)Q_1(\beta) = \lambda^2 \quad \text{with} \quad Q_i(\beta) = r + \lambda - \beta(r - \delta_i) - \frac{1}{2}\beta(\beta-1)\sigma^2 \tag{2.39}$$

for $i = 0, 1$, and $\gamma_2 < 0 < 1 < \gamma_1$ are explicitly given by:

$$\gamma_j = \frac{1}{2} - \frac{r - \delta_1}{\sigma^2} - (-1)^j \sqrt{\left(\frac{1}{2} - \frac{r-\delta_1}{\sigma^2}\right)^2 + \frac{2(r+\lambda)}{\sigma^2}} \tag{2.40}$$

for every $j = 1, 2$. Observe that we should have $C_3(\theta) = C_4(\theta) = 0$ in (4.2), since otherwise $W(s,\theta) \to \pm\infty$ as $s \downarrow 0$, that must be excluded by virtue of the obvious fact that the value function in (2.27) is bounded under $s \downarrow 0$, for any $\theta = 0, 1$ fixed. The latter fact also follows from the property that 0 cannot be reached in a finite time by the process S under $\theta = 0, 1$, that is expressed by the condition of (2.34).

Then, using the structure of the coupled system of ordinary differential equations in (2.30) and applying the conditions of (2.31) and (2.35) to the functions in (2.36)–(2.37) with $C_3(i) = C_4(i) = 0$, $i = 0, 1$, we obtain that the following equalities:

$$C_j(0)Q_0(\beta_j) = C_j(1)\lambda \quad \text{for } j = 1, 2 \tag{2.41}$$

$$C_1(0)a^{\beta_1}(0) + C_2(0)a^{\beta_2}(0) = a(0) - K \tag{2.42}$$

$$C_1(0)\beta_1 a^{\beta_1}(0) + C_2(0)\beta_2 a^{\beta_2}(0) = a(0) \tag{2.43}$$

$$D_1(1)a^{\gamma_1}(1) + D_2(1)a^{\gamma_2}(1) + G(a(1)) = a(1) - K \tag{2.44}$$

$$D_1(1)\gamma_1 a^{\gamma_1}(1) + D_2(1)\gamma_2 a^{\gamma_2}(1) + a(1)G'(a(1)) = a(1) \tag{2.45}$$

hold. Observe that, since the point $a_*(0)$ belongs to the corresponding continuation region when $\theta = 1$, the function in (2.36) should be continuously differentiable, and thus the equalities:

$$C_1(1)a^{\beta_1}(0) + C_2(1)a^{\beta_2}(0) = D_1(1)a^{\gamma_1}(0) + D_2(1)a^{\gamma_2}(0) + G(a(0)) \tag{2.46}$$

$$C_1(1)\beta_1 a^{\beta_1}(0) + C_2(1)\beta_2 a^{\beta_2}(0) = D_1(1)\gamma_1 a^{\gamma_1}(0) + D_2(1)\gamma_2 a^{\gamma_2}(0) + a(0)G'(a(0)) \tag{2.47}$$

are satisfied. Hence, solving the system in (2.41)–(2.47), by means of straightforward computations, we obtain that the solution of the free-boundary problem in (2.30)–(2.31) and (2.34)–(2.35) is given by:

$$W(s, 0; a_*(0)) = \sum_{j=1}^{2} \frac{(\beta_{3-j} - 1)a_*(0) - \beta_{3-j}K}{\beta_{3-j} - \beta_j} \left(\frac{s}{a_*(0)} \right)^{\beta_j} \tag{2.48}$$

and

$$W(s, 1; a_*(0)) = \sum_{j=1}^{2} \frac{(\beta_{3-j} - 1)a_*(0) - \beta_{3-j}K}{\beta_{3-j} - \beta_j} \frac{Q_0(\beta_j)}{\lambda} \left(\frac{s}{a_*(0)} \right)^{\beta_j} \tag{2.49}$$

for $0 < s < a_*(0)$, as well as

$$\begin{aligned} W(s, 1; a_*(1)) &= G(s) \\ &+ \sum_{j=1}^{2} \frac{(\gamma_{3-j} - 1)a_*(1) - \gamma_{3-j}(K + G(a_*(1))) + a_*(1)G'(a_*(1))}{\gamma_{3-j} - \gamma_j} \left(\frac{s}{a_*(1)} \right)^{\gamma_j} \end{aligned} \tag{2.50}$$

for $a_*(0) \le s < a_*(1)$. Here, the couple $a_*(\theta)$, $\theta = 0, 1$, is determined as a unique solution of the system of equations:

$$\sum_{j=1}^{2} \frac{(\beta_{3-j} - 1)a(0) - \beta_{3-j}K}{\beta_{3-j} - \beta_j} \frac{Q_0(\beta_j)}{\lambda} = G(a(0))$$
$$+ \sum_{j=1}^{2} \frac{(\gamma_{3-j} - 1)a(1) - \gamma_{3-j}(K + G(a(1))) + a(1)G'(a(1))}{\gamma_{3-j} - \gamma_j} \left(\frac{a(0)}{a(1)}\right)^{\gamma_j} \tag{2.51}$$

and

$$\sum_{j=1}^{2} \frac{(\beta_{3-j} - 1)a(0) - \beta_{3-j}K}{\beta_{3-j} - \beta_j} \frac{\beta_j Q_0(\beta_j)}{\lambda} = a(0)G'(a(0))$$
$$+ \sum_{j=1}^{2} \frac{(\gamma_{3-j} - 1)a(1) - \gamma_{3-j}(K + G(a(1))) + a_*(1)G'(a(1))}{\gamma_{3-j} - \gamma_j} \gamma_j \left(\frac{a(0)}{a(1)}\right)^{\gamma_j} \tag{2.52}$$

(cf. [16, Sec. 2]). Using the corresponding verification assertion from [16, Theorem 2], that can be also proved by means of the arguments similar to the ones used in the proof of Lemma 3.1 below, we may therefore conclude that the value functions in (2.27) take the form:

$$W_*(s, 0) = \begin{cases} W(s, 0; a_*(0)), & \text{if } 0 < s < a_*(0) \\ s - K, & \text{if } s \ge a_*(0) \end{cases} \tag{2.53}$$

and

$$W_*(s, 1) = \begin{cases} W(s, 1; a_*(0)), & \text{if } 0 < s < a_*(0) \\ W(s, 1; a_*(1)), & \text{if } a_*(0) \le s < a_*(1) \\ s - K, & \text{if } s \ge a_*(1) \end{cases} \tag{2.54}$$

where the expressions for $W(s, \theta; a_*(0))$, $\theta = 0, 1$, and $W(s, 1; a_*(1))$ are given by (2.48)–(2.49) and (2.50), respectively, under the assumption that $\delta_0 > \delta_1$.

Remark 2.2. Since the set of stopping times over which the supremum is taken in (2.27) is larger than that in (2.7), it is easily seen that the inequalities $V_*(s, \theta) \le W_*(s, \theta)$ hold, so that $W_*(s, \theta)$ is an upper bound for $V_*(s, \theta)$, for every $\theta = 0, 1$. It thus follows from the easily proved convexity of the function $\pi \mapsto V_*(s, \pi)$ on $[0, 1]$ that for the function $\overline{W}(s, \pi)$ defined by:

$$\overline{W}(s, \pi) = W_*(s, 0)(1 - \pi) + W_*(s, 1)\pi \tag{2.55}$$

the inequalities:

$$\overline{W}(s, \pi) \ge V_*(s, 0)(1 - \pi) + V_*(s, 1)\pi \ge V_*(s, \pi) \tag{2.56}$$

hold for all $(s, \pi) \in (0, \infty) \times [0, 1]$. Moreover, by virtue of the Markovian structure of the problem in (2.7) for the process (S, Π) from (2.4) and (2.5), taking into account the comparison results for solutions of stochastic differential equations, we conclude that the value function $\pi \mapsto V_*(s,\pi)$ is increasing on $[0,1]$, for each $s>0$ fixed, under the assumption that $\delta_0 > \delta_1$. The latter fact directly implies that the inequality $V_*(s,\pi) \le W_*(s,1)$ is satisfied, so that the standard comparison arguments yield that $b_*(\pi) \le a_*(1)$ holds for all $(s,\pi) \in (0,\infty) \times [0,1]$.

3. Main Results

In this section, we reduce the operator from (2.22) to the normal form and prove the corresponding verification assertion.

3.1. *Verification lemma*

In order to find the normal form of the operator from (2.22) and formulate the associated optimal stopping and free-boundary problem, we follow the arguments of [11] and use the one-to-one correspondence transformation of processes proposed by A. N. Kolmogorov in [19]. For this, let us define the process $Y = (Y_t)_{t\ge 0}$ by:

$$Y_t = \frac{S_t^{-\eta}\Pi_t}{1-\Pi_t} \quad \text{with} \quad \eta = \frac{\delta_0 - \delta_1}{\sigma^2} \tag{3.1}$$

for all $t \ge 0$. Then, it follows from (2.4)–(2.5) that the process S takes the form:

$$dS_t = \left(r - \delta_0 - (\delta_1 - \delta_0)\frac{S_t^{\eta} Y_t}{1 + S_t^{\eta} Y_t} \right) S_t dt + \sigma S_t d\overline{B}_t \quad (S_0 = s) \tag{3.2}$$

and, by means of Itô's formula, we get that the process Y admits the representation:

$$dY_t = \left(\frac{\lambda(1 - S_t^{2\eta} Y_t^2)}{S_t^{\eta} Y_t} - \frac{\eta}{2}(2r - \delta_0 - \delta_1 - \sigma^2) \right) Y_t dt \quad \left(Y_0 = y \equiv \frac{s^{-\eta}\pi}{1-\pi} \right) \tag{3.3}$$

for any $(s,\pi) \in (0,\infty) \times (0,1)$. It is seen from the equation in (3.3) that the process Y started at $y>0$ is of bounded variation. It follows from the relation in (3.1) that there exists a one-to-one correspondence between the processes (S,Π) and (S,Y). Hence, for any $\pi \in (0,1)$ fixed, the value function $V_*(s,\pi)$ from (2.7) is equal to that of the optimal stopping problem:

$$U_*(s,y) = \sup_{\tau} E_{s,y}[e^{-r\tau}(S_\tau - K)^+] \tag{3.4}$$

where $E_{s,y}$ denotes the expectation under the assumption that the two-dimensional Markov process (S,Y) from (3.2) and (3.3) starts at some $(s,y) \in (0,\infty)^2$. The supremum in (3.4) is taken over all stopping times τ with respect to the natural filtration of (S,Y), which clearly coincides with $(\mathcal{F}_t)_{t\ge 0}$. It thus follows from (2.19) that there exists a function $g_*(y) \ge K$, for $y>0$, such that the optimal stopping time in the problem of (3.4) is of the form:

$$\tau_* = \inf\{t \ge 0 \mid S_t \ge g_*(Y_t)\}. \tag{3.5}$$

Standard arguments then show that the infinitesimal operator $\mathbb{L}_{(S,Y)}$ of the process (S,Y) from (3.2) and (3.3) acts on an arbitrary twice continuously differentiable locally bounded function $F(s, y)$ according to the rule:

$$(\mathbb{L}_{(S,Y)}F)(s,y) = \left(\left(r - \delta_0 - (\delta_1 - \delta_0)\frac{s^\eta y}{1 + s^\eta y} \right) sF_s + \frac{1}{2}\sigma^2 s^2 F_{ss} + \left(\frac{\lambda(1 - s^{2\eta}y^2)}{s^\eta y} - \frac{\eta}{2}(2r - \delta_0 - \delta_1 - \sigma^2) \right) yF_y \right)(s,y) \quad (3.6)$$

for all $(s, y) \in (0, \infty)^2$. We are now ready to formulate the associated free-boundary problem for the unknown value function $U_*(s, y)$ from (3.4) and the boundary $g_*(y)$ from (3.5):

$$(\mathbb{L}_{(S,Y)}U)(s,y) = rU(s,y) \quad \text{for} \quad 0 < s < g(y) \quad (3.7)$$

$$U(s,y)|_{s=g(y)-} = g(y) - K \quad (\textit{instantaneous stopping}) \quad (3.8)$$

$$U(s,y) = (s-K)^+ \quad \text{for} \quad s > g(y) \quad (3.9)$$

$$U(s,y) > (s-K)^+ \quad \text{for} \quad s < g(y) \quad (3.10)$$

where the condition in (3.8) is satisfied for all $y > 0$. Moreover, we assume that the following conditions:

$$U(s,y)|_{s=0+} = 0 \quad (\textit{natural boundary}) \quad (3.11)$$

$$U_s(s,y)|_{s=g(y)-} = 1 \quad (\textit{smooth fit}) \quad (3.12)$$

hold and the one-sided derivative:

$$U_y(s,y)|_{s=g(y)-} \quad \text{exists} \quad (3.13)$$

for all $y > 0$. Note that the condition of (3.11) can be used because 0 cannot be reached in a finite time by the process S in the model of (3.2)–(3.3).

We further search for solutions of the *parabolic-type* free-boundary problem in (3.7)–(3.10) satisfying the conditions in (3.11)–(3.13) and such that the resulting boundary is continuous and of bounded variation. Since such free-boundary problems cannot, in general, be solved explicitly, the existence and uniqueness of classical as well as viscosity solutions of the related variational inequalities and their connection with the optimal stopping problems have been extensively studied in the literature (see, e.g. [9, 4, 20] or [23]).

We continue with the following *verification* lemma related to the free-boundary problem in (3.7)–(3.13).

Lemma 3.1. *Assume that the function $U(s, y; g_*(y))$ and the continuous monotone boundary $g_*(y)$ such that $K < \underline{g}(y) \leq g_*(y)$ form a unique solution of the free-boundary problem in* (3.7)–(3.10) *and satisfying the conditions of* (3.11)–(3.13). *Here, the function $\underline{g}(y)$ is defined as the inverse to $\underline{g}^{-1}(s) = (\delta_0 s - rK)s^{-\eta}/$*

$(rK - \delta_1 s)$ for each $s > rK/(\delta_0 \vee \delta_1)$ with $\eta = (\delta_0 - \delta_1)/\sigma^2$. Then, the value function of the optimal stopping problem in (3.4) takes the form:

$$U_*(s,y) = \begin{cases} U(s,y;g_*(y)), & \text{if } 0 < s < g_*(y) \\ s - K, & \text{if } s \geq g_*(y) \end{cases} \tag{3.14}$$

and $g_*(y)$ provides the optimal stopping boundary for (3.5), for all $(s,y) \in (0,\infty)^2$.

Proof. Let us denote by $U(s,y)$ the right-hand side of the expression in (3.14). Hence, applying the change-of-variable formula with local time on surfaces from [24] to $e^{-rt}U(s,y)$ and $g_*(y)$, and taking into account the smooth-fit condition in (3.12), we obtain

$$e^{-rt}U(S_t,Y_t) = U(s,y) + \int_0^t e^{-ru}(\mathbb{L}_{(S,Y)}U - rU)(S_u,Y_u)I(S_u \neq g_*(Y_u))du + M_t \tag{3.15}$$

where the process $M = (M_t)_{t \geq 0}$ defined by:

$$M_t = \int_0^t e^{-ru}U_s(S_u,Y_u)\sigma S_u d\overline{B}_u \tag{3.16}$$

is a continuous square integrable martingale under $P_{s,y}$ with respect to $(\mathcal{F}_t)_{t\geq 0}$.

It follows from the equation in (3.7) and the conditions of (3.8)–(3.10) that the inequality $(\mathbb{L}_{(S,Y)}U - rU)(s,y) \leq 0$ holds for any $(s,y) \in (0,\infty)^2$ such that $s \neq g_*(y)$, as well as $U(s,y) \geq (s-K)^+$ is satisfied for all $(s,y) \in (0,\infty)^2$. Note that the former inequality is equivalent to the assumption that $\underline{g}(y) \leq g_*(y)$ holds for all $y > 0$. Recall the assumption that the boundary $g_*(y)$ is continuous and monotone and the fact that both $g_*(y)$ and the process Y from (3.1) are of bounded variation. We thus conclude that the time spent by the process S at the boundary $g_*(Y)$ is of Lebesgue measure zero, so that the indicator that appears in (3.15) can be ignored. Hence, the expression in (3.15) with the structure of the stopping time in (3.5) yields that the inequalities:

$$e^{-r\tau}(S_\tau - K)^+ \leq e^{-r\tau}U(S_\tau,Y_\tau) \leq U(s,y) + M_\tau \tag{3.17}$$

hold for any stopping time τ of the process (S,Y) started at $(s,y) \in (0,\infty)^2$.

Let $(\tau_n)_{n\in\mathbb{N}}$ be an arbitrary localizing sequence of stopping times for the processes M. Taking in (3.17) the expectation with respect to the measure $P_{s,y}$, by means of Doob's optional sampling theorem, we get that the inequalities:

$$E_{s,y}[e^{-r(\tau\wedge\tau_n)}(S_{\tau\wedge\tau_n} - K)^+] \leq E_{s,y}[e^{-r(\tau\wedge\tau_n)}U(S_{\tau\wedge\tau_n},Y_{\tau\wedge\tau_n})] \leq U(s,y) + E_{s,y}[M_{\tau\wedge\tau_n}] = U(s,y) \tag{3.18}$$

hold for all $(s,y) \in (0,\infty)^2$. Hence, letting n go to infinity and using Fatou's lemma, we obtain:

$$E_{s,y}[e^{-r\tau}(S_\tau - K)^+] \leq E_{s,y}[e^{-r\tau}U(S_\tau,Y_\tau)] \leq U(s,y) \tag{3.19}$$

for any stopping time τ and all $(s, y) \in (0, \infty)^2$. By virtue of the structure of the stopping time in (3.5), it is readily seen that the inequalities in (3.19) hold with τ_* instead of τ when $s \geq g_*(y)$.

It remains to show that the equalities are attained in (3.19) when τ_* replaces τ for $(s, y) \in (0, \infty)^2$ such that $s < g_*(y)$. By virtue of the assumption that the function $U(s, y)$ and the boundary $g_*(y)$ satisfy the conditions of (3.7) and (3.8), it follows from the expression in (3.15) and the structure of the stopping time in (3.5) that the equalities:

$$e^{-r(\tau_* \wedge \tau_n)} U(S_{\tau_* \wedge \tau_n}, Y_{\tau_* \wedge \tau_n}) = U(s, y) + M_{\tau_* \wedge \tau_n} \tag{3.20}$$

hold for all $(s, y) \in (0, \infty)^2$ and any localizing sequence $(\tau_n)_{n \in \mathbb{N}}$ of M. Observe that it follows from the structure of the process S in (2.1) that the variables $e^{-r\tau_*} S_{\tau_*}$ and $e^{-r\tau_*} U(S_{\tau_*}, Y_{\tau_*})$ are equal to zero on the event $\{\tau_* = \infty\}$ ($P_{s,y}$-a.s.). Therefore, taking the expectations in (3.20) and letting n go to infinity, we use the fact that the process $(M_{\tau_* \wedge t})_{t \geq 0}$ is a uniformly integrable martingale and apply the Lebesgue dominated convergence theorem to obtain the equalities:

$$E_{s,y}[e^{-r\tau_*}(S_{\tau_*} - K)^+] = E_{s,y}[e^{-r\tau_*} U(S_{\tau_*}, Y_{\tau_*})] = U(s, y) \tag{3.21}$$

for all $(s, y) \in (0, \infty)^2$, which together with the inequalities in (3.19) directly imply the desired assertion. □

3.2. *The case of partial information*

We are now in a position to formulate the main assertion of the paper, which follows from a straightforward combination of Lemmas 2.1 and 3.1 above and the standard change-of-variable arguments. More precisely, after obtaining the solution $U_*(s, y)$ with $g_*(y)$ of the free-boundary problem in (3.7)–(3.10), which satisfies the conditions of (3.11)–(3.13), we put $y = s^{-\eta}\pi/(1 - \pi)$, in order to get the solution of the initial perpetual American call option pricing problem under partial information stated in (2.3).

Theorem 3.1. *Suppose that the assumptions of Lemma* 3.1 *hold with* $\delta_0 > \delta_1$. *Then, in the perpetual American call option pricing problem of* (2.3) *and* (2.7) *for the underlying asset price process* S *from* (2.1)–(2.2), *the value function takes the form:*

$$V_*(s, \pi) = \begin{cases} U_*(s, s^{-\eta}\pi/(1 - \pi)), & \text{if } 0 < s < g_*(s^{-\eta}\pi/(1 - \pi)) \\ s - K, & \text{if } s \geq g_*(s^{-\eta}\pi/(1 - \pi)) \end{cases} \tag{3.22}$$

and the optimal exercise boundary $b_*(\pi)$ *in* (2.19) *satisfying* (2.20)–(2.21) *is uniquely determined as the inverse to* $b_*^{-1}(s) = s^\eta g_*^{-1}(s)/(1 + s^\eta g_*^{-1}(s))$ *for each* $s > rK/\delta_0$ *with* $\eta = (\delta_0 - \delta_1)/\sigma^2$. *Moreover, the functions* $V_*(s, \pi)$ *and* $b_*(\pi)$ *are monotone (increasing) and* $K < \underline{b}(\pi) \leq b_*(\pi)$ *holds with* $\underline{b}(\pi) = rK/(\delta_0 + (\delta_1 - \delta_0)\pi)$ *for all* $\pi \in [0, 1]$.

Remark 3.1. In order to construct an upper estimate for the value function $V_*(s,\pi)$ from (3.22), let us define the boundary $\widetilde{a}(\pi)$ as the unique root of the equation:

$$W_s(a(\pi),0;a_*(0))(1-\pi)+W_s(a(\pi),1;a_*(0))\pi=1 \tag{3.23}$$

and define the function:

$$h(\pi)=\widetilde{a}(\pi)-\widetilde{W}(\widetilde{a}(\pi),\pi) \tag{3.24}$$

for each $\pi\in[0,1]$. It follows from the structure of the strictly increasing functions $s\mapsto W(s,\theta;a_*(0))$ from (2.48)–(2.49) with $a_*(\theta)$, $\theta=0,1$, given by (2.51)–(2.52) that $h(\pi)$ is decreasing on the interval $[\widetilde{a}(1)-\widetilde{W}(\widetilde{a}(1),1),K]$ with $h(0)=K$. It is shown by means of straightforward computations that the function $\widetilde{W}(s,\pi)$ defined by:

$$\widetilde{W}(s,\pi)=\begin{cases} W(s,0;a_*(0))(1-\pi)+W(s,1;a_*(0))\pi, & \text{if } 0<s<\widetilde{a}(\pi)\\ s-h(\pi), & \text{if } s\geq\widetilde{a}(\pi)\end{cases} \tag{3.25}$$

surprisingly solves the partial differential equation in (2.23) above for $0<s<\widetilde{a}(\pi)$ and $\pi\in(0,1)$. Taking into account the condition of (3.23) and the fact that $0<h(\pi)\leq K$, by means of the arguments of Lemma 3.1, we may therefore conclude from Theorem 3.1 that the function $\widetilde{W}(s,\pi)$ from (3.25) represents a uniformly upper bound for the initial value function $V_*(s,\pi)$ from (2.7), so that $V_*(s,\pi)\leq\widetilde{W}(s,\pi)$ holds for all $(s,\pi)\in(0,\infty)\times[0,1]$.

4. Conclusions

In this section, we provide closed form estimates for the value function and the exercise boundary, and make some concluding remarks concerning analytic properties of the solution of the free-boundary problem, under certain relations between the parameters of the model.

4.1. *Solution in a particular case*

Let us now introduce a function $\widehat{U}(s,y)$ and a boundary $\widehat{g}(y)$ as a solution of the free-boundary problem consisting of the differential equation:

$$\begin{aligned}&(\mathbb{L}_{(S,Y)}U-rU)(s,y)\\ &\quad=\left(\frac{\lambda(1-s^{2\eta}y^2)}{s^\eta y}-\frac{\eta}{2}(2r-\delta_0-\delta_1-\sigma^2)\right)yU_y(s,y)\quad\text{for}\quad 0<s<g(y)\end{aligned} \tag{4.1}$$

instead of that in (3.7), for each $y>0$ fixed, and the boundary conditions of (3.8)–(3.10) as well as (3.11)–(3.12). The general solution of the resulting *homogeneous ordinary* differential equation in (4.1) takes the form:

$$U(s,y)=\sum_{j=1}^{2}A_j(y)s^{\alpha_j}F(\psi_{j1},\psi_{j2};1-(-1)^j2\varphi_0;-s^\eta y) \tag{4.2}$$

where $A_j(y)$, $j = 1, 2$, are some arbitrary continuously differentiable functions, so that the condition in (3.13) is satisfied, as well as

$$\alpha_j = \frac{1}{2} - \frac{r - \delta_0}{\sigma^2} - (-1)^j \eta \varphi_0 \quad \text{and} \quad \psi_{kl} = 1 - (-1)^k \varphi_k - (-1)^l \varphi_l \tag{4.3}$$

with

$$\varphi_i = \frac{1}{\eta} \sqrt{\frac{\delta_i^2}{\sigma^4} + \delta_i \left(1 - \frac{2r}{\sigma^4}\right) + \left(\frac{r}{\sigma^2} + \frac{1}{2}\right)^2} \quad \text{and} \quad \eta = \frac{\delta_0 - \delta_1}{\sigma^2} \tag{4.4}$$

for every $i = 0, 1$ and $j, k, l = 1, 2$. Here, $F(\alpha, \beta; \gamma; x)$ denotes Gauss' hypergeometric function, which is defined by means of the expansion:

$$F(\alpha, \beta; \gamma; x) = 1 + \sum_{m=1}^{\infty} \frac{(\alpha)_m (\beta)_m}{(\gamma)_m} \frac{x^m}{m!} \tag{4.5}$$

for $\gamma \neq 0, -1, -2, \ldots$ and $(\gamma)_m = \gamma(\gamma + 1) \cdots (\gamma + m - 1)$, $m \in \mathbb{N}$, where Γ denotes Euler's Gamma function. Note that the series in (4.5) converges under all $|x| < 1$, and the appropriate analytic continuation into (certain parts of) the complex plane can be obtained through the the same representation for any $\alpha, \beta, \gamma \in \mathbb{R}$ given and fixed. Moreover, the function in (4.5) admits the integral representation:

$$F(\alpha, \beta; \gamma; x) = \frac{\Gamma(\gamma)}{\Gamma(\beta)\Gamma(\gamma - \beta)} \int_0^1 t^{\beta - 1}(1 - t)^{\gamma - \beta - 1}(1 - tx)^{-\alpha} dt \tag{4.6}$$

whenever $\gamma > \beta > 0$ (see, e.g. [1, Chapter XV] and [2, Chapter II]).

Observe that, under the assumption that $\delta_0 > \delta_1$ holds, we should have $A_2(y) = 0$ in (4.2), since otherwise $U(s, y) \to \pm\infty$ as $s \downarrow 0$, that must be excluded by virtue of the obvious fact that the value function in (3.4) is bounded under $s \downarrow 0$, for any $y > 0$ fixed. The latter fact also follows from the property that 0 is a natural boundary for the process S, that is expressed by the condition of (3.11). Then, applying the conditions of (3.8) and (3.12) to the function in (4.2) with $A_2(y) = 0$, we get that the following equalities:

$$A_1(y) g^{\alpha_1}(y) F(\psi_{11}, \psi_{12}; 1 + 2\varphi_0; -g^\eta(y) y) = g(y) - K \tag{4.7}$$

$$\alpha_1 A_1(y) g^{\alpha_1}(y) F(\psi_{11}, \psi_{12}; 1 + 2\varphi_0; -g^\eta(y) y) - \eta A_1(y) g^{\alpha_1 + \eta}(y) y \\ \times \frac{(1 + \psi_{11})(1 + \psi_{12})}{1 + 2\varphi_0} F(1 + \psi_{11}, 1 + \psi_{12}; 2(1 + \varphi_0); -g^\eta(y) y) = g(y) \tag{4.8}$$

hold for each $y > 0$ fixed. Hence, solving the system of (4.7)–(4.8), we get that the solution of the free-boundary problem of (4.1) with (3.8) and (3.11)–(3.12) is given by:

$$U(s, y; \widehat{g}(y)) = (\widehat{g}(y) - K) \left(\frac{s}{\widehat{g}(y)}\right)^{\alpha_1} \frac{F(\psi_{11}, \psi_{12}; 1 + 2\varphi_0; -s^\eta y)}{F(\psi_{11}, \psi_{12}; 1 + 2\varphi_0; -\widehat{g}^\eta(y) y)} \tag{4.9}$$

for all $0 < s < \widehat{g}(y)$, where $\widehat{g}(y)$ satisfies the equation:

$$\frac{(1+\psi_{11})(1+\psi_{12})}{1+2\varphi_0}\,\frac{F(1+\psi_{11},1+\psi_{12};2(1+\varphi_0);-g^{\eta}(y)y)}{F(\psi_{11},\psi_{12};1+2\varphi_0;-g^{\eta}(y)y)} = \frac{(\alpha_1-1)g(y)-\alpha_1 y}{\eta(g(y)-K)g^{\eta}(y)y} \tag{4.10}$$

for any $y > 0$ fixed. The uniqueness of the solution of (4.10) as well as the condition of (3.10) are verified using the properties of Gauss' hypergeometric function in (4.5).

4.2. *Some remarks and examples*

Corollary 4.1. *Suppose that the assumptions of Theorem* 3.1 *are satisfied. Then, using the same arguments as in the proof of Lemma* 3.1 *above, it is shown that the function:*

$$\widehat{U}(s,y) = \begin{cases} U(s,y;\widehat{g}(y)), & \text{if } 0 < s < \widehat{g}(y) \\ s-K, & \text{if } s \geq \widehat{g}(y) \end{cases} \tag{4.11}$$

with $U(s,y;\widehat{g}(y))$ *from* (4.9) *coincides with the value function of the optimal stopping problem:*

$$\begin{aligned} \widehat{U}(s,y) = \sup_{\tau} E_{s,y}\Bigg[& e^{-r\tau}(S_\tau - K)^+ \\ & - \int_0^{\tau} e^{-rt}\left(\frac{\lambda(1-S_t^{2\eta}Y_t^2)}{S_t^{\eta}Y_t} - \frac{\eta}{2}(2r-\delta_0-\delta_1-\sigma^2)\right) \\ & \times Y_t\widehat{U}_y(S_t,Y_t)I(S_t < \widehat{g}(Y_t))dt\Bigg] \end{aligned} \tag{4.12}$$

and $\widehat{g}(y)$ *from* (4.10) *provides the hitting boundary for the stopping time:*

$$\widehat{\tau} = \inf\{t \geq 0 \,|\, S_t \geq \widehat{g}(Y_t)\} \tag{4.13}$$

which turns out to be optimal in (4.12). *Note that the functions* $\widehat{U}(s,y)$ *and* $\widehat{g}(y)$ *can also be considered as estimates for the true value function* $U_*(s,y)$ *and the boundary* $g_*(y)$ *from* (2.7) *and* (2.19), *for all* $(s,y) \in (0,\infty)^2$.

Example 4.1. Let us finally consider the case in which $\lambda = 0$. This means that $\Theta_t = \Theta_0$ for all $t \geq 0$, where Θ_0 is a random variable taking two values 1 and 0 with probabilities $P(\Theta_0 = 1) = \pi$ and $P(\Theta_0 = 0) = 1 - \pi$ for $\pi \in [0,1]$. This assumption reflects the situation in which the issuing firm does not change the dividend policy which is inaccessible to a usual small investor during the whole infinite time interval. The same model appears by solving the Bayesian sequential testing problem for two simple hypotheses about the unknown local drift of an observed Wiener process (see, e.g. [27, Chapter IV, Sec. 2] or [25, Chapter VI, Sec. 1]). In that case, π and $1-\pi$ play the role of a priori probabilities of the statistical hypotheses $H_1 : \Theta_0 = 1$ and $H_0 : \Theta_0 = 0$, respectively. It follows directly from the structure of the expressions in (4.12) and (4.13) that the functions $\widehat{U}(s, y)$ and $\widehat{g}(y)$ coincide with the value function $U_*(s, y)$ and the boundary $g_*(y)$ of the initial optimal stopping problem of (3.4) and (3.5), under the additional assumption that $\delta_0 + \delta_1 = 2r - \sigma^2$ is satisfied.

Remark 4.1. It follows from the assumptions of Corollary 4.1 and Example 4.1 that the boundary $\widehat{g}(y)$ from the equation in (4.10) is continuously differentiable on $(0, \infty)$. Hence, since $\widehat{U}(s, y) = U_*(s, y)$ and $\widehat{g}(y) = g_*(y)$ holds for all $(s, y) \in (0, \infty)^2$ in that case, by means of straightforward computations applied to the expression in (4.9), it is shown using the equation of (4.10) that the smooth-fit condition:

$$(U_*)_y(s, y)|_{s=g_*(y)-} = 0 \tag{4.14}$$

is satisfied for all $y > 0$ under the assumption that $\lambda = 0$ and $\delta_0 + \delta_1 = 2r - \sigma^2$. Thus, taking into account the expression in (3.12), which holds for $U_*(s, y)$ at $g_*(y)$ in this case, and the one-to-one correspondence given by (3.1), we conclude from (4.14) that the smooth-fit condition:

$$(V_*)_\pi(s, \pi)|_{s=b_*(\pi)-} = 0 \tag{4.15}$$

with $b_*(\pi) = g_*(s^{-\eta}\pi/(1 - \pi))$ is satisfied for all $\pi \in (0, 1)$. This property can be explained by the fact that the continuous process S intersects the continuous boundary $g_*(Y)$ and thus $b_*(\Pi)$ with a positive probability.

Acknowledgments

The paper was initiated when the author was visiting Imperial College London in January 2007. The author is grateful Mark Davis, Lane Hughston, and Mihail Zervos for warm hospitality and valuable comments. The financial support from European Science Foundation (ESF) through the grant number 1505 of the programme Advanced Mathematical Methods for Finance (AMaMeF) is gratefully acknowledged. The author thanks Peter Carr, Robert Dalang, Monique Jeanblanc, Andreas Kyprianou, Hans Rudolf Lerche, and Goran Peskir for useful discussions. The results of the paper were presented at the Workshop on Financial Derivatives and Risk Management held at the Fields Institute for Research in Mathematical Sciences in Toronto in May 2010. The financial support from the Thematic Program on Quantitative Finance is gratefully acknowledged.

References

[1] M. Abramovitz and I. A. Stegun, *Handbook of Mathematical Functions with Formulas, Graphs, and Mathematical Tables* (National Bureau of Standards, Wiley, New York, 1972).

[2] H. Bateman and A. Erdélyi, *Higher Transcendental Functions* (Mc Graw-Hill, New York, 1953).

[3] M. Beibel and H. R. Lerche, A new look at optimal stopping problems related to mathematical finance, *Statistica Sinica* **7** (1997) 93–108.

[4] A. Bensoussan and J. L. Lions. *Applications of Variational Inequalities in Stochastic Control* (North Holland, Amsterdam, 1982; French Edition, 1978).

[5] D. C. Brody, L. P. Hughston and A. Macrina, Information-based asset pricing, *International Journal of Theoretical and Applied Finance* **11** (2008) 107–142.

[6] R. C. Dalang and M.-O. Hongler, The right time to sell a stock whose price is driven by Markovian noise, *Annals of Applied Probability* **14** (2004) 2167–2201.

[7] R. J. Elliott, L. Aggoun and J. B. Moore, *Hidden Markov Models: Estimation and Control* (Springer, New York, 1995).

[8] R. J. Elliott and C. A. Wilson, The term structure of interest rates in a hidden Markov setting, *Hidden Markov Models in Finance*, R. S. Mamon and R. J. Elliott, eds. (Springer, New York, 2007) 15–30.

[9] A. Friedman, *Stochastic Differential Equations and Applications, Volumes I, II* (Academic Press, New York, 1976).

[10] P. V. Gapeev and M. Jeanblanc, Pricing and filtering in a two-dimensional dividend switching model, *International Journal of Theoretical and Applied Finance* **13**(7) (2010) 1001–1017.

[11] P. V. Gapeev and A. N. Shiryaev, On the sequential testing problem for some diffusion processes, *Stochastics: An International Journal of Probability and Stochastic Processes* **83**(4–6) (2011) 519–535.

[12] P. V. Gapeev and A. N. Shiryaev, Bayesian quickest detection problems for some diffusion processes, arXiv:1010.3430v1 [math.ST] (25 pp).

[13] R. Geske, The pricing of options with stochastic dividend yield, *Journal of Finance* **33**(2) (1978) 617–625.

[14] B. I. Grigelionis and A. N. Shiryaev, On Stefan's problem and optimal stopping rules for Markov processes, *Theory of Probability and its Applications* **11** (1966) 541–558.

[15] X. Guo, An explicit solution to an optimal stopping problem with regime switching, *Journal of Applied Probability* **38** (2001) 464–481.

[16] X. Guo and Q. Zhang, Optimal selling rules in a regime switching model, *IEEE Transactions on Automatic Control* **50** (2005) 1450–1455.

[17] Z. Jiang and M. R. Pistorius, On perpetual American put valuation and first-passage in a regime-switching model with jumps, *Finance and Stochastics* **12** (2008) 331–355.

[18] A. Jobert and L. C. G. Rogers, Option pricing with Markov-modulated dynamics, *SIAM Journal on Control and Optimization* **44** (2006) 2063–2078.

[19] A. N. Kolmogorov, On analytic methods in probability theory, *Selected Works of A. N. Kolmogorov, Volume II, Probability Theory and Mathematical Statistics*, A. N. Shiryaev, ed. (Kluwer, Dordrecht, 1992).

[20] N. V. Krylov, *Controlled Diffusion Processes* (Springer, New York, 1980).

[21] R. S. Liptser and A. N. Shiryaev, *Statistics of Random Processes I* (Springer, Berlin, 1977).

[22] H. P. McKean, Appendix: A free boundary problem for the heat equation arising from a problem of mathematical economics, *Industrial Management Review* **6** (1965) 32–39.

[23] B. Øksendal, *Stochastic Differential Equations. An Introduction with Applications* (Fifth edition, Springer, Berlin, 1998).

[24] G. Peskir, A change-of-variable formula with local time on surfaces, *Séminaire de Probabilité XL*, Lecture Notes in Mathematics **1899** (Springer, 2007) 69–96.

[25] G. Peskir and A. N. Shiryaev, *Optimal Stopping and Free-Boundary Problems* (Birkhäuser, Basel, 2006).

[26] R. Rishel, Whether to sell or hold a stock, *Communications in Information and Systems* **6** (2001) 193–202.

[27] A. N. Shiryaev, *Optimal Stopping Rules* (Springer, Berlin, 1978).
[28] A. N. Shiryaev, *Essentials of Stochastic Finance* (World Scientific, Singapore, 1999).
[29] A. N. Shiryaev and A. A. Novikov, On a stochastic version of the trading rule "Buy and Hold", *Statistics and Decisions* **26** (2008) 289–302.
[30] M. H. Vellekoop and J. W. Nieuwenhuis, Efficient pricing of derivatives on assets with discrete dividends, *Applied Mathematical Finance* **13** (2006) 265–284.

OPTIMAL INVESTMENT ON FINITE HORIZON WITH RANDOM DISCRETE ORDER FLOW IN ILLIQUID MARKETS*

PAUL GASSIAT and HUYÊN PHAM

Laboratoire de Probabilités et Modèles Aléatoires
University Paris Diderot
Site Chevaleret, Case 7012
75205 Paris Cedex 13, France

MIHAI SÎRBU

Department of Mathematics
University of Texas at Austin
Austin, TX 78712, USA

We study the problem of optimal portfolio selection in an illiquid market with discrete order flow. In this market, bids and offers are not available at any time but trading occurs more frequently near a terminal horizon. The investor can observe and trade the risky asset only at exogenous random times corresponding to the order flow given by an inhomogenous Poisson process. By using a direct dynamic programming approach, we first derive and solve the fixed point dynamic programming equation satisfied by the value function, and then perform a verification argument which provides the existence and characterization of optimal trading strategies. We prove the convergence of the optimal performance, when the deterministic intensity of the order flow approaches infinity at any time, to the optimal expected utility for an investor trading continuously in a perfectly liquid market model with no-short sale constraints.

Keywords: Liquidity modelling; discrete order flow; optimal investment; inhomogenous Poisson process; dynamic programming.

1. Introduction

Financial modeling very often relies on the assumption of continuous-time trading. This is essentially due to the availability of the powerful tool of stochastic integration, which allows for an elegant representation of continuous-time

*This chapter was originally published under the same title in *International Journal of Theoretical and Applied Finance*, Vol. 14, No. 1, 17–40 (2011). Singapore: World Scientific Publishing.

trading strategies, and the analytic tractability of the stochastic calculus, typically illustrated by Itô's formula. Sometimes this assumption may not be very realistic in practice: illiquid markets provide a prime example. Indeed, an important aspect of market liquidity is the time restriction both on trading and observation of the assets. For example, in power markets, trading occurs through a brokered OTC market, and the liquidity is really thin. There could be a possible lack of counterparty for a given order: bids and offers are not available at any time, and may arrive randomly, while the investor can observe the asset only at these arrival times. Moreover, in these markets, because of the physical nature of the underlying asset, trading activity is really low far from the delivery, and is higher near the delivery.

In this paper, we propose a framework that takes into account such liquidity features by considering a discrete order flow. In our model, the investor can observe and trade over a finite horizon only at random times given by an inhomogenous Poisson process encoding the quotes in this illiquid market. To capture the high frequency of trading in the neighborhood of the finite horizon, we assume that the deterministic intensity of this inhomogenous Poisson process approaches infinity as time gets closer to the finite horizon. This is *the crucial feature* of our model, which allows us to compare trading strategies using *expected utility from terminal wealth.*

Optimal investment problems with random discrete trading dates were studied by several authors. Rogers and Zane [8] and Matsumoto [5] considered trading times associated to the jump times of a Poisson process, but assumed that the price process is observed continuously, so that trading strategies are actually in continuous-time. Recently, Pham and Tankov [6] (see also [2]) investigated an optimal portfolio/consumption choice problem over an infinite horizon, where the asset price, essentially extracted from a Black-Scholes model, can be observed and traded only at the random times corresponding to a Poisson process with constant intensity.

Compared to the model of Matsumoto [5], which is closest to our work, the present paper contributes to different levels. First, we allow for a general utility function, as opposed to power/log utility, and the underlying continuous-time asset price process is no longer a Brownian motion but an inhomogenous Lévy process. Second, in our framework, the traded asset is observed only at the sequence of Poisson arrivals, and not continuously. As we prove later in Lemma 4.1, in this Markov model actually continuous and discrete observations lead to the same solutions. However, this is not obvious from [5], so Lemma 4.1 is a part of our contribution. However, the main contribution of our model is the possibility to account for more and more frequent trading near maturity. The total wealth of an agent can be only defined at the trading times, so we believe that the model we present here is the only case of time-illiquidity where it actually makes sense to consider *expected utility from terminal wealth* (see Remark 3.1). If the trading intensity is constant (or does not satisfy the hyper-intensity condition (2.1) below), then total wealth cannot be defined at the terminal time horizon since the agent will usually not be able to liquidate his position at maturity.

In order to analyze our model of portfolio selection, we use a direct dynamic programming approach. We first derive the fixed point dynamic programming equation

(DPE) and provide a constructive proof for the existence of a solution to this DPE in a suitable functional space by means of an iterative procedure. Then, by proving a verification theorem, we obtain the existence and characterization of optimal policies. We also provide an approximation of the optimal strategies that involves only a finite number of iterations. Finally, we address the natural question of convergence of our optimal investment strategy/expected utility when the arrival intensity rate becomes large at all times. We prove that the value function converges to the value function of an agent who can trade continuously in a perfectly liquid market with no-short sale constraints. A related convergence result was recently obtained by Kardaras and Platen [4] by considering continuous-time trading strategies approximated by simple trading strategies with constraints, but with asset prices observed continuously. Here we face some additional subtleties induced by the discrete observation filtrations: the illiquid market investor has less information coming from observing the asset, compared to the continuous-time investor, but he/she has the additional information coming from the arrival times, which is lacking in the perfectly liquid case.

The rest of the paper is organized as follows. Section 2 describes the illiquid market model with the restriction on the trading times, and sets up all the assumptions of the model. We formulate in Sec. 3 the optimal investment problem, and solve it by a dynamic programming approach and verification argument. Finally, Sec. 4 is devoted to the convergence issue when the deterministic intensity of arrivals is very large at all times.

2. The Illiquid Market Model and Trading Strategies

We consider an illiquid market in which an investor can trade a risky asset over a finite horizon. In this market, bids and offers are not available at any time, but trading occurs more frequently near the horizon. This is typically the case in power markets with forward contracts. This market illiquidity feature is modelled by assuming that the arrivals of buy/sell orders occur at the jumps of an inhomogeneous Poisson process with an increasing deterministic intensity converging to infinity at the final horizon. In order to obtain an analytically tractable model, we further assume that the discrete-time observed asset prices come from an unobserved continuous-time stochastic process, which is independent of the sequence of arrival times. We may think about the continuous time process as an asset price process based on fundamentals independent of time-illiquidity, which would be actually observed if trading occurred at all times.

More precisely, fixing a probability space $(\Omega, \mathcal{G}, \mathbb{P})$ and a finite horizon $T < \infty$, we consider the fundamental unobserved positive asset price $(S_t)_{0 \leq t \leq T}$. An investor can observe and trade the asset *only* at some exogenous random times $(\tau_n)_{n \geq 0}$, $\tau_0 = 0$, such that $(\tau_n)_{n \geq 0}$ and $(S_t)_{0 \leq t \leq T}$ are independent under the physical probability measure $\mathbb{P}$.

In order to obtain a stochastic control problem of Markov type for the utility maximization problem below, we assume an exponential-Lévy structure and some regularity/integrability conditions on the continuous-time positive price process S. More precisely, we assume that

$$S_t = \mathcal{E}(L)_t, \quad 0 \le t \le T,$$

where the process $(L_t)_{0 \le t \le T}$ is a semimartingale on $(\Omega, \mathcal{G}, \mathbb{P})$ with independent increments and jumps strictly greater than minus one. We use $\mathcal{E}(L)$ to denote the Doléans-Dade stochastic exponential of L. The assumption $\Delta L > -1$ ensures that the asset S, as well as its left-limit S_-, are strictly positive at all times. It is well known that a semimartingale with independent increments has *deterministic predictable characteristics*, see e.g. [3]. We then assume that the Lévy-Khintchin-Itô decomposition of L has the form
(**HL**)

$$L_t = \int_0^t b(u)\, du + \int_0^t c(u)\, dW_u + \int_0^t \int_{-1}^\infty y(\mu(du, dy) - \nu(du, dy)), \quad 0 \le t \le T,$$

where $(W_t)_{0 \le T}$ is a Brownian motion on $(\Omega, \mathcal{G}, \mathbb{P})$ independent on the jump measure μ with deterministic compensator ν, and integrable large jumps, i.e.

$$\int_0^T \int_{-1}^\infty y\, \nu(dt, dy) < \infty.$$

The deterministic functions $b : [0, T] \to \mathbb{R}, c : [0, T] \to (0, \infty)$, satisfy

$$\int_0^T |b(u)| du < \infty, \quad \text{and} \quad \int_0^T c^2(u) du < \infty.$$

Since in our model the asset S is not observed at the terminal time T, there is no loss of generality if we assume that $S_T = S_{T-}$, which can be translated in terms of predictable characteristics as $\nu(\{T\}, (-1, \infty)) = 0$. We will make this assumption for the rest of the paper.

We denote by

$$Z_{t,s} = \frac{S_s - S_t}{S_t} = \left\{ e^{(L_s - L_t - \frac{1}{2}\int_t^s c^2(u)\, du)} \prod_{t < u \le s} e^{-\Delta L_u}(1 + \Delta L_u) \right\} - 1,$$
$$0 \le t \le s \le T,$$

the return between times t and s (if trading is allowed at both times) and denote by

$$p(t, s, dz) = \mathbb{P}[Z_{t,s} \in dz]$$

the distribution of the return.

The sequence of observation/trading times is represented by the jumps of an inhomogeneous (and independent of S) Poisson process $(N_t)_{t \in [0,T]}$ with deterministic intensity function $t \in [0, T) \to \lambda(t) \in (0, \infty)$, such that:

$$\int_0^t \lambda(u)du < \infty, \quad (\forall)\ 0 \le t < T \quad \text{and} \quad \int_0^T \lambda(u)du = \infty. \tag{2.1}$$

The simplest way to actually define such an inhomogeneous Poisson process is to consider a homogeneous Poisson process M with intensity equal to one, independent of S, and define

$$N_t = M_{\int_0^t \lambda(u)du} \quad \text{for } 0 \le t < T. \tag{2.2}$$

Condition (2.1) is crucial in our illiquidity modelling, and ensures that the probability of having no jumps between any interval $[t, T], t < T$, is null, and so the sequence (τ_n) converges increasingly to T almost surely when n goes to infinity. We also know that the process of jump times $(\tau_n)_{n\ge0}$ is a homogeneous Markov chain on $[0, T)$, and its transition probability admits a density given by:

$$\mathbb{P}[\tau_{n+1} \in ds \,|\, \tau_n = t] = \lambda(s)e^{-\int_t^s \lambda(u)du} 1_{\{t\le s<T\}} ds, \tag{2.3}$$

(which does not depend on n).

An investor trading in this market can only observe/trade the asset S at the discrete arrival times τ_n. Therefore, the only information he/she has is coming from observing the two-dimensional process $(\tau_n, S_{\tau_n})_{n\ge0}$. Taking this into account, we introduce the discrete observation filtration $\mathbb{F} = (\mathcal{F}_n)_{n\ge0}$, with $\mathcal{F}_0$ trivial and

$$\mathcal{F}_n = \sigma\{(\tau_k, Z_k) : 1 \le k \le n\}, \quad n \ge 1, \tag{2.4}$$

where we denote by

$$Z_n = Z_{\tau_{n-1},\tau_n}, \quad n \ge 1,$$

the observed return process valued in $(-1, \infty)$.

In this model a (simple) trading strategy is a real-valued $\mathbb{F}$-adapted process $\alpha = (\alpha_n)_{n\ge0}$, where α_n represents the amount invested in the stock over the period $(\tau_n, \tau_{n+1}]$ after observing the stock price at time τ_n. Assuming that the money market pays zero interest rate, the observed wealth process $(X_{\tau_n})_{n\ge0}$ associated to a trading strategy α is governed by:

$$X_{\tau_{n+1}} = X_{\tau_n} + \alpha_n Z_{n+1}, \quad n \ge 0, \tag{2.5}$$

where X_0 is the initial capital of the investor. In order to simplify notation, we fix once and for all an initial capital $X_0 > 0$ and denote by $\mathcal{A}$ the set of trading strategies α such that the wealth process stays nonnegative:

$$X_{\tau_n} \ge 0, \quad n \ge 1. \tag{2.6}$$

For the rest of the paper, we will call *simple* these trading strategies where trading occurs only at the discrete times $\tau_n, n \ge 0$.

Remark 2.1. *Constrained strategies.* From assumption (**HL**) we conclude that for each $0 \le t < s \le T$ the distribution $p(t, s, dz)$ has full support on $[-1, \infty)$, so

Z_n has also full support on $[-1, \infty)$. Taking this into account and using (2.5), the admissibility condition (2.6) on $\alpha \in \mathcal{A}$ means that we have a no-short sale constraint (on both the risky and savings account asset):

$$0 \leq \alpha_n \leq X_{\tau_n}, \quad \text{for all } n \geq 0. \tag{2.7}$$

Moreover, since $Z_n > -1$ a.s. for all $n \geq 1$, the wealth process associated to $\alpha \in \mathcal{A}_0$ is actually strictly positive:

$$X_{\tau_n} > 0, \quad n \geq 0.$$

For technical reasons, some related to the asymptotic behavior in Sec. 4.1, we need to define some continuous time filtrations along with the discrete filtration $\mathbb{F}$. To avoid confusion, we will denote by $\mathbb{G}$ (with different parameters) all continuous-time filtrations. In this spirit, we define the filtration $\mathbb{G} = (\mathcal{G}_t)_{0 \leq t \leq T}$ generated by observing continously the process S and the arrival times as

$$\mathcal{G}_t = \sigma\{(S_u, N_u), 0 \leq u \leq t\} \vee \mathcal{N}, \quad 0 \leq t \leq T, \tag{2.8}$$

where N is the inhomogenous Poisson process in (2.2) and $\mathcal{N}$ are all the null sets of $\mathcal{G}$ under the historical measure $\mathbb{P}$. We would like to point out that, because of the Lévy structure of the joint process (S, N), the filtration $\mathbb{G}$ is right continous, so it satisfies the *usual conditions*. In addition, we have the strict inclusion:

$$\mathcal{F}_n \subset \mathcal{G}_{\tau_n} \quad \text{for all } n \geq 1.$$

We make an additional assumption on the model, which, among others, precludes arbitrage possibilities:

(**NA**)

$$\int_0^T \frac{b^2(u)}{c^2(u)} du < \infty.$$

Under this assumption we can then define the probability measure $\mathbb{Q}$ by

$$\frac{d\mathbb{Q}}{d\mathbb{P}} = e^{-\int_0^T \frac{b(u)}{c(u)} dW_u - \frac{1}{2}\int_0^T \left(\frac{b(u)}{c(u)}\right)^2 du}.$$

Under $\mathbb{Q}$, the process N has the same law as under $\mathbb{P}$, and $(\tau_n)_{n \geq 0}$ and $(S_t)_{0 \leq t \leq T}$ are still independent under $\mathbb{Q}$. Moreover, the process S is a positive $(\mathbb{Q}, \mathbb{G})$-local martingale so a supermartingale. This means that the discrete-time process $(S_{\tau_n})_{n \geq 0}$ is a $(\mathbb{Q}, \mathbb{F})$ supermartingale as well.

Remark 2.2. *Embedding in a continuous-time wealth process.* Given $\alpha \in \mathcal{A}$ with corresponding wealth process $(X_{\tau_n})_n$ in (2.5), let us define the continuous time process $(X_t)_{0 \leq t < T}$ by

$$\begin{aligned} X_t &= X_{\tau_n} + \alpha_n Z_{\tau_n, t}, \quad \tau_n < t \leq \tau_{n+1}, \ n \geq 0, \\ &= X_0 + \int_0^t H_u dS_u, \quad 0 \leq t < T, \end{aligned} \tag{2.9}$$

where H is the simple and $\mathbb{G}$-predictable process

$$H_t = \sum_{n=0}^{\infty} \frac{\alpha_n}{S_{\tau_n}} \mathbb{I}_{\{\tau_n < t \leq \tau_{n+1}\}}, \quad 0 \leq t < T,$$

representing the number of shares invested in the risky asset. From (2.7) and since $S_t > 0$, so $Z_{\tau_n,t} > -1$, $n \geq 0$, we notice that the continuous time process X is strictly positive: $X_t > 0$ for $0 \leq t < T$. Moreover, since S is a $(\mathbb{Q}, \mathbb{G})$-local martingale, we also see that $(X_t)_{0 \leq t < T}$ is a $(\mathbb{Q}, \mathbb{G})$-local martingale, hence a super-martingale up to T. Consequently, we also have $X_{t-} > 0$ for $0 \leq t < T$. The definition of X_{τ_n} in (2.5) is consistent with (2.9), so $(X_{\tau_n})_{n \geq 0}$ is a positive $\mathbb{F}$-supermartingale under $\mathbb{Q}$. Therefore, for each $\alpha \in \mathcal{A}$ we may define the terminal wealth value by:

$$X_T = \lim_{n \to \infty} X_{\tau_n} = \lim_{t \nearrow T} X_t = X_0 + \sum_{n=0}^{\infty} \alpha_n Z_{n+1},$$

and, since $S_T = S_{T-}$ we also have

$$X_T = X_0 + \int_0^T H_u dS_u,$$

where the integrand H is related to the simple trading strategy α as described above. The supermartingale property implies the budget constraint

$$\mathbb{E}^{\mathbb{Q}}[X_T] \leq X_0.$$

The continuous time wealth process X has the meaning of a shadow wealth process: it is not observed except for at times τ_n, $n \geq 0$. The no-short sale constraints (2.7) is translated in terms of the number of shares held as

$$0 \leq H_t S_{t-} \leq X_{t-}, \quad 0 \leq t < T. \tag{2.10}$$

We denote by $\mathcal{X}$ the set of all wealth processes $(X_t)_{0 \leq t \leq T}$ given by (2.9), by using simple trading strategies under the no-short sale constraint (2.7)/(2.10). We denote by $\bar{\mathcal{X}}$ the set of all positive wealth processes $(X_t)_{0 \leq t \leq T}$ given by (2.9), by using *general* $\mathbb{G}$-predictable and S-integrable processes H satisfying (2.10). We clearly have $\mathcal{X} \subset \bar{\mathcal{X}}$.

For technical reasons, it is sometimes convenient to regard trading strategies equivalently in terms of proportions of wealth. For any continuous time wealth process $X \in \bar{\mathcal{X}}$ associated to a trading strategy H satisfying (2.10), let us consider the process $\pi = (\pi_t)_{0 \leq t \leq T}$, defined by: $\pi_t = H_t S_{t-}/X_{t-}$, and notice that π is valued in $[0, 1]$ by (2.10). We stress the dependence of the wealth on the proportion π, and denote by $X^{(\pi)} = X$, which is then written in a multiplicative way as

$$X^{(\pi)}_{\cdot} = X_0 \mathcal{E}\Big(\int_0^{\cdot} \pi \frac{dS}{S_-}\Big) = X_0 \mathcal{E}\Big(\int_0^{\cdot} \pi dL\Big), \tag{2.11}$$

where $\mathcal{E}$ is the Doléans-Dade operator. Denote by $\mathcal{D}(\mathbb{G})$ the set of all $\mathbb{G}$-predictable processes π valued in $[0, 1]$. It is then clear that

$$\bar{\mathcal{X}} = \{X^{(\pi)} \,|\, \pi \in \mathcal{D}(\mathbb{G})\}.$$

3. Optimal Investment Problem and Dynamic Programming

We investigate an optimal investment problem in the illiquid market described in the previous section. Let us consider an utility function U defined on $(0,\infty)$, strictly increasing, strictly concave and C^1 on $(0,\infty)$, and satisfying the Inada conditions: $U'(0^+) = \infty, U'(\infty) = 0$. We make the following additional assumptions on the utility function U:

(**HU**) (i) there exist some constants $C > 0$ and $p \in (0,1)$ such that

$$U^+(x) \le C(1 + x^p), \quad (\forall)\ x > 0$$

where $U^+ = \max(U, 0)$

(ii)there exist some constants $C' > 0$ and $p' < 0$ such that

$$U^-(x) \le C'(1 + x^{p'}), \quad (\forall)\ x > 0,$$

where $U^- = \max(-U, 0)$.

The above assumptions include most popular utility functions, in particular those with constant relative risk aversion $1 - p > 0$, in the form $U(x) = (x^p - 1)/p, x > 0$.

Given the chosen positive initial wealth $X_0 > 0$, we consider the optimal investment problem:

$$V_0 = \sup_{\alpha \in \mathcal{A}} \mathbb{E}[U(X_T)] = \sup_{X \in \mathcal{X}} \mathbb{E}[U(X_T)]. \tag{3.1}$$

Remark 3.1. As noted in the Introduction, the hyper-intensity condition (2.1) allows us to define the terminal wealth X_T. Without such a condition, while one could always define the continuous-time wealth process X as in Remark 2.2 for mathematical convenience, the terminal wealth X_T does not have economic meaning. Therefore, the condition (2.1) appears as necessary if one wants to compare portfolios using expected utility from terminal wealth, as we do here.

Our aim is to provide an analytic solution to the control problem (3.1) using direct dynamic programming, i.e. *first* solve the Dynamic Programming Equation (DPE) *analytically* and *then* perform a *verification* argument. Therefore, there is no need to either define the value function at later times or to prove the Dynamic Programming Principle (DPP).

The Lemma below provides the intuition behind the (DPE):

Lemma 3.1. *Assume* (**HL**) *holds true. Let $\alpha \in \mathcal{A}$ and let $(X_{\tau_n})_{n \ge 0}$ be the wealth process associated with the trading strategy α. Consider a measurable function $v : [0,T) \times (0,\infty) \to \mathbb{R}$. For a fixed $n \ge 0$, if $v(\tau_{n+1}, X_{\tau_{n+1}}) \in L^1(\Omega, \mathcal{G}, \mathbb{P})$, then*

$$\mathbb{E}[v(\tau_{n+1}, X_{\tau_{n+1}}) \,|\, \mathcal{F}_n] = \int_{\tau_n}^{T} \int_{(-1,\infty)} \lambda(s) e^{-\int_{\tau_n}^{s} \lambda(u) du} v(s, X_{\tau_n} + \alpha_n z) p(\tau_n, s, dz) ds,$$

where the above equality holds $\mathbb{P}$-a.s.

Proof. Assumption (**HL**) together with the independence of S and N ensures that for all $n \geq 0$, the (regular) distribution of (τ_{n+1}, Z_{n+1}) conditioned on $\mathcal{F}_n$ is given as follows:

(1) $\mathbb{P}[\tau_{n+1} \in ds \,|\, \mathcal{F}_n] = \lambda(s)e^{-\int_{\tau_n}^s \lambda(u)du} ds$

(2) further conditioning on knowing the next arrival time τ_{n+1}, the return Z_{n+1} has distribution

$$\mathbb{P}[Z_{n+1} \in dz \,|\, \mathcal{F}_n \vee \sigma(\tau_{n+1})] = p(\tau_n, \tau_{n+1}, dz).$$

We then get

$$\begin{aligned}
\mathbb{E}[v(\tau_{n+1}, X_{\tau_{n+1}})|\mathcal{F}_n] &= \mathbb{E}[\mathbb{E}[v(\tau_{n+1}, X_{\tau_n} + \alpha_n Z_{n+1})|\mathcal{F}_n \vee \sigma(\tau_{n+1})]|\mathcal{F}_n] \\
&= \mathbb{E}\left[\int_{(-1,\infty)} v(\tau_{n+1}, X_{\tau_n} + \alpha_n z)p(\tau_n, \tau_{n+1}, dz)|\mathcal{F}_n\right] \\
&= \int_{\tau_n}^T \int_{(-1,\infty)} \lambda(s)e^{-\int_{\tau_n}^s \lambda(u)du} v(s, X_{\tau_n} + \alpha_n z)p(\tau_n, s, dz)ds.
\end{aligned}$$

□

Taking into account the above lemma, we can now *formally* write down the Dynamic Programming Equation as

$$\begin{aligned}
v(t,x) &= \sup_{a \in [0,x]} \int_t^T \int_{(-1,\infty)} \lambda(s)e^{-\int_t^s \lambda(u)du} v(s, x + az)p(t, s, dz)ds, \\
&= \sup_{\pi \in [0,1]} \int_t^T \int_{(-1,\infty)} \lambda(s)e^{-\int_t^s \lambda(u)du} v(s, x(1 + \pi z))p(t, s, dz)ds, \quad (3.2)
\end{aligned}$$

for all $(t,x) \in [0,T) \times (0,\infty)$ together with the natural terminal condition

$$\lim_{t \nearrow T, x' \to x} v(t, x') = U(x), \quad x > 0. \quad (3.3)$$

It appears that the right space of functions to be looking for a solution of (3.2) and (3.3) is actually the space $\mathcal{C}_U([0,T) \times (0,\infty))$ of measurable functions w on $[0,T) \times (0,\infty)$, such that

(1) $w(t,.)$ is concave on $(0,\infty)$ for all $t \in [0,T)$, and

(2) for some $C = C(w) > 0$, we have

$$U(x) \leq w(t,x) \leq C(1+x), \quad \forall\,(t,x) \in [0,T) \times (0,\infty). \quad (3.4)$$

For any $w \in \mathcal{C}_U([0,T) \times (0,\infty))$, we consider the measurable function $\mathcal{L}w$ on $[0,T) \times (0,\infty)$ defined by:

$$\mathcal{L}w(t,x) = \sup_{\pi \in [0,1]} \int_t^T \int_{(-1,\infty)} \lambda(s)e^{-\int_t^s \lambda(u)du} w(s, x(1+\pi z))p(t, s, dz)ds. \quad (3.5)$$

Lemma 3.2 below shows that the operator

$$\mathcal{L} : \mathcal{C}_U([0,T) \times (0,\infty)) \to \mathcal{C}_U([0,T) \times (0,\infty)),$$

is well defined. Therefore, we are looking for a solution $w \in \mathcal{C}_U([0,T) \times (0,\infty))$ to the DPE:

$$\begin{cases} \mathcal{L}w = w \\ \lim_{t \nearrow T, x' \to x} w(t,x') = U(x). \end{cases} \tag{3.6}$$

In order to solve the DPE and perform the verification argument, we need some technical details collected in the subsection below:

3.1. *A supersolution of the DPE and other technical details*

Lemma 3.2. *Assume that* (**HL**) *holds. For any* $w \in \mathcal{C}_U([0,T) \times (0,\infty)), \mathcal{L}w$ *also belongs to* $\mathcal{C}_U([0,T)\times(0,\infty))$. *For each* $(t,x) \in [0,T)\times(0,\infty)$ *the supremum in* (3.5) *is attained at some* $\pi(t,x)$ *which can be chosen measurable in* (t,x).

Proof. Given $w \in \mathcal{C}_U([0,T) \times (0,\infty))$, let us consider the measurable function $\widehat{w}$ defined on $[0,T) \times (0,\infty) \times [0,1]$ by:

$$\widehat{w}(t,x,\pi) = \int_t^T \int_{(-1,\infty)} \lambda(s) e^{-\int_t^s \lambda(u)du} w(s, x(1+\pi z)) p(t,s,dz) ds,$$

so that $\mathcal{L}w(t,x) = \sup_{\pi \in [0,1]} \widehat{w}(t,x,\pi)$. Under (**HL**), there exists some positive constant C (which can be chosen actually as $C = e^{\int_0^T |b(u)|du}$), s.t.

$$\int_{(-1,\infty)} |z|\, p(t,s,dz) \le C, \quad 0 \le t \le s < T. \tag{3.7}$$

Thus, for w satisfying (3.4), we see that $\hat{w}$ is well-defined on $[0,T) \times (0,\infty) \times [0,1]$ and satisfies:

$$-\infty \le \widehat{w}(t,x,\pi) \le C(1+x), \quad \forall\, (t,x,\pi) \in [0,T) \times (0,\infty) \times [0,1], \tag{3.8}$$

for some positive constant $C > 0$. Moreover, for each $(t,x) \in [0,T) \times (0,\infty)$, we have

$$\widehat{w}(t,x,0) \ge U(x). \tag{3.9}$$

As a matter of fact, one can easily see that $\widehat{w}(t,x,\pi)$ is actually finite for any $\pi \in [0,1)$ and may only equal negative infinity for $\pi = 1$. Consequently, for fixed $(t,x) \in [0,T)\times(0,\infty)$, $\widehat{w}(t,x,.)$ is a proper one-dimensional concave function defined on $[0,1]$ (concavity follows easily from that of w). In addition, using the linear growth (3.4) together with Fatou lemma, we obtain that $\pi \in [0,1] \to \widehat{w}(t,x,\pi)$ is upper semicontinuous (this refers to the endpoints $\pi = 0, 1$ since the function is continuous on $(0,1)$ being finite and concave). Therefore $\mathcal{L}w(t,x) = \max_{\pi \in [0,1]} \widehat{w}(t,x,\pi)$, where the maximum is attained at some $\pi = \pi(t,x)$ which can be chosen measurable in (t,x), see e.g. Ch. 11 in [1]. In addition, since $\pi \to \widehat{w}(t,x,\pi)$ is continuous on $(0,1)$, the function $\mathcal{L}w$ has the additional representation

$$\mathcal{L}w(t,x) = \sup_{\pi\in[0,1]\cap\mathbb{Q}} \widehat{w}(t,x,\pi),$$

which shows that $\mathcal{L}w$ is measurable. The concavity of $w(t,.)$ implies the concavity of $(x,a) \in \{(x,a) \in (0,\infty)\times\mathbb{R} : a \in [0,x]\} \to \widehat{w}(t,x,a/x)$ for all $t \in [0,T)$. This easily implies that $\mathcal{L}w(t,.)$ is also concave on $(0,\infty)$ for all $t \in [0,T)$. Finally, it is clear from (3.8) and (3.9) that $\mathcal{L}w$ satisfies also the growth condition:

$$U(x) \le \mathcal{L}w(t,x) \le C(1+x), \quad \forall\,(t,x) \in [0,T)\times(0,\infty). \qquad \square$$

The next lemma constructs a supersolution $f \in C_U([0,T)\times(0,\infty))$ for the DPE:

Lemma 3.3. *Assume that* (**HL**), (**NA**) *and* (**HU**) *hold. Define*

$$f(t,x) = \inf_{y>0}\{\mathbb{E}[\tilde{U}(yY_{t,T})] + yx\} \quad (t,x) \in [0,T]\times(0,\infty),$$

where

$$Y_{t,T} = e^{-\int_t^T \frac{b(u)}{c(u)}dW_u - \frac{1}{2}\int_t^T\left(\frac{b(u)}{c(u)}\right)^2 du}, \tag{3.10}$$

and $\tilde{U}$ is the Fenchel-Legendre transform of U:

$$\tilde{U}(y) = \sup_{x>0}[U(x) - xy] < \infty, \quad \forall y > 0. \tag{3.11}$$

Then, f lies in the set $C_U([0,T)\times(0,\infty))$, and satisfies

$$\begin{cases} \mathcal{L}f \le f \\ \lim\limits_{t\nearrow T, x'\to x} f(t,x') = U(x). \end{cases} \tag{3.12}$$

Proof. Jensen's inequality gives $\mathbb{E}[\tilde{U}(yY_{t,T})] \ge \tilde{U}(y)$, so

$$f(t,x) \ge \inf_{y>0}\{\tilde{U}(y) + yx\} = U(x).$$

From the definition of f we know that

$$f(t,x) \le \mathbb{E}[\tilde{U}(yY_{t,T})] + yx, \quad (\forall)\, y > 0. \tag{3.13}$$

Fix a $y_0 > 0$. We denote by

$$\mathcal{G}'_t = \sigma\{(S_u - S_t, N_u - N_t),\ t \le u \le T\},$$

the information accumulated from time t to maturity T by observing continuously the asset S and the arrival times (the jumps of N). Jensen's inequality together with Assumption (**HU**)(i) shows that

$$\mathbb{E}[\tilde{U}(y_0Y_{t,T})] = \mathbb{E}[\tilde{U}(y_0\mathbb{E}[Y_{0,T}\,|\,\mathcal{G}'_t])] \le \mathbb{E}[\mathbb{E}[\tilde{U}(y_0Y_{0,T})\,|\,\mathcal{G}'_t]] = \mathbb{E}[\tilde{U}(y_0Y_{0,T})] < \infty,$$

so

$$f(t,x) \le \mathbb{E}[\tilde{U}(y_0 Y_{t,T})] + y_0 x \le C(1+x) \quad (\forall)\,(t,x) \in [0,T] \times (0,\infty).$$

This shows that $f \in \mathcal{C}_U([0,T) \times (0,\infty))$. Using assumption (**HU**) (both (i) and (ii)) we obtain that there exist constants $\tilde{C} > 0$, $q < 0$ and $0 < q' < 1$ such that

$$\tilde{U}^+(y) \le \tilde{C}(1+y^q), \quad \tilde{U}^-(y) \le \tilde{C}(1+y^{q'}), \quad (\forall)\,y > 0.$$

Using the defintion of $Y_{t,T}$ (which is log-normal) and the explicit moments of log-normal random variables we obtain that

$$\sup_{0 \le t < T} \mathbb{E}[|\tilde{U}(yY_{t,T})|^2] < \infty.$$

This means that the collection $(\tilde{U}(yY_{t,T}))_{0 \le t < T}$ of random variables is uniformly integrable, so

$$\lim_{t \nearrow T} \mathbb{E}[\tilde{U}(yY_{t,T})] = \tilde{U}(y), \quad (\forall)\,y > 0.$$

We can now use this in (3.13) to deduce that

$$U(x) \le \liminf_{t \nearrow T, x' \to x} f(t,x') \le \limsup_{t \nearrow T, x' \to x} f(t,x') \le \tilde{U}(y) + xy, \quad (\forall)\ y > 0.$$

Taking the infimum over y we obtain the terminal condition. For each fixed t, the function $f(t,\cdot)$ is finite and concave on $(0,\infty)$, so the only thing left to check is the supersolution property. Fix $0 \le t \le s \le T$ and $x > 0$. Denote by $h(z) = \mathbb{E}[\tilde{U}(zY_{s,T})]$ and fix $y > 0$ and $\pi \in [0,1]$. By the very definition of the function f we have that

$$f(s, x(1+\pi Z_{t,s})) \le h(yY_{t,s}) + x(1+\pi Z_{t,s})yY_{t,s}.$$

Using independence and the definition of h, we obtain

$$\begin{aligned}\mathbb{E}[f(s,x(1+\pi Z_{t,s}))] &\le \mathbb{E}[h(yY_{t,s}) + x(1+\pi Z_{t,s})yY_{t,s}] \\ &= \mathbb{E}[\tilde{U}(yY_{t,s}Y_{s,T})] + \mathbb{E}[x(1+\pi Z_{t,s})yY_{t,s}] \le \mathbb{E}[\tilde{U}(yY_{t,T})] + xy.\end{aligned}$$

Taking the inf over all y and recalling the definition of $f(t,x)$ we obtain

$$f(t,x) \ge \mathbb{E}[f(s,x(1+\pi Z_{t,s}))] = \int_{(-1,\infty)} f(s,x(1+\pi z))p(t,s,dz)$$

for all π and s. For a fixed π, we can integrate over s to obtain

$$f(t,x) \ge \int_t^T \int_{(-1,\infty)} \lambda(s) e^{-\int_t^s \lambda(u)du} f(s,x(1+\pi z))p(t,s,dz)ds,$$

and then taking the supremum over π we obtain $f(t,x) \ge (\mathcal{L}f)(t,x)$, so the proof is complete. Due to the linear growth condition of f and recalling (3.7), all expectations/integrals above are well defined, but may be negative infinity. In other words, the positive parts in all expectations/integrals are actually integrable. □

Remark 3.2. The whole analysis in this paper extends to the case when the Brownian part of the process L is degenerate, as long as the jumps have full support on $(-1,\infty)$ and the jump measure allows for a martingale measure with density process Y that can replace the definition (3.10) in the corresponding proofs. In other words, the assumptions (**HL**) and (**NA**) can be relaxed to include the situation when the drift can be removed by changing the jump measure appropriately, if the Gaussian part is missing.

It turns out that, for the verification arguments below, we also need an assumption on the integrability of jumps.

(**HI**): (i) there exists $q > 1$ such that

$$\int_0^T \int_0^\infty ((1+y)^q - 1 - qy)\nu(dt, dy) < \infty.$$

(ii) If the utility function U satisfies $U(0) = -\infty$, then there exists $r < p' < 0$ (where p' is given in (**HU**)(ii)) such that

$$\int_0^T \int_{-1}^0 ((1+y)^r - 1 - ry)\nu(dt, dy) < \infty.$$

(iii) there are no predictable jumps, i.e. $\nu(\{t\}, (-1,\infty)) = 0$ for each t.

Remark 3.3. Using convexity, it is an easy exercise to see that assumption (**HI**) (i) can actually be rephrased as $\nu_q([0,T]) < \infty$, and assumption (**HI**) (ii) as $\nu_r([0,T]) < \infty$ where

$$\nu_l(dt) = \int_{-1}^\infty \sup_{\pi\in[0,1]} ((1+\pi y)^l - 1 - l\pi y)\nu(dt, dy).$$

We now prove a crucial uniform integrability condition, but before that we denote by $\mathcal{T}$ the set of random times $0 \le \tau < T$ which are stopping times with respect to the filtration $\mathbb{G}$.

Lemma 3.4. *Assume that* (**HL**), (**HU**), (**NA**) *and* (**HI**) *hold.*

(1) *For any $X \in \bar{\mathcal{X}}$, the family $(f^+(\tau, X_\tau))_{\tau\in\mathcal{T}}$ is uniformly $\mathbb{P}$-integrable.*
(2) *For any $X \in \bar{\mathcal{X}}$, the family $(U^-(X_\tau))_{\tau\in\mathcal{T}}$, is uniformly $\mathbb{P}$-integrable.*

Proof. Assume $\nu_l([0,T]) < \infty$ for some l. Consider $X = X^{(\pi)} \in \bar{\mathcal{X}}$ for some $\pi \in \mathcal{D}(\mathbb{G})$, and recall that

$$dX_t^{(\pi)} = \pi_t X_{t-}^{(\pi)} dL_t, \quad 0 \le t \le T. \tag{3.14}$$

In order to simplify notation, we suppress the upper indices of X. We apply Itô formula to $(X_t)^l$ to conclude that

$$X_t^l = x^l + \int_0^t (X_{u-})^l \left(l\pi_u b(u) + \frac{l(l-1)}{2} c^2(u)\pi^2(u) \right) du$$
$$+ \int_0^t \int_{-1}^{\infty} (X_{u-})^l ((1+\pi_u y)^l - 1 - l\pi_u y)\nu(du, dy) + \text{“}\textit{local martingale}\text{”}$$

Fix a stopping time $\tau \in \mathcal{T}$. If T_n' is a sequence of localizing stopping times for the local martingale part, denote by $T_n = T_n' \wedge \{\inf t : (X_t)^l \geq n\}$. Observe that $T_n \nearrow T$ a.s. since X_- is locally bounded and locally bounded away from zero. We then have, for each $0 \leq t < T$,

$$\begin{aligned} \mathbb{E}[(X_{t\wedge\tau\wedge T_n})^l] &= x^l + \mathbb{E}\Bigg[\int_0^{t\wedge\tau\wedge T_n} (X_{u-})^l \Bigg\{ \left(l\pi_u b(u) + \frac{l(l-1)}{2} c^2(u)\pi^2(u) \right) du \\ &\quad + \int_{-1}^{\infty} ((1+\pi_u y)^l - 1 - l\pi_u y)\nu(du, dy) \Bigg\} \Bigg] \\ &\leq x^l + \mathbb{E}\Bigg[\int_0^{t\wedge\tau\wedge T_n} (X_{u-})^l \Bigg\{ \left(|\, lb(u)| + \frac{|\, l(l-1)|}{2} c^2(u) \right) du + \nu_l(du) \Bigg\} \Bigg] \end{aligned} \tag{3.15}$$

Since $(X_{u-})^l \leq n$ for $0 \leq u \leq \tau \wedge T_n$ and $\nu_l([0,T]) < \infty$, we conclude that

$$\mathbb{E}[(X_{t\wedge\tau\wedge T_n})^l] < \infty, \quad 0 \leq t < T. \tag{3.16}$$

In addition, since the paths of the process X^l are RCLL and $\nu_l(\{u\}) = 0$ for each $0 \leq u \leq T$ (because of (**HI**) part (iii)), we have that, for each $0 \leq t < T$, with $\mathbb{P}$-probability one

$$\begin{aligned} &\int_0^{t\wedge\tau\wedge T_n} (X_{u-})^l \left\{ \left(|\, lb(u)| + \frac{|l(l-1)|}{2} c^2(u) \right) du + \nu_l(du) \right\} \\ &\quad = \int_0^{t\wedge\tau\wedge T_n} (X_u)^l \left\{ \left(|lb(u)| + \frac{|l(l-1)|}{2} c^2(u) \right) du + \nu_l(du) \right\} \\ &\quad \leq \int_0^t (X_{u\wedge\tau\wedge T_n})^l \left\{ \left(|lb(u)| + \frac{|l(l-1)|}{2} c^2(u) \right) du + \nu_l(du) \right\}. \end{aligned}$$

Replacing this in (3.16) and using Fubini, we obtain

$$\mathbb{E}[(X_{t\wedge\tau\wedge T_n})^l] \leq x^l + \int_0^t \mathbb{E}[(X_{u\wedge\tau\wedge T_n})^l] \left\{ \left(|lb(u)| + \frac{|l(l-1)|}{2} c^2(u) \right) du + \nu_l(du) \right\}. \tag{3.17}$$

Now, using (3.16) and $\nu_l([0,T]) < \infty$, we can apply Gronwall in (3.17) to conclude that $\mathbb{E}[(X_{t\wedge\tau\wedge T_n})^l] \leq M(l) < \infty$, for each $0 \leq t < T$, where $M(l)$ does not depend on τ or n. Letting $n \to \infty$ and $t \to T$, by Fatou, we obtain $\mathbb{E}[(X_\tau)^l] \leq M(l)$ for each stopping time $\tau \in \mathcal{T}$.

We can finish the proof considering $l = q$ for item (i) and $l = r$ for item (ii), and also using the upper bound $f(t, x) \leq C(1 + x)$ as well as Assumption (**HU**) part (ii). □

Remark 3.4. In case $U(0) = -\infty$, we can follow the arguments in the proof of Lemma 3.4 for the case $\pi = 1$ and $l = r$ (taking into account that $X_t = X_0 S_t$ for $0 \leq t < T$) to conclude that

$$\mathbb{E}[(S_t)^r] = \mathbb{E}[(1 + Z_{0,t})^r] < \infty \quad \text{for } 0 \leq t < T.$$

(we assumed that $S_0 = 1$ above, and we also used that the times $0 \leq t < T$, because are deterministic, belong to $\mathcal{T}$). The same argument actually works if we start at any time $0 \leq t < T$, so we have

$$\mathbb{E}[(1 + Z_{t,s})^r] = \int_{(-1,\infty)} (1 + z)^r p(t, s, dz) < \infty, \quad \text{for } t \leq s < T.$$

3.2. *Construction of a solution for the DPE*

We provide a constructive proof for the existence of a solution of (3.6) using an iteration scheme. Let us define inductively the sequence of functions $(v_m)_m$ in $\mathcal{C}_U([0, T) \times (0, \infty))$ by:

$$v_0 = U, \quad v_{m+1} = \mathcal{L}v_m, \quad m \geq 0.$$

Lemma 3.5. *Assume* (**HL**), (**NA**), *and* (**HU**). *Then the sequence of functions* v_m *satisfies*

$$v_m \leq v_{m+1} \leq f, \quad m \geq 0.$$

Proof. We do the proof by induction. We obviously have $U = v_0 \leq v_1$. In addition, since the operator $\mathcal{L}$ is monotone and $U \leq f$ we have

$$v_1 = \mathcal{L}U \leq \mathcal{L}f \leq f,$$

so the statement is true for $m = 0$. Assume now the statement is true for m. We use again the monotonicity of $\mathcal{L}$ to get

$$v_{m+2} = \mathcal{L}v_{m+1} \geq \mathcal{L}v_m = v_{m+1}, \quad v_{m+2} = \mathcal{L}v_{m+1} \leq \mathcal{L}f \leq f,$$

so the proof is finished. □

Under the conditions of the above lemma, the nondecreasing sequence $(v_m)_m$ converges pointwise, and we may define

$$v^* = \lim_{m \to \infty} v_m \leq f. \tag{3.18}$$

We show next that v^* satisfies the fixed point DP equation.

Theorem 3.1. *Assume that* (**HL**), (**NA**), (**HU**) *and* (**HI**) *hold. Then,* v^* *is solution to the fixed point DP* (3.6).

Proof. Fix $\pi \in [0,1]$. We know by construction that

$$v_{m+1}(t,x) \geq \int_t^T \int_{(-1,\infty)} \lambda(s) e^{-\int_t^s \lambda(u)du} v_m(s, x(1+\pi z)) p(t,s,dz) ds.$$

If $0 \leq \pi < 1$, then $v_m(s, x(1+\pi z) \geq U(x(1-\pi))$ so the integral on the right-hand side is clearly finite. If $\pi = 1$, according to Remark 3.4, the integral on the right-hand side is still finite for each $m \geq 0$. Therefore, we can let $m \nearrow \infty$ and use the monotone convergence theorem to obtain

$$v^*(t,x) \geq \int_t^T \int_{(-1,\infty)} \lambda(s) e^{-\int_t^s \lambda(u)du} v^*(s, x(1+\pi z)) p(t,s,dz) ds.$$

Since this happens for each π, taking the supremum over π we get $v^* \geq \mathcal{L}v^*$. Conversely, for $\varepsilon > 0$ there exists m such that $v^*(t,x) - \varepsilon \leq v_{m+1}(t,x)$ and (because of convexity the maximum is attained) $\pi^m(t,x)$ such that

$$v_{m+1}(t,x) = \int_t^T \int_{(-1,\infty)} \lambda(s) e^{-\int_t^s \lambda(u)du} v_m(s, x(1+\pi^m(t,x)z)) p(t,s,dz) ds.$$

Since $v_m \leq v^*$ it follows that

$$\begin{aligned} v^*(t,x) - \varepsilon &\leq \int_t^T \int_{(-1,\infty)} \lambda(s) e^{-\int_t^s \lambda(u)du} v^*(s, x(1+\pi^m(t,x)z)) p(t,s,dz) ds \\ &\leq \mathcal{L}v^*(t,x). \end{aligned}$$

Letting $\varepsilon \to 0$ we obtain $v^* = \mathcal{L}v^*$. Finally, since $U(t,x) \leq v^*(t,x) \leq f(t,x)$ and the function f satisfies the boundary condition (3.3) by Lemma 3.3, we conclude that v^* is a solution to the fixed point DP equation (3.6). □

Remark 3.5. The previous theorem shows the existence of a fixed point to the DP equation (3.6), and gives also an iterative procedure for constructing a fixed point. In the next subsection, we shall prove that such a fixed point is equal to the value function v, which implies in particular the uniqueness for the fixed point equation (3.6).

3.3. *Verification and optimal strategies*

Consider the solution v^* to the fixed point DP equation (3.6), constructed in Theorem 3.1. We now state a verification theorem for the fixed point equation (3.6), which provides the optimal portfolio strategy in feedback form.

Theorem 3.2. *Assume that* (**HL**), (**NA**), (**HU**) *and* (**HI**) *hold. Then,*

$$V_0 = v^*(0, X_0),$$

and an optimal control $\hat{\alpha} \in \mathcal{A}$ is given by

$$\hat{\alpha}_n = \hat{\pi}(\tau_n, \hat{X}_{\tau_n})\hat{X}_{\tau_n}, \quad n \geq 0, \tag{3.19}$$

where $\hat{\pi}$ is a measurable function on $[0,T) \times (0,\infty)$ solution to

$$\hat{\pi}(t,x) \in \arg\max_{\pi \in [0,1]} \int_t^T \int_{(-1,\infty)} \lambda(s) e^{-\int_t^s \lambda(u)du} v^*(s, x(1+\pi z)) p(t,s,dz) ds,$$

and $(\hat{X}_{\tau_n})_{n \geq 0}$ is the wealth given by

$$\hat{X}_{\tau_{n+1}} = \hat{X}_{\tau_n} + \hat{\alpha}_n Z_{n+1}, \quad n \geq 0,$$

and starting from $\hat{X}_0 = X_0$.

Proof. Consider $\alpha \in \mathcal{A}$ and the corresponding positive wealth process $(X_{\tau_n})_{n\geq 0}$. From Lemma 3.4, we know that

$$\mathbb{E}[|v^*(\tau_n, X_{\tau_n})|] < \infty, \quad (\forall)\ n \geq 0.$$

We apply Lemma 3.1 to get for any $n \geq 0$:

$$\begin{aligned}\mathbb{E}[v^*(\tau_{n+1}, X_{\tau_{n+1}})|\mathcal{F}_n] &= \int_{\tau_n}^T \int_{(-1,\infty)} \lambda(s) e^{-\int_{\tau_n}^s \lambda(u)du} v^*(s, X_{\tau_n} + \alpha_n z) p(\tau_n, s, dz) ds \\ &\leq \mathcal{L}v^*(\tau_n, X_{\tau_n}) = v^*(\tau_n, X_{\tau_n}),\end{aligned} \tag{3.20}$$

so the process $\{v^*(\tau_n, X_{\tau_n}), n \geq 0\}$ is a $(\mathbb{P}, \mathbb{F})$-supermartingale. Recalling that $v^*(t,.) \geq U$ we obtain

$$\mathbb{E}[U(X_{\tau_n})] \leq \mathbb{E}[v^*(\tau_n, X_{\tau_n})] \leq v^*(0, X_0), \quad (\forall)\ n \geq 0.$$

Now, by Lemma 3.4, the sequence $(U(X_{\tau_n}))_n$ is uniformly integrable. By sending n to infinity into the last inequality, we then get

$$\mathbb{E}[U(X_T)] \leq v^*(0, X_0).$$

Since α is arbitrary, we obtain $V_0 \leq v^*(0, X_0)$.

Conversely, let $\hat{\alpha} \in \mathcal{A}$ be the portfolio strategy given by (3.19), and $(\hat{X}_{\tau_n})_{n\geq 0}$ the associated wealth process. Then, by the same calculations as in (3.20), we have now the equalities:

$$\begin{aligned}\mathbb{E}[v^*(\tau_{n+1}, \hat{X}_{\tau_{n+1}})|\mathcal{F}_n] &= \int_{\tau_n}^T \int_{(-1,\infty)} \lambda(s) e^{-\int_{\tau_n}^s \lambda(u)du} v^*(s, X_{\tau_n} + \hat{\alpha}_n z) p(\tau_n, s, dz) ds \\ &= \mathcal{L}v^*(\tau_n, \hat{X}_{\tau_n}) = v^*(\tau_n, \hat{X}_{\tau_n}), \quad n \geq 0,\end{aligned}$$

by definition of $\mathcal{L}$ and $\hat{\alpha}$. This means that the process $\{v^*(\tau_n, \hat{X}_{\tau_n}), n \geq 0\}$ is a $(\mathbb{P}, \mathbb{F})$-martingale, and so:

$$\mathbb{E}[v^*(\tau_n, \hat{X}_{\tau_n})] = v^*(0, X_0), \quad (\forall)\, n \geq 0.$$

From the bounds $U \leq v^* \leq f$ and Lemma 3.4, we know that the sequence $(v^*(\tau_n, \hat{X}_{\tau_n}))_n$ is uniformly integrable. By sending n to infinity into the last equality, and recalling the terminal condition for v^*, we then get

$$\mathbb{E}[U(\hat{X}_T)] = v^*(0, X_0).$$

Together with the inequality, $V_0 \leq v^*(0, X_0)$, this proves that $V_0 = v^*(0, X_0)$ and $\hat{\alpha}$ is an optimal control. □

An identical verification argument to the proof of Theorem 3.2 can be performed for an investor starting at time t with initial capital x: this way we prove that v^* is actually the value function of the control problem. In addition, this shows that the Dynamic Programming Equation (3.6) has a unique solution. For the sake of avoiding the heavy notation associated with strategies starting at time t, we decided to only do the verification for time $t = 0$.

The Proposition below shows that actually we can approximate the optimal control, and not only the maximal expected utility, using a finite number of iterations. The approximate optimal control is actually very simple, since after the mth arrival time all the wealth is invested in the money market. In addition, a stochastic control representation for the iteration v_m is provided.

Proposition 3.1. *Assume that* (**HL**), (**NA**), (**HU**) *and* (**HI**) *hold. Then*

$$v_m(0, X_0) = \sup_{\alpha \in \mathcal{A}_m} \mathbb{E}[U(X_T)], \tag{3.21}$$

where $\mathcal{A}_m$ is the set of admissible controls $\alpha = (\alpha_n)_{\geq 0} \in \mathcal{A}$ such that all money is invested in the money market after m arrivals, i.e. $\alpha_n = 0$ for $n \geq m$.

For any $0 \leq n \leq m-1$, consider the measurable function $\hat{\pi}^n(\cdot,\cdot)$ defined by

$$\hat{\pi}^n(t,x) = \arg\max_{\pi \in [0,1]} \int_t^T \int_{(-1,\infty)} \lambda(s) e^{-\int_t^s \lambda(u)du} v_{m-n-1}(s, x(1+\pi z)) p(t,s,dz)ds,$$

so that

$$v_{m-n}(t,x) = \int_t^T \int_{(-1,\infty)} \lambda(s) e^{-\int_t^s \lambda(u)du} v_{m-n-1}(s, x(1+\pi^n(t,x)z)) p(t,s,dz)ds.$$

Define in feedback form the admissible strategy $\hat{\alpha}^m \in \mathcal{A}_m$ by $\alpha_n^m = \hat{\pi}^n(\tau_n, \hat{X}^m_{\tau_n})\hat{X}^m_{\tau_n}$ for $0 \leq n \leq m-1$ and $\alpha_n^m = 0$ for $n \geq m$, where the wealth processes $(\hat{X}^m_{\tau_n})_{n \geq 0}$ is given by

$$\hat{X}^m_{\tau_{n+1}} = \hat{X}^m_{\tau_n} + \hat{\alpha}^m_n Z_{n+1}, \quad 0 \leq n \leq m-1, \quad \hat{X}^m_{\tau_n} = \hat{X}^m_{\tau_m}, \;\; n \geq m,$$

starting from the initial wealth X_0. Then $\alpha^m \in \mathcal{A}_m$ is an optimal control for (3.21).

Proof. The proof is based on similar arguments to the proof of Theorem 3.2. Namely, for each $\alpha \in \mathcal{A}_m$, one can use Lemma 3.1 to conclude that $(v_{m-n}(\tau_n, X_n))_{n=0,1,\ldots,m}$ is a supermartingale and, for the particular choice of the control α^m described above we actually have that $(v_{m-n}(\tau_n, \hat{X}_n^m))_{n=0,1,\ldots,m}$ is a true martingale. Since $v_0(t,x) = U(x)$ and for each $\alpha \in \mathcal{A}_m$ the wealth process X is constant after the arrival time τ_m, it is easy to finish the proof. □

Theorems 3.1 and 3.2 together show how we can compute by iterations the maximal expected utility and the optimal control. Since the control problem is finite-horizon in time and infinite horizon in n, taking into account Proposition 3.1, the iteration procedure represents exactly the approximation of the infinite horizon problem by a sequence of finite horizon problems.

4. Convergence in the Illiquid Market Model

So far, we have considered the optimal investment problem (3.1) for a *fixed* arrival rate function $\lambda : [0,T) \to [0,\infty)$ satisfying condition (2.1). To emphasize the dependence on the arrival rate, let us denote by V_0^λ the value in (3.1). When the arrival rate is very large *at all times* (in some sense to be precised), one would expect that V_0^λ is very close to the optimal expected utility of an agent who can trade at all times (therefore continuously) in the asset S. It is also expected that the constraint (2.7), which is *implicitly* contained in the admissibility condition (2.6) in the time-illiquid case, becomes and *explicit* no-short sale constraint (2.10) in the continuous time limit. This section is devoted to proving that this is actually true.

First, we need to define the optimization problem for the agent who can trade continuously. We remind the reader that continuous time trading strategies can be defined by (2.9). We denote by $\mathcal{X}^S$ the set of positive wealth processes $(X_t)_{0\le t\le T}$ given by (2.9), by using $\mathbb{G}^S$-predictable and S-integrable processes H satisfying the no-short sale constraint (2.10). The filtration $\mathbb{G}^S = (\mathcal{G}_t^S)_{0\le t\le T}$ is defined by

$$\mathcal{G}_t^S = \sigma\{S_s, 0 \le s \le t\} \vee \mathcal{N},$$

and represents the information one can get from following the asset S. Because of the Lévy structure of S, $\mathbb{G}^S$ satisfies the usual conditions. We also denote by $\mathcal{D}(S)$ the set of all $\mathbb{G}^S$-predictable processes π valued in $[0,1]$. It is then clear that

$$\mathcal{X}^S = \{X^{(\pi)} \,|\, \pi \in \mathcal{D}(S)\}.$$

The optimization problem for an agent trading continuously, under no-short selling constraints can be formulated as

$$V_0^M = \sup_{X\in\mathcal{X}^S} \mathbb{E}[U(X_T)] = \sup_{\pi\in\mathcal{D}(S)} \mathbb{E}[U(X_T^{(\pi)})]. \tag{4.1}$$

The main result of this section is:

Theorem 4.1. *Under Assumptions* (**HL**), (**NA**), (**HU**) *and* (**HI**), *consider a sequence* $(\lambda_k)_k$ *of intensity functions such that each* λ_k *satisfies* (2.1), *and*

$$\lambda_k(t) \to \infty \quad \text{as } k \to \infty, \quad \forall t \in [0, T]. \tag{4.2}$$

Then $V_0^{\lambda_k} \to V_0^M$ *as* $k \to \infty$, *where* V_0^M *is defined by* (4.1).

In order to prove Theorem 4.1, we first have to put all the optimization problems (3.1) on *the same physical probability space*, independent of the intensity function λ. This is an easy task actually. We consider a probability space $(\Omega, \mathcal{G}, \mathbb{P})$ supporting two independent processes: the continuous time stock price process $(S_t)_{0\leq t\leq T}$ (which has all the desired properties) and a Poisson process $(M_t)_{0\leq t<\infty}$ with intensity equal to one. After that, for each intensity function λ we define the nonhomogenous Poisson process N^λ (actually its sequence of jumps) by (2.2). Therefore, for different intensities, we still have the same physical space. We now denote by $\mathbb{F}^\lambda$ and $\mathbb{G}^\lambda$ the discrete and continuous time filtrations on $(\Omega, \mathcal{G}, \mathbb{P})$ defined by (2.4) and (2.8) corresponding to the intensity λ, and by τ_n^λ the associated jump times.

The main obstacle in proving Theorem 4.1 is the fact that the filtration $\mathbb{F}^\lambda$ only observes the process S at the arrival times, while the filtration $\mathbb{G}^S$ used by the investor in (4.1) observes the stock continuously. This problem is overcome in three steps.

Step 1: First, we show that in (3.1), the discrete-time filtration $\mathbb{F}^\lambda = (\mathcal{F}_n^\lambda)_{n\geq 0}$ can be replaced by the larger filtration $(\mathcal{G}^\lambda_{\tau_n^\lambda})_{n\geq 0}$. In other words, due to the Markov structure of the model, an investor who can only trade at the discrete arrival times, cannot improve his/her expected utility by continuously observing the evolution of the stock between the arrival times. This is done in Lemma 4.1 below.

Lemma 4.1. *Fix an intensity function* λ *and define*

$$V_0^{\lambda,c} := \sup_{\alpha\in\mathcal{A}_c^\lambda} \mathbb{E}[U(X_T)], \tag{4.3}$$

where $\mathcal{A}_c^\lambda$ *is the set of simple admissible strategies* $\alpha = (\alpha_n)_{n\geq 0}$ *with continuous observation, which means that for each* $n \geq 0$ *we have* $\alpha_n \in \mathcal{G}^\lambda_{\tau_n^\lambda}$ *and* α *satisfies the constraint* (2.7) *for the wealth process* $(X_{\tau_n})_{n\geq 0}$ *defined by* (2.5).

Then, under Assumptions (**HL**), (**NA**), (**HU**) *and* (**HI**), *we have* $V_0^{\lambda,c} = V_0^\lambda$.

Proof. Assumption (**HL**) together with the independence of S and N ensures that for all $n \geq 0$, the (regular) distribution of (τ_{n+1}, Z_{n+1}) conditioned on $\mathcal{G}^\lambda_{\tau_n^\lambda}$ is given by:

(1) $\mathbb{P}[\tau_{n+1}^\lambda \in ds \,|\, \mathcal{G}^\lambda_{\tau_n^\lambda}] = \lambda(s)e^{-\int_{\tau_n}^s \lambda(u)du}ds$
(2) Further conditioning on knowing the next arrival time τ_{n+1}^λ, the return Z_{n+1} has distribution

$$\mathbb{P}[Z_{n+1} \in dz \,|\, \mathcal{G}^\lambda_{\tau_n^\lambda} \vee \sigma(\tau_{n+1}^\lambda)] = p(\tau_n^\lambda, \tau_{n+1}^\lambda, dz).$$

Therefore, in Lemma 3.1, one can replace the filtration $\mathbb{F}^\lambda$ by the larger filtration $(\mathcal{G}^\lambda_{\tau^\lambda_n})_{n\geq 0}$ and obtain that, for each $\alpha \in \mathcal{A}^\lambda_c$ we have

$$\mathbb{E}[v(\tau^\lambda_{n+1}, X_{\tau^\lambda_{n+1}}) \,|\, \mathcal{G}^\lambda_{\tau^\lambda_n}]$$
$$= \int_{\tau^\lambda_n}^T \int_{(-1,\infty)} \lambda(s) e^{-\int_{\tau^\lambda_n}^s \lambda(u)du} v(s, X_{\tau^\lambda_n} + \alpha_n z) p(\tau^\lambda_n, s, dz) ds.$$

After that, one can just follow the verification arguments in the proof of Theorem 3.2 to show that

$$V_0^{\lambda,c} = v^{*,\lambda}(0, X_0),$$

which ends the proof. □

Step 2: We define the continuous time filtration $\mathbb{G}^\infty = (\mathcal{G}^\infty_t)_{0\leq t\leq T}$ which contains all the information from the arrival times right at time zero. This corresponds to an investor who knows in advance all the jumps of the homogeneous Poisson process M and also observes continuously the stock S up to time t:

$$\mathcal{G}^\infty_t = \mathcal{G}^S_t \vee \sigma(M_u \,:\, 0 \leq u < \infty), \quad 0 \leq t < T.$$

Because the information added is independent, the process S is still a semimartingale with respect to the larger filtration $\mathbb{G}^\infty$, which satisfies the usual conditions as well. Using again the independence property, Lemma 4.2 below shows that if the investor in (4.1) has the additional information in $\mathbb{G}^\infty$, he/she cannot improve the maximal expected utility.

Lemma 4.2. *Consider the set $\bar{\mathcal{X}}_c$ of wealth processes defined by* (2.9) *where the general integrand H is $\mathbb{G}^\infty$-predictable, S-integrable and satisfies* (2.10). *Define*

$$V_0^\infty := \sup_{X\in\bar{\mathcal{X}}_c} \mathbb{E}[U(X_T)].$$

Then $V_0^\infty = V_0^M$.

Proof. Since $\mathcal{X}^S \subset \bar{\mathcal{X}}_c$, we obviously have $V_0^M \leq V_0^\infty$. Now take some arbitrary $X \in \bar{\mathcal{X}}_c$ associated to a no-short sale trading strategy H, which is $\mathbb{G}^\infty$-predictable. Consider the $\mathbb{G}^S$-predictable projection of H: $\hat{H}_s = \mathbb{E}[H_s \,|\, \mathcal{G}^S_{s-}]$, $t \leq s \leq T$. We then have (see e.g. Lemma 2.2.4 in [7])

$$\hat{X}_t := \mathbb{E}[X_t|\mathcal{G}^S_t] = X_0 + \int_0^t \hat{H}_u dS_u, \quad 0 \leq t \leq T.$$

This means that the process $\hat{X}$ lies in $\mathcal{X}^S$. Since U is concave, we get by the law of iterated conditional expectations and Jensen's inequality

$$\mathbb{E}[U(X_T)] = \mathbb{E}[\mathbb{E}[U(X_T) \,|\, \mathcal{G}^S_T]] \leq \mathbb{E}[U(E[X_T \,|\, \mathcal{G}^S_T])] = \mathbb{E}[U(\hat{X}_T)] \leq V_0^M.$$

We conclude from the arbitrariness of X in $\bar{\mathcal{X}}_c$. □

Step 3: Once we prove the step above and transform the Merton problem in a utility maximization problem with no short-sale constraints under the filtration $\mathbb{G}^\infty$, we can basically follow the arguments in Theorems 3.1, 3.3 and 4.1 in [4], to finish the proof. In order to use the ideas in [4] we still need the following technical lemma.

Lemma 4.3. *Consider a sequence $(\lambda_k)_k$ of intensity functions such that each λ_k satisfies* (2.1), *and*

$$\lambda_k(t) \to \infty \quad \text{as } k \to \infty, \quad \forall\, t \in [0,T].$$

Then, the jump times $\{(\tau_n^k)_n, k \in \mathbb{N}\}$ of $\{N^{\lambda_k}, k \in \mathbb{N}\}$, satisfies up to a subsequence (in k),

$$\sup_n |\tau_{n+1}^k - \tau_n^k| \to 0 \quad \text{a.s. when } k \to \infty. \tag{4.4}$$

Proof. Consider subdivisions $0 = t_0^k < \cdots < t_{M_k}^k = T$ such that $\sup_{i=0,\ldots,M_k-1}(t_{i+1} - t_i) \le 1/2k$. By Fatou's lemma, $\lim_{l\to\infty} \int_s^t \lambda_l(u)du = \infty$ for all $0 \le s < t \le T$, so up to a subsequence indexed by l_k we can assume that

$$\sum_{i=0}^{M_k-1} \exp\left(- \int_{t_i^k}^{t_{i+1}^k} \lambda_{l_k}(u)du \right) \le 2^{-k}, \quad \forall\, k \ge 0.$$

Now, from the relations

$$\begin{aligned}
\mathbb{P}[\sup_n |\tau_{n+1}^{l_k} - \tau_n^{l_k}| > 1/k] &\le \sum_{i=0}^{M_k-1} \mathbb{P}[\exists\, n, \tau_n^{l_k} \le t_i^k < t_{i+1}^k < \tau_{n+1}^{l_k}] \\
&= \sum_{i=0}^{M_k-1} \mathbb{P}[N_{t_i^k}^{\lambda_{l_k}} = N_{t_{i+1}^k}^{\lambda_{l_k}}] \\
&= \sum_{i=0}^{M_k-1} \exp\left(- \int_{t_i^k}^{t_{i+1}^k} \lambda_{l_k}(u)du \right),
\end{aligned}$$

we see that for all $\epsilon > 0$,

$$\begin{aligned}
\sum_{k=0}^{\infty} \mathbb{P}[\sup_n |\tau_{n+1}^{l_k} - \tau_n^{l_k}| > \epsilon] &\le \sum_{k<\epsilon^{-1}} \mathbb{P}[\sup_n |\tau_{n+1}^{l_k} - \tau_n^{l_k}| > \epsilon] + \sum_{k\ge\epsilon^{-1}} 2^{-k} \\
&< \infty,
\end{aligned}$$

and thus by Borel-Cantelli we have

$$\sup_n |\tau_{n+1}^{l_k} - \tau_n^{l_k}| \to 0 \quad \text{a.s. when } k \to \infty,$$

which ends the proof of the lemma. □

Proof of Theorem 4.1. Using Lemma 4.3 and taking further subsequences of any sequence, it is enough to prove Theorem 4.1 under the additional assumption (4.4).

We first represent continuous time trading strategies with no short sale constraints in terms of proportion of wealth, for the larger filtration $\mathbb{G}^\infty$. For any continuous time wealth process $X \in \bar{\mathcal{X}}_c$ associated to a trading strategy H satisfying (2.10), we still denote by $\pi_t = H_t S_{t-}/X_{t-}$, and notice that the process $(\pi_t)_{0 \le t \le T}$ is valued in $[0,1]$ by (2.10). We also denote by $X^{(\pi)}$ the process defined by (2.11) and define $\mathcal{D}^\infty$ to be the set of all $\mathbb{G}^\infty$-predictable processes π valued in $[0,1]$. It is then clear that

$$V_0^\infty = \sup_{\pi \in \mathcal{D}^\infty} \mathbb{E}[U(X_T^{(\pi)})].$$

Using Lemmas 4.1 and 4.2 we have, for each intensity function λ that

$$V_0^\lambda = V_0^{\lambda,c} \le V_0^\infty = V_0^M. \tag{4.5}$$

Let now $\pi \in \mathcal{D}(S) \subset \mathcal{D}^\infty$ be a (proportional) trading strategy in (4.1) and let $(\lambda_k)_k$ a sequence of intensity functions as in Theorem 4.1. We will follow the arguments in [4] to approximate this continuous time trading strategy by a sequence of simple strategies $\alpha^k \in \mathcal{A}_c^{\lambda_k}$, which are discrete, but *use information from continuous observations*. First, according to Lemmas 3.4 and 3.5 in [4], there exists a sequence $\pi^m \in \mathcal{D}(S)$ such that each π^m is LCRL (left continuous with right limits) and such that

$$uc\mathbb{P} - \lim_{m \to \infty} X^{(\pi^m)} = X^{(\pi)},$$

so, in order to approximate π we can actually assume it is LCRL. Here, by $uc\mathbb{P}$-convergence, we mean the usual convergence of processes in probability, uniformly on $[0,T]$.

Next, let us define

$$\pi_n^k = \pi_{\tau_n^{\lambda_k}+}, \quad n \ge 0,$$

where $\pi_{t+} = \lim_{u \searrow t} \pi_t$. Because the filtration $\mathbb{G}^{\lambda^k}$ satisfies the usual conditions we have that the process $(\pi_{t+})_{0 \le t \le T}$ is optional with respect to $\mathbb{G}^{\lambda_k}$ for each k. Since, in addition, $\tau_n^{\lambda_k}$ are stopping times with respect to $\mathbb{G}^{\lambda_k}$ we obtain that, for each k,

$$\pi_n^k \in \mathcal{G}^{\lambda^k}_{\tau_n^{\lambda_k}}, \quad k \ge 0. \tag{4.6}$$

Therefore, if we define, for each fixed k the discrete-time wealth process by

$$X_{\tau_{n+1}^{\lambda_k}} = X_{\tau_n^{\lambda_k}}(1 + \pi_n^k Z_{n+1}), \quad n \ge 0, \tag{4.7}$$

and denote by $\alpha_n^k = \pi_n^k X_{\tau_n^{\lambda_k}}$ we have $\alpha^k = (\alpha_n^k)_{n \ge 0} \in \mathcal{A}_c^{\lambda_k}$. To each of the above defined α^k, we can associate by Remark 2.2 a continuous time simple integrand H^k which is $\mathbb{G}^{\lambda_k}$-predictable and the continuous time wealth process $(X_t^k)_{0 \le t \le T}$. The fundamental observation is now that all H^k are predictable with respect to the same "large" filtration $\mathbb{G}^\infty$. Using this universal filtration, we can now follow the proof of Theorem 3.1 in [4], which actually works for stochastic partitions under condition (4.4), to conclude that

$$X^{(\pi)} = uc\mathbb{P} - \lim_{k\to\infty} X^k.$$

Therefore, we can approximate any continuous time strategy in the Merton problem (4.1) by simple trading strategies $\alpha^k \in \mathcal{A}_c^{\lambda_k}$. The rather obvious details on how approximation of strategies leads to approximation of optimal expected utility are identical to the arguments in [4] Sec. 4, and are omitted: this means that for all $\pi \in \mathcal{D}(S)$, $\mathbb{E}[U(X_T^{(\pi)})] = \lim_k \mathbb{E}[U(X_T^k)]$, and so $V_0^M \leq \liminf_k V_0^{\lambda_k,c}$. Together with (4.5), this concludes the proof of Theorem 4.1. □

Acknowledgments

H. Pham would like to thank Peter Leoni (Electrabel) for interesting discussions on this illiquidity market modelling. The research of M. Sîrbu was supported in part by the National Science Foundation under Grant DMS-0802681. All the authors would like to thank the anonymous referee for the suggestions which led to an improvement of the paper.

References

[1] D. Bertsekas and S. Shreve, *Stochastic Optimal Control: The Discrete-Time Case* (Academic Press, 1978).

[2] A. Cretarola, F. Gozzi, H. Pham and P. Tankov, Optimal consumption policies in illiquid markets, to appear in *Finance and Stochastics*.

[3] J. Jacod and A. Shiryaev, *Limit Theorems for Stochastic Processes*, 2nd edn. (Springer-Verlag, 2003).

[4] K. Kardaras and E. Platen, Multiplicative approximation of wealth processes involving no-short-sale strategies via simple trading, preprint, http://arxiv.org/abs/0812.0033 (2008).

[5] K. Matsumoto, Optimal portfolio of low liquid assets with a log-utility function, *Finance and Stochastics* **10** (2006) 121–145.

[6] H. Pham and P. Tankov, A model of optimal consumption under liquidity risk with random trading times, *Mathematical Finance* **18** (2008) 613–627.

[7] E. Pardoux, Filtrage nonlinaire et EDPS associes, *Lect. Notes in Maths. St Flour 1989* **1464** (1991) 67–163.

[8] C. Rogers and O. Zane, A simple model of liquidity effects, in *Advances in Finance and Stochastics: Essays in Honour of Dieter Sondermann*, eds. K. Sandmann and P. Schoenbucher (Springer, Berlin, 2002), pp. 161–176.

OPTIMAL TRADE EXECUTION UNDER GEOMETRIC BROWNIAN MOTION IN THE ALMGREN AND CHRISS FRAMEWORK*

JIM GATHERAL

Department of Mathematics, Baruch College, CUNY
One Bernard Baruch Way,
New York, NY 10010, USA

ALEXANDER SCHIED

Department of Mathematics, University of Mannheim
A5, 6, 68131 Mannheim, Germany

With an alternative choice of risk criterion, we solve the HJB equation explicitly to find a closed-form solution for the optimal trade execution strategy in the Almgren–Chriss framework assuming the underlying unaffected stock price process is geometric Brownian motion.

Keywords: HJB; optimal execution; risk measures; market impact.

1. Introduction

A problem of fundamental practical importance to algorithmic traders is how to optimally split up a large trade so as to minimize the effect of market impact. In a pair of seminal papers [2, 3], Almgren and Chriss showed how to frame this problem as a tradeoff between expected execution cost and risk; in their framework, execution costs are increasing (in fact linear) in the trading rate and the choice of risk criterion is variance (or more precisely, quadratic variation). Under these assumptions, there is a closed-form analytical solution to the optimal execution problem which turns out to be static. In particular, adaptive trade schedules that depend on the current level of the stock price are suboptimal.

A key question that then arises is to what extent the optimality of the static solution in the Almgren and Chriss framework depends on detailed modeling assumptions, specifically their assumption that the unaffected stock price process

*This chapter was originally published under the same title in *International Journal of Theoretical and Applied Finance*, Vol.14, No.3, 353–368 (2011). Singapore: World Scientific Publishing.

is arithmetic Brownian motion (ABM). In particular, if the true underlying process is geometric Brownian motion (GBM), how suboptimal would it be to follow the static strategy derived under the ABM assumption?

Under the GBM assumption for the unaffected stock price process with variance as risk criterion, the optimal execution problem does not appear to be analytically tractable. On the other hand, Peter Forsyth and his collaborators [8, 9] have investigated this version of the problem by solving the HJB equation numerically. They find that under the GBM assumption, the optimal trading rate increases with the stock price and that the cost-risk efficient frontier is almost identical under ABM and GBM assumptions. Thus, if the true underlying process is GBM, the static solution obtained by solving the problem under the ABM assumption is not very suboptimal.

In this paper, by adopting a different risk criterion, we find that we can solve the optimal execution problem under geometric Brownian motion analytically, obtaining an explicit closed-form expression for the trading rate. We are then able to make precise statements about properties of the optimal strategy under the GBM assumption, and explicitly compare the optimal strategy under GBM with the optimal strategy for the risk criterion under ABM.

2. The Optimal Trade Execution Problem

We use the following continuous-time formulation of the market impact model proposed by Almgren and Chriss [2, 3] and Almgren [1]. We assume that the number of shares in the trader's portfolio is described by an absolutely continuous trajectory $t \mapsto x_t$. Given this trading trajectory, the price at which transactions occur is

$$\widetilde{S}_t = S_t + \eta \dot{x}_t + \gamma(x_t - x_0) \tag{2.1}$$

where η and γ are constants and S_t is the unaffected stock price process. The term $\eta \dot{x}_t$ corresponds to the *temporary* or *instantaneous impact* of trading $\dot{x}_t dt$ shares at time t and only affects this current order. The term $\gamma(x_t - x_0)$ corresponds to the *permanent price impact* that has been accummulated by all transactions until time t. As mentioned earlier, in the original Almgren-Chriss model, the unaffected stock price follows a Bachelier process, or arithmetic Brownian motion (ABM),

$$S_t = S_0(1 + \sigma W_t), \tag{2.2}$$

where W is a standard Brownian motion. Here we will consider the case in which S is a geometric Brownian motion (GBM),

$$S_t = S_0 e^{\sigma W_t - \frac{1}{2}\sigma^2 t}. \tag{2.3}$$

Let us now consider a *trade execution strategy* in which an initial long or short position of X shares is liquidated by time T. The asset position of the trader at time t is described by an absolutely continuous and adapted curve x_t satisfying the boundary condition $x_0 = X$ and $x_T = 0$. In such a strategy, $\dot{x}_t dt$ shares are bought at price $\widetilde{S}_t$ at each time t. Thus, the *costs* arising from the strategy x are

$$\begin{aligned}\mathcal{C}(x) &:= \int_0^T \widetilde{S}_t \dot{x}_t dt = \int_0^T S_t \dot{x}_t dt + \eta \int_0^T \dot{x}_t^2 dt + \gamma \int_0^T x_t \dot{x}_t dt + \gamma X^2 \\ &= -XS_0 - \int_0^T x_t dS_t + \eta \int_0^T \dot{x}_t^2 dt + \frac{\gamma}{2} X^2.\end{aligned}$$

The *optimal trade execution problem* consists in minimizing a certain objective function, which may involve both cost and risk terms, over the class of admissible trading strategies x with side conditions $x_0 = X$ and $x_T = 0$.

The easiest case corresponds to taking the expected costs,

$$\mathbb{E}[\mathcal{C}(x)] = -XS_0 + \frac{\gamma}{2} X^2 + \eta \mathbb{E}\left[\int_0^T \dot{x}_t^2 dt\right], \tag{2.4}$$

as cost criterion. In this case, which was first considered by Bertsimas and Lo [6] in a discrete-time setting, a simple application of Jensen's inequality shows that the unique optimal strategy x^* is characterized by having the constant trading rate

$$\dot{x}_t^* = -\frac{X}{T},$$

regardless of the choice of the unaffected price process. When, as is usually assumed in practice, time is parameterized in volume time, such a constant trading rate corresponds to a VWAP strategy, where VWAP stands for volume-weighted average price.

2.1. *An alternative risk criterion*

In this paper, we compute optimal strategies for a new risk criterion. Specifically, we choose to quantify the risk associated with a trading strategy as the time-averaged value-at-risk (VaR) associated with the P&L of the position. This choice of risk criterion closely mimics the practice at investment banks of imposing a daily risk capital charge on trading portfolios proportional to value-at-risk (VaR). Moreover, in contrast to VaR itself, which is a time-inconsistent risk measure, time-averaged VaR is time-consistent. At each point in time, we will compute the value-at-risk associated with the position $x_t \geq 0$. Ignoring permanent impact and under the GBM assumption, this value-at-risk is proportional to $x_t S_t$. Thus, under the GBM assumption, we choose our risk term to be the expectation of the time-average

$$\widetilde{\lambda} \int_0^T x_t S_t dt \tag{2.5}$$

of the risk measurements taken until the liquidation of our position. To solve the optimal liquidation problem, we study the minimization of an objective function of the form

$$\mathbb{E}[\mathcal{C}(x)] + \widetilde{\lambda}\mathbb{E}\left[\int_0^T x_t S_t dt\right]$$
$$= -XS_0 + \frac{\gamma}{2}X^2 + \mathbb{E}\left[\eta\int_0^T \dot{x}_t^2 dt + \widetilde{\lambda}\int_0^T x_t S_t dt\right] \qquad (2.6)$$

for some constant $\widetilde{\lambda} > 0$. More precisely, for $\lambda := \widetilde{\lambda}/\eta$ we will consider the problem

$$\text{minimize } \mathbb{E}\left[\int_0^T (\dot{x}_t^2 + \lambda x_t S_t)dt\right] \text{ over all strategies } x \in \mathcal{X}(T, X), \qquad (2.7)$$

where $\mathcal{X}(T, X)$ consists of all adapted and absolutely continuous strategies that satisfy the side conditions $x_0 = X > 0$ and $x_T = 0$ and the integrability conditions $\int_0^T \dot{x}_t^2 dt < \infty$ P-a.s. and $\mathbb{E}[\int_0^T |x_t S_t| dt] < \infty$.

Remark 2.1 (Permanent price impact). The choice (2.5) of risk term corresponds to approximating the time average of value-at-risk (VaR), neglecting the effect on the stock price of permanent impact. This approximation is therefore valid when the permanent impact coefficient γ is either zero or small. In Sec. 3.1 we will add another risk term in (2.7) so as to take care of nonvanishing permanent impact.

Remark 2.2 (Risk measures alternative to VaR). The general form (2.5) of our risk term can also be motivated when risk is monitored by means of an alternative risk measure ρ such as the *mean-standard deviation risk measure*,

$$\rho(Y) = \mathbb{E}[-Y] + \alpha\sqrt{\mathbb{E}[Y^2] - \mathbb{E}[Y]^2},$$

or coherent risk measures such as *average value-at-risk* (AVaR, also called *conditional value-at-risk* (CVaR) or *expected shortfall* (ES)); see [5, 7]. The only property ρ needs to satisfy is positive homogeneity,

$$\rho(cY) = c\rho(Y) \quad \text{for } c \geq 0.$$

With such a risk measure ρ we will measure the risk that the P&L of the currently held asset position would incur after a certain time span t_0 has passed. Thus, when $x_0 \geq 0$ shares of the risky asset are held at time $t = 0$, the P&L is $x_0(S_{t_0} - S_0)$, and the risk will be assessed as

$$\rho(x_0(S_{t_0} - S_0)) = x_0\rho(S_{t_0} - S_0) = x_0 S_0 \rho(e^{\sigma W_{t_0} - \frac{1}{2}\sigma^2 t_0} - 1).$$

When the risk of $x_t \geq 0$ is assessed at a later time $t > 0$ by means of the standard time-shift ρ_t of the risk measure ρ, we obtain

$$\rho_t(x_t(S_{t+t_0} - S_t)) = x_t\rho_t(S_{t+t_0} - S_t) = x_t S_t \rho(e^{\sigma W_{t_0} - \frac{1}{2}\sigma^2 t_0} - 1). \qquad (2.8)$$

Thus, the risk of $x_t \geq 0$ is assessed as $x_t S_t \widetilde{\lambda}$, where $\widetilde{\lambda} = \rho(e^{\sigma W_{t_0} - \sigma^2 t_0/2} - 1)$ is independent of t. Taking a time average thus also yields a risk term of the form (2.5).

When taking ρ specifically as value-at-risk at confidence level $\alpha \in (0,1)$,

$$\rho(Y) = \mathrm{VaR}_\alpha(Y) = \inf\{m \in \mathbb{R} \mid P[-Y \le m] \ge \alpha\},$$

we find that

$$\begin{aligned}\widetilde{\lambda} &= \rho(e^{\sigma W_{t_0} - \frac{1}{2}\sigma^2 t_0} - 1) = \mathrm{VaR}_\alpha(e^{\sigma W_{t_0} - \frac{1}{2}\sigma^2 t_0} - 1) \\ &= 1 - e^{-\sigma\sqrt{t_0}\Phi^{-1}(\alpha) - \sigma^2 t_0/2},\end{aligned} \tag{2.9}$$

where $\Phi(x) = \frac{1}{\sqrt{2\pi}}\int_{-\infty}^{x} e^{-y^2/2}dy$.

Remark 2.3 (The risk term for arithmetic Brownian motion). Let us discuss how our risk criterion changes when we use ABM, $S_t = S_0(1 + \sigma W_t)$, instead of GBM. In this case, the P&L of the position $x_t \ge 0$ is $x_t(S_{t+t_0} - S_t) = x_t S_0 \sigma W_{t_0}$. Instead of (2.8) we hence get

$$\rho_t(x_t(S_{t+t_0} - S_t)) = x_t S_0 \rho(\sigma W_{t_0}). \tag{2.10}$$

The risk term thus becomes

$$\widehat{\lambda} S_0 \int_0^T x_t dt, \tag{2.11}$$

where $\widehat{\lambda} = \sigma\rho(W_{t_0})$. In the special case $\rho = \mathrm{VaR}_\alpha$, we get

$$\widehat{\lambda} = \sigma\rho(W_{t_0}) = \sigma\sqrt{t_0}\Phi^{-1}(\alpha). \tag{2.12}$$

Comparing this expression with (2.9), we see that

$$\widehat{\lambda} = \widetilde{\lambda} + O(\sigma^2 t_0) \quad \text{when } \sigma\sqrt{t_0} \ll 1. \tag{2.13}$$

3. Solution of the Optimal Execution Problem

Here is our first main result:

Theorem 3.1. *The unique optimal trade execution strategy attaining the infimum in* (2.7) *is*

$$x_t^* = \left(\frac{T-t}{T}\right)\left[X - \frac{\lambda T}{4}\int_0^t S_s ds\right] \tag{3.1}$$

Moreover, the value of the minimization problem in (2.7) *is given by*

$$\begin{aligned}\mathbb{E}\left[\int_0^T ((\dot{x}_t^*)^2 + \lambda x_t^* S_t)dt\right] &= \frac{X^2}{T} + \frac{1}{2}\lambda T X S_0 \\ &\quad - \frac{\lambda^2}{8\sigma^6} S_0^2 \left(e^{\sigma^2 T} - 1 - \sigma^2 T - \frac{1}{2}\sigma^4 T^2\right).\end{aligned} \tag{3.2}$$

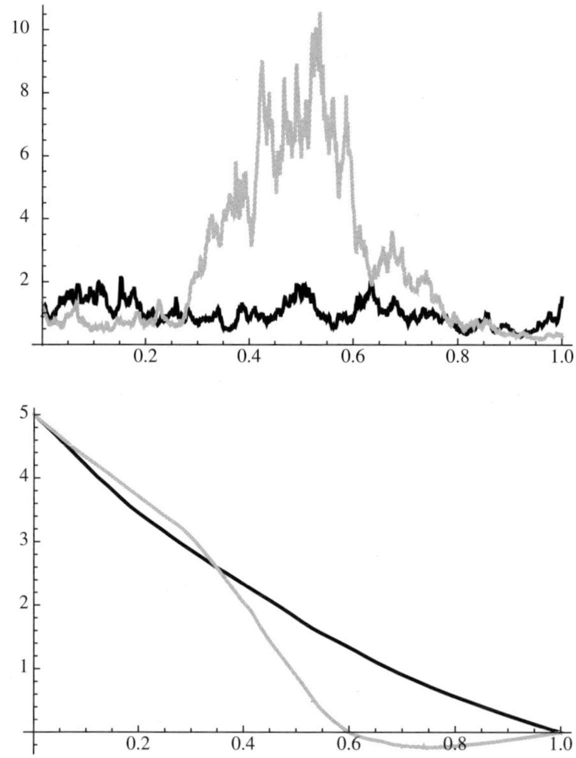

Fig. 1. Two realizations of GBM and the corresponding optimal strategies.

Remark 3.1. Note that, as illustrated in Fig. 1, when selling stock the strategy x^* in (3.1) is *aggressive in-the-money* in the sense that it involves trading at a higher (slower) speed $v_t^* = -\dot{x}_t^*$ when stock prices increase (decrease). In particular, if the stock price becomes very high, it can be optimal to liquidate completely before time T. In this case, the optimal strategy (3.1) can actually become negative (see Fig. 1). Such negative values of the strategy would be problematic since the interpretation of (2.5) as a risk term would be lost. But, as discussed in Sec. 4, a sign change of the optimal strategy is highly unlikely to happen in practice with reasonable parameters. The minimization problem (2.7) with strategies constrained to stay nonnegative will be solved in a forthcoming paper.

Theorem 3.1 relies on a formulation of the minimization problem (2.7) within the framework of stochastic optimal control. To this end, we parameterize strategies x by their rate of trading $v_t := -\dot{x}_t$ and introduce the class $\mathcal{V}(T, X)$ of all progressively measurable processes $(v_t)_{0 \le t \le T}$ for which

$$x_t^v := X - \int_0^t v_s ds, \quad 0 \le t \le T, \tag{3.3}$$

belongs to $\mathcal{X}(T, X)$. The value function $C(T, X, S)$ of our problem can then be expressed as

$$C(T, X, S_0) = \inf_{v \in \mathcal{V}(T,X)} \mathbb{E}\left[\int_0^T v_t^2 dt + \lambda \int_0^T x_t^v S_t dt\right], \tag{3.4}$$

where we assume that the starting point S_0 of S is deterministic. Due to the state dependence of the class $\mathcal{V}(T, X)$ of admissible control processes, the problem (3.4) is a *finite-fuel control problem.*

Heuristic arguments suggest that $C(T, X, S)$ should satisfy the following Hamilton–Jacobi–Bellman (HJB) PDE:

$$C_T = \frac{1}{2}\sigma^2 S^2 C_{SS} + \lambda SX + \inf_{v \in \mathbb{R}} (v^2 - vC_X). \tag{3.5}$$

Indeed, assuming that C is sufficiently smooth, dynamic programming suggests that

$$C(T - t, x_t^v, S_t) + \int_0^t v_s^2 ds + \lambda \int_0^t x_s^v S_s ds$$

should be a submartingale for every $v \in \mathcal{V}(T, X)$ and a martingale as soon as v is optimal. Thus, an application of Itô's formula suggests (3.5). In addition, the fuel constraint $\int_0^T v_t dt = -X$ required from strategies in $\mathcal{V}(T, X)$ suggests that the value function C should satisfy a singular initial condition of the form

$$\lim_{T \downarrow 0} C(T, X, S) = \begin{cases} 0 & \text{if } X = 0, \\ +\infty & \text{if } X \neq 0. \end{cases} \tag{3.6}$$

The intuitive explanation for this initial condition is that a state with a nonzero asset position with no time left for its liquidation means that the liquidation task has not been performed, so that this state should receive an infinite penalty. See also [12] for similar effects in exponential-utility maximization for order execution. As a first step in proving Theorem 3.1, one can check easily that the right-hand side of (3.2) solves the singular initial value problem (3.5), (3.6):

Lemma 3.1. *The function*

$$C^*(T, X, S) = \frac{X^2}{T} + \frac{1}{2}\lambda TXS - \frac{\lambda^2}{8\sigma^6} S^2 \left(e^{\sigma^2 T} - 1 - \sigma^2 T - \frac{1}{2}\sigma^4 T^2\right), \tag{3.7}$$

is a classical solution of the singular initial value problem (3.5), (3.6). *Moreover, the strategy x^* defined in* (3.1) *satisfies the side conditions $x_0^* = X$ and $x_T^* = 0$. Its trading rate $v_t^* = -\dot{x}_t^*$ is such that*

$$\begin{aligned} v_t^* &= \frac{x_t^*}{T - t} + \frac{1}{4}\lambda S_t (T - t) = \frac{1}{2} C_X^*(T - t, x_t^*, S_t) \\ &= \arg\min\{v^2 - vC_X^*(T - t, x_t^*, S_t) \,|\, v \in \mathbb{R}\}. \end{aligned} \tag{3.8}$$

The proof of this lemma is straightforward. It allows us to prove Theorem 3.1 by means of the following verification argument.

Proof of Theorem 3.1. We first show that

$$C^*(T, X, S_0) \le \mathbb{E}\left[\int_0^T (v_t^2 + \lambda x_t^v S_t)dt\right] \tag{3.9}$$

for any given $v \in \mathcal{V}(X,T)$, where C^* is as in (3.7). To this end, we may clearly assume that the right-hand side of (3.9) is finite. Then in particular $\mathbb{E}[\int_0^T v_s^2 ds] < \infty$ since the admissibility of v includes the the integrability condition $\mathbb{E}[\int_0^T |x_t^v S_t| dt] < \infty$. Note that the fuel constraint $\int_0^T v_s ds = X$ and Jensen's inequality imply that in addition

$$|x_t^v| = \left|\int_t^T v_s ds\right| \le \sqrt{(T-t)\int_0^T v_s^2 ds} \in L^2(\mathbb{P}). \tag{3.10}$$

We next define

$$\tau_n := \inf\left\{0 \le t \le T \,\middle|\, \int_0^t v_s^2 ds \ge n\right\} \wedge T$$

with the convention that $\inf \emptyset = +\infty$. Then (3.10) yields that

$$|x_{t\wedge\tau_n}^v| \le \sqrt{n(T-t)}. \tag{3.11}$$

For $0 < t < T$, Itô's formula and the fact that C^* satisfies the HJB equation (3.5) yield that

$$\begin{aligned}
&C^*(T - t\wedge\tau_n, x_{t\wedge\tau_n}^v, S_{t\wedge\tau_n}) - C^*(T, X, S_0) \\
&\quad = \int_0^{t\wedge\tau_n} C_S^*(T-s, x_s^v, S_s)dS_s \\
&\quad\quad + \int_0^{t\wedge\tau_n} \Big[- C_T^*(T-s, x_s^v, S_s) - v_s C_X^*(T-s, x_s^v, S_s) \\
&\quad\quad + \frac{1}{2}S_s^2 C_{SS}^*(T-s, x_s^v, S_s)\Big]\, ds \\
&\quad \ge \int_0^{t\wedge\tau_n} C_S^*(T-s, x_s^v, S_s)dS_s - \int_0^{t\wedge\tau_n} [v_s^2 + \lambda x_s^v S_s]ds. \qquad (3.12)
\end{aligned}$$

Differentiating (3.7), we have

$$\begin{aligned}
&C_S^*(T-s, x_s^v, S_s) \\
&\quad = \frac{\lambda}{2}(T-s)x_s^v - \frac{\lambda^2}{4\sigma^2}S_s\left(e^{\sigma^2(T-s)} - 1 - \sigma^2(T-s) - \frac{1}{2}\sigma^4(T-s)^2\right).
\end{aligned}$$

By (3.11), the absolute value of the first term on the right is bounded by $\frac{\lambda}{2}\sqrt{n}(T-s)^{3/2}$ for $s \le t\wedge\tau_n$, and so $\int_0^{t\wedge\tau_n} C_S^*(T-s, x_s^v, S_s)dS_s$ is a true martingale. Taking expectations in (3.12) thus yields

$$C^*(T, X, S_0) \le \mathbb{E}[C^*(T - t \wedge \tau_n, x^v_{t\wedge\tau_n}, S_{t\wedge\tau_n})] + \mathbb{E}\left[\int_0^{t\wedge\tau_n} (v_s^2 + \lambda x_s^v S_s)ds\right]. \tag{3.13}$$

It follows from our assumptions on v that

$$\lim_{n\uparrow\infty}\lim_{t\uparrow T}\mathbb{E}\left[\int_0^{t\wedge\tau_n} (v_s^2 + \lambda x_s^v S_s)ds\right] = \mathbb{E}\left[\int_0^{T} (v_s^2 + \lambda x_s^v S_s)ds\right].$$

Next, (3.10) yields that

$$|C^*(T - t \wedge \tau_n, x^v_{t\wedge\tau_n}, S_{t\wedge\tau_n})| \le \int_0^T v_s^2 ds + \frac{\lambda}{2}T^{3/2}\sqrt{\int_0^T v_s^2 ds}\max_{0\le s\le T}|S_s| + C\left(1 + \max_{0\le s\le T}|S_s|^2\right),$$

where C is a suitable constant. Again by (3.10), the right-hand side is integrable and we obtain that

$$\lim_{n\uparrow\infty}\lim_{t\uparrow T}\mathbb{E}\left[C^*(T - t \wedge \tau_n, x^v_{t\wedge\tau_n}, S_{t\wedge\tau_n})\right] = \mathbb{E}\left[\lim_{t\uparrow T} C^*(T - t, x_t^v, S_T)\right] = 0.$$

Hence, (3.13) implies our claim (3.9).

Our next goal is to show that we get an equality in (3.9) if we take $v = v^*$, where v^* is as in (3.8) for x^* as in (3.1). First, however, we need to show that $v^* \in \mathcal{V}(T, X)$. But this is easy since

$$|x_t^*| \le X\left(\frac{T-t}{T}\right) + \frac{\lambda}{4}(T-t)t\max_{0\le s\le T}|S_s| \le X\left(\frac{T-t}{T}\right)^2 + \frac{\lambda T^2}{16}\max_{0\le s\le T}|S_s|.$$

It thus follows that $\mathbb{E}[\int_0^T |x_t^* S_t|dt] < \infty$ and in turn that $v^* \in \mathcal{V}(T, X)$.

Finally, we note that (3.8) implies that we get an $\mathbb{P}$-a.s. identity in (3.12) when choosing $v = v^*$. This implies an identity in (3.13) and in turn an identity in (3.9). Therefore v^* is an optimal strategy. In fact, v^* is the only strategy for which an identity in (3.12) holds $\mathbb{P}$-a.s. Therefore the inequality in (3.13) must be strict when $v \ne v^*$ and t and n are sufficiently large. This shows that v^* is indeed the only optimal strategy.

3.1. *Including the effect of permanent impact*

We now study the problem

$$\text{minimize } \mathbb{E}\left[\int_0^T (\dot{x}_t^2 + \kappa^2 x_t^2 + \lambda x_t S_t)dt\right] \text{ over } x \in \mathcal{X}(T, X), \tag{3.14}$$

where κ is a positive constant. This problem arises, for instance, when instead of the unaffected stock price S_t we consider a stock price

$$\widehat{S}_t = S_t + \gamma(x_t - x_0)$$

including the effect of permanent price impact when computing time-averaged VaR in (2.5). We have the following result.

Theorem 3.2. *The unique optimal strategy for* (3.14) *is*

$$x_t^* = \sinh((T-t)\kappa)\left[\frac{X}{\sinh(T\kappa)} - \frac{\lambda}{2\kappa}\int_0^t \frac{S_s}{1+\cosh((T-s)\kappa)}ds\right] \tag{3.15}$$

Moreover, the value of the minimization problem is given by

$$\mathbb{E}\left[\int_0^T ((\dot{x}_t^*)^2 + (\kappa x_t^*)^2 + \lambda x_t^* S_t)dt\right] = \kappa X^2 \coth(T\kappa) + \frac{\lambda X S_0}{\kappa}\tanh\left(\frac{T\kappa}{2}\right) - \frac{\lambda^2 S_0^2 e^{\sigma^2 T}}{4\kappa^2}\int_0^T \left[\tanh\left(\frac{t\kappa}{2}\right)\right]^2 e^{-\sigma^2 t}dt. \tag{3.16}$$

Remark 3.2. The rightmost integral in (3.16) cannot easily be computed in explicit form. By means of a computer algebra system such as Mathematica it is possible to obtain a lengthy representation in terms of hypergeometric functions.

The strategy of proving Theorem 3.2 is similar to proving Theorem 3.1. We parameterize strategies x again by their rate of trading $v_t := -\dot{x}_t$ belonging to the class $\mathcal{V}(T,X)$. The value function $\Gamma(T,X,S)$ of our problem can then be expressed as

$$\Gamma(T,X,S_0) = \inf_{v\in\mathcal{V}(T,X)} \mathbb{E}\left[\int_0^T v_t^2 + (\kappa x_t^v)^2 + \lambda x_t^v S_t dt\right]. \tag{3.17}$$

Similar heuristic arguments as above suggest that $\Gamma(T,X,S)$ should satisfy the following HJB equation:

$$\Gamma_T = \frac{1}{2}\sigma^2 S^2 \Gamma_{SS} + \kappa^2 X^2 + \lambda S X + \inf_{v\in\mathbb{R}}(v^2 - v\Gamma_X) \tag{3.18}$$

with singular initial condition

$$\lim_{T\downarrow 0}\Gamma(T,X,S) = \begin{cases} 0 & \text{if } X = 0, \\ +\infty & \text{if } X \neq 0. \end{cases} \tag{3.19}$$

A tedious, though straightforward, computation then shows that this singular initial value problem is solved by

$$\Gamma^*(T,X,S) := \kappa X^2 \coth(T\kappa) + \frac{\lambda X S}{\kappa}\tanh\left(\frac{T\kappa}{2}\right) - \frac{\lambda^2 S^2 e^{\sigma^2 T}}{4\kappa^2}\int_0^T \left[\tanh\left(\frac{t\kappa}{2}\right)\right]^2 e^{-\sigma^2 t}dt.$$

Moreover, the strategy x^* defined in (3.15) satisfies the side conditions $x_0^* = X$ and $x_T^* = 0$. Its trading rate $v_t^* = -\dot{x}_t^*$ is such that

$$\begin{aligned} v_t^* &= x_t^* \kappa \coth(\kappa(T-t)) + \frac{\lambda S_t}{2\kappa} \cdot \frac{\sinh(\kappa(T-t))}{1+\cosh(\kappa(T-t))} \\ &= x_t^* \kappa \coth(\kappa(T-t)) + \frac{\lambda S_t}{2\kappa} \tanh\left(\frac{\kappa(T-t)}{2}\right) \\ &= \frac{1}{2}\Gamma_X^*(T-t, x_t^*, S_t) \\ &= \arg\min\{v^2 - v\Gamma_X^*(T-t, x_t^*, S_t) \,|\, v \in \mathbb{R}\}. \end{aligned} \tag{3.20}$$

Having noticed these facts, one can repeat the verification argument from the proof of Theorem 3.1 with the appropriate modifications to obtain a proof for Theorem 3.2. The details are left to the reader.

Remark 3.3. As before, the optimal strategy involves trading at a higher (slower) rate $v_t^* = -\dot{x}_t^*$ when stock prices increase (decrease).

4. Sensitivity of Risk-Adjusted Cost to Strategy

Motivated by the form (3.8) of the optimal strategy, consider the one-parameter family of trading strategies with trading rate

$$v^\beta(t) = \frac{x_t}{T-t} + \beta S_t(T-t)$$

The choice $\beta = \lambda/4$ then corresponds to the optimal strategy.

Neglecting permanent impact (or alternatively with $\gamma = 0$), a straightforward computation gives the risk-adjusted expected cost (as of time $t = 0$) of this strategy as

$$\begin{aligned} C^\beta(T, X, S_0) &= \int_0^T dt \left\{ \mathbb{E}\left[\left(\frac{x_t}{T-t} + \beta(T-t)S_t\right)^2\right] + \lambda \mathbb{E}[S_t x_t] \right\} \\ &= \frac{X^2}{T} + \frac{\lambda}{2} S_0 X T + \left(\beta^2 - \beta\frac{\lambda}{2}\right) \frac{2S_0^2}{\sigma^6} \left\{ e^{\sigma^2 T} - 1 - \sigma^2 T - \frac{1}{2}\sigma^4 T^2 \right\}, \end{aligned} \tag{4.1}$$

which is minimized when

$$\beta = \frac{\lambda}{4} =: \beta^\star$$

consistent with our earlier claim. The choice $\beta = 0$ corresponds to a VWAP execution.

As discussed earlier in Remark 2.3, under the ABM assumption, the risk term corresponding to time-average VaR becomes

$$\widehat{\lambda}\int_0^T x_t S_0 dt \tag{4.2}$$

and so to solve the optimal liquidation problem, we must study the minimization of a slightly different objective function of the form

$$\text{minimize } \mathbb{E}\left[\int_0^T (\dot{x}_t^2 + \lambda x_t S_0) dt\right] \text{ over } x \in \mathcal{X}(T, X). \tag{4.3}$$

It is straightforward to verify that the optimal strategy that solves (4.3) is the static version of the dynamic strategy (3.8) obtained by replacing S_t with its expectation $\mathbb{E}[S_t] = S_0$, a strategy qualitatively similar to the popular Almgren-Chriss optimal strategy.

Remark 4.1. In the GBM framework, had we chosen to model price impact in the following multiplicative way instead of the additive definition (2.1):

$$\widetilde{S}_t = S_t[1 + \eta\dot{x}_t + \gamma(x_t - x_0)], \tag{4.4}$$

the costs of a strategy $x \in \mathcal{X}(T, X)$ would become

$$\mathcal{C}(x) = \int_0^T \widetilde{S}_t x_t dt = -XS_0 - \int_0^T x_t dS_t + \eta\int_0^T S_t \dot{x}_t^2 dt + \gamma\int_0^T S_t x_t \dot{x}_t dt.$$

Adding our risk term (2.5) would then lead to the problem of minimizing

$$\mathbb{E}\left[\int_0^T S_t(\eta\dot{x}_t^2 + \gamma x_t \dot{x}_t + \widetilde{\lambda} x_t) dt\right] \tag{4.5}$$

over $x \in \mathcal{X}(T, X)$. Since S is a martingale, the expectation in (4.5) is equal to

$$\mathbb{E}\left[S_T \int_0^T (\eta\dot{x}_t^2 + \gamma x_t \dot{x}_t + \widetilde{\lambda} x_t) dt\right],$$

the minimization of which is equivalent to the ABM minimization problem (4.3) (generalized to include permanent market impact). The optimal strategy is thus also static.

This motivates us to define another one-parameter family of static strategies, independent of S_t:

$$v_0^\beta(t) = \frac{x_t}{T - t} + \beta S_0(T - t)$$

Once again, the choice $\beta = \lambda/4$ corresponds to the optimal strategy.

Another straightforward computation gives the expected cost (as of time $t = 0$) of this strategy as

$$
\begin{aligned}
C_0^{\beta}(T, X, S_0) &= \int_0^T dt \left\{ \mathbb{E}\left[\left(\frac{x_t}{T-t} + \beta(T-t)S_0 \right)^2 \right] + \lambda S_0 \mathbb{E}[x_t] \right\} \\
&= \frac{X^2}{T} + \frac{\lambda}{2} S_0 X T + \left(\beta^2 - \beta \frac{\lambda}{2} \right) S_0^2 \frac{T^3}{3}. \qquad (4.6)
\end{aligned}
$$

Now define the characteristic timescale[1]

$$
T^{\star} = \sqrt{\frac{X}{\beta^{\star} S_0}} = \sqrt{\frac{4X}{\lambda S_0}}
$$

and choose the liquidation time T to be $T^{\star}$. Further define $\theta := \beta/\beta^{\star}$. Substitution into (4.6) gives

$$
C_0^{\beta}(T^{\star}, X, S_0) = \frac{X^2}{T^{\star}} \left(3 + \frac{\theta^2 - 2\theta}{3} \right) \qquad (4.7)
$$

which is minimized when $\theta = 1$ (i.e. when $\beta = \beta^{\star}$).

With $T = T^{\star}$, the optimal trading rate under ABM becomes

$$
v^A(t) = \frac{x_t}{T-t} + \frac{X}{T^2}(T-t) = \frac{2X}{T}\left(1 - \frac{t}{T}\right) \qquad (4.8)
$$

and the optimal trading rate under GBM becomes

$$
v^G(t) = \frac{x_t}{T-t} + \frac{X}{T^2}\frac{S_t}{S_0}(T-t) \qquad (4.9)
$$

[here we assume implicitly that we use the same parameter λ for both GBM and ABM, which can be justified by (2.13)].

We observe that with this particular choice of liquidation time, the cost function $C_0^{\beta}(T^{\star}, X, S_0)$ has a sharp minimum with respect to the parameter θ which parameterizes the sensitivity of the trading rate to the stock price. In particular, the risk-adjusted cost of a VWAP execution ($\theta = 0$) is 1/9 (or over 10%) greater than the risk-adjusted cost of an optimal execution.

Moreover, for reasonable values of $\sigma^2 T \ll 1$, there is almost no difference in expected costs and risks between the optimal strategies under ABM and GBM assumptions. We can see this directly by comparing (4.1) and (4.6) and noting that $\mathbb{E}[S_t^2] = S_0^2(1+\epsilon)$ with $\epsilon \ll 1$. Intuitively, although the optimal strategy is stock price-dependent under GBM assumptions but not under ABM assumptions, when $\sigma^2 T \ll 1$, the difference in optimal frontiers is tiny because the stock-price S_t cannot diffuse very far away from S_0 in the short time available. Equivalently, as in Fig. 2, there can only be a small difference in optimal trading rates under the two assumptions.

[1] $T^{\star}$ is a critical point of the cost function and so for T close to $T^{\star}$ the cost is approximately independent of T.

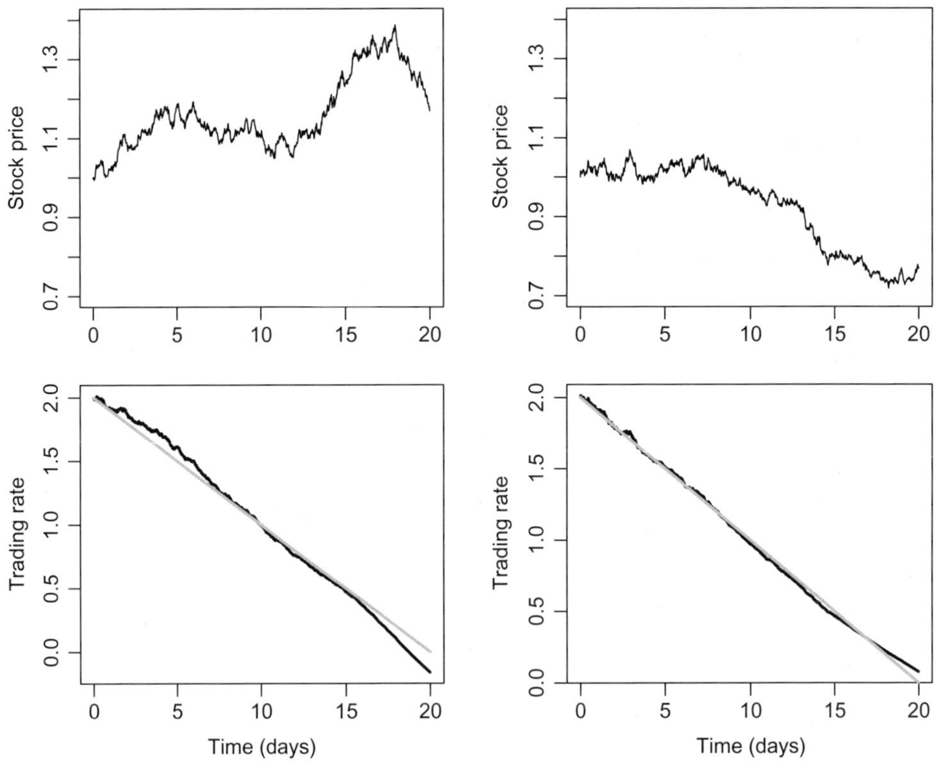

Fig. 2. The upper plots show rising and falling stock price scenarios respectively; the trading period is 20 days and daily volatility is 4%. The lower plots show the corresponding optimal trading rates from (4.8) and (4.9); the optimal trading rate under ABM is in gray and the optimal trading rate under GBM is in black. Even with such extreme parameters and correspondingly extreme changes in stock price, the differences in optimal trading rates are minimal.

In particular, since the expected costs and risks are almost identical under ABM and GBM, so must be the optimal frontiers, confirming the observations of [8, 9]. This observation also formally justifies the original choice of Almgren and Chriss [2, 3] of ABM as a modeling assumption. Another corollary is that with $\sigma^2 T \ll 1$, the cost function $C^{\beta}(T^{\star}, X, S_0)$ associated with the one-parameter family of strategies under the GBM assumption is also very sensitive to the parameter θ.

From (4.8) and (4.9), we see that the typical deviation of the optimal trading rate $v^G(t)$ under GBM from its static counterpart is roughly

$$v^G(t) - v^A(t) = \frac{X}{T^2}\frac{S_t - S_0}{S_0}(T - t) \sim \frac{X}{T}\sigma\sqrt{T}.$$

which is tiny, again consistent with Fig. 2. On the other hand, in practice, a typical aggressive-(passive-)in-the-money strategy may double(halve) the trading rate if the stock price goes in-the-money by more than one standard deviation, a strategy that is extremely suboptimal in this framework.

The sharp minimum in (4.7) thus appears to contrast with the numerical results of [8] where the risk criterion is variance but is consistent with the numerical results of [9] where the risk criterion is quadratic variation.

4.1. *Numerical example*

In Fig. 2, we plot the optimal trading rates in two scenarios, one where the stock price is rising and one where the stock price is falling. We assume that liquidation of a stock position takes place over 20 trading days and that the underlying stock has a *daily* volatility of 4%. The price of risk λ is chosen such that the characteristic time $T^\star$ is 20 days. Obviously these are extreme parameters that are only rarely applicable in practice. It is immediately apparent from the plots of the optimal trading strategies that the difference between the optimal strategy under GBM and ABM assumptions is minimal, even with these extreme parameters. With more reasonable volatilities and trading horizons, the differences in practice between the optimal trading rates is negligible.

5. Summary and Conclusions

In summary, with an alternative financially-motivated choice of risk criterion, we have found an explicit closed-form solution to the optimal execution problem in the Almgren and Chriss framework when the underlying stock price follows geometric Brownian motion. We find that if the liquidation horizon is chosen optimally, the minimum of the cost function is rather sharp in contrast to the results of [8] with a pre-commitment mean-variance objective function but consistent with the results of [9] with a mean-quadratic-variation objective function. One practical consequence of this is that, in the Almgren and Chriss framework, trading at a rate significantly different from the optimal rate is significantly suboptimal.

We also find that for even quite extreme choices of volatility and trading horizon, there is very little difference between the optimal trading rates under ABM and GBM assumptions and thus the difference in efficient frontiers is also very small.

Acknowledgments

We wish to thank Nicholas Westray for his helpful comments on an initial draft of this paper.

References

[1] R. Almgren, Optimal execution wizth nonlinear impact functions and trading-enhanced risk, *Applied Mathematical Finance* **10** (2003) 1–18.
[2] R. Almgren and N. Chriss, Value under liquidation, *Risk Magazine* December, 1999.
[3] R. Almgren and N. Chriss, Optimal execution of portfolio transactions, *Journal of Risk* **3** (2000) 5–39.

[4] R. Almgren and J. Lorenz, Adaptive arrival price, in *Algorithmic Trading III: Precision, Control, Execution*, B. R. Bruce, ed. (Institutional Investor Journals, 2007).

[5] P. Artzner, F. Delbaen, J.-M. Eber and D. Heath, Coherent measures of risk, *Mathematical Finance* **9** (1999) 203–228.

[6] D. Bertsimas and A. Lo, Optimal control of execution costs, *Journal of Financial Markets* **1** (1998) 1–50.

[7] H. Föllmer and A. Schied, *Stochastic Finance: An Introduction in Discrete Time*, third edition (de Gruyter, Berlin, 2011).

[8] P. Forsyth, A Hamilton–Jacobi–Bellman approach to optimal trade execution, preprint, available at http://www.cs.uwaterloo.ca/~paforsyt/optimal_trade.pdf (2009).

[9] P. Forsyth, J. Kennedy, T. S. Tse and H. Windcliff, Optimal trade execution: A mean-quadratic-variation approach, preprint, available at http://www.cs.uwaterloo.ca/~paforsyt/quad_trade.pdf (2009).

[10] J. Gatheral, No-dynamic-arbitrage and market impact, *Quantitative Finance* **10**(7) (2010) 749–759.

[11] A. Schied and T. Schöneborn, Risk aversion and the dynamics of optimal trading strategies in illiquid markets, *Finance and Stochastics* **13** (2009) 181–204.

[12] A. Schied, T. Schöneborn and M. Tehranchi, Optimal basket liquidation for CARA investors is deterministic, *Applied Mathematical Finance* **17**(6) (2010) 471–489.

[13] T. Schöneborn, Trade execution in illiquid markets. Optimal control and multi-agent equilibrium, Ph.D. thesis, TU Berlin (2008).

THE HEAT-KERNEL MOST-LIKELY-PATH APPROXIMATION*

JIM GATHERAL and TAI-HO WANG
Department of Mathematics, Baruch College, CUNY
One Bernard Baruch Way, New York, NY 10010, USA

In this article, we derive a new most-likely-path (MLP) approximation for implied volatility in terms of local volatility, based on time-integration of the lowest order term in the heat-kernel expansion. This new approximation formula turns out to be a natural extension of the well-known formula of Berestycki, Busca and Florent. Various other MLP approximations have been suggested in the literature involving different choices of most-likely-path; our work fixes a natural definition of the most-likely-path. We confirm the improved performance of our new approximation relative to existing approximations in an explicit computation using a realistic S&P500 local volatility function.

Keywords: Most-likely-path; heat kernel expansion; implied volatility; local volatility model; asymptotic expansion.

1. Introduction

Derivatives practitioners face two key problems that involve the parameterization of prices of vanilla options. The first problem is that, given the prices of vanilla options for a discrete set of strikes and expirations, the practitioner would like to be able to price options with other strikes and expirations. For this, the observed option prices need to be interpolated and extrapolated. This is typically achieved in practice by parameterizing the implied volatility surface; there is then a deterministic mapping (via the Black-Scholes formula) between implied volatilities returned by the parametric formula and option prices. The main issue here is that nobody has yet devised an implied volatility surface parameterization that is arbitrage-free. More recently, there has been a trend to parameterize the Dupire local volatility surface directly–so long as local variance is positive, there can be no static arbitrage. The problem then becomes one of fast calibration, or how to quickly compute vanilla option prices given the parameterized local volatility function.

*This chapter was originally published under the same title in *International Journal of Theoretical and Applied Finance*, Vol.15, No.1, 1250001-1–18 (2012). Singapore: World Scientific Publishing.

The second problem is how to price exotic options given the prices of vanilla options. In this case, the practitioner is aiming for fast calibration of a complex model (typically involving stochastic volatility) with realistic dynamics to given option prices. Through techniques such as Markovian projection, this problem can again be reduced to one of fast calibration of a local volatility surface to given option prices.

It is possible to generate an entire volatility surface by solving the Dupire forward PDE using numerical PDE techniques (see [1] for example). However, numerical PDE solutions are often too slow for fast calibration and in higher dimensions, completely impractical. Ideally, practitioners would like a more direct and faster method for generating the implied volatility surface from a parameterized local volatility function, even better if this method provides insight into the connection between local volatility and implied volatility functions, both of which encode the same information. The most-likely-path approach (as in [5, 8, 9]) is such a method, offering both fast computation and natural intuition. Moreover, the most-likely-path approach has a natural and straightforward generalization to higher dimensions.

In the foregoing, as in [8], we will assume that the local volatility function is smooth enough to give an estimator of the most-likely-path type a chance to be competitive with a PDE solver. For example local volatility functions used by practitioners as well as local volatility functions generated from more sophisticated models (such as stochastic volatility models) typically fall into this class.

To make this precise, we assume the underlying asset S satisfies

$$dS_t = S_t\, \sigma_\ell(S_t, t)\, dW_t = a(S_t, t)\, dW_t.$$

under the risk-neutral probability measure (zero interest rates and dividends are assumed). Also, we denote the log-spot by $x_t := \log(S_t/S_0)$ in terms of which the local volatility function becomes

$$\sigma(x_t, t) := \sigma_\ell(S_0\, e^{x_t}, t).$$

For notational simplicity, the terms a, σ_ℓ and σ will be used interchangeably. We define the log-strike k of a European call or put option with strike K by $k := \log(K/S_0)$.

As is well-known, the market price of a call option with strike K and expiration T is often quoted in terms of the Black-Scholes implied volatility $\sigma_{\mathrm{BS}}(K,T)$ defined through the implicit relation:

$$C_{\mathrm{BS}}(K, \sigma_{\mathrm{BS}}(K,T), T) = \mathbb{E}[(S_T - K)^+],$$

where $C_{\mathrm{BS}}(\cdot)$ denotes the Black-Scholes formula and the expectation is taken under the risk-neutral measure.

Our problem then is to find an approximate expression for the implied volatility $\sigma_{\mathrm{BS}}(K,T)$ in terms of the local volatility function $\sigma(x_t, t)$.

Local volatilities can be computed directly from option prices using the Dupire equation (see [5] for example). Re-expressing option prices in terms of the Black-Scholes formula and implied volatility, with $w(k,T) := \sigma_{\mathrm{BS}}(k,T)^2\, T$, the following simple formula follows directly from the Dupire equation:

$$\sigma^2(k,T) = \frac{\frac{\partial w}{\partial T}}{1 - \frac{k}{w}\frac{\partial w}{\partial k} + \frac{1}{4}(-\frac{1}{4} - \frac{1}{w} + \frac{k^2}{w^2})(\frac{\partial w}{\partial k})^2 + \frac{1}{2}\frac{\partial^2 w}{\partial k^2}}. \tag{1.1}$$

If it were possible to invert (1.1) exactly, our problem would be solved. In the present paper, we proceed as follows:

In Sec. 2, we use the Chapman-Kolmogorov equation to express the transition density as a convolution of transition densities over small time-steps, each of which is approximated by the lowest order term in the heat-kernel expansion. The resulting multidimensional integral is then approximated using Laplace's method which gives rise to a variational boundary value problem. The solution to this problem, termed the variational most-likely-path, leads to a simple approximate expression for the European call price. By matching exponents of this approximate European option price with the exponent in the corresponding Black-Scholes expression, we deduce an approximate expression for Black-Scholes implied volatility in terms of local volatility. In Sec. 3, we show how to solve the variational problem using a fixed-point iterative procedure. We further show that our approximation is a natural extension of the well-known formula due to Berestycki, Busca and Florent, an extension that moreover behaves correctly under a deterministic time-change. In Sec. 4, we use our approximation to compute implied volatility smiles in a realistic local volatility model. The accuracy of our new method is then demonstrated through comparison with numerical PDE and other existing approximations. Finally, in Sec. 5, we summarize and conclude.

1.1. *Prior literature*

In [2], Berestycki, Busca and Florent (BBF) derived an approximate formula for implied volatility in terms of the local volatility by approximating (1.1) for short times and explicitly solving the resulting nonlinear PDE. In our notation, the BBF formula reads

$$\frac{1}{\sigma_{\mathrm{BS}}(k,T)} \approx \frac{1}{k}\int_0^k \frac{dy}{\sigma(y,0)}. \tag{1.2}$$

By a simple change of variable, the BBF formula may be re-expressed suggestively for our purposes as

$$\frac{1}{\sigma_{\mathrm{BS}}(k,T)} \approx \frac{1}{T}\int_0^T \frac{dt}{\sigma(k\frac{t}{T},0)}. \tag{1.3}$$

In words, the BBF formula approximates implied volatility as the harmonic mean of local volatility along the straight-line path from the log-spot $x_0 = 0$ to the log-strike $x_T = k$. Note however that on the right-hand side of (1.3), the local volatility function is "frozen" at time $t = 0$.

On the other hand, the following formula again from [5, Eq. (3.5), p. 28] is exact:

$$\sigma_{\text{BS}}^2(k,T) = \frac{1}{T}\int_0^T \frac{\mathbb{E}[\sigma_t^2 S_t^2 \Gamma_{\text{BS}}]}{\mathbb{E}[S_t^2 \Gamma_{\text{BS}}]} dt, \tag{1.4}$$

where Γ_{BS} is the Black-Scholes gamma, i.e. $\Gamma_{\text{BS}} = \frac{\partial^2 C_{\text{BS}}}{\partial s^2}$, and the instantaneous volatility σ_t is some arbitrary stochastic process (subject to some general technical conditions). For the details of the derivation of (1.4), we refer the reader to Chap. 3 of [5]. For the purposes of the present paper, we choose σ_t to be the deterministic local volatility function $\sigma(x_t, t)$, in which case the expectations in the integrand of (1.4) may be rewritten in terms of integrations over the transition density $p(\cdot)$ for S_t as

$$\frac{\mathbb{E}[\sigma_t^2 S_t^2 \Gamma_{\text{BS}}]}{\mathbb{E}[S_t^2 \Gamma_{\text{BS}}]} = \int \sigma^2(x,t)\, q(x,t;k,T) dx,$$

where, as explained in detail in [5],

$$q(x,t;k,T) = \frac{p(t,x)\, S_t^2 \Gamma_{\text{BS}}}{\mathbb{E}[S_t^2 \Gamma_{\text{BS}}]}$$

is the density of a pinned diffusion that peaks on a line joining the stock price at inception to the strike price at expiration. The problem with equation (1.4) is that though it is exact, it is implicit in the sense that the transition densities $p(\cdot)$ and the Black-Scholes gammas Γ_{BS} themselves depend on the implied volatilities $\sigma_{\text{BS}}(\cdot)$. This leads us to look for approximations.

The idea of the *most-likely-path* (MLP) approach is to approximate the expectation in (1.4) by evaluating the random process at a specific path $\tilde{x}(t)$, an approximation reminiscent of the maximum likelihood estimator. The most-likely-path implied volatility approximation is then obtained by averaging the local volatility function along the most likely path:

$$\sigma_{\text{BS}}^2(k,T) \sim \frac{1}{T}\int_0^T \sigma^2(\tilde{x}(t), t) dt.$$

In the literature, there is no agreement on the best choice of most-likely-path. To assess the relative accuracy of our new approximation, we will focus on two particular versions of the most likely path approximation: A popular choice in [9] due to Reghai and a naïve extension of equation (1.3).

1.2. *Adil Reghai's most-likely-path approximation*

Reghai's approximation in [9] may be written as follows:

$$\sigma_{\text{BS}}^2(k,T) = \frac{1}{T}\int_0^T \sigma^2(\tilde{x}(t), t) dt \tag{1.5}$$

with

$$\tilde{x}(t) = \frac{w(t)}{w(T)} k + \frac{w(t)}{2}\left(1 - \frac{w(t)}{w(T)}\right)$$

and

$$w(t) = \int_0^t \sigma^2(\tilde{x}(s), s)ds.$$

In this case, the distribution of the underlying at time t is approximated as lognormal so that the most-likely-path $\tilde{x}(t)$ is the mode of the normal process followed by the log-spot pinned at $(0,0)$ and (k,T) with time-dependent volatility $\sigma(\tilde{x}(t),t)$. This definition of most-likely-path is still implicit but the fixed-point algorithm described in [9] for computing $\tilde{x}(t)$ starting from an initial guess (for example, the straight line $x_0(t) = k\,t/T$ from log-spot to log-strike) typically converges within very few iterations. Again, the approximation made here is that the underlying is lognormal, which it is clearly not in general.

1.3. *A naïve extension of the BBF formula*

A natural extension of (1.3) that also involves integration along a path from the current spot at inception to the strike at expiration is the following:

$$\frac{1}{\sigma_{\mathrm{BS}}(k,T)} \approx \frac{1}{T}\int_0^T \frac{dt}{\sigma\left(k\frac{t}{T},t\right)} = \int_0^1 \frac{d\alpha}{\sigma\left(\alpha\,k,\alpha T\right)}. \tag{1.6}$$

In this approximation, which we will refer to as *BBFe*, implied volatility is approximated as the harmonic mean of local volatility along the straight-line path (in log-space) between the log-spot at inception $(0,0)$ and the log-strike at expiration (k,T). Note that all we have done here is to "unfreeze" the local volatility function which in (1.3) is "frozen" at time $t=0$, as previously discussed.

2. Most-Likely-Path from the Heat-Kernel Expansion

Recall that the underlying asset S follows the local volatility model (zero interest rates and dividends)

$$dS_t = S_t\sigma_\ell(S_t,t)dW_t = a(S_t,t)dW_t = S_t\sigma(x_t,t)dW_t. \tag{2.1}$$

Let $p(t,S_t;u,S_u)$, $t<u$, be the transition probability density associated with the local volatility model (2.1). The price C of a European call struck at K, with expiry at T is given by the expectation under risk neutral probability

$$C(s_0,K,T) = \mathbb{E}[(S_T-K)^+|S_0=s_0] = \int p(0,s_0,T,s)(s-K)^+ds. \tag{2.2}$$

In Sec. 2 of [7], the authors use the heat kernel expansion for the transition density p and then apply Laplace's asymptotic formula to obtain an asymptotic expansion for the implied volatility in local volatility models for small time to maturity. In this section we follow the same line of argument but refine it a bit as follows. Instead of approximating the transition density at maturity T in one step as in the prior literature, we apply the Chapman-Kolmogorov equation to decompose the transition density from current time to maturity into many tiny steps. We then approximate the transition density for each such consecutive tiny step by the lowest order term in its corresponding heat kernel expansion. The price we pay for such a decomposition is that the expression (2.2) for the call price now involves a multidimensional integral. Laplace's asymptotic formula is applied to the resulting multidimensional integral to generate an asymptotic expansion for the call price.

To be more precise, we partition the time horizon $[0, T]$ into disjoint subintervals as $t_0 < t_1 < t_2 < \cdots < t_n$ with $t_0 = 0$ and $t_n = T$. For simplicity we further assume that the time intervals between the sampling slots are equal, i.e., $t_i - t_{i-1} = \Delta t = \frac{T}{n}$, for $i = 1, \ldots, n$. According to the Chapman-Kolmogorov equation, the transition density $p(0, S_0; T, S_T)$ satisfies

$$p(0, S_0; T, S_T) = \int \cdots \int p(0, S_0; t_1, S_1) p(t_1, S_1; t_2, S_2) \cdots \\ p(t_{n-1}, S_{n-1}; T, S_T) dS_1 \cdots dS_{n-1}.$$

The expression (2.2) for the call price is then transformed into the following n-dimensional integral:

$$C = \int \cdots \int \left\{ \prod_{i=1}^{n-1} p(t_{i-1}, S_{i-1}; t_i, S_i) dS_i \right\} p(t_{n-1}, S_{n-1}; t_n, S_n)(S_n - K)^+ dS_n. \tag{2.3}$$

The following heat kernel expansion for transition density p is well-known (see for instance [7] and the references therein): for $t < t'$,

$$p(t, x; t', y) = \frac{e^{-\frac{d^2(x,y,t)}{2(t'-t)}}}{\sqrt{2\pi(t'-t)a(y,t')}} \left(\sum_{i=0}^{k} H_i(t, x, y)(t'-t)^i \right) [1 + O_{k+1}(t, x; t', y)],$$

where

$$d(x, y, t) = \int_x^y \frac{d\xi}{a(\xi, t)},$$

$$H_0(t, x, y) = \sqrt{\frac{a(x,t)}{a(y,t)}} e^{-\int_x^y \frac{d_t(\eta,y,t)}{a(\eta,t)} d\eta} = \sqrt{\frac{a(x,t)}{a(y,t)}} e^{\int_x^y \int_\eta^y \frac{a_t(\xi,t)}{a^2(\xi,t)a(\eta,t)} d\xi d\eta},$$

$$H_1(t, x, y) = \frac{H_0(t, x, y)}{d(x, y, t)} \int_x^y \frac{1}{H_0(t, \eta, y)} \left[\frac{a^2}{2} \frac{\partial^2 H_0}{\partial x^2} + \frac{\partial H_0}{\partial t} \right] \frac{d\eta}{a(\eta, t)}.$$

Here we note that $d(x, y, t)$ is the (signed) geodesic distance between x and y in the Riemannian metric induced by $\frac{1}{a(\cdot,t)}$ and the H_i's are called heat kernel coefficients. It is known that under certain technical conditions, the heat kernel expansion converges to the transition density p uniformly on every compact interval (see Sec. 3.4 in [7] for a treatment in one dimension). For our purposes, the following condition is imposed:

- $\sigma(x,t)$ is smooth and bounded with bounded derivatives in x, t. (2.4)

For our argument, we shall only need the first two terms H_0 and H_1. Moreover, under the conditions (2.4), the error terms $\mathcal{O}_k$, $k = 1, 2$, in the heat kernel expansion are bounded in the sense that, for any x and y in a compact set, and for any t and t' with $t < t'$, there exists a constant $A_k > 0$ such that $|\mathcal{O}_k(t, x; t', y)| \leq A_k(t' - t)^k$. Define, for $n > 1$,

$$p_n^0(t, x; t', y) = \frac{1}{(2\pi\Delta t)^{\frac{n}{2}}} \int \left(\prod_{i=1}^{n} \frac{e^{-\frac{d^2(x_{i-1}, x_i, t_{i-1})}{2\Delta t}}}{a(x_i, t_i)} H_0(t_{i-1}, x_{i-1}, x_i) \right) \mathcal{D}x, \tag{2.5}$$

$$\hat{p}_n(t, x; t', y) = \frac{1}{(2\pi\Delta t)^{\frac{n}{2}}} \int \left(\prod_{i=1}^{n} \frac{e^{-\frac{d^2(x_{i-1}, x_i, t_{i-1})}{2\Delta t}}}{a(x_i, t_i)} [H_0(t_{i-1}, x_{i-1}, x_i) + H_1(t_{i-1}, x_{i-1}, x_i)\Delta t] \right) \mathcal{D}x, \tag{2.6}$$

where $\mathcal{D}x = \prod_{i=1}^{n-1} dx_i$.

Remark 2.1. Note that $\hat{p}_n$ in (2.6) is an analogue of p_n^0 in (2.5) but to one order higher in Δt. In Lemma 2.1, we prove the convergence of the call price approximation using $\hat{p}_n(\cdot)$ to the true call price given by the local volatility model (2.1). Our results in later sections use only H_0 and neglect H_1 and so are formally only to lowest order in T and have the same asymptotic order of convergence as the BBF approximation. However, for a realistic local volatility function such as that considered in Section 4, our most-likely-path approximation is very much superior to the BBF approximation.

Now if we use (2.5) and (2.6) respectively to approximate the transition density, we obtain (different) approximations to the call price C. The following lemma permits us to characterize the asymptotic behavior of these two approximations as $n \to \infty$.

Lemma 2.1. *For $k = 0, 1$, let*

$$\widetilde{C}_k = \frac{1}{(2\pi\Delta t)^{\frac{n}{2}}} \int_\Omega e^{-\frac{D(\mathbf{S},\mathbf{t})}{\Delta t}} W_k(\mathbf{S}, \mathbf{t}) d\mathbf{S}, \tag{2.7}$$

where $\mathbf{t}$ refers to the partition $\mathbf{t} = \{0 = t_0 < t_1 < \cdots < t_n = T\}$, $\mathbf{S} = (S_1, \ldots, S_n)$, and

$$D(\mathbf{S}, \mathbf{t}) = \frac{1}{2} \sum_{i=1}^{n} d^2(S_{i-1}, S_i, t_{i-1}),$$

$$W_k(\mathbf{S},\mathbf{t}) = (S_n - K)\prod_{i=1}^{n}\frac{\widetilde{H}_k(t_{i-1},t_i,S_{i-1},S_i)}{a(S_i,t_i)},$$

$$\widetilde{H}_0 = H_0, \quad \widetilde{H}_1 = H_0 + H_1\Delta t,$$

$$\Omega = \{\mathbf{S} = (S_1,\ldots,S_n) : S_n \geq K\}.$$

If (2.5) is used to approximate the transition density, the following bounds on the call price are obtained.

$$[1 - A_1\Delta t]^n\widetilde{C}_0 \leq C \leq [1 + A_1\Delta t]^n\widetilde{C}_0. \tag{2.8}$$

On the other hand, if (2.6) is used to approximate the transition density, the following bounds on the call price are obtained

$$[1 - A_2(\Delta t)^2]^n\widetilde{C}_1 \leq C \leq [1 + A_2(\Delta t)^2]^n\widetilde{C}_1. \tag{2.9}$$

Proof. Since the proofs for both sets of inequalities in (2.9) are similar, we shall prove (2.8) only. Recall that since

$$p(t,x;t',y) = \frac{e^{-\frac{d^2(x,y,t)}{2(t'-t)}}}{\sqrt{2\pi(t'-t)}}\frac{H_0(t,x,y)}{a(y,t')}[1 + \mathcal{O}_1(t,x;t',y)],$$

we have the following upper and lower bounds for p.

$$p(t_{i-1},S_{i-1};t_i,S_i) \geq \frac{e^{-\frac{d^2(S_{i-1},S_i,t_{i1})}{2\Delta t}}}{\sqrt{2\pi\Delta t}}\frac{H_0(t_{i-1},S_{i-1},S_i)}{a(S_i,t_i)}[1 - A_1\Delta t],$$

$$p(t_{i-1},S_{i-1};t_i,S_i) \leq \frac{e^{-\frac{d^2(S_{i-1},S_i,t_{i1})}{2\Delta t}}}{\sqrt{2\pi\Delta t}}\frac{H_0(t_{i-1},S_{i-1},S_i)}{a(S_i,t_i)}[1 + A_1\Delta t].$$

The proof is immediate by replacing each of the transition densities in (2.3) with their upper and lower bounds and integrating over Ω.[1] □

Remark 2.2. The difference between (2.8) and (2.9), which correspond to approximating the transition density p by the heat kernel expansion up to zeroth order or first order respectively, is that (2.9) shows that the approximation $\widetilde{C}_1$ tends to the true option price C as $n \to \infty$ in contrast to (2.8).

Precisely, from (2.8), as $n \to \infty$, $\lim_{n\to\infty}[1 \pm A_1\Delta t]^n = e^{\pm A_1 T}$ so

$$e^{-A_1 T}\lim_{n\to\infty}\widetilde{C}_0 \leq C \leq e^{A_1 T}\lim_{n\to\infty}\widetilde{C}_0$$

[1]More precisely, we integrate over a compact subset of Ω where the heat kernel expansion and the corresponding bounds hold, such that the contribution to the integral from the complement of this subset is arbitrarily small. This principle of not feeling the boundary is explained in detail in for example Appendix A of [7].

whereas (2.9) gives

$$C = \lim_{n\to\infty} \widetilde{C}_1$$

since $\lim_{n\to\infty}[1 \pm A_2(\Delta t)^2]^n = 1$. For the most-likely-path approximation presented in this paper, we only need $\widetilde{C}_0$. Once again, there is no guarantee of asymptotic convergence of our approximation to the true implied volatility for large T.

To compute $\widetilde{C}_0$, we need to perform the n-dimensional integration in (2.7). We approximate this n-dimensional integral as $\Delta t \to 0^+$ using the following Laplace asymptotic formula:

Lemma 2.2. (*Laplace asymptotic formula*) *Let Ω be a closed set in $\mathbb{R}^n$ with nonempty and smooth boundary $\partial\Omega$. Suppose ϕ is a continuous function in Ω and attains its minimum uniquely on the boundary $\partial\Omega$ at $x^* \in \partial\Omega$ and, given any $\epsilon > 0$, there exists $\delta > 0$ such that $\phi(x) \geq \phi(x^*) + \delta$ for all $x \in \Omega\backslash B_\epsilon(x^*)$, where $B_\epsilon(x^*) = \{x : |x - x^*| < \epsilon\}$ is the open ball of radius ϵ centered at x^*. Assume that f is an integrable function in Ω, i.e., $\int_\Omega |f(x)|dx < \infty$ and that f vanishes identically in Ω^c and on the boundary $\partial\Omega$ but the inward normal directional derivative of f at x^* is nonzero. Then we have the asymptotic expansion as $\tau \to 0^+$*

$$\int_\Omega e^{-\frac{\phi(x)}{\tau}} f(x)dx = (2\pi)^{\frac{n-1}{2}} \tau^{\frac{n+3}{2}} e^{-\frac{\phi(x^*)}{\tau}} \left[\frac{\nabla f(x^*) \cdot \nabla \phi(x^*)}{\sqrt{\det \partial_{\mathbf{t}}^2 \phi(x^*)} |\nabla \phi(x^*)|^3} + \mathcal{O}(\tau) \right], \tag{2.10}$$

where $\partial_{\mathbf{t}}^2 \phi(x^*)$ is the Hessian of ϕ in the tangential direction to Ω at x^*.

Proof. See for instance Sec. 8.3 in Bleistein and Handelsman [3]. □

With the aid of the Laplace asymptotic formula (2.10) in Lemma 2.2 applied to the multidimensional integral in (2.7), $k = 0$, the following theorem is immediate.

Theorem 2.1. *For any given positive integer n, the European out of the money call option price C struck at K with expiry T in the local volatility model (2.1) has the following upper and lower bounds:*

$$(1 - A_1\Delta t)^n \widehat{C}(\mathbf{S}^*, \mathbf{t}) \leq C(s_0, K, T) \leq (1 + A_1\Delta t)^n \widehat{C}(\mathbf{S}^*, \mathbf{t}), \tag{2.11}$$

where

$$\widehat{C}(\mathbf{S}^*, \mathbf{t}) := \frac{T^{\frac{3}{2}}}{\sqrt{2\pi}} e^{-\frac{n}{T}D(\mathbf{S}^*, \mathbf{t})} \frac{U(\mathbf{S}^*, \mathbf{t})}{n^{\frac{3}{2}}},$$

$\mathbf{S}^* = (S_1^*, \ldots, S_n^*)$ *is a solution to the constrained optimization problem*

$$\min_{\mathbf{S}} D(\mathbf{S}, \mathbf{t}) = \min_{\mathbf{S}} \frac{1}{2} \sum_{i=1}^{n} d^2(S_{i-1}, S_i, t_{i-1}) \tag{2.12}$$

subject to the constraints $S_n = K$ *and* $S_i \geq 0$, *for* $i = 1, \cdots, n-1$, *and*

$$U(\mathbf{S}, \mathbf{t}) = \frac{1}{\sqrt{\det \partial_{\mathbf{t}}^2 D(\mathbf{S}^*)}} \frac{a^2(S_n, t_{n-1})}{d^2(S_{n-1}, K, t_{n-1})} \prod_{i=1}^{n} \frac{H_0(t_{i-1}, S_{i-1}, S_i)}{a(S_i, t_i)},$$

$\partial_{\mathbf{t}}^2 D(\mathbf{S}^*)$ *is the Hessian of* D *in the tangential direction of the set* $\Omega = \{\mathbf{S} = (S_1, \ldots, S_n) : S_n \geq K\}$ *at* $S^* \in \partial\Omega$.

In the limit $n \to \infty$, or equivalently as $\Delta t = T/n \to 0$,

$$d(S_{i-1}, S_i, t_{i-1}) \sim \frac{\Delta S_i}{a(S_{i-1}, t_{i-1})}$$

where $\Delta S_i = S_i - S_{i-1}$, so in this limit

$$\frac{1}{2\Delta t} \sum_{i=1}^{n} d^2(S_{i-1}, S_i, t_{i-1}) \sim \frac{1}{2} \sum_{i=1}^{n} \left[\frac{\frac{\Delta S_i}{\Delta t}}{a(S_{i-1}, t_{i-1})} \right]^2 \Delta t.$$

Then, in the limit $\Delta t \to 0$, the minimization problem (2.12) gives rise to the following variational problem:

$$\min_{S(t)} \frac{1}{2} \int_0^T \left[\frac{S'(t)}{a(S(t), t)} \right]^2 dt$$

subject to $S(0) = s_0$ and $S(T) = K$. The Euler-Lagrange equation associated with the variational problem is given by the second order ordinary differential equation:

$$-\left[\frac{S'}{a(S,t)} \right]' + \frac{a_t(S,t)}{a(S,t)} \frac{S'}{a(S,t)} = 0.$$

Therefore, the optimal path satisfies the boundary value problem:

$$\begin{cases} -\left[\dfrac{S'}{a(S,t)} \right]' + \dfrac{a_t(S,t)}{a^2(S,t)} S' = 0, \\ S(0) = s_0, \quad S(T) = K. \end{cases} \tag{2.13}$$

Definition 2.1. (Variational most likely path) The unique solution of the boundary value problem in (2.13) is called the *variational most likely path* (*variational MLP*).

Corollary 2.1. *The European call option price C struck at K with expiry T in the local volatility model* (2.1) *has the following approximation: there exists a function $A(T)$ converging to 1 as $T \to 0$ such that*

$$C(s_0, K, T) = A(T)\frac{T^{\frac{3}{2}}}{\sqrt{2\pi}} e^{-\frac{1}{2}\int_0^T [\frac{S'(t)}{a(S(t),t)}]^2 dt} U(s_0, K, T)[1 + \mathcal{O}(T)], \tag{2.14}$$

where $S(t)$ is the variational most likely path, i.e., the unique solution to the boundary value problem (2.13), *and U is given by*

$$U(s_0, K, T) = \lim_{n\to\infty} \frac{U(\mathbf{S}^*, \mathbf{t})}{n^{\frac{3}{2}}}.$$

Proof. The result follows by replacing the exponent in (2.11) by its limit as $n \to \infty$. □

We now state our main result.

Theorem 2.2. *Assume the dynamic of the underlying asset S_t under risk neutral probability measure is governed by the local volatility model* (2.1) *and the local volatility function $\sigma(x,t)$ satisfies the conditions* (2.4). *Then the implied volatility σ_{BS} has the following expansion as $T \to 0^+$,*

$$\sigma_{\mathrm{BS}}(K, T) = \sigma_{\mathrm{BS},0}(1 + \mathcal{O}(T)),$$

with

$$\sigma_{\mathrm{BS},0} = \left(\frac{\sqrt{T}}{|k|} \sqrt{\int_0^T \left[\frac{S'(t)}{a(S(t),t)}\right]^2 dt} \right)^{-1}, \tag{2.15}$$

where $S(t)$ is the variational most-likely-path (MLP) given by (2.13).

Proof. Recall the following asymptotic expansion for Black-Scholes formula (see for instance Lemma 2.5 of [7]):

$$\begin{aligned} C_{\mathrm{BS}}(s_0, K, T, \sigma_{\mathrm{BS}}) &= \sqrt{\frac{s_0 K}{2\pi}} e^{-\frac{(\log K - \log s_0)^2}{2\sigma_{\mathrm{BS}}^2 T}} \frac{\sigma_{\mathrm{BS}}^3 T^{\frac{3}{2}}}{(\log K - \log s_0)^2} [1 + \mathcal{O}(T)] \\ &= \sqrt{\frac{s_0 K}{2\pi}} e^{-\frac{k^2}{2\sigma_{\mathrm{BS}}^2 T}} \frac{\sigma_{\mathrm{BS}}^3 T^{\frac{3}{2}}}{k^2} [1 + \mathcal{O}(T)] \end{aligned} \tag{2.16}$$

and from Corollary 2.1, we have

$$C(s_0, K, T) = A(T)\frac{T^{\frac{3}{2}}}{\sqrt{2\pi}} e^{-\frac{1}{2}\int_0^T [\frac{S'(t)}{a(S(t),t)}]^2 dt} U(s_0, K, T)[1 + \mathcal{O}(T)], \tag{2.17}$$

Matching the exponential terms in (2.16) and (2.17) we obtain

$$\frac{1}{\sigma_{\mathrm{BS},0}} = \frac{\sqrt{T}}{|k|} \sqrt{\int_0^T \left[\frac{S'(t)}{a(S(t),t)}\right]^2 dt},$$

proving the result. □

3. Solution of the Variational Problem

Recall that the variational MLP is the unique solution of equation (2.13):

$$-\left[\frac{S'}{a(S,t)}\right]' + \frac{a_t(S,t)}{a^2(S,t)}S' = 0,$$

with boundary conditions

$$S(0) = s_0; \quad S(T) = K.$$

We begin by changing variables in (2.13) to $x(t) := \log S(t)/s_0$, $a(S(t),t) = S(t)\sigma(x(t),t)$ and rearranging to obtain

$$\frac{d}{dt}\left(\log\left(\frac{x'(t)}{\sigma(x(t),t)}\right)\right) = \partial_t \log \sigma(x,t)|_{x=x(t)} =: f(x(t),t) \tag{3.1}$$

with boundary conditions $x(0) = 0$, $x(T) = k$ and where once again the log-strike $k := \log K/s_0$.

Remark 3.1. Note that for any given closed-form parameterization of the local volatility surface, $f(\cdot)$ is known in closed-form. $f(\cdot)$ is a measure of the time-inhomogeneity of the local volatility surface. In particular, if the local volatility function is time-independent, $f(\cdot) = 0$.

Integrating (3.1), we obtain in the general case

$$\frac{x'(t)}{\sigma(x(t),t)} = A\exp\left\{\int_0^t f(x(s),s)ds\right\}. \tag{3.2}$$

The constant A may be determined by the condition

$$x(T) = k = \int_0^T x'(t)dt = A\int_0^T dt\sigma(x(t),t)\exp\left\{\int_0^t f(x(s),s)ds\right\},$$

so (3.2) may in turn be rearranged to give

$$x'(t) = k\frac{\sigma(x(t),t)\exp\{\int_0^t f(x(s),s)ds\}}{\int_0^T dt\sigma(x(t),t)\exp\{\int_0^t f(x(s),s)ds\}}. \tag{3.3}$$

Integrating (3.3) gives

$$x(t) = k\frac{\int_0^t du\sigma(x(u),u)\exp\{\int_0^u f(x(s),s)ds\}}{\int_0^T du\sigma(x(u),u)\exp\{\int_0^u f(x(s),s)ds\}}. \tag{3.4}$$

Remark 3.2. Equation (3.4) leads to an efficient fixed-point algorithm for solving for the variational most likely path reminiscent of Reghai's algorithm in [9]. The natural choice of first guess is just the straight line

$$x_0(t) = k\frac{t}{T}.$$

Remark 3.3. Note that

$$\frac{S'(t)}{a(S(t),t)} = \frac{x'(t)}{\sigma(x(t),t)} = A\exp\left\{\int_0^t f(x(s),s)ds\right\},$$

so the value of the variational problem may be expressed as

$$\frac{1}{2}\int_0^T \left[\frac{S'(t)}{a(S(t))}\right]^2 dt = \frac{A^2}{2}\int_0^T \exp\left\{2\int_0^t f(x(s),s)ds\right\} dt \tag{3.5}$$

with

$$A = \frac{k}{\int_0^T dt\sigma(x(t),t)\exp\{\int_0^t f(x(s),s)ds\}}.$$

By substituting (3.5) into (2.15) we obtain

Lemma 3.1. *In terms of the local volatility $\sigma(x,t)$, equation* (2.15) *may be rewritten as*

$$\sigma_{\mathrm{BS},0} = \frac{\frac{1}{T}\int_0^T \sigma(x(t),t)\exp\{\int_0^t f(x(s),s)ds\}dt}{\sqrt{\frac{1}{T}\int_0^T \exp\{2\int_0^t f(x(s),s)ds\}dt}} \tag{3.6}$$

where $x(t)$ is (*the logarithmic version of*) *the variational most likely path.*

3.1. *Time-separable local volatility*

Suppose the local volatility function is time-separable so that $\sigma(x,t) = \sigma(x)\theta(t)$ for some functions $\sigma(\cdot)$ and $\theta(\cdot)$. Then by the definition of $f(\cdot)$,

$$f(x,t) = \frac{\theta'(t)}{\theta(t)}.$$

In particular

$$\exp\left\{\int_0^t f(x(s),s)ds\right\} = \frac{\theta(t)}{\theta(0)}$$

and Eq. (3.2) becomes

$$\frac{x'(t)}{\sigma(x(t))\theta(t)} = A\frac{\theta(t)}{\theta(0)}.$$

With $\phi(x) = \int_0^x \frac{d\xi}{\sigma(\xi)}$, the solution is

$$x(t) = \phi^{-1}\left(\phi(k)\frac{\int_0^t \theta^2(s)ds}{\int_0^T \theta^2(s)ds}\right). \tag{3.7}$$

Thus, in the time-separable case, with this choice of $x(t)$, our lowest order approximation for the implied volatility reads

$$\sigma_{\mathrm{BS},0} = \frac{\frac{1}{T}\int_0^T \sigma(x(t))\theta(t)dt}{\sqrt{\frac{1}{T}\int_0^T \theta^2(t)dt}}. \tag{3.8}$$

In particular, if $\sigma(x,t) = \sigma(x)$ is time-homogeneous, $\theta(\cdot)$ is constant, and

$$\sigma_{\mathrm{BS},0} = \frac{1}{T}\int_0^T \sigma(x(t))dt. \tag{3.9}$$

At first sight, (3.9) seems to differ from the familiar BBF formula (1.2) of Berestycki, Busca and Florent derived in [2] and again in [7]. A straightforward computation confirms that the BBF formula and (3.9) are in fact equivalent.

Of course, the time-separable case can be reduced to the time-homogeneous case by the simple deterministic time-change

$$\tau(t) = \int_0^t \theta^2(s)ds.$$

Note that the variational MLP (3.7) in the time-separable case is just the time-changed version of the variational MLP in the time-homogeneous case. It follows that our approximation has the correct behavior under a deterministic time-change. Consequently, the numerical accuracy of our approximation is just as great in the time-separable case as it is in the time-homogeneous case. Specifically, were we to repeat the numerical experiments of [7] (where the time-inhomogeneous local volatility function chosen was time-separable), we would find that the accuracy of our new approximation was equal to that of the BBF formula in the time-homogeneous case. Moreover, as is well-known, the BBF formula is typically highly accurate in the time-homogeneous case.

4. Numerical Experiment

In [7], the authors performed numerical experiments that demonstrated the high accuracy of the BBF formula when the local volatility function is time-homogeneous. In the previous section, we established that our new approximation is exactly time-changed BBF in the case of time-separable local volatility. Thus, the accuracy of the BBF formula in the time-homogeneous case is inherited by our new formula in the time-separable case. This motivates us to test the variational MLP approximation with a local volatility function that is both much more realistic and more difficult than those considered in [7]; difficult in the sense that this volatility function explodes at $t = 0$. Specifically, consider the following SVI[2] parameterization of

[2]For details of this parameterization see [6].

the local volatility surface:

$$\sigma^2(k,t) = a + b\left\{\rho\left(\frac{k}{\sqrt{t}} - m\right) + \sqrt{\left(\frac{k}{\sqrt{t}} - m\right)^2 + \sigma^2 t}\right\}$$

with

$$\begin{aligned} a &= 0.0012, \\ b &= 0.1634, \\ \sigma &= 0.1029, \\ \rho &= -0.5555, \\ m &= 0.0439. \end{aligned} \tag{4.1}$$

Thus the local variance $\sigma^2(k,t)$ on each time slice (or expiration) t is parameterized as SVI, effectively a hyperbola in the log-strike k. In practice, to avoid numerical

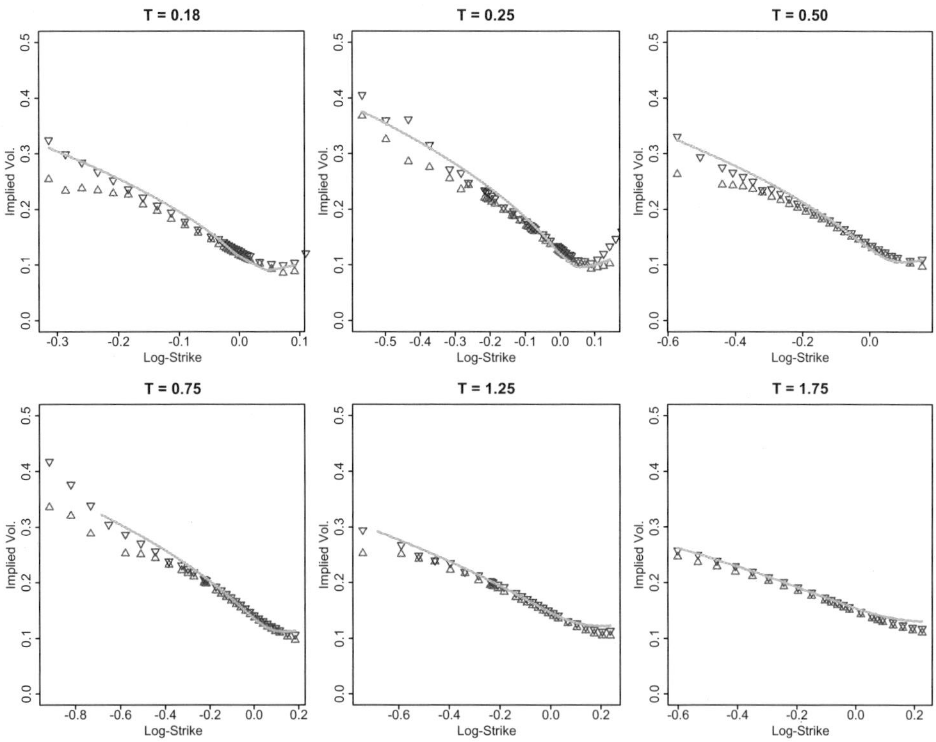

Fig. 1. Solid lines are from PDE computations, triangles are market SPX bid and offered vols as of September 15, 2005. It is clear that our local volatility function generates a realistic implied volatility surface.

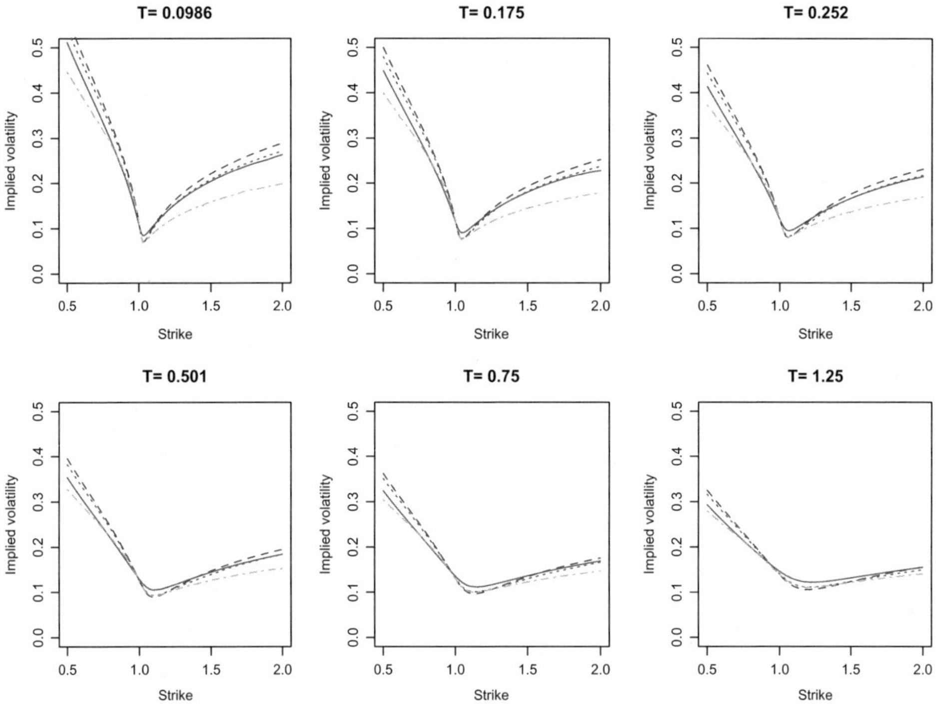

Fig. 2. The solid lines are from PDE computations, the dotted lines are $\sigma_{\mathrm{BS},0}$, the dash-dotted lines are Reghai and the dashed lines are BBFe. Expirations shown are actual SPX market expirations as of September 15, 2005.

problems, we freeze the local volatility function for times $t \leq 1/250$ years, roughly one trading day.

Remark 4.1. Because the local volatility surface (4.1) is singular at $t = 0$, small-time expansions such as those of [7] cannot work.

In Fig. 1, we plot implied volatilities from numerical PDE computations against actual SPX bid and offered implied volatilities as of September 15, 2005, the day before triple-witching.[3] We confirm by inspection that the SVI parameterization (4.1) of the local volatility surface generates a realistic implied volatility surface.

In Figs. 2 and 3, we plot the variational MLP approximation $\sigma_{\mathrm{BS},0}$ from (3.6) against the smile generated by a numerical PDE computation from (4.1) and the smiles corresponding to the Reghai and BBFe most-likely-path approximations from (1.5) and (1.6) respectively. We note that our new approximation dominates the alternative most-likely-path approximations; for each expiration, the smile generated by the variational MLP approximation is closer to the (true) smile generated

[3]This is the same volatility surface as the one plotted in Fig. 3.2 on p. 36 of [5].

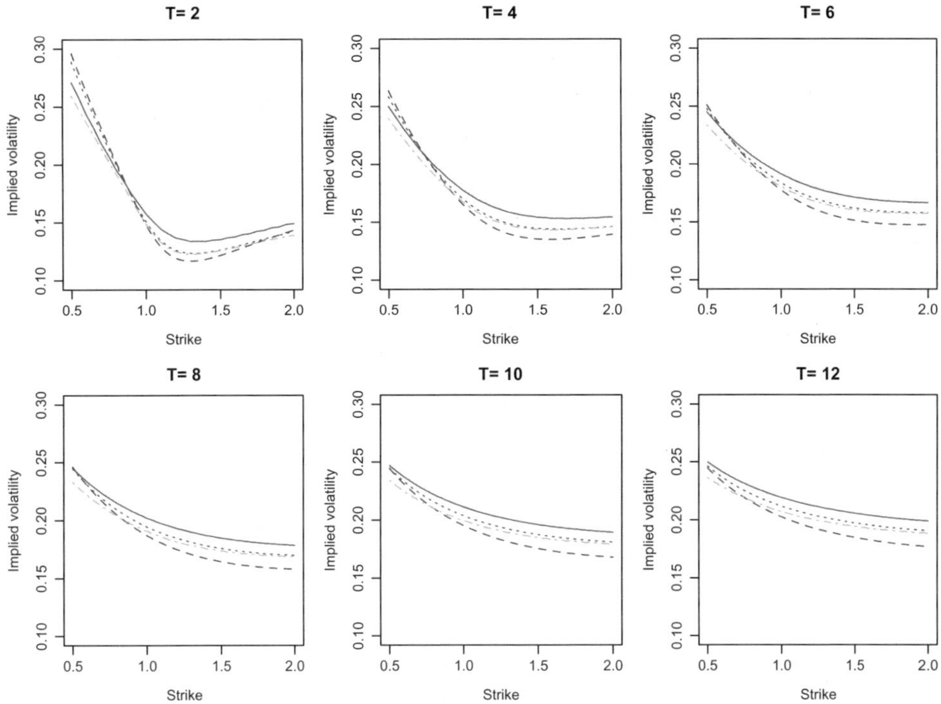

Fig. 3. The solid lines are from PDE computations, the dotted lines are $\sigma_{\mathrm{BS},0}$, the dash-dotted lines are Reghai and the dashed lines are BBFe. Expirations are from 2 to 12 years.

by numerical PDE computation than the alternatives. We note that BBFe does better than Reghai for shorter expirations and Reghai does better than BBFe for longer expirations (but again, variational MLP does better than either).

On closer inspection of the smiles, we may observe that for all three most-likely-path approximations, there is consistently a large approximation error at the cusp of the smile. As noted in [8], this is because the most-likely-path technique fails when there is substantial curvature in the local volatility function. In that case, fixing a time t, one cannot reasonably approximate an integration over all possible prices of the underlying x_t by one point, the most-likely point $\tilde{x}(t)$. Appropriately approximating the integration over x_t may substantially improve accuracy. The price to be paid for this improved accuracy is in computational effort and indeed, a brute-force numerical PDE computation may often be faster (and of course even more accurate). In contrast, the fixed-point algorithm we proposed to compute our variational MLP estimate is very fast, typically converging within 3 or 4 iterations.

5. Summary and Conclusion

We have derived a new most-likely-path estimate which we call *variational MLP* for approximating the implied volatility surface given a local volatility function.

The variational MLP estimate is a natural extension of the BBF formula that moreover behaves correctly under a deterministic time-change, in contrast to prior definitions of most-likely-path. We have further shown by explicit computation using a realistic parameterization of the SPX local volatility function, that the variational MLP estimate outperforms two competing definitions of most-likely-path: a popular definition due to Adil Reghai and a naïve extension of the BBF formula.

How to improve the accuracy of our variational MLP estimate by for example better approximating the integration over x_t is left for future research.

Acknowledgments

We are very grateful to Julien Guyon and Vladimir Lucic for sharing their results and for valuable discussions. The first author also thanks Nick Constanzino and his collaborators at Penn State University for sending an early version of their paper. The second author is grateful to Professor Gérard Ben Arous of Courant Institute for insightful and valuable comments and discussions. All errors are our responsibility. Finally, we are particularly grateful to the referee whose valuable comments helped us correct some inaccuracies and improve our presentation.

References

[1] R. Achdou and O. Pironneau, Computational methods for option pricing, *SIAM* (2005).
[2] H. Berestycki, J. Busca and I. Florent, Asymptotics and calibration of local volatility models, *Quantitative Finance* **2** (2002) 61–69.
[3] N. Bleistein and R. A. Handelsman, *Asymptotic Expansions of Integrals* (Dover Publications, 1986).
[4] W. Cheng, N. Costanzino, J. Liechty, A. Mazzucato and V. Nistor, Closed-form asymptotics and numerical approximations of 1D parabolic equations with applications to option pricing, *SIAM Journal on Financial Mathematics* **2** (2011) 901–934.
[5] J. Gatheral, *The Volatility Surface: A Practitioner's Guide* (Wiley Finance, 2006).
[6] J. Gatheral, A parsimonious arbitrage-free implied volatility parameterization with application to the valuation of volatility derivatives, Presentation at Global Derivatives & Risk Management, Madrid (2004), available at www.math.nyu.edu/fellows_fin_math/gatheral/madrid2004.pdf.
[7] J. Gatheral, E. P. Hsu, P. Laurence, C. Ouyang and T.-H. Wang, Asymptotics of implied volatility in local volatility models, forthcoming in *Mathematical Finance* (2011)
[8] J. Guyon and P. Henry-Labordère, From local to implied volatilities, SSRN preprint (2010).
[9] A. Reghai, The hybrid most likely path, *Risk Magazine* April (2006).

FORWARD AND FUTURE IMPLIED VOLATILITY*

PAUL GLASSERMAN

Graduate School of Business
Columbia University
New York, NY 10027, USA

QI WU

Department of Applied Physics and Applied Mathematics
Columbia University, New York, NY 10027, USA

We address the problem of defining and calculating forward volatility implied by option prices when the underlying asset is driven by a stochastic volatility process. We examine alternative notions of forward implied volatility and the information required to extract these measures from the prices of European options at fixed maturities. We then specialize to the SABR model and show how the asymptotic expansion of the bivariate transition density in Wu (forthcoming) allows calibration of the SABR model with piecewise constant parameters and calculation of forward volatility. We then investigate empirically whether current option prices at multiple maturities contain useful information in predicting future option prices and future implied volatility. We undertake this investigation using data on options on the euro-dollar, sterling-dollar, and dollar-yen exchange rates. We find that prices across maturities do indeed have predictive value. Moreover, we find that model-based forward volatility extracts this predicative information better than a standard "model-free" measure of forward volatility and better than spot implied volatility. The enhancement to out-of-sample forecasting accuracy gained from model-based forward volatility is greatest at longer forecasting horizons.

Keywords: Forward volatility; implied volatility surface; time-dependent SABR model; currency options; volatility forecasting.

1. Introduction

This paper investigates the concept of forward implied volatility in option prices with a specific application to stochastic volatility and currency markets. The term "forward implied volatility" or simply "forward vol" is used, broadly, to refer to

*This chapter was originally published under the same title in *International Journal of Theoretical and Applied Finance*, Vol.14, No.3, 407–432 (2011). Singapore: World Scientific Publishing.

future levels of volatility consistent with current market prices of options. The values of many path-dependent options, including cliquets and barrier options, are commonly interpreted through levels of volatility implied at some future date and, often, at some future level of the underlying asset. Similarly, the price of a forward-starting option is sensitive to the anticipated level of volatility at the forward start date and strike price of the option.

Forward volatility builds on the notions of spot implied volatility and forward rates, but with important differences. Spot implied volatility is unambiguous, in the sense that, given all other contract terms and market parameters, there is precisely one value of volatility at which the Black-Scholes formula will match a finite, strictly positive price observed in the market. In a term structure setting, bond prices at any two maturities completely determine the forward rate between those maturities through a static arbitrage argument without any assumptions on the evolution of interest rates.

But forward vol is not uniquely determined by the absence of arbitrage and the market prices of standard calls and puts at a finite set of maturities. This is a special case of the fundamental ill-posedness of the derivatives valuation problem: calls and puts determine, at best, the marginal distribution of the underlying asset at fixed dates, but pinning down a specific model requires the joint distribution across multiple dates. Resolving the ambiguity requires additional information or assumptions. For example, in fitting a volatility surface based on Dupire [13], practitioners often add smoothness constraints to select a calibration. The main alternative is to posit a model for the dynamics of the underlying asset, and this is the approach we follow. Once calibrated to standard European options at two or more maturities, the model implies a value of forward volatility at all but the last maturity, for each level of the model's state variables. Thus, a forward implied volatility is implied by a combination of market prices and model choice.

We work within a stochastic volatility setting generally and the SABR model of Hagan, Kumar, Lesniewski, and Woodward [20] specifically. The SABR model is widely used to fit slices of the volatility surface, particularly for currency and interest rate options, so it is natural to extend this application to extract forward volatilities. Our approach is made feasible by the asymptotic expansion derived in Wu [26] for the bivariate transition density of the underlying and its stochastic volatility in the SABR model. The original expansion of Hagan *et al.* [20] provides highly accurate implied volatilities at a single maturity; but calibration to multiple maturities and the calculation of forward volatilities requires the joint transition density of the two state variables analyzed in Wu [26]. Henry-Labordere [22] and Hagan, Lesniewski, and Woodward [21] also derived approximations to the bivariate transition density, but these are less amenable to the computations we undertake here.

Before focusing on the SABR model, we examine alternative notions of forward implied volatility in the presence of stochastic volatility. Alternative notions differ, for example, in the information on which they condition. Passing from a forward implied volatility at a given level of the underlying and its stochastic volatility to one conditioned only on the underlying requires integrating over the conditional distribution of the stochastic volatility. We also examine various ways of taking expectations of future levels of implied volatility as measures of forward volatility. This discussion clarifies alternative interpretations of "forward vol," which is often used loosely in practice. The calculations required for the alternative interpretations are, here again, made possible in the SABR setting by the results in Wu [26].

Having defined and calculated notions of forward volatility, we test our approach on market data and examine whether forward vol has predictive power in forecasting future levels of implied volatility. We use data from August 2001 to June 2009, provided by a major derivatives dealer, on over-the-counter currency options on the euro-dollar, sterling-dollar, and dollar-yen exchange rates. The data is in the form of constant-maturity quotes. From quotes on 6-month options and 9-month options, for example, we calculate 3-month volatilities, six months forward. We then compare these with spot implied volatilities observed six months later. As one benchmark, we use the current level of implied volatility to forecast future volatility. Another benchmark is provided by a "model-free" forward volatility associated with a deterministic but time-varying volatility function. We compare in-sample forecasts and out-of-sample forecasts using rolling regressions. For both, we find that model-based forward vol outperforms the benchmarks.

There is no simple theoretical link between forward volatility and future volatility. Forward volatility depends only on a model's dynamics under a pricing measure, whereas the evolution of implied volatility depends on the dynamics under both the pricing measure and the empirical measure. A link between the two requires, at a minimum, a model that describes dynamics under both measures. One would then expect that the relationship between forward vol and expected future vol involves a risk premium and a convexity correction, as is usually the case when a forward value is used to predict a future value. We therefore do not suggest that forward volatility should be an unbiased predictor of future implied volatility, even in theory. Nevertheless, the fact that the forward vols we calculate enhance the ability to predict future vols lends support and adds value to the approach we take. It also confirms the view that market prices of options at different maturities contain information relevant to predicting future option prices. More details on modeling implied volatility in general can be found in Gatheral's book [19]. Specific examples of dynamic volatility models can be found in Schönbucher [25], Cont and Da Fonseca [11], Buehler [7], Carr and Wu [10], Schweizer and Wissel [24], Carmona and Nadtochiy [9], Gatheral [18], and Bergomi's series of papers on "smile dynamics" [3]–[6].

The rest of this paper is organized as follows. In Sec. 2, we detail various notions of forward volatility. In Sec. 3, we present our calibration method, using time-varying parameters to fit the SABR model to multiple maturities. Section 4 applies Wu [26] and numerical integration to calculate forward vol in the calibrated SABR model. Section 5 presents our empirical results.

2. Notions of Forward Implied Volatility

Depending the set of information utilized for evaluation of future state variables, we introduce three notions of model-based forward implied volatilities, namely the fully-conditional, the partially-conditional, and the expected forward implied volatility. Throughout, we focus on stochastic volatility models and define all model-based notions through the Black model's volatility parameter. Expectations in this section are all taken under relevant forward measures.

2.1. *Spot and forward Black implied volatility*

Let the forward price process of an underlying asset be $F(t)$, and let its instantaneous volatility process be $\alpha(t)$. Further let the parameters of the concerned stochastic volatility model be θ and let the model's joint transition density from t to T be $p(t, f, \alpha; T, F, A)$ with f, α and F, A denoting values of random variables $F(t), \alpha(t)$ at t and T respectively.

A standard European call on $F(t)$ has payoff

$$(F(T) - K)^+, \quad K > 0, \quad t < T$$

where t is the evaluation time, usually understood as "now" and set to zero, and T is the option maturity. Under the Black model, F follows geometric Brownian motion, and the option price is given by:

$$\mathbb{E}[(F(T) - K)^+ | F(t)] = F(t)N(d_+) - KN(d_-)$$
$$\text{with } d_\pm = \frac{\log(F(t)/K) \pm \frac{1}{2}\sigma^2(T-t)}{\sigma\sqrt{T-t}} \tag{2.1}$$

Let V^{Mkt} be the market price of the call and let σ be its Black implied volatility, the unique volatility parameter under which V^{Mkt} matches the call price in the Black model (2.1).

Now consider a forward starting European call on $F(t)$ with payoff

$$(F(T_2) - kF(T_1))^+, \quad k > 0, \quad t < T_1 < T_2$$

where k is the strike ratio, t is still the evaluation time, T_1 is the option starting time and T_2 is the option maturity. Conditional on T_1 and denoted by $V^{\text{Black}}(T_1, T_2, k, \sigma)$, its price under the Black model becomes:

$$V^{\text{Black}}(T_1, T_2, k, \sigma) = F(T_1)N(d_+) - kF(T_1)N(d_-)$$
$$\text{with } d_\pm = \frac{\log(1/k) \pm \frac{1}{2}\sigma^2(T_2 - T_1)}{\sigma\sqrt{T_2 - T_1}}$$

Let $V^{\text{Model}}(T_1, T_2, k, \theta)$ be the T_1-conditional expectation of this payoff under the concerned stochastic volatility model. The model-based notion of T_1-into-T_2 forward Black implied volatility is defined as the unique volatility parameter in the Black model under which $V^{\text{Model}}(T_1, T_2, k, \theta)$ matches $V^{\text{Black}}(T_1, T_2, k, \sigma)$:

$$\sigma \text{ s.t. } V^{\text{Model}}(T_1, T_2, k, \theta) = V^{\text{Black}}(T_1, T_2, k, \sigma)$$

where

$$V^{\text{Model}}(T_1, T_2, k, \theta) := \mathbb{E}[(F(T_2) - kF(T_1))^+ | F(T_1), \alpha(T_1)]$$

is calculated under the dynamics of the stochastic volatility model with calibrated parameter θ. When the concerned model is the SABR stochastic volatility model, $V^{\text{Model}}(T_1, T_2, k, \theta)$ becomes $V^{\text{SABR}}(T_1, T_2, k, \alpha, \beta, \rho, \nu)$. The case of a put can be defined analogously.

The thus-defined forward Black implied volatility is a T_1-dependent quantity. In particular, it is a function of future state variables $F(T_1)$ and $\alpha(T_1)$ in the concerned stochastic volatility model, which are unknown at time t. From now on, we shorten it to "Blk-Fwd-IV" and denote it by

$$\Sigma(T_1, T_2, k | F(T_1), \alpha(T_1)) \tag{2.2}$$

to explicitly reflect its T_1 dependency.

Depending on the set of information utilized to evaluate $F(T_1)$ and $\alpha(T_1)$ in (2.2), we arrive at three notions of forward implied volatilities — fully conditional, partially conditional, and expected.

2.2. *Fully-conditional*

The "Fully-Conditional Forward Implied Volatility" refers to the Blk-Fwd-IV when $F(T_1), \alpha(T_1)$ in Σ are evaluated at some chosen positive real values F_1, A_1. Denoted by Σ^{flcd} and shortened to "Flcd-Fwd-IV", the fully-conditional forward implied volatility is:

$$\Sigma^{\text{flcd}}(T_1, T_2, k, F_1, A_1) := \Sigma(T_1, T_2, k \,|\, F(T_1) = F_1, \alpha(T_1) = A_1) \tag{2.3}$$

Given a fixed strike ratio k and a fixed future period $[T_1, T_2]$, fully-conditional forward implied volatility is a function of future underlying level F_1 and future instantaneous volatility A_1. Its two dimensional property is analogous to that of a spot implied volatility surface which is understood as a function of today's underlying level and option tenor.

When computing Σ^{flcd} in (2.3), one first fixes both F_1 and A_1 at some chosen positive real values, then uses the model's full joint transition density from T_1 to T_2 to obtain an option price under the concerned model as

$$\iint_{\mathbb{R}^2_+} (F_2 - kF_1)^+ p(T_1, F_1, A_1; T_2, F_2, A_2) dF_2 dA_2$$

and inverts this price to a Black volatility using the same value of F_1.

Upon calibrating the model to the market's spot implied volatility curves at both T_1 and T_2, the Flcd-Fwd-IV incorporates market information regarding the T_2 states conditional on starting at F_1, A_1, and it does so through the model's full joint transition density from T_1 to T_2.

2.3. *Partially-conditional*

The "Partially-Conditional Forward Implied Volatility" is defined similarly through the Blk-Fwd-IV where only $F(T_1)$ in Σ is evaluated at some chosen positive real value F_1 and the volatility state variable $\alpha(T_1)$ is integrated out using the model's conditional joint transition density from t to T_1, conditional on $F(T_1)$ being F_1.

Denoted by Σ^{ptcd} and shortened to "Ptcd-Fwd-IV", the partially-conditional forward implied volatility is:

$$\Sigma^{\text{ptcd}}(t, T_1, T_2, k, F_1) := \mathbb{E}[\Sigma(T_1, T_2, k \,|\, F(T_1), \alpha(T_1)) \,|\, F(T_1) = F_1] \tag{2.4}$$

Alternatively, it could be defined by first taking the expectation of forward Black implied variance Σ^2 and then taking the squared root of the resulting expectation:

$$\Sigma^{\text{ptcd}}(t, T_1, T_2, k, F_1) := \sqrt{\mathbb{E}[\Sigma^2(T_1, T_2, k \,|\, F(T_1), \alpha(T_1)) \,|\, F(T_1) = F_1]} \tag{2.5}$$

(2.4) and (2.5) differ from each other only by a convexity adjustment. However, our focus will be on the alternative dependence on the variables F and A, rather than on this distinction.

Given a fixed strike ratio k and a fixed future period $[T_1, T_2]$, partially-conditional forward implied volatility is a one-dimensional function of future underlying level F_1 with future instantaneous volatility integrated out.

When computing Σ^{ptcd}, one first fixes F_1, then, for each value of the volatility state A_1 in its support $\mathbb{R}_+$, one obtains the corresponding Flcd-Fwd-IV using the joint transition density from T_1 to T_2 as in the fully-conditional case, and finally the Ptcd-Fwd-IV is obtained by integrating these Flcd-Fwd-IVs against the F_1-conditional joint transition density from t to T_1:

$$p(t, f, \alpha; T_1, A_1 \,|\, F_1) := \frac{p(t, f, \alpha; T_1, F_1, A_1)}{\int_{\mathbb{R}_+} p(t, f, \alpha; T_1, F_1, A_1) dA_1}$$

as:

$$\int_{\mathbb{R}_+} \Sigma^{\text{flcd}}(t, T_1, T_2, k, F_1, A_1) p(t, f, \alpha; T_1, A_1 \,|\, F_1) dA_1$$

Upon model calibration, the Ptcd-Fwd-IV not only reflects market information regarding the T_2 states conditional on starting at F_1, A_1 as in the Flcd-Fwd-IV case, but also partially incorporates through the model market information from the period $[t, T_1]$ to eliminate the uncertainty, from an evaluation point of view, of the future volatility state $\alpha(T_1)$ at T_1. It does so through the full joint transition density from T_1 to T_2 and the F_1-conditional joint transition density from t to T_1.

2.4. *Expected*

The "Expected Forward Implied Volatility" goes one step further than the partially conditional case, and is defined by integrating both of the T_1 state variables $F(T_1), \alpha(T_1)$ in Σ against the model's full joint transition density from t to T_1.

Denoted by Σ^{expt} and shortened to "Expt-Fwd-IV", the expected forward implied volatility is no longer a function of T_1 states and it is:

$$\Sigma^{\text{expt}}(t, T_1, T_2, k) := \mathbb{E}[\Sigma(T_1, T_2, k \,|\, F(T_1), \alpha(T_1))] \tag{2.6}$$

Similar to the partially-conditional case, it could also be defined alternatively as:

$$\Sigma^{\text{expt}}(t, T_1, T_2, k) := \sqrt{\mathbb{E}[\Sigma^2(T_1, T_2, k \,|\, F(T_1), \alpha(T_1))]} \tag{2.7}$$

up to a convexity difference.

When computing Σ^{expt}, one follows the same procedure as in the partially-conditional case except neither F_1 nor A_1 is fixed when computing Flcd-Fwd-IV. Instead, one obtains Flcd-Fwd-IV for each pair of F_1 and A_1 in its support $\mathbb{R}^2_+$, and then integrates these Flcd-Fwd-IVs against the full joint transition density from t to T_1 as:

$$\iint_{\mathbb{R}_+} \Sigma^{\text{flcd}}(t, T_1, T_2, k, F_1, A_1) p(t, f, \alpha; T_1, F_1, A_1) dF_1 dA_1$$

instead of using the F_1-conditional one.

The Expt-Fwd-IV utilizes full joint transition probabilities from both periods $[T_1, T_2]$ and $[t, T_1]$, thus fully incorporates market information regarding state variables at both the starting point T_1 and the ending point T_2.

2.5. *Model-free*

The following model-free quantity is sometimes used (see, e.g., Corte, Sarno, and Tsiakas [12], Egelkraut and Garcia [14] and Egelkraut, Garcia, and Sherrick [15]) as a measure of market implied forward volatility

$$\Sigma^{\text{mdfr}}(t, T_1, T_2, K) := \sqrt{\frac{(\sigma^{\text{Mkt}}(t, T_2, K))^2 \times (T_2 - t) - (\sigma^{\text{Mkt}}(t, T_1, K))^2 \times (T_1 - t)}{T_2 - T_1}} \tag{2.8}$$

where σ^{Mkt} denote market quotes of spot implied volatilities and Σ^{mdfr} denotes this model-free notion which is shortened to "Mdfr-Fwd-IV". As a "model-free" concept, Σ^{mdfr} in (2.8) is not a function of state variables at any of the future times. When computing it, one simply follows its definition.

3. Model Specification and Calibration

Having introduced various notions of forward volatility, we turn to the SABR model, its tenor-dependent parameters and model calibration.

3.1. *Piecewise-constant parameters*

The original SABR model has constant parameters and specifies a forward price process $F(t)$ and an instantaneous volatility $\alpha(t)$ process under the T-forward measure

$\mathbb{Q}^T$. For $0 < t < T$,

$$
\begin{aligned}
&dF(t) = \alpha(t)F^{\beta}(t)dW_1(t); \qquad &F(0) = f\\
&d\alpha(t) = \nu\alpha(t)dW_2(t); \qquad &\alpha(0) = \alpha\\
&\mathbb{E}^{\mathbb{Q}^T}[dW_1(t)dW_2(t)] = \rho dt;
\end{aligned}
$$

where the model parameters are:

$$\theta := (\alpha, \beta, \rho, \nu)$$

We further denote the dependence of the model's joint transition density on the model parameters explicitly by:

$$p(t, f, \alpha; T, F, A; \theta)$$

The constant-parameter setting is adequate for calibrating θ to an implied volatility curve at one fixed tenor T. In practice, market participants use different parameters for different maturities and recalibrate frequently, so parameters depend on T and t.

Let us denote the parameters' dependence on T by:

$$\theta(T) := (\alpha, \beta, \rho, \nu)(T)$$

Plain vanilla options are traded only on a finite set of tenors

$$0 < T_1 < T_2 < \cdots < T_N$$

at any time t, so we use a piecewise-constant (in T) parameterization. For a fixed date t, where $0 < t < T_1$, the parameter vector becomes a parameter matrix,

$$
\theta(T) := \begin{cases} \theta_0, & t < T \leq T_1 \\ \theta_{i-1}, & T_{i-1} < T \leq T_i \\ \theta_{N-1} & T_{N-1} < T \leq T_N \end{cases} \tag{3.1}
$$

$$\text{where } \theta_i = (\alpha_i, \beta_i, \rho_i, \nu_i), \ \ i = 0, 1, \ldots, N-1$$

and the tenor-dependent SABR model then reads:

$$
\begin{aligned}
&dF(t, T_i) = \alpha(t)[F(t, T_i)]^{\beta_i}dW_1(t); \qquad &F(0, T_i) = f_i\\
&d\alpha(t, T_i) = \nu_i\alpha(t, T_i)dW_2(t); \qquad &\alpha(0, T_i) = \alpha_i\\
&\mathbb{E}^{\mathbb{Q}^{T_i}}[dW_1(t)dW_2(t)] = \rho_i dt;
\end{aligned} \tag{3.2}
$$

Accordingly, the dependence of the model's transition density on parameters becomes piecewise-constant:

$$
\begin{aligned}
&p(t, f, \alpha; T_1, F_1, A_1; \theta_0)\\
&p(T_{i-1}, F_{i-1}, A_{i-1}; T_i, F_i, A_i; \theta_{i-1}), \quad i = 2, \ldots, N-1\\
&p(T_{N-1}, F_{N-1}, A_{N-1}; T_N, F_N, A_N; \theta_{N-1})
\end{aligned} \tag{3.3}
$$

In the case where only the parameter dependence need to be stressed, we use the shortened notion:

$$p(t, T_1; \theta_0) \quad \text{and} \quad p(T_{i-1}, T_i; \theta_{i-1}), \quad i = 2, \ldots, N$$

3.2. *Synchronizing underlying and measure*

A standard SABR model describes the dynamics of a forward price process $F(t, T_i)$ maturing at a particular T_i. Forward prices associated with different maturities are martingales with respect to different forward measures defined by different zero-coupon bond prices $B(t, T_i)$ as numéraires. This raises consistency issues on both the underlying and the pricing measure when we work with multiple option maturities simultaneously.

We address this issue by consolidating all dynamics into those of $F(t, T_N), \alpha(t, T_N)$ in (3.2) whose tenor is the longest among all, and express all option prices at different tenors in one terminal measure $\mathbb{Q}^{T_N}$ which is the one associated with the zero-coupon bond price $B(t, T_N)$. We may do so because we assume

- No-arbitrage between spot price of a security $S(t)$ and all of its forward prices $F(t, T_i), i = 1, \ldots, N$ at all trading time t;
- Zero-coupon bonds are risk-less assets whose prices $B(t, T_i), i = 1, 2, \ldots, N$ have positive values.

A consequence of the first assumption is the standard relation

$$F(t, T_i) = \frac{S(t)}{B(t, T_i)}, \quad i = 1, 2, \ldots, N,$$

at any trading time t. Forward prices $F(t, T_i)$ at shorter maturities $T_1, \ldots, T_{N-1}$ could then be expressed in terms of the common underlying $F(t, T_N)$ as:

$$F(t, T_i) = F(t, T_N)\frac{B(t, T_N)}{B(t, T_i)}, \quad 1 \le i \le N - 1. \tag{3.4}$$

The second assumption reflects the that fact that we do not model interest rates as stochastic processes. This is a simplifying assumption in the context of currency options. For models that do model interest rates stochastically in the currency option context, see Amin and Jarrow [1] and Piterbarg [23]. Although volatilities of domestic and foreign interest rates could be important forces affecting currency options, we deem it reasonable to make this assumption for option tenors that are not too long.

To price a call option on $F(\cdot, T_i)$ with strike price K_j and maturity T_i, we use (3.4) and some simple algebra to arrive at

$$\begin{aligned} V(t, T_i, K_j) &= B(t, T_N)\mathbb{E}^{\mathbb{Q}^{T_N}}[(F(T_i, T_N) - \mathcal{K}_j^i)^+ \mid \mathcal{F}_t] \\ &\qquad \text{where } \mathcal{K}_j^i := \frac{K_j}{B(T_i, T_N)}. \end{aligned} \tag{3.5}$$

In other words, we convert an option on $F(\cdot, T_i)$ to an option on $F(\cdot, T_N)$.

3.3. *Bootstrapping vs. global optimization*

Since model parameters are piecewise constant in maturity, at each date t they can be calibrated through either a bootstrapping algorithm (in which the piecewise constant parameters are calibrated sequentially) or one based on global optimization (in which they are calibrated simultaneously). In either case, we recalibrate at each date t and do not seek to calibrate simultaneously across different dates t, only across different maturities T.

At any time of calibration t, let σ^{Mkt} be the market-quoted implied volatilities of liquid European options and let σ^{Model} be implied volatilities obtained by inverting option prices under the SABR model. For a given set of model parameters $\theta(T)$ as in (3.1), let $f(t, \theta(T))$ be the l_2 difference of implied volatility surface between market quotes and those obtained from the SABR model,

$$f(t, \theta(T)) := \sum_{i=1}^{N} \sum_{j=1}^{M_i} |\sigma^{\text{Model}}(t, T_i, K_j) - \sigma^{\text{Mkt}}(t, T_i, K_j)|^2 (t, \theta(T))$$

The model is globally calibrated (at date t) when a set of optimal parameters, denoted by $\theta^*(T)$,

$$\theta^*(T) := \begin{cases} \theta_0^*, & t < T \leq T_1 \\ \theta_{i-1}^*, & T_{i-1} < T \leq T_i \\ \theta_{N-1}^* & T_{N-1} < T \leq T_N \end{cases}$$

$$\text{where } \theta_i^* = (\alpha_i^*, \beta_i^*, \rho_i^*, \nu_i^*), \quad i = 0, 1, \ldots, N-1$$

is found over its feasible region Ω^N with Ω being

$$\Omega := (0, +\infty) \times (0, 1) \times (-1, 1) \times (0, +\infty)$$

such that f is minimized:

$$\theta^*(T) := \underset{\theta(T) \in \Omega^N}{\text{argmin}}\, f(t, \theta(T))$$

- Bootstrapping

The bootstrapping calibration is carried out sequentially in N steps according to option tenors. First obtain θ_0^* such that $f(t, \theta_0)$ is minimized for implied volatility curve at T_1 quoted at time t. Next given θ_0^*, obtain θ_1^* such that $f(t, [\theta_0^*; \theta_1])$ is minimized for tenor T_1. The procedure goes on until the last tenor T_N where θ_{N-1}^* is obtained such that $f(t, [\theta_0^*; \ldots; \theta_{N-2}^*; \theta_{N-1}])$ is minimized given the previous $N-1$ optimal parameter curves $[\theta_0^*; \ldots; \theta_{N-2}^*]$.

Step 1: At tenor T_1, find θ_0^* such that:

$$\theta_0^* := \underset{\theta_0 \in \Omega}{\text{argmin}} f(t, \theta_0)$$

Step 2: At tenor T_2, find θ_1^* given θ_0^* from step 1 such that:

$$\theta_1^* := \underset{\theta_1 \in \Omega}{\operatorname{argmin}} f(t, [\theta_0^*; \theta_1])$$

$$\vdots$$

Step N: At tenor T_N, find θ_{N-1}^* given $[\theta_0^*; \ldots; \theta_{N-2}^*]$ from step 1 to $N-1$ such that:

$$\theta_{N-1}^* := \underset{\theta_{N-1} \in \Omega}{\operatorname{argmin}} f(t, [\theta_0^*; \ldots; \theta_{N-2}^*; \theta_{N-1}])$$

- Global Optimization

  Calibration based on global optimization seeks $\theta_0^*, \theta_1^*, \ldots, \theta_{N-1}^*$ all at the same time such that

$$[\theta_0^*, \theta_1^*, \ldots, \theta_{N-1}^*] := \underset{[\theta_0, \theta_1, \ldots, \theta_{N-1}] \in \Omega^N}{\operatorname{argmin}} f(t, [\theta_0, \theta_1, \ldots, \theta_{N-1}])$$

In the empirical studies we undertake later in Sec. 5, we use global optimization for model calibrations. When evaluating f in either the bootstrapping calibration or that based on global optimization, σ^{Model} are obtained by inverting model prices of European options according to (3.5) which, in practice, are calculated by integrating payoffs against transition densities in (3.3). At tenor T_1,

$$V(t, T_1, K_j) = B(t, T_N) \iint_{R_+^2} (F_1 - \mathcal{K}_j^i)^+ p(t, T_1; \theta_0) dF_1 dA_1 \tag{3.6}$$

and generally at tenor $T_i, i = 2, \ldots, N$,

$$V(t, T_i, K_j) = B(t, T_N) \iint_{R_+^2} \left[\cdots \left[\iint_{R_+^2} (F_i - \mathcal{K}_j^i)^+ p(T_{i-1}, T_i; \theta_{i-1}) dF_i dA_i \right] \cdots \right] \times p(t, T_1; \theta_0) dF_1 dA_1 \tag{3.7}$$

4. Computing Conditional Expectations

Have specified the model and articulated its calibration, we now provide details on using the truncated series expression of the density obtained in Wu [26] of the model's joint transition density for fast computation of expectations and conditional expectations that arise in both model calibration and calculation of various forward implied volatility measures.

4.1. *Conditional expectations*

In model calibration, computing spot implied volatilities from the model requires computing option prices as in (3.6) and (3.7):

$$\begin{aligned} &\mathbb{E}^{\mathbb{Q}^{T_N}} [(F(T_i) - \mathcal{K}_j)^+ \mid F_{i-1}, A_{i-1}] \\ &\quad = \iint_{R_+^2} (F_i - \mathcal{K}_j)^+ p(T_{i-1}, T_i; \theta_{i-1}) dF_i dA_i \end{aligned} \tag{4.1}$$

at each tenor $T_i, i = 1, \ldots, N$ for each equivalent strike $\mathcal{K}_j, j = 1, \ldots, M_i$.

Once the model is calibrated, computing model-based forward implied volatilities in (2.3), (2.4)–(2.5) and (2.6)–(2.7) also boils down to computing:

$$\begin{aligned} &\mathbb{E}^{\mathbb{Q}^{T_N}}[(F(T_i) - kF(T_{i-1}))^+ \mid F_{i-1}, A_{i-1}] \\ &\quad = \iint_{R_+^2} (F_i - kF_{i-1})^+ p(T_{i-1}, T_i; \theta_{i-1}) dF_i dA_i \end{aligned} \tag{4.2}$$

over any speriod $[T_{i-1}, T_i], i = 2, \ldots, N-1$.

4.2. *Numerical integration*

In both (4.1) and (4.2), we need to evaluate two-dimensional integrations of payoff functions that depend on state variables at T_i or at both T_{i-1} and T_i. To include both cases, we consider payoff functions depending on two arbitrary temporal points t and T with $t < T$ and denote values of state variables by f, α at t and F, A at T.

Let

$$\Phi(F(T), F(t))$$

be an arbitrary payoff function of $F(T)$ and $F(t)$ and let $I_{(f,\alpha)}(t, T, \theta)$ be its time-t conditional expectation which is:

$$\begin{aligned} I_{(f,\alpha)}(t, T, \theta) &:= \mathbb{E}[\Phi(F(T), F(t)) | F(t) = f, \alpha(t) = \alpha] \\ &= \iint_{\Omega(F,A)} \Phi(F, f) p(t, f, \alpha; T, F, A; \theta) dF dA \end{aligned} \tag{4.3}$$

Both (4.1) and (4.2) could then be cast as instances of $I_{(f,\alpha)}(t, T, \theta)$.

Asymptotic expansions of the joint transition density $p(t, f, \alpha; T, F, A; \theta)$ have been obtained analytically in Wu [26] to the nth order as:

$$p_n(t, f, \alpha; T, F, A; \theta) = \frac{1}{\nu T F^\beta A^2} \sum_{k=0}^{n} (\nu\sqrt{T})^k \hat{p}_k(\tau, u, v) \quad \text{where}$$

$$\tau := \frac{T-t}{T}; \quad u := \eta(F) = \frac{f^{1-\beta} - F^{1-\beta}}{\alpha(1-\beta)\sqrt{T}}; \quad v := \zeta(v) = \frac{\ln(\alpha/A)}{\nu\sqrt{T}}$$

where $\hat{p}_k(\tau, u, v)$ are obtained recursively in [26]. As demonstrated in [26], the expansion to its second order p_2 is a quite accurate approximation of p for a wide range of model parameters and values of state variables as well.

When computing (4.3), we will first replace $p(t, f, \alpha; T, F, A; \theta)$ by the asymptotic expansion to 2nd order whose analytical form is $p_2(t, f, \alpha; T, F, A; \theta)$ obtained in [26] for an approximation of (4.3) and then evaluate the resulting approximation either by a direct numerical integration or through quadrature rules. We do not recommend using just the first-order expansion. The difference between p_1 and p_2 is that most of the tail details of the density function are captured by p_2 but not p_1, without which skew and/or smile features of implied volatility are hard to capture correctly. Quoted from Eq. (40) in [26], $p_2(t, f, \alpha; T, F, A; \theta)$ reads:

$$
\begin{aligned}
p_2(t, f, \alpha; T, F, A; \theta) &= \frac{1}{\nu T F^{\beta} A^2}[\hat{p}_0 + \nu\sqrt{T}\hat{p}_1 + \nu^2 T \hat{p}_2](\tau, u, v, \theta), \quad \text{with} \\
\hat{p}_0(\tau, u, v, \theta) &= \frac{1}{2\pi\tau\sqrt{1-\rho^2}} \exp\left[-\frac{u^2 - 2\rho u v + v^2}{2\tau(1-\rho^2)}\right] \\
\hat{p}_1(\tau, u, v, \theta) &= g_1(\tau, u, v, \theta)\hat{p}_0(\tau, u, v, \theta) \\
\hat{p}_2(\tau, u, v, \theta) &= g_2(\tau, u, v, \theta)\hat{p}_0(\tau, u, v, \theta)
\end{aligned} \tag{4.4}
$$

where g_1 and g_2 are given by:

$$
\begin{aligned}
g_1(\tau, u, v) &= \frac{a_{11} + a_{10}/\tau}{2(-1+\rho^2)} \\
g_2(\tau, u, v) &= \frac{a_{23}\tau + a_{22} + a_{21}/\tau + a_{20}/\tau^2}{24(1-\rho^2)^2}
\end{aligned}
$$

To save space, we refer the reader to Eq. (42) in [26] for explicit expressions for the polynomial functions a_{11}, a_{10} and $a_{23}, a_{22}, a_{21}, a_{20}$.

A straightforward way of using this analytical result is to plug (4.4) into (4.3) and use one's favorite routine for a direct numerical integration, such as a trapezoidal rule with sub-intervals of equal size where the integral is taken over a truncated domain $\Omega(F, A)$ of the support of the original variable F, A, which is $\mathbb{R}_+^2$. The computing time required for each approximate double integral in (3.7) is quadratic in the number of grid points, and the total time required for (3.7) is linear in the number of maturities N.

If one is not tightly constrained by CPU time or computer memory, direct numerical integration with a sufficiently fine discretization of the domain of integration achieves high accuracy and is reasonably fast. This is how we carry out our model calibrations in the empirical studies we undertake in Sec. 5. It takes about 1–10 milliseconds for an evaluation of (4.3) on a 1000 by 1000 grid. Similar integrals have to be calculated repeatedly in the course of calibration.

To accelerate the calculation, the Gaussian structure in the density expansion can be exploited. In the transformed variables τ, u, v, the leading order density $\hat{p}_0$ is a bivariate Gaussian distribution and corrections at the next two orders $\hat{p}_1, \hat{p}_2$ are of a product form of polynomial functions g_1, g_2 and the leading order $\hat{p}_0$.

In the following, we derive expressions of $I_{(f,\alpha)}(t, T, \theta)$ in the transformed variables τ, u, v that are convenient for Gaussian-quadrature-based numerical integration to compute (4.3).

First, let us express the original integration variables F, A in terms of u, v as:

$$
\begin{aligned}
F &= \eta^{-1}(u) = [f^{1-\beta} - \alpha(1-\beta)\sqrt{T}\cdot u]^{\frac{1}{1-\beta}} \\
A &= \zeta^{-1}(v) = \alpha \cdot \exp(-\nu\sqrt{T}\cdot v)
\end{aligned} \tag{4.5}
$$

Plugging (4.5) into (4.4) and after some algebra, we consolidate p_2 in τ, u, v as:

$$p_2(t, f, \alpha, T, F, A, \theta) = J^2_{(f,\alpha)}(\tau, u, v, \theta) \times \hat{p}_0(\tau, u, v) \quad \text{where,}$$
$$J^2_{(f,\alpha)}(\tau, u, v, \theta) := \frac{1 + \nu\sqrt{T} \times g_1(\tau, u, v, \theta) + (\nu\sqrt{T})^2 \times g_2(\tau, u, v, \theta)}{\nu T \times (\eta^{-1}(u))^{\beta} \times (\zeta^{-1}(v))^2} \tag{4.6}$$

With (4.6) plugged into (4.3), we then express $I_{(f,\alpha)}(t, T, \theta)$ in τ, u, v as:

$$I_{(f,\alpha)}(t, T, \theta) \approx \iint_{\Omega(u,v)} H_{(f,\alpha)}(\tau, u, v, \theta) \times \hat{p}_0(\tau, u, v) du dv \quad \text{where,}$$
$$H_{(f,\alpha)}(\tau, u, v, \theta) = \Phi(\eta^{-1}(u), f) \times J^2_{(f,\alpha)}(\tau, u, v, \theta) \times (\eta^{-1}(u))' \times (\zeta^{-1}(v))' \tag{4.7}$$

Finally, we slightly enlarge the domain of integration $\Omega(u, v)$ to a rectangular one such that it covers $\Omega(u, v)$ which is usually a curved one. Then we are ready to apply a two-dimensional Gaussian quadrature rule to (4.7) as $I_{(f,\alpha)}(t, T, \theta)$ now becomes an integration of a bivariate Gaussian kernel $\hat{p}_0$ against an analytical function H whose expression is explicit and differentiable with respect to u, v. For instance, let the slightly-enlarged rectangular domain be

$$\Omega'(u, v) = [\underline{u}, \overline{u}] \times [\underline{v}, \overline{v}]$$

then (4.7) can be evaluated as

$$\begin{aligned} I_{(f,\alpha)}(t, T, \theta) &\approx \int_{\underline{v}}^{\overline{v}} \int_{\underline{u}}^{\overline{u}} H_{(f,\alpha)}(\tau, u, v, \theta) \times \hat{p}_0(\tau, u, v) du dv \\ &\approx \sum_i \sum_j W_{ij} \times H_{f,\alpha}(\tau, u_i, v_j, \theta) \times \hat{p}_0(\tau, u_i, v_j) \end{aligned}$$

where one could choose the weights W_{ij} according to a particular quadrature rule.

5. Application to Currency Options

Having laid out the framework, we now report empirical findings based on currency option market data. We first examine whether the term structure of today's option prices across multiple tenors contains predictive information about future option prices. We then examine the relative predictive merits of spot volatility, model-based forward volatility, and model-free forward volatility. We test both in-sample and out-of-sample performance.

5.1. *Data description*

Option quotes in the foreign exchange market are expressed as Garman-Kohlhagen [17] implied volatilities for fixed tenors and for fixed Garman-Kohlhagen deltas. The deltas at which implied volatilities are quoted can be converted to strikes.

Our data covers options on the euro-dollar, sterling-dollar and dollar-yen rates from September 24, 2001 to June 16, 2009 and includes daily quotes at four tenors — 3 months, 6 months, 9 months, 1 year — and five strikes — the 10 and 25 put delta, the at-the-money call, and the 10 and 25 call deltas. For each of the three currency pairs, the data set consists of 20 time series, each corresponding to a fixed tenor and delta, and we have 60 such quoted time series in total.

Our data also includes domestic and foreign LIBOR rates, spot exchange rates, forward exchange rates, and the relevant option strikes calculated according to the Garman-Kohlhagen deltas, at the same calender dates as those of the option quotes. Table 1 summarizes the statistics of the data set.

5.2. *Model calibration*

We use the global optimization method of Sec. 3.3 for calibration. On each calendar date, we use quoted implied volatility curves at two relevant option tenors to calibrate the model. Within the calibration algorithm, we use the trust-region-reflective method in [8] for global optimization with the objective function being the l_2 difference between the ten implied volatility quotes, five at each of the two tenors, and those from the model-generated ones. We further supplement the objective function with a Tikhonov regularization term, see Chapter 5 of [16], in terms of the l_2 norm of the model parameters, to stabilize convergence.

The optimization algorithm is stopped when either one of the following three criteria is met: the residual norm is less than 10^{-6}, relative changes in the Jacobian of the objective function are less than 10^{-6}, or the maximum number of iterations (set at 10000) is reached.

When calculating the model-based implied volatilities, we use a 1000 by 1000 grid for numerical integration of joint transition densities against payoff functions, whenever conditional expectations are involved. On a 2.93 GHz Xeon workstation, each calibration takes 30 seconds to 3 minutes to converge, and each 2-dimensional numerical integration takes 1–10 milliseconds.

The most CPU-intensive components within the optimization process are the total number of searching iterations for the optimization to converge, the inversion of option prices to implied volatilities whenever needed, and the calculation of model prices at the second tenor given a set of tenor-dependent parameters, due to the nested nature of this step. Table 2 reports performances of all calibrations.

5.3. *Regressions*

After calibrating the model, we calculate both the model-based expected forward implied volatilities, Expt-Fwd-IV, and the model-free ones, Mdfr-Fwd-IV, at all five deltas (P10d, P15d, ATM, C25d, C10d), all three forward horizons (3-into-6 months, 6-into-9 months, and 9-into-12 months), and for all three currency pairs on a given calender day.

When calculating forward implied volatilities using today's calibrated model, we use absolute strikes from those of the future spot implied volatilities at the relevant Garman-Kohlhagen deltas. Next, we assemble time series from future spot quotes

Table 1. Summary statistics of currency option spot implied volatility quotes.

	P10d				P25d				ATM				C25d				C10d			
	Mean	Std	Min	Max	Mean	Std	Min	Max	Mean	Std	Min	Max	Mean	Std	Min	Max	Mean	Std	Min	Max
EURUSD																				
3M	10.81	3.75	5.57	28.75	10.22	3.31	5.23	25.66	10.06	3.11	5.04	24.50	10.42	3.22	5.10	25.64	11.17	3.56	5.41	28.22
6M	10.99	3.52	5.96	26.01	10.32	3.02	5.60	23.11	10.14	2.82	5.42	22.25	10.55	2.94	5.57	23.31	11.37	3.35	5.96	25.98
9M	11.09	3.40	6.06	24.73	10.38	2.87	5.66	21.89	10.18	2.66	5.55	20.90	10.60	2.80	5.79	22.00	11.48	3.23	6.25	24.96
1Y	11.18	3.37	6.23	24.36	10.41	2.78	5.76	21.10	10.19	2.57	5.61	20.00	10.64	2.70	5.91	21.12	11.57	3.17	6.42	24.21
GBPUSD																				
3M	10.20	4.48	5.66	32.61	9.47	3.80	5.23	28.86	9.13	3.34	5.00	26.00	9.29	3.21	5.11	24.57	9.83	3.34	5.48	24.32
6M	10.31	4.15	6.04	28.09	9.53	3.42	5.60	24.52	9.17	2.97	5.39	22.00	9.35	2.85	5.57	20.96	9.93	3.02	5.99	22.54
9M	10.39	4.05	6.23	27.47	9.58	3.28	5.77	23.24	9.19	2.81	5.57	20.60	9.40	2.70	5.78	20.15	10.01	2.92	6.23	22.13
1Y	10.46	4.04	6.33	27.22	9.61	3.20	5.85	22.65	9.20	2.72	5.65	20.00	9.43	2.62	5.93	19.97	10.08	2.88	6.42	22.16
USDJPY																				
3M	12.96	5.04	7.56	42.63	11.21	3.74	6.85	33.73	9.97	2.78	6.13	27.65	9.53	2.33	5.81	24.73	9.76	2.30	5.72	24.63
6M	13.08	4.68	8.08	37.22	11.08	3.22	7.14	28.08	9.71	2.26	6.36	22.05	9.24	1.89	6.00	19.34	9.48	1.95	6.01	19.36
9M	13.18	4.51	8.48	34.24	11.02	2.96	7.35	24.88	9.57	2.01	6.46	18.92	9.09	1.70	6.07	16.30	9.38	1.83	6.10	16.29
1Y	13.31	4.45	8.76	32.29	11.00	2.80	7.34	22.94	9.48	1.86	6.53	17.17	9.00	1.60	6.15	14.67	9.35	1.77	6.09	14.77

Note: The four columns under each currency pair report the mean (Mean), standard deviation (Std), minium (Min) and maximum (Max) of the quoted implied volatilities at 10-delta put (P10d), 25-delta put (P25d), at-the-money (ATM), 25-delta call (C25d), and 10-delta call (C10d). The units are absolute values of implied volatility, expressed in percentage points. The range of the data is from August 9, 2001 to June 16, 2009, consisting 2049 data points. The first column denotes option tenors under relevant currency pair and the first row denotes deltas.

Table 2. Summary statistics of model calibrations.

	Tenor T_1										Tenor T_2									
	P10d		P25d		ATM		C25d		C10d		P10d		P25d		ATM		C25d		C10d	
	Mean	Std	Mean	Std	Mean	Std	Mean	Std	Mean	Std	Mean	Std	Mean	Std	Mean	Std	Mean	Std	Mean	Std
EURUSD																				
3M6M	0.84	0.88	0.59	0.77	0.52	0.49	0.47	0.42	0.61	0.60	2.37	1.70	5.91	5.68	4.52	5.64	0.95	1.17	1.34	1.61
6M9M	0.93	1.00	0.65	0.89	0.62	0.63	0.66	0.60	0.79	0.86	1.96	1.47	4.70	4.70	3.83	4.14	1.00	0.99	1.23	1.03
9M1Y	1.01	1.04	0.66	0.92	0.60	0.69	0.69	0.64	0.89	0.93	1.53	1.25	3.76	3.92	3.14	3.39	1.06	1.35	1.09	0.89
GBPUSD																				
3M6M	1.93	1.81	1.79	1.48	0.97	0.83	0.46	0.42	1.38	1.05	0.76	1.11	1.64	3.06	1.74	2.61	1.47	1.85	0.93	1.10
6M9M	1.85	1.88	1.70	1.53	0.87	0.79	0.50	0.59	1.40	1.32	0.80	1.14	1.61	2.96	1.62	2.53	1.40	1.76	0.88	1.10
9M1Y	1.75	1.21	1.96	1.14	1.67	0.90	0.98	0.72	0.79	0.95	0.74	0.77	1.43	1.76	1.22	1.30	1.30	1.34	0.61	0.50
USDJPY																				
3M6M	0.51	0.69	0.12	0.20	0.25	0.29	0.21	0.32	0.23	0.19	0.23	0.14	0.94	0.46	0.85	0.52	0.19	0.30	0.17	0.27
6M9M	0.95	0.76	0.50	0.93	0.58	0.88	0.35	0.46	0.47	0.68	0.28	0.46	0.94	0.56	1.05	0.49	0.78	1.04	0.37	0.63
9M1Y	1.10	0.87	0.62	1.10	0.70	1.04	0.43	0.62	0.62	0.78	0.32	0.64	0.83	0.68	1.06	0.52	0.95	1.11	0.44	0.73

Note: Each column reports the mean (Mean) and standard deviation (Std) of residual errors of model calibrations in units of absolute values of implied volatilities, expressed percentage points. Residual errors are from daily calibrations from August 9, 2001 to April 8, 2009, consisting of 2000 days. At each day, implied volatility quotes from two relevant tenors (Tenor T_1, Tenor T_2), each with 5 data points at 5 deltas (P10d, P25d, ATM, C25d, C10d), are inputs to the calibration. The first column denotes the relevant option tenors with "M" denoting month and "Y" denoting "year".

(Fut-Spot-IV), the two forward ones (Expt-Fwd-IV, Mdfr-Fwd-IV), and today's spot quotes (Tdy-Spot-IV) for regressions.

In both in-sample and out-of-sample tests, we take Fut-Spot-IV as dependent variable and use Expt-Fwd-IV, Mdfr-Fwd-IV and Tdy-Spot-IV as explanatory variables. For in-sample tests, regression performance is measured by the root-mean-square-absolute-error (RMSAE) and R^2 values. For out-of-sample tests, error metrics are root-mean-square-absolute-error (RMSAE) and root-mean-square-percentage-error (RMSPE).

In-sample tests are reported in Table 3. We carry out 135 regressions: for a given forecasting horizon, delta, and currency pair, we have three individual regressions. The dependent variable is the future spot implied volatility time series and the explanatory variables are the vector series of Expt-Fwd-IV curve, Mdfr-Fwd-IV curve and Tdy-Spot-IV curve, all involving five deltas for the same horizon and

Table 3. Summary statistics of in-sample regressions.

	Tdy-Spot-IV Curve		Mdfr-Fwd-IV Curve		Expt-Fwd-IV Curve	
	RMSAE	R^2	RMSAE	R^2	RMSAE	R^2
3M6M	0.0024	0.6495	0.0022	0.6738	0.0016	0.8521
6M9M	0.0046	0.4465	0.0036	0.5394	0.0016	0.7552
9M1Y	0.0065	0.3950	0.0058	0.5167	0.0021	0.6852
P10d	0.0105	0.4826	0.0094	0.5553	0.0042	0.7098
P25d	0.0044	0.4923	0.0038	0.5692	0.0017	0.7386
ATM	0.0025	0.4995	0.0020	0.5819	0.0010	0.7622
C25d	0.0022	0.5026	0.0018	0.5880	0.0009	0.7810
C10d	0.0029	0.5077	0.0023	0.5888	0.0012	0.7842
EURUSD	0.0042	0.5383	0.0030	0.6672	0.0013	0.8474
GBPUSD	0.0042	0.5015	0.0037	0.5745	0.0017	0.7662
USDJPY	0.0052	0.4511	0.0049	0.4883	0.0024	0.6519

Note: Entries report in-sample regression performance in terms of the root-mean-squared-absolute-error (RMSAE) in unites of absolute values of implied volatilities, expressed in percentage points, and its associated R^2 values. The dependent variable is the future spot implied volatility (Fut-Spot-IV) series. The explanatory variables are vector series of implied volatility curve from today's spot one (Tdy-Spot-IV curve), the model-free forward one (Mdfr-Fwd-IV curve), and the model-based expected forward one (Expt-Fwd-IV curve) at all 5 deltas for a relevant horizon and currency pair. The first 3 rows summarize statistics according to the forecasting horizons. Each entry of RMSAE and R^2 is the arithmetic mean of 15 individual ones from regression at all 5 deltas and all 3 currency pairs for a shared horizon. The second 5 rows summarize results according to the deltas. Each entry is the arithmetic mean of 9 individual ones from regressions at all 3 horizons and all 3 currency pairs for a shared delta. The last 3 rows summarize results according to the currency pairs and the average is taken over 15 individual ones from all 3 horizons and all 5 deltas for a shared currency pair. The first column denotes the relevant groups and the first row denotes relevant explanatory variables.

currency pair. The length of data are 1934 from March 16, 2009 to September 24, 2001 for all 3M6M cases, 1868 from December 12, 2008 to September 24, 2001 for all 6M9M cases and 1802 from September 11, 2008 to September 24, 2001 for all 9M1Y cases.

All in-sample regressions are summarized into three groups according to the forecasting horizon, delta and currency pair. In the horizon group, we report the arithmetic mean of RMSAE and R^2 over fifteen individual regressions from all five deltas and all three currency pairs for a shared horizon. In the delta group, we report the arithmetic mean over nine individual regressions from all three horizons and all three currency pairs at a shared delta. And in the currency pair group, the reported RMSAE and R^2 is taken over fifteen individual ones from all three horizons and all five deltas of the shared currency pair.

Out-of-sample tests are reported in Tables 4 and 5. The dependent variables and the explanatory variables are the same as in the in-sample case.

Table 4 reports out-of-sample forecasting results from 135 one-day-ahead rolling regressions with a one year rolling window where for a given forecasting horizon, delta, and currency pair, three regressions are carried out. In the rolling regressions, both absolute volatility differences and relative percentage changes between the one-day-ahead out-of-sample forecasts and the actual ones are recorded to compute the RMSAE in absolute differences of volatility points and RMSPE in relative percentage changes.

Table 5 then summarizes the forecasting enhancements of Expt-Fwd-IV over Mdfr-Fwd-IV and Tdy-Spot-IV into the same three groups as in the in-sample case and using the same arithmetic averages.

5.4. *Observations and conclusions*

5.4.1. *Predicative information embedded in the option quotes*

Findings regarding the predictive information embedded in the liquid options are summarized below. We begin with overall observations on the predictive information in current option prices before distinguishing the relative performance of alternative predictors:

- Today's option prices do contain predicative information about future prices, and this holds true for all forecasting horizons, at all deltas, and on all currency pairs;
- Forecasts of future implied volatility are more predictive, other things equal, for shorter forecasting horizons than longer horizons;
- Forecasts of future implied volatility are most predicative for the euro-dollar pair, with sterling-dollar second, and dollar-yen last.

The first point is supported by the overall observation in the tables that a significant amount of predicative information regarding Fut-Spot-IV has been extracted from today's option quotes using all three explanatory variables. This is evidenced by both in-sample and out-of-sample tests. In the in-sample tests, 76%, 58% and

Table 4. Summary statistics of out-of-sample regressions.

	Expt-Fwd-IV Curve					Mdfr-Fwd-IV Curve					Tdy-Spot-IV Curve				
	P10d	P25d	ATM	C25d	C10d	P10d	P25d	ATM	C25d	C10d	P10d	P25d	ATM	C25d	C10d
EURUSD															
3M6M	0.75	0.57	0.48	0.48	0.54	1.50	1.10	1.02	1.20	1.70	1.75	1.25	1.13	1.32	1.92
6M9M	0.53	0.39	0.32	0.31	0.34	4.16	2.44	1.96	2.35	3.87	3.02	1.82	1.50	1.82	3.00
9M1Y	0.66	0.54	0.50	0.51	0.60	3.23	1.86	1.45	1.58	2.43	3.52	2.10	1.58	1.62	2.19
GBPUSD															
3M6M	0.50	0.37	0.31	0.29	0.30	7.29	4.03	2.68	2.48	3.09	2.18	1.37	1.06	1.05	1.27
6M9M	0.60	0.44	0.36	0.33	0.34	1.01	0.70	0.59	0.64	0.81	1.21	0.79	0.64	0.66	0.83
9M1Y	1.90	1.10	0.72	0.60	0.63	11.15	3.82	1.72	1.21	1.11	15.50	4.67	1.94	1.45	1.42
USDJPY															
3M6M	1.34	0.65	0.41	0.35	0.40	6.52	3.08	1.59	1.16	1.11	5.77	2.82	1.55	1.15	1.14
6M9M	1.28	0.75	0.53	0.47	0.51	11.50	3.21	1.19	0.83	0.86	6.41	1.98	0.94	0.78	0.84
9M1Y	1.90	1.10	0.72	0.60	0.63	11.15	3.82	1.72	1.21	1.11	15.50	4.67	1.94	1.45	1.42

Note: Entries report out-of-sample regression performance in terms of the root-mean-squared-absolute-error (RMSAE) in unites of absolute values of implied volatilities, expressed in percentage points. The dependent variable is the future spot implied volatility at each of the 3 horizons, 5 deltas, and 3 currency pairs. The explanatory variables are vector series of implied volatility curve from today's spot one (Tdy-Spot-IV curve), the model-free forward one (Mdfr-Fwd-IV curve), and the model-based expected one (Expt-Fwd-IV curve) at all 5 deltas for a relevant horizon and currency pair. Each regression uses one year rolling window and the differences between the one-day-ahead forecasts and the actual ones are recorded to compute the RMSAE. The first column denotes explanatory variables at different horizon and currency pair and the first row denotes explanatory variables at different delta.

Table 5. Summary statistics of forecasting enhancements of model-based forward implied volatilities.

	Enhancement of Expt-Fwd-IV over Tdy-Spot-IV						Enhancement of Expt-Fwd-IV over Mdfr-Fwd-IV					
	RMSAE			RMSPE			RMSAE			RMSPE		
	Expt	Spot	Ehmt	Expt	Spot	Ehmt	Expt	Mdfr	Ehmt	Expt	Mdfr	Ehmt
3M6M	0.51	1.78	1.27	35.60%	128.67%	93.06%	0.51	2.64	2.12	35.60%	149.10%	113.50%
6M9M	0.50	1.75	1.25	43.46%	115.18%	71.72%	0.50	2.41	1.91	43.46%	142.45%	99.00%
9M1Y	0.85	4.06	3.22	73.25%	267.08%	193.83%	0.85	3.24	2.39	73.25%	217.06%	143.81%
P10d	1.05	6.10	5.05	56.73%	258.08%	201.35%	1.05	6.39	5.34	56.73%	258.81%	202.08%
P25d	0.65	2.39	1.73	51.24%	179.11%	127.87%	0.65	2.67	2.02	51.24%	182.12%	130.88%
ATM	0.48	1.36	0.88	48.25%	142.73%	94.48%	0.48	1.55	1.07	48.25%	142.99%	94.75%
C25d	0.44	1.25	0.82	46.93%	134.55%	87.62%	0.44	1.41	0.97	46.93%	130.85%	83.92%
C10d	0.48	1.56	1.08	47.73%	137.06%	89.33%	0.48	1.79	1.31	47.73%	132.92%	85.19%
EURUSD	0.50	1.97	1.47	41.86%	129.86%	88.00%	0.50	2.12	1.62	41.86%	130.51%	88.65%
GBPUSD	0.58	2.40	1.82	52.07%	172.03%	119.96%	0.58	2.82	2.24	52.07%	168.91%	116.85%
USDJPY	0.77	3.22	2.45	56.61%	209.04%	152.43%	0.77	3.34	2.56	56.61%	209.19%	152.58%

Note: Entries report out-of-sample forecasting enhancements of model-based expected forward implied volatility measure (Expt-Fwd-IV), shortened to "Expt", over today's spot implied volatility (Tdy-Spot-IV), shortened to "Spot", and the model-free forward implied volatility measure (Mdfr-Fwd-IV), shortened to "Mdfr", in terms of both the root-mean-squared-absolute-error (RMSAE) in unites of absolute values of implied volatilities, expressed in percentage points and the root-mean-squared-percentage-error (RMSPE). Enhancements are summarized according to forecasting horizons (3M6M, 6M9M, 9M1Y), implied volatility deltas (P10d, P25d, ATM, C25d, C10d) and currency pairs (EURUSD, GBPUSD, USDJPY). For the horizon group, enhancements are calculated as the arithmetically average of absolute differences of RMSAE and RMSPE from table 3 over 15 individual ones across all 5 deltas and 3 currency pairs for the same horizon. For the delta group, the average is over 9 individual ones across all 3 horizons and 3 currency pairs. And for the currency pair group, it is over 15 individual ones across all 3 horizons and 5 deltas. The first column denotes the relevant groups. The left half of the table summarizes forecasting enhancements of Expt-Fwd-IV over Tdy-Spot-IV and the right half Expt-Fwd-IV over Mdfr-Fwd-IV.

50% of Fut-Spot-IV variance is explained respectively by Expt-Fwd-IV, Mdfr-Fwd-IV, and Tdy-Spot-IV, where, in each case, the results are averaged over all forward horizons, all deltas and all currency pairs. In the out-of-sample tests, 0.62, 2.53 and 2.76 volatility points, on average, in RMSAE occurred respectively using Expt-Fwd-IV, Mdfr-Fwd-IV, and Tdy-Spot-IV as explanatory variables.

The second point above is evidenced by the fact that regression performance is better at the short end of the forecasting horizons than at the long end, as one would expect. In the in-sample tests, 73%, 56% and 54% of Fut-Spot-IV variance is explained for 3M6M, 6M9M and 9M1Y respectively, each of which are averaged over all three explanatory variables, all five deltas, and all three currency pairs for a given forecasting horizon. In the out-of-sample tests, 1.64, 1.55 and 2.71 volatility points in RMSAE occurred respectively.

The third point is also evident from the regression results. In particular, we observe 68%, 61% and 53% of Fut-Spot-IV variance is explained in-sample for EURUSD, GBPUSD and USDJPY respectively and 1.53, 1.93 and 2.44 volatility points occurred respectively in out-of-sample RMSAE, each of which is averaged over all three explanatory variables and over all five deltas and all three forecasting horizons.

5.4.2. *Relative performance of forecasts*

Our findings regarding the relative merits of each of the explanatory variables on extracting this embedded inforation are summarized below.

- Model-based forward implied volatility extracts substantially more information from today's prices for prediction of future spot prices, and this holds true for all forecasting horizons, at all deltas, and in all currency pairs;
- The improvement from using model-based forecasts is greater at longer forecasting horizons;
- The improvement is greatest for the dollar-yen pair, with sterling-dollar next, and euro-dollar last.

The first point is evidenced by the observation that regressions using Expt-Fwd-IV as explanatory variable produce the largest R^2 values and the smallest RMSAE in in-sample tests and the smallest RMSAE and RMSPE in out-of-sample test, compared to those using Tdy-Spot-IV and Mdfr-Fwd-IV as explanatory variables.

In terms of in-sample performance, this enhancement of Expt-Fwd-IV over Mdfr-Fwd-IV is as large as 72% in RMSAE and 65% in R^2 across the three forecasting horizons, 55% in RMSAE and 37% in R^2 across five deltas, and finally 56% in RMSAE and 33% in R^2 across three currency pairs. Comparing Expt-Fwd-IV to Tdy-Spot-IV, this enhancement is as large as 75% in RMSAE and 91% in R^2 across horizons, 61% in RMSAE and 62% in R^2 across deltas, and finally 68% in RMSAE and 57% in R^2 across currency pairs.

Out-of-sample performance is consistent with this observation. Forecasts using Expt-Fwd-IV have the smallest RMSAE which is 0.62 in volatility points and the smallest RMSPE which is 50%, averaged over all out-of-sample forecasting horizons, all deltas and all currency pairs. The averaged RMSAE and RMSPE is 2.76 and 169% for Mdfr-Fwd-IV. And for Tdy-Spot-IV it is 2.53 and 170%. Thus on average, the out-of-sample forecasting enhancement of Expt-Fwd-IV over Mdfr-Fwd-IV is 2.14 volatility points in RMSAE and 119% in RMSPE. The enhancement of Expt-Fwd-IV over Tdy-Spot-IV and is 1.91 volatility points in RMSAE and 119% in RMSPE.

The second and third point are evidenced by the fact that the out-of-sample forecasting enhancements of Expt-Fwd-IV over Tdy-Spot-IV and Mdfr-Fwd-IV are the largest for the longest forecasting horizon (9M1Y) and are the largest for the dollar-yen pair among all three currency pairs under investigation.

Across horizons, these enhancements are 1.27, 1.25, 3.22 in RMSAE and 93%, 71%, 194% in RMSPE for Expt-Fwd-IV over Tdy-Spot-IV at 3M6M, 6M9M, 9M1Y respectively. And for Expt-Fwd-IV over Mdfr-Fwd-IV, they are 2.12, 1.91, 2.39 in RMSAE and 114%, 99%, 144% in RMSPE respectively.

Across currency pairs, these enhancements are 1.47, 1.82, 2.45 in RMSAE and 88.00%, 119.96%, 152.43% in RMSPE for Expt-Fwd-IV over Tdy-Spot-IV in EURUSD, GBPUSD, USDJPY respectively. And for Expt-Fwd-IV over Mdfr-Fwd-IV, they are 1.62, 2.24, 2.56 in RMSAE and 88.65%, 116.85%, 152.58% in RMSPE respectively.

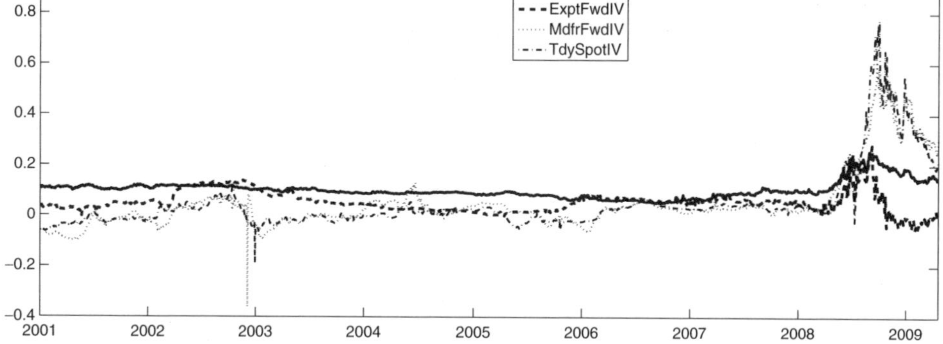

Fig. 1. The illustrative case is with respect to the euro-dollar pair (EURUSD) for 3 months-into-6 months (3M6M) forecasting horizon at 25 call delta (C25d). The picture shows time series plots of one-day-ahead one-year rolling out-of-sample forecasts using future spot implied volatility (FutSpotIV) as dependent variable. The explanatory variables are vector series of implied volatility curve at all five deltas from the model-based expected forward one, the model-free forward one and today's spot one.

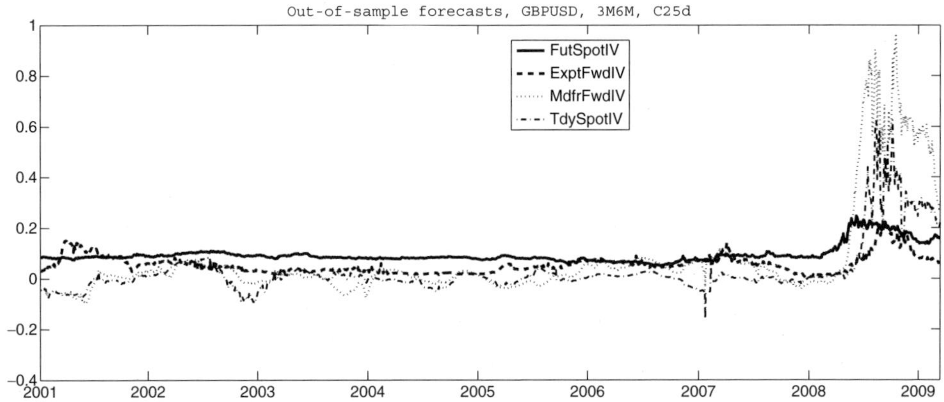

Fig. 2. The illustrative case is with respect to the sterling-dollar pair (GBPUSD) for 3 months-into-6 months (3M6M) forecasting horizon at 25 call delta (C25d). The picture shows time series plots of one-day-ahead one-year rolling out-of-sample forecasts using future spot implied volatility (FutSpotIV) as dependent variable. The explanatory variables are vector series of implied volatility curve at all five deltas from the model-based expected forward one, the model-free forward one and today's spot one.

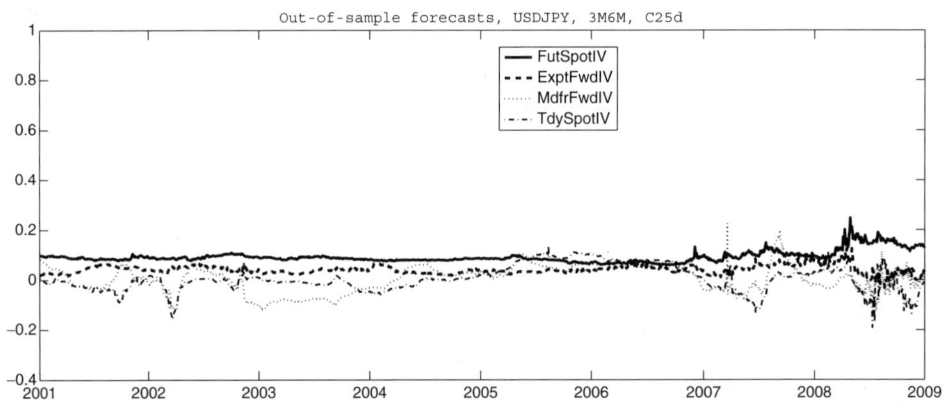

Fig. 3. The illustrative case is with respect to the dollar-yen pair (USDJPY) for 3 months-into-6 months (3M6M) forecasting horizon at 25 call delta (C25d). The picture shows time series plots of one-day-ahead one-year rolling out-of-sample forecasts using future spot implied volatility (FutSpotIV) as dependent variable. The explanatory variables are vector series of implied volatility curve at all five deltas from the model-based expected forward one, the model-free forward one and today's spot one.

As illustrative examples, Figs. 1–3 plot forecasts of 6-month implied volatility as forecast three months earlier against the actual spot 6-month implied volatility three months later. The figures show the EURUSD, GBPUSD, and USDJPY pairs, respectively, for 25 call delta options.

6. Conclusions

In this paper, we have addressed three aspects of forward implied volatility. First, we have formalized alternative definitions of forward implied volatility in the context of a stochastic volatility model, and distinguished three model-based notions that differ in the information they use from the term structure of current market prices of options. We then specialized to the SABR model and show how the asymptotic expansion of the bivariate transition density in Wu [26] allows calibration of the SABR model with piecewise constant parameters and calculation of forward implied volatility. A similar approach could be followed using the Heston model or any other tractable stochastic volatility model. We have focused on the SABR model because of its widespread use in fitting implied volatility smiles.

Finally, we have investigated empirically whether today's option prices contain predictive information regarding the future option prices and to what degree various notions of forward implied volatility extracts this information. Using currency option data, our first finding is that option prices across maturities do contain predictive information in forecasting future spot volatility. Our second finding is that model-based forward implied volatility measures extract this predicative information more effectively than a model-free forward measure and more effectively than today's spot implied volatility. The enhancement from using model-based forecasts is greater at longer horizons and greater for the dollar-yen pair than the euro-dollar and sterling-dollar pairs.

Acknowledgments

This work is supported by NSF grant DMS0914539. The authors would like to thank Credit Suisse for providing the data.

References

[1] K. I. Amin and R. A. Jarrow, Pricing foreign currency options under stochastic interest rates, *Journal of International Money and Finance* **10** (1991) 310–329.

[2] G. Bakshi, C. Cao and Z. Chen, Empirical performance of alternative option pricing models, *Journal of Finance* **52** (1997) 2003C2049.

[3] L. Bergomi, Smile Dynamics I, *Risk* April (2004).

[4] L. Bergomi, Smile Dynamics II, *Risk* March (2005).

[5] L. Bergomi, Smile Dynamics III, *Risk* March (2008).

[6] L. Bergomi, Smile Dynamics IV, *Risk* December (2009).

[7] H. Buehler, Consistent variance curve models, *Finance and Stochastics* **10** (2006) 178–203.

[8] R. H. Byrd, R. B. Schnabel and G. A. Shultz, Approximate solution of the trust region problem by minimization over two-dimensional subspaces, *Mathematical Programming* **40** (1988) 247–263.

[9] R. Carmona and S. Nadtochiy, Local volatility dynamic models, *Finance and Stochastics* **13** (2008) 1–48.

[10] P. Carr and L. Wu, Stochastic skew in currency options, *Journal of Financial Economics* **86** (2007) 213–247.

[11] R. Cont and J. da Fonseca, Dynamics of implied volatility surfaces, *Quantitative Finance* **12** (2002) 45–60.

[12] P. D. Corte, L. Sarno and I. Tsiakas, Spot and forward volatility in foreign exchange, FEA 2009 Bergen Meetings Paper (2009).

[13] B. Dupire, Pricing with A Smile, *Risk* January (1994).

[14] T. M. Egelkraut and P. Garcia, Intermediate volatility forecasts using implied forward volatility: The performance of selected agricultural commodity options, *Journal of Agricultural and Resource Economics* **31** (2006) 508–528.

[15] T. M. Egelkraut, P. Garcia and B. J. Sherrick, The term stucture of implied forward volatility: Recovery and informational content in the corn options market, *American Journal of Agricultural Economics*, February (2007) 1–11.

[16] H. W. Engl, M. H. and A. Neubauer, *Regularization of Inverse Problems* (Springer-Verlag, New York, 1996).

[17] M. Garman and S. Kohlhagen, Foreign currency option values, *Journal of International Money and Finance* **2** (1983) 231–237.

[18] J. Gatheral, Consistent modeling of SPX and VIX options, *5th World Congress of the Bachelier Finance Society*, London July (2008).

[19] J. Gatheral, *The Volatility Surface: A Practitioner's Guide* (John Wiley and Sons, New Jersey).

[20] P. S. Hagan, D. Kumar, A. S. Lesniewski and D. E. Woodward, Managing smile risk, *Wilmott Magazine*, September (2002) 84–108.

[21] P. S. Hagan, A. S. Lesniewski and D. E. Woodward, Probability distribution in the SABR model of stochastic volatility, preprint (2005).

[22] P. Henry-Labordere, A general asymptotic implied volatility for stochastic volatility models, working paper (2005).

[23] V. Piterbarg, A multi-currency model with FX volatility skew, working paper (2005).

[24] M. Schweizer and J. Wissel, Term structures of implied volatilities: Absence of arbitrage and existence results, *Mathematical Finance* **18** (2008) 77–114.

[25] P. Schönbucher, A market model for stochastic implied volatility, working paper, (1999).

[26] Q. Wu, Series expansion of SABR joint density, *Mathematical Finance*, forthcoming.

ABSOLUTELY CONTINUOUS COMPENSATORS*

SVANTE JANSON

Uppsala University, Department of Mathematics
P.O. Box 480, SE-751 06 Uppsala, Sweden

SOKHNA M'BAYE

Département de de Mathématiques
École Normale Supérieure de Cachan
61 Avenue du Président Wilson
94235 Cachan Cedex, France

PHILIP PROTTER

Statistics Department, Columbia University
New York, NY 10027, USA

We give sufficient conditions on the underlying filtration such that all totally inaccessible stopping times have compensators which are absolutely continuous. If a semimartingale, strong Markov process X has a representation as a solution of a stochastic differential equation driven by a Wiener process, Lebesgue measure, and a Poisson random measure, then all compensators of totally inaccessible stopping times are absolutely continuous with respect to the minimal filtration generated by X. However Çinlar and Jacod have shown that all semimartingale strong Markov processes, up to a change of time and slightly of space, have such a representation.

Keywords: Compensator; dual predictable projection; Doob-Meyer decomposition; credit risk; martingale; hazard rate.

1. Introduction

The celebrated Doob-Meyer Decomposition Theorem states that if X is a submartingale, then it can be written in the form $X = M + A$ where X is a local martingale and A is a unique, càdlàg increasing predictably measurable process with $A_0 = 0$. (See, for example, [27].) A non-exploding point process $N = (N_t)_{t\geq 0}$ is trivially a submartingale, and hence we know there exists an increasing, predictable

*This chapter was originally published under the same title in *International Journal of Theoretical and Applied Finance*, Vol.14, No.3, 407–432 (2011). Singapore: World Scientific Publishing.

process A such that $N - A$ is a local martingale. A special case which is of interest in the theory of Credit Risk is the case

$$1_{\{t \geq R\}} - A_t = \text{ a martingale} \tag{1.1}$$

The process A in (1.1) is known as *the compensator of the stopping time* R, by an abuse of language. It is common in applications to assume, often without mention, that A has absolutely continuous paths. That is, one often assumes *a priori* that (1.1) is of the form

$$1_{\{t \geq R\}} - \int_0^t \lambda_s ds = \text{ a martingale} \tag{1.2}$$

for some adapted process λ. The process λ is often referred to as the *hazard rate* and has intuitive content as the instantaneous likelihood of the stopping time R occurring in the next infinitesimal time interval. Of course this is not true in general, and for example in the theory of credit risk K. Giesecke and L. Goldberg have given a natural example where it does not hold [12, C3, p. 7]. The goal of this paper is to give simple and natural conditions on the generating underlying filtration to show when the compensators of *all* of the totally inaccessible stopping times are absolutely continuous; that is, to give sufficient conditions on the filtration such that they all have hazard rates.

2. Prior Results

Previous work has been restricted to giving conditions on a given stopping time in relation to the underlying filtration that ensures the compensator is absolutely continuous. Perhaps the most well known of these conditions is that of Ethier and Kurtz [9], which we restate here. One can consult, for example [27], for the definition in general of a compensator (or dual predictable projection, as it is also known) $(\tilde{A}_t)_{t \geq 0}$ of any integrable, increasing process $(A_t)_{t \geq 0}$ with respect to a given filtration $\mathbb{G}$. In particular if A is also adapted, then $A - \tilde{A}$ is a martingale.

Theorem 2.1 (Ethier–Kurtz Criterion). *Let $\mathbb{G} = (\mathcal{G}_t)_{t \geq 0}$ be a given filtration satisfying the usual hypotheses (see [27] for the "usual hypotheses.") Let A be an increasing (not necessarily adapted) and integrable cádlág process, with $A_0 = 0$. Let $\tilde{A}$ be the $\mathbb{G}$ compensator of A. If there is a constant K such that for all $0 \leq s \leq t$*

$$E\{A_t - A_s | \mathcal{G}_s\} \leq K(t - s) \text{ a.s.} \tag{2.1}$$

then the compensator of A has absolutely continuous paths, a.s. That is, it is of the form $\tilde{A}_t = \int_0^t \lambda_s ds$.

An extension of Theorem 2.1 to necessary and sufficient conditions for the $\mathbb{G}$ compensator to have such an intensity process is given in the Cornell PhD thesis of Zeng [29]. A trivial extension is to replace the constant K with an increasing predictable process $(K_t)_{t \geq 0}$, and then the inequality (2.1) becomes:

$$E\{A_t - A_s | \mathcal{G}_s\} \leq K_s(t - s) \text{ a.s.} \tag{2.2}$$

and of course the conclusion in Theorem 2.1 still holds. Zeng [29, p. 14] did a little better:

Theorem 2.2 (Zeng). *Let A be an increasing (not necessarily adapted) and integrable measurable process, with $A_0 = 0$. Let $\tilde{A}$ be the compensator of A. Then $d\tilde{A}_t \ll dt$ if and only if there exists an increasing and integrable measurable process D with $D_0 = 0$, such that $d\tilde{D}_t \ll dt$ and for all $t \geq 0, h \geq 0$,*

$$E\{A_{t+h} - A_t|\mathcal{G}_t\} \leq E\{D_{t+h} - D_t|\mathcal{G}_t\} \tag{2.3}$$

and if equality holds, then we have $\tilde{A} = \tilde{D}$.

Another observation is perhaps useful to make. Once a stopping time has an absolutely continuous compensator in a given filtration, say $\mathbb{G}$, then if it is also a stopping time for a smaller filtration it also has an absolutely continuous compensator in the smaller filtration. Actually one can obtain a more precise result, which is established in the book of Jacobsen [14]. Yor has informed us that the same result was established in 1978 [4, Proposition 3, p. 278, and comments following]. We provide here an elementary proof of this result, and *inter alia* we slightly extend the result (as presented in [14]).

Theorem 2.3. *Let R be a $\mathbb{G}$ stopping time with compensator given by $\int_0^t \lambda_s dc(s)$ for some $\mathbb{G}$ adapted process λ, where $\mathbb{G}$ satisfies the usual hypotheses. Here $s \mapsto c(s)$ is non random, continuous, and non-decreasing. Let $\mathbb{F}$ be a subfiltration of $\mathbb{G}$ also satisfying the usual hypotheses, and suppose R is also an $\mathbb{F}$ stopping time. Then the $\mathbb{F}$ compensator of R is given by $\int_0^t {}^o\lambda_s dc(s)$.*[1] *That is we have*

$$\begin{aligned} &\textit{If } 1_{\{t\geq R\}} - \int_0^t \lambda_s dc(s) = \textit{a martingale in } \mathbb{G} \\ &\textit{then } 1_{\{t\geq R\}} - \int_0^t {}^o\lambda_s dc(s) = \textit{a martingale in } \mathbb{F}. \end{aligned} \tag{2.4}$$

Proof. Let

$$M_t = 1_{\{t\geq R\}} - \int_0^t \lambda_s dc(s). \tag{2.5}$$

Then M is a $\mathbb{G}$ martingale. Since $\lambda_s \geq 0$, the optional projection ${}^o\lambda_s$ exists with $0 \leq {}^o\lambda_s \leq \infty$. For every s, $E^o\lambda_s = E\lambda_s$, and thus, by Fubini's theorem, $E\int_0^\infty {}^o\lambda_s\, dc(s) = E\int_0^\infty \lambda_s\, dc(s) = E1_{\{R<\infty\}} < \infty$. Thus, $A_t = \int_0^t {}^o\lambda_s\, dc(s)$ is an

[1]Note that for fixed s, ${}^o\lambda_s = E\{\lambda_s|\mathcal{F}_s\}$ a.s.; the optional projection gives a method to define the projection via conditional expectation for all $s \geq 0$ simultaneously. Since λ is positive, the optional projection exists. See [27] for more details.

integrable increasing continuous adapted process; in particular, ${}^o\lambda_s < \infty$ for a.e. s a.s. We define

$$L_t = 1_{\{t\geq R\}} - A_t = 1_{\{t\geq R\}} - \int_0^t {}^o\lambda_s\, dc(s). \tag{2.6}$$

If $0 \leq s \leq t$ and H is bounded and $\mathcal{F}_s$ measurable, then, by Fubini's theorem and the fact that for fixed r, ${}^o\lambda_r = E\{\lambda_r|\mathcal{F}_r\}$ a.s.,

$$\begin{aligned} E\big(H(L_t - L_s)\big) &= E\big(H1_{\{t\geq R>s\}}\big) - \int_s^t E\big(HE(\lambda_r|\mathcal{F}_r)\big)\, dc(r) \\ &= E\big(H1_{\{t\geq R>s\}}\big) - \int_s^t E(H\lambda_r)\, dc(r) \\ &= E\big(H(M_t - M_s)\big) = 0. \end{aligned} \tag{2.7}$$

Hence the uniformly integrable process L_t is an $\mathbb{F}$ martingale. This gives the $\mathbb{F}$ canonical decomposition of the $\mathbb{F}$ submartingale $1_{\{t\geq R\}}$ as $1_{\{t\geq R\}} = L_t + A_t$, and thus A is the $\mathbb{F}$ compensator of $1_{\{t\geq R\}}$. □

We include for emphasis the following obvious but important (and well known) corollary:

Corollary 2.1. *Let R be a $\mathbb{G}$ stopping time with compensator given by $\int_0^t \lambda_s ds$ for some $\mathbb{G}$ adapted process λ, where $\mathbb{G}$ satisfies the usual hypotheses. Let $\mathbb{F}$ be a subfiltration of $\mathbb{G}$ also satisfying the usual hypotheses, and suppose R is also an $\mathbb{F}$ stopping time. Then the $\mathbb{F}$ compensator of R is given by $\int_0^t {}^o\lambda_s ds$. That is we have*

$$\begin{aligned} &\textit{If } 1_{\{t\geq R\}} - \int_0^t \lambda_s ds = \textit{a martingale in } \mathbb{G} \\ &\textit{then } 1_{\{t\geq R\}} - \int_0^t {}^o\lambda_s ds = \textit{a martingale in } \mathbb{F}. \end{aligned} \tag{2.8}$$

Theorem 2.3 and its Corollary 2.1 show that once there is a filtration $\mathbb{H}$ such that a stopping time R is totally inaccessible, if R has an AC compensator in $\mathbb{H}$, then it has an AC compensator in any smaller filtration $\mathbb{G}$ as well. In particular Dellacherie's result (Theorem 2.4 below) implies that *the law of R is absolutely continuous (ie, has a density) as well.* We recall Dellacherie's result here for the reader's convenience. A proof can be found in [27, p. 120].

Theorem 2.4 (Dellacherie's Theorem). *Let R be a nonnegative random variable with $P(R = 0) = 0, P(R > t) > 0$ for each $t > 0$. Let $\mathcal{F}_t = \sigma(t \wedge R)$, the minimal filtration which renders R a stopping time. Let F denote the law of R. That is, $F(x) = P(R \leq x)$ for $x \geq 0$. Then the compensator $A = (A_t)_{t\geq 0}$ of the* *process* $1_{\{R \geq t\}}$ *is given by*

$$A_t = \int_0^{t \wedge R} \frac{1}{1 - F(u-)} dF(u).$$

If F *is continuous, then* A *is continuous,* R *is totally inaccessible, and* $A_t = -\ln(1 - F(R \wedge t))$.

One may ask if, once a compensator of a totally inaccessible stopping time R is a.s. singular with respect to Lebesgue measure, does that propagate down to smaller filtrations, and in particular does it imply that the law of the stopping time is singular as well? The next example shows that this is not true in general.

Example 2.1. Let B be a standard one dimensional Brownian motion with natural filtration $\mathbb{F}$ and with a local time at zero $L = (L_t)_{t \geq 0}$. Define the change of time

$$\tau_t = \inf\{s > 0 : L_s > t\}.$$

Then $(\tau_t)_{t \geq 0}$ is a family of $\mathbb{F}$ stopping times. We can form the time changed filtration $\mathbb{G}$ given by $\mathcal{G}_t = \mathcal{F}_{\tau_t}$ for $t \geq 0$. Let N be an independent Poisson process for a large filtration $\mathbb{H}$ that contains $\mathbb{G}$ as a subfiltration. Then the family $(L_t)_{t \geq 0}$ are stopping times for $\mathbb{H}$, and

$$N_{L_t} - L_t = \text{a local martingale for the filtration } \tilde{\mathbb{H}}$$

where $(\tilde{\mathcal{H}_t}) = (\mathcal{H}_{L_t})_{t \geq 0}$. Since L is Brownian local time at zero, it has paths which are singular with respect to Lebesgue measure, a.s. However by Tanaka's formula we have

$$|B_t| = \int_0^t \text{sign}(B_s) dB_s + L_t$$

and therefore $E(L_t) = E(|B_t|) = \sqrt{\frac{2}{\pi}}\sqrt{t}$.

Next let

$$R = \inf\{s > 0 : N_{L_s} \geq 1\},$$

and R is a stopping time for the filtration $\tilde{\mathbb{H}}$. Then $1_{\{t \geq R\}} - L_{t \wedge R} =$ a martingale for the filtration $\tilde{\mathbb{H}}$, and the compensator of R is $L_{t \wedge R}$ which inherits the singular nature of the paths of L. Since the compensator of R is continuous, R is totally inaccessible. The point of this is, however, is that the compensator of R has paths which are a.s. singular with respect to Lebesgue measure whereas the law F of R satisfies

$$F(t) = P(R \leq t) = E(1_{\{R \leq t\}}) = E(L_{t \wedge R}),$$

which is absolutely continuous, since $t \mapsto E(L_t) = \sqrt{\frac{2}{\pi}}\sqrt{t}$ is absolutely continuous. Therefore by Dellacherie's theorem the compensator of R in the minimal filtration that makes it a stopping time is absolutely continuous.

Corollary 2.2. *Let R be a stopping time for a filtration $\mathbb{H}$, and suppose there is a subfiltration $\mathbb{G}$ such that R is totally inaccessible, and that the compensator of $1_{\{t\geq R\}}$ is given by $\int_0^t \lambda_s dc(s)$ where $s \mapsto c(s)$ is non random, continuous, and non-decreasing. Let F denote the law of R. Then $dF(s) \ll dc(s)$. In particular if $c(s) = s$, then F is absolutely continuous; if $s \mapsto dc(s)$ is singular with respect to Lebesgue measure, then F is also singular.*

Corollary 2.3. *Let R be a stopping time for a filtration $\mathbb{H}$. Suppose there is a subfiltration $\mathbb{G}$ such that R is totally inaccessible, and that the compensator of $1_{\{t\geq R\}}$ is given by $\int_0^t \lambda_s dc(s)$ where $s \mapsto c(s)$ is non random, continuous, and non-decreasing. Then for any sub-subfiltration $\mathbb{F}$ where R is still a stopping time, R will still be totally inaccessible, and its compensator will be absolutely continuous with respect to dc. In particular, a compensator cannot be singular of this form for a filtration $\mathbb{G}$ and then become absolutely continuous for a subfiltration $\mathbb{F}$.*

3. Filtration Level Results

In their seminal paper of 1981, Çinlar and Jacod [6, Theorem 3.33, p. 206] showed that any $\mathbb{R}^d$ valued strong Markov process which is a Hunt process, and which is also a semimartingale, up to a change of time via an additive functional "clock," can be represented as the solution of a stochastic differential equation driven by dt, dW_t, and $n(ds, dz)$; where W is a standard multidimensional Brownian motion, and n is a standard Poisson random measure with mean measure given by $ds\nu(dz)$.

Therefore we assume as given a strong Markov Hunt process semimartingale which can be represented on a space $(\Omega, \mathcal{F}, \mathbb{F}, P^x)$ where $\mathbb{F} = (\mathcal{F}_t)_{t\geq 0}$, as follows:

$$\begin{aligned} X_t = X_0 &+ \int_0^t b(X_s)ds + \int_0^t c(X_s)dW_s \\ &+ \int_0^t \int_{\mathbb{R}} k(X_{s-}, z)1_{\{|k(X_{s-},z)|\leq 1\}}[n(ds, dz) - ds\nu(dz)] \\ &+ \int_0^t \int_{\mathbb{R}} k(X_{s-}, z)1_{\{|k(X_{s-},z)|>1\}}n(ds, dz) \end{aligned} \tag{3.1}$$

We let P^μ denote the probability measure governing X where the law of X_0 is μ, and $\mathbb{F}^\mu$ denote the filtration containing $\mathbb{F}$ but such that $\mathcal{F}_0^\mu$ contains all of the P^μ null sets. Our goal is to prove that the predictable compensator process A, of the process $1_{\{t\geq R\}}$ where R is a given but arbitrary totally inaccessible stopping time, has absolutely continuous paths a.s. The next theorem makes this precise.

Theorem 3.1. *For any totally inaccessible stopping time R on the space $(\Omega, \mathcal{F}, \mathbb{F}^\mu, P^\mu)$ the predictable increasing process A, with $A_0 = 0$, such that $1_{\{t\geq R\}} - A_t = M_t$ is a martingale, has the form $A_t = \int_0^t \lambda_s ds$ for some adapted process λ.*

Proof. It is now perhaps mostly forgotten, but most of the ingredients for the proof of this theorem are contained in an old paper of Meyer [24]; see also [23]. The idea is to recall that for each law P^μ, each square integrable martingale M with $M_0 = 0$ is null, if it is orthogonal to all martingales of the form

$$C_t^n = g_n(X_t) - g_n(X_0) - \int_0^t Lg_n(X_s)ds \tag{3.2}$$

where L is the infinitesimal generator of the underlying strong Markov process X, and the functions g_n are a suitable sequence of functions that are "nearly Borel" measurable, belong to the domain of L, and each Lg_n is bounded. Next let D^n be the sequence of (still square integrable) martingales obtained by an orthogonalization procedure under P^μ, for the sequence C^n. Let M denote an arbitrary and chosen square integrable martingale under P^μ. Then M can be represented as a sum of stochastic integrals with respect to the collection D^n, and hence $\langle M, M\rangle$ is absolutely continuous with respect to the collection $\langle D^n, D^n\rangle$, hence also absolutely continuous with respect to the collection $\langle C^n, C^n\rangle$. We next choose constants λ_n such that $E(\sum_n \lambda_n \langle C^n, C^n\rangle_t) < \infty$ for all $t > 0$, and we let

$$K_t = \sum_n \lambda_n \langle C^n, C^n\rangle_t. \tag{3.3}$$

Thus, $\langle M, M\rangle$ is absolutely continuous with respect to K.

In the case of the martingale M which is the compensated indicator function of the stopping time R: $M_t = 1_{\{R\geq t\}} - A_t$, with A continuous (which is equivalent to R being totally inaccessible), then we have that

$$[M, M]_t = \sum_{s\leq t} (\Delta M_s)^2 = 1_{\{t\geq R\}}.$$

We conclude that $\langle M, M\rangle_t = A_t$. Thus $\langle M, M\rangle = A$ is also continuous, and we conclude that $\langle M, M\rangle$ is absolutely continuous with respect to the continuous part of K. The continuous part of K, however, is a version of the continuous additive functional H of the Lévy system of X, as given in (3.4) which follows this proof.

Therefore $A = \langle M, M\rangle$ must be absolutely continuous with respect to H. Finally for a Markov process X of the type given in (3.1), because the compensator of the Poisson random measure is absolutely continuous, we know that dH_t is also absolutely continuous with respect to dt. This completes the proof. □

Remark. Theorem 3.1 gives a sufficient condition for compensators of all totally inaccessible stopping times to be absolutely continuous, within a semimartingale Hunt process framework. One might ask for necessary and sufficient conditions. The same proof plus a use of Lévy systems can provide this result, given in Corollary 3.1. The connection to Lévy systems was recently recalled in the work of Guo and Zeng [13], and examples of intensities arising in the field of Credit Risk can be found there and in their references, as well as in [12] and [19], for example. See also [18]. Examples of intensities arising in the field of Survival Analysis can be found in the book of Fleming and Harrington [10].

Corollary 3.1. *Let $X = (\Omega, X, P^\mu)$ be a semimartingale Hunt process with a Lévy system (K, H), where K is a kernel on $\mathbb{R}$ and H is a continuous additive functional, given by the following relationship:*

$$E^\mu\left(\sum_{0<s\leq t} f(X_{s-}, X_s)1_{\{X_{s-}\neq X_s\}}\right) = E^\mu\left(\int_0^t dH_s \int_{\mathbb{R}} K(X_s, dy) f(X_s, y)\right) \tag{3.4}$$

Then all totally inaccessible stopping times have absolutely continuous compensators if and only if the continuous additive functional of equation (3.4) is absolutely continuous with respect to Lebesgue measure, a.s. That is, if and only if $dH_s \ll ds$ a.s.

Proof. The representation of a semimartingale Markov process given in equation (3.1) assumes there has already been a time change, if necessary, to arrive at a Poisson random measure with compensator $ds\,\nu(dx)$. Here we are not making that assumption. The results contained in (for example) [24] and [3] show that for the additive functional H of the Lévy system, any representation such as (3.1) must have that the compensator of the corresponding "Poisson random measure" will be absolutely continuous in the t variable with respect to H. The additive functional H is not necessarily unique within the framework of Lévy systems, but any other version will be mutually absolutely continuous with respect to it. Therefore by the proof of Theorem 3.1 we have that all totally inaccessible times have compensators that are absolutely continuous with respect to dt if $dH_t \ll dt$.

For the necessity, suppose that every totally inaccessible stopping time has absolutely continuous compensator. Since C^n in (3.2) jumps only when X jumps, and the jumps of the Hunt process X can be covered by a countable collection of totally inaccessible stopping times, it follows that $d\langle C^n, C^n\rangle_t \ll dt$. Hence, by (3.3), $dK_t \ll dt$. In particular K_t is continuous and is thus a version of the additive functional H, so $dH_t \ll dK_t \ll dt$. □

A useful result related to Theorem 3.1 is the following. Jacod and Skorohod [17] define a *jumping filtration* $\mathbb{F}$ to be a filtration such that there exists a sequence of stopping times $(T_n)_{n=0,1,\ldots}$ increasing to ∞ a.s. with $T_0 = 0$ and such that for all $n \in \mathbb{N}, t > 0$, the σ-fields $\mathcal{F}_t$ and $\mathcal{F}_{T_n}$ coincide on $\{T_n \leq t < T_{n+1}\}$. We then have:

Theorem 3.2. *Let $N = (N_t)_{t\geq 0}$ be a point process without explosions that generates a quasi-left continuous jumping filtration, and suppose there exists a process $(\lambda_s)_{s\geq 0}$ such that*

$$N_t - \int_0^t \lambda_s ds = a\ martingale. \tag{3.5}$$

Let $\mathbb{D} = (\mathcal{D}_t)_{t\geq 0}$ be the (automatically right continuous) filtration generated by N and completed in the usual way. Then for any $\mathbb{D}$ totally inaccessible stopping time R we have that the compensator of $1_{\{t\geq R\}}$ has absolutely continuous paths, a.s.

Proof. By Theorem 2.2 of [17] we know that $\{R < \infty\} \subset \bigcup_{n\geq 1}\{R = T_n\}$, a.s. This implies that $1_{\{t\geq R\}} \leq N_t$. We write

$$N_t = 1_{\{t\geq R\}} + (N_t - 1_{\{t\geq R\}}) = 1_{\{t\geq R\}} + C_t \tag{3.6}$$

Let us now take compensators of both sides of (3.6), and let A denote the compensator of $1_{\{t\geq R\}}$, and $\tilde{C}$ denote the compensator of C. We want to show $dA_t \ll dt$. Then the compensators version of equation (3.6) becomes

$$\int_0^t \lambda_s ds = A_t + \tilde{C}_t \tag{3.7}$$

since taking compensators is a linear operation. Since both dA_t and $d\tilde{C}_t$ are positive measures on $\mathbb{R}_+$, it follows that $dA_t \ll \lambda_t dt$ and $d\tilde{C}_t \ll \lambda_t dt$. □

Corollary 3.2. *Let N be a Poisson process with parameter λ, and R be a totally inaccessible stopping time on the minimal filtration generated by N. Then the compensator*[2] *of R has paths which are absolutely continuous.*

A result which is related to Theorem 3.2, but does not involve a hypothesis on the filtration, is the following. For convenience we define $\Delta Z_\infty = 0$; hence $\{\Delta Z_R > 0\} \subseteq \{R < \infty\}$.

Theorem 3.3. *Suppose Z is an increasing process which has an absolutely continuous compensator*[3]*; that is, suppose there exists a nonnegative adapted process λ such that $\int_0^t \lambda_s ds$ = the dual predictable projection of Z (i.e., the compensator of Z). Let R be a totally inaccessible stopping time such that $P(\Delta Z_R > 0 \cap \{R < \infty\}) = P(R < \infty)$, i.e., $\Delta Z_R > 0$ a.s. on $\{R < \infty\}$. Then R has an absolutely continuous compensator. That is, there exists a nonnegative adapted process μ such that $1_{\{t\geq R\}} - \int_0^t \mu_s ds$ = a martingale.*

Proof. Let

$$\begin{aligned} \Lambda_1 &= \{\Delta Z_R \geq 1\}, \\ \Lambda_n &= \left\{\frac{1}{n} \leq \Delta Z_R < \frac{1}{n-1}\right\}, \quad n \geq 2, \\ Y_t^n &= 1_{\{t\geq R_{\Lambda_n}\}}. \end{aligned} \tag{3.8}$$

[2]The compensator of a stopping time R refers to the compensator of the increasing process $1_{\{t\geq R\}}$.
[3]We do not need to assume Z is adapted here, only measurable; in the literature this is known as a *raw* increasing process.

In the preceding we have used the standard notation for a stopping time R and an event Λ that

$$R_\Lambda(\omega) = \begin{cases} R(\omega) & \text{if} \quad \omega \in \Lambda \\ \infty & \text{if} \quad \omega \notin \Lambda \end{cases}$$

We have that $nZ_t - Y_t^n$ is again an increasing process, and if we observe that

$$nZ_t = (nZ_t - Y_t^n) + Y_t^n, \tag{3.9}$$

then by taking compensators of both sides in (3.9) we have, by the same argument as in the proof of Theorem 3.2, that the compensator of Y^n is absolutely continuous. Therefore we can write the compensator of Y^n as $\int_0^t \mu_s^n ds$. Furthermore, $1_{\{t\geq R\}} = \sum_{n=1}^\infty Y_t^n$ and thus the compensator A of $1_{\{t\geq R\}}$ is

$$A_t = \sum_{n=1}^\infty \int_0^t \mu_s^n ds = \int_0^t \left(\sum_{n=1}^\infty \mu_s^n \right) ds \tag{3.10}$$

by the Fubini–Tonelli theorem, and the theorem is proved. □

4. Related Results

In this section we relate the results of the preceding part of the paper to some situations that arise in Mathematical Finance Theory. Indeed, it is often the case in Finance that one begins with a system $(\Omega, \mathcal{F}, P, \mathbb{F}, X)$ and then one changes to an equivalent probability measure Q such that X is a sigma martingale (or less generally, a local martingale) under Q. We will say that a probability measure Q has **Property AC** if all totally inaccessible stopping times have absolutely continuous compensators under Q.

Theorem 4.1. *Suppose that $(\Omega, \mathcal{F}, P, \mathbb{F}, X)$ is a given system, and that there exists an equivalent probability measure $Q^\star$ (which can be P itself) such that $Q^\star$ has Property AC. If $\mathcal{Q}$ is the set of all probability measures equivalent to P, we have that Property AC holds under any $Q \in \mathcal{Q}$.*

Proof. Suppose $Q^\star \in \mathcal{Q}$, and let $R \in \mathcal{Q}$, so that R is equivalent to $Q^\star$. Let τ be a totally inaccessible stopping time, so that we can write

$$1_{\{t\geq\tau\}} - \int_0^t \lambda_s ds = \text{ a martingale, } \quad \text{under } Q^\star.$$

By the predictable version of the Meyer–Girsanov theorem (see, eg, [27, p. 135])

$$
\begin{aligned}
Z &= \frac{dR}{dQ^\star} \\
Z_t &= E_{Q^\star}\left\{ \frac{dR}{dQ^\star} \middle| \mathcal{F}_t \right\} \\
M_t &= 1_{\{t\geq T\}} - \int_0^t \lambda_s ds \\
M_t &= \left(1_{\{t\geq T\}} - \int_0^t \lambda_s ds - \int_0^t \frac{1}{Z_{s-}} d\langle Z, M\rangle_s \right) + \int_0^t \frac{1}{Z_{s-}} d\langle Z, M\rangle_s
\end{aligned}
\tag{4.1}
$$

and we have the term in parentheses on the right side of (4.1) is a martingale under R. Therefore the compensator of τ under R is $\int_0^t \lambda_s ds + \int_0^t \frac{1}{Z_{s-}} d\langle Z, M\rangle_s$, and is absolutely continuous as soon as $d\langle Z, M\rangle_t \ll dt$. We next note that

$$[M, M]_t = \sum_{s\leq t} (\Delta M_s)^2 = 1_{\{t\geq T\}}$$

since M has only one jump, and it is of size one. Since compensators are unique, this means that $\langle M, M\rangle_t = \int_0^t \lambda_s ds$, since $\langle M, M\rangle_t$ is the compensator of $[M, M]$, and it exists since $[M, M]_t \in L^1$. Moreover we also know that $\langle Z, M\rangle_t$ exists, and by the Kunita–Watanabe inequality (see, eg, [27, p. 150]) we have that $d\langle Z, M\rangle_t \ll d\langle M, M\rangle_t \ll dt$, a.s. The result follows. □

A topic that has achieved importance recently in the theory of Credit Risk is that of the Expansion of Filtrations. See, for example, [2], [7], or [20]. In the case of initial expansions, we can expand using Jacod's criterion (see [15] or [27, p. 371]) by adding a random variable L to the filtration $\mathbb{F}$ at time 0, provided that for each $t \geq 0$ the (regular) conditional distribution of L given $\mathcal{F}_t$, denoted $\Upsilon_t(\omega, dx)$, is such that $\Upsilon_t(\omega, dx) \ll \eta_t(dx)$, where $\eta_t(dx)$ is a σ-finite measure. (The key part is that $\eta_t(dx)$ does not depend on ω.) It is shown [15, 27] that we can in general replace $\eta_t(dx)$ with $\eta(dx)$ which does not depend on t. We define q_t^x to be a càdlàg martingale such that $\Upsilon_t(\omega, dx) = q_t^x \eta(dx)$. Finally, we let $\mathcal{G}_t^0 = \mathcal{F}_t \vee \sigma(t \wedge L)$, and $(\mathcal{G}_t)_{t\geq 0}$ be the completed, right continuous version of the filtration $\mathbb{G}^0$.

We return to considering the probability measure P only; the results generalize immediately to all measures $Q^\star \in \mathcal{Q}$ by Theorem 4.1.

Theorem 4.2. *Suppose we expand the filtration $\mathbb{F}$ by adding a random variable L initially, where its conditional distribution $\Upsilon_t(\omega, dx) \ll \eta_t(dx)$ for some σ-finite measure $\eta_t(dx)$. Suppose also that P has Property AC. Then P has Property AC for all $\mathbb{F}$ totally inaccessible stopping times under the expanded filtration $\mathbb{G}$. That is, for any $\mathbb{F}$ totally inaccessible stopping time R, the compensator of R when computed for $\mathbb{G}$ will still be absolutely continuous.*

Proof. Let τ be an $\mathbb{F}$ totally inaccessible stopping time and recall that $M_t = 1_{\{t\geq\tau\}} - \int_0^t \lambda_s ds$ is our decomposition for the filtration $\mathbb{F}$. Jacod's theorem [15, Théorème (2.5)] gives that, for some predictable process k_s^x and with $\langle\cdot,\cdot\rangle$ computed always in $\mathbb{F}$,

$$\langle q^x, M\rangle_t = \int_0^t k_s^x q_{s-}^x d\langle M, M\rangle_s, \quad \text{when } q_{t-}^x > 0, \quad \text{for } \eta\text{-a.e. } x,$$

$$M_t - \int_0^t k_s^L d\langle M, M\rangle_s = \text{ a martingale in } \mathbb{G}. \tag{4.2}$$

Since $M_t = 1_{\{t\geq\tau\}} - \int_0^t \lambda_s ds$ in $\mathbb{F}$, we have that the compensator of $1_{\{t\geq\tau\}}$ in $\mathbb{G}$ is again absolutely continuous, since as we saw in the proof of Theorem 4.1, $d\langle M, M\rangle_t$ is absolutely continuous. □

We have an analogous result for progressive expansions. Using the notation and results presented in [27, Chap. VI, Sec. 3], we let L be a positive random variable that avoids all $\mathbb{F}$ stopping times. That is, $P(L = \nu) = 0$ for all $\mathbb{F}$ stopping times ν. Since constants are stopping times, we note that this implies that L has a continuous distribution function. By Dellacherie's theorem (Theorem 2.4) we have that this implies L is totally inaccessible, at least in the minimal filtration that turns L into a stopping time; see further Lemma 4.2 below.

We let $Z_t = {}^o1_{\{L>t\}}$, where the o superscript denotes optional projection onto the $\mathbb{F}$ filtration. We let $A^L = (A_t^L)_{t\geq 0}$ denote the (predictable) compensator of $1_{\{t\geq L\}}$ for the filtration $\mathbb{F}$. (The process $1_{\{t\geq L\}}$ need not be adapted in order to have a compensator.) We then have that the Doob–Meyer decomposition of Z in $\mathbb{F}$ is $Z_t = M_t^L - A_t^L$, where M_t^L is defined by $M_t^L \equiv Z_t + A_t^L$.

Recall that a random time L is called an **honest time** if it is the end of an optional set. More precisely a random variable L is called **honest** if for every $t \leq \infty$ there exists an $\mathcal{F}_t$ measurable random variable L_t such that $L = L_t$ on $\{L \leq t\}$. (See, e.g., [27, p. 381–382] for more on honest times.) If L is honest, we let $\mathbb{F}^L$ be the filtration defined by

$$\mathcal{F}_t^L = \{\Gamma : \Gamma = (A \cap \{L > t\}) \cup (B \cap \{L \leq t\}) \text{ for some } A, B \in \mathcal{F}_t\}. \tag{4.3}$$

(It is easy to see that $\mathbb{F}^L$ is a filtration satisfying the usual hypotheses when L is honest, see [27, Theorem VI.17].) We note that this definition of $\mathbb{F}^L$ is not the standard one. In [27] it is called the filtration $\mathbb{G}$. The standard definition of $\mathbb{F}^L$ (which does not require L to be honest) is as follows, and to avoid confusion, we denote it $\mathbb{K}^L$:

$$\mathcal{K}_t^L = \{\Gamma \in \mathcal{F} : \text{there exists } \Gamma_t \in \mathcal{F}_t : \Gamma \cap \{L > t\} = \Gamma_t \cap \{L > t\}\}$$

(Thus $\mathcal{F}_t^L \subseteq \mathcal{K}_t^L$.) The filtration $\mathbb{F}^L$ is called the **progressive expansion** of $\mathbb{F}$ under L. We assume that L is honest, and consider the filtration $\mathbb{F}^L$. It is easy to see that L becomes a stopping time for $\mathbb{F}^L$. ($\mathbb{F}^L$ is the smallest expansion of $\mathbb{F}$ that makes L a stopping time.)

Theorem 4.3. *Let L be a positive honest random variable which avoids all $\mathbb{F}$ stopping times. If P has Property AC for $\mathbb{F}$, then for any totally inaccessible $\mathbb{F}$ stopping time τ, the compensator of τ in $\mathbb{F}^L$ is again absolutely continuous.*

Proof. We begin by assuming that τ is a totally inaccessible $\mathbb{F}$ stopping time. It is shown in [27, Theorem VI.18] that for a square integrable martingale X, its decomposition under $\mathbb{F}^L$, is given by

$$X_t = \left(X_t - \int_0^{t\wedge L} \frac{1}{Z_{s-}} d\langle X, M^L\rangle_s + 1_{\{t\geq L\}} \int_L^t \frac{1}{1-Z_{s-}} d\langle X, M^L\rangle_s\right)$$

$$+ \left(\int_0^{t\wedge L} \frac{1}{Z_{s-}} d\langle X, M^L\rangle_s - 1_{\{t\geq L\}} \int_L^t \frac{1}{1-Z_{s-}} d\langle X, M^L\rangle_s\right).$$

In our case, the $\mathbb{F}$ martingale X is equal to M, where $M_t = 1_{\{t\geq\tau\}} - \int_0^t \lambda_s ds$. But we already know that $d\langle M, M\rangle_t \ll dt$, whence again by the Kunita–Watanabe inequality we have that $d\langle X, M^L\rangle_t \ll d\langle X, X\rangle_t = d\langle M, M\rangle_t \ll dt$, and the result follows for all totally inaccessible stopping times τ. □

Theorem 4.3 shows the AC property only for $\mathbb{F}$ stopping times τ. In order to extend it to $\mathbb{F}^L$ stopping times, we need two lemmas (and an extra condition). Note that the first part of Lemma 4.1(i) is a special case of the Lemma in [27, p. 378] (with essentially the same proof).

Lemma 4.1. *Let T be a stopping time for $\mathbb{F}^L$. Then:*

(i) *There exists an $\mathbb{F}$ stopping time S such that $T \wedge L = S \wedge L$ a.s. If T is $\mathbb{F}^L$ totally inaccessible, then S can be chosen to be $\mathbb{F}$ totally inaccessible.*
(ii) *There exists a sequence $(S_n)_{n\geq 1}$ of $\mathbb{F}$ stopping times such that $[T] \subseteq [L] \cup \bigcup_{n=1}^{\infty} [S_n]$ a.s. If T is $\mathbb{F}^L$ totally inaccessible, then all S_n can be chosen to be $\mathbb{F}$ totally inaccessible.*

Proof. The process $U_t = 1_{\{t>T\}}$ is $\mathbb{F}^L$ predictable, so by [27, Theorem VI.17], there exist two $\mathbb{F}$ predictable processes H and K such that

$$U = H1_{[0,L]} + K1_{(L,\infty)}.$$

Define

$$R_0 = \inf\{t \geq 0 : H_t \neq 0\}$$

and, for rational $r > 0$,

$$R_r = \inf\{t > r : K_t \neq 0\}.$$

These are $\mathbb{F}$ stopping times. If $T < L$, then $H = 0$ on $[0, T]$ and $H = 1$ on $(T, L]$, so $R_0 = T$. If $T > L$, then $K = 0$ on $(L, T]$ and $K = 1$ on (T, ∞), so $R_r = T$ for every $r \in (L, T)$. Consequently, $[T] \subseteq [L] \cup \bigcup_{r\geq 0}[R_r]$, and the first assertion in (ii) follows by rearranging the countable set of stopping times $(R_r)_{r\geq 0}$ into a sequence $(S_n)_{n\geq 1}$.

Furthermore, if $T \geq L$, then $R_0 \geq L$, and thus $T \wedge L = R_0 \wedge L$, so the first part of (i) follows with $S = R_0$.

Now suppose that T is totally inaccessible. Each $\mathbb{F}$ stopping time R_r can be decomposed into two $\mathbb{F}$ stopping times as $[R_r] = [R_r^a] \cup [R_r^i]$ with R_r^a accessible and R_r^i totally inaccessible [27, p. 104]. Then R_r^a is also for $\mathbb{F}^L$ an accessible stopping time, and since T is totally inaccessible, $P(T = R_r^a) = 0$. Hence $[T] \subseteq [L] \cup \bigcup_{r\geq 0}[R_r^i]$ a.s. and we can replace R_r by R_r^i above. □

Lemma 4.2. *L is a totally inaccessible stopping time for $\mathbb{F}^L$.*

Proof. L is a stopping time by the definition of $\mathbb{F}^L$.

Suppose that T is a $\mathbb{F}^L$ predictable stopping time, and let T_n be a sequence of $\mathbb{F}^L$ stopping times that announces T, i.e., $T_n \nearrow T$ and $T_n < T$ for all n when $T > 0$ [27, Sec. III.2]. By Lemma 4.1, there exist $\mathbb{F}$ stopping times S_n such that $T_n \wedge L = S_n \wedge L$. Let $S = \liminf S_n$; this is an $\mathbb{F}$ stopping time. On the set $\{0 < T \leq L\}$, each $T_n < T \leq L$, so $T_n \wedge L = T_n$ and $S_n = T_n$; thus $S = T$. Further, on $\{T = 0\}$, trivially each $T_n = 0 < L$ a.s., so $S_n = 0$ and $S = 0 = T$ a.s. Hence, $S = T$ a.s. on $\{T \leq L\}$. Consequently,

$$P(T = L) = P(S = T = L) \leq P(S = L) = 0,$$

because S is an $\mathbb{F}$ stopping time. Since T is an arbitrary $\mathbb{F}^L$ predictable stopping time, this shows that L is totally inaccessible. □

We can now extend Theorem 4.3 to $\mathbb{F}^L$ totally inaccessible stopping times, but we need an extra condition.

Theorem 4.4. *Let L be a positive honest random variable which avoids all $\mathbb{F}$ stopping times, and suppose that P has Property AC for $\mathbb{F}$. Then P has Property AC for $\mathbb{F}^L$ if and only if the compensator A^L of L in $\mathbb{F}$ is absolutely continuous on $[0, L]$.*

Proof. By the Jeulin–Yor theorem [22, 13], the $\mathbb{F}^L$ compensator of L is $\int_0^{t\wedge L} \frac{1}{Z_{s-}} dA_s^L$. Hence this compensator is absolutely continuous if and only if A_t^L is absolutely continuous on $[0, L]$.

The necessity of this condition is now clear, since L is totally inaccessible by Lemma 4.2.

Conversely, suppose that this condition holds so that L has an absolutely continuous compensator. Let T be a totally inaccessible stopping time for $\mathbb{F}^L$. By Lemma 4.1, there exists a sequence $(S_n)_{n\geq 1}$ of totally inaccessible $\mathbb{F}$ stopping times such that $[T] \subseteq [L] \cup \bigcup_{n=1}^{\infty}[S_n]$. For notational convenience, let $S_0 = L$, so $[T] \subseteq \bigcup_{n=0}^{\infty}[S_n]$.

By assumption (for $n = 0$) and Theorem 4.3 (for $n \geq 1$), each S_n has an absolutely continuous compensator A_L^n for $\mathbb{F}^L$; we write $A_t^n = \int_0^t \lambda_s^n \, ds$. Let $T_n = T$ if $T = S_k$ for some $k \leq n$, and $T_n = \infty$ otherwise. Then T_n is a stopping time with $[T_n] \subseteq \bigcup_{k=0}^n [S_k]$, and it follows that T_n has a compensator B^n for $\mathbb{F}^L$ such that $\sum_{k=0}^n A_t^k - B_t^n$ is an increasing process; thus $B_t^n = \int_0^t f_s^n \, ds$ with $0 \leq f_s^n \leq \sum_{k=0}^n \lambda_s^k$; in particular the compensator B^n of T^n is absolutely continuous. It now follows by monotone convergence that B^n converges to the compensator B of T for $\mathbb{F}^L$, and thus this compensator too is absolutely continuous. □

The condition that A^L be absolutely continuous on $[0, L]$ seems, unfortunately, to be rather restrictive. As we see in Example 4.1 below, in several natural examples, A^L is, on the contrary, singular, which by the proof above implies that the $\mathbb{F}^L$ compensator of L is singular, and thus that P does *not* have Property AC for $\mathbb{F}^L$. Nevertheless, Theorem 4.3 still applies, and more generally, the $\mathbb{F}^L$ compensator of every totally inaccessible $\mathbb{F}^L$ stopping time T such that $P(T = L) = 0$ is absolutely continuous.

Problem 4.1.

(i) Does there exist an honest time L (for some $(\Omega, \mathcal{F}, P, \mathbb{F})$) such that A^L is absolutely continuous a.s.?

(ii) In particular, does there exist such an honest time for the natural filtration of a standard Brownian motion?

We note that the relatively recent work of Nikeghbali [26] makes the positive resolution of Problem 4.1 seem unlikely.

Remark 4.1. It is easily seen that A^L always is continuous, since otherwise the set of jump times would be an $\mathbb{F}$ predictable set and thus there would exist a predictable $\mathbb{F}$ stopping time R such that $P(\Delta A_R^L > 0) > 0$. But then $E(\Delta 1_{\{t \geq L\}})_R = E\Delta A_R^L > 0$ so $P(L = R) > 0$, a contradiction.

Example 4.1. Typical examples of honest times are last exit times. For a simple example, consider a standard Brownian motion B_t with its standard filtration $\mathbb{F}$, and let $L = \sup\{t \leq 1 : B_t = 0\}$. Then L is an honest time, and $P(L = T) = 0$ for every stopping time T (by the strong Markov property of B, which implies that a.s. either $B_T \neq 0$ or $B_{T+t} = 0$ for some sequence of $t \searrow 0$). Since L belongs to the predictable set $\{t : B_t = 0\}$, the compensator dA^L is a.s. supported by this set, but this set has Lebesgue measure 0, so dA^L is a.s. singular.

In fact [1, 28], a simple calculation shows that for $t < 1$, $Z_t = P(L > t|\mathcal{F}_t) = 2\Phi(-|B_t|/\sqrt{1-t})$, where Φ is the standard normal distribution function, and $dA_t^L = \sqrt{\frac{2}{\pi(1-t)}} dL_t^0$, where L^0 is the local time at 0.

Several similar examples with singular A^L are treated in [1] and [28], for example $\sup\{t < 1 : B_t \in F\}$ for a given finite set F, $\sup\{t < \tau_1 : B_t = 0\}$ with $\tau_1 = \inf\{t > 0 : B_t = 1\}$, and $\sup\{t : |B_t^{(3)}| \geq 1\}$ where $B^{(3)}$ is a three-dimensional

Brownian motion and thus $|B^{(3)}|$ is a BES(3) process (see also [11] for this exit time).

The results above are easily extended by induction to the case of the filtration $\mathbb{F}^{\{L^1,L^2,\ldots\}}$ extended by a finite or infinite, strictly increasing sequence $(L_n)_{n=1}^N$ of positive honest variables that avoid all $\mathbb{F}$ stopping times; cf. [8, pp. 190–191]. We omit the details. One could also consider a more general setting, where for example L^{i+1} is honest only for $\mathbb{F}^{L^i}$, instead of requiring it and all subsequent random times to be honest for $\mathbb{F}$, or the case where the L^i need not be required to be strictly increasing. We do not treat these cases here. The necessary theory to do so is available, however, within the book of Jeulin [21].

Acknowledgments

We wish to thank an anonymous referee for his or her careful reading of the paper, along with excellent suggestions to improve the exposition. P. Protter is supported by NSF Grant DMS-0906995.

References

[1] J. Azéma, T. Jeulin, F. B. Knight and M. Yor, Le Théorème d'Arrêt en une Fin d'Ensemble Prévisible, *Séminaire de Probabilités (Strasbourg)*, Vol. 27 (Springer-Verlag, Berlin, 1993), pp. 133–158.

[2] C. Blanchet-Scaillet and M. Jeanblanc, Hazard rate for credit risk and hedging defaultable claims, *Finance and Stochastics* **8** (2004) 145–159.

[3] A. Benveniste and J. Jacod, Systèmes de Lévy des Processus de Markov, *Invent. Math.* **21** (1973) 183–198.

[4] P. Brémaud and M. Yor, Changes of filtrations and of probability measures, *Z. Wahrscheinlichkeitstheorie verw. Gebeite* **45** (1978) 269–295.

[5] U. Çetin, R. Jarrow, P. Protter, and Y. Yildirim, Modeling credit risk with partial information, *Annals of Applied Probability* **14** (2004) 1167–1178.

[6] E. Çinlar and J. Jacod, Representation of semimartingale markov processes in terms of wiener processes and poisson random measures, in *Seminar on Stochastic Processes* (Birkhäuser, Boston, 1981), pp. 159–242.

[7] D. Coculescu and A. Nikeghbali, Hazard processes and martingale hazard processes, preprint (2009).

[8] C. Dellacherie and P.-A. Meyer, *Probabilités et Potentiel, Chapitres XVII à XXIV: Processus de Markov (fin), Compléments de Calcul Stochastique* (Hermann, Paris, 1992).

[9] S. Ethier and T. G. Kurtz, *Markov Processes: Characterization and Convergence*, 2nd edition (Wiley, New York, 2005).

[10] T. R. Fleming and D. P. Harrington, *Counting Processes and Survival Analysis* (Wiley, New York, 1991).

[11] R. K. Getoor, The brownian escape process, *Ann. Probab.* **7**(5) (1979) 864–867.

[12] K. Giesecke and L. Goldberg, The market price of credit risk: The impact of asymmetric information, Working Paper, Stanford University (2008).

[13] X. Guo and Y. Zeng, Intensity process and compensator: a new filtration expansion approach and the Jeulin–Yor formula, *Annals of Applied Probability* **18** (2008) 120–142.

[14] M. Jacobsen, *Point Process Theory and Applications: Marked Point and Piecewise Deterministic Processes* (Birkhäuser, Boston, 2005).

[15] J. Jacod, Grossissement Initial, Hypothèse (H'), et Théorème de Girsanov, *Grossissements de Filtrations: Exemples et Applications*, *Lecture Notes in Mathematics*, Vol. 1118 (Springer-Verlag, Berlin, 1985), pp. 15–35.

[16] J. Jacod and A. N. Shiryaev, *Limit Theorems for Stochastic Processes*, second edition (Springer-Verlag, Heidelberg, 2003).

[17] J. Jacod and A. V. Skorohod, Jumping filtrations and martingales with finite variation, *Séminaire de Probabilités (Strasbourg)*, Vol. 28 (Springer-Verlag, Berlin, 1994), pp. 21–35.

[18] R. Jarrow and P. Protter, Structural versus reduced form models: A new information based perspective, *Journal of Investment Management* **2** (2004) 34–43.

[19] R. Jarrow, P. Protter, and A. D. Sezer, Information reduction via level crossings in a credit risk model, *Finance and Stochastics* **11** (2007) 195–212.

[20] M. Jeanblanc and Y. Le Cam, Progressive enlargement of filtrations with initial times, *Stochastic Processes and Their Applications* **119** (2009) 2523–2543.

[21] T. Jeulin, *Grossissements de Filtrations: Exemples et Applications*, Lecture Notes in Math., Vol. 1118 (Springer-Verlag, Berlin, 1985).

[22] T. Jeulin and M. Yor, Grossissement d'une Filtration et Semimartingales: Formules Explicites, *Séminaire de Probabilités XII (Strasbourg)*, *Lecture Notes in Mathematics*, Vol. 649 (Springer-Verlag, Berlin, 1978), pp. 78–97.

[23] P.-A. Meyer, Intégrales stochastiques III, *Séminaire de Probabilités I (Strasbourg)*, *Lecture Notes in Mathematics*, Vol. 39 (Springer-Verlag, Berlin, 1967), pp. 118–141.

[24] P.-A. Meyer, Une Mise au Point sur les Systèmes de Lévy. Remarques sur l'exposé de A. Benveniste, *Séminaire de Probabilités VII (Strasbourg)*, *Lecture Notes in Mathematics*, Vol. 321 (Springer-Verlag, Heidelberg, 1973), pp. 25–32.

[25] P.-A. Meyer and J. B. Walsh, Quelques Applications des Résolvantes de Ray, *Inventiones Math.* **14** (1971) 143–166.

[26] A. Nikeghbali, Enlargements of filtrations and path decompositions at non stopping times, *Probability Theory and Related Fields* **136** (2006) 524–540.

[27] P. Protter, *Stochastic Integration and Differential Equations*, Second edition, version 2.1 (Springer-Verlag, Heidelberg, 2005).

[28] M. Yor, *Some Aspects of Brownian Motion. Part II. Some Recent Martingale Problems.* Lectures in Mathematics ETH Zürich (Birkhäuser Verlag, Basel, 1997).

[29] Y. Zeng, Compensators of Stopping Times, PhD thesis, Mathematics Department, Cornell University (2006).

CONIC FINANCE AND THE CORPORATE BALANCE SHEET*

DILIP B. MADAN

Robert H. Smith School of Business
Van Munching Hall, College Park, MD 20742, USA

WIM SCHOUTENS

Department of Mathematics, K.U. Leuven
Celestijnenlaan 200 B, B-3001 Leuven, Belgium

Markets are modeled as passively accepting a convex cone of cash flows that contain the nonnegative cash flows. Different markets are modeled using different cones that reflect the clientele of the market. Conditions are established to exclude the possibility of arbitrage between markets. Operationally these cones are defined by a positive expectation under a concave distortion of the distribution function of the cash flow delivered to market. Under conic finance firms may access risky assets and risky liabilities but regulatory bodies need to ensure that sufficient capital is put at stake to make the risk of excess loss acceptable to taxpayers. Firms approach equity markets for funding and can come into existence only if they can raise equity capital sufficient to meet regulatory requirements. Firms that are allowed to exist may approach debt markets for favorable funding opportunities. The costs of debt limit the amount of debt. Firms with lognormally distributed and correlated assets and liabilities are analysed for their required capital, their optimal debt levels, the value of the option to put losses back to the taxpayer, the costs of debt and equity, and the level of finally reported equity in the balance sheet. The relationship between these entities and the risk characteristics of a firm are analyzed and reported in detail.

Keywords: Concave distortions; clientele effects; capital requirements; taxpayer put option; liability valuation; two price markets; bid and ask prices.

1. Introduction

Financial markets are generally modeled as counterparties for market participants permitting such entities to trade in both directions, buy from or sell to the market at the going market price. Though market participants are seen as optimizing

*This chapter was originally published under the same title in *International Journal of Theoretical and Applied Finance*, Vol.14, No.5, 587–610 (2011). Singapore: World Scientific Publishing.

agents, the financial market itself passively accepts a range of so-called traded cash flows. When we analyze the behavior of economic agents in market economies, the counterparty to each transaction by an economic agent is not another economic agent, but the market. These are the basic tenets of the modeling of markets in general equilibrium as set out for example in Arrow and Hahn [1], and Debreu [7]. By virtue of accepting trades in both directions the set of cash flows acceptable to the market, at the margin, has both the cash flow and its negative being acceptable. Furthermore the sum of acceptable cash flows is also acceptable as is any positive multiple of such a cash flow. The set of cash flows acceptable at the margin is then by virtue of these properties, a linear subspace of the space of all possible cash flows. Such a model of marketed cash flows has been central to the no arbitrage theory of financial markets as described for example in Duffie [9].

The above view of markets is central to much of modern financial analysis and it is central to the law of one price and the no arbitrage theory of markets with its many implications. We modify this view of markets in just one respect. We permit what may be called the law of two prices by allowing the terms of trade with the market to depend on the direction of trade. When buying from the market one pays the ask price but when we sell to the market we receive the lower bid price. The market buys at bid and sells at ask. As a consequence the set of cash flows just acceptable to the market is no longer closed under negation. That is, the negative of an acceptable cash flow may not be acceptable. We shall, however, continue to treat it as closed under addition and scaling. With our revised view of markets we address a number of issues arising in the construction of the corporate balance sheet. Our focus in marking to market is that of marking to two-price markets as opposed to marking to markets where the law of one price prevails.

Furthermore, traditionally a corporation accesses random cash flows as assets and finances the purchase in debt and equity markets (Merton [20–22]). The firm is characterized by a nonnegative but random asset value that is unchanged by financing choices (Modigliani and Miller [23]). Debt is issued to capture tax advantages that are limited by exposure to default. Furthermore, there may be additional costs associated with bankruptcy (Leland [17], Leland and Toft [18]). We now expand this view by modeling a corporation as accessing both random cash flows as assets and another set of potentially unbounded random cash flows as liabilities. For examples one may take long short hedge funds, insurance liabilities and a variety of swap contracts. Such a model has recently been proposed in Madan [19] and studied further in Eberlein and Madan [10].

It now becomes possible that liabilities may dominate the assets and the firm cannot be permitted to exist as a limited liability entity if it is insufficiently capitalized. We follow Madan [19] and determine the required capital levels as a function of the risk structure of the firm. In this paper we model an all-equity firm as approaching in the first instance the equity market with a view to raising this required capital. We show that it is now possible that the markets in equity capital turn out to be unwilling to supply this exogenously required and predetermined level of capital. In such cases the firm cannot come into existence. Hence, contrary to the structure of firms in the Modigliani and Miller [23] model, financial markets determine the size of the real economy by a precise computation that we illustrate and demonstrate. The size of the real economy and the number of risk structures that are allowed to exist depends critically on the interaction between risk exposures, their associated capital requirements and the subsequent willingness of capital markets to fund these requirements. Our first result establishes these conditions for corporate existence.

The capital at stake is worked out in the first instance as a level of precautionary cash reserves designed to absorb potential losses. In a traditional balance sheet this level of reserves is related to the level of equity in place. Hence capital is aligned with traditional measures of equity capital. However, one of the effects of limited liability is as follows. Once a firm is allowed to exist as a limited liability entity, it accesses for free the option to put excessive losses back to the economy. Equity is now a call option even in the absence of debt and reflects the value of this put. Equity as a measure of capital is then contaminated by the value of this put option. It must be stripped of this contamination to get back to a proper measure of capital. This contamination of equity as capital is an important observation resulting from our model.

The value of this put option is an asset of the firm that should be reported on its balance sheet and is held by the equity holders. It was valued recently for the major US banks in Eberlein and Madan [10] as at the end of the calendar year 2008. Additionally, the firm may also decide to issue debt securities. In our model, unlike that of Leland [17] and Leland and Toft [18] there need not be any tax advantages to debt. Debt is issued to access favorable financing terms by designing securities that appeal to investors in debt markets. This is essentially a clientele effect that gets quantified by our two-price markets. Furthermore in our two-price markets we make explicit the costs of issuing debt. Given these explicit costs to issuing debt, described here in some detail, the extent of debt issued is limited. Our firms issue the maximum allowable debt and the optimal debt level is reached on meeting a funding constraint. Our second result defines this optimal debt level that prevails even in the absence of tax advantages.

The static model of Leland [17] has been generalized to a dynamic version by a number of authors, including Hilberink and Rogers [13], Goldstein *et al.* [12] and Chen and Kou [5]. A dynamic extension of our approach requires the use of dynamic versions of risk acceptability as described in Peng [24], Delbaen *et al.* [8], Jobert and Rogers [15] and Cohen and Elliott [4]. We leave such extensions for future research concentrating first on the static case.

Our plan is to first formally define our two-price financial markets. We then take a stochastic balance sheet seen as the joint random process for assets and liabilities and show how one may compute the capital required for existence. The second step is to determine whether the firm can exist as an all-equity firm. If it can exist, we value the limited liability option to put excessive losses back to the taxpayer or the general economy. Finally we determine the amount of debt the firm will issue.

From the inputs of balance sheet risk characteristics that describe the joint probability law of the random assets and liabilities, we determine as outputs,

- the required capital,
- the indicator variable for firm existence and if this is unity,
  - — we determine the value of the option to put losses to the taxpayer, and
  - — finally the debt level,
- the corporate balance sheet displaying the value of the taxpayer put, the explicit costs of financing and its optimal structure.

Though the required capital and the value of the taxpayer put have been defined in earlier papers, notably Madan [19] and Eberlein and Madan [10], this paper is the first to model different markets using different cones. Importantly, cones defined by concave distortions are observed to be free of arbitrage. The paper goes on to define the conditions for firm existence, optimal debt levels and provides a full description of the balance sheet for the two-price market world, where the two prices are supported by a rigorous theoretical and analytically tractable foundation.

The relevance of such marking to two-price markets and the role of potentially unbounded liabilities has been all the more enhanced by the events of the recent financial crisis. Nonetheless, the basic principles are broadly relevant quite generally. We go on to construct a variety of selectively generated bivariate Gaussian stochastic balance sheets and we report on the relationships between a firm's risk characteristics and its final balance sheet.

The outline of the rest of the paper is as follows. Section 2 describes our model for financial markets. In Sec. 3 we present the methods for computing capital required for existence. Section 4 explains how to value the option to put losses to the taxpayer if the firm is allowed to exist. The determination of the debt level is detailed in Sec. 5. Section 6 presents a typical balance sheet recognizing all the items analyzed here. The analysis of our selectively generated balance sheets is presented in Sec. 7. Section 8 concludes.

2. Modeling Financial Markets

We model markets as satisfying the law of two prices as opposed to one price. In keeping with the classical model for markets, economic agents may trade prospective cash flows with the market in any amount at the going bid or ask price. The market sells at the ask price and buys at the bid price so agents buy at ask and sell at bid. The bid price is below the ask price. Since one may trade any amount the set of cash flows that one may deposit in the market at a zero net cost as a consequence includes any positive multiple of such a cash flow. Hence this set of cash flows is closed under scaling by a positive constant. Furthermore, if two different cash flows may be deposited at zero cost in the market then one may also deposit the sum. The set of cash flows that one may deposit in the market at a zero cost is then closed under addition. It follows that the set of zero cost cash flows economic agents may deposit in the market is a convex cone. We further recognize that any agent may deposit in any market at zero cost any nonnegative cash flow. The convex cone of cash flows acceptable to a market therefore contains the set of nonnegative cash flows. Markets therefore accept at zero cost a set of risks that satisfy the axioms for acceptable risks as set out in Artzner *et al.* [2], and studied further in Carr *et al.* [3], Jaschke and Kuchler [14] and Follmer and Schied [11].

The classical market of liquid markets with its law of one price allows one to trade in both directions at the same price and so the boundary of these cash flows is closed under negation. This property makes the set of cash flows acceptable to the market a half space defined as the set of all cash flows with positive expectation under a single risk neutral and unique probability measure Q. These are the so-called positive alpha trades. Once we pass to the law of two prices we lose closure under negation for the cash flows that are on the boundary or are just acceptable at the margin. We then have just a convex cone containing the nonnegative cash flows but no longer a half space associated with one risk neutral measure.

The structure of this convex cone of cash flows acceptable to the market at zero cost may be understood more clearly on noting that every convex set is also equivalently defined by the intersection of all the half spaces that contain it. Such a result also holds for convex cones. Since our cone of acceptable cash flows contains the nonnegative cash flows, there exists a whole collection $\mathcal{M}$ of probability measures $Q \in \mathcal{M}$, with the property that a cash flow is acceptable to the market at zero cost just if its expectation is positive under each measure $Q \in \mathcal{M}$. Without loss of generality we may take the set $\mathcal{M}$ of measures to be a convex set as we may always include all the convex combinations. Every market is then defined by a convex cone of zero cost cash flows acceptable to the market, and this cone has associated with it a convex set of probability measures $Q \in \mathcal{M}$ with acceptability equivalently defined as positive expectation under each $Q \in \mathcal{M}$. We therefore refer to financial markets for the law of two prices as conic, given that they are defined by convex cones of acceptable cash flows.

We may model different markets using different convex cones of acceptable cash flows. For two markets we may have cones of acceptable zero cost cash flows $\mathcal{A}_1$, $\mathcal{A}_2$ with associated sets of measures $\mathcal{M}_1, \mathcal{M}_2$. One may then wonder if the two markets may be arbitraged by buying some cash flow at the ask price from one market and selling it to the other market at its higher bid price. Now for any cash flow X we determine the markets ask price $a(X)$ by noting that

$$a(X) - X \in \mathcal{A}$$

or equivalently that

$$a(X) - E^Q[X] \geq 0, \quad \text{all } Q \in \mathcal{M},$$

and so

$$a(X) = \sup_{Q \in \mathcal{M}} E^Q[X].$$

Similarly one shows that

$$b(X) = \inf_{Q \in \mathcal{M}} E^Q[X].$$

Now provided the set of supporting measures $\mathcal{M}_1, \mathcal{M}_2$ have a common element $\overline{Q}$ then

$$a_1(X) \geq E^{\overline{Q}}[X] \geq b_2(X)$$

and the bid price of market two is never above the ask price of market one. Hence one may employ different cones to conceptualize different markets provided the set of supporting measures have a nonempty intersection. One may show by classic separation arguments, separating $\mathcal{A}_1$ from $-\mathcal{A}_2$ that this condition for the absence of arbitrage is also necessary.

Models for arbitrage free markets may be constructed by specifying intersecting sets of supporting measures. Cherny and Madan [6] define such explicit cones that depend solely on the probability law of the cash flow being assessed. We view the market much like the Walrasian auctioneer in competitive economic analysis where a positive excess demand was not acceptable. Here a cash flow insufficiently positive to the market is not acceptable to it. The market like the auctioneer has no prior positions to consider and just focuses on the probability law and decides on the cash flow acceptability. The result is an operational first model leading to explicit rules for the construction of balance sheets and the necessary disparate valuations of assets and liabilities. More complex cones of acceptability may subsequently be constructed but they would preserve many of the qualitative properties for corporate balance sheets described here.

For the explicit construction of such cones of based on the probability law one may proceed by linking acceptability to a positive expectation under a concave distortion of its distribution function. One may take any concave distribution function on the unit interval $\Psi(u)$, $0 \leq u \leq 1$ and define a random variable X with distribution function $F(x)$ to be acceptable provided

$$\int_{-\infty}^{\infty} x d\Psi(F(x)) \geq 0.$$

In this case the set of supporting measures consist of all equivalent probabilities with densities Z such that

$$E[(Z-a)^+] \leq \Phi(a), \quad \text{for all } a \geq 0$$

where $\Phi(a)$ is the conjugate of Ψ,

$$\Phi(a) = \sup_{u \in [0,1]} (\Psi(u) - ua).$$

Alternatively Cherny and Madan [6] show that once attention is restricted to the distribution function or its inverse then the set of supporting measures may be described as densities on the unit interval with distortion bounded anti derivatives.

Cherny and Madan [6] introduced parametric families of distortions $\Psi^{\gamma}(u)$, that define a decreasing sequence of cones as one raises γ with the limit as γ goes to infinity being just the nonnegative cash flows. Observing that expectations under concave distortions are also expectations under the measure change $\Psi^{\gamma\prime}(F(x))$ they suggested that for x tending to negative infinity and $F(x)$ tending to zero, one should induce loss aversion by ensuring that $\Psi^{\gamma\prime}(u)$ tends to infinity as u tends to zero. Similarly as x tends to positive infinity and u tends to unity one should ensure against being enticed by large gains by requiring that $\Psi^{\gamma\prime}(u)$ tends to zero. A suggested distortion that has these properties is the distortion termed *minmaxvar* for which

$$\Psi^{\gamma}(u) = 1 - (1 - u^{\frac{1}{1+\gamma}})^{1+\gamma}.$$

We generalize this distortion to a two parameter one that allows different rates of convergence to infinity and zero at the left and right end points of the unit interval defined by

$$\Psi^{\lambda,\gamma}(u) = 1 - (1 - u^{\frac{1}{1+\lambda}})^{1+\gamma}.$$

For this distortion the rate of loss aversion is determined by λ while the absence of gain enticement is controlled by γ. We call this distortion *minmaxvar*2 for its two parameters. We could model different markets using different levels of loss aversion and absence of gain enticement. However, we have to enquire first whether the sets of supporting measures associated with different distortions have a nonempty intersection, thereby ensuring the absence of arbitrage opportunities between markets.

For this we first show how one evaluates bid and ask prices using distortions. For the bid price one must have that

$$Y = X - b$$

is acceptable. This requires that

$$\int_{-\infty}^{\infty} y d\Psi(F_Y(y)) \geq 0.$$

Note now that

$$F_Y(y) = F_X(y + b)$$

and so we must have that

$$\int_{-\infty}^{\infty} y d\Psi(F_X(y + b)) = \int_{-\infty}^{\infty} (x - b) d\Psi(F_X(x)) \geq 0,$$

or that

$$b(X) = \int_{-\infty}^{\infty} x d\Psi(F_X(x)).$$

From the relationship between suprema and infima we observe that

$$\begin{aligned} a(X) &= -b(-X) \\ &= -\int_{-\infty}^{\infty} x d\Psi(F_{(-X)}(x)). \end{aligned}$$

Let $\Psi(u)$ be a distortion. Suppose we have another distortion $\widetilde{\Psi}(u)$. Now if there exists a distribution function of a random variable X, $F(x)$ such that we may buy this random variable at the ask price for Ψ and sell to $\widetilde{\Psi}$ at the bid for a profit then we have an arbitrage. Let a denote the ask price of Ψ while b is the bid for $\widetilde{\Psi}$. For $a < b$ we have arbitrage.

Now the bid and ask prices for $\widetilde{\Psi}, \Psi$ are respectively (noting that $F_{(-X)}(x) = 1 - F(-x)$)

$$b = \int_{-\infty}^{\infty} x d\widetilde{\Psi}(F(x))$$

$$a = -\int_{-\infty}^{\infty} x d\Psi(1 - F(-x))$$

We may also write that

$$b = \int_0^1 F^{-1}(u)\widetilde{\Psi}'(u)du$$

while

$$\begin{aligned} a &= \int_0^1 F^{-1}(1-u)\Psi'(u)du \\ &= \int_0^1 F^{-1}(u)\Psi'(1-u)du. \end{aligned}$$

Let $G(u) = F^{-1}(u)$ and note that G is an increasing function. We may write the difference between ask and bid prices as

$$\begin{aligned} a - b &= \int_0^1 G(u)(\Psi'(1-u) - \widetilde{\Psi}'(u))du \\ &= -\int_0^1 G'(u)(1 - \Psi(1-u) - \widetilde{\Psi}(u))du \\ &\geq 0 \end{aligned}$$

The last inequality follows on noting that for all concave distortions $\Psi(u) \geq u$ and so $\Psi(1-u) + \widetilde{\Psi}(u) \geq 1$. Hence we have established the following proposition.

Proposition 2.1. *The set of measures supporting concave distortions have a nonempty intersection and arbitrage is excluded when modeling different markets using different concave distortions.*

Our model for corporate entities in real economies sees the corporations as interacting with a variety of stakeholders. Corporations have a multitude of complementary and competing interests at issue with a variety of stakeholders. We quote from John and Senbet [16], "The pay-off structure of the claims of different classes of stakeholders are different. The degree of alignment of interests with those of the agents in the firm who control the major decisions in the firm are also different. This gives rise to potential conflicts among stakeholders, and these incentive conflicts have come to be known as "agency (principal-agent) problems." Left alone, each class of stakeholders pursues its own interest which may be at the expense of other stakeholders. We can classify agency problems on the basis of conflicts among particular parties to the firm, such as conflicts between stockholders (principals) and management (agent) ("managerial agency" or "managerialism"), between stockholders (agents) and bondholders ("debt agency"), between the private sector (agent) and the public sector ("social agency"), and even between the agents of the public sector (e.g. regulators) and the rest of society or taxpayers ("political agency")."

We distinguish in our study and formulation of a corporation four separate stakeholders, the stockholders, the debtholders, the firm itself or its internal managers and decision makers, and the external taxpayer who provides limited liability to the firm even if it was debt free. We take the view that the counterparties of the corporation are not particular stockholders, bondholders, managers, and taxpayers but stock markets, bond markets, markets for managerial talents and markets for the creation of limited liability entities. Each of these markets decides on the residual risks it will hold as appropriate and these are given by potentially different convex cones of random variables that we denote by $\mathcal{A}_S$, $\mathcal{A}_D$, $\mathcal{A}_M$, and $\mathcal{A}_T$.

By modeling the counterparties as passive markets ready to trade on prespecified terms that vary with the trade direction we essentially abstract from agency problems and game theoretic issues studied extensively in the corporate finance literature. This is in keeping with classical competitive analysis where markets announce the terms of trade and agents optimize without concern for being gamed by an impersonal market. The relevance of such a construction depends on the relative atomicity of individuals in markets. We therefore focus our attention on the balance sheet issues of competitive markets as opposed to strategic issues analyzed elsewhere.

We take all four cones to be determined by different parameter settings for the distortion *minmaxvar*2. The taxpayers have the most loss aversion and the highest absence of gain enticement and we suppose that for them $\gamma = \lambda = 0.75$. The managers of a firm we take to be somewhat more tolerant of losses than taxpayers but they are induced by gains and so we suppose $\lambda = 0.5$ and $\gamma = 0.25$. The debt holders are tolerant of losses but unlike equity holders and firm managers they are not enticed by gains and prefer to see their principal back. They have a cone with $\lambda = 0.1$ but $\gamma = 0.2$. Equity holders however are both tolerant of losses and enticed by gains with $\gamma = \lambda = 0.025$.

In this way we formulate the widest cone for the equity market which will deliver the highest bid prices and the lowest ask prices and the smallest spreads. However for claims like bonds with a bounded up side the debt market may offer better valuations. For example for a geometric Brownian motion model for the underlying value process with a 20% volatility and a one year maturity the equity market provides a liability valuation for a 100 dollar face value bond at the ask price of 88 for a 5% interest rate. The debt market gives a corresponding ask price of 91.47. These market valuations capture through the varied cones the preferences of different markets for different securities as expressed in the bid and ask prices they then offer.

We now have a complete specification of the four markets the corporation has to interact with and we can compute the bid and ask prices for cash flows traded in each market. We may write all prices as distorted expectations of cash flows and we abbreviate and write

$$de(X, \lambda, \gamma) = \int_{-\infty}^{\infty} x d\Psi^{\lambda,\gamma}(F_X(x)).$$

3. Determining Required Capital

We have remarked that the classic Mertonian firm has no need for capital reserves as the value of the option to put losses back on the taxpayer or economy is zero by construction. The worst that happens is that assets go to zero wiping out debt and equity holders but there are no adverse consequences for the general economy. Debt holders may worry about there being sufficient equity capital as a reserve protecting against their loss exposure. Our concern is not with protecting debt holders and nor should this be the concern of regulatory bodies.

We recognize that corporations may access random and potentially unbounded liabilities with the possibility that come year end, or whatever suitable horizon one works with, we find that the random liabilities exceed assets in place and losses either fall on counterparties in the economy who are not made whole, or there is an explicit bail out with counterparties being made whole by the general taxpayer and then the losses fall uniformly across the community of taxpayers. Every limited liability entity accessing random and potentially unbounded liabilities should ensure that there is a sufficient stake up front from the organizers of the enterprise or else the enterprise should not be allowed to exist and get the limited liability status.

The up-front stake is reserve cash capital whose purpose is to cover losses if and when they should arise. The regulatory body granting the limited liability has to consider the total cash flow that is being accessed and this should be acceptable to taxpayers. For random assets $A(T)$ and random liabilities $L(T)$ with a capital stake of M^* we have to ensure that

$$M^* e^{rT} + A(T) - L(T) \in \mathcal{A}_T.$$

A simple computation reveals (see Madan [19]) that

$$M^* = -e^{-rT} de(A(T) - L(T), \lambda_T, \gamma_T). \tag{3.1}$$

Given a model for the evolution of the random or stochastic components of the balance sheet or the joint law for $A(T)$, $L(T)$ and the parameters of the taxpayer cone one may determine the capital M^* that must be placed at stake to get the limited liability license from the taxpayers making the proposed business generally economically acceptable. From the viewpoint of the general economy the base law for $A(T), L(T)$ to be distorted is a risk neutral law for one has to ensure at a minimum a positive expectation after risk compensation. Hence we shall define acceptability by distorting risk neutral laws. The actual funds the firm has to raise in the capital markets will turn out to exceed

$$M^* + A(0) - L(0).$$

By way of a simple example helpful in illustrating the issues involved consider the model of geometric Brownian motion for the random assets and liabilities with correlated Brownian motions. Risk neutrally we suppose that

$$\begin{aligned} A(t) &= A(0)e^{rt+\sigma_A W_A(t) - \frac{\sigma_A^2}{2}t} \\ L(t) &= L(0)e^{rt+\sigma_L W_L(t) - \frac{\sigma_L^2}{2}t} \\ dW_A dW_L &= \rho dt \end{aligned}$$

For an annual horizon ($T = 1$) with equal volatilities of 25% , a 50% correlation, an interest rate of 3% and starting values of 100, 90 for assets and liabilities we determine M^* for the taxpayer cone parameters $\lambda = \gamma = 0.75$ at 17.2399 dollars as per equation (3.1). The capital to be raised in the markets for this firm to exist or start operations is then 27.2399.

4. Firm Existence and the Value of the Taxpayer Put

Though required capital and the value of the taxpayer put have been defined in earlier work, the question of equity markets granting existence to a firm by agreeing to fund the required capital is addressed here for the first time. We begin by considering first the possibility of an all-equity firm approaching the equity markets for funding. The equity market has high tolerance for losses and may be easily enticed by gains. For this reason we model the equity market with a wide cone and $\lambda_S = \gamma_S = 0.025$. We could take zero values and then we have a single risk neutral measure and no bid ask spread. We allow for a small spread and relate this spread to the cost of entering financial markets. In a liquid market there are no costs to entering the market as the round trip cost is zero given that we trade in both directions at the same price. For markets with two prices, bid and ask, defined by cones of acceptable cash flows you sell to market at bid but you have to buy back at ask and the difference is a cost that must be funded up-front. The difference may be held as cash reserves in recognition of the expected cost of reversing the trade.

These costs address the separate treatment of assets and liabilities when transacting in two-price markets. On the asset side one unwinds by selling to market and one receives the bid price. On the liability side however one unwinds by buying from market and this takes place at the ask price. Hence all assets are to be marked at their bid prices while all liabilities are to be marked at their ask prices. When we issue liabilities like stocks or bonds we receive for them the bid price, but we mark then up to the ask price we expect to pay for an unwind. The difference is a cost we incur and hold as reserve.

The firm approaches the equity market with a final limited liability cash flow of $V(T)$, for a maturity of say $T = 5$, where

$$V(T) = (M^* e^{rT} + A(T) - L(T))^+.$$

The bid price from the equity market is given by

$$bJ = de(V(T), \lambda_S, \gamma_S)$$

while the ask price will be

$$aJ = -de(-V(T), \lambda_S, \gamma_S).$$

We receive bJ but mark the liability at aJ and the funds raised must provide us with

$$M^* + A(0) - L(0) + aJ - bJ.$$

Our conditions for firm existence are then as follows.

Proposition 4.1. *The all-equity firm can come into existence provided*

$$M^* + A(0) - L(0) + aJ - bJ \leq bJ. \tag{4.1}$$

We mentioned in the last section that the funds required would exceed $M^* + A(0) - L(0)$ and the excess is the cost of equity measured by $aJ - bJ$.

If the equity market is perfectly liquid and satisfies the law of one price then $aJ - bJ = 0$ and bJ is the risk neutral price of $V(T)$ that is a call option on $A(T) - L(T)$ with strike $-M^* e^{rT}$. The value of this call exceeds the intrinsic value of $M^* + A(0) - L(0)$ by the value of the option to put losses back to the economy and so the firm will have sufficient capital and it can come into existence. Non existence requires a conic equity market with a positive spread between aJ and bJ. As one reduces the size of the equity market cone, the spread $aJ - bJ$ rises while bJ falls and we expect that for any prespecified capital level one has nonexistence if the equity market gets too conservative. In general with fairly liquid equity markets, one may set conservative capital requirements and the equity market will fund the firm. There is then not much conflict between regulatory capital requirements and the equity market. However one should be careful about such a leniency offered by liquid equity capital markets as the approval is actually coming from a leveraging of the limited liability put built into the liquid stock price. More on this shortly. From this perspective some conic structure in equity market cones is a desirable feature.

For our example, we have $bJ = 35.4621$ and $aJ = 39.0824$ and the left hand side of the above inequality is 30.8602. As a result the all-equity firm can come into existence. On the other hand if equity markets were more averse to losses and less responsive to gains with $\lambda_S = 0.05$, $\gamma_S = 0.05$ then $bJ = 33.8428$ and the left hand side is 34.5178 and the equity market will not fund the firm at the required level. Hence the firm has insufficient funds to come into existence.

We believe we are the first in providing conditions for firm existence that interact risk exposures, with regulatory capital requirements and the funding appetites of equity markets. We ask and answer the important question of when an all-equity firm has possibly insufficient equity to continue operations. In this regard we make clear that though our conditions appear as conditions for cash reserves and not equity as traditionally defined, we are in fact speaking of traditional equity. This is seen by considering the case of a balanced fund with $A(0) = L(0)$, a liquid equity market with $aJ = bJ$, in which case we have $aJ = J = bJ = M^*$ and the so called cash reserve is the equity.

Interestingly we address the question of insufficient equity in the absence of debt. This is because limited liability brings to the table creditor counterparties and other stakeholders like workers pensions who face a loss of value when the limited liability kicks in. It is a weak point to argue that all these counterparties voluntarily entered into contracts with a party subject to credit risk and they should have, could have or would have priced this risk into their contracts. Therefore they took a bet and in this case they lost, so why worry about it. The same goes for losses put by equity holders to debt holders, so why worry about it. In fact the same goes for charlatans issuing stock with theft being the only business in mind. The protection of properly functioning capital markets requires that we not allow a widespread distribution of high value puts for free. Furthermore, having a sufficient equity stake actually meant putting up funds to back losses and not putting up inflated stock prices coming out of high risk investments leveraging the firm's limited liability put option. Equity capital is not just a stock price. In fact it should be stripped of any implied value of the limited liability put. This put is not the asset whose value we seek to maximize, and its value is in the stock price. In a more dynamic context generalizations of our principles would lead to conditions requiring on occasion the closure of all-equity entities as insufficiently capitalized for the risk exposures undertaken. What we present here are the beginnings of a framework for corporate existence.

Given existence, the firm acquires for free the option to put excessive losses back to the taxpayer. This option has the payoff

$$(-M^* e^{rT} - A(T) + L(T))^+.$$

This option is an asset of the firm to be valued at the bid price for the market to which it could be sold. If we temporarily suppose that this is the equity market, the bid price is 9.8789. We later relax this assumption in Sec. 7 where we construct the reported balance sheet.

5. Determining Debt Levels

If a firm cannot exist as an all-equity firm, we show later under conservative assumptions that it cannot exist by issuing debt as well. This is an important result for when its conditions are in place one has a built in stop to existence shopping. The question of managing to raise the required funds by partitioning cash flows into a variety of structures and raising the money from partitioned clienteles is then curtailed. Of course the details for such shopping prohibitions and their interactions with a variety of structures and their market cones is a subject for a detailed future study. Here we just consider the traditional debt and equity markets. There are also various forms of debt and we consider just one. Assuming we have a firm that can exist as an all-equity firm, we consider debt issues of pure discount bonds with a face value F and maturity of $T = 5$ years. On a debt issue of face value F the cash flow to bond holders is

$$CFD = \min(V(T), F)$$

while equity holders receive

$$JD = (V(T) - F)^+.$$

The bid prices for these securities in the bond and equity markets are

$$\begin{aligned} bD &= de(CFD, 0.1, 0.2) \\ bJD &= de(JD, 0.025, 0.025) \end{aligned}$$

while the ask prices are

$$\begin{aligned} aD &= -de(-CFD, 0.1, 0.2) \\ aJD &= -de(-JD, 0.025, 0.025) \end{aligned}$$

For a debt issue at level F the funds raised must cover the cost of such an issue and we require that

$$M^* + A(0) - L(0) + aJD - bJD + aD - bD \leq bD + bJD. \tag{5.1}$$

We first note that if the equity and debt markets had the same cone of acceptable risks then the bid and ask prices for debt bD, aD and equity with debt, bJD, aJD add up to the corresponding all-equity prices bJ, aJ. There are then no advantages to issuing debt when evaluated at the bid or the ask. In general as the bid prices are computed as an infimum over expectations taken with respect to a set of measures and ask prices are supremums we have that

$$bD + bJD \leq bJ$$

$$aD + aJD \geq aJ$$

When the cones are the same in both the debt and equity markets we may observe the required equalities as follows. Let $X = CFD$ and $Y = JD$. The distribution function of $J = X + Y$ for values $a < F$ is just $F_Y(a)$. Hence we note that for $a < F$,

$$F_J(a) = F_Y(a).$$

For values $a > F$ the probability that

$$\begin{aligned} P(V = X + Y < a) &= P(X < a - F) \\ &= F_X(a - F) \end{aligned}$$

Hence we have that

$$\begin{aligned} bJ &= \int_0^F a d\Psi(F_Y(a)) + \int_F^\infty a d\Psi(F_X(a - F)) \\ &= \int_0^F a d\Psi(F_Y(a)) + \int_0^\infty (F + x) d\Psi(F_X(x)) \\ &= \int_0^F a d\Psi(F_Y(a)) + F(1 - \Psi(F_Y(F_-))) + \int_0^\infty x d\Psi(F_X(x)) \\ &= bD + bJD. \end{aligned}$$

A similar argument supports the additivity of ask prices under the same cone.

When the cone of the debt market is smaller and the set of supporting measures larger than for the equity market the sum of the bid prices for debt and equity with debt will be lower than the all-equity bid price and similarly the sum of the ask prices will be larger than aJ. Now the value of a firm is the cost of acquiring the firm or a comparable firm. This value is given by the ask prices and we value all our liabilities, debt and equity at the ask prices. From this perspective there is an advantage to issuing debt and appealing to the higher pricing of liabilities in the debt market with a view to raising the value of the firm. The amount of debt one can issue is however limited by the constraint (5.1) as eventually the cost of debt rises and one hits the boundary of the constraint with insufficient funds available to cover the reserve costs of debt issue.

Proposition 5.1. *When the debt market is more conservative than the equity market as represented by a debt market distortion $\widetilde{\Psi}(u)$ that everywhere dominates the equity market distortion $\Psi(u)$ then the firm value measured by the sum of aD plus aJD is increasing in the face value of debt. Hence the optimal debt is defined by equality*

$$M^* + A(0) - L(0) + aJD - bJD + aD - bD = bD + bJD. \tag{5.2}$$

This result displays optimal debt in the absence of tax advantages. The advantage to debt arises from the clientele effects of debt markets modeled by strictly more conservative cones.

We shall now use the fact that for positive random variables X with distribution function $G(x)$ the bid and ask prices, $b(X)$, $a(X)$ respectively are

$$b(X) = \int_0^\infty (1 - \Psi(G(x)))dx$$

$$a(X) = \int_0^\infty \Psi(1 - G(x))dx.$$

To observe that firm value increases with the face value of debt offered we note that the ask price of debt for a face value F and a firm value distribution function $H(v)$ and density $h(v)$ is given by

$$aD(F) = \int_0^F \widetilde{\Psi}(1 - H(v))dv$$

while the ask price of equity given debt is

$$aJD(F) = \int_0^\infty \Psi(1 - H(F + v))dv$$

The derivative of firm value with respect to the face value of debt is

$$\begin{aligned} aD'(F) + aJD'(F) &= \widetilde{\Psi}(1 - H(F)) + \int_0^\infty \Psi'(1 - H(F + v))h(F + v)dv \\ &= \widetilde{\Psi}(1 - H(F)) - \Psi(1 - H(F)) \\ &\geq 0 \end{aligned}$$

where the last inequality follows from the assumption of debt markets being more conservative.

We define by $g(F)$ the funding gap for debt at face value F as

$$g(F) = M^* + A(0) - L(0) + aD(F) + aJD(F) - 2(bD(F) + bJD(F)).$$

For an all-equity firm that is allowed to exist we have that

$$g(0) < 0.$$

We now observe that the derivative of this funding gap is positive as

$$\begin{aligned} g'(F) &= aJD'(F) + aD'(F) - 2(bD'(F) + bJD'(F)) \\ &= \widetilde{\Psi}(1 - H(F)) - \Psi(1 - H(F)) - 2(1 - \widetilde{\Psi}(H(F)) - (1 - \Psi(H(F))) \\ &= \widetilde{\Psi}(1 - H(F)) - \Psi(1 - H(F)) + \widetilde{\Psi}(H(F)) - \Psi(H(F)) \\ &\geq 0. \end{aligned}$$

It follows that if the funding gap is initially positive at zero debt it will grow as debt is introduced and so if a firm cannot exist as an all-equity firm, it cannot exist with positive debt. Furthermore, for a firm that is allowed to exist with a negative initial funding gap at zero debt, there will be at most one solution to the equation for a zero funding gap as the derivative is universally positive. We also observe that as F tends to infinity the funding gap tends to

$$g(\infty) = M^* + A(0) - L(0) + \int_0^\infty \widetilde{\Psi}(1 - H(v))dv - 2\int_0^\infty (1 - \widetilde{\Psi}(H(v)))dv.$$

This is the funding gap for financing as an all-equity firm in the debt market and we suppose this funding gap is positive for a sufficiently conservative debt distortion $\widetilde{\Psi}$.

Proposition 5.2. *Assuming the funding is negative at zero debt at infinity there is exactly one solution to the equation for a zero funding gap and we have a formula for the optimal debt F^* in terms of the distribution function of firm value given by*

$$M^* + A(0) - L(0) + \int_0^{F^*} \widetilde{\Psi}(1 - H(v))dv + \int_0^\infty \Psi(1 - H(F^* + v))dv$$
$$= 2[\int_0^{F^*} (1 - \widetilde{\Psi}(H(v)))dv + \int_0^\infty (1 - \Psi(H(F^* + v)))dv]. \quad (5.3)$$

In our example the highest level of debt that can be funded is a face value of 23. At this level the ask price of the debt security is 14.3752 and the value of equity with debt at this level is 26.2107. The increase in the value of the firm is 1.5035.

6. Balance Sheet Construction

We now present the construction of the balance sheet to be reported. We begin with the complete markets balance sheet with all items valued under the single risk neutral measure and the value of the tax payer put recognized as an asset of the firm. In this case we have for the assets, $M + A_0 + P$ where P is the value of the put option. On the liability side we have L_0 and the value of the all-equity firm J or equivalently in the presence of debt we write the value of debt D and the value of equity with debt JD. The balance sheet reflects the equality

$$M + A_0 + P = L_0 + D + JD. \quad (6.1)$$

We next recognize that in our incomplete markets the debt and equity are carried on the books at the ask price for their respective markets and their cones. These are the cones $\mathcal{A}_D$, $\mathcal{A}_S$. We have to raise the extra funds in reserves and this is accomplished by adding the difference between the mark and the complete market value to both sides of equation (6.1) to get the equality

$$M + aD - D + aJD - JD + A_0 + P = L_0 + aD + aJD. \quad (6.2)$$

However, both the debt and equity markets deliver their bid prices instead of the complete markets value. We thus add the difference to cash reserves for the assets and to equity for the liabilities.

Proposition 6.1. *In two-price markets with regulatory capital and reserve requirements the corporate balance sheet reflects the equity level JR and the following equality,*

$$M + aD - bD + aJD - bJD + A_0 + P = L_0 + aD + JR$$
$$JR = aJD + D - bD + JD - bJD.$$

The value of equity plus debt equals net assets plus cash reserves made up of externally required capital plus reserves associated with the cost of financing, and the value of the tax payer put.

We now make a final adjustment to the value of the taxpayer put. Currently it stands as valued at the base risk neutral measure. We illustrated earlier in Sec. 4, a value taken at the bid price for the equity market cone $\mathcal{A}_S$. However, this put option is not an explicitly traded contract in the equity market. It comes into existence when the firm is created by its owner managers who then organize the financing structure. The value one may realize for it may then have to come from the managerial market where the cones are narrower and the bid price in this market could be lower. If we mark this put option value down to its managerial bid price then we reduce the reported equity down by the mark down in this put option value. This value is given in our example by 3.8490. The complete markets value was 10.7166.

Proposition 6.2. *If the option to put losses back into the economy is valued in the managerial market with a wider cone then the reported equity is*

$$aJD + D - bD + JD - bJD - (P - bP)$$

where P is the complete markets put value and $bP$is the bid price in the managerial market. On the assets side we have

$$M + aD - bD + aJD - bJD + A_0 + bP.$$

The rest of the liability side includes

$$L_0 + aD.$$

In our example the final balance sheet is as presented in Table 1 with zero coupon debt issued at a face value of 23 for a five year maturity.

7. Gaussian Balance Sheet Models

We investigate the relationships between the risk characteristics of the balance sheet and seven outputs of interest in the corporate balance sheet, for firms that are allowed to exist on account of being able to raise enough capital in the equity markets. These outputs are the level of required capital (RC) as determined by the taxpayer cone. The cost of debt in the debt market (CD), the cost of equity post

Table 1.

Assets		Liabilities	
Required Capital	17.2400	Risky Liabilities	90
Cost of Debt	3.6541	Debt	14.3752
Cost of Equity	2.9811	Equity	23.3490
Risky Assets	100		
Taxpayer Put	3.8490		
Total	127.7242		127.7242

debt issue in the equity market (CJD), the value of the taxpayer put as valued in the managerial market (bP), the face value of debt issued (F) and the level of debt (aD) and reported equity (JR) as they appear in the final balance sheet.

We investigate these matters here for firms with a Gaussian model underlying the randomness in assets and liabilities. The initial asset level is set at 100. For the initial level of liabilities we take 5 settings of 10, 25, 50, 75, and 90. We allow for three levels of the interest rate at 2.5%, 5%, and 10%. The maturity of the debt has three levels of 5, 10 and 15 years. For the asset and liability volatilities we take three levels each of $0.15, 0.3$, and 0.6. The correlations are set at 7 levels, of -0.75, -0.5, -0.25, 0, 0.25, 0.5, and 0.75. In all we have $5 * 3 * 3 * 3 * 3 * 7 = 2835$ potential Gaussian balance sheets.

Apart from the firm's risk characteristics we have to specify the structure of the taxpayer, debt market, equity market and managerial market cones of market acceptable risks. These are given by the level of λ, and γ, the coefficients for loss aversion and absence of gain enticement in the respective markets. For our first cone the values of λ in the four markets are 0.75, 0.1, 0.025, and 0.5 respectively for the taxpayer, debt, equity and managerial markets. The corresponding values for γ are 0.75, 0.2, 0.025, and 0.25.

Our second set of cones just opens up the taxpayer cone to levels of λ, γ set at 0.5 instead of 0.75. Finally in our third cone we set the taxpayer cone back to the level of 0.75 for λ, γ and narrow the debt market cone to $\lambda = 0.15$ and $\gamma = 0.3$.

For our first set of cones, and for each of our 2835 potential balance sheets we first simulate 100000 scenarios for the random assets and liability levels at year end. The required capital is then determined in accordance with equation (3.1). We then evaluate whether the firm can raise sufficient capital to actually come into existence as defined by equation (4.1). Unlike the Mertonian world, not all firms are allowed to exist. For our first cone we found that 1536 out of 2835 firms are allowed to exist. For a more generous taxpayer cone with λ, γ at 0.5, the number of firms allowed to exist goes up marginally by an additional 36 firms to 1572 firms. We therefore concentrate attention on the first and third of our sets of market cones, that differ in the size of the debt market cone with the third being narrower. We find that the presence of risky liabilities helps the existence of firms as it reduces the need for funding from equity markets and helps meet the required constraint (4.1). For firms with the level of risky liabilities at 90 only 9 failed to meet the criterion for existence. For the lower levels of risky liabilities at 75, 50, 25 and 10 the numbers that failed to exist were 18, 207, 498, and 567 respectively. Our further analysis is restricted to the 1536 firms that come into existence and we report on the results using the first and third set of market cones that we shall refer to as the base debt cone and the narrow debt cone.

For these existing firms we determine the face value of debt (F) issued at the maturity in question in accordance with equation (5.1). We may then determine the cost of debt (CD), the cost of equity post debt (CJD), the managerial bid price for the taxpayer put option (bP), the level at which debt is marked (aD), and the level of reported equity (JR). For each of these six items plus the required capital (RC) we analyze by regression the effects of liability levels ($L0$), the effects of interest rates (r), the maturity (T), the asset volatility (σ_A), the liability volatility (σ_L) and the level of correlation (ρ). The levels of $L0$, r, T, σ_A, σ_L and ρ are proxied by dummy variables to give six sets of explanatory variables with respectively $5, 3, 3, 3, 3$ and 7 variables. There were not enough surviving firms at $L0 = 10$ and so we used 4 dummy variables in the regressions on the liability levels for the levels 25, 50, 75 and 90. In each case we regressed all 7 variables of interest RC, CD, CJD, bP, F, aD and JR on dummy variables for the levels of $L0$, r, T, σ_A, σ_L and ρ. The result of these regressions consists of 6 matrices of coefficients of dimension $4, 3, 3, 3, 3$ and 7 by 7. The six matrices are in duplicate, one for the base debt cone, and the other

Table 2.

		Base Debt Cone						
		RC	CD	CJD	bP	F	aD	JR
L0	25	0.0000	3.0300	5.9528	2.5761	74.8590	29.7513	56.8077
	50	7.1308	6.2414	9.0916	6.9418	84.2417	28.2410	51.1646
	75	29.3785	10.1627	8.4676	8.6433	168.5517	42.8434	38.8087
	90	49.6467	12.7974	8.1586	9.3860	251.7783	54.9764	35.0123
Rates	0.025	30.2075	9.8804	8.3886	8.2418	105.5077	43.2405	41.1340
	0.05	30.2075	9.8804	8.3886	8.2418	145.7898	43.2405	41.1340
	0.1	30.2075	9.8804	8.3886	8.2418	273.1544	43.2405	41.1340
Maturity	5	32.9358	5.8773	6.3635	5.8837	51.7452	31.2133	45.1717
	10	28.9968	10.1601	8.5285	8.6476	133.7709	44.4108	40.6999
	15	29.0714	13.0609	9.9992	9.8716	322.8031	52.4627	38.0798
Asset volatility	0.15	21.3583	12.8691	2.4846	6.0353	290.2499	58.8456	13.6782
	0.3	26.9301	11.6751	6.2584	7.8972	156.2029	46.3954	33.9654
	0.6	43.8629	4.5066	17.4367	11.1233	64.6597	22.0671	80.1789
Liability volatility	0.15	15.6652	4.3827	9.4584	9.4606	51.8031	12.6045	48.9847
	0.3	22.5585	7.5737	8.4260	8.2435	90.8424	27.1817	44.8979
	0.6	46.2398	15.4835	7.6203	7.3985	325.5177	76.9724	32.7650
Correlation	−0.75	37.7327	10.7703	9.4322	9.4178	145.4134	46.6149	51.0996
	−0.5	35.1163	10.4304	9.3150	9.1396	144.1350	45.0482	49.0750
	−0.25	32.5555	10.1041	9.1736	8.8543	154.7413	43.5242	46.4759
	0	29.9649	9.9746	8.7852	8.4182	175.4633	43.0040	42.3206
	0.25	27.6438	9.5100	8.1835	7.7945	179.8620	41.4185	37.6992
	0.5	24.3729	9.5191	6.8968	7.0161	238.3385	42.2528	29.5037
	0.75	18.7601	8.2061	5.7770	6.0304	213.7006	38.9918	23.0275

Table 3.

		Narrow Debt Cone						
		RC	CD	CJD	bP	F	aD	JR
L0	25	0.0000	2.7533	6.1534	2.5761	54.8441	22.3922	64.0907
	50	7.1308	5.7737	9.4882	6.9418	56.5391	21.9256	57.4090
	75	29.3785	9.4736	9.1071	8.6433	91.9500	34.2929	47.3097
	90	49.6467	12.0118	8.9557	9.3860	119.7148	44.6666	45.3335
Rates	0.025	30.2075	9.2266	9.0087	8.2418	57.0269	34.6283	49.7127
	0.05	30.2075	9.2266	9.0087	8.2418	76.7749	34.6283	49.7127
	0.1	30.2075	9.2266	9.0087	8.2418	142.4085	34.6283	49.7127
Maturity	5	32.9358	5.4150	6.7393	5.8837	35.4641	22.9687	53.3298
	10	28.9968	9.4472	9.1690	8.6476	81.2380	35.6212	49.4172
	15	29.0714	12.3013	10.8101	9.8716	151.9978	43.7118	46.8820
Asset volatility	0.15	21.3583	12.1203	3.2822	6.0353	125.9105	47.9619	24.6107
	0.3	26.9301	10.8422	6.9968	7.8972	101.3787	36.7127	43.5536
	0.6	43.8629	4.1590	17.7249	11.1233	43.4219	17.2138	84.9727
Liability volatility	0.15	15.6652	4.1130	9.7300	9.4606	32.7671	9.2893	52.3018
	0.3	22.5585	7.0489	8.9019	8.2435	58.5406	20.3788	51.6518
	0.6	46.2398	14.4636	8.5941	7.3985	159.2784	63.2847	46.4064
Correlation	−0.75	37.7327	9.9711	10.1163	9.4178	94.7232	36.2449	61.3545
	−0.5	35.1163	9.6555	9.9782	9.1396	92.4561	35.2787	58.7328
	−0.25	32.5555	9.3517	9.8171	8.8543	90.5124	34.3930	55.4981
	0	29.9649	9.2641	9.4174	8.4182	91.2354	34.4404	50.8060
	0.25	27.6438	8.8516	8.7849	7.7945	89.0907	33.4803	45.5804
	0.5	24.3729	8.9709	7.4870	7.0161	94.0135	34.8204	36.9781
	0.75	18.7601	8.0449	6.2487	6.0304	92.5629	33.1436	29.1861

for the narrow debt cone. The columns for RC and bP are the same for the base debt cone and the narrow debt cone as these values are independent of the debt market cone. The results are presented in Tables 2 and 3 for the base debt cone and the narrow debt cone respectively. We comment on the relationship of each of the seven independent variables on the set of six regressors in turn.

The required capital (RC) rises with the level of risky liabilities, and is independent of rates and maturity. Furthermore, the level of capital required rises with asset and liability volatility and decreases with an increase in the correlation.

The cost of debt rises with the level of risky liabilities, is independent of rates, and rises with maturity. The cost of debt decreases with asset volatility and rises with the volatility of the liabilities. It is invariant to correlation.

The cost of equity post debt also rises with the level of risky liabilities, is insensitive to rates and rises with maturity. It rises with asset volatility and declines somewhat with the volatility of liabilities. It also falls somewhat with correlation.

The value of the taxpayer put rises with the level of risky liabilities and maturity and is insensitive to rates. It rises with asset volatilities, falls with liability volatility and correlation.

The face value of debt issued rises with the level of risky liabilities, and is positively related to rates and maturity. It falls with asset volatilities and rises with liability volatility and correlation.

The marked value of debt however, rises with the level of risky liabilities, is insensitive to rates, and rises with maturity. It falls with asset volatility, rises with liability volatility and falls with correlation.

The level of reported equity falls with the level of risky liabilities, is insensitive to rates, and falls with maturity. It is positively related to asset volatility, negatively related to liability volatility and decreases with correlation.

The face values of debt issued are uniformly substantially reduced when the debt cone is narrowed.

8. Conclusion

Markets are modeled as passively accepting a convex cone of cash flows. These cones contain the set of nonnegative cash flows as they are acceptable to all. Different markets are conceptualized as accepting different cones reflecting varying clienteles. Conditions are established to exclude the possibility of arbitrage between markets. Operationally these cones are defined by a positive expectation under a concave distortion of the distribution function of the cash flow delivered to market. Different cones are then constructed using different distortions. A two parameter family of distortions is introduced that calibrates the level of loss aversion in markets and the level of the absence of gain enticement.

Firms or corporations are seen as accessing risky assets and risky liabilities where the latter may dominate the former. As a consequence capital requirements are set by taxpayers via their regulatory bodies to ensure that sufficient capital is put at stake by the creators of a firm. This capital level must be such that the residual risk of excess loss is acceptable to the taxpayer cone. The taxpayer cone reflects the highest level of loss aversion and the highest level of absence of gain enticement. Firms approach equity markets that have the lowest level of risk aversion and the highest level of gain enticement and can come into existence if they can raise sufficient equity capital.

Firms that are allowed to exist approach debt markets using securities particularly attractive to such markets to generate favorable funding opportunities. Debt is however costly as it is marked at the ask price of the debt market though the securities issued raise just the bid price. The difference is the cost of debt and this rises as the debt level is increased and sets a limit to the amount of debt a firm may issue. This constraint on covering the cost of debt coupled with the clientele effects of debt markets determines the optimal level of debt.

Firms with lognormally distributed and correlated assets and liabilities are analyzed for their required capital, their optimal debt levels, the value of the option to put losses back to the taxpayer, the costs of debt and equity, and the level of finally reported equity in the balance sheet. The relationship between these entities and the risk characteristics of a firm are analyzed and reported in detail.

Acknowledgements

We would like to thank Phillipe Artzner, Gurdip Bakshi, Peter Carr, Freddy Delbaen, Ernst Eberlein, Damir Filipović, Thomas Gehrig, Ed Kane, Eckhard Platen, Martijn Pistorious, Martin Schweizer, Lemma Senbet, Haluk Unal, and Juan Jorge Vicente Alvarez for discussions on the subject matter of this paper. Errors remain our responsibility.

References

[1] K. J. Arrow and F. H. Hahn, *General Competitive Analysis* (Holden Day, San Francisco, 1971).

[2] P. Artzner, F. Delbaen, J. Eber and D. Heath, Definition of coherent measures of risk, *Mathematical Finance* **9** (1998) 203–228.

[3] P. Carr, H. Geman and D. B. Madan, Pricing and hedging in incomplete markets, *Journal of Financial Economics* **62** (2001) 131–167.

[4] S. N. Cohen and R. J. Elliott, A general theory of finite state backward stochastic difference equations, arXiv:0810.4957v1 [math.PR] (2008).

[5] N. Chen and S. G. Kou, Credit spreads, optimal capital structure, and implied volatility with endogenous default and jump risk, *Mathematical Finance* **19** (2009) 343–378.

[6] A. Cherny and D. B. Madan, New measures of performance evaluation, *Review of Financial Studies* **22** (2009) 2571–2606.

[7] G. Debreu, *Theory of Value* (Wiley, New York, 1959).

[8] F. Delbaen, S. Peng and E. Rosazza Gianin, *Department of Mathematics*, Representation of the penalty term of dynamic concave utilities, Working Paper, ETH, Zurich (2008).

[9] D. Duffie, *Dynamic Asset Pricing Theory*, 3rd edn. (Princeton University Press, Princeton, New Jersey, 2001).

[10] E. Eberlein and D. B. Madan, Capital requirements, and taxpayer put option values for the major US banks, Working Paper, Robert H. Smith School of Business (2009).

[11] H. Föllmer and A. Schied, *Stochastic Finance: An Introduction in Discrete Time* (Walter de Gruyter, Berlin, 2004).

[12] R. S. Goldstein, N. Ju and H. E. Leland, An EBIT-based model of optimal capital structure, *Journal of Business* **47** (2001) 483–512.

[13] B. Hilberink and L. C. G. Rogers, Optimal capital structure and endogenous default, *Finance and Stochastics* **6** (2002) 237–263.

[14] S. Jaschke and U. Küchler, Coherent risk measures and good deal bounds, *Finance and Stochastics* **5** (2001) 181–200.

[15] A. Jobert and L. C. G. Rogers, Valuations and dynamic convex risk measures, *Mathematical Finance* **18**(1) (2008) 1–22.

[16] K. John and L. Senbet, Corporate governance and board effectiveness, Working Paper, Leonard N. Stern School, New York University (1998).

[17] H. E. Leland, Corporate dect value, bond covenants and optimal capital structure, *Journal of Finance* **49** (1994) 1213–1252.

[18] H. E. Leland and K. B. Toft, Optimal capital structure, endogenous bankruptcy, and the term structure of credit spreads, *Journal of Finance* **51** (1997) 987–1019.

[19] D. B. Madan, Capital requirements, Acceptable risks and profits, *Quantitative Finance* **9** (2009) 767–773.

[20] R. C. Merton, Theory of rational option pricing, *Bell Journal of Economics and Management Science* **4** (1973) 141–183.

[21] R. C. Merton, On the pricing of corporate debt: The risk structure of interest rates, *Journal of Finance* **29** (1974) 449–470.

[22] R. C. Merton, An analytic derivation of the cost of loan guarantees and deposit insurance: An application of modern option pricing theory, *Journal of Banking and Finance* **1** (1977) 3–11.

[23] F. Modigliani and M. H. Miller, The cost of capital, corporate finance and the theory of investment, *American Economic Review* **48**(3) (1958) 261–297.

[24] S. Peng, Dynamically consistent nonlinear evaluations and expectations, *Preprint No. 2004-1, Institute of Mathematics*, Shandong University. Also available at http://arxiv.org/abs/math/0501415 (2005).

OPTIMAL EXERCISE OF AN EXECUTIVE STOCK OPTION BY AN INSIDER*

MICHAEL MONOYIOS and ANDREW NG

Mathematical Institute, University of Oxford
24–29 St Giles', Oxford, OX1 3LB, United Kingdom

We consider an optimal stopping problem arising in connection with the exercise of an executive stock option by an agent with inside information. The agent is assumed to have noisy information on the terminal value of the stock, does not trade the stock or outside securities, and maximises the expected discounted payoff over all stopping times with regard to an enlarged filtration which includes the inside information. This leads to a stopping problem governed by a time-inhomogeneous diffusion and a call-type reward. We establish conditions under which the option value exhibits time decay, and derive the smooth fit condition for the solution to the free boundary problem governing the maximum expected reward, and derive the early exercise decomposition of the value function. The resulting integral equation for the unknown exercise boundary is solved numerically and this shows that the insider may exercise the option before maturity, in situations when an agent without the privileged information may not. Hence we show that early exercise may arise due to the agent having inside information on the future stock price.

Keywords: Optimal stopping; executive stock options; enlargement of filtration; free boundary.

1. Introduction

In this paper we model the exercise decision of an insider who is granted an executive stock option (ESO). The agent is an employee who is granted a single American-style option on a stock of his employing company. This executive is barred from trading the stock, does not trade other securities either, and has some inside information on the future evolution of the stock at the terminal date of the option. The executive is modelled as risk-neutral, so has a linear utility function, and hence maximises the discounted expectation under the physical measure P of the option payoff at the exercise time. We do not endow the agent with risk-averse preferences as we wish

*This chapter was originally published under the same title in *International Journal of Theoretical and Applied Finance*, Vol.14, No.1, 83–106 (2011). Singapore: World Scientific Publishing.

to focus exclusively on the role of inside information on the exercise decision, and this is also the reason for assuming away all other trading opportunities, as well as other contractual complications that are common in ESOs, such as a vesting period, resetting of strikes, partial exercise opportunities, job termination, and so on.

The exercise time is a stopping time with respect to an enlarged filtration formed by augmenting a filtration $\mathbb{F}$ with the σ-algebra of a random variable L, which corresponds to noisy information on the value of the stock at the option maturity time T. Writing the stock dynamics under the enlarged filtration $\mathbb{F}^L$, the stock price is governed by a time-inhomogeneous diffusion with state and time-dependent drift and constant volatility, and we are faced with an optimal stopping problem governed by the time-inhomogeneous diffusion. The enlargement of filtration, leading to a state and time-dependent drift, leads to the theoretical possibility of early exercise. We establish that early exercise can occur and provide a numerical computation of the early exercise boundary.

We establish the equivalence between the optimal stopping problem and a free boundary PDE. We further establish that the value function governing the maximum expected reward exhibits time decay for suitably low realisations of L, and for zero interest rate, regardless of L. In these cases we prove that the value function satisfies the smooth-fit condition at the free boundary, and from this we derive the early exercise decomposition of the value function into a European-style payoff and an early exercise premium. This leads to an integral equation characterising the free boundary, which is solved numerically. The numerical results show that the insider can indeed exercise the ESO prior to maturity in situations in which an executive without the inside information would not. Hence, we show that privileged information can also be a factor contributing to the early exercise of ESOs.

The rest of the paper is as follows. Section 2 describes the model and the optimal stopping problems for an insider and a non-insider. Section 3 contains our main results. We analyse the value function of the insider's discounted ESO value as a function of log-stock price. We use ideas of stochastic flows to establish convexity and monotonicity of the value function, derive the free boundary PDE, conditions under which the ESO value exhibits time decay, and the smooth fit condition at the exercise boundary. We use these results to derive an early exercise decomposition for the ESO value, and a resulting integral equation for the exercise boundary. The properties are well-known in standard American option problems with constant parameters under a martingale measure, but our problem is rather non-standard, containing a time-inhomogeneous drift term not equal to the interest rate, since valuation is performed under the physical measure. We solve the integral equation numerically and present results which show that the insider can be induced to early exercise by possessing privileged information. Section 4 concludes.

2. The Model

We have a single stock price process $S = (S_t)_{0\leq t\leq T}$ defined on a complete probability space $(\Omega, \mathcal{F}, P)$ equipped with a filtration $\mathbb{F} = (\mathcal{F}_t)_{0\leq t\leq T}$ that satisfies the usual conditions of right-continuity and completeness. A $(P, \mathbb{F})$-Brownian motion $B = (B_t)_{0 \le t \le T}$ drives the stock price, which follows the geometric Brownian motion

$$dS_t = \mu S_t dt + \sigma S_t dB_t,$$

where μ and $\sigma > 0$ are known constants. There is a constant risk-free interest rate $r \geq 0$.

It will be sometimes be more convenient to work with the log-stock price $X := \log S$, satisfying

$$X_t = X_0 + \gamma t + \sigma B_t, \quad 0 \le t \le T, \tag{2.1}$$

where $\gamma := \mu - \sigma^2/2$.

Our financial agent (an executive) is an employee of the firm whose stock price is S, and is awarded at time zero a single American-style call option on the stock with maturity T. We assume that the agent is barred from trading S or outside securities, that there is no opportunity for partial exercise of the option, and we take the agent's preferences to be risk-neutral, so he maximises the expected discounted payoff under the objective probability measure P. Grasselli and Henderson [6] or Rogers and Scheinkman [16] focus on the effects of risk aversion and outside trading on early and block exercise. We do not introduce contractual complications that sometimes feature in ESOs, as done by Sircar and co-authors [12, 13, 18]. We exclude the above features of ESOs in order to focus exclusively on the impact of inside information on the agent's optimal stopping problem of when to exercise the option. In particular, we can examine a case in which the absence of inside information results in no early exercise, and we can then show that the introduction of additional information can lead to early exercise, and we compute the early exercise boundary numerically. Even with the simplifications that we make, we shall see that we are nevertheless faced with a non-standard American problem with a time-inhomogeneous diffusion for the stock, so that many standard properties of the value function are not known a priori and have to be established. These properties include monotonicity and convexity in the log-stock price, time decay, and the smooth fit condition (continuity of the first spatial derivative) at the optimal exercise boundary.

The agent has inside knowledge at time zero of an $\mathcal{F}$-measurable random variable L, corresponding to noisy knowledge of the terminal log-stock price X_T. We shall sometimes refer to this agent as the *insider* or the *executive*. We shall also consider an agent whose information is represented by the filtration $\mathbb{F}$, so who does not have the privileged information. This agent will sometimes be referred to as the *regular agent* or as the *non-executive*.

The random variable L will be given by

$$L = aX_T + (1-a)\epsilon, \quad 0 < a < 1, \tag{2.2}$$

where ϵ is a standard normal random variable independent of $\mathbb{F}$. Hence, the executive's information flow is represented by the enlarged filtration $\mathbb{F}^L = (\mathcal{F}_t^L)_{0 \le t \le T}$, defined by

$$\mathcal{F}_t^L := \mathcal{F}_t \vee \sigma(L), \quad 0 \le t \le T.$$

See Danilova *et al.* [1] for similar examples of such inside information within the context of partial information investment problems. The dynamics of the log-stock price with respect to the enlarged filtration are given by classical enlargement of filtration methods (see Yor [19]) in the following lemma.

Lemma 2.1. *With respect to the enlarged filtration* $\mathbb{F}^L$, *the dynamics of the log-stock price are*

$$dX_t = \frac{1}{T_a - t}\left(\gamma(T_a - T) + \frac{L}{a} - X_t\right)dt + \sigma dB_t^L,$$

where B^L *is an* $\mathbb{F}^L$*-Brownian motion and* T_a *is the modulated time defined by*

$$T_a := T + \left(\frac{1-a}{a\sigma}\right)^2, \quad 0 < a < 1. \tag{2.3}$$

Proof. Classical enlargement of filtration results (Theorem 12.1 in Yor [19]) imply that the $\mathbb{F}$-Brownian B has a semi-martingale decomposition with respect to $\mathbb{F}^L$ of the form

$$B_t = B_t^L + \int_0^t \nu(L,u)du, \quad 0 \le t \le T,$$

with B^L an $\mathbb{F}^L$-Brownian motion, and the process $(\nu(L,t))_{0\le t\le T}$, is called the *information drift*, given by the logarithmic derivative of the conditional density of L given $\mathcal{F}_t$. This results in

$$B_t = B_t^L + \int_0^t \frac{L - a(X_0 + \gamma T + \sigma B_u)}{a\sigma(T_a - u)}du, \quad 0 \le t \le T, \tag{2.4}$$

and combining this with (2.1), the lemma follows. □

2.1. *The optimal stopping problems*

Denote by $\mathcal{T}$ the set of all stopping times with respect to the filtration $\mathbb{F}$, and by $\mathcal{T}^L$ the set of all stopping times with respect to the enlarged filtration $\mathbb{F}^L$. Introduce the following subsets of $\mathcal{T}$ and $\mathcal{T}^L$:

$$\mathcal{T}_{t,T} := \{\tau \in \mathcal{T} \,|\, P(\tau \in [t,T]) = 1\}, \quad 0 \le t \le T < \infty,$$
$$\mathcal{T}^L_{t,T} := \{\tau \in \mathcal{T}^L \,|\, P(\tau \in [t,T]) = 1\}, \quad 0 \le t \le T < \infty.$$

Of course, we have $\mathcal{T}_{0,T} \equiv \mathcal{T}$ and $\mathcal{T}^L_{0,T} \equiv \mathcal{T}^L$.

The executive stock option is an American call with strike $K \ge 0$. If exercised at time $\tau \in [0,T]$, the discounted payoff at time zero is Y_τ, where $Y = (Y_t)_{0\le t\le T}$ is the *reward process*, defined by

$$Y_t := e^{-rt}(e^{X_t} - K)^+, \quad 0 \le t \le T,$$

assumed to satisfy

$$E\left[\sup_{0\leq t\leq} Y_t\right] < \infty.$$

The insider's (that is, the executive's) optimal stopping problem is to find a stopping time $\tau^* \in \mathcal{T}^L$ to achieve the maximal expected reward

$$V_0(L) := \sup_{\tau\in\mathcal{T}^L} E[Y_\tau \,|\, \mathcal{F}_0^L].$$

Notice that the supremum is over stopping times of the enlarged filtration $\mathbb{F}^L$, so we emphasise this with the conditioning on the enlarged initial σ-field $\mathcal{F}_0^L$. The maximal expected reward $V_0(L)$ is thus an $\mathcal{F}_0^L$-measurable random variable (though from the perspective of the insider, L is a known constant) and the relevant dynamics of the state variable X are given by Lemma 2.1. When no confusion arises we suppress the dependence on L of V_0.

The non-executive faces a similar optimal stopping problem, but over $\mathbb{F}$-stopping times, so in this case X is given by (2.1). We denote the non-executive's maximal expected reward at time zero by

$$V_0^0 := \sup_{\tau\in\mathcal{T}} E[Y_\tau],$$

where the expectation is conditional upon the (assumed trivial) σ-algebra $\mathcal{F}_0$.

2.2. *Benchmark case: $\mu \geq r$ and no inside information*

For $\mu \geq r$, the reward process Y is a $(P, \mathbb{F})$-submartingale, so the regular agent's value for the American ESO coincides with the European value: $V_0^0 = E[Y_T]$. In particular, the exercise time $\tau = T$ is optimal for the regular agent. This slightly artificial conclusion derives from the fact that there are no trading opportunities for the regular agent and also that the agent has a linear utility function. This result serves as a useful benchmark for us. Given the same trading opportunities (none) and the same preferences for the insider as the regular agent, our main goal is to show that inside information on the stock can result in early exercise, because the drift of the stock becomes time and price-dependent.

2.3. *The insider's problem*

In this section we analyse the optimal stopping problem for the insider. The log-stock price follows the time-inhomogeneous diffusion of Lemma 2.1, which we write as

$$dX_t = \beta(t, X_t)dt + \sigma dB_t^L, \tag{2.5}$$

where $\beta(t, x) \equiv \beta(t, x; L)$ is given by

$$\beta(t, x) = \frac{C - x}{T_a - t}, \quad C := \gamma(T_a - T) + \frac{L}{a}. \tag{2.6}$$

Given an initial condition $X_t = x \in \mathbb{R}$, for $t \in [0, T]$, the solution to (2.5) is the Gaussian process $(X_u)_{t\le u\le T}$ given by

$$X_u = x + \beta(t,x)(u-t) + \sigma(T_a - u)\int_t^u \frac{1}{T_a-\rho}dB^L_\rho, \quad 0 \le t \le u \le T. \tag{2.7}$$

In particular, the transition density $p(t, x; u, y)$ for moving from $X_t = x$ to $X_u \in dy$ at $u \ge t$ is given explicitly by

$$p(t,x;u,y) = \frac{1}{\Sigma(t;u)\sqrt{2\pi}}\exp\left[-\frac{1}{2}\left(\frac{y-m(t,x;u)}{\Sigma(t;u)}\right)^2\right], \quad x, y \in \mathbb{R}, \quad 0 \le t \le u \le T, \tag{2.8}$$

where $m(t, x; u)$ and $\Sigma(t; u) > 0$ are given by

$$m(t,x;u) = x + \beta(t,x)(u-t), \quad \Sigma^2(t;u) = \sigma^2\left(\frac{T_a-u}{T_a-t}\right)(u-t). \tag{2.9}$$

For a starting time $t \in [0, T]$ the maximal expected discounted payoff is given by the $\mathbb{F}^L$-adapted process

$$\begin{aligned} V_t \equiv V_t(L) &:= \operatorname*{ess\,sup}_{\tau\in\mathcal{T}^L_{t,T}} E[e^{-r(\tau-t)}(e^{X_\tau}-K)^+ \,|\, \mathcal{F}^L_t] \\ &= e^{rt}\operatorname*{ess\,sup}_{\tau\in\mathcal{T}^L_{t,T}} E[Y_\tau \,|\, \mathcal{F}^L_t], \quad 0 \le t \le T. \end{aligned}$$

We are thus led to consider the $\mathbb{F}^L$-adapted process U defined by

$$U_t \equiv U_t(L) := \operatorname*{ess\,sup}_{\tau\in\mathcal{T}^L_{t,T}} E[Y_\tau \,|\, \mathcal{F}^L_t], \quad 0 \le t \le T, \tag{2.10}$$

satisfying $U_t = e^{-rt}V_t$ a.s., for any $t \in [0, T]$.

Classical optimal stopping theory (Appendix D of Karatzas and Shreve [11]) characterises the solution to the optimal stopping problem (2.10) as follows. There exists a non-negative càdlàg $(P, \mathbb{F}^L)$-supermartingale $U = (U_t)_{0\le t\le T}$, the *Snell envelope* of Y, such that U is the smallest $(P, \mathbb{F}^L)$-supermartingale that dominates Y, with $U_T = Y_T$ a.s. A stopping time $\tau^* \in \mathcal{T}^L$ is optimal for the problem (2.10) starting at time zero if and only if $U_{\tau^*} = Y_{\tau^*}$ a.s., and the stopped supermartingale U^{τ^*} defined by $U^{\tau^*}_t := U_{\tau^*\wedge t}, 0 \le t \le T$, is a $(P, \mathbb{F}^L)$-martingale. The smallest optimal stopping time in $\mathcal{T}^L_{t,T}$ for the problem (2.10) is τ^*_t, defined by

$$\tau^*_t := \inf\{\rho \in [t,T] \,|\, U_\rho = Y_\rho\} \wedge T, \quad 0 \le t \le T.$$

3. The Value Function

We are interested in the optimal stopping problem with reward process

$$Y_t = e^{-rt}(e^{X_t} - K)^+ =: f(t, X_t),$$

where $f : [0,T] \times \mathbb{R} \to \mathbb{R}^+$ is the continuous non-negative function given by

$$f(t,x) := e^{-rt}(e^x - K)^+,$$

and where $(X_u)_{t\le u\le T}$ is the solution (2.7) of (2.5) with $X_t = x$ deterministic, for $t \in [0,T]$. For a fixed value of the random variable L, say $L = \ell \in \mathbb{R}$, we define the value function $F : [0,T] \times \mathbb{R} \to \mathbb{R}^+$ by

$$F(t,x) \equiv F(t,x;\ell) := \sup_{\tau\in\mathcal{T}^L_{t,T}} E[f(\tau, X_\tau) \,|\, X_t = x, L = \ell]. \tag{3.1}$$

Then, in a very general continuous-time Markov setting, F is a continuous function and the process $U = (F(t,X_t))_{0\le t\le T}$ is the Snell envelope of $Y = (f(t,X_t))_{0\le t\le T}$ (see for instance El Karoui *et al.* [5]).

The insider's value process for the ESO is $(V(t,S_t;L))_{0\le t\le T}$, where $V : [0,T] \times \mathbb{R}^+ \to \mathbb{R}^+$ is given by

$$V(t,s) \equiv V(t,s;\ell) := \sup_{\tau\in\mathcal{T}^L_{t,T}} E[e^{-r(\tau-t)}(S_\tau - K)^+ \,|\, S_t = s, L = \ell],$$

and we suppress dependence on L when no confusion arises. Hence the value functions F and V are related according to

$$e^{-rt}V(t,s(x)) = F(t,x), \quad \text{with } s(x) := e^x.$$

The (smallest) optimal stopping time for the problem (3.1) starting at time $t \in [0,T]$ with $X_t = x$ is $\tau^*(t,x)$ given by

$$\begin{aligned}\tau^*(t,x) &= \inf\{\rho \in [t,T] \,|\, F(\rho,X_\rho) = f(\rho,X_\rho)\}\\ &= \inf\{\rho \in [t,T] | V(\rho,S_\rho) = (S_\rho - K)^+\}.\end{aligned}$$

The *continuation region* $\mathcal{C}$ is defined by

$$\begin{aligned}\mathcal{C} &:= \{(t,x) \in [0,T) \times \mathbb{R} \,|\, F(t,x) > f(t,x)\}\\ &= \{(t,s) \in [0,T) \times \mathbb{R}^+ \,|\, V(t,s) > (s-K)^+\}.\end{aligned}$$

Since F, V are continuous, $\mathcal{C}$ is open. This suggests (and we show below) that there is function $x^* : [0,T] \to \mathbb{R}$ (respectively, $s^* : [0,T] \to \mathbb{R}^+$), the critical log-stock price (respectively, critical stock price) or optimal early exercise boundary, such that the option is exercised the first time the log-stock price exceeds $x^*(t)$. Since it is never optimal to exercise if the stock is below the strike K, we must have $x^*(t) \ge \log K$ for all $t \in [0,T]$.

We shall characterise the early exercise boundary and the value function F as a solution to a free boundary problem, and we also establish the smooth fit condition at the boundary that is common in many optimal stopping problems. This is not guaranteed and in general needs to be verified on a case by case basis. This is the situation we are faced with here, as we are dealing with a non-standard American option problem involving a stock with a state and time-dependent drift.

3.1. *Convexity and monotonicity of the value function in x*

We wish to show that the value function F is increasing and convex in x. Although these properties do not necessarily imply similar properties for the ESO value V in the stock price, they will be sufficient to allow us to characterise the exercise boundary and establish bounds on the derivative F_x, which are ingredients we need to obtain the free boundary PDE and the smooth fit condition satisfied by F. These then lead easily to a corresponding free boundary PDE and smooth fit condition for V.

We shall utilise ideas of stochastic flows applied to the log-stock price. We write $X(x)$ for the log-stock price with initial condition $X_0 = x$, considered as the solution to a diffusion SDE with time and state-dependent drift. In Lemma 3.1, we show that the map $x \to X(x)$ is non-decreasing, and give a condition on the drift β of X for this map to be convex in x. This condition is indeed satisfied in our specific model. From the properties of $x \to X(x)$ we deduce the corresponding properties for the map $x \to F(\cdot, x)$.

Note that for a diffusion with time and state dependent drift, properties such as monotonicity and convexity in the initial condition are not automatic, so the obvious properties of the map $x \to X(x)$ under $\mathbb{F}$ do indeed need to be shown to hold under $\mathbb{F}^L$.

An alternative to our approach would be to use a technique due to El Karoui *et al.* [4]. They prove convexity of standard American option prices with respect to stock price (so evaluated under a martingale measure) in diffusion models with deterministic interest rate. They also employ ideas of stochastic flows, first to show the property for European prices, then, adapting an iterative procedure found in El Karoui [3], they extend the result to American prices. This approach can be shown to work in our model, since the European option value can be written as an integral with respect to the transition density of X, given in (2.8).[1] Indeed, we adapt this technique later for part of our analysis of the time decay property of the American ESO value: see the proof of Theorem 3.3.

In principle one might try to use our techniques to prove convexity and monotonicity of ESO value function V in the starting stock price $S_t = s$, for any $t \in [0, T]$. This does not appear to be straightforward using our methods, because it does not appear easy to prove that the map $s \to S(s)$ is increasing and convex for a general diffusion. Indeed, we shall see in Remark 3.1 that, when we use the explicit solution (2.7) for $X(x)$, the map $x \to X(x)$ is indeed increasing and convex, but that the map $s \to S(s)$ is increasing but not convex.

It is well known that convexity of American option prices with respect to stock price does not immediately follow from the convexity of the payoff process when the return distribution of the stock depends on the stock price, as shown by Merton [14] (Theorem 10 and the counter-example in Appendix 1). Other authors

[1]We thank an anonymous referee for pointing this out.

have also analysed convexity of American option values with respect to stock price. Ekstrom [2] used stochastic time changes and a limiting argument based on approximating American option by a Bermudan option, and Hobson [7] utilised coupling methods. Similar to [4], these papers consider standard American pricing problems under a risk-neutral measure, with a deterministic rate of interest. We have a rather non-standard problem where the stock price drift is not the interest rate, and in addition is both state and time-dependent. For these reasons, we cannot directly read off the required properties of the value function from these papers.

For simplicity consider a starting time $t = 0$. The same ideas apply to any starting time $t \in [0, T]$. Consider the log-stock price with initial condition $X_0 = x$, and write $X \equiv X(x)$, following

$$X_t(x) = x + \int_0^t \beta(u, X_u(x))du + \sigma B_t^L, \quad 0 \le t \le T. \tag{3.2}$$

We may choose versions of $(X_t(x))_{0 \le t \le T}$ which for each $t \in [0, T]$ and each $\omega \in \Omega$ are diffeomorphisms in x from $\mathbb{R} \to \mathbb{R}$. That is, the map $x \to X(x)$ is smooth.

Define

$$b(t, x) := \frac{\partial}{\partial x}\beta(t, x), \quad D_t(x) := \frac{\partial}{\partial x}X_t(x). \tag{3.3}$$

Lemma 3.1. *The map $x \to X(x)$ is increasing, and if $\beta_{xx}(t, x) \ge 0$, also convex.*

Proof. We have

$$D_t(x) = \exp\left(\int_0^t b(u, X_u(x))du\right) > 0,$$

so $x \to X(x)$ is increasing.

Define $c(t, x) := b_x(t, x) = \beta_{xx}(t, x)$. Then

$$\frac{\partial}{\partial x}D_t(x) = D_t(x)\int_0^t c(u, X_u(x))D_u(x)du,$$

which is non-negative if $c(t, x) \ge 0$ for all $(t, x) \in [0, T] \times \mathbb{R}$. Then $x \to X(x)$ is convex. □

Remark 3.1. Lemma 3.1 holds for a general diffusion with a time and state-dependent drift. Alternatively, with the explicit solution (2.7) we can directly compute

$$D_t(x) = 1 - \frac{t}{T_a} > 0, \quad \frac{\partial}{\partial x}D_t(x) = 0,$$

which directly shows that $x \to X(x)$ is increasing and convex. The same method applied to the map $s \to S(s)$ (the stock price with initial condition $S_0 = s > 0$) gives

$$\frac{\partial}{\partial s}S_t(s) = \frac{S_t(s)}{s}\left(1 - \frac{t}{T_a}\right) > 0, \quad \frac{\partial^2}{\partial s^2}S_t(s) = -\frac{S_t(s)}{s^2}\left(1 - \frac{t}{T_a}\right)\frac{t}{T_a} < 0,$$

so that $s \to S(s)$ is increasing, but not convex (though this does not necessarily imply that $s \to V(\cdot, s)$ is not convex).

Theorem 3.1. *The map $x \to F(t,x)$ is increasing for any $t \in [0,T]$. Suppose $\beta_{xx}(t,x) \geq 0$. Then the map $x \to F(t,x)$ is convex for any $t \in [0,T]$.*

Proof. We set $t = 0$ without loss of generality. Then $F(x) \equiv F(0,x)$ is given by

$$F(x) = \sup_{\tau \in \mathcal{T}^L} E[e^{-r\tau}(\exp(X_\tau(x)) - K)^+ \,|\, \mathcal{F}_0^L], \tag{3.4}$$

and where $X_0(x) = x$. Let $\tau^*(x) \in \mathcal{T}^L$ denote the optimal stopping time for the problem in (3.4). Then we may write

$$F(x) = E[e^{-r\tau^*(x)}(\exp(X_{\tau^*(x)}(x)) - K)^+],$$

where for brevity we have suppressed the conditioning on $\mathcal{F}_0^L$.

Since the map $x \to X(x)$ is increasing, we have, for $x_0 < x_1$,

$$(\exp(X_{\tau^*(x_0)}(x_0)) - K)^+ < (\exp(X_{\tau^*(x_0)}(x_1)) - K)^+.$$

Multiply both sides by $e^{-r\tau^*(x_0)}$, take expectations, and use the fact that $\tau^*(x_0)$ is sub-optimal for the starting state x_1, to obtain

$$F(x_0) < E[e^{-r\tau^*(x_0)}(\exp(X_{\tau^*(x_0)}(x_1)) - K)^+] \leq F(x_1),$$

which shows that $x \to F(x)$ is non-decreasing.

To establish convexity, define $x_\lambda := \lambda x_0 + (1-\lambda)x_1$ for $x_0 < x_1$ and $\lambda \in [0,1]$. Using the property that $x \to X(x)$ is convex, we have that $x \to (\exp(X(x)) - K)^+$ is also convex. Hence

$$\begin{aligned}(\exp(X_{\tau^*(x_\lambda)}(x_\lambda)) - K)^+ &\leq \lambda(\exp(X_{\tau^*(x_\lambda)}(x_0)) - K)^+ \\ &\quad + (1-\lambda)(\exp(X_{\tau^*(x_\lambda)}(x_1)) - K)^+.\end{aligned}$$

Multiplying by $\exp(-r\tau^*(x_\lambda))$, taking expectations and using the fact that $\tau^*(x_\lambda)$ is sub-optimal for the starting states $x_i, i = 0,1$, we obtain

$$F(x_\lambda) \leq \lambda F(x_0) + (1-\lambda)F(x_1),$$

so $x \to F(x)$ is convex. □

3.2. *Free boundary problem for the value function*

As F is increasing and convex, the exercise boundary $x^*(t)$ divides the domain of F into the continuation region $\mathcal{C}$ and the stopping region $\mathcal{S}$, given by

$$\mathcal{C} = \{(t,x) \in [0,T) \times \mathbb{R} \,|\, x < \log x^*(t)\} = \{(t,s) \in [0,T) \times \mathbb{R}^+ \,|\, s < s^*(t)\},$$

with $\mathcal{S} = \mathcal{C}^c$.

Define the extended generator $\mathcal{L}$ of X by

$$\mathcal{L}g(t,x) := g_t(t,x) + \beta(t,x)g_x(t,x) + \frac{1}{2}\sigma^2 g_{xx}(t,x).$$

Denote the closure of the continuation region by $\bar{\mathcal{C}}$.

Theorem 3.2. *The value function F in* (3.1) *solves, in $\bar{\mathcal{C}}$, the free boundary problem*

$$\begin{aligned} \mathcal{L}F(t,x) &= 0, && (t,x) \in \mathcal{C}, \\ F(t,x) &> e^{-rt}(e^x - K), && (t,x) \in \mathcal{C}, \\ F(t,x^*(t)) &= e^{-rt}(e^{x^*(t)} - K), && 0 \le t \le T, \\ F(T,x) &= e^{-rT}(e^x - K)^+, && x \in \mathbb{R}. \end{aligned}$$

Proof. This is by standard methods (Theorem 2.7.7 in Karatzas and Shreve [11]). □

3.3. *The exercise boundary is non-increasing*

We now analyse the time decay of the ESO value, that is, that the map $t \to V(t,s)$ is non-increasing, for any $t \in [0,T]$ and $s \in \mathbb{R}^+$. This property will imply that the exercise boundary is a non-increasing function of time. Recall the $\mathcal{F}_0^L$-measurable random variable C in (2.6).

Theorem 3.3. (1) *If $C \le \log K$ then the map $t \to V(t,s)$ is non-increasing.*
(2) *If the interest rate is zero, then $t \to V(t,s)$ is non-increasing for any value of C.*

Time decay for American-style claims cannot be expected to hold in general when the price dynamics are governed by a time-inhomogeneous process, as pointed out by Ekstrom [2]. He describes a drastic counter-example, in which volatility can jump from zero to a positive value at some future time. Time decay is often taken for granted, as longer-dated options have all the exercise opportunities of shorter-dated claims, so holds in time-homogeneous models. For this reason, there seems to be very little analysis of this property in the literature.

Theorem 3.3 states that the time decay property always holds for zero interest rate. The same holds for standard American pricing problems (under a martingale measure) in diffusion models (see [2]). Regardless of the interest rate, time decay for the ESO holds for suitably low realisations of the random variable L. Indeed, $C < \log K$ corresponds (modulo the noise in the inside information, governed by the parameter $a \in (0,1)$) to knowledge that the stock price will end up below the strike. With this knowledge, it is intuitively plausible that the insider would exercise the option early, knowing that it will end up out of the money, and this would make the ESO less valuable as time progresses.

We shall use this property below to establish that the exercise boundary is non-increasing, which is an ingredient in our subsequent proof of the smooth pasting condition. An alternative to our approach would be to use an iterative procedure due to Muthuraman [15], which seeks to solve American option problems using a sequence of problems each with known exercise boundary, and with successively better approximations to the true boundary. This would be a good topic for future research, and might be able to show that the smooth pasting condition holds.[2] In particular, this would imply that in fact the exercise boundary is non-increasing and that the time decay property is valid.

Proof. [Proof of Theorem 3.3] The dynamics of the stock price with respect to the enlarged filtration $\mathbb{F}^L$ are

$$dS_t = S_t[\alpha(t,S_t)dt + \sigma dB_t^L], \quad \alpha(t,s) = \beta(t,\log s) + \frac{1}{2}\sigma^2. \tag{3.5}$$

Using the Tanaka-Meyer formula (Jeanblanc *et al.* [9], Chapter 4) applied to the semi-martingale S, we have

$$\begin{aligned}e^{-ru}(S_u-K)^+ &= e^{-rt}(S_t-K)^+ - r\int_t^u e^{-r\rho}(S_\rho-K)^+d\rho + \int_t^u e^{-r\rho}\mathbb{1}_{\{S_\rho>K\}}dS_\rho\\ &\quad+\frac{1}{2}\int_t^u e^{-r\rho}dL_\rho^K(S), \quad 0\le t\le u\le T,\end{aligned}$$

where $L^K(S)$ denotes the local time of S at level K. We take expectation given $S_t = s$ (and of course, implicitly, given $L = \ell$, with this dependence suppressed). It is not hard to verify that the stochastic integral is a $(P,\mathbb{F}^L)$ martingale, and we obtain, on using the dynamics (3.5),

$$\begin{aligned}&E[e^{-ru}(S_u-K)^+\,|\,S_t=s]\\ &\quad= e^{-rt}(s-K)^+ + E\left[\int_t^u e^{-r\rho}[(\alpha(\rho,S_\rho)-r)S_\rho + rK]\mathbb{1}_{\{S_\rho>K\}}d\rho\,\middle|\,S_t=s\right]\\ &\qquad+\frac{1}{2}E\left[\int_t^u e^{-r\rho}dL_\rho^K(S)\,\middle|\,S_t=s\right], \quad 0\le t\le u\le T.\end{aligned} \tag{3.6}$$

We proceed formally for the moment, and indicate further below how to make the following argument rigorous. The local time may be represented as

$$L_t^K(S) = \int_0^t \delta(S_\rho-K)d\langle S\rangle_\rho, \quad 0\le t\le T,$$

where $\delta(\cdot)$ is the Dirac delta function. We shall give meaning to this heuristic expression further below. Using this representation of $L^K(S)$ we convert (3.6) into

$$\begin{aligned}&E[e^{-r(u-t)}(S_u-K)^+\,|\,S_t=s] - (s-K)^+\\ &\quad= E\left[\int_t^u e^{-r(\rho-t)}\mathcal{A}(\rho,S_\rho)d\rho\,\middle|\,S_t=s\right], \quad 0\le t\le u\le T,\end{aligned} \tag{3.7}$$

[2]We thank an anonymous referee for pointing us towards this reference.

where

$$\mathcal{A}(t,s) := [(\alpha(t,s) - r)s + rK]\mathbb{1}_{\{s>K\}} + \frac{1}{2}\sigma^2 s^s \delta(s-K), \quad 0 \le t \le T, \quad s \in \mathbb{R}^+.$$

Jacka and Lynn [8] use a similar construction to (3.7), but for smooth payoff functions, to analyse time decay of optimal stopping problems governed by diffusions.

Now consider two times t_0, t satisfying $0 \le t_0 < t \le T$. Suppose that $(t,s) \in \mathcal{C}$. Let $\tau^*(t,s)$ denote the optimal stopping time for starting state (t,s) and define $v \ge 0$ by $\tau^*(t,s) =: t + v$. Applying (3.7) between t and $t+v$, we obtain

$$0 < V(t,s) - (s-K)^+ = E\left[\int_t^{t+v} e^{-r(\rho-t)}\mathcal{A}(\rho, S_\rho)d\rho \,\middle|\, S_t = s\right]. \tag{3.8}$$

Since t_0+v is in general sub-optimal for the starting state (t_0, s), the same argument applied over $[t_0, t_0+v]$ gives

$$V(t_0,s) - (s-K)^+ \ge E\left[\int_{t_0}^{t_0+v} e^{-r(\rho-t_0)}\mathcal{A}(\rho, S_\rho)d\rho \,\middle|\, S_{t_0} = s\right]. \tag{3.9}$$

From (3.8) and (3.9) we see that if $\mathcal{A}(t,s)$ is non-increasing in t, then we will have

$$V(t_0,s) - (s-K)^+ \ge V(t,s) - (s-K)^+ > 0,$$

implying that value function is non-increasing in time.

The condition that $\mathcal{A}(t,s)$ is non-increasing in t translates to

$$\frac{(C - \log s)}{(T_a - t)^2}\mathbb{1}_{\{s>K\}} \le 0.$$

This condition is clearly satisfied whenever $s \le K$. When $s > K$ (which is the case whenever $(t,s) \in \mathcal{C}$) it will always be satisfied for $C \le \log K$, and with the outline below of how to make the above arguments fully rigorous, this proves the first statement in the theorem.

To be fully rigorous, one must give precise meaning to the representation of the local time in terms of the Dirac delta function. This can be done in the classical manner in which the generalised Itô formula for convex functions is established, by approximating the Dirac delta function $\delta(x)$ by a sequence of probability densities with increasing concentration at the origin. This type of argument can be found in Secs. 3.6 and 3.7 of Karatzas and Shreve [10] and is outlined below.

One defines a sequence of probability density functions (or mollifiers, positive C^∞ functions with compact support that integrate to 1) $(\varphi_n(x))_{n\in\mathbb{N}}$ as well as a sequence of functions $(u_n(x))_{n\in\mathbb{N}}$, given by

$$u_n(x) := \int_{-\infty}^{x}\int_{-\infty}^{y} \varphi_n(z-K)dzdy, \quad x \in \mathbb{R}, \ n \ge 1,$$

such that the following limiting relations hold:

$$\lim_{n\to\infty} u_n(x) = (x-K)^+, \quad \lim_{n\to\infty} u_n'(x) = \lim_{n\to\infty} \int_{-\infty}^{x} \varphi_n(z-K)dz = \mathbb{1}_{\{x>K\}},$$

as well as

$$\lim_{n\to\infty} \int_{\mathbb{R}} u_n''(x)g(x)dx = \lim_{n\to\infty} \int_{\mathbb{R}} \varphi_n(x-K)g(x)dx \int_{\mathbb{R}} \delta(x-K)g(x)dx = g(K),$$

for any Borel function $g(\cdot)$. Thus, in the limit as $n\to\infty$, the function $\varphi_n(\cdot)$ takes on the same properties as the Dirac delta.

One now applies the same arguments that led to (3.7) with $u_n(x)$ in place of $(x-K)^+$, so we are able to use the Itô formula because the u_n are C^2. This gives

$$E[e^{-r(u-t)}u_n(S_u) \,|\, S_t = s] - u_n(s) = E\left[\int_t^u e^{-r(\rho-t)}\mathcal{A}_n(\rho, S_\rho)d\rho \,\middle|\, S_t = s\right],$$

where

$$\mathcal{A}_n(t,s) := \alpha(t,s)su_n'(s) + \frac{1}{2}\sigma^2 s^s u_n''(s) - ru_n(s), \quad 0 \le t \le T, \;\; s \in \mathbb{R}^+.$$

With this is place one looks for conditions such that $\mathcal{A}_n(t,s)$ is non-increasing in t, and finally takes the limit as $n\to\infty$, drawing the same conclusions as before.

To prove the second part of the theorem, we need to establish that when $C > \log K$, then time decay holds provided $r=0$, since we already know that time decay is valid for $C \le \log K$, regardless of r. We do this by adapting a procedure found in El Karoui *et al.* [4], first considering the time decay of a European ESO, and then invoking a variant of an iterative procedure originally due to El Karoui [3] which allows one to infer that the American ESO will inherit whatever time decay property holds for the European ESO.

The European ESO value for starting state $(t,s) \in [0,T] \times \mathbb{R}^+$ and maturity $u \le T$ is given by

$$V^E(t,s;u) = E[e^{-r(u-t)}(S_u - K)^+ \,|\, S_t = s],$$

where the dependence on a given value of L is suppressed as usual. A straightforward computation using the transition density (2.8) gives

$$V^E(t,s;u) = e^{-r(u-t)}[e^{b(t,s;u)}\Phi(z(t,s;u)) - K\Phi(z(t,s;u) - \Sigma(t;u))],$$

where $\Phi(\cdot)$ is the standard cumulative normal distribution function and

$$b(t,s;u) = m(t,\log s;u) + \frac{1}{2}\Sigma^2(t;u), \quad z(t,s;u) = \Sigma(t;u) + \frac{m(t,\log s;u) - \log K}{\Sigma(t;u)},$$

with m, Σ defined in (2.9). Differentiation with respect to t gives

$$\frac{\partial V^E}{\partial t}(t,s;u) = e^{-r(u-t)}\left[\left(r + \frac{\partial m}{\partial t} + \Sigma\frac{\partial \Sigma}{\partial t}\right)e^b\Phi(z) - rK\Phi(z-\Sigma) + K\frac{\partial \Sigma}{\partial t}\Phi'(z-\Sigma)\right],$$

where we have suppressed arguments of functions for brevity. Since Φ and Φ' are positive and $\partial\Sigma/\partial t$ is negative, the last two terms on the right-hand side are negative, so the European ESO value will be guaranteed to be non-increasing with time provided that

$$r + \frac{\partial m}{\partial t}(t, \log s; u) + \Sigma(t;u)\frac{\partial \Sigma}{\partial t}(t;u) \leq 0.$$

This condition translates to

$$C - \log s \geq r\frac{(T_a - t)^2}{T_a - u} - \frac{1}{2}\sigma^2(T_a - u).$$

Suppose $r = 0$. We are ultimately interested in when the American ESO value will exhibit time decay, and since $V(t,s) = 0$ for $s \leq K$, we only consider the case when $s > K$. Then, for the European ESO value to exhibit time decay in the region $s > K$ we require

$$C - \log s \geq -\frac{1}{2}\sigma^2(T_a - u), \quad \text{when } s > K. \tag{3.10}$$

Since the right-hand side is negative, the condition will be guaranteed if $C \geq \log K$. Hence we conclude that for $r = 0$ and $s > K$, $\partial V^E/\partial t(t,s;u) \leq 0$ if $C \geq \log K$.

To complete the proof we now invoke the iterative procedure of El Karoui *et al.* [4] to infer a property for the American option from the corresponding property for the European value.

Denote the payoff of the option by $h(s) = (s-K)^+$. Denote by $(S_u(t,s))_{t\leq u\leq T}$ the stock price process given initial condition $S_t = s$, for $t \in [0,T]$. Recall that the American ESO value is given by

$$V(t,s) = \sup_{\tau\in\mathcal{T}^L_{t,T}} E[e^{-r(\tau-t)}h(S_\tau(t,s))], \quad 0 \leq t \leq T, \ \ s > 0.$$

For fixed (t,s) the process $(e^{-r(u-t)}V(u, S_u(t,s)))_{t\leq u\leq T}$ is the smallest supermartingale that dominates $(e^{-r(u-t)}h(S_u(t,s)))_{t\leq u\leq T}$. We now construct V by an iterative procedure found in [4], adapted to the situation in hand.

For any continuous Borel function $g : [0,T]\times\mathbb{R}^+ \to \mathbb{R}$, we define

$$(R_u g)(t,s) := E[e^{-r(u-t)}g(u, S_u(t,s))], \quad 0 \leq t \leq u \leq T, \ \ s > 0.$$

So, in particular, we have $V^E(t,s;u) = (R_u h)(t,s)$ and this is decreasing in t for $r = 0$, $s > K$ and $C \geq \log K$.

Define the operator

$$(\mathcal{K}g)(t,s) := \sup_{u\in[t,T]} (R_u g)(t,s), \quad 0 \le t \le T, \;\; s > 0.$$

It is straightforward to see that $\mathcal{K}h$ also exhibits time decay. Moreover, for $r = 0$ and $s > K$, $\mathcal{K}h \ge h$ if $C \ge \log K$, by virtue of the Jensen inequality, since we have for any $u \in [t,T]$:

$$\begin{aligned}(\mathcal{K}h)(t,s) \ge (R_u h)(t,s) &= e^{-r(u-t)} E[(S_u(t,s) - K)^+] \\ &\ge e^{-r(u-t)} (E[S_u(t,s)] - K)^+ \\ &= e^{-r(u-t)} \left(s \exp\left[\beta(t, \log s)(u-t) + \frac{1}{2}\Sigma^2(t;u) \right] - K \right)^+ .\end{aligned}$$

Then, if $r = 0$, we see that $(\mathcal{K}h)(t,s) \ge h(s)$ provided that

$$\beta(t, \log s)(u-t) + \frac{1}{2}\Sigma^2(t;u) \ge 0.$$

This is (3.10), so for $s > K$ will hold whenever $C \ge \log K$.

Since $\mathcal{K}h \ge h$, we have $\mathcal{K}^{n+1}h \ge \mathcal{K}^n h$, where $\mathcal{K}^n$ denotes the n-fold iterate of $\mathcal{K}$. We can thus define

$$w := \lim_{n\to\infty} \mathcal{K}^n h = \sup_{n\in\mathbb{N}} \mathcal{K}^n h.$$

It is easy to see that w inherits the properties of $\mathcal{K}h$, so w also exhibits time decay.

The remainder of the proof follows the same reasoning as Theorem 9.4 in El Karoui *et al.* [4], to establish that w is the smallest fixed point of $\mathcal{K}$ dominating h, and hence that w coincides with V, so that V also displays time decay when $r = 0$ and $C \ge \log K$. Since V displays time decay when $C \le \log K$, we conclude that time decay holds for all values of C when $r = 0$. This ends the proof. For completeness, here is the argument.

We have $w \ge \mathcal{K}^{n+1} w = \mathcal{K}(\mathcal{K}^n w)$. Letting $n \to \infty$, we obtain $w \ge \mathcal{K}w$. The reverse inequality is trivial.

If u is a fixed point of $\mathcal{K}$ dominating h, then $u = \mathcal{K}^n u \ge \mathcal{K}^n h$. Letting $n \to \infty$, we obtain $u \ge w$.

Fix (t,s) and consider $Z_u = e^{-r(u-t)} w(u, S_u(t,s))$. For $0 \le t \le u_1 \le u_2 \le T$, we have

$$\begin{aligned}E[Z_{u_2} \mid \mathcal{F}^L_{u_1}] &= e^{-r(u_1-t)} E[e^{-r(u_2-u_1)} w(u_2, S_{u_2}(t,s)) \mid \mathcal{F}^L_{u_1}] \\ &= e^{-r(u_1-t)} (R_{u_2} w)(u_1, S_{u_1}(t,s)) \\ &\le e^{-r(u_1-t)} (\mathcal{K}w)(u_1, S_{u_1}(t,s)) \\ &= Z_{u_1}.\end{aligned}$$

Thus, Z is a supermartingale dominating $e^{-r(u-t)} h(S_u(t,s))$, and so must dominate $e^{-r(u-t)} V(u, S_u(t,s))$ as well. In particular, $w(t,s) = Z_0 \ge V(t,s)$.

For the reverse inequality, we observe from the supermartingale property for $e^{-r(u-t)}V(u, S_u(t,s))$ that $(R_u V)(t,s) \leq V(t,s)$, and hence $\mathcal{K}V \leq V$. Therefore, V is a fixed point of $\mathcal{K}$, and being a fixed point of $\mathcal{K}$, V must dominate w. Hence, V and w coincide, and so V inherits the properties of w, and we are done.

□

Lemma 3.2. *Suppose the map $t \to V(t,s)$ is non-increasing. Then the exercise boundary $s^*(t)$ is non-increasing, for $t \in [0,T]$.*

Proof. Choose $(t,s) \in \mathcal{C}$ for some $s \in \mathbb{R}^+$ and consider t_0 satisfying $0 \leq t_0 < t \leq T$. By assumption, $V(t_0, s) \geq V(t,s)$, and therefore

$$V(t_0, s) - (s-K)^+ \geq V(t,s) - (s-K)^+ > 0, \quad 0 \leq t \leq T,$$

so that (t_0, s) is also in $\mathcal{C}$. That is, for $t_0 < t$, we have that $s < s^*(t)$ necessarily implies that $s < s^*(t_0)$, and this can only be true if $s^*(t_0)$ is at least as big as $s^*(t)$, that is, $s^*(t_0) \geq s^*(t)$. □

This lemma implies that $x^*(t) = \log s^*(t)$ is also non-increasing.

3.4. *Smooth fit condition*

In this subsection we establish the smooth-fit condition for F. There are three ingredients in the proof: convexity of F in x (Theorem 3.1), a "regularity" property of the exercise boundary x^* (Lemma 3.3) and a result (Lemma 3.4) which allows us to establish a lower bound for F_x just below the exercise boundary.

The smooth-fit condition for F is as follows. The proof is given at the end of this subsection, after establishing some auxiliary lemmas.

Theorem 3.4. *Suppose the exercise boundary is non-increasing. Then the value function satisfies the smooth fit condition, that is*

$$F_x(t, x^*(t)) = e^{-rt}e^{x^*(t)} \Leftrightarrow V_s(t, s^*(t)) = 1, \quad \textit{for all } t \in [0,T).$$

When the exercise boundary is non-increasing, we have the regularity result below characterising the boundary. It states that if the log-stock price process starts arbitrarily close to the boundary, then it will hit the boundary in the next instant. This is in the spirit of the definition of a regular boundary point in the context of the Dirichlet problem (see Definition 4.2.9 and Theorem 4.2.12 in [10]).

Lemma 3.3. *Suppose the exercise boundary is non-increasing. Denote by $\tau^*(t,x)$ the optimal stopping time for $F(t,x)$, for some $(t,x) \in [0,T) \times \mathbb{R}$. Then, we have*

$$\lim_{\epsilon \to 0} \tau^*(t, x^*(t) - \epsilon) \to t, \quad \text{a.s.,} \ 0 \leq t \leq T.$$

Proof. Without loss of generality, set the starting time to zero, write $X(x) \equiv X(0,x)$ for the value of the log-stock price given $X_0 = x$, as well as $\tau^*(x) \equiv \tau^*(0,x)$ and $x^*(0) \equiv x^*$. For $\epsilon > 0$, since the exercise boundary is non-increasing we have

$$\tau^*(x^* - \epsilon) \leq \inf\{\rho \in [0,T) \,|\, X_\rho(x^* - \epsilon) \geq x^*\}. \tag{3.11}$$

From the solution (2.7) for $X(x)$ and the Law of the Iterated Logarithm for Brownian motion (Section I.16 of Rogers and Williams [17]), we have

$$\sup_{0 \leq u \leq \rho} X_u(x) > x, \quad \text{a.s.},$$

for every $\rho > 0$. Hence there exists a sufficiently small $\epsilon > 0$ such that

$$\sup_{0 \leq u \leq \rho} X_u(x^* - \epsilon) \geq x^*, \quad \text{a.s.}$$

Hence the right-hand side of (3.11) tends to zero as $\epsilon \to 0$, and this completes the proof. □

The next ingredient we need for the proof of smooth fit is the following lemma.

Lemma 3.4. *Let $(t,x) \in [0,T) \times \mathbb{R}$ and denote by $X(t,x)$ the log-stock price with initial condition $X_t = x$. Denote by $(\tau_\epsilon)_{\epsilon>0}$ a family of $\mathcal{T}^L_{t,T}$-stopping times converging to t almost surely as $\epsilon \to 0$. Then $X(t,x)$ satisfies*

$$\lim_{\epsilon \to 0} \frac{1}{\epsilon}(\exp(X_{\tau_\epsilon}(t,x)) - \exp(X_{\tau_\epsilon}(t,x-\epsilon))) = e^x, \quad \text{a.s.}$$

Proof. Without loss of generality, consider a starting time $t = 0$. The same ideas apply to any starting time $t \in [0,T)$. Write $X(x) \equiv X(0,x)$ for the log-stock price with initial condition $X_0 = x \in \mathbb{R}$. For $\epsilon > 0$, define

$$\Delta_u(\epsilon) := \frac{1}{\epsilon}(\beta(u, X_u(x)) - \beta(u, X_u(x-\epsilon))), \quad 0 \leq u < T. \tag{3.12}$$

Using (3.2), we have

$$\frac{1}{\epsilon}(e^{X_{\tau_\epsilon}(x)} - e^{X_{\tau_\epsilon}(x-\epsilon)}) = \frac{1}{\epsilon} e^{X_{\tau_\epsilon}(x-\epsilon)} \left[\exp\left\{\epsilon\left(1 + \int_0^{\tau_\epsilon} \Delta_u(\epsilon) du\right)\right\} - 1\right].$$

Using Taylor's expansion, we get

$$\frac{1}{\epsilon}(e^{X_{\tau_\epsilon}(x)} - e^{X_{\tau_\epsilon}(x-\epsilon)}) = e^{X_{\tau_\epsilon}(x-\epsilon)}\left(1 + \int_0^{\tau_\epsilon} \Delta_u(\epsilon) du + O(\epsilon)\right),$$

where $O(\epsilon)$ denotes terms of order ϵ or higher. Observe that

$$\lim_{\epsilon \to 0} \Delta_u(\epsilon) = b(u, X_u(x)) D_u(x), \quad 0 \leq u \leq T, \quad \text{a.s.},$$

where b, D are defined in (3.3). Then, using the fact that $\lim_{\epsilon \to 0} \tau_\epsilon = 0$ (since we have set $t = 0$) and $e^{X_{\tau_\epsilon}(x-\epsilon)} = e^x$ a.s. completes the proof. □

Note that if the drift β was constant or a deterministic function of time, then the lemma would follow directly from the fact that Δ in (3.12) is equal to zero.

We now prove the smooth fit condition.

Proof. [Proof of Theorem 3.4 (Smooth fit)] It entails no loss of generality if we set $r = 0$ and $t = 0$, but significantly simplifies notation. Write $F(x) \equiv F(0, x)$ and $x^* \equiv x^*(0)$. Then $F(x) = (e^x - K)$ for $x \geq x^*$, so $F_x(x^*+) = e^{x^*}$.

On the other hand, from Theorem 3.1 we know that the mapping $x \to F(x)$ is increasing and convex, so $F_x(x^*-) \leq e^{x^*}$. Hence it suffices to show that

$$F_x(x^*-) \geq e^{x^*}.$$

As before let $\tau^*(x)$ denote the optimal stopping time for starting state x. Since $\tau^*(x - \epsilon)$ is suboptimal for $F(x)$, we have

$$\begin{aligned} F(x) - F(x-\epsilon) &\geq E[(\exp(X_{\tau^*(x-\epsilon)}(x)) - K)^+ - (\exp(X_{\tau^*(x-\epsilon)}(x-\epsilon)) - K)^+] \\ &\geq E[(e^{X_{\tau^*(x-\epsilon)}(x)} - e^{X_{\tau^*(x-\epsilon)}(x-\epsilon)})\mathbb{1}_{\{X_{\tau^*(x-\epsilon)}(x-\epsilon) \geq \log K\}}], \quad (3.13) \end{aligned}$$

where we have use the fact that $x \to X(x)$ is increasing.

By Lemma 3.3 and the fact that it is never optimal to exercise below the strike, we have

$$\lim_{\epsilon \to 0} \mathbb{1}_{\{X_{\tau(x^*-\epsilon)}(x^*-\epsilon) \geq \log K\}} = \mathbb{1}_{\{X_0(x^*) \geq \log K\}} = 1, \quad \text{a.s.} \tag{3.14}$$

Also, by Lemma 3.4, we have

$$\lim_{\epsilon \to 0} \frac{1}{\epsilon}(e^{X_{\tau(x^*-\epsilon)}(x^*)} - e^{X_{\tau(x^*-\epsilon)}(x^*-\epsilon)}) = e^{x^*}, \quad \text{a.s.} \tag{3.15}$$

Using (3.14) and (3.15) and noting that all terms inside the expectation in (3.13) are uniformly integrable, Theorem II.21.2 in Rogers and Williams [17] gives

$$\lim_{\epsilon \to 0} \frac{1}{\epsilon}[F(x^*) - F(x^* - \epsilon)] \geq e^{x^*},$$

which completes the proof. □

3.5. *The early exercise decomposition*

We now transform the state space from log-stock price to stock price in order to state the early exercise decomposition for the ESO value function V, given by $e^{-rt}V(t, s) = F(t, \log s)$. With this change of variable the smooth fit condition becomes $V_s(t, s^*(t)) = 1$ and the PDE for F in the continuation region transforms to $\mathcal{L}^S V - rV = 0$, where $\mathcal{L}^S$ is the extended generator of S, given by

$$\mathcal{L}^S = \frac{\partial}{\partial t} + \alpha(t, s)s\frac{\partial}{\partial s} + \frac{1}{2}\sigma^2 s^2 \frac{\partial^2}{\partial s^2}, \quad \alpha(t, s) = \beta(t, \log s) + \frac{1}{2}\sigma^2. \tag{3.16}$$

We then have the following decomposition for V.

Theorem 3.5. *The value function V of an executive stock option with strike K and maturity T has the following decomposition into a European option value and an early exercise premium:*

$$V(t,s) = e^{-r(T-t)}E[(S_T - K)^+ \mid S_t = s] + p(t,s), \quad (t,s) \in [0,T] \times \mathbb{R}^+, \tag{3.17}$$

where

$$p(t,s) := \int_t^T e^{-r(u-t)}E[((r - \alpha(u,S_u))S_u - rK)\mathbb{1}_{\{S_u > s^*(u)\}} \mid S_t = s]du, \tag{3.18}$$

is the early exercise premium.

Proof. The smooth fit condition implies that F_x is continuous. We have that F_{xx} is continuous in the continuation region and equal to e^{-rt+x} in the stopping region. Though the second derivative might not be continuous across the exercise boundary we may nevertheless apply the generalised Itô formula for convex functions to F, to obtain the Doob-Meyer decomposition of the Snell envelope:

$$\begin{aligned} F(T,X_T) &= F(t,X_t) + \sigma \int_t^T F_x(u,X_u)dB_u^L \\ &+ \int_t^T e^{-ru}\left[\left(\beta(u,X_u) + \frac{1}{2}\sigma^2 - r\right)e^{X_u} + rK\right]\mathbb{1}_{\{X_u > x^*(u)\}}du, \quad 0 \le t \le T, \end{aligned}$$

where we have used $F(t,x) = e^{-rt}(e^x - K)$ for $x > x^*(t)$. Now take expectation conditional on $X_t = x$ (and of course given a known value of L), change variables from X to S, and (3.18) follows. □

3.6. *Integral equation for early exercise boundary*

The integral equation for the early exercise boundary follows by setting $s = s^*(t)$ in (3.18), yielding the following corollary. To be explicit we restore the dependence on the random variable L. For $L = \ell$, denote the insider's exercise boundary by $s_\ell^*(t)$. Using $V(t, s_\ell^*(t)) = s_\ell^*(t) - K$, we obtain:

Corollary 3.1. *For $L = \ell \in \mathbb{R}$, the insider's exercise boundary s_ℓ^* satisfies, for $0 \le t \le T$,*

$$\begin{aligned} s_\ell^*(t) &= K + e^{-r(T-t)}E[(S_T - K)^+ \mid S_t = s^*(t), L = \ell] \\ &+ \int_t^T e^{-r(u-t)}E[\mathbb{1}_{\{S_u > s_\ell^*(u)\}}((r - \alpha(u,S_u))S_u - rK) \mid S_t = s_\ell^*(t), L = \ell]du. \end{aligned}$$

3.7. *Numerical solution of early exercise boundary equation*

The algorithm used to numerically solve the integral equation in Corollary 3.1 is as follows. For a fixed $t \in [0,T]$ and $\ell \in \mathbb{R}$, we treat the computations of the expectations as European option prices, with stock price dynamics under $\mathbb{F}^L$ given by

$$dS_u = \alpha(u,S_u)S_u du + \sigma S_u dB_u^L,$$

with α defined in (3.16).

These are computed by solving the associated Black-Scholes style PDE using a central difference scheme, for a sufficiently wide range of $s_\ell^*(t)$. We discretise the interval $[0, T]$ and use the trapezoidal rule to approximate the integral, solving the discretised integral equation using the fixed point method. The exercise boundary is computed by backward recursion with the starting value $s_\ell^*(T) = K$.

Figure 1 shows the insider's exercise boundaries when the stock appreciation rate μ is higher than the interest rate. The insider possesses noisy log-stock price knowledge with $L = a \log 80$ with $a = 0.5, 0.6, 0.7$, so the insider knows that the ESO is likely to be at-the-money at maturity with varying degrees of certainty.

The impact of inside information in this case is clear. Recall that it is not optimal for the regular agent to exercise early when $\mu \geq r$.[3] This conclusion is altered for the insider, who has greater certainty than the regular agent that the option will expire out of the money, and this induces early exercise. We also observe that the exercise boundary is lower as a increases towards 1, and the privileged information becomes less noisy. The insider becomes more certain that the option will expire worthless and early exercise is induced at lower thresholds.

Figure 2 shows the regular trader's and insider's exercise boundaries when $\mu < r$. The insider possesses noisy log-stock price knowledge where $L = 0.5 \log S_T$ with $S_T = 78, 80, 82, 90$.

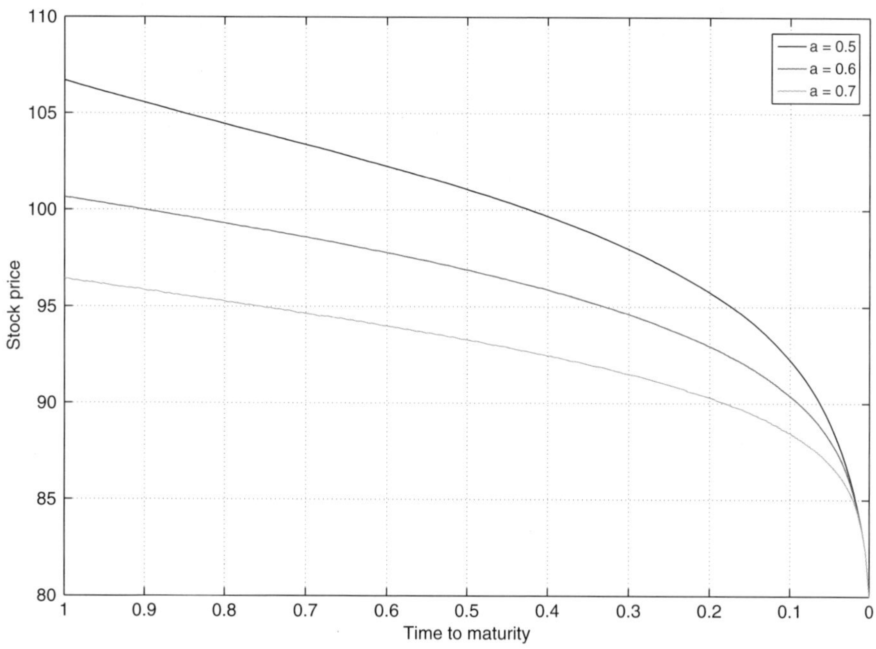

Fig. 1. Insider's exercise boundaries for $L = a \log 80$ with different values of the noise coefficient a, $r = 0.01$, $\mu = 0.02$, $\sigma = 0.2$, $T = 1$, $K = 80$.

[3]Indeed, attempts to solve for the regular agent's exercise boundary numerically when $\mu \geq r$ leads to divergence when executing the fixed point method.

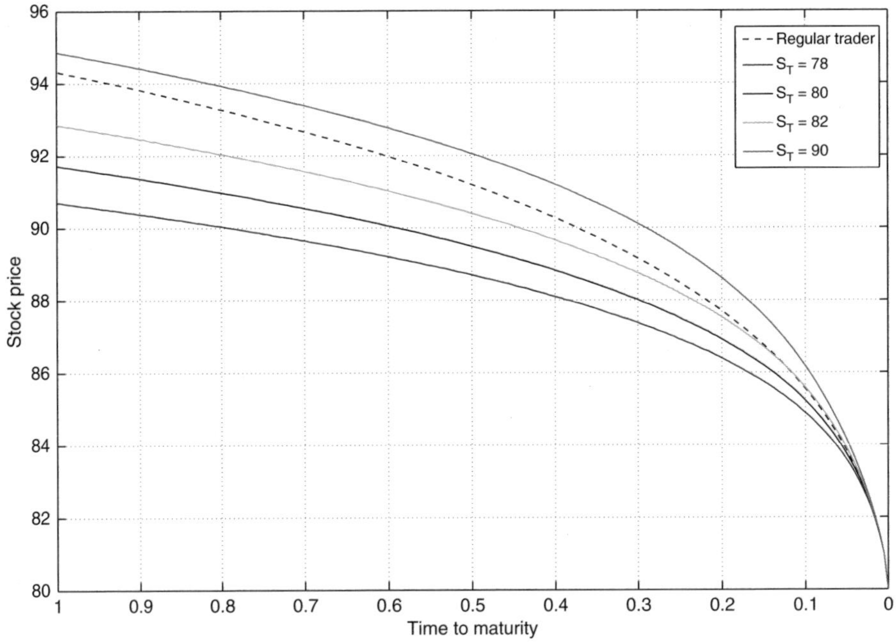

Fig. 2. Regular trader's and insider's exercise boundaries for $L = 0.5 \log S_T$ with different values of S_T, $r = 0.01$, $\mu = 0$, $\sigma = 0.2$, $T = 1$, $K = 80$.

For $S_T = 78$ and $S_T = 80$, the insider has a lower exercise boundary than the regular agent due to his pessimistic inside information, in a similar vein to the results in Fig. 1. For $S_T = 82$, the insider knows that the ESO is likely to be in-the-money, yet still exercises the ESO earlier than the regular agent. Although the fact that the ESO is likely to end up in-the-money tends to delay exercise, there is a competing effect of a lower variance in the stock price as perceived by the insider, and this induces earlier exercise. For the case $S_T = 90$, the privileged information is sufficiently optimistic so that the insider exercises later than the regular trader.

This suggests that inside information has two potentially competing effects: a reduced variance of the stock price that hastens exercise and a directional effect, which can hasten or delay exercise.

4. Conclusions

Using an initial enlargement of filtration to augment a Brownian filtration with noisy information on the value of a stock at the maturity time of an ESO, we have analysed the stopping decision faced by an insider who does not trade the stock or other securities. This shows that the insider can exercise the ESO before maturity, in situations in which a regular agent would not. This involved establishing fundamental properties of the value function (notably convexity, time decay and smooth fit) when the price process is a time-inhomogeneous diffusion.

This paper has set a framework in which such questions can be studied. An interesting direction for future work is to add trading opportunities in outside assets and risk aversion for the agent.

Acknowledgments

We thank Peter Bank, Kasper Larsen, Goran Peskir, Martin Schweizer, Mihalis Zervos, two anonymous referees and participants at the Workshop on Foundations of Mathematical Finance (Fields Institute, 2010) for helpful suggestions.

References

[1] A. Danilova, M. Monoyios and A. Ng, Optimal investment with inside information and parameter uncertainty, *Math. Financ. Econ.* **3** (2010) 13–38.

[2] E. Ekström, Properties of American option prices, *Stochastic Process. Appl.* **114** (2004) 265–278.

[3] N. El Karoui, Les aspects probabilistes du contrôle stochastique, in *Ninth Saint Flour Probability Summer School — 1979* (Saint Flour, 1979), Vol. 876 of Lecture Notes in Math. (Springer, Berlin, 1981), pp. 73–238.

[4] N. El Karoui, M. Jeanblanc-Picqué and S. E. Shreve, Robustness of the black and scholes formula, *Math. Finance* **8** (1998) 93–126.

[5] N. El Karoui, J.-P. Lepeltier and A. Millet, A probabilistic approach to the reduite in optimal stopping, *Probab. Math. Statist.* **13** (1992) 97–121.

[6] M. Grasselli and V. Henderson, Risk aversion and block exercise of executive stock options, *J. Econom. Dynam. Control* **33** (2009) 109–127.

[7] D. G. Hobson, Volatility misspecification, option pricing and superreplication via coupling, *Ann. Appl. Probab.* **8** (1998) 193–205.

[8] S. D. Jacka and J. R. Lynn, Finite-horizon optimal stopping obstacle problems and the shape of the continuation region, *Stochastics Stochastics Rep.* **39** (1992) 25–42.

[9] M. Jeanblanc, M. Yor and M. Chesney, *Mathematical Methods for Financial Markets*, Springer Finance (Springer-Verlag, London Ltd., London), 2009.

[10] I. Karatzas and S. E. Shreve, *Brownian Motion and Stochastic Calculus*, Vol. 113 of Graduate Texts in Mathematics, 2nd edn. (Springer-Verlag, New York, 1991).

[11] I. Karatzas and S. E. Shreve, *Methods of Mathematical Finance*, Vol. 39 of Applications of Mathematics (New York), (Springer-Verlag, New York, 1998).

[12] T. Leung and R. Sircar, Accounting for risk aversion, vesting, job termination risk and multiple exercises in valuation of employee stock options, *Math. Finance* **19** (2009) 99–128.

[13] T. Leung and R. Sircar, Exponential hedging with optimal stopping and application to employee stock option valuation, *SIAM J. Control Optim.* **48** (2009) 1422–1451.

[14] R. C. Merton, Theory of rational option pricing, *Bell J. Econom. and Management Sci.* **4** (1973) 141–183.

[15] K. Muthuraman, A moving boundary approach to American option pricing, *J. Econom. Dynam. Control* **32** (2008) 3520–3537.

[16] L. C. G. Rogers and J. Scheinkman, Optimal exercise of executive stock options, *Finance Stoch.* **11** (2007) 357–372.

[17] L. C. G. Rogers and D. Williams, *Diffusions, Markov Processes and Martingales*, Vol. 1, Cambridge Mathematical Library (Cambridge University Press, Cambridge, 2000). Foundations, Reprint of the 2nd edn. (1994).

[18] R. Sircar and W. Xiong, A general framework for evaluating executive stock options, *J. Econom. Dynam. Control* **31** (2007) 2317–2349.

[19] M. Yor, *Some Aspects of Brownian Motion, Part II*, Lectures in Mathematics ETH Zürich, Birkhäuser Verlag, Basel, 1997, Some recent martingale problems.

INITIAL INVESTMENT CHOICE AND OPTIMAL FUTURE ALLOCATIONS UNDER TIME-MONOTONE PERFORMANCE CRITERIA*

M. MUSIELA

BNP Paribas, 10 Harewood Avenue,
London NW1 6AA, United Kingdom

T. ZARIPHOPOULOU

Oxford-Man Institute of Quantitative Finance
Eagle House, Walton Well Road, Oxford OX2 6ED, United Kingdom

The Mathematical Institute
University of Oxford, Oxford, United Kingdom

Departments of Mathematics and IROM
The University of Texas at Austin
1 University Station, Austin, TX 78712, USA

The paper offers a new perspective on optimal portfolio choice by investigating how and to what extent knowledge of an investor's desirable initial investment choice can be used to determine his future optimal portfolio allocations. Optimality of investment decisions is built on the so-called forward investment performance criteria and, in particular, on the time-monotone ones. It is shown that for this class of forward criteria the desired initial allocations completely characterize the future optimal investment strategies. The analysis uses the connection between a nonlinear equation, satisfied by the local risk tolerance, and the backward heat equation. Complete solutions are provided as well as various examples.

Keywords: Portfolio management; forward investment performance; time consistency; utility theory.

1. Introduction

The powerful and elegant theory of expected utility yields optimal portfolio choices for risk averse investors in stochastic market environments. In the classical continuous time framework, introduced in [5], the investor's preferences are assigned at the end of the trading horizon. The optimal investment strategy is, then, the one that

*This chapter was originally published under the same title in *International Journal of Theoretical and Applied Finance*, Vol.14, No.1, 61–81 (2011). Singapore: World Scientific Publishing.

delivers the maximal expected (indirect) utility of terminal wealth. Recently, the authors proposed an alternative approach to optimal portfolio choice which is based on the so-called forward investment performance criterion (see, among others, [8]). In this approach, the investor does not choose her risk preferences at a single point in time, as it is the case in the Merton model, but has the flexibility to revise them dynamically.

From the methodological point of view, one of the fundamental differences between the two approaches is that the investor specifies her utility at the beginning of the trading horizon and not at the end. Whether one works in the traditional or the alternative framework, the specification of the terminal, or initial, risk preferences remains a challenging task. In the context of forward portfolio choice, this question was recently examined in [6]. Therein, one shows how the investor's preferences may be inferred from desirable distributional properties of future investment targets. An important consequence of this methodology is that the individual risk preferences are calibrated to the specific market environment and the investment opportunities this environment offers. This is in contrast to the classical framework in which the utility function is assigned exogenously, in isolation to the market in which the investor operates. Inference of risk preferences from similar probabilistic criteria has been also proposed and analyzed in a static model by Sharpe and his coauthors in [3, 4, 11, 12].

Herein, we provide an additional point of view on portfolio choice and the *specification* of the investor's risk preferences. The analysis is built on an entirely different perspective which is, from one hand, quite unorthodox with respect to the classical academic ideas but, on the other, it appears to be much closer to the rationale applied in investment practice. Specifically, instead of requiring that the investor knows his risk preferences at the beginning of the investment horizon, it is assumed that he is able to specify the portfolio allocations that are desirable to him at initiation. The motivation to consider this direction comes mainly from the fact that the concept of utility is quite elusive and difficult to quantify.

The inspiration comes from a paper* written by Black ([2]) on similar ideas. One reads:

> ... "Utility" is a foreign concept for most individuals, and the traditional way of mapping an individual's utility function is to ask him about his preferences among a number of gambles.
>
> Instead of stating his preferences among various gambles, the individual can specify his consumption function and his initial investment function. He can give the rate at which he would consume his wealth at various times in the future as a function of the amount of his wealth at those times. And he can tell how much he would invest currently in the market portfolio as a function of his current wealth.

*The authors are thankful to Peter Carr who brought this manuscript to their attention.

> It is possible to eliminate the individual's utility function entirely from these equations, giving a set of equations involving only his investment function and his consumption function....

Therein, an infinitesimal analysis is proposed for the specification of the future optimal investment and consumption policies once their initial values are chosen. The case when these initial choices are proportional to the investor's wealth is solved in detail.

In this paper, we build on the same ideas and extend the results in various directions. We allow for both more general initial allocations and asset prices.[†] However, we do not incorporate intermediate consumption. Optimality is considered with respect to the forward investment performance criteria and, specifically, for time-monotone ones. For such families of dynamic risk preferences, we show how knowledge of the initial desired allocation can be used to recover all future portfolio processes, the associated wealth process and, finally, the investment criterion with respect to which they (portfolio and wealth) are optimal.

We note that the entire analysis bypasses the need to know the risk preferences. Indeed, we will see that risk preferences are identified only at the end, when one seeks the criterion with respect to which the already constructed processes are optimal. The solution approach is based on a deep connection between the so-called local risk tolerance function and harmonic functions as well as on the specification of a measure whose bilateral Laplace transform yields the latter. This measure becomes the defining element for all quantities of interest. We show how the initial desired allocation reveals it. A by-product of this analysis is the specification of the set of initial allocations that lead to well defined future investment choices. One can say that this is the set of feasible initial investment choices.

We conclude mentioning that the choice to use forward performance criteria is a natural consequence of their suitability to address the questions posed herein which are formulated "forward" in time. The specific choice of time-monotone performances was motivated by the facts that, from one hand, similar monotone criteria were used in [2] and, from the other, this class offers substantial tractability that helps us producing explicit solutions. Our knowledge of forward performance processes that are non-monotone is still limited. On the other hand, even the monotone case presents various challenges and offers a number of interesting, if not intriguing, insights. As a first step towards addressing the questions posed by Black, the family we use herein seems to offer a rich enough framework to produce meaningful solutions and to provide strong motivation for further research in this direction.

The paper is organized as follows. In Secs. 2 and 3 we introduce the model and pose the portfolio choice problem. In Sec. 4 we provide auxiliary results on the representation of the local risk tolerance function and its connection with harmonic

[†]For convenience, we assume that there is a single risky asset but the results easily extend to the multi-asset case.

solutions. In Sec. 5 we provide the main results and answers to the questions in consideration. We conclude with various examples in Sec. 6.

2. The Model and the Investment Performance Criterion

The market environment consists of a riskless bond and a stock. The stock price, $S_t, t \geq 0$, is modelled as an Itô process following

$$dS_t = S_t(\mu_t dt + \sigma_t dW_t), \tag{2.1}$$

with $S_0 > 0$. The process W_t is a standard Brownian motion, defined on a filtered probability space $(\Omega, \mathcal{F}, \mathbb{P})$. The coefficients μ_t and $\sigma_t, t \geq 0$, are $\mathcal{F}_t$-adapted processes. The riskless asset, the savings account, has the price process $B_t, t \geq 0$, satisfying

$$dB_t = r_t B_t dt,$$

with $B_0 = 1$, and for a nonnegative, $\mathcal{F}_t$-adapted interest rate process r_t. The market coefficients μ_t, σ_t and r_t are taken to satisfy the appropriate integrability conditions.

We define the process $\lambda_t, t \geq 0$, by

$$\lambda_t = \frac{\mu_t - r_t}{\sigma_t}, \tag{2.2}$$

and we throughout assume that it is bounded by a deterministic constant $c > 0$, i.e., for all $t \geq 0, |\lambda_t| \leq c$. We will be occasionally referring to this process as the market price of risk.

Starting at $t = 0$ with an initial endowment $x \in \mathbb{R}$, the investor invests, at any time $t > 0$, in the two assets. The present value of the amounts invested in the bond and the stock are denoted, respectively, by π_t^0 and π_t.

The present value of her current total investment is, then, given by $X_t^\pi = \pi_t^0 + \pi_t, t \geq 0$. Using (2.1) we have that it satisfies

$$dX_t^\pi = \sigma_t \pi_t (\lambda_t dt + dW_t), \tag{2.3}$$

with $X_0 = x$. The investment policies π_t, $t \geq 0$, will play the role of control processes and are taken to satisfy the usual assumptions of being self-financing, $\mathcal{F}_t$-progressively measurable and satisfying the integrability condition $E(\int_0^t |\sigma_s \pi_s|^2 ds) < +\infty, t > 0$. We denote the set of admissible strategies by $\mathcal{A}$.

Recently, a selection criterion for investment strategies in $\mathcal{A}$ was introduced in [8] (see, also, [10]). It is represented by a process, the so-called forward investment performance. This criterion is defined for all times and complements the traditional one which is based on the maximal expected utility of terminal wealth (value function process), defined only on $[0, T], T < +\infty$.

As the definition below states, a strategy is deemed optimal if it generates a wealth process whose average performance is maintained over time. In other words, the average performance of this strategy at any future date, conditional on today's information, preserves the performance of this strategy up until today. Any strategy that fails to maintain the average performance over time is, then, sub-optimal. The intuition behind these requirements comes from the analogous properties of the value function process, namely, its martingality along optimal policies and its supermartingality away from the optimum. We refer the reader to [8] for a detailed discussion on the new approach.

Definition 2.1. An $\mathcal{F}_t$-adapted process $U(x,t)$ is a forward investment performance if for $t \geq 0$ and $x \in \mathbb{D}, \mathbb{D} \subseteq \mathbb{R}$:

(i) the mapping $x \to U(x,t)$ is strictly concave and increasing,
(ii) for each $\pi \in \mathcal{A}$, $E(U(X_t^\pi,t))^+ < \infty$, and

$$E(U(X_s^\pi,s)\,|\,\mathcal{F}_t) \leq U(X_t^\pi,t), \quad s \geq t, \tag{2.4}$$

(iii) there exists $\pi_t^* \in \mathcal{A}$, for which

$$E(U(X_s^{\pi^*},s)\,|\,\mathcal{F}_t) = U(X_t^{\pi^*},t), \quad s \geq t. \tag{2.5}$$

Remark 2.1. Intuitively speaking, $U(x,t)$ represents the stochastic utility that is generated by the policy of investing all wealth in the riskless asset across time. Note that even though this is a riskless strategy, it generates nondeterministic utility, for it is implemented in a stochastic environment. Note, also, that this interpretation is directly aligned with the fact that the bond has been chosen as the numeraire.

Characterizing the class of processes which satisfy the above definition is a challenging problem. An important result in this direction, introduced recently in [9], is a stochastic partial differential equation for the investment performance process, namely,

$$dU(x,t) = \frac{1}{2}\frac{(\lambda_t U(x,t) + a_x(x,t))^2}{U_{xx}(x,t)}dt + a(x,t)dW_t, \tag{2.6}$$

where $a(x,t)$ is an $\mathcal{F}_t$-progressively measurable process and λ_t, $t \geq 0$, as in (2.2).

The *volatility process* $a(x,t)$ is the novel element of the forward approach in portfolio choice. This input is up to the investor to choose, in contrast to the classical formulation in which the volatility coefficient of the value function process is uniquely determined.

The above SPDE was derived under various assumptions on existence, uniqueness and regularity of the involved processes. Except for the case of zero volatility which was completely solved in [6] (see, also, [1]), results to whether (2.6) provides a necessary and/or sufficient condition for its solution, $U(x,t)$, to satisfy the above definition are lacking. These questions are being currently studied by various authors. While such theoretical results are not yet available, concrete examples for various cases of non-zero volatility processes can be found in [9].

Herein, we do not examine such issues. Rather, we investigate how information about preferred personal portfolio choice can be used to build a framework for investment advice across time.

3. The Portfolio Selection Problem Under Time-Monotone Performance Criteria

We consider an individual who starts today with some initial wealth and faces investment decisions in upcoming times. The investor specifies his initial desired investment allocation between the two accounts.

We are interested in the following questions:

- How does the investor's initial investment choice affect, and to what extent determine his future allocations?
- Is there an investment criterion that is consistent with these policies, in that these portfolios — initial and future — are optimal with respect to it?
- Are all initial investment choices admissible in the sense that they lead to feasible future investment allocations and, in general, to a well-posed portfolio choice problem?

We will study these questions focusing on the class of investors who have time-monotone investment criteria, specifically, when the process $U(x,t)$ is time-decreasing. This is the simplest class of forward investment performance processes which, nevertheless, offers rich intuition and valuable insights. It is easy to see that this case corresponds to the zero volatility choice, $a(x,t) = 0, t \geq 0$, in the performance SPDE (2.6).

To ease the exposition, we first provide some auxiliary results on monotone investment performance processes. These results can be found in [8] and are presented herein without a proof. To this end, we recall that such processes are represented as a compilation of market related input with a deterministic function of space and time. Specifically, for $t \geq 0, U(x,t)$ is given by

$$U(x,t) = u(x, A_t), \tag{3.1}$$

where $u(x,t)$ is increasing and strictly concave in x, and satisfies the fully nonlinear equation

$$u_t = \frac{1}{2}\frac{u_x^2}{u_{xx}}. \tag{3.2}$$

The process A_t depends only on market movements up to current time t and is given by

$$A_t = \int_0^t \lambda_s^2 \, ds, \tag{3.3}$$

with λ_t, $t \geq 0$, as in (2.2).

In [8] it was also shown that the investor's optimal wealth and optimal portfolio processes, denoted respectively by X_t^* and $\pi_t^*, t \geq 0$, satisfy an *autonomous system* (cf. (3.7)) of stochastic differential equations whose coefficients depend functionally on the spatial derivatives of u. Specifically its coefficients can be expressed in terms of the so-called local risk tolerance function defined by

$$r(x,t) = -\frac{u_x(x,t)}{u_{xx}(x,t)}. \tag{3.4}$$

Another important result therein is that the above function satisfies an *autonomous equation* (*cf.* (3.5)). The autonomous system and equation will play pivotal role in our analysis as explained in the sequel.

The results below can be found in Propositions 6 and 9 in [8]. Because later on we will be working with different cases of the spatial domain, we use, for the moment, the generic notation $\mathbb{D}$.

Theorem 3.1. (i) *Let* $u(x,t)$ *solve* (3.2) *and* $r(x,t)$ *be as in* (3.4). *Then, for* $(x,t) \in \mathbb{D}\times[0,+\infty)$, $r(x,t)$ *solves*

$$r_t + \frac{1}{2}r^2 r_{xx} = 0. \tag{3.5}$$

(ii) *Define the process*

$$R_t^* = r(X_t^*, A_t), \tag{3.6}$$

with $A_t, t \geq 0$, *as in* (3.3) *and consider the system*

$$\begin{cases} dX_t^* = r(X_t^*, A_t)\lambda_t(\lambda_t dt + dW_t) \\ dR_t^* = r_x(X_t^*, A_t)dX_t^*, \end{cases} \tag{3.7}$$

with $X_0^* = x$ *and* $R_0^* = r(x,0)$. *Assume that* X_t^* *and* R_t^* *solve* (3.7) *and define* $\pi_t^*, t \geq 0$, *by*

$$\pi_t^* = \frac{\lambda_t}{\sigma_t} R_t^*. \tag{3.8}$$

Then π_t^* *generates* X_t^* *and, moreover, is optimal under the criterion* $U(x,t)$ *given in* (3.1).

Returning to the problem we want to analyze herein, let us assume that the investor specifies her initial desired allocation as functions of her wealth, say $\pi_0^*(x)$ and $x - \pi_0^*(x)$, for each wealth level $x \in \mathbb{D}$. The questions posed at the beginning of the section can be, then, formulated as follows:

- How does the form of $\pi_0^*(x)$ affect and, to what extent, determine the future allocation processes $\pi_t^*, t > 0$?
- How can one infer the investor's performance criterion, $u(x, A_t), t \geq 0$, with respect to which the policies π_t^*, $t \geq 0$, are optimal?
- What is the class of admissible initial allocations $\pi_0^*(x)$, i.e. initial allocations that generate future optimal investment policies $\pi_t^*, t > 0$, that belong to the set of admissible policies $\mathcal{A}$?

Theorem 3.1 gives valuable insights which will be central in our solution approach. Firstly, note that solving the above system essentially bypasses the need to specify the investment criterion. Indeed, knowing the function $r(x,t)$ and solving (3.7) yields directly the optimal processes X_t^* and π_t^*. This is in contrast to the classical setting in which one starts with the specification of terminal utility, then finds the value function process and, in turn, recovers the optimal policies.

We will utilize the results of the above theorem as follows. Firstly note that the investor's initial preferred allocation $\pi_0^*(x)$ yields the initial condition $r(x,0)$, as (3.6) and (3.8) indicate. The function $r(x,0)$ together with equation (3.5), specifies $r(x,t), t > 0$. The latter and its spatial derivatives give the functional coefficients in (3.7) which, in turn, yield the processes X_t^* and R_t^*. The optimal allocation and the associated investment criterion, π_t^* and $U(x,t)$, are, then, recovered from (3.8) and (3.1), respectively.

In order to execute these steps, one needs to solve equation (3.5) and the system (3.7), and to construct the function u. We discuss these problems next. We start with auxiliary results for solutions to (3.5) and (3.2).

4. Analysis

We focus on specific classes of solutions to equation (3.5) and (3.2), namely, positive solutions of (3.5) and strictly concave and increasing solutions of (3.2). We stress that, for the moment, we do *not* assume that these solutions are related to each other as (5.4) might indicate (as well as the titles of the subsections below). This connection will be discussed at the end of the section. For now we treat the two equations separately.

We recall the backward heat equation,

$$h_t + \frac{1}{2}h_{xx} = 0. \tag{4.1}$$

We consider strictly increasing solutions to the above equation and construct the associated solutions to (3.5) and (3.2) by appropriate nonlinear and integral transformations (see Propositions 4.1 and 4.3). The motivation to involve (4.1) comes from the fact that its harmonic solutions have very explicit, and quite useful for the investment problem at hand, representations. These representation results are also discussed in this section.

As in the previous section, we use $\mathbb{D}$ to denote the generic spatial domain of the function r.

4.1. *Local risk tolerance and harmonic functions*

We start with a result that relates solutions of (4.1) and (3.5).

Proposition 4.1. *Let $h : \mathbb{R} \times [0,+\infty) \to \mathbb{D}$ be a strictly increasing solution to* (4.1) *and define $r : \mathbb{D} \times [0,+\infty) \to \mathbb{R}^+$ by*

$$r(x,t) = h_x(h^{(-1)}(x,t),t). \tag{4.2}$$

Then r solves (3.5).

Proof. Differentiating (4.2) yields

$$h_t(x,t)r_x(h(x,t),t) + r_t(h(x,t),t) = h_{xt}(x,t)$$

and

$$h_{xx}(x,t)r_x(h(x,t),t) + h_x^2(x,t)r_{xx}(h(x,t),t) = h_{xxx}(x,t).$$

Therefore,

$$h_{xt}(x,t) + \frac{1}{2}h_{xxx}(x,t) = r_t(h(x,t),t) + \frac{1}{2}h_x^2(x,t)r_{xx}(h(x,t),t),$$

where we used (4.1). Differentiating the latter and using the above we deduce

$$r_t(h(x,t),t) + \frac{1}{2}h_x^2(x,t)r_{xx}(h(x,t),t) = 0,$$

and we easily conclude. □

Remark 4.1. In portfolio choice, a quantity that occasionally appears is the reciprocal of the local risk tolerance that is called, in analogy, the local risk aversion,

$$\gamma(x,t) = \frac{1}{r(x,t)}.$$

Direct differentiation of $\gamma(x,t)$ and use of (3.5) yield that $\gamma(x,t)$ satisfies the equation

$$\gamma_t + \frac{1}{2}(\gamma^m)_{xx} = 0 \quad \text{with } m = -1. \tag{4.3}$$

Equation (4.3) is a porous medium[‡] equation (PME) with negative exponent m. Frequently, for $m < 1$, PME is referred to as a fast diffusion equation and various properties of its solution are different than the ones when $m > 1$. We refer the reader to [13] and [14] for an extensive study on this equation.

4.2. *Representation of strictly increasing harmonic functions*

We continue with representation results for strictly increasing solutions to (4.1). They appeared recently in [6] and we refer the reader therein for the related proofs. Here, we only highlight the main findings and representative cases.

The key idea in constructing monotone solutions to (4.1) is to use the classical representation result of Widder for positive harmonic functions. This result, recalled below (see, also, [15]), states that every positive solution of (4.1) can be represented in terms of the bilateral Laplace transform of a finite positive Borel measure, denoted hereafter by ν. We will be using the notation $\mathcal{B}(\mathbb{R})$ to denote the set of Borel measures in $\mathbb{R}$.

[‡]The porous medium equation is a nonlinear heat equation of the form $f_t = \Delta(f^m)$ (or more generally of the form $f_t = \Delta(F(f))$).

Widder's theorem is not directly applicable in the portfolio problem we study because the solutions h we consider might not be positive. Indeed, as we will see in the next section, these solutions will be ultimately used to construct the investor's optimal wealth which is not necessarily positive (see, for instance, Examples 6.1). However, Widder's theorem can be applied to the spatial derivative h_x which is a positive harmonic solution, as it follows from direct differentiation of (4.1) and the monotonicity of h.

We introduce the following set of measures,

$$\mathcal{B}^+(\mathbb{R}) = \left\{ \nu \in \mathcal{B}(\mathbb{R}) : \forall B \in \mathcal{B}, \nu(B) \geq 0 \text{ and } \int_{\mathbb{R}} e^{yx} \nu(dy) < \infty, x \in \mathbb{R} \right\}. \tag{4.4}$$

Theorem 4.1 (Widder). *Let $g(x,t), (x,t) \in \mathbb{R} \times [0, +\infty)$, be a positive solution of* (4.1). *Then, there exists $\mu \in \mathcal{B}^+(\mathbb{R})$ such that g is represented as*

$$g(x,t) = \int_{\mathbb{R}} e^{yx - \frac{1}{2}y^2 t} \mu(dy). \tag{4.5}$$

As the results in the sequel show, there is an interesting interplay between the *support* and the *integrability properties* of the measure ν, and the *range* of the solution h. We will see that, in turn, this interplay affects the range of the local risk tolerance, the range and the limiting behavior of the differential input and, finally, the range of the investor's optimal wealth process. We stress that h is defined, throughout, for *all* $(x,t) \in \mathbb{R} \times [0, +\infty)$. It is the range of h that varies as the underlying measure changes.

To this end, we introduce the following subsets of $\mathcal{B}^+(\mathbb{R})$,

$$\mathcal{B}_0^+(\mathbb{R}) = \{\nu \in \mathcal{B}^+(\mathbb{R}) \text{ and } \nu(\{0\}) = 0\},$$
$$\mathcal{B}_+^+(\mathbb{R}) = \{\nu \in \mathcal{B}_0^+(\mathbb{R}) : \nu((-\infty, 0)) = 0\}$$

and

$$\mathcal{B}_-^+(\mathbb{R}) = \{\nu \in \mathcal{B}_0^+(\mathbb{R}) : \nu((0, +\infty)) = 0\}.$$

It is throughout assumed that the trivial case $\nu(\mathbb{R}) = 0$ is excluded.

In what follows, C represents a generic constant whose special choices lead to simplified expressions which we will use for our examples (cf. (4.7) and (4.8) below).

Proposition 4.2. (i) *Let $\nu \in \mathcal{B}^+(\mathbb{R})$. Then, the function h defined for $(x,t) \in \mathbb{R} \times [0, +\infty)$ by*

$$h(x,t) = \int_{\mathbb{R}} \frac{e^{yx - \frac{1}{2}y^2 t} - 1}{y} \nu(dy) + C \tag{4.6}$$

is a strictly increasing solution to (4.1).

Moreover, if $\nu(\{0\}) > 0$, or $\nu(-\infty, 0) > 0$ and $\nu(0, +\infty) > 0$, or $\nu \in \mathcal{B}_+^+(\mathbb{R})$ and $\int_{0^+}^{+\infty} \frac{\nu(dy)}{y} = +\infty$, or $\nu \in \mathcal{B}_-^+(\mathbb{R})$ and $\int_{-\infty}^{0^-} \frac{\nu(dy)}{y} = -\infty$, then $Range(h) = (-\infty, +\infty)$, for $t \geq 0$.

On the other hand, if $\nu \in \mathcal{B}^{+}_{+}(\mathbb{R})$ *with* $\int_{0+}^{+\infty} \frac{\nu(dy)}{y} < +\infty$ *then* $Range(h) = (C - \int_{0+}^{+\infty} \frac{\nu(dy)}{y}, +\infty)$, *for* $t \geq 0$. *For* $C = \int_{0+}^{+\infty} \frac{\nu(dy)}{y}$, *we have*

$$h(x,t) = \int_{0+}^{\infty} e^{yx - \frac{1}{2}y^2 t} \mu(dy), \tag{4.7}$$

with $\mu(dy) = \frac{\nu(dy)}{y}$. *Similarly, if* $\nu \in \mathcal{B}^{+}_{-}(\mathbb{R})$ *with* $\int_{-\infty}^{0^-} \frac{\nu(dy)}{y} > -\infty$ *then* $Range(h) = (-\infty, C - \int_{-\infty}^{0^-} \frac{\nu(dy)}{y})$, *for* $t \geq 0$. *For* $C = \int_{-\infty}^{0^-} \frac{\nu(dy)}{y}$, *we have*

$$h(x,t) = \int_{-\infty}^{0^-} e^{yx - \frac{1}{2}y^2 t} \mu(dy), \tag{4.8}$$

with $\mu(dy) = \frac{\nu(dy)}{y}$.

(ii) *Conversely, let* $h : \mathbb{R} \times [0, +\infty) \to \mathbb{R}$ *be a strictly increasing solution to* (4.1). *Then, there exists* $\nu \in \mathcal{B}^{+}(\mathbb{R})$ *such that* h *is given by* (4.6).

Moreover, if $Range(h) = (-\infty, +\infty), t \geq 0$, *then it must be either that* $\nu(\{0\}) > 0$, *or* $\nu(-\infty, 0) > 0$ *and* $\nu(0, +\infty) > 0$, *or* $\nu \in \mathcal{B}^{+}_{+}(\mathbb{R})$ *and* $\int_{0+}^{+\infty} \frac{\nu(dy)}{y} = +\infty$, *or* $\nu \in \mathcal{B}^{+}_{-}(\mathbb{R})$ *and* $\int_{-\infty}^{0^-} \frac{\nu(dy)}{y} = -\infty$.

On the other hand, if for some $x_0 \in \mathbb{R}$, $Range(h) = (x_0, +\infty)$ (*resp.* $Range(h) = (-\infty, x_0)$), $t \geq 0$, *then it must be that* $\nu \in \mathcal{B}^{+}_{+}(\mathbb{R})$ *with* $\int_{0+}^{+\infty} \frac{\nu(dy)}{y} < +\infty$ (*resp.* $\nu \in \mathcal{B}^{+}_{-}(\mathbb{R})$ *with* $\int_{-\infty}^{0^-} \frac{\nu(dy)}{y} > -\infty$).

The proof of the above result can be found in Proposition 9 in [6].

4.3. *Differential input and harmonic functions*

Next, we discuss how strictly concave and increasing solutions of (3.2) can be constructed from strictly increasing solutions to (4.1). We stress that the harmonic function appearing in (4.9) and (4.11) is not necessarily the same with the one in Sec. 4.2. We use, with a slight abuse, the same notation only for simplicity.

In order to facilitate the exposition, we compress some of the different cases and assumptions on the measure. We also omit the case *Range*$(h) = (-\infty, 0)$.

Proposition 4.3. *Let* h *be a strictly increasing harmonic function and* ν *its associated measure* (*cf.* (4.6) *and* (4.7)). *We have the following cases*:

(i) *Let* ν *be such that* $Range(h) = (-\infty, +\infty)$. *Then,* $u : \mathbb{R} \times [0, +\infty) \to \mathbb{R}$ *defined by*

$$u(x,t) = -\frac{1}{2} \int_0^t e^{-h^{(-1)}(x,s) + \frac{s}{2}} h_x(h^{(-1)}(x,s), s) ds + \int_0^x e^{-h^{(-1)}(z,0)} dz, \tag{4.9}$$

with h *given in* (4.6), *is strictly increasing and concave in its spatial argument and satisfies equation* (3.2).

(ii) *Let ν be such that Range$(h) = (0, +\infty)$ and satisfying, in addition, $\nu((0,1]) = 0$ and $\int_{1+}^{+\infty} \frac{\nu(dy)}{y-1} < +\infty$. Then $u\colon \mathbb{R}^+ \times [0,+\infty) \to \mathbb{R}$ is given by (4.9), for $x \in \mathbb{R}^+$, and satisfies*

$$\lim_{x \to 0} u(x,t) = 0, \quad \textit{for } t \geq 0. \tag{4.10}$$

If, on the other hand, $\nu((0,1]) > 0$ and/or $\int_{1+}^{+\infty} \frac{\nu(dy)}{y-1} = +\infty$, we have

$$u(x,t) = -\frac{1}{2}\int_0^t e^{-h^{(-1)}(x,s)+\frac{s}{2}} h_x(h^{(-1)}(x,s),s)ds + \int_{x_0}^x e^{-h^{(-1)}(z,0)}dz, \tag{4.11}$$

for (arbitrary) $x_0 > 0$, with

$$\lim_{x \to 0} u(x,t) = -\infty, \quad \textit{for } t \geq 0. \tag{4.12}$$

For each $t \geq 0$, the Inada conditions

$$\lim_{x \to -\infty} u_x(x,t) = +\infty \quad \textit{and} \quad \lim_{x \to +\infty} u_x(x,t) = 0$$

and

$$\lim_{x \to 0} u_x(x,t) = +\infty \quad \textit{and} \quad \lim_{x \to +\infty} u_x(x,t) = 0 \tag{4.13}$$

are satisfied for the cases (i) *and* (ii), *respectively.*

In [6] one also shows that the converse of the above statements is also true, namely, if u is a strictly increasing and concave solution to (3.2) (and certain limiting properties hold) then, there exists an associated solution h to (4.1) with the appropriate representation characteristics (see Propositions 10, 14 and 15 in [6]).

4.4. *Local risk tolerance and differential input*

So far we have seen that solutions to (3.5) and (3.2) are directly related and can be constructed by harmonic solutions (see (4.2) and (4.9)). How are, then, $r(x,t)$ and $u(x,t)$ related to each other if they "correspond" to the same harmonic function?

Given that the measure ν is the defining element of $h(x,t)$ it is immediate that $r(x,t)$ and $u(x,t)$ must be associated with the same measure. This, in turn, implies that the initial conditions $r(x,0) = h(h^{(-1)}(x,0),0)$ and $u(x,0) = \int_0^x e^{-h^{(-1)}(z,0)}dz$ must be compatible. Direct differentiation yields that

$$-\frac{u_x(x,0)}{u_{xx}(x,0)} = r(x,0). \tag{4.14}$$

Further differentiation in (5.11) and use of (5.9) will yield that the above relation is also propagated to all positive times, namely, for $t > 0$,

$$-\frac{u_x(x,t)}{u_{xx}(x,t)} = r(x,t). \tag{4.15}$$

5. Synthesis

We are now ready to address the questions posed in Sec. 3. We introduce the process M_t, $t \geq 0$,

$$M_t = \int_0^t \lambda_s dW_s, \tag{5.1}$$

with λ_t as in (2.2). We also introduce a stricter than (4.4) assumption on the measure ν, specifically,

$$\int_{\mathbb{R}} e^{yx+\frac{1}{2}y^2 t}\nu(dy) < \infty, \quad t \geq 0. \tag{5.2}$$

This condition is not needed for the representation results of the previous section but it is crucial in establishing the appropriate integrability, and, in turn, admissibility of the candidate optimal investment process.

We start with the case when the investor's initial wealth is unconstrained, $x \in \mathbb{R}$. For the reader's convenience, we rewrite some of the formulae derived earlier. On the other hand, we do not write explicitly the conditions on the measure that yield full range of the solution h, for they are already listed in the first part of Proposition 4.2. We also take $C = 0$ in (4.6).

Theorem 5.1. *Let $\pi_0^* : \mathbb{R} \to \mathbb{R}^+$ be the investor's initial desired allocation in the risky asset and let the function $r_0 : \mathbb{R} \to \mathbb{R}^+$ be given by*

$$r_0(x) = \frac{\sigma_0}{\lambda_0}\pi_0^*(x). \tag{5.3}$$

Let us assume that the autonomous equation

$$r_0(h_0(x)) = h_0'(x) \tag{5.4}$$

has a solution $h_0 : \mathbb{R} \to \mathbb{R}$ of the form

$$h_0(x) = \int_{\mathbb{R}} \frac{e^{yx} - 1}{y}\nu(dy), \tag{5.5}$$

where ν satisfies (5.2) and is such that $Range(h_0) = (-\infty, +\infty)$.

Let $h : \mathbb{R}\times[0, +\infty) \to \mathbb{R}$ be given by

$$h(x,t) = \int_{\mathbb{R}} \frac{e^{yx-\frac{1}{2}y^2 t} - 1}{y}\nu(dy) \tag{5.6}$$

and define the processes X_t^* and π_t^*, $t \geq 0$, by

$$X_t^* = h(h^{(-1)}(x, 0) + A_t + M_t, A_t) \tag{5.7}$$

and

$$\pi_t^* = \frac{\lambda_t}{\sigma_t} h_x(h^{(-1)}(X_t^*, A_t), A_t), \tag{5.8}$$

with A_t and M_t, $t \geq 0$, as in (3.3) *and* (5.1), *respectively. Consider the function* $r : \mathbb{R} \times [0, +\infty) \to \mathbb{R}^+$ *defined by*

$$r(x,t) = h_x(h^{(-1)}(x,t), t) \tag{5.9}$$

and the process

$$R_t^* = r(X_t^*, A_t). \tag{5.10}$$

Finally, define $u : \mathbb{R} \times [0, +\infty) \to \mathbb{R}$ *by*

$$u(x,t) = -\frac{1}{2}\int_0^t e^{-h^{(-1)}(x,s)+\frac{s}{2}} r(x,s)ds + \int_0^x e^{-h^{(-1)}(z,0)}dz, \tag{5.11}$$

where r and h are as in (5.9) *and* (5.6), *respectively. Then,*

(i) *the portfolio π_t^* generates the wealth process X_t^*,*
(ii) *the processes X_t^* and R_t^* solve the autonomous system* (3.7),
(iii) *the policy π_t^*, $t \geq 0$, is the optimal portfolio process for the forward investment performance criterion*

$$U(x,t) = u(x, A_t), \tag{5.12}$$

with $u(x,t)$ as in (5.11).

Proof. (i) Let $N_t = h^{(-1)}(x,0) + A_t + M_t$. Applying Itô's formula to X_t^* yields

$$\begin{aligned} dX_t^* &= h_x(N_t, A_t)dN_t + \lambda_t^2\left(h_t(N_t, A_t) + \frac{1}{2}h_{xx}(N_t, A_t)\right)dt \\ &= h_x(N_t, A_t)\lambda_t(\lambda_t dt + dW_t) + \lambda_t^2\left(h_t(N_t, A_t) + \frac{1}{2}h_{xx}(N_t, A_t)\right)dt. \end{aligned}$$

From Proposition 4.2 we recall that h solves the heat equation (4.1). Therefore, the above simplifies to

$$dX_t^* = h_x(N_t, A_t)\lambda_t(\lambda_t dt + dW_t).$$

On the other hand,

$$\begin{aligned} h_x(N_t, A_t) &= h_x(h^{(-1)}(h(h^{(-1)}(x,0) + A_t + M_t, A_t), A_t), A_t) \\ &= h_x(h^{(-1)}(X_t^*, A_t), A_t) \end{aligned} \tag{5.13}$$

and using (2.3) and (5.8) we easily conclude.

(ii) The above calculations yield that X_t^* satisfies the first equation in (3.7). For the second equation we have

$$\begin{aligned} dR_t^* &= dr(X_t^*, A_t) \\ &= \lambda_t^2\left(r_t(X_t^*, A_t) + \frac{1}{2}r^2(X_t^*, A_t)r_{xx}(X_t^*, A_t)\right)dt + r_x(X_t^*, A_t)dX_t^*. \end{aligned}$$

Proposition 4.1 and (5.9) yield that the function $r(x,t)$ solves equation (3.5). Thus, the above drift vanishes and the assertion follows.

(iii) This part has several assertions to be established. The arguments are lengthy and the calculations rather tedious. Moreover, most of them follow from arguments used in the proof of Theorem 4 in [6]. For these reasons, we only highlight the main steps.

To this end, we first need to show that the policy in consideration π_t^*, $t \geq 0$, defined in (5.8) and rewritten for convenience,

$$\pi_t^* = \frac{\lambda_t}{\sigma_t} h_x(h^{(-1)}(X_t^*, A_t), A_t)$$

is admissible. Its $\mathcal{F}_t$-measurability follows trivially. To show the integrability property $E(\int_0^t |\sigma_s \pi_s|^2 ds) < \infty$, $t > 0$, we use (4.6) and that $h_x(x,t) = \int_{\mathbb{R}} e^{yx - \frac{1}{2}y^2 t} \nu(dy)$, as it follows by direct differentiation and Tonelli's theorem. Writing

$$\begin{aligned} &(h_x(h^{(-1)}(X_t^*, A_t), A_t))^2 \\ &\quad = \int_{\mathbb{R}} \int_{\mathbb{R}} e^{(y_1+y_2)(h^{(-1)}(x,0)+A_t+M_t) - \frac{1}{2}(y_1^2+y_2^2)A_t} \nu(dy_1)\nu(dy_2), \end{aligned}$$

using (5.8), (5.2) and the uniform bound on the market risk premium we conclude.

To show that $U(x,t)$ is a forward investment performance process, it suffices to check that u given in (5.11) solves (3.2) and that $E(U(X_t^*, t)^+) < +\infty$. Finally, one needs to show that the policy is optimal. For this, one needs to prove that the drift of the process $u(X_t^*, A_t)$ vanishes. □

Next, we state the results for the semi-infinite case. Due to space limitations, we compress some arguments.

Theorem 5.2. *Let $\pi_0^* : \mathbb{R}^+ \to \mathbb{R}^+$ be the investor's initial desired allocation in the risky asset. Define the function $r_0 : \mathbb{R}^+ \to \mathbb{R}^+$ as in (5.3) and assume that equation (5.4) has a solution $h_0 : \mathbb{R} \to \mathbb{R}^+$ of the form*

$$h_0(x) = \int_{0+}^{+\infty} e^{yx} \nu(dy), \tag{5.14}$$

with $\nu \in \mathcal{B}_+^+(\mathbb{R})$ with $\int_{0+}^{+\infty} \frac{\nu(dy)}{y} < +\infty$ and satisfying (5.2). Let $h : \mathbb{R} \times [0, +\infty) \to \mathbb{R}^+$ be given by

$$h(x,t) = \int_{0+}^{+\infty} e^{yx - \frac{1}{2}y^2 t} \nu(dy). \tag{5.15}$$

Then the processes X_t^* and π_t^*, $t \geq 0$, given by

$$X_t^* = h(h^{(-1)}(x,0) + A_t + M_t, A_t) \quad \text{and} \quad \pi_t^* = \frac{\lambda_t}{\sigma_t} h_x(h^{(-1)}(X_t^*, A_t), A_t)$$

are optimal. Moreover, $X_t^* > 0, t \geq 0, a.e.$ Let $r : \mathbb{R}^+ \times [0, +\infty) \to \mathbb{R}^+$ be given by $r(x,t) = h_x(h^{(-1)}(x,t), t)$.

If $\nu((0,1])=0$ *and* $\int_{1+}^{+\infty}\frac{\nu(dy)}{y-1}<+\infty$, *define* $u\colon \mathbb{R}^+\times[0,+\infty)\to\mathbb{R}$ *by*

$$u(x,t)=-\frac{1}{2}\int_0^t e^{-h^{(-1)}(x,s)+\frac{s}{2}}r(x,s)ds+\int_0^x e^{-h_0^{(-1)}(z)}dz, \tag{5.16}$$

while if $\nu((0,1])>0$ *and/or* $\int_{1+}^{+\infty}\frac{\nu(dy)}{y-1}=+\infty$, *define*

$$u(x,t)=-\frac{1}{2}\int_0^t e^{-h^{(-1)}(x,s)+\frac{s}{2}}r(x,s)ds+\int_{x_0}^x e^{-h_0^{(-1)}(z)}dz, \tag{5.17}$$

for some fixed $x_0>0$. *Then,* X_t^* *and* π_t^* *are optimal with respect to the forward investment criterion* $U(x,t)=u(x,A_t)$ *with* $u(x,t)$ *as above.*

The above theorems give answers to the questions we put forward in Sec. 2. Indeed, the desired initial allocation $\pi_0^*(x)$ yields the initial risk tolerance $r_0(x)$. If equation (5.4) has a solution that can be represented in the appropriate integral form, then the measure ν is identified. From there, one readily constructs the harmonic function $h(x,t)$.

Using $h(x,t)$, $h_x(x,t)$, the market input processes A_t and M_t, and formulae (5.7) and (5.8) we find the processes X_t^* and $\pi_t^*, t>0$. From $h(x,t), h_x(x,t)$, (5.9) and (5.11), one, also, finds the differential input $u(x,t)$ and, in turn, the time-monotone investment performance criterion from (5.12). The theorems yield that the processes X_t^* and π_t^* are optimal with respect to the forward investment process $U(x,t)=u(x,A_t)$.

Conditions (5.5) and (5.14) yield the *admissibility* requirement for the desired initial allocations.

5.1. *Inferring risk preferences from desired asset allocations*

The analysis herein highlights how risk preferences can be entirely inferred from the investor's allocations. This is in contrast to the traditional approach in portfolio theory in which one first specifies the utility and then determines the optimal policies. Herein, one takes the reverse route.

Indeed, the investment criterion is found by (5.12) as long as the market risk premium is specified (cf. (3.3)) and the function $u(x,t)$ is known. The latter is given by (5.11) (resp. (5.16) and (5.17)) which requires knowledge of $h(x,t)$ and $r(x,t)$. Both functions are specified once the measure ν is known, as it is manifested in (5.6) (resp. (5.15)) and (5.9). The measure is found by (5.4) and (5.5).

It is worth mentioning an alternative way which provides a direct construction of $u(x,t)$ from $r(x,t)$ which entirely bypasses the use of $h(x,t), t>0$. This result carries useful insights, for it essentially shows how risk preferences can be recovered simply by propagating the initial risk preferences along the inverted characteristic curves whose slope is half of the local risk tolerance. On the other hand, the slope of these curves is directly related to the optimal portfolio itself as it can be seen from (5.8). In other words, the construction below alludes to the fact that the investment performance process $U(x,t)$ can be directly constructed from the optimal portfolio process π_t^* by inverting the appropriate stochastic characteristic curves. This idea was recently explored by El Karoui.

The arguments that follow are non-formal and are presented only to highlight the approach. The main idea comes from the fact that the fully nonlinear equation (3.2) can be equivalently written as the one below if one takes into account (4.15). Similarly, the initial condition in (5.18) comes from (4.14).

To this end, let us assume that the function $r(x,t)$ is known for $t \geq 0$ and consider the equation

$$u_t + \frac{1}{2} r(x,t) u_x = 0 \quad \text{with} \quad u_0(x) = \int_0^x e^{-h_0^{(-1)}(z)} dz, \tag{5.18}$$

with $h_0(x)$ as in (5.5).

Classical results in the theory of first-order linear partial differential equations yield the solution via the so-called *method of characteristic curves* (see, for example, Chapter 2 in [17]). Specifically, let $x \in \mathbb{D}$ and consider the solution $\mathcal{X}^x(t)$ of the equation

$$\frac{d\mathcal{X}^x(t)}{dt} = \frac{1}{2} r(\mathcal{X}^x(t), t) \quad \text{with} \quad \mathcal{X}^x(0) = x. \tag{5.19}$$

Differentiating the function $u(\mathcal{X}^x(t), t)$ with respect to t and using (5.18) yields

$$\frac{d}{dt} u(\mathcal{X}^x(t), t) = 0.$$

In turn, for all $t > 0$,

$$u(\mathcal{X}^x(t), t) = u(\mathcal{X}^x(0), 0) = u_0(x), \tag{5.20}$$

which essentially tells us that the solution remains constant along each characteristic curve. One, then, sees that $u(x,t)$ can be found from the above equality and the initial condition. For illustration, we present an example of this construction in the first example below.

6. Examples

In this section we provide some representative examples for both the unconstrained and constrained wealth cases. For the sake of simplicity we present the results in terms of the initial risk tolerance and not the initial allocation in (5.3). This is only to eliminate the multiplicative constant $\frac{\lambda_0}{\sigma_0}$.

6.1. *Domain*$(r) = (-\infty, +\infty)$

• $r_0(x) = 1$

Equation (5.4) has the solution $h_0(x) = x$. From (5.5) we easily deduce that $\nu = \delta_0$, where δ_0 is a Dirac measure at 0. Then (5.6) yields $h(x,t) = x$. In turn, (5.7) and (5.8) give

$$X_t^* = x + A_t + M_t \quad \text{and} \quad \pi_t^* = \frac{\lambda_t}{\sigma_t}.$$

On the other hand, (5.9) implies $r(x,t) = 1$. From (5.11) we deduce

$$u(x,t) = -\frac{1}{2}\int_0^t e^{-x+\frac{s}{2}}ds + \int_0^x e^{-z}dz = 1 - e^{-x+\frac{t}{2}}. \tag{6.1}$$

The associated investment performance process is given by $U(x,t) = 1 - e^{-x+\frac{1}{2}A_t}$ (this class of forward processes has been extensively analyzed; see, for example, [7] and [18]).

For completeness, we also construct $u(x,t)$ using (5.18) and the method of characteristics. Using the form of $h_0(x)$ we easily deduce that the initial condition in (5.18) becomes $u_0(x) = 1 - e^{-x}$. Moreover, the characteristic curves (cf. (5.19)) are given by

$$\frac{d\mathcal{X}^x(t)}{dt} = \frac{1}{2} \quad \text{with } \mathcal{X}^x(0) = x,$$

which implies that

$$\mathcal{X}^x(t) = x + \frac{1}{2}t.$$

Therefore, (5.20) yields

$$u(\mathcal{X}^x(t), t) = u\left(x + \frac{1}{2}t, t\right) = 1 - e^{-x},$$

and by inverting the arguments, (6.1) follows.

• $r_0(x) = \sqrt{a^2x^2 + b^2}; a, b > 0$

The solution of (5.4) is given by $h_0(x) = \frac{b}{a}\sinh(ax)$. Formula (5.5) corresponds to $\nu = \frac{b}{2}(\delta_a + \delta_{-a})$, $a, b > 0$, and $\delta_{\pm a}$ are Dirac measures at $\pm a$. In turn, $h(x,t) = \frac{b}{a}e^{-\frac{1}{2}a^2t}\sinh(ax)$ and $h^{(-1)}(x,t) = \frac{1}{a}\ln(\frac{a}{b}xe^{\frac{1}{2}a^2t} + \sqrt{\frac{a^2}{b^2}x^2e^{a^2t} + 1})$. This, in turn, yields $h_x(h^{(-1)}(x,t),t) = \sqrt{a^2x^2 + b^2e^{-a^2t}}$. The optimal processes in (5.7) and (5.8) turn out to be

$$X_t^* = \frac{b}{a}e^{-\frac{1}{2}a^2A_t}\left(\sinh\left(\ln\left(\frac{a}{b}x + \sqrt{\frac{a^2}{b^2}x^2e^{a^2t} + 1} + a(A_t + M_t)\right)\right)\right)$$

and

$$\pi_t^* = \frac{\lambda_t}{\sigma_t}\sqrt{a^2(X_t^*)^2 + b^2e^{-a^2A_t}}.$$

If $a = 1$, (5.11) gives

$$u(x,t) = \frac{1}{2}\left(\ln(x + \sqrt{x^2 + b^2 e^{-t}}) - \frac{e^t}{b^2} x(x - \sqrt{x^2 + b^2 e^{-t}}) - \frac{t}{2}\right) - \frac{1}{2}\ln b,$$

while, if $a \neq 1$,

$$u(x,t) = \frac{\sqrt[a]{a}}{a^2 - 1} e^{\frac{1-a}{2}t} \frac{b^2 e^{-at} + a(1+a)(ax^2 + x\sqrt{a^2x^2 + b^2 e^{-a^2 t}})}{(ax + \sqrt{a^2 x^2 + b^2 e^{-a^2 t}})^{1+\frac{1}{\alpha}}} - \frac{\sqrt[a]{a}}{a^2 - 1} b^{1-\frac{1}{a}}.$$

Further results on this case can be found in [16]. This two-parameter class is quite rich and leads to the popular utilities — power, logarithmic and exponential — for limiting values of the parameters a and b (see Remark 6.2 at the end of this section).

• $r_0(x) = f(F^{(-1)}(x))$ with $F(x) = \int_0^x e^{\frac{1}{2}z^2} dz$, $x \in \mathbb{R}$ and $f = F'$
Equation (5.4) has the solution $h_0(x) = F(x)$ which corresponds to the measure $\nu(dy) = \frac{1}{\sqrt{2\pi}} e^{-\frac{1}{2}y^2} dy$. Then, $h(x,t) = F(\frac{x}{\sqrt{t+1}})$. Using that $h^{(-1)}(x,t) = \sqrt{t+1}F^{(-1)}(x)$ we obtain that $h_x(h^{(-1)}(x,t),t) = \frac{1}{\sqrt{t+1}} f(F^{(-1)}(x))$.

The optimal processes are given by

$$X_t^* = F\left(\frac{F^{(-1)}(x) + A_t + M_t}{\sqrt{A_t + 1}}\right)$$

and

$$\pi_t^* = \frac{1}{\sqrt{A_t + 1}} f\left(\frac{F^{(-1)}(x) + A_t + M_t}{\sqrt{A_t + 1}}\right).$$

We deduce (after tedious calculations that are omitted) that

$$u(x,t) = k_1 F(F^{(-1)}(x) - \sqrt{t+1}) + k_2$$

with $k_1 = e^{-\frac{1}{2}}$ and $k_2 = e^{-\frac{1}{2}} \int_{-1}^{0} e^{\frac{1}{2}z^2} dz$.

6.2. *Domain*$(r) = (0, +\infty)$ *or* $[0, +\infty)$

• $r_0(x) = \gamma x$, $\gamma > 1$
Equation (5.4) yields $h_0(x) = \frac{1}{\gamma} e^{\gamma x}$. From (5.5) we then have $\nu = \delta_\gamma$. Therefore, $h(x,t) = \frac{1}{\gamma} e^{\gamma x - \frac{1}{2}\gamma^2 t}$, $h^{(-1)}(x,t) = \ln(\gamma x)^{\frac{1}{\gamma}} + \frac{1}{2}\gamma t$ and $h_x(h^{(-1)}(x,t),t) = \gamma x$. In turn, (5.7) and (5.8) yield

$$X_t^* = x \exp\left(\left(\gamma - \frac{1}{2}\gamma^2\right) A_t + \gamma M_t\right) \text{ and } \pi_t^* = \gamma \frac{\lambda_t}{\sigma_t} X_t^*.$$

Since $\nu((0,1]) = 0$, u is given by

$$u(x,t) = -\frac{1}{2}\int_0^t \gamma x e^{-(\ln(\gamma x)^{\frac{1}{\gamma}} + \frac{1}{2}\gamma s) + \frac{s}{2}} ds + \int_0^x (\gamma z)^{-\frac{1}{\gamma}} dz = \frac{\gamma^{\frac{\gamma-1}{\gamma}}}{\gamma - 1} x^{\frac{\gamma-1}{\gamma}} e^{-\frac{\gamma-1}{2}t},$$

(cf. part (ii) in Proposition 4.3).

• $r_0(x) = \gamma x, \gamma \in (0,1)$

This example is the same as the above. The only difference is that now $\nu((0,1]) \neq 0$. Thus, u is given by (5.17) for $x_0 > 0$,

$$u(x,t) = -\frac{1}{2}\int_0^t \gamma x e^{-(\ln(\gamma x)^{\frac{1}{\gamma}} + \frac{\gamma}{2}s) + \frac{s}{2}} ds + \int_{x_0}^x (\gamma z)^{-\frac{1}{\gamma}} dz$$

$$= -\frac{\gamma^{\frac{\gamma-1}{\gamma}}}{1-\gamma} x^{\frac{\gamma-1}{\gamma}} e^{\frac{1-\gamma}{2}t} + \frac{\gamma^{\frac{\gamma-1}{\gamma}}}{1-\gamma} x_0^{\frac{\gamma-1}{\gamma}}.$$

• $r_0(x) = x$

Equation (5.4) yields $h_0(x) = e^x$ which corresponds to $\nu = \delta_1$. Then, $h(x,t) = e^{x-\frac{1}{2}t}$, $h^{(-1)}(x,t) = \ln x + \frac{1}{2}t$, and $h_x(h^{(-1)}(x,t),t) = x$. In turn,

$$X_t^* = x \exp\left(\frac{1}{2}A_t + M_t\right) \quad \text{and} \quad \pi_t^* = \frac{\lambda_t}{\sigma_t} X_t^*.$$

Since $\nu((0,1]) \neq 0$, u is given by (4.11) for $x_0 > 0$,

$$u(x,t) = -\frac{1}{2}\int_0^t x e^{-(\ln x + \frac{1}{2}s) + \frac{s}{2}} ds + \int_{x_0}^x \frac{1}{z} dz = \ln \frac{x}{x_0} - \frac{t}{2}.$$

Remark 6.1. The examples in 6.2 are the ones examined in an infinitesimal setting in [2].

Remark 6.2. It is worth noticing that the examples in 6.2 can be thought as limiting cases of the parameters a and b in $r_0(x) = \sqrt{a^2x^2 + b^2}$. Indeed, the first two correspond to $b = 0$ and $\gamma = a$ while the last one to $b = 0$ and $\gamma = 1$. The first example in 6.1 can be also thought as a limiting case, namely, for $a = 0$ and $b = 1$.

Acknowledgments

The authors thank the Fields Institute for its hospitality and partial support during the "Kick-off Workshop" under the auspices of the semester-long program in Financial Mathematics (January–June, 2010). They also thank an anonymous referee whose comments were very helpful in improving the first version of the paper. T. Zariphopoulou acknowledges partial support from the Oxford-Man Institute of Quantitative Finance and the NSF grant DMS-RTG-0636586.

References

[1] F. Berrier, L. C. Rogers and M. Tehranchi, A characterization of forward utility functions, preprint (2009).

[2] F. Black, Individual investment and consumption under uncertainty, in *Portfolio Insurance*: *A Guide to Dynamic Hedging*, D. L. Luskin (Ed.) (New York, John Wiley and Sons, 1998), 207–225.

[3] D. G. Goldstein, E. J. Johnson and W. F. Sharpe, A new way to measure consumer risk preferences, working paper (2008).

[4] D. G. Goldstein, E. J. Johnson and W. F. Sharpe, Choosing outcomes versus choosing products: Consumer-focused retirement investment advice, *Journal of Consumer Research* **35** (2008) 440–456.
[5] R. Merton, Lifetime portfolio selection under uncertainty: The continuous-time case, *The Review of Economics and Statistics* **51** (1969) 247–257.
[6] M. Musiela and T. Zariphopoulou, Portfolio choice under space-time monotone performance criteria, *SIAM Journal on Financial Mathematics* **1** (2010) 326–365.
[7] M. Musiela and T. Zariphopoulou, Optimal asset allocation under forward exponential criteria, *Markov Processes and Related Topics: A Festschrift for Thomas. G. Kurtz*, IMS Collections, Institute of Mathematical Statistics **4** (2008) 285–300.
[8] M. Musiela and T. Zariphopoulou, Portfolio choice under dynamic investment performance criteria, *Quantitative Finance* **9**(2) (2009) 161–170.
[9] M. Musiela and T. Zariphopoulou, Stochastic partial differential equations in portfolio choice, in *Contemporary Quantitative Finance: Essays in Honour of Eckhard Platen*, C. Chiarella and A. Novikov (Eds.) (Springer Verlag, 2010), pp. 195–216.
[10] M. Musiela and T. Zariphopoulou, Investments and forward utilities, preprint (2006).
[11] W. F. Sharpe, D. G. Goldstein and P.W. Blythe, The distribution builder: A tool for inferring investor's preferences, preprint (2000).
[12] W. F. Sharpe, Expected utility asset allocation, *Financial Analysts Journal* **63**(5) (2007) 18–30.
[13] J.-L. Vasquez, *The Porous Medium Equation* (Oxford University Press, 2006).
[14] J.-L. Vasquez, Smoothing and decay estimates for nonlinear parabolic equations of porous medium type, preprint (2005).
[15] D. V. Widder, *The Heat Equation* (Academic Press, 1975).
[16] T. Zariphopoulou and T. Zhou, Investment performance measurement under asymptotically linear local risk tolerance, *Mathematical Modeling and Numerical Methods in Finance, Handbook of Numerical Analysis*, A. Bensoussan and Q. Zhang (Eds.) (North Holland, 2009), pp. 227–254.
[17] E. Zauderer, *Partial Differential Equations of Applied Mathematics* (John Wiley & Sons, 1983).
[18] G. Žitković, A dual characterization of self-generation and exponential forward performances, *Annals of Applied Probability* **19**(6) (2009) 2176–2210.

PERFORMANCE OF ROBUST HEDGES FOR DIGITAL DOUBLE BARRIER OPTIONS[‡]

JAN OBŁÓJ[*,†] and FRÉDÉRIK ULMER[*]

[*]*Mathematical Institute, University of Oxford*
24-29 St Giles, Oxford OX1 3LB, United Kingdom

[†]*Oxford-Man Institute of Quantitative Finance*
Eagle House, Walton Well Road,
Oxford OX2 6ED, United Kingdom

We analyze the performance of robust hedging strategies of digital double barrier options of Cox and Obłój (2011) against that of traditional hedging methods such as delta and delta/vega hedging. Digital double barrier options are financial derivative contracts which pay out a fixed amount on the condition that the underlying asset remains within or breaks into a range defined by two distinct barrier levels. We perform the analysis in hypothetical forward markets driven by models with stochastic volatility and jumps, calibrated to the AUD/USD foreign exchange rate market. Our findings are strikingly unanimous and suggest that, in the presence of model uncertainty and/or transaction costs, robust hedging strategies typically outperform in a substantial way model-specific hedging methods.

Keywords: Robust hedging; evaluation of hedging strategies; Skorokhod embedding; digital double barrier option; risk adjusted performance.

1. Introduction

One way to see the fundamental idea of Black and Scholes [4], which gave momentum to the whole financial industry, is that pricing is done through hedging. The unique fair price for a payoff at some future date is equal to the capital needed to replicate, through trading, its cashflow. In this idea is embedded an assumption of a fixed model for the dynamics of the price process. The price and, more importantly, the hedging strategy depend crucially on this model. Naturally, they also depend on a number of simplifying assumptions about transaction costs, dividends, interest

[‡]This chapter was originally published under the same title in *International Journal of Theoretical and Applied Finance*, Vol.15, No.1, 1250003-1–34 (2012). Singapore: World Scientific Publishing.

rates, etc. However, if the trader can have a feel for the impact of the latter, it is very hard to estimate the impact of wrong modelling assumptions. This issue was accentuated through the crisis in 2008 and resulted in a growing interest in robust hedging strategies as alternatives to model-specific hedging strategies.

The generic idea behind robust hedging is as follows. One starts with the market input, namely the prices of liquidly traded options. Using these options and trading strategies in the underlying S, one looks for the cheapest superhedge (and/or most expensive subhedge) for an exotic option which works under any dynamics of S, possibly under some generic assumptions (e.g. continuity of paths of S). The bounds are tight if one can further construct a model which matches the market input and in which the superhedge (resp. subhedge) is a perfect hedge.

One of the methods to obtain such robust hedging strategies is based on the Skorokhod embeddings and pathwise inequalities (see Hobson [20] and Obłój [30, 31]). The underlying ideas go back to Hobson [21] and Brown *et al.* [5] and they were more recently explored in depth by Cox and Obłój [10, 11]. In there, the authors developed robust pricing and hedging for digital double touch and double no-touch barrier options. Digital double barrier options are financial derivative contracts, most commonly traded in the foreign exchange markets, which pay out a fixed amount on the condition that the underlying asset remains within or breaks into a range defined by two distinct barrier levels.

The aim of this paper is to compare the performances of the robust hedging methods of Cox and Obłój [10, 11] against that of some model-specific hedging strategies. A preliminary comparison was carried out in [10] where the authors concluded that for Heston dynamics and in the presence of transaction costs, robust hedging may well outperform delta/vega hedging. At least three interesting avenues for further research were also suggested. First, the methods in [10, 11] were developed under the assumption of continuous paths and one should explore what happens when the true model has jumps. Second, Cox and Obłój only considered deta/vega hedging with fixed rebalancing frequency and a better benchmark would be set by a strategy with random, delta-dependent, rebalancing times. Finally, methods of [10, 11] are tailored to forward markets and extending them to spot markets is a challenging problem.

In this paper we deal with the first two of these three questions. We present a comprehensive analysis of the performance of robust versus classical hedging strategies of digital double touch and double no-touch barrier options under a number of market scenarios, which include stochastic volatility and jumps. We analyze risk-adjusted performance using standard deviation, VaR, CVaR and maximum loss as risk measures as well as expected utility when needed. Market assumptions and parameters are calibrated to AUD/USD foreign exchange rate market on 14 January 2010. Our findings are strikingly homogeneous: robust hedging strategies tend to outperform classical delta or delta/vega hedging strategies under nearly all market scenarios.

The remainder of the paper is structured as follows. In the following section we describe our setup: Sec. 2.1 discusses market scenarios which drive the dynamics of the underlying, Secs. 2.2 and 2.3 present robust hedging strategies and classical hedging strategies respectively, and finally Sec. 2.4 introduces risk measures used to evaluate the performance of different hedging strategies. Then in Sec. 3 we describe our findings and Sec. 4 concludes. Appendix A contains tables and figures which summarize our results and Appendix B has a short discussion of the numerical procedures employed in our simulations.

2. Market Models and Hedging Strategies

The aim of this paper is to compare the performances of the robust hedging methods of Cox and Obłój [10, 11] when applied to digital double touch options and digital double no-touch options against that of some model-specific hedging methods. We want to consider a situation when the trader is uncertain about the real dynamics and will either decide to use a robust hedge or some Black-Scholes-based delta or delta/vega hedge. We will simulate their hedging performance in a number of market scenarios and examine the distributions of hedging errors of the considered hedging strategies. This methodology and setup have several important ingredients, which are now described in detail: market scenarios, robust hedging, classical hedging strategies and risk-adjusted performance measures of hedging errors.

2.1. *Market scenarios*

We assume a trader sells or buys for a premium p a one-year digital double barrier option with continuously monitored barriers $\underline{b}$ and $\overline{b}$ written on an underlying process $S := \{S_t : t \geq 0\}$ which has zero cost of carry. We consider both digital double touch option, which pays one on the event $\{\min_{t\leq 1} S_t \leq \underline{b} \;\&\; \max_{t\leq 1} S_t \geq \overline{b}\}$ and zero otherwise, and digital double no-touch option, which pays one on the event $\{\min_{t\leq 1} S_t > \underline{b} \;\&\; \max_{t\leq 1} S_t < \overline{b}\}$ and zero otherwise. The premium p is set to the Black-Scholes price corresponding to the implied volatility of the at-the-money call option at time $t = 0$. We think of this as the price dictated by the market. The values of the premium are reported in Tables A.1–A.5. We stress that changing p is equivalent to a constant additive shift of hedging errors (of all strategies) and does not affect our relative performance comparisons.

We assume that transactions in the asset S carry a 4 bps cost and that buying or selling call or put options carries a 100 bps cost. Both rates are applied to the volume traded (i.e. the number of units traded multiplied by the unit price) and approximate the proportional transaction costs observed in the real-life market data set used below. We further assume that there are 250 trading days in one year.

We consider three base scenarios for the dynamics of S: a diffusion process driven by the Black-Scholes model [4], a diffusion process with stochastic volatility and finite activity jumps driven by the Bates model [3] and a pure-jump Lévy process with stochastic volatility and infinite activity jumps driven by the Variance Gamma with CIR stochastic clock model [7]. All modelling is done under the risk-neutral measure so that S is a martingale (since it has zero cost of carry). We summarize these models hereafter.

Black-Scholes (BS) model [4] assumes that S is the solution to the following stochastic differential equation:

$$\frac{\mathrm{d}S_t}{S_t} = \sigma \mathrm{d}W_t, \tag{2.1}$$

where $\sigma > 0$ is a constant referred to as the volatility of S and (W_t) is a Brownian motion.

Bates model [3] describes the dynamics of S via the following stochastic differential equations:

$$\begin{cases} \dfrac{\mathrm{d}S_t}{S_t} = -\lambda\mu_j \mathrm{d}t + \sqrt{v_t}\mathrm{d}W_t^{(1)} + J_t \mathrm{d}L_t, \\ \mathrm{d}v_t = \kappa(\theta - v_t)\mathrm{d}t + \zeta\sqrt{v_t}\mathrm{d}W_t^{(2)}, \end{cases} \tag{2.2}$$

with

$$\begin{cases} \mathrm{d}\langle W^{(1)}, W^{(2)}\rangle_t = \rho \mathrm{d}t, \quad \mathbb{E}(\mathrm{d}L_t) = \lambda \mathrm{d}t, \\ \log(1 + J_t) \sim \mathcal{N}\left(\log(1+\mu_j) - \dfrac{1}{2}\sigma_J^2, \sigma_J^2\right), \end{cases} \tag{2.3}$$

where $(W_t^{(1)})$ and $(W_t^{(2)})$ are correlated Brownian motions with correlation coefficient ρ, (L_t) is an independent Poisson process with intensity $\lambda > 0$ and J_t are lognormally, identically and independently distributed over time with mean μ_j.

Variance Gamma with CIR stochastic clock (VGSV) model [7] considers S given by:

$$S_t = S_0 \exp(X(Y(t)) - Y(t)\psi_X(-i)), \tag{2.4}$$

where $X(Y(t))$ is a Variance Gamma process $X(t)$ with parameters C, G and M (cf. Madan and Seneta [26] and Carr *et al.* [6]) time-changed with an integral of a CIR process (cf. [12]): $Y(t) = \int_0^t y(u)\mathrm{d}u$,

$$\mathrm{d}y(u) = \kappa(\eta - y(u))\mathrm{d}u + \lambda\sqrt{y(u)}\mathrm{d}W(u), \tag{2.5}$$

where (W_u) is a standard Brownian motion independent of all other processes used in the model. $\psi_X(u)$ in (2.4) is the characteristic exponent of X, which is the logarithm of the characteristic function of X_1 (see Carr *et al.* [6, 7]) and is given by

$$\psi_X(u) = C\log\left(\frac{GM}{GM + (M-G)iu + u^2}\right). \tag{2.6}$$

The market and model parameters we used are based on real-life global spot foreign exchange interbank market data observed on 14 January 2010 for the AUD/USD foreign exchange spot rate. We calibrated the models to bid and ask implied volatility quotes on standard European options on AUD/USD for different maturities and spot delta points,[1] without premium adjustment. This way, we obtain realistic parameters for our models and we also have different models which all match market observed prices so each of them could potentially drive the true dynamics and the trader should consider all these models.

As a result of the calibration, we have $S_0 = 0.9308$ for all models whilst the other model parameters are summarized below:

$$\text{BS: } \sigma = 0.1506.$$

$$\text{Bates: } \begin{cases} v_0 = 0.0107, & \kappa = 0.9952, \quad \theta = 0.0451, \quad \zeta = 0.4074, \\ \rho = -0.4031, & \lambda = 1.2563, \quad \mu_j = -0.0112, \quad \sigma_j = 0.0695. \end{cases} \tag{2.7}$$

$$\text{VGSV: } \begin{cases} C = 17.2562, & G = 41.9420, \quad M = 50.5294, \\ \kappa = 4.7198, & \lambda = 4.7295, \quad \eta = 1.6226. \end{cases}$$

The calibrated models are then used to drive our hypothetical market scenarios and generate option prices available to the trader. At any time $t \geq 0$, the trader is given prices of call and put options co-maturing with the barrier option and at strike prices evenly spaced from 0.641 to 1.153 with an increment of 0.0005, thereby obtaining 1,024 call option prices from which we derive a volatility smile.[2] These prices are computed using the same model which drives the evolution of S. As a result of our calibration, under Bates and VGSV models, the initial prices are close to our market data (naturally BS model only produces a flat volatility surface).

In addition to the three models above, we consider two rather unrealistic models which are designed to examine the performance of various hedging strategies when the volatility of the underlying dramatically and suddenly changes, e.g. due to the arrival of some unforeseen news. The new values of volatility are chosen here in an arbitrary manner to obtain a significant change whilst remaining within the interval commonly observed in practise for the volatility of the underlying.

BS HV model is the BS model described above, only σ at time $t > 0$ is set to 0.4518 (which is three times its value at time $t = 0$).

BS LV model is the BS model described above, only σ at time $t > 0$ is set to a value of 0.1.

In both models, the initial European option prices in the market are computed using the BS model with a constant $\sigma = 0.1506$ and are thus mispriced, which

[1]A total of 176 data points: 11 options (strikes ranging between 5Δ put to 35Δ put strike, ATM and from 35Δ call strike to 5Δ call strike) for each of 16 maturities ranging from 1 week to 1 year.
[2]The lower and upper bounds of the range of strike prices approximate the strike prices of options from our real-life market data set at delta strikes 5Δ put and 5Δ call, respectively.

reflects the unforeseen nature of the news. Prices at $t > 0$ are computed using the appropriate value of σ.

2.2. *Robust hedging strategies*

Robust hedges of digital double barrier options described in [10, 11] are quasi-static. They involve a carefully chosen initial position in co-maturing European vanilla options (at most 7 among the 1024 options available to the trader), cash and forward, and at most two dynamic forward transactions when barriers are breached. The nature of the hedge depends on the position of the barriers relative to the spot and market prices of European options. For example, if $\overline{b}$ is very far from the spot compared with $\underline{b}$ then it is shown that the optimal robust hedge for the digital double touch options is in fact the one developed in [5] for a one-touch option struck at $\overline{b}$. Although this is a possible case, we are interested here in examining the strategies which are genuinely new in [10, 11] and tailored to double barrier options. We consider four possible positions: long or short in digital double touch or double no-touch option. For each of these, we set barrier levels so that we are in the *typical* case when the genuine double barrier hedging strategy should be used.[3] More precisely, we have the following four scenarios:

(i) *The trader sells a digital double touch option with barriers* $\underline{b} = 0.85$ *and* $\overline{b} = 1.01$. The optimal robust super-hedge is type *III* in [10]. The initial portfolio is composed of $\alpha_i > 0$ calls with strike $K_i, i = 1, 2$ and $\alpha_j > 0$ puts with strike $K_j, j = 3, 4$ where $0 < K_4 < \underline{b} < K_3 < K_2 < \overline{b} < K_1$. The dynamic part involves at most two forward transactions. If $\overline{b}$ is reached first the trader sells β_1 forwards and if then the price reaches $\underline{b}$ they buy β_3 forwards. Alternatively, if $\underline{b}$ is reached first the trader buys β_2 forwards and then if the price reaches $\overline{b}$ they sell β_4 forwards. The choice of α_i, β_i ensures superreplication. We refer to [10] for details and explicit formulae. The optimal hedge $\overline{H}^{III}_{DT}$ is found by minimizing the price over all admissible strikes K_1, K_2, K_3, K_4 and the optimal values are reported in Table A.1.

(ii) *The trader sells a digital double no-touch option with barriers* $\underline{b} = 0.85$ *and* $\overline{b} = 1.01$. The optimal robust super-hedge is type *I* in [11]. It is simply given by $\overline{H}^{I}_{DNT} = \mathbf{1}_{S_T \in (\underline{b}, \overline{b})}$, i.e. the superhedge is static and consists simply of buying digital options paying 1 when $\underline{b} < S_T < \overline{b}$.

(iii) *The trader buys a digital double touch option with barriers* $\underline{b} = 0.875$ *and* $\overline{b} = 0.985$. The optimal robust sub-hedge is type *I*, described explicitly in [10] to which we refer for the exact formulae. The initial portfolio has judiciously chosen amounts of: cash, forward, long positions in calls with strikes $K_2 < \underline{b}$, $K_3 \in (\overline{b}, \underline{b})$ and $K_1 > \overline{b}$ and in a digital call struck at $\underline{b}$, and short positions

[3] The particular choice of barrier levels, as long as it guarantees we are in the interesting case, does not seem to affect our results qualitatively, cf. [35].

in calls with strikes $\underline{b}$, $\overline{b}$ and in a digital call struck at $\overline{b}$. The dynamic part is analogous to the one in $\overline{H}^{III}_{DT}$ described above, i.e. it involves forward transactions when the barriers are first breached. The value of K_3 is given as a function of K_1 and K_2, and the optimal hedge $\underline{H}^{I}_{DT}$ is hence found by maximizing the price over admissible values of K_1, K_2. The optimal values are reported in Table A.3.

(iv) *The trader buys a digital double no-touch option with barriers* $\underline{b} = 0.71$ *and* $\overline{b} = 1.1$. The optimal robust sub-hedge is type *II* in [11]. The initial portfolio consists of -1 (cash) and is long $1/(\overline{b}-K_2)$ calls with strike K_2 and $1/(K_1-\underline{b})$ puts with strike K_1, for arbitrary $\underline{b} < K_1 < K_2 < \overline{b}$. The dynamic component involves at most one transaction: the trader sells $1/(\overline{b}-K_2)$ forwards when $\overline{b}$ is breached first or buys $1/(K_1-\underline{b})$ forwards if $\underline{b}$ is breached first. The optimal hedge $\underline{H}^{II}_{DNT}$ is found by maximising the price over admissible values of K_1, K_2 and the optimal values are reported in Table A.4.

Three out of four strategies described above require the trader to monitor barrier crossings continuously. In practice this may be hard or costly. We consider thus the following strategies:

(i) ***Robust hedge exact*:** the trader implements the optimal robust hedge, as described above. They monitor continuously the breaching of the barriers.[4]

(ii) ***Robust hedge*** $\boldsymbol{N}$**:** the trader implements the optimal robust hedge, as described above, but only monitors the breaching of the barriers N times, at even intervals, during the life of the option. This means that they may carry out the relevant forward transactions with some delay.

We consider the cases where $N = 250$ and $N = 1000$, corresponding to monitoring daily and every six hours, respectively, during the life of the option.

Let us examine the distribution of hedging errors resulting from robust hedging under continuous monitoring of barrier crossing. Denote $O(S)_T$ the payoff of the digital double barrier option at maturity. The trader sells or buys the option for p, as discussed in Sec. 2.1, whereas the (frictionless) correct price[5] at time zero is $p^* = \mathbb{E}[O(S)_T]$. The trader then sets up the initial portfolio $F(S_T)$ prescribed by their super- or sub- hedge for an initial premium $p^{RH} = \mathbb{E}[F(S_T)]$ and pays transaction costs ϵ_0. Typically, $p^{RH} > p^*$ if the trader sold the digital double barrier option and $p^{RH} < p^*$ if they bought it. When barriers are breached the trader enters

[4]The continuous monitoring of the breaching of the barriers is approximated by monitoring the breaching of the barriers at each one of the 200,000 time steps used for the simulation of the underlying price.

[5]In any given scenario the underlying and option prices are generated by an arbitrage free model under a risk neutral measure. Broadly speaking, this measure is unique since the market is complete when all European options and the underlying can be traded with no transaction costs. Frictionless prices are then uniquely specified as the risk-neutral expectation of the payoffs.

into forward transactions. At maturity T, the trader thus holds

$$\Pi = \gamma(-O(S)_T + F(S)_T + V_T + p - p^{RH}) - \epsilon_0 - \epsilon_1, \tag{2.8}$$

where $\gamma = 1$ or -1 if the trader respectively sold or bought the digital double barrier option and V_T is the payoff from the self-financing dynamic trading (i.e. forward transactions) which carried (aggregated) transaction costs ϵ_1. We have

$$\mathbb{E}[\Pi] = \gamma(p - p^*) - \epsilon_0 - \epsilon_1, \quad \text{and} \quad \Pi \geq \gamma(p - p^{RH}) - \epsilon_0 - \epsilon_1.$$

The mean of Π is thus the same as that of an unhedged position less the transaction costs. However, these transaction costs are small, as we will see, since they come from single transactions as opposed to continuous rebalancing. On the other hand, Π is bounded below, which may be a greatly appealing feature and will be rewarded by risk measures.

If barrier crossing is monitored discretely (*Robust hedge N*) then Π in (2.8) has an additional error term which has zero mean but is not theoretically bounded. In practice this term is very small, as one would expect, but it does affect the risk profile of hedging errors.

2.3. *Benchmark (classical) hedging strategies*

We want to benchmark the robust hedging strategies described above against classical delta or delta/vega hedging. The trader needs to decide on a model-specific hedge facing uncertainty about the market conditions and hence the model. As in [10], we assume they settle for the simplest (and possibly most universal, see e.g. El Karoui *et al.* [15]) solution, i.e. they construct the delta and delta/vega hedges within the Black-Scholes framework using the same Black-Scholes volatility input which is used to determine the option price p at time $t = 0$. We consider the following strategies:

(i) ***No hedging***: the trader does not set up any replicating portfolio after the sale of the digital double barrier option and the position is left unhedged until expiry.

(ii) ***Delta N(ΔN)***: the trader delta hedges the digital double barrier option by rebalancing the replicating portfolio N times, at even intervals, during the life of the option.

(iii) ***Delta/vega N(Δ/𝒱N)***: the trader delta/vega hedges the digital double barrier option and rebalances the position N times, at even intervals, during the life of the option. When rebalancing the trader aims to keep his portfolio consisting of the digital double barrier option and the hedging portfolio delta- and vega-neutral by trading ATM options, the asset and the risk-free bond.

We consider the cases where $N = 250$ and $N = 1000$, corresponding to rebalancing daily and every six hours, respectively, during the life of the option.

We also examine modifications of the *delta N* and *delta/vega N* hedging strategies intended to improve their performance in the presence of transaction costs.

One of the most popular methods to improve delta or delta/vega hedging in markets with transaction costs is the utility-based stochastic optimization approach first proposed by Hodges and Neuberger [22]. They define the price of an option as that which results in the investor achieving the same terminal utility as when not trading the option. Mohamed [28], Clewlow and Hodges [9], and Martellini and Priaulet [27] studied the performance of the utility-based approach and showed that it achieves very good empirical performance. In this project, however, we do not implement this approach because it would have been too computationally intensive. Instead, we looked for methods that provide a closed-form formulae and are, in spirit and in results, reasonably good approximations to the utility-based stochastic optimization approach.

Whalley and Wilmott [36] performed an asymptotic analysis of the stochastic optimization problem under small transaction costs and proposed a closed-form formula that can be used to arrive at an approximately optimal trading rule for delta hedging. More precisely, assuming the trader has an exponential utility function with absolute risk aversion γ, [36] showed that it is optimal for the hedger to not rebalance their delta hedge when the current delta of their replicating portfolio is within a given bandwidth centred about the target delta Δ_t^{BS} derived in the Black-Scholes framework. In the case of zero interest rates the formula simplifies considerably and the bandwidth is given by

$$\Delta_t = \Delta_t^{BS} \pm \left(\frac{3}{2\gamma}\right)^{\frac{1}{3}}. \tag{2.9}$$

Zakamouline [37] compared the risk-adjusted performances of different optimised hedging strategies and found that the Whalley and Wilmott method gives very good results considering its ease of use. We obtained similar results as a by-product of our simulations.

We were not able to find any analogous asymptotic analysis of the stochastic optimization problem under transaction costs applicable to vega hedging. We chose to implement a rule similar to (2.9), which is rather widespread in practice: a fixed vega band rule. The trader does not rebalance their vega hedge as long as

$$\mathcal{V}_t = \mathcal{V}_t^{BS} \pm H, \tag{2.10}$$

where $\mathcal{V}_t^{BS}$ is the Black-Scholes vega at time t and H is a constant. The more risk-averse the hedger is, the lower H should be. The higher transaction costs are, the higher H should be. Apart from those two intuitions, the optimal H must be found either by running the simulation with many different values of H and selecting the value achieving the highest risk-adjusted performance or by applying a rule of thumb. We believe the former would give an unfair advantage to vega hedging and would not be representative of a practical trading rule, as we would be setting in advance the parameters of the true distribution of the underlying and selecting the best value of H for that specific distribution. Instead, we decided to use a rule of thumb, which is closer to the way the trading rule would be applied in practice. The idea is to set the maximum loss due to volatility movements the trader is willing to incur between rebalancing and infer the corresponding value of H. Let us assume that the trader sells a digital double barrier option for a premium p and is not willing to incur a loss exceeding $x\%$ of this premium between any rebalancing. Let us further assume that the trader believes that the volatility of the asset can move by up to $\Delta\sigma$ in one day during the life of the option. We may then compute H as follows: $H = xp/\Delta\sigma$. In our implementation, we chose $x = 50\%$ and $\Delta\sigma = 0.1$ after having experimented with different values and found these chosen values to provide significant improvements in performance. Summarizing, in addition to the *delta N* and *delta/vega N* hedging strategies previously described, we have two additional strategies:

(iv) ***Optimized delta*** $\boldsymbol{N(\Delta + N)}$**:** identical to *delta N*, only the trader implements the aforementioned delta trading rule (2.9). The trader's absolute risk aversion (ARA) level is assumed equal to 1.

(v) ***Optimized delta/vega*** $\boldsymbol{N(\Delta/\mathcal{V} + N)}$**:** identical to *delta/vega N*, only the trader uses the delta and vega trading rules (2.9) and (2.10) described above.

2.4. *Performance measures*

We run Monte Carlo simulations, each with 200,000 simulated paths and 200,000 time steps and carry out in parallel the twelve hedging strategies described above. In order to compare the performances of the simulated hedging strategies, we consider their expected profit and their risk. We record the distribution of hedging errors for each of the hedging strategies and mean-correct them in the spirit of the control variate approach suggested in Hull and White [24] (see also Davis *et al.* [14] or [10]). The procedure is detailed in Appendix B.3 and the adjustments (Adj[6]) are reported. We call these the *realized hedging errors* and compute their sample mean (Mean), standard deviation (SD), skewness (Skew), kurtosis (Kurt), minimum (Min) and maximum (Max).

We chose the sample mean of the hedging errors as an obvious measure of expected profit. Note that the sample mean for *no hedging* is simply the difference between the sell/buy price[7] and the true price. The means for other strategies additionally capture the average level of transaction costs paid by each strategy as well as its exposure to mispriced European options (the latter only happens in the BS HV and BS LV models).

With respect to measuring the risk, there is no obvious unique choice. The distributions of the hedging errors for the considered hedging strategies substantially deviate from the normal distribution and, as a result, it would be misleading to only use the sample standard deviation as a measure of risk. Instead, we chose as risk measures the maximum observed loss, the Value-at-Risk (VaR) and the Conditional

[6]Abbreviations given in parenthesis are used in Tables A.1–A.5.
[7]Recall that it was set to the BS price with the at-the-money call option implied volatility.

Value-at-Risk (CVaR). Both VaR and CVaR measures were computed at the 99% confidence level and with a time horizon equal to the life of the digital double barrier option. These measures are typically used in practice to assess the economic capital of unfunded transactions such as the sale of an exotic option. We examine those risk measures in combination rather than in isolation when subjectively assessing the risk of a particular hedging strategy. To illustrate, whenever a hedging strategy H1 achieves lower VaR, CoVaR and maximum loss measures than another strategy H2, we conclude that H1 is less risky than H2. Furthermore, if that same H1 achieves an expected return equal to or higher than H2, we conclude that H1 achieves a higher risk-adjusted performance than H2.

We recall that VaR(α) of a portfolio at a confidence level α is given by the smallest number l such that the probability that the portfolio loss exceeds l is not greater than $(1-\alpha)$. The Conditional Value-at-Risk (CVaR), also called expected shortfall, is given by

$$\mathrm{CVaR}(\alpha) = \frac{1}{1-\alpha}\int_{\alpha}^{1} \mathrm{VaR}(u)\mathrm{d}u \tag{2.11}$$

and has the advantage of being a convex risk measure, see Artzner *et al.* [2] or Föllmer and Schied [17].

Finally, to complement the above, we compute the trader's expected utility assuming a negative exponential utility function: $U(X) = 1 - e^{-\gamma X}$ for two values of absolute risk aversion $\gamma = 1$ and $\gamma = 2$. These values are reported as EUM and EUH respectively.

Observe that all the statistics and risk measures considered are either invariant or monotone under a constant shift of the distribution and hence the choice of the initial premium p does not affect the relative performance of hedging strategies.

All the computations are done under the risk-neutral measure (RNM), which is uniquely specified through the calibration procedure to the market data. It may be argued that for risk assessment one should use the real-world (physical) measure (RWM) and not the pricing measure. However, we are here concerned with the relative evaluation of different hedging methods and there are good reasons to do it under the RNM. Firstly, a canonical example for an underlying here would be the exchange rate for a pair of stable currencies with very similar domestic interest rates. In such a situation one might expect a drift close to zero, even under the RWM, making the RNM a plausible guess for the RWM. Secondly, to estimate the dynamics under the RWM one would have to turn to time series of historical prices. Such model estimation may be inaccurate, drift estimation poses a significant difficulty (see e.g. Monoyios [29]) and one would have to assess how sensitive the results are with respect to e.g. drift misspecification. Further, we think here of a situation of model uncertainty when the trader has doubts about future dynamics. In such a case, using historical prices to forecast future dynamics does not seem appropriate. The RNM in contrast has the benefit of being well specified and calibrated to prices of future payoffs. Naturally, these are interesting problems that merit independent research and we leave it for future investigations.

3. Results

We discuss now the risk-adjusted performance of hedging strategies under different market scenarios applying the methodology described above. We refer to Tables A.1–A.5 for the detailed results of our simulations.

We begin by looking at how the robust hedging strategies performed relative to traditional hedging methods in the ideal case for the latter, namely when the underlying is driven by the Black-Scholes model. In this case there is no model misspecification and the only error in delta-hedging is due to discrete rebalancing and transaction costs. One might expect the robust hedges not to be competitive in such a scenario. Indeed, for a long position in a digital double touch (DT) option and a short position in a digital double no-touch (DNT) option, classical strategies, especially *delta N* or *optimized delta N* hedges, tend to outperform robust hedges with the exception that robust strategies achieve lower maximum observed losses. In contrast, for a short position in a DT option and a long position in a DNT option, the situation is reversed and the robust strategies achieved a higher risk-adjusted performance than all considered traditional hedging methods. We note, however, that the standard deviation of the hedging errors for robust strategies is between 2 and 3 times greater than that of a typical classical hedging strategy.

If we now look at the results for Bates and VGSV models, we find that the robust hedging strategies lead to an often dramatic reduction in risk relative to traditional hedging methods, whilst achieving similar or higher expected profits.[8] Robust hedges for a short position in a DT option and short or long position for a DNT option outperformed all other considered hedging strategies on a risk-adjusted basis. The results are less conclusive for a long position in a DT option. Here, the $\Delta+$ 1000 strategy under the Bates model and the $\Delta/\mathcal{V}+1000$ strategy under the VGSV model achieved significantly higher means than robust hedges (the differences are small and equal 3.7% and 0.5% of option's premium respectively). They performed worse on risk measures and achieved similar values for the expected utility.

The standard deviation of hedging errors for robust strategies was either comparable to that of classical hedges (short or long DT option) or higher by around 30% (long DNT option) up to a factor of 2 (short DNT option). Finally, in terms of expected utility, for higher risk aversion (EUH) robust strategies typically decisively outperformed classical strategies, while achieving higher or similar expected utility for lower risk aversion (EUM). We emphasise that both Bates and VGSV models have jumps and these results show that the robust strategies, originally designed

[8]To compare the means of hedging errors we run paired t-test at a 99% confidence level. We say that a strategy has a significantly higher mean if this is true for both raw and mean-adjusted hedging errors (cf. Appendix B.3).

for markets with continuous paths, perform remarkably well also in the presence of jumps.

We now turn to market scenarios with dramatic changes of volatility: BS HV and BS LV. Robust hedges use market traded European options to construct the static parts of the hedge. At time $t = 0$, these options are underpriced in BS HV and overpriced in BS LV. We would thus expect robust hedges to perform well or poorly under BS HV/LV depending on whether they go long or short European options. Naturally, a similar reasoning applies to delta/vega hedges. Our results confirm this intuition. Under BS HV for a short position in a DT option and a long position in a DNT option and under BS LV for a short position in a DNT option, robust hedges decisively outperformed all other hedging strategies. For a long position in a DT option under BS LV, robust hedges outperformed delta hedges but comparison with delta/vega strategies is inconclusive: robust hedges came first under our three risk measures but delta/vega hedges achieved higher means and expected utility. We note finally that in all four situations the hedging errors of robust strategies had a considerably larger standard deviation than other strategies (about 2 to 3 times larger up to 5 times larger for the long position in DNT option under BS HV). This is mainly due to comparatively large maximal hedging errors (gains) attained by robust strategies.

Table A.5 contains the simulation results for the remaining four cases: long DT or short DNT under BS HV and short DT or long DNT under BS LV. In these cases, both the robust hedges and the delta/vega hedges had a worse risk-adjusted performance than delta hedges or *no hedging*. This was to be expected: frictionless delta hedging would be guaranteed to super/sub-replicate (cf. El Karoui *et al.* [15]) while robust or delta/vega hedging methods have to lead to an expected loss. Remarkably, in all four cases, we find that robust hedges achieved a better risk-adjusted performance than delta/vega hedging. As previously, the hedging errors of robust strategies had higher standard deviations than other strategies but this was less pronounced: of the order of 1.5 to 2 times higher, except for the short position in DNT under BS HV where other strategies had almost zero variance.

In all market scenarios and for all positions, the distribution of hedging errors resulting from the robust methods is significantly positively skewed. In other words, robust hedging tends to lead to poor returns more frequently than good returns, but the poor returns are small whilst the good returns are large. In contrast, the distribution of hedging errors for traditional hedging methods is typically negatively skewed, leading to the opposite conclusion regarding the frequency and size of poor and good returns.

Figures A.1–A.4 show the cumulative distribution functions of the hedging errors achieved by some of the simulated hedging strategies. Those figures highlight how the hedging errors are practically bounded on the loss side for the robust hedges whilst all the traditional hedging methods have important left tails. The figures also highlight the extent to which the probability of large returns is much higher for the robust hedges than for the traditional ones: the right tails of the cumulative distribution functions for the traditional methods converge to 1 on the right-hand side of the figures much faster than those of the robust methods.

Finally, we examine in more detail the effect of jumps and discrete monitoring of barrier crossing, both of which violate assumptions in [10, 11], on the performance of robust hedges. We are interested in how well the theoretical property of super- or sub-hedging is preserved and hence we need to examine the left tail of the distribution of hedging errors. For the short position in a DNT option the robust hedge is fully static and hence invariant to these factors. The hedging error is bounded below, as in (2.8), which is clearly visible in Fig. A.2. Jumps in the underlying alone do not affect the performance of the robust hedge of a short position in a DT option or a long position in a DNT option, see [10, 11]. However, the hedging error is no longer bounded below because the discrete monitoring of barrier crossing introduces an additional error term to (2.8). We see this in Figs. A.1 and A.4 — robust hedges exhibit a small left tail. It is, however, roughly similar in all four figures, which confirms that jumps in the underlying do not introduce an additional error. We see also that the tail grows with the decrease of monitoring frequency, which is summarised by worsening risk measures, cf. Tables A.1 and A.4. Lastly, in Fig. A.3 we see the cumulative distribution function of hedging errors from a long position in a digital double touch option. In this case the theory indicates that the robust hedging strategy is sensitive to the assumption of continuity of paths. This is confirmed by our simulations. Under BS and BS LV robust hedging errors exhibit a small left tail which grows with decreasing monitoring frequency. Under Bates and VGSV models the left tail becomes more pronounced and the changing frequency of monitoring has little effect, indicating that the presence of jumps is a more important factor. This is confirmed by the risk measures computed in Table A.3.

We conclude that the introduction of jumps in the underlying and the discrete monitoring of barrier crossing may affect the performance of robust hedges, along the lines predicted by the theory. We stress, however, that in our simulations this effect is of second order compared with the differences between robust and classical hedges and all our main findings above apply equally well to all considered versions of the robust hedges.

4. Conclusions and Further Research

The results of our simulations, as described above, are strikingly unanimous. We compared the hedging errors resulting from robust hedging strategies of Cox and Obłój [10, 11] and from Black-Scholes delta or delta/vega hedges with fixed or optimally adjusted rebalancing times. In the vast majority of considered market scenarios and trader's positions, robust hedges achieved an expected return similar to or higher than the best classical hedge whilst delivering an often dramatic reduction in risk measured with VaR, CVar and Maximum Loss. The hedging errors of robust strategies typically have higher variance than classical model-specific hedges but this is mainly due to infrequent large gains.

Theoretical properties of robust hedging strategies of digital double barrier options were developed in [10, 11] assuming continuity of paths of the underlying and continuous monitoring of barrier crossings. Our market scenarios included models with finite and infinite activity jumps component and we implemented robust strategies with discrete monitoring of barrier crossings. Results of our simulations indicate the robust hedges are truly robust, even with respect to these two simplifying assumptions in [10, 11].

We believe that our results present convincing evidence of the benefits of robust hedging methods. Nevertheless, the setup of our paper was restrictive in two ways. Firstly, we only considered an underlying with zero cost of carry. This may be appropriate for futures markets or currency pairs with the same domestic and foreign interest rates but not in all generality. Implementation of robust hedging methods of [10, 11] for generic spot markets and a numerical analysis of their performance remains, in our view, an important research avenue. Secondly, all our analysis apply to a single position in a digital double barrier option. It remains an open problem whether, and how, this discussion may be extended to a portfolio of options.

Appendix A. Tables and Figures

Table A.1. Simulation results (cf. Sec. 2.4) for the short position in the considered digital double touch barrier option.

Strategy	Mean	SD	Skew	Kurt	Min	Max	VaR	CVaR	EUM	EUH	Adj
BS model; $p = 0.1644$; Robust Strategy: $\overline{H}_{DT}^{III}$, $K_1 = 1.0425$, $K_2 = 0.9805$, $K_3 = 0.8795$, $K_4 = 0.819$											
No Hedging	0.0000	0.37	−1.8	4.3	−0.84	0.16	0.84	0.84	−0.09	−0.47	−0.0010
Δ 250	−0.0209	0.07	−1.8	39.1	−1.80	1.25	0.24	0.38	−0.02	−0.06	−0.0011
Δ 1000	−0.0397	0.05	−4.6	99.1	−1.95	0.94	0.19	0.30	−0.04	−0.09	−0.0011
$\Delta/\mathcal{V}$ 250	−0.0549	0.07	−2.0	35.6	−1.83	1.21	0.28	0.43	−0.06	−0.13	−0.0011
$\Delta/\mathcal{V}$ 1000	−0.0999	0.07	−2.0	23.1	−2.04	0.78	0.30	0.41	−0.11	−0.24	−0.0011
$\Delta +$ 250	−0.0092	0.10	−1.2	19.0	−1.93	1.14	0.30	0.44	−0.01	−0.04	−0.0011
$\Delta +$ 1000	−0.0101	0.08	−1.3	23.5	−2.10	1.29	0.24	0.35	−0.01	−0.03	−0.0011
$\Delta/\mathcal{V} +$ 250	−0.0248	0.10	−0.9	15.0	−1.85	1.14	0.31	0.46	−0.03	−0.08	−0.0023
$\Delta/\mathcal{V} +$ 1000	−0.0266	0.09	−0.9	15.1	−2.25	1.27	0.26	0.37	−0.03	−0.07	−0.0026
Robust 250	−0.0081	0.20	1.7	6.2	−0.45	2.47	0.23	0.26	−0.03	−0.08	−0.0006
Robust 1000	−0.0081	0.20	1.8	6.5	−0.29	2.45	0.18	0.20	−0.03	−0.08	−0.0006
Robust Exact	−0.0081	0.20	1.8	6.5	−0.15	2.45	0.14	0.14	−0.03	−0.08	−0.0006
BS HV model; $p = 0.1644$; Robust Strategy: $\overline{H}_{DT}^{III}$, $K_1 = 1.0425$, $K_2 = 0.9805$, $K_3 = 0.8795$, $K_4 = 0.819$											
No Hedging	−0.5316	0.46	0.8	1.7	−0.84	0.16	0.84	0.84	−0.86	−2.93	−0.0027
Δ 250	−0.5482	0.45	−1.8	8.7	−9.68	2.25	2.15	2.59	−1.03	−520.56	−0.0026
Δ 1000	−0.5621	0.45	−1.9	8.8	−7.05	0.77	2.19	2.64	−1.04	−10.92	−0.0028
$\Delta/\mathcal{V}$ 250	0.4405	0.51	−1.5	7.1	−8.64	2.94	1.29	1.73	0.22	−65.23	−0.0026
$\Delta/\mathcal{V}$ 1000	0.3355	0.59	−1.6	6.6	−6.40	1.51	1.65	2.13	0.08	−2.52	−0.0027
$\Delta +$ 250	−0.5439	0.46	−1.9	9.0	−9.58	2.21	2.16	2.61	−1.03	−430.30	−0.0025
$\Delta +$ 1000	−0.5468	0.45	−2.0	9.2	−6.96	0.78	2.16	2.62	−1.00	−10.28	−0.0027
$\Delta/\mathcal{V} +$ 250	0.4925	0.46	−1.6	7.8	−8.45	2.99	1.07	1.51	0.29	−43.63	−0.0026
$\Delta/\mathcal{V} +$ 1000	0.4804	0.46	−1.7	8.0	−6.04	1.90	1.11	1.57	0.28	−0.48	−0.0027
Robust 250	0.6414	1.34	3.8	29.4	−1.13	31.90	0.42	0.50	0.23	0.23	−0.0006
Robust 1000	0.6414	1.34	3.9	29.8	−0.56	31.97	0.27	0.31	0.23	0.26	−0.0007
Robust Exact	0.6414	1.34	3.9	30.0	−0.15	31.92	0.14	0.14	0.24	0.26	−0.0006

Table A.1. (*Continued*)

Strategy	Mean	SD	Skew	Kurt	Min	Max	VaR	CVaR	EUM	EUH	Adj
Bates model; $p = 0.1831$; Robust Strategy: $\overline{H}_{DT}^{III}$, $K_1 = 1.046$, $K_2 = 0.978$, $K_3 = 0.8845$, $K_4 = 0.8105$											
No Hedging	0.0179	0.37	−1.8	4.3	−0.82	0.18	0.82	0.82	−0.07	−0.42	0.0000
Δ 250	0.0029	0.25	−1.9	15.7	−4.90	3.58	0.90	1.23	−0.04	−0.37	0.0005
Δ 1000	−0.0100	0.25	−2.0	15.9	−4.48	3.55	0.90	1.24	−0.05	−0.40	0.0006
$\Delta/\mathcal{V}$ 250	−0.0240	0.23	−1.8	18.4	−4.99	3.52	0.84	1.15	−0.06	−0.38	0.0728
$\Delta/\mathcal{V}$ 1000	−0.0532	0.23	−1.9	17.9	−4.51	3.55	0.89	1.20	−0.09	−0.45	0.0728
$\Delta + 250$	0.0107	0.25	−2.0	15.2	−4.63	3.47	0.91	1.25	−0.03	−0.32	0.0006
$\Delta + 1000$	0.0098	0.25	−2.0	16.3	−4.58	3.07	0.89	1.22	−0.03	−0.37	0.0004
$\Delta/\mathcal{V} + 250$	−0.0056	0.23	−1.7	17.1	−4.97	3.66	0.82	1.13	−0.04	−0.32	0.0763
$\Delta/\mathcal{V} + 1000$	−0.0071	0.22	−1.7	18.2	−4.47	3.27	0.79	1.10	−0.04	−0.29	0.0763
Robust 250	0.0099	0.26	3.9	39.0	−1.16	7.35	0.26	0.32	−0.02	−0.08	−0.0033
Robust 1000	0.0099	0.26	4.0	40.6	−1.19	7.39	0.20	0.23	−0.02	−0.07	−0.0033
Robust Exact	0.0099	0.26	4.1	41.5	−0.16	7.42	0.16	0.16	−0.02	−0.07	−0.0033
VGSV model; $p = 0.1895$; Robust Strategy: $\overline{H}_{DT}^{III}$, $K_1 = 1.0445$, $K_2 = 0.979$, $K_3 = 0.8845$, $K_4 = 0.811$											
No Hedging	0.0675	0.33	−2.3	6.3	−0.81	0.19	0.81	0.81	−0.00	−0.22	0.0000
Δ 250	0.0580	0.22	−1.4	20.7	−5.42	4.04	0.70	1.01	0.03	−0.31	−0.0108
Δ 1000	0.0565	0.22	−0.8	64.1	−7.83	11.24	0.68	0.99	0.02	−31.47	−0.0107
$\Delta/\mathcal{V}$ 250	0.0347	0.19	−1.4	30.1	−5.41	4.04	0.64	0.95	0.01	−0.32	0.0127
$\Delta/\mathcal{V}$ 1000	0.0300	0.19	−0.7	101.0	−7.81	11.14	0.64	0.95	−0.00	−30.35	0.0127
$\Delta + 250$	0.0615	0.22	−1.5	19.4	−5.39	4.24	0.70	1.01	0.03	−0.29	−0.0078
$\Delta + 1000$	0.0612	0.22	−0.8	55.6	−6.33	11.06	0.69	0.99	0.03	−1.62	−0.0078
$\Delta/\mathcal{V} + 250$	0.0453	0.19	−1.2	26.2	−5.51	4.23	0.60	0.91	0.02	−0.35	0.0256
$\Delta/\mathcal{V} + 1000$	0.0447	0.19	−0.2	87.2	−6.25	11.04	0.58	0.88	0.02	−1.38	0.0267
Robust 250	0.0599	0.23	2.9	24.8	−1.23	5.53	0.19	0.27	0.04	0.04	0.0196
Robust 1000	0.0599	0.23	3.0	26.2	−0.81	5.53	0.12	0.17	0.04	0.04	0.0198
Robust Exact	0.0599	0.23	3.0	26.6	−0.13	5.53	0.12	0.12	0.04	0.04	0.0198

Table A.2. Simulation results (cf. Sec. 2.4) for the short position in the considered digital double no-touch barrier option.

Strategy	Mean	SD	Skew	Kurt	Min	Max	VaR	CVaR	EUM	EUH	Adj
BS model; $p = 0.0295$; Robust Strategy: $\overline{H}^I_{DNT}$											
No Hedging	0.0000	0.17	−5.5	31.4	−0.97	0.03	0.97	0.97	−0.02	−0.12	0.0005
Δ 250	−0.0085	0.05	−2.8	70.9	−1.17	1.55	0.21	0.32	−0.01	−0.02	0.0005
Δ 1000	−0.0161	0.04	−5.1	63.5	−1.22	0.88	0.19	0.27	−0.02	−0.04	0.0005
$\Delta/\mathcal{V}$ 250	−0.0357	0.06	−3.6	43.8	−1.21	1.41	0.28	0.39	−0.04	−0.08	0.0005
$\Delta/\mathcal{V}$ 1000	−0.0673	0.08	−2.8	14.5	−1.44	0.69	0.38	0.47	−0.07	−0.16	0.0005
$\Delta +$ 250	−0.0045	0.06	−2.2	47.8	−1.58	1.52	0.25	0.36	−0.01	−0.02	0.0007
$\Delta +$ 1000	−0.0051	0.05	−2.7	44.0	−1.07	1.18	0.19	0.28	−0.01	−0.01	0.0008
$\Delta/\mathcal{V} +$ 250	−0.0330	0.07	−3.5	36.5	−1.41	1.43	0.32	0.44	−0.04	−0.08	0.0005
$\Delta/\mathcal{V} +$ 1000	−0.0580	0.08	−2.9	16.4	−1.30	0.99	0.38	0.47	−0.06	−0.14	0.0005
Robust 250	−0.0097	0.49	0.4	1.2	−0.41	0.59	0.41	0.41	−0.13	−0.49	0.0005
Robust 1000	−0.0097	0.49	0.4	1.2	−0.41	0.59	0.41	0.41	−0.13	−0.49	0.0005
Robust Exact	−0.0097	0.49	0.4	1.2	−0.41	0.59	0.41	0.41	−0.13	−0.49	0.0005
BS LV model; $p = 0.0295$; Robust Strategy: $\overline{H}^I_{DNT}$											
No Hedging	−0.2125	0.43	−1.2	2.4	−0.97	0.03	0.97	0.97	−0.37	−1.40	0.0009
Δ 250	−0.2314	0.26	−1.2	3.7	−2.53	0.99	0.96	1.16	−0.31	−0.89	0.0007
Δ 1000	−0.2483	0.28	−1.1	3.2	−2.84	1.14	0.97	1.14	−0.34	−0.98	0.0006
$\Delta/\mathcal{V}$ 250	−0.1851	0.26	−1.1	3.8	−2.51	1.06	0.92	1.12	−0.25	−0.71	0.0009
$\Delta/\mathcal{V}$ 1000	−0.2265	0.29	−1.0	3.1	−2.80	1.17	0.98	1.16	−0.31	−0.92	0.0009
$\Delta +$ 250	−0.2214	0.27	−1.2	3.8	−2.34	0.92	0.98	1.16	−0.30	−0.86	0.0006
$\Delta +$ 1000	−0.2224	0.26	−1.2	3.6	−2.33	1.45	0.94	1.11	−0.30	−0.84	0.0005
$\Delta/\mathcal{V} +$ 250	−0.1773	0.27	−1.2	3.9	−2.50	1.02	0.93	1.12	−0.24	−0.70	0.0009
$\Delta/\mathcal{V} +$ 1000	−0.2034	0.28	−1.0	3.3	−2.44	1.45	0.95	1.12	−0.28	−0.80	0.0009
Robust 250	−0.0434	0.48	0.5	1.3	−0.41	0.59	0.41	0.41	−0.16	−0.55	0.0003
Robust 1000	−0.0434	0.48	0.5	1.3	−0.41	0.59	0.41	0.41	−0.16	−0.55	0.0003
Robust Exact	−0.0434	0.48	0.5	1.3	−0.41	0.59	0.41	0.41	−0.16	−0.55	0.0003

Table A.2. (*Continued*)

Strategy	Mean	SD	Skew	Kurt	Min	Max	VaR	CVaR	EUM	EUH	Adj
Bates model; $p = 0.0228$; Robust Strategy: $\overline{H}^{I}_{DNT}$											
No Hedging	−0.0920	0.32	−2.4	6.8	−0.98	0.02	0.98	0.98	−0.17	−0.66	0.0000
Δ 250	−0.1020	0.29	−1.2	20.3	−5.50	8.95	1.10	1.34	−0.17	−1.22	−0.0004
Δ 1000	−0.1102	0.29	−1.4	20.2	−5.46	8.35	1.11	1.36	−0.18	−1.11	−0.0006
$\Delta/\mathcal{V}$ 250	−0.1307	0.26	−0.9	26.1	−5.77	8.40	1.04	1.31	−0.19	−1.65	−0.0574
$\Delta/\mathcal{V}$ 1000	−0.1623	0.27	−1.2	24.6	−5.78	7.78	1.10	1.38	−0.23	−1.55	−0.0579
Δ + 250	−0.0975	0.29	−1.3	18.2	−5.31	8.98	1.09	1.31	−0.16	−0.86	−0.0003
Δ + 1000	−0.0983	0.29	−1.3	18.7	−4.76	8.66	1.08	1.30	−0.16	−0.81	−0.0004
$\Delta/\mathcal{V}$ + 250	−0.1270	0.26	−1.0	20.8	−5.62	7.73	1.03	1.28	−0.18	−1.19	−0.0574
$\Delta/\mathcal{V}$ + 1000	−0.1507	0.27	−1.2	22.1	−5.34	8.14	1.07	1.33	−0.21	−1.18	−0.0579
Robust 250	−0.1022	0.47	0.7	1.5	−0.43	0.57	0.43	0.43	−0.22	−0.69	−0.0036
Robust 1000	−0.1022	0.47	0.7	1.5	−0.43	0.57	0.43	0.43	−0.22	−0.69	−0.0036
Robust Exact	−0.1022	0.47	0.7	1.5	−0.43	0.57	0.43	0.43	−0.22	−0.69	−0.0036
VGSV model; $p = 0.0208$; Robust Strategy: $\overline{H}^{I}_{DNT}$											
No Hedging	−0.1087	0.34	−2.2	5.9	−0.98	0.02	0.98	0.98	−0.20	−0.75	0.0000
Δ 250	−0.1161	0.31	−1.5	11.9	−5.77	4.28	1.21	1.44	−0.19	−1.26	0.0149
Δ 1000	−0.1178	0.31	−1.3	18.9	−5.87	8.71	1.21	1.46	−0.20	−1.56	0.0149
$\Delta/\mathcal{V}$ 250	−0.1373	0.27	−1.6	15.0	−5.79	4.19	1.15	1.39	−0.20	−1.26	−0.0092
$\Delta/\mathcal{V}$ 1000	−0.1418	0.27	−1.4	26.4	−5.90	8.80	1.15	1.42	−0.21	−1.57	−0.0093
Δ + 250	−0.1140	0.31	−1.5	11.2	−5.73	4.23	1.17	1.38	−0.19	−1.16	0.0118
Δ + 1000	−0.1145	0.30	−1.5	11.8	−5.52	4.95	1.17	1.39	−0.19	−1.07	0.0120
$\Delta/\mathcal{V}$ + 250	−0.1355	0.27	−1.5	13.6	−5.72	3.97	1.12	1.34	−0.20	−1.13	−0.0091
$\Delta/\mathcal{V}$ + 1000	−0.1387	0.27	−1.6	14.8	−5.47	5.05	1.12	1.35	−0.20	−1.06	−0.0091
Robust 250	−0.1189	0.46	0.8	1.7	−0.43	0.57	0.43	0.43	−0.23	−0.72	0.0003
Robust 1000	−0.1189	0.46	0.8	1.7	−0.43	0.57	0.43	0.43	−0.23	−0.72	0.0003
Robust Exact	−0.1189	0.46	0.8	1.7	−0.43	0.57	0.43	0.43	−0.23	−0.72	0.0003

Table A.3. Simulation results (cf. Sec. 2.4) for the long position in the considered digital double touch barrier option.

Strategy	Mean	SD	Skew	Kurt	Min	Max	VaR	CVaR	EUM	EUH	Adj
BS model; $p = 0.3896$; Robust Strategy: $\underline{H}^I_{DT}$, $K_1 = 1.1525$, $K_2 = 0.7385$											
No Hedging	−0.0000	0.49	0.5	1.2	−0.39	0.61	0.39	0.39	−0.11	−0.44	0.0031
Δ 250	−0.0230	0.08	−0.6	32.2	−2.54	2.01	0.25	0.38	−0.03	−0.06	0.0017
Δ 1000	−0.0425	0.05	−3.4	79.9	−2.14	1.53	0.20	0.30	−0.04	−0.10	0.0019
$\Delta/\mathcal{V}$ 250	−0.0628	0.08	−0.8	28.9	−2.57	1.95	0.30	0.43	−0.07	−0.15	0.0017
$\Delta/\mathcal{V}$ 1000	−0.1145	0.08	−1.6	19.8	−2.27	1.48	0.33	0.43	−0.12	−0.27	0.0019
$\Delta +$ 250	−0.0110	0.10	−0.1	17.2	−2.49	2.17	0.29	0.41	−0.02	−0.05	0.0016
$\Delta +$ 1000	−0.0120	0.08	−0.5	16.6	−1.49	1.66	0.24	0.33	−0.02	−0.04	0.0019
$\Delta/\mathcal{V} +$ 250	−0.0272	0.10	−0.2	16.7	−2.66	1.99	0.31	0.43	−0.03	−0.08	0.0025
$\Delta/\mathcal{V} +$ 1000	−0.0291	0.08	−0.6	16.6	−1.79	1.55	0.25	0.34	−0.03	−0.07	0.0027
Robust 250	−0.0297	0.32	1.0	2.8	−0.45	1.99	0.35	0.36	−0.08	−0.25	0.0014
Robust 1000	−0.0297	0.32	1.0	2.8	−0.38	1.94	0.32	0.33	−0.08	−0.25	0.0015
Robust Exact	−0.0297	0.32	1.0	2.8	−0.30	1.94	0.30	0.30	−0.08	−0.25	0.0015
BS LV model; $p = 0.3896$; Robust Strategy: $\underline{H}^I_{DT}$, $K_1 = 1.1525$, $K_2 = 0.7385$											
No Hedging	−0.2437	0.35	2.0	5.1	−0.39	0.61	0.39	0.39	−0.34	−0.90	0.0012
Δ 250	−0.2664	0.14	−1.9	11.1	−1.84	0.81	0.77	0.96	−0.32	−0.79	0.0013
Δ 1000	−0.2859	0.14	−1.8	10.1	−2.06	0.82	0.78	0.95	−0.35	−0.87	0.0013
$\Delta/\mathcal{V}$ 250	−0.0964	0.13	−2.3	14.4	−1.63	1.01	0.58	0.78	−0.11	−0.27	0.0005
$\Delta/\mathcal{V}$ 1000	−0.1303	0.14	−2.1	12.3	−1.90	0.98	0.62	0.79	−0.15	−0.36	0.0005
$\Delta +$ 250	−0.2529	0.16	−1.6	8.7	−1.77	0.79	0.79	0.97	−0.30	−0.76	0.0013
$\Delta +$ 1000	−0.2536	0.15	−1.6	8.8	−1.82	0.85	0.76	0.93	−0.30	−0.75	0.0012
$\Delta/\mathcal{V} +$ 250	−0.0720	0.14	−1.8	10.1	−1.58	0.98	0.58	0.76	−0.09	−0.21	0.0019
$\Delta/\mathcal{V} +$ 1000	−0.0728	0.14	−1.8	10.5	−1.77	1.07	0.55	0.72	−0.09	−0.21	0.0020
Robust 250	−0.1299	0.26	1.7	5.3	−0.40	0.79	0.33	0.34	−0.17	−0.43	0.0011
Robust 1000	−0.1299	0.26	1.7	5.3	−0.35	0.74	0.31	0.32	−0.17	−0.43	0.0011
Robust Exact	−0.1299	0.26	1.7	5.3	−0.30	0.70	0.30	0.30	−0.17	−0.43	0.0011

Table A.3. (*Continued*)

Strategy	Mean	SD	Skew	Kurt	Min	Max	VaR	CVaR	EUM	EUH	Adj
Bates model; $p = 0.4083$; Robust Strategy: $\underline{H}^I_{DT}$, $K_1 = 1.153$, $K_2 = 0.689$											
No Hedging	−0.0820	0.47	0.7	1.5	−0.41	0.59	0.41	0.41	−0.19	−0.62	0.0000
Δ 250	−0.1007	0.29	0.8	14.2	−3.87	8.60	0.79	1.02	−0.15	−0.47	−0.0000
Δ 1000	−0.1156	0.28	0.8	17.3	−3.54	9.33	0.80	1.03	−0.17	−0.49	−0.0001
$\Delta/\mathcal{V}$ 250	−0.1320	0.26	0.4	17.6	−3.96	7.97	0.85	1.09	−0.18	−0.54	−0.0973
$\Delta/\mathcal{V}$ 1000	−0.1682	0.25	0.2	21.1	−3.88	8.52	0.89	1.12	−0.22	−0.64	−0.0975
Δ + 250	−0.0915	0.29	0.9	13.7	−3.96	8.62	0.78	0.99	−0.14	−0.44	−0.0000
Δ + 1000	−0.0926	0.28	0.8	10.7	−3.38	5.50	0.77	0.98	−0.14	−0.42	−0.0001
$\Delta/\mathcal{V}$ + 250	−0.1070	0.26	0.6	16.8	−4.02	8.06	0.80	1.02	−0.15	−0.47	−0.0908
$\Delta/\mathcal{V}$ + 1000	−0.1087	0.25	0.4	12.9	−3.97	5.28	0.79	1.00	−0.15	−0.44	−0.0916
Robust 250	−0.1108	0.32	1.2	4.2	−1.31	3.61	0.61	0.70	−0.17	−0.46	−0.0051
Robust 1000	−0.1108	0.31	1.2	4.2	−1.31	3.61	0.61	0.70	−0.17	−0.46	−0.0051
Robust Exact	−0.1108	0.31	1.2	4.2	−1.31	3.63	0.61	0.69	−0.17	−0.46	−0.0051
VGSV model; $p = 0.4145$; Robust Strategy: $\underline{H}^I_{DT}$, $K_1 = 1.149$, $K_2 = 0.693$											
No Hedging	−0.1540	0.44	1.1	2.2	−0.41	0.59	0.41	0.41	−0.26	−0.77	0.0000
Δ 250	−0.1667	0.27	0.2	11.9	−5.88	3.63	0.91	1.17	−0.23	−1.42	0.0091
Δ 1000	−0.1685	0.27	0.5	28.8	−6.00	10.97	0.91	1.17	−0.23	−1.91	0.0093
$\Delta/\mathcal{V}$ 250	−0.1928	0.24	−0.1	17.4	−5.98	3.43	0.89	1.16	−0.25	−1.60	−0.0258
$\Delta/\mathcal{V}$ 1000	−0.1982	0.23	0.3	48.8	−6.11	10.89	0.89	1.16	−0.26	−2.17	−0.0257
Δ + 250	−0.1625	0.27	0.4	10.5	−4.84	3.87	0.89	1.11	−0.22	−0.78	0.0048
Δ + 1000	−0.1629	0.27	0.7	27.6	−5.13	11.23	0.89	1.11	−0.22	−0.89	0.0049
$\Delta/\mathcal{V}$ + 250	−0.1783	0.24	0.1	13.9	−4.81	3.61	0.86	1.09	−0.23	−0.78	−0.0296
$\Delta/\mathcal{V}$ + 1000	−0.1790	0.23	0.6	43.4	−4.96	11.08	0.85	1.08	−0.23	−0.86	−0.0307
Robust 250	−0.1828	0.28	1.4	4.8	−1.10	3.17	0.56	0.62	−0.24	−0.63	−0.0158
Robust 1000	−0.1828	0.28	1.4	4.8	−1.11	3.17	0.55	0.61	−0.24	−0.63	−0.0157
Robust Exact	−0.1828	0.28	1.4	4.8	−1.11	3.17	0.55	0.61	−0.24	−0.63	−0.0158

Table A.4. Simulation results (cf. Sec. 2.4) for the long position in the considered digital double no-touch barrier option.

Strategy	Mean	SD	Skew	Kurt	Min	Max	VaR	CVaR	EUM	EUH	Adj
BS model; $p = 0.6722$; Robust Strategy: $\underline{H}^{II}_{DNT}$, $K_1 = 0.7615$, $K_2 = 0.997$											
No Hedging	−0.0000	0.47	−0.7	1.5	−0.67	0.33	0.67	0.67	−0.13	−0.61	0.0002
Δ 250	−0.0277	0.08	−1.6	46.1	−3.02	1.64	0.27	0.43	−0.03	−0.07	−0.0008
Δ 1000	−0.0533	0.05	−3.1	122.3	−2.05	2.60	0.22	0.34	−0.06	−0.12	−0.0007
$\Delta/\mathcal{V}$ 250	−0.0761	0.08	−2.3	45.0	−3.06	1.60	0.34	0.51	−0.08	−0.19	−0.0008
$\Delta/\mathcal{V}$ 1000	−0.1412	0.08	−2.5	30.3	−2.31	2.42	0.43	0.55	−0.16	−0.35	−0.0007
$\Delta +$ 250	−0.0133	0.10	−0.8	19.1	−3.04	1.64	0.31	0.46	−0.02	−0.05	−0.0009
$\Delta +$ 1000	−0.0151	0.08	−1.0	17.0	−1.75	1.54	0.24	0.36	−0.02	−0.05	−0.0008
$\Delta/\mathcal{V} +$ 250	−0.0662	0.10	−1.5	25.5	−3.02	1.55	0.36	0.53	−0.07	−0.17	−0.0009
$\Delta/\mathcal{V} +$ 1000	−0.1120	0.09	−1.7	14.2	−1.85	1.21	0.41	0.54	−0.12	−0.28	−0.0008
Robust 250	−0.0070	0.23	5.0	44.7	−0.58	5.55	0.23	0.27	−0.03	−0.08	−0.0009
Robust 1000	−0.0070	0.23	5.2	46.8	−0.31	5.67	0.16	0.18	−0.03	−0.08	−0.0009
Robust Exact	−0.0070	0.23	5.2	47.5	−0.09	5.62	0.09	0.09	−0.03	−0.08	−0.0008
BS HV model; $p = 0.6722$; Robust Strategy: $\underline{H}^{II}_{DNT}$, $K_1 = 0.7615$, $K_2 = 0.997$											
No Hedging	−0.6660	0.08	12.3	151.5	−0.67	0.33	0.67	0.67	−0.95	−2.82	−0.0003
Δ 250	−0.6857	0.66	−1.9	8.0	−7.66	0.52	3.16	3.66	−1.88	−55.33	−0.0001
Δ 1000	−0.7027	0.68	−2.0	8.1	−7.64	0.25	3.26	3.75	−2.01	−68.52	0.0003
$\Delta/\mathcal{V}$ 250	0.7148	0.61	−1.2	5.3	−5.57	1.99	1.29	1.68	0.37	−0.15	−0.0003
$\Delta/\mathcal{V}$ 1000	0.6123	0.68	−1.5	6.1	−5.45	1.71	1.72	2.16	0.24	−1.50	−0.0002
$\Delta +$ 250	−0.6824	0.66	−1.9	8.1	−7.66	0.54	3.14	3.66	−1.87	−57.69	−0.0002
$\Delta +$ 1000	−0.6871	0.67	−2.0	8.2	−7.64	0.24	3.18	3.69	−1.91	−62.45	0.0001
$\Delta/\mathcal{V} +$ 250	0.7163	0.61	−1.2	5.3	−5.77	2.01	1.26	1.67	0.37	−0.19	−0.0004
$\Delta/\mathcal{V} +$ 1000	0.6219	0.67	−1.4	6.0	−5.13	1.69	1.65	2.11	0.26	−1.22	−0.0003
Robust 250	1.8606	3.97	3.7	26.1	−1.70	87.92	0.62	0.76	0.28	0.20	0.0109
Robust 1000	1.8606	3.97	3.7	26.1	−0.92	88.21	0.35	0.42	0.29	0.27	0.0109
Robust Exact	1.8606	3.97	3.7	26.1	−0.09	88.21	0.08	0.08	0.29	0.28	0.0112

Table A.4. (*Continued*)

Strategy	Mean	SD	Skew	Kurt	Min	Max	VaR	CVaR	EUM	EUH	Adj
Bates model; $p = 0.6466$; Robust Strategy: $\underline{H}^{II}_{DNT}$, $K_1 = 0.809$, $K_2 = 1.0065$											
No Hedging	0.0057	0.48	−0.6	1.4	−0.65	0.35	0.65	0.65	−0.12	−0.59	0.0000
Δ 250	−0.0169	0.39	−1.1	9.2	−5.53	5.69	1.28	1.67	−0.12	−1.59	−0.0001
Δ 1000	−0.0366	0.39	−1.1	10.5	−6.03	7.53	1.30	1.71	−0.15	−2.88	−0.0003
$\Delta/\mathcal{V}$ 250	−0.0575	0.35	−1.0	11.7	−5.61	5.72	1.19	1.59	−0.14	−1.43	0.1116
$\Delta/\mathcal{V}$ 1000	−0.1052	0.35	−1.1	13.6	−6.17	7.49	1.28	1.67	−0.20	−2.98	0.1118
Δ + 250	−0.0063	0.39	−1.1	8.8	−5.56	5.68	1.27	1.67	−0.11	−1.34	−0.0001
Δ + 1000	−0.0082	0.39	−1.0	9.9	−5.89	7.60	1.26	1.66	−0.11	−1.63	−0.0003
$\Delta/\mathcal{V}$ + 250	−0.0502	0.35	−1.0	11.5	−5.60	5.65	1.19	1.58	−0.13	−1.25	0.1118
$\Delta/\mathcal{V}$ + 1000	−0.0837	0.35	−1.0	12.9	−6.02	7.15	1.23	1.63	−0.17	−1.88	0.1119
Robust 250	−0.0019	0.46	9.0	145.1	−2.08	17.03	0.32	0.40	−0.05	−0.16	−0.0057
Robust 1000	−0.0019	0.45	9.1	147.6	−1.06	17.03	0.24	0.27	−0.05	−0.16	−0.0057
Robust Exact	−0.0019	0.45	9.1	147.9	−0.16	16.88	0.16	0.16	−0.05	−0.16	−0.0058
VGSV model; $p = 0.6377$; Robust Strategy: $\underline{H}^{II}_{DNT}$, $K_1 = 0.806$, $K_2 = 1.0075$											
No Hedging	0.0428	0.47	−0.8	1.6	−0.64	0.36	0.64	0.64	−0.08	−0.47	0.0000
Δ 250	0.0280	0.35	−0.6	10.4	−5.75	6.39	1.04	1.40	−0.05	−1.22	−0.0484
Δ 1000	0.0250	0.35	−0.6	11.2	−5.65	5.91	1.04	1.40	−0.05	−1.03	−0.0487
$\Delta/\mathcal{V}$ 250	−0.0049	0.30	−0.5	15.1	−5.89	6.26	0.92	1.27	−0.06	−1.34	−0.0155
$\Delta/\mathcal{V}$ 1000	−0.0120	0.30	−0.5	16.5	−5.80	5.76	0.93	1.28	−0.07	−1.14	−0.0157
Δ + 250	0.0326	0.35	−0.7	9.4	−5.02	6.10	1.04	1.39	−0.04	−0.52	−0.0432
Δ + 1000	0.0319	0.34	−0.6	10.3	−4.44	7.65	1.03	1.37	−0.04	−0.44	−0.0433
$\Delta/\mathcal{V}$ + 250	−0.0016	0.29	−0.5	13.6	−4.40	6.14	0.91	1.25	−0.05	−0.38	−0.0093
$\Delta/\mathcal{V}$ + 1000	−0.0068	0.29	−0.5	16.1	−4.56	7.80	0.92	1.25	−0.06	−0.45	−0.0094
Robust 250	0.0354	0.43	8.2	112.1	−1.74	11.39	0.21	0.35	−0.01	−0.08	−0.0048
Robust 1000	0.0354	0.43	8.3	113.9	−1.03	11.39	0.14	0.21	−0.01	−0.07	−0.0047
Robust Exact	0.0354	0.43	8.3	114.6	−0.14	11.39	0.14	0.14	−0.01	−0.07	−0.0047

Table A.5. Additional simulation results (cf. Sec. 2.4) for all the position in the considered digital double touch barrier options under BS HV/LV models.

Strategy	Mean	SD	Skew	Kurt	Min	Max	VaR	CVaR	EUM	EUH	Adj
Short DT; BS LV model; $p = 0.1644$; Robust Strategy: $\overline{H}_{DT}^{III}$, $K_1 = 1.0425$, $K_2 = 0.9805$, $K_3 = 0.8795$, $K_4 = 0.819$											
No Hedging	0.1447	0.14	−7.0	49.4	−0.84	0.16	0.84	0.84	0.12	0.19	−0.0002
Δ 250	0.1319	0.08	3.8	28.5	−0.49	1.60	−0.05	−0.03	0.12	0.22	−0.0002
Δ 1000	0.1204	0.07	3.7	27.4	−0.16	1.57	−0.05	−0.04	0.11	0.21	−0.0002
$\Delta/\mathcal{V}$ 250	−0.0714	0.07	4.2	35.6	−0.69	1.40	0.14	0.15	−0.08	−0.16	0.0011
$\Delta/\mathcal{V}$ 1000	−0.0930	0.07	3.8	32.7	−0.41	1.34	0.16	0.17	−0.10	−0.21	0.0010
Δ + 250	0.1404	0.09	3.2	21.6	−0.48	1.53	−0.02	0.01	0.13	0.23	−0.0002
Δ + 1000	0.1402	0.09	3.1	21.1	−0.46	1.56	−0.03	−0.01	0.13	0.23	−0.0002
$\Delta/\mathcal{V}$ + 250	−0.0562	0.11	1.5	11.0	−0.87	1.37	0.27	0.29	−0.06	−0.14	−0.0015
$\Delta/\mathcal{V}$ + 1000	−0.0566	0.11	1.2	9.3	−0.69	1.35	0.27	0.29	−0.06	−0.14	−0.0012
Robust 250	−0.0261	0.17	2.0	6.7	−0.33	0.91	0.18	0.20	−0.04	−0.10	0.0000
Robust 1000	−0.0261	0.17	2.0	6.8	−0.26	0.88	0.16	0.17	−0.04	−0.10	0.0000
Robust Exact	−0.0261	0.17	2.0	6.8	−0.14	0.86	0.14	0.14	−0.04	−0.10	0.0000
Short DNT; BS HV model; $p = 0.0295$; Robust Strategy: $\overline{H}_{DNT}^{I}$											
No Hedging	0.0295	0.00	1.0	1.0	0.03	0.03	−0.03	−0.03	0.03	0.06	0.0000
Δ 250	0.0286	0.03	2.3	13.7	−0.13	0.64	0.01	0.02	0.03	0.05	0.0001
Δ 1000	0.0278	0.03	2.7	17.8	−0.11	0.77	0.00	0.01	0.03	0.05	0.0001
$\Delta/\mathcal{V}$ 250	−0.4240	0.03	0.3	3.8	−0.59	−0.06	0.48	0.48	−0.53	−1.34	0.0000
$\Delta/\mathcal{V}$ 1000	−0.4372	0.02	−0.2	2.4	−0.60	−0.23	0.49	0.50	−0.55	−1.40	0.0000
Δ + 250	0.0289	0.03	2.5	14.8	−0.06	0.68	0.01	0.02	0.03	0.05	0.0000
Δ + 1000	0.0287	0.03	2.8	18.0	−0.03	0.78	0.00	0.01	0.03	0.05	0.0001
$\Delta/\mathcal{V}$ + 250	−0.4239	0.03	0.4	3.7	−0.56	−0.07	0.48	0.49	−0.53	−1.34	0.0000
$\Delta/\mathcal{V}$ + 1000	−0.4367	0.03	−0.2	2.7	−0.63	−0.24	0.50	0.51	−0.55	−1.40	0.0000
Robust 250	−0.2650	0.35	2.0	4.9	−0.41	0.59	0.41	0.41	−0.37	−0.99	0.0002
Robust 1000	−0.2650	0.35	2.0	4.9	−0.41	0.59	0.41	0.41	−0.37	−0.99	0.0002
Robust Exact	−0.2650	0.35	2.0	4.9	−0.41	0.59	0.41	0.41	−0.37	−0.99	0.0002

Table A.5. (*Continued*)

Strategy	Mean	SD	Skew	Kurt	Min	Max	VaR	CVaR	EUM	EUH	Adj
Long DT; BS HV model; $p = 0.3896$; Robust Strategy: $\underline{H}^{I}_{DT}$, $K_1 = 1.1525$, $K_2 = 0.7385$											
No Hedging	0.4003	0.41	−1.4	3.0	−0.39	0.61	0.39	0.39	0.26	0.31	0.0021
Δ 250	0.3867	0.41	2.0	9.5	−2.26	5.98	0.17	0.24	0.27	0.42	0.0036
Δ 1000	0.3761	0.39	2.1	9.9	−1.44	5.12	0.06	0.10	0.27	0.42	0.0037
$\Delta/\mathcal{V}$ 250	−0.8327	0.38	1.7	8.2	−3.04	4.51	1.39	1.46	−1.44	−5.52	0.0020
$\Delta/\mathcal{V}$ 1000	−0.9272	0.31	2.1	9.8	−2.30	3.30	1.29	1.33	−1.63	−6.33	0.0021
$\Delta + 250$	0.3899	0.42	2.0	9.6	−2.48	5.81	0.17	0.23	0.27	0.42	0.0037
$\Delta + 1000$	0.3877	0.41	2.2	10.0	−1.22	5.72	0.06	0.09	0.28	0.43	0.0037
$\Delta/\mathcal{V} + 250$	−0.7829	0.41	1.5	7.0	−3.16	4.60	1.37	1.44	−1.35	−5.10	0.0020
$\Delta/\mathcal{V} + 1000$	−0.7925	0.39	1.6	7.0	−2.28	3.58	1.25	1.28	−1.35	−5.06	0.0021
Robust 250	0.0816	0.72	4.8	45.4	−0.90	21.23	0.51	0.56	−0.06	−0.27	0.0023
Robust 1000	0.0816	0.71	4.9	46.2	−0.59	21.23	0.41	0.43	−0.05	−0.25	0.0024
Robust Exact	0.0816	0.71	4.9	46.5	−0.32	21.23	0.31	0.31	−0.05	−0.25	0.0024
Long DNT; BS LV model; $p = 0.6722$; Robust Strategy: $\underline{H}^{II}_{DNT}$, $K_1 = 0.7615$, $K_2 = 0.997$											
No Hedging	0.2330	0.29	−2.8	8.6	−0.67	0.33	0.67	0.67	0.16	0.17	0.0000
Δ 250	0.2131	0.10	2.8	18.7	−0.72	1.96	−0.04	-0.01	0.19	0.34	0.0001
Δ 1000	0.1946	0.09	2.6	16.4	−1.20	2.00	−0.05	-0.03	0.17	0.31	0.0000
$\Delta/\mathcal{V}$ 250	−0.0718	0.11	3.1	19.3	−1.06	1.69	0.23	0.26	−0.08	−0.18	0.0001
$\Delta/\mathcal{V}$ 1000	−0.1091	0.09	2.7	17.6	−1.57	1.65	0.28	0.31	−0.12	−0.26	0.0000
$\Delta + 250$	0.2256	0.12	2.3	13.7	−0.66	1.92	−0.02	0.01	0.20	0.35	−0.0001
$\Delta + 1000$	0.2250	0.11	2.2	12.5	−0.71	1.68	−0.03	-0.01	0.20	0.35	0.0000
$\Delta/\mathcal{V} + 250$	−0.0633	0.12	2.9	17.3	−0.98	1.41	0.24	0.27	−0.07	−0.16	−0.0001
$\Delta/\mathcal{V} + 1000$	−0.0872	0.11	2.6	16.3	−1.04	1.60	0.27	0.30	−0.10	−0.21	−0.0000
Robust 250	−0.0237	0.16	3.2	13.2	−0.33	1.93	0.14	0.17	−0.03	−0.09	0.0001
Robust 1000	−0.0237	0.16	3.2	13.4	−0.22	2.05	0.11	0.13	−0.03	−0.09	0.0001
Robust Exact	−0.0237	0.16	3.2	13.4	−0.09	2.07	0.09	0.09	−0.03	−0.09	0.0001

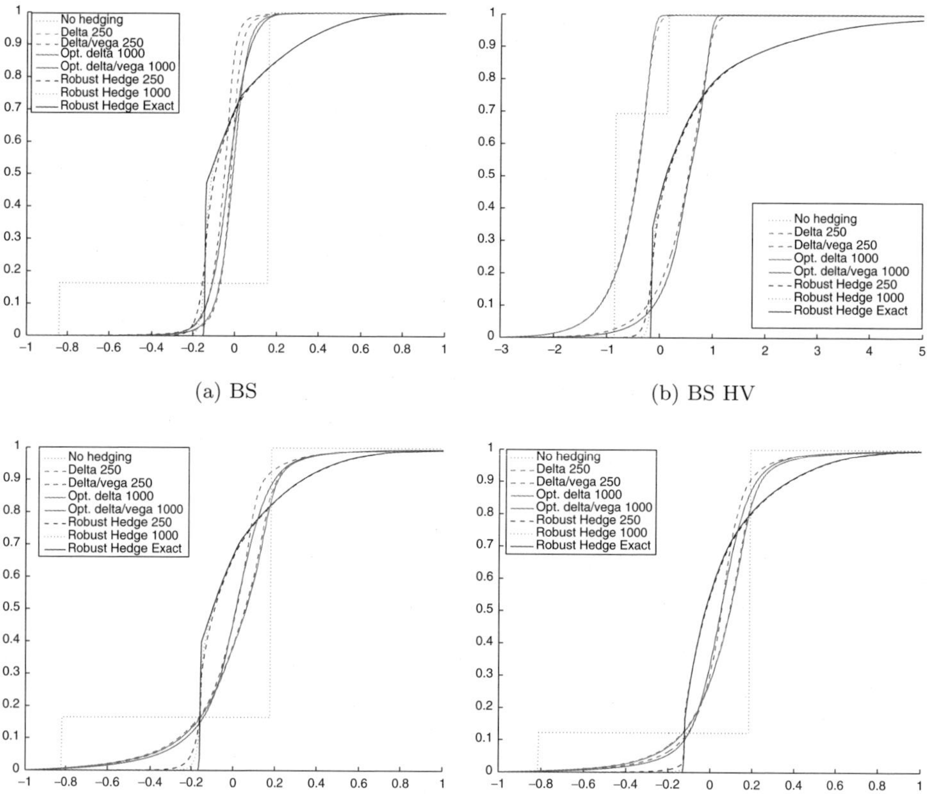

(a) BS

(b) BS HV

(c) Bates

(d) VGSV

Fig. A.1. Cumulative distribution function of hedging errors achieved on the short position in the digital double touch barrier option under each one of the considered models for the underlying process. Please note that the figure appears in colour in the electronic version of the paper.

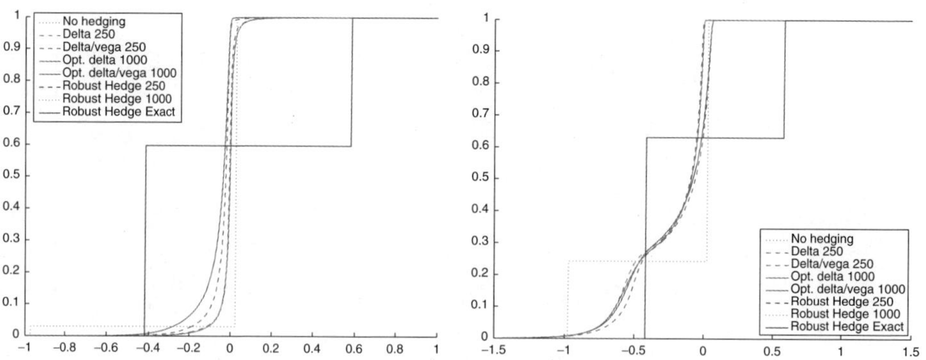

(a) BS

(b) BS LV

Fig. A.2. Cumulative distribution function of hedging errors achieved on the short position in the digital double no-touch barrier option under each one of the considered models for the underlying process. Please note that the figure appears in colour in the electronic version of the paper.

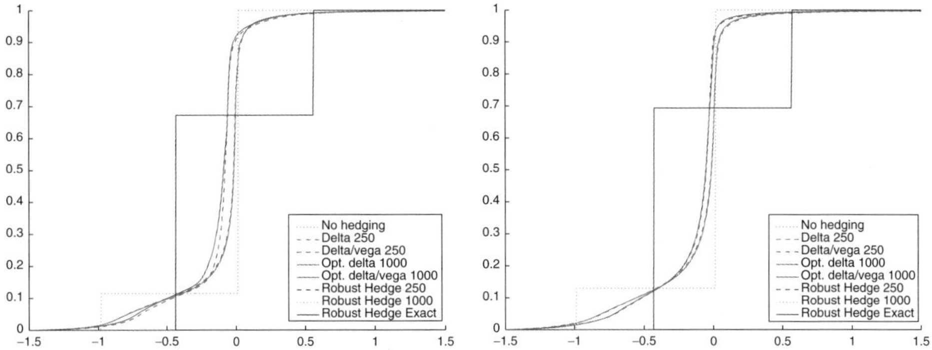

(c) Bates (d) VGSV

Fig. A.2. (*Continued*)

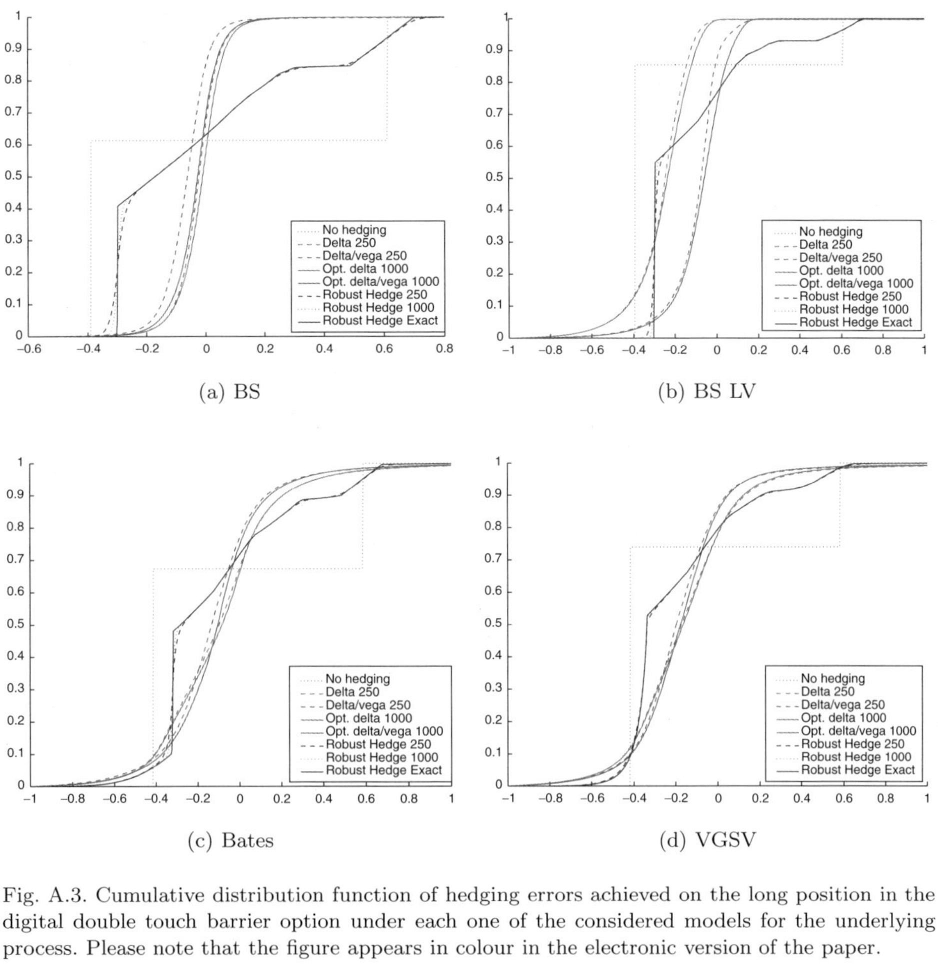

(a) BS (b) BS LV

(c) Bates (d) VGSV

Fig. A.3. Cumulative distribution function of hedging errors achieved on the long position in the digital double touch barrier option under each one of the considered models for the underlying process. Please note that the figure appears in colour in the electronic version of the paper.

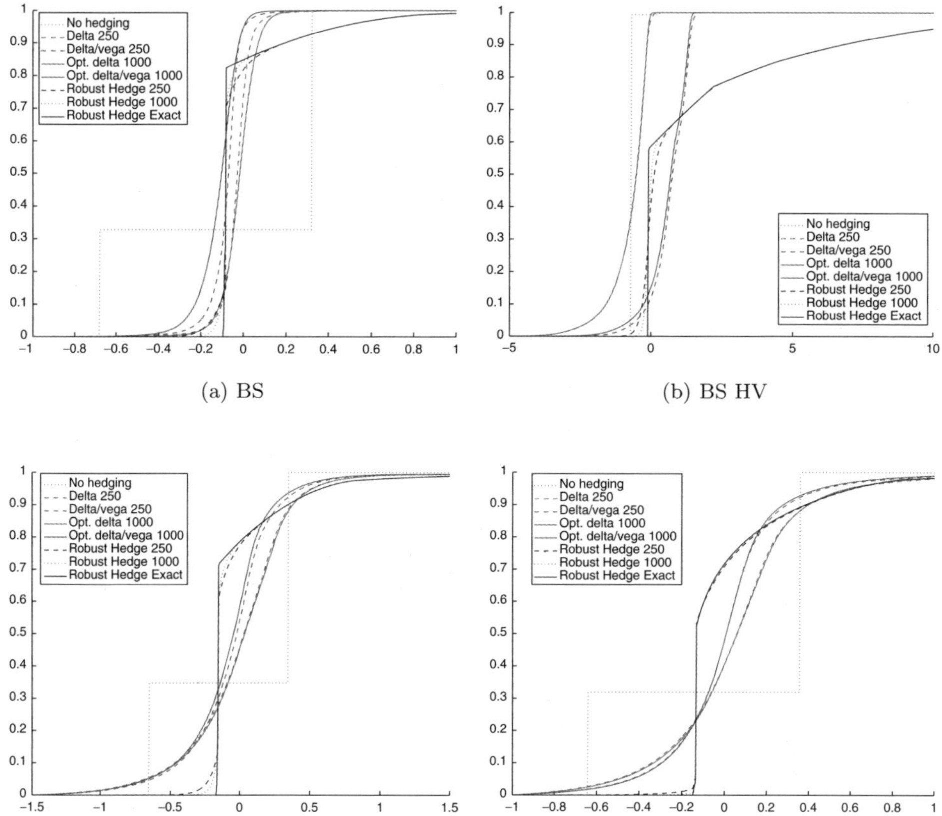

(a) BS (b) BS HV (c) Bates (d) VGSV

Fig. A.4. Cumulative distribution function of hedging errors achieved on the long position in the digital double no-touch barrier option under each one of the considered models for the underlying process. Please note that the figure appears in colour in the electronic version of the paper.

Appendix B. Summary of Numerical Methods

B.1. *Calibration*

As mentioned in Sec. 2.1, the parameters of the considered models were based on real-life global spot foreign exchange interbank market data observed on 14 January 2010 for the AUD/USD foreign exchange spot rate. We calibrated the models to bid and ask implied volatility quotes on standard European options on AUD/USD for different maturities and spot delta points, without premium adjustment. We excluded from the data set the market quotes for options with maturity of one day as their prices are potentially subject to microstructure effects that would only create unwanted noise in our calibration procedure.

The calibration was performed by minimising the weighted sum of squared pricing errors. The pricing error was taken to equal the difference between the model option price and the market ask price if the model option price was higher than the market ask price, to the difference between the model option price and the market bid price if the model option price was lower than the market bid price, and to zero if the model option price was within the market bid and ask prices. For each maturity considered, we used market call option prices for strikes higher than the at-the-money strike and market put option prices for strikes lower than or equal to the at-the-money strike.

To avoid putting excessive weight on near-the-money options relative to out-of-the-money ones and on long-term options relative to short-term ones, we used the weighting scheme suggested by [23], whereby an optimal weighting matrix is estimated using the variance of the normalized option prices. The normalized option price is defined as being equal to the option price divided by the spot price in percentage points. The variance of the normalized option prices at each level of moneyness and maturity is estimated using a nonparametric regression and the weight for the pricing error at that moneyness and maturity is given by the reciprocal of that estimated variance. As both the VGSV and Bates models may be regarded as time-changed Lévy processes (see [8]) and the stochastic time parameters have little influence on short-dated option prices relative to the Lévy parameters, we split the overall calibration procedure into two steps: we first ran the calibration routine on all model parameters against the short-dated maturities in order to arrive at better estimates for the Lévy process parameters; we then ran the calibration routine again against all the maturities in the data set, only this time we set the Lévy process parameters to the values estimated in the first calibration run.

The Black-Scholes model is calibrated to the ATM mid implied volatilities derived from the bid and ask market quotes for options of maturity equal to that of the digital double barrier option (one year).

B.2. *Computing prices and Greeks*

In our simulations we needed to compute the prices, deltas and vegas of the digital double barrier options under the BS model. To this end we implemented a Crank-Nicolson finite difference scheme (see [13]). We used a finite difference grid with 1,000 uniform time steps and restricted the grid in the spatial dimension to the region $S \in [\underline{b}, \overline{b}]$ where we concentrated via coordinate transformation the number of spatial points towards the barrier levels (see [34] for a description on how well chosen coordinate transformations can generally improve the stability, accuracy and solver convergence rate of finite difference calculations) and where the number of spatial steps was chosen so that the spatial step size in the original coordinate be 5E-5 $\times$ S_0. Restricting the spatial region was motivated by the observation that in the region $S \in (0, \underline{b}]$ a digital double touch option is equivalent to a digital up-and-in single barrier option with barrier at $\overline{b}$ and a digital no-touch option is knocked out, and in the region $S \in [\overline{b}, \infty)$ a digital double touch option is equivalent to a digital down-and-in single barrier option with barrier at $\underline{b}$ and a digital no-touch option is knocked out. Analytical formulae for the pricing of digital single barrier options are known (see [32]) and we derived the formulae for the delta and vega of those options by direct differentiation of the price with respect to the relevant variable. In solving the Black Scholes PDE, we may thus apply the finite difference scheme to the region $S \in [\underline{b}, \overline{b}]$ and use the aforementioned equivalences and analytical formulae to compute the relevant values on the boundaries $S = \underline{b}$ and $S = \overline{b}$ of the finite difference grid as well as the price, delta and vega of the digital double barrier option outside the region $S \in [\underline{b}, \overline{b}]$. In order to concentrate the spatial grid towards the barriers, we used the one-dimensional and time-independent coordinate transformation suggested in [34] summarised as follows. Denote ξ the new spatial coordinate and write $S = S(\xi)$ as the equation defining the original space coordinate in terms of the new one. We used a uniformly spaced grid in the coordinate ξ such that $\xi_{n+1} - \xi_n = \Delta\xi$ is constant. We then have that $\Delta S(\xi) = J(\xi)\Delta\xi$ where $J(\xi) = \mathrm{d}S(\xi)/\mathrm{d}\xi$ is the global Jacobian of the transformation. As suggested in [34], we defined $J(\xi)$ as follows:

$$J(\xi) = A\left[\sum_{k=1}^{n}(\alpha_k^2 + (S(\xi) - B_k)^2)^{-1}\right]^{-1/2},$$

where we set $\alpha_1 = \alpha_2 = (\overline{b} - \underline{b})/50$. We used a standard ODE integrator to integrate $J(\xi)$ numerically to yield the transformation $S(\xi)$ by setting $S(\xi = 0) = \underline{b}$ as an initial condition. The normalization constant A was found by adjusting A iteratively until the second boundary condition $S(\xi = 1) = \overline{b}$ was met (this is guaranteed to happen because $S(\xi = 1)$ is monotically increasing with A). This finite difference scheme generates option values on the entire grid and we computed the deltas at each grid node by direct discretisation at negligible additional computational cost. In order to avoid accuracy and computational speed issues, we did not use the same type of direct discretisation for the vegas and instead we computed them by solving the PDE governing the vega dynamics using the same type of finite difference scheme used to solve the PDE governing the price dynamics.

In order to compute the prices of market call and put options under the Bates and VGSV models, we used the COS pricing method (see [16]), which is based on Fourier-cosine series expansions and is computationally fast and accurate. We applied the COS pricing method with 5,000 grid points and used the truncation ranges suggested in [16] with $L = 30$ (using the notation in [16]).

With respect to the simulation of sample price paths followed by the underlying asset under the Bates model, we used the quadratic exponential (QE) scheme proposed by [1] to simulate a process driven by the Heston stochastic volatility model ([19]) and added a jump term and an additional jump-related martingale correction (the jumps are independent from all other stochastic variables). Our scheme under the Bates model may then be expressed as follows:

$$\begin{aligned}\log S(t+\Delta t) = \log S(t) + K_0^* + K_1 v(t) + K_2 v(t+\Delta t) \\ + \sqrt{K_3 v(t) + K_4 v(t+\Delta t)}Z \\ + L\left(\log(1+\mu_j) - \frac{1}{2}\sigma_j^2\right) + \sigma_j\sqrt{L}Z_j - \mu_j\lambda\Delta t,\end{aligned} \tag{B.1}$$

where the first line of (B.1) is the expression of a QE scheme for a Heston process and the second line is what is added to that scheme to simulate the jumps. Z and Z_j are standard Gaussian random variables and L is a Poisson random variable with mean parameter $\lambda\Delta t$. Z, L and Z_j are independent of each other and of all other random variables in the model. The term $-\mu_j\lambda\Delta t$ in (B.1) is the martingale correction related to the presence of jumps. The expressions for K_0^*, K_1, K_2, K_3 and K_4 are lengthy and we refer the reader to [1] for their definitions in the case of the QE scheme for martingale processes.

In order to simulate sample paths of the underlying asset price under the VGSV model, we first need to simulate the rate of time change $y(t)$ in (2.5). We did so by sampling from the exact transition law of the CIR process, as described in [18]. The distribution of $y(t)$ given $y(s)$, for $s < t$, is a noncentral chi-square distribution (see [12]), up to a scale factor, and is given by

$$\mathbb{P}(y(t) \leq x|y(s)) = F_{\chi'^2}\left(\frac{x\eta(s,t)}{e^{-\kappa(t-s)}}; d, y(s)\eta(s,t)\right), \tag{B.2}$$

where

$$d = \frac{4\kappa\theta}{\zeta^2}, \quad \eta(s,t) = \frac{4\kappa e^{-\kappa(t-s)}}{\zeta^2(1-e^{-\kappa(t-s)})}, \tag{B.3}$$

and $F_{\chi'^2}(z,\nu,\lambda)$ denotes the cumulative distribution function for a non-central chi-square distribution with ν degrees of freedom and non-centrality parameter λ, which is given by

$$F_{\chi'^2}(z,\nu,\lambda) = e^{-\lambda/2}\sum_{j=0}^{\infty}\frac{(\lambda/2)^j}{j!2^{\nu/2+j}\Gamma(\nu/2+j)}\int_0^z z^{\nu/2+j-1}e^{-x/2}\mathrm{d}x, \tag{B.4}$$

where $\Gamma(x)$ denotes the gamma function. (B.4) indicates that for any $\nu > 0$ a non-central chi-square random variable may be represented as an ordinary chi-square random variable with a random number of degrees of freedom. Following a scheme suggested by [33], we use this property to sample from a noncentral chi-square random variable by first generating a Poisson random variable L and then, conditional on L, sampling a chi-square random variable with $\nu + 2L$ degrees of freedom.

Now, to simulate the VGSV process from time $t = 0$ to time $t = T$ for some $T > 0$, we considered the time discretizations $\mathcal{T}_1 = \{t_i = iT/n, i = 0, 1, \ldots, n\}$ for some $n \in \mathbb{N}^*$ and $\mathcal{T}_2 = \{t_j = jT/nm, j = 0, 1, \ldots, nm\}$ for some $m \in \mathbb{N}^*$. In our application, we chose n = 200,000 and m=1. $t_i \in \mathcal{T}_1$ is a time at which the VGSV process is computed, whilst $t_j \in \mathcal{T}_2$ is a time at which the operational time is computed. We simulated the rate of time change $y(t)$ at each time $t_j \in \mathcal{T}_2$ following the method described above, starting from $y(0) = 1$. We then computed the operational time $Y(t) = \int_0^t y(s)\mathrm{d}s$ at each time $t_i \in \mathcal{T}_1$ by approximating the integration of the process y from 0 to t_i as follows

$$Y(t_i) = \int_0^{t_i} y(s)\mathrm{d}s \approx \sum_{j=0}^{im} y_{t_j}. \tag{B.5}$$

We then used the fact that the VG process X may be expressed as the difference between two independent gamma processes (see [25]) to write the value of the VGSV process at time $t_i \in \mathcal{T}_1$ is $X(Y(t_i)$ as follows:

$$X(Y(t_i)) = \gamma_p(Y(t_i); \mu_p, \nu_p) - \gamma_n(Y(t_i); \mu_n, \nu_n), \tag{B.6}$$

where $\mu_p = C/M$, $\nu_p = C/M^2$, $\mu_n = C/G$ and $\nu_n = C/G^2$. We thus simulated the VG process at time $Y(t_i)$ by simulating the two independent gamma processes γ_p and γ_n at time $Y(t_i)$ and by computing their difference. The gamma process $\gamma := \{\gamma(t; \mu, \nu) : t \geq 0\}$ with mean rate μ and variance rate ν is a continuous-time process with stationary, independent gamma increments such that for any $h > 0$

$$\gamma(t+h; \mu, \nu) - \gamma(t; \mu, \nu) \sim \mathcal{G}\left(\frac{\mu^2 h}{\nu}, \frac{\nu}{\mu}\right), \tag{B.7}$$

where $\mathcal{G}(\alpha, \beta)$ denotes the gamma distribution with density $f(x) = \frac{x^{\alpha-1}e^{-x/\beta}}{\beta^\alpha \Gamma(\alpha)}$. Noting that $\mu_p^2/\nu_p = \mu_n^2/\nu_n = C$, $\nu_p/\mu_p = 1/M$ and $\nu_n/\mu_n = 1/G$, we have

$$\gamma_p(t+\Delta t; \mu_p, \nu_p) - \gamma_p(t; \mu_p, \nu_p) \sim \mathcal{G}\left(C\Delta t, \frac{1}{M}\right), \tag{B.8}$$

$$\gamma_n(t+\Delta t; \mu_n, \nu_n) - \gamma_n(t; \mu_n, \nu_n) \sim \mathcal{G}\left(C\Delta t, \frac{1}{G}\right). \tag{B.9}$$

By setting $t = t_i$ and $\Delta t = Y(t_{i+1}) - Y(t_i)$ in (B.8) and (B.9) one obtains the equations required to compute the increments of the time-changed VG process.

B.3. *Mean adjustment of the hedging errors*

When analyzing the performance of hedging strategies Hull and White [24] suggested to mean-adjust them i.e. to add a constant to the whole vector of hedging errors of any given strategy so that the final mean is equal to the theoretical mean. This control variate approach, subsequently used e.g. by Davis *et al.* [14], makes it possible to decouple the object of interest (say influence of transaction costs) from the noise of Monte Carlo simulations. Since the MC noise could affect differently each strategy and *a priori* impact fine relative comparison between them, we decided to adopt this approach in this paper and proceeded as follows:

- For the BS, BSHV and BSLV models we computed the theoretical mean of each hedge using the finite difference scheme for the digital double barrier option and explicit formulae for European options and then adjusted the empirical mean of the hedging strategy (without transaction costs) to that value.

- For Bates an VGSV models we only compute the digital double barrier option price using MC. Hence we assumed that the *no hedging* strategy has the appropriate mean and adjusted all other strategies to this value.

For each strategy the size of the mean adjustment is reported in the column (Adj) in Tables A.1–A.5. *A posteriori*, we observe that these are very small numbers, mainly of order of 10^{-3}. Our results and conclusions stay the same with or without the mean adjustment. We link this to the fact that we are able to run 200000 MC paths as opposed to e.g. 1000 in [14].

References

[1] L. Andersen, Efficient simulation of the Heston stochastic volatility model, http://ssrn.com/abstract=946405, 2006.

[2] P. Artzner, F. Delbaen, J.-M. Eber and D. Heath, Coherent measures of risk, *Mathematical Finance* **9**(3) (1999) 203–228.

[3] D. S. Bates, Jumps and stochastic volatility: Exchange rate processes implicit in Deutsche Mark options, *The Review of Financial Studies* **9**(1) (1996) 69–107.

[4] F. Black and M. Scholes, The pricing of options and corporate liabilities, *Journal of Political Economy* **81**(3) (1973) 637.

[5] H. Brown, D. Hobson and L. C. G. Rogers, Robust hedging of barrier options, *Mathematical Finance* **11**(3) (2001) 285–314.

[6] P. Carr, H. Geman, D. B. Madan and M. Yor, The fine structure of asset returns: An empirical investigation, *The Journal of Business* **75**(2) (2002) 305–332.

[7] P. Carr, H. Geman, D. B. Madan and M. Yor, Stochastic volatility for Lévy processes, *Mathematical Finance* **13**(3) (2003) 345–382.

[8] P. Carr and L. Wu, Time-changed Lévy processes and option pricing, *Journal of Financial Economics* **71**(1) (2004) 113–142.

[9] L. Clewlow and S. D. Hodges, Optimal delta-hedging under transactions costs, *Journal of Economic Dynamics and Control* **21**(8–9) (1997) 1353–1376.

[10] A. M. G. Cox and J. Obłój, Robust hedging of double touch barrier options, *SIAM J. on Financial Mathematics* **2**(1) (2011) 141–182.

[11] A. M. G. Cox and J. Obłój, Robust pricing and hedging of double no-touch options, *Finance and Stochastics* **15**(3) (2011) 573–605.

[12] J. C. Cox, J. E. Ingersoll Jr and S. A. Ross, A theory of the term structure of interest rates, *Econometrica* **53**(2) (1985) 385–407.

[13] J. Crank and P. Nicolson, A practical method for numerical evaluation of solutions of partial differential equations of the heat-conduction type, *Advances in Computational Mathematics* **6**(1) (1996) 207–226.

[14] M. H. A. Davis, W. Schachermayer and R. G. Tompkins, Pricing, no-arbitrage bounds and robust hedging of instalment options, *Quantitative Finance* **1**(6) (2001) 597–610.

[15] N. El Karoui, M. Jeanblanc-Picqué and S. E. Shreve, Robustness of the Black and Scholes formula, *Mathematical Finance* **8**(2) (1998) 93–126.

[16] F. Fang and C. W. Oosterlee, A novel pricing method for European options based on Fourier-cosine series expansions, *SIAM Journal on Scientific Computing* **31**(2) (2008) 826–848.

[17] H. Föllmer and A. Schied, *Stochastic Finance*, extended edition, Vol. 27 of de Gruyter Studies in Mathematics (Walter de Gruyter & Co., Berlin, 2004).
[18] P. Glasserman, *Monte Carlo Methods in Financial Engineering* (Springer-Verlag, 2003).
[19] S. L. Heston, A closed–form solution for options with stochastic volatility with applications to bond and currency options, *The Review of Financial Studies* **6**(2) (1993) 327–343.
[20] D. Hobson, The Skorokhod Embedding Problem and Model-Independent Bounds for Option Prices, in R. A. Carmona, E. Çinlar, I. Ekeland, E. Jouini, J. A. Scheinkman and N. Touzi, editors, *Paris-Princeton Lectures on Mathematical Finance 2010*, Vol. 2003 of Lecture Notes in Math. (Springer, 2010), pp. 267–318.
[21] D. G. Hobson, Robust hedging of the lookback option, *Finance and Stochastics* **2**(4) (1998) 329–347.
[22] S. D. Hodges and A. Neuberger, Optimal replication of contingent claims under transaction costs, *Review of Futures Markets* **8**(2) (1989) 222–239.
[23] J. Huang and L. Wu, Specification analysis of option pricing models based on time–changed Lévy processes, *Journal of Finance* (2004) 1405–1439.
[24] J. Hull and A. White, The use of the control variate the use of the control variate technique in option pricing, *Journal of Financial and Quantitative Analysis* **23** (1988) 237–251.
[25] D. B. Madan, P. P. Carr and E. C. Chang, The variance gamma process and option pricing, *Review of Finance* **2**(1) (1998) 79–105.
[26] D. B. Madan and E. Seneta, The variance gamma (VG) model for share market returns, *The Journal of Business* **63**(4) (1990) 511–524.
[27] L. Martellini and P. Priaulet, Competing methods for option hedging in the presence of transaction costs, *The Journal of Derivatives* **9**(3) (2002) 26–38.
[28] B. Mohamed, Simulations of transaction costs and optimal rehedging, *Applied Mathematical Finance* **1**(1) (1994) 49–62.
[29] Michael Monoyios, Optimal hedging and parameter uncertainty, *IMA J Management Math.* **18**(4) (2007) 331–351.
[30] J. Obłój, The Skorokhod embedding problem and its offspring, *Probability Surveys* **1** (2004) 321–392.
[31] J. Obłój, Skorokhod embedding, In R. Cont, editor, *Encyclopedia of Quantitative Finance* (Wiley, 2010), pp. 1653–1657.
[32] M. Rubinstein and E. Reiner, Unscrambling the binary code, *Risk* **4**(9) (1991) 75–83.
[33] L. O. Scott, Simulating a multi–factor term structure model over relatively long discrete time periods, In *Proceedings of the IAFE First Annual Computational Finance Conference* (1996).
[34] D. Tavella and C. Randall, *Pricing Financial Instruments: The Finite Difference Method* (John Wiley & Sons New York, 2000).
[35] F. Ulmer, Performance of robust model-free hedging via Skorokhod embeddings of digital double barrier options, Master's thesis, Mathematical Institute, University of Oxford (2010).
[36] A. E. Whalley and P. Wilmott, An asymptotic analysis of an optimal hedging model for option pricing with transaction costs, *Mathematical Finance* **7**(3) (1997) 307–324.
[37] V. Zakamouline, Optimal hedging of option portfolios with transaction costs, http://ssrn.com/abstract=938934 (2006).

CDO TERM STRUCTURE MODELLING WITH LÉVY PROCESSES AND THE RELATION TO MARKET MODELS*

THORSTEN SCHMIDT

Department of Mathematics
Chemnitz University of Technology
Reichenhainer Str. 41, 09126 Chemnitz, Germany

JERZY ZABCZYK

Institute of Mathematics of the Polish Academy of Sciences
Sniadeckich 8, POB 21, 00-956, Warszawa 10, Poland

This paper considers the modelling of collateralized debt obligations (CDOs). We propose a top-down model via forward rates generalizing Filipović, Overbeck and Schmidt (2009) to the case where the forward rates are driven by a finite dimensional Lévy process. The contribution of this work is twofold: we provide conditions for absence of arbitrage in this generalized framework. Furthermore, we study the relation to market models by embedding them in the forward rate framework in spirit of Brace, Gatarek and Musiela (1997).

Keywords: Collateralized debt obligations; loss process; single tranche CDO; term structure of forward spreads; Lévy processes; market models; Libor rate.

1. Introduction

A *collateralized debt obligation* (CDO) is a security backed by a pool of credit risky securities. There are issued notes on so-called tranches of the CDO which are characterized by different levels of credit riskiness or, in financial terms, seniorities. In this work we consider a general model for the evolution of tranche prices similar in spirit to the forward rate approach of Heath *et al.* [9] and derive conditions under which the model is free of arbitrage.

For practical applications, market models are of a high importance. In this kind of models, traded securities have a finite set of maturities while in the forward rate approach all possible maturities are considered. For the pricing of options respectively calibration of the model one imposes a simple dynamics for suitable

*This chapter was originally published under the same title in *International Journal of Theoretical and Applied Finance*, Vol.15, No.1, 1250008-1–19 (2012). Singapore: World Scientific Publishing.

quantities and uses the conditions for absence of arbitrage which results in tractable pricing formulas.

The main goal of this work is to provide conditions which guarantee the absence of arbitrage in a general class of models and to study market models embedded in this framework. The new contribution of this work is the following: first, we consider models where the driving random process is a Lévy process, generalizing Filipović *et al.* [8]. We derive general drift conditions which ensure that the market is free of arbitrage. In a next step we consider market models similar to those in Eberlein *et al.* [3]. However, we embed the market models in the forward rate models and derive the resulting drift conditions. The risk-free case studied in Brace *et al.* [2] turns out to be a special case.

2. Collateralized Debt Obligations

Consider a complete filtered probability space $(\Omega, \mathcal{F}, (\mathcal{F}_t)_{t\geq 0}, \mathbb{P})$ satisfying the usual conditions. Mathematically speaking, a collateralized debt obligation is a derivative on a portfolio of N credit risky securities. With each security there is an associated nominal and we assume that the total nominal is one. Denote the process of accumulated losses over time by $L = (L_t)_{t\geq 0}$. Then L is a pure-jump process which jumps upward at defaults of the securities in the pool and the jump size is the occurring loss. As the total nominal is one, $L_t \in [0,1]$ for all $t \geq 0$. A special case, quite often considered in practice, is when the loss on each default is a constant. By $\mathcal{I} \subset [0,1]$ we denote the set of attainable loss fractions and we assume that $\mathcal{I} = [0,1]$. The case where $\mathcal{I}$ is finite may be considered analogously, see Filipović *et al.* [8].

Similar to Filipović *et al.* [8] we consider (T,x)-*bonds* as basic constituents: a (T,x)-bond pays $1_{\{L_T\leq x\}}$ at maturity T, for $x \in \mathcal{I}$. Its price at time t is denoted by $P(t,T,x)$. For $x = 1$ we obtain that $P(t,T,1) =: P(t,T)$ equals the risk-free bond. In Eberlein *et al.* [3], Sec. 6.1, it is shown how to extract (T,x)-bonds from observed CDO quotes under common assumptions.

Pricing CDOs with (T,x)-bonds. We consider (T,x)-bonds as they are sufficient to provide prices for CDOs and similar derivatives as we will show in this section. First of all, (T,x)-bonds are sufficient for pricing European derivatives on the loss process. Indeed, consider a payoff $h(L_T)$ such that

$$h(L_T) = h(1) - \int_0^1 h'(y) 1_{\{L_T \leq y\}} dy.$$

Linearity of prices on contingent claims implies that the price at time t of the derivative offering $h(L_T)$ at T is given by the following functional of (T,x)-bonds

$$h(1)P(t,T) - \int_0^1 h'(y) P(t,T,y) dy.$$

A more general result holds true. Investing in CDOs is done via a so-called *single-tranche CDO* (STCDO), sometimes also called tranche credit default swap.

A STCDO is represented by its lower and upper detachment points, x_1 and x_2, with $0 \leq x_1 < x_2 \leq 1$. The investor receives coupon payments at times $T_1, \ldots, T_n$. In exchange to this, the investor covers a certain part of the occurring losses in each period. Set

$$H(x) := (x_2 - x)^+ - (x_1 - x)^+ = \int_{(x_1,x_2]} 1_{\{x \leq y\}} dy.$$

Then, investing in the STCDO with swap rate S is equivalent to the following payment stream:

(1) *Payment leg.* The investor receives $SH(L_{T_i})$ at times $T_i, i = 1, \ldots, n$.
(2) *Default leg.* The investor pays $-dH(L_t) = H(L_{t-}) - H(L_t)$ at any time where $\Delta L_t \neq 0$.

In Filipović *et al.* [8] it is shown that the value of the STCDO at time t can be derived solely on the basis of (T, x)-bonds. In the case where risk-free and risky (T, x)-bonds are independent, it follows from Lemma 4.1 therein that the value of the STCDO at time t is given by

$$V(t, S) = \int_{(x_1,x_2]} \left(S \sum_{i=1}^{n} P(t, T_i, y) + P(t, T_n, y) - P(t, T_0, y) \right.$$
$$\left. + \int_{T_0}^{T_n} f(t, u) P(t, u, y) du \right) dy,$$

where $f(t, u)$ denotes the risk-free forward rate. Setting $V = 0$ and solving for S gives the par-spread for this investment. Market prices of STCDOs are typically quoted via the par-spread.

3. Arbitrage-Free Term Structure Movements

In this article we consider term structure movements of (T, x)-bonds given by

$$P(t, T, x) = 1_{\{L_t \leq x\}} \exp\left(- \int_t^T f(t, u, x) du \right), \tag{3.1}$$

where $f(t, T, x)$ is the (T, x)-*forward rate* prevailing at t. Let us assume that

(A1) $L_t = \sum_{s \leq t} \Delta L_s$ is càdlàg, non-decreasing, adapted, pure jump process, which admits an absolutely continuous compensator $\nu^L(t, dx)dt$ satisfying $\int_0^t \nu^L(s, \mathcal{I}) ds < \infty$ (finite activity).

As shown in Filipović *et al.* [8], under (A1), the indicator process $(1_{\{L_t \leq x\}})_{t \geq 0}$ is cádlág and has intensity

$$\lambda(t, x) = \nu^L(t, (x - L_t, 1]). \tag{3.2}$$

That is,

$$M_t^x = 1_{\{L_t \le x\}} + \int_0^t 1_{\{L_s \le x\}} \lambda(s,x)ds \tag{3.3}$$

is a martingale. Moreover, $\lambda(t,x)$ is decreasing and continuous in x with $\lambda(t,1) = 0$.

Consider a d-dimensional Lévy process Z. Denote by $\langle \cdot, \cdot \rangle$ the scalar product in $\mathbb{R}^d$, by $\cdot^\top$ the transpose and by $|\cdot|$ the respective norm on $\mathbb{R}^d$. It is well-known that a Lévy-process can be decomposed as

$$Z_t = mt + W_t + \int_0^t \int_{|z|\le 1} z(\mu(ds,dz) - \nu(dz)ds) + \int_0^t \int_{|z|>1} z\mu(ds,dz), \tag{3.4}$$

where $m \in \mathbb{R}^d$, W is a d-dimensional Wiener process with covariance matrix Σ and μ is the random measure of jumps with its $\mathbb{P}$-compensator $\nu(dz)ds$. That is, for any Borel set B of $\mathbb{R}^+$ and any Borel set Λ of $\mathbb{R}^d$, μ denotes the number of jumps in the time interval B which have sizes in Λ,

$$\mu(\omega; B, \Lambda) = \sum_{s\in B} 1_\Lambda(\Delta Z_s).$$

The process Z has exponential moments if the Laplace transform is always finite. Then the Laplace transform satisfies $\mathbb{E}(e^{-\langle u, Z_t\rangle}) = e^{tJ(u)}$ for all $u \in \mathbb{R}^d$ with

$$J(u) = -\langle m, u\rangle + \frac{1}{2}\langle \Sigma u, u\rangle + \int_{\mathbb{R}^d} (e^{-\langle u,z\rangle} - 1 + 1_{\{|z|\le 1\}}(z)\langle u, z\rangle)\nu(dz). \tag{3.5}$$

We assume throughout that the (T,x)-forward rate is given by

$$\begin{aligned} f(t,T,x) = f(0,T,x) &+ \int_0^t a(s,T,x)ds + \int_0^t \langle b(s,T,x), dZ_s\rangle \\ &+ \int_0^t \int_{\mathcal{I}} c(s,T,x;y)\mu^L(ds,dy) \end{aligned} \tag{3.6}$$

where μ^L is the random measure associated to the jumps of L. By $[L,Z]$ we denote the covariation of L and Z. Let

$$B := \left\{ u \in \mathbb{R}^d : \int_{|z|>1} e^{-\langle u,z\rangle}\nu(dz) < \infty \right\}.$$

Additionally, we use the following assumptions.

(A2) For each T, x the processes a, b, and c are assumed to be predictable and have bounded trajectories. Furthermore, $c(\cdot, T, 1; y) = 0$ for all $y \in \mathcal{I}$.

(A3) $[L, Z]_t = 0$ for all $t \ge 0$.

(A4) For any $r > 0$ the function $u \mapsto \int_{|z|>1} e^{-\langle u,z\rangle}\nu(dz)$ is bounded on $\{u \in \mathbb{R}^d : |u| \le r\} \cap B$.

(A5) For each (T,x) there exists $K(T,x)$ such that

$$\sup_{0\le s\le T, y\in\mathbb{R}^d} c(s,T,x;y) \le K(T,x).$$

The assumption on c in (A2) states that losses in the considered portfolio do not influence the risk-free rate. This assumption can be relaxed but at the cost of further notation. Assumption (A3) is natural from a modelling point of view: jumps in L influence f only through c and not via a dependence of L and Z.

Contagion. This framework allows for two kinds of *contagion*, i.e. feedback of the loss process L on the forward rates: first, a direct contagion via simultaneous jumps of L and f; when $\Delta L_t \neq 0$, (A3) gives that $\Delta f(t,T,x) = c(t,T,x;\Delta L_t)$. Second, a kind of indirect contagion via letting the model parameters a, b, and c be explicit functions of the loss path L.

It is well-known that then the market of (T,x)-bonds is free of arbitrage if

$$(D_t P(t,T,x))_{0\le t\le T} \quad \text{are local martingales for all } (T,x), \tag{3.7}$$

where D is the discounting process given by

$$D_t = e^{-\int_0^t r_s ds} = e^{-\int_0^t f(s,s,1)ds}.$$

The goal of this section is to give conditions which are sufficient for (3.7) to hold.

Default-free market. The default-free forward rate, $f(t,T)$, is given by

$$f(t,T) = f(t,T,1).$$

We also denote $a(t,T) = a(t,T,1)$ and $b(t,T) = b(t,T,1)$. In the case of default free markets, the following was shown in Jakubowski and Zabczyk [11], Theorem 3.1.

On one side, (A2) and the no-arbitrage condition

$$D_t P(t,T) \quad \text{are local martingales for all } 0\le t\le T; \tag{3.8}$$

imply that for any $u \le T$

$$\int_t^u b(t,v)dv \in B \quad \text{for almost all } t\in[0,u]. \tag{3.9}$$

On the other side, if (A2), (A3) and (3.9) hold, then (3.8) is equivalent to

$$\int_t^s a(t,u)du = J\left(\int_t^s b(t,u)du\right) \tag{3.10}$$

for almost all $0\le t\le s\le T$.

The drift conditions. Now we are in the position to state the model for the defaultable market and derive the drift conditions. Recall that we consider a market consisting of (T,x)-bonds.

Theorem 3.1. *Assume that* (A1)–(A4) *hold.*

(i) *If* (A5) *holds, it follows from* (3.7) *that*

$$\int_t^s b(t,v,x)dv \in B \tag{3.11}$$

for any $0\le t\le s$ *on* $\{L_t \le x\}$, $\mathbb{Q}\otimes dt$*-a.s.*

(ii) *If* (3.11) *holds, then* (3.7) *is equivalent to*

$$\int_t^s a(t,u,x)du = J\Big(\int_t^s b(t,u,x)du\Big)$$

$$+ \int_{\mathcal{I}} \Big(e^{-\int_t^s c(t,u,x;y)du} - 1\Big) 1_{\{L_t + y \leq x\}} \nu^L(t,dy) \tag{3.12}$$

$$f(t,t,x) = f(t,t) + \lambda(t,x) \tag{3.13}$$

for any $0 \leq t \leq s$, *where* (3.12) *and* (3.13) *hold on* $\{L_t \leq x\}$, $\mathbb{Q} \otimes dt$*-a.s.*

Proof. Set

$$p(t,T,x) := \exp\bigg(-\int_t^T f(t,u,x)du\bigg),$$

such that $P(t,T,x) = 1_{\{L_t \leq x\}} p(t,T,x)$. Recall the martingale M^x from (3.3). Then

$$d(D_t P(t,T,x)) = D_t p(t-,T,x) dM_t^x - D_t p(t-,T,x)\lambda(t,x) 1_{\{L_t \leq x\}} dt$$
$$+ 1_{\{L_{t-} \leq x\}} d(D_t p(t,T,x)) + d[1_{\{L_t \leq x\}}, D_t p(t,T,x)]. \tag{3.14}$$

Denote $a^*(t,T,x) := \int_t^T a(t,u,x)du$, $b^*(t,T,x) := \int_t^T b(t,u,x)du$, and similarly $c^*(t,T,x;y) := \int_t^T c(t,u,x;y)du$. We first compute the last term in (3.14). Note that the process $(1_{\{L_t \leq x\}})_{t \geq 0}$ jumps at most once, from 1 to 0, at the first time when L crosses the barrier x. Hence,

$$\begin{aligned}
[1_{\{L_\cdot \leq x\}}, D_\cdot p(\cdot,T,x)]_t &= \sum_{0 \leq s \leq t} \Delta 1_{\{L_s \leq x\}} \Delta(D_s p(s,T,x)) \\
&= -\sum_{0 \leq s \leq t} 1_{\{L_{s-} \leq x, L_s > x\}} \Delta(D_s p(s,T,x)) \\
&= -\int_0^t \int_{\mathcal{I}} 1_{\{L_{s-} \leq x\}} D_s p(s-,T,x) 1_{\{L_{s-} + y > x\}} \\
&\quad \times (e^{-c^*(s,T,x;y)} - 1) \mu^L(ds,dy),
\end{aligned} \tag{3.15}$$

where we used in the last step that by (A3), Z and L do not have simultaneous jumps. Regarding the remaining term in (3.14), we obtain from (3.1) and (3.6), by the Itô-formula, that

$$1_{\{L_{t-} \leq x\}} d(D_t p(t,T,x))$$

$$= D_t p(t-,T,x) 1_{\{L_{t-} \leq x\}} \bigg((f(t,t,x) - r_t - \langle b^*(t,T,x), m \rangle - a^*(t,T,x))dt$$

$$+ \frac{1}{2} b^*(t,T,x)^\top \Sigma b^*(t,T,x) dt + \int_{\mathbb{R}^d} [e^{-b^*(t,T,x)^\top z} - 1 + b^*(t,T,x)^\top z] 1_{\{|z| \leq 1\}}$$

$$\times \mu(dt, dz) + \int_{\mathbb{R}^d} [e^{-b^*(t,T,x)^\top z} - 1]1_{\{|z|>1\}}\mu(dt, dz)$$

$$+ \int_{\mathcal{I}} 1_{\{L_{t-} \leq x\}}[e^{-c^*(t,T,x;y)} - 1]\mu^L(dt, dy)\Bigg) + d\tilde{M}_t \tag{3.16}$$

where $\tilde{M}$ is a local martingale and we used the decomposition (3.4). Inserting (3.15) and (3.16) in (3.14) we obtain, using $1_{\{L_{t-} \leq x\}}p(t-, T, x) = P(t-, T, x)$, that

$$\begin{aligned} d(D_t P(t,T,x)) = D_t P(t-,T,x)\Bigg(& dM_t^x - \lambda(t,x)1_{\{L_t \leq x\}}dt \\ & \times (f(t,t,x) - r_t - \langle b^*(t,T,x), m\rangle - a^*(t,T,x))dt + \frac{1}{2}b^*(t,T,x)^\top \\ & \times \Sigma b^*(t,T,x)dt + \int_{\mathbb{R}^d} [e^{-b^*(t,T,x)^\top z} - 1 + b^*(t,T,x)^\top z]1_{\{|z|\leq 1\}} \\ & \times \mu(dt, dz) + \int_{\mathbb{R}^d} [e^{-b^*(t,T,x)^\top z} - 1]1_{\{|z|>1\}}\mu(dt, dz) \\ & + \int_{\mathcal{I}} 1_{\{L_{t-}+y \leq x\}}(e^{-c^*(t,T,x;y)} - 1)\mu^L(dt, dy)\Bigg) + d\tilde{\tilde{M}}_t \end{aligned} \tag{3.17}$$

with a local martingale $\tilde{\tilde{M}}$. First we study (i). From (3.17) we obtain that

$$\begin{aligned} D_t P(t,T,x) &= D_0 P(0,T,x) + A(t) + \tilde{\tilde{\tilde{M}}}_t + \int_0^t \int_{\mathbb{R}^d} D_s P(s-,T,x) \\ &\quad \times (e^{-b^*(s,T,x)^\top z} - 1 + b^*(s,T,x)^\top z)1_{\{|z|\leq 1\}}\mu(ds, dz) \\ &\quad + \int_0^t \int_{\mathbb{R}^d} D_s P(s-,T,x)(e^{-b^*(s,T,x)^\top z})1_{\{|z|>1\}}\mu(ds, dz) \\ &\quad - \int_0^t \int_{\mathbb{R}^d} D_s P(s-,T,x)1_{\{|z|>1\}}\mu(ds, dz) \\ &\quad + \int_0^t \int_{\mathcal{I}} D_s P(s-,T,x)1_{\{L_{s-}+y\leq x\}}(e^{-c^*(s,T,x;y)} - 1)\mu^L(ds, dy) \\ &=: D_0 P(0,T,x) + A(t) + \tilde{\tilde{\tilde{M}}}_t + I_1(t) + I_2(t) - I_3(t) + I_4(t). \end{aligned} \tag{3.18}$$

Here $\tilde{\tilde{\tilde{M}}}_t$ is a local martingale and $A(t)$ is a dt integral and thus they both are locally integrable processes. The no-arbitrage condition (3.7) implies that the sum of all those six processes is a local martingale and in particular the sum

$$I_1(t) + I_2(t) - I_3(t) + I_4(t)$$

is locally integrable. We consider each term separately. Since $(D_tP(t,T,x))_{0\le t\le T}$ is a nonnegative local martingale, it is a supermartingale and hence

$$\sup_{0\le s\le T} \mathbb{E}(D_sP(s-,T,x)) \le \sup_{0\le s\le T} \mathbb{E}(D_sP(s,T,x)) \le \mathbb{E}(D_0P(0,T,x)) < \infty \tag{3.19}$$

the last expectation being finite by (3.7). The process

$$I_3(t) := \int_0^t \int_{\mathbb{R}^d} D_sP(s-,T,x)1_{\{|z|>1\}}\mu(ds,dz)$$

is locally integrable. To see this let (τ_n) be an increasing sequence of stopping times dominated by T. Then

$$\begin{aligned}\mathbb{E}&\left(\int_0^{\tau_n} \int_{\mathbb{R}^d} D_sP(s-,T,x)1_{\{|z|>1\}}\mu(ds,dz)\right)\\ &\le \mathbb{E}\left(\int_0^{T} \int_{\mathbb{R}^d} D_sP(s-,T,x)1_{\{|z|>1\}}\mu(ds,dz)\right)\\ &= \int_0^{T} \int_{\mathbb{R}^d} \mathbb{E}(D_sP(s-,T,x))\,1_{\{|z|>1\}}\nu(dz)ds. \end{aligned}\tag{3.20}$$

Since the integrands are nonnegative, we obtain with (3.19) that

$$\begin{aligned}\mathbb{E}&\left(\int_0^{\tau_n} \int_{\mathbb{R}^d} D_sP(s-,T,x)1_{\{|z|>1\}}\mu(ds,dz)\right)\\ &\le T\mathbb{E}(D_0P(0,T,x))\nu(\{z\in\mathbb{R}^d : |z|>1\}) < \infty.\end{aligned}$$

Next, we consider I_4. By (A5)

$$|e^{-c^*(s,T,x;y)} - 1| \le e^{TK(T,x)} + 1 =: \tilde{K}(T,x)$$

and hence

$$\begin{aligned}\mathbb{E}&\left(\int_0^{\tau_n} \int_{\mathbb{R}^d} D(s)P(s-,T,x)1_{\{L_{s-}+y\le x\}}|e^{-c^*(s,T,x;y)} - 1|\mu^L(ds,dy)\right)\\ &\le \tilde{K}(T,x)\mathbb{E}\left(\int_0^{T} \int_{\mathbb{R}^d} 1_{[0,\tau_n]}(s)D(s)P(s-,T,x)1_{\{L_{s-}+y\le x\}}\mu^L(ds,dy)\right)\\ &\le \tilde{K}(T,x)\int_0^{T} \int_{\mathbb{R}^d} \mathbb{E}(D(s)P(s-,T,x))\,\nu^L(s,dy),\end{aligned}$$

which is finite by (3.19), (A1) and the second part in (A5). Summarizing, the no-arbitrage condition (3.7) implies that the sum $I_1 + I_2$ is locally integrable. However

$$\begin{aligned}I_1 + I_2 &= \int_0^t \int_{\mathbb{R}^d} (e^{-b^*(s,T,x)^\top z} - 1 + b^*(s,T,x)^\top z)1_{\{|z|\le 1\}}\mu(ds,dz)\\ &+ \int_0^t \int_{\mathbb{R}^d} e^{-b^*(s,T,x)^\top z}1_{\{|z|>1\}}\mu(ds,dz).\end{aligned}$$

Since both integrands are nonnegative, this sum is locally integrable if and only if both summands are locally integrable and so $\int_0^t \int_{\mathbb{R}^d} e^{-b^*(s,T,x)^\top z} 1_{\{|z|>1\}} \mu(ds, dz)$ is locally integrable. Therefore, for a localizing sequence τ_n

$$\mathbb{E} \int_0^T \int_{\mathbb{R}^d} e^{-b^*(s,T,x)^\top z} 1_{\{s \le \tau_n\}} 1_{\{|z|>1\}} \mu(ds, dz) < +\infty.$$

Equivalently

$$\mathbb{E}\left[\int_0^{\tau_n} \left(\int_{|z|>1} e^{-b^*(s,T,x)^\top z} \nu(dz) \right) ds \right] < +\infty.$$

This implies (3.11) and assertion (i) follows.

We consider now (ii). Note that $D_t p(t-, T, x) > 0$. Compensating in (3.16) the integrals with respect to the random measures μ and μ^L, collecting the "dt"-terms and dividing by $D_t p(t-, T, x) > 0$ gives

$$\begin{aligned} 1_{\{L_t \le x\}} \Bigg[& f(t,t,x) - r_t - \lambda(t,x) - \langle b^*(t,T,x), m \rangle - a^*(t,T,x) \\ & + \frac{1}{2} b^*(t,T,x)^\top \Sigma b^*(t,T,x) + \int_{\mathbb{R}^d} [e^{-b^*(t,T,x)^\top z} - 1 + 1_{\{|z|\le 1\}} b^*(t,T,x)^\top z] \nu(dz) \\ & + \int_{\mathcal{I}} 1_{\{L_t + y \le x\}} (e^{-c^*(t,T,x;y)} - 1) \nu^L(t, dy) \Bigg] dt. \end{aligned} \tag{3.21}$$

Dp being a local martingale is equivalent to having a vanishing drift. From (3.21) we obtain the following condition:

$$\begin{aligned} 0 = & f(t,t,x) - r_t - \lambda(t,x) - a^*(t,T,x) + J(b^*(t,T,x)) \\ & + \int_{\mathcal{I}} (e^{-c^*(t,T,x;y)} - 1) 1_{\{L_t + y \le x\}} \nu^L(t, dy), \end{aligned} \tag{3.22}$$

$dt \otimes \mathbb{Q}$-almost surely for all $T \ge t$. Let $N \in \mathcal{B}(\mathbb{R}^+) \otimes \mathcal{F}$ be the set of all (t, ω) for which (3.22) holds. For $(t, \omega) \in N$ we choose $T = t$ and hence obtain (3.13) as $J(0) = 0$. The remaining terms give (3.12), where both equations hold only on N, i.e. $dt \otimes \mathbb{Q}$-almost surely.

For the converse, we need to show that the drift conditions imply that all discounted (T, x)-bonds are local martingales. For fixed x, the drift conditions imply that the "dt"-terms in (3.17) vanish (compare (3.21)) and hence $(D_t P(t,T,x))_{0 \le t \le T}$ are local martingales. The conclusion follows. □

Theorem 3.1 states that, under the no-arbitrage condition (3.7), the *drift* $a(t,\cdot,x)$ of the forward rates is determined by the *volatility* $b(t,\cdot,x)$ and the *contagion* $c(t,\cdot,x;\cdot)$. Besides this, (3.12) gives an implicit relation between $f(t,t,x)$ and L_t or more precisely its compensator; the relationship between λ and the compensator ν is given in (3.2).

In Filipović *et al.* [8] it is shown how to construct a conditional Markov process which satisfies the drift conditions when the filtration is generated by a Brownian motion. The extension to the case where the background filtration is generated by a Lévy process is studied in Schmidt and Tappe [15].

There is a rich literature on drift conditions in the defaultable and default-free case, see for example Björk *et al.* [1], Musiela and Rutkowski [12], Filipović [6], Schmidt [14], Özkan and Schmidt [13] and Huehne [10].

4. Market Models

For practical applications it is important to realize, that (T,x)-bond prices are neither available for all maturities nor for all levels x. This chapter is devoted to the study of a *market model* where this assumption is relaxed. We start by deriving dynamics of (T_k,x_i)-rates in Sec. 4.1, and consider market models of the forward rate and the (T_k,x_i)-rate in Secs. 4.2 and 4.3, respectively. The drift condition derived in Theorem 3.1 is, however, still sufficient for absence of arbitrage. Recall that $(L_t)_{t\geq 0}$ was the loss process of the CDO and $P(t,T,x) = 1_{\{L_t\leq x\}}p(t,T,x)$ with $p(t,T,x)>0$.

We fix a tenor structure $0<T_1<\cdots<T_n$ and a barrier structure $0=x_1<\ldots<x_m=1$. Set $\mathcal{S} := \{T_1,\ldots,T_n\}\times\{x_0,\ldots,x_m\}$. The considered market model consists of all (T,x)-bonds with $(T,x)\in\mathcal{S}$. As $x_m=1$, the market also contains risk-free bonds. Throughout we assume that the initial term structure, denoted in (T,x)-bonds, is strictly positive and decreasing in T and increasing in x.

Definition 4.1. Set $\delta_k := T_{k+1}-T_k$. The rate

$$L(t,T_k,x_i) := 1_{\{L_t\leq x_i\}}\frac{1}{\delta_k}\left(\frac{p(t,T_k,x_i)}{p(t,T_{k+1},x_i)}-1\right)$$

is called (T_k,x_i)*-rate*. For all $0\leq t\leq S\leq T$ and $x\in\mathcal{I}$,

$$F(t,S,T,x) := 1_{\{L_t\leq x\}}\frac{p(t,S,x)}{p(t,T,x)} \tag{4.1}$$

defines the (S,T,x)*-forward bond price.*

The $(T_k,1)$-rate is the so-called LIBOR-rate. It is a default-free and has been studied in many papers, see e.g. Filipović [7]. Defaultable LIBOR-rates have been studied in Eberlein *et al.* [4]. In this paper we follow Brace *et al.* [2] and embed the (T_k,x_i)-rates in the framework of continuous forward rates and obtain sufficient conditions for absence of arbitrage. In Eberlein *et al.* [3] (T_k,x)-rates are studied directly; however they do not consider a discrete structure for the loss levels.

4.1. *Dynamics of (T_k, x_i)-rates*

In this section we derive the dynamics of (T_k, x_i)-rates when the drift condition (3.12) is satisfied. This result generalizes Eberlein and Özkan [5] and Huehne [10]. Recall that $b^*(t,T,x) = \int_t^T b(t,u,x)du$.

Theorem 4.1. *Assume that* (A1)–(A4) *and* (3.12) *hold and consider* $(T_k, x_i) \in \mathcal{S}$. *On* $\{L_{t-} \le x_i\}$ *we have that*

$$dL(t,T_k,x_i) = \frac{1+\delta_k L(t-,T_k,x_i)}{\delta_k}\bigg(D(t,T_k,T_{k+1},x_i) - \frac{\delta_k L(t-,T_k,x_i)}{1+\delta_k L(t-,T_k,x_i)}\lambda(t,x_i)\bigg)dt + d\tilde{M}_t, \tag{4.2}$$

where the drift term attributed to the compensated jumps and the quadratic variation of the diffusive part is

$$\begin{aligned} &D(t,T_k,T_{k+1},x_i)\\ &\quad := \int_{\mathbb{R}^d} (e^{\langle b^*(t,T_{k+1},x_i)-b^*(t,T_k,x_i),z\rangle} - e^{-\langle b^*(t,T_k,x_i),z\rangle} + e^{-\langle b^*(t,T_{k+1},x_i),z\rangle} - 1)\nu(dz)\\ &\qquad + \int_{\mathcal{I}} (e^{c^*(t,T_{k+1},x_i;y)-c^*(t,T_k,x_i;y)} - e^{-c^*(t,T_k,x_i;y)} + e^{-c^*(t,T_{k+1},x_i;y)})1_{\{L_t+y\le x_i\}}\\ &\qquad \times \nu^L(t,dy) + \langle \Sigma(b^*(t,T_{k+1},x_i) - b^*(t,T_k,x_i)), b^*(t,T_{k+1},x_i)\rangle \end{aligned} \tag{4.3}$$

and $\tilde{M} = \tilde{M}(T_k,x_i)$ *is the local martingale*

$$\begin{aligned} d\tilde{M}_t &:= L(t-,T_k,x_i)dM_t^x + \frac{1+\delta_k L(t-,T_k,x_i)}{\delta_k}\\ &\quad \times \bigg(\int_{\mathbb{R}^d} (e^{\langle b^*(t,T_{k+1},x_i)-b^*(t,T_k,x_i),z\rangle} - 1)(\mu(ds,dz) - \nu(dz)ds)\\ &\quad + \int_{\mathcal{I}} (e^{c^*(t,T_{k+1},x_i;y)-c^*(t,T_k,x_i;y)} - 1)1_{\{L_{t-}+y\le x_i\}}(\mu^L(ds,dy) - \nu^L(dy)ds)\\ &\quad + \langle b^*(t,T_{k+1},x_i) - b^*(t,T_k,x_i), dW(t)\rangle\bigg). \end{aligned} \tag{4.4}$$

Proof. Fix $0 < S < T$. First, we derive the dynamics of the pre-default (S,T,x)-forward bond price process

$$g(t,S,T,x) := \frac{p(t,S,x)}{p(t,T,x)}. \tag{4.5}$$

With x, S and T fixed we denote $A(t) := \int_S^T a(t,u,x)du$, $B(t) := \int_S^T b(t,u,x)du$, and $C(t;y) := \int_S^T c(t,u,x;y)du$. By (4.5) and the dynamics of the forward rate f

given in (3.6), the stochastic Fubini theorem yields

$$\begin{aligned} g(t,S,T,x) &= e^{\int_S^T \left(f(0,u,x)+\int_0^t a(s,u,x)ds+\int_0^t \langle b(s,u,x),dZ_s\rangle+\int_0^t\int_{\mathcal{I}} c(s,u,x;y)\mu^L(ds,dy)\right)du} \\ &= g(0,S,T,x)e^{\int_0^t A(s)ds+\int_0^t \langle B(s),dZ(s)\rangle+\int_0^t\int_{\mathcal{I}} C(s;y)\mu^L(ds,dy)}. \end{aligned}$$

The Itô-formula gives an expression for the dynamics of g:

$$\begin{aligned} dg(t,S,T,x) &= g(t-,S,T,x)(A(t)+\langle B(t),dZ(t)\rangle)dt \\ &\quad+\frac{1}{2}g(t-,S,T,x)\langle \Sigma B(t),B(t)\rangle dt \\ &\quad+(g(t,S,T,x)-g(t-,S,T,x)-g(t-,S,T,x)\langle B(t),\Delta Z(t)\rangle) \\ &=: dI_1(t)+dI_2(t)+dI_3(t). \end{aligned} \tag{4.6}$$

The decomposition of Z in (3.4) yields

$$\begin{aligned} dI_1(t) &= g(t-,S,T,x)\left(A(t)+\langle B(t),m\rangle\right)dt+g(t-,S,T,x)\langle B(t),dW(t)\rangle \\ &\quad+\int_{\|z\|\le 1} g(t-,S,T,x)\langle B(t),z\rangle(\mu(dt,dz)-\nu(dz)dt) \\ &\quad+\int_{\|z\|>1} g(t-,S,T,x)\langle B(t),z\rangle\mu(dt,dz). \end{aligned}$$

By (A3), L and Z have no joint jumps and therefore

$$\begin{aligned} dI_3(t) &= g(t-,S,T,x)(e^{\langle B(t),\Delta Z(t)\rangle+C(t,\Delta L(t))}-1)-g(t-,S,T,x)\langle B(t),\Delta Z(t)\rangle \\ &= \int_{\mathbb{R}^d} g(t-,S,T,x)(e^{\langle B(t),z\rangle}-1-\langle B(t),z\rangle)\mu(dt,dz) \\ &\quad+\int_{\mathcal{I}} g(t-,S,T,x)(e^{C(t;y)}-1)\mu^L(dt,dy), \end{aligned}$$

Inserting this expressions in (4.6) we obtain

$$\begin{aligned} \frac{dg(t,S,T,x)}{g(t-,S,T,x)} &= \left(A(t)+\langle B(t),m\rangle+\frac{1}{2}\langle \Sigma B(t),B(t)\rangle\right)dt+\langle B(t),dW(t)\rangle \\ &\quad+\int_{\mathbb{R}^d}(e^{\langle B(t),z\rangle}-1)(\mu(dt,dz)-\nu(dz)dt) \\ &\quad+\int_{\mathbb{R}^d}(e^{\langle B(t),z\rangle}-1-1_{\{\|z\|\le 1\}}\langle B(t),z\rangle)\nu(dz)dt \qquad (4.7) \\ &\quad+\int_{\mathcal{I}}(e^{C(t;y)}-1)\mu^L(dt,dy). \qquad (4.8) \end{aligned}$$

As $L(t,T_k,x) = 1_{\{L_t\le x\}}\delta_k^{-1}(g(t,T_k,T_{k+1},x)-1)$, we have that

$$dL(t,T_k,x) = \delta_k^{-1}(g(t-,T_k,T_{k+1},x)-1)d1_{\{L_t\le x\}} + 1_{\{L_{t-}\le x\}}\delta_k^{-1}dg(t,T_k,T_{k+1},x) \\ + d[1_{\{L_t\le x\}},\delta_k^{-1}(g(t,T_k,T_{k+1},x)-1)].$$

Note that $d1_{\{L_t\le x\}} = dM_t^x - 1_{\{L_t\le x\}}\lambda(t,x)dt$ and, similar to (3.15),

$$\begin{aligned} &d[1_{\{L_t\le x\}},\delta_k^{-1}(g(t,T_k,T_{k+1},x)-1)] \\ &\quad = \delta_k^{-1}\int_{\mathcal{I}}(1_{\{L_{t-}+y\le x\}} - 1_{\{L_{t-}\le x\}})g(t-,T_k,T_{k+1},x) \\ &\qquad \times (e^{C(t,T_k,T_{k+1};y)}-1)\mu^L(dt,dy). \end{aligned}$$

Summarizing, we obtain the following dynamics of L,

$$\begin{aligned} dL(t,T_k,x) = {} & L(t-,T_k,x)(dM_t^x - \lambda(t,x)dt) \\ & + 1_{\{L_{t-}\le x\}}\frac{\delta_k L(t-,T_k,x)+1}{\delta_k}\Bigg[\bigg(A(t)+\langle B(t),m\rangle + \frac{1}{2}\langle \Sigma B(t),B(t)\rangle \\ & + \int_{\mathbb{R}^d}(e^{\langle B(t),z\rangle}-1-1_{\{\|z\|\le 1\}}\langle B(t),z\rangle)\nu(dz)\bigg)dt \\ & + \langle B(t),dW(t)\rangle + \int_{\mathbb{R}^d}(e^{\langle B(t),z\rangle}-1)(\mu(dt,dz)-\nu(dz)dt) \\ & + \int_{\mathcal{I}}(e^{C(t;y)}-1)\mu^L(dy,dt) \\ & + \int_{\mathcal{I}}(1_{\{L_{t-}+y\le x\}} - 1_{\{L_{t-}\le x\}})(e^{C(t;y)}-1)\mu^L(dt,dy)\Bigg]. \end{aligned} \tag{4.9}$$

Compensating the remaining μ^L terms and collection all ds-terms and using (3.5) gives the drift term of L,

$$\begin{aligned} & -L(t-,T_k,x)\lambda(t,x) + 1_{\{L_{t-}\le x\}}\frac{\delta_k L(t-,T_k,x)+1}{\delta_k} \\ & \times\left[A(t)+J(-B(t)) + \int_{\mathcal{I}}\left(e^{C(t;y)}-1\right)1_{\{L_t+y\le x\}}\nu^L(t,dy)\right]. \end{aligned} \tag{4.10}$$

In the next step we will use the drift condition (3.12) to work further on this expression. Recall that

$$B(t) = \int_S^T b(t,u,x)du = b^*(t,T,x) - b^*(t,S,x),$$

such that (3.5) gives

$$\begin{aligned}
J(-B(t)) &= -\langle m, b^*(t,S,x)\rangle + \langle m, b^*(t,T,x)\rangle \\
&\quad + \frac{1}{2}\langle \Sigma(b^*(t,T,x) - b^*(t,S,x)), (b^*(t,S,x) - b^*(t,T,x))\rangle \\
&\quad + \int_{\mathbb{R}^d} (e^{-\langle b^*(t,S,x)-b^*(t,T,x),z\rangle} - 1 + 1_{\{\|z\|\le 1\}} \\
&\quad \times \langle b^*(t,S,x) - b^*(t,T,x), z\rangle)\nu(dz) \\
&= J(b^*(t,S,x)) - J(b^*(t,T,x)) + \langle \Sigma(b^*(t,T,x) - b^*(t,S,x)), b^*(t,T,x)\rangle \\
&\quad + \int_{\mathbb{R}^d} (e^{-\langle b^*(t,S,x)-b^*(t,T,x),z\rangle} - e^{-\langle b^*(t,S,x),z\rangle} + e^{-\langle b^*(t,T,x),z\rangle} - 1)\nu(dz)
\end{aligned}$$

With $A(t) = a^*(t,T,x) - a^*(t,S,x)$ the drift condition (3.12) gives

$$\begin{aligned}
A(t) &= J(b^*(t,T,x)) - J(b^*(t,S,x)) \\
&\quad + \int_{\mathcal{I}} (e^{-c^*(t,T,x;y)} - e^{-c^*(t,S,x;y)})1_{\{L_t+y\le x\}}\nu^L(t,dy).
\end{aligned}$$

Hence,

$$\begin{aligned}
&A(t) + J(-B(t)) + \int_{\mathcal{I}} (e^{C(s;y)} - 1)1_{\{L_t+y\le x\}}\nu^L(t,dy) \\
&\quad = \langle \Sigma(b^*(t,T,x) - b^*(t,S,x)), b^*(t,T,x)\rangle \\
&\qquad + \int_{\mathbb{R}^d} (e^{\langle b^*(t,T,x)-b^*(t,S,x),z\rangle} - e^{-\langle b^*(t,S,x),z\rangle} + e^{-\langle b^*(t,T,x),z\rangle} - 1)\nu(dz) \\
&\qquad + \int_{\mathcal{I}} (e^{c^*(t,T,x;y)-c^*(t,S,x;y)} - e^{-c^*(t,S,x;y)} + e^{-c^*(t,T,x;y)})1_{\{L_t+y\le x\}}\nu^L(t,dy).
\end{aligned} \tag{4.11}$$

Inserting this in (4.10) and using the dynamics of L in (4.9) we obtain the result. □

As byproduct of the above proof we obtain the dynamics of the (S,T,x)-forward rate.

Corollary 4.1. *Assume* (A1)–(A4) *and* (3.12) *holds and* $(T_k, x_i) \in \mathcal{S}$ *with* $k < n$. *Then, on* $\{L_{t-\le x_i}\}$,

$$\frac{dF(t,T_k,T_{k+1},x_i)}{F(t-,T_k,T_{k+1},x_i)} = (-\lambda(t,x_i) + D(t,T_k,T_{k+1},x_i))dt + d\tilde{\tilde{M}}_t \tag{4.12}$$

with D *from* (4.3) *and the local martingale* $\tilde{\tilde{M}}$ *given in* (4.13).

Proof. Noting that $F(t, T_k, T_{k+1}, x_i) = 1_{\{L_t \le x_i\}} g(t, T_k, T_{k+1}, x_i)$ with g defined in (4.5), we obtain the dynamics of F via

$$dF(t, T_k, x_i) = g(t-, T_k, T_{k+1}, x_i) d1_{\{L_t \le x_i\}} + 1_{\{L_{t-} \le x_i\}} dg(t, T_k, T_{k+1}, x_i) + d[1_{\{L_t \le x_i\}}, g(t, T_k, T_{k+1}, x_i)].$$

As above we have that

$$d[1_{\{L_t \le x_i\}}, g(t, T_k, T_{k+1}, x_i] = \int_{\mathcal{I}} (1_{\{L_{t-}+y \le x_i\}} - 1_{\{L_{t-} \le x_i\}}) g(t-, T_k, T_{k+1}, x_i)(e^{C(t,T_k,T_{k+1};y)} - 1)\mu^L(dt, dy).$$

With (4.8) and (4.11) we obtain the stated dynamics. Here

$$d\tilde{\tilde{M}}_t := dM_t^x + \int_{\mathbb{R}^d} (e^{\langle b^*(t,T_{k+1},x_i) - b^*(t,T_k,x_i), z\rangle} - 1)(\mu(dt, dz) - \nu(dz)dt) + \int_{\mathcal{I}} (e^{(c^*(t,T_{k+1},x_i;y) - c^*(t,T_k,x_i;y))} - 1) 1_{\{L_{t-}+y \le x_i\}} (\mu^L(dt, dy) - \nu^L(dy)dt) + \langle b^*(t, T_{k+1}, x_i) - b^*(t, T_k, x_i), dW(t)\rangle. \tag{4.13}$$

□

4.2. *Forward rate modelling*

In practical applications one needs a simple structure of the (T_k, x_i)-rates which is analysed in this section. For notational convenience, we consider forward bond prices instead of (T_k, x_i)-rates themselves. A result for the (T_k, x_i)-rate can be obtained in a similar way. Recall from (3.3) that $\lambda(t, x)$ was the intensity that $1_{\{L_t \le x\}}$ jumps to zero at t. Let $\eta(t) := \inf\{1 \le i \le n : T_{i+1} > t\}$. In the following model the forward rate is driven by the Lévy process Z through the functions β_k; the reaction on the loss process L can be adjusted through the functions γ_k. These may depend on the loss occurring at t, ΔL_t, and the current loss level L_{t-} itself. We need the following assumption:

(A6) For each $(T_k, x_i) \in \mathcal{S}$ the functions $\beta_{ki} : \mathbb{R}^+ \to \mathbb{R}^d$, $\gamma_{ki} : \mathbb{R}^+ \times \mathcal{I} \times [0, 1] \to \mathbb{R}$ are measurable and bounded.

Proposition 4.1. *Assume* (A1)–(A6) *hold. Forward bond prices given on* $\{L_t \le x_i\}$ *by*

$$\frac{dF(t, T_k, T_{k+1}, x_i)}{F(t-, T_k, T_{k+1}, x_i)} = \alpha_{ki}(t)dt + \langle \beta_{ki}(t), dW(t)\rangle + \int_{\mathbb{R}^d} (e^{\langle \beta_{ki}(t), z\rangle} - 1)\mu(dt, dz) + \int_{\mathcal{I}} (e^{\gamma_{ki}(t, L_{t-};y)} - 1) 1_{\{L_{t-}+y \le x_i\}} \mu^L(dt, dy), \tag{4.14}$$

$(T_k, x_i) \in \mathcal{S}$, $k < n$ *and zero on* $\{L_t > x_i\}$ *constitute an arbitrage-free market if*

$$\alpha_{ki}(t) = -\lambda(t, x_i) + \sum_{j=\eta(t)}^{k} \langle \beta_{ji}(t), \Sigma\beta_{ki}(t)\rangle$$
$$+ \int_{\mathbb{R}^d} \left(e^{\langle \beta_{ki}(t), z\rangle} + (e^{-\langle \beta_{ki}(t), z\rangle} - 1) \prod_{j=\eta(t)}^{k-1} e^{-\langle \beta_{ji}(t), z\rangle} - 1 \right) \nu(dz)$$
$$+ \int_{\mathcal{I}} \left(e^{\gamma_{ki}(t, L_{t-}; y)} + (e^{-\gamma_{ki}(t, L_{t-}; y)} - 1) \prod_{j=\eta(t)}^{k-1} e^{-\gamma_{ji}(t, L_{t-}; y)} \right) 1_{\{L_t + y \le x_i\}}$$
$$\times \nu^L(t, dy)$$

for all $(T_k, x_i), (T_{k+1}, x_i) \in \mathcal{S}$.

In this way the (T, x)-forward bond price explicitly relates to $\lambda(t, x)$ and ν^L. With this result at hand pricing of typical derivatives on the forward rate can be done in a standard way. The input parameters for the modeler are β_{ki}, γ_{ki} as well as Σ, ν and ν^L while the α_{ki} are determined as above to ensure that the model is free of arbitrage.

Proof. The idea is to identify b (see (3.6)) from the dynamics of F and then show that the drift condition (3.12) holds with the chosen α: a comparison of (4.14) with Corollary 4.1 and (4.13) yields that

$$\beta_{ki}(t) = \int_{T_k}^{T_{k+1}} b(t, u, x_i)du \quad \text{and} \quad \gamma_{ki}(t, L_{t-}; y) = \int_{T_k}^{T_{k+1}} c(t, u, x_i; y)du.$$

The drift in (4.12) yields that

$$\begin{aligned} \alpha_{ki}(t) &= -\lambda(t, x_i) + \langle \Sigma\beta_{ki}(t), b^*(s, T_{k+1}, x_i)\rangle \\ &\quad + \int_{\mathbb{R}^d} (e^{\langle \beta_{ki}(t), z\rangle} + e^{-\langle b^*(t, T_k, x_i), z\rangle}(e^{-\langle \beta_{ki}(t), z\rangle} - 1) - 1)\nu(dz) \\ &\quad + \int_{\mathcal{I}} (e^{\gamma_{ki}(y, L_{t-})} + e^{-c^*(t, T_k, x_i; y)}(e^{-\gamma_{ki}(y, L_{t-})} - 1))1_{\{L_t + y \le x_i\}}\nu^L(dy). \end{aligned} \tag{4.15}$$

We have that $\beta_{ki}(t) = b^*(t, T_{k+1}, x_i) - b^*(t, T_k, x_i)$ and we use the freedom to specify $b(t, T, x_i) \equiv 0$ whenever $t > T$. This in turn gives that for $T_j < t < T_{j+1}$

$$\beta_{ji}(t) = \int_{T_j}^{T_{j+1}} b(t, u, x_i)du = \int_{t}^{T_{j+1}} b(t, u, x_i)du = b^*(t, T_{j+1}, x_i)$$

such that

$$b^*(t, T_{k+1}, x_i) = \sum_{j=\eta(t)}^{k} \beta_{ji}(t). \tag{4.16}$$

Analogously,

$$c^*(t, T_{k+1}, x_i; y) = \sum_{j=\eta(t)}^{k} \gamma_{ji}(t, L_{t-}; y). \tag{4.17}$$

Inserting this in (4.15) gives the claim. □

4.3. (T_k, x_i)-rate modelling

In this section we study the case where instead of the forward price process the (T_k, x_i)-rate has a simple structure. As in the previous setting we consider the lognormal case including jumps. For simplicity we assume $\nu = 0$, i.e. the dynamics is only driven by a Brownian motion and L. In turn we will obtain the result from Brace *et al.* [2] as a special case. Finally, we also give the results for market models in a single-name credit risky case.

(A7) Assume $\nu(dx) = 0$ and that for each $(T_k, x_i) \in \mathcal{S}$ the functions $\beta_{ki} : \mathbb{R}^+ \to \mathbb{R}^d$, $\gamma_{ki} : \mathbb{R}^+ \times \mathbb{R}^+ \to \mathbb{R}$ are measurable and bounded.

Proposition 4.2. *Assume* (A1)–(A4) *and* (A7) *hold.* (T_k, x_i)*-rates given by*

$$dL(t, T_k, x_i) = L(t-, T_k, x_i)(\alpha_{ki}(t)dt + \langle \beta_{ki}, dW(t)\rangle) + \frac{1 + \delta_k L(t-, T_k, x_i)}{\delta_k} \times \int_{\mathcal{I}} \left(e^{\gamma_{ki}(y, L_{t-})} - 1\right) 1_{\{L_{t-}+y \le x_i\}} \mu^L(ds, dy) \tag{4.18}$$

for all $(T_k, x_i) \in \mathcal{S}$ *and zero otherwise constitute an arbitrage-free market if*

$$\alpha_{ki}(t) = -\lambda(t, x_i) + \sum_{j=\eta(t)}^{k} \frac{1 + \delta_j L(t-, T_j, x_i)}{\delta_j L(t-, T_j, x_i)} \langle \beta_{ji}(t), \Sigma \beta_{ki}(t)\rangle + \frac{1 + \delta_k L(t-, T_k, x_i)}{\delta_k L(t-, T_k, x_i)} \cdot \int_{\mathcal{I}} \left(e^{\gamma_{ki}(t;y)} + (e^{-\gamma_{ki}(t, L_{t-};y)} - 1) \prod_{j=\eta(t)}^{k-1} e^{-\gamma_{ji}(t, L_{t-};y)} \right) 1_{\{L_t+y \le x_i\}} \nu^L(dy) \tag{4.19}$$

for all $(T_k, x_i) \in \mathcal{S}$.

With this result at hand pricing of typical derivatives on the (T_k, x_i)-rates can be done in a standard way, see for example Sec. 6 in Brace *et al.* [2]. As previously, the input parameters for the modeler are λ, β_{ki} and γ_{ki} while the α_{ki} are determined as above to ensure that the model is free of arbitrage.

Proof. We proceed similar to the proof of Proposition 4.1. A comparison of (4.18) with (4.4) yields that

$$\beta_{ki}(t) = \frac{1 + \delta_k L(t-, T_k, x_i)}{\delta_k L(t-, T_k, x_i)} (b^*(t, T_{k+1}, x_i) - b^*(t, T_k, x_i)) \tag{4.20}$$

such that

$$b^*(t,T_{k+1},x_i) = b^*(t,T_k,x_i) + \beta_{ki}(t)\frac{\delta_k L(t-,T_k,x_i)}{1+\delta_k L(t-,T_k,x_i)}$$
$$= \sum_{j=\eta(t)}^{k} \beta_{ji}(t)\frac{\delta_j L(t-,T_j,x_i)}{1+\delta_j L(t-,T_j,x_i)},$$

compare (4.16). Furthermore, we have that $\gamma_{ki}(y,L_{t-}) = C(t,T_k,T_{k+1}x_i;y)$ and hence (4.17). From the drift term in (4.2) we obtain that

$$\alpha_{ki}(t) = -\lambda(t,x_i) + \frac{1+\delta_k L(t-,T_k,x_i)}{\delta_k L(t-,T_k,x_i)} D(t,T_k,T_{k+1},x_i).$$

With (4.20) and (4.17)

$$D(t,T_k,T_{k+1},x_i)$$
$$= \frac{\delta_k L(t-,T_k,x_i)}{1+\delta_k L(t-,T_k,x_i)}\langle \Sigma\beta_{ki}(t), b^*(t,T_{k+1},x_i)\rangle$$
$$+ \int_{\mathcal{I}} \left(e^{\gamma_{ki}(t,L_{t-};y)} + (e^{-\gamma_{ki}(t,L_{t-};y)} - 1) \prod_{j=\eta(t)}^{k-1} e^{-\gamma_{ji}(t,L_{t-};y)} \right) 1_{\{L_t+y\le x_i\}} \nu^L(dy)$$

and we conclude as in Proposition 4.1. □

Remark 4.1. With $x_m = 1$ and $c(\cdot,T,1;y) = 1$ (from Assumption (A2)) gives the risk-free Libor market model as a special case and (4.19) equals Eq. (2.6) in Brace *et al.* [2]. Also a doubly stochastic model for single-name credit risk as in Huehne [10] is a special case: consider the doubly stochastic random time τ which has an intensity $(\lambda_t)_{t\ge 0}$. Choose $L_t := \frac{1}{2}1_{\{\tau\le t\}}$. Then, with $x_1 = \frac{1}{2}$, one has that the rates of defaultable bond satisfying, on $\{\tau > t\}$,

$$\frac{d\bar{L}(t,T_k)}{\bar{L}(t-,T_k)} = \bar{\alpha}_k(t)dt + \langle \bar{\beta}_k(t), dW(t)\rangle \tag{4.21}$$

and zero otherwise constitute an arbitrage-free market if

$$\bar{\alpha}_k(t) = -\lambda(t) + \left\langle \bar{\beta}_k(t), \sum_{j=\eta(t)}^{k} \frac{\delta_j \bar{L}(t-,T_j)}{1+\delta_j \bar{L}(t-,T_j)}\bar{\beta}_j(t) \right\rangle. \tag{4.22}$$

Acknowledgment

Support by the Polish Ministry of Science and Education projects: 5 1P03A 03429 “Stochastic evolution equations with Lévy noise” and N N201 419039 “Stochastic equations in infinite dimensional spaces”is gratefully acknowledged. We thank the Fields Institute for the kind support as well as Frank Gehmlich and an anonymous referee for their helpful comments.

References

[1] T. Björk, G. B. Di Masi, Y. Kabanov and W. J. Runggaldier, Towards a general theory of bond markets, *Finance and Stochastics* (1997) 141–174.

[2] A. Brace, D. Gatarek and M. Musiela, The market model of interest rate dynamics, *Mathematical Finance* **7** (1997) 127–155.

[3] E. Eberlein, Z. Grbac and T. Schmidt, Market models driven by Lévy processes, working paper (2010).

[4] E. Eberlein, W. Kluge and P. J. Schönbucher, The Lévy Libor model with default risk, *Journal of Credit Risk* **2**(2) (2006) 3–42.

[5] E. Eberlein and F. Özkan, The Lévy LIBOR model, *Finance and Stochastics* **9** (2005) 327–348.

[6] D. Filipović, *Consistency Problems for Heath-Jarrow-Morton Interest Rate Models*, Vol. 1760, Lecture Notes in Mathematics (Springer Verlag, Berlin Heidelberg New York, 2001).

[7] D. Filipović, *Term Structure Models: A Graduate Course* (Springer Verlag, Berlin Heidelberg New York, 2009).

[8] D. Filipović, L. Overbeck and T. Schmidt, Dynamic CDO term structure modelling, *Mathematical Finance* **21** (2011) 53–71.

[9] D. Heath, R. A. Jarrow and A. J. Morton, Bond pricing and the term structure of interest rates, *Econometrica* **60** (1992) 77–105.

[10] F. Huehne, Defaultable Lévy Libor rates and credit derivatives, *International Journal of Theoretical and Applied Finance* **10** (2007) 407–435.

[11] J. Jakubowski and J. Zabczyk, Exponential moments for HJM models with jumps, *Finance Stoch.* **11**(3) (2007) 429–445.

[12] M. Musiela and M. Rutkowski, *Martingale Methods in Financial Modelling* (Springer, Berlin, 1997).

[13] F. Özkan and T. Schmidt, Credit risk with infinite dimensional Lévy processes, *Statistics and Decisions* **23** (2005) 281–299.

[14] T. Schmidt, An infinite factor model for credit risk. *International Journal of Theoretical and Applied Finance* **9** (2006) 43–68.

[15] T. Schmidt and S. Tappe, General cdo term structure modelling: existence and monotonicity, working paper (2010).

INDEX